The Insider's Guide to the Colleges

34th Edition

2 0 0 8

**Compiled and Edited
by the Staff of
*The Yale Daily News***

St. Martin's Griffin
New York

Readers with comments or questions should address them to Editors, *The Insider's Guide to the Colleges*, c/o *The Yale Daily News*, 202 York Street, New Haven, CT 06511-4804.

Visit *The Insider's Guide to the Colleges* Web site at www.yaledailynews.com/books.

The editors have sought to ensure that the information in this book is accurate as of press time. Because policies, costs, and statistics do change from time to time, readers should verify important information with the colleges.

ISBN-13: 978-0-312-36689-6
ISBN-10: 0-312-36689-2

First Edition: July 2007

10   9   8   7   6   5   4   3   2   1

Contents

Preface

Welcome to the 2008 edition of *The Insider's Guide to the Colleges*. The college process may seem overwhelming, but you are beginning your search on the right foot simply by picking up this book. In this 34th edition of the Guide, we provide you with the tools necessary to give you an advantage in the hectic college-choosing process. Our primary objective is to paint an accurate picture of what day-to-day life is like for college students at each school. In each write-up, we rely on hours of personal interviews with actual college students so you can get a true sense of the school and its students.

We tell you what we would have wanted to know when we were in your shoes. College is an experience of meeting hundreds of peers in your first few weeks, of dining halls where the lines are long and the food is bad, and of making friends who skip class to help you out when you're in trouble. It's about pulling all-nighters on papers due the next morning or engaging in late-night talks until the sun comes up. It's about trying things you never thought you would, and probably will never have the chance to do again. It's about driving halfway across the country to see your football team win, walking onto a sports team knowing you'll probably get cut, or volunteering at the local elementary school when you still have 300 pages of reading to do. College is gallons of coffee, stress, and laughter.

But first you need to choose a school. Among the thousands of colleges that span the continent, you can apply to no more than a handful. Maybe you have a vague idea of what you are looking for, but how do you begin to narrow your choices?

This is where *The Insider's Guide* comes in. For this 34th edition, we've revamped our entire book to ensure that it provides an accurate portrayal of life at each of the 326 colleges and universities in United States and Canada. We give you the inside scoop on these places, directly from the students who attend these institutions. We research each school in *The Insider's Guide* by interviewing friends, friends of friends, and a random selection of students at each school. This gives *The Insider's Guide* a unique perspective from students whose opinions we trust. It also means that we are only as accurate as our sources. Though we have worked hard to make each article factually correct and current, the college experience is unique for every individual—after all, one student's closet-sized dorm room is another student's palace.

In addition to articles on each college, *The Insider's Guide* includes a number of special features to help you in your search. "The College Finder" gives you a rundown on various schools according to selected attributes. "Getting In" takes you step-by-step through the intricacies of the admissions process. In "The College Spectrum," we discuss some of the most important factors to consider when choosing between schools, as well as give you a look at current trends in college life. "Introduction for International Students" provides some tips on applying to American schools if you live outside of the United States, while "Disabled Student Services" introduces students with learning or physical disabilities to issues they should be aware of when applying to college. We have also included "Terms You Should Know," a glossary to help you decode confusing college slang. This year, our editors have added a new "What to Bring" checklist to the book, a quiz to find out what college is right for you, as well as a "Travelogue," for an inside look at one student's life studying abroad. And of course, we've included our ever-popular "Editors' Choice," a ranking of schools in categories ranging from ugliest school colors to biggest rivalries. These lists are based on research, statistics, student interviews, as well as our own assessments. Our hope is that the feature might offer you a new perspective or introduce you to a school you might not have considered.

We know how stressful the college process is. After all the hard work of preparing and applying, acceptance letters or rejections often appear to have been decided at random. It may sound difficult, but try not to worry. The majority of students love college. In part, this is because they chose a school that was right for them. But remember, every single college will provide you with new people to meet, new freedoms to explore, and new experiences to enjoy and learn from. So whatever college you end up going to, take it from us: four years go fast, so make the most of it!—*Dana Schuster & Nathaniel Puksta*.

Editors-in-Chief
Nathaniel Puksta
Dana Schuster

Managing Editor
Jay Buchanan

Executive Editors
Alexandra Bicks
Lauren Ezell
Ryan Galisewski
Keneisha Sinclair
Lindsay Starck
Janet Xu

Associate Editors
Kimberly Chow
Christine Geiser
Amy Koenig
Dorota Poplawska
Suzanne Salgado
Laura Sullivan
Janet Yang

Statistical Editor
Jessica Rubin

Staff Writers
Angelica Baker
Elizabeth Bewley

Becky Bicks
Stephanie Brockman
Robert Casey
Catherine Cheney
Shaughnessy Costigan
Eliza Crawford
Cara Dermody
Jesse Dong
Danny Friedman
Caroline Garner
Gerardo Giacoman
Jennifer Hansen
Michelle Katz
Jongwook Kim
Melissa-Victoria King
Kristin Knox
Lee Komeda
Emily Matykiewicz
Xiaohang Liu
Jamie Redman
Catherine Reibel
Taylor Ritzel
Juliann Rowe
Xiaochen Su
Ariel Shepherd-Oppenheim
Emily St. Jean
Victoria Wild
Christina White
Jeffrey Zuckerman

Acknowledgments

We would like to give particular thanks to Meredith Mennitt and Tom Mercer, our editors at St. Martin's Press. Without their organizational and creative vision, the 2008 *Guide* would never have been published. To Susan Zucker and Emad Haerizadeh, we give considerable thanks for their time and patience at *The Yale Daily News*. We would also like to thank all the interviewees, who were kind enough to let us get a personal peek into their lives and their colleges: without you, this book would not have been possible. Finally, a special thanks to those Yalies who 34 years ago decided to devote their time and energy toward creating a helpful guide for high-schoolers about to go to college. We hope you enjoy.

Avi Bajpai
Jason Rodriguez
Sarah Barasch.
Nicole Willey
Rebecca Richardson
Lissa Yu
Jason Buursma
Emily Gabranski
Rebecca Lange
Lily Gordon
Taylor Lawch
Caroline Finigan
Andrey Dragun
Robin Friebur
Greg Pearlman
Allyson Rees
Matt Brodie
Stephanie Heath
Kelly Royer
Allison Loeb
Cory Malone
Matthew Pincus
Steven Bartus

Elise Goodreault
Chrissy Taylor
Tanya Donovan
Cayley Coulbourne
Alex Terry
Aditi Bhaskar
Britt Eichner
Daniel Goldbard
Michael Hadley
Brian Luu
Caitlin Howitt
Danny Karp
Lauren Finzer
Danny Berring
Nisha Gadgil
Winston Lofton
Scott Keyes
Kaitlyn Kasinkas
Katherine Gay
Jennifer Koshliek
Lauren Hartnett
Charles Gordon
Gabriella Kula

Jamie Landau
Bret Chaness
Shawn Achtman
John R. Waldeisen
Xiaole Mao
Lauren Nucci
Monica Tulchinsky
Kristen Mowery
Sameer Honward
Daniel Skilone
Marian Hamilton
Leah Bellshaw
Liz Lam
Leane Nguyen
Christine Smith
Mae Huo
Kate Dillon
Helen Zhou
Robin Zhou
Jenny Pirela
Sanin Sanjay Mody
Brian Matthews

How to Use This Book

How We Select the Colleges

One of the most difficult questions we wrestle with here at *The Insider's Guide* is which schools to include in the upcoming edition. From more than 2,000 four-year institutions nationwide, we cover only **323** colleges. We examine a number of criteria in deciding which colleges to select, but our first priority is always the quality of academics offered by the institution. Another key factor in our decisions is the desire to offer a diversity of options in *The Insider's Guide*. Thus we have included schools from all 50 states as well as top institutions in Canada and most recently England, due to growing demand. In deciding which schools to include, we also take into account the range of extracurricular options. Each year we review our list of schools, research potential additions, and try to include new schools that we have not had the space to write about before.

We have made a point to review the largest state-affiliated institutions because of the significant number of students who apply and matriculate to their states' schools. These universities tend to offer an especially wide-range of opportunities. We have also made every effort to include a broad cross-section of the smaller colleges because of the unique kind of education they offer. The smaller the school, the more we tend to consider the quality of the student body. Many of these small schools are top liberal arts colleges, generally clustered in the Northeast, that offer a broad but personalized education. To add to the diversity of schools reviewed by *The Insider's Guide*, we have also included selections from the most prominent technical schools and creative and performing arts schools. These schools provide a more specialized education that combines general knowledge with a specialty in a particular field. The sampling of schools in this category is by no means conclusive, and we encourage students interested in specialized institutions to explore their options more deeply through additional research.

In sum, this book covers the colleges we believe to be among the most noteworthy in both the United States and Canada. This does not imply in any way that you cannot get a good education at a school not listed in the Guide. We strongly encourage students to use strategies discussed within this book to explore the wide variety of schools that we did not have space to explore here, including community colleges, state schools, international schools, and professional schools. Nor does this mean that you are guaranteed a blissful and prosperous four years if you attend one of these schools. Rather, we believe that every school in the Guide offers students the raw materials for constructing an excellent education.

It's All Up to You

Now that you have picked up a copy of *The Insider's Guide*, it's up to you how to use it. A few dedicated readers' pore through the book from start to finish, determined to gain the most complete understanding of the college process and the schools that are out there. Others flip through the Guide for only a few minutes to look at **FYIs** from schools that interest them or read funny quotes taken from nearby colleges. Another good strategy is to use the College Finder, **Top Ten lists**, and statistics that begin each article to learn more about colleges that you may not have heard of before. It might be worthwhile to read up on colleges that you wouldn't initially consider—you just may find yourself intrigued by the student perspectives. Take advantage of the opening features of the book—they are designed to help you zero in on schools that meet your search criteria. You can also explore these beginning sections to learn what is unique and important about schools you are already considering. We encourage all these approaches. Above all, we hope that the Guide is fun to read, educational, and makes the college process just a little less stressful.

While our **Top Ten Lists** use a mix of statistics and subjectivity to provide an alternative perspective on the schools we include, we have avoided the temptation to pigeonhole the colleges with some kind of catch-all rating system, or worse, to numerically rank them from first to last. Our reason is that the "best" college for one person may come near the bottom of the list for another. Each student has his or her own particular set of wants and needs, so it would be impossible for us to objectively rank the schools from "best" to "worst." Whereas most rankings focus solely on academic factors, the college experience is a balance of academics, social life, extracurricular, and living.

Even so, some may wonder why we don't rate the colleges solely on the basis of academic quality. We think that attempting to come up with such a ranking is both impossible and undesirable. There are too many variables—from the many factors that contribute to the quality of a department and school as a whole to the articulateness and accessibility of the professor who happens to be your academic advisor. Furthermore, it's useless to try to compare a college of 2,000 students with a university of 10,000 (or a university of 10,000

with a state school of 40,000 for that matter) on any basis other than individual preference. Despite these reasons not to, some reportedly reputable sources such as national magazines often insist on publishing numerical rankings of colleges. We advise you not to take these lists too seriously. Oftentimes the determining factor in the rankings is a statistic such as "percent of alumni who donate money," something that means very little to most college applicants.

For 34 years, *The Insider's Guide* has been dedicated to the belief that the best rankers of schools are students themselves, not magazine writers. Our goal, therefore, is to help you train your eye so that you can select the college that is best for you. Remember, we may describe, explain, interpret, and report—but in the end, the choice is always yours.

Getting In

Applying to college can seem as intimidating as the thickness of this book. In the spring of your sophomore year of high school your Aunt Doris, whom you have not seen in seven years, pinches your cheek and asks you where you are going to college. How the heck should I know? you think to yourself. That fall, your mom tells you that the girl down the street with the 4.0 grade point average is taking the SAT prep course for the fifth time to see if she can get a perfect score and win thousands in scholarship money. You reply that you are late for school. You keep ducking the subject, but the hints come with increasing regularity. Not only has dinnertime become your family's "let's talk about Joe's college options" hour, but friends at school are already beginning to leaf through college catalogs. Soon you find the guidance counselor's office crowded with your wide-eyed peers, and it's clear they aren't asking for love advice. Panicking, you decide to make an appointment with the counselor yourself.

When you first talk to your counselor, preferably in the early part of your junior year, you may have just begun to feel comfortable in high school, let alone prepared to think about college. The entire prospect seems far away, but choosing the right school for you takes a good amount of thought and organization—and a visit to your counselor is a solid start. You may even be wondering if college is the path you want to take after high school. And you're not alone. A good number of people choose to take a year or two off to work or travel before pursuing a college education.

One important resource in making a decision about any post-graduation plans is your counselor. College counselors have a wealth of information and experience from which to draw, and they can help you lay out a plan for whatever direction you wish to take. If you decide that college is your next step, you will have a lot options. Though many schools are surveyed in this book, we have not included technical schools, professional schools, or community colleges, all of which also offer numerous opportunities. With research of your own and the aid of your counselor, you should be able to find a school that will give you what you're looking for.

In your hunt for the best college, it is wise to do a little exploring of your own before sitting down with your counselor. Counselors can be invaluable advisors and confidants throughout the college admissions process, but sometimes counselors inadvertently limit your search by only recommending noncompetitive schools, or, conversely, by assuring you that you'll get into whichever school you want. A few may even try to dissuade you from applying to colleges that you are seriously considering. These cases aren't common, but they do happen. Regardless of your counselor's perspective, it is best if you already have an idea of what you are looking for, as it will help both you and your advisor sort out all the options. In the end, always follow your instincts.

As you begin to wade through the piles of brochures, ask yourself questions. What factors about a school make a difference to you? What do you want in a college? A strong science department? A Californian landscape? A small student body? A great social life? Although each college is a mix of different features, it is wise to place your academic needs first. Check out the general academic quality of the school, as well as what kind of programs they offer. Since many college students change their majors repeatedly before finally settling down, look for schools with good programs in various areas of interest to you.

Of course, it's impossible to think of all the angles from which you should approach your college search. You can't predict what your interests will be three or four years from now, or what things will prove most important to you at the college you attend. After all, those realizations are a big part of what the college experience is all about. But by taking a hard look at yourself now, and proceeding thoughtfully, you can be confident that you are investigating the right colleges for the right reasons.

As you begin the search, schools will start to seek you out as well. In the early winter of your junior year you'll receive your PSAT scores, and unless you request otherwise, your mailbox will soon become inundated with letters from colleges around the country. The College Search Service of the College Board provides these schools with the names and addresses of students who show promise and the schools crank out thousands of form letters to send, often to students who they feel are underrepresented in their student population.

While sorting through these masses of glossy brochures, you'll probably notice that most of them contain lofty quotes and pictures of a diverse, frolicking student body. The only way to find out if these ideals are actually truths is to visit the college. But before that, you can verify some of what you read by comparing it to nationally published articles and statistics. You will probably find the colleges that most interest you through your own research, and the majority of these schools wait for you to contact them before they send information. In that case, create a form letter that briefly expresses your interest in the college and requests materials. You'll get your name on their mailing list and they'll appreciate the fact that you took the initiative.

Throughout this process, make sure to listen to those who know you well and often have sound advice to share—namely, your parents and elder siblings. Besides having some ideas of schools you might enjoy attending, your parents also have great insight into how your education can and will be financed. If you come to an early understanding with your family about prospective colleges and financial concerns, things will move much more smoothly down the road. Be warned, though, the college search can be one of the most trying times in any parent-child relationship. Typically parents become more involved in the process than students would want. The best advice we can give is to remember that calm, patient discussions are a better tactic than yelling matches.

When consulting others about your college search, it is helpful to keep a few things in mind. Every piece of advice you receive will be a reflection of someone's own life experiences, and it is likely to be highly subjective. Most adults will suggest schools located in regions they know or colleges they have visited or attended themselves. Also, opinions are often based on stereotypes that can be false, outdated, or just misleading. Still, the more people you talk to, the better perspective you will gain on the colleges you are considering. Once you have a few outside ideas, this book can give you some inside information. If you like what you have heard about a particular school, follow up with some research and find out if it's still a place that calls to you.

As you approach the time when your final college list must be made, you will probably have visited college fairs and attended various college nights. Real-life representatives from the schools are always good to meet. Talking to current college students is an even more important step, as is visiting the schools that make it to your last list. During these encounters, ask the questions that are on your mind. Be critical and observant. When it's time for the final leg of the college selection process, you'll be calm and satisfied if you know you've really looked hard into yourself and all your options.

Visit

Whether your list of schools has been set for months or fluctuates on a daily basis, college visits are a great way to narrow down your choices and prioritize your list of options. Try to plan campus visits so that you'll be finished by the fall of your senior year, especially if you are considering early application programs. Additionally, aim to see as many schools that interest you as possible—there's no better way to get a feel for where you'd like to spend the next four years of your life.

When you visit a campus, try to keep in mind why you are there. You have probably already seen the college viewbook with glossy pictures of green lawns and diverse groups of students in seminar-size classes. Now is the time to find out what the campus is really like. Is the student population truly that diverse? Do people really gather and play Frisbee on plush green lawns? What do the dorms actually look like? And most importantly, do you feel comfortable there?

If you are visiting a campus for an interview, make sure you schedule one in advance. Making the decision not to interview on campus may be a good one, however. While some schools require an on-campus interview, some insiders recommend that you request an alumni interview instead. Alumni interviews tend to be more significant in your application and less grueling than on-campus interviews. In any case, make sure you check a school's policy regarding interviews before you arrive, and schedule your visit accordingly.

While some prefer to visit colleges over summer vacation, we think the best time to visit is during the academic year, when regular classes are in session. During the summer months very few students are on campus, so it will be much more difficult to get a feel for the student culture and vibrancy (or lack thereof). For this reason, you'll also want to avoid exam periods and vacations. During the academic year, your questions about the campus are much more likely to be answered. You'll get a feel for the type of people at the school, and you'll get an idea of what it is like to be a student living on campus. It's important to get a good sense of what your daily life will be like if you end up attending the school.

Before you look at any college, take a little time to prepare. Perhaps you will want to come up with some kind of system to evaluate the schools you will visit. Putting together a list of characteristics that are important to you will make it easier to compare one school to the next, whether they be academics, the size of the campus, or the surrounding area's vibrancy and atmosphere.. Make sure you jot down some notes on the schools during and after your trips. Although colleges may seem easy to differentiate at the time, your impressions of each may blur together when you are back at home, sitting in front of 10 identical-looking applications.

An overnight stay with undergraduates can provide you with a more inside look at campus life. Most admissions offices have students on call who are happy to show you around campus, take you to some classes and parties, and let you crash in their dorms. If you have friends there, they are good resources as well. Either way, staying with students will help you see what an undergraduate's academic and social life is really like. One student said, "I found that it didn't matter much if I stayed over or not, as long as I got to talk to students. But if you do stay over, Thursday or Friday night is the best time." Sometimes it is hard to connect with students during a single day when everybody is rushing around to classes. Try to spend a night late in the week when students will have more time for you and the nightlife will be more vibrant. It is always possible that you will end up with hosts that are difficult to relate to or socially withdrawn. Don't let a bad hosting experience completely dictate your feelings about the college—just do everything you can to get out into the student body and explore what the school has to offer.

Keep in mind that college life doesn't consist entirely of classes. Sample the food, which is, after all, a necessity of life. Check out the dorms. Take the campus tour. Although you are sure to be inundated with obscure facts about the college that may not interest you, it can be useful to have a knowledgeable guide to show you the buildings themselves and the campus as a whole. If you have any questions, do not hesitate to ask. Tour guides are often students, and are a great resource for any information you want about the school.

Should you bring your parents along? Maybe. Some students prefer to leave them at home. Although parents don't mean any harm, they can sometimes get in the way. Your discomfort at having them around you when you're trying to get along with new students may cloud your opinion of a school. However, most students do bring along at least one family member. If you go this route, don't completely discount the advice or opinions they may have about the school. Parents can be great resources to bounce ideas off of, particularly regarding the pros and cons of the various colleges you have seen. You might want to take the campus tour with them, and then break-away to explore the campus on your own and talk with students one-on-one. When you enter college your parents will not be there with you, so it's a good idea to get a feel for what that will actually be like.

Most importantly, keep in mind your sense of the campus atmosphere. How does it feel to walk across the main quad? Does the mood seem intellectual or laid-back? Do T-shirts read "Earth Day Every Day" or "Coed Naked Beer Games"? Look for postings of events; some campuses are alive and vibrant while others seem pretty dead. Check your comfort level. Imagine yourself on the campus for the next four years and see how that makes you feel. Focus on these characteristics while you are on campus— you can read about the distribution requirements when you get back home. Most of all, enjoy yourself! The campus visit is an exciting peek into a world that will soon be your own.

The Interview

Just about every college applicant dreads the interview. It can be the most nerve-wracking part of the college application process. But relax—despite the horror stories you might have heard, the interview will rarely make or break your application. If you are a strong candidate, don't be overly self-assured; if your application makes you look like a hermit, be lively and personable. Usually the interview can only help you, and at some schools it is nothing more than an informational session. "I was constantly surprised at how many questions they let me ask," one applicant reported.

Consider the interview your chance to highlight the best parts of your application and explain the weaker parts without being whiny or making excuses. Are your SAT scores on the low side? Does your extracurricular section seem a little thin? An interview gives you the opportunity to call attention to your successes in classes despite your scores, or explain that of the three clubs you listed, you founded two and were president of the third.

There are a few keys to a successful interview.

1. The first and most important is to stand out from the crowd. Keep in mind that the interviewer probably sees half a dozen or more students every day, month after month. If you can make your interviewer laugh, interest him or her in something unusual you have done, or somehow spice up the same old questions and answers, you have had a great interview. Don't just say that you were the president of something; be able to back up your titles with interesting and genuine stories.

2. Do not try to be something you are not. Tell the truth, and give the interviewer a feel for who you really are—your passions, your strengths, and your challenges. By doing so, you will be more relaxed and confident. Even if you feel that the "real you" isn't that interesting or amazing, take time to reflect on your high school experience—the stories that surface in your mind may just surprise you.

3. A few days before the actual interview, think about some of the questions you might be asked. Some admissions officers begin every interview by asking, "Why do you want to go to this school, and why should we let you?" You should not have memorized speeches for every answer, but try not to get caught off guard. Make sure you really know why you want to attend this college. Even if you are not sure, think of a few plausible reasons and be prepared to give them. Students often make the mistake of giving a canned answer, which is okay since most answers are similar, but admissions officers look to admit students who want to take advantage of all that is available at their school. Your answer must include the three essential elements of a good reply: your interests, whether academic or extracurricular; what you believe the school will provide; and how and why you are excited about the opportunity to take advantage of them. Other common questions include those about your most important activities, what you did with your summers, and what vision you may have for your future.

4. A note of caution: If your interview takes place after you have submitted your application, the interviewer might ask you questions about some of the things you included. One student wrote on his application that he read *Newsweek* religiously. During his interview, the admissions officer asked the student about a story in a recent issue of the magazine. The student had no idea what the interviewer was talking about. He was not accepted. So be ready to back up your claims. It is always an excellent idea to indicate that you have a special interest in something, but make sure the interest is genuine—you may wind up in an hour-long conversation on the topic. Do not start talking about how you love learning about philosophy if you have only dabbled in it once. Do not try to use big words simply to sound impressive during what should be just a friendly chat. An open, thoughtful manner can do as much as anything else to impress your interviewer.

5. Being spontaneous in a contrived situation usually amounts to having a successful interview. If you are nervous, that's okay. Said one applicant, "I felt sick and I didn't eat for a day before the interview." The most common misconception is that admissions officers are looking for totally confident individuals who know everything and have their entire future planned out. Almost the opposite is true. An admissions officer at a selective private college said, "We do not expect imitation adults to walk through the door. We expect to see people in their last year or two of high school with the customary apprehensions, habits, and characteristics of that time of life." Admissions officers know students get nervous. They understand. If everything in your life is not perfect, do not be afraid to say so when appropriate. For example, if the conversation comes around to your high school, there is no need to cover up if problems do exist. It is okay to say you did not think your chemistry lab was

well equipped. An honest, realistic critique of your school or just about anything else will make a better impression than false praise ever could. Even more, someone with initiative who overcomes adversity is often more appealing than a person who goes to the "right" high school and coasts along.

6. If something you say does not come out quite right, try to react as you would with a friend. If the interviewer asks about your career plans, it is all right to say that you are undecided. As a high school student, no one expects you to have all the answers—that is why you are going to college. Above all, remember that the admissions officer is a person interested in getting to know you as an individual. A person who may be a parent to someone, a friend of someone's, a sibling of someone's. They empathize. As one interviewer explained, "I'm not there to judge the applicants as scholars. I'm just there to get a sense of them as people."

7. Do not get so worried about saying all the right things that you forget to listen carefully to the interviewer. The purpose of the interview is not to grill you, but to match you with the school in the best interest of both. Sometimes the interviewer will tell you, either during the interview or in a follow-up letter, that you have little chance of getting in. If she says so or implies it, know that such remarks are not made lightly. On the other hand, if she is sincerely encouraging, listen to that, too. If an interviewer suggests other schools for you to look into, remember that she is a professional and take note. Besides, many interviewers appreciate a student's ability to listen as well as to talk.

8. Your interviewer might ask you whether you have a first choice, particularly if her college is often seen as a backup. If the school is really not your first choice, fudge a little. Mention several colleges, including the one you are visiting, and say you have not made up your mind yet. Your first choice is your business, not theirs. If the school really is your first choice, though, feel free to say so, and give a good reason why. A genuine interest can be a real plug on your behalf.

9. Also know that you can direct the conversation. Do not worry about occasional lapses as some interviewers wait to see how you will react to a potentially awkward situation. Take advantage of the pause to ask a question, or bring up a relevant topic that really interests you. It is your job to present the parts of you and your background that you want noted.

10. Selective colleges need reasons to accept you. Being qualified on paper is not always enough. Think of the interviewer's position: "Why should we accept you instead of thousands of other qualified applicants?" The answer to that question should be evident in every response you give. Use the interview to play up and accentuate your most memorable qualities. Show flashes of the playful sense of humor that your English teacher cites in his recommendation; impress the interviewer with the astute eye for politics about which your history teacher raves.

11. Too many applicants are afraid to talk confidently about their accomplishments. If the interviewer is impressed by something, do not insist that it was not much, or he might believe you. If he is not impressed by something you think is important, tactfully let him know that he should be. But do not, under any circumstances, act like you are too good for the college. One well-qualified applicant to a leading college was turned down when the interviewer wrote, "It obviously isn't going to be the end of his world if he doesn't get in. And it won't be the end of our world, either." If there is any quality you want to convey, it is a sincere interest in the school.

12. Almost all interviewers will eventually ask, "Do you have any questions about our school?" Come to the interview armed with a good question or two, and not one whose answer is easily found in the college's viewbook or on the school Web site. Do not ask if they have an economics department, for example—ask the average class size in introductory economics courses. It may help to do some extra preparation ahead of time. Are you interested in studying abroad? If so, know what kind of programs the school offers and ask a few questions about them. If you are excited to learn more about the school and have already done some homework, it goes a long way in the eyes of the interviewer. Also, if the interviewer is an alumnus, a good question is to ask what they would have done differently during their time at the college. You can be sure that they will need a moment of reflection, and you'll have time to relax!

13. You will probably wonder what to wear. This is no life or death decision, but remember that your appearance is one of the first things the interviewer will notice about you. Wear something you will be comfortable in—a jacket and a tie or a nice dress are fine. Do not, however, be too casual. Faded jeans and a T-shirt will give the impression that you are taking the interview too lightly. But, if your interview is at Starbucks as opposed to someone's office building, take their choice in location as a cue for dress.

14. One crucial point: Keep your parents a thousand feet and preferably a thousand miles away from the interview session. It will be harder to relax and be genuine with an additional set of eyes on you, and you might hold back some interesting information. When parents sit in, interviews tend to be short, boring, and useless. If the interviewer feels you cannot handle an hour without your parents, she might be concerned about your ability to survive the pressures of college life. Take the risk of hurting your parents' feelings and ask them to wait outside.

    Once the interview is over, it is perfectly all right for your parents to ask any questions they may have if the interviewer walks with you back to the waiting room. Even if this makes you uncomfortable, do not let it show. Admissions officers can learn as much about you by the way you treat your parents as they do in the interview. The interviewer is not judging your parents. As long as you conduct yourself calmly and maturely, you have got nothing to worry about.

15. It is a good idea to send a thank you note after the interview. It doesn't need to be extensive, just let the interviewer know that you appreciate the time she or he spent with you and enjoyed learning more about the school. While it doesn't seem like much, a simple note can leave a lasting impression. Be sure to say something specific to your interview. If you shared a laugh or if the interviewer mentioned something about his or her job, try to slip something personal into the note. All of this advice applies for interviews given by alumni as well as those conducted by admissions staff. Alumni interviewers sometimes carry slightly less weight with the admissions office, but they are valuable contacts with the schools and should not be taken lightly. Expect on-campus interviews to be a bit more formal than alumni interviews.

What if you do not have an interview at all? Perhaps you live too far away, and you cannot get to the school itself. Or, perhaps you feel that your lack of poise is serious enough that it would work against you in any interview you had. Talk it over with your guidance counselor. In general, geographic isolation is a valid excuse for not having an interview, and most colleges will not hold it against you. Ask if they will allow a phone interview instead. Yet, if the college is fairly close and makes it clear that applicants should have an on-campus interview if at all possible, make the effort to go. Otherwise, the college will assume that for some reason you were afraid to interview, or worse, that you simply did not care enough to have one. If the prospect is genuinely terrifying, schedule your first interview for a safety school, or ask your guidance counselor to grant you a practice interview. You might discover that the process is not as horrible as you originally thought.

The Tests

Whether you are an Olympic hopeful, a musical prodigy, or a third-generation legacy, you cannot avoid taking standardized tests if you want to go to college. Approximately 90 percent of all four-year institutions now require some type of admissions test. Certainly tests do not tell the whole story; grades, recommendations, extracurricular activities, the application essays, and personal interviews round out the picture. However, standardized test scores are often the only uniform criteria available to admissions committees. They are meant to indicate the level of education you have had in the past, as well as your potential to succeed in the future.

Virtually all of the nation's colleges require applicants to submit SAT I or ACT scores. In addition, some colleges will ask their applicants for SAT II subject test scores. If you are an international student with a native language other than English (or recently moved from an education system using a foreign language), you may be required to take the TOEFL as well. If you take AP tests or are in an IB program, your scores could help you earn college credit if they agree with the score requirements of the college you are applying to. Does all this seem overwhelming to you? Read this section and hopefully we can help you understand each test a little better.

The Scholastic Aptitude Test (SAT) is the most widely chosen admissions test by college applicants. Administered by the Educational Testing Service (ETS) and created by the College Board, the SAT I: Reasoning Test currently has a math section, a critical reading section, and a writing section. A nearly four-hour test, there are a total of 10 sections; two are writing, three are verbal, three are math, and there is an unscored variable section (math or critical reading) thrown in somewhere. The new math section has been upgraded to include material up through Geometry and Algebra II, and, to your benefit, you are allowed to use calculators. It has five-choice multiple-choice questions and questions where you produce the answer yourself. In the critical reading section, you will find sentence completions and short and long passages with reading comprehension questions.

The SAT I scores the math, critical reading, and writing sections separately on a 200 to 800 scale. Therefore, your combined score can be a minimum of 600 and a maximum of 2400. One disadvantage with the SAT I is that you are penalized for wrong answers, so avoid guessing haphazardly. However, if you can eliminate a few answer choices, it is often better to guess than to leave the question blank. The average score for each section is a 500 based on the recentered scale that the ETS implemented starting in 1995. When the SAT was originally calibrated, it was done so that the average score for the math and verbal sections would each be 500. Over several decades, the average dropped—some say as a result of the declining American education system. However, others argue that the perceived "decrease" is not surprising considering that today's over two million SAT-takers are much more representative of American education as a whole than the 10,000 primarily affluent prep-school students who took the test when it was implemented in 1941. As a result, the scoring was recentered in 1995 in order to redistribute scores more evenly along the 200 to 800 scale. All colleges and scholarship institutions are aware of this new scoring calibration, so even though it may be easier to get that rare 800 section score, your percentile rank among other students who took the exam will not change.

There are five ways to register for the SAT. The two most common methods are to complete an online registration at www.college-board.com or mail in a registration form, which you can get from your high school counselor's office. If you've registered for an SAT Program test before, you can complete the registration over the phone. For those students living outside of the United States, U.S. territories, and Puerto Rico, there is an option to fax in your registration. International students have the option of registering through a representative found in the International Edition of the SAT Registration Bulletin. The SAT is administered seven times a year in the domestic areas, and six times a year overseas.

Before you take the test, be sure to take advantage of two services offered by the College Board upon registration. The first is called the Student Search Service and allows universities, colleges, and scholarship programs to get general information about you, as well as what range your score falls into. You will receive a flood of information about different universities, colleges, and scholarship programs in the mail in addition to information regarding financial aid opportunities. While you'll begin to see most of these letters as junk mail, some of them will help you come up the list of colleges to which you intend to apply. As a second service the College Board will mail your test scores to a maximum of four specified schools or scholarship programs for free. You can send additional score reports for a fee. Be aware that if you have taken the SAT I more than once, all of your previous scores will be sent when reporting to schools and scholarship programs. If you have second thoughts and want to cancel your scores, you must do so by the Wednesday following your exam via e-mail, fax, or mail.

The American College Test (ACT) was required mostly by colleges in the southern and western regions of the country, but is now accepted by most colleges across the nation. The exam covers English, reading, mathematics, and science reasoning in the format of 215 multiple-choice questions. It also offers an optional writing component. One distinguishing feature of the ACT is that it measures what you have learned in the high school curriculum rather than your aptitude.

The ACT, unlike the SAT I, does not deduct any points for incorrect answers, so be sure to fill in every bubble. You will receive a score on a scale of 1 to 36 for each of the four subject areas; your Composite score is just an average of the four scores rounded to the nearest whole number. Based on the over 1.1 million students who choose to take the test, the average Composite score is around 21. Registration is much like the SAT I, with a mail-in option, online registration at www.act.org, or telephone preregistration. There is a stand-by registration option for those who forget to register. As far as score reporting goes, you can choose up to six schools or scholarship programs on your registration to have the scores sent to for free. The great thing about the ACT is that you can choose to send just one testing date's scores instead of having your whole history of scores sent, as is done with the SAT I.

Many of the more selective colleges also require up to three SAT II exams, formerly called Achievement Tests. Available subjects include English, a variety of foreign languages, math, history, and several of the sciences. Due to the changes in the SAT I: Reasoning Test, there is no longer a writing exam available. One thing about the SAT II is that you don't have to choose which tests you want to take until you're at the test center on the test date. The scores are reported on a 200 to 800 scale, but Score Choice is no longer an option. Score Choice had allowed students to put their subject tests on hold until they had decided which scores to send to universities, colleges, and scholarship agencies. It posed problems in giving those who could pay for more tests an unfair advantage and also in that students would often forget to send their scores later on. The College Board abandoned this option in 2002; now all SAT II scores are reported, but only your highest in each subject will be taken into consideration.

The Test of English as a Foreign Language (TOEFL) is an English proficiency test provided for international students who want to study in the United States, Canada, or other English-speaking countries. It is administered on the computer or by paper-and-pencil depending on the location you choose. The scale for your total score is from 0 to 300 along with a score of 0 to 6 for the essay, which is scored separately. The TOEFL will test your listening, structured writing, and reading skills—giving a better picture of your English to the schools you apply to. Advanced Placement (AP) exams are another animal altogether since their purpose is not to get you into college, but instead to earn you credits once you get there. Administered in May, each test covers a specific subject area and scores you from 1 to 5. Different schools require different scores for granting college credit. Some will offer credit but still require you to take classes in a subject that you aced on the AP exams. Since the tests require in-depth knowledge of specific subjects, do not put off studying for them. It is generally a good idea to take the exam in a particular subject the May right after you have finished (or are in the midst of finishing) a course in that area. Not only can you get college credit with a high score, but you can also help your college applications with AP exams taken before your senior year.

If you attend an International Baccalaureate (IB) school, you might be able to receive college credit for your coursework depending on your score. A score of 4 or 5 are the required minimum by a college for credit and/or placement, but many institutions require a higher score of 6 or 7. Although not as popularly embraced by colleges and universities across the nation for giving college credit, they will definitely recognize you for the rigorous work you have completed in the program.

You may have already taken the PSAT/NM-SQT, which is usually administered to sophomores or juniors through their high school. This is a great practice exam for the SAT I because it has a lot of the same type of questions. It is also a good way to qualify for merit scholarships if you get a high score. The PSAT changed its format in the fall of 2004 to complement the new SAT I in 2005.

The most reliable way to keep up-to-date on test dates, sites, and registration deadlines is through your high school guidance office. After the PSAT, you will be on your own about when and where you take the tests. Find out way ahead of time which ones are required by the colleges you are interested in; deadlines have a way of sneaking up on you. It is a good idea to begin taking the tests by the spring of your junior year. If you take the SAT I in March or May of your junior year and do not do as well as you think you should, you will have a couple of other opportunities to improve your score. The required SAT II exams should be taken by June of your junior year so that if you decide to apply to an early-action or early-decision program, you will have completed the required testing.

Avoid postponing required testing until November, December, or January of your senior year. One new college student, who put off his exams until the last minute, recalled his college freshman faculty advisor saying to him, "I just don't understand it . . . you went to one of the best high schools in Chicago and did very well. How could your SAT scores have been so low?" He told her how lucky he felt just getting into college; he had contracted a nasty flu and thrown up before, during, and after the test! On the other hand, do not repeat tests over and over. The ETS reports that students can gain an average of 25 points on both the math and verbal sections of the SAT I if they take the test a second time. Two or three shots at the SATs should be sufficient. If you've got the time and money, you may want to consider taking a prep course given by a professional test-preparation service. National test-prep companies like Kaplan and the Princeton Review, as well as dozens of local companies, attempt to give helpful tips on how to take tests for those willing to shell out hundreds of dollars. If you do decide to take a prep course, take it seriously. You may have six or seven high school classes to worry about, but you cannot hope to get your money's worth if you do not attend all of the sessions and complete the homework in these prep courses.

Many people choose not to take practice courses. A good student who is confident about taking tests can probably do just as well studying on his or her own. Practice exams are available online and in commercially marketed practice books. Get acquainted with the tests you plan to take beforehand; you should not have to waste time during your exam re-reading instructions and trying to figure out what to do. It's a good idea to even simulate an actual test by timing yourself with no interruptions on a real test that was previously administered.

The College Board puts out a book called *10 Real SATs* that proves to be one of the most effective ways to prepare for the SAT I. True to its title, the book has official SATs from the past, along with hints, test-taking strategies, and exercises to help you improve your test score. The ACT has a similar book called *Getting into the ACT* with two complete exams plus ACT's own analyses and explanations designed to help you with the test. Getting the chance to practice exams in a real test-like situation (no phones, family, or friends to distract you) will help you to get a keener sense of the overall structure of the test and help you work faster during the actual exam. It might also help you relax!

Do not cram the night before the exam. Get plenty of sleep and relax. "My teacher encouraged us to go out and have a good time the day before," recalled one first-year college student. "So I went to the movies as a distraction. I think it worked!" On the day of the test, eat a full breakfast that isn't too heavy, dress comfortably, and do not forget to bring two pieces of ID, a calculator, a couple of number two pencils, and a pencil sharpener. Make sure you are up early and know where you will be taking the test as well as how to get there. The test center may be overcrowded, there may be no air-conditioning or heat, and a hundred construction workers may be drilling outside the nearest window—be prepared for anything!

The key to success on any of these exams is to keep calm. During the exam, keep track of how many problems there are and allot time accordingly. Read and attempt to answer every question since you do not get more credit for the hard ones than the easy ones. If you are stuck on a question, try to eliminate as many answers as possible and select from the remaining choices. Only if you really have no clue about the question should you leave it blank on the SAT. Just remember to also leave a blank on your answer sheet!

A word of warning: Do not even think about cheating. It is not worth it, and your chances of getting caught and blackballed from college are high. To weed out cheaters, the ETS uses the mysterious K-index, a statistical tool that measures the chance of two students selecting the same answers. If your K-index is suspect, a form letter goes out to the colleges you are interested in, delaying your score until you retake the exam or prove your innocence. Know that looking at another person's test is not the only activity that the ETS considers cheating. Going back to finish work on a previous section is also against the rules. Do not tempt fate—a low score is better than no score at all.

At the beginning of this section, we stressed that standardized tests are important. How important? It varies depending on the school you are applying to. At many state schools, admission depends almost entirely on test scores and grades; if you score above the cutoffs, you are in. With the more selective schools, scores are usually only one of many important factors in the admissions process. According to the dean of admissions at Harvard University, "If scores are in the high 500 to low 700 range, they probably have a fairly small impact on our decisions." Each of the schools in this book lists a mean score range for the SAT I. Remember that there are students who score below this range and above this range that were accepted to that college. Unless you score far below or far above the mean of your desired college, most likely your SAT I score will not make or break your chances of getting in. If you attended an inner-city school or a school in an area of the country where education standards are below the norm, your apparent deficit might, in fact, indicate a strength—as long as you are above the minimum levels.

Many students mistakenly believe that the SAT is the only test that "really matters" in competitive college admissions. In fact, SAT II scores taken as a whole are usually of equal importance. Colleges will often view these scores as a more accurate predictor of future performance than the SAT I. Aside from tests, it is important to remember that your high school record is weighed heavily. If you bomb your admissions tests, but have decent grades, there's a chance that your high school performance can outweigh the bad test scores. However, a poor GPA is hard to overlook, even if your scores are high. Remember that your admissions test scores are just a portion of the whole picture you present to the colleges. So try your best to make it advantageous for you and don't worry if you don't get a perfect score!

The Application

It's the fall of your senior year of high school. You've done your research, and found a few schools that you're interested in. You've taken the standardized tests, you've visited the campuses, and you may even have had some on-campus interviews. You still have one major hurdle ahead of you, however: The Application. Though the piles of paperwork may seem daunting, with some advance planning you can make the application process as painless as possible.

First, you have to decide where you want to apply. You should have this done no later than the first few weeks of your senior year. After talking to students and visiting campuses, try to narrow down your original list of colleges to somewhere between five and 15. Applying to any more schools than this is probably overkill. Not only is it a waste of time to apply to more schools than necessary, it is also a waste of money to apply to any school you won't be happy attending—application processing fees can run as high as $65 per school. However, you want to apply to enough schools that you'll be sure to get accepted somewhere.

It's also important to think about the selectivity of the schools you apply to. Don't be scared to apply to your dream school

even if your SAT score or GPA is a bit low. On the other hand, make sure to apply to at least one or two "safety schools," where you'll be both happy and stand an excellent chance of getting accepted. A good rule of thumb is to apply to at least one "reach" school, a school that may be a long-shot to get into, but one where you'd love to go, at least one "safety school," and a few schools in between.

After you've listed the schools where you'll apply, get the applications and figure out when each of them are due. It may be a good idea to make a list of deadlines, both early and regular, and hang it somewhere in your room. Many schools allow you to download their applications from their Web sites. Others send them to you in the mail; if this is the case, make sure you request the application in plenty of time to fill it out carefully and send it in. Whatever you do, make sure you get your applications in on time. Many schools won't even look at applications they receive late, so make deadlines a priority.

Different schools accept applications in a variety of ways. A brief description of the major types of applications follows:

- *Rolling Admissions:* Most large public schools and many less-selective colleges accept "rolling applications," which means they process applications continuously, in the order they receive them. You hear back from the school a few weeks after you send in your application. Though these schools often accept applications into the spring, it is important to send in your application early because admittance often becomes more challenging as these schools accept more and more students. Try to send in applications to schools with rolling deadlines as early as you can.

- *Regular Decision:* Colleges that don't offer rolling admissions typically require all your application materials to be sent by a specific date, usually in December or sometimes in January. The applications are processed and evaluated all at the same time, so while it is still an excellent idea to send in your application materials as early as possible, there is no automatic advantage to applying as soon as you can, as there is with rolling admissions. Whereas with rolling admissions, you'll hear back from the college within a few weeks, with regular decision all applicants hear back from the school at the same time. Many schools have separate parts of the application with different deadlines, so be prepared to organize your calendar so as not to miss any deadlines. Acceptances and rejections get mailed in early April.

- *Early Decision:* Some schools offer an "early decision" option as part of their regular decision program. However, a recent push by presidents of several top universities (including Harvard, Stanford, Yale and others) is working to erode this option since it hurts economically disadvantaged students who would need to compare financial aid packages in making their decision. Typically available at more selective colleges, the early-decision program allows you to apply to one school by mid-October or November, and will respond to you by mid-December either with an acceptance, a rejection, or a deferral. An acceptance to a school under an early decision program is binding. This means that when you apply early decision, you sign a contract stating that you absolutely commit to attending that school if you are accepted. Rejections are final. A deferral means that the admissions committee will wait to make a decision about your application until they see what the regular pool of applicants is like. If you are deferred from an early decision acceptance but are accepted with the regular pool, the contract is no longer binding, and you may choose to attend a different school. Failure to comply with the agreement can lead to unpleasant consequences like being blackballed from other schools.

  Early decision does have some advantages. By expressing a clear interest in one school, you may gain some advantage in admissions, and if accepted you'll already know where you're going to school in December. However, by no means feel that you need to apply to a school under an early decision commitment. You should not apply to a school early decision unless you are totally, completely, positively sure that the school is your first choice, and you should not apply early decision if you feel like your credentials will improve significantly during your first semester of your senior year. Rejections under early decision are final, so if you think your application will be stronger after another semester, you should wait until you can provide the best application possible.

- *Early Action:* Early action has become an increasingly common option at schools across the country. Like early decision, early action offers applicants a chance to find out in December if they've been admitted. However, the acceptance is not binding; if you get accepted to another school in April that you would prefer to attend, you're welcome to do so. This provides a convenient alternative for students who want to hear back from a school as soon as possible, but aren't ready to commit to attending a particular school right away. Some institutions, such as Stanford and Yale, now offer single-choice early action programs. Under these plans acceptance is still non-binding, but students may not submit an early application (early action or early decision) to any other institution. This allows early applicants to compare financial aid packages from the regular round of admissions before making a decision.

Once you know when your applications will be due, it's time to start filling out the paperwork. There are a few general guidelines to follow. First, read the entire application carefully before you begin. Plan what you are going to say in each section before you write anything. It is a great idea to make a photocopy of the application to "practice" on before you fill out the official form. Always fill out or type the application yourself. If you're going to hand-write the application, try to use the same pen for the entire thing, to remain consistent in ink color and thickness. If you're going to use a printer, use a standard font like Times New Roman or Arial, and use the best printer you can find. Presentation and neatness count. If the application specifically suggests that you handwrite anything, be sure to do so, but draft exactly what you're going to write on scrap paper so that you don't have to make any corrections on the actual application.

More and more colleges nationwide are coming to accept the Common Application in lieu of applications specifically tailored for their schools. With a standard format and several general essays, you can fill out this application—online or on paper—once and submit to any of the participating schools. It makes the application process somewhat less burdensome and time-consuming, although you may still want to consider tweaking essays to better fit the demands of each individual college.

Applications are usually divided up into several sections. All of them are important, and you should use all of them to your advantage. The following explanations of the application sections include some things you should remember when filling out your application:

- *Personal Information:* This section is fairly straightforward. It asks for general information about you, your school, and your family. Since all applications will ask for pretty much the same information, it's a good idea to keep it all on an index card so that you can easily reference it whenever you need to. This section often includes a question about race. Though this question is optional, you can go ahead and answer it; it won't hurt you, and the answer could help you. If you do answer, don't try to "stretch the truth;" answer it the way you would on a census form. Legal debates about affirmative action have gotten a lot of attention in recent years, but you still should not worry about answering this question.

- *Standardized Tests:* This is another relatively easy section to fill out. Most applications require you to fill in your tests scores here, but also require you to have copies of your scores sent from the testing companies to the admissions offices. Make sure you do this in enough time for the test scores to arrive at the admissions office well before applications are due. Also, be sure you pay attention to which tests are required by your school. Some schools don't require test scores at all, others require either SAT and SAT II or ACT scores, still others specify which they want. Be sure your school receives all of the scores that it needs.

- *Extracurricular Activities:* This is the first section where your personality and accomplishments can shine through; be sure to make the most of it. Your extracurriculars allow the admissions office to see what you do when you're not studying. Sports, clubs, publications, student government, jobs, and volunteer positions are examples of some of the activities that fall into this category. Make sure to follow directions carefully when filling out this section. Some schools want you to write your activities directly on the form; others allow you to attach a typed list to the application instead. If you have the option to type a list it's a good idea to do so, even if the rest of your application is handwritten. It looks neater, you'll have more space for all your activities, and you can just print out a copy of the list for each school that requests it. Just make sure to adapt the list to the particular requirements of the school. If the application instructs you to list your activities in chronological order, do so. Otherwise it is best to list activities in order of their importance to you.

A few final words about extracurriculars—quality is more important than quantity. It is infinitely better to have long-term involvement and leadership positions in a few activities than it is to join a thousand groups to which you devoted only an hour a month. Admissions officers can tell when you're just trying to pad your résumé with activities. They look more highly on passion and commitment to a few activities that reflect who you are and what interests you. You're also more likely to stand out to admissions officers if you have dedicated your time to an activity or subject that few others have explored. Admissions officers come across countless tennis captains and student-body presidents, but few national kayaking champions.

- *Transcript:* Your transcript is a window into your academic history. Admissions officers look at your grades and class rank, and they also look at the types of classes you've taken. A high GPA is important, but so is the number of AP or Honors courses you've had. Colleges look for students who challenge themselves. At this point you can't go back and fix that C you got in freshman biology, but you can do a few things to make your transcript look as good as possible. First, make sure everything is accurate. Check that your grades are correct, and that every honors class you have taken is listed as such. Second, remember that colleges will see your grades from senior year. Don't pad your schedule with blow-off courses; make sure to continue to take challenging classes. Try not to let yourself develop a serious case of "senioritis," because admissions committees will think that you don't take academics seriously. Also, if you received a poor grade in a particular class because of a certain situation, or you struggled all of sophomore year because someone you loved passed away, feel free to write an additional essay explaining any vast discrepancies. Lastly, request transcripts from your school as soon as you can. They can take a while to print, and you don't want your application to be late because you did not get your transcript in time.

• *Recommendations:* Many schools request letters of recommendation from teachers, coaches, or other adults who know you well. These letters let the admissions officers see how others view you and your potential. Most people will be happy to write a good recommendation for you. If a teacher doesn't feel comfortable recommending you, he or she will most likely not agree to write a letter for you. So don't worry about a teacher trashing you behind your back; it probably won't happen.

Do think carefully about whom you choose to write these letters, though. You want to choose teachers who know you personally and with whom you have a good relationship. It's a good idea to choose teachers in your strong subjects, but it's also important to demonstrate some diversity of interest. For example, it is better to have your English teacher and your physics teacher write recommendations than it is to have two math teachers write them. Whomever you choose, make sure to provide them with plenty of time to write and revise a strong recommendation. You may even want to contact them before the summer of your senior year and let them know you'd like them to write on your behalf. That will give them ample time to write a shining letter! Many colleges want your teachers to send recommendations in separate from the rest of your application. If so, don't forget to give teachers a stamped and addressed envelope in which to send it. Be assertive; there's nothing wrong with reminding your teachers about the recommendation, and asking before the deadline if they'd gotten it done. Most teachers are careful about these deadlines, but it does not hurt to make sure.

Additionally, most recommendation forms have a line asking you to waive your right to see the recommendation. You should probably sign it. Signing the waiver shows confidence that your teachers respect you and gives the recommendation more credibility. Finally, though most schools only require two recommendations from teachers, some allow you to send additional recommendations from others who know you well. Though by no means required or necessary, this is a good opportunity for students with significant activities outside of school-affiliated activities to get people like coaches, art tutors, or employers to say something helpful. Don't go overboard on these though; one extra recommendation is more than enough. Content is more important than the person who writes

it. It's not impressive to get your state senator to write a recommendation for you if he's never met you before.

• *The Essay:* The college essay strikes fear in the hearts of high school seniors every fall, but you should not think about it as something scary. Instead, consider it an opportunity to show your wonderful, special, unique personality while telling the admissions officers a bit about yourself. If you give yourself plenty of time and have some fun with it, it can actually be the most enjoyable part of your application.

Think about your topic carefully, but do not kill yourself trying to come up with a topic that you think an admissions officer will like. It's always a good idea to write about something that is meaningful to you. If you feel strongly about the topic it will show through in your writing, and that will catch an admissions officer's attention. Too many students write about a class project or winning the state championship—try to describe any experiences that are less common. You want your personality and your passion to shine through. Though it might seem obvious, it's worth restating that you should be sure to answer whatever question the application asks. Sometimes you can reuse an essay for more than one school, but don't try to make an essay fit a topic just so you don't have to write another one. And be prepared to write several different essays if you're applying to a lot of schools.

Once your topic is chosen, give yourself enough time to write a good rough draft. It's sometimes intimidating to begin writing, but just put your pen to paper and start. It doesn't matter what your draft looks like at first; you'll have plenty of time to correct and edit it later. Since the essay is the part of the application where you can be yourself, write in a way that feels natural to you, whether that's humorous or serious or something completely different. You should never submit a first draft to a college. Revise your essay a few times, both for style and for content. If the application gives you a word limit, stick to it.

Once you feel confident about the essay, it's a good idea to have a teacher, parent, older sibling, or counselor look over it for you. They can both help you find technical mistakes in spelling and grammar, and can point out places where you could be more clear in your content. By all means have others help you out with your essay in these ways, but under no circumstances should you ever, ever let anyone else write your essay for you. Not only is this dishonest, admissions officers read thousands of essays every year, and so have a good eye for essays that do not seem to be written by a particular student. Once your essay has been drafted, revised, edited, and perfected, you can either hand-write it on the application form, or, if the school allows, you can attach a typed version to the form.

Once your application is complete, put a stamp on the envelope, and pat yourself on the back. Your application was honest, well thought-out, neat, and will show the admissions committee who you are. Though you might want to call the admissions office in a week or so to make sure they've received all your materials, there is not much left to stress out about. Once the application is in the mail it's out of your hands, so kick back, relax, and enjoy the end of your senior year. You deserve it.

The Wait

There is probably nothing anybody can say to you at this point to make you feel secure and confident regarding your applications. Your worries of the last few months about application deadlines and teacher recommendations are now petty concerns, replaced with the general unease that comes with the uncertain ground of your fate resting in somebody else's hands. Your applications are in the mail (and by now they have arrived at various admissions offices across the state and country.) You hope they did, anyway. You are finished with the applications, but have only just begun the long road of anxiety.

Well, all is not lost. While it is nearly impossible to distract you from the near-constant pressure of the uncertainty regarding your future, we can at least let you know a little more about what is going on in the office.

Your application will arrive and most likely be put into an anonymous-looking, plain envelope. It will then be given to the admission officer who is in charge of your district or school. In some larger schools, you will not get much individual attention: There are often grade and SAT/ACT score cutoffs that they use to determine who gets admitted. In smaller, private schools that can afford it, your application will be considered much more closely. Generally, your application will be read by up to three or four officers. Some schools use a numbering system to rate your academic record, your standardized test scores, and your extracurricular activities. There are some "bonus points" that you may end up with for uncontrollable variables such as your economic or racial background, or your relationship to an alumnus of the school.

Mostly, your application will speak for itself. While some schools weigh academics over extracurriculars, others might want to see high levels of community involvement or strong standardized test scores. This is where things are entirely out of your control. Each school is looking for a diverse group of students. The schools keep their academic standards relatively high, while looking for people from every possible background with every possible interest. If there happen to be 20 other students just like you from Houston, Texas, with 1350 SATs, a 3.5 GPA, roles in several school plays, and playing time on the varsity basketball team, all 20 will probably not be accepted. Likewise, if you happen to be the only student applying with an 1100 SAT, 2.8 GPA, and work founding a nonprofit organization to help teach English to needy children in Africa, you would probably look more unique and attractive to the admissions officer. It is fantastically frustrating, but in the end much of this process is out of your control. You are not only competing to be good enough for a school, but you are competing against everybody else who is applying to the school. When the decision has been made, the myth is generally true: Big, thick envelopes often have big admit letters inside. The thin ones often bring bad news. You will probably be receiving a mix of these, so don't let a poor first response get you down. You may end up knowing the decision before the envelope ever reaches your mailbox. Each year, more schools are experimenting with letting students find out their acceptance status online.

The good news is that thin envelopes sometimes bring news of a place on the wait list. The last thing you want to do in this situation is anger the admissions office. Surely, a place on the wait list is disappointing. There are only two things that can help you get off, however. First and foremost, the best you can hope for is a lot of luck. Your eventual admission depends a lot on how many people reject their offers of admission. The second factor is how you act: Admissions offices do like to see people eager to attend their school. A simple letter stating your excitement about the school and your eagerness to attend may help nudge things in your direction. Anything pestering or negative directed at the admissions office will ensure you a rejection letter.

Admissions officers are quick to admit that they turn away an incredible number of qualified applicants every year; enough, in fact, to more than fill two separate classes of equal strength. The decision process, therefore, often seems arbitrary. You may end up on the wait list of one of your safety schools, and find yourself accepted at the strongest school you applied to. You simply cannot know what is going to happen until you receive the letters. In the end, you should choose the school where you feel most comfortable. If you can afford to, visit the schools you are considering. Otherwise, try to call students there and get a better feel for the campus. Even if one school has a better name than another, you may not be as happy there. There is no absolute way to measure your potential happiness at a school, and although it may not seem this way now, you will probably be happy anywhere you end up. The best advice we can offer you is to follow your instincts. If you get some kind of feeling about a school, go with it! There is no better reason out there to make a decision.

For now, sit back and relax. It's your senior year, your very last semester in high school. While you can't start failing your classes now, there is plenty of room left for you to chill out. Do what you can to forget about your applications (and stress about work) and instead think about how you can make the most out of your last couple months of high school. Be proud that your applications are finished and go out and have some fun!

The Money

Best case scenario: you get into the college of your dreams. Worst case scenario: you get into the college of your dreams and you realize you cannot pay for it. With many of the nation's most expensive colleges quickly passing the $30,000 annual tuition mark, adding up to $120,000+ for a four-year education, it is no wonder that many students are talking as much about finances as they are about SAT scores. Although few families can afford this expensive price tag, especially if there is more than one member of the family attending college, there are many resources to aid families in paying for college. You should never hesitate to apply to a college simply because of its "sticker price." Many colleges

meet most, if not all, of a family's financial need with a combination of scholarships, grants, loans, and work-study programs.

The most important step you can take as a student is to openly discuss your family's financial situation at the outset of your college search. Talk about how much your family is able to pay for college, how much your parents are willing to take out in loans, and other financial topics. By initiating this discussion with your family, you are showing them that you are both responsible and sensitive to your family's financial situation.

Your biggest advantage in the financial aid game is to be organized. As you will find out, there are many forms that you must fill out in order to even begin applying for financial aid. Getting organized helps you to see exactly where you stand in the financial aid process. The money is not going to land on your doorstep, so you have to be proactive in looking for it. There are plenty of resources available to you, but you have to know where to look for it.

A good place to start is with your college guidance counselor. Counselors have the knowledge and experience in helping students like yourself get into college and pay for college. Oftentimes, they receive information from colleges regarding scholarships and will post them around the school. Take note of these announcements and fill out the applications as soon as possible. The applications can be time consuming, but if you are well-organized, there should be no problem. The following Web sites also provide useful information for students seeking financial aid: www.finaid.org and www.fastweb.com. The more persistent and diligent you are in your search, the better your chances will be for finding the resources you need.

The best sources for financial aid are the colleges themselves. Colleges oftentimes earmark large sums of money specifically for financial aid. Many colleges also receive money from federal and private sources for financial aid purposes. Scholarships come in a variety of forms, including need-based, and merit or achievement awards. You will need to look at what types of financial aid the schools that you are considering offer. Be aware of which colleges offer only need-based financial aid packages and which colleges offer merit and/or achievement scholarships. The policies and practices at each school can vary significantly, so it is important that you have the information you need.

Carefully read the bulletins provided by the colleges you are considering. If you have any questions, e-mail or call the admissions office or financial aid office right away. Find out what the colleges' admissions policies are regarding financial aid applicants. Some of the nation's wealthier schools have need-blind admissions, which means that you are considered for admission without taking into account your family's ability to pay. However, at some schools, financial need may play a part in the final admission decision, especially in borderline cases where preference may be given to those with the ability to pay. Even if you do not think you can afford it, apply to the school and for the financial aid. Then, just wait and see. You might be pleasantly surprised. Sometimes it is cheaper to attend a more expensive college because they often provide superior aid packages. Of course this is not always the case, but it does prove that you should never decide against a school because of money until you have a financial aid offer (or rejection) in your hand.

As a financial aid applicant, you will soon notice all that paperwork involved. Most schools require you to file a standardized need analysis form to determine an expected family contribution (EFC). Depending on the school, the form will either be the College Board's Profile form or the U.S. Department of Education's Free Application for Federal Student Aid (FAFSA), or in some cases, both. The school will also have its own financial form for you to fill out, which you have to send along with the family's income tax forms for verification. The school will determine a reasonable family contribution for one year. (The student is also usually expected to contribute at least $1,000 from summer earnings.) To come up with an estimate, a formula established by Congress is used. The formula takes into account family income, expenses, assets, liabilities, savings accounts, and other data. The cost of attendance minus this expected family contribution yields an approximate financial need. The school then designs a financial aid package that may consist of a low-interest, federally guaranteed loan, a work-study job, and a combination of different types of grants. This would lead one to believe that all packages would be similar, yet this is not always the case. Even though all schools receive the same input data, they do not all use the same formula. The family contribution will thus vary slightly, but there should not be a big difference. The difference in aid packages comes mainly from the way the school issues money. Some schools may require you to get more loans, or they might give you more money.

Some schools will always make better offers than others. Some wealthier schools guarantee to meet the full "demonstrated" need of every applicant that they accept. At other colleges, however, the financial aid package may leave an "unmet" need that you will have to cover on your own. In unfortunate cases like these, students can bear the extra financial burden or choose a college that gives them a better offer.

There are a few things that you can do to improve your chances of receiving an adequate financial aid package from a school. First of all, be efficient in getting all of the forms in as early as possible. Some schools have a limited supply of funds available for financial aid, and the earlier they look at your application, the better your chance of receiving a larger share. Getting your forms in early shows a good-faith effort on your part, and schools are more likely to be cooperative with you if they feel you are being cooperative with them. Another thing you can do is write a letter to the financial aid office explaining any special family circumstances that are not reflected on the financial aid forms. If you do not let the school know about such situations, there is no way they can take them into account.

If a school offers you a financial aid package that you consider inadequate despite your best efforts to let them know about your family situation, all is still not lost. After you have been accepted at the school, make a polite call to the school's financial aid office. If you noted any special circumstances either on the financial aid form or in a separate letter, ask if they took them into account when determining the award. Sometimes letters or comments get overlooked in the haste to get the aid awards out on time. If they say they took the circumstances into account, or if you did not mention any, tell them you would really like to attend the school but do not think it will be possible without more aid. If another school has offered you more aid, mention that, especially if the school is a competitor of the one you're talking to. Calling may not help, but they are not going to withdraw your acceptance once you are in.

If you are eligible for money on the basis of need, then the school may list some federal government assistance. The first of the types of federal government assistance are grants. Grants do not have to be paid back, unlike loans, but they are also harder to obtain. The federal government offers two grants: the Federal Pell Grant and the Federal

Supplemental Education Opportunity Grants. You have to demonstrate "exceptional" financial need for either, but the latter is harder to obtain since the government does not guarantee as much. A Pell Grant is as high as $2,340, and the FSEOG is as high as $4,000 annually.

The federal government also offers lower-interest loans. If you demonstrate "exceptional" financial need, you may be eligible for a Perkins Loan, which can be loaned at 5 percent interest up to a maximum of $3,000. There are two types of Stafford Loans, one subsidized and the other unsubsidized. The subsidized Stafford Loan is only for people who demonstrate financial need, and it has a cap of 8.25 percent interest. The government pays for the interest while you are in school and during the grace period after you graduate. The unsubsidized loan is for those who do not demonstrate financial need, and they have to pay interest the whole time. There is also a new loan called the Federal Direct Student Loan which is just like the Stafford except that the lender is the federal government and not a bank.

There is also a federal government sponsored loan for parents called the PLUS loan. It is particularly valuable for those who qualify for little or no financial aid. Each year, parents are allowed to borrow the full amount of tuition less any financial aid the student receives. The loan requires good credit, repayment while the child is still in school, and interest rates that are not far from market rates. Still, it can help to ease the burden on middle-class families.

You will also probably be required to take a job through the federal work-study program. Many applicants worry that working part-time will detract from studying or, equally important, playtime. Yet, if you work on campus, you certainly will not be the only one: Most colleges report that about half of their students hold term-time jobs. It is possible to take a full load of courses, participate in extracurricular activities, and work 10 or 15 hours per week, all while maintaining a good grade point average. Although freshmen tend to get the least exciting jobs on campus, in later years you may well find yourself working on interesting research, in a lab, or in a library job.

Many private colleges also provide scholarships based on academic, athletic, or artistic ability. As competition among colleges for the best students intensifies, more and more colleges are offering lucrative merit awards to well-qualified students. There are many excellent schools, including many state universities, that offer merit scholarships in ever-increasing numbers. The best sources for information are your high school counselor and state Department of Education.

Be sure not to overlook the millions of dollars of aid available from private sources. Organizations ranging from General Motors to the Knights of Columbus offer money for college, often as prizes to assist students from your community. Sometimes large companies offer scholarships to children of their employees, so have your parents find out if their employers have such programs. There are also several scholarships out there related to specific majors, religions, or even ethnic heritage. Or if you scored very high on the PSAT, you could be in the running for a National Merit Scholarship. There is often a catch to merit-based awards, however: If you qualify for awards from private sources, your school will often deduct some or all of the amount from any need-based aid you receive.

The only other significant source of federal aid available that is not based on need is the ROTC (Reserve Officers Training Corps) scholarship program. Thousands of dollars are available annually for students willing to put in several years in a branch of the armed forces. Sometimes they will even repay a portion of the federal government loans.

More and more, federal aid is being reserved exclusively for the very needy. Many families with incomes over $35,000 who qualify for PLUS loans must now pass a needs test to get Stafford Loans. Yet, if you play your cards right, your family should not have to undergo severe financial hardship to put you through school.

Advice for Transfers

If you are already in college and are thinking about transferring to another school, the preceding advice is mostly old news to you. Theoretically you know what to do now, but there are actually a number of new considerations that all potential transfers should keep in mind.

There are plenty of reasons students cite for transferring. Perhaps you don't feel comfortable in the social or political environment at your school. Maybe your academic interests have changed, and the programs available at your current college are not extensive enough. It could also be an issue of being too far from or close to home. Whatever the reason, it's important to figure out what it is about your college experience that doesn't work, so you can find one that does.

You're about to embark on a daunting and sometimes disappointing process, so be sure to think it through beforehand. It can be easy to blame your school if you are unhappy. But issues with the college experience itself, such as roommate problems or work overload, may be the real source of your dissatisfaction. If so, you may be able to work out these troubles without transferring.

Don't assume that you'll necessarily be happy at another university. One student left Stanford in search of "greener pastures." Instead, she found New England "cold, gray, and without pastures at all." According to another student, "It's a big risk. You have to really want to leave where you are or really want to go where you will be." There are no guarantees that you will be better off at another school, and the process itself may make things even less satisfactory for you. You might want to take a semester or two off to reevaluate your situation, or think about giving a more wholehearted effort at making your current situation work.

Most schools accept transfer students who have up to two years of credit at another university. It may be safer, however, to transfer after your first year, because your old university will be more likely to take you back if you change your mind. One student advised that it is better to take a leave of absence from your original school than to withdraw completely.

The application process is also slightly different for transfer students. Be aware that colleges tend to consider a transfer student in a different light from a high school senior. To your advantage, admissions officers tend to look upon transfer applicants as mature and motivated candidates who have the potential to make a significant impact on campus. However, few students tend to leave top private universities, so the acceptance rate for transfers at top schools is much, much lower than that for first-time applicants. The situation can be different at larger state schools.

Each school looks for different students, but grades, recommendations, and the essay that explains why you want to transfer are usually the three most important parts of the application. Make sure that you find classes with professors who will be able to write you good recommendations. Standardized test scores and extracurriculars are less important. One exception to this may be if you decide to take time off and do something exceptional during your time away from school. Keep in mind that your college transcript is incredibly important. As much as you might want to leave your school, do not ease up on your academics. If staying an extra semester will help boost your academic record, you may want to consider holding off on your move.

Because colleges will expect you to prove that you have developed during your first year or two of college and to show why you absolutely cannot stay at your old school, your essay (and interview if you can arrange one) is critical. Be definite and clear about your reasons for transferring and what you expect to find in a new environment. Academic reasons are best; personal ones are only as convincing as you can make them. It also helps if the department in which you want to major is under-subscribed at the new school.

Make sure you know a lot about the school you are applying to. Not only will this show through in your application, but you will also be much more prepared for the experience ahead. If what you need is an active, social campus in which to get involved, then make sure that you will be guaranteed on-campus housing. If you are going to need financial aid, check and see that it will be available for transfer students. Also, be sure you look into how your credits will transfer at the new school. Will you get credit towards a major, or only towards graduation? If you don't have a major already picked out, it can be very difficult to graduate in four years.

Before submitting the paperwork, make sure that you are confident in your decision to transfer, and be ready for anything. It's important to have a backup plan for the upcoming year in case you don't get accepted. Come up with a plan for what you do with a year off, or be prepared to make another run at getting the most out of your school. If everything does work out for you, make sure you have covered all of the bases before you commit to the new school. Making the decision to transfer is not a walk in the park, but you shouldn't let this deter you. If you are truly unhappy with your current situation, it can be a very rewarding and worthwhile route.

The College Spectrum

Current Trends and Comparing Colleges

At first glance, the sheer number of colleges included in this book might seem a bit overwhelming—clearly you would never consider applying to over 300 schools. Since colleges and their student bodies vary in so many ways, it can be difficult to identify schools at which you would feel comfortable. One piece of advice is to be aware of the general social, political, and academic trends many schools are currently experiencing. Issues such as affirmative action, the fairness of standardized testing, expanding financial aid, and the early application programs have become heated topics of discussion on countless college campuses. It can be helpful to figure out where certain schools stand in terms of these trends. Another way to get some perspective on different colleges is to identify where they stand in terms of various criteria—to figure out where they fall on a continuum we call the College Spectrum. Most importantly, it is not our place to judge which types of schools are best, but instead to present a variety of perspectives and observations that can help you with the decision-making process. Here are some of the many areas in which you can compare different schools.

Size

The total undergraduate enrollments of the schools in this book range from 26 at California's Deep Springs College to nearly 40,000 at Ohio State University. Considering the size of the campus you want to attend is helpful in the initial narrowing-down process; the feel of a school can be very dependent on the number of students around. There are two main parts of your experience that will be affected by the size of the school you choose: academics and social life.

Academically, class size and the accessibility of senior faculty are two important areas of comparison that tend to vary between large and small schools. In this case, smaller colleges decidedly have the advantage simply because a smaller population usually translates into smaller classes. Students at small schools have great opportunities for one-on-one student-faculty interaction. At large schools, students are more likely to complain of impersonal instruction and "being treated as a Social Security number."

To make up for this apparent disadvantage, many larger schools offer special programs intended to create a more intimate sense of community among professors and students. Different universities have different approaches. Some offer honors programs for a limited number of students, and some house all the students who are in special programs together. Generally, students in such programs all take the same or similar courses—most of which are small, discussion-oriented classes. Bear in mind that many honors and special programs are highly selective; do your best to make a realistic assessment of your chances to be accepted. Additionally, don't be *snowed* by the glossy pictures in admissions booklets: If you are considering a large university, take a close look at the quality of its special programs. Very often, there is a gap between the description of the program in the brochures and the reality. If you are seriously considering one of these programs, try to speak with an undergraduate currently participating in the program—he or she may be able to paint a more realistic picture of what it is like. Another important factor to remember is that no matter how large a school is, not all of the classes it offers will be huge and over-crowded, and some of the huge classes will break into smaller discussion groups. Thus, although most schools do have some very large classes, you can almost always find small ones of interest. In this case however, it is important to remember that in bigger schools, it is often difficult to get into small classes as an underclassman.

Also, pay attention to who teaches the classes. At most liberal arts colleges, only professors do. Many large universities pad their student-faculty ratios by including graduate students, or they advertise discussion classes that turn out to be taught by people who are still working toward a Ph.D. By reading guides such as this one and by talking to students, you can find out roughly how many graduate students teach and whether or not senior professors teach undergraduates at all. Keep in mind that having younger, less experienced professors teach is not always a bad thing. Many times, courses taught by graduate students allow for a rapport between teachers and students that does not develop with some of the stodgier old professors. However, if graduate students appear to dominate the teaching, even if only for the freshman year, you should definitely consider this as you make your decision. These facts will also give you a sense of how much personal attention the typical undergraduate student receives from the administration.

For highly specialized fields that require extensive facilities, the resources at small schools are generally limited. For facilities not associated with academics, such as the gym or the library, size and showiness are not nearly as important as accessibility. You will not care how many racquetball courts the gym has as long as one is available when you want to play and it's not a three-mile walk away. Instead of asking how many volumes there are in the library, find out whether everyone has full access to all its resources, and if the library holds long hours. While the facilities at smaller schools may be less impressive than those at big universities, they are often more accessible to undergraduates.

Social life, too, is affected by the size of the school. Consider carefully what kind of social life you plan to have and which type of school would be more conducive to your interests. The set-up of freshman housing will play a significant role in your social experience; your first-year roommates and hall-mates often become some of your closest friends. It's likely that the people you associate with will also be determined by your extracurricular interests—a sports team, a student newspaper, or student government. This tends to be especially true for universities that do not provide more than one year of campus housing.

The key is finding your own comfortable niche within any school. While there are usually more niches to be discovered in large colleges, finding yours may require some initiative. The larger the school, the more subgroups there are likely to be within the student body. Frats and sororities tend to be more abundant and popular on bigger campuses. An advantage to being a member of a very large community is that the supply of new faces never runs out. If you get tired of one circle of friends, you can always find another. But it is also important to keep in mind that when you are on your own in the midst of all those unfamiliar people, it is also possible to feel very lonely. On the other hand, small environments can be more welcoming and friendly. Small schools often have a greater sense of community and people can find that making friends is easier. Some students find that small schools can be a little too small, because "everybody knows everybody else's business."

One common misconception about smaller schools is that they are inevitably more homogenous and have less school pride or spirit. On the contrary, many of them, especially the more selective ones, have just as many different types of people as do most large universities, only in smaller numbers. Although larger schools, especially those with a big emphasis on athletics, may have tremendous school spirit, smaller ones foster their own brand of pride, usually stemming from rich tradition and a strong sense of community.

Schools come in all different sizes. No matter how big or small a school is, make sure it prioritizes what is important to you. Be sure to keep in mind both academic and social consequences of the size of your school: Both have the potential to drastically change your college experience.

Location

At some point, if not right away, you will find yourself thinking about the towns in which each of your college choices are located. Can you see yourself living there for four years? What sounds more appealing to you—a college where your dorm is surrounded by towering oak trees, or a college with easy access to shops and malls? Before you answer these questions, be sure you really understand the difference between urban and rural settings, and more importantly, how this difference will impact your college experience.

Often, what some students perceive to be "city life," "suburban life," or "life on the farm" is not the reality of what living at a college in one of these areas would be like. Many factors need to be considered in order to get an accurate idea of how location will affect your whole college experience.

Whether you've found your way through corn fields for eighteen years, or you've wandered around Times Square by yourself since you were ten, going away to college, while exciting and rewarding, can also be an intimidating experience. Many people arrive at school the very first day completely oblivious to the opportunities and the challenges of being out of their town, their state, or their region. If you are from a rural area and are considering the big move to the city, expect adjustment (to noise, traffic, people, crime, the hectic pace), but try not to make or accept any assumptions about "the horrors" of city life. If you are from an urban area and are considering the peace and quiet of a smaller school tucked in the woods somewhere, also expect adjustment (to relatively silent nights, no movie theater or department store, the slower pace), but also try not to make or accept any assumptions about "life with the cows." Your thoughts about the location of the school should be balanced by the fact that every school will inherently have some sort of community; is this community, along with the city the school is located in, right for you?

College is a great time to try new things, including a new location—a new city, a new state, maybe a whole new region of the United States or even Canada. In general, you do need to be aware of certain broad characteristics of each type of campus. At a campus in a big city, for example, there is a greater chance that on-campus nightlife will be non-existent, as everyone will head to clubs and bars to relax. Yet after a week of academic work, extracurricular activities, dorm parties, visiting speakers, football games, and the multitude of other school-sponsored events, being in an urban environment means there is still the option of seeing a Broadway show or going to a world-renowned museum. As for a campus in a smaller town, the exact opposite may be true. Without anything to do around town, students will have all of their activities and create all of their own nightlife on campus. While you may sometimes wish you did have the major clubs and bars, the tight-knit community that forms among students at the school may very well more than compensate for those longings. Whichever setting you do end up choosing should depend on your own reflections on how you would feel in those surroundings.

Another point to consider is how comfortable you would be living so close to or so far away from home. Does leaving the Pacific Ocean for the Atlantic Ocean sound like a real adventure, or does being even two hours away from your family make your hands start to tremble? Are you at a point in your life where you still want to be with all of your friends going to the same school near your hometown, or can you not wait for all of your new friends and your "whole new life" far from home? Distance is one of those factors that requires thinking about everything in context. Your life will change in college, whether you pack your bags to travel far away or keep your room at home. Anywhere you end up, even if you do stay close to home, your old relationships will change at least a little bit. Make sure you are honest with yourself about your reasons for choosing a particular school. It may be helpful to talk to current students at the school to get a sense of where they came from and what they think about the location. It may also be helpful to fold a piece of paper in half and come up with a list of positives about the location of the school on one side, and negatives on the other. Include everything that will affect your life: the weather, the people, the travel expenses, and the homesickness, without forgetting to take into account the school's own community. Life at college will require at least some adjustment, but it may be that exact adjustment which completes your college experience.

Private vs. Public

The question of whether to attend a public or private school is best answered through a cost-benefit approach. Don't worry, we know you haven't had Econ 101, so consider this a free lesson. Let's first divide the universities in the United States. into three categories: large private, public, and small private.

The most obvious distinction between a private and a public university is the price tag. As the cost of a private school education continues to climb, public school is becoming an increasingly attractive option. However, in recent years the tuition gap has significantly diminished for those who are eligible for financial aid, as private schools have allocated increasingly more funds to aid packages. These packages are almost always a combination of loans and grants, meaning that they do not always diminish the cost of college, but simply postpone it to a future date.

Most top-tier private institutions have adopted need-blind admissions policies which mean that they admit regardless of your ability to pay and then work with you to create a financial aid package that will allow you to attend. Princeton led the pack in this respect by announcing that it would replace loans with outright grants; soon many other colleges followed suit.

Smaller private schools, however, do not have the high-powered endowments necessary to fund such need-blind policies. In this area, public universities definitely have an advantage. Subsidized by state taxpayers, they offer an outstanding education at a fraction of its actual cost—everyone is basically a financial aid recipient.

If you do decide to break the bank and attend a private school, you will often be rewarded with smaller class size and greater student-teacher interaction. There is, however, a not-so-obvious advantage to the small private colleges. At larger private or state universities much of the teaching duty has been increasingly placed on the shoulders of ill-equipped, barely comprehensible, and many times foreign teaching assistants (graduate students). Additionally, at large private universities, professors must devote a significant amount of time to research in order to stay ahead in their field. Small private colleges offer teaching environments in which the professors are not burdened with this dictum of publish or perish; they can devote all their time to teaching the material instead of contributing to it.

At college you will learn as much from your fellow students as you will from your professors, so it's important to consider the quality and diversity of the student body. It might be said that private universities offer the best socio-economic racial mix because state schools reserve the majority of their spaces for state residents. Also, highly selective private colleges have an intellectual atmosphere rarely matched at state universities. This is an important consideration because at any good college, public or private, much of the valuable learning takes place outside of the classroom.

When deciding which type of school to attend, make sure that you look beyond its label as either public or private. While some applicants consider attending a state university second-best when compared to an elite private school, others make a public institution their first choice. It is important to consider department-specific academic strengths along with the overall reputation of the university as whole. Public schools such as UC Berkeley, UCLA, and University of Michigan rank among some of the top academic institutions, public or private, in the country. In

the end, you should never be swayed too much by a school's private or public designation. Instead, try to choose the school that's best suited to you.

Coed or Single-Sex?

Since coeducation became the norm at American universities in the 1960s, the number of single-sex schools in the nation has dropped significantly. There are only four men's colleges remaining in this book: Deep Springs College, Hampden-Sydney College, Morehouse College, and Wabash College. The students here chose to attend mainly because of their belief that the absence of the opposite sex allows greater dedication to academics and a friendlier, more fraternal atmosphere. Tradition and conservatism prevail at these all-male institutions, and men that work best in these atmospheres find themselves very content.

Women's colleges have similar reasons for existence as all-male colleges, but with a few twists. There are many more women's colleges, as the whole movement for women's education came later and is still firmly rooted in feminine beliefs. The most famous all-female schools are the Seven Sisters, a group of seven Northeastern colleges that self-organized in 1927 to promote single-sex education. The seven sisters—Barnard, Bryn Mawr, Mount Holyoke, Radcliffe (now folded into Harvard), Smith, Vassar (now coed), and Wellesley—hoped to compete with the image of the Ivy League schools. Interestingly, it was not until 1978 that all seven schools had female presidents.

Most women who attend single-sex colleges cite the supportive, nurturing environment as their college's asset. In an arguably male-dominated culture, women's schools provide a learning environment where there is support for developing one's female identity, no academic competition with men, and numerous leadership opportunities. Women's colleges are usually very liberal, with focus on current events and debates on different points of view.

There is no debate, however, about the fact that life at a single-sex institution is very different from life at a coed one. Because single-sex schools tend to be smaller, there are often fewer academic programs and resources than at larger coed colleges. Also, the atmosphere is somewhat contrived, since one of the sexes is missing. There are always outlets through which students can find the opposite sex, such as "brother universities," but the social life and vivacity of the campus is usually at a much "calmer" level than coed schools. For students who want the best of both worlds, there are a few colleges that are part of coed consortia. Women at Mount Holyoke and Smith can take classes at the neighboring Amherst and Hampshire Colleges and the University of Massachusetts, the women at Barnard are paired with the coed Columbia University, and Bryn Mawr allows its female students to explore academic offerings at Haverford and Swarthmore Colleges.

Besides the actual experience, another thing to keep in mind is a certain stigma attached to many single-sex schools. Since the majority of these schools are extremely liberal, they are generally known for strong activism in women's and gay rights. This reputation exists despite the more conservative nature of some of the top academic single-sex schools. Whether accurate or not, this is another factor to consider in your choice.

Single-sex atmospheres can be ideal for some students, but not everyone seeks out such a college experience. Most college-bound seniors end up enrolling in coeducational schools, an environment that requires little adjustment. Issues of coed bathrooms and dormitories may come to the fore, but there are many different housing options, and administrators work to make you comfortable. So after choosing whether a single-sex or coed college is right for you, wait for your institution to send you information on handling all the details.

Advising and Tutoring

The first few weeks of college can be confusing. There are placement tests to take, forms to fill out, questions about AP credits to ask, and parents to kiss goodbye. Many freshmen are often unaccustomed to the breadth of courses from which to choose. Also, it's hard to plan your academic year when you're in the midst of meeting new friends, moving into your dorm room, trying to go to as many parties as possible, and asking out that cute German down the hall. However, do not be daunted.

Almost all colleges provide students with faculty advisors for at least the first year. Their function is twofold: they can both rubber stamp your schedule and be used as reference for everything from course selection to general questions about the college. Though most students agree that faculty advisors are usually only good for placing their John Hancocks on your schedule, there are a few who are adamant that faculty advisors do have some value. If you do not know what you want to major in from day one, don't worry, your advisor can help you plan your schedule and think things through.

If you still have unanswered questions, ask upperclassmen (often the best source for good, quick information). They can point you towards interesting classes, often-overlooked majors, and talented professors—but remember their advice is very much based on their personal experiences. For more detailed, department-specific questions about graduation/major requirements, ask a faculty member in that department.

Once you have chosen your classes, remember that this is only half the battle! Fortunately, most colleges and universities offer tutoring resources free of charge to help you succeed. If you find yourself in a large class with a professor who rushes through the most important points in the last five minutes of lecture or have a foreign TA who can barely speak English, you should consider getting a tutor. Professors' office hours are usually insufficient for detailed explanations. Even the brightest students can benefit from going over the subject matter once per week.

Many times tutors are graduate students or particularly advanced undergraduates proficient in that specific academic discipline. Having recently learned the material, they can often make it more accessible than a weathered professor who had taught it for decades. When exam time rolls around, look to upperclassmen for old study guides and more general insight into acing specific courses.

A Minority Perspective

As a minority student or a person of color, there might well be some additional factors to consider in your decision. You may, for example, be searching for a school with a high population of students from a particular background or for a school with high overall diversity. A school with a large minority population may prove to be more supportive and even more comfortable. Regardless of size, a strong minority community can be helpful during the next four years and can even help reduce racism and ignorance on some campuses.

Another factor to consider is the general attitude of both the administration and the student body. Unfortunately, racism still exists at many colleges, but do not assume a defensive attitude while visiting schools. Instead, be aware of possible situations and attitudes that may make you feel excluded and uncomfortable. What might have seemed like a diverse college in the brochures may not seem so open-minded after all. Take note of how integrated the minority community is, and what the school does to recognize and support other cultures. Some schools may foster a pressure to conform; if the school has a large population of a certain race, there may be a distinct sense of separatism. For some this may provide a stronger sense of belonging, while for others it will only increase the stress of college life.

To determine the true attitude of the administration, look at how it attempts to support the minority communities. Some schools assign ethnic counselors to help minority students adjust to college life. Some students appreciate this; others resent it. One student reported that her school was doing so much to accommodate her minority status she felt separated rather than integrated. Many students, however, get used to the idea of special resources and ultimately find them supportive. Another thing to look at is the extracurricular life. What kinds of organizations are there for specific minority groups or minority students in general? The school may have cultural centers and politically oriented associations that focus on the traditional arts and dances of their culture.

For African-American students, an important decision may be whether to attend a predominantly black college over another school. Despite the improving financial situations of most private black colleges, you are likely to find better facilities and larger academic departments at other schools. Unfortunately, the continuing decline of federal funding is likely to exacerbate this situation, since black colleges rely heavily on such resources. Nevertheless, many students choose to attend a predominantly black college for many of the same reasons other students choose to attend a single-sex school. Some black students find them a more congenial and accepting community that is more conducive to personal growth. Likewise, students often have a better chance to attain key leadership positions at a college where they do not have minority status. At a predominantly black school, the African-American experience is one of the central issues on campus. What does it mean to be a black person in 21st century America? Of what importance is African-American heritage? At predominantly black schools, these questions are addressed in a manner and with a fervor unrivaled by other institutions.

In this book, we include reports on five of the best-known predominantly black schools in the United States: Howard University in Washington, D.C.; Spelman and Morehouse Colleges in Georgia; Florida A&M University; and Tuskegee University in Alabama. For a more complete listing, we suggest you consult The Black Student's Guide to Colleges, written by Barry Beckham and published by Beckham House. Another school with an ethnic majority is the University of Hawaii, which is predominantly made up of Asian students.

Ultimately, you have to decide where you will feel most comfortable. Whatever your choice, it is important to remember that your ethnicity is an integral part of yourself and is not something you should have to compromise in choosing a school.

Sexual Minorities

The first question that a gay, lesbian, bisexual, or transgender student should ask when considering choosing a college is the same one that straight students ask: where will I be the most comfortable and happiest for four years? Students planning on being openly gay at college will want to choose a campus where they can come out to their roommates, friends, and even professors without worrying about the consequences. But how can you tell after one or two trips to a college whether or not you'll get a positive reception?

The good news is that, as one transfer student put it, "there are sensitive people everywhere—at large schools and small ones." Another student said she sought out a campus with diversity, guessing that a diverse population "would create more understanding." Beyond these general statements, however, there are other aspects of campus life to observe. Check out a school's listing of organizations, for instance. A school with several gay alliances and clubs, for example, probably has a more accepting environment, even if you don't think you'll end up being active in any of them. One student pointed out that the surrounding community can be just as important. "Knowing that there were gay bars and events in the town made me more comfortable in my choice." The more town-gown interaction there is, the more important it is that a prospective student feels comfortable being gay in that city. A lesbian student who chose a Quaker school commented that she "guessed the school's principles would attract a more accepting student body." In other words, there are countless characteristics that imply a college's atmosphere welcomes gay students.

In looking for a school, all students search for a place with unlimited options. As a gay, lesbian, or even questioning student, the best college is going to be one where your opportunities are not constrained by your sexual orientation. As one gay member of a fraternity pointed out, "I wanted to join a frat in college, so it was important that I found a place where my sexuality wouldn't be as big a deal. At a school where the Greek scene isn't predominant, it's been easier to be openly gay." In other words, there are countless schools where gay and lesbian students participate in every aspect of campus life—and fortunately it isn't too hard to track them down. This is not to say life for gay students is always perfect; gay students do risk running up against prejudices, but it is reassuring to know that gay and lesbian students at large and small schools, public and private, have managed to find their niche, be active members of the undergraduate community, and simply have a good time.

Politics

How politically active a campus is may affect how comfortable you are there. You will find that many schools have clubs of all alignments, and political journals of all bents as well, from the left-wing liberals to the Green Party to the ultra-conservatives. Generally these partisan organizations are most active in presidential election years. If this is what you're interested in, you will have no trouble finding your political niche.

Forty years ago, political activism permeated college campuses. Today, the number of students strongly involved in politics on campus is generally a minority. One student remarked that a majority of her fellow students stay away from politics for social reasons:

many people at her university look down on those with strong convictions because they assume them to be closed-minded. Instead of joining political organizations, many students channel their activism into volunteer programs that confront specific problems such as urban blight or environmental destruction. Usually the small liberal arts schools are the most politicized colleges. "At my school, you don't just put your name on name tags, you put your cause, your oppressor, your god, and your sexual orientation," said one student. Before selecting a school, you may want to see if it has a political forum that brings in outside speakers and organizes discussions and lectures.

Although only a few years ago campus activism was moving towards being institutionalized and domesticated, recent events, such as the September 11 attacks and the war in Iraq, have provoked an increasing amount of activity on behalf of students. Student protests, petitions, and marches have garnered much support as well as media recognition. Additionally certain incidents and issues, particularly those involving racism and sexuality, receive community-wide attention. On Columbus Day at one school, for example, indignant students covered sidewalks with brightly colored chalked polemics against racism and genocide. The gay- and lesbian-rights activists at a different school sponsor a kiss-in where same-sex couples cluster around the campus' central promenade and neck. Gay rights, AIDS awareness, and race-related issues are commonly on the collegiate slate of activist causes. Today, to be politically correct (PC)—manifested by a tolerance for others' ideas and political affiliations and an attempt to be inoffensive to any and all groups in speech as well as in print—is something of a secondary issue. Although PC was a hot topic on campus in the nineties, the debates on the spelling of "woman" and whether your roommate is disabled or "differently abled" seem to have faded.

However the PC movement's focus on the implications of language has pushed people—particularly educators—to reconsider the lens through which academic disciplines are typically approached. Many schools now require students to take courses that focus on non-Western cultures, or courses aimed at raising sensitivity to minority issues and concerns. More and more schools have started classifying "Women and Gender Studies" as a major, as well as "Latin-American Studies" and "African-American Studies." Courses and programs exploring Native American Studies have also begun to emerge.

As a general rule of thumb, the more liberal the campus, the more concerned students are about political issues. If you enjoy informal political debates or thrive on dinner conversations about the Middle East or Title IX athletics, you might want to consider a more liberal school, even if you are a radical Republican.

By visiting a college you can quickly pick up on how important politics are to the student body. Read posters and skim student newspapers to gauge whether or not the political climate on that campus is right for you. The best schools may be those that can absorb all viewpoints, so that no matter what you think, there will be others who will embrace your thoughts, challenge them, or respect your decision not to vocalize them.

Preprofessionalism vs. Liberal Arts

Preprofessionalism is a term you will see repeated throughout this book. Not all curriculums are the same, and whether you will receive either a preprofessional or liberal arts education is determined both by the school you attend and the major you choose there.

Majors that do not lead directly to a specific career fall into the liberal arts category. Even if a student plans to be an accountant, for example, he or she might get a liberal arts degree in philosophy or English, and then go on to study accounting at the appropriate professional school. The goal of a liberal arts education is to teach students how to think creatively and analytically, preparing them to pursue any career.

There are pros and cons to both tracks. Some argue that a liberal arts education is the key to a solid education and to becoming a well-rounded individual. Others believe that a liberal arts degree can be a waste of four years and thousands of dollars for those who already have their career plans mapped out. Students from a liberal arts background may also have a more difficult time securing a job immediately after graduating, as they tend to lack both experience and specific skills. Many preprofessional programs require students to take general education courses in liberal arts departments. In fact, almost all colleges insist that you take some courses outside your chosen field.

If you don't yet know your interests well enough to decide now which option is for you, you may be pleased to learn that the largest colleges and universities have both liberal arts and preprofessional students. The University of Michigan, for example, has a strong undergraduate school of business; many students in Michigan's liberal arts school also plan to go into business eventually but are pursuing a B.A. in a more general field first. The case is similar with Cornell.

If you do know what you want from a school in terms of career preparation, then you may prefer to attend a preprofessional institution. But keep in mind that getting a liberal arts education and getting a good job are not mutually exclusive. Moreover many report that the learning environment at a preprofessional university is more competitive, and would therefore not be as enjoyable to a student who enjoys the intellectual exchange more common to liberal arts campuses.

In the past two decades there has also been a revival of interest in ROTC (Reserve Officers Training Corps) programs. These scholarships from the four branches of the armed forces help pay for tuition, books, and room and board during college. When you graduate, you are committed to anywhere between four and eight years of reserve or active duty, depending on the program. As the supply of financial aid declines and the cost of college education continues to climb, more and more students are coming to see ROTC scholarships as worthwhile. However, be very thorough when investigating ROTC programs at different schools. Some colleges tend to be more antimilitary, and you may find yourself part of a controversial program. Even so, the benefits of the program can be substantial for a student who joins after careful consideration and research.

Greek Life and Other Social Options

When choosing a college, you are choosing a place in which to live and learn. In this way the social life at colleges becomes a large factor in choosing your school and many people claim that when they visited colleges, the people they met made them love or hate the campus more than any other aspect. You will find that sometimes you just click with the students at a particular school. Although most schools are large enough to ensure you will find your social niche, it is also important to consider how the overall social atmosphere will affect you while you are there.

Collegiate life in the United States often conjures images of a social scene dominated exclusively by fraternities and sororities. While this is true of some schools, there are many schools where Greek life is either nonexistent or less central to college life than some would believe. Greek life can run the gamut from a dominating institution to a relatively unknown and tame element of college life. It is also true that while many fraternities and sororities have high levels of membership, some of the numbers are dropping across the country. This is due mostly to increasingly strict policies on campuses to curb hazing as well as alcohol abuse that has made Greek life so infamous in today's media.

Although the most widely publicized side of Greek organizations has to do with their partying habits, belonging to a Greek organization is not just for those who like to party. In fact, many organizations have reformed their policies to reduce or eliminate such practices as pledge hazing and many require that Greeks be dry at official functions (although that does not mean they cannot party together outside of meetings).

Beyond being a social group, Greek organizations offer many advantages to students including a nationwide network of alumni, community service opportunities and housing (which is often very difficult to find for upperclassmen). The emphasis on community service is particularly important to most Greek organizations and most chapters have an office dedicated specifically to organizing the chapter to participate in local charitable activities. On some campuses, the fraternities and sororities are the most active social-service organizations.

In terms of housing considerations, most organizations are on campus and thus are financially supported by the school, national chapter, and students. Because of this, Greek houses are some of the nicest housing available, often as free standing buildings with manicured lawns and beautifully decorated interiors. However, an increasing trend among colleges is to kick Greek organizations off campus. This trend is especially marked among fraternities that gain the reputation of being unkempt and raucous. Without campus funding, many of the organizations lose large amounts of their financial support and thus cannot run as well as those that are on campus.

Whether Greek life appeals to you or not, it is essential to know just how influential the Greek organizations are at each school you are considering. At some campuses, not rushing could seriously limit your social options. On the other hand, there are many schools where fraternities and sororities are most certainly not part of campus life and are regarded as conformist. There are also schools, especially among the Ivy League, where although Greek life is present, there is a strong residence system that fills many of the social functions that Greek organizations occupy elsewhere. As a rule of thumb, Greek life is more dominant at the largest schools where practical concerns keep the organizations strong and smallest at the most specialized schools where campus life is intimate enough that smaller social organizations may prove stifling.

However, even at the most Greek-dominated campuses, there are always other social outlets. Your interests will largely determine who your friends are. Therefore, you should choose a school that has groups that represent your interests. Greek organizations, athletics, cultural organizations, or theater groups will all be part of your college experience. The people you meet in these organizations often become some of your closest friends. Ultimately, the best way to tell if a school's social scene is right for you is to visit the campus or talk to friends who go there. Most college applicants worry that they will not find people like themselves when they get to college, but when they get there realize that making friends was much easier than expected. Find what you think will be the right combination of organizations, Greek or otherwise, and you will meet the right people.

Security

Security as an issue on college campuses is not simply a response to a few well-publicized campus murders. Although the tragedies at some colleges are by no means insignificant, crime in general is increasing on campuses across the country. In response to this trend, federal legislation has made it mandatory for all colleges receiving federal aid (which is almost every one) to publish crime statistics in several categories. At your request, the appropriate office (usually the public relations or admissions offices) at any college or university should release to you the crime count for the last calendar year. Many colleges have also taken measures to beef up security. If you visit a campus and notice very stringent security measures (at the University of Pennsylvania, for example, you have to show your ID just to get into the quadrangle), remember that this means two things: there is a need for security measures, and the administration is responding to this need.

There are a number of features that any safety-conscious campus should have. Doors to individual dorm rooms and to the building entrances should be equipped with locks. All walkways should have bright lights, not only so that you can see, but so friends and classmates would be able to see you from a distance in case of danger. Another important security measure is a safety phone system with one-touch access to an emergency line. Each safety phone should have a distinct light to make it easily recognizable at night. Ideally, there should be enough units so that you are never more than a half a block from a phone. For getting around campus late at night, colleges should provide bus service or student safety escorts, free of charge. At least one of these services should be available 24-hours-a-day and should travel to every possible destination on campus. Every school should employ some type of security guard, whether unarmed monitors in or near the dorms or full-time police officers responsive solely to students and the affairs of the college.

Security problems are not limited to urban campuses. Some rural schools have crime rates as high as the urban ones. The sad truth is that most non-violent crimes are committed by other students, not outsiders. Why is campus crime such an issue now? College students are ideal targets—they keep expensive stereo and computer equipment in poorly guarded areas, and they often walk alone across dark, seemingly safe campuses.

It is important to understand that you cannot judge the safety of a campus simply by eyeing it from the safe confines of a brochure. Yet, by using a little common sense and preventive measures, the security problems of a given school should not prevent you from attending. By making yourself aware of potential problems and following the school's security guidelines, you can improve your chances of enjoying a safe four years.

Whether you are an art major, a computer science major, or an expert procrastinator, computers will be an important part of your college experience. Looking up information for that research paper due in 12 hours, searching for your classmate's e-mail address in the online directory, and downloading the next problem set from the class Web site are just a few examples of the countless ways that computers are a part of everyday life on campus. With that in mind, here are a few things to look for when evaluating a college's computing facilities:

24-Hour Computer Clusters: Make sure that there are at least a few accessible computer clusters to rely on when your computer or printer stops cooperating once you finally sit down to start your homework. Many people also like to work on their papers in computer clusters to get away from the distractions of their own room. Easily accessible clusters with numerous, fast computers are always a plus.

Macs vs. PCs: Although compatibility issues are largely a thing of the past, the networks at some schools may be preferentially built for Macs or PCs. If you are looking into bringing your computer, double-check that your school provides adequate support for your machine.

Support Staff: Another important thing to consider is the availability of computer assistants. Many schools hire students or other staff to troubleshoot the problems you may encounter with networking, hardware, or software licensed by the school. This can be especially helpful at the beginning of each semester when you have to register your computers with the school network and install the necessary software.

Internet and E-mail Access: Nearly every school now provides Ethernet access from dorm rooms and e-mail accounts that you can use during both the semester and your breaks. Another feature to look for is the availability of wireless Ethernet at your school, which is also becoming more and more universal—even in classrooms. In addition to getting rid of an extra wire on your desk, it also allows you to check your e-mail or chat with your roommate from anywhere on campus.

Academic Usage of the Internet: Professors at most schools now use the Internet (in some form) as an important resource for their classes. Being able to find class notes, handouts, homework assignments, or even taped lectures posted on a Web site can be an aspect to consider when choosing a class or a school. Although not every professor at every school is willing to put extensive course information online, finding a school where it is more common will help make your life slightly easier over the next four years.

A Final Note About Quality of Life

If you started at the first page and you've read up to here, you are probably thinking there are just way too many things to think about in choosing a college! Certainly, you already have many reasons why, right off the bat, you would add a college to, or eliminate a college from, your list. Perhaps the school has the best zoology program in the nation. Or maybe you have always wanted to be in the stands cheering as your school's basketball team wins the championship game. Either way, a final but crucial criterion for your decision is the overall quality of life you can expect to have at college.

Everyone goes to college to learn more, right? Yes, of course. Continuing your academic education will provide you with even more ways of thinking as well as more opportunities after graduation. You have to remember, though, college is someplace you will be for three or more years of your life. Academics are the most important reason to go to college, but when it comes down to everyday life, the college you choose will basically be your new world. Everything from extracurricular activities to housing, social life, and even weather will affect the way you eat, dress, study, and relax. Don't consider UMass if you can't stand the cold; and don't go to Florida State if the heat makes you miserable. Have you always thought about joining a fraternity or a sorority, and there just aren't any on campus? Or perhaps your favorite weekend activity is to curl up on a chair in a coffee shop; is the college in such a small town that there is no coffee shop? What about the housing situation? Could you see yourself coming "home" every day to that closet-sized room you share with three other students? Speaking of the other students, would you be comfortable being around them—or any of the people walking down the street? All of these factors can and will make a difference in how you feel about a school. The best way to really get an idea of what it would be like to be a student at the college is to visit the school, maybe stay over for a night or two, talk to the students around you, and browse through the student newspaper. Do you like what you see and how it feels to be there?

As you figure out what you like about a college, you may also want to check that those aspects of the school will still be there when you enroll. When the economy is doing poorly, an increasing number of schools, both public and private, will face a shortage of funds; administrations at the schools have no choice but to make budget cuts. Without adequate funding, programs or even entire departments may be eliminated, the number of tenured professors may be reduced, campus renovations and additions may be delayed, extracurricular activities and sports teams may be cut, or worse yet, a combination of all of these possibilities may take place. If you are the star of your high school's varsity swimming team and want to continue swimming in college, check with the coach or the current swimmers to make sure the team is not rumored to be next on the list of programs to be cancelled. If you know that you want to major in biomedical engineering, make sure the department is big enough so that it is not one of the smaller and less popular departments that would be first to go. As recent newspaper headlines will tell you, even the best-endowed schools are tightening their purse strings.

We hope that we have given you a stronger sense as to what to think about and what to focus on as you continue to search for the college that's right for you. Just remember, in the end you are the one who will be attending the college, so you should be the one who is happy. Best of luck!

Introduction for International Students

International students looking to apply to colleges in the United States may discover a daunting and unfamiliar path ahead of them. Unlike in many other countries, admission to U.S. colleges depends not only on grades and scores, but on the whole package: what you have done outside of schoolwork, what your teachers have to say about you, and what you have to say about yourself. In addition to the typical trials of the application process, students from abroad may also have to deal with linguistic and cultural differences, scarce resources, and communication delays that their American-counterparts do not. Yet you should not let yourself be deterred by these challenges—some basic planning can eliminate many potential obstacles and pave the way to a unique and rewarding college experience.

An "international student" formally refers to anyone who is applying to American universities from an address outside of the United States. This means U.S. citizens and permanent residents applying from abroad are still placed in the international category. Many colleges review this applicant pool differently from the domestic applicants—admissions committees might place less emphasis on SAT scores, for example. Many schools also look for geographical and cultural diversity, which could work in your favor if only a few students are applying from your country, or against you if there are many other applicants.

With these advantages and disadvantages in mind, here are some tips about the application process that might be especially helpful. You should also read the **Getting In** section of this book for more general information. The best advice is: get started early. Deadlines for American universities can be as early as November for fall admissions. As one student said, "make sure you take care of everything well ahead of time—last minute surprises are harder to deal with abroad."

Pre-Application Preparations

If you decide that you want to go to an American university, start getting involved. While extracurricular activities are not taken seriously in many countries, American universities place emphasis on what you achieve outside of the classroom. Extracurricular experiences can include a variety of activities such as taking piano lessons, writing for the newspaper, doing volunteer work, or working part-time. These activities might highlight your leadership, talent, or determination. If your school does not offer many extracurricular activities, look for opportunities to get involved in the community or take the initiative to organize something yourself. When application time rolls around, be sure to list everything to which you have devoted your time.

Academically, international students might want to think about taking Advanced Placement (AP) tests and courses related to them if they are not already following the International Baccalaureate (IB) program. Although not required for college admission, AP exams will measure the level of your knowledge in the subject as compared to American high school students. As an added bonus, high scores might let you bypass some classes in college or accelerate and graduate early. Arranging to take an AP test internationally might be difficult; try to see if an American school in your area will arrange it. If you can take it and you have recently completed a course corresponding to one of the tests, it would be a risk-free way to increase your chances at admission—students can choose whether to report individual AP scores. Students studying under the IB system, and even students that do not take either of these tests, might be able to negotiate for acceleration in their first year of college. Acceleration policies, however, vary greatly from college to college.

Deciding that you want to go to college in the United States and figuring out where to apply might be the rocky starting point for many international students because of the relative lack of information. Research, however, is an essential part of the college application process and what many internationals said they wished they had spent more time doing. The United States is a huge country, and it will make a difference whether you are in California or Massachusetts, whether you are in a city or a rural area. There are also a large number of schools with excellent programs, beyond the names that people outside of the United States would recognize. If you have a college guidance counselor in your school who is knowledgeable about admissions to U.S. schools, take advantage of the resource. However, many advisors are not. One international student, now a senior, warned, "don't trust your high school counselors too much; they probably don't know as much about the schools you're applying to as you might assume they do—including application deadlines."

If your advisor is unable to offer you the help you need, seek out a counselor outside of the school. You might also want to speak with someone who has recently gone through a similar decision-making process, or talk to an American expatriate. Libraries and the Internet are prime sources of information. College Web sites provide accurate, up-to-date information, and sometimes feature special application guidelines for international students. If possible, try to visit the colleges. It will probably make a big difference in your opinion of each school.

You may also want to consider the size of the international population at the schools you are deciding between. Colleges with a larger number of students from abroad tend to have more organizations and activities geared toward international students. These schools will likely have more extensive resources available for you at the administrative level as well. However this may not be an important factor in your decisions, and it all depends on what kind of college environment you are looking for.

Testing

Most American colleges require international students to take the SAT (Scholastic Aptitude Test), a selection of SAT II tests, and the TOEFL. The Educational Testing Service (ETS) has many international test sites, although the tests might still be hard to come by in certain countries. Students from such diverse countries as Israel, Japan, and Guatemala all attested that signing up was easy, particularly with online registration. However, some people might have to travel hours out of the way to get to the testing center. To avoid any unnecessary travel, register for these tests early before popular testing centers fill their seats. To find out where the nearest testing center is located, write to ETS or visit their Web site.

Many colleges require the TOEFL (Test of English as a Foreign Language) if English is not your first language or the language of instruction in your high school. While taking another test might seem like a hassle, TOEFL is easier than the SAT and could work to your advantage since many schools will substitute a TOEFL score for the SAT Verbal score. If you are satisfied with your SAT Verbal scores, you should probably not bother taking TOEFL—although a near perfect score could never hurt. The newly instituted SAT Essay section will pose a further hurdle to non-native English speakers, and while colleges are likely to take your native abilities into account when making admissions decisions, the essay will undoubtedly require more test preparation on the part of international students.

Application Package

In getting teachers to write recommendations for you, be sure to approach those who not only know your work, but know you and are willing to write enthusiastically about you. International teachers tend to be more reluctant to award superlatives or write a personalized recommendation than their American counterparts. If you went to a school taught in a non-English language, you can ask the teachers to write you recommendations in English, have them translated, or send them to the colleges to have them translated. It is often better to have the recommendations translated in your own country than to send them to colleges to be translated by someone there. You might offer to work with your teacher to translate the letter into English, especially if you have a higher level of proficiency.

The essay is a personal reflection of yourself and an opportunity to have the different parts of your application come together. Think of what will be interesting to the admissions officers reading the essay, and allow for more creativity than might be acceptable in college applications in your own country. Many internationals choose to write about living in different countries or experiencing cultural differences, which might be more interesting than the fact that you won a national academic award—the latter point can be listed elsewhere in the application. You want to give the admissions officers a strong sense of who you are and how you will add to the college community.

Financial Aid and Visas

While some large and wealthy colleges can afford to be need-blind in their admission of international students, the consensus is that there is very little financial aid available for non-U.S. citizens and residents. If you will definitely need aid, you should research the financial aid policy of each college before applying. Depending on which country you are from, you might be able to look to sources in your home country for financial support. If, on the other hand, you are an American citizen applying from abroad, the financial aid process is the same as for any other American student.

As soon as you mail off that final college application, most of your hard work will be over. Although regulations differ from country to country, you shouldn't have any problems obtaining a student visa once you are accepted to a U.S. school. The visa will allow you to work inside the university, but be forewarned that finding an outside job will be very difficult.

International students face a number of challenges when applying to U.S. universities, but some advance research and planning can help make the process as painless as possible. There are numerous benefits to pursuing an American education—you'll have a vast array of academic options, enjoy access to high-tech facilities, and be exposed to students with backgrounds quite different from your own. Attending a U.S. college is a chance to expand your horizons, and you shouldn't let the application obstacles hold you back. One international student summed it up by saying, "Although it is an endless process, it is worth it!"

Students with Disabilities

Deciding on a college is a daunting time for every student, but those with one or more disabilities will have an additional set of factors to keep in mind throughout the application process. As you research, visit, and apply to different colleges you'll need to dig a little deeper to ensure that the schools you are considering are places where you will feel comfortable for the next four years. Doing some extra preparation early on will also help to ease the transition to college when the time comes.

There are a broad range of disabilities for which students seek assistance at the college level, including mobility disabilities, learning disabilities, attention deficit disorder, autism, and hearing loss or visual impairments. If you have one or more of these disabilites, it is important to know that the laws governing disability services at the high school level are not the same laws that apply to universities. Secondary schools abide by the Individuals with Disabilities Education Act, which requires them to seek out students with disabilities and accommodate them as fully as possible. On the other hand, colleges fall under the general Americans with Disabilities Act, which means they must only provide reasonable accommodations for those in need. "Reasonable" is a pretty vague term though, and you'll find that services vary widely from school to school.

For this reason, the campus visit will be a crucial part of your college search process—you'll need to examine the campus and its resources up close to determine whether it will be a good fit for your strengths and needs. Most schools have a designated office for students with disabilities. This will be the best place to find information about what services the school offers and how you can access them.

Before setting out for campus visits though, you'll probably want to make a few phone calls. Ruth Bork, Director and Dean of the Disability Resource Center at Northeastern University, advises students with mobility disabilities or hearing impairments to contact the admissions office before arriving for a campus tour. This way the admissions office can ensure the tour route is completely accessible, or hire an interpreter, Bork explained. A little advance planning will allow you to get the most out of the tour and get a sense of the school's overall commitment to providing services for the disabled.

You should also plan to stop by the school's office for students with disabilities, and may want to make an appointment with the director or coordinator in advance. Having a detailed discussion about your situation with someone in charge will help you determine if the school would be a good fit for you. The college Web site should have all the specific staffing and contact information you'll need to schedule such a meeting.

When you finally do arrive on campus, here are some suggestions to make the visit as helpful as possible:

If You Have a Physical Disability:

The most important thing is to take a hard look at the ways in which the campus is or is not handicapped accessible. Make sure that you can enter all of the buildings without assistance. Find out where the elevators are located and whether you will need a special key to use them. If you have a special automobile, find out if and how you'll be able to use it around campus. Schools often provide on-campus shuttles—check whether you can make use of these. Take a look at the surrounding area and off-campus transportation as well.

Wheelchair users need to check that there are adequate ramps throughout the campus. Schools that are truly committed to making their campuses accessible for wheelchair users will not only have many ramps available, but those ramps will be attractive and blend in naturally with the immediate environment. Make sure the ramps have safe borders running along each edge and provide adequate "turn around" room at the bottom. Doorways should be wide enough to pass through comfortably, and classrooms need to have appropriate and adequate spaces for wheelchairs. Be warned, many older universities have buildings that are still not wheelchair accessible, so try to determine how much of a problem this will be. If you see someone with a physical disability on your visit, consider asking his or her opinion concerning the accessibility of the campus.

If You Have a Learning Disability:

The office for students with disabilities should be able to answer all of your questions about the specific services and resources available. Before you stop by, it's a good idea to think about your particular strengths and weaknesses, as well as the kind of support you will need at the university level. Assessing your situation ahead of time will allow you to ask more focused questions when you arrive and get a better sense of whether your needs can be fully accommodated.

There are a number of special services and resources that colleges may provide to LD students. These can include note-takers, tutors, extended time on tests, alternative testing situations, and special computers. You may want to ask about the school's policies in regards to distributional requirements. Some colleges allow students with documented disabilities to take lighter course loads or make substitutions for required classes. Most importantly, do not be afraid to be honest about your learning needs; most school officials and fellow students will be more than happy to help.

Other resources that may be available to you include interpreters, books-on-tape, readers, and special technological equipment. Some schools are more wired than others, so try to get a feel for how advanced the equipment is. It's also important to check your comfort level while you're at the office. A welcoming and conveniently-located center will make you much more likely to use the services offered there.

When you do decide on a college, there will be some additional logistics to work through to ensure that you can access the services and resources you'll need. In order to receive accommodations from the office, you will have to provide documentation of your disability. This most likely means arranging an assessment, so be sure to find out from the school exactly what paperwork is required.

Always remember that whether or not you disclose that you have a disability is totally up to you. By law, schools cannot demand such information. Either way—whether or not you disclose that you have a disability—you should be able to find a school that can accommodate your needs and compliment your strengths.

Essay: Study Abroad

Three students, three countries and three unique and unforgettable experiences! The following students recount their time abroad in different parts of the globe.

> **Name:** Anne Cui
>
> **University/college:** Mount Holyoke College
>
> **Major:** Art History & International Relations
>
> **Year of college you studied abroad:** Junior (2006)
>
> **Place you studied abroad:** Beirut, Lebanon
>
> **Subject/field studied:** Arabic
>
> **Program name:** SINARC Institute, Lebanese American University
>
> **Extremely random thing you most enjoyed about your experience:** All forms of the cheap eatery, Barbar – especially Juicy Barbar. They sell shawarma and smoothies to die for.

Beirut is the gem of the Middle East and one of the most diverse places on Earth! It's common to encounter fully veiled women, high-fashion clad men, Christians, Muslims, and foreigners chatting together on the same street. The Lebanese, in fact, are the most hospitable people I've ever met—you definitely won't have trouble making new friends. The Lebanese also love to take visitors out to enjoy Beirut's infamous nightlife. Be prepared; the city never sleeps! If you study abroad in Beirut, you better be prepared to work hard and play even harder.

I participated in a rigorous language program that required ample amounts of homework, but time passes by quickly when you're studying Arabic in a cafe overlooking the Mediterranean. LAU is a mere 10-minute walk from the Corniche (a famous walkway by the coastline), but the campus itself is so lush and beautiful that most students just sit outdoors to do their reading assignments. Being from California, I adjusted to life on LAU's campus quite easily. Like my own college in the states, it boasts a diverse group of international students and I became friends with students from all over the world and from all walks of life. My academic experience was further enriched by series of lectures given about Middle Eastern culture and history, but you can just as easily learn about politics outside the classroom. Your Lebanese friends will undoubtedly discuss politics with you any time, any place. I've had some of the most intellectually stimulating conversations in clubs and rooftop bars—something I've missed since returning home!

Although Beirut is rich in cultural and religious sites, I took advantage of my study abroad experience to also travel to many other cities in Lebanon, all of which contain out-of-this-world historical sites (castles and grottos, to name a few) and nearby Syria. Neighboring Middle Eastern countries and cities are easily accessible by bus or plane. However, flights to Beirut are expensive so if you are thinking about studying in Lebanon, be sure to make travel plans early. American carriers do not fly into Beirut so it's not the easiest place to access in the world, but the country is worth all the effort.

> **Name:** Shadee Malaklou
>
> **University/college:** Duke University
>
> **Major:** Cultural Anthropology & Women's Studies
>
> **Year of college you studied abroad:** American University in Cairo (AUC)
>
> **Place you studied abroad:** Cairo, Egypt
>
> **Subject/field studied:** Cultural Anthropolgy & Women's Studies
>
> **Program name:** Study Abroad (direct exchange program)
>
> **Extremely random thing you most enjoyed about your experience:** Crashing an Egyptian wedding on the cornice (alongside the Nile) in Cairo.

The stereotypical Study Abroad advice is this: regardless of where you go, you will love your experiences abroad. As trite as this saying goes, it's true . . . even for an austere country like Egypt.

Egypt is not a country for the faint of heart or for partiers. Most likely, instead of drinking, you will melt away your sorrows on a tobacco pipe, or "sheesha." And it's for the better; Egyptian hard liquor is rumored to blind you.

Egypt is a dirty but beautiful country, and its people are still growing accustomed to foreigners. Sailboats down the Nile and trips to the "Khan," or bazaar, are popular tourist attractions in Cairo. The Pyramids at Giza are only a twenty-minute cab drive away, and with a little "backshish" (or tip) you can even climb them. "Koshari," a carbohydrate-based food, is the food of the masses and it is easy to eat cheap in Cairo.

In Egypt, you will be living amongst a rather empoverished community. In my opinion, it is the ultimate study abroad experience. You will still make friends, and you will still find a way to have a good time (despite the shortage of alcohol), but you will also learn a tremendous amount about yourself and about the world in which you live. Indeed, the luxuries of the first world are a far-off change from an Egyptian lifestyle.

Name: Laura Gutowski

University/college: Yale University

Major: History

Year of college you studied abroad: Spring 2006 (Junior Year)

Place you studied abroad: King's College London

Subject/field studied: History, Geography, French

Program name: JTA directly to KCL

Extremely random thing you most enjoyed about your experience: Snakebites: If you don't know what those are, you'll just have to go to London to find out.

London is the most amazing city on earth, and King's is the best place to be in the city. The campus is right in the middle of town by Trafalgar Square, and surrounded by world-class museums, shopping, and entertainment. I aimed to visit one new site each afternoon over the six months I was there,

and I still couldn't even come close to going to everything I wanted to see!

The people are incredible, and the culture in London is unlike anywhere else. Studying there gives you literally hundreds of perks, including huge discounts for food and drinks and free admission to all museums. Plus if you go to London through King's College, you're really living and studying with British students, unlike most other programs where you are surrounded by study abroad kids. I got to be great friends with people from all over the United Kingdom, and was thus able to hear their views and really discuss issues with them that would have been impossible in any other program. Of course since I was an actual student at King's, the workload was the same as at any prestigious university, but well worth it because of all I got out of having tutorials with only one other student and professor.

One of the major advantages of being in London is the ease of traveling all over Europe from there. Trains and buses are simple to take throughout the UK, and more importantly plane fares are absurdly inexpensive—I took one flight to Berlin for 1 pence, and another to Dublin for 7 pence, though with taxes it ended up being a whopping $4.99. Between the cheapness of travel and the extraordinarily long breaks, I was able to visit 18 different countries pretty thoroughly, including getting the chance to see the winter Olympics. By studying in London you not only take advantage of the city itself, but the whole continent!

To dispel a few common myths: I spent *far* less during my semester in London (including travel) than I ever did back at my university in the states, so avoid being tricked into thinking it's too expensive for you. Also, it doesn't rain much at all; London is in a drought and I used my umbrella only a handful of times. So don't let the legends stop you from having the most amazing experience of your life in the UK!

Terms You Should Know

Advanced Placement (AP)—College credit earned by students while still in high school. Many high schools offer specially designed AP courses that prepare students for the College Board's AP Exams. Administered in May, they can qualify students who score well for advanced standing when they enroll in college.

all-nighter—As in, "pulling an all-nighter." The process by which students attempt to learn a semester's worth of course material or crank out a paper of considerable length in a short period, often 24 to 48 hours. Cola, coffee, and/or caffeine pills are the staples of most all-night cramming sessions.

American College Test (ACT)—Test administered to high school juniors and seniors by the American College Testing Program. Traditionally it has been used as an admissions criterion primarily by Midwestern schools. Some Southern and Western schools use it as well.

American College Testing Program (ACTP)—The organization that produces the American College Test (ACT) and the Family Financial Statement (FFS). Many Midwestern universities use the ACT and the FFS in admissions instead of the SAT and the Financial-Aid Form (FAF). (See also "Family Financial Statement" and "Financial-Aid Form").

arts and sciences (also called liberal arts)—A broad term that encompasses most traditional courses of study, including the humanities, social sciences, natural sciences, mathematics, and foreign languages. A liberal arts college is also a college of arts and sciences. (See also "humanities" and "social sciences").

candidate's reply date—The May 1 deadline, observed by most selective colleges, by which the applicant must respond to an offer of admission, usually with a nonrefundable deposit of several hundred dollars. Colleges that require students to respond by May 1 in almost all cases notify them of their acceptance on or before April 15.

College Board—The organization that sponsors the SAT, the SAT IIs, the Advanced Placement tests, and the Financial-Aid Form (FAF). College Board admissions tests are developed and administered by the Educational Testing Service (ETS). (See also "Advanced Placement" and "Financial-Aid Form").)

Common Application—A form produced by a consortium of over 250 colleges that may be filled out and sent to member colleges in lieu of each school's individual application.

comprehensive exams (comps)—Also known as "generals," these tests, administered by some colleges (usually during the senior year) are designed to measure knowledge gained over a student's entire college career. Schools that give comps usually require students to pass the test in their major field in order to graduate.

computing assistant (CA)—A university employee, often an undergraduate, who helps students with all varieties of computing problems, from how to use a word processor to how to download games from the network.

consortium—A group of colleges affiliated in some way. The extent of the association can vary widely. Some consortiums—usually among colleges in close proximity—offer a range of joint programs that may include cross-registration, interlibrary loans, residential exchanges, and coordinated social, cultural, and athletic events.

co-op job—A paid internship, arranged for a student by his or her college, that provides on-the-job training, usually in an occupation closely related to the student's major.

core curriculum—A group of courses all students in a college must take in order to graduate. Core curricula are becoming widespread.

crew (rowing)—A sport, more familiar to those who live on or near either coast than to those from the South and Midwest, in which teams of two, four, or eight oarsmen or oarswomen race in long, narrow boats, usually on inland waterways. Crew is very "Ivy," quite popular at many schools, and usually requires no high school experience.

deferral—A college's postponement of the decision to accept or reject an early-action applicant. The applicant's file is entered in with those of regular-action candidates and is reviewed once again, this time for a final decision.

distribution requirements—Requirements stipulating that students take courses in a variety of broad subject areas in order to graduate. The number and definition of subject areas and the number of courses required in each varies from school to school. Typical categories include the humanities, social sciences, fine arts, natural sciences, foreign languages, and mathematics. Unlike a core curriculum, distribution requirements do not usually mandate specific courses that students must take. (See also "humanities," "social sciences," and "core curriculum").

drunk dial—To make a phone call to an old boyfriend or girlfriend, former hook-up (see below), or current love interest in an inebriated state.

dry—as in "dry campus." A school that does not allow alcohol for any students in its dorms or other campus facilities.

early action—A program that gives students early notification of a college's admissions decision. Unlike early decision, it does not require a prior commitment to enroll if accepted. Early action has become increasingly popular and is now available at many colleges covered in this book. Recently a few institutions, including Stanford and Yale, have switched to "single-choice" early action programs. These plans work the same way as regular early action, except that students cannot apply early anywhere else. Deadlines for both types of early-action applications are usually in late fall, with notification in December, January, or February. An applicant accepted under early action usually has until May 1, the candidate's reply date, to respond to the offer of admission. (See also "early decision" and "candidate's reply date").

early decision—A program under which a student receives early notification of a college's admissions decision if the student agrees in advance to enroll if accepted. Students may apply early decision to only one college; it should be a clear first choice. Application deadlines for early decision are usually in November, with decision letters mailed by mid-December.

Ethernet—A direct, high-speed means of access to the World Wide Web and the Internet, as well as a way to keep in touch with friends via e-mail. Most campuses are either "wired" with Ethernet, or will be in the near future.

family contribution—The amount of money that a family can "reasonably" be expected to pay toward a student's education, as determined by one of the two standardized needs-analysis forms. (See also "Financial-Aid Form" and "Family Financial Statement").

Family Financial Statement (FFS)—The financial-needs analysis form submitted to the American College Testing Program (ACTP), which, like the FAF, determines the expected family contribution. Colleges that use the American College Test (ACT) for admissions purposes usually require a copy of the FFS report from students applying for financial aid. (See also "American College Testing Program," "family contribution," and "Financial-Aid Form").

Facebookstalk—The process of stalking the likes of a crush, former high school sweetheart, or ex-boyfriend's girlfriend through facebook.com (See also "facebook.com).

fee waiver—Permission, often granted upon request, for needy students to apply for college admission without having to pay the application fee.

Financial-Aid Form (FAF)—The financial-needs analysis form submitted to the College Board by students applying for financial aid. Like the Family Financial Statement (FFS), it yields the expected family contribution. Colleges that require the Scholastic Assessment Test (SAT) for admission typically use the FAF as the basis for financial-aid awards. (See also "Family Financial Statement," "family contribution," and "College Board").

financial-aid package—The combination of loans, grants, and a work-study job that a school puts together for a student receiving financial aid.

five-year plan—The practice of stretching a four-year degree program over a five-year period.

four-one-four—An academic calendar consisting of two regular four-month semesters with a short "winter" or "January" term in between. Variations include four-four-one and three-three-two. In most cases, these numbers refer to the number of courses a student is expected to complete in each segment of the year, although at some schools they refer to the number of months in each segment.

freshman 15—A reference to the number of pounds students often gain during the freshman year. Usually caused by a combination of too little exercise, unlimited helpings in the dining hall, too many late-night runs for pizza, and over consumption of alcoholic beverages.

government aid—Money that federal or state governments make available to students, most of which is administered through the colleges on the basis of need. Government aid can come in the form of grants, loans, and work-study jobs. Stafford Loans (formerly Guaranteed Student Loans) and PLUS parent loans of up to $2,625 and $4,000 per year, respectively, are made available through commercial lending institutions. For further information on government aid programs, contact the state and federal departments of education.

grade inflation—A situation in which average work is consistently awarded a higher letter grade than it would normally earn. At most schools, the grade for average work is about B–/C+. But in classes or entire colleges with grade inflation, it can be as high as B or even B+.

Greek system—The fraternities and sororities on a particular campus. They are called "Greek" because most take their names from combinations of letters in the Greek alphabet.

gut—A course widely known to be very easy, often with enrollments well into the hundreds. Guts are traditionally favorites among second-semester seniors.

hook up—To enjoy a person's nonplatonic company, often used in reference to a one-night event. A very vague term that can range from an innocent kiss to sex, depending on usage.

humanities—Subjects in which the primary focus is on human culture. Examples include philosophy, language, and literature. (See also "social sciences").

independent study—A course, usually in a student's major field, in which he or she studies independently and meets one-on-one with a professor on a topic of the student's choosing. Some colleges require an independent study essay or research paper for graduation.

interdisciplinary major—A major that combines two complementary subjects from different fields, such as biology and psychology. Students completing these majors take courses in each area as well as courses that explicitly join the two.

International Baccalaureate (IB)—A high school program found across the world which, like AP courses, can earn a student advanced standing upon college enrollment.

intramurals—Athletic leagues informally organized within a college. Students are free from the burden of tryouts and play with and against fellow classmates.

jungle juice—A potent mix of liquor (often grain alcohol) and juice served at college parties out of a large watercooler. Freshmen who underestimate the juice's power due to its fruity taste, inevitably regret consumption the morning after.

language requirement—A rule at many colleges that requires students to study a foreign language before graduation. Two years on the college level are usually required, although credit from Advanced Placement or SAT IIs often allows students to bypass the requirement.

legacy—An applicant whose mother or father is a graduate of a particular school. Students with legacy status are often given preferential treatment in admissions.

merit scholarship—A financial grant for some part of college costs, usually awarded for academic achievement or special skill in an extracurricular activity and not based on need. Private corporations and many colleges offer merit scholarships.

need-based aid—Money awarded solely on the basis of need, usually administered through the colleges. Some schools agree to pay the difference between their total fees and the expected family contribution; others pay only part of it, leaving some "unmet" need. Most financial-aid packages consist of some combination of three components: grants, loans, and work-study jobs. Some of the money comes from the college's own resources, although part is financed by federal and state governments. (See also "government aid").

need-blind admissions—A policy in which the applicant's ability to pay does not affect the college's consideration of his or her application. Some schools with need-blind admissions also guarantee to meet the full demonstrated financial need of all accepted applicants as determined by one of the two standardized needs-analysis forms; others do not. (See also "family contribution," "Financial-Aid Form," and "Family Financial Statement").

office hours—A period during which a professor agrees to be available in his or her office for the purpose of talking with students about their coursework. Professors are not always required by their colleges to have office hours, but most do anyway.

open admissions—A policy under which any applicant with a high school diploma is accepted. State universities that have this policy usually limit open admission to state residents.

parietals—Regulations that govern the times when students of one sex may visit dorms or floors housing the opposite sex. Usually found only at the most conservative schools nowadays.

pass/fail or CR/F or CR/D/F—An option offered by some schools in certain classes. A student may enroll in a class and simply receive credit or failure (or a D in "CR/D/F") for it on his or her transcript instead of a specific grade; God's gift to college students everywhere.

PLUS parent loans—A component of the Stafford Loan, for parents. (See also "government aid").

pre-frosh—A visiting high school student, potential college recruit, or admitted student who has yet to enroll.

problem set—An annoying weekly assignment you're inevitably faced with in any given science or quantitative class. This thankless task will keep you up 'til 2 a.m. Sunday nights but can count for 1/50 of your grade or one-half. Previously known as homework.

quad—An abbreviation for "quadrangle"; many dorm complexes are built in squares (quadrangles) with a courtyard in the middle. Quad can also refer to a suite of dormitory rooms in which four students live together.

quarter system—An academic calendar under which the school year is divided into four quarters, three of which constitute a full academic year. Less common than the semester system, it is most often used by large universities with extensive programs in agricultural and technical fields.

resident advisor/assistant (RA)—A student, usually an upperclassman, who lives in a dorm and helps to maintain regulations and enforce school policy, as well as offering advice and support to dorm residents. RAs receive compensation from the school for their services, usually in the form of free room and board.

rolling admissions—A policy under which a college considers applications almost immediately after receiving them. Decision letters are mailed within a month after the application is filed. Colleges with rolling admissions continue to accept applications only until the class is filled, so it is best to apply early.

Scholastic Assessment Test (SAT)—Test administered to high school juniors and seniors by the College Board of the Educational Testing Service, with math, verbal, and written-language sections. Used as an admissions criterion at most colleges nationwide.

senior project—Many majors at many colleges require seniors to complete a special project during their senior year. This could involve a thesis (anywhere from 15 to 100 pages), a research project, some sort of internship, or all of the above. Some colleges offer seniors a choice between taking comps or doing a project. (See also "comps.")

sexile—There are two people in the bedroom you share with your roommate, and you are not one of them. Hopefully you have a common room with a comfortable couch.

social sciences—Subjects that deal systematically with the institutions of human society, most notably economics and political science. The behavioral sciences, which include psychology, sociology, and anthropology, are often included in this group as well.

study break—An institutionalized form of procrastination involving food and talk. Often informally arranged—"I'm sick of calculus, let's take a study break at——" (insert name of local hangout)—but can be sponsored by RAs, cultural groups, or even school administrators. Some nights, study breaks can take more of your time than the actual studying.

teaching assistant (TA)—A graduate student who assists a professor in the presentation of a course. Usually the professor gives two to four lectures a week for all the students in the class; the TAs hold smaller weekly discussion sections.

facebook.com—An online directory launched in 2004 that connects individuals through college networks. Invaluable tool for procrastinators.

three-two program (3–2)—A program in which students can study three years at one school, followed by two at another, more specialized school. Upon completion, many of these programs award both the bachelor's and the master's degrees.

town-gown relations—The contact between a college (students, employees, buildings) and its host town (citizens, businesses, local government) and the set of issues around which this contact revolves. Such issues include taxes, traffic, local employment practices, and government services like road maintenance, sewage, and trash collection.

townie—A resident of a college town or city who is not enrolled in the college, but who might sit beside you at the local pub. Often involves a them-versus-us mentality.

trimesters—An academic calendar that divides the school year into three terms of approximately equal length. Schools on the trimester system generally have one term before the winter break and two after.

tutorial major (also self-designed or special major)—A program offered by many schools in which a student can plan his or her own major, combining the offerings of two or more traditional majors, usually in consultation with a faculty member. An example is Medieval studies, in which the student might study the history, literature, philosophy, and art of the period, taking courses from a number of departments. (See also "interdisciplinary major").

waiting list—A list of students who are not initially accepted to a certain school, but who may be admitted later, depending on the number of accepted students who enroll. Most colleges ultimately accept only a fraction of the students on the waiting list, who are notified during the summer.

work-study—Campus jobs, for financial-aid recipients, that are subsidized by the federal government. Work-study jobs are a component of most need-based financial-aid packages. Students typically work 10 to 20 hours a week to help finance their education.

Editors' Choice

Most Blondes

University of Southern California
University of Mississippi
Southern Methodist University
Pepperdine University
University of Texas at Austin
Vanderbilt University
University of South Carolina
University of Georgia
Florida State University
University of Virginia

Easiest Course Load

Seton Hall University
Hofstra University
University of Hawaii
Arizona State University
University of Alaska-Fairbanks
Keene State University
Salve Regina University
Texas Tech University
University of California Santa Cruz
Hampshire College

Biggest Jock Schools

University of Florida
Clemson University
University of Notre Dame
Ohio State University
Texas A&M University
University of North Carolina Chapel Hill
University of Connecticut
United States Naval Academy
Penn State University
University of Michigan

Most Difficult Requirements

Reed College
University of Chicago
California Institute of Technology
Columbia University
United States Military Academy at West
    Point
Parsons School of Design
University of California Berkeley
Princeton University
United States Coast Guard Academy
Massachusetts Institute of Technology

Most Millionaire Graduates

Stanford University
Northwestern University
Duke University
Southern Methodist University
University of Texas at Austin
Yale University
Brown University
Harvard University
Duke University
Princeton University

Best Local Restaurants

The University of Texas at Austin
University of California Berkeley
Brown University
New York University
Boston University
Northwestern University
University of Washington
University of Miami
Georgetown University
Amherst College

Schools That Never Sleep

New York University
Massachusetts Institute of Technology
California Institute of Technology
Cooper Union
Yale University
University of Chicago
Parsons School of Design
University of California Irvine
Cornell University
University of California Santa Barbara

Strongest Undergraduate Focus

Princeton University
Stanford University
Occidental College
Mt. Holyoke College
Williams College
Smith University
California Polytechnic Institute
Carleton College
Tulane University
Baylor University

Place most likely to find your spouse (getting an MRS. Degree as they call it)

Southern Methodist University
University of California Santa Barbara
University of South Carolina
University of Mississippi
Auburn University
Middlebury College
Connecticut College
Wheaton College (Illinois)
Brigham Young University
Penn State University

Happiest Students

Yale University
University of Pennsylvania

Pomona College
DePaul University
Whitman College
Tufts University
Wesleyan College
Brown University
Claremont McKenna
Bowdoin College

Best Study Abroad Programs

St. John's University
University of Montana
Colgate University
Colby College
Carleton College
Lewis & Clark
Bates College
Elon University
Duke University
University of California Los Angeles

Most Behind the Times

Oral Roberts University
College of William and Mary
University of North Dakota
Beloit College
Iowa State
Michigan Tech
Rutgers
Davidson College
Union College
George Mason

Best College Town

University of California / Berkeley
University of California / Los Angeles
University of Texas / Austin
Tulane University
Parsons School of Design
University of Michigan
Univesity of Miami in Ohio
University of Wisconsin
Boston College
Georgetown University

Biggest Rivalries

Harvard/Yale
West Point/Naval Academy
Stanford/University of California Berkeley
University of Southern California/University
    of California Los Angeles
University of Texas Austin/Texas Tech
    University
Duke/University of North Carolina Chapel Hill
University of South Carolina/Clemson
    University
Leigh University/Lafayette College
University of Alabama/Auburn University
Ohio State/University of Michigan

Craziest mascot

Harvard University (Cantab)
Xavier University (Blue Blob)
Syracuse University (Orangemen)
Western Kentucky State (Red Blob—
    Hilltoppers)

Connecticut College (Camels)
University of California Irvine (Anteaters)
Purdue University (Boilermakers)
Texas Christian University (Horned Frogs)
Franklin and Marshall (The Diplomats)
Knox college (Prairie Fire)

Ugliest school colors

Bowling Green State University (Brown and
    Orange)
Clemson University (Burnt Orange and
    Purple)
Rice University (Blue and Gray)
University of Washington (Purple
    and Gold)
Florida State University (Maroon and Dark
    Gold)
Mississippi State University (Maroon)
University of Tennessee (Bright Orange and
    White)
University of Wyoming (Brown and Gold)
Auburn University (Burnt Orange and Navy
    Blue)
Beloit College ("The Gold")

The College Finder

Regions

New England:
Connecticut
Maine
Massachusetts
New Hampshire
Rhode Island
Vermont
Eastern Canada

Mid-Atlantic:
Delaware
District of Columbia
Maryland
New Jersey
New York
Pennsylvania
West Virginia

Midwest:
Illinois
Indiana
Iowa
Kansas
Kentucky
Michigan
Minnesota
Missouri
Nebraska
North Dakota
Ohio
South Dakota
Wisconsin

Southeast:
Alabama
Arkansas
Florida
Georgia
Lousiana
Mississippi
South Carolina
North Carolina
Tennessee
Virginia

West:
Alaska
Arizona
California
Colorado
Hawaii
Idaho
Montana
New Mexico
Nevada
Oklahoma
Oregon
Texas
Utah
Washington
Wyoming
Western Canada

Schools with 1,500 Undergraduates or Fewer

New England:
College of the Atlantic
Marlboro College
Bennington College
United States Coast Guard Academy
Hampshire College
Bard College

Mid-Atlantic:
St. John's College
Trinity College
Haverford College
Bryn Mawr College
Swarthmore College
Goucher College
The Cooper Union for the
 Advancement of Science and Art
Sarah Lawrence College
The Juilliard School

Midwest:
Wabash College
Centre College
Cornell College
Earlham College
Knox College
Kalamazoo College
Alma College
Beloit College
Lake Forest College
St. Mary's College
Lawrence University
Principia College

Southeast:
New College of Florida
Randolph-Macon Women's College
Sweet Briar College
Hollins University
Agnes Scott College
Milsaps College
Hampden-Sydney College
Wofford College
Birmingham-Southern College

West:
Deep Springs College
Harvey Mudd College
Mills College
California Institute of the Arts
Scripps College
California Institute of Technology
Pitzer College
Claremont McKenna College
Whitman College
Reed College
University of Dallas
Hendrix College
Whittier College

1,501–3,000 Undergraduates

New England:
Connecticut College
Trinity College
Wesleyan University
Bowdoin College
Bates College
Colby College
Wheaton College
Amherst College
Babson College
Simmons College
Clark University
Mount Holyoke College
Williams College
Wellesley College
Smith College
The College of the Holy Cross
Worcester Polytechnic Institute
Rhode Island School of Design
Middlebury College
Salve Regina University

Mid-Atlantic:
Catholic University
Drew University
Stevens Institute of Technology
Manhattanville College

Hamilton College
Hobart and William Smith Colleges
Alfred University
St. Lawrence University
St. Bonaventure University
Union College
Barnard College
Skidmore College
Vassar College
Clarkson University
Colgate University
Franklin and Marshall
Susquehanna University
Allegheny College
Muhlenberg College
Lafayette College
Dickinson College
Gettysburg College

Midwest:
Wheaton College
Grinnell College
Rose-Hulman Institute of Technology
DePauw University
Albion College
Macalester College
Carleton College
Gustavus Adolphus College
St. Olaf College
Kenyon College
College of Wooster
Ohio Wesleyan University
Wittenberg University
Denison University
Oberlin College

Southeast:
Tuskegee University
Rollins College
Florida Southern University
Stetson University
Florida Institute of Technology
Spelman College
Morehouse College
Furman University
Rhodes College
Washington and Lee University
University of Richmond

West:
Pomona College
Occidental College
University of Redlands
St. Mary's College of California
Pepperdine University
Colorado College
Colorado School of Mines
University of Tulsa
Lewis and Clark College

Willamette University
Trinity University
Rice University
University of Puget Sound

Over 20,000 Undergrads

New England:
University of Toronto

Mid-Atlantic:
University of Maryland / College Park
Rutgers/ The State University of New Jersey
Temple University
Penn State University

Midwest:
University of Illinois / Urbana-Champaign
Indiana University / Bloomington
Purdue University
Iowa State University
University of Iowa
University of Kansas
University of Michigan
Michigan State University
University of Minnesota
Ohio State University
University of Wisconsin, Madison

Southeast:
Florida State University
University of Florida
University of Georgia
North Carolina State University
Virginia PolyInstitute of Technology
   University

West:
University of Arizona
Arizona State University
University of California / San Diego
University of California / Davis
University of California / Berkeley
University of California / Los Angeles
University of Colorado / Boulder
Texas Institute of Technology University
Texas A&M University
University of Texas, Austin
Brigham Young University
University of Washington
University of British Columbia
University of Western Ontario

Single Sex Schools

Female:
Mills College
Scripps College
Agnes Scott College
St. Mary's College
Mount Holyoke College
Spelman College
Barnard College
Smith College
Wellesley College
Trinity College (D.C.)
Bryn Mawr
Randolph-Macon Women's College
Sweet Briar College
Hollins University
Simmons College
Wells College

Male:
Deep Springs College
Wabash College
Hampden-Sydney College
Morehouse College

Predominantly Male Schools (>66%)

The Cooper Union for the Advancement of
   Science and Art
Florida Institute of Technology
California Institute of Technology
Harvey Mudd College
United States Coast Guard Academy
Rochester Institute of Technology
Georgia Institute of Technology
Stevens Institute of Technology
Rensselaer Polytechnic Institute
Worcester Polytechnic Institute
Rose-Hulman Institute of Technology
Clarkson University
Colorado School of Mines
United States Air Force Academy
United States Naval Academy
United States Military Academy
Michigan Technological University

Predominantly Female Schools (>66%)

California Institute of the Arts
Sarah Lawrence College
Adelphi University
City University of New York / Hunter College
Manhattanville College
Eugene Lang College/ New School
Bennington College
Howard University
Rhode Island School of Design
Salve Regina University

High Minority Enrollment (>35%)

New England:
Yale University
Massachusetts Institute of Technology
Wellesley
Harvard University

Mid-Atlantic
Howard University
Johns Hopkins University
Rutgers
Princeton University
CUNY/ City College
CUNY/ Hunter College
CUNY/ Queens College
The Cooper Union for the Advancement of Science and Art
New York University

Midwest
University of Illinois, Chicago
Loyola University
DePaul University

Southeast
Tuskegee University
Florida A & M University
University of Miami
Morehouse College
Spelman College

West
University of California / Riverside
University of California / Irvine
University of California / Los Angeles
University of California / Berkeley
Stanford University
University of California / Davis

University of California / San Diego
University of South Carolina
California State University / Fresno
California Institute of Technology
Pepperdine University
University of California / Santa Barbara
University of California / Santa Cruz
Occidental College
University of Hawaii
New Mexico State University
University of New Mexico
University of Houston
Rice University
Whittier College

Schools Accepting <25% of Applicants

The Juilliard School
Yale University
United States Naval Academy
Harvard University
United States Military Academy
The Cooper Union for the Advancement of Science and Art
Stanford University
Princeton University
Columbia University
United States Air Force Academy
California Institute of the Arts
Massachusetts Institute of Technology
Brown University
Dartmouth College
Amherst College
Williams College
Pomona College
California Institute of Technology
University of Pennsylvania
Duke University
Washington University St. Louis
Rice University
Claremont McKenna College
Georgetown University
United States Coast Guard Academy
University of California / Los Angeles
Middlebury College
Bowdoin College

Schools Accepting 25–40%

University of California / Berkeley
Swarthmore College
University South Carolina

Pepperdine University
Barnard College
Wesleyan College
Tufts University
Haverford College
Cornell University
Carleton College
Vassar College
Hunter College
Northwestern
University of Notre Dame
Washington and Lee
Bates College
Boston College
Colgate University
Hamilton College
Bucknell College
Rhode Island School of Design
College of William and Mary
Connecticut College
Johns Hopkins University
New York University
Vanderbilt University
Oberlin College
Emory University
Trinity College
Bard College
Colby College
Wellesley College
Babson College
University of Virginia
Harvey Mudd College
California Poly Institute of Technology San
   Luis Obispo
George Washington University
Kenyon College
Pitzer College
Macalester College
Brandeis University
University of Chicago
University of Richmond
Lehigh University
Carnegie Mellon University
CUNY/ Queens College
University of California / San Diego
University of Miami
Northeastern University
Elon University
SUNY / Binghamton
Denison University
Colorado College
University of Tennessee, Knoxville
College of the Holy Cross
Sarah Lawrence College
Franklin and Marshall College
Reed College
Occidental College
Tulane University
University of Delaware

Wheaton College
Muhlenberg College
Gettysburg College
Spelman College
Howard University
Bryn Mawr College
Wake Forest University
Union College
University of Rochester
The College of New Jersey
Skidmore College
Kansas State University
Stevens Institute of Technology
Scripps College
Wabash College
University of Pittsburg
Dickinson College
Rhodes College
University of Maryland, College Pk
Fordham University
University of Connecticut
Whitman College
SUNY / Stony Brook

Large Fraternity/Sorority Systems (More than 30%)

Albion College
Birmingham-Southern College
Bucknell College
Case Western Reserve University
Centre College
Colgate University
Cornell College
Dartmouth College
Denison University
DePauw University
Emory University
Franklin and Marshall College
Furman College
Gettysburg College
Hamilton College
Hampden-Sydney College
Lehigh University
Millsaps College
Massachusetts Institute of Technology
Northwestern University
Ohio Wesleyan University
Rensselaer Polytechnic Institute
Rhodes College
Rollins College
Rose-Hulman Institute of Technology
Stevens Institute of Technology
Texas Christian University

Tulane University
University of Richmond
University of the South / Sewanee
University of Virginia
Vanderbilt University
Wabash College
Wake Forest University
Washington and Lee University
Whitman College
Willamette University
College of William and Mary
Wofford College

St. John's/St. Benedict
St. Mary's College
St. Olaf College
United States Naval Academy
University of Notre Dame
United States Air Force Academy
United States Coast Guard Academy
Wabash College
Wellesley College
Wheaton College

Schools with No Fraternity or Sororities

Alfred College
Amherst College
Barnard College
Bates College
Bennington College
Boston College
Bowdoin College
Brigham Young
Bryn Mawr College
Carleton College
Clark University
College of the Atlantic
Connecticut College
The Cooper Union for the Advancement of
    Science and Art
Drew University
Earlham College
Georgetown University
Goucher College
Hampshire College
Harvard University
Hendrix College
Hobart and William Smith
College of the Holy Cross
The Juilliard School
Kalamazoo College
Lewis and Clark College
Macalester College
Marlboro College
Mills College
Mount Holyoke College
New College of Florida
Oral Roberts University
Pitzer College
Principia College
Reed College
Rice University
Skidmore College
Smith College

Schools with Very High Graduation Rates

Amherst College
Barnard College
Bates College
Boston College
Bowdoin College
Brandeis University
Brown University
Bryn Mawr College
Bucknell College
California Institute of Technology
Carleton College
Carnegie Mellon University
Case Western Reserve University
Centre College
Claremont McKenna
Colby College
Colgate University
Colorado College
Columbia University
Connecticut College
Cornell University
Dartmouth College
Deep Springs College
Dickinson College
Duke University
Emory University
Fairfield University
Franklin and Marshall College
Furman College
Georgetown University
Grinnell College
Hamilton College
Harvard University
Harvey Mudd College
Haverford College
College of the Holy Cross
James Madison
Johns Hopkins University
The Juilliard School
Kenyon College
Lafayette College

Lehigh University
Macalester College
Miami University, Ohio
Middlebury College
Massachusetts Institute of
    Technology
Muhlenberg College
Northwestern University
New York University
Penn State University
Pomona College
Princeton University
Rensselaer Polytechnic Institute
Rhode Island School of Design
Skidmore College
Smith College
St. Olaf College
SUNY Binghamton
Swarthmore College
The College of New Jersey
Trinity College
Tufts University
University of Pennsylvania
United States Military Academy
United States Naval Academy
Union College
University of Illinois /
    Urbana-Champaign
University of Chicago
University of Michigan
University of Notre Dame
University of Richmond
University of Rochester
University of Virginia
Vanderbilt University
Vassar College
Villanova University
Wake Forest University
Washington and Lee University
Washington University / St. Louis
Wellesley College
Wesleyan University
Whitman College
College of William and Mary
Worcester Poly Institute of
    Technology
Yale University

Tuition Under $6,000

The Evergreen State College
University of British Columbia
McGill University

$6,000–$11,999

Mid-Atlantic
SUNY / Albany
CUNY/ City College
CUNY/ Queens College
SUNY / Stony Brook
CUNY/ Hunter College

Midwest
University of South Dakota
Bowling Green University
University of Southern Illinois / Carbondale
University of Kentucky
Marshall University

Southeast
University of Southern Alabama
University of Mississippi
Mississippi State University
Tuskegee University

West
University of Nevada / Reno
University of Hawaii
University of Wyoming

$12,000–$17,999

New England
The College of New Jersey
Rutgers
University of Delaware
University of Massachusetts /
    Amherst
University of Maine / Orono

Mid-Atlantic
SUNY / Binghamton
Howard University
West Virginia University
George Mason University
Temple University
Virginia Polytechnic Institute and State
    University

Midwest
University of Idaho
Illinois State University
University of Kansas
Kent State University
Iowa State University
Ohio University

University of Iowa
Kansas State University
University of Kansas

Southeast
University of Arkansas
Louisiana State University
University of Alabama
Florida A & M University
University of Florida
Spelman College
Florida State University
University of Tennessee, Knoxville
North Carolina State University
Morehouse College
University of Georgia
University of Missouri / Columbia

West
Hendrix
Oral Roberts University
Colorado State University
Texas A&M University
Texas Institute of Technology
University of Texas / Austin
University of Nebraska
Arizona State University
California Poly Institute of Technology San
    Luis Obispo
University of Houston
University of Montana
University of Utah
University of New Mexico
California State University / Chico
University of Arizona
California State University / Fresno
New Mexico State University
Oklahoma State University
University of Alaska / Fairbanks
University of Oklahoma

$18,000–$23,999

New England
University of Rhode Island
University of Connecticut
Quinnipiac University
University of New Hampshire
Seton Hall University
Marlboro College

Mid-Atlantic
Penn State University
University of Maryland, College Pk

University of Pittsburg
St. Bonaventure University
Hofstra University
The Juilliard School
Rochester Institute of Technology
Drexel University

Midwest
Ohio State University
Michigan State University
University of Illinois, Chicago
Indiana University, Bloomington
Purdue University
University of Minnesota
DePaul University
University of Wisconsin, Madison
Wheaton College
Alma College
University of Cincinnati
Miami University, Ohio
Valparaiso University
University of Illinois / Urbana-Champaign
Marquette University
Wabash College
Cornell College
St. John's/St. Benedict
Lawrence University
Principia College

Southeast
Hampden-Sydney
Agnes Scott College
Randolph-Macon Women's College
Centre College
College of William and Mary
Hollins University
Sweet Briar College
Birmingham-Southern College
Millsaps College
Florida Southern University
New College of Florida
Elon University
University of South Carolina /
    Columbia
Georgia Institute of Technology
Centre College
Rhodes College

West
University of Tulsa
University of Washington
Colorado School of Mines
University of Dallas
Texas Christian University
Trinity University
Baylor University
Rice University

Insider's Quiz

What kind of college is right for you?

On a Saturday afternoon you can find me . . .
- a. Cheering on our football team with 10,000 of my closest friends
- b. As a jail guard for the schoolwide capture the flag game.
- c. Is it the afternoon already? Off to the library stat!
- d. Yelling at pedestrians not to step on my sidewalk chalk mural.

What's your biggest college hookup fear?
- a. That everyone I've ever kissed is in the same circle of friends.
- b. I'll never run into the person again.
- c. It'll be purely physical. Intellectual conversation is the best foreplay of all.
- d. Accidentally hooking up with a jock.

How do you take your coffee?
- a. Frozen, blended with whipped cream. It's got to travel well.
- b. They only serve one type where I'm from.
- c. Strong.
- d. Low-fat organic soy milk latte with a shot and a half of sugar free sustainable hazelnut syrup . . . . No cup. I have my mug.

Where is your favorite place to party?
- a. Where the football team is, celebrating its big win.
- b. At my best friend's house. Everyone at school comes to our parties, I guess because we all fit into one house.
- c. I'm not picky. I study so much I'll take any chance I get to party.
- d. Anywhere there's a hookah.

What adjective would your best friend use to describe you?
- a. Spirited
- b. Sociable
- c. Studious
- d. Socially Conscious

Where's your favorite place to shop?
- a. My school's store. They have the best selection of team sweatshirts.
- b. The town mall. They have a GAP and J.Crew. Enough said.
- c. Online. I have too much homework to do and too many club meetings and practices to attend to have time to go to the mall.
- d. The thrift store. I'm so not about mass market.

In ten years, you see yourself
- a. At your school's homecoming weekend, remembering the good ol' days.
- b. Married to your high school sweetheart and living in your hometown.
- c. Thinking your hard work has finally paid off.
- d. Being an artist or an activist.

After four years of high school, I feel . . .
- a. Trapped! I've been with these people for way too long. I hate that everyone knows everything about my life!
- b. Sad. I've formed such good friendships and wish I had more time here.
- c. As though I'm at an intellectual standstill. I need more of an academic challenge!
- d. Like my talents and capabilities have gone unappreciated for way too long. Who cares that I did not do well in science or geography class?

During lunchtime in high school, I usually . . .
- a. Leave campus. The cafeteria is too limiting, I need more choices!
- b. Usually? I always eat with the same group of people and always at the same table.
- c. Can't waste time having a sit-down meal. Lunch period is my only free time to meet with teachers or study partners. I need to feel like I've accomplished something!
- d. Take the time to sit down, relax, and discuss . . .

What is your favorite music to listen to on the way to school in the morning?
- a. AC/DC's "You Shook Me All Night Long."

b. "Lean on Me"—it may be corny but it's got a good message
c. No better way to start the school day than with Beethoven.
d. It's not even worth naming it. I'm sure you've never heard of them anyway.

My favorite high school teacher . . .
   a. Was my gym teacher, she knew how to keep us energized.
   b. Knew me very well. It's important to form close relationships with educators.
   c. Always kept us thinking. His/her class was difficult, but I learned a lot!
   d. Truly understood me for who I am, and always saw my hidden talents.

Results

What kind of college is right for you?

One where . . .

If you answered mostly (a.) College spirit rules

If you answered mostly (b.) Everybody knows your name

If you answered mostly (c.) You work hard, play hard—that is, if you ever leave the library

If you answered mostly (d.) Your creative side can shine

Insider's Packing List

Things to bring:

- Jumbo pack of energy drinks
- Red cups
- Clorox wipes
- Airborne
- Hotpot
- Shower shoes
- Febreeze
- Tool kit
- A photo of your family
- A photo of your high school friends
- Costumes
- 1 nice dress
- iPod
- One beer light (at least)
- Christmas lights
- Duct tape
- Twister
- Deck of cards
- Dice
- Iron
- Layers
- Compact umbrella
- Brita
- Cough drops
- ATM card
- Checkbook
- Stamps
- Stationery
- USB
- A white t-shirt to write on
- Shot glass
- Magnetic poetry
- Boardgames
- Fan
- Feather boa
- Cowboy hat
- Homemade cookies
- Picnic blanket
- Sweatshirt blanket
- Clorox bleach pen
- Sticky tack
- Energy saving light bulb
- Condoms
- Cute facebook photo
- Hand sanitizer
- Bottle opener
- Corkscrew
- Fake ID
- Waterguns
- Water balloons
- Tide to Go
- Thai bowls
- Annie's Mac & Cheese
- Sexy underwear
- Bathing suit
- One pair of shoes that you don't mind ruining
- One pair of shoes that you'd hate to ruin
- SS #—memorized
- US Weekly subscription
- Handcuffs
- Hookah
- Vibrator
- Best high school friends' emails and school addresses
- Costco card
- Frisbee
- Markers
- DVDs
- Organized jewelry holder
- Lots of towels
- A pair of aviators
- Hair straightener
- Plastic utensils
- Volleyball/Basketball/Baseball . . . pretty much, anything you can throw
- A Day Minder
- 1-Subject notebooks
- Body paint
- Mirror
- Punch bowl
- Wig

Things to leave at home:

- Varsity jackets
- High school yearbooks
- Pleasure reading
- More than 2 stuffed animals
- A high school sweetheart
- SAT scores
- Trophies
- Your virginity
- Stamp/baseball card/Absolut ad collections
- Overly-descriptive away messages
- Dry-clean only clothes
- A "College" T-shirt

A Word About Statistics

You want to narrow your search, size up a school quickly, or check out your chances of getting admitted? Statistics are a useful place to start when you are browsing colleges, and they are also helpful in creating that perfect list of reach, mid-range, and safety schools to which you will apply. A statistical profile precedes every college in the *Insider's Guide*. The colleges themselves provide the data. The letters "NA" (not available) either represents data that the school did not report, or figures under one percent. For the most up-to-date information, as well as for all data not included in the *Insider's Guide*, you should contact the colleges directly.

As a rule, the statistics provided are from the most recent year for which the college has information. In most cases, this means either the 2005–2006 or 2006–2007 academic year. In general, percentages have been rounded to the nearest whole-number percent. Statistically speaking, there is no significant difference between an acceptance rate of 30 percent and 30.4 percent; in fact, even a difference of 3 to 5 percent would hardly be noticeable.

Below the name of each school the **address** and undergraduate **admissions phone number** are listed; this is the contact information that a school's admissions office prefers applicants to use when corresponding.

A **Web site URL** and admissions office e-mail address is listed for each school, so you can correspond over e-mail and get a quick sense of the school online.

Founded is the year that the school first accepted students.

The designation **private or public** refers to private schools versus publicly-funded state schools.

Religious affiliation indicates whether a school is affiliated in any way with a particular religious establishment. This affiliation may vary from traditional school history to strong religious and cultural sentiments in the student population and administration.

Location describes the setting of the college, which is either rural, suburban, small city, or urban. This description gives only a general idea of the surroundings.

Undergraduate enrollment is the number of full-time undergraduate students for the most recent year available at the time of publication, whereas **Total enrollment** gives the total number of students, including part-time and full-time undergraduates, graduate students, and professional students. Often the ratio of undergraduate to graduate students gives an indication of the relative emphasis an institution places on each.

Percent male/female (M/F) gives the percentage of undergraduates of each sex.

Percent minority is the percentage of enrolled students who indicated on their applications that they consider themselves members of a minority group. This figure is broken down by percentages of students in four broad minority groups—**African-American, Asian-American, Hispanic, and Native-American**—to give a measure of the ethnic diversity of the school. Many students of different ethnicities, such as international students and biracial students, are not included in this section. You may want to contact the college directly for more specific information.

Percent in-state/out-of-state is the percentage of enrolled undergraduates who are residents of the state in which the school is located. For Canadian schools, the percentage is that of students from within Canada. This figure gives an approximation of the regional diversity of the school. Obviously, the in-state numbers will usually be much higher for public schools than for private schools, although in most cases, states provide incentives for private schools to take in-state students.

Percent pub HS is, of course, the percentage of students whose secondary education took place in a public school.

On-campus housing gives the percentage of students living in school-controlled housing. Be prepared to seek off-campus housing arrangements early if a school's housing percentage is less than 90 percent or if no figure is listed.

The figures for membership in **sororities** and **fraternities** represent the approximate percentage of male students joining fraternities and female students joining sororities, as reported by the administration. Fraternity and sorority enrollment over 25 or 30 percent usually indicates a strong Greek system. Note that fraternity and sorority figures do not include non-Greek exclusive clubs or secret societies.

Number of applicants is the number of completed first-year undergraduate applications received by the university.

The **percent accepted** figure is the number of applicants accepted for the most recent entering freshman class (in this case, usually the class of 2012) divided by the total number of applicants. This is an imperfect measure of a college's selectivity, and does not necessarily reflect academic quality, since many factors can influence acceptance rates. One example of this is that some schools with reputations for being easy after admission tend to attract larger numbers of applicants. For another example, public schools offer lower tuition to in-state residents, which is an attractive incentive for those applicants. Even winning sports teams can increase application numbers. There are many other factors that can influence the quality and size of the applicant pool even from year to year. Despite these caveats, the percent accepted figure is a revealing statistic. Colleges that accept relatively small numbers of applicants are usually in the best position to maintain high academic standards. When the acceptance rate is less than one-third, you can be assured that the school is one of the best around.

Percent accepted who enroll is the number of students who enroll divided by the number of students accepted. This figure, commonly called the "yield" by the admissions offices, is another way to assess how well a school attracts qualified applicants. Since many applicants have to decide between several schools, the yield is a good indicator of which schools are first-choice and which are "safety" schools. The latter usually have yields below 40 percent. The main use of yields is to compare colleges that have similar applicant pools. State universities tend to have high yields because some applicants are in-state students who do not apply elsewhere.

Entering class includes the number of first-years and transfers on campus at the beginning of the year.

Transfers reports the number of students who were accepted for transfer to that institution each year. The transfers accepted is a better indication of an applicant's chances of gaining admission than the actual number of transfers matriculated, since often the number of transfers accepted is large compared to the number of matriculating transfer students. Keep in mind that

"NA" here does not mean that there were no transfers, only that the schools did not report a number. Of course, not every school accepts transfer students, but those that do may restrict the number or have as many students leaving as transferring. Many big state schools are known for accepting lots of transfers from local community colleges. For these reasons, the number of transfers is not a good measure of a school's popularity.

Early decision or early action acceptance rate is a recent addition to the *Insider's Guide*. There has been a growing population of students applying early to college to demonstrate commitment or to increase chances of admission. A school's policy for early admission may include "early action" (EA) or "early decision" (ED). Both programs have application due dates far in advance of regular admission, so check with the school to make sure your application will arrive on time. Remember that while early action is advance acceptance with the option of applying and matriculating elsewhere, early decision requires a commitment to matriculate and to rescind all outstanding applications to other schools. The fact that these programs exist should not exert any pressure on an applicant to commit to an institution early, and many institutions in fact prefer to use regular or rolling admissions.

The **application deadline** is the final deadline for completed applications (except for second-term grade reports and late admissions tests) for freshman students. Early decision and early action programs have different deadlines, and rolling admissions may have priority deadlines after which an application is at a disadvantage. Transfer student applications usually are due one or two months after freshman applications. Nevertheless, submitting your application early gives the admissions committee more time to become familiar with your application and increases your chance of getting in.

The College Board prefers schools to use the **middle 50% SAT** range when discussing scores. The range represents where half of a particular school's new freshman students' scores fell. A mathematics range of 550 to 650 would mean that half the incoming freshmen had SAT mathematics scores between 550 and 650. The middle 50 percent range are the numbers between the twenty-fifth and seventy-fifth percentile boundaries; someone whose SAT score falls on the seventy-fifth percentile scored higher than 75 percent of the people who took that particular test.

The same applies for someone whose score falls on the twenty-fifth percentile; the median is a score at the fiftieth percentile. Therefore, if your SAT score falls within the middle 50 percent range, you are on par with the SAT scores of last year's successful applicants. This does not mean that you have a 50–50 chance of getting in. Instead, view this figure as an indication of your own competitiveness against the overall applicant pool that the school evaluates. Because the new SAT essay section was not implemented until the spring of 2005, many schools did not have statistical information based on the new range available. However, these numbers will likely become available next year.

Schools in the South and Midwest often prefer the American College Test (ACT). We report the **middle 50% ACT** range as well as the SAT for this reason. The scale for this test is 1 to 36, and the middle 50 percent range for this test means the same as it does for the SAT.

Most popular majors lists the top three majors among the seniors in the most recent graduating class for which the college has data. Remember, though, that popularity is not necessarily a measure of quality. Also, the exact number of students majoring in any given field can vary widely from year to year. Certain schools, however, are well-known for specific programs (e.g., criminology, biomedical engineering, government, journalism).

The **Retention** rate is the percentage of first-year students who remain enrolled at a given institution for their second (sophomore) year. This statistic is an indicator of the quality of life, resources, and general satisfaction of the students at a particular college. Like the statistics on percent accepted who enroll, these numbers are most useful in comparisons between schools of the similar academic caliber, size, and student body.

The **Graduation** rate represents the percentage of students who graduate successfully over a certain time period: for example, "70 percent in five years." Different institutions will report this statistic over four-, five-, or six-year periods. Many students take five years to obtain their bachelor's degree. Contact a school directly to find out how long the average student takes to complete the requirements for his or her degree. Generally students are more likely to take over four years to graduate in public schools than private schools.

Tuition and fees and **Room and board** figures are given for the most recent year available. In cases where costs differ for in-state and out-of-state students, both figures are listed. Also, many public schools charge tuition that varies with the course load taken. Remember that these figures are meant as an estimate of the cost for a year at a given institution, and do not include travel, book, and personal expenses. These figures tend to increase every year. Use these figures as a relative index of how expensive one college is compared to another. For Canadian schools, these figures are reported in Canadian dollars.

For **financial aid, first-year** figures, schools are asked to report the percentage of the entering class receiving need-based financial assistance from the institution out of those applying for aid. In some cases, though, schools responded with the total percentage of students on financial aid. This does not include students receiving only merit-based scholarships, federal loans not given out by the institution, and students who did not apply for aid. These figures are most relevant for comparing similar institutions. Questions about schools' particular financial aid programs should be addressed directly to their financial aid offices.

Varsity or club athletes represents the percentage of students who play a varsity or club sports at the college. Like the fraternity and sorority figures, this statistic helps to give an impression of the general composition of the student body and campus life.

Finally, **Library** figures list the physical number of volumes possessed by the college library system. This includes book, audio and video recordings, but not microreproductions or volumes available through cooperation with other libraries.

A Note About Some Statistics We Do Not Include

Previous editions of the *Insider's Guide* included a percentage of international students. Since the international student percentage was generally under nine percent, the figure was dropped in favor of others that would better serve the audience. International students should not feel slighted by this.

Mean SAT and ACT numbers were also eliminated, as not enough schools reported the numbers to warrant their listing. The trend seems to be to list the middle 50% range of scores to give an idea of the broader composition of the student body.

Other statistics an applicant might wish to research independently are: the percentage of students involved in community service, the average loan debt of a typical graduate, the number of transfers from a community college at your state university, or the percentage of graduates who continue their education within five years of graduation.

Alabama

Auburn University

Address: Auburn, 108
Mary Martin Hall,
Auburn University,
AL 36849
Phone: 334-844-4000
E-mail Address:
admissions@auburn.edu
Web site URL:
http://www.auburn.edu
Year Founded: 1856
Private or Public: public
Religious affiliation: none
Location: small city
**Regular Application
Deadline:** 2-Aug
Number of Applicants:
16,238
Percent Accepted: 72%
**Percent Accepted who
enroll:** 35%
Number Entering: 4,092
**Number of Transfers
Accepted each Year:** 1,842
Mean SAT: 1,129
Mean ACT: 24

Middle 50% SAT range:
1,020–1,230 (writing not
included)
Middle 50% ACT range:
22–27
**Early admission program
(EA/ ED/ NA):** ED
ED or EA Acceptance Rate:
NA
**Full time Undergraduate
enrollment:** 19,367
Total enrollment: 22,612
Percent Male: 47%
Percent Female: 53%
Total Percent Minority: 19%
Percent African-American:
12%
**Percent Asian/Pacific
Islander:** 2%
Percent Hispanic: 3%
Percent Native-American:
1%
Percent Other: 1%
**Percent in-state / out of
state:** 61%/39%

Percent from Public HS:
86%
Retention Rate: 84%
Graduation Rate: 63%
**Percent in On-campus
housing:** 14%
**Percent affiliated with
Greek system:** 23%/34%
**Percent Varsity or Club
Athletes:** NA
**Number of official
organized extracurricular
organizations:** 300
3 Most popular majors:
Business/Marketing,
Engineering, Education
Student/Faculty ratio: 18:01
Tuition and Fees:
$15,496.00
**In State Tuition and Fees (if
different):** $5,496.00
Cost for Room and Board:
$7,564.00
**Percent receiving Financial
aid, first-year:** NA

Less than an hour's drive east of Montgomery, the plains of Alabama give rise to Auburn University. The school, whose athletics department has produced stars like Charles Barkley and Bo Jackson, boasts some of the region's top veterinary and engineering programs. But it is the student body that will most likely catch the eye of a passer-by, especially if he or she hails from more northern lands. "Southern hospitality is alive and well here," and this charm mixed with fun and academics keeps Auburn students smiling.

Bed and Breakfast (and Lunch and Dinner)

Auburn students electing to live on campus can choose from four clusters of residence halls, but the housing is not guaranteed to anyone, even freshmen. The more popular living areas are the Hill and the Quad, and dorms are either women-only or coed by floor. Many in-state students and upperclassmen chose to live off campus in one of the several apartment complexes near campus. Since many students opt not to live in dorms, Auburn provides an apartment guide and some helpful tips for students shopping the off-campus market. Tiger Transit is available to get students from point A to point B, and the Off Campus Association "gets you a good deal on utilities."

There is no shortage of food options on campus. The two main dining areas, Terrell Dining Hall and War Eagle Food Court, are located at the southern and northern ends of the campus, respectively. Both have an assortment of fast food and local restaurants that cater to students on the go. Auburn offers a variety of meal plans to meet a wide range of needs, and the Tiger Card can be used "like a debit card" at local eateries and grocery stores. Students deposit funds into the account and use the swipes until the balance dwindles down again.

Students choosing to eat on campus can get all the basic sandwiches and burgers, or they can go for a smoothie at Chillers in War Eagle Court. The town of Auburn offers the traditional fare of Ruby Tuesdays and family dining along with some establishments appealing to the younger crowd. Students frequent the Mellow Mushroom for a more gourmet pizza and head to Moe's for "the best burritos in town."

Cracking the Books

Auburn University was the first land-grant college in the Southeast, and to this day its engineering and agriculture departments remain strong. But the University has become more diverse in its faculty and currently offers undergraduate degrees in 12 schools—agriculture, architecture, business, education, engineering, forestry and wildlife, human sciences, liberal arts, nursing, pharmacy, science and mathematics, and veterinary medicine. Moreover, the University recently began a Bachelor of Wireless Engineering program which represents first degree of this type in the nation. Students select their major at the end of the second year, but changing majors is not difficult with the help of Auburn's advising system.

> **"Most professors are more than willing to help you out. All you have to do is ask."**

The University offers plenty of options for study abroad. Auburn itself has over 20 distinct programs, or students can participate in approved programs from other universities. One student who returned from a summer in Florence, a popular destination for art students, said "transferring credits was really easy."

While Auburn students put in their time in Draughton Library (open 24 hours a day during finals), they do not often complain of being tremendously overworked. "Some students skip classes and don't work that hard," but workload largely depends on the course of study. If an Auburn Tiger is having some difficulties in the classroom, he or she can usually find plenty of help. "Most profes-

sors are more than willing to help you out. All you have to do is ask."

Auburn professors have earned a reputation of being accessible and invested in their students' educations, but the same cannot always be said about teaching assistants. Especially in math and science courses, students said some TAs have problems speaking clear English, which can make learning more difficult.

In preparation for life after graduation, Auburn provides advice and information for students interested in graduate or professional school. A senior in the College of Science and Math said her adviser has helped her not only navigate Auburn's undergraduate curriculum, but also gave her tips for applying to graduate schools. The University brings in representatives from schools throughout the region to speak to students about opportunities after graduation.

Frivolity, Fraternities and Football

The social scene is alive and well at Auburn no matter what time of year, but students have different preferences for the seasons. During the fall, students don their best orange and blue to support their Tigers on the field at Jordan-Hare Stadium. The on-campus stadium is regularly filled to capacity of over 85,000 raucous fans screaming "War Eagle," and the surrounding areas are teeming with tailgates for each home game. Don't be surprised to see Auburn students dressed up for this Saturday afternoon affair. The game is a place to be seen as well as show school spirit. The fun continues, especially after a win, at Toomer's Corner after the final snap.

The stadium is bursting at the seams when in-state rival Alabama comes to town the Saturday before Thanksgiving for the Iron Bowl. Students must make sure they get their tickets early if they want a seat at this perennial sell-out event.

Many students hit the fraternity parties Friday and Saturday nights. A significant chunk of the student body is Greek, but "parties are open for the most part." In contrast to most other SEC schools, there are no sorority houses at Auburn. The sisterhoods have halls in dorms, mostly populated with sophomore members, and a chapter room. Greek organizations keep a lively party environment with formal dances and band parties.

The Auburn police are usually present at larger organized events, but there is not a visible crackdown on underage drinking as long as students act responsibly. The police are strict on drunk driving. Since most students at Auburn come with cars and many live off campus, there is a volunteer designated-driver program to make sure every student makes it home safely.

In the spring semester, students focus their revelry on off-campus locales—apartments or downtown bars. College Park Apartments usually has something going on during the weekends. For good drink deals, of-age students head to Buffalo's for a brew and then to Quixote's, where "there is always a good band playing." While the town restaurants might let things slide, bars have no problem carding, and they can be quite difficult to get into at times.

Apart from the night life, students engage in many social activities and student groups on campus. Students can try their hand at radio broadcasting on WEGL, do community service through Habitat for Humanity or Kiwanis Club, partake in theater and singing groups, and do just about anything else that might be of interest.

Getting Your Bearings

Two important landmarks on campus for new students are the Foy Student Union and the Haley Center. These two buildings are the hubs of basic student life on campus. Foy contains the War Eagle Food Court, a CD and game store, study lounges, student organization offices, an ATM, and a mail drop. The Haley Center houses a cafeteria, lecture halls, and the campus bookstore. The one thing these buildings don't have is parking, which can be a "nightmare" on campus. Since most students are in-state or from surrounding areas, they drive to school from home, and having a car is "a big plus on the weekends for road trips to the beach."

Go to one football game, and it's easy to see the tradition that pervades the Auburn campus. Some students are third- or fourth-generation Tigers, but that should not scare away newcomers to the South. With pleasant weather and people, it is easy to understand why Auburn is one of the most popular universities in the region.—*Adam Weber*

FYI

If you come to Auburn, you'd better bring "your country music collection."

What's the typical weekend schedule? "Drink, drink, drink, go to a football game, drink, drink, and pass out."

If I could change one thing about Auburn, I'd "move it to a more metropolitan area."

Three things every Auburn student should do before graduating are "get every single flavor of milkshake at Cheeburger Cheeburger, participate in the cheesy 'Hey Day,' and run in the Cake Race."

Birmingham-Southern College

Address: Birmingham-Southern College, 900 Arkadelphia Rd, Birmingham, AL 32254

Phone: 205-226-4696

E-mail Address: admission@bsc.edu

Web site URL: http://www.bsc.edu

Year Founded: 1856

Private or Public: private

Religious affiliation: United Methodist

Location: urban

Regular Application Deadline: Rolling

Number of Applicants: 2,198

Percent Accepted: 57%

Percent Accepted who enroll: 23%

Number Entering: 292

Number of Transfers Accepted each Year: 54

Mean SAT: 1,197

Mean ACT: 27

Middle 50% SAT range: 1,570–1,940

Middle 50% ACT range: 23–28

Early admission program (EA/ ED/ NA): NA

ED or EA Acceptance Rate: NA

Full time Undergraduate enrollment: 1,207

Total enrollment: 1,256

Percent Male: 36%

Percent Female: 64%

Total Percent Minority: 22%

Percent African-American: 14%

Percent Asian/Pacific Islander: 2%

Percent Hispanic: 1%

Percent Native-American: 1%

Percent Other: 4%

Percent in-state / out of state: 67%/33%

Percent from Public HS: 65%

Retention Rate: NA

Graduation Rate: 74%

Percent in On-campus housing: 77%

Percent affiliated with Greek system: 51%/50%

Percent Varsity or Club Athletes: NA

Number of official organized extracurricular organizations: 70

3 Most popular majors: Business/Marketing, Biology, Visual and Performing Arts

Student/Faculty ratio: 10:01

Tuition and Fees: $23,040.00

Cost for Room and Board: $7,740.00

Percent receiving Financial aid, first-year: 92%

Birmingham-Southern College prides itself on its reputation as a top-notch university, and the students here work hard to live up to BSC's expectations. Students manage the intense workload and credit the "loads of personal attention" to their success and survival.

"Life-long Learners"

As a four-year liberal arts college, Birmingham-Southern seeks to send out well-rounded, well-educated, and cultured leaders. As such, the academic requirements cover a broad range of subjects and interests. Freshmen have to take two "First-Year Foundations" courses in order to acclimate themselves to the college environment as well as to take their first steps as "life-long learners." Over the course of four years, students at BSC must accumulate at least one unit each of art, lab science, history, literature, a non-native language, humanities, philosophy and religion, writing, math, and social science. After fulfilling these core courses, students must take two additional credits in humanities and one additional credit in math or science. Although there are no pre-

professional majors, many take a difficult course set aimed at medical or law school. English, Business, and Education are, not surprisingly, extremely popular majors. Math and Science majors are rarer but remain a presence on campus. A highly selective honor program is also available to the most motivated and qualified students at BSC. The program offers accelerated courses and small seminars with an interdisciplinary approach. Those interested in the program are encouraged to apply as early as spring of their senior year in high school.

BSC requires its students to go even farther above and beyond the minimal requirements, and make use of its unique "interim" period. The interim period, the "1" portion of Birmingham-Southern's 4-1-4 year, is a month-long period between the school's two four-month semesters in which students are free to explore one specific interest. One student used one of her four interim periods to design a course as a teacher assistant in an urban school environment. The student explained, "I decided how long I was in the classroom, what types of activities I would

do, how I would be graded . . . all of that."
Although some students thought that the interim period can be a "pain," many say it
also provides the opportunity to travel
abroad without worrying about falling off a
four-year track.

With all that Birmingham-Southern requires, "the workload can be tough;" however, students have advisors at their disposal
and a strong support system. Professors are
generally described as "great" and "absolutely approachable." Classes with good
reputations may be tricky to obtain for freshmen (it's not easy getting that first-choice
class), but amazing classes are definitely
available. "[My professor] set up a fake crime
scene . . . roped it off, had a chalk outline of
the body, fake blood everywhere . . ." said a
student about his Forensic Science course.
"We had to walk around, take it apart . . . all
the way to conviction." The bottom line remains: people at BSC take academics pretty
seriously, and as one student affirmed, "people do what they've got to do."

Outside the Classroom—Like Wonderbread?

Despite the high academic expectations, BSC
students know how to balance the books
with some much needed down time. With
Birmingham in their backyard and a variety
of clubs and activities to choose from, students have a wide array of weekend options.
Prospective students should be aware, however, that Birmingham-Southern has a definite Greek feel. "The frat scene is definitely
the dominant social scene here . . . the rush
process starts during the summer," a freshman explained, "but the formal rush doesn't
happen until the third week of school or so."
The downside of having such a close-knit
and supporting Greek system is that "what
Greek organization you belong to has a large
impact on who you're going to be friends
with." As one student remarked, "It's sad in
my opinion that in the cafeteria, people still
sit at certain tables based on what fraternity,
sorority, or sports team he/she is on." Still,
students are quick to point out that the
Greek life isn't for everybody at BSC—and
that's okay. The Student Government Association sponsors movie-nights out, for example, and clubs such as "Chaos" and "Platinum"
are a short drive away. And as most students
have cars on campus—"if you don't, you can
always mooch off someone else," according
to one student—transportation is usually not
a huge issue.

Big annual activities include the Greek-
sponsored "Philanthropy Party" as well as
the Entertainment Festivals (E-Fest in BSC
vernacular) where local talents are show-
cased each semester. Students also note attempts by administration and other students
to broaden the cultural aspects on campus.
Although diversity at Birmingham-Southern
may prove a disappointment to some (minority enrollment has been documented at
around twenty percent, but students generally deemed geographic and class diversity
to be somewhat lacking), clubs such as the
BSC Step Team are giving a different feel to
the pervasive—as one student termed it,
"Wonderbread—white and rich"—culture of
the school.

> "We know how to do things—be it
> academics, partying, or whatever—
> right here."

Another extracurricular option is intramurals, also known as IMs. Flag football, inner
tube water polo, and dodgeball are just a few
examples of available intramural activities.
"People play [IMs] and they can get pretty
competitive, but everybody realizes it's just
IMs and we're all out of shape," said one BSC
student. In addition to IMs, students can
cheer for their school's teams. While
Birmingham-Southern does not have a football team, they "live vicariously through
[University of] Alabama and Auburn [Univer-
sity]." The basketball and baseball games are
well-attended, and "it's a face-painted, t-shirt
wearing, screaming, jumping good time."
One student summed it up saying, "We know
how to do things—be it academics, partying,
or whatever—right here."

Living and Dining

"Dorms are . . . well, dorms" one junior explained, "you can't expect too much."
Freshmen guys live in New Men's, while
freshmen girls live in either Cullin Daniels
or Margaret Daniels. A student revealed
that "New Men's is pretty nasty, but it's a
cool experience." The freshmen dorms
have two people to a room and communal
bathrooms. Other options include a four
room-four person suite, a four room-eight
person suite, or two doubles connected by
a bathroom. Housing situations improve with
both seniority and GPA—those with seniority
and higher GPAs pick first. Residential

Advisors (RAs) are on each floor of the freshmen dorms, ready to help with any problems. However, RAs are also meant to enforce the rules: "Level of strictness varies from person to person . . . they're there to enforce the rules through fines mostly." Students sometimes choose to forgo dorm life for student apartments on campus or the Sorority Townhouses and Fraternity Row. Other notable buildings and locations on campus include the science building (which was remodeled only about three years ago), the humanities building, and the Southern Methodist Center. The Center recently built a new facility on the former Frat Row (the new Row is only two years old.) "The [Frats] are a hangout area . . . as well as the Caf, and the Cellar." The Cellar, a coffee house, is a popular place for both relaxing

and studying. The cafeteria, or "Caf" as BSC students call it, has just been recently revamped and is "a definite improvement" over the old cafeteria, and now boasts a Subway, a KFC, a soul food bar, a grille, and a salad stand. Students living on campus have to purchase a meal plan; the choices range from light, medium, and hearty, which differ in numbers of meals provided.

Coming to Birmingham-Southern is coming into a great tradition of excellence. With its mixture of Division I sports, academics, and bridges into the business world, Birmingham promises to provide not only an unforgettable college experience, but connections for life. "We produce the best and the brightest—but not only that, once you're a part of the BSC family, those ties never die. [That] sounds so sappy, but it's true."—*Melody Pak*

FYI

If you come to BSC, you'd better bring "your leg muscles, it's hilly."

The typical weekend schedule includes: "Friday: some sort of party Friday night, Saturday: football games, sports, party on Saturday night, Sunday: really low key."

If I could change one thing about BSC, I'd "bring more diversity."

Three things every student at BSC should do before graduating are "spend half of your day trying to figure out what you did the night before, make love, and still pass with a 3.5 or higher."

T u s k e g e e   U n i v e r s i t y

Address: Tuskegee, PO Box 1239, Tuskegee, 36088

Phone: 334-727-8500

E-mail Address: adminweb@tusk.edu

Web site URL: http://www.tuskegee.edu

Year Founded: 1881

Private or Public: private

Religious affiliation: none

Location: rural

Regular Application Deadline: rolling

Number of Applicants: NA

Percent Accepted: 81%

Percent Accepted who enroll: 44%

Number Entering: NA

Number of Transfers Accepted each Year: NA

Mean SAT: 890

Mean ACT: 19

Middle 50% SAT range: V:390–500, M:380–490

Middle 50% ACT range: 17–21

Early admission program (EA/ ED/ NA): NA

ED or EA Acceptance Rate: NA

Full time Undergraduate enrollment: NA

Total enrollment: 2,420

Percent Male: 45%

Percent Female: 55%

Total Percent Minority: 78%

Percent African-American: 78%

Percent Asian/Pacific Islander: 0%

Percent Hispanic: 0%

Percent Native-American: 0%

Percent Other: NA

Percent in-state / out of state: 41%/59%

Percent from Public HS: NA

Retention Rate: 70%

Graduation Rate: 50%

Percent in On-campus housing: 55%

Percent affiliated with Greek system: 11%

Percent Varsity or Club Athletes: NA

Number of official organized extracurricular organizations: 36

3 Most popular majors: Electrical, Electronics and Communications Engineering

Student/Faculty ratio: 12:01

Tuition and Fees: $14,615

Cost for Room and Board: $6,783

Tuskegee University has historically been home to many generations of African-American men and women searching for an outstanding academic experience in addition to a unique cultural enrichment. Tuskegee's close-knit student community lives and studies in one of the country's most historic African-American universities.

Changing Tradition

Tuskegee affords its undergraduates the opportunity to pursue a true liberal arts education through the College of Liberal Arts and Education. Although it was founded with the intention of giving African-Americans a more technical, career-specific education to give them an edge in specific job markets, the curriculum has gradually changed to ally Tuskegee with other liberal arts schools. Still, some traditions remain: all freshmen are required to take an orientation course, which consists of history of the University, including the mandatory reading of Booker T. Washington's *Up from Slavery*, and advice for adapting to college life. Freshmen will also discover that their other basic requirements include two semesters each of English and math.

The university includes five colleges in total: the College of Agriculture, Environmental and Natural Sciences; the College of Business and Information Science; the College of Engineering, Architecture and Physical Sciences; the College of Veterinary Medicine, Nursing, and Allied Health; and the College of Liberal Arts and Education. Thus, despite the shift towards a more liberal-arts-oriented academic environment, many Tuskegee students are engineering or science majors. The school often receives acclaim for its pre-vet, pre-med and nursing programs, and students confirm high numbers of enrollees in each of these disciplines. Lower level lectures tend to enroll between 40 and 50 students, but the average class size overall ranges from 20 to 30 students. Students like the class size, and report that "whatever class size you prefer, you can usually pick accordingly." The smaller class sizes and conservative use of TAs keep student-faculty interaction high. Students generally give Tuskegee's academics a high rating. There were those who disagreed, remarking that "it can be easy to feel lost in the larger classes that don't have TAs," but on the whole, many agreed that the school is "demanding but rewarding." Tuskegee's history is clearly visible around its campus. A senior commented that "It's very cool, some of the brick buildings were built by students when the school was founded."

Still Living in the Past

The residential life on campus is one of students' more frequent complaints. In addition to being "ancient" and "without much furniture," dorms are not coed and students are required to live on campus both freshman and sophomore years. The older dorm buildings have a reputation for being in poor physical condition, and one student called the dorms "older than rocks." "You had better bring things that make you feel at home," said one undergrad, because "there's no real cozy feeling." The on campus apartment situation is slightly better; the Commons apartments offer students the amenities of a kitchen in addition to rooms that they can make their own with decoration. Students' biggest problem, however, is with the university housing regulations. Because of the school's conservative nature, men's and women's dorms are separated by a 10-minute walk to prevent students from visiting those of the opposite gender. The university staff also keeps a close eye on dorms; students are not allowed to be on the "wrong" side of campus after 11 p.m. and, if caught, face punishment.

Many upperclassmen choose to move off campus. One student said of the coed policies, "I love my campus, but I had to leave it because of the rules." Students tend to meet in the student union, which contains a movie theater, a grill, a game room and offices for student organizations. The student cafeteria is another popular meeting place, and serves as a place where Tuskegee's many clubs and organizations can meet to bring students together. Some of the biggest clubs are the state clubs, which unite students hailing from the same state to plan activities relating to their home turf. African-American groups like the National Society of Black Engineers and several prominent fraternities and sororities are also present on campus. There is an active chapter of ROTC, which helps some students to fund their education. Students are active in community service, and the nearby hospital employs a number of Tuskegee students.

Football and basketball games generate great excitement at Tuskegee. In particular, the rivalry with Morehouse College and Alabama State University tends to draw the largest crowds to sporting events.

Homecoming is one of the biggest social events of the year. The week-long tradition incorporates performances by student groups, the Miss Tuskegee Gala and a number of pep rallies to boost school spirit. In the spring, the school hosts "Springfest," an event drawing many students together for shows, concerts and a dance.

The Typical Tuskegee Student

While the Greek system is a strong presence on campus, students report that they do not feel an urge to rush. There is little animosity between the fraternities, but they reportedly have a "friendly rivalry." Officially, alcohol is prohibited on campus and students who are caught with it face fines or other penalties. As a result, drinking generally tends to occur off campus. Students said they considered the town of Tuskegee "slow," but most agree that it has most of the things necessary for college life. And, as one student put it, "Tuskegee has a lot of potential to grow," adding, "but you come for the school, not the town." Tuskegee students also added that their campus is safe,

with a large body of security officers and a closely monitored electronic keycard system.

> "The town of Tuskegee offers nothing except seclusion from the modern world, but you learn a lot trapped in the wilderness."

Tuskegee is more than just an academic college experience; it is also one of cultural and historical enrichment. The schools' fundamental mission remains an avid part of why students attend, and the school's community and tradition are enough to overcome some of its more conservative and comparatively strict policies. The experience tends to bind people in a lasting way. As one student said, "There are a lot of good people here and you can meet a lot of great minds—not to mention we're friends for life. People might complain about things here, but in the end, you don't want to leave."—*Melissa Chan and Staff*

FYI

If you come to Tuskegee, you'd better bring "a car to survive here because the nearest mall is 20 minutes away. The town of Tuskegee offers nothing except seclusion from the modern world, but you learn a lot trapped in the wilderness."

What's the typical weekend schedule? "Go to a football game if we're playing at home and then party at a fraternity at night."

If I could change one thing about Tuskegee I'd "change the administration. It seems to have no respect or regard for the students, the registration process takes three days, and the dorms are really run-down."

The three things every student should do before graduating from Tuskegee are "try the food at the Chicken Coop, go to Homecoming, and visit the George Washington Carver Museum on campus."

The University of Alabama

Address: University of Alabama, PO Box 870132, Tuscaloosa, AL 35487-0132
Phone: 205-348-5666
E-mail Address: admissions@ua.edu
Web site URL: http://www.ua.edu
Year Founded: 1831
Private or Public: public
Religious affiliation: none
Location: suburban
Regular Application Deadline: Rolling
Number of Applicants: 10,700
Percent Accepted: 70%
Percent Accepted who enroll: 50%
Number Entering: 4,378
Number of Transfers Accepted each Year: 2,104
Mean SAT: 1,131
Mean ACT: 24

Middle 50% SAT range: 1,000–1,260
Middle 50% ACT range: 21–27
Early admission program (EA/ ED/ NA): NA
ED or EA Acceptance Rate: NA
Full time Undergraduate enrollment: 19,237
Total enrollment: 23,878
Percent Male: 47%
Percent Female: 53%
Total Percent Minority: 16%
Percent African-American: 11%
Percent Asian/Pacific Islander: 1%
Percent Hispanic: 2%
Percent Native-American: 1%
Percent Other: 1%
Percent in-state / out of state: 73%/27%

Percent from Public HS: 90%
Retention Rate: 86%
Graduation Rate: 62%
Percent in On-campus housing: 29%
Percent affiliated with Greek system: 23%
Percent Varsity or Club Athletes: 6%
Number of official organized extracurricular organizations: 228
3 Most popular majors: Finance, Nursing, NA
Student/Faculty ratio: 19:01
Tuition and Fees: $15,294.00
In State Tuition and Fees (if different): $5,278.00
Cost for Room and Board: $5,380.00
Percent receiving Financial aid, first-year: 32%

With four buildings that survived the Civil War (Gorgas House, Barnard Hall, the Rotunda, and the President Mansion), the graceful architecture and serene campus might be awe-inspiring to a new freshman arriving at Alabama. As one student said, "The campus is just so beautiful, it really can be a very peaceful place." But before you can say the words "Roll Tide," the semester propels forward into football season, with the first games taking place in the month of September.

You would have to try really hard to leave "Bama" without knowing the significance of the Iron Bowl, "Bear" Bryant, and why Alabama must always beat Auburn in any competition. But, students agree that athletic traditions and rivalries hardly define the UA experience. "It's just a great school in so many different ways."

Academics

Overall, students at Alabama seem pretty satisfied with the academic opportunities. "There's pretty much any major you could ever want" and a fair amount of minor options too. In addition to completing the re-

quirements for each individual major, students must also complete the core curriculum requirements for graduation. These requirements force students to take courses in a variety of areas, such as humanities and fine arts, history, social/behavioral sciences, natural science and mathematics, foreign languages or computers, and writing. "The requirements actually aren't that hard to fill," says one student. "By the time you've taken all the classes that look interesting to you, you realize that you're really knocking out the core requirements."

But for those not satisfied with Alabama's offerings, the New College program, though "relatively small and relatively new," allows admitted students to design their own majors and minors. The program is considered "pretty intense," requiring, in addition to the University requirements for graduation, extra language classes, New College seminars, and independent study. The program boasts that it promotes more independent thinking and allows students a closer relationship with his or her advisor.

Another option for Alabama students who desire "more of a challenge" in their academic pursuits is the Honors College, which is divided up into three programs: the Computer-Based Honors Program, the International Honors Program, and the University Honors Program. The trailblazing Computer-Based Honors Program accepts about 40 students each year, and allows undergraduates of any major the opportunity to work one-on-one with faculty members in computer-oriented research. The students "really jump in" with an intense course freshmen year in computing concepts. The International Honors Program helps students incorporate an international flair into their major, grooming the students for a study-abroad experience. The University Honors Program is the largest of the programs, with approximately 10 percent of the undergraduate population taking part. The program seeks to provide a higher level of education to Alabama students; admission is primarily based on ACT or SAT scores, and honors students are required to maintain their GPAs throughout college.

Bama Life

Students agree that the housing available on campus is adequate, but not luxurious by any means, and most will say that the primary motivating factor for living on campus is convenience. They say that it is "very easy for walking to class," while off-campus students complain that, "it's hard to decide which is worse, traffic or parking." Students who choose to live off-campus generally do so either to live in their Greek houses or to have more independence in an apartment or house. One student commented that "guys are more inclined to get houses" because "there's not really a nice guys dorm."

Freshmen in the past have not been required to live on campus, but beginning in fall 2006, all students are required to spend their first year on campus. One student whole-heartedly endorsed this change, saying "it's a great way to meet new people. A lot of Alabama kids already come here with friends from home, so if you want to branch out, the dorms are a way to do it." Ask current students for the lowdown on which dorms are the best, but right now the new Riverside Residential Complex seems to be the hottest ticket on campus. The dorm complex primarily houses honors college students and freshmen, and includes two- and four-bedroom suites, which each have a kitchenette and a living room. Students say that it is "unbelievably nice" and even has an Einstein Brothers Bagel place, a small grocery store, and a pool. Also scheduled to be

open by fall 2006 is Bryant Hall, which will mostly house male athletes.

Students on campus most often dine at the Ferguson Center, where they can choose from fast-food options like Blimpie, Burger King, and Chick-Fil-A, or a variety of pizza, soups, sandwiches, sushi, salads, and other hot dishes. Other on-campus dining locations include a coffee shop in the Gorgas Library (a favorite study spot), and quick eateries in Tutwiler, Burke, Paty halls, and the Riverside Residential Center. Students on the whole seem to be satisfied with the options overall—"You can always find something different"—though one student remarked that the options can get boring. "You get tired of having the same stuff all the time, but that's just what it's like at every college. The nice thing is that if you want to go out to eat, you always can."

All freshmen are required to participate in the freshman meal plan. First-year students can choose from one of three meal plans, and then are also charged $300 a semester in Dining Dollars. After freshman year, students are allowed more flexibility in which meal plan they choose, with five different meal options available. Dining Dollars can be used at all on-campus dining locations, at all vending machines, and at off-campus locations like Domino's, Buffalo Phil's, and The Crimson Cafe. Students seem to think the dining system a fair one: "The good thing is that you don't lose your Dining Dollars if you don't spend them all in a semester." At the end of the year, students can request a refund for any remaining Dining Dollars. After the rush season, many students also choose to dine at their fraternity or sorority houses, and there is a meal plan that accommodates for that change.

The Diversity Question

Students today seem to be more or less divided over the current state of race relations at Bama, but one doesn't have to look far into the past to see that the university has come a long way. On June 11, 1963, Alabama Governor George Wallace made his infamous "stand at the schoolhouse door" in an attempt to prevent desegregation of the University. Federal marshals had to be called in, and the two African-American students were ultimately admitted.

Though students say that "all people are welcome at Alabama" and that they have "never seen any signs of racial discrimination on campus," students will also admit that the "social life can be segregated." One place that this de facto segregation is most apparent is in the Greek system. The fraternities and sororities at Alabama are "mostly homogenous," and the Greek systems for whites and for minorities are even managed by different organizations. But these divisions, too, seem to be breaking down with time, as one student noted that "Greek life at Alabama is becoming more and more diverse every day."

In Their Free Time

By far the most prevalent extracurricular activity for students is the Greek system, with over 20 percent belonging to a University-recognized fraternity or sorority. There are three different governing bodies for the Greek system, each with its own timeline for rush. The Inter-Fraternity Council oversees some 28 fraternities in their rush, which takes place in the first weeks of freshman year. The Alabama Panhellenic Association governs the women's sororities and holds rush in August before the start of classes freshman year. The National Pan-Hellenic Council, which oversees the seven minority-dominated fraternities and sororities, begins its rush season after the first semester of school.

Students generally disagree over how large the divide between Greeks and "independents" (non-Greeks) is, and it seems to depend on the individual character of each person. "Some people have lots of independent friends, but I just don't have any," one student said. Students agree, though, that while the Greek system may have seemed super-important freshman year, by senior year it is not that big of a deal. "As you get older, the distance between people in fraternities and sororities and people not in them lessens."

Other activities that students take part in are intramural sports—"even that competition can get pretty intense"—the school newspaper, *The Crimson White*; and "countless community service opportunities." While Alabama is "not considered a very political campus, per se" there are some activist options for students who are more politically minded.

Fun and Games

In the fall semester, football more or less dominates the weekend social scenes, with games most weekends and tons of parties surrounding each game. The highlights of the season are definitely the two most important games: homecoming and the Iron Bowl. "Homecoming is a crazy experience" at the University of Alabama. "You have to see it to believe it." The event is met with droves of alumni and fans, a huge bonfire the night before the game, music, food, fireworks, and parties. "You might even say the spectacle is more important than who wins the game." That is, unless Alabama is playing against Auburn University. Auburn, located just a few hours away, is Alabama's biggest rival. "You learn in your first days here that you're not supposed to like Auburn," says one student. The two teams match off every year in the "Iron Bowl," an annual game that has been played since 1893. The competition even extends beyond football, into community service areas with competitions like the "Beat Auburn Beat Hunger" food drive.

> "You learn in your first days here that you're not supposed to like Auburn"

Off-campus, students find Tuscaloosa to be a "nice, medium-sized town," with "everything you need," but "not big enough for you to get lost." The Jupiter is the "best place to see concerts" in town, and students often frequent the "fun, run-down little bars" surrounding campus. For the first years of college, it seems that the fraternity houses, which often invite bands to play for their parties, are social hubs, but "as students get older, they tend to prefer to go to bars over the frats."

But, as one student put it, "the best part of the social scene is just in the everyday, individual interactions." Whether it's in their classwork, extracurricular activities, or in the football stadium, Bama students really seem to enjoy what they do. "Coming here was one of the best decisions I've ever made. It's just a really fun place to be."—*Susanna Moore*

FYI
If you come to Alabama, you'd better bring "a red-and-white shaker for the football games."
What is the typical weekend schedule? "Band party Friday, game Saturday, rest on Sunday."
If I could change one thing about Alabama, I'd "improve campus parking."
Three things every student at Alabama should do before graduating are "go to the Paul 'Bear' Bryant Museum, go to the homecoming bonfire, get involved with a community-service activity."

University of South Alabama

Address: University of S. Alabama, 307 University Boulevard, Mobile, AL 36688-0002	**Mean SAT:** NA	**Percent in-state / out of state:** NA
Phone: 251-460-6141	**Mean ACT:** 23	**Percent from Public HS:** 92%
E-mail Address: admiss@usouthal.edu	**Middle 50% SAT range:** NA	
	Middle 50% ACT range: 19–24	**Retention Rate:** 72%
Web site URL: http://www.southalabama.edu	**Early admission program (EA/ ED/ NA):** NA	**Graduation Rate:** 40%
	ED or EA Acceptance Rate: NA	**Percent in On-campus housing:** 16%
Year Founded: 1963	**Full time Undergraduate enrollment:** 10,078	**Percent affiliated with Greek system:** 14%
Private or Public: public	**Total enrollment:** 12,814	**Percent Varsity or Club Athletes:** NA
Religious affiliation: none	**Percent Male:** 40%	
Location: small city	**Percent Female:** 60%	**Number of official organized extracurricular organizations:** 185
Regular Application Deadline: 11-Sep	**Total Percent Minority:** 30%	
Number of Applicants: 2,906	**Percent African-American:** 19%	**3 Most popular majors:** NA
Percent Accepted: 93%		**Student/Faculty ratio:** 13:01
Percent Accepted who enroll: 50%	**Percent Asian/Pacific Islander:** 3%	**Tuition and Fees:** $7,620.00
Number Entering: 1,433	**Percent Hispanic:** 2%	**In State Tuition and Fees (if different):** $3,810.00
Number of Transfers Accepted each Year: 1,527	**Percent Native-American:** 1%	**Cost for Room and Board:** $4,428.00
	Percent Other: 5%	

Located in Mobile, Alabama, the University of South Alabama—"USA" or "South" to students—combines the conservative hospitality of the South with the warm sunny climate of the Gulf Coast. Mobile itself is an historic port city and boasts wildlife-rich deltas and estuaries, antebellum homes with hanging Spanish moss, its own popular Mardi Gras celebration, and of course, twenty-one golf courses and a variety of nearby beaches. The university, located in the heart of the city, caters to both traditional and non-traditional students alike and offers a variety of degree options for adults of any age returning to earn their bachelors' degrees.

Academics: Something for Everyone

The University of South Alabama offers a variety of special programs to accommodate the diverse groups that comprise its student body. Those maintaining at least a 3.5 GPA in high school can apply for the university Honors Program, which includes participation in small honors seminars and the completion of an Honors Senior Project. Each honor student is assigned a faculty mentor from the department of his or her major; these mentors offer advice on everything from course selection to future careers within the field, and both mentor and student participate in group community service projects. New students jump into college life through USA's First Year Experience Program, in which all freshmen living in the dorms are required to participate. The program includes a mandatory freshman seminar designed to teach "effective study skills, exam preparation, college level research skills, writing effectively, and student health issues," among other topics, as well as tutors, a campus meal plan, and access to student RAs who can offer advice and counsel about campus life. In addition, many USA courses in a variety of disciplines are offered online, allowing students to attend class from home and submit homework in their pajamas.

A branch campus of the university in Fairhope, Alabama, located in Baldwin County—USABC—also offers undergraduate, graduate, and non-degree courses and opportunities for public service involvement for students who, for a variety of reasons, might prefer a different location. This branch campus primarily supports undergraduate majors in business, both elementary and secondary education, nursing, and adult inter-disciplinary studies. USABC is not a residential campus—students enrolling here generally commute from their homes in Baldwin County—and boasts its own computer lab and performance center but shares the libraries and other research resources with the main university campus across Mobile Bay.

> "The university, located in the heart of the city, caters to both traditional and non-traditional students alike."

All students must fulfill the core curriculum before graduation, which requires taking several courses in each of the major academic disciplines—humanities and fine arts; natural sciences and mathematics; and history, social, and behavioral sciences—as well as two classes in written composition. South is divided into nine different colleges encompassing a variety of fields of study. Those related to healthcare—the Colleges of Medicine, Nursing, and Allied Health Professions—are considered to be particularly strong and rigorous. The joint BS/MS degree programs in these majors are popular, but to gain admission, students must have GPAs in the 3.8 range and apply during their junior year.

BYOB

South's architecture is fairly nondescript like many college campuses built in the late twentieth century. One student described it as "nothing fancy . . . built to last, not to look pretty." Few students live in the dorms all four years, but for those who do, it can be a rewarding experience and provide the opportunity to meet many new friends quickly. "Living in dorms is a terrific way to meet people," enthused one junior. "Most of the people I hang out with now I met freshman year in dorms." The residence halls offer various rooming options in the form of suites and apartments; for first-time students, the most popular options are the Epsilon and Delta two-person suites with private baths. All students living on campus are required to purchase a meal plan, but limited weekend operating hours for the on-campus eateries can reportedly cause frustration. USA also offers married students housing in the form of unfurnished single-family houses in the neighborhood of Hillsdale Heights.

Most of South's 13,300 students come from nearby cities and towns in Alabama, making the university primarily a commuter school in which much of the student body drives to class every day. Many clubs, for example, hold meetings in the afternoons to accommodate members who leave campus in the evening. Because of this, the campus activities and night life can be somewhat lacking; as one student complained, "there is no campus life at South!" However, the university is taking steps to correct this problem, and programs such as the Freshman Year Experience help new students to make friends and connections. The RAs in each dorm occasionally sponsor activities to foster a community spirit, and interested students can join intramural sports and other organizations to stay involved.

The social scene that does exist at USA revolves around the Greek system, and most events that take place on campus are sponsored by one of the college's 8 sororities and 10 fraternities. Although total membership is not huge, the Greeks have a strong presence on campus, due mainly to their widespread involvement in other clubs and organizations. Because South's campus is officially dry (although, as one student put it, this is true "in name only"), the frats do not usually supply alcohol at their parties, so Greek and non-Greek partiers alike are encouraged to bring their own beverages.

No Football?!?

Unique in the football-dominated region of the Southeast, the University of South Alabama has no football team, and many students lament the resulting lack of school spirit. Instead of football, the crowd-pleasing sports to watch are men's and women's varsity basketball; die-hard Jaguar fans can also watch these games live via Internet streaming. Students can also indulge their competitive sides in an assortment of intramural sports based out of USA's state-of-the-art Intramural Field Complex, including inner tube water polo, soccer, flag football, basketball, volleyball, and softball. The Student Recreation Center is home to two basketball courts, a weight-lifting room, a track, and a game room containing table tennis and a pool table as well as free South-Fit aerobics and dance classes. The university has also recently announced plans to build a brand-new recreation center with additional facilities.

South also boasts a sizeable Student Center

that hosts lounge areas, a computer lab, office space for student groups, a big-screen TV, a variety of small eateries located in the Market area, and a large ball room that can be reserved for student use. Jaguar Productions, the Student Activities Board, meets here as well, and provides a relatively popular way for students to become involved with the university and help to plan campus-wide concerts, film screenings, lectures, vacation trips, and more. Over 190 clubs and organizations also offer a chance to meet fellow students and include everything from pre-professional organizations to groups for sports, music, meteorology, and video gaming enthusiasts. Jag TV, USA's student-run television station, is broadcast in all of the residence halls and other buildings throughout the campus.

The University of South Alabama offers numerous benefits to its many students, from its location in the welcoming Deep South city of Mobile to its variety of special degree and enrichment programs. Non-traditional students especially find its continuing education programs to be accommodating and flexible, while those living in the residential dorms appreciate the social atmosphere and the friendly RAs. The university's shortcomings, most notably a lack of school spirit, can be overcome through a determination to stay involved, and South's recent efforts to this end have made strides in improving the sense of community.—*Kristin Knox*

FYI

If you come to USA, you better bring "a desire to get involved and make the most of the college experience."

What is the typical weekend schedule? "Go to a frat party at night, catch up on work during the day."

If I could change one thing about USA, it would be "the lack of a football team."

Three things every student at USA should do before graduating are "play oozeball (volleyball in a knee-deep mud pit), go to an event in the Mitchell Center, and take advantage of the fine-arts offerings."

Alaska

Address: University of Alaska, Fairbanks, PO Box 757480, Fairbanks, AK 99775-7480

Phone: 907-474-7500

E-mail Address: admissions@uaf.edu

Web site URL: http://www.uaf.edu

Year Founded: 1917

Private or Public: public

Religious affiliation: none

Location: urban

Regular Application Deadline: 2-Jul

Number of Applicants: 1,777

Percent Accepted: 74%

Percent Accepted who enroll: 69%

Number Entering: 1,000

Number of Transfers Accepted each Year: 611

Mean SAT: 1,045

Mean ACT: 21

Middle 50% SAT range: 900–1,190

Middle 50% ACT range: 18–25

Early admission program (EA/ ED/ NA): NA

ED or EA Acceptance Rate: NA

Full time Undergraduate enrollment: 4,684

Total enrollment: 5,751

Percent Male: 40%

Percent Female: 60%

Total Percent Minority: 36%

Percent African-American: 3%

Percent Asian/Pacific Islander: 4%

Percent Hispanic: 3%

Percent Native-American: 19%

Percent Other: 7%

Percent in-state / out of state: 87%/13%

Percent from Public HS: NA

Retention Rate: 74%

Graduation Rate: 32%

Percent in On-campus housing: 27%

Percent affiliated with Greek system: NA

Percent Varsity or Club Athletes: 8%

Number of official organized extracurricular organizations: 93

3 Most popular majors: Psychology

Student/Faculty ratio: 13:01

Tuition and Fees: $12,888.00

In State Tuition and Fees (if different): $4,518.00

Cost for Room and Board: $5,580.00

Percent receiving Financial aid, first-year: 34%

Originating as a federal Agricultural Experiment Station in the northernmost frontier of the United States, the University of Alaska at Fairbanks today continues its legacy of cutting-edge research in a unique arctic environment. Through the gradual accumulation of government grants and support, Alaska's largest university has developed into an institution that prides itself on its ability to teach specialized skills to students in a very distinctive setting.

Scientific Significance

Since its founding in 1917, the University of Alaska at Fairbanks has acquired an array of resources from the government in order to further its progress in the world of research. After its humble beginnings as a land-grant institute, UAF eventually gained sea-grant and space-grant status—signs of the importance of its scientific polar research. Additionally, its unique location in the middle of Alaska led Congress in 1946 to establish the Geophysical Institute, which is renowned for its studies of the geological world in Polar Regions and which also maintains the Poker Research Flat Range, the only university-owned rocket-launching facility in the world. Indeed, for the brave souls that can withstand the bitterly cold winters in this harsh arctic tundra, UAF provides excellent opportunities for students to interact with the exceptional environment surrounding them.

Arctic Adventures

One of the main factors that differentiates UAF from other schools is its setting just 200 miles south of the Arctic Circle. UAF does not joke when it boasts about its "360-million-plus-acre classroom." Many of the majors that are offered make use of the university's vast environmental resources: Geophysics majors may find themselves measuring tectonic plate motions in Denali National Park; Oceanography majors might conduct research on the *R/V Alpha Helix*, one of the Seward Marine Center's research vessels; a Natural Resources Management student could end up developing and promoting Alaska's reindeer industry—the list goes on. Above this, one of the most unique opportunities students have is the ability to work right alongside the world's brightest scientists at any of the top-notch research institutes that call UAF home. In fact, many professors are "from all over the country, including Ivy League schools, since the research here is not available in science programs elsewhere."

The educational route that students take is in large part framed by the Baccalaureate Core, which requires a range of credits in six different areas: Communication, Perspectives on the Human Condition, Mathematics, Natural Sciences, Library and Information Research, and Upper-Division Communication. Although most students agree that the Core provides the foundation upon which students begin to build their knowledge, some find it a little bit strict (38-39 core credits needed). The classes can get quite large, and sometimes it is hard to get into your first choice course. In the end, though, UAF's eight colleges—Engineering and Mines, Liberal Arts, Natural Science and Mathematics, Rural and Community Development, Education, Fisheries and Ocean Sciences, Management, Natural Resources and Agricultural Sciences—still manage to provide flexibility by covering a broad spectrum of fields, offering 164 degrees and 24 certificates in over 100 disciplines. The professors will assist students "as long as you communicate with them one on one."

All Bundled Up

The most obvious shared trait evident amongst the student body is their similar taste in fashion: everyone wears winter hats, scarves, and jackets. Although one student opines that the culture is "very bad because we're always late to get all the latest trends in clothing and music," another counters that at least all the students have the latest in winter-weather clothing. The characteristic student can be as variable as the arctic weather. On one hand, there are a handful of traditional party-types, who scour the campus for the liveliest events. One student believes that "because it is dark most of the

winter, a lot of people drink more than usual." On the other hand, "a lot of people [at UAF] do not drink—but instead are outdoorsy and down-to-earth." The drinking that does occur usually takes place in the many student apartments on campus. Freshmen are required to live in dorms for their first year.

> **"The characteristic student can be as variable as the arctic weather."**

Though UAF was founded in the 20th century, it already has a number of traditions that continue their legacy each year. "Starvation Gulch", started in 1923 by the founding president, Charles Bunnell, involves a ceremony with the building of very large bonfires— "some of the piles the size of a small house"— that signify the "passing of knowledge" from upperclassmen to the incoming freshmen. Many campus groups fight over the possession and control of the "Tradition Stone", a block of concrete with a sign that was placed on a pile of beer bottles in defiance of an alcohol ban instituted in the 50s.

Close-knit Community

Though many of the campus buildings may be aesthetically unappealing, one student quaintly characterizes the campus as "90s meets Gotham." Filled with a mix of "square/blah" and more-modern buildings, the tight layout of the campus—one student posits that it might be to "increase the 'warmth' of the community"—contains a number of wonderful structures. The Elmer E. Rasmuson Library now holds more than 1.75 million volumes and contains a specialized collection of "Alaska and Polar Regions" materials. The Wood Center, created "as a solution to cabin fever," serves as the center of the student community. Housing a ballroom, adjoining conference rooms, an eight-lane bowling alley ("Polar Alley"), and a number of eateries, the facility is frequented by many students. Pizza Piazza, in particular, is a popular hangout spot for students. Additionally, the Upper Campus views of the stunning Brookes Mountain range more than make up for any lack of architectural beauty.

Polar Pastimes

Though the thermometer can hit extremely low readings during the winter, students try to take advantage of what they can. Within heated buildings, the Alaska Gravity Works Juggling Club spends time "throwing things in the air and periodically let them hit the ground." The Space and Robotics clubs cater towards the many students that have a passion for science. Students can also participate in a video game tournament sponsored by the VICE Club. In the great Alaskan outdoors, students take advantage of the ski slopes and trails, which the Trails Club maintains.

Athletes make the most of the fairly limited varsity-level athletic offerings. The UAF "Nanooks" (polar bears) have had particular success in cold-weather sports such as skiing and hockey. Even the more traditional basketball team has had its successes: it won the Division I Top of the World Classic in 2002. Alone in national prominence, however, is the Nanook rifle team, which dominates the national circuit with eight NCAA titles in the past 13 years. As a testament to the team's success, UAF will be hosting the 2007 NCAA Championships for the first time ever. Most students, however, rally around the hockey team as they compete each season. Of course, for those looking for a more leisurely experi-ence, the UAF intramurals program offers 19 sports ranging from 2-person volleyball to hoop shooting to the IM classic, broomball.

Northern Nuance

The single-most important factor that UAF students emphasize is Alaska's beautiful arctic landscape and natural resources. With gorgeous summer days filled with twenty-four hours of sunshine, and winter nights dazzled by the flashing of the Aurora Borealis in the sky, UAF's setting in rural Alaska provides its students with an out-standing learning environment. The biggest complaint one might have of the University of Alaska at Fairbanks, however, is the extreme cold and harsh winters. At times, the thermometer readings can hit as low as −65—but as one student declared, "Don't let that scare you out of the experience, be-cause it's sure to be one you'll never forget." Indeed, UAF students take the climate in stride; it is a testament to the hearty charac-ter of the student body that you can always find a scantily-clad student posing alongside a time/temperature sign that flashes forty below zero.—*Wookie Kim*

FYI

If you come to UAF, you'd better bring "lots of entertainment and no clothing; the only quality winter clothes are sold here."

What's the typical weekend schedule? "Each night starts out with calling or Myspacing friends to see where the parties are. Bowling, sledding, bonfires, cabin parties, clubbing, concerts, drag shows . . ."

If I could change one thing about UAF, I'd "make it less cold!"

Three things every student at the University of Alaska at Fairbanks should do before graduating are: "sled at midnight under the Northern Lights, eat moose meat, and join the forty-below club."

Arizona

"A SU is more than just a party school . . . seriously." Although its former ranking as one of the nation's ten top party schools has helped propagate that image for years, Arizona State has recently upped its efforts to increase its academic and intellectual appeal. More than ever, ASU students are involved, professional, and know how to have a damn good time.

English 101, Psych 101, Latin Salsa 101

Like most four-year colleges, ASU demands that its students fulfill certain general education requirements before entering into a specific major. Thus, some of the freshman and sophomore intro lecture classes can have up to 600 students. While some of these classes meet in sections, others opt for a more technologically adept method: internet conferences. Students meet weekly in small groups over the internet to discuss topics addressed in class. Participation in these online groups then contributes to the overall grade for the course. Seems too detached from the teacher? Students assure that "the higher up you get, the more attention they pay to you."

After students complete their general education requirements, they are free to focus on classes that go towards their major. Students do not have to declare a major at any designated time, although most choose to do so at the end of sophomore year. Picking a major allows a student to apply to a special pre-professional program in his or her area of interest, such as nursing, business, journalism, or art. These programs become the focus of the remaining two years, and provide students with useful connections after they graduate.

In addition to general education and major-oriented classes, students can also take cool electives for credit, as well as more arbitrary classes just out of curiosity. One student, for example, insisted that her Latin Salsa course is the hottest possible way to earn two credits. Other popular classes include Intro to Mass Communication, Psychology 101, and Political Science with Professor Kinney, an American government specialist. Since courses are often crowded, they stand out when the professor makes an effort to involve the students. Overall, students say that most of the professors are excellent and feel that their experiences have been positive.

What about That Reputation?

ASU students appreciate their academics, but have no fear, they still know how to have their fun. Even if they are busy becoming broadcasters and engineers, Sun Devils can't help but love the Arizona heat. According to one student, "The only reason we have a reputation as a party school is because it is just SO BEAUTIFUL at night!" In Tempe, a city where temperatures rarely go below sweatshirt level, students tend to be "pretty night-lifey." And Tempe police, many of whom are ASU alumni, are reportedly lenient when it comes to busting underage drinking. With the frat houses encircling the campus and most of the upperclassman housing not far beyond, "there is a lot of opportunity to do whatever you want." The frat scene is huge, and basically open to everyone. Older students frequent bars on Mill Avenue, the main drag of restaurants and nightclubs near campus. Favorites include Dos Gringos, Four Peaks, and Flip-Flop, all of which are within a couple blocks. In fact, as one student says excitedly, "Hooters is only a quarter mile away!" But "whatever you want" can also include staying in for the night or choosing a more subdued option. Cultural performances and concerts come to Gammage Auditorium, Frank Lloyd Wright's breathtaking last building. Sometimes, students drive to Phoenix to catch a concert or a play. So, while many students regularly take advantage of the weather-always-permitting nightlife, plenty of others prefer to maintain healthy sleep patterns and legal levels of alcohol consumption.

Back to Reality

One thing you will not find at ASU is dorm parties. The freshmen dorms, located in the middle of the campus, are under the supervision of RAs who have recently increased their efforts to prevent drinking in the dorms, instituting bag and ID checks upon entry into the buildings. Despite that, dorm life can mean anything from "crazy anarchy" to pleasant afternoons sitting on the balcony, overlooking the dorm's courtyard. Housing quality varies, although most of the dorms are "huge." But once a freshman is assigned to a building, he or she can apply to switch. Often freshmen choose to live in dorms according to their preliminary area of academic interest, living with others who will probably apply to the same pre-professional program. After the first year nearly everybody lives off-campus, simply because there is not enough room provided by the school. Most students have cars even though "parking is horrible 95 percent of the time." Cars also come in handy for going longer distances than just to class; students often drive to nearby Phoenix, or even to the Grand Canyon.

> "ASU is more than just a party school . . . seriously."

As for food, "dining halls," in the traditional sense of the term, do not really exist at ASU. There is a cafeteria-style eatery in one of the residence halls, which complements the more popular Memorial Union. The Memorial Union houses several chains like Taco Bell and Burger King, as well as an increasing number of healthier alternatives (in response to a recent barrage of student complaints). ASU has also developed a good relationship with local grocery stores and other businesses, which allow students to bill purchases from those establishments directly to their student account. Additionally, Tempe boasts hundreds of great restaurants, many of which are aimed at student tastes and budgets.

Desert Life

"We're just a really big school in the middle of the desert, and there aren't many big schools in the middle of the desert." Although applicants might find the 57,000-strong ASU enrollment daunting, students insist that they quickly find their place and adjust to the smaller communities built through the freshman dorms, academic programs, and extracurricular activities: "There are a lot of people, but it seems small because you are in your own part of campus, so you see people around randomly." ASU's colossal student body allows for an amount and variety of clubs, jobs, and intramural sports that would not be possible at a smaller school. ASU's award-winning newspaper, The State Press, as well as student-run Sun Devil TV reach thousands of people every day. For non-hardcore athletes, IM sports invite everyone to try something random and sweaty, while more intense students can play various levels of club sports through school and city teams. Post-graduation jobs are also fairly easy to find, either in Tempe or Phoenix. Positions range from telecommunications to freelance journalism to working in one of the many shops around campus, most of which are geared towards college students.

While IMs are great fun, watch out when it comes to taking ASU's varsity teams lightly. Sports at ASU "are AWESOME!" As a Pac 10 school, ASU draws substantial crowds for almost all of its sporting events, especially football and basketball. Many students purchase season passes to the stadiums, allowing them to cheer on the Sun Devils as often as possible. The biggest sports event of the year is the annual football game between ASU and the University of Arizona, a rivalry that one student describes as "massive." When ASU hosts the game, students sign up to camp out and defend the giant "A" that stands on a nearby hill, to prevent U of A fanatics from painting it U of A colors.

That "A" serves other important, symbolic purposes as well. According to tradition, the A, which is normally gold, must be painted white by the freshmen for a week at the beginning of the school year. During the year its colors "reflect the mood on campus," whether it be red, white, and blue around September 11, or rainbow during Pride Week. Every fall ASU also holds its annual "Homecoming FestDevil," a week-long themed extravaganza of concerts, parties, an activities fair, the Lantern Walk, and of course, the Homecoming Parade. School spirit runs high at ASU—students are overwhelmingly glad to be there. And who wouldn't be, considering the ever-gorgeous weather, the ridiculous variety of night time activities, and the consistently strong pre-professional training programs? The only drawback, according to one student, is the "airheadedness" that gives students the uncomfortable feeling that they are "walking down a runway when [they] go to class." But rest assured, beautiful people, beautiful landscape, and Latin Salsa classes for credit makes the Arizona college experience very memorable.—*Sophie Perl*

FYI
If you come to ASU, you'd better bring "a lot of money—tuition and dorms are really expensive."
What's the typical weekend schedule? "Go to sporting events, party hearty, sleep, and work."
If I could change one thing about ASU, it would be "to increase the amount of available student parking."
Three things that every student at ASU should do before graduating are "find and visit the secret garden, skip at least a week's worth of a single class, and paint the A white."

University of Arizona

Address: University of Arizona, PO Box 210040, Tucson, AZ 85721-0040

Phone: 520-621-3237

E-mail Address: admissions@arizona.edu

Web site URL: http://www.arizona.edu

Year Founded: 1885

Private or Public: public

Religious affiliation: none

Location: urban

Regular Application Deadline: 2-Apr

Number of Applicants: 16,609

Percent Accepted: 80%

Percent Accepted who enroll: 45%

Number Entering: 6,009

Number of Transfers Accepted each Year: 2,770

Mean SAT: 1,115

Mean ACT: 23

Middle 50% SAT range: 990–1,230

Middle 50% ACT range: 20–26

Early admission program (EA/ ED/ NA): NA

ED or EA Acceptance Rate: NA

Full time Undergraduate enrollment: 28,442

Total enrollment: 36,805

Percent Male: 47%

Percent Female: 53%

Total Percent Minority: 35%

Percent African-American: 3%

Percent Asian/Pacific Islander: 6%

Percent Hispanic: 16%

Percent Native-American: 2%

Percent Other: 8%

Percent in-state / out of state: 63%/37%

Percent from Public HS: 90%

Retention Rate: 79%

Graduation Rate: 59%

Percent in On-campus housing: 20%

Percent affiliated with Greek system: 10%

Percent Varsity or Club Athletes: NA

Number of official organized extracurricular organizations: 350

3 Most popular majors: Education, Political Science, Psychology

Student/Faculty ratio: 18:01

Tuition and Fees: $14,800.00

In State Tuition and Fees (if different): $4,594.00

Cost for Room and Board: $7,850.00

Percent receiving Financial aid, first-year: 35%

The University of Arizona Wildcats spend their four years living the ideal of "fun in the sun." Located in the desert oasis of Tucson, Arizona (an hour from the Mexican border), students bask in 300 days of sunshine as they scurry between sporting events and classes. Quality academics and a large student body provide for nearly every degree and extracurricular interest.

If You Want It, You Got It

A student would be hard pressed to find something he or she didn't love among the 120 undergraduate degree programs offered at Arizona. Majors like accounting, theatre arts, and Wildlife, Watershed and Rangeland Resources, provide a mere glimpse at the incredible variety of academic options available to Wildcats. Taming the freedom of the student body is the notorious "Gen. Ed." requirement. Gen. Ed. is made up of three tiers of classes, including Traditions and Cultures, Individuals and Societies, and the feared Natural Sciences. Gen. Ed. classes can be annoying and packed with 150 to 300 students, but students say that they fulfill the requirements with minimal discomfort.

Psychology, Communications, Political Science and Business are the most popular majors. Students wishing to take the more rigorous academic route subscribe to the engineering department's five-year program. One student warned, however, that, "as a general rule it seems that all of the hard science classes and engineering courses are the toughest on campus."

Arizona boasts one of the nation's top business schools, the Eller College of Management. One student proudly stated, "The Eller School is one of the most well known departments in the country and is perennially one of the top business schools in the country." Brainy Wildcats enjoy a special Honors College that demands no lower than a 3.5 GPA. Competition for admission is fierce, but the select few enjoy smaller classes, a support structure of 90 advisors and 11 staff members, private residence halls, and $40,000 annually for student research projects. Although for the majority of Wildcats the classes can be large and the student-teacher ratio overwhelming, students agree that, "grading is done fairly and the professors are always willing to listen if you have a question."

Going Greek

Outside of the classroom, most Wildcats spend time at the restaurants and bars located on University and Fourth Avenue. Students report that they value their fake IDs, but those without still have ample opportunity for underage drinking at Tucson house parties and along Frat Row.

Arizona administrators can be tough, however, on those caught drinking, as one student revealed. "There is no tolerance for underage drinking on campus, and if caught there is a mandatory program that all students must attend." Worse, still is the Red Tag Policy, which declares that for six months post party-breakup students must hang a red tag in the window and limit visitors to the number of housemates. Luckily, students report that "the Student Senate is currently trying to amend the situation" and Wildcats have plenty of opportunities for good clean fun.

Greek life is "the dominant social scene on campus," consisting of 21 sororities and 29 fraternities. Undergrad Greeks agree that Arizona Greek life offers members a support system, a community service group, and a post-grad network system, not to mention a full calendar of mixers and socials. Nearly 1,500 men and women rush, and getting a bid can be stressful. Yet, as one sorority girl advised, "Don't worry about everything. If it's right, it will happen."

Where'd Everybody Go?

With all that sunshine, students freely frolic about the entire campus. But the most popular spot is the student union. "The union is the main place people go if they have time. There are restaurants and rooms for people to sit and study or sleep." There are two unions: the Main Union in central campus; and the Student Union Memorial Center Park on the west side of campus. The newly built Student Union is a $60 million dollar, 450,000 square feet structure, with amenities like a bookstore, a post office, and even an arcade. Although everyone frequents the unions, University Drive, "a street right next to campus with restaurants, bars and shopping," is another hot spot for student activity. The campus is safe and full of friendly Wildcats, but students are warned to retain common sense as they travel around.

Dorms at Arizona vary significantly from "some really nice ones to some really bad dorms." The housing system offers students coed dorms, women-only dorms, sorority and fraternity housing, apartments for sin-

gle students, special housing for disabled students, and even special housing for international students. For the adventurous, the Coronado dorm is "the biggest dorm on campus and every year it leads all the other dorms in evictions." The RAs at Arizona are described as "cool." "Their major role," one student explained, "is to make sure nothing horrible happens . . . and they usually organize activities to let everyone get to know each other."

Although the insides of dorms vary, students report that the architecture is exactly the same: "everywhere you go, brick red buildings, everywhere." The most famous building on campus is the Old Main, built upon the University's founding in 1885. But one student noted that, "there is always construction of some kind on campus and new buildings are always popping up," leaving hope for a campus mini-makeover in the near future.

In terms of food, students can choose from a variety of meal plans offering fast food and restaurant fare. When describing student union food, one student reported that, "there are several different meal plans to choose from, but the food generally stinks." In response to whether the dining hall is better or worse than other schools, a student offered, "There is only one. So there isn't much choice in the matter."

> **"A big city, Tucson can still be looked at as a college town."**

Perhaps the bad dining is the reason "there is a huge off-campus life." "The majority of upper classmen live in the neighborhoods surrounding campus," one student explained. Whatever the reason, students are well received by the nearby towns. "The university is one of the largest employers in town, and it seems that the population supports the university as much as it can. . . . A big city, Tucson can still be looked at as a college town."

Wildcat Fever

Sports rule at the University of Arizona, and basketball is king. One student reported that, "Yesterday, there was a basketball game against North Carolina. The game started at 11, and there were students lining up at 10 the night before to get in." But all those denied basketball tickets have football, baseball, and softball games, not to mention numerous intramurals, to attend. Wildcats are an active bunch, so if they're not outside enjoying the sun, they're sweating it out at the student recreation center, which one student said is "nice, but it is always packed." In true Arizona fashion, plans to expand the popular rec center are already in progress.

The University of Arizona offers every student opportunities for academics, extracurricular activities, and socializing. School spirit permeates every aspect of life—school pride, sports, student organizations and popular events like Spring Fling and Homecoming make life at Arizona unforgettable. With so much to offer, a wise Wildcat advised, "Make the most of your time here."—*Eliza Crawford*

FYI

If you come to Arizona, you'd better bring "suntan lotion."

What is the typical weekend schedule? "Friday nights you usually go out [and party], Saturdays are sporting events and more partying, and Sundays are usually recovery days [when] you get all your work for the week done."

If I could change one thing about Arizona, I'd "lower the faculty to student ratio, some of the lower level class sizes are pretty big."

Three things every student at Arizona should do before graduating are "attend a Wildcat basketball game, sunbathe in January, make the most of your time here."

Arkansas

Hendrix College

Address: Hendrix, 1600 Washington Ave, Conway, AR 72032
Phone: 800-277-9017
E-mail Address: adm@hendrix.edu
Web site URL: http://hendrix.edu
Year Founded: 1876
Private or Public: private
Religious affiliation: United Methodist
Location: suburban
Regular Application Deadline: rolling
Number of Applicants: 1,086
Percent Accepted: 85%
Percent Accepted who enroll: 37%
Number Entering: NA
Number of Transfers Accepted each Year: NA
Mean SAT: NA

Mean ACT: 27
Middle 50% SAT range: 560–690V, 560–660M
Middle 50% ACT range: 25–31
Early admission program (EA/ ED/ NA): NA
ED or EA Acceptance Rate: NA
Full time Undergraduate enrollment: 1,010
Total enrollment: 1,010
Percent Male: 44%
Percent Female: 56%
Total Percent Minority: 11%
Percent African-American: 4%
Percent Asian/Pacific Islander: 3%
Percent Hispanic: 3%
Percent Native-American: 1%
Percent Other: 6%

Percent in-state / out of state: 55%/45%
Percent from Public HS: 80%
Retention Rate: 87%
Graduation Rate: 60%
Percent in On-campus housing: 83%
Percent affiliated with Greek system: 0%
Percent Varsity or Club Athletes: NA
Number of official organized extracurricular organizations: 72
3 Most popular majors: Biology, English, Psychology
Student/Faculty ratio: 11:01
Tuition and Fees: $22,616
Cost for Room and Board: $6,310.00
Percent receiving Financial aid, first-year: 56%

Located in Conway, Arkansas, Hendrix College is in a tiny, Methodist-affiliated liberal arts school with an openly liberal student body. Yet despite the elitism you might expect at an "oasis of liberalness" in the middle of conservative Arkansas, Hendrix is a down-to-earth college where "the atmosphere is just awesome, and the people are so friendly." Just because you haven't heard of this Southern school, don't pass it over without a closer look—the outstanding academics and intimate size make Hendrix a perfect fit for many.

Journeys and Explorations

Universally, students are delighted with the quality of Hendrix academics, the hallmark of which is the faculty-student interaction permitted by its small student body (just over 1000 undergraduates and no graduate school). "The academic life," one sopho-more said, "is by far my favorite aspect of Hendrix. I'm a pretty big fan of the faculty. I haven't had a bad teacher yet and I've had some amazing ones."

A small college, of course, means that there are fewer majors available (29) and fewer course options. Yet students are satisfied with the tradeoff, reporting that their classes are intimate (the average class size being 15) and they know their professors well. One sophomore said that her classes have been evenly split between lectures and seminars, but that even her lectures are no larger than 30 students. In all classes, active student participation is emphasized. "One of the things I've noticed about my classes," a freshman said, "is that there's a lot more open discussion than at what most people would consider a college environment."

Though there are no noticeably weak academic programs here, Hendrix's strong suits are traditional fields such as English, politics, and biology, with pre-med being a popular choice. Hendrix has many core requirements that it believes constitute a broad liberal arts education. But as one sophomore said, "While a lot of students at other schools dread core requirements, students often have fun here taking core classes no matter how unrelated to their major they are. I'm currently in a natural history lab where we take fun field trips to forests." Plus, because the school is so small, many upper-level courses are available to freshmen and sophomores.

Hendrix places heavy emphasis on integrating freshmen into the social and academic life of the college immediately upon arrival. A mandatory course for all freshmen, "Journeys," introduces students to important works by Plato, Confucius and other philosophers all in one year. Less popular is the required orientation "Explorations," which focuses on introducing freshmen to the campus by creating small groups led by a faculty member and a sophomore guide.

The college welcomes freshmen to Hendrix life in more ways than just academics. Every student participates in an orientation trip before even arriving on campus; one freshman described his trip up to the Buffalo River, where his group went canoeing for two days with upperclassmen, who "kind of showed us the ropes." Indeed, because Hendrix is so small, college life thrives on interaction between upperclassmen and freshmen.

"Hippies and Gays"?

One junior described a "weird kind of dual stereotype" about the Hendrix student body. On the one hand, he said, Hendrix is the most academically challenging school in the state and the object of many Arkansans' aspirations, but on the other, "there is the image of Hendrix as an out of control party school with hippies and gays running rampant." Students say neither stereotype is truly accurate, though they do agree that many diverse opinions and beliefs are expressed openly on the Hendrix campus.

The school's Methodist background and religious life play an important part of many students' lives at Hendrix. One freshman described "countless religious groups at Hendrix, lots of Catholics and other religions who have their organizations on campus." And though political leanings here are "predominantly liberal," one student assures

that "you'll find your conservatives and socialists and other groups there too."

Still, there isn't much geographic diversity, and students who are from out-of-state sometimes find themselves isolated. "There's a lot of southerners, a fair amount from Little Rock and Arkansas," a sophomore said. "All the non-southern people sort of clump together. It's a very regional school in that sense."

Partying Under Strict Scrutiny

Hendrix may have a miniscule student body and lack fraternities or sororities, but students repeatedly emphasized that they still manage to have a bustling social life. Residential dorm parties are the major attraction on weekend nights. Each dorm has its own personality and reputation, and in a fake rush week every year they mimic fraternities and pretend to recruit new "taps." "There's definitely one spot—Martin Hall, one of the dorms—where every Wednesday, Friday and Saturday you can pretty much guarantee there will be people drinking," one student said.

Students frequently complain about the way the Hendrix administration deals with partying. "In recent years, there's been a very notable and organized effort by the administration to crack down on parties," one student said. As part of its efforts, the administration has attempted to cloister all student partying in one house, the Cottage, or in the Brick Pit, an open space in the middle of campus where college police can easily manage students. Other Hendrix-approved social events including a dance competition called Shirttails at the end of the first week of school, for which all the male freshmen "do this sort of dance, usually a little raunchy, where they're just wearing their boxer shorts and an Oxford shirt. They perform it in front of these judges, and the winners get a pizza party."

The insularity and closeness of Hendrix social life—and the jumping through hoops required to throw parties on campus—lead a number of students to escape campus on the weekends, usually to Little Rock, the closest major city. Conway provides a few movie theatres and restaurants near campus, and Hendrix puts on some concerts and theatrical productions throughout the year, but partying seems to be the central focus of student social lives.

Beyond complaints about the administration's alcohol policies, students also cited inflexible and difficult housing regulations and poor access to health services as further problems. In fact, a number of students mentioned the uncaring administration as their biggest gripe with Hendrix. "I was lucky, and housing flowed for me," a sophomore said, "but there's a facebook.com group about getting screwed over by the administration." "The president is highly unpopular, as well as the new dean of students," another sophomore noted. "The students aren't afraid to speak up and try to do something about it, but it is very hard to get pro-student laws passed as the board of trustees is a bunch of conservative Methodists."

An Unusual School Spirit

Although extracurricular involvement varies widely among students, there are several influential organizations on campus. The Student Senate deals with campus issues and gives students a voice. "They struggle with the administration every once in a while," a freshman said. But despite occasional problems, they "really do care about the students and try to get stuff done."

Another popular activity is writing for and editing the student newspaper, *The Profile*, which has a regular staff of 50 and an editorial staff of 10-15. For a small school, Hendrix boasts an impressive array of other extracurricular options, from political groups like the Young Democrats and the Progressive Student Alliance to musical ensembles such as the jazz band, pep band, and wind ensemble.

At Hendrix, approximately 200 students are athletes, on eight men's teams and nine women's teams. Students say that they show a great deal of school spirit, but that winning is not necessarily important to Hendrix culture. "We're not going to be real upset if the basketball team doesn't do that well this year. We care because our friends might be on it, but we don't care because we want Hendrix to win—we care about the people and not about the competition," one student said. Describing the easygoing nature of Hendrix athletics, one junior said, "We're probably best known for our Ultimate Frisbee team, the Flying Squirrels."

A Close Community

The sense that every Hendrix student knows everyone else constitutes a great deal of the school's appeal, but also its drawbacks. Several students said they felt claustrophobic after being on campus a year. "Last year, I found that a lot of my friends, one way or another, thought about leaving," a sophomore said. "But the feeling is that this year, my friends are more settled in. It's just anxiety over change."

> "Whatever bias or opinions or preconceived notions you have about anything will be challenged at Hendrix."

Many students come to Hendrix for financial reasons, citing its strong financial aid package as a major appeal. But once they've arrived on campus and have gotten over some of its problems, most thrive in its intimate atmosphere. "I don't think twice when I meet new people," a sophomore said. "I almost think, well, they're at Hendrix, they have to be good people."

Above all, Hendrix prizes an active academic life and personal, social, and academic development. As one student put it, "Whatever bias or opinions or preconceived notions you have about anything will be challenged at Hendrix."—*Yotam Barkai*

FYI

If you come to Hendrix, you'd better bring "flip-flops, a Ryan Adams CD, and a healthy appreciation for mob flicks."

What is the typical weekend schedule? "Friday, there's usually some sort of party going on, and the campus usually tries to have some other activity going on (a play at the theater or a movie). Saturdays are pretty much up in the air—unless there's a soccer game, there's usually not that much on campus. We do a lot of studying."

If I could change one thing about Hendrix, I'd "loosen the rules regarding partying and social life and alcohol."

Three things every student at Hendrix should do before graduating are "break into the greenhouse, check out the Ozarks, and get thrown into the fountain for your birthday."

University of Arkansas

Address: University of Arkansas, Office of Admissions, 232 Hunt Hall, University of Arkansas, Fayetteville, Arkansas, 72701

Phone: 479 575 5346 or 800 377 UofA

E-mail Address: UofA@uark.edu

Web site URL: http://www.uark.edu

Year Founded: 1871

Private or Public: Public

Religious affiliation: None

Location: Small City

Regular Application Deadline: 15-Aug

Number of Applicants: 12,044

Percent Accepted: 54%

Percent Accepted who enroll: 56%

Number Entering: 4,583

Number of Transfers Accepted each Year: ~1,000

Mean SAT: 1,149

Mean ACT: 25

Middle 50% SAT range: 1040–1,280

Middle 50% ACT range: 22–28

Early admission program (EA/ ED/ NA): EA

ED or EA Acceptance Rate: 77.0%

Full time Undergraduate enrollment: 12,175

Total enrollment: 17,938

Percent Male: 50%

Percent Female: 50%

Total Percent Minority: 20%

Percent African-American: 5.3%

Percent Asian/Pacific Islander: 2.5%

Percent Hispanic: 2.5%

Percent Native-American: 1.8%

Percent Other: 7.9%

Percent in-state / out of state: 79%/21%

Percent from Public HS: NA

Retention Rate: 81%

Graduation Rate: 56%

Percent in On-campus housing: 28%

Percent affiliated with Greek system: 29%

Percent Varsity or Club Athletes: NA

Number of official organized extracurricular organizations: 290

3 Most popular majors: Marketing, Finance, Journalism

Student/Faculty ratio: 18:01

Tuition and Fees: $13,942.00

In State Tuition and Fees (if different): $5,808.00

Cost for Room and Board: $6,522.00

Percent receiving Financial aid, first-year: 70%

For it's A-A-A-R-K-A-N-S-A-S for Arkansas! Fight! Fight! Fi-i-i-ght!" Don't even think about setting foot in Fayetteville, Arkansas, without knowing the words to the Razorback fight song. Athletics aren't just for the jocks at this Southern university. If you are looking for a community with school pride, are unsure if you want to rush Pi Beta Phi or just go to their parties, and are interested in anything from engineering to agriculture, the University of Arkansas is calling your name.

Welcome to Fayetteville

Located in the Ozark Mountains, Fayetteville is the home of 345 acres of University of Arkansas campus. The city has a population of approximately 60,000 people for now, but Northwest Arkansas is considered the sixth-fastest-growing region in the United States, according to the U.S. Census.

Upon arrival in Fayetteville, freshmen are introduced to their academic advisers, who "really know what they're doing," according to one senior. During orientation period, freshmen are clued in to all university policies and academic requirements. "It's hard to fall through the cracks freshman year," students said. "There are advisers and older students who really take pride in helping the younger ones." Make sure you ask about Advanced Placement status in classes, or how to "clep-out" of the University's second-language requirement by taking proficiency tests or foreign language classes. Oftentimes high school AP credits can cut down your "core" course load. The completion of core classes is required for graduation, and according to a senior, the readily-accessible advisers are helpful in "letting us know exactly what we need" in order to graduate on time.

By sophomore year undergrads are usually enrolled in a specific college at the University of Arkansas. Students may choose between the Dale Bumpers College of Agricultural, Food & Life Sciences, the School of Architecture, the Fulbright College of Arts & Sciences, the Sam M. Walton College of Business, the College of Education and Health Professions, and the College of Engineering, depending on the student's academic interests. With 216 academic degree programs, UA covers virtually all academic bases.

Most students are quick to say that the professors are all easy to reach, and hold convenient office hours, oftentimes meeting students for coffee on campus. However, as the freshmen core courses (such as Chemistry and Communications) are usually numbered at around 300 or 400 students, they are mostly taught by Teaching Assistants, not actual professors. One senior business major explained, "Once you get more into your major by junior and senior year, you get more of the professors, and people who actually wrote the books you are reading."

Deemed the hardest major at Arkansas by a number of students, engineering is only a hair less harrowing than molecular biology. Nonetheless, students claim that the difficulty of the subjects really shouldn't deter any undergrads from taking them. "Help is really just around the corner," one sophomore said. "I have tutors in a few subjects, and they are really flexible, and helpful around midterms and finals especially."

Life as a Razorback

While students are required to live on campus their freshman year, this is certainly not viewed as a bad thing. The dorms are described as "traditional" and "spacious" but beware: they are not all created equal. Humphreys (aka "the Hump-Dump") is coed and in the middle of campus. However, it has no air-conditioning and is "miserable" at the beginning of school because "it can get pretty hot here in Arkansas." A better dorm is Pomphret, which "everyone who lives there loves" and "they have a lot of fun." Its location isn't as convenient, however, as it sits at the "very bottom of a great big hill." (Don't come to Fayetteville without good walking shoes; students say "we have a ton of huge hills!")

By sophomore year many students choose to live off campus in any of Fayetteville's many apartment complexes. The city is "overflowing" with them, and the crowding in the city has also created a huge parking problem. Students call the city parking "awful" and "downright impossible." Luckily for future classes, the city just built the biggest parking deck in the state of Arkansas, which holds 550 automobiles.

Greeks and Non-Greeks

Sophomore year is also the first year that students who choose to "Go Greek" can live in their fraternity and sorority houses. While Greek life is a large part of the Arkansas social scene, it is certainly not something that students feel pressured to join. "If you do it, great, but if you don't want to do it, that's great too," one Razorback senior commented. Greek or not, students can still attend frat parties, where the serving of alcohol to minors is reportedly "not a problem whatsoever." Students who live in off-campus apartments and houses often open up their houses for parties and keggers, and offer a stress-free night for students who are underage.

The Greek houses are also all on campus, making party-hopping very convenient. With Sorority Row on Maple Street and Fraternity Row on Stadium Drive, undergrads don't have to look far for a "typical huge, beautiful, southern-style Greek house" offering plenty of cold beer and Southern hospitality.

Students are quick to add that there are no lines drawn between dorm-dwellers and off-campus renters. UA offers over $100 million of financial aid each year, and many students receive this in the form of free room and board. The cafeterias received mixed reviews from Razorback undergrads. While some students lived on campus for four years and "never got tired of it" others don't think they will "step foot into a dining hall" for a whole year, even if they live in the dorms.

On campus or off, students mix and mingle the nights away on Fayetteville's Dickson Street. Running straight through campus, the street offers so many bars and clubs that "it's hard to keep up with the new names and owners," explains one seasoned senior. Go to George's Majestic Lounge and rub elbows with University of Arkansas alums recounting the nights they spent at the waterhole 50 years ago. Gypsy, Alligator Ray's and Grubb's are just a few of the places that shouldn't be missed during an educational stint in Razorback Country. Even underage students can party with the rest of them on certain nights. Clubs and bars often offer 18-and-over nights, and on big weekends (think Homecoming Weekend versus South Carolina, or 'Bama and Texas games) the whole street is closed off.

"Suuuey, Hogs"

A University of Arkansas education is incomplete without the inclusion of Arkansas athletics. Their unstoppable track program, which has won 17 consecutive indoor titles, and their powerhouse football and basketball teams, are just a few examples of nationally dominant Razorbacks sports. "The weekends are all about sporting events," students explain. "You have to get real geared up for the game, and no matter what, you MUST know the fight songs."

> **"Arkansas sporting events are huge, women's or men's, it's just a culture."**

With no professional sports teams to root for in the area, the entire Fayetteville community supports their hogs on game day. From the parquet in the Bud Walton Arena to the green grass of the Donald W. Reynolds Razorback Stadium, the thrill of victory (and the stench of keg beer) lingers in the sweet Southern air. Arkansas sports aren't simple weekend entertainment for UA Students. Students reported that "Arkansas sporting events are huge. Women's or men's, it's just a culture."

If a Division I athletic career isn't a personal option, undergrads can still quench their competitive spirits within the confines of HPER (the UA Health, Physical Education, and Recreation building). The $14 million facility is the largest in the area and features 10 racquetball courts, four basketball gyms, an indoor track, an Olympic-size swimming pool, a climbing wall, men's and women's saunas, a computer lab, thousands of lockers, and a human performance lab.

Greek or non-Greek, on campus or off, athlete or academic, Razorbacks are all about one thing: having one hell of a time. If you are looking for a school with tons of school pride nestled in a true Southern college city, then University of Arkansas is the place to be. When you are leaving home, don't forget to pack your Razorback football jersey. You won't regret it.—*Meredith Hudson*

FYI

If you come to Arkansas, you'd better bring "your car or enough money to buy one."

What's the typical weekend schedule? "Friday: hit up a frat party; Saturday: go crazy at the football game, head to the bars at night; Sunday: sleep in, catch up on studying."

If I could change one thing about the University of Arkansas, I would "send more funds to the science department instead of to athletics. Sometimes we lack a sufficient amount of chemicals to perform chemistry experiments."

Three things every student should do before graduating are "attend a Razorback football game and 'call the hogs,' take a class that is taught in Old Main, and eat at Herman's restaurant."

California

Address: Cal Tech, 1200 East California Boulevard, Mail Code 1-94, Pasadena, CA 91125
Phone: (626) 395-6341
E-mail Address: ugadmissions@admissions.caltech.edu
Web site URL: www.caltech.edu
Year Founded: 1891
Private or Public: Private
Religious affiliation: None
Location: Suburban
Regular Application Deadline: 3-Jan
Number of Applicants: 3,330
Percent Accepted: 17%
Percent Accepted who enroll: 37%
Number Entering: 214
Number of Transfers Accepted each Year: varies

Mean SAT: NA
Mean ACT: NA
Middle 50% SAT range: NA
Middle 50% ACT range: NA
Early admission program (EA/ ED/ NA): EA
ED or EA Acceptance Rate: NA
Full time Undergraduate enrollment: 864
Total enrollment: 864
Percent Male: 70%
Percent Female: 30%
Total Percent Minority: 44%
Percent African-American: 1%
Percent Asian/Pacific Islander: 37%
Percent Hispanic: 6%
Percent Native-American: 0%
Percent Other: NA
Percent in-state / out of state: 31%/69%

Percent from Public HS: 70%
Retention Rate: 97%
Graduation Rate: 90%
Percent in On-campus housing: 92%
Percent affiliated with Greek system: 0%
Percent Varsity or Club Athletes: 50%
Number of official organized extracurricular organizations: 165
3 Most popular majors: Engineering, Physical Science, Biological Sciences
Student/Faculty ratio: 3:01
Tuition and Fees: $29,595
Cost for Room and Board: $9,102
Percent receiving Financial aid, first-year: 70%

If you're serious about science or math, the California Institute of Technology (Caltech) is the place for you. Located in sunny Southern California, Caltech is considered to be by far the best and most rigorous school for students seeking to pursue studies in math and science. With building clusters designed completely around the famous Fibonacci Sequence, students are constantly reminded of Caltech's technical prowess. Nobel Prize winners and laureates come from all over the world to conduct their research and teach at Caltech while rubbing elbows with some of the most brilliant students in the world. The result? A mathematically beautiful campus in a temperate climate with highly intelligent students.

486 Credits to Go

The admissions material makes it blatantly clear that Caltech's curriculum is extremely lopsided. There is a core curriculum that requires all undergraduates, or "techers," to take five terms of math, five terms of physics, and classes like chemistry, biology and science writing. Of course, students are also expected to take at least 12 courses in the humanities and social sciences. The course load can become so rigorous that Caltech requires students to take three terms of physical education in order to give their brains a break. All in all, techers need a whopping 486 credit units to graduate.

Although you "theoretically" can major in literature or history, you would still have to take five terms of math and physics. Such strict requirements are why "techies" are often attracted to the school. "If you're absolutely sure that you want to be a scientist or engineer, come to Caltech," one student said. Perhaps most notably, Caltech has produced many famous physicists and engineers over the years, many of whom have gone on to work at the neighboring Jet Propulsions Laboratory, run by Caltech and responsible for feats like the Mars Rover Project.

"Caltech has some wonderful benefits in terms of access to professors and research. But you have to know that you will pay in hard work for the great access to research you will get," said another student. It is not uncommon for students to spend more than 12 hours a day going to classes and working on the assignments. To make matters more intense, many students also take advantage of the tremendous number of undergraduate research opportunities, opportunities to work with Nobel Laureates and Field Medalists, which means there's often no time for sleep. "It's not unusual to see students up until 4 a.m., even frosh taking pass/fails—sleep is a very precious commodity," said a student.

3 to 1

Caltech has less than one thousand undergraduates—that's across four years combined. That means there's a greater sense of community than in your typically faceless state universities. Yet some students complain about the lack of diversity. While there are plenty of Asians, almost as many as Caucasians, the number of Hispanic and African-American students is dismal in comparison.

Additionally, because of the school's emphasis on engineering and the hard sciences, the incoming classes tend to be heavily dominated by men, sometimes in greater ratios than 3:1. "For girls, the odds are good, but the goods are odd. For guys, the odds are terrible and the goods are all screwed up," one student said. In a curious phenomenon that is mostly contained at Caltech, students said, the few "datable" girls are quickly swamped by swarms of boys, and many attract a loyal following and fan base. Others are simply too busy to even think about dating or the opposite sex.

360 Degree Rotation

Right after "Frosh Camp," an all-expense-paid "vacation" for the entire freshman class to the San Jacinto Mountains begins a week called Rotation. The week is spent having dinner and various social events at the seven undergraduate houses. "Rotation lasts through the first week of classes, and is designed to help Frosh choose Houses and Houses choose Frosh," said one upperclassman. Since each House has its own personal-

ity, students tend to gravitate towards some over others. And Houses act like Caltech's version of fraternities, serving as focuses for most of the campus's social activities.

"The weather here is great, the people are incredibly intelligent, and the campus is beautiful," said one student. This observation sums up the perks of going to Caltech, of which weather and the campus aren't to be overlooked. The California weather is simply priceless when all your friends who went off to stuffy schools in the Northeast are freezing as they trudge through the snow to their classes. The Southern California weather is Mediterranean in nature, mild in winter and summer, and with little precipitation.

Furthermore, the campus is a diverse milieu of architectural styles that is easy on the eye. With a well-kept ground and green grass everywhere, it's tempting to just nap the afternoon away under a tree. The Spanish and modern buildings really bring out the contrast of this small campus, a quarter mile by a quarter mile (you can reach any point on campus in around five minutes).

And how about the food? Well, aside from quips about how some students are too busy to eat, Caltech provides incoming students with a meal plan that includes five lunch and dinner meals per week. Lunch is usually at the cozy and centralized Chandler dining hall, which has various booths like fast food and deli, while dinners are at the various Houses. Of course, students get sick of the food eventually, and many venture out to the restaurants in Pasadena to satisfy their hunger.

30 Pumpkins Frozen in Liquid-Nitrogen

So what do techers do for fun? Well, like Ditch Day, pranks are a revered tradition. One popular prank is "the annual Pumpkin Drop, when we freeze 30 pumpkins in liquid nitrogen and drop them off of Millikan Library, the tallest building on campus, in an amazing display of gravitation." In the classic Caltech fashion, many of the pranks end up employing some engineering or science ingenuity, like rewiring the scoreboard at Caltech-MIT sports games.

While there are a few parties off campus, the social scene primarily centers around the Houses. A party can usually be found at one of the Houses every week, although, again, Caltech isn't your normal party school. While drinking and perhaps even greater vices are tolerated, students are careful not to overindulge as problem sets and lectures are always looming over their heads. "For some people, the social structure is stifling rather than familial," said one student. Other than the Houses, there are not many outlets for other social events, as fraternities and sororities were supplanted by the current system.

> **"Caltech is not a 'party school,' but it is the nation's playground for math and science."**

"Caltech is not a 'party school,' but it is the nation's playground for math and science," another student said. Yet on weekends, techers can be found all over town. Caltech is located in the upscale suburbs of Pasadena, which is itself a suburb of the greater Los Angeles metropolitan area. The houses near Caltech are often occupied by professors and feature quaint Mediterranean architecture.

The city of Pasadena really is a paradise, with low crime and a high concentration of PhDs (not surprisingly). Within walking distance of campus is Old Town Pasadena, with countless shops and restaurants lining Colorado Blvd, where the famous annual Rose Parade passes through. Just a short drive away is more shopping and leisure at Long Beach, Rodeo Drive and Beverly Hills, and Venice Beach, as well as the San Gabriel Mountains, which has great hiking. Also nearby is the serene Huntington Gardens, with a museum that contains one of the few remaining Gutenberg Bibles.

Caltech isn't the right school for everyone. For those who go there, the ability to balance work, play and exploration is crucial for success and sanity. But if you want to be surrounded by the best in math, science and engineering, whether it's a gold medalist in the International Mathematical Olympiad or a professor who is the world's leader in the development of a mustard weed (the model plant Arabidopsis), Caltech is the place to be.—*Jerry Guo*

FYI
If you come to Caltech, you'd better bring "a copy of 'Calculus' by Apostol."
What is the typical weekend schedule? "About 4 hours of play, 24 hours of sleep; the rest is homework."
If I could change one thing about Caltech, "it would be the coed bathroom."
Three things every student at Caltech should do before graduating are "visit the underground tunnels, get ponded, and live in Avery."

California Institute of Arts

Address: California Institute of the Arts, 24700 McBean Parkway, Valencia, CA 91355
Phone: 800-545-2787
E-mail Address: asmiss@calarts.edu
Web site URL: www.calarts.edu
Year Founded: 1961
Private or Public: private
Religious affiliation: none
Location: suburban
Regular Application Deadline: Rolling
Number of Applicants: NA
Percent Accepted: 12%
Percent Accepted who enroll: 25%
Number Entering: NA
Number of Transfers Accepted each Year: NA
Mean SAT: NA
Mean ACT: NA

Middle 50% SAT range: NA
Middle 50% ACT range: NA
Early admission program (EA/ ED/ NA): NA
ED or EA Acceptance Rate: NA
Full time Undergraduate enrollment: 850
Total enrollment: 850
Percent Male: 56%
Percent Female: 44%
Total Percent Minority: 30%
Percent African-American: 7%
Percent Asian/Pacific Islander: 10%
Percent Hispanic: 12%
Percent Native-American: 1%
Percent Other: NA
Percent in-state / out of state: NA
Percent from Public HS: NA

Retention Rate: 80%
Graduation Rate: 74% in four, 80% in six
Percent in On-campus housing: 40%
Percent affiliated with Greek system: 0%
Percent Varsity or Club Athletes: NA
Number of official organized extracurricular organizations: NA
3 Most popular majors: Art, Directing and Theatrical Production, Film/Video
Student/Faculty ratio: 7:01
Tuition and Fees: $29,300.00
Percent receiving Financial aid, first-year: 66%

At California Institute of Arts, the word "traditional" is all but taboo. CalArts distinguishes itself with its cutting-edge approach to art, as well as its free-thinking students—the combination of which can lead to endless possibilities. "CalArts is very laid-back and very progressive, so if you really want to do something artistic or otherwise, there's a good chance you can, as long as you're willing to put enough work into it," said a vocal performance student. For the right student, CalArts offers a dynamic, creative environment where the inspiration (and the workload) never seems to end.

A New Form of Art

Many students said they love the fact that CalArts prides itself on the avant-garde nature of its art. In fact, they cited it as one of the most important components of their education. "CalArts is really the best school for experimental graphic design . . . [but it's] not good for people who are interested in advertising or corporate design," noted a second year student. "If you like anything traditional, don't bother applying, because if you do, you will regret it," one first-year lighting

design student noted. "But if you are adventurous and up for a challenge, CalArts is for you."

Furthermore, the curriculum allows students to fully engage with their art. A fourth-year live-action film student raved about the world of possibilities available to undergraduates. "[I was] able to practice my art right away without having to wait years to pick up a camera," he said. And, of course, some of the best opportunities that CalArts students have are in the form of artistic collaborations between different departments. For example, musicians may arrange for a choreographed dance during a recital. In one instance, described by a CalArtian, a horn student had an artist paint during his recital. Collaborations take place on a larger scale, as well, such as a theater production that combines student expertise in everything from lighting and props to scenery, acting and film.

Within one of the six CalArtian schools—Art, Dance, Film, Writing, Music and Theater—students enroll in general classes as well as ones specific to their specialty within the school. And while everyone has a unique experience within these classes, students agree that the CalArtian curriculum is highly dependent on a well-developed knowledge of art. "Before coming to CalArts, make sure you really know exactly what you want out of this school or you might find yourself a little lost," one third year student warned.

> **"Come to this school if you are self-motivated and serious about your pursuit and want to broaden your mind without being pigeonholed."**

Some students said it can be all too easy for students to get good grades while completing only the minimum workload. While many students are constantly immersed in their art—to the exclusion of almost everything else—there are also a few who seem to have too much free time. However, CalArts provides a wealth of opportunities to offer a sufficiently dedicated student. One current music-performance student suggested, "Come to this school if you are self-motivated and serious about your pursuit and want to broaden your mind without being pigeonholed. . . . Avoid it, please, if all you want is to fulfill the 'social requirement' that you should attend college after high school."

Academics (With a Twist)
In addition to an intensive study in the arts, CalArts students pursue more traditional academic studies within the context of the Critical Studies program. Within the Critical Studies Department, students study a wide variety of subjects, from philosophy to psychology to physics—but almost always with a CalArtian spin. Rather than take a traditional physics or biology class, for example, students take courses with titles like "The Reproduction of Sound" or "Biology and Music." While some complained that Critical Studies classes detract from the time available to spend on art, most did not seem to feel constrained by the workload. Most Critical Studies courses require students to keep a journal about the specific course, in addition to the several papers assigned throughout the semester.

One of the many unique aspects of CalArts is the method by which undergraduates are labeled. Students are classified by the degree they are pursuing (either a Bachelor's in Fine Arts or Master's in Fine Arts) and their year. For example, a second-year undergraduate would not be referred to as a sophomore, but rather as a BFA2 (more specifically, a student in the first semester of their second year would be a BFA2-1). Students attribute this system to the fact that almost all classes, except those within the Critical Studies department, contain a mixture of undergraduate and graduate students.

According to some students, the mixture gives undergraduates a unique opportunity to learn from the more experienced students. "The grad students are generally really helpful," one photography student said. "They have really good work—it's inspiring."

Students agreed that instructors are readily available. One BFA3 raved about the "talented teachers who also really care about you." And as a first-year in fine arts described, "students and faculty are very friendly, sweet, and at times wacky or eccentric." And, in the spirit of the laid-back CalArts attitude, students call their instructors by their first names.

A CalArtian Campus
The campus is centered around the "Main Building," where the majority of classes are held. One student, citing its "long, dark, maze-like corridors" described the edifice as a "giant art-producing casino." It includes a cafeteria and three theaters within its four floors, along with a basement known as the "sub-level." The sub-level is well-known for its "designated 'anything goes' area for student graffiti in the building," and students come both to add their own designs to the wall and to admire the works of past students, including a number of celebrities. A number of buildings scattered around the Main Building serve to support the pursuit of art in other ways. Many provide space for students to work, perform and display their art.

While many first year students prefer to live on campus, third- and fourth-year students rarely decide to live in the dorms. Once students become more familiar with the area, they tend to move into Valencia, the suburban home of CalArts, or even (car-permitting) Los Angeles. The two campus dormitories are constructed in a U-shape around a communal area that includes a pool (in which "clothing is optional") as well as plenty of grassy areas for students to hang out, study, and enjoy the California sun. One of these dorms, Chouinard, primarily houses underclassmen in suites of two large doubles connected by a bathroom. The other, Ahmanson, offers an apartment-style living option for upperclassmen as well as graduate students.

Students' opinions on the food offered at CalArts varied considerably. "I actually like the food served at our café, Bon Appetit, a lot," asserted an acting major. Raved another, "the breakfast burritos rock!" However, not all students gave such glowing reviews of their dining options. Many complained that the food is too expensive without the meal plan. Still, more said that they simply dislike it. Fortunately, while not all dorms have their own kitchenettes, they are all equipped with "a tiled area with a counter," well-suited (with the addition of a microwave and mini-fridge) for a makeshift kitchen.

Despite the sub-par cuisine, the majority of student complaints are directed at Valencia, the town in which CalArts is located. Valencia, far from being the traditional college town, exemplifies Californian suburbia. The college itself is located in a largely residential area, complete with gated communities and the omnipresent strip mall. Public transportation is practically nonexistent, making cars a very valuable asset, if not an absolute necessity. Furthermore, students complained of a lack of cultural events in the area. Indeed, one graphic design major noted, "If you want anything interesting, you need to go into L.A., and who has time with these class loads?"

Parties: From Thursday Fun to Halloween Madness

Social life at CalArts is squeezed in between (or during) classes, rehearsals, and—for the vast majority of CalArtians—homework, projects, work, work, and more work. "The weekends are usually dead," one music major said, adding "People don't hang out too much because they are either always busy, or at some sort of performance." Yet, as another student pointed out, "Saturdays and Sundays are full of concerts or student recitals."

The acknowledged high point of campus social life, according to CalArts students, is the Thursday evening art openings. In addition to showcasing the work of individual students, the events offer free drinks to students of age and often feature live music performances. "You get to look at art, dance and let loose after a hard week of classes," one first-year student said.

If Thursday night is the regular party slot, the campus nevertheless manages to shake things up significantly with events such as the annual Halloween Show, a famous (or infamous) campus tradition. The show never fails to draw in huge crowds from the community and is known for its rowdiness. As a current third year in music technology put it, "You will have quite a few interesting stories to tell afterward. . . . They will mostly likely contain references to people who are naked and/or drunk or otherwise under the influence of something."

CalArts is certainly not an institution for everyone. It draws passionate, highly-motivated students interested in pursuing the non-traditional aspects of art. A successful match, however, produces artists who are as much devoted to their craft as they are to their school. "I truly love CalArts, and everything it has done for me in terms of my music, and my life as a whole," said one musical arts student. "I am going to have a hard time separating myself from this place."—*Stephanie Brockman*

FYI
If you come to CalArts, you'd better bring a "water gun, hacky sack, bubbles, a feather . . ."
What is the typical weekend schedule? "Work work work on your art! (maybe a job . . .) Paint, draw, dance, write, sing, play, animate, monologue, shoot, edit etc."
If I could change one thing about CalArt, I'd "make more resources [available] such as color printers."
Three things that every student at CalArts should do before graduating are "write in the sublevel, go to a gallery opening and be naked in public."

California State University System

With over 400,000 students on 23 campuses, The California State University system stakes its claim as one the largest and most diverse university systems in the United States. Brought together by the Donahue Higher Education Act of 1960, these state schools offer a wide range of academic and social experiences. They include the first public university in California, San Jose State University, and CSU Channel Islands, opened in the fall of 2002. From the metropolitan Los Angeles campus to rural CSU Sonoma to the coastal San Diego State, the individual campuses that make up the system are distinctive and vary greatly. San Diego State University, known for its party atmosphere and close proximity to fine beaches, is the largest campus, with about 31,000 full-time students. Maritime Academy and CSU Monterey Bay are the smallest, with total enrollments of 450 and 1,960 respectively.

UC Who?

Although often overshadowed by the better-known University of California system, the CSU system offers many features that the UC system does not. With campuses located throughout the state, the CSU system allows many Californians the option of commuting to a college close to home. For students concerned with the high costs of financing higher education, the tuition of the California State Universities are half that of UC schools, while still providing larger and better resources than two-year junior colleges. Even for an out-of-state student seeking California weather, the CSU system is still an attractive deal.

So Many Choices . . .

All CSU schools offer financial aid and over 60 percent of the students are currently receiving aid. The larger campuses offer Divi-

sion I varsity sports, while the smaller schools are in Division II. All campuses have organized club and intramural sports. Each campus differs greatly and prospective students should research the academic focus, size, location, and student makeup of each campus before deciding. To help high school students decide which of the 23 campuses is right for them, Cal State has implemented a specialized Web site named CSUMentor System (www.csumentor.edu). This site is very helpful and anyone interested in CSU should check it out.

A Focus on Undergrads

The most popular undergraduate majors in the system are business and management, social science, and interdisciplinary studies. At the graduate level, education, business, and management majors top the list. The CSU system gives out more degrees in business, computer science, and engineering than all other California schools combined, reflecting the career-oriented focus of the programs.

> "Unlike the research-oriented UC system, CSU schools concentrate most of their resources on undergraduate teaching."

Unlike the research-oriented UC system, CSU schools concentrate most of their resources on undergraduate teaching. Although the professors are less prestigious, it is for this reason that they can spend less of their efforts maintaining their reputation and more time focused on teaching. As tuition skyrockets at private colleges, the CSU system's offer of a good education at a reasonable price looks better and better.—*Seung Lee and Staff*

California Polytechnic State University/San Luis Obispo

Address: Cal Poly Tech San Luis Obispo, 1 Grand Avenue, San Luis Obispo, CA 93407
Phone: 805-756-2311
E-mail Address: admissions@calpoly.edu
Web site URL: http://www.calpoly.edu
Year Founded: 1901
Private or Public: public
Religious affiliation: none
Location: suburban
Regular Application Deadline: 1-Dec
Number of Applicants: NA
Percent Accepted: 47%
Percent Accepted who enroll: 29%
Number Entering: NA
Number of Transfers Accepted each Year: NA
Mean SAT: NA
Mean ACT: NA

Middle 50% SAT range: 1,080–1,290
Middle 50% ACT range: 23–28
Early admission program (EA/ ED/ NA): NA
ED or EA Acceptance Rate: NA
Full time Undergraduate enrollment: 17,671
Total enrollment: 17,671
Percent Male: NA
Percent Female: NA
Total Percent Minority: 23%
Percent African-American: 1%
Percent Asian/Pacific Islander: 11%
Percent Hispanic: 10%
Percent Native-American: 1%
Percent Other: NA
Percent in-state / out of state: NA

Percent from Public HS: NA
Retention Rate: 91%
Graduation Rate: 21% in four, 68% in six
Percent in On-campus housing: 20%
Percent affiliated with Greek system: NA
Percent Varsity or Club Athletes: NA
Number of official organized extracurricular organizations: 375
Most popular majors: Civil Engineering, Mechanical Engineering
Student/Faculty ratio: 20:01
Tuition and Fees: $17,671.00
Cost for Room and Board:
Percent receiving Financial aid, first-year: 32%

A manageable distance from both San Francisco and Los Angeles, California Polytechnic State University San Luis Obispo (often known as CalPoly) can be said to have the best of all worlds: Northern and Southern California, many academic and extracurricular options, and a balance between urban and suburban environments.

Out of the Classroom and Beyond Four Years

One of the best parts of CalPoly's academic program is its emphasis on engaging students with real-world experience. CalPoly's official motto is "Learn by doing," and students often find themselves doing just that at school. Notable projects have included the business plans for Jamba Juice, the San Luis Obispo public transportation system, and urbandictionary.com, and many courses involve hands-on projects that require implementation in the community or field at large. One student described a final project he did for a marketing class, which involved surveying several hundred people and writing a detailed marketing proposal for a local company.

At the same time, several students complained about the difficulty of getting into courses required for graduation, particularly general education classes. In addition to their major-related courses, students are required to take general education classes distributed across communication, science and technology, arts and humanities, social, political, economic institutions, life understanding and technology. The administration's effort to keep overall course sizes lower has made getting into these classes more difficult, but this often forces students to choose between sacrificing summers to take supplementary coursework or remaining at CalPoly for a fifth year to finish remaining requirements.

Students apply to CalPoly with an academic major in mind, and enrolled students say that this has helped to shape their college experience. "People are really focused on what they want to do, and that helped me to make connections right away," raved one third-year student. Some of the stronger academic programs students described were the engineering, accounting, and business majors; one senior also named architecture and construction management programs as being very strong. Students from different disciplines describe the academic experience at CalPoly very differently, with some students complaining of "more schoolwork than I ever could have imagined" and others describing their classes as "ridiculously easy." Some of the easier college majors identified were the recreational administration and marketing programs.

Building a Beautiful Campus

"They're doing all kinds of construction," said one student of the CalPoly campus. The aerospace department recently received a new building, and current projects include a second recreation center and expansion of the football field. Popular student hangout areas include the business building and the University Union. Students convene at the student union on Thursdays at 11am for "UU Hour," during which most students do not have class and the student union sponsors bands.

> "People are really focused on what they want to do, and that helped me to make connections right away."

Like at many public universities, the school only provides housing freshman year, although there are separate facilities for transfer students and a set of on-campus apartments for second years. Students may select to be in dorms based on major if they choose, and buildings change in personality each year. One student described the mixed dorm FYC (First Year Connection) as being the most fun, but acknowledged that the major-affiliated dorms can provide valuable connections. CalPoly is a dry campus, and alcohol is prohibited in the dorms; one student described RAs as being "strict, but can be cool about rules if you get to know them."

Students living in dormitories must purchase a meal plan, and students may eat at a number of on-campus dining facilities, including the recently opened Garden Grille, which serves restaurant-like options. Be warned however, one student described campus food as being "among the top 10 worst in the country." Nearby off-campus eating options include JD Boones Smoke-

house and Woodstocks pizza, both of which are frequented by students. The vast majority of students are quick to move off campus after freshman year, and the city of San Luis Obispo provides a number of reasonably-priced housing options. Many of them are farther away, however, and can make owning a car to get to class a necessity.

Close to the Beach and the Mountains

When not studying, many CalPoly students were quick to name the beach as a frequent destination. With Pismo and Avila beach short distances away and a reasonably warm temperature year-round, sand and surf time is a regular extracurricular activity.

Unlike at many public schools, the CalPoly student body is not engulfed in its sports teams. "Football games are free and we have a tiny stadium," remarked one student, and, although the Mustangs have several NCAA Division I teams, most students express little or no interest in attending collegiate sports events. Instead, the social scene is largely dominated by clubs. One notable club was the Central Pacific Ski Club, a larger organization recently kicked off campus for drinking, but was previously known to take three to four hundred students skiing several times a year. Other club options include Poly Escapes, which takes students on trips all over the state, the Rose Bowl Float Building Club, which devotes its time to producing a float for the Rose Bowl, and a number of popular professional clubs sponsored by the school. The student body also rallies around "Open House," a weekend-long event put on for prospective students including a tractor pull, parade and rodeo.

Students say differing things about CalPoly's student body. One student described the student body as having a lot less diversity than he anticipated when enrolling at CalPoly. "Sometimes it feels like just a lot of rich white kids," said one graduating senior, while another student remarked that the relaxed and diverse student environment was her favorite part about CalPoly.

CalPoly has a Greek community, but it's not prominent and "the University has been cracking down on the frats, bigtime," kicking several of the larger fraternities off campus and threatening the same to others.

Alternatively on weekend nights, students go to off-campus parties and bars. Popular bars include Bulls, McCarthy's (known for being the biggest purchaser of Jameson's whiskey in the country) and the Frog and Peach Pub (formerly owned by Scott and Lacey Peterson). Each Thursday night, downtown is blocked off for the weekly Farmer's Market, which many students attend to enjoy good food and inexpensive drinks.

CalPoly offers its students a valuable way to spend four (or five) exciting years in a beautiful California environment, and prospective students can also look forward to taking advantage of the many academic, social and local opportunities the college provides.—*Stephanie Teng*

FYI

If you come to CalPoly, you'd better bring "a swimsuit or a surfboard."

If I could change one thing about CalPoly, I'd "change the locals' perception of CalPoly students."

What's the typical weekend schedule? "Friday: hit the bars and clubs and then off campus parties; Saturday: beach during the day and then fraternity parties at night; Sunday: Frank's Famous Hot Dogs for breakfast burritos, do some homework and then barbecue for the rest of the day or night."

Three things every student should do before graduating are "a bulls sweat on their birthday, see sunrise on the beach at Pismo Beach, and hike Bishop's Peak."

California State University / Chico

Address: Cal State Chico, 400 W. First Street, Chico, CA 95929-0722
Phone: 800-542-4426
E-mail Address: info@csuchico.edu
Web site URL: http://www.csuchico.edu
Year Founded: 1887
Private or Public: public
Religious affiliation: none
Location: rural
Regular Application Deadline: 1-Dec
Number of Applicants: NA
Percent Accepted: 90%
Percent Accepted who enroll: 22%
Number Entering: NA
Number of Transfers Accepted each Year: NA
Mean SAT: 973
Mean ACT: 20

Middle 50% SAT range: 890–1,140
Middle 50% ACT range: 18–23
Early admission program (EA/ ED/ NA): NA
ED or EA Acceptance Rate: NA
Full time Undergraduate enrollment: 14,927
Total enrollment: 14,927
Percent Male: 47%
Percent Female: 53%
Total Percent Minority: 21%
Percent African-American: 2%
Percent Asian/Pacific Islander: 6%
Percent Hispanic: 12%
Percent Native-American: 1%
Percent Other: NA

Percent in-state / out of state: NA
Percent from Public HS: NA
Retention Rate: 82%
Graduation Rate: 16 in four, 51 in six
Percent in On-campus housing: 13%
Percent affiliated with Greek system: 2%
Percent Varsity or Club Athletes: NA
Number of official organized extracurricular organizations: NA
3 Most popular majors: NA
Student/Faculty ratio: 21:01
Tuition and Fees: $12,690.00
Percent receiving Financial aid, first-year: 43%

For students who want to experience the relaxed yet festive atmosphere of a true "college town," California State University at Chico may be the ideal school. The University is located in the northern part of California in a city that can best be described as "a small town located in the middle of nowhere." However, what Chico State lacks in location, it makes up for in the friendliness of the students and faculty and the type of open welcome that only a small town can provide.

Personable Academics

CSU Chico offers over 100 majors in a number of distinct colleges, including Agriculture; Behavioral and Social Sciences; Business; Communication and Education; Engineering; Computer Science and Construction Management; Humanities and Fine Arts; and Natural Sciences. Students must fulfill a number of general education courses in order to graduate. These requirements include 12 units of Area A, or "Skills," 27 units of Areas B–E, or "Breadth," and 9 units of upper division courses. The comprehensive GEs reveal that CSU isn't all about social life; in fact, the curriculum can be quite challenging. One student was quick to point out that "Chico has recently become a lot tougher academically."

"Most faculty members are very close with their students. It's a great benefit."

However the administration at Chico makes a concerted effort to create an enjoyable academic experience, and it shows in CSU's comparatively high retention rate. One of the most impressive facets of the academic system is student-professor relationships. One student boasts that "most faculty members are very close with students. It's a great benefit." This type of relationship is made possible thanks to small class sizes, the average class being only 27 students. Another benefit is the ease with which students are able to select classes they want—registration takes place through personal Portal accounts. Another option for the high-achieving Chico student is the honors program. This program is made available to incoming freshman with a 3.5 GPA or higher. If admitted into the program students receive academic luxuries like individual attention from professors, small classes, and off-campus Honors Houses. For those students just looking for an easy A, Chico has obliged them with classes like "American Sports in Film" and "Lifetime Fitness."

Middle of Nowhere . . . So What?

Students don't really seem to mind the isolated location; instead they take advantage of being set among the foothills of the beautiful Sierra Nevada Mountains. Most are more than pleased with their scenic surroundings—"it's really picturesque!" exclaimed one student. Chico boasts a plethora of clubs and organizations, many that reap the benefits from its surrounding areas. The "Chico Snow Club is a bunch of people who party and go snow boarding," and the Adventure Outings organization is a university-sponsored program that promotes outdoor expeditions. Expeditions like white-water rafting and hiking trips are among the most popular. Along with being near the sixth-largest waterfall in the country, Chico students pride themselves on their annual tubing event along the Sacramento River. Though the Labor Day event is quite dangerous and can lead to arrests, some still brave the adventure.

One Big Slumber Party

The largest freshman dorm is also the tallest building in all of Chico. Whitney Hall is nine stories high and houses both lots of first-years and the only dining hall. Students can also use their meal cards at eateries around campus, such as the recently revamped Bell Memorial Union. The housing department is planning to add a new dining center as well as additional residence space. Reviews of the existing dorms are better than average. Most students are assigned doubles and the rest live in triples and are happy with their living situation. Both alcohol rules and security are reportedly tight. Moreover, when entering the dorm, students must check in themselves and any visitors they may have. Since it is a dry campus, students are not allowed to bring alcohol into their rooms. Officials look through any bags the student is carrying to ensure the rules are not broken. To further enforce the strict alcohol rules, two RAs live on each floor. Upperclassmen usually move off campus into apartments or houses. One student noted that "compared to many other colleges, off-campus housing in Chico is dirt-cheap."

Go Wildcats!

Chico students have a strong sense of pride in their athletic teams, and with good reason—in a recent year, 10 of their 13 athletic teams saw postseason playoffs. The basketball and baseball games are among the most popular and well-attended. Most student attention is focused on intramural competition, and the two most popular and competitive IMs are flag football and soccer. The gym facilities are only decent, so most students opt for an off-campus gym membership. For those who enjoy outdoor activites, Bidwell Park is a popular destination. The park offers a number of swimming holes as well as trails for biking, jogging and hiking.

Students recently passed a referendum to build a state-of-the-art recreation center, which is scheduled to open in fall 2008. There will also be a new Student Services Center opening in fall 2007. For those who enjoy the arts, BMU auditorium and Chico Performances attract many top acts.

Parties Done Right

If there is one thing a Chico student knows how to do, it is how to party. Just check the Five and Ivy liquor store on any given Tuesday, Thursday, Friday, or Saturday; there is often a line that winds its way out into the street. Ivy Street is also made popular by all the Greek Houses located within close proximity. The Greek system is the predominant force in the Chico social scene. Approximately 40 percent student body belongs to a fraternity or a sorority. However, the Greeks aren't the only ones having a good time. There are plenty of other party options like house parties or downtown bars to keep the students entertained.

A perfect end to a long night of fiestas is Franky's Pizza; another late-night food option is Tacos de Acapulco, which is "the best Mexican food in Chico, but it only tastes good when you are drunk!" While Chico students party on regular days, they go out for holidays as well—including Labor Day's "tubing" and Halloween. In the end, Chico students enjoy a vibrant social life, vast academic options, and close personal attention from professors, all in the picturesque setting of Northern California.—*Kelly Cooper*

FYI
If you come to Chico State, you'd better bring "a spirit for the outdoors."
What's the typical weekend schedule? "Friday: bars; Saturday: party, hiking; Sunday: relax."
If I could change one thing about Chico State, I'd "make the drinking rules more lenient."
Three things every student at Chico State should do before graduating are "float down the river, go to the Farmer's Market, and participate in an Adventure Outing."

California State University/ Fresno

Address: Cal State Fresno, 5150 N. Maple, Fresno, CA 93740	**Mean ACT:** 19	**Percent in-state / out of state:** 98%/2%
Phone: 559-278-2261	**Middle 50% SAT range:** 800–1,060	**Percent from Public HS:** NA
E-mail Address: vivian_franco@csufresno.edu	**Middle 50% ACT range:** 16–22	**Retention Rate:** 82%
Web site URL: http://www.csufresno.edu	**Early admission program (EA/ ED/ NA):** NA	**Graduation Rate:** 12% in four, 45 in six
Year Founded: 1911	**ED or EA Acceptance Rate:** NA	**Percent in On-campus housing:** 6%
Private or Public: public	**Full time Undergraduate enrollment:** 18,951	**Percent affiliated with Greek system:** 7%
Religious affiliation: none	**Total enrollment:** 18,951	**Percent Varsity or Club Athletes:** NA
Location: urban	**Percent Male:** 42%	**Number of official organized extracurricular organizations:** 250
Regular Application Deadline: 2-Apr	**Percent Female:** 58%	**3 Most popular majors:** Business, Health Services, Liberal Arts
Number of Applicants: NA	**Total Percent Minority:** 51%	
Percent Accepted: 69%	**Percent African-American:** 5%	**Student/Faculty ratio:** NA
Percent Accepted who enroll: 28%	**Percent Asian/Pacific Islander:** 14%	**Tuition and Fees:** $13,209.00
Number Entering: NA	**Percent Hispanic:** 31%	**Percent receiving Financial aid, first-year:** 60%
Number of Transfers Accepted each Year: NA	**Percent Native-American:** 1%	
Mean SAT: 950	**Percent Other:** NA	

If you come to the city of Fresno on a typical Saturday afternoon, you might be engulfed in a sea of red. "The whole town comes out" for University tailgates and football games, taking over the campus and celebrating their successful team. But California State University, Fresno, or "Fresno State," has even more to offer than great athletics. The student body invests pride in not only its strong agriculture programs, but a wide range of popular academic offerings, ranging from criminology and education to preparations for jobs in the health profession. Students looking for a state school that provides diversity, a "laid-back but ambitious" atmosphere, and plenty of opportunities for involvement in the heart of California should give Fresno State a closer look.

Not Just an Ag School

Students at Fresno State are required to take a wide range of specific classes over their first two years to fulfill their General Education credits. These courses, which are classified as Foundation, Breadth, Integration and Multicultural/International, are designed to give undergraduates a broad base of knowledge along with their specialized areas of study. Foundation covers oral and written communication, critical thinking, and quantitative reasoning; breadth includes physical and life sciences and arts and humanities; integration courses are upper-division versions of these offerings; and the Multicultural/International requirements provide insights into international relations and countries around the world. Some students say that as far as GE classes are concerned, "if you show up and do your work, you'll be fine," but others complain that the requirements "are a real pain—I feel like I'm wasting my time taking so many of these courses when I would rather have more focus on my interests."

Students feel that Fresno State offers a good liberal arts background—the most popular majors include teaching and business. On the other hand, one senior griped that "the sciences are not well-developed or taken care of—the humanities are more straightforward." One of the school's most distinguishing features are its agriculture programs, though, since Fresno is perfectly situated in the richly-cultivated San Joaquin Valley and includes a 1,011-acre University Farm. In particular, students mention the viticulture program, which teaches participants about winemaking in the school's very own vineyard. Overall, students report that, while grading is fair and people don't do much work on the weekends, "a lot of people get really stressed out around midterms and finals, maybe because they skip classes during the semester."

Underclassmen also complained about being able to sign up for their courses, saying that "seniors are given top priority, and freshmen are last, which can really make it difficult getting into some of the courses you want." However, few had problems with inordinately large class sizes, since many classes are capped at 30, and the occasional large lecture class has around 200 members. Students praised their professors for being "helpful and available," although many feel people don't take as much advantage of office hours as they should. One senior stated, "My professor was really surprised when I came to his office—apparently, it doesn't happen that often." The school also offers many tutoring options, such as a writing lab, that struggling students use to keep their grades up.

Variety of Social Options

A great deal of Fresno's social scene centers around the football team. Weekend games are elaborate events that entail rowdy tailgates in the campus parking lots, cheering yourself hoarse in the stands, and usually after-parties in the frats. The frats and sororities have a "pretty big presence on campus, and their parties are popular." They often have themed parties, such as "Pimps and Hos" and toga parties. In general, "the police don't shut them down unless things are really out of control."

Another big party sector at Fresno State is present in the apartments near campus, where many students choose to live. One freshman girl who lives in the apartments confessed that "on the weekends, no one sleeps." Students say that, in general, "everyone drinks—from what I've seen, maybe two people don't," and smoking is not uncommon, but anything harder than that is rare. There have been a few binge-drinking incidents, but "people are usually just social drinkers, not drinking to get hammered."

There are "tons of places around campus to eat or go shopping—I think every major store or restaurant on the West Coast is present here," said a junior girl. Some students venture farther off campus to areas like the

Tower District, which offers a more unique experience with its thrift stores and clubs, even though it "isn't as advertised as it should be."

Fresno State's University Student Union (USU) also provides students with entertainment a little closer to home, including a food court, a post office, a lounge, and a recreation center complete with bowling, billiards, video games, and more. The University also puts on a number of events throughout the year. The new Save Mart Center often hosts concerts, counting Prince and Britney Spears among its recent attractions. Big annual events include Vintage Days, when the University invites local bands and offers activities like wine tasting, and the Top Dog Awards, when students are recognized for contributions to the school and community. However, "the sad thing is that few students really care that much about these events. The school needs to step it up and get better attractions if they want a lot of people to come."

While "it's difficult to describe a typical Fresno student because there's so much diversity," many people are from the Fresno County area, and nearly everyone is from California. Guys are "usually into sports" and girls are a "happy medium between really fashionable and laid-back." In general, "people here are really cool and chill," and there aren't problems with making friends. Students feel that there is a very strong feeling of diversity on campus, because it has a large Hispanic population, as well as many Asian-Americans and African-Americans. However, one student felt the school's international population was decreasing, in particular because of tensions after September 11, 2001.

Living in Fresno

Students who choose to live in the dorms can decide between the community and the suite options. In the community-style dorms, there is a guys' side and a girls' side to each floor, separated by a common lounge area, with two bathrooms and two RA's. In the suites, six people share a common room and a bathroom. All the rooms are doubles, often with bunk beds. The dorms are dry, and "the RA's are very strict if they catch you with alcohol." On the other hand, "they will take care of you if you're in bad shape after a night of partying, so you shouldn't be afraid of going to them for help." People "spend a lot of time hanging

out in the dorms," where "they leave their doors open and people can just walk in and talk if they want to." But, if you want on-campus housing, you'd better be on top of the applications, because "they fill up very quickly—in fact, some people are still living in a hotel because there were more people who wanted to live in the dorms than the school anticipated."

A lot of students choose to move off campus into apartments, which are plentiful, close to campus and affordable. One girl said enthusiastically that "it gives me more freedom, plus the social scene out here is great." However, students caution against discounting the dorms right away, since that's where many of them met their friends. It's also easy to move off campus into Greek housing, which is another popular option.

A meal plan is not required, but there are quite a few options if you choose to purchase one. There is one central dining hall, the Residence Dining Facility, which some students not-so-affectionately nickname "RD-Barf." However, others say the food "isn't that bad—I was expecting much worse—but I eat the same thing every day." Meal plans can include flex points which students use to buy food at the Student Union restaurants, which include Panda Express, Subway, and Taco Bell.

The dominant theme of the campus architecture is "old and brick," but there are new buildings scattered around as well. Students say proudly that "a lot goes into campus maintenance," resulting in picturesque lawns and greenery. Fresno State has been undergoing a lot of renovation recently, and the Henry Madden Library has been expanded and finished just in the past year.

> **"Fresno State *is* the city of Fresno!"**

Students say that "just about everyone has a car, and if you don't have one, you're probably getting one next semester." A lot of people make weekend trips to Cal Poly San Luis Obispo, which is about an hour and a half away, and others even drive north to the Bay Area or south to Los Angeles, since Fresno is directly in-between the two locations. Cars are also useful since a sizeable portion of the student body (students estimate as much as 25 percent) commutes from their homes in the Fresno area. While it doesn't mean that the campus is dead on the weekends, "it can get kind of quiet sometimes." Fresno State offers a good opportunity for students looking for an education close to home.

All in all, "Fresno State *is* the city of Fresno," since both have developed together. The school is such a dominant presence in the area, providing jobs and opportunities for the community, that "although Fresno is not really a college town, the city really does a lot to make things nicer for college kids." Students report feeling safe walking around campus and the surrounding area, as well as enjoying the support of the many local businesses, which "always have Fresno State posters and paraphernalia up."

Go Bulldogs
If you haven't noticed already, "Sports are huge here!" The football team's successes have "really boosted school spirit," encouraging the school and "what seems like everyone who lives in Fresno County" to come out to the games and support the Bulldogs. Other popular sports are basketball and baseball. The school supports its athletic teams with stunning facilities, such as the new Save Mart Center, two gyms, and a new two-story fitness center that includes an indoor track and pool. You don't have to be a stellar athlete to get in on the action, though, because "intramural sports are also really popular," encouraging many students to play everything from inner-tube water polo to ultimate Frisbee.

Fresno State also boasts a large number of student organizations, which range from the Bulldogger Rodeo Club to the Meat Science Club. Some of the most popular include the Campus Crusade for Christ, the Salsa Club, and the various cultural organizations. Generally, "people are very committed to their extracurricular activities, and there are a ton to choose from!" In addition, "almost everyone has a job because so many of us are paying our own college tuition." Competition for on-campus jobs can be tough, but there are so many businesses in the surrounding area that "if you want a job, you'll be able to find one somewhere." Students don't report much of a problem balancing their jobs with schoolwork on the whole.

If you're a California student looking for a school not too far from home that will offer myriad opportunities for your next four years, Fresno State may be the perfect school for you. Along with its strong agricultural tradition, Fresno also provides its students with good preparation in other disciplines, giving them a wide field of experience with which to face the world after college. Just don't forget your Bulldog spirit!—*Kimberly Chow*

FYI
If you come to Fresno State, you'd better bring "all of your red clothing to show your Bulldog spirit!"
What's the typical weekend schedule? "College night on Thursday, going to bars, a football or basketball game, chilling."
If I could change one thing about Fresno State, I'd "make the nightlife better—there isn't a lot for people under 21, and frat parties get old."
Three things every student at Fresno should do before graduating are: "Go to a football game, go to the Tower District, and go snowboarding or tubing at Sierra Summit."

The Claremont Colleges

The Claremont Colleges are a cluster of five small liberal arts colleges and two graduate schools, nestled in a suburban valley about 35 miles east of Los Angeles. The member colleges are Claremont McKenna, Harvey Mudd, Pitzer, Pomona, and Scripps, as well as Claremont Graduate University and Keck Graduate Institute, both of which are separate from the undergraduate colleges. Each college is independent, with its own faculty, campus, and academic focus. However, the schools' being adjacent to one another gives their respective students the best of both worlds: the feel of a small college with the resources of a large university.

Academic Integration
Cross-registration of classes between the colleges is easy and commonplace. The five

campuses make up about 12 blocks total, so commuting is not a problem. Since each college has a particular academic focus and expertise, students can take advantage of specialized instructions in almost every subject. Claremont McKenna offers over 25 majors with strengths in economics, government, and international relations. Harvey Mudd specializes in science and engineering with the option of a five-year master's program. Pitzer offers liberal arts majors with an emphasis on social and behavioral sciences. Pomona offers a variety of majors in arts, humanities, and social and natural sciences with a para-professional bent. Scripps is a liberal arts college for women. All the libraries are integrated as is the campus bookstore.

Campuswide Activities

The Claremont Colleges are also linked through athletic, social, and extracurricular activities. Pitzer and Pomona together comprise a NCAA Division III team, while Claremont McKenna, Harvey Mudd, and Scripps make up another. However, most athletic competition is usually among one another. Parties thrown in one college draw people from the other colleges. And there are several all-college parties thrown throughout the year. Many student organizations are comprised of undergrads from all the colleges, including *The Claremont Collage*, the student daily newspaper; the Claremont Colleges Model U.N.; and the Claremont Shades, an a cappella group. The Claremont Center is the hub for social groups, organizations, and administrations on each campus, and orchestrates the activities of all five schools.

As integrated as the five colleges are, they still retain distinct characteristics, and prospective students should look to find the right fit. As one student summed it up, "It's really a matter of your academic interests as well as your personality. There is something for everyone at each of the colleges, but one college will definitely be the best fit."—*Seung Lee*

Claremont/McKenna College

Address: Claremont McKenna, 890 Columbia Avenue, Claremont, CA 91711

Phone: 909-621-8088

E-mail Address: admission@claremontmckenna.edu

Web site URL: http://admission.claremontmckenna.edu

Year Founded: 1946

Private or Public: private

Religious affiliation: none

Location: suburban

Regular Application Deadline: 2-Jan

Number of Applicants: 3,587

Percent Accepted: 22%

Percent Accepted who enroll: 37%

Number Entering: 306

Number of Transfers Accepted each Year: ~20

Mean SAT: NA

Mean ACT: NA

Middle 50% SAT range: 1,350–1,550

Middle 50% ACT range: 28–35

Early admission program (EA/ ED/ NA): ED

ED or EA Acceptance Rate: ~60%

Full time Undergraduate enrollment: 1,064

Total enrollment: 1,069

Percent Male: 53%

Percent Female: 47%

Total Percent Minority: 38%

Percent African-American: 4.4%

Percent Asian/Pacific Islander: 15.4%

Percent Hispanic: 11.6%

Percent Native-American: 0.4%

Percent Other: 6.2%

Percent in-state / out of state: 38%/62%

Percent from Public HS: NA

Retention Rate: 98%

Graduation Rate: 88%

Percent in On-campus housing: 95%

Percent affiliated with Greek system: NA

Percent Varsity or Club Athletes: 33%

Number of official organized extracurricular organizations: 200+

3 Most popular majors: Economics, Government, InterNAtioNAl Relations

Student/Faculty ratio: 9:01

Tuition and Fees: $33,210.00

Cost for Room and Board: $10,740.00

Percent receiving Financial aid, first-year: 46%

For any student who wishes they could have the nurturing, close-knit environment of many liberal arts schools on the East Coast but balks at the thought of New England weather, Claremont-McKenna College offers the best of both coasts. Located at the foot of the San Gabriel Mountains in the suburban town of Claremont, California, the college is roughly three hours from Las Vegas and less than an hour away from Los Angeles. Somewhat closer, however, are the four other schools that comprise the Claremont consortium. This close proximity to other colleges gives Claremont-McKenna the feel of a larger university, despite its relatively small undergraduate enrollment of just over 1,100 students. In addition, students have the chance to utilize the resources—from dining halls to parties—of their neighboring institutions. Whether to take advantage of that larger community or to remain within the cozy campus of Claremont-McKenna is the personal choice of each student; every "CMC-er" can attend a college that is truly whatever size they wish.

Academics on Lockdown

Claremont-McKenna's academic requirements, on the other hand, are somewhat less fluid. Students must fulfill eleven General Education (GE) requirements that include taking required classes in four disciplines—including science and mathematics, literature, social sciences and humanities—as well as show proficiency in a foreign language and satisfy a physical education requirement. The nine or ten additional requirements for each major leave underclassmen with relatively little freedom of choice when it comes to their course loads. One freshman lamented, "It's stricter than I'd like it to be. As a freshman, you're pretty much locked in because you have to get these requirements out of the way. It's frustrating not being able to take some of the really good courses that you know are out there."

The upside to the broad range of mandated classes, however, is that by the end of their sophomore year, when it is recommended that GE requirements be completed, CMC students have a rich educational base from which to select their major. "They really emphasize a liberal arts education here. They want you to be grounded in a wide range of things before you decide what you want to study. You really have to test

everything out," said one student who is a fan of the broad range of requirements. The college is known for its exceptional programs in government and economics. According to one student, the government professors are "the most well-known on campus."

"We aren't so big in the sciences," remarked one student. "At least half the people I know are majoring in econ." Nonetheless, students who pursue the pre-med course of study still perform well above the national average; last year, 70% of them were accepted to medical school.

Before students can choose a major, however, they must register for classes. The process is still done manually and can seem fairly arbitrary, with students being assigned a time to register for classes and sometimes finding themselves at the mercy of their scheduled time slot. "The people who get the times earlier in the day definitely benefit from that," one student said. "Class sizes are also kept small, which can be a problem." Yet perseverance, combined with the friendly atmosphere for which the school is known, can often overcome the inconvenience of registration. "If you really want to take a class, you can," one freshman said. "I just showed up to all the classes I wanted to take and the professors were willing to let me in."

Additionally, students may take advantage of programs, classes and majors offered at the other four colleges. Undergraduates have the ability to cross-register for off-campus courses, and if they choose an off-campus major from another school's department they may submit their required senior thesis to the sponsoring college's department in lieu of writing their CMC thesis.

While cross-registering can give Claremont-McKenna the feel of a larger college, students agree that the school's small size usually makes for a decidedly intimate and personal classroom experience. "My largest class has 20 students, and we're really on a family member basis with our teachers. We go to dinner with them pretty often," said one student. In addition to forming friendships outside the classroom, faculty members and students have generally good academic relationships. One freshman observed that while much of the grading for his classes is done on a curve, his teachers are not unreasonable when it comes to distribution of A's. "The teachers really want you to do well. No one is out to trick you, but there also are no easy teachers. It's really up to the student."

No Frats? Who Cares?

While CMC's lack of Greek life sets it apart from many other college campuses, the social scene hardly suffers as a result. In fact, with four other schools close by, students say that people who are eager to go out are never at a loss for a party—in fact, they have five different campus party scenes to choose from. "When one campus is hosting an especially big or good party, everyone else from the Five C's will go there too. There's a lot of interaction between schools," said one student.

"Every Thursday, there's a huge themed party," explained another. "We've had a resort theme, rock star night, a black and white party. Harvey-Mudd even threw a foam party—and they made their own foam." These theme parties are organized by the upperclassmen in individual dorms but are usually held outside. Dorms even have funds earmarked for buying alcohol for such events, a practice that is indicative of the administration's view towards alcohol on campus. One student says, "The alcohol policy is very, very lax. Officially the school doesn't condone it, but it's certainly very lax. The school provides a keg to anyone over the age of 21 who wants to host a party, and they are then responsible for carding at parties. But that rarely happens."

The general consensus on campus is that the campus security staff is primarily there to protect students rather than break up parties or arrest anyone who's underage and imbibing. In fact, the campus has what is known as "a red cup policy"—as long as students carry their alcohol around campus in a cup rather than a bottle, they run into very few problems with the administration. While students feel that "the social scene does center around drinking," Claremont-McKenna makes an extra effort to plan social events like movie nights for non-drinkers. "There's an entire committee set up on campus that plans weekly sober activities. I mean, drinking is a big part of being at CMC. But if you don't, it's no big deal."

Sticking to "The Five C's"

In general, the school's social scene extends only as far as the campuses of the other Five C's; students report trips to Claremont, or "the village," as relatively rare—especially for anyone looking to go out. "We don't really go to bars in Claremont. I don't know if

there are any bars in Claremont," one student commented.

While the relations between town residents and students are thought to range from "non-existent" to "fine," students sometimes spot "townies" or "drunk Claremont high school kids" at campus parties. In general, however, students have limited but cordial contact with Claremont residents and choose to stick close to home; this sentiment is supported by the overwhelming majority of students, about 95 percent, who opt to live on campus all four years.

Despite the popularity of campus living arrangements, not every student is as enthusiastic about the campus itself. As one student said, "Everything is in really good shape, but I just can't stand the architecture. It's all stucco, and the campus is made up of all these one or two-story buildings. It's really different in that regard from East Coast Schools."

Even so, many students are content to stay on campus as much as possible, though one student deemed a car (or at least a friend with one) as "definitely a necessity." This campus-centric outlook applies to many aspects of student life. Rather than eat at restaurants in Claremont itself, most students opt to swipe at one of any of the five college's dining halls—Harvey-Mudd has Steak Night every Sunday, "the best dining halls are at Scripps and Pomona," and free snacks are served each night at 10:30 p.m. While the student center, ironically called "The Hub," is not a very popular gathering spot, many students enjoy hanging out on the school's social North Quad, which is also home to dorms. "People spend a lot of time out there, which makes life for people that live there kind of tough." In comparison, Mid Quad dorms are known as the slightly more subdued social areas and South Quad, comprised of three towers, is "generally pretty quiet." Students who do not drink have the option to live in a substance-free dorm, Stark Hall.

> **"We're the frat boys with no frats, according to the kids at the other Five C's."**

Dorms are assigned via a lottery system, with some students having the option to retain their room from year to year. Each year, the Dean of Students chooses a junior or senior to live in each dormitory as a resident assistant. While students did not report having especially close relationships with these RAs, they are generally well-liked by their advisees. "They're cool people," said one freshman. "We don't really hang out with them, but it's not like they pop in to our rooms every few hours to make sure we aren't doing anything bad."

Claremont-McKenna students often branch out from their dorms and make the trip "literally across the street" to their neighboring schools for social events like the aforementioned foam party. "It's really like one huge campus. If your school is too small for you, you can always expand it to include any of the others."

California Dreamin'

Indeed, even students who claim to see a lack of diversity in their student body had a difficult time identifying the "stereotypical" Claremont-McKenna student. "We're the frat boys with no frats, according to kids at the other Five C's," one student ultimately decided. "And the stereotypical CMC girl? Well, we don't know. We don't date the girls from CMC." Ultimately, whatever their background, Claremont-McKenna students have come to their school to take part in world-class academics while also reaping the benefits of a vibrant party scene. And the California sunshine doesn't hurt either.— *Angelica Baker*

FYI

If you come to CMC, you'd better bring "an air-conditioning unit, a keg, and a skateboard—that seems to be the preferred method of transportation on-campus."

The typical weekend schedule includes "a theme party on Thursday night, studying on Friday, look around campus for the millions of people playing beer pong on Saturday night and spend Sunday recovering and studying."

If I could change one thing about CMC, I'd "make it a little bit bigger. The campus can get small really quickly."

Three things everyone should do before graduating are "get thrown in 'the pond' on your birthday, win a beer pong tournament, and learn how to skateboard."

Harvey Mudd College

Address: Harvey Mudd, 301 Platt Blvd, Claremont, CA 91711

Phone: 909.621.8011

E-mail Address: admission@hmc.edu

Web site URL: www.hmc.edu

Year Founded: 1955

Private or Public: private

Religious affiliation: none

Location: suburban

Regular Application Deadline: 16-Jan

Number of Applicants: 2,119

Percent Accepted: 30%

Percent Accepted who enroll: 28%

Number Entering: 180

Number of Transfers Accepted each Year: 10

Mean SAT: NA

Mean ACT: 31

Middle 50% SAT range: V:680–760, M:740–790

Middle 50% ACT range: NA

Early admission program (EA/ ED/ NA): ED

ED or EA Acceptance Rate: 40%

Full time Undergraduate enrollment: 730

Total enrollment: 730

Percent Male: 71%

Percent Female: 29%

Total Percent Minority: 29.2%

Percent African-American: 1.4%

Percent Asian/Pacific Islander: 19.3%

Percent Hispanic: 8%

Percent Native-American: 0.5%

Percent Other: 2.1%

Percent in-state / out of state: 45%/ 55%

Percent from Public HS: 70%

Retention Rate: 93%

Graduation Rate: 85%

Percent in On-campus housing: 97%

Percent affiliated with Greek system: 0%

Percent Varsity or Club Athletes: NA

Number of official organized extracurricular organizations: ~300

3 Most popular majors: Engineering, Physics, Computer Science

Student/Faculty ratio: 9:01

Tuition and Fees: $33,425.00

Cost for Room and Board: $10,993.00

Percent receiving Financial aid, first-year: 80%

Strolling past its basic concrete buildings—covered in "warts" (random, purposeless square protrusions), one might never recognize the intense learning that occurs within the walls of Harvey Mudd. Harvey Mudd's no-frills exterior projects its hard working interior. It is no secret: Harvey Mudd is no walk in the park. Though listed as a liberal arts school, Mudd's curriculum is geared towards the scientifically inclined.

The school offers only seven majors: physics, math, computer science, engineering, chemistry, biology, and math / CS. These heavily technical majors are earned through an intense four years of work. When asked about gut courses, one Mudd student responded, "To tell you the truth, I've never even heard that phrase before. I think that's just a foreign concept here. You come here with the assumption that all your classes will be hard."

No Guts, But Such Glory

Students agree that classes are hard but believe that Mudd's programs make it worthwhile. At such a science-concentrated school, students are able to obtain research opportunities not present at other schools. Another part of the Harvey Mudd experience is the clinic program. Designed to give students hands-on experience in their future professions, the clinic program introduces many out of classroom skills vital to work survival. Corporations such as Kodak or Techtronics contact the school with particular problems, and groups of five or so students join together to solve them. Their creations are working prototypes that often eventually become products employed by the companies. The clinic program is far from an elite activity for only the brightest at Mudd.

In fact, all students majoring in a related area are required to participate in a clinic. Another trademark of the Harvey Mudd experience is intense academic study. A typical day for a student would include three or four classes, which for most unfortunate freshmen, start at eight or nine a.m. Nights are often consumed by the eight or ten hours of homework that professors assign. At Mudd, the majority of exams are given as take home tests, which often take hours to complete. Mudders don't hide the fact that for them, college does mean a lot of work.

All Work and All Play

With such an intense academic program, it is not surprising that Mudders are also strong believers in the idea of "play as hard as you work." They may be passionate students, but when the weekend arrives the social scene comes alive on campus. With a budget of $38,000 per semester devoted entirely to entertainment, weekends are filled with original and creative parties. Everything from tequila nights and roses for all the girls to Nevada night and parties with batting cages, Mudders really know how to brighten the twilight hours.

But if partying isn't your scene, there is still a place for you at Harvey Mudd. Students are split into dorms based on detailed questionnaires that determine a student's studying style and social habits. Each dorm carries its own personality and a separate social circle. Do you love sports? You'll find yourself at home in the North Dorm, the stereotypically "jock dorm." Of a quieter mind? Down in South Dorm a more serene atmosphere exists for those who prefer the peace. Living amongst the more socially tame are unique and quirky groups such as the unicyclers. Mudd's slightly bizarre claim to fame is the high percentage of unicyclers that circle the campus. For an unbeknownst reason, travel by one wheel is of abnormal popularity—just another example of Mudd's diverse personality. One student ventured to admit, "There are definitely some strange people here. During one of the speeches given at orientation it was said that, 'All of us have some nerd tendencies, but just to varying degrees.' "

Spacious Living

Housing for this eclectic collection of science lovers isn't too shabby at all. Nearly all students live on campus, in one of Mudd's seven residence halls. The residences are divided into the Quad and the Outdoor dorms. Sontag Hall, which opened in fall 2004, offers a kitchen in each suite for those who tire of dining hall fare. The spacious rooms come in various styles, from suites to singles and doubles, and are furnished with the basics for student life. With an average of only four students to each bathroom, the inevitable fight for the shower each morning may only be a small standoff, rather than a full-on battle. Freshmen enjoy the benefit of being integrated within upperclassmen in dorms, providing them with interaction with those who may help them assimilate to campus life.

Amongst these upperclassmen is the ever-present authority figure, a college residential advisor. Known as proctors at Mudd, RAs play a slightly less fearful role, their presence more as a parental figure than policeman. "Their job is not to make sure people don't drink, but to make sure people don't hurt themselves. The school lets the students take care of each other and take care of themselves," one freshman stated.

The community lifestyle is instilled in students as soon as they reach campus. Each freshman is assigned an upperclassman sponsor who takes them through orientation, on shopping trips, and generally helps them through the first couple of days of college. Beyond that, throughout the year students find themselves taking care of one another. As one student put it, "You're all writing the same paper at four in the morning, so you look out for each other."

There is, however, some faculty support as well. When first arriving at Mudd, each student is given a freshman advisor who helps students choose classes and signs off on schedules through the third semester. Afterward, students are given a choice as to which faculty member they want as an academic advisor. In addition to the academic advisor, students also have a humanities advisor, who guides them through the task of fulfilling Mudd's high humanities requirements.

In May 2005 the school opened a new dining area, Hoch-Shanahan Dining Commons, to replace the Platt Campus Center's eating facilities. Those with after-hours munchies can hit up Jay's Place, a late-night lounge with pool tables, snacks, and music that also opened in 2005.

The Fab Five

Harvey Mudd, though a very science oriented school, is listed as a liberal arts college, and has the graduation requirements to back that claim. A third of the average student's classes will be more humanities oriented classes. In fact, ten courses of humanities beyond the freshman classes are required for any degree, four or five of which must be in the same concentration. Five of the classes must also be on campus.

Which brings up the question, five on campus? Where else would they be from? At Mudd class selection is not limited to the science heavy course manual. Harvey Mudd also has the unique quality of being a part of the Claremont College System, or 5C system. As one of five schools in this southern Californian town, its students can cross reg-

ister for courses at any of the other four colleges. Can't find a course that goes in depth into Russian literature at Mudd? Simply go across the street to Scripps or to nearby Pomona to find the classes Mudd may be lacking.

Classes aren't the only things students in the 5C system share. Everything from gym facilities to dining halls are communal. When Mudd students sometimes find the menu repetitive (it's cycled every four weeks) or slightly greasy, they simply can head to one of the other four dining halls. Sports teams are also a group effort. Harvey Mudd's NCAA athletic teams are formed in collaboration with Claremont McKenna and Scripps, while Pitzer and Pomona make up another team. Most club sports, and other extracurricular activities for that matter, are shared between the five schools.

The 5C system also provides a broader social scene, allowing students to go beyond the tiny Harvey Mudd campus. With a ratio of females to males that one student jokingly pointed out was, "nothing significant to a ton," Mudd men may find relationships a little hard to come by were it not for Scripps, an all female college, just across the street. Coupling within Mudd students is also difficult because of the school's small town feel. With such a small class, gossip travels fast. To avoid the chatter of curious classmates, most students look to one of the other four colleges to find romance.

> "It's going to be hard, you should come here knowing that you're going to work hard; but just know that everything you put into it, you'll get out of it. No matter what, you'll find your place here."

Despite the work, Mudd students are proud of where they are. What makes it all worth it? One student answered, "The fun and knowing everyone here will be doing something cool." Students looking at Harvey Mudd should recognize that, "its going to be hard, you should come here knowing that you're going to work hard, but just know that everything you put into it, you'll get out of it. No matter what, you'll find your place here."—*Vivian Hsu*

FYI

If you come to Harvey Mudd, you better bring "an air conditioner. It's hot!"

What is the typical weekend schedule? "Friday: classes, a relaxed afternoon with some work, the dorm BBQ for dinner, and parties through the night starting at nine. Saturday: a late brunch, homework or sports or clubs to fill the day, dinner at another college because it isn't too good on Saturday then off to parties. Sunday: a late rise and homework . . . all day."

If I could change one thing about Harvey Mudd, I'd "want there to be more attractive women."

Three things every student at Harvey Mudd should do before graduating are "pull off a big prank, get whirled or showered, and go to Long Tall Glasses (a formal where the drinks are served from, you guessed it, long tall glasses!)."

Pitzer College

Address: Pitzer, 1050 N. Mills Ave., Claremont, CA 91711

Phone: 909-621-8129

E-mail Address: admission@pitzer.edu

Web site URL: www.pitzer.edu

Year Founded: 1963

Private or Public: private

Religious affiliation: none

Location: suburban

Regular Application Deadline: 1-Jan

Number of Applicants: 3,436

Percent Accepted: 37%

Percent Accepted who enroll: 18%

Number Entering: 247

Number of Transfers Accepted each Year: ~20

Mean SAT: NA

Mean ACT: NA

Middle 50% SAT range: V 570–680, M 570–650

Middle 50% ACT range: NA

Early admission program (EA/ ED/ NA): ED

ED or EA Acceptance Rate: NA

Full time Undergraduate enrollment: 916

Total enrollment: 958

Percent Male: 41%

Percent Female: 59%

Total Percent Minority: 57.2%

Percent African-American: 6.5%

Percent Asian/Pacific Islander: 12%

Percent Hispanic: 14.7%

Percent Native-American: 0.4%

Percent Other: 23.6%

Percent in-state / out of state: 57%/43%

Percent from Public HS: NA

Retention Rate: 89%

Graduation Rate: 76%

Percent in On-campus housing: 70–72%

Percent affiliated with Greek system: 0%

Percent Varsity or Club Athletes: 12%

Number of official organized extracurricular organizations: 84

3 Most popular majors: Psychology, English and World Literature, Sociology

Student/Faculty ratio: 12:01

Tuition and Fees: $34,038.00

Cost for Room and Board: $9,670.00

Percent receiving Financial aid, first-year: 50%

I n the unique setting of the Claremont Colleges is Pitzer College, reputedly "the most carefree" and "the most liberal" of the five. The number one thing you should know about Pitzer, according to its students, is that stereotypes are not always correct. Whether you've heard that Pitzer students are actively concerned about social justice, pot smokers, or laidback hippies, they caution that, for the most part, people who come to Pitzer are surprised by how it differs from its various reputations. The bottom line is that "things at Pitzer are changing a lot," and while students may complain about the surprising level of apathy or protest the hippie stereotype, "Pitzer is designed to be a place free of restrictions so, if you have the initiative, you can basically do whatever you want to follow your dreams."

Lots of Freedom

Pitzer's academic requirements, simply known as "Objectives," are comprised of two courses in the humanities, two in the social and behavioral sciences, one in the natural sciences, and one in mathematics, with a community service, or "social responsibility," and an interdisciplinary requirement. In other words, "you get a tremendous amount of freedom to explore your own interests due to the lack of structured curriculum." In fact, they say that "one of Pitzer's greatest attractions is that it lets you pursue subjects outside the norm." A very popular option among students is the ability to create your own major, which in the past has led to majors such as "Political Psychology," "Social Responsibility and the Arts," and "Nature, Meditation, and Healing."

Most students at Pitzer major in the humanities, with political science, psychology and sociology being three of the most popular choices, but "a lot of people choose the good environmental studies program" as well. The sciences are reputedly "pretty rigorous," but the joint science program that Pitzer shares with Claremont McKenna and Scripps is "really good." The workload is "very manageable if you had a good college preparatory experience," and some classes, particularly some of the Freshman Seminars, are dismissed as being "much too easy," a phenomenon that is described as "weird, because it's not an easy school to get into."

The small class sizes are a big draw for the Claremont schools, with classes usually capped at around 30 students, and most classes enrolling fewer. A student marveled, "Even Introduction to Biology, a traditionally huge class at other schools, only had forty people in it." However, a common complaint is that the low cap causes classes to fill up quickly, a problem especially for the freshmen, who enroll last. One junior lamented, "It can get very competitive when it comes time to sign up for classes—I've been trying to get in this one class for three years and haven't been able to." On the other hand, students pointed out that it's also not difficult to go to the class after the semester has started and talk to the professor: "Most of the time, they'll let you into the classes you want."

One of the best aspects of Pitzer, students say, is its place in the community of the Claremont Colleges. Students are encouraged to cross-register at Pomona, Claremont McKenna, Harvey Mudd, and Scripps, giving them a wide range of options that Pitzer doesn't offer by itself. It's only a 15-minute walk from one side of the Claremont Colleges campus to the other, so access to the other colleges is convenient and rewarding. A freshman said that "you can find a class in pretty much anything you're interested in somewhere in the five colleges." Even with this added benefit, however, a freshman girl still feels that "the classes that Pitzer offers are more creative and original compared to the other Claremonts."

Tearing Down the Stereotypes

One student claimed, "Everyone here is always bashing Bush and smoking weed." Another defended Pitzer as typical college environment, saying "there is substance abuse here just like you'll find at pretty much every other college in the nation." Students agree that marijuana and alcohol are very present on campus, but opinions differ on whether it is more than anywhere else or if Pitzer is just the victim of an exaggerated reputation. It's true that sometimes "hundreds of students from the 5-C's, but mostly Pitzer," are present at "Smoke Force" gatherings on Wednesday nights, when students gather to flip a coin on a map of the Claremont Colleges, then smoke weed where the coin lands.

The school has taken steps to address the problem of drinking on campus with forums about its abuse, but for the most part, Pitzer's policies are "ambivalent" about substances. A senior said that "the official rules are that there is no drinking under 21 and no illegal drug use, but the actual rules are that it's a closed-door policy: if there's no noise or smell, then the RA can't intrude. There's no policing." One student cautioned against getting the wrong impression of the school, though, saying that "as long as you're well-adjusted and come in with the knowledge that there will be these temptations, you won't be any more affected than you would at another college."

The social scene is "very laidback" at Pitzer, and few students leave the Claremont campus often because "there's always something to do at one of the 5-C's". At least once a weekend, events range from music, which is "more pop and hip-hop at the other colleges than at Pitzer, which has a relaxed, coffeehouse vibe," to "occasional laser-tag at Claremont McKenna." "A lot of partying goes on in people's rooms and suites in the dorms," while "the few people who live in off-campus apartments throw larger-scale parties," said a sophomore. Few people have cars because "you definitely don't need one to get around campus" and "most people don't usually go into L.A. because there's so much to do here."

Pitzer "definitely has a very liberal feel— there might be five conservatives here out of a thousand students," but more right-leaning students can find others who share their beliefs in the other 5-C colleges. While most students are from California and are mostly white or Latino, they found difficulty characterizing the typical Pitzer student, and many expressed dissatisfaction at this inability. One girl said ruefully that "the school claims to be socially active and progressive, but the people I've met here don't fulfill that image, and neither does the school." Others speculated that "Pitzer is trying to increase its endowment by getting wealthier, more mainstream students who just don't fit its traditional image." One student expressed frustration at "the general lack of motivation and commitment to Pitzer's ideals." A senior summed it up by saying, "You really should come to Pitzer with a strong sense of initiative and social justice, which are very important here if you have goals and want to make a difference in the world, but I've been both disillusioned and happy with the activist community here."

Living in Claremont

Freshmen are mostly housed in Sanborn Hall, which along with Holden Hall is of the long-hallway design, with every two double rooms connected by a bathroom. These doubles "are pretty standard size-wise for college" and feature fast internet connections and enough room for a microwave, a fridge, lofted beds, a sink, and a medicine cabinet. In the third residence hall, Mead, the rooms are suites for either four or eight people, and any suite above the first floor has a balcony, sometimes with a view of the mountains. Due to a housing crunch that makes it difficult for seniors to find housing, Pitzer often helps them find local apartments for "reasonable prices." However, in 2007, the existing dorms will have been razed and the new dorms will be complete as part of Pitzer's Residential Life Project. The new dorms will be the first in the nation to fulfill certain environmental sustainability and low-energy standards, and as a senior put it, "We talk so much about the environment and social justice that it would be hypocritical not to meet these standards." Other environmental sustainability projects on campus include the Green Bike Raffle, which allows winners to borrow a bike to get around campus for the year, and bottle redemption and recycling programs.

Within the residence halls, students can elect to stay in Hush Hall, which features 24 hours of quiet, the substance-free hall, where the students do not drink or smoke, or the Involvement Tower, where the students are especially involved in the school or the community. One senior even described how he and his friends created a Game Hall one year with the theme hall charters that Pitzer offers—it was designated for people to play anything from tag to Monopoly.

Students who live on campus are required to have a meal plan, and reviews of Pitzer's dining hall, McConnell, vary. Some praise the variety of vegetarian fare, and others complain that "it's okay, but always the same," but everyone agrees that "if you don't like it, you can go to any of the other five dining halls on campus, as well as the seven different on-campus restaurants." Meal plans vary, so students can elect to have fewer meals and more flex dollars to use at places like Pitzer's Grove House, which is a popular place to grab a bite at the café, meet with clubs, or just hang out. Other popular places to have a quiet moment to yourself or talk with friends include Pitzer's Arboretum, the orange grove, and "the Mounds," which are "hilly lawns."

The city of Claremont, where the 5-C's are located, is "very wealthy" and "definitely not oriented towards a college crowd, since everything closes early and the town sleeps." It offers some nice restaurants, but they're on the pricey side. The result is that "some kids never leave campus," instead participating in the myriad of activities and events that the colleges offer. "Many good speakers come to the 5-C's," said a sophomore, describing the recent visit of a documentary filmmaker who held open forums and panels to discuss his work, among other guests.

The most heralded Pitzer event every year is Kohutek, a multiple-day music and arts festival that originated in the 70's when the community gathered with a lot of hype to watch the Kohutek comet, which turned out to be indiscernible. Pitzer continues the tradition today as "a tongue-in-cheek way to make fun of ourselves and of science for trying to make predictions," said a senior. It draws bands like The Roots and OAR. The Bob Marley festival every fall is also a big attraction for the Pitzer community.

Concerned Students

"Pitzer's philosophy of freedom extends to extracurriculars as well as academics," commented a senior. "There's a club for every interest and the school will give you money to start something if you aren't already represented." Students at Pitzer are "not really into sports at all, since we share a team with Pomona and most of the training and coaching goes on there." The Women's Center and the Arts Collective have large followings, as well as the Student Activities Committee and the Student Senate. Many students have jobs, mostly on campus, which range from working in the admission office to the Grove House. Many students are also involved in protesting the destruction of the Bernard Field Station, activism which has even led to students "chaining themselves to the building." A member of the Eco Club and other environmental activism groups complained that "it's the same seven or eight people in all of my clubs—I feel like a lot of people here just are too apathetic to fit the traditional image of Pitzer's concerned students." He summed up his view of the activist's plight at Pitzer by saying, "You can do or accomplish anything here—you just have to take charge, but it's hard to get people to help you."

> "The only things holding me back at Pitzer are my own level of passion and commitment—no one's going to stop me."

"The warm, friendly people here and the degree of freedom that Pitzer offers really make it worth staying," said a freshman. Whether Pitzer's changing image is simply due to unstoppable nationwide trends or whether it's time for a new generation of students to revive the "Vietnam War-protesting, environmentally-conscious hippie" stereotype of the 1960's and 70's, there's a lot that this unique school has to offer. As a freshman put it, "The only things holding me back at Pitzer are my own level of passion and commitment—no one's going to stop me."—*Kimberly Chow*

FYI
If you come to Pitzer, you'd better bring "a sense of initiative so you can take control of your own education and ideals."
What's the typical weekend schedule? "Parties at the other 5-C's on Thursday and Friday nights, a musical event, playing Frisbee, maybe going into L.A., and studying on Sunday."
If I could change one thing about Pitzer, I would change "the level of student apathy—I really wish the average student would care more about the environment and stop sinking into the Southern California lifestyle."
Three things every student at Pitzer should do before graduating are: "Go to the hot springs, have an internship with a social justice group in L.A., and go on a Pitzer Outdoor Adventures trip."

Pomona College

Address: Pomona, 550 N. College Avenue, Claremont, CA 91711
Phone: 909-621-8134
E-mail Address: admissions@pomona.edu
Web site URL: http://www.pomona.edu
Year Founded: 1887
Private or Public: private
Religious affiliation: none
Location: suburban
Regular Application Deadline: 3-Jan
Number of Applicants: NA
Percent Accepted: 18%
Percent Accepted who enroll: 39%
Number Entering: NA
Number of Transfers Accepted each Year: 14
Mean SAT: 1,460
Mean ACT: 32

Middle 50% SAT range: 1,370–1,420
Middle 50% ACT range: 29–34
Early admission program (EA/ ED/ NA): ED
ED or EA Acceptance Rate: NA
Full time Undergraduate enrollment: 1,545
Total enrollment: 1,545
Percent Male: 50%
Percent Female: 50%
Total Percent Minority: 33%
Percent African-American: 8%
Percent Asian/Pacific Islander: 14%
Percent Hispanic: 11%
Percent Native-American: less than 1%
Percent Other: NA
Percent in-state / out of state: 33%/67%

Percent from Public HS: NA
Retention Rate: 98%
Graduation Rate: 94%
Percent in On-campus housing: 98%
Percent affiliated with Greek system: 3%
Percent Varsity or Club Athletes: NA
Number of official organized extracurricular organizations: 289
3 Most popular majors: Economics, English Language and Literature
Student/Faculty ratio: 8:01
Tuition and Fees: $29,650.00
Cost for Room and Board: $10,851.00
Percent receiving Financial aid, first-year: 53%

At Pomona College, you'll find "nerds in paradise." Touted as one of the top liberal arts colleges on the West Coast, Pomona attracts highly motivated students. The school, located in an idyllic Southern California setting an hour outside of Los Angeles, is situated in the intimate family of the five Claremont Colleges. Here, students find a welcoming community, top-notch academics and the freedom and resources to pursue individual passions. As one student put it, "People are extremely happy at Pomona; we work hard, but we're quirky and know how to make the most of the sunny days."

Studying and Surfing
Pomona's requirements were recently changed from a more rigorous list to the Breadth Requirements, which "allow for more freedom." Students must take a physical education activity, an intermediate-level foreign language or its approved equivalent, and one course from each of these areas: Creative Expression; Social Institutions and Human Behavior; History, Values, Ethics and Cultural Studies; Physical and Biological Sciences; and Mathematical Reasoning. Freshmen must also take a Critical Inquiry Seminar, "a 15-person writing class held around a table." Students say that the requirements are "extremely easy to fulfill; basically, you take five classes that are interesting and you're done." While the math and sciences are reputedly more difficult than the humanities, Pomona offers many classes designed for people who don't intend to major in those subjects, like "Math in Many Cultures" and "Statistics for Politicians."

One of the great attractions of the Claremont College system, or the "5-C's", as the consortium is called, is the ability to register at any of the five colleges: Pomona, Claremont McKenna, Harvey Mudd, Pitzer and Scripps. A senior girl mentioned taking advantage of the Japanese program at Pomona, which is the only college offering it, but cross-registering at Scripps for an art history course on Japanese prints. Some of the most popular courses on the Pomona campus include "Asian Traditions" with professor Yamashita, who "knew everyone's name on the second day, even though it was a 55-person lecture," and "Altered States of Consciousness" with anthropology professor Jennifer Perry, in which students "learn about everything from drumming and shamans to drugs and meditation."

"Our professors are one of the top reasons to go to Pomona," a sophomore said.

"They will help you with whatever you need, have lunch with you, invite you to their houses and even to go surfing with them." In addition, almost all classes are readily accessible for all students. "I've only ever had problems getting into classes my freshman and sophomore years, and that was only for the really popular classes that I got to take later anyway," a senior said. "All you need to do is take the initiative and talk to the professor." And just how big are these popular classes? "Most of my classes have less than 20 people in them; 40 people is on the larger side," a junior said.

> **"While we're all really smart and motivated, there's no cutthroat competition"**

A sophomore guy explained: "What mainly sets Pomona students apart from many around the country is that while we're all really smart and motivated, there is no cutthroat competition. I've never even heard of people getting upset about other people's grades—it's not a high-stress situation."

A Warm Community
"The best part of Pomona is the welcoming atmosphere that envelops you the minute you step onto campus as a freshman," claimed a senior. It's true that Pomona goes to great lengths to make sure that incoming students make a smooth transition. Students raved about Pomona's "Sponsor Program," in which groups of 10 to 20 freshmen live in a hall with two sophomore "sponsors" who are there to help them and be their friends and mentors, not to get them in trouble, for their whole first year. Students go out, participate in intramural sports, and just spend time with their sponsor groups. "Your sponsor group becomes your family," said a senior girl. "I'm still close with them now after three years." Freshmen also go on Orientation Adventure trips when they first arrive. These four-day excursions include backpacking, sailing, kayaking and surfing, and help new students make even more friends.

"There's a big party culture here on weekends," a sophomore said. "If you go looking for it, you can usually hear it right away." Few students venture off the 5-C campus because "there's a ton to do right here," including official parties sponsored by the colleges, events put on by the various organizations, and parties held in the dorms. At the college-sponsored parties, which are usually held in the outdoor courtyards, "the college will pay for a couple kegs, so people can drink and hang out comfortably." Many students just hang out in dorm rooms, where "most people are drinking." There is a substance-free activities committee that puts together events like "mocktail parties" (with dry cocktails) and movie showings for those who don't drink, though, and students say "the number of people who don't is larger than most people think."

Some of the big annual events put on by Pomona include "Harwood Halloween" and "Smiley 80's," which are held in those specific dormitories. When "Death by Chocolate" comes around on the last day of classes before reading period, "the school spends an absurd amount of money on chocolate; there's a fondue fountain, candy, cake, hot chocolate, you name it." If you're used to a cooler climate, don't despair: On Snow Day, the Friday before winter exams start, "a snow machine creates a big square of snow on the quad for students to have snowball fights and build snowmen."

"Most people here are really friendly," said a freshman. "I can drop into people's rooms anytime, and since it's such a small campus, I know a lot of people." It's not at all uncommon to see students waving as they pass each other, relaxing together on the pristine lawns, or even playing a variety of sports while drinking beer as part of what students call "Beer League": "You have to have a cup in your hand while you play, then when you do something athletic like hitting a home run, you drink from it." Regardless of how they bond with their classmates, Pomona students are classified as "really smart, but not arrogant, and with some idea of how to be social." On campus, "nearly everyone is very liberal and intensely politically correct, and everybody has a passion." A sophomore said that "many different states and countries are represented, and the school does a good job of attracting people of different ethnic groups, but I feel like many of these people are middle to upper-class. The school, while it does have pretty good financial aid and work-study programs, could do more to attract a more diverse socioeconomic base."

Roosting with the Sagehens

On South Campus, which houses mostly underclassmen, the room organization is in long hallways with rooms on each side. Most freshmen are in doubles, but more than a third have singles. On North Campus, "many rooms open onto nice courtyards" and "if you get a good room draw number, you can end up with a suite and apartment-style living with a common room and kitchen." By junior and senior year, most people have singles. Rooms are described as "the nicest dorm rooms I've ever seen" and "very spacious, with lots of closet space." Although some buildings don't have air conditioning, "it doesn't matter too much except for a couple weeks at the beginning and end of the year." Other options include school-affiliated cottages right across the street from campus, and a few people each year choose to live off-campus.

There are a variety of housing options to choose from, including the "party dorm, which is made of cinder blocks," substance-free housing, and Oldenborg, the language dorm, where there is a hall for each of the six languages offered. In the Oldenborg dining hall, different tables allow students to practice using the languages in a conversational setting. There's no lack of dining options, since Pomona has one each on North and South Campus in addition to Oldenborg, and meal plans are also accepted at the other 5-C campuses, so "there's enough variety for everyone." Flex dollars, a part of some meal plans, can be applied at the "Coop Fountain" in the Smith Campus Center, as well as at the Sagehen Café, which offers "more upscale restaurant-style dining." The fare is described as "pretty good for college food, and you can always go to the other colleges if you're tired of Pomona. Sushi night at Scripps is especially good."

Students say that "the RAs write people up more regularly on South Campus than North, although the overall campus substance policy is non-interventionist: if you aren't causing any problems, the administration won't crack down." Hard alcohol is against the rules on South Campus, and it must be closed on North Campus. Beer and mixed drinks are allowed everywhere, and so are open containers when walking around campus.

Claremont Village, the surrounding town, is described as "like a retirement community, there's so little to do." "The stores close by about six o'clock," complained a girl, "but enough going on on-campus that it doesn't matter." While there are plans to introduce more student-friendly businesses to the Claremont area, students don't even find much cause to go into L.A. often. A

Metrolink station is a couple blocks from campus, but most people who go into the city for concerts, museums or the nightlife use their cars.

More than 47 Interests

"Everyone is passionate about something, and many people start their own organizations on campus to reflect those passions," a senior said. Some of the prominent organizations on campus include Pomona Student Union, which hosts debates and invites speakers, the Women's Union, which does "cool events like screening documentaries and improv comedy workshops," and On the Loose, an outdoors group that rents hiking, camping, backpacking and surfing equipment to students. There are many on-campus jobs available as well.

While "sports tend to be somewhat marginalized and forgotten at Pomona," the Pomona-Pitzer Sagehens enjoy a loyal following in their many sports, especially when they play the Harvey Mudd-Scripps-Claremont McKenna team. "Some of the school's Division III teams are excellent, especially women's volleyball and men's soccer," a senior said. Club sports are very popular, with lacrosse, rugby and Ultimate Frisbee getting the most praise. For the less athletically inclined but still enthusiastic, "In-tramural sports are really fun; we even started an IM soccer team with my professor, who played on the team with us and his kids."

Sagehens definitely have time for fun and quirkiness. One of the school's most mysterious traditions is that of the number 47, which has popped up in countless unlikely places: Pomona's highway exit is number 47; there were 47 students enrolled at the time of Pomona's first graduating class in 1894; and there are 47 letters in the dedication plaque on Mudd-Blaisdell Hall, which was completed in 1947. The number 47 even appears in many Star Trek episodes thanks to co-producer and writer Joseph Menosky '79.

"This place is like Eden," a student said. "Not only is the campus beautiful, but the attitude of the students and faculty helps us make the best of the great education we get here." While the laid-back Southern California atmosphere is evident as you stroll around campus, so is an air of focus and purpose. A senior explained, "We know how to balance work with fun." Another student explained, "At an opening talk at the beginning of the year, the vice president of the college put on Mickey Mouse ears as he welcomed us to 'The Happiest Place on Earth.' How could you not be happy when you have amazing professors, wonderful friends and the bright California sun?"—Kimberly Chow

FYI

If you come to Pomona, you'd better bring "a unique passion about something that distinguishes you from everyone else, because it can be easy to relax too much and become just another face in the crowd here."

At Pomona, the typical weekend schedule consists of "chilling with friends in someone's room on Thursday night, going to a dance party on Friday night, playing Frisbee during the day, going to a big party hosted by one of the colleges on Saturday night, and catching up on work all Sunday."

If I could change one thing about Pomona, "I would have the administration spend the college's money more wisely, like on social issues, instead of paying for so many extravagant student events."

Three things every student at Pomona should do before graduating are "take a class with less than five people in it; go on Ski-Beach day, when you ski in the morning then go to the beach afterwards; go to Joshua Tree National Park."

S c r i p p s   C o l l e g e

Address: Scripps, 1030 Columbia Ave., Claremont, CA 91711-3948
Phone: 800-770-1333
E-mail Address: admission@scrippscollge.edu
Web site URL: www.scrippscollege.edu
Year Founded: 1926
Private or Public: private
Religious affiliation: none
Location: suburban
Regular Application Deadline: 1-Jan
Number of Applicants: 1,873
Percent Accepted: 45%
Percent Accepted who enroll: 28%
Number Entering: 233
Number of Transfers Accepted each Year: varies
Mean SAT: NA
Mean ACT: NA

Middle 50% SAT range: 1,900–2,175
Middle 50% ACT range: NA
Early admission program (EA/ ED/ NA): ED
ED or EA Acceptance Rate: 40%
Full time Undergraduate enrollment: 878
Total enrollment: 899
Percent Male: 0%
Percent Female: 100%
Total Percent Minority: 42%
Percent African-American: 3%
Percent Asian/Pacific Islander: 13%
Percent Hispanic: 5%
Percent Native-American: 1%
Percent Other: 20%
Percent in-state / out of state: 41%/58%

Percent from Public HS: 60%
Retention Rate: 88%
Graduation Rate: 0.74%
Percent in On-campus housing: 96%
Percent affiliated with Greek system: 0%
Percent Varsity or Club Athletes: 0.01%
Number of official organized extracurricular organizations: 200
3 Most popular majors: Psychology, Studio Art, English
Student/Faculty ratio: 11:01
Tuition and Fees: $33,700.00
Cost for Room and Board: $10,100.00
Percent receiving Financial aid, first-year: 52%

One of the first things that come to the students' minds when describing Scripps College is its intimate community coupled with a great location outside of Los Angeles. Scripps is the only single-sex school among the Claremont Colleges, offering a highly reputable education to about 800 female students. Although, students are quick to point out that they chose Scripps because of the great education and numerous opportunities it offers, not because of its all-female student body. So if you want to spend four years in a college that has perfect weather, Mediterranean architecture, a proximity to a large city, and reputable academics, maybe take a closer look at Scripps.

An All-Female School

One of the advantages of going to an all-female school is its "very warm, friendly atmosphere." According to one student, "A lot of kids here went to high schools with as many or even more people. That's why we didn't feel at the beginning that college life was so overwhelming." Her sentiments are echoed by other members of the student population. "The small student body makes it a great and really close community," added one.

Despite the small enrollment, however, Scripps is located right next to the other four Claremont Colleges, all of which are coeducational. As a result, being an all-female school does not mean that there is no interaction with male students. In fact, since students often register for classes in the other colleges, there are plenty of opportunities to make friends with people in the other colleges, both male and female. "Scripps is like part of a much larger campus. You get to go to other colleges all the time, so you don't have to worry about Scripps being an all-female college," said a student. One undergrad pointed out that, as a single-sex school, Scripps receives "differing, condescending attitudes from other colleges in the consortium," but most people agree that the consortium system works very well for Scripps' social atmosphere.

The City of Trees and PhDs

As an upscale suburb for Los Angeles, Claremont is also known as the "City of Trees and PhDs," thanks to a high concentration of professors working in the city's universities. The older neighborhoods of Claremont take pride in their shade-covered streets, making Scripps "a delightful place to live in."

The primary shopping center is at the Village, a collection of small shops and restaurants located at walking distance of the Claremont Colleges. Some students complain about the overpriced shopping, but they generally agree that, "the Village is indispensable for college life." Whenever they crave a little more excitement than the Village, students can jump on a train and visit Los Angeles. Although downtown Los Angeles is still about 30 miles away, it only takes ten minutes for Scripps students to walk to the MetroLink station, a railway system that connects directly to Los Angeles Union Station.

Within the Claremont Colleges, Scripps' own campus is very small. It extends over about three blocks and is only built around one single quad, the Jaqua Quadrangle. Nevertheless, the small campus adds even more to the college's intimacy, and according to the students, "the Mediterranean Revival architecture that dominates the campus feels very welcoming to us."

Sharing is Fun!

Scripps is generally ranked among the top 30 liberal arts colleges by *US News and World Report*. It is a relatively selective college, accepting less than 50 percent of the applicant pool. "Above all else, people come to Scripps because it has a strong academic program," said a student.

By sharing facilities with the other colleges of the consortium, Scripps, despite its small size, offers its students the level of resources and opportunities of a large university. "The departments here are often interrelated to the same departments of the other colleges," said one junior. "For example, Scripps College has a Joint Science Department with Pitzer and Claremont McKenna." This close relationship between the colleges maximizes the resources of the consortium, letting the students explore a greater number of opportunities.

Just like most other liberal arts colleges, Scripps has an interdisciplinary Core Program, which focuses on critical thinking. The Core is divided into three different courses. Core I teaches the students about the relationship between knowledge and cultures. Core II lets the students to choose between different courses that offer in-depth studies of topics introduced in Core I.

Core III focuses on innovation and requires the students to come up with a self-designed project as part of the course. According to a student, "Core I is important. It builds the foundations for future undergraduate work. Core II is not as beneficial, as it is too narrow. My section, at least, did not seem to end up anywhere. Core III is a wonderful experience. It makes one feel potent and encourages applying what you've learned."

In addition, the students are also required to fulfill the general requirements, which include one class each in fine arts, letters, writing, natural science, social science, race and ethnic studies, and mathematics. Students also have to take three semesters of a foreign language. These rather extensive requirements enable the students to acquire knowledge and skills in a variety of fields, an important goal of the college.

Scripps' classes are generally small, having less than 20 students, which lets students interact frequently with their professors. Since there are no teaching assistants, the professors devote a significant part of their time to office hours in order to help their students. "I interact a lot with professors outside of class," one undergrad explained. "I go to office hours frequently, have done an internship with one professor, and have gone to conferences with some others."

Kicking it with the Consortium

Scripps provides its students with great dorm rooms. "The average dorm room is spacious, elegantly furnished, and clean." Each dorm also has a browsing room, a small quiet library that forbids male entrance.

> "During Friday and Saturday, there are generally several parties going on in different colleges, but if you just restrict yourself to Scripps, you might not find anything interesting during the weekends."

Scripps athletes participate in competitions with Claremont McKenna and Harvey Mudd as one single team. Scripps does have its own clubs, but many larger organizations draw members from the entire consortium.

The weekend life is similarly conjoined with that of the other colleges. Students usually go to parties in any of the Claremont Colleges, since Scripps' small size usually does not make for extremely exciting parties.

According to one student, "During Friday and Saturday, there are generally several parties going on in different colleges, but if you just restrict yourself to Scripps, you might not find anything interesting during the weekends." But lack of social life said, one student still cited the biggest disadvantage of being at Scripps as being that "they make you leave after four years."— *Xiaohang Liu*

FYI

What is the typical weekend schedule? "Friday: party. Saturday: party, L.A. Sunday: work, work, and work."

If you come to Scripps, you'd better bring "a stapler!"

If I could change one thing about Scripps, I'd "have more diversity."

Three things every student at Scripps should do before graduating are "to play glow-in-the-dark Frisbee on the lawn at midnight, attend candlelight dinners, and participate in the Humanities Institute"

Deep Springs College

Address: Deep Springs, HC 72 Box 45001, Deep Springs, CA via Dyer NV 89010-9803

Phone: 760-872-2000

E-mail Address: apcom@deepsprings.edu

Web site URL: http://www.deepsprings.edu

Year Founded: 1917

Private or Public: private

Religious affiliation: none

Location: rural

Regular Application Deadline: 16-Nov

Number of Applicants: 200

Percent Accepted: 7%

Percent Accepted who enroll: 92%

Number Entering: 13

Number of Transfers Accepted each Year: 0

Mean SAT: 1,490

Mean ACT: NA

Middle 50% SAT range: 1,450–1,600

Middle 50% ACT range: NA

Early admission program (EA/ ED/ NA): NA

ED or EA Acceptance Rate: NA

Full time Undergraduate enrollment: 26

Total enrollment: 26

Percent Male: 100%

Percent Female: 0%

Total Percent Minority: NA

Percent African-American: NA

Percent Asian/Pacific Islander: NA

Percent Hispanic: NA

Percent Native-American: NA

Percent Other: NA

Percent in-state / out of state: 20%/80%

Percent from Public HS: 50%

Retention Rate: 100%

Graduation Rate: NA

Percent in On-campus housing: 100%

Percent affiliated with Greek system: 0%

Percent Varsity or Club Athletes: NA

Number of official organized extracurricular organizations: 1

Most popular major: Liberal arts

Student/Faculty ratio: 4:01

Tuition and Fees: $0.00

In State Tuition and Fees (if different): $0.00

Cost for Room and Board: $0.00

Though it was founded in 1917, Deep Springs hasn't lost any of its novelty appeal as the years have gone on. If anything, this all-male, tuition-free, 26-student bastion of service, labor and academics only seems to become more and more of a curiosity for college-bound students in the know.

The college, surely, is unique. But students protest that the school is often sensationalized or romanticized. "I think Deep Springs has too much mystique," a second-year Deep Springer said. Even with the isolation, the intensity of the curriculum, and the opportunity to participate in a working ranch, students at Deep Springs are in the end just college students, albeit ones who are particularly adept at lassoing cattle.

Boys Will Be Boys

Located in a desert valley approximately the size of Manhattan, Deep Springs' campus— with its 26 students, plus faculty and staff— is the sole sign of human existence for miles around. And while the college's rule prohibiting use of drugs and alcohol may differ from a more typical college experience, it is the isolation policy that really sets it apart.

Students do not leave the campus (which they interpret as the valley) during the academic term except for college business, religious services or emergencies. Visitors are few and far between, and the school's phone system functions off a spotty two-way radio, making communication with the outside world unreliable. "Some people get really lonely," one Deep Springer said.

And while dealing with the same 25 people day in and day out can be trying at times, the seclusion helps students form especially close relationships. "I couldn't stand the tininess of the community and the isolation at first, but it's a community that grows on you."

One caveat: that community, of students at least, does not include a single female member. While making the campus coed is a subject of both practical and philosophical debate, Deep Springs is still all-male, and will probably remain so for some time. "I think everyone at Deep Springs misses girls . . . I mean, we like them," a student said. But the absence of women does allow the men to form relationships without the same pressures of romantic interests, and also places less emphasis on gender roles. "There were very macho guys who would be very intent on making a good pastry," a graduate remembered.

So, other than being male and able to deal with seclusion, what makes for a good Deep Springer? Ultimately, the backbone of Deep Springs is its commitment to service and a promise that applicants make in exchange for their tuition-free two years. "We really are oriented towards people who will use their talents to make a difference in the world." While the school is not particularly ethnically or racially diverse, "it's no different from any other small liberal arts school," in that it strives to embrace diversity of all kinds—including socioeconomic and intellectual—even if it is not quite representative of the national population. No two Deep Springers are alike, except that, as one student pointed out, "I think everybody there was willing to take a risk on Deep Springs."

Edutain Me
The "risk" of Deep Springs is largely up to the students' shaping. The school is run by a philosophy of self-governance. Each student is a member of one of four standing committees that run the workings of the college: Applications, Communications, Curriculum, or Review and Reinvitation. There are also a variety of elected positions, from the more mundane (archivist, treasurer) to the more

unusual (the "dragonslayer," or the fire chief).

Additionally, the entire student body meets every Friday night to discuss whatever issues arise. These meetings average four hours, but can last anywhere from three to 10. When they aren't too burned out by the proceedings, students will often end the meetings with "edutainment," which in past years has included games of sardines, communal Choose Your Own Adventure and wrestling matches.

> **"You never have to be frustrated that some decision is being made that you have no say in."**

While it is a huge undertaking, students value the self-government aspect for the autonomy it provides. "We make mistakes a lot of the time, but you never have to be frustrated that some decision is being made that you have no say in," one second-year student said. It also involves an incredible time commitment in an already very busy schedule, but one that is intensely satisfying. "It is a trade-off, and I think on the whole it's probably worth it."

My Professor, My Neighbor
As far as academics, Deep Springs is, unsurprisingly, again unique. While many of the course titles—"Nietzsche," "Hemingway and Faulkner," "Poetry and the Uses of History"—sound like they could come out of any school's course catalogue, it is not at every (or almost any) other college that you could find yourself in basically a private tutorial. With an average class size of four students, Deep Springs offers a particularly intimate intellectual environment.

Because of the small library (23,000 volumes—"very, very frustrating") and limited laboratory facilities, Deep Spring's greatest strength is in the humanities, perhaps at the expense of social and natural sciences. The only required courses for students are "Composition" and "Public Speaking," otherwise the classes are up to the discretion of the Curriculum committee and the faculty's ideas.

Deep Springs has three long-term professors, with one each in humanities, social sciences, and natural sciences and mathematics. The long-term professors stay at the school for up to six years, while three to four visiting scholars or artists come to campus each semester. All faculty and staff live on campus, and some often hold class at their houses. At night, a lit porch light is taken as a sign that a professor is home and open to student visitors.

Saddle Up, Office Cowboy

After spending a morning with "Advanced Molecular Biology" or "Appalachian Social History," students spend the afternoon on the second component of their education: educational labor. Deep Springs functions as a working cattle ranch, with approximately 300 head of cattle. It is also an alfalfa farm (152 acres of alfalfa produce 350 tons of alfalfa hay) and a garden, complete with a fruit orchard, a greenhouse, a chicken coop, composting worm pits, a grape arbor, a half-acre of potatoes and a corn field.

The only required position is Boarding House Crew, which consists of more thankless tasks like washing dishes, mopping, taking out the trash, and sorting slop and compost. Each student must serve on BH for two terms, but the rest is open to a variety of labor options. The butcher, one of the more desirable positions, slaughters approximately two cows each term, as well as sometimes slaughtering chicken, sheep and pigs. He also spends time making sausage, cold-smoked ribs, bacon and other products for the college. The dairy boys milk the four cows (Ruth, Lilith, Persephone and Olivia) twice daily to provide fresh milk for breakfast and dinner. The "Student Cowboy" supervises the birthing, branding, inoculating and castrating of the calves; his counterpart, jokingly referred to as the "Office Cowboy," works with administrative tasks.

One of the most tangible benefits of the labor program is the food. Meals are served regularly at 7:30 a.m., 12:30 p.m. and 6 p.m. Besides the fresh milk and meat, the meals often also feature organic vegetables from the garden. But meal quality varies. "The thing is, the students cook it," one first-year said. "There are occasionally meals that are really terrible, and there are occasionally meals that are really, really amazing."

On the whole, despite BH duty (which "is valuable in itself"), students gain an understanding and appreciation of labor. And while many of the skills they pick up at the ranch may not be directly transferable to the outside world, they are nonetheless satisfying. "I'm decent at riding a horse now, and I got really, really good at branding calves during calving season," one student boasted.

Home on the Range

"It's hard to cordon off one part of your life and call it your 'social life,' " a second-year student commented. With a dynamic like Deep Springs', everything from intense philosophical debate to baling hay can count in some way as sociable. But when the students really want to relax, they are uniquely situated to explore yet more outdoorsy options. From swimming in the nearby reservoir to horseback riding to running, the desert provides plenty of opportunity for physical recreation, including weekend expeditions to places such as Death Valley and an abandoned mining town. Students particularly enjoy hiking ("you could walk for three days and never see another human being"), and every year at least a couple embark on what is half-jokingly called "the Death March": an attempt to hike around the entire rim of Deep Springs Valley in a week.

Inside activities still take an unconventional track. While there is plenty of hanging out in the dining hall late at night making nachos and sitting around watching movies (cheesy teen flicks have been a traditional favorite), there are no clubs or student groups, per se. Since the student body is so intimate, student "groups" are often more casual assemblies of people who pick up a topic they are interested in and drop it once they feel it is fully explored. In the past, students ran a Tolkien reading group; now, they run a Walter Benjamin one.

Finally, though students admit their Saturday night may be a bit different from that at other colleges ("Obviously the party scene is a little bit more limited"), they still know how to get down. "Boojies," the Deep Springs version (nonalcoholic, all-male) of dance parties, allow students to blow off steam and flex their dance floor muscle. Only in this case the dance floor is frequently the floor of the dairy barn ("We'd string up little Christmas lights and turn the music up real loud and kick the cows out"). Larger-scale, planned boojies occur about once a month, but smaller ones often break out spontaneously, frequently initiated by someone running through the library and suggesting a boojie study break.

Boojies are just another example of how these 26 students put a Deep Springs twist on a classic college experience. Because when it comes down to it, Deep Springers are basically college kids; in fact, the majority usually go on to four year universities such as Harvard, Brown and the University of Chicago after earning their two-year associate degree. "The people here are basically normal people," a student pointed out. "Obviously very smart, very ambitious, very driven, very focused. But basically what Deep Springs is is this community of people that are engaged in this common interest of intellectual inquiry." And the amazing view of the Sierras out the dorm room window doesn't hurt.—*Claire Stanford*

FYI

If you come to Deep Springs, you better bring "as little as possible—every year we challenge the new students to come with just the clothes on their backs."

What's the typical weekend schedule? "Typical weekends don't exist . . . on Saturday, I took a two-hour walk with my philosophy professor down a desert road, helped prepare lunch, and then shot cans of tomato paste with the cook and his son for three hours before a bonfire that night."

If I could change one thing about Deep Springs, I'd "make it more monastic."

Three things every student at Deep Springs should do before graduating are "go to a slaughter, play with the little kids because they're wonderful, and definitely slide naked down the Eureka sand dunes on a full moon."

Mills College

Address: Mills, 5000 MacArthur Boulevard, Oakland, CA 94613
Phone: 510-430-2135
E-mail Address: admission@mills.edu
Web site URL: http://www.mills.edu/admission/undergraduate/index.php
Year Founded: 1852
Private or Public: private
Religious affiliation: none
Location: urban
Regular Application Deadline: 1-Mar
Number of Applicants: 1,122
Percent Accepted: 74.5%
Percent Accepted who enroll: 27.5%
Number Entering: 333
Number of Transfers Accepted each Year: 215
Mean SAT: NA
Mean ACT: NA

Middle 50% SAT range: 970–1,230
Middle 50% ACT range: 20–26
Early admission program (EA/ ED/ NA): EA
ED or EA Acceptance Rate: 79%
Full time Undergraduate enrollment: 881
Total enrollment: 1,410
Percent Male: 0%
Percent Female: 100%
Total Percent Minority: 33%
Percent African-American: 9%
Percent Asian/Pacific Islander: 11%
Percent Hispanic: 13%
Percent Native-American: 1%
Percent Other: 12%

Percent in-state / out of state: 80%/20%
Percent from Public HS: 80%
Retention Rate: 75%
Graduation Rate: 67%
Percent in On-campus housing: 55%
Percent affiliated with Greek system: 0%
Percent Varsity or Club Athletes: NA
Number of official organized extracurricular organizations: 43
3 Most popular majors: English, Psychology, PLEA
Student/Faculty ratio: 11:01
Tuition and Fees: $31,190.00
Cost for Room and Board: $10,290.00
Percent receiving Financial aid, first-year: 84%

Mills College, an all-female liberal arts college in Oakland, California, has been committed to women's education for over 150 years. In fact, Mills made news in 1990 when the board of trustees voted to admit males to the undergraduate program. Students, outraged, immediately adopted the slogan "Better Dead than Coed." They mounted protests, officially shutting down the campus, and they refused to resume their normal lives until the board of trustees reversed their decision. Eventually, the trustees conceded, and Mills reinforced its position as a school dedicated to women's education. That take-charge spirit is characteristic of Mills students, who are still a group of empowered women committed to making the most of their education.

Blaze Your Own Trail

Historically, Mills is a school of "firsts": the first women's college to the west of the Rockies, the first women's college to offer a computer science major and a 4+1 MBA degree, and even one of the first liberal arts colleges to offer a modern dance degree. Mills students agree that their academic experience is completely "what you make of it." One student noted that it's possible to "slack" through a semester, but said that it is equally possible to have a hard semester by taking classes from hard professors—it's all up to the individual.

The general education requirement at Mills consists of 36 credits in what the school calls three "outcome categories": skills, perspectives, and disciplinary experiences. The skills category includes classes in written communication, quantitative reasoning, and information technology skills. Perspectives courses include women and gender, multicultural, and interdisciplinary studies. Classes in arts criticism, historical perspectives, natural sciences, and human behavior comprise the disciplinary exercises category. Despite the variety of academic requirements at Mills, many students complain about the lack of diversity in the choice of classes, saying they wish there were "more fun and random classes." Fortunately, for those seeking classes outside the box, UC Berkeley and other Bay Area schools welcome Mills students to cross-register in some of their programs.

Some of the most popular Mills majors are English, psychology, and Political, Legal, and Economic Analysis. Several students complained about the school having recently dropped the theater major. "The theater department was dropped because there weren't enough people majoring in it," one student explained. And although there's still a theater club on campus, those looking to major in theater arts may be disappointed. For those Mills women anxious to get a head start on advanced degrees, the school has six dual degree programs, in which students can get masters degrees in Business Administration, Public Policy, Infant Mental Health, Interdisciplinary Computer Science, Engineering, and Mathematics. Another specialized degree program at Mills is its Nursing Leadership Program, which consists of two years of liberal arts followed by two years of nursing school.

The Hills of Mills

Living at Mills is like, as one student put it, living in a "gorgeous oasis" with "beautiful architecture." Currently, the campus is undergoing a significant amount of renovations, such as a new environmentally friendly "green" science building. Mills women agree that their dorms are "very nice." Freshmen live in singles or doubles in two residences right in the middle of campus, and their housing is not too shabby. "One of our buildings, Orchard Meadow, is considered one of the nicest dorms on campus," one freshman boasted. There are a total of five residence halls at Mills. Upperclasswomen can choose among on-campus apartments, townhouses, or house co-ops.

The main dining hall at Mills is called Founders Commons, and it is set atop a hill. Students generally agree that the food is "fairly good for a college." The cafeterias are independently owned, and, to the relief of many Californians, "there are always vegetarian and vegan options." In addition to dining halls, Mills has a teashop that serves hot breakfast and "quick meals like hamburgers," along with a popular coffee shop, Café Susie's.

Unfortunately, Oakland has no real "college-town feel." In fact, some students even go so far as to say that, "the area around campus does not feel very safe." Nonetheless, Mills has its own shuttle system and even a bus stop outside its front gate, making it easy to get on and off campus. In fact, there are several restaurants and shops off campus that are popular with Mills women, especially the Italian favorite, La Fiesta Pizza. And, for those looking to escape from Oakland entirely, San Francisco and all its distractions are just a car or shuttle ride away.

Friendly Feminists

Outside of the classroom, Mills women are famous for being friendly and sociable. One freshman enthused that, "On the first day of college, I sat down at tables at the cafeteria where I didn't know anyone, and was warmly welcomed!" The student body of Mills is notoriously ethnically and culturally diverse. One American Caucasian woman even went so far as to say that, "Sometimes I feel like a minority."

The women of Mills also have their own unique take on age diversity. 24 percent of the undergraduate population is made up of "resumers," or students over the age of 23. Resumers are usually students who have taken time off from their studies to pursue careers or raise families. Resumers have their own apartments on campus that welcome spouses and children. Yet, far from being secluded from the rest of the population, students universally proclaim that there is no real division on campus between resumers and regular undergraduates, since friendships form between women of all ages.

> "Most Mills women are usually feminists and interested in women's rights—or at least, they become so after four years here!"

The integration of resumers into the community is just one aspect of Mills' openness and tolerance of differences. This includes sexual orientation, too. "There is . . . a lesbian stereotype," one student said, "but although there are many lesbians on campus, it is often hard to tell whose toast is buttered which way." No matter one's sexual preference, "most Mills women are usually feminists and interested in women's rights—or at least, they become so after four years here!"

Partying Without Guys?

Mills women agree that their school is not by any means a party school. Most students go out on weekend nights, and because many students don't have classes on Fridays, weekends tend to include Thursdays. There are a few popular campus-wide parties, including the Fetish Ball, which discourages clothing. Alcohol has little presence on campus. One freshman noted that she has seen "very little drinking in the freshman dorms." Even once you hit the age of 21, "even then it has to be done behind closed doors," one student explained. Students do note that drugs, mostly pot, are a lot more prevalent on campus than alcohol.

Be warned, Mills women don't often get a chance to mingle with members of the opposite sex. In fact, most couples around the school are female-female. Mills allows men to stay overnight in the dorms for up to seven nights each month, which is good news for students with boyfriends at other

schools. Mills' graduate school, on the other hand, *is* coed, and Berkeley and Stanford are not too far away, so students say that if you're really looking for men, they're not too hard to find if you're willing to make a small trek.

Fun and Games

Athletics are admittedly not Mills' main focus, and, not surprisingly, the school doesn't have a football team. However, as a Division III school, Mills has six varsity sports: cross country, crew, soccer, swimming, tennis, and volleyball. Students generally seem happy that more inexperienced athletes are allowed to participate since some of the pressure is off. As one Mills woman put it, "We take pride in what we've got." If varsity sports aren't your thing, you can get a workout by playing club sports, or by taking yoga and swimming classes at the gym.

Off the field, there are a plethora of student clubs and organizations, some favorites of which are the Animé Club, Horror Movie Club, Superhero Club, and the Gay/Lesbian Alliance. Mills women say that there is definitely something for everybody to be involved in, and if not, students are encouraged to start new organizations. Many students also get on-campus jobs, like serving food in the campus cafeteria.

A Tradition of Empowerment

In a school rooted in tradition, Mills students say that one of their favorite rites of passage is Paint Night. Students assign a color to each class year, and on Paint Night, which takes place in the spring, seniors storm the campus and paint surfaces the color of their class. This tradition, fun and silly as it is, ties into Mills' continual emphasis on fostering strong women, ready to use their education to make a difference in the world around them. Still stubbornly single-sex, Mills continues to be a place where students and administration both remain believers in the power of all-women's schools.—*Becky Bicks*

FYI
If you come to Mills you'd better bring "an open mind."
What's the typical weekend schedule? "Enjoying weekend brunch, relaxing during free time, and evening on-campus activities."
If I could change one thing about Mills, I'd "make the campus more accessible, offering a shuttle to and from the airport at break time."
Three things every student at Mills should do before graduating are "explore the whole campus, get an on-campus job, eat the dining hall waffles for breakfast."

Occidental College

Address: Occidental, 1600 Campus Road, Los Angeles, CA 90041
Phone: 800-825-5262
E-mail Address: admission@oxy.edu
Web site URL: http://www.oxy.edu/Admission.xml
Year Founded: 1887
Private or Public: private
Religious affiliation: none
Location: urban
Regular Application Deadline: 10-Jan
Number of Applicants: 5,309
Percent Accepted: 42%
Percent Accepted who enroll: 21%
Number Entering: 515
Number of Transfers Accepted each Year: 50
Mean SAT: NA
Mean ACT: NA

Middle 50% SAT range: 1,200–1,360, 1,820–2,020
Middle 50% ACT range: 26–30
Early admission program (EA/ ED/ NA): ED
ED or EA Acceptance Rate: 9%
Full time Undergraduate enrollment: 1,820
Total enrollment: 1,839
Percent Male: 43%
Percent Female: 57%
Total Percent Minority: 36.7%
Percent African-American: 6.6%
Percent Asian/Pacific Islander: 13.5%
Percent Hispanic: 15.6%
Percent Native-American: 1%
Percent Other: 0%
Percent in-state / out of state: 49%/51%

Percent from Public HS: 60%
Retention Rate: 92%
Graduation Rate: 84%
Percent in On-campus housing: 70%
Percent affiliated with Greek system: 15%
Percent Varsity or Club Athletes: 25%
Number of official organized extracurricular organizations: 109
3 Most popular majors: Psychology, Economics, English
Student/Faculty ratio: 10:01
Tuition and Fees: $33,689.00
Cost for Room and Board: $9,042.00
Percent receiving Financial aid, first-year: 74%

Nestled in the green suburbs of northeast L.A., Occidental College is a gem of a liberal arts college dedicated to recruiting students of diverse backgrounds. An "Urban Oasis," Oxy is one of the oldest colleges on the West Coast, and strives to provide motivated students with opportunities to work together and with the resources of L.A. to forge educational paths all their own.

Academics at the Core

Occidental's core curriculum encourages students to explore a wide variety of subjects; the core "creates more open-minded, pluralistic individuals," said one senior. It "enables students to take different classes, sometimes outside of their major, to understand and partake in different disciplines so that they can further develop their knowledge." One-third of a student's education is devoted to this core. Requirements include classes in foreign languages, the sciences (including a lab science), the arts, and "a social studies-type requirement where you have to take a minimum of three classes from different geographical areas,"

a student described. One particular core class is a year-long freshman writing requirement; "the core [writing] class is really nice because we are in a dorm with the other people in the core, so we form a close bond," said a freshman. Popular majors at Oxy include economics, which is highly competitive as "Oxy students want to make a lot of money after they leave," commented a senior, and biology, for whose majors the college offers many research opportunities.

Class size generally ranges from small to medium, and even in the few larger classes, there is ample communication between students and professors. Getting into the class you want is relatively easy, especially for upperclassmen, because professors are often willing to add extra students. There are places reserved for freshmen in all entry-level courses, and the system for priority is fair: freshmen are placed in numerical order in terms of priority for getting into a class, and this order switches around at the start of the second semester.

In general, students find that the workload at Occidental is pretty heavy, and though it can depend on the classes you are taking, it is manageable if you budget your time well. If you need help, there are many resources within the college and the peer community. Professors are required to hold office hours, and the Center for Academic Excellence, located in the college library, has advisors available in nearly every subject, five nights a week.

Always Getting Involved

Oxy students may work hard, but the academic atmosphere is relaxed enough that it does not impede students' involvement in extracurriculars. Quite the contrary: Occidental is home to an incredibly active and involved student community. "Everyone that I meet is part of a larger organization on campus; people want to get involved," said a freshman. There are over 100 organizations—quite a lot for a student population of only about 1,800! These groups cover all possible areas of student interest on the diverse campus. From the Asian-Pacific Islander Alliance to the American Medical Students Association, Oxy students create their own opportunities to explore L.A., tutor younger students, engage in student government, political activism, and venture into the outdoors.

> "Everyone that I meet is part of a larger organization on campus; people want to get involved."

There are club sports teams, and despite their popularity among Oxy athletes, one freshman said that, "right now, club sports are having trouble getting field space," and it is the club sports that suffer. The college has installed a new FieldTurf surface on the football field to allow for use by club sports, so the problem has not gone unaddressed.

Chill Out, With Choices

Wherever your interests lie, there are many social activities offered to Oxy students in their free time, and not just on weekends: cultural, social and educational events are offered daily by clubs or the college. There frequently movies are offered by different departments, and the ICC (Inter-Cultural Community) hosts weekly events open to the public.

A typical Oxy weekend "can be bland," one senior admits, but if you make the effort, there are a lot of things to do. Drinking can be prominent at parties, and many students feel that marijuana is common on campus. The Greek system isn't big, and "the frats rarely throw parties because they're always on probation." Occidental parties usually occur in off-campus houses. The school has taken measures to limit on-campus pre-parties, notorious for hard alcohol, but binge drinking can still be found. "The pressure is not too bad, but freshmen are usually targets for peer pressure," a student remarked. One freshman agreed: "Sometimes it does feel like all anyone wants to do is sit in a room and drink." In the end, it is a student's decision whether or not to drink. If students choose not to, "you can find people who don't want to drink and want to do something else besides go to a party," this freshman remarked. Recently, the college has been successful in preparing "wonderful themed parties" free of charge, which spices up the usual routine of mingling with your friends in one another's houses and dorm rooms.

L.A. Livin'

When it comes to social life, if all else fails, there is always L.A. "One wonderful thing about Oxy is that it is so close to L.A. that students can enjoy off-campus life when the parties aren't so happening," said a student. Oxy's array of student activities meshes well with Los Angeles' great weather, and the resources really add to campus life as both a bridge and an escape to the real world. Students leave campus to attend parties off campus, eat (especially on the weekends), and go to the beach. The weather is a huge draw for many Oxy kids—when East Coasters are beginning to bundle up for fall and winter, Oxy students are still sunning themselves while studying and hanging out! The campus is relatively close to Pasadena; students can take the college's Bengal Bus to Old Town Pasadena, LA's Westside, Santa Monica, or the Glendale Galleria, but having a car is a definite plus. "Bumming rides off of people is fine," remarked a student, "until you miss dinner on Friday and no one wants to get food." Some students complain that Old Town Pasadena can be expensive, but if you know where to go, you won't break the bank.

A Beautiful and Diverse Campus

It's hard not to see Occidental's appeal when you visit the campus glistening and green in the L.A. sun. One student described the Beaux-Arts architecture as "very Grecian, yet modern," and it retains a definite California flavor in the terra cotta rooftops. Everything is within walking distance and the view is amazing from the hillside on which Oxy is perched. Campus and the surrounding area are well patrolled, and students consistently report feeling very safe. The freshman dorms get mixed reviews, described as both "decent" and not "overwhelmingly too small." Upperclassmen "can live anywhere on campus, depending on their room draw number," said a senior, and while only some halls have air conditioning, all will eventually get it as Oxy updates the facilities. While the majority of students live on campus, there are many options for off-campus living, and the school provides a wealth of information about available apartments, including the apartment style residence hall for upperclassmen that is under construction.

Occidental students praise not only their physically beautiful campus, but also the very diverse, active, and friendly student community. A lot of students come from multiracial backgrounds, but race is not the only type of diversity here at Oxy. "Diversity ranges from ethnicity to socio-economic background to hobbies to types of music," remarked one student. With such varied interests, Oxy students enrich their community by being involved in the many, varied activities offered. In addition, "the things that Oxy lacks—art studio space, field space, etc.—are made up in the friendliness of the people who go here," gushed a freshman.

At Oxy, students experience diversity on all fronts: in academics, in the people they meet, in the activities they do, and in the events offered by the relationship between the college and the city. With all these things to offer, Oxy is an invigorating and inviting place to spend four years.—*Samantha Wilson*

FYI

If you come to Occidental, you'd better bring "shower sandals and a lot of room decorations."
What is the typical weekend schedule? "Friday, Farmers' Market for dinner, a movie or party of the week either on or off campus; Saturday, go to brunch at 12 p.m., do some homework, go shopping, or trek to the beach to "study," and finally head out to L.A. for a club."
If I could change one thing about Occidental, I'd "make the campus bigger with more facilities for students that are open 24 hours."
Three things every student at Occidental should do before graduating are "go tunneling, hike Mt. Fiji, and attend the 'Sex on the Beach' party."

Pepperdine University

Address: Pepperdine, 24255 Pacific Coast Highway, Malibu, CA 90263
Phone: 310-506-4392
E-mail Address: admission-seaver@pepperdine.edu
Web site URL: http://seaver.pepperdine.edu/admission/
Year Founded: 1937
Private or Public: private
Religious affiliation: Church of Christ
Location: suburban
Regular Application Deadline: 16-Jan
Number of Applicants: NA
Percent Accepted: 28%
Percent Accepted who enroll: 34%
Number Entering: NA
Number of Transfers Accepted each Year: 102
Mean SAT: NA

Mean ACT: 26
Middle 50% SAT range: 1,130–1,350
Middle 50% ACT range: 24–29
Early admission program (EA/ ED/ NA): NA
ED or EA Acceptance Rate: NA
Full time Undergraduate enrollment: 3,281
Total enrollment: 6,898
Percent Male: 43%
Percent Female: 57%
Total Percent Minority: 31%
Percent African-American: 8%
Percent Asian/Pacific Islander: 10%
Percent Hispanic: 11%
Percent Native-American: 2%
Percent Other: NA

Percent in-state / out of state: 52%/48%
Percent from Public HS: NA
Retention Rate: 89%
Graduation Rate: 80%
Percent in On-campus housing: 62%
Percent affiliated with Greek system: 50%
Percent Varsity or Club Athletes: NA
Number of official organized extracurricular organizations: 50
Most popular majors: Advertising, Psychology
Student/Faculty ratio: 12:01
Tuition and Fees: $24,326.00
Cost for Room and Board: $9,500.00
Percent receiving Financial aid, first-year: 43%

Located in scenic Malibu, California, Pepperdine University bills itself as a Christian university committed to the highest standards of academic excellence and Christian values. Combining ethical ideals of the Christian faith with high academic standards, Pepperdine's mission rests on its belief that spiritual commitment demands the highest standards of academic excellence. With its emphasis on international perspective, broad education, and religious devotion, Pepperdine seeks to create individuals with a solid grasp of both their duties to the world and their duties to themselves.

Spiritual and Academic Commitment

George Pepperdine, who founded the university in 1937, was a devout member of the Churches of Christ, and thus constructed a college that would teach students to lead lives of purpose, service, and leadership. Accepting students from all faiths and races, the University seeks to extend its ideals to all students.

Pepperdine University enrolls 8,300 students and is comprised of five colleges and schools. Originally, George Pepperdine had vision of a small, primarily undergraduate university. Seaver College, the undergraduate residential college of letters, arts, and sciences, is the embodiment of that vision. Every year, it matriculates 3,000 of Pepperdine's students.

In 1971, Pepperdine became a university with the addition of the School of Law. Shortly following this development, a grant by Mrs. Frank Seaver allowed the university to move from its location in south-central Los Angeles to its current 830-acre campus in Malibu.

Pepperdine's academic reputation and its beautiful campus has been the subject of much acclaim, and as a result, its selectivity has been significantly rising over the past few years. In 2005, Seaver experienced one of its largest applicant pools ever, with 7,800 applicants and 837 freshmen and transfer students enrolled. "I think Pepperdine is getting more and more academically ambitious students," one senior said. "Good thing for the reputation, maybe not so much for the people who have to compete with them!"

The bachelor's degree is offered in 38 fields of study, and high-achieving students are given the opportunity to study for a master's degree in one of seven areas. In addition to focusing on a particular major, the university encourages students to develop as broadly educated persons and take classes in unfamiliar terrains. In keeping with George Pepperdine's original goals, it also requires that students take three terms of religious classes. "The religious classes are pretty much what you would expect," one student said. "Not exactly the most exciting things in the world." Other students, however, said that the classes are "pretty interesting."

> "Be smart. Be religious. Be conservative. Be good looking. You'll fit in."

Aside from the larger general education lectures, classes are usually small. "That's probably Pepperdine's biggest weakness and greatest strength." While students maintain close relationships with professors, one junior complained, "Sometimes you get a little sick of seeing the same people over and over again . . . after a few years, I actually want my lectures back!"

In addition, the small class structure works extremely well if the professor is engaging, but if he or she is not, then the class becomes disproportionately unbearable. As one student stated, "I think the small classes are hit or miss, because if you like your class, then you love it, and if you don't like it, then you *really* don't like it."

Location, Location, Location

Students rarely, if ever, complain about their on-campus housing. "I never thought I'd say this, but the dorms are absolutely beautiful," admitted one student. Even during freshman year, when other universities give their freshmen sub-par housing, Pepperdine pampers its students. It houses four freshmen in a suite of two bedrooms, each suite filled with such amenities as a common area and a daily-cleaned bathroom. Despite these amenities, however, many students do choose to move off campus after freshman year. "It's about having the space and the freedom to move around," said one off-campus student.

As beautiful as the view is, many students claim that Pepperdine's student body can rival it. "We have the best-looking student population in the entire United States!" one student boasted enthusiastically. This confidence can be shown by the fact that many wear little more than a bathing suit while tanning on or nearby campus.

But although "Malibu is beautiful," "it isn't a college town. Sure, we live in great dorms with a great view of the ocean, but if you don't love the beach, you'll definitely need a car." With Monica, Westwood, and Los Angeles about half an hour away, students are often tempted with an easy escape on weekends. However, Southern California's terrible traffic often puts a damper on students' impromptu getaways. Because the getaways might take an hour to reach, students tend to stay on campus and go to parties which "aren't too difficult to find."

International Perspective

Many students agree that Pepperdine's study abroad program sets it apart from other Christian universities. Seaver College students are offered year-round residential programs in Germany, England, Italy, Argentina, and various other countries. Having established its study abroad program in 1963, Pepperdine has worked hard to expand and enhance its students' experiences abroad. Pepperdine believes that by encouraging students to study abroad and by making the transfer process painless, students will be more likely to venture out and gain an international perspective. If students decide not to study abroad during the school year, they may study abroad during the summer. Additionally, students are encouraged to partake in language programs at Pepperdine over the summer to complete their language requirements. According to the school's center for international programs, over half of all Seaver College students go overseas during their college career. "Inter-national programs and study abroad opportunities are Pepperdine's greatest strength. I went to South America and Asia and didn't have to worry about credits or anything. They take really good care of you."

Political Activism

Students claim that there isn't much political activism in either direction. While some democratic or republican organizations may hang a banner here and there, students do not often discuss politics. One female student stated, "I often protest Pepperdine's conservatism. As a liberal arts education, you'd expect them to be more liberal about homosexuality and women's rights. But they aren't." Another student noted that the College Republicans are much more popular than the Young Democrats, though neither of the two draw much support, which he felt was indicative of Pepperdine's apolitical nature.

Despite this, however, Pepperdine has a strong history of community service. For example, it had the top acceptance rates in its region for the selective Teach for America program. While the program only accepts 30 percent of its students, over 50 percent of Pepperdine applicants were accepted.

Of course, Pepperdine isn't above having a good joke now and then. Pepperdine won the NCAA National Collegiate Men's Volleyball Championship last year, beating the UCLA Bruins at an away tournament. This scored them a visit to the White House, where they proceeded to present President Bush with an honorary surfboard.—*Danny Friedman*

FYI
If you come to Pepperdine, you'd better bring "your best Gucci sunglasses."
What's the typical weekend schedule? "The usual—partying, studying, taking advantage of the beach."
If I could change one thing about Pepperdine, I'd "get rid of the hugely conservative atmosphere! C'mon, people, we need a little diversity now and then."
Three things every student at Pepperdine should do before graduating are "One, get a great tan; two, go abroad; three, take advantage of being on the most beautiful campus in the world!"

St. Mary's College of California

Address: St. Mary's, PO Box 4800, Moraga, CA 94575-4800

Phone: 800-800-USMC

E-mail Address: smcadmit@stmarys-ca.edu

Web site URL: www.stmarys-ca.edu

Year Founded: 1863

Private or Public: private

Religious affiliation: Roman Catholic

Location: suburban

Regular Application Deadline: 15-Jan

Number of Applicants: 4,991

Percent Accepted: 70%

Percent Accepted who enroll: 17.0%

Number Entering: 610

Number of Transfers Accepted each Year: 347

Mean SAT: 1,680

Mean ACT: NA

Middle 50% SAT range: 1,510–1,840

Middle 50% ACT range: NA

Early admission program (EA/ ED/ NA): EA

ED or EA Acceptance Rate: NA

Full time Undergraduate enrollment: 2,835

Total enrollment: 3,962

Percent Male: 0.37%

Percent Female: 63%

Total Percent Minority: 42%

Percent African-American: 7%

Percent Asian/Pacific Islander: 10%

Percent Hispanic: 19%

Percent Native-American: 1%

Percent Other: NA

Percent in-state / out of state: 89%/11%

Percent from Public HS: 56.00%

Retention Rate: 82%

Graduation Rate: 0.65

Percent in On-campus housing: 60%

Percent affiliated with Greek system: 0%

Percent Varsity or Club Athletes: NA

Number of official organized extracurricular organizations: 43

3 Most popular majors: Business Administration, Communications, Liberal Arts and Sciences

Student/Faculty ratio: 11:01

Tuition and Fees: $29,050

Cost for Room and Board: $10,566

Percent receiving Financial aid, first-year: 58%

At St. Mary's, students won't hesitate to tell you that their location is "perfect." This small Catholic college, located in a picturesque valley sheltered from the metropolises of Berkeley and San Francisco, also offers easy access to these cities at any time. Along with the cosmopolitan experience, St. Mary's offers a tradition of solid academics and athletics, as well as a supportive environment that encourages its students to seek out new ways of learning and helping the community—all principles rooted firmly in the philosophy of its founding Christian Brothers.

The Big Picture

St. Mary's boasts a number of strong programs. Applicants can choose to study in the following schools: The School of Liberal Arts, the School of Science, the School of Economics and Business Administration, the School of Education, or the School of Intercollegiate Nursing. Within these programs, except for the School of Nursing, students pick from a variety of different majors, the most popular of which are business, communications and social sciences. However, students point out other interesting choices, such as the undergraduate teacher's preparation program that gives students their teaching credentials and a Masters of Education in five years. Some students believe that St. Mary's most unique opportunity is the Integral Program of liberal arts. While only a handful of students enroll in the program, it allows them to spend all four years in rigorous and well-rounded classes taught in small seminar and tutorial settings with "discussions around round tables." Academics are truly an area in which the small size of St. Mary's becomes especially valuable. The average class size is 21 students, and professors are usually known on a first-name basis. One student even boasted, "We all exchanged phone numbers in my class, and my professor called me at home to make sure I was okay when I was sick."

St. Mary's seeks to develop the whole student, a sentiment reflected in the college's General Requirements, which asks that all students take twelve classes from three distinct groups: Religious Studies, Collegiate Seminars, and the Area Requirements in humanities, empirical science, and the social sciences. There are also requirements in language proficiency, diversity, and writing. Within the broad spectrum of courses offered, students say that in general, it's easy to fulfill the various requirements. One senior explained, "I took two music theory classes, which counted for the General Requirements. It wasn't my area of study, but I like listening to music, so it was enjoyable and fulfilled an area." On the other hand, other students pointed out that the number of required courses makes it difficult to change from one major to another. A second senior admitted that she must spend an extra semester taking courses after her class has graduated because she changed majors in her junior year.

> "We all exchanged phone numbers in my class, and my professor called me at home to make sure I was okay when I was sick."

"Jan-term," or the January Term, is a distinctive aspect of St. Mary's academic calendar. St. Mary's operates on a 4-1-4 system. This means that students take four course credits in both the fall and spring terms, but have four weeks in between to explore subjects outside of their majors in one full-credit class. It's a time that "pretty much everyone looks forward to" and students have the opportunity to study abroad, pursue a unique on-campus class, take a course from another 4-1-4 college, or participate in an independent study project. Some choices the college offers for on-campus courses include "The Semiotics of Buffy the Vampire Slayer (and other Female Heroes)," "The Sixties through Film," and "Chocolate, Waffles, and Other Belgian Passions." One student raved that she got to "spend 10 days at the Sundance Film Festival" as part of her Jan-term course, as well as take field trips to Buddhist temples around the Bay Area as part of her "What is Buddhism?" course.

Living in Moraga

St. Mary's guarantees housing only to freshmen and sophomores while juniors and seniors must enter a lottery if they want housing. Even so, students say "people who want it generally get it." Freshmen live in doubles or triples that are "a little cramped" with sinks in the rooms and a bathroom down the hall. Sophomores live in suites with combinations of doubles and singles and a common room with a "nice bathroom." Upperclassmen who get lucky in the lottery are provided with on-campus townhouses that include bathrooms, kitchens, and living rooms.

Freshmen dorms are single-sex by floor, and for underclassmen, there is a Resident Advisor or a Resident Director on every floor; upperclassmen have one per building. "They vary in terms of strictness," but policies often get more lenient as the students get older. One student explained that the policies for the townhouses is more like "see no evil, smell no evil, as long as you're being legal and safe," while for the freshmen, they crack down harder for alcohol violations or having the opposite sex in the rooms past 2 a.m.

There is one dining hall on campus, where students classify the food as "not great" and "pretty standard for college food, although people tend to complain a lot." One student confessed that "during sophomore year, when I had to have a meal plan, I ate in the dining hall about three times the whole year." While the dining hall may not receive the best reviews, there are other on-campus options, including "The Brickpile," which has burgers and fries, and a café, at which it is possible to redeem "flex dollars." Flex dollars are part of some meal plans and allow students to purchase à la carte. Students living on campus are required to purchase a meal plan but the plans vary by the number of meals per week and amount of flex dollars.

Some students choose to move off campus into apartments in downtown Moraga, and others find housing in the neighboring towns of Lafayette and Walnut Creek. However, these options can be a lot pricier, although comfortable and convenient. Student housing discounts are available and make it easier for students who want a slightly more vibrant setting to be able to afford it. Moraga in itself is "not the most exciting place," but students find it pretty easy to make the short trips to have dinner and see shows in San Francisco and Berkeley or go shopping in Walnut Creek. These excursions range from 10 to 45 minutes away by car or the Bay Area Rapid Transit train system. In Moraga, the nearest grocery stores and restaurants to campus are five to 10 minutes away by car. Many students also choose to take the bus, which stops by the campus regularly and is free with a St. Mary's ID card. But one girl complained that "I feel a bit isolated because the bus makes it harder to go places at night."

Relaxing Between Activities

Students classify St. Mary's as "not a party school . . . but people have fun here." There are no fraternities or sororities, so most of the social scene is in the dorms, especially the townhouses, which are "where the party's at" for upperclassmen. The freshman dorms are dry, and alcohol is strictly off-limits for everyone under 21, so freshmen usually hang out in each other's rooms and watch movies. Regardless, students feel that "many people drink, although there's not a lot of pressure to join in." The school also hosts many events, ranging from concerts to various speakers, and everyone is invited to attend, most often in the Soda Center, at the center of campus. The most attended dance every year is Oasis, a Hawaiian-themed party held on the quad. There are other dances too, like the Halloween Dance, but "mostly freshmen go to them."

St. Mary's students pride themselves on a diversity of political opinion and thought, saying that while "the Liberals are more vocal, the Republican club is definitely growing." However, other students said that they haven't noticed much socioeconomic diversity around the campus, seeing mostly white middle-class students from around the Bay Area. Students speculated that "the average St. Mary's girl is blonde, rich, and perky," while guys are "more geeky and outgoing," but hasten to add that there are many exceptions. One student proudly cited the college's efforts to increase the diversity of the school by making it easier for lower-income students to attend, referring to the LaSallian Catholic Brothers' mission of teaching and serving the disadvantaged.

In general, "people are really friendly here," and it's not uncommon to see students relaxing on the quad or talking at the picnic tables on warm California days. People meet many friends in their dorms, but "people in the same clubs tend to hang out together," such as those who work on *The Collegian*, the college newspaper, or those who play on sports teams. Overall, the atmosphere is easygoing, explained a senior, saying, "Classes tend to intermix a lot, and it's really easy to meet people" in other grades. In addition, people don't feel that the Catholic presence at St. Mary's is overbearing at all; in fact, one student feels that "the school's greatest untapped resource is its network of Brothers."

Go Gaels!

Any St. Mary's student will tell you that the school is fiercely proud of its sports teams, even though the football program was recently canceled. St. Mary's boasts NCAA Division I teams in 15 sports, including baseball, basketball, and soccer, and the school works hard to recruit talented athletes from California and from around the country. St. Mary's has seen action at March Madness and at the Sweet Sixteen of the NCAA tournament with its strong men's basketball and women's volleyball teams. Many students come out to support these up-and-coming teams by joining the "Gael-Force," the school's pep squad, which has a special section reserved at every home game so that the legions of loyal fans can cheer on their teams.

The school also offers a myriad of club and intramural sports, which "can sometimes get pretty intense, but are a lot of fun." While students don't hesitate to step out on the fields, some students feel that the gym, weight room, the fields and some of the other athletics facilities could use a facelift. Overall, "it's really hard to find a student who's just involved in class," as the groups present on campus range from the school newspaper and the Intervarsity Christian Fellowship to Best Buddies, which pairs students with disabled kids from the community, and Italian club. Many students also join clubs affiliated with their particular majors. In addition, a lot of students at St. Mary's spend time working. The college offers various on-campus jobs, but many students venture into the surrounding area. Babysitting is one of the most popular jobs for girls, due to the rich suburban atmosphere of Moraga and neighboring Orinda and Lafayette.

There is a strong sense of tradition and serenity as you walk across the St. Mary's campus among the mission-style buildings bathed in the California sunshine. At St. Mary's, students can find a refreshing blend of an intimate liberal arts education and the Catholic mission of developing the many parts of an individual.—*Kimberly Chow*

FYI

If you come to St. Mary's, you better bring "a good attitude towards the small Catholic school atmosphere."

What is the typical weekend schedule? "Hang out with your roommates and have dinner and watch a movie on Friday; on Saturday, go to Berkeley or San Francisco; and on Sunday, relax, do homework and laundry.

If I could change one thing about St. Mary's, I'd "make it easier for students who don't have cars, because the bus is inadequate for really going out at night and on the weekends."

Three things every student should do before graduating from St. Mary's are "hike up to the cross at midnight, sneak into the catacombs, and get to know a Brother."

Stanford University

Address: Stanford, Bakewell Building, 355 Galvez Street, Stanford, CA 94305

Phone: 650-723-2091

E-mail Address: admission@stanford.edu

Web site URL: http://www.stanford.edu

Year Founded: 1885

Private or Public: private

Religious affiliation: none

Location: suburban

Regular Application Deadline: 15-Dec

Number of Applicants: 22,333

Percent Accepted: 10.88%

Percent Accepted who enroll: 67.4%

Number Entering: 1,648

Number of Transfers Accepted each Year: 72

Mean SAT: NA

Mean ACT: NA

Middle 50% SAT range: 2,000–2,300

Middle 50% ACT range: 28–33

Early admission program (EA/ ED/ NA): EA

ED or EA Acceptance Rate: 18.9%

Full time Undergraduate enrollment: 6,422

Total enrollment: 17,747

Percent Male: 0.52%

Percent Female: 48%

Total Percent Minority: 53%

Percent African-American: 10%

Percent Asian/Pacific Islander: 24%

Percent Hispanic: 11%

Percent Native-American: 2%

Percent Other: 6%

Percent in-state / out of state: 46%/54%

Percent from Public HS: 62%

Retention Rate: 98%

Graduation Rate: 0.95%

Percent in On-campus housing: 90%

Percent affiliated with Greek system: 15%

Percent Varsity or Club Athletes: NA

Number of official organized extracurricular organizations: 650

Most popular majors: Economics, Political Science

Student/Faculty ratio: 6:01

Tuition and Fees: $33,419

Cost for Room and Board: $10,367

Percent receiving Financial aid, first-year: 100%

Whether they're running madly from fountain to fountain, participating in a campus-wide makeout session during the first full moon of the year, or enjoying the mild California weather, Stanford students will tell you they know how to have fun. But they still find time in their busy schedules to fit in demanding course loads, community service, sports, and music, all while maintaining a social life. An hour away from San Francisco in the affluent dotcom community of Palo Alto, some of the nation's top students have found a school that will support their interests and goals, however quirky or lofty they may be. Beneath this laidback, West Coast "summer camp" atmosphere, lays the university's strong commit-ment to balancing a prominent research institution with a strong undergraduate academic experience.

Balancing Act

To fulfill the 180 units required for graduation, which includes requirements for the major, writing and rhetoric, humanities, science, math, culture studies, and a year of foreign language, Stanford students generally take four or five units a quarter. The Stanford year is divided into quarters, which makes for three marking periods during the academic year and one during the summer. Because of this arrangement, students said they often find that their midterm period extends from "the second week of classes until dead week [the week before finals]." But many said they enjoy the quarter system, in part because it allows them both to explore more classes and be done quickly with classes they dislike. Although IHUM, the humanities requirement for freshmen and sophomores, got mixed reviews due to occasional "overambitious" or "irrelevant" subject matters, most agreed that they benefited from PWR, the writing and rhetoric requirement. Overall, students said the general requirements, or "GERs," are very flexible and often fulfill themselves; in fact, one sophomore said his history class fulfilled four at once.

Freshman classes are generally large, ranging from 100 to 200 students, but there are always discussions sections, as well as opportunities for more specialized seminars. Although academic concentrations are categorized as either "fuzzy" (the humanities) or "techie" (science and math), students said they love that Stanford is so evenly divided among different disciplines. Some of the most popular include human biology, economics, and psychology. Professor Dement got high marks for his course on "Sleep and Dreams" while Robert Sapolsky attracts many undergrads to his neurology courses. Students touted the small introductory seminars as particularly engaging, especially when they offer the opportunity to get to know "ridiculously important and famous" experts in the field. Opportunities to interface with professors are not difficult to find if you make an effort, one junior explained, and developing a relationship can lead to research positions or simply the chance to discuss your studies with a world specialist. One biology major confessed that what he likes most about Stanford is its ability to be "an amazing research institution, while simultaneously giving a lot of emphasis to teaching."

> "If someone told you they never get stressed they'd be lying to you."

"If someone told you they never get stressed they'd be lying to you here," a sophomore said. "It's a way of life, but it's definitely a manageable level of stress, and it makes it that much more enticing to blow off steam on weekends." Most Stanford students appear to have found the balance between work and play that allows them to take advantage of their many academic resources, as well as the pleasant weather. And they agree that people usually collaborate when studying; one girl emphasized that she had "never met anyone who wouldn't give you their full help right when you asked."

Camp Stanford

Many upperclassmen describe their freshman year as "Camp Stanford." "It's basically an amazing time the whole year, doing crazy things with your dorm like scavenger hunts in San Francisco and Secret Snowflake, when you dare each other to do things like lick the RA's toes," one male student said. "I tried on a $3,000 dress at Neiman Marcus." While it's not uncommon for freshmen to go out en masse to frat parties and campus events, upperclassmen said they usually go out in smaller groups of their close friends and meet up with residents of other buildings. But the more the merrier for Full Moon on the Quad, the time of year when the freshmen and seniors rush out at midnight to swap spit (and probably mono, one student commented). A good number of students in all grades drink, and in freshman dorms it can run to excess when "people don't know what their limits are since they just studied all through high school." Pot is less common, and hard drugs are "just about nonexistent, at least as far as I've seen." The 15 frats and 11 sororities on campus often host parties, but "you definitely don't need to join in order to have fun," one girl said. "They're there if you want them, but there's no pressure at all."

Some students said they were surprised at "how normal people are" at Stanford; "Instead of being totally awkward like I was expecting, people are very well-rounded and have good social networks of close friends and acquaintances," a junior commented. Most seem to have found a healthy balance between intense studying and having fun. "People are very focused on work, but they can still relax and go out to parties," a girl said. "People will do well in school, but they won't talk about it too much, like they won't bring up academics in conversation but they'll flow with it if it comes up and have interesting ideas." While the student body is perceived as being mostly upper-middle class, there is an impressive amount of diversity. Undergraduates hail from 68 foreign countries and minorities are well-represented. Politically, the campus is less stratified; students tend to lean towards the left, and one of the most recent campus protests occurred when President George W. Bush visited campus.

Among the Palm Trees

The attractive, sprawling campus is predominantly Spanish-style architecture and landscaping, featuring red tiles, adobe, and palm trees—lots of palm trees. But underneath its uniform exterior, Stanford seems to offer every housing option imaginable, including "all-frosh, freshman-sophomore, and four-class" residence halls for first years, then upperclassmen dorms that include small houses, mid-sized dorms, apartments, and suites. After freshman year, students enter the "Draw," in which they form groups of friends and enter the lottery, hoping to get a good number so they have a better chance of getting the living situation they desire. Out of the three years, two are "preferred" in the lottery while one year is "un-preferred," and students automatically receive a worse draw number. There is a lot of "Draw-ma" when it comes to forming groups or when the housing students receive is too far away or doesn't have a good social scene, but "people tend to be pretty happy, or at least neutral, about where they end up." One sophomore raved about the open kitchen and chef in her house on "The Row," the nice strip of houses, fraternities, and sororities on one end of campus, while one junior said his four-class dorm wasn't nearly exciting as his freshman residence, which was "wild and chaotic 24-7."

A more controversial element of the housing system is the "theme house" option, through which students choose a house based on language, culture, or academic interest. In Casa Zapata, the Chicano/Latino theme house, for example, 50 percent of residents are of that particular ethnic heritage, while the other 50 percent are not. While some students have said the theme houses are a great chance to live with those who share their cultures, others have protested that the houses both divide the undergraduate population and oblige the half of the house that aren't of that heritage to "live with people who didn't necessarily choose to live with them."

Dorms often play host to consumption of alcohol, although not usually in a raucous party setting, and "the RAs are usually very cool about it, even letting you have kegs, although some houses are stricter than others and you aren't allowed to bring anything into the hall." Campus police will sometimes enforce the rule of no open containers outside the dorms. The dining hall food—which students eat when living in the dorms—gets pretty good reviews for being generally tasty and including many vegetarian and vegan options, but "you can definitely get tired of it after a few weeks because it doesn't change much," one freshman lamented. Students can also apply their meal plans to a variety of on-campus eateries, including CoHo coffeehouse, Subway, and the Treehouse. Stanford attracts many speakers, in the past few years featuring the Dalia Lama, Elie Wiesel, and Cameron Diaz, among others.

Stanford is often called a "bubble" because of its self-sufficiency—it even has its own zip code. Palo Alto doesn't get high marks as a college town, although most students don't seem to mind since "everything you need in terms of entertainment is on campus." But the quiet, predominantly wealthy city does offer an array of Asian restaurants, the sandwich chain Pluto's, and the Cheesecake Factory, as well as bowling and ice skating. Once in a while, students take the local Caltrain for about an hour to get to San Francisco. This metropolis offers a wealth of entertainment and culture, from concerts in small nightclubs to browsing through tie-dye shirts and used books in the legendary Haight-Ashbury district.

Find Your Passion

"A lot of us used to be athletes in high school," one sophomore said. "And even though only the very best go on to play for Stanford, it's a very active campus on the whole." When they aren't playing IMs—the most popular of which are Frisbee, volleyball, and basketball—you can find Cardinals working out at the new Arrillaga gym or running outside. But they're not afraid to take to the sidelines, and "people often spend their Saturdays cheering on their friends at their sports events." Much of the campus comes out for football and basketball games; some fanatical male supporters have even been known to paint the Stanford letters on their chests and get the outlines sunburned on their skin. The combined excellence of Stanford's Division I programs has earned it the Director's Cup for success in college athletics for the past 12 years in a row.

When they aren't at the gym making the "athletic, attractive campus" even more so, Stanford students get involved in "as many activities as you could imagine." "There is every kind of dance group, publication, a cappella, cultural, religious, or club sport organization there is," a political science major said. Community service groups are particularly popular, allowing undergraduates the opportunity to venture off campus and tutor in underprivileged neighborhoods or work with the homeless. Undergrads can even stay on campus and help Stanford employees with their English skills in a program called Habla la Noche.

"Everyone here has something they really care about," one Cardinal reflected. And it seems to be true. You have your world-class athletes, community service movers and shakers, dedicated researchers, and political activists, and yet, "this amazing person is just the kid down the hall from you who you can have late-night conversations with and who got dared to do something outrageous during Secret Snowflake." The opportunities that Stanford students enthusiastically enumerated featured not only the challenging academics and fine research facilities; but they also praised their fellow undergrads: "The caliber of people here, not necessarily just the professors, but also the students, is amazing," a sophomore said. "You learn so much from the people around you."—*Kimberly Chow*

FYI

If you come to Stanford, you'd better bring "a more laidback attitude, but a desire to do something meaningful."

What's the typical weekend schedule? "Friday go out to dinner in Palo Alto, then go to a frat or hang out with friends in one of the houses; Saturday morning sleep in, then go to a sports event or do community service, then go to a room party; Sunday hit the books during the day, but if you have time, go to FLICKS at 10PM to watch a movie and throw paper at each other."

If I could change one thing about Stanford, "I'd make Palo Alto more of a college town; even though staying on campus is fine, it would be nice if places stayed open later and there was more to do."

Three things every student at Stanford should do before graduating are "Go fountain-hopping, when you run from fountain to fountain on campus with a group of your friends or dorm and get really wet; get to know a big-name professor; do Sophomore College, when you come a few weeks early for your second year and either take a small class you're interested in or travel to locations like the Galapagos Islands."

University of California System

The University of California, a system of public colleges established to educate high-achieving California high school students, offers strong academic departments on nine distinctive campuses—Berkeley, Davis, Irvine, Los Angeles, Merced, Riverside, San Diego, Santa Barbara, and Santa Cruz. San Francisco also belongs to the UC system, instructing graduate students in the health sciences. Each college enrolls a large undergraduate body, ranging from 13,700 students at Santa Cruz to 25,000 students at Los Angeles. UC conducts some of the most important research in the country, employing 49 Nobel laureates in faculty and research positions, and maintains America's second-largest library collection with over 20 million volumes.

Distinctive Atmospheres

Often the strongest distinctions between the UCs lie in their attractive locations and unique academic specialties. As the first UC campus, Berkeley displays a tradition of academic excellence in all curricular areas—an achievement matched today by the wide-ranging strengths of UCLA. Both schools reside on energetic but peaceful campuses within urban areas. Academically rigorous and known for its college system, UC San Diego offers a strong biology program that includes the only ABET-accredited bioengineering major of any UC. It is situated near the ocean in La Jolla, a short distance north of San Diego. Santa Barbara, whose faculty recently won several Nobel prizes in the sciences, is rising in the academic world as an up-and-coming research power. Davis, founded under the name "University Farm," spans over 5,000 acres in the California central valley. It leads agricultural research with exceptional strengths in many quantitative fields. Irvine, with unique acclaim in technological and scientific instruction, rests in a coastal region of Orange County, five miles from the ocean. Santa Cruz features somewhat less-known prowess in physics, mathematics, and astronomy/astrophysics, along with strong political science and art departments. Its location near Monterey Bay allows for quick getaways to San Francisco, Berkeley, and San Jose. Advertising breadth of study, Riverside has an attractive, scenic campus placed a short distance from Los Angeles. Constructed in 2005, Merced overlooks the Sierra Nevada Mountains in Northern California, and rests just a short distance from Yosemite National Park. It is expected to introduce new fields of engineering such as nanobioengineering, materials engineering, and bioelectronic engineering.

Wide-Ranging Strengths
UC offers many strong departments, whereas most private universities only have the resources to develop strengths in a few. The diversity of smaller academic fields also sets UC apart. Student groups can be tailored to a narrow field of interest while maintaining a large group of members. However, the astounding number of educational opportunities means students often need personal initiative to find the groups that interest them: "There's so much to do, but no one's going to hand it to you," noted one undergraduate.

Interaction between students of the different campuses proceeds in a few ways. An academic exchange program allows qualified students to spend a semester at another campus, allowing students to explore subject areas not offered at their school. Student organizations organize events with multi-campus participation. Informally, road trips are an exciting way to visit friends at other UC schools.

Diversity Concerns
Since a court case formally ended affirmative action within the University of California's admissions criteria, some concerns of racial imbalance have surfaced. The percentage of minority enrollment has decreased noticeably. To address these issues, the University of California has established the "President's Task Force" to implement ways to improve racial balance. With the flourishing diversity of California, the University of California cannot be far away from its goal.

All Interests Represented
The University of California offers unparalleled breadth and strength of subject areas and active research at all campuses allows for any level of investigation or study. The opportunity an ambitious student has to explore or to focus on an area in depth is virtually unlimited within the UC System. Interested students can undoubtedly find intellectual enthusiasm and a vibrant atmosphere on each campus.—*Eric Klein*

University of California / Berkeley

Address: UC Berkeley, 110 Sproul Hall, Berkeley CA, 94720

Phone: 510-642-3175

E-mail Address: ouars@berkeley.edu

Web site URL: http://www.berkeley.edu

Year Founded: 1868

Private or Public: public

Religious affiliation: none

Location: Urban

Regular Application Deadline: 1-Dec

Number of Applicants: 41,750

Percent Accepted: 26%

Percent Accepted who enroll: 4,101

Number Entering: NA

Number of Transfers Accepted each Year: 3,020

Mean SAT: 1,324

Mean ACT: NA

Middle 50% SAT range: 580–710V, 620–740M

Middle 50% ACT range: NA

Early admission program (EA/ ED/ NA): NA

ED or EA Acceptance Rate: NA

Full time Undergraduate enrollment: 23,447

Total enrollment: NA

Percent Male: 46%

Percent Female: 54%

Total Percent Minority: 55.5%

Percent African-American: 3%

Percent Asian/Pacific Islander: 41%

Percent Hispanic: 11%

Percent Native-American: 0.5%

Percent Other: 7%

Percent in-state / out of state: 89%/11%

Percent from Public HS: 85

Retention Rate: 96

Graduation Rate: 61

Percent in On-campus housing: 35%

Percent affiliated with Greek system: 10 Frats/10 Sor

Percent Varsity or Club Athletes: NA

Number of official organized extracurricular organizations: 300

3 Most popular majors: Computer Engineering, English Lit and Language, Political Science

Student/Faculty ratio: 15:01

Tuition and Fees: $25,338 (tuition and fees)

In State Tuition and Fees (if different): $6,654 (required fees, no actual tuition)

Cost for Room and Board: $13,074

Percent receiving Financial aid, first-year: 48%

The University of California, Berkeley is a long name for a college, so the lucky students who do manage to land a spot here affectionately call it "Cal." Sprawling over 1,232 acres that overlook the San Francisco Bay, Berkeley is home to over 23,500 undergraduates and boasts a long history of preeminent scholars and academic breakthroughs. It is no wonder that Berkeley is consistently named among one of the top public universities in the nation.

Let There Be Light—and A's

First chartered in 1868, Berkeley was the founding campus of the University of California system. Now, it offers more than 100 majors, each of which belongs to one of the six undergraduate colleges and schools scattered across the campus. The six undergraduate colleges consist of the College of Chemistry, College of Engineering, College of Environmental Design, College of Letters and Science, College of Natural Resources and the Haas School of Business. The College of Letters and Science boasts more than 70 majors from Peace & Conflict Studies to Scandinavian. On the other hand, those wishing to be in the Haas School of Business will find that the enrollment is capped at 700, and only sophomores may apply for the two-year program. Freshmen must first enroll at the College of Letters and Science and declare their major as "pre-business administration." In addition, some majors, like economics, are called "impacted majors," and require an application for admittance.

Requirements vary according to each college and major. However, there are three University requirements that all students must take to receive a bachelor's degree—Entry Level Writing, American History and American Institutions. The latter two requirements are to ensure that all students "have a basic understanding of U.S. history and governmental institutions." All University requirements can be satisfied with high-school classes.

Class sizes vary from the very small to the extremely large. One student recalled her Astronomy 10 experience, which included 700 students. However, that doesn't mean that individualized attention isn't possible. She remembered, "All of my professors have strongly encouraged students to come visit them in office hours, including my astronomy professor who would remember the names of students who had visited him as he called on them amongst 699 other students during lectures."

"Anyone who says they are in the schools of chemistry or engineering is sort of automatically deemed very smart," a third-year student said. Lower-level science courses are often called "weed classes" because they seem designed to weed out students who may not be so committed to the scientific path.

Students seem to agree that grading at Berkeley is hard, but fair. "We have one professor who wrote the textbook and is known to give difficult exams where the mean is failing," one student said. 'I do believe that grading at Berkeley is fair. It's not hard to get a B . . . The curve never hurts you." But as another student explained, "It's difficult for everyone to do well because there are so many smart people." His peer agreed: "I think science midterms are hard as hell, but as long as you're doing better than most of the class, you'll at least get a B."

Living in the Bay

Berkeley now guarantees housing for students for two years, instead of just one. Undergraduates have a variety of housing options. All students may apply for residence halls, which mostly consist of doubles and triples. Unit 1, Unit 2, Unit 3 and the Clark Kerr Campus together house about 4,800 students. Those wishing to live in single-sex dorms can choose either the Bowles for male students or Stern for females. Freeborn Hall is a substance-free dorm. In addition, within this system there are six themed residence halls such as African American or Women in Science & Engineering. In addition, juniors, seniors and new transfers may apply for one of the two university apartment complexes, Channing Bowditch or Yoritada Wada.

Most students agree that living in the dorms is a great experience, if only for the social aspect. One first-year who lived in the Units said, "My dorm is more social . . . People who are in Clark Kerr/Foothill/Stern are in a quieter environment, they're not as socially focused as the people in the Units."

Despite the new change in housing guarantees, most upperclassmen do move off-campus. Many students find that housing co-ops are the easiest way to go. There are 20 co-ops in Berkeley—17 houses and four apartments—and the costs are very reasonable. About $3,000 a semester will snag you a room with food, utilities and furniture included. A downside to the co-op is that all members are expected to contribute 5 hours per week to the upkeep of the buildings, including chores like mopping and cooking. Students can also find their own houses and apartments around the Berkeley area, although affordable housing can be run-down. All in all, for most Berkeley students, moving off campus isn't as big a deal as it may be for students in other colleges. "Distance-wise, it's pretty much the same thing," one third-year said.

The Berkeley meal plan system is based on points. Standard meal plans are included in room and board and offer about 1,250 points a semester; although you can also purchase more points at any time. Even though the city of Berkeley itself offers a myriad of restaurant choices, the dining hall system seems lackluster. One student put it frankly when he explained that, "the dining halls are not the best. Students don't rave about them."

Blue and Gold Weekends

Berkeley students definitely do not lack things to do on the weekends. "On the weekends, many undergrads go to football games (and many don't), study in cafés or at the library, go out to clubs in Berkeley or San Francisco, or to house, co-op, or frat parties," said one Peace and Conflict Studies major. "Frat parties seem to dominate the social scene," commented another student, "but there is the occasional house party." Dorm parties are not all that frequent, mainly due to the presence of the RA's and security monitors. Upperclassmen frequent bars and clubs around the area, like Blake's.

There are also plenty of social opportunities for those who do not drink, such as theater, musical performances, talks and lectures, cheap movies, and even speed-dating. The city of San Francisco also provides a great source for entertainment.

Although alcohol doesn't seem like a big deal on campus, drugs, especially pot, is prevalent. "Come on, it's Berkeley," one student said. "People smoke weed on the streets." Another student noted wryly, "Last month a co-op got headlines for sending 12 people to the hospital because they ate too many special brownies."

Extracurricular activities also take up a lot of students' time. There are over 350 registered student organizations on campus, with the majority of them falling in the academic, professional and service sectors. "The Greek life and athletic program are thriving here, but so are political activism, theater and dance, and the Rubber Band Club," a student said.

12 percent of the Berkeley population—approximately 3,000 students—goes Greek. There are three councils that govern the 55 fraternities and sororities, with an additional 12 multicultural Greek organizations that do not belong to a council. However, Greek life isn't the be-all-end-all. The overwhelming majority seems to agree that "Greek life is pretty popular, but you don't have to pledge to be let in the party scene."

The Times Are A-Changin'?

Berkeley has two great reputations—its academic prowess and its student activism. Students differ in their opinions of whether the academic competitiveness helps the overall college atmosphere. As one student said, "Everyone sees everyone else as competition." However, another disagreed, stating that the academic environment actually helps the college: "It's great to know people that like other things and think differently."

The 1960s, especially the Free Speech Movement, has garnered Berkeley a reputation for being the academic haven for student activism. Even though times have changed, politics has only done so to a small extent. Student activism is still alive and well. "Yesterday there was a two-hour rally—with press—called 'Save the Oaks.' It is exactly what it is, saving the beautiful oaks on campus," one student said.

A 2005 poll by the Berkeley NewsCenter revealed that only a slight majority of freshmen identified themselves as liberal, while about 39% said that they were "middle of the road." However, that doesn't mean that there is not a vocal minority. One third-year noted that, "one of the largest groups, surprising to many, is Berkeley College Republicans."

The shift in political beliefs might be gradual, but the ethnic makeup of Berkeley has changed drastically from the 1960s. Now, Asians make up the largest group, comprising more than 45 percent of the population. Some students deride Proposition 209, which ended affirmative action, for the lack of underrepresented minorities. "It is especially frustrating that the student demographics are not at all representative of the population of the state of California," said one third-year. "When you walk around campus it's hard to not notice that the majority of students are Asian," another student explained. Others also complain that there aren't a lot of out-of-state students, which is hardly surprising given the fact that non-residents are accepted at about half the rate of residents. Nevertheless, one out-of-state student said that, "Adjusting isn't too difficult. The weather's really nice—we just had a blizzard in my hometown!"

Golden Bear Is Ever Watching

Berkeley sponsors 27 sports, including crew, cross-country and women's volleyball, and it has claimed 62 national championships to date. Berkeley students truly redefine the term "student-athlete," as 48% of them hold a GPA above 3.0.

Berkeley's main athletic rival is Stanford, which can be evidenced in its fight song, in which the Golden Bear "fiercely growls" at the "lowly Stanford Red." The Stanford-Berkeley football game is easily the biggest athletic event of the year, and is simply referred to as the "Big Game." The Big Game stretches all the way back to 1892, when former U.S. President Herbert Hoover was team manager for Stanford. The 1910 Big Game saw the first ever "card stunt," which depicted the Stanford Axe and a big C on a white background. Nowadays, 10 different card stunts are performed per year, with computer technology aiding in the process.

The Stanford Axe is another Big Game tradition, but it actually stems from a 1899 baseball game between Stanford and Berkeley. On the eve of this game, Stanford students used an axe to chop up a straw man in blue and gold. However, the very next day, Berkeley pulled a stunning upset over their rival and managed to steal the axe. In 1933, both schools agreed that the Stanford Axe should be mounted on a plaque and given as a trophy to the winner of the Big Game.

Nobel Laureates ONLY!

Visiting Berkeley, one might notice that there are certain parking spots marked "NL Parking Only." These are actually spots reserved for Nobel Laureates, and they are well-needed—Berkeley has the sixth largest number of Nobel Laureates out of all the universities in the world.

> "Berkeley is a tough school. Be prepared."

In the world of public universities, Berkeley's rich history, academic reputation, and social opportunities is truly unparalleled.

The availability of such resources can be equally part of Berkeley's allure as it is part of its challenge. As one student said, "Berkeley is a tough school. Be prepared." Another student reflected, "Berkeley has opened me up and helped me learn about myself. I'm thankful I got in and am thoroughly enjoying my time here." But perhaps one molecular biology and economics double-major summed it up the best: "I love Berkeley, with all its bad and good things."—*Janet Xu*

FYI
If you come to Berkeley, you'd better bring "something blue and gold!"
What is the typical weekend schedule? "Go to a frat party or a bar on Thursday and Friday night, go to the city or see a game on Saturday, and study all day Sunday."
If I could change one thing about Berkeley, I'd "get rid of the unpredictable and sometimes annoying weather . . . and if they can form an inner tube water polo team I'd be satisfied."
Three things every student should do before graduating from Berkeley is: "Live in the dorms, nap on the Glade, and eat in as many restaurants as possible."

University of California / Davis

Address: UC Davis, 1 Shields Avenue, Davis, CA 95616
Phone: 530-752-2971
E-mail Address: undergraduateadmissions@ucdavis.edu
Web site URL: http://www.ucdavis.edu
Year Founded: 1905
Private or Public: public
Religious affiliation: none
Location: suburban
Regular Application Deadline: 1-Dec
Number of Applicants: 30,079
Percent Accepted: 61%
Percent Accepted who enroll: 4,381
Number Entering: NA
Number of Transfers Accepted each Year: NA
Mean SAT: 1,164
Mean ACT: 24

Middle 50% SAT range: 500–630V, 560–670M
Middle 50% ACT range: 21–27
Early admission program (EA/ ED/ NA): NA
ED or EA Acceptance Rate: NA
Full time Undergraduate enrollment: 23,329
Total enrollment: NA
Percent Male: 45%
Percent Female: 55%
Total Percent Minority: 64%
Percent African-American: 3%
Percent Asian/Pacific Islander: 41%
Percent Hispanic: 11%
Percent Native-American: 1%
Percent Other: 8%
Percent in-state / out of state: 97%/3%

Percent from Public HS: 85%
Retention Rate: 90%
Graduation Rate: 42%
Percent in On-campus housing: 19%
Percent affiliated with Greek system: 9 Frats/ 8 Sor
Percent Varsity or Club Athletes: NA
Number of official organized extracurricular organizations: 364
Most popular majors: Economics, Psychology
Student/Faculty ratio: 19:01
Tuition and Fees: $26277 (tuition and fees)
In State Tuition and Fees (if different): $7,593 (in fees)
Cost for Room and Board: $11,239
Percent receiving Financial aid, first-year: 51%

When most people consider the prestigious University of California system, they normally think of UC Berkeley and UC Los Angeles. Nestled in the heart of California's Central Valley, however, lies another UC campus; UC Davis offers its students a rigorous academic program, lush green scenery, and an active social life.

More Than Just Farming
The University of California at Davis is one of the larger public schools in the country, boasting a diversity of students and a wealth of academic programs. With this comes all the advantages and drawbacks of a large school. The breadth and variety of courses of study is almost unparalleled, but students say they often have difficulty

getting into popular and required classes—underclassmen can find themselves on waiting lists.

"Chemistry and biology can be a real pain to get into," one clinical nutrition major said, while several students cited the Communications I course as a prerequisite course that fills up quickly. Most low-level classes are taught lecture style, with many professors deferring to Power Point slides. These classes also usually meet in smaller sections taught by teaching assistants, although one student said it is sometimes difficult to find TAs whose first language is English. Despite the size of lecture, students describe professors as accessible and eager to talk to students.

Davis is broken down into three "colleges," which encompass the different academic departments: Agricultural and Environmental Sciences, Biological Sciences, Letters and Science, and Engineering. Undergraduates apply to specific college programs when applying to Davis, and each has a unique set of general education requirements. The University permits students to change majors after the first quarter, but some say switching to a different college is difficult. Students cited the political science, biology and communications majors as being particularly popular, while others mentioned the difficulty of some chemistry and computer science courses. True to its mascot, the "Aggie," Davis also offers an exceptionally strong Agricultural Sciences program.

UC Davis is on the quarter system, with three quarters falling during the traditional academic year and one during summer. One junior complained, "It's a bit overwhelming, since once midterms roll around, they seem to never stop." She also pointed out, however, that "students can be out of a class they hate in just 10 weeks."

Living It Up on Campus

On-campus housing is primarily occupied by freshmen. There is a wide variety of options, however: single-sex, coed, and theme housing are all available. The alcohol policy for on-campus housing is zero tolerance, but some students said that the enforcement of these policies can be relaxed if you happen to get a laid-back RA. As for eating on-campus, students select a meal plan with a number of "points" they think appropriate to their needs, and one point is swiped per meal. The dining commons put on theme dinner nights throughout the year, but descriptions of the food ranged from "nothing to write home about" to "much improved from several years ago." The Segundo dorm has a new dining commons, and students say "it is the best." Midnight snackers may also add "late night points," to purchase the pizza, cookies and snack food sold in the dining commons until midnight each night.

Sophomores can live in the dorms, but as they receive last priority, most choose to live off campus. Students described the process of finding off-campus housing as being very easy, with "a lot of beautiful neighborhoods to choose from" and a "very tight relationship between Davis and the community." This housing is generally apartments, but students may also find houses in Davis to rent and share.

> "Granted there are those who wear really thick glasses or super fancy clothes, [but] our student body is pretty average."

The Davis campus itself offers a number of facilities. A popular hangout location is the MU Games Area, which features bowling, pool, and air hockey. Other students enjoy spending time at the Quad between classes, where various extracurricular meet and advertise. Davis has also recently constructed a facility called the ARC, a large, modern gym for students; a new pool is also in the works. A football stadium is also being built because UC Davis football is going to be Division I soon.

What to Do with the Time

The peak of undergraduate social life is on Thursday, Friday, and Saturday nights. The fraternities and sororities frequently throw parties, particularly in the beginning of the year. For students wanting to get off campus, Cantina, a local bar, is a "relaxed place to hang out and drink." To combat binge drinking, the school administration has implemented a "0-3" campaign, encouraging students to limit alcohol intake to zero to three drinks. Concerts and shows occasionally come to the Mondavi Center, and a few of the local clubs periodically host social events. The University annually hosts Picnic Day, which is an event featuring food, informational booths, and recreational activities for students, alumni, and the Davis community.

Several students complained that Davis isn't noted for its nightlife—"it's a ghost town after seven," according to one senior. Others, however, mentioned its "charming" atmosphere, with a variety of unique shops. The city of Davis is strict about its recycling policies and prohibits the construction of cinderblock superstores like Wal-Mart, which keeps the area green and plush. A favorite off-campus restaurant is "Fuji Cafe," an all-you-can-eat sushi buffet, which is so popular that students line up outside half an hour before opening to secure seats and tables. The local movie theater also offers $4 movies on Tuesday evenings to lure students.

Situation Normal

Students described the student population as "pretty relaxed," and standard attire is generally jeans and sweatshirts. "Granted there are those who wear really thick glasses or super fancy clothes, but our student body is pretty average," remarked one student. Another commented on the lack of racial diversity, however, as the student body is largely comprised of Caucasian and Asian students. Almost everyone has a car, which is critical for getting out of Davis and for taking weekend trips to Lake Tahoe and the San Francisco Bay Area, which are each a little over an hour's drive away.

Varsity sports do not have a huge presence on campus, but a student organization called the Aggie Pack arranges giveaways like tube socks and burritos to increase student attendance at games and meets. Students are fairly active, however, in intramural sports, including water polo and flag football. There are a significant number of student organizations to get involved in, and students say it is easy to have a full extracurricular schedule. Some of the larger student organizations include the Christian fellowships, student government, and the honor societies. Others choose to rush the Greek organizations, which maintain a strong presence during the beginning of the year to recruit new members. "You basically get attacked by Greek fliers on your way to class when the year starts," one junior said. Popular student jobs include the library and dining commons, and most student employment is contained to campus jobs. Overall, Davis is a great way to get a sterling University of California education while living in a tightly knit, small town community with a laid-back atmosphere.—*Stephanie Teng*

FYI
If you come to UC Davis, you'd better bring "a bike with fenders."
What's the typical weekend schedule? "Studying during the day (usually on the grass in the sun, yes even now in February), parties at night."
If I could change one thing about UC Davis, "I'd get rid of the professors that can't speak clear enough English."
Three things every student at UC Davis should do before graduating are "go to Picnic Day at least once," "learn to rock climb at the ARC," and "join the Aggie Pack for a football game."

University of California / Irvine

Address: UC Irvine, 240 Administration, Irvine, CA 92697
Phone: 949-824-6703
E-mail Address: admissions@uci.edu
Web site URL: http://www.uci.edu
Year Founded: 1965
Private or Public: public
Religious affiliation: none
Location: urban
Regular Application Deadline: 1-Dec
Number of Applicants: NA
Percent Accepted: 60%
Percent Accepted who enroll: 21%
Number Entering: NA
Number of Transfers Accepted each Year: NA
Mean SAT: 1,214
Mean ACT: NA

Middle 50% SAT range: 1,110–1,310
Middle 50% ACT range: NA
Early admission program (EA/ ED/ NA): NA
ED or EA Acceptance Rate: NA
Full time Undergraduate enrollment: 19,930
Total enrollment: NA
Percent Male: 49%
Percent Female: 51%
Total Percent Minority: 64%
Percent African-American: 2%
Percent Asian/Pacific Islander: 49%
Percent Hispanic: 12%
Percent Native-American: 0%
Percent Other: NA
Percent in-state / out of state: NA

Percent from Public HS: 84%
Retention Rate: 93%
Graduation Rate: 42 in four; 80 in six
Percent in On-campus housing: 34%
Percent affiliated with Greek system: 18%
Percent Varsity or Club Athletes: NA
Number of official organized extracurricular organizations: 378
Most popular majors: Computer Science, Economics
Student/Faculty ratio: 19:01
Tuition and Fees: $24,825.00
In State Tuition and Fees (if different): $6,141.00
Percent receiving Financial aid, first-year: 47%

L ocated in the heart of Southern California, UC Irvine gives students a chance to experience a diverse set of academic and social experiences without the congestion of Los Angeles living. The school boasts a terrific location, with beaches and the city just a short drive away, and combined with strong academics and a wide range of extracurricular opportunities, a UC Irvine "Anteater" can expect a meaningful college experience.

The Grind of Learning

Like many of the other University of California campuses, UC Irvine has a sizeable undergraduate population and the majority of undergraduate courses are taught as large lectures breaking into smaller sections by teaching assistants, even beyond the introductory level. Teaching assistants "vary in quality by subject," but many noted that the professors are "outstanding." One such professor cited by several students for his sociology classes and extreme liberalism was Professor Chuck O'Connell. "I loved his class because he's not afraid to challenge things that he thinks are wrong," raved one senior. As far as class sizes go, "there never seem to be enough of the popular classes to go around." Enrollment in these classes is generally distributed based on seniority, so upperclassmen had far fewer complaints about class size than underclassmen, although many students complained that enrollment limitations can make graduating within four years difficult.

In addition to major requirements, students have to fulfill a number of general education requirements (otherwise known as "breadth requirements"), including language, math, and world and culture classes. Popular majors include engineering and biology, although they are also notoriously hard. In recent years, the University has faced major budget cuts, which has resulted in reduction of many class offerings. One senior mentioned that she thinks administration gives preferential funding to the science majors, noting "every time requirement cuts come along, these cuts are only ever applied to the 'soft' sciences."

Socially Greek

Several students described the on-campus social scene as being divided into two groups: "frat" and "not frat." One junior estimated that approximately 30 percent of students "go Greek" although this number includes ethnic, academic, and service-based fraternities as well. Another student said she thought the Greek presence on campus was "not overwhelming, but they do host most of the larger campus parties." The parties in general are "not that great," but students also have the option of going to the fraternities or several of the local clubs, including Irvine and Costa Mesa. Although the University prohibits alcohol in dorms, several undergraduates said that it is not difficult to find alcohol on campus or to get away with having it.

For those not inclined to join fraternity or sorority life, the University does offer a variety of other extracurricular activities. Once a quarter, the registered organizations on campus host a central curricular bazaar, and several popular clubs include the snowboarding club, student government, and multicultural organizations. One student said that "it seems like everyone is involved in campus life in one way or another," and the many opportunities to participate in different parts of campus offer chances to meet other students as well as to be involved.

Several students mentioned that the school has a notoriously high Asian population—some say UC Irvine's informal name is "University of Chinese Immigrants"—but others said that they felt the student body was "very diverse." One junior noted the significantly lower in-state tuition costs and higher out-of-state admissions standards ensure that a large percentage of the student body hails from California. Another mentioned that she found students to be "friendly and eager to meet you" and many students agreed that they thought it was easy to build lasting relationships while at UC Irvine.

Athletics and Traditions

UC Irvine has an underemphasized athletic program—although a number of students participate in varsity athletics, the school does not have a football team, and as one junior said, "The games are sparsely populated even at their fullest." Some of the more popular sports include basketball and volleyball.

More common is gym attendance and participation in intramural sports, which include the traditional team sports in addition to some of the less conventional, including wrestling, flag football and badminton. Anyone can field a team in one of three divisions: recreational, intermediate and competitive; the gym's facilities are "pretty nice," as the non-varsity athlete gym is only a couple of years old.

One of the most significant yearly traditions at UC Irvine is Welcome Week, during which incoming freshmen are oriented to college life at Irvine. During this time, the school hosts one of its largest parties, the annual foam party, but students can expect all sorts of activities during this intensive week at the beginning of each academic year.

Transitioning into Irvine

On-campus housing is only guaranteed for first-year students, and consequently, most undergraduates move off-campus after freshman year. The dorms themselves are grouped into "Phase One," "Phase Two" and "Phase Three" based on how recently they were built. Although assignments are made randomly, each Phase generally takes on the personality of its residents, who are clustered on the basis of lifestyle and roommate preferences. The dorms are patrolled by Resident Assistants (RAs), and students said RA strictness varied a lot based on the individual, although one student said she found the "housing staff to be really well trained and they care a lot about the residents." Still, another acknowledged that "dorming is a one-time experience and by the end of freshman year, most people are ready to move on." With regards to food, one off-campus student said, "We often complained about the food, but after we moved out, we missed it terribly." Undergraduates living in the dorms are required to take out meal plans allotting meals on a weekly basis, but many upperclassmen also purchase off-campus plans, which can range from offering a quarterly number of meals to a punch card allowing students to mix and match meals in the cafeterias.

> "Unfortunately, a lot of college students find themselves homeless at one point in their college careers."

The surrounding area offers both apartments and houses as options, but students said it can be a difficult transition into off-campus housing. Real estate is currently very expensive in Irvine, and competition for nearby housing is frequently very "stiff." One fourth year student lamented, "Unfortunately, a lot of college students find themselves homeless at one point in their college careers," although another said, "As long as you look hard enough, everyone knows they will find something."

The city of Irvine itself is reputed to be one of the safest cities in the nation, due to its "very active police force," according to one student. Students indicated, however, that it cannot boast to be much of a college town. "The clubs are very expensive and not very good," said one student, while another remarked that, "Irvine is a city of strip malls and chain stores and not much else." Still, students wishing to find things to do off campus are usually able to do it. A high proportion of the undergraduates own cars, which are "necessary to get around Southern California," and Los Angeles and San Diego are both manageable distances away.— *Stephanie Teng*

FYI
If you could come to Irvine, you'd better bring "a good attitude and motivation to find things."
What's the typical weekend schedule? "Thursday and Friday: go out and party; Saturday wake up late kick back and go to the gym or hang out, Saturday night is low key; Sunday: study and catch up on work for the week."
If I could change one thing about UC Irvine, I'd "add more culture to the city of Irvine."
Three things every student at Irvine should do before graduating are "take a class taught by Professor O'Connell, participate in at least one IM sport, and get out of Irvine to visit the greater Southern California area."

University of California / Los Angeles

Address: UC LA, 405 Hilgard Avenue, Los Angeles, CA 90095
Phone: 310-825-3101
E-mail Address: ugadm@saonet.ucla.edu
Web site URL: http://www.ucla.edu/
Year Founded: 1919
Private or Public: public
Religious affiliation: none
Location: urban
Regular Application Deadline: 1-Dec
Number of Applicants: NA
Percent Accepted: 26%
Percent Accepted who enroll: 39%
Number Entering: NA
Number of Transfers Accepted each Year: NA
Mean SAT: 1,284
Mean ACT: 27
Middle 50% SAT range: 1,180–1,410

Middle 50% ACT range: 24–30
Early admission program (EA/ ED/ NA): NA
ED or EA Acceptance Rate: NA
Full time Undergraduate enrollment: 25,432
Percent Male: 44%
Percent Female: 56%
Total Percent Minority: 56%
Percent African-American: 3%
Percent Asian/Pacific Islander: 38%
Percent Hispanic: 15%
Percent Native-American: 0%
Percent Other: NA
Percent in-state / out of state: NA
Percent from Public HS: 80%
Retention Rate: 97%

Graduation Rate: 59 in four; 89 in six
Percent in On-campus housing: 40%
Percent affiliated with Greek system: 26%
Percent Varsity or Club Athletes: NA
Number of official organized extracurricular organizations: 700
3 Most popular majors: Economics, Political Science, Psychology
Student/Faculty ratio: 17:01
Tuition and Fees: $24,825.00
In State Tuition and Fees (if different): $6,141.00
Percent receiving Financial aid, first-year: 53%

Surrounded by Bel Air, Beverly Hills and the Santa Monica Mountains, a picturesque Southern California campus is home to one of the UC's premier academic institutions. With a huge undergraduate population of over 35,000, UCLA offers a panoply of academic, athletic and extracurricular opportunities for every type of student. UCLA distinguishes itself from universities of similar size and reputation through its expressed commitment to undergraduate education.

First-Rate Academics

In spite of their university's size, UCLA students do not report feeling neglected. While students claim that classes fill up quickly, very few are unable to take their top choices. "It is also great if you are an athlete or an honors student, because you get to pick your classes before everyone else," explained one junior. In addition, most describe accessible professors and small class sizes in upper-level courses. These qualities make UCLA academically competitive with the top universities in the country, and give its students a sense of community in such a large institution.

A unique aspect of academics at UCLA is the modified quarter system that consists of three ten-week periods. Students take three sets of classes each academic year compared with the normal two at universities on the semester system. Although students like to complain about the General Education (GE) requirements, which include courses in departments they do not necessarily major in, they often grudgingly admit that it opens their eyes to subjects they never thought they would be interested in. At the completion of the GE requirements, students take prerequisite courses for the major they plan on applying to. Engineering and business-economics are two majors with a competitive application process, while increasingly popular majors are economics, chemistry, and particularly biology. "More and more students are becoming interested in pursuing science degrees as the UCLA Med School is becoming more and more competitive," says one freshman.

The course load around finals week often takes its toll on students' sanity, but don't be frightened during finals week when loud, desperate yelps are heard from the street late at night. The traditional Midnight Yells take place every night during finals to offer therapy for those who need to release their test-taking anxiety. The event has become a social, stress-relieving fanfare, and in years past it has gotten out of control with students burning furniture in the street.

Party LA-Style

The social scene at UCLA during the weekends is dominated by the fraternities and sororities. At such a large school these are popular social niches that make the social scene less intimidating. "It isn't necessary to be in a frat or sorority; it just makes the school a little smaller for you," explained one sophomore. In-demand underclass girls need not join a sorority to be involved in the weekend Greek scene. This is less true for underclass boys, who have a harder time gaining entrance to Greek parties if they are not in a fraternity themselves.

Alternatives to Greek life include apartment parties and local bars within walking distance. However, being underage can be a problem even with fake identification. "Tons of people use fake IDs all the time, but I got arrested and you have to deal with the LAPD if you get caught," said one embarrassed freshman.

UCLA students often venture off campus for social events, as many of them are from the area and have cars. Some students choose to go home for the weekend, treating UCLA more like a commuter school. On the other hand, there are nights on the L.A. strip when there is no dearth of lively hot spots teeming with attractive college students. Even trips to Mexico are not unheard of, with the border only a couple of hours away.

Eat, Sleep, and Be Merry

The residential plan for UCLA students is quite varied. Freshmen live in one of four high-rise dormitories. These buildings are described by some as madhouses due to the number of excited, bewildered and reportedly drunk freshmen. One freshman describes the dorms as "chaotic, unorganized, and uncomfortable." Upperclassmen look back on these dorms with nostalgia from the tamer confines of university-owned apartment buildings. Such accommodations are more like hotels, many with picnic and volleyball areas. For those not living in a fraternity or sorority house, another option is finding an apartment in one of the local neighborhoods, such as Santa Monica, Culver City or Westwood. Private apartments are often luxurious compared to the freshman dorms and Greek houses, but may be farther from campus.

The food at the dining halls in UCLA seems to get mixed reviews. While students can hang out and eat at places like Taco Bell, the dining-hall prepared food is reportedly lackluster. The UCLA meal plan does provide much flexibility because one can hang out in the Ackerman Union for hours, studying, socializing and taking advantage of the fast-food dining options. Some enjoy the meal plan because they can use allotted funds at many other eateries on campus.

Being a Bruin

What does it mean to be a UCLA Bruin? Well, whatever you want it to mean. If you're an athlete, you find yourself at a highly competitive Division I school with plenty of campus recognition. UCLA has been named "The Number One Jock School" by *Sports Illustrated* within the past five years and has enjoyed many victories on the part of their sports teams. The University has won over 80 NCAA championships in basketball, football, volleyball, and water polo. Home football games are always an occasion for an enthusiastic display of school spirit, especially when the Bruins play UCLA's rival, USC.

There are plenty of community service opportunities and a countless number of clubs, societies, and club sports on and off campus. Moreover, at such a large and diverse school, students have access to interesting jobs on campus. "What makes this place different from other schools is the opportunity we have to work on research projects and get involved with faculty that are well-known in their fields," boasts one female junior.

> **People find relief in the laid-back mentality pervasive in the sun-soaked Southern California atmosphere of UCLA.**

Another aspect students consistently mention is the L.A. mindset. "I love UCLA but it was not what I expected. I was a little shocked. I guess I didn't prepare myself for the L.A. mentality," said one sophomore boy. The "L.A. mentality" is a Hollywood-infused, fast-paced, image-oriented social stance that is both loved and hated. Whether students embrace it or reject it, this attitude has found its way into the UCLA campus dynamic. While many are disgusted by the superficiality, with its make up, hair bleach, and who-you-know name-dropping, they find relief in the laid-back mentality pervasive in the sun-soaked Southern California Coast.—*Nate Puksta*

FYI
If you come to UCLA you'd better bring "a parking pass and a really good fake ID."
What is the typical weekend schedule? "An overnight getaway with a fraternity or sorority, nights out at the local bars, or a quiet weekend of hanging out and studying."
If I could change one thing about UCLA, I would "make it more open to different kinds of people."
Three things every student at UCLA should do before graduation are "attend a USC vs. UCLA football game, eat at Diddy Reese's famous cookie shop, and cruise the Sunset Strip."

University of California/Riverside

Address: UC Riverside, 1120 Hinderaker Hall, Riverside, CA 92521
Phone: 951-827-3411
E-mail Address: discover@ucr.edu
Web site URL: http://www.ucr.edu
Year Founded: 1954
Private or Public: public
Religious affiliation: none
Location: urban
Regular Application Deadline: 1-Dec
Number of Applicants: 19,982
Percent Accepted: 83%
Percent Accepted who enroll: 22%
Number Entering: 3,594
Number of Transfers Accepted each Year: 3,350
Mean SAT: 1,048
Mean ACT: 21

Middle 50% SAT range: 910–1,170
Middle 50% ACT range: 18–23
Early admission program (EA/ ED/ NA): NA
ED or EA Acceptance Rate: NA
Full time Undergraduate enrollment: 14,571
Total enrollment: 16,573
Percent Male: 48%
Percent Female: 52%
Total Percent Minority: 81%
Percent African-American: 7%
Percent Asian/Pacific Islander: 41%
Percent Hispanic: 25%
Percent Native-American: 0%
Percent Other: 8%
Percent in-state / out of state: 99%/1%

Percent from Public HS: 88%
Retention Rate: 86%
Graduation Rate: 64%
Percent in On-campus housing: 27%
Percent affiliated with Greek system: 4%
Percent Varsity or Club Athletes: NA
Number of official organized extracurricular organizations: 250
3 Most popular majors: Psychology, Business, Social Sciences
Student/Faculty ratio: 18:01
Tuition and Fees: $25,264.00
In State Tuition and Fees (if different): $6,590.00
Cost for Room and Board: $10,200.00
Percent receiving Financial aid, first-year: 62%

While sometimes overshadowed by the other University of California schools, UC Riverside is known for its convenient location, diverse academics, and its vibrant student population. UC Riverside offers a wide array of majors ranging from Global Studies and Entomology to Dance and Creative Writing.

As its name suggests, the campus is in the large city of Riverside and near the famous forests and mountains of Southern California. This allows students many getaways to shopping centers, movie theaters, and various other distractions conveniently located near the campus, as well as giving nature lovers the opportunity to explore right in the backyard of their dormitories.

Higher Education's Little Asia

When asked about the typical student activities at UC Riverside, all students, no matter of what background, come up with the same response, "of course, the ethnic organizations! The Chinese, Vietnamese, Japanese, and Korean-Student Associations are all very strong in both numbers and influence over the entire campus at-mosphere." UC Riverside is one of the few American colleges where the Asian population claims the absolute majority. Although most of the Asian population are 2nd, 3rd, or even 4th generation of Asian Americans and many do not even know how to speak anything besides English, their connections with their Asian heritages have yet to wane. However, the Asians are willing to share their cultural heritage with the rest of the school. As one Caucasian student pointed out, "compared to the other colleges in America, the students of Riverside know much more about Asia, its people, and its customs, and its society. That comes from the existence of the large Asian population in the campus."

Because of the abundant Asian population, activities relating to Asian life have exploded near UC Riverside. For example, large numbers of Asian restaurants flourish near the campus, driven by student demand. One Caucasian student noticed, "because of all the Asian stuff near the campus, it feels like all the non-Asian people at UC Riverside became more and more Asian, and you know, once we graduate, its going to feel like we automatically graduate with a degree in Asian Studies."

Of course, there are also options not involving Asian cultures. Athletic clubs and scientific and political organizations are in abundant existence and Greek life is also very influential. There are also many newspapers and magazines on the campus and journalism is one of the most popular majors at UC Riverside. As one senior male student said, "The student life here is so vibrant, and the professors are really nice; I really feel like I can fit in really well in the school no matter what my background is."

Although UCR does not have academic renown at the national level, students often find the coursework more challenging then it first appears. One student complained, "You know, I thought since it was so easy getting into this school, it was going to be easy to get A's in all of my classes. But I was deceived! I am having a hard time in my classes not because the material is hard but because the curves in the classes are working against me because the average of the classes is driven up so much by really studious people, meaning that there is so little grade inflation." The competitive nature of Riverside academics is disproportionate to its high admission rate.

L.A.? Not L.A.?

Riverside is located east of Los Angeles, within the driving distance of its downtown, yet it is known for its quietness and closeness to natural environment. The San Bernardino Mountains are just east of the town and the Los Angeles National Forest north and west of the campus. Other than shops and eateries, there are relatively few manmade attractions to be noted in the city itself. The surrounding wilderness, however, offers plenty for students to explore. To get away from campus, students can camp out in the woods (assuming that it is not closed due to wildfire) or take skiing and

snowboarding lessons. As one Colorado student remarked, "San Bernardino Mountains are great! I don't even have to go back home to snowboard, it really reminds me of home. Plus, it is a great way to show off my skills because most of the people in Southern California can't even ski or snowboard at all."

Many Riverside students own cars. This is especially true for the many students who commute daily to the campus from as far as northern San Diego County. Cars allow students to visit Los Angeles as often as possible, for its shopping, parks and beaches. Also many live within the confines of the city.

> **"It's good everybody in my suite is gone for the weekend, it's finally quiet and I can get down to studying."**

But living next to Los Angeles and the natural environment has its downside as well. The foul industrial and automobile smog from Los Angeles, America's second-largest urban center, constantly floods the UC Riverside campus. Also, the frequent wildfires in the nearby forests bring large amounts of flying ash into the campus, darkening the sky from sunny to "cloudy." As a result of the poor air quality and proximity to home, students drive away from the campus almost every weekend, leaving one student to remark, "The campus is almost 50% empty every weekend; people are mostly going home, some are in L.A." Nonetheless, the people remaining on campus are generally not bothered by the mass exodus. As one student eagerly said, "It's good everybody in my suite is gone for the weekend, it's finally quiet and I can get down to studying." After all, academics are what really matters in all colleges including UC Riverside.—*Xiaochen Su*

FYI
If you come to UCR, you better bring "summer clothes (because you'll need them until the middle of November) and a car!"
The typical weekend schedule at UCR is "going home because all of my friends do."
If I could change one thing about UCR, I would change "the poor air quality."
The three things you have to do before graduating from UCR are "go to L.A., learn to ski, and learn about Asia from practical experience."

University of California / San Diego

Address: UC San Diego, 9500 Gilman Dr., 0021, La Jolla, CA 92093
Phone: 858-534-4831
E-mail Address: admissionsinfo@ucsd.edu
Web site URL: www.ucsd.edu
Year Founded: 1959
Private or Public: public
Religious affiliation: none
Location: Urban
Regular Application Deadline: 1-Dec
Number of Applicants: 40,418
Percent Accepted: 49%
Percent Accepted who enroll: 22%
Number Entering: 4,589
Number of Transfers Accepted each Year: 4,824
Mean SAT: 1,239
Mean ACT: 25

Middle 50% SAT range: 1,140–1,360
Middle 50% ACT range: 23–29
Early admission program (EA/ ED/ NA): NA
ED or EA Acceptance Rate: NA
Full time Undergraduate enrollment: 20,679
Total enrollment: 24,208
Percent Male: 48%
Percent Female: 52%
Total Percent Minority: 68%
Percent African-American: 1%
Percent Asian/Pacific Islander: 39%
Percent Hispanic: 11%
Percent Native-American: 0%
Percent Other: 17%
Percent in-state / out of state: 97%/3%

Percent from Public HS: NA
Retention Rate: 95%
Graduation Rate: 85%
Percent in On-campus housing: 35%
Percent affiliated with Greek system: 10%
Percent Varsity or Club Athletes: 3%
Number of official organized extracurricular organizations: 250
3 Most popular majors: Economics, Microbiology, Political Science
Student/Faculty ratio: 19:01
Tuition and Fees: $25,372.00
In State Tuition and Fees (if different): $6,888.00
Cost for Room and Board: $9,657.00
Percent receiving Financial aid, first-year: 55%

What do you think of when you imagine what college life will be like? An academically challenging school; a university with a mild, sunny climate; or maybe a college with many extracurricular activities to offer? If any of the above descriptions fits your requirements for what a college experience should entail, the University of California San Diego (UCSD) is certainly a university to put on your list. No matter who you ask, they respond that UCSD is an "all-around great school" whose "professors are really interesting" and whose people "are definitely UCSD's strongest attraction." At UCSD, "everyone seems to take it pretty chill" but are still brilliant and focused on their goals. Oh, and did we forget to mention that it is located on one of the most pristine beaches in America?

Life in the Fast Lane

At UCSD, students switch classes every quarter rather than every semester, like most schools in America. Although some give it mixed reviews, most UCSD students seem to like the quarter system. When asked about the fast-paced academic schedule, one sophomore replied, "You know, it's really not that bad. If you are in a class you particularly don't like, wait a few weeks and you'll be done with it!" On the other hand, some students complain that "the quarter system doesn't allow [them] to fully get immersed in some of [their] subjects" and that "as soon as you are done with a midterm or final, another one hits you in the face a week or two later."

UCSD's academic requirements also inspire varied reactions among students. While many think that the lengthy time commitment to fulfill the writing requirement or humanities requirement is a complete waste, most students questioned feel that because UCSD has so many choices for classes, getting the general education requirements out of the way really isn't that much of an annoyance. According to some, picking classes is really simple and "quite convenient." Everything is done online, and students can see if classes are filled up even before they try to sign up for them. Many students did indicate that one downside of UCSD is the class sizes; as one student put it, "I feel like I need a megaphone and binoculars to participate in class sometimes." While this is a problem for popular majors like biology, chemistry and psychology, many students seem to feel "comfortable" in their classes. The University boasts some of the best science, research and engineering on the West Coast. Consistently at the top of its class in technology and science research, UCSD proves to be a powerful academic institution with "rigorous and challenging" courses to satisfy even the brightest and most talented students. "Every day I am constantly reminded of the academic splendor that UCSD offers. Its students are actually very serious about their work and know how to get things done."

Picking the Right College (and the Right TA)

UCSD is divided up residentially and academically into six colleges. Revelle College focuses on science and mathematics, while Muir College and Warren College emphasize humanities and liberal arts, respectively. Marshall College's emphasis is on public policy, and Roosevelt College focuses on international policy; the creatively named Sixth College emphasizes service and cultural learning. Upon applying to UCSD, each student applies to whichever college they would prefer to live and study in, and the University "usually does a great job of allocating people properly." Each college has unique graduation requirements so as to "maximize the efficiency of your undergraduate experience." Although some majors prove stronger or more rigorous than others, the competition is pretty much "evenly distributed throughout the colleges and majors."

"Everyone is extremely competitive, but every major also has its slackers." As if classes at UCSD weren't hard enough, the professors and TAs seem to make things slightly more inconvenient by speaking "a different dialect of English." As one student put it, "professors and TAs may speak English, but their accents speak something else." Apparently, this really only is a problem in the math and science departments (as it is in many schools) and can be easily avoided if you "learn to pick the right professor or TA for lecture and section."

Dance, Yoga, Pilates, Oh My!

With all this talk about requirements and TAs, don't be fooled into thinking UCSD is all work and no play. The students definitely know how to have a good time, how to stay in shape, and most of all, how to relax. At UCSD, students are serious about their bodies, as well as their appearance. The gym seems to be a very common meeting place. "People will go to the gym before and after parties, when they wake up in the morning, even between study breaks," one sophomore commented on the amount the students went to the gym. "I guess it's because our athletic center offers so many fun programs like pilates, yoga and all kinds of dance classes." With year-round ability to hit the surf, it's clear why the gym is a popular place to meet people, get work done, and of course, tone and shape the gorgeous student bodies.

> "There are so many trophy girls here that some times I look at them and say, 'How is it possible for you to look that gorgeous!?'"

Some UCSD students feel that because "there is sometimes a lack of party scene at the school," the gym becomes an easy "outlet for time-wasting." When asked if the people were generally good-looking at UC San Diego, one student immediately responded with: "Yeah. Definitely. There are so many trophy girls here that some times I look at them and say, 'How is it possible for you to look that gorgeous!?'"

"GO GREEK!" . . . And Other Activities

While many UC San Diego students consider going to the beach as their main extracurricular activity, as one student put it, "extracurriculars are perhaps the most important thing to your experience at UCSD. There are so many activities that one can participate in whether it be the Surf Club, the huge LGBT community, or a frat or sorority." One student commented that "the gay and lesbian society is really big here. There may not be that many openly gay people on campus, but their presence is definitely felt." Perhaps the most popular club or activity is fraternity or sorority life. Perhaps due to the fact that the party scene at UCSD is considered small, the Greek life often takes over social events and gatherings. Greek life at UCSD is seen more as a way to get to know people than as a "place to get trashed and be exclusive," commented one sorority sister. The main attraction to Greek life at UCSD is "really to form a close bond of friends that all share the same mindset." "Meeting new people is very hard at UCSD, so it is important to sign up for everything you possibly can and being in a frat or sorority is definitely a good way to find people that interest you," one junior said when asked why being in sororities is very popular. UCSD Greek life does seem atypical in one regard. Most frats and sororities don't throw a lot of wild parties and, despite having the stereotypical sorority or frat member here and there, "UCSD Greek life really seems to be a little more down to earth."

Location, Location, Location

Although having a car to get around the UCSD campus is definitely not necessary, many UCSD students report that wheels are essential for the not-so-unusual (and often much-needed) escape from campus life. One freshman noticed that "many people have cars or live really close to campus so they end up going home a lot and not being around." She commented that because her roommate lived 10 minutes away, she would go home "all the time, even for dinner." Because so many people have cars on campus or live close to UCSD, the campus can "sometimes feel like an empty place." For students who do not have cars though, there is an extensive transportation system of buses that take students anywhere in a 10-mile radius for free. There is also a campus transport system that shuttles students to nearby grocery stores and malls. Being situated in the heart of La Jolla, Calif., (one of the state's wealthiest cities) proves to be a nuisance as well as a blessing. Many students wish they were not located in the quiet neighborhood because "parties are often shut down or not allowed due to noise restriction." There also "isn't a lot going on at any time because the average age is, like, 45." UCSD's location does definitely provide some great benefits. "The beach is beautiful, there is great shopping, and overall, there is very little crime," one senior said.

Overall, students rave about the University of California at San Diego. While top-notch academics, amazingly "chill and beautiful" people, great weather and a decent social life all make UCSD an attractive college, in the end what really charms high school students across America can only be described by the old real estate adage: "location, location, location."—*Nate Puksta*

FYI

If you come to UCSD, you'd better bring "a planner or calendar so you can write down all the appointments you made for clubs to join during freshman year."

What is the typical weekend schedule? "Party Friday night, sleep through half the day on Saturday, go out on Saturday night not to a party, sleep through half the day on Sunday, then go to the beach and cram on Sunday night."

If I could change one thing about UCSD, I'd "get rid of the writing general education requirement—no one likes it and no one learns anything!"

Three things that every student should do before graduating UCSD are "get drunk at the Sun-God Festival, take 'The Psychology of Human Sexuality,' and GO GREEK!"

University of California / Santa Barbara

Address: UC Santa Barbara, 1210 Cheadle Hall, Santa Barbara, CA 93106
Phone: 805-893-2485
E-mail Address: appinfo@sa.ucsb.edu
Web site URL: www.ucsb.edu
Year Founded: 1909
Private or Public: public
Religious affiliation: none
Location: suburban
Regular Application Deadline: 1-Dec
Number of Applicants: 39,854
Percent Accepted: 53%
Percent Accepted who enroll: 19%
Number Entering: 4,096
Number of Transfers Accepted each Year: 5,460
Mean SAT: 1,178
Mean ACT: 25

Middle 50% SAT range: 1,070–1,310
Middle 50% ACT range: 22–28
Early admission program (EA/ ED/ NA): NA
ED or EA Acceptance Rate: NA
Full time Undergraduate enrollment: 18,058
Total enrollment: 21,016
Percent Male: 43%
Percent Female: 57%
Total Percent Minority: 0.41%
Percent African-American: 0.03%
Percent Asian/Pacific Islander: 0.17%
Percent Hispanic: 0.2%
Percent Native-American: 0.01%
Percent Other: 6%
Percent in-state / out of state: 98%/2%

Percent from Public HS: 87%
Retention Rate: 91%
Graduation Rate: 75%
Percent in On-campus housing: 31%
Percent affiliated with Greek system: 11%
Percent Varsity or Club Athletes: NA
Number of official organized extracurricular organizations: 487
3 Most popular majors: Biology, Economics, Psychology
Student/Faculty ratio: 17:01
Tuition and Fees: $25,694.00
In State Tuition and Fees (if different): $7,010.00
Cost for Room and Board: $11,493.00
Percent receiving Financial aid, first-year: 63%

Set against the backdrop of the golden Santa Ynez Mountains, overlooking the blue Pacific Ocean, and surrounded by fresh green palm fronds that ripple gently in the sea breeze, the University of California, Santa Barbara always stuns its visitors with its spectacular natural beauty. Students take advantage of their seaside location as they whiz along to class on the vast network of campus bike trails or enjoy a bonfire on the beach before heading out to parties in Isla Vista. Although students enjoy a notoriously thriving social life that has led some to refer to the school as the "University of Casual Sex and Beer" (UCSB), the university offers much more, including a stellar faculty, plentiful research opportunities, and a relaxed atmosphere that allows for academics to be challenging without being super-competitive.

Yes, We Do Study Sometimes

"The academics are really strong here," said one student. "More than people give it credit for." Students are divided into three main schools: the College of Letters and Science, the College of Engineering, and the College of Creative Studies. There are a lot of "pretty broad" requirements that all students regardless of major must fulfill, in areas such as writing, language, western culture, nonwestern culture, and science. Top choices for majors include biology (particularly marine biology), philosophy, engineering (one of the hardest majors) and global studies. The school boasts several Nobel Prize-winning faculty and other professors who are highly distinguished in their fields.

Competition within classes varies according to major, and is probably most intense in the sciences where a large number of pre-meds are all vying for the top grades. According to one student, "I love the laid-back atmosphere. I don't feel that it's overly competitive—it never gets to the point you hear about at other schools where people are stealing each other's binders." Another student disagreed, saying that students "sometimes bring materials into closed-book tests and don't get caught, which makes the atmosphere unnecessarily competitive. I wish the school regulated that kind of thing more effectively." Competition to get into classes can be tricky, especially for the more popular majors, but students say it helps to come in with extra credits from high school in order to gain a higher standing in the course selection process.

As at most colleges, introductory level classes have hundreds of students, while higher-level classes are smaller. "Because classes are so big, you really have to make an effort to get to know your professors," commented one junior. All professors and TAs have office hours, though students generally agree that not a lot of people take advantage of this system. The workload varies between classes and majors, but one student estimated that to get Bs, people must study about two hours for each day of classes. Said one sophomore, "I feel like I always have work to do and it's never-ending! But some people seem to get it all done quickly and then go out and party every night. It really depends on the classes and the students."

California Nights

Everyone overwhelmingly agrees that UCSB is a notorious party school. "That's probably because we're all crammed into one place," said one student, in reference to Isla Vista. "I.V.," a party zone often referred to as the "most densely populated square mile west of the Mississippi" is a little close-knit community right off campus where student apartments are packed up next to each other. House parties are probably the most common kind of party, particularly along Del Playa; frats also host parties, but it's often difficult for guys to get in if they don't already know someone in the fraternity. Some people prefer to hang out in small groups with friends in their rooms, drinking, watching movies, or just winding down after a long week of classes.

For non-drinkers, the school's Alternative Program Board arranges dances, movie nights by the lagoon, concerts, and other musical events such as debuting new freshman bands. The Magic Lantern also screens movies in one of the nearby theatres, and even though there are not often a lot of drama events that people attend, there is a well-liked improv comedy group that performs on Friday nights. One sophomore reports, "The dance teams and clubs get together and put on performances for benefits or other activities. And one of the frats puts on a huge show every year. There are definitely other things to do—you don't have to come here and party, though it's certainly an option!"

The alcohol policy on campus is similar to most schools, but regulations are rarely enforced. Recently, USCB has been trying to gain more jurisdiction over what goes on in Isla Vista, but "people are fighting it, because this is where we live!" Said one junior, "Everyone knows what's going on. Professors plan exams around Halloween weekend so that 'people don't come in hungover,' and they always throw a lot of beer jokes into their lectures." Another student noted that there have been some new policies regarding the usual Halloween craziness, such as the rule that all kegs and music must now be indoors. Since about a quarter of I.V. is home to families, older residents, and others, the administration tries to work to achieve a healthy relationship between the various factions of the Isla Vista community.

In addition to Halloween, special annual parties include a large and raucous St. Patrick's Day celebration, summertime Fiesta, and Fight Night at one of the frats, where students box in the basketball arena. Each of the residence halls also holds an annual All-Hall Ball, where students go to a formal dance held at one of the nearby hotels. Generally speaking, there will always be something going on at UCSB, whether alcohol-related or not, and students have a wide array of activities to choose from when deciding upon their weekend plans.

Surfer Guys and O.C. Girls

When asked to describe the general population of UCSB, most students respond with one word: "surfer." The guys especially are part of the "surfer crowd—you know, like cargo shorts, t-shirts, sunglasses, maybe a hooded sweatshirt if the weather is cool." Girls have been described as walking "right out of the O.C, complete with highlighted hair, huge sunglasses, short skirts, and Uggs. "When popped collars were popular, absolutely everyone had a popped collar," said one student. "And people are very fashion-conscious ... Abercrombie, Gucci, Chanel, you name it." While this kind of culture is the norm for many students, some find it rather troubling. "It's definitely a high-income school," noted one freshman. "That's probably why the Greek life is so popular here, because so many people can afford it. It does make me feel uncomfortable once in a while."

Still, everyone agrees that the students are all very friendly, welcoming people. With such a large student population and large classes, however, sometimes it can be hard to meet people. According to one student, "TAs try to promote interaction among the students in discussion sections, but even so, it can be really hard to meet other kids if you're not involved in an extracurricular activity." Many recommend the freshman summer program as a way to meet people. The dating scene is typical of most colleges, where "dating" doesn't really exist since most romantic interactions take the form of one of two extremes: either random hook-ups or long-term relationships.

The school is not typically described as being diverse. Students say that their school is known for being a basically Caucasian campus. "There are a lot of culturally/ethnically based clubs and organizations," said one student. "But the actual diversity here is pretty low." In terms of geography, most students are from California. "I've only ever met three people who are from outside the state," one junior commented.

Life Along The Beach

The majority of freshmen opt to live in the dorms for at least their first year (often moving out to I.V. for their second or third year) because everyone tends to feel that dorm life is an essential part of the college experience and it's an easy way to meet people. "The dorms are kind of small, but the quality is good, and the food isn't bad," said one freshman. The Santa Cruz dorms are located closest to the beach and are usually considered to be the "most fun." Students who move to I.V. in later years love it, saying that "there are always people coming and going, and it's not as loud as you'd think it would be."

When asked to describe the campus itself, one student observed that it is "very spread out. There are a lot of empty green spaces." The campus is slowly renovating its older buildings, particularly those in the science and engineering departments. The Marine Biology building is especially beautiful, with one side of the building designed to look like a lighthouse and a room at the top with windows that offer a 360-degree view of the surrounding area. The backdrop of the campus is the beautiful blue Pacific Ocean, and many of the dorms look out over the water. Several students also commented on the horseshoe-shaped lagoon, a quiet area where people can read, study, have picnics, and watch the wildlife. The student population is very active, so there are often runners taking a jog around the lagoon and down along the beach. Other favorite places on campus include the University Center, which is a great central meeting place right next to the bookstore with computers, restaurants, and a corner store for snacks, as well as the strip, the library, and the rec center. Most students agree that the campus is pretty safe at night, and members of the campus security team are always around to escort students back to their dorms if they feel anxious about walking back alone.

In the neighborhood immediately surrounding the campus, students can take advantage of off-campus eateries such as the famous Freebirds (open 24 hours) for delicious burritos and nachos, Pita Pit, Starbucks, Chili's, Borders, a Japanese restaurant, and more. "Some places are a little far, and if you don't want to walk, we have a free bus system," explained one sophomore. There is also a convenient cab system from downtown Santa Barbara to I.V.

Get Involved

Varsity sports do not enjoy a huge following on campus (USCB does not have a football team), although the soccer team is "pretty good." The biggest (and sometimes the only) sports fans are the members of Gauchos Locos, a club that goes to every sporting event and tries to spark more school spirit. Although students may not watch the games, they do often participate in sports through intramurals. Soccer, softball, volleyball, and lacrosse are always popular. Students may also stay active in the Rec Center, which boasts a field with artificial grass, several outdoor pools, two weight rooms for non-athletes, racquetball courts, a climbing wall, and a roller hockey arena. Some unique club sports include kayaking, snorkeling, scuba diving, sailing, surfing, and skiing.

> "Not a lot of campuses are located on a beach, and where else can you have surfing and skiing within such a close distance?"

There are a number of other clubs and organizations on campus where students can pursue individual interests and meet people with similar passions. One of the more prominent is the Community Affairs Board, a service-based organization. Many people in dorms participate in the Hall Council, a group that throws events for the dorms. Sororities and fraternities are popular, as are ethnic clubs and some religious organizations. People also enjoy a break-dancing club, a swing and ballroom dance club, shows put on by a Filipino urban dance group, and performances by a cappella groups, who usually perform at fund raisers and variety shows.

California Dreamin'

Students say that they enjoy the closeness of the community at UCSB, particularly in I.V., and that the entire campus is permeated by a "warm, homey, kick-back kind of feeling." Said one student, "One of the most unique aspects of our school is the location.

Not a lot of campuses are located on a beach, and where else can you have surfing and skiing within such a close distance?" Many people say that they are pleasantly surprised when they arrive at USCB to discover that there is more to the school than wild, drunken parties at beachfront apartments (although the party scene is definitely dynamic). When asked if she would choose USCB again if she had to do it all over, a senior responded, "Yeah, I think I would. It's pretty cool here. It's a closer-knit community and a smaller town than UCLA with all the benefits of a California setting, so really, why not?"—*Lindsay Starck*

FYIs
If you come to UCSB, you'd better bring "a pair of Rainbow sandals, a bike, and a swimsuit."
What's the typical weekend schedule? "Friday night party or see a movie, Saturday go to the beach and then go to I.V., and Sunday get work done."
If I could change one thing about UCSB, "I'd reduce the emphasis on drinking—even the professors are almost encouraging it! It kind of makes you feel dumb if you don't party as much as everyone else."
Three things every UCSB student should do before graduating are "have a bonfire on the beach, try a Freebirds burrito, party in I.V. on Halloween."

University of California / Santa Cruz

Address: UC Santa Cruz, 1156 High St., Santa Cruz, CA 95064
Phone: 831-459-4008
E-mail Address: admissions@cats.ucsc.edu
Web site URL: www.ucsc.edu
Year Founded: 1965
Private or Public: public
Religious affiliation: none
Location: suburban
Regular Application Deadline: 1-Dec
Number of Applicants: NA
Percent Accepted: 80%
Percent Accepted who enroll: 17%
Number Entering: NA
Number of Transfers Accepted each Year: NA
Mean SAT: NA
Mean ACT: 24
Middle 50% SAT range: V:500–630, M:520–640

Middle 50% ACT range: 22–28
Early admission program (EA/ ED/ NA): NA
ED or EA Acceptance Rate: NA
Full time Undergraduate enrollment: 13,941
Total enrollment: NA
Percent Male: 47%
Percent Female: 53%
Total Percent Minority: 48%
Percent African-American: 3%
Percent Asian/Pacific Islander: 20%
Percent Hispanic: 15%
Percent Native-American: 1%
Percent Other: NA
Percent in-state / out of state: 97%/3%
Percent from Public HS: 85%

Retention Rate: 89%
Graduation Rate: 69%
Percent in On-campus housing: 48%
Percent affiliated with Greek system: 2%
Percent Varsity or Club Athletes: NA
Number of official organized extracurricular organizations: 129
3 Most popular majors: Business/Managerial Economics, Classics and Classical Languages, Literature
Student/Faculty ratio: 19:01
Tuition and Fees: NA
Cost for Room and Board: NA
Percent receiving Financial aid, first-year: 48%

Though it is known among Californian high school students as one of the easier University of California campuses to be admitted to, UCSC nonetheless offers one of the best educations of all public universities in the country. A school of almost 15,000 people located in a small coastal town directly south of San Francisco and San Jose, UCSC offers students a liberal arts-oriented education along with a quiet and picturesque, yet friendly environment.

UCSC models its system after other, earlier UC schools. With its large freshman class of more than 3000, 61 majors, and the quarter system unique to the UC schools, UCSC allows its students to pursue exactly what they wish with extensive support from faculty and fellow students.

A Relaxing Experience in Education

Once the most famous aspect of the UCSC education was its pass/fail grading system. The only difference between an A+ and a D– were the words in the evaluations of the students written by professors. The evaluations were usually not accessible to potential employers and the graduate school admission officers, causing the system to be finally revamped and replaced by the A through F used in most schools.

> "People just fall asleep in the back of the lecture hall as soon as the professor starts talking; no worries, the professor doesn't see them."

However, the impact of the pass/fail system continues. Students can take up to one-quarter of their classes pass/fail. At the same time, UCSC is known for its minimal course requirements, allowing students to take most of their classes in the fields they are interested in. Also, almost all incoming freshmen receive large amounts of UCSC course credits for almost all of their AP scores above 3, allowing many freshmen to enter UCSC as sophomores in their first year. Therefore, as one freshman pointed out, the amount of courses students actually have to try hard is at UCSC "next to nothing, so I can do extracurricular activities for hours even during weekdays."

As a result of such a relaxing academic atmosphere, it is not difficult to find some of the most carefree students in the entire University of California system at UCSC. Because the Core classes of a UCSC education consist of writing-focused large lecture classes of more than a hundred students and unbelievably favorable curves, some students find classes a little less challenging than they'd like. As one freshman remarked, "People just fall asleep in the back of the lecture hall as soon as the professor starts talking; no worries, the professor doesn't see them."

However, once students choose majors, the classes can become fairly small in size and very competitive. Students can also get a personal touch from the professors in these small, often seminar-like classes. One freshman remarked on her class atmosphere, "The people are all pretty friendly and the RA's [equivalent to Teaching Assistants] are very cool." It is a common feeling that the personal academic feel of UCSC increases as the time of study increases.

Real Definition of Coed

UCSC's campus consists of many residential colleges, each consisting of several large dorm buildings. In each of the residential/academic colleges, there are several hundred students and separate facilities such as gym/exercise area and dining halls. It is said that there are large differences in the quality of facilities from college to college, especially in terms of dining hall food. As one girl pointed out, "The food at my college (Crown) is pretty good but there are other places that are best avoided." Also, each college has their own education principle and emphasizes different subjects. Thus, the Core classes in different colleges all have different themes and thus are taught differently.

It should be noted that even with such great dorms, UCSC students do not usually just live within the bubble that is the university itself. With its closeness to the city of Santa Cruz and its relatively relaxing academic atmosphere, UCSC students find large amount of time to explore the city they are part of. One freshman said, "I haven't gone downtown very often, but it seems neat." Most students have cars, and even though it is difficult to get a parking permit on campus, it is also not uncommon for students to leave UCSC and Santa Cruz all together on weekends and long holiday breaks for trips to such places as Golden Gate Bridge in San Francisco and Yosemite National Park. Students find great pleasure in exploring all the tourist spots in and around Santa Cruz or Northern California in general.

"Go Banana Slugs?"

Students complain sometimes that there is relatively little to do on campus, even on the weekends. According to many students, one of the great drawbacks of UCSC is its lack of a football team. "We are just missing out on college football!" one male student said with dismay. "There is so little school spirit here, because we have no decent sports teams!" another student noted with sorrow. For those who enjoy tailgating sports team, UCSC is not the choice.

Greek life is also close to nonexistent in UCSC; sororities and fraternities do not have their own houses. There is no obvious "rush" for sororities and fraternities and not many students join the few choices that are available. When asked why UCSC students do not care about Greek life, one student responded, "What's the point? The parties are not good without hot girls, and there are no good-looking girls here." Another student interjected, "Haven't you heard of the saying? 'Nine of ten Californian girls are hot, the tenth goes to UCSC.'" Apparently, female beauty is not prevalent at UCSC. The male students describe the typical female students at UCSC as lacking. But the female students returned the favor with equally negative terms to describe the typical UCSC guy.

Also, even though clubs and organizations of any kind and any interests are available to students, participation is usually sporadic and the presence of the majority of the campus organizations is not obvious enough to be known among the majority of the student body. This is why so many UCSC students typically spend weekends outside of campus in the city or driving through Northern California. As one student remarked, "what's the point of staying on campus on the weekend? The parties are lame, the clubs are dead, and the homework is done."—*Xiaochen Su*

FYI
If you come to UCSC, you better bring "a warm jacket, an open mind, and a pair of walking shoes."
What's the typical weekend schedule? "Sleeping, eating, homework, hanging out with people"
If you could change one thing about UCSC, I'd have "slightly larger shower stalls."
Three things every student at UCSC should do before graduating are "satisfy all the requirements, not suck at life, and have a major."

The University of the Redlands

Address: University of Redlands, 1200 East Colton Avenue PO Box 3080, Redlands, CA 92373-0999

Phone: 909-748-8187

E-mail Address: admissions@redlands.edu

Web site URL: www.redlands.edu

Year Founded: 1907

Private or Public: private

Religious affiliation: none

Location: small city

Regular Application Deadline: 1-Mar

Number of Applicants: 3,480

Percent Accepted: 65.3%

Percent Accepted who enroll: 27%

Number Entering: 613

Number of Transfers Accepted each Year: varies

Mean SAT: 1,175

Mean ACT: 24

Middle 50% SAT range: 1,080–1,260

Middle 50% ACT range: 22–26

Early admission program (EA/ ED/ NA): NA

ED or EA Acceptance Rate: NA

Full time Undergraduate enrollment: 2,313

Total enrollment: 2,477

Percent Male: 42%

Percent Female: 58%

Total Percent Minority: 23%

Percent African-American: 3%

Percent Asian/Pacific Islander: 3%

Percent Hispanic: 11%

Percent Native-American: 1%

Percent Other: 5%

Percent in-state / out of state: 30%/70%

Percent from Public HS: NA

Retention Rate: 85%

Graduation Rate: 60%

Percent in On-campus housing: 67%

Percent affiliated with Greek system: 3%

Percent Varsity or Club Athletes: NA

Number of official organized extracurricular organizations: 105

3 Most popular majors: Psychology, Liberal Studies, Business

Student/Faculty ratio: 11:01

Tuition and Fees: $28,776.00

Cost for Room and Board: $9,360.00

Percent receiving Financial aid, first-year: 81.7%

Boasting an enviable location in the midst of Southern California, the Univeristy of the Redlands lays at the base of the magnificent San Bernardino Mountains. The desert landscape is indicative of the great weather year round—"it goes below zero only a few days every winter"—but also serves as a reminder that a Redlands experience without a car can quickly turn into a very isolated one. Most students find a way to get around the small city and many say they appreciate the college's small size, citing the 600-student entering class size and the 12:1 student-faculty ratio as proof that they are more than just numbers here. "Coming from a small high school, I feel like Redlands has helped make the transition a very smooth one," says one junior. "Almost all of my professors know my name and I often see them outside of class." With a beautiful campus, small classes, and professors who are interested in teaching, Redlands seems to offer a good deal; that is if you're willing to pick up the tab.

When Nature Calls—Being Aware of Your Surroundings

The Redlands campus has been used as a set for recent films such as "Rules of Attraction" and "Joy Ride," but even if the college grounds are attractive, it's the surroundings that stand out the most, for they offer great opportunities for students to interact with nature. Students recognize their surroundings as full of opportunities for wildlife observation, rock climbing, hiking, mountain biking, photography, or just camping out. To this end, Redlands helps organize "Outdoor Programs" which may last from as short as a weekend afternoon to a month during the summer. "Going out on the hot air balloon was the coolest experience ever!" recalls one student. Other available excursions include bungee jumping, skiing, snowboarding, skydiving, and surfing.

For those who wish to take their own initiative, Redlands has everything the casual outdoorsman needs: tents, sleeping bags, backpacks, and rain gear are all available to students for free. Although a credit card is required as deposit, students generally agree that the rental shop is very accessible. "As long as you plan a few days in advance, you can usually get what you need."

> **Redlands has everything the casual outdoorsman needs . . . for free.**

Unfortunately, while its surroundings may be a paradise for the outward bound, the small city of Redlands (population approximately 60,000) does not have much to offer. The town is a little far from central campus, but almost everyone either owns a car or knows someone who does. The trolley system that operates during the mornings and afternoons doesn't run during the nights, but it's usually easy to catch a ride. Downtown Redlands boasts many of the most popular fast food shops, as well as some fancier Italian restaurants and coffee shops which students and townspeople frequent. Besides going downtown, students use their cars to "catch a late night snack or go shopping at the nearby outlet malls." One student agrees that "Redlands will definitely get dull very quickly if you don't get out often." He suggested that he and his friends often go into downtown Los Angeles or San Diego, which are only about an hour away. Some upperclassmen also go to Las Vegas— about five hours away.

Making Service a Way of Life
Although students often reveal their concern for the lack of economic diversity at Redlands, one thing that can be said about the kids here is that they know how to get their hands dirty to serve others. Community service is integrated into the curriculum and students must complete a combination of service instruction and outreach requirements. While some students serve at the local high schools, others use their summers or May terms to go as far as Africa. One senior recalls her experience with helping victims of Hurricane Katrina as "one of the most enriching experiences of my entire life." She added, "I felt like I was really making a difference in people's lives and I really want to go back." The same student agreed that Redlands seems to attract a more service-oriented crowd, "but it's not like a huge deal for everyone."

A Bold Academic Experiment
The flagship of the Redlands academic experience is the Johnston Center for Integra-

tive Studies. Requiring a supplemental application, the center admits a limited number of the incoming freshman class. Students in the Johnston Center have unparalleled control over their education. Students may create their own major and choose their own courses. They are also allowed to write contracts for individual courses, leaving it to the students to decide how they will go about meeting their educational needs and which requirements they will fulfill. Quizzes may be substituted for longer tests or papers, and vice-versa. It's also possible to increase or decrease the credits for many courses by contracting to do more or less work.

However, as is true of many things, there's a catch: each contract must be negotiated between the student and the professor and complete academic freedom is more of an aspiration than a reality. All Redlands students are also expected to graduate with sufficient "depth" and "breadth" in their studies. "The distributional requirements are complex and pretty burdensome," points out a freshman. "I think it's a little easier for the Johnston kids because they don't have to take any particular courses, but for those in the LAF [Liberal Arts Foundation], there's not that much freedom because you have to be worrying about your requirements so much."

Unlike large research universities, Redlands is focused on teaching. Students express a lot of respect for their faculty and really like the individualized attention. "My expectations have been surpassed over and over again," says one student. Another student adds: "Having such small classes helps me keep motivated. I feel like I know my professors and my professors know me. I also know who I'm working with and that makes me feel much more comfortable. I don't think I'd be as motivated if I were taking larger classes at a bigger school." Most people refer to their peers as "competent" or "smart", but generally agree that the school "does not attract the biggest minds. Most kids care about their classes and study, but their interest rarely goes beyond the classes they're taking. This is not the kind of place where you'll find people discussing philosophy all day, although politics seem to be a common dinner table topic."

One aspect of Redlands that is appreciated by almost everyone in the community is the strong emphasis that is placed on study abroad. Although the focus is often on European countries to the exclusion of other regions of the world, there are ample opportunities for Redlands students to study a semester or a whole year abroad through a university-approved program. The most popular study abroad destination is Salzburg, Germany. Credit and financial aid are easily transferable. Students hoping to spend less time abroad may also opt to take one of the courses during the "May term." The May term refers to one month of intensive study, usually undertaken abroad. Courses during the May term include "Japanese Gardens" and "Economics in Buenos Aires."

Housing for All Tastes

Redlands doesn't approach housing in a "one-size-fits-all" fashion. While all undergraduates are guaranteed a room on-campus, every year students can choose to live one of the dozen or so different halls. Each one of these housing complexes has its own perks and advantages. Some of them, like East Hall, are for freshmen only, while Cortner Hall and Melrose Hall tend to have more upperclassmen. Melrose, with its extended quiet hours, is also seen as a good fit for the more studious. On the other hand there's North Hall, the closest to the gymnasium and thereby host to many of Redlands' jocks. Some of the halls are same-sex, but most are co-ed.

"Most people seem to be happy with their living conditions," says one junior. "The most common complaint about housing is that some halls are not air-conditioned and it can get extremely hot during the summer." Students are advised to bring a fan—or several. "It was pretty bad the first few weeks of the fall semester," notes a freshman. "However, for most of the year the weather was just perfect." Still, those who hail from colder weather may often be less excited. SNOW (Students in Need of Winter) is a student group that brings together all those who are interested in following the ski season in the nearby Rockies.

Besides the regular housing options, students may also elect to live at one of the fraternity or sorority houses. Although there are several Greek organizations around campus, they don't seem to dominate the social scene. "Generally, there are a few guys who are really into it, but Greek life just isn't as big as you would expect." Students estimate that less than ten percent of their peers have donned Greek letters.

It's Not Just About the Academics

Redlands offers a fairly wide variety of extracurricular activities and student groups. Opportunities for giving back to the community are plentiful through volunteer groups and there are many student-run religious and cultural organizations as well. The university also has an outstanding debate society, often placing among the top in the country. In fact, debate is valued so much at Redlands that the university offers merit scholarships for outstanding debaters.

Everyone has an opportunity to play sports—at some level—at Redlands. "It's fairly easy to be a walk-on at Redlands if you played in high school," says one junior who plays for the basketball team. "Some kids certainly get recruited, but some sports membership may be almost half walk-ons." The most popular club sports include golf, lacrosse, ultimate frisbee and ice hockey. There is also an equestrian club.

While many find Redlands too small by the end of their four years, most enjoy the tight-knit community it affords. Within that community, some complain of "a total lack of diversity," and one student remarked that the stereotypical Redlands student was "your average intellectual rich white kids from the West Coast." This does seem to be changing, as Redlands has been recruiting more widely and applications have been increasing significantly in recent years. For all its insularity, Redlands seems to be about unexpected surprises. Whether students enjoy uncovering these hidden treasures will dictate whether they survive their four years out in the oasis of the Californian desert.—*Gerardo Giacoman*

FYI

If you come to Redlands, you'd better bring: "a car or a friend who has one; also, bring a fan—or several in case your housing unit is not air-conditioned."

What's the typical weekend schedule? "Fraternity parties are prevalent during the weekends, but with the recent crackdown on alcohol consumption, weekend nights usually involve chilling/ hanging out with friends, or getting out of Redlands to find a real party."

If I could change one thing about Redlands, I'd "move it closer to Las Vegas and fight the formation of social cliques."

Three things that every student should do before graduating are: "attend the festival of lights, make a 2 a.m. Del Taco run, drive to Mexico for Spring Break."

University of Southern California

Address: USC, University Park,
Los Angeles, CA 90089
Phone: 213-740-1111
E-mail Address:
admitusc@usc.edu
Web site URL: www.usc.edu
Year Founded: 1880
Private or Public: private
Religious affiliation: none
Location: urban
**Regular Application
Deadline:** 11-Jan
Number of Applicants:
33,979
Percent Accepted: 25%
**Percent Accepted who
enroll:** 32%
Number Entering: 2,763
**Number of Transfers
Accepted each Year:** 2,071
Mean SAT: 1,374
Mean ACT: 30
Middle 50% SAT range:
1,280–1,460

Middle 50% ACT range:
28–32
**Early admission program
(EA/ ED/ NA):** NA
ED or EA Acceptance Rate:
NA
**Full time Undergraduate
enrollment:** 16,449
Total enrollment: 33,000
Percent Male: 50%
Percent Female: 50%
Total Percent Minority: 41%
Percent African-American:
6%
**Percent Asian/Pacific
Islander:** 21%
Percent Hispanic: 13%
Percent Native-American:
1%
Percent Other: NA
**Percent in-state / out of
state:** 66%/34%
Percent from Public HS: 55%
Retention Rate: 96%

Graduation Rate: 84%
**Percent in On-campus
housing:** 36%
**Percent affiliated with
Greek system:** 18%
**Percent Varsity or Club
Athletes:** NA
**Number of official
organized extracurricular
organizations:** 645
3 Most popular majors:
Business Administration/
Management;
Communications Studies/
Speech Communication
and Rhetoric
Student/Faculty ratio: 10:01
Tuition and Fees: $33,314
Cost for Room and Board:
$10,144
**Percent receiving Financial
aid, first-year:** 40%

S et in sun-drenched Southern California, in the heart of "The City of Angels," the University of Southern
California has a distinctly West Coast
atmosphere that would be hard to find anywhere else. "Everyone here is so incredibly
stylish. It's almost competitive," remarked
one USC freshman. Indeed, fashion may be
important to the trendsetters at this school,
but a large and diverse student body can satisfy the interests of anyone. The theme of
taking pride in appearance extends to the
USC campus itself. The stunning and well-
kept campus has often appeared in film as
other colleges, including Harvard in
"Legally Blonde." USC's campus, although in
the middle of the inner city, is surprisingly
quiet and safe; the campus is fenced-off from
the city, and all entrances are guarded, allowing a peaceful environment for intellectual
pursuits.

An Academic Challenge
The College of Letters, Arts and Sciences offers a variety of majors to all undergraduates, but some decide to choose majors
from some of the 17 professional schools at
USC. Some of the most famous schools

include the School of Cinema-Television,
the Annenberg School for Communication,
the Marshall Business School, and the
Viterbi School of Engineering. Undergraduates must apply to enter a major program at
any of these schools, but transferring between schools or double-majoring between
two is common.

The School of Cinema-Television, enrolling
900 students total, boasts acclaimed faculty
and top-notch equipment. In one popular
introductory film course, class members
watch screenings of new or unreleased films
and hear analysis from "the highest paid
professor at the school," who receives rave
reviews from his students. "It's not just a lecture, it's an experience," explained one undergrad.

The Marshall School offers one of the
most highly-ranked business programs in
the country and a variety of internships in
Los Angeles. As a distinctive feature of the
Marshall program, leadership laboratory
classes simulate the business world to give
students hands-on experience. Between the
School of Letters, Arts and Sciences and the
professional schools, one student remarked
that "there are classes here for anything you

could ever imagine." Adding a minor or a second major to a degree is common and encouraged for those with the motivation to take on the additional course work.

Even though many introductory classes are large and lecture-style, any curious student has "good opportunities to meet the professor." Also, lectures are broken up into TA-led discussion sections and extra practice sessions that provide opportunities for clarification and extra help. With these sources of additional instruction available, students rarely need private tutoring: "You would have to be new to chemistry and speak another language to need a tutor." The only reported problems with TAs occur in the math department, and then only with English skills—"I've heard horror stories," reports one student. Writing classes tend to be small and interactive.

> "Everyone is so incredibly stylish. It's almost competitive."

For the General Education requirement, USC students are required to take at least one course in each of six categories: Western Cultures and Traditions, Global Cultures and Traditions, Scientific Inquiry, Science and its Significance, Arts and Letters, and Social Issues. In addition, all students must fulfill a two-part writing requirement, as well as a class in diversity. Some of these requirements, however, can be met with AP credit. Students seem to enjoy their GE classes, which they usually begin their freshman year. They find the courses "really valuable" and the requirements unobtrusive. What bothers students, however, is that many of the GE classes are led by TAs.

When it comes time to hit the books, productive students choose to study in some of USC's large libraries. The private study rooms in the main library are especially popular. These small rooms contain all the essentials for group work (whiteboard, computer, large table) and can be reserved in advance. Another library makes use of a hierarchical floor system, in which students on each floor remain quieter than the room below it. The top room is strictly "for reading only."

Mixed Diversity

Racial diversity at USC is described as "well-balanced." Geographical diversity at USC comes from the presence of out-of-state students—nearly half of the student body hails from outside of California, but only "a few" international students can be found. The reputation of USC students as "rich white kids" has all but disappeared. The opportunity that USC affords draws in some of the most highly sought-after students from the West Coast. Students are ambitious, talented, and academic: "I've met some amazing people . . . really, really great people," gushed one Trojan.

Livin' Large

Students at USC praise its housing for its many newly renovated dorms. Even though a student may be assigned a small dorm room, like some found in Marks Tower, the rooms generally feature updated amenities. "New/North" (New Residential College and North Residential College) is the most social dorm on campus, decidedly opposite from "the Honors Dorm," where it can be sometimes "hard to meet people." Students can even opt to live with other students from their professional school so that a floor may house only business or cinema students, for example. A detailed housing form helps to ensure successful roommate matches. For those who favor regular house-cleaning and room service to the traditional dorm experience, a USC-rented hotel provides a luxurious (though pricey) option.

Though they're serious about maintaining their authority, Residential Advisors are generally liked. Some students even go so far as to call their RAs their "best friends." A required one-on-one meeting between student and RA at the beginning of the year helps solve any initial problems and clear up questions. For academic advising, undergraduates consult faculty advisors, to which students are assigned by major.

On campus, USC students have their pick from several dining options that prepare quality fare. Undergrads can choose from three cafeterias: Parkside serves near-gourmet quality food; at Café 84, meals are cooked to order; and EVK has a reputation for good breakfasts, though its other meals are "nothing exciting."

Partying like a Trojan

Students agree that social life at USC centers around "The Row," where fraternities and sororities are located. "I think the thing that surprised me the most was how dominant the Greek system is on a student's social life. It seems like every night revolves around the fraternities that are having parties," commented one undergrad. Guys often feel the pressure to join Greek life more than girls do. "If you want to be social and you're a guy, join a frat," remarked one student.

RAs strictly enforce the no-alcohol policy in dorms: "If they catch you, they have to write you up for it." Other options for nightlife can be found in the surrounding Los Angeles community, but an automobile is a necessity: "if you want to go out to dinner or anything like that, you need a car." Some students find personal vehicles indispensable for leaving campus, but for most, having access to a car is enough.

Away from the Classroom

Apart from social life, USC students are involved in literally hundreds of student groups. Student government, such as Student Senate, is especially popular. A cappella, dance, and improv comedy groups are a favored form of entertainment for any weekend night. Religious organizations have many active members and frequently schedule trips and activities.

Jobs are readily available even for those not on a work study financial aid plan. Students find it easy to work during the school year, as on-campus employers "are pretty good about working with your schedule."

USC students place high value on personal fitness, as the gym is always packed. For those looking for more organized activities, intramural sports offer an attractive alternative. These competitions most frequently take place between Greek houses, but intramurals organized according to dormitory are also popular. Men's club soccer, club rugby, and club Ultimate Frisbee rank among the most competitive of the club sports. Regardless of the sport, physical activity seems to be a key part of the Trojan spirit.

Being such a large, competitive university, USC is home to Army, Navy, and Air Force ROTC detachments. Officers-in-training can be seen in uniform around campus or in physical training.

Tribute to Troy

The strong sense of community among Trojans is a major draw for potential students. No one attending a USC football game can ignore the fans' love for the school. In the fall, USC football games are "huge." The award-winning USC marching band, which makes elaborate formations on the football field during halftime, is awe-inspiring.

A key part of the Trojan spirit involves adopting an aversion to anything and everything UCLA. Although the rivalry between USC and UCLA seems vicious, most see it as an excuse for USC students to show pride in their school. One student concedes that "UCLA is otherwise a great school. The rivalry is just fun and unifying."

It often comes down to particulars when comparing the two schools. On food, one student feels that "UCLA's food beats SC's food like SC beat Oklahoma. No contest." The general consensus is that USC gives more personal attention and aims for practicality in most disciplines.

Internship-seekers and graduates soon find that alumni do not leave their pride behind with the school. The number of jobs and internships available through alumni connections is often referred to as the "Trojan Network." Students find the availability of work in the Los Angeles film industry especially valuable.

With the great number of connections available to USC graduates, it would seem that students just need to graduate in order to be successful. But don't get the wrong impression—USC is by no means a cakewalk. USC students study just as hard as students at any other prestigious university. "It seems like everyone is genuinely happy," one student noted, undoubtedly due to an ideal mix of work and play. If you are looking for a rigorous education with a fun-loving atmosphere at a school you can be proud of, the Trojan life may be calling for you.—*Eric Klein*

FYI
If you come to USC you'd better bring "an air conditioner—the dorms get hot in the summer."
What is the typical weekend schedule? "Go to a frat party on Thursday, drive into L.A. on Friday night, attend a football or basketball game on Saturday, and study on Sunday."
If I could change one thing about USC, I'd "popularize alternatives to Greek life."
Three things every student at USC should do before graduating are "go to the USC-UCLA football game, shop on Melrose, and see a performance at the Staples Center."

Whittier College

Address: Whittier College, 13046 Philadelphia Street, Whittier, California 90608
Phone: 562-907-4870
E-mail Address: admission@whittier.edu
Web site URL: www.whittier.edu
Year Founded: 1887
Private or Public: private
Religious affiliation: none
Location: suburban
Regular Application Deadline: rolling
Number of Applicants: NA
Percent Accepted: 58%
Percent Accepted who enroll: 19%
Number Entering: NA
Number of Transfers Accepted each Year: NA
Mean SAT: 1,072
Mean ACT: 23

Middle 50% SAT range: 960–1,180
Middle 50% ACT range: 22–24
Early admission program (EA/ ED/ NA): EA
ED or EA Acceptance Rate: NA
Full time Undergraduate enrollment: 1,325
Total enrollment: 1,327
Percent Male: 46%
Percent Female: 54%
Total Percent Minority: 53%
Percent African-American: 4%
Percent Asian/Pacific Islander: 8%
Percent Hispanic: 27%
Percent Native-American: 1%
Percent Other: NA
Percent in-state / out of state: 30% out

Percent from Public HS: NA
Retention Rate: 72%
Graduation Rate: 55%
Percent in On-campus housing: NA
Percent affiliated with Greek system: 26%
Percent Varsity or Club Athletes: NA
Number of official organized extracurricular organizations: 68
3 Most popular majors: Business Management, Child Development, English
Student/Faculty ratio: 13:01
Tuition and Fees: $29,860.00
Cost for Room and Board: $8,620.00
Percent receiving Financial aid, first-year: 62%

W hittier College, a small, diverse liberal arts college, is spread out over 75 acres in California, only about 12 miles southeast of the city of Los Angeles. Originally a Quaker institution, Whittier is now a secular school, but some of its original Quaker values, like emphasis on the individual and the diversity of the student body, remain an integral part of the Whittier experience.

Founding "Friends"

Whittier College began as a Quaker academy established by the Religious Society of Friends in 1887, the same year that they founded the town of Whittier itself. Although the Quaker heritage is visible in such things as the name of the weekly student newspaper, the *Quaker Campus*, there does not seem to be a large focus on the legacy of the founding Friends. One student even went so far as to have said that, despite the school's reputation as a former Quaker haven, "They don't force much on to us about Quakers."

Fewer Students, More Options

With such a small student body, Whittier is able to offer smaller, more intense classes.

The average class size is about 17, which fosters the development of real relationships between students and professors. As one student said, "It's nice to be able get to know your teachers." However, limiting the number of students in each classroom does create other issues. "Some of the classes are hard to get in to because of how small they are and the order of how [students] register," a junior complained.

Besides regular classes, students at Whittier can design their own major in the Whittier Scholars Program (WSP). Members of the WSP work closely with professors and other students to build their own curriculums, whether by creating their own major or fashioning a course of study around an existing one. Students can even incorporate off-campus experiences like study abroad and internships into their course of study, a large academic draw to Whittier.

Another way for students to expand their academic horizons is Whittier's one-month term in January. The courses offered for the "Jan Term" often cover more "fun" and interesting subjects, including classes that even integrate travel or other types of hands-on experiences into the session.

Some of the most popular options include a class on death and dying, involving a trip to the morgue, or a trip to help clean up New Orleans. Students generally enjoy Jan Term. "I love the Jan Term classes!" one Whittier student enthused.

"I love the Jan Term classes!"

Splendid Spectrum: Sports, Societies, and Student Groups

From small-town charm to the bustling activity of nearby Los Angeles, Whittier's 75-acre campus has no shortage of ways to stay busy outside of the classroom. There are tons of extracurricular activities to get involved in, from editing the *Quaker Campus*, to working on the Whittier College Radio station. And, if you can't find the club for you, never fear—the Whittier Office of Student Activities specializes in helping students create their own clubs or groups.

On a typical weekend, a lot of people spend time partying with societies, special fraternity-type organizations unique to Whittier. The societies host numerous social events and remain an important part of Whittier's history and traditions. Founded in the 1920s, the societies are behind most of the biggest parties on campus. If that's not your scene, never fear—students also report that there are plays, movies, and concerts on campus to entertain them. And, for the more adventurous, L.A. has a whole world of restaurants, museums, and shopping to amuse even the pickiest of procrastinators.

In terms of sports, Whittier has 22 Division III varsity teams on which students keep busy, the most popular of which is definitely lacrosse. Aside from the varsity teams, students can choose from a multitude of intramural sports, often played outside in the region's year-round temperate climate.

Overall, students agree that they can find whatever they want in Whittier's diverse campus. Although students may venture to downtown Los Angeles or the nearby Pacific coastline, they need not look beyond their own community for exciting opportunities among familiar faces.—*Suzanne Salgado*

FYI

If you come to Whittier, you'd better bring "pictures, posters, decorations and anything that gives you a sense of comfort from home."

What's the typical weekend schedule? "Get up at noon or so, do whatever you can on Saturday, and then Sunday is homework day."

If I could change one thing about Whittier it would be "make smaller classes easier to get in to."

Three things every student at Whittier should do before graduating are "study abroad, get involved, and take advantage of the free services and fun events provided for students"

Colorado

Address: Colorado College, 14 E. Cache La Poudre St., Colorado Springs, CO 80903

Phone: 719-389-6344

E-mail Address: admission@coloradocollege.edu

Web site URL: www.coloradocollege.edu

Year Founded: 1874

Private or Public: private

Religious affiliation: none

Location: urban

Regular Application Deadline: 16-Jan

Number of Applicants: 4,386

Percent Accepted: 34%

Percent Accepted who enroll: 33%

Number Entering: 492

Number of Transfers Accepted each Year: 81

Mean SAT: NA

Mean ACT: NA

Middle 50% SAT range: 1,240–1,400

Middle 50% ACT range: 27–30

Early admission program (EA/ ED/ NA): both

ED or EA Acceptance Rate: 39%

Full time Undergraduate enrollment: 1,939

Total enrollment: 1,998

Percent Male: 43%

Percent Female: 57%

Total Percent Minority: 14%

Percent African-American: 2%

Percent Asian/Pacific Islander: 4%

Percent Hispanic: 7%

Percent Native-American: 1%

Percent Other: 4%

Percent in-state / out of state: 26%/74%

Percent from Public HS: 58%

Retention Rate: 94%

Graduation Rate: 83%

Percent in On-campus housing: 76%

Percent affiliated with Greek system: 23%

Percent Varsity or Club Athletes: NA

Number of official organized extracurricular organizations: 92

Most popular majors: Economics, English

Student/Faculty ratio: 10:01

Tuition and Fees: $32,124.00

Cost for Room and Board: $8,052.00

Percent receiving Financial aid, first-year: 91%

C olorado College boasts a distinctive academic system and an amazing locale, as it is surrounded by some of the biggest and most beautiful mountains in North America. The college is admired not only for its solid academic foundation, but also for the wealth of outdoor opportunities available to students and for its intimate, close-knit community.

One by One

One of Colorado College's most unique and intriguing distinctions is the Block Plan, an academic system characterized by intense, focused study on one class for three and a half weeks. "The Block Plan, above anything else, is the reason I came to CC," said one student. "I love the total immersion learning." The word most commonly used to describe the system is "intense," as classes meet every day for three hours: each day of class on the Block Plan is the equivalent of a week's worth of classes on a normal semester schedule. In total, there are eight blocks per year at CC, and each block is separated by a four-day weekend. "The block breaks are a fantastic reprieve," commented one student. "You have absolutely nothing hanging over your head." Another benefit of the system is the lack of a finals week, because students have one final at the end of each block.

Students acknowledge that the Block Plan seems intimidating at first, but they say it isn't as overwhelming as it sounds because there are no other subjects, papers, or homework to worry about. One outstanding advantage of the system is that it facilitates field trips, field study and classes held outside the traditional campus setting. Because the professor and the students of the course are only focusing on that one subject, "professors have the opportunity to take students away for a week or for a block anywhere in the world." A disadvantage of the system, said one student, "is that it can be frustrating if you don't like the class you're in. Still, all you have to do is get through a couple of weeks, and then you're done. It makes the prospect of a calculus class much easier to tolerate."

At the Bidding Block

The average class size at CC is 13 students, and all classes are capped at 25. The small class size and intimacy fostered by this kind of setting encourage discussion, thereby promoting a strong student-faculty connection. Professors are extremely approachable, especially because of the fact that "this class is their life for that period of time." One student said that several of her friends have gone over to professors' houses for breakfast or dinner, and that everyone calls the professors by their first names. "Because you develop such a close relationship with them, you learn more about them as human beings instead of as lecturers in front of a big class at a larger university."

Students also develop close relationships with their classmates. Although this often leads to lasting friendships, it may sometimes lead to an unofficial phenomenon referred to as "block friends." According to one student, a "block friend" is someone whom another student gets to know really well during the block, but when the block is over and everyone is suddenly immersed into a completely new subject with completely different people, the student may never see that friend again. "The block plan, no matter how much I love it, can be a little socially staggering," he observed.

Competition between students in class is "nonexistent" because of the discussion-based setting. Because students are all going through the material together, there is a "community atmosphere" in which "you're not competing with kids for a grade, you're working with them to get the grade." Said one student, "There is definitely a certain sense of camaraderie; you're so immersed in your subject and so is the person next to you, and no one else on campus is taking that class at that time, so you're sharing a unique experience."

More than a third of the student body graduates with a degree in the natural sciences, which is the main reason why the university calls itself "a liberal arts and sciences" college. Registration for classes is a bidding process in which every student is allotted a certain number of points based on seniority. Some classes are difficult to get into, and seniors have a better chance of getting in simply because they can bid more on each class. Intro psychology is an extremely popular class, perhaps partly because each student gets a live rat at the beginning of the block (the next three weeks are focused on training that rat). Another interesting course is the biology and comparative literature class, in which students read the works of a famous butterfly expert and spend the block traveling the country and following the same path he did while tracking butterflies. Most students call the bidding system "fair," even though "it takes some strategy." All in all, people quickly get used to the Block Plan and swear that they couldn't imagine going back to the semester schedule.

Living in the Mountains

The College requires students to live on campus for the first three years, and most students choose to stay for all four. Freshmen and sophomores are usually housed in traditional dormitories, while upperclassmen have the additional option of apartment-style complexes and larger, older houses. A handful of the houses have themes that change every year, with a couple of current houses being the Mountain House (with a strong focus on the outdoors) and the Animal House (an animal appreciation group where everyone has a pet). There are also several language houses, which provide residence options for students who are studying those languages. The "mediocre" dining hall food rates a seven out of 10 for most students, but they can also use both of the different meal plan options (dining dollars and flex points) at restaurants like the charming on-campus cafe called Herb'n Farm.

The College's architecture is described as "varied," and "somewhat random," though two particularly beautiful and interesting buildings are Shove Chapel (modeled after Westminster Abbey) and the new science center, which continuously monitors the inside and outside atmospheres, self-adjusting to changes in light and temperature. The building is surrounded by different kinds of rocks that have been flown in from all over the world, making it a popular site for geology classes.

When the Weekend Rolls Around

Students at Colorado College enjoy a thriving social scene throughout the year, though the action definitely peaks on the four-day block breaks. Because almost all students live on campus, a lot of the partying occurs in dorms and residence buildings. One popular annual party is the Anything But Clothes party, where students come dressed in trash bags and cardboard boxes. Said one student, "We're not a dry campus, so people aren't flocking away to do all their partying."

The Greek system is a part of the social life, but it certainly doesn't dominate, and students claim that the best parties are those at houses where live bands are playing. Drinking is prevalent, as it is on most college campuses, but "it's not hard to avoid and it's not pushed or pressured on anyone." A few students observed that the use of pot is more common at CC than at a lot of other schools. One prominent group on campus, the Other Choices club sponsors alcohol and drug free activities that are always an enjoyable alternative to the party scene.

When it comes to clubs and student organizations, says one student, "We've got it all." There are three major a cappella groups, a popular improv group called TWIG, and a lot of other musical, cultural, political, and random groups (such as the Carnivore Club). Intramurals are huge ("really fun and really low-key"), even for less common sports such as dodgeball and broomball. Experience isn't necessary; as one student said enthusiastically, "I haven't played soccer since third grade, and this year I'm on Team Awesome!" As far as varsity sports go, the nationally-ranked hockey team has the biggest following; said one student, "Every time I see the hockey players down the hall after I've just seen them on TV, I'm always a little starstruck."

> "On the weekend all the hard-core people climb Pike's Peak at 10, make it to the top by sunrise, and then climb back down."

One major organization is the Outdoor Recreation Committee, which hosts outdoor activities and excursions throughout the year, including the freshman orientation backpacking trip. "It's a great way to meet new people, and the upperclassmen who lead the trip give you really good insight as to what the school is like," said one current freshman. The ORC deals with "everything wilderness—the organization gets lots of funding, and you can rent out

everything from skis to sleeping bags." One student summarized student extracurriculars at CC by saying, "Everyone is really active here. That's one of the things I love about it."

Also praised is the general tendency of CC students to be outgoing and incredibly friendly. "It seems like you're always getting hugs from people," commented one student. On the whole, people are pretty easygoing and casual both in dress and attitude. "We're nice people," said one student. "I walk across campus every day and I smile at nearly every person I see and just about every person smiles back at me." When asked to give a general characterization of the student body, most students said that the school had a little bit of everything and that anyone can find friends with similar interests. Another student described the students as "upper- to middle-class white hippies who are probably from one of the coasts and who are really empathetic to social and political issues." One major issue is the current lack of ethnic diversity, consistently cited as a concern of both the students and the administration.

Location, Location, Location

"You can never overlook our location," several students declared. The mountains, rivers, forests and canyons surrounding the University add a whole new aspect to college life. Students have the opportunity to take the afternoon to go fly fishing, hiking in a canyon, white-water rafting, kayaking, skiing, snowboarding, mountain climbing, or virtually any other outdoor activity they can think of. "On the weekend all the hard-core people climb Pike's Peak at 10, make it to the top by sunrise, and then climb back down," said one student. "The area is a huge selling point for the people who come here," said another. "I've lived in Colorado all my life, so I've always taken the skiing and snowboarding culture for granted. But my peers from out of state want to ski and snowboard at every possible moment." Everyone at CC, whether or not they were born in the area, takes full advantage of the rich natural surroundings and appreciates the beautiful views from the dorm room windows. One interviewee responded to the first phone call with, "Is it OK if I call you back in like 10 minutes? There are some gorgeous clouds over the mountains right now and I just want to run down and take a few pictures."

All in all, students feel that they made the

right choice in coming to Colorado College. The Block Plan is great (the block breaks are even better), the students are friendly, and the sunny skies and the beautiful mountains provide the perfect backdrop to the campus. "I love it here," concluded one student. "It truly is a fabulous place to become educated."—*Lindsay Starck*

FYI

If you come to Colorado College, you'd better bring: "skis and a sleeping bag."
What's the typical weekend schedule? "A little homework, a little partying, a little adventure."
If I could change one thing about Colorado College, "I'd make the cafeteria staff more friendly."
Three things every student at Colorado College should do before graduating are: "take a class
    off-campus, go salsa dancing, and ski or snowboard."

Colorado School of Mines

Address: Colorado School of Mines, 1600 Maple St., Golden, CO 80401
Phone: 303-273-3220
E-mail Address: admit@mines.edu
Web site URL: www.mines.edu
Year Founded: 1874
Private or Public: public
Religious affiliation: none
Location: suburban
Application and Admissions Information: 0.01
Regular Application Deadline: 2-Jun
Number of Applicants: 3,142
Percent Accepted: 84%
Percent Accepted who enroll: 29%
Number Entering: 787
Number of Transfers Accepted each Year: 151
Mean SAT: 1,240
Mean ACT: 28

Middle 50% SAT range: 1,200–1,380
Middle 50% ACT range: 25–30
Early admission program (EA/ ED/ NA): NA
ED or EA Acceptance Rate: NA
Full time Undergraduate enrollment: 3,209
Total enrollment: 4,056
Percent Male: 76%
Percent Female: 24%
Total Percent Minority: 15%
Percent African-American: 1%
Percent Asian/Pacific Islander: 5%
Percent Hispanic: 8%
Percent Native-American: 1%
Percent Other: 7%
Percent in-state / out of state: 75%/25%

Percent from Public HS: 90%
Retention Rate: 84%
Graduation Rate: 66%
Percent in On-campus housing: 35%
Percent affiliated with Greek system: 40%
Percent Varsity or Club Athletes: NA
Number of official organized extracurricular organizations: 126
3 Most popular majors: engineering, physical sciences, computer science
Student/Faculty ratio: 15:01
Tuition and Fees: $22,250.00
In State Tuition and Fees (if different): $9,656.00
Cost for Room and Board: $7,100.00
Percent receiving Financial aid, first-year: 92%

Looking at the landscapes of the Rocky Mountains, the glorious foliage and the breathtakingly mountainous terrain, it is very easy to overlook Golden, Colorado, an uneventful town harboring about 15,000 people. However, to 3,200 Colorado School of Mines students, this is home. Offering 15 degree programs of which eight contain the word "engineering," Mines is strongly slanted towards the technical disciplines. Even for the most optimistic and open-minded college student, the School of Mines is "lame at first," as one senior described, but the expansive scenery and unique student body eventually become a welcoming home.

Golden Academics in Golden

According to most students, Mines does not have enough parties to really call the party scene a scene, but the parties are not what guides most students to apply to the school. Academics are clearly the main attraction at the School of Mines. The extremely rigorous curriculum challenges students with a "basically prescribed" schedule of classes for the first three years, including extensive mathematics, from calculus through differential equations, as well as physics, economics, and computer programming. A typical freshman schedule includes classes (and class-related meetings) from eight to five, three times a week, and a marginally lighter load on the off-days; 15 credit hours is standard for most freshmen. Professors are generally very knowledgeable, but also have a reputation as being very demanding. Nonetheless, on the whole, the teaching staff is considered unmatched and many students cite the "opportunities for interactions with professors" as one of Mines's key advantages.

Another program mandated by the school is its EPICS program, an acronym for Engineering Practices Introductory Course Sequence. With EPICS, students are given real-world engineering problems and are asked to find innovative solutions to those problems. Additionally, in the summer following their sophomore or junior year, students participate in a Field Session program where they are introduced to skills unique to their particular area of specialization.

According to one student, the University strives to teach "the stuff you really need to be an engineer." However, students point to a lack of well-taught liberal arts classes as being the school's weakest point. With engineering as the unequivocal focus of the university, few resources are dedicated to other disciplines. Mines does have an unusually high dropout rate—around 16 percent. Of these students, most transfer to Colorado State University and other state colleges around the country. For those who remain, most are satisfied with the rigor and quality of their education. As one student put it, "it is gratifying to see how much work you actually get done by the end of each term."

Beyond the Classroom?

According to one junior, the party scene at Mines is "best thought of as a desert country . . . a quiet, lonely realm with sporadic oases of people and alcohol." Another student complained that there is "no social atmosphere and the frats are lame." Perhaps some of the trouble with social life at Colorado School of Mines lies in the fact that dorms are primarily for freshmen. After their first year, most established Miners find housing elsewhere. However all of the traditional residence halls were recently revamped, and the school has built four new Greek houses in the past few years. A new apartment-style housing complex called Mines Parks offers something in between traditional dorm life and off-campus living. Housing is not a problem in Golden either. Students can easily find reasonably-priced apartments or housing for rent within five or ten minutes of the campus. With most people in apartments, parties are usually small groups of friends hanging out at various locations off campus, as opposed to large, campus-wide parties. One senior said that the best change for Mines would be to "open [the party scene] more to freshmen and let them get involved." Although the social scene at Mines may not be as raucous as at other schools, one student stated that, "I have class with the same people, I study with the same people, I eat dinner with the same people. CSM helps to build a real sense of community and friendship that I couldn't find anywhere else."

Mines also offers a growing athletic program. The football team has seen four consecutive winning seasons, and was ranked among the top 10 Division II programs in the country in 2005. In 2006, the school broke ground on a new $25 million recreation center with facilities for club, recreational, and varsity athletics. Intramural and club sports are fairly popular among students, with about 70 percent of undergrads participating.

What About the Coors Brewery?

Given the lack of gathering places on campus, the Coors Brewery, which also calls Golden, Colorado, home, serves to fill this void (literally). The brewery packs with Miners "Monday, Tuesday, Wednesday . . . every night." One student described the brewery phenomenon as the "cultural and social center of CSM." While the brewery traditionally serves free beer at the conclusion of a half-hour-long tour, with a Mines identification card, students can take "the short tour" on their way to three free servings of Colorado's best beer. Drinkers and non-drinkers should not stray from the Coor's experience, advised one Mines junior. "It is the brewery that captures the best of CSM's social life."

For students wishing to evade the enduring call of barley and hops, the University offers a number of highly patronized alternatives. The Fellowship of Christian Athletes (or FCA) attracts many students, and athletic participation is not a prerequisite. While the FCA is a religious organization, its activities are mostly social events and community service projects. One student said that while religion (specifically Christianity) is a "big deal on campus," those who do not observe are not isolated from other students. Additionally, a large number of students associate through club sports. Although "homework is still the varsity sport of the weekends," rugby and soccer are the perennial favorites among the Miners.

Let's Party—Mines-Style
Noting the dominance of engineering in Colorado School of Mines academics, it is not surprising that the grandest production of the University is also engineering-related. In the first week of April, the school hosts "E-Days," short for—of course—Engineering Days. During this well-respected and highly anticipated event, the university presents a carnival-type fair demonstrating the newest engineering technologies. Besides a healthy dose of engineering, E-Days also boasts a spectacular pyrotechnics show. In fact, Mines is famous for their spectacular fireworks, bringing local and national bands, alumni, and students from neighboring colleges to their E-Days festival.

Beyond the Mines
When not celebrating their E-Days, Colorado School of Mines, due to its geographical location, provides numerous escapes for its students. Major cities are within a short driving distance. Denver and Boulder are within 15 minutes, while Colorado Springs is about 30 minutes away. Activities such as skiing and kayaking are frequent forms of amusement for Mines students. A senior said, "There is always something available to do, just not always time."

> **"I would definitely come back. Great education, great people, great friends!"**

Clearly, Colorado School of Mines is a departure from the traditional state school education. By centering engineering as the locus of the Mines experience, the University may have narrowed its curriculum, but it has produced a praiseworthy and noteworthy academic experience. Even with a few complaints about social life, Mines students are satisfied with their college experiences. As one senior put it, "Colorado is a great place, and I like CSM." Another stated, "I would definitely come back for a second time. Great education, great people, great friends!" Those who are looking to call themselves Mines students should nevertheless heed the warning of a CSM veteran: "I would like to have known how hard it would be once I got here. The school is great but very hard."—*Anatoly Brekhman*

FYI
If you come to CSM, you'd better bring "a calculator and get ready to study hard!"
A typical weekend schedule at CSM includes "homework, going to the Coors Brewery, and doing more work."
If I could change one thing about CSM, "I'd get the freshmen more into parties."
Three things every student at CSM should do before graduating are "go to E-Days for the fireworks, get to know a professor well, and take a non-engineering class."

Colorado State University

Address: Colorado State, Office of Admissions, 8020 Campus Delivery, Fort Collins, CO 80523-8020

Phone: 970-491-6909

E-mail Address: admissions@colostate.edu

Web site URL: www.colostate.edu

Year Founded: 1870

Private or Public: public

Religious affiliation: none

Location: small city

Regular Application Deadline: 1-Jul

Number of Applicants: 11,310

Percent Accepted: 86%

Percent Accepted who enroll: 42%

Number Entering: 5,460

Number of Transfers Accepted each Year: varies

Mean SAT: NA

Mean ACT: NA

Middle 50% SAT range: 1,010–1,210

Middle 50% ACT range: 22–26

Early admission program (EA/ ED/ NA): NA

ED or EA Acceptance Rate: NA

Full time Undergraduate enrollment: 18,801

Total enrollment: 26,723

Percent Male: 48%

Percent Female: 52%

Total Percent Minority: 12.3%

Percent African-American: 1.5%

Percent Asian/Pacific Islander: 3.1%

Percent Hispanic: 6.2%

Percent Native-American: 1.5%

Percent Other: 0%

Percent in-state / out of state: 82%/18%

Percent from Public HS: NA

Retention Rate: 82%

Graduation Rate: 63%

Percent in On-campus housing: 30%

Percent affiliated with Greek system: 8%

Percent Varsity or Club Athletes: 2%

Number of official organized extracurricular organizations: 330

3 Most popular majors: Business Administration, Psychology, Human Development and Family Studies

Student/Faculty ratio: NA

Tuition and Fees: $16,245.00

In State Tuition and Fees (if different): $4,717.00

Cost for Room and Board: $6,602.00

Percent receiving Financial aid, first-year: 36%

Colorado State University is nestled between the edge of the Great Plains and the foothills of the Rocky Mountains in the mid-size city of Fort Collins, Colorado. Enjoying an average of 300 sunny days per year and ranked as one of the "Best Places to Live" in the western US by *Money Magazine*, Fort Collins is home to vast green spaces coupled with low stress and lower crime rates, and the students of CSU are well aware of the advantages of living in this "outdoor lovers' paradise". Besides enjoying the beauty of their surroundings, under- and upperclassmen alike appreciate their school's rigorous academics at a reasonable cost as well as the numerous opportunities to get involved in a wide array of extracurricular and athletic activities.

Decisions, Decisions

When applying to CSU, students must apply for acceptance into one of eight academic departments—Agricultural Sciences, Applied Human Sciences, Business, Engineering, Liberal Arts, Forestry and Natural Resources, and Veterinary Medicine and Biomedical Sciences—and select their major before arriving on campus. However, as many

as a third of the freshman class opts to take advantage of the "open option" programs that postpone the choice of a major until the beginning of sophomore year. Various individual departments offer this alternative in addition to the university-wide program that allows undecided freshmen to take courses in a variety of subject areas before committing to only one. The school also offers an honors program that provides enrichment for 190 students and features smaller honors sections in key courses within each major, priority housing in the honors dormitory, early class registration, and research opportunities with members of the faculty.

Class registration at CSU can easily be done online, but students unable to reach their computers early enough on registration day might find themselves shut out of some necessary courses and rearranging their schedules to take them the next year instead. Smaller classes (40% have less than 20 students) naturally fill up more quickly and the competition to gain entrance can be quite fierce; larger classes (20% have 50 or more students) are generally quite easy to get into. These larger lectures can offer frustrations of their own, however, as many of the freshman introductory classes must accommodate up-wards of 200 to 300 students. While the amount of work assigned in any class can pile up, most of these introductory 100-level classes are known for being relatively easy. One of the most popular courses offered—and one that fills up very quickly on registration day—is "Psychology of Human Sexuality," which hosts a "porn day" during which the entire class watches a porno-graphic video for an hour in order to study and discuss its psychological implications. In order to graduate, all CSU students must take a course in English composition, although it is possible to test out of this requirement by scoring well on an AP or departmental exam. A wide variety of course options are available for fulfilling the other areas of the core cur-riculum, and students generally agree that it is relatively painless to do so.

At the Foot of the Mountains

Freshmen at CSU are required to live on campus, and the school does honor housing requests on a first-come, first-serve basis, so submitting dorm preferences early is a good idea. Each of the 10 residence halls has its own theme and offers related "Living Learn-ing Communities" that provide tutoring and study groups in its focus academic area: In-gersoll, for example, is the science dorm, Newsom the honors dorm, Allison is engi-neering, and Edwards serves the pre-veterinarians. There are also dorms with non-academic reputations: Corbett is the "Party Dorm", and most of the athletes live in The Towers. In spite of the fact that many students consider on-campus living to be en-joyable, "the food is pretty terrible and the rooms are not good", and so most move into off-campus housing after their first or sec-ond year. Huge apartment complexes such as Ram's Pointe and Ram's Village are lo-cated conveniently close to campus and cater primarily to sophomores, as upper-classmen tend to "realize that those places aren't much better than the dorms were and find a house or a better apartment". The ar-chitecture of the dorms and other buildings at CSU tends to vary in aesthetics; the older part of campus seems built in the design of the old Spanish Missionary style, while other areas call to mind classical revivalist or "some kind of nasty '70's non-style", al-though these latter buildings have been un-dergoing recent renovations to improve their appearance. The Lory Student Center is a popular place to hang out for CSU students and boasts restaurants, student lounges fea-turing video arcades, TVs, and pool tables, a ballroom, a theater and the campus box of-fice, and stores offering everything from textbooks and school supplies to haircuts and bicycle repairs. When this monolithic fa-cility was renovated several years ago, *The New York Times* ranked it as one of the 10 best student centers in the country.

> "Fort Collins's 300 days of sunshine keep students—particularly those that love the outdoors—smiling."

CSU has a firm alcohol policy and the on-campus dorms are strictly dry, but even so, alcohol often makes its way onto school property and into students' bedrooms. There are RAs on every hall to watch over their student charges, but most are not terri-bly severe and instead favor a policy of gen-eral oversight to stringently enforcing every rule. Binge drinking indeed is somewhat of a problem at CSU, and "at least one frat per year gets shut down for getting an underage girl sent to the hospital." With the exception of marijuana, which is somewhat popular, recreational drugs do not make much of an appearance here, and the use of harder sub-stances is very rare.

Fort Collins offers a particularly vibrant bar scene, which tends to attract many CSU students. There are bars with specials every night of the week, although the most popu-lar evenings for bar hopping tend to be Tues-days and Thursdays, and seniors frequent these establishments more often than the underclassmen, who often prefer the party scene offered by the frats. As one student summed up, "you can see herds of freshmen walking off campus at night looking for par-ties, but the older classes usually just stay home or go to friends' houses."

Freshmen and upperclassmen living on campus can choose from one of six different meal plans that offer a great deal of flexibil-ity and include the option of eating at the all-you-can-eat residence hall dining center as well as any of the restaurants housed in the Lory Student Center. Nevertheless, students are lukewarm in their enthusiasm for the food quality in the on-campus retail facilities and often end up traveling beyond the cam-pus borders to find a satisfying meal.

Most students, particularly those from nearby towns and cities, bring their cars to campus, and those that do not have a vehicle are definitely in the minority. Although the majority do remain at CSU during the weekends, a notable minority use their cars to go home or visit nearby Denver, sixty-five miles away, for a couple of days.

Indeed, most of CSU's 20,500 undergraduates do come from within the state and are well used to Colorado's chilly winters, which in Fort Collins can reach a low of 15°F in January. Nevertheless, there are still plenty of girls who wear "mini skirts and fuzzy boots" around campus as they attempt to strike a compromise between fashion and warmth. The student body stereotypically tends to be "upper middle class and white" and sports perhaps a lower level of diversity than might be common at other universities. The Greek scene remains prevalent and drives much of the party scene, and in the weeks before rush, advertisements for the various fraternities and sororities flood the campus.

Ram-ping Up the Involvement

Football is the major player in the CSU sports arena and much of the university's sense of school spirit derives from it, although as one student admits, "The team isn't very good". Spirit organizations—the cheerleading squad, the marching band, and Cam the Ram, the university's costumed mascot—support the team on game days and pull the crowd into the action. On the other hand, the varsity volleyball and lacrosse teams boast a great deal of talent but lack the attention given to football. Intramural sports are extremely popular, especially among freshmen and upperclassmen living on campus, and can become quite competitive depending on the level of ability. Everything from football to soccer to innertube water polo is offered, and students who want to play a sport that has not been organized are encouraged to start a new league for it. The Campus Rec center provides basketball courts, exercise rooms, an inline skating arena, a racquetball court, a pool and spa, a track, and a boxing area, among many other facilities, and is popular among athletes and non-athletes alike. The only disadvantage to this altar to exercise is that it often becomes very busy and overly crowded.

Outside of athletics, CSU hosts over 300 recognized clubs, organizations, and performance groups, and as with IMs, any student who finds that his or her interests are not already represented can found a new one. The student government—Associated Students of Colorado State University (or ASCSU)—is a popular extracurricular activity that makes it easy to become involved with the university through voluntary committees and associate positions as well as running for office in campus-wide election. Both the college radio station, KCSU, and the student-run TV channel Campus Television attract their share of the university audience, and the *Rocky Mountain Collegian* keeps undergraduates informed about recent news. In addition, the Curfman Gallery at the Lory Student Center offers several rotating art exhibits every year, and undergraduates can become involved in choosing and displaying the works. Volunteering off campus is also a popular pastime for CSU students, and opportunities abound to become involved with many different projects in Fort Collins and beyond. A bi-annual event called the Centertainment allows campus organizations to showcase themselves and man informational displays while interested students browse their options for extracurricular involvement.

Here Comes The Sun

Students at Colorado State University benefit from the multitude of offerings presented by their college, from the abundance of in-depth courses to the wide variety of extracurricular options, and although the food may not be gourmet or the architecture artistic, CSU undergraduates are generally quite positive about their experience. From the Lory Student Center to the themed dorms to the popular gymnasium, the amenities available on campus compare favorably with those of other universities, and Fort Collins's 300 days of sunshine keep students—particularly those that love the outdoors—smiling.—*Kristin Knox*

FYI

If you come to CSU, you'd better bring "a car—students who don't have them are definitely in the minority."

What's the typical weekend schedule? "Sleep till noon, go skiing or biking, have dinner with friends, go out."

If I could change one thing about CSU, it would be "the food options in the dining halls."

Three things every student at CSU should do before graduating are "hang out in the student center, hike to the Aggies sign above Fort Collins, and go into the Old Town on Friday night."

The United States Air Force Academy

Address: US Air Force Academy, HQ USAFA/RRS, 2304 Cadet Drive, Suite 200, USAF Academy, CO 80840
Phone: 719-333-2520
E-mail Address: rr_webmail@usafa.af.mil
Web site URL: www.usafa.af.mil
Year Founded: 1954
Private or Public: public
Religious affiliation: none
Location: suburban
Regular Application Deadline: 1-Feb
Number of Applicants: 9,255
Percent Accepted: 19%
Percent Accepted who enroll: 77%
Number Entering: 1,266
Number of Transfers Accepted each Year: NA
Mean SAT: 1,309
Mean ACT: 28

Middle 50% SAT range: 1,190–1,390
Middle 50% ACT range: NA
Early admission program (EA/ ED/ NA): NA
ED or EA Acceptance Rate: NA
Full time Undergraduate enrollment: 4,524
Total enrollment: 4,524
Percent Male: 82%
Percent Female: 18%
Total Percent Minority: 21%
Percent African-American: 4%
Percent Asian/Pacific Islander: 8%
Percent Hispanic: 7%
Percent Native-American: 2%
Percent Other: NA
Percent in-state / out of state: 6%/94%
Percent from Public HS: NA
Retention Rate: 87%

Graduation Rate: 76%
Percent in On-campus housing: 100%
Percent affiliated with Greek system: 0%
Percent Varsity or Club Athletes: NA
Number of official organized extracurricular organizations: 110
3 Most popular majors: Business Administration/ Management; Engineering, General; Social Sciences, General
Student/Faculty ratio: 8:01
Tuition and Fees: $0.00
In State Tuition and Fees (if different): $0.00
Cost for Room and Board: $0.00
Percent receiving Financial aid, first-year: 0%

The United States Air Force Academy is not for the weak. Acceptance into the school is just the first difficulty you face when becoming a cadet—and at the USAFA you are not a student, you are a cadet. Cadets are challenged both in and out of the classroom and are pressured by strict rules, but the benefits of going to the USAFA are immense. You get to enjoy seclusion in the Colorado wilderness, you get paid to go to a great school, you become part of a closely-knit squad, and—the best part—you get to fly.

Adjusting to a New Life

Almost all cadets would agree that the first year at the USAFA is the most difficult one. Freshmen, also known as "doolies" by the upperclassmen, have to adjust to many lifestyle changes. The USAFA's strict daily regimen is difficult for all cadets, but the freshmen have it the worst, since they have to live in the most cramped rooms and have the least privileges. Freshmen come to the USAFA during the summer to partake in Basic Cadet Training, a five-week long "boot camp" where cadets learn basic military skills, and get yelled at by their superiors.

Cadets are randomly divided into 36 squadrons of 120 each. The squadrons include students from all four years and determine where a cadet will live. The squadrons allow for cadets to become close with a small group. Although everyone lives in the squadrons, the living arrangements are different: Freshmen generally have three roommates while sophomores and juniors have two and seniors have one.

Besides these inequalities in rooming, the other big difference between the underclassmen and upperclassmen is the weekend privileges. Only seniors are allowed to have a car at school, though, be warned, it cannot be a motorcycle. Because of seniors' access to transportation, they are more likely to get the opportunity to party at neighboring colleges such as Colorado University Bolder and Colorado State University. In addition to the difficulties with transportation, freshmen are also more vulnerable to the strict prohibitions against underage drinking, and getting caught with alcohol can lead to expulsion. Upperclassmen are also allowed to leave campus more frequently, and to stay out longer when they do.

Lastly, the freshmen are prohibited from the food court, where cadets can buy pizza and subs if they are tired of the cafeteria food, which is automatically deducted from cadets' pay, but one cadet simply described the food the Academy offers as "horrible." Although upperclassmen can get dinner at the food court, lunch is a mandatory meal, served to everyone at the same time. There is only one cafeteria—and unlike the cafeteria at any other school, the one at USAFA has windows protected by bombproof glass.

Studytime

The USAFA is a highly competitive school. In fact, many cadets find the academics to be a lot harder than the physical elements of being in the Air Force. One cadet remarked, "the Air Force is tough, but mainly because of how much we have to do for class." Many are athletes, or were athletes in high school, and said they were not used to such rigorous academic focus, though the average SAT score for admits is 1309. Once they get in, they are competing with the other students for good grades since everything is graded on a curve, "even if said otherwise," one cadet explained.

> **"The Air Force is tough, but mainly because of how much we have to do for class."**

A typical cadet will spend around 20 hours a week on schoolwork. Most class sizes range from 15 to 20 people, which allows students to get to know their professors, who are both civilian and military and many are quite famous—one professor was the leading expert on the Columbia Space Shuttle Accident. Because of the USAFA's unique standing as a highly academically competitive military school, the opportunities are endless for those who graduate from the Academy.

Students are required to have at least 132 credit hours to graduate, but most end up having far more. Most cadets either major in engineering or management, which each have their own reputations. One cadet remarked, "The engineering majors are geeks, the computer science majors don't even bother looking for dates, and the management majors don't bother doing homework because it is more of a recommendation than a requirement." Indeed the management major is considered the easy major while the engineering major is considered the harder major. And obviously, the Air Force is also famous for its "Aero" and "Astro"—that's Aeronautics and Astrophysics departments for you non-cadets.

EXTRAcurricular

Sports are very popular at the Air Force, and actually everyone plays at least one intramural sport, because it is mandatory. Some cadets find this requirement to be just another addition to their academic workload, while others take extracurricular activities very seriously, causing some sports to become very competitive. At the USAFA, you can play just about any sport you wish, ranging from ultimate Frisbee to soccer. However, the facilities for non-varsity athletes have been known to get crowded.

Varsity sports are very prevalent at the academy, with about one fourth of all cadets playing a varsity sport—and the teams are known to take a lot of pride in their sport. The mainstream sports, such as football and basketball, get large support from the school, with cadets actually required to go to every home football game, another requirement that meets with mixed reviews. One cadet remarked that "people are either totally into the game or they wish they weren't there and complain the whole time."

Most cadets were athletes in high school so are somewhat prepared for the military training at the USAFA, and participating in varsity sports counts as part of the military requirement. But after sports, classroom, and military requirements, cadets aren't left with a lot of free time. Luckily, they don't have to worry about making money; they are banned from any outside employment because attending the Air Force is considered a job, as it is a military school and provides students with a salary.

Overall, the USAFA is one of the best colleges out there for those who want to make a difference. You learn the skills you need to survive both the battlefield and the workplace, and make valuable connections for whichever path you eventually take. So if you are willing to put in the effort, the USAFA would be a wonderful choice.—*Benjamin Dzialo*

FYI

If you come to the USAFA, you'd better bring "motivation to stay . . . everything else is issued to you."

What's the typical weekend schedule? "A weekend would consist of whatever we do not get to do during the week. About half of the weekends have some kind of training on the Saturday morning that everyone has to be back for but, after that is done, the weekend is free for whatever."

If I could change one thing about the USAFA, "I'd get rid of the noncommissioned officer (NCO) presence here. The Air Force Academy is training cadets to be commissioned officers, and NCOs have no part in the training of cadets."

Three things every cadet at the USAFA should do before graduating are "remain standing and cheering for the football team even though it is the end of the fourth quarter and the team is losing by over three touchdowns, use your uniform to pick up the opposite sex, and deploy overseas to see what you are getting into."

University of Colorado / Boulder

Address: University of CO, Boulder, 552 UCB, Boulder, CO 80309-0552
Phone: 303-492-6301
E-mail Address: apply@colorado.edu
Web site URL: www.colorado.edu
Year Founded: 1876
Private or Public: public
Religious affiliation: none
Location: urban
Regular Application Deadline: 16-Jan
Number of Applicants: 18,173
Percent Accepted: 88%
Percent Accepted who enroll: 35%
Number Entering: 5,647
Number of Transfers Accepted each Year: 1,965
Mean SAT: NA
Mean ACT: 25

Middle 50% SAT range: 1,060–1,320
Middle 50% ACT range: 23–28
Early admission program (EA/ ED/ NA): NA
ED or EA Acceptance Rate: NA
Full time Undergraduate enrollment: 24,710
Total enrollment: 28,624
Percent Male: 53%
Percent Female: 47%
Total Percent Minority: 15%
Percent African-American: 2%
Percent Asian/Pacific Islander: 6%
Percent Hispanic: 6%
Percent Native-American: 1%
Percent Other: 0%
Percent in-state / out of state: 69%/31%

Percent from Public HS: NA
Retention Rate: 84%
Graduation Rate: 66%
Percent in On-campus housing: 26%
Percent affiliated with Greek system: 8%
Percent Varsity or Club Athletes: 4%
Number of official organized extracurricular organizations: 300
3 Most popular majors: English, Physiology, Psychology
Student/Faculty ratio: 16:01
Tuition and Fees: $23,539.00
In State Tuition and Fees (if different): $5,643.00
Cost for Room and Board: $8,300.00
Percent receiving Financial aid, first-year: 39%

Situated in the foothills of the Rocky Mountains, the University of Colorado at Boulder presents students with unbounded opportunities to explore every aspect of college life. "CU-Boulder" simply has it all. Passionate outdoors-types can take advantage of the hundreds of miles of trails for running, biking, and hiking that surround the campus. Or, daredevils can hit the slopes at over 20 ski resorts located in the vicinity. Such limitless exploration goes far beyond the outdoors, however. With over 3,400 courses in 150 fields of study, the University offers students endless ways to pursue their academic interests. The presence of four Nobel-prize winners and seven MacArthur Fellowship recipients among the faculty further reinforces CU-Boulder's ranking by the Institute of Higher Education as the 11th best public school in the world. The unique "hippy" flavor of the town of Boulder entertains students with its laidback but fun atmosphere. In short, CU-Boulder combines the best of many worlds, offering rigorous academic discipline in a free-spirited environment.

Open-ended Opportunity

The first thing that students mention when referring to CU-Boulder is its freedom. With a plethora of course offerings, students may choose from thousands of courses to satisfy their intellectual desires. To help students streamline their interests, the university is divided into 7 different colleges. While most take the common Arts and Sciences track, many students also enroll in the Leeds School of Business and the School of Engineering and Applied Science. The other colleges are in Architecture and Planning, Education, Journalism and Mass Communication, and Music. Students' majors vary widely, but the three most popular majors from the Fall 2005 term were psychology, integrative physiology, and English.

Without a doubt, accommodating over 28,000 students at CU-Boulder is no small task. Though 47 percent of all undergraduate course sections enroll under 20 students, and 85 percent enroll fewer than 50 students, students do express a frustration with the size of some classes. "I hate the big lectures!" exclaimed one current sophomore. Another frequent complaint is the core curriculum requirement. The curriculum is divided between "skills acquisition" (foreign language, quantitative reasoning, writing, and critical thinking) and "content areas of study" (history, diversity, United States, literature, natural science, contemporary society, and values). Nonetheless, as at most colleges, the requirements "lessen as you progress through the years."

While finding a niche at such a large institution might seem intimidating to many incoming freshmen, CU-Boulder does provide opportunities for personalized attention. One unique aspect of the university is the presence of RAPs (Residential Academic Programs) that allow undergraduates to share experiences with others who have common interests. The sense of community engendered by the RAPs is bolstered by the fact that select relevant courses are located in the respective halls and special events are planned just for the program. RAPs are centered on numerous concepts, including, but not limited to: Environmental Science (Baker), Diversity (Hallett), Humanities (Farrand), Honors (Kittredge), American West (Sewall), and International (Smith Hall).

Beyond the RAPs, CU-Boulder offers an Honors Program for exceptionally motivated students, providing specialized curriculum and advising from faculty members. Also, the Norlin Scholars Program, a merit-based award of $3,000 per year, helps talented students achieve their goals with individual guidance.

For those looking for diverse experiences outside of Colorado, the university offers an extensive study-abroad program in locations ranging from Perugia, Italy to Valparaiso, Chile to Cape Town, South Africa, to Ulaanbaatar, Mongolia.

Adventuresome Architecture

With over 200 "architecturally-pleasing" rural-Italian style buildings, students have plenty to gape at besides the Rocky Mountains. A common "hotspot" on campus is Norlin Quadrangle, a broad grassy area where students can go to study, meet up with friends, or simply relax and enjoy the nice weather. One student comments that Norlin Quad is "nice and open, has lots of sunshine, and is simply a nice place where you can just lie down and see the Flatirons." Slacklining—tightrope walking across climbing ropes, usually tied between two trees—is an interesting pastime commonly seen on the Quad. Other often-frequented buildings on campus include Macky Auditorium and the Norlin Library, which, with 11 million volumes, boasts the "largest library collection in the Rocky Mountain region."

> **"Everyone's really laid back."**

Charles Z. Klauder designed most of the buildings on campus in a distinctive rural-North Italian fashion. The red-tiled roofs and rough walls evoke an impression of being in the mountainous regions of Northern Italy—a particularly relevant ambiance for a university placed at the base of the Rockies.

Hippie Heaven

"Everyone's really laid back," explains one student, referring to the student body. When asked about the basic composition of the general population, most people name "Hippie" and "frat guy" as the common student types that exist at CU-Boulder. In terms of music and culture, many students list the Grateful Dead and Phish among their favorite bands. In addition, there is a recognizable presence of marijuana on campus, albeit amongst a smaller group of people.

Drinking is ubiquitous. Though the university's stated policy disallows drinking in the dorms, enforcement of the rules is characteristic of the school as a whole—laid back. The "two-strikes" policy comes as a result of CU-Boulder's campaign as one of the first schools in the nation to systematically address student alcohol abuse. Nonetheless, drinking provides much entertainment for CU-Boulder students, especially at the fraternities and sororities that are located on "The Hill," a favorite district for students.

Recreational Respites

Located on the Eastern slope of the Rocky Mountains at an altitude of 5,400 feet, the university has the natural rocky formations as its backyard. The miles and miles of trails allow students to hike, bike, climb, or snowshoe for hours on end. During the warmer months of the year, students can opt to go whitewater rafting or kayaking on the Colorado River.

But for those who aren't willing to make the trek out to the mountains, there is plenty to do on campus. The Colorado Buffaloes football team is a source of shared pride for nearly all CU-Boulder students. Playing in Folsom Stadium, the football team draws huge crowds during games against perennial opponents such as the Nebraska Cornhuskers. The Colorado Buffaloes also boast a strong cross-country running team, and they have produced world-class runners such as Adam Goucher and Dathan Ritzenhein.

For students who are less competitive, the intramurals program offers an array of exciting and relaxed sports to play. Among the many options, the Ultimate Frisbee team is generally regarded as a highly-competitive and successful group. Other IMs include Whiffleball, Broomball, and inner-tube Water Polo.

Free Future

As successful as it has been thus far, CU-Boulder still desires to improve as an institution. The "Quality for Colorado" investment plan hopes to emphasize "quality growth" rather than enrollment growth, by such things as reducing the size of the freshman class, improving the average preparation of entering freshmen, and increasing financial aid. In August of 2006, the stunning $31 million, 66,000 square-foot ATLAS (Alliance for Technology, Learning, and Society) Center opened, heralding a new age of advanced technological resources for student use. Finally, in September of 2006, the dedication of the new Wolf Law Building occurred. With a gigantic new law library and two high-tech courtrooms, the Law Building will be a landmark building for generations to come.

In general, CU-Boulder looks towards the future. Faculty members have won 4 Nobel Prizes in the last 2 decades, and have advanced the scientific knowledge of mankind in many respects. In fiscal year 2005, the school received $258 million in sponsored research awards from organizations such as the National Sciences Foundation, NASA, and the Department of Health and Human Services. With its strong, forward-looking academic program and an environment that promotes the freedom to explore, CU-Boulder provides the perfect experience for students looking to excel in new and old frontiers.—*Wookie Kim*

FYI
If you come to CU, you better bring "a tent and a beer funnel."
What's the typical weekend schedule? "Go camping, watch the football game, and drink beer."
If I could change one thing about CU, "I'd make the campus less hilly."
The three things that every student should do before graduating from CU are "hike the Flatirons, attend a frat party, and go to a CU football game."

University of Denver

Address: University of Denver, 2197 S. University Blvd., Denver, CO 80208
Phone: 303-871-2036
E-mail Address: admission@du.edu
Web site URL: www.du.edu
Year Founded: 1864
Private or Public: private
Religious affiliation: none
Location: urban
Regular Application Deadline: 16-Jan
Number of Applicants: 4,038
Percent Accepted: 73%
Percent Accepted who enroll: 33%
Number Entering: 1,103
Number of Transfers Accepted each Year: 387
Mean SAT: 1,180
Mean ACT: 26
Middle 50% SAT range: 1,070–1,290

Middle 50% ACT range: 23–28
Early admission program (EA/ ED/ NA): EA
ED or EA Acceptance Rate: 56%
Full time Undergraduate enrollment: 4,877
Total enrollment: 9,192
Percent Male: 45%
Percent Female: 55%
Total Percent Minority: 20%
Percent African-American: 2%
Percent Asian/Pacific Islander: 5%
Percent Hispanic: 7%
Percent Native-American: 1%
Percent Other: 5%
Percent in-state / out of state: 47%/53%
Percent from Public HS: NA

Retention Rate: 89%
Graduation Rate: 72%
Percent in On-campus housing: 45%
Percent affiliated with Greek system: 20%
Percent Varsity or Club Athletes: 3.90%
Number of official organized extracurricular organizations: 120
3 Most popular majors: Business, Communications, Psychology
Student/Faculty ratio: 10:01
Tuition and Fees: $30,372.00
Cost for Room and Board: $8,351.00
Percent receiving Financial aid, first-year: 44%

Revise: The "oldest independent university in the Rockies" is undergoing a face-lift. Students agree that the focus of the school has shifted noticeably in the past several years. The existing emphasis on community leadership and involvement is being matched by a set of construction projects aimed at centralizing and modernizing the campus. The administration has also cracked down on the wild Greek scene. The result? A mellow, focused, and more academically oriented feel pervades the school that was known for its tradition of good times, great skiing and rousing school events.

Personalized Academics

To start off their time at DU, freshmen are required to take a medley of courses, including a foreign language, oral communication, math, computer science, and English. Most students are in agreement that the core curriculum lets them explore the school's strengths before choosing a major. "My favorite class to date was definitely my freshman year Spanish class, no question," one sophomore said. The student-to-faculty ratio is an impressive 14 to 1, and many commented on the personal attention received from teachers. The result is that students enjoy very small class sizes and foster "interactive" relationships with professors. TAs are a concept foreign to DU students, except in a few science courses. DU also boasts a freshman-mentoring program, which assigns all entering freshmen a faculty mentor to see them through the major decisions of the first year. After freshman year, students split their range of studies in various directions, from Arts and Literature to Creative Expression.

Popular majors include business, reflecting DU's impressive Business School; psychology; and biology. Science majors are generally considered more difficult, and include killer courses in organic chemistry and cellular biology.

For all majors, DU makes an effort to foster a merit-based academic feel on campus from the very start. Freshmen can apply to be in the Pioneer Leadership Program the summer before they arrive. This highly selective program fits into their curriculum as a minor, applicable to any primary major later on. Equally selective is the Honors Program, which offers students with a 3.4 GPA or higher who apply to the program access to special lectures and seminars. The Pioneer Leadership and Honors Program students live on special, separate floors in freshman housing.

Another popular offering is the Interterm Program, which provides students with intensive programs between the formal academic quarters, both based at DU and abroad. Past Interterm opportunities, which are available in the fall, winter and spring recesses, have included An Economic History of the Caribbean taught on St. Kitts and Nevis in the West Indies, a course on the European Union on location in London, and a course on gaming and gambling taught from the casinos of Las Vegas.

Students at DU generally like the academic term system, which divides the school year into quarters. Some complain that it is a bit fast paced at times, leaving "no room for screwing up." The daily workload is manageable, and more than two or three classes per day are rare.

DU students are motivated and engaged, but not over-the-top intense. One student describes academics as "strong, but nothing I can't handle. I'm challenged, but not killing myself over work on a daily basis." The University has tried to unify and raise the quality of the academic experience by, for the last four years, requiring all students to have a laptop computer. Classes make use of online discussion groups, note taking and in-class Internet access.

Central and Modern

"Copper is big here," commented one DU student when describing the campus. A nice blend of fresh, modern architecture and older structures makes for a very pleasant campus feel. The red brick tower of University Hall meets the low lines of Pembrose Library, while pathways snake through manicured lawns and green open spaces. The wide Colorado sky and view of the Rockies add to the picturesque feel of the campus. The university prides itself on its accomplishments in enhancing the beautiful surroundings as well, with additions such as the beautiful Humanities Gardens near the center of campus. Students call the campus "very central and modern," and praise the large capital project devoted to the recently completed residence hall and science center. Recent construction projects are part of the University's efforts to move much of DU's satellite campus, Park Hill, closer to the action on the central grounds. The Ritchie Center for Sports and Wellness is another highly visible landmark, as well as a state-of-the-art athletic facility for varsity athletes and gym-rats alike.

The campus is manageably sized, so that "it never takes more than 10 or so minutes to get to class, at the extreme," one student said. Freshmen and sophomores are required to live on campus. Freshmen are housed in two dormitories, Johnson-McFarlane, or J-Mac, and Centennial Halls. Both buildings are air-conditioned and made up of suites with kitchenettes. Centennial Halls is the home of Special Interest floors, which group students by interests such as substance free, business, math/science, all male or all female, and the Honors Program. Members of the Pioneer Leadership Program and others live in J-Mac, generally regarded as the "dorkier" of the two freshman residences. The dorms are variously described as "decent," and "kinda gross." Freshmen live with RAs on each floor, who keep tabs on alcohol, which is forbidden, and noise violations. A new residence hall, Nagel Hall, is scheduled to open in 2008. Designed to keep more upperclassmen on campus, the dorm will feature singles, doubles, and apartments.

Students eat in cafeterias located in both of the freshman dorms, and the upperclassman dorm. After freshman year, many sophomores choose to eat in their fraternity or sorority, and there are few upperclassmen in the cafeterias at all. DU offers a "point system" allowing students extra meal points with which they can eat in local restaurants and "get a Starbucks fix."

Greek Festivities

The area around campus is "residential and cute," made up of mostly student houses. There is a small, "adequate" commercial area a few blocks from campus, and downtown Denver is only a 10-minute drive from campus. A majority of students have cars on campus, and they are permitted for freshmen. The social life at DU has many ties to the Greek system, and more than 20 percent of students are members of the eight fraternities and five sororities. As the campus continues with renovations, many of the Greek facilities will be among those revamped. Those inside the Greek system say that "it does not entirely dominate the social scene, but it is strong," and say that there are "tons of alternative, non-Greek weekend options," though some are more adamant that the Greek system "is the social scene." Students lament the increased frequency with which house parties are broken up, and say that the party scene has begun to shift towards "bar parties," where a group will rent a bar, and allow anyone over 18 (those under 21 get a wristband) to enter and enjoy dancing and drinking. Traditional fraternity events at the ever popular SAE, Lambda Chi Alpha, and Sigma Chi fraternities include annual theme parties, such as Western, Pajama, and Principals and Schoolgirls. All formal events are Greek-based. One of the major non-Greek events is the yearly Winter Carnival, a hugely popular campuswide event in January.

Involved and Evolving

Like all universities of its size, DU has a long list of interesting extracurricular possibilities, from public service organizations to professional honors societies and dance troupes. The student newspaper, *The Clarion*, is a popular involvement, and the Alpine Club is known for organizing frequent outdoor excursions.

The student body at DU is "not extremely diverse," and one student commented that with regards to breaking the stereotype that it's a school of rich kids, "they try but it's pretty white, fairly preppy, not a lot of punks." The 15 percent of the student body of minority background does not fail to make an impression on campus, however, forming a strong community within a community through ethnic clubs and organizations.

One student remarked that arts opportunities are not at the forefront at DU, but that with the completion of the new music building on central campus, which includes a larger theater space, students will no longer "need to be in the know to hear about the arts."

Winter Sports Rule

Skiing is a huge campus pastime and "those who don't ski can feel a little excluded," as many students hit the slopes every weekend throughout the winter. Aside from skiing, DU offers many athletic choices to the sports-minded. Club sports are popular. They do not make any cuts and are "a lot of fun" for all involved. DU also fosters strong varsity sports teams, the most popular of which is its successful hockey team, followed by the lacrosse, soccer and swim teams. There is generally "good turnout" to games, though hockey is unquestionably king. Division I hockey games take the place of football games, as DU has no football team, and the annual game against rival Colorado College is "not to be missed."

> **"Those who don't ski can feel a little excluded."**

Traditions such as the enthusiasm for the hockey team unify DU as it continues to establish itself as a rising academic institution. Students are as relaxed and ready to take advantage of its opportunities to hit the slopes and fraternity row as they are to hit the books.—*Charlotte Taft*

FYI
If you come to the University of Denver, you'd better bring "a fake ID."
What is the typical weekend schedule? "Rest up, go out, squeeze in the homework."
If I could change one thing about DU, "I'd change the rules about social activities—make them less anal about breaking up house parties."
The three things that every student should do before graduating from the University of Denver are "travel around the area because Colorado is beautiful, realize what downtown has to offer, and go to the Colorado College-DU hockey game."

Connecticut

Connecticut College

Address: Connecticut College, 270 Mohegan Avenue, New London, CT 06320

Phone: 860-439-2200

E-mail Address: admission@conncoll.edu

Web site URL: www.connecticutcollege.edu

Year Founded: 1911

Private or Public: private

Religious affiliation: none

Location: small city

Regular Application Deadline: 15-Dec

Number of Applicants: 4,278

Percent Accepted: 151.9%

Percent Accepted who enroll: 30%

Number Entering: 491

Number of Transfers Accepted each Year: 45

Mean SAT: 1,364 or 2,054

Mean ACT: 28

Middle 50% SAT range: 1,310–1,440 or 1,970–2,160

Middle 50% ACT range: 26–30

Early admission program (EA/ ED/ NA): ED

ED or EA Acceptance Rate: NA

Full time Undergraduate enrollment: 1,757

Total enrollment: 1,757

Percent Male: 40%

Percent Female: 60%

Total Percent Minority: 13%

Percent African-American: 3.8%

Percent Asian/Pacific Islander: 3.6%

Percent Hispanic: 5.5%

Percent Native-American: 0%

Percent Other: 7.5%

Percent in-state / out of state: 92%/8%

Percent from Public HS: 86.4%

Retention Rate: 91%

Graduation Rate: 86%

Percent in On-campus housing: 98.5%

Percent affiliated with Greek system: NA

Percent Varsity or Club Athletes: 50%

Number of official organized extracurricular organizations: 70

3 Most popular majors: English, Economics, Government

Student/Faculty ratio: 10:01

Tuition and Fees: $37,640.00

Cost for Room and Board: $7,600.00

Percent receiving Financial aid, first-year: 40%

Connecticut College is a small liberal arts college nestled above the historic Thames River. Its close-knit community fosters a sense of vibrancy through a tradition of student interaction. Undergraduates run nearly everything on campus, from social events to the judicial board. Bound by their sense of honor and tradition, the students here take the initiative, and it pays off. At Conn College, a student can follow his interests in a "small community where you can feel like you know everyone . . . [where] you really get to know people."

The Essential Liberal Arts Program

The academic program at Connecticut College is typical of most liberal arts colleges. It is geared toward a "really well-rounded education" for everyone, while providing students with "a very good variety" of options. Every student has to fulfill the General Education Requirements before she can declare a major. The requirements are designed to engage students in the various fields of the liberal arts. There are seven areas, including Mathematics and Logic, Creative Arts, and Historical Studies, in which every student must take a course. There is also a foreign language requirement of one or two semesters. The students generally find the requirements easy to complete, given the variety of ways to complete them, and most finish by the end of their sophomore year when they have to declare a major. Once free of obligations, students have a lot of freedom with their schedules, and take whatever suits their fancy. Thus, it is not surprising to the students here that the most popular class is "Experimental Dance."

There are nearly 40 majors or minors to choose from at Connecticut College. Psychology is the most popular option, and Conn College boasts a well-developed psychology department. It is the only department that offers graduate-level courses. Other popular majors are English, dance and international relations. The pre-med program, described as "extremely difficult, but well worth it in the end," is also very popular. Students can also design their own majors with special approval. Although Conn College is a liberal arts college without an engineering program, there are still some design-it-yourself engineering students who work with the opportunities that Conn College offers and supplement with summer courses elsewhere. Connecticut College also offers six competitive interdisciplinary certificate programs that include internships between junior and senior year.

A series of freshman seminars—small classes devoted to the intense study of one subject—premiered for the class of 2009. It is too early to gauge the quality of the program, but the students seemed very excited about the opportunity to study in-depth in a class of about 10 students. "Glow," a seminar devoted to the study of bioluminescence, includes a trip to Puerto Rico over break. Connecticut College prides itself on its close relationships between students and faculty. The largest lectures contain just over 100 students, but students are encouraged to participate even in classes of that size. One professor passed back tests to a class of about 100 students, handing out each test by name. Beyond introduction-level courses, the class size drops considerably. One girl exclaimed, "I love [the professors]! They know my name. I have dinner with them."

Booze, Music, and Fun: Conn College on the Weekends

The social scene at Connecticut College is both vibrant and insular. Very few students stray off campus during the weekends, so all of the activity happens on campus and in the dorms. Drinking is a common theme at many of the parties on campus. One student suggested that as many as three-fourths of the students "drink in some form;" the rest "have one beer a week or don't drink at all." Since the campus is relatively small, it is easy to get around, and many people spend their nights "literally going dorm to dorm looking for the biggest party." Because of the Honor Code, the campus safety has a lenient alcohol policy, and campus safety only intervenes if "people are out of control."

There is no pressure for students to drink, though, and there are many alternatives to drinking. The college organizes events every weekend, including game nights, concerts, conversational desserts, and movie nights. Those who do not want to drink and party can just as easily watch a movie, knit (at the Stitch and Bitch club), or discuss philosophy over some pizza. It is not surprising for a group of international students to get together on the weekend and cook an ethnic meal for a group of students. Thursday Night Events (TNEs) are especially popular, as they showcase the musical talents of the students. Friday Night Live also brings student and upcoming bands for free concerts. Other popular pastimes include theater and a cappella. With countless student-run organizations on campus, it seems that "the school is almost completely student-run." Because of this, the student government is very involved and influential. "Whatever you're interested in, you can find a group for it, or you can make a group for it."

Sports are not very big at Conn College, where the mascot is a camel. The Division I sailing team is the most successful team at the college and continually ranks as one of the top sailing teams in the nation. Conn also offers a variety of Division III varsity sports. This is not to say they don't take their sports seriously; the athletes are all "really dedicated" and they "just don't do [sports] for the hell of it." Connecticut College sports a number of intramural and club sports for those who want to play recreationally.

The typical Conn College student is "involved in 10 things at once, always with a close group of friends." The students take great pride in their initiative and ability: "There's always something special about a student that comes here that only they can offer." Although the student body is not racially diverse—it is "predominantly white"—it varies greatly in the "personalities, life goals and interests" of the students. Students take a lot of pride in their college and their residence halls. Every year, the entire campus takes part in the Camelympics, which one student claims is "the best event all year." The event spans two days of competition ranging from spelling bees and board games to dodge ball and ultimate Frisbee. Another popular event, named "Floralia" after a Roman holiday, is described as a "Conn Woodstock," where local and student bands come together in the spring for a day-long music festival.

The Honor Code

The Honor Code is one of Connecticut College's distinctive features, and one of the most important parts of the students' lives. The honor code covers both academic and residential life, and it ensures that every student is responsible for him or herself. The only person who can write up a student is the House Fellow, a position taken by another student. For serious offenses, students are taken to the Judicial Board, or J-Board, to which some students are elected. The faculty puts a lot of trust in the students' ability to be responsible for themselves. One student estimates that a remarkable 90 percent of damage is reported and paid for by students. The Honor Code also extends to academics, and professors trust that the students will not cheat. Some professors even give out take-home exams. Normal exams are unproctored, so each student is able to make his or her own exam schedule during exam week. The students laud the Honor Code, proclaiming, "it brings out the best in you."

> The honor code covers both academic and residential life, and it ensures that every student is responsible for himself.

Most students stay on campus during the weekends. A few go to Providence, Boston or New York City, which are all a reasonable distance away from campus by car or by train. The nearby city of New London seems a less desirable destination. The Camel Van, which can take students off campus, provides rides every hour. Although some students described it as a bit of a hassle, it is the best way to get out for students who don't own cars. Also, the Van has expanded service in the past year, to much praise. Although the city boasts some restaurants and the Garde Arts Theater, most students find enough to do on campus, so they don't feel the need to go outside very often. One student says that "people don't hang out in New London," when the campus provides everything a student needs.

Isolated Campus, Looking Outward

The dorms generally receive high marks from the students, though the quality of the rooms on campus varies. Some of the older dorms are "outdated" and "run-down," but many of the parties are held in them for that reason. Most freshmen are given doubles, but there are some triples and quads. There is a lottery for upperclassman housing, and most that request singles get them. One student said "if you're expecting a lot of luxury, you won't get it, but there are quality spaces." The residence halls foster the community spirit that is so prevalent at Conn. One girl explained how almost everyone keeps his or her door unlocked and open, and she can "have a casual conversation on [the] way to the bathroom." There are also a number of special-interest dorms: quiet, substance-free, single-sex, and cultural housing are all available. A remarkable display of housing satisfaction is shown in the fact that over 98 percent of students live on campus all four years.

The food at Connecticut College is "not the best food you can have," but the students like the variety. There are always vegetarian options, and one girl especially liked "make-your-own stir fry a couple nights a week." There is one main dining hall, and four smaller ones. The bakery received high marks for fresh bagels and Tollhouse pie, a concoction described as "a big pie of chocolate chip cookies." There are even a snack shop and a bar on campus, for late-night food and drink excursions.

Some students griped about a Conn College bubble, but admitted that the draw of the school for them was the close-knit community. One freshman said, "if someone is looking for somewhere they can leave, I wouldn't recommend Conn College to them." For all the energy and activity of the student body, the campus does tend to feel small. But although there is a feeling of isolation in some ways, the students of the college are very concerned with the outside world. Many of the students are international, and half of the junior class studies abroad. "Community service is huge" for the students, with many going into nearby New London to tutor or participate in community action. While this allows undergraduates to immerse themselves in the local community, many students still feel their interaction with the city is "limited."

Most students love the campus. "Really beautiful" stone buildings coexist with more modern structures, including the newest dorm complex, nicknamed the Plex. Stretching across the middle of the campus is the expansive green, a popular place for people to meet and hang out. The college also boasts an expansive Arboretum, which most students said is the "most beautiful spot on campus," especially when New England fall foliage is at its peak. The campus satisfies most students, and although it feels "a little small, it's easy to get everywhere." The small, intimate setting of Connecticut College fosters the strong bonds felt by students and faculty alike.—*Ryan Galisewski*

FYI

If you come to Connecticut College, you'd better bring: "a Beirut table, snow boots, and athletic gear."

What's the typical weekend schedule? "Thursday—Thursday Night Event, mingle in the student center; Friday—go out to dinner, go to Friday Night live open mic show; Saturday—party night, go out from dorm to dorm and get drunk; Sunday—do homework and catch up from Saturday evening."

If I could change one thing about Connecticut College, I'd "renovate the athletic center."

Three things every student at Connecticut College should do before graduating are "participate in the Fishbowl—when seniors do a naked run from one side of the campus to the other, ring the gong outside of the Cummings Art Building, and dance on the tables in Cro's Nest."

Fairfield University

Address: Fairfield, 1073 North Benson Road, Fairfield CT 06824-5195
Phone: 203-254-4100
E-mail Address: admis@mail.fairfield.edu
Web site URL: www.fairfield.edu
Year Founded: 1942
Private or Public: private
Religious affiliation: Jesuit
Location: suburban
Regular Application Deadline: 15-Jan
Number of Applicants: NA
Percent Accepted: NA
Percent Accepted who enroll: NA
Number Entering: NA
Number of Transfers Accepted each Year: NA

Mean SAT: 1,181
Mean ACT: 25
Middle 50% SAT range: NA
Middle 50% ACT range: NA
Early admission program (EA/ ED/ NA): NA
ED or EA Acceptance Rate: NA
Full time Undergraduate enrollment: 4,008
Total enrollment: 5,091
Percent Male: NA
Percent Female: NA
Total Percent Minority: NA
Percent African-American: NA
Percent Asian/Pacific Islander: NA
Percent Hispanic: NA
Percent Native-American: NA
Percent Other: NA

Percent in-state / out of state: NA
Percent from Public HS: NA
Retention Rate: NA
Graduation Rate: NA
Percent in On-campus housing: NA
Percent affiliated with Greek system: NA
Percent Varsity or Club Athletes: NA
Number of official organized extracurricular organizations: NA
3 Most popular majors: NA
Student/Faculty ratio: 13:01
Tuition and Fees: $31,450.00
Cost for Room and Board: $9,980.00

Fairfield University is a mid-sized Catholic university located in the picturesque town of Fairfield, CT, and overlooking the Long Island Sound. Dubbed "J.Crew U," it is a place where preppy, party lovers in search of a quality education can feel at home.

A Jesuit Education

Fairfield is proud of its Jesuit tradition, evidence of which is seen in its high-quality academic programs. The university offers lucrative scholarships to top-notch incoming freshmen and high-achieving sophomores are invited to apply to the prestigious Honors Program. The program allows students to replace certain distribution requirements with an interdisciplinary, writing intensive program. Most students must complete core courses in five areas: natural sciences and mathematics; history and social/behavioral sciences; philosophy, religious studies, and ethics; English and visual/performing arts; and modern or classical languages. Fairfield is divided into four schools: Arts and Sciences, Business, Nursing, and the Graduate School. Students consider Biology, International Studies, Art History, Religious Studies, Sociology, Accounting and Finance, and Mechanical Engineering to all be popular and strong programs. The New Media major, similar to film studies, is gaining popularity thanks in part to the CinFest Fairfield festival that showcases the work of many students in the major.

Fairfield students love how their school's small size allows them to get individualized attention. Introductory lectures often have no more than 40 people and most seminars have less than twelve. Professors are described as very knowledgeable and helpful. As one student said, they "are really concerned and devoted to the students' education." Students say the workload is the right balance- not too easy, but very manageable. "I like that we're challenged but we have a lot of time to get our work done," said one girl. The Fairfield administration and faculty are also very devoted to giving as many students as possible the opportunity to study abroad. Not only can upperclassmen elect to take the classic term or full year abroad, but all students can have an abroad experience through a variety of programs that take place during January intercession, March break, and the summer. Popular programs are in Italy, Ireland, Russia, Australia, and Nicaragua.

The Beach, The Mirror, and D-I Athletics

Fairfield students are not too busy fulfilling their core requirements or traveling abroad to engage in their favorite activity in their favorite location. As one freshman explained, "Fairfield is a big party school, there's usually something to do every night." Fairfield has a thriving party scene despite the fact that there are no fraternities and sororities because of "The Beach," a four mile strip of land along the Long Island Sound where houses are rented by about 200 seniors. The Beach is the center of Fairfield night life, though the townhouses where many juniors live are another extremely popular location. The infamous partying that takes place at the Beach has historically caused a strain on town-gown relations. It seems that Connecticut suburbanites are not too keen on hearing hundreds of college students partying into the

wee hours of the night. The Fairfield administration is now trying to exercise greater control over the partying at the Beach, causing students to bring their socializing back to the campus proper or out of town to nearby cities such as Bridgeport, New Haven, and New York City, which is just a MetroNorth ride away.

Students do not spend all their time drinking at the Beach. "At any party you go to, alcohol is pretty dominant, like at most colleges, but people are involved in a lot of other stuff, too," explained one student. Since Fairfield is a Catholic university, campus ministry programs with community service focuses are popular extracurricular activities. Other activities include glee club, improv groups, FUSA: the Fairfield student government, and cultural groups. Campus publications include *The Mirror*, the independent student run newspaper, as well as a variety of literary magazines and arts publications.

> "All Fairfield students dress alike, and it really annoys a lot of people."

Though Fairfield students aren't as into athletics as students at other Division I schools, watching the men's basketball team play at the Arena at Harbor Yard in Bridgeport is sometimes a popular activity. Fairfield usually does very well in men's and women's soccer, and women's volleyball, often getting to the NCAA tournament. Despite these facts, school spirit isn't that high at Fairfield and there are more students involved in intramural sports than there are spectators at most games.

The Scoop on J.Crew U

Since Fairfield is a Catholic school in Connecticut, most students are Christians from surrounding New England states. And as the nickname would suggest, many people at Fairfield think of their fellow students as being very preppy, wealthy, and white. As one girl explained, "the typical Fairfield student is pretty laid back, preppy, smart, and usually a partier." "All Fairfield students dress alike, and it really annoys a lot of people," complained one freshman. The university is working hard to change the stereotype of having a homogenous population. Diversity is slowly, but steadily increasing in the student body and the Center for Multicultural Relations is the home to a number of popular cultural groups and programs. Whether they fit into the idea of the typical Fairfield student or not, few students can complain about the physical appearance of their fellow students, and most say that Fairfield has a very attractive student body. And despite the fact that the administration recently got quite upset when a student group handed out condoms, hookups are very predominant.

To Live in a Townhouse

Students at Fairfield are guaranteed housing for all four years. Most underclassmen live in either the Quad or the Orient. The living arrangements for freshmen are often a bit cozy, to say the least. "When I first got here I found my dorm to be a lot smaller than I thought it was going to be and I'm not even in a forced triple. It's grown on me though and I like it. Some dorms are bigger than others, some are better, it just varies," summed up one freshman. Underclassmen's dreams of one day getting to live in the school-sponsored, condominium-style townhouses or the Beach allow them to put up with cramped living spaces. Housing on the Beach is not affiliated with the university, but it is one of the most popular and wished for options.

Despite their unique housing options, Fairfield students say that their food is typical college cafeteria fare. Fairfield has two dining halls, one for freshmen and one for upperclassmen. Some students complain that there is not much variety from day to day in the types of food offered, but not everyone is complaining. "I like that they have stir-fry with a lot of options so you can cook your own food. You can also eat at one restaurant and one café but you have to pay money for it, it's not on the plan," explained one girl.

Overall, Fairfield students have high praise for their school and think that potential students will love it, too. Whether you want to live on the beach, study abroad, or be educated in the Jesuit tradition, they are confident that Fairfield University would be a great place for you.—*Keneisha Sinclair*

FYI

If you come to Fairfield, you'd better bring "a car—it's essential."

What is the typical weekend schedule? "Friday and Saturday, pregame in the dorms and then go to the townhouses or the Beach. Sunday, sleep."

If I could change one thing about Fairfield, I'd "make registration be online instead of in person."

Three things every student should do before graduating from Fairfield are "go to a beach party, study abroad, and live in a townhouse."

Quinnipiac University

Address: Quinnipiac, 275 Mount Carmel Avenue, Hamden, CT 06518
Phone: 203-582-8600
E-mail Address: NA
Web site URL: www.quinnipiac.edu
Year Founded: 1929
Private or Public: private
Religious affiliation: none
Location: suburban
Regular Application Deadline: 1-Feb
Number of Applicants: NA
Percent Accepted: NA
Percent Accepted who enroll: NA
Number Entering: NA
Number of Transfers Accepted each Year: NA

Mean SAT: 1,115
Mean ACT: 24
Middle 50% SAT range: NA
Middle 50% ACT range: NA
Early admission program (EA/ ED/ NA): EA
ED or EA Acceptance Rate: NA
Full time Undergraduate enrollment: 5,400
Total enrollment: 7,950
Percent Male: NA
Percent Female: NA
Total Percent Minority: NA
Percent African-American: NA
Percent Asian/Pacific Islander: NA
Percent Hispanic: NA
Percent Native-American: NA

Percent Other: NA
Percent in-state / out of state: NA
Percent from Public HS: NA
Retention Rate: NA
Graduation Rate: NA
Percent in On-campus housing: 64%
Percent affiliated with Greek system: NA
Percent Varsity or Club Athletes: NA
Number of official organized extracurricular organizations: 70
3 Most popular majors: NA
Student/Faculty ratio: 16:01
Tuition and Fees: $27,600.00

Q uinnipiac University is a small school with huge vocational opportunities. Set in a picturesque area of New England, the University offers a rural-campus feel and family-like faculty that create an all-around homey feel. While Sleeping Giant State Park looms over the campus and provides a popular hiking spot, students can still enjoy the urban nightlife of neighboring New Haven. While the majority of students come from Connecticut and surrounding New England states, they may be pleasantly surprised by the setting. As one student said, "The combination of nature and urban convenience is a major bonus for Quinnipiac."

Campus Commuters

If you're looking for a school that complements the New England fall, this is the place. Directly across the street sits a large state park which, according to one sophomore, "looks like a patchwork quilt in the fall." An elegant pine-grove path meanders through campus providing a scenic walk to class, the library, or the new gym. When asked to describe the campus, one sophomore said: "It looks like a little village. Everything is pretty close together and within walking distance. It's very picturesque too!" Another student noted, "Students literally get mad if you litter or sometimes even walk on the grass. . . . It is THAT nice."

Although the campus may feel like a small village, many of the buildings are architecturally modern or even futuristic. Recently renovated, the gym now contains a suspended indoor track hanging over new tennis courts. The library also has a modern feel with a whole wall made of glass that makes it easy to enjoy the winter scenery while studying cozily in the warm library. The dorms may not be quite as elegant as the gym and library, but nonetheless students had few complaints. Freshman dorms are the smallest, but still not cramped. They are coed and accessible to all the essential campus buildings.

Freshman bathrooms are communal, but upperclassmen suites each have their own. Suites after freshman year vary in size from three to 10 students. Some students move off campus as juniors, but all seniors live off campus. As far as dining goes, students generally give high marks to their Café, which has recently received a remodeling of the seating area. One student remarked: "The Café is amazing even though people complain a lot about it. I mean, the chefs make most of the food right in front of you. It's like a mall food court; there are a bunch of different stations. I've eaten at a lot of different colleges and our Café is by far the best I've seen and eaten in."

Many students at Quinnipiac either have cars or are hankering for them. Since freshmen are not allowed to have cars on campus, some find themselves saying, "I hate waiting for shuttles and taxis when I want to get off campus; I can't wait until next year." One student emphasized, however, that cars are not a requirement: "You definitely do not need a car to have fun here. Half the time the upperclassmen take the shuttle into New Haven anyway so they don't have to drive wasted."

Partying

A lot of Quinnipiac partying takes place in nearby New Haven, but there is plenty of fun on campus, too. According to most students, it is only a minor setback that kegs are not allowed on campus. "It's not a big deal. We usually just drink in our rooms until we want to go to the bars anyway." The Greek scene is not hugely dominating at Quinnipiac, so weekend festivities revolve around the various bars surrounding campus. However, with two fraternities and three sororities and around 300 members, the frat scene certainly has a distinct presence on campus. An additional fraternity will be added this year. As one sorority member said, "We're small but we're still here!"

> **"The combination of nature and urban convenience is a major bonus for Quinnipiac."**

One favorite hot spot off campus, especially for girls, is Toad's Place in New Haven located next to the Yale University campus. Just 10 minutes away from Quinnipiac, Toad's has dance parties every Wednesday and Saturday and often good bands on other nights. One freshman said, "Toad's is my favorite place on Saturday nights because I get to meet hot Yale boys." While upperclassmen tend to get off-campus more, this is mostly because of the accessibility of cars rather than the limitations of being underage. Consensus among underclassmen is that fake IDs are common and rarely scrutinized. But even if students don't make it off campus on the weekend there are usually options for partying on campus. For those who prefer dry events, there are also plenty of options. As one student said, "[The] student programming board puts on tons of free campus events all weekend every weekend for kids who don't want to party or just want to have some sober fun."

Students at Quinnipiac love to talk about the tradition of May weekend. Every year in May the school spends large amounts of money for fun events like concerts. One senior said: "The entire campus turns in to a drunken carnival. People run around and go crazy. It's my favorite weekend of the year."

Other social events include the school's basketball and hockey games. Both teams are quite good and the school gets excited for home games, although many students resent the lack of a football team and stadium. Other varsity sports are not as popular, but many students participate in intramural sports. "It's a great way to meet people and actually get some decent exercise," one sophomore said.

Preparing for a Job

Quinnipiac does not offer a liberal arts education, but rather provides students with training in various career paths. Among these options, Quinnipiac has gained a solid reputation in the health sciences, although these majors also seem to be the most difficult. A junior physical therapy major said, "Even though I know I'm working harder on the weekends while my friends are out partying, it's worth it knowing I can get a good job right out of college."

There are a few other majors that also receive high marks. As one student related, "The health science majors are extremely popular, and the business school and communications schools are both phenomenal. The communications school has an amazing group of teachers who are so experienced in their fields, they are on television news talks shows . . . literally every week." Students in all majors, however, note very experienced and accessible faculty members. "Teachers can be really good and even if they aren't they are usually always accessible." Classes tend to be quite small, but most students have found it relatively easy to get in to the classes they want. Teachers are often flexible about letting students in even when the classes are full. Among the more interesting electives, students mention a popular art class in which students hike outdoors and make natural sculptures inspired by existing works of art. The outdoor sculptures are displayed along the campus's central pathway for all the students to admire. Outside of class time, Quinnipiac students find themselves very busy, with more than 65 student groups and clubs on campus and strong emphases on student leadership. These opportunities led one student to gush, "The student activities are amazing." By providing a rigorous pre-professional education within a small close-knit and spirited community, Quinnipiac is, in the words of one student, "a perfect fit for so many of us. I would never choose to go anywhere else."—*Quinn Fitzgerald*

FYI

If you come to Quinnipiac you'd better bring "a car and a fake ID."

What is the typical weekend schedule? "Sleeping in, homework, campus events, bars."

If I could change one thing about Quinnipiac, "it would be the lack of student enthusiasm for on-campus events."

Three things every student at Quinnipiac should do before graduating are "hike through Sleeping Giant State Park; become a leader of a team, club, or organization; and go crazy on May weekend with the rest of campus."

Trinity College

Address: Trinity, 300 Summit Street, Hartford, CT 06106
Phone: 860-297-2180
E-mail Address: admissions.office@trincoll.edu
Web site URL: www.trincoll.edu
Year Founded: 1823
Private or Public: private
Religious affiliation: none
Location: urban
Regular Application Deadline: 2-Jan
Number of Applicants: NA
Percent Accepted: 43%
Percent Accepted who enroll: 27%
Number Entering: NA
Number of Transfers Accepted each Year: NA
Mean SAT: 1,299
Mean ACT: 28

Middle 50% SAT range: V:600–690, M:610–700
Middle 50% ACT range: 27–29
Early admission program (EA/ ED/ NA): ED
ED or EA Acceptance Rate: NA
Full time Undergraduate enrollment: NA
Total enrollment: 2,203
Percent Male: 50%
Percent Female: 50%
Total Percent Minority: 0%
Percent African-American: 6%
Percent Asian/Pacific Islander: 6%
Percent Hispanic: 5%
Percent Native-American: 0%
Percent Other: NA

Percent in-state / out of state: 18%/82%
Percent from Public HS: 44%
Retention Rate: 92%
Graduation Rate: 83%
Percent in On-campus housing: 95%
Percent affiliated with Greek system: 36%
Percent Varsity or Club Athletes: NA
Number of official organized extracurricular organizations: 105
3 Most popular majors: Economics, History, Political Science and Government
Student/Faculty ratio: 11:01
Tuition and Fees: $35,130
Cost for Room and Board: $8,970
Percent receiving Financial aid, first-year: 40%

Even though Trinity College was founded in 1823 and boasts some of the earliest examples of Gothic architecture in America, this college is not afraid of innovation. With a fresh curriculum and a large handful of renovated buildings, Trinity students enjoy constant improvements in both facilities and academics. Located in Hartford, Connecticut's capital, Trinity offers a small community feeling in an urban setting, where friendliness is a common attribute. As one sophomore said, "I was surprised in a good way, because it is so easy to fit in; you can always find a group of friends."

Small Class Conundrum

Trinity offers a wide range of classes and attracts students with a variety of interests.

Though Trinity is one of the best liberal arts schools in the country, students are not deterred from pursuing science majors. Students must fulfill their distribution requirements by taking classes from five general areas: humanities, the arts, natural sciences, social sciences, and numerical and symbolic reasoning. Within each area, students are free to choose whichever classes interest them. As one sophomore declared, "I took an environmental studies course for a requirement, which I never would have chosen myself, and ended up loving it!" Students find that the requirements improve their academic experience and give just enough freedom for finding classes.

Part of Trinity's close-knit community feeling stems from the seminar classes each freshman is required to take. First-years take a seminar and live with the same group of students, fostering strong relationships and forming a comfortable environment from the very beginning of their Trinity experience. One junior commented, "these seminars are not traditional classes; they focus on unique topics and have a budget to plan activities like going to the Bushnell Theater for a show or eating out at a local restaurant." Trinity can be characterized by this focus on small classes and close student-faculty relationships.

The most popular majors on campus are history, economics, and political science, which offer more classes than smaller majors such as classics or computer science. Trinity also started a new Human Rights Program and has unique classes under such disciplines as Queer Studies and Community Action. Though students are pleased with the range of courses, they comment that competition for entry into the most popular classes such as philosophy of sports or fitness classes severely limits their availability, especially to underclassmen. A current freshman moaned, "There is a lot of competition to get into classes. Most people settle for classes in their major that they need to take; only a few get to take the ones they really want."

> Professors will even give you their cell phone number. They are willing and eager to help you with anything.

Regardless of the classes' popularity, students universally agree that the small-class environment has made for a wonderful academic experience. Students regularly eat dinner with their professors and one claimed that "professors will even give you their cell phone number. They are willing and eager to help you with anything," Yes, the academic experience fulfills students' expectations of rigor, but students say that is just "part of what they do here; there is still plenty of time to socialize." Though some students strive to make the dean's list, others find that academics are not a dominant part of life. Professors are fair with grading, and as a savvy junior remarked, "school is just about as hard as you make it."

Community of Bantams

After freshmen year, when the students all live together in a quad, they have the ability to choose their roommates and even request themed housing. Housing for upperclass-

men is integrated with a variety of buildings, including the coveted new Prassel dorm. Though freshman dorms are currently being renovated, a sophomore insisted that "dorms get bigger after freshman year with a little more to choose from, like the option of having a living room."

The RA system provides yet another way for students to form relationships with figures of authority and guidance. Though RAs are responsible for students following dorm policies and act as mediators between students and the administration, students praise the system and are happy about the bond forged between them and their RAs. "We have fantastic RAs. They are trusting and make sure you are safe, but are not an overbearing presence. They want to keep you out of trouble with authority." The college prohibits alcohol in rooms with underage students and restricts everyone from possessing hard alcohol, but students claim that the policies are not strictly enforced.

Among old gothic architecture, a beautiful chapel, and a Victorian-style English Department building, Trinity students find new modern facilities that add even more to the college's character. Recently, students have been able to enjoy the addition of an entirely new dorm complex and a community hockey rink, while anticipating a new Trinity commons area and the renovation of some of the older buildings. When the weather is nice, students flock to the quad to socialize or play frisbee with their friends between classes and, when it's crunch time, students take advantage of quiet study spots such as Gallows Hill with comfy couches and free coffee.

The main dining hall, where most students eat on the weekdays, provides another place to meet students and socialize. There are two places available to eat other than the main dining hall, one serving a variety of sandwiches and the other burgers and fries. Students pay a fee, choosing from three levels, at the beginning of the year and budget from that set amount of money. The food receives neither great praise nor terrible complaints and is occasionally surpassed by those venturing to restaurants in West Hartford or looking for a cheap meal at Timothy's, a local favorite.

Party If You Please

Trinity students agree that the social scene on campus revolves around Vernon Street, the home of the college's rowdy fraternities. A male freshman cautioned that "some are hard to get into if you don't have girls, but

you can always find a party on the weekend."
The frats also host annual themed parties
such as Tropical, a party ranked in Playboy
Magazine, where the students bring in sand,
and Foam, where a frat house is filled with—
believe it or not—foam. Some other favorite
party spots include the football house or one
of the cultural houses. Students usually
party from Thursday through Saturday, and
drinking remains a very prominent part of
the campus social life.

If these parties aren't enticing enough to
relieve students' weekday stresses, they
may find themselves at one of the student-
run coffeehouses or attending an event
hosted by "The Fred." The Fred Pfiel Community Project is a group of students who
host daily events such as comedians or
arts shows as an alternative to drinking.
Though Trinity is a small school and most
of the social scene is integrated, mostly
upperclassmen can be found in The Tap,
while underclassmen search for local bars
that don't card. Drinking may be a part
of campus culture, but "not in the absence
of other options," claimed a well-rounded
sophomore.

One student rejoiced that "though there
are school policies regulating alcohol consumption, everyone drinks; it happens in
everyone's room." Pot is also fairly common
on campus, though the harder drugs are
scarce. Luckily, regardless of students' preferences of how to have fun, all rave about
the general friendliness and ease of finding
their own comfort zone.

Change of Heart-ford

Students disagree about the role the surrounding city of Hartford plays in their educational and social experience at Trinity. All
students either own cars or have access to a
friend's for shopping trips to the Westfarms
Mall or food runs down the Berlin Turnpike.
One junior warned, "I would never walk
around campus at night alone" and that the
surrounding area can either be "really nice
or really sketchy." Others comment about
living in the "Trinity bubble," where it's really easy to forget the city and only use campus resources.

The administration and student-run volunteer groups strive to close the gap between
the college "bubble" and the Hartford community. An involved sophomore described
taking a class called Child Development,
where students design a public policy project, "we had to identify a problem relating to
child development in Hartford, speak to community members, formulate a solution, and
present proposals to the community that
were later implemented." The school also offers classes on Hartford to further familiarize
the students with the city and perhaps inspire
them to invest time in promoting its growth.

Squashing Opponents

Step aside, football; the eight-time national
championship squash team draws the largest
crowd on this campus. Though both sports
enjoy support from their dedicated fans,
squash remains Trinity's true claim to fame.
A spirited senior said that "around campus
you can sense the trinity pride," which carries over into other extracurricular activities as well. Everyone is involved on this
campus, whether a student competes as a
varsity athlete, on the intramural fields, or
just cheers on a friend.

In addition to sports, Trinity students participate in a variety of clubs, from the student
newspaper *The Tripod*, to student government, a wide range of volunteer groups, and
even a cat alliance, which cares for cats
roaming the campus. Do It Day, a campus-
wide volunteer initiative, provides another
outlet for students to get involved in the community by participating in activities such as
painting a nursing home or planting flowers
outside hospitals. There is an activity here for
all interests, and as one sophomore explained, "people here are so over-involved,
you hardly find anyone who only has one
commitment."

Students at Trinity brag about their close
relationships with amazing, compassionate
professors, show their Bantam spirit through
devotion to a myriad of activities, and save
their best tropical attire to debut for weekend
revelry. With so much to do, schedules are
usually packed, but most students wouldn't
have it any other way.—*Cara Dermody*

FYI
If you come to Trinity, you'd better bring "a pair of Uggs, a car, and a high squash IQ."
What is the typical weekend schedule? "Most spend the afternoon watching movies or playing
   sports, followed by pregaming for a long night at a frat or attending a concert with friends."
If I could change one thing about Trinity, "I'd bring back a dating scene."
The three things every student at Trinity should do before graduating are "Go to a squash game, get
   thrown into Trinity's fountain, and climb the bell tower."

United States Coast Guard Academy

Address: US Coast Guard Academy, 31 Mohegan Avenue, New London, CT 06320-8103
Phone: 860-444-8500
E-mail Address: NA
Web site URL: http://www.cga.edu/
Year Founded: 1931
Private or Public: private
Religious affiliation: none
Location: suburban
Regular Application Deadline: 2-Mar
Number of Applicants: 3,000
Percent Accepted: 24%
Percent Accepted who enroll: 70%
Number Entering: 504
Number of Transfers Accepted each Year: NA
Mean SAT: 1,262
Mean ACT: 27
Middle 50% SAT range: 1,180–1,390

Middle 50% ACT range: 25–29
Early admission program (EA/ ED/ NA): EA
ED or EA Acceptance Rate: NA
Full time Undergraduate enrollment: 996
Total enrollment: 996
Percent Male: 72%
Percent Female: 28%
Total Percent Minority: 14%
Percent African-American: 3%
Percent Asian/Pacific Islander: 5%
Percent Hispanic: 5%
Percent Native-American: 1%
Percent Other: NA
Percent in-state / out of state: 6%/94%
Percent from Public HS: 77%
Retention Rate: 86%

Graduation Rate: 64%
Percent in On-campus housing: 100%
Percent affiliated with Greek system: 0%
Percent Varsity or Club Athletes: 70% varsity
Number of official organized extracurricular organizations: NA
3 Most popular majors: Engineering, General; Oceanography, Chemical and Physical; Political Science and Government, General
Student/Faculty ratio: 9:01
Tuition and Fees: $0.00
In State Tuition and Fees (if different): $0.00
Cost for Room and Board: $0.00
Percent receiving Financial aid, first-year: 0%

The United States Coast Guard Academy provides its students with the discipline and skills useful for all tracks of life, turning its cadets into the leaders of the future. With military employment following graduation and several opportunities for development while in the Academy, cadets receive much more than a four-year education. The USCGA holds firm to its rigorous academic curriculum, strong athletics programs, and varied extracurricular offerings. Each graduate leaves the Academy with a sense of accomplishment that inevitably leads to post-graduation success.

Core Values

The United States Coast Guard Academy boasts much more than a commanding name and intimidating reputation. Founded as the Revenue Cutter School of Instruction in 1876, the USCGA offers an impressive combination of tradition, rigor, and discipline that has shaped leaders of America for over a century. In fact, the leadership skills developed during the four years at USCGA are what many cadets refer to as the best aspect of the Academy. The USCGA's set of core values is three-fold, emphasizing honor, respect and devotion to duty. These values form the foundation for all programs in the Academy. The lofty reputation of the Academy often intimidates potential students, discouraging them from applying to the undergraduate program. However, prospective candidates should be encouraged "to consider the broad range of opportunities that the Academy has to offer, and acknowledge the diverse student body that enjoys the benefits of the USCGA."

The USCGA draws a student body that is about 70 percent male and 30 percent female. All cadets receive equal treatment with respect to academics, housing and athletic training. The promise of equal opportunities at the Academy is one of the most treasured aspects of the institution, as reported by many cadets. The USCGA provides an equal playing field whether a cadet is male or female, first-class or fourth-class. You might ask: What is the difference between a first-class and a fourth-class cadet? How can delineating classes exist within a system of fair play?

All freshmen at the Academy are called

fourth-class cadets, and each year students climb one rung on the ladder. Each class has special roles and duties at the Academy; this reflects the hierarchical structure of military life and prepares cadets for post-graduation military employment. Fourth-class cadets can be compared to understudies, learning the ropes of military life and closely following examples of the more experienced. Third-class cadets are assigned to advise one or two fourth-class cadets, while second-class cadets assume the responsibility of Assistant Division Officers, leading the younger cadets during training. Finally, first-class cadets have the opportunity to become Regimental Staff Officers, Company Commanders, Department Heads, and Division Officers. This specific regimentation at the Academy prepares cadets for the structured system of military duty and creates a progressive path towards increased responsibility, learning and opportunity. At the end of four years, first-class cadets have had the experience of being followers, mentors, assistant leaders and commanders. Each of these roles provides a wide range of opportunities for growth and enrichment unique to the mission of the Academy.

The Typical Day

With such a close parallel to military structure and core values, it is hardly surprising that discipline plays a tremendous role in the lives of cadets at the USCGA. Although cadets' names and roles change from year to year, the typical weekday schedule "falls equally upon all cadets alike." The wake-up alarm sounds at "0600" and breakfast quickly follows. Academic instruction begins promptly at 0800 and ends at 1200 for lunch. Classes then resume after lunch and end for the day at 1600. The Academy's curriculum offers a Bachelor of Science degree for all students. Classes are often competitive, though many cadets enjoy the academic challenges laid before them. The classroom setting encourages cadets to think quickly, observe objectively and analyze deeply. Most classes do not exceed 40 students, and this fosters close relationships between students and professors, as well as interactive learning. The Academy has set core requirements, which students often complete during their first two years.

The USCGA ensures the well-roundedness of its cadets, whether they are in the classroom or on the field. Sports period runs from 1600 to 1800, and the school encourages all of its cadets to pursue athletics. The majority of its cadets to pursue athletics. The majority of students play for a varsity team, though some cadets take sports less seriously and wish there was less emphasis on it at the Academy. In addition to intramural and varsity sports, a cadet may choose from 18 other clubs and activities. These range "from glee club to aviation club to ski club to pep band." Cadets may develop a wide variety of talents and delve into many of their special interests.

> "The friends you meet here will be the ones you keep for the rest of your life."

Sports period doesn't end the day for cadets. Buffet dinner follows from 1700 to 1900. Then, 1900 marks the beginning of military period, and from 2000 until 2200 is study hour. Sleep becomes an option only at 2200, and all cadets must be in bed by 2400. Cadets must stay on the base during the week, and the Academy requires its students to live on the base all four years. Cadets say that living "on base" gives them a strong sense of unity with the whole student body, and this is valued very highly. Cadets report that homesickness does not often occur because of the strong bonds that cadets form while living, training and learning together. One sophomore cadet reports that "the best thing about the Academy is the people you are surrounded by. The friends you meet here will be the ones you keep for the rest of your life."

Life Beyond the Coast

Cadets need not apply for jobs after graduation, since the Academy assures them of a career with the United States Coast Guard. Immediately following graduation, cadets receive positions as Deck Watch Officers or Engineers in Training for their first two-year tour. This embarks them on a military journey that further develops their minds, bodies and spirits. The work ethic taught at the USCGA prepares cadets for a successful life within the military or in civilian surroundings.

Alumni of the Academy also make their mark on the outside world, often receiving honors in fields such as medicine, business and law. They attribute much of their success to the training at the USCGA and often come back to the Academy for lectures and conferences. A strong alumni network really kindles the spirit at the Academy and illustrates the fact that the Academy's core values continue to thrive in the minds of its cadets long after graduation.

The job security that the USCGA offers is one of the most attractive features of the Academy. After the first tour, cadets can apply for advanced-degree programs financed by the U.S. Coast Guard. Flight school is another appealing option for many graduates. Pay and benefits, including full medical and dental plans, continue during any tenure of employment with the Coast Guard. Cadets admit that many of them choose the USCGA because it ensures them job security when they finally embark into the world.

Graduating from the USCGA is not the end for cadets, but rather the beginning of a fruitful career of military life and much more. The USCGA asks a lot of its students but gives back just as much, if not more.—*Aleksandra Kopec*

FYI

If you come to the U.S. Coast Guard Academy, you'd better bring "a sense of humor for the many disciplining challenges you will encounter."

What is the typical weekend schedule? "Live large while freedom reins. Leisure time increases as cadets get closer to graduation, but getting off the base is something most cadets try to do during the weekend. Maybe a little bit of studying on Sunday would ease the workload for the rest of the week, but it is important to get outside the gates and enjoy yourself."

If I could change one thing about the U.S. Coast Guard Academy, I'd "give cadets the option to get into bed before 10 p.m."

Three things every student at the U.S. Coast Guard Academy should do before graduating are "go to the Caribbean for five weeks on a 300-foot sailboat, experience swab summer—a rigorous orientation program prior to the beginning of freshman year, and become part of an athletic team."

University of Connecticut

Address: U Conn, 2131 Hillside Road, Unit 3088, Storrs, CT 06269-3088-3088
Phone: 860-486-3137
E-mail Address: beahusky@uconn.edu
Web site URL: http://www.uconn.edu
Year Founded: 1881
Private or Public: public
Religious affiliation: none
Location: rural
Regular Application Deadline: 2-Feb
Number of Applicants: NA
Percent Accepted: 51%
Percent Accepted who enroll: 32%
Number Entering: NA
Number of Transfers Accepted each Year: NA
Mean SAT: 1,189
Mean ACT: NA

Middle 50% SAT range: V:530–630, M:560–660
Middle 50% ACT range: 23–27
Early admission program (EA/ ED/ NA): EA
ED or EA Acceptance Rate: NA
Full time Undergraduate enrollment: NA
Total enrollment: 16,006
Percent Male: 49%
Percent Female: 51%
Total Percent Minority: 17%
Percent African-American: 5%
Percent Asian/Pacific Islander: 7%
Percent Hispanic: 5.0%
Percent Native-American: 0%
Percent Other: NA
Percent in-state / out of state: 77%/23%

Percent from Public HS: 87%
Retention Rate: 93%
Graduation Rate: 74%
Percent in On-campus housing: 71%
Percent affiliated with Greek system: 15%
Percent Varsity or Club Athletes: NA
Number of official organized extracurricular organizations: 303
3 Most popular majors: Registered Nurse Training, Political Science and Government, Psychology
Student/Faculty ratio: 17:01
Tuition and Fees: $22,786
In State Tuition and Fees (if different): $8,842
Cost for Room and Board: $8,850
Percent receiving Financial aid, first-year: 48%

A small, unassuming town with a permanent population of around 11,000 people, Storrs, Conn., is a cartographer's speck. But a well-known university with a premiere sports program has put Storrs on the map. Over the past decade, the University of Connecticut has distinguished itself academically and athletically as one of the best public universities in New England.

No Place Like Home

Three-fourths of UConn undergraduates call the Nutmeg State home. But despite the lack of geographic diversity, the student body is composed of individuals with a wide variety of backgrounds and interests: "There is a broad range of personalities that would allow any student to blend in fairly easily—from people that love to drink to people who are dedicated to studying." One consequence of a predominately New England student body is a fierce Yankee-Red Sox rivalry that often gets heated when October rolls around. Even the closest of roommates may find themselves temporarily torn apart. "Two years ago, when the Yanks were playing the Sox in the playoffs, the quad was filled," one senior remembers. "It was divided between the Sox and Yankee fans yelling at each other in the middle of the night." Playoffs time aside, students say that most people are open and friendly: "Obviously there are some exceptions, but everyone here is pretty cool." Because UConn boasts such a large student population—over 16,000 undergraduates—there is a group of people for everyone. By the same token, it can be easy to be lost in the mix: "You can stay to yourself and not meet anyone if you want and nobody will stop you. You just have to put yourself out there to make friends." Many freshmen rush fraternities and sororities; UConn, which has a detailed anti-hazing policy, oversees around 30 organizations on campus. But making friends is not contingent upon being a Greek.

Close Quarters

The real estate bubble has already burst at UConn. In recent years, the University has had to deal with serious housing shortages that have forced some students to move off campus. Unanticipated high rates of matriculation have resulted in too many students and too few rooms. Underclassmen, however, are guaranteed housing. Most freshmen live in either North or Northwest—don't be fooled by the similar names. The former is an old, rundown building known as "the jungle"; the latter is new and nice. Both dorms' rooms aren't particularly spacious and are usually shared by up to three people. After their first year or two, many students opt to move off campus into apartments but even those "are a hike from classes and tough to get into." In short, housing is hardly one of UConn's strong points. "Unfortunately, housing has been an on and off problem at UConn," one upperclassman said. "If you're lucky enough to have a first pick and end up in Northwest, the all-freshman housing is pretty good quality. . . . On the other hand,

though, you could end up like me, in an all-girls dorm with an awful dining hall on the farthest end of campus possible. It was a much less convenient freshman experience but still a great one."

Something for Everyone

With over 100 majors and programs to choose from, undergraduates can study virtually anything. In addition to courses required for the major, students must take a certain number of General Education classes in a variety of disciplines including art, science and philosophy, affording a basic, well-rounded education. GE classes tend to be large but on average, class size ranges from 27 to 34 students. For those seeking smaller classes and a more challenging workload, UConn offers an honors program. By junior year, students interested in applying to one of the University's nine specialized schools, such as the Physical Therapy, Pharmacy or Business School, must do so: "Specialized programs like the Business School and School of Education are really prominent, apparently." Yet, the majority of students are in the College of Liberal Arts and Sciences.

> "There is a broad range of personalities that would allow any student to blend in fairly easily—from people that love to drink to people who are dedicated to studying."

The difficulty of classes depends largely on the major. Engineering courses are considered tough while human development and family studies is thought to be one of the easier majors. Some of the more acclaimed classes include David Miller's General Psychology I, which despite starting at 8 a.m. is always well-attended. "He is so good that kids want to get up and go to it," one student said. "He always starts off the class with a music video and sometimes he dresses up as former famous psychologists." Other popular courses include Children's Literature, in which students read books like Goodnight Moon, Where the Wild Things Are, Alice in Wonderland, and Hip Hop Culture.

Work Hard, Play Harder

UConn has a reputation of a party school, which is well-deserved. Though the campus is billed as dry, when the weekend arrives, students don't shy from putting down the books and picking up the bottle. Underclassmen often head to the Celeron Square Apartments or make the trek to the off-campus Carriage House: "It's a fairly long path, but when you are buzzed or drunk, it goes by quickly." Those over 21—or with IDs that say they are—hit up the local bars, including Civic Pub and Huskies. Fraternities and sororities figure prominently into the party scene as well. Many have houses off campus, where they throw keggers. The Rugby House is also a weekend hotspot. Despite the occasional debauchery, students are adept at balancing school work with their social life and one senior is quick to point out that while UConn is a party school, "it's also a great place to gain a good education."

Top Dogs

UConn is perhaps best known for its sports teams. The men's and women's basketball teams have established themselves as perennial powerhouses, contending annually for national championships and making household names out of the likes of Emeka Okafor and Diana Taurasi. Come winter every year, Huskymania takes over. The campus is transformed into a frenzy as students pile into Gampel Pavilion and the nearby Hartford Civic Center to cheer on their Huskies. Tickets are not easy to come by, but the University recently instituted a lottery system to cut down on students camping out in front of the ticket booth: "People would just line up in their tents down the street. I actually saw people bring their TVs and Playstations."

Success has not been limited to the hardwood, however. The football team, which plays in the newly constructed, 40,000-set Rentschler Field, captured the Motor City Bowl two years ago in just its second season in Division I-A. The men's and women's soccer teams and field hockey team have all made deep runs in NCAA tournaments in the last few years. UConn also promises a wide range of intramural sports from bowling to badminton to dodge ball. The competition is intense—even to get on a team: "IMs are pretty big. The slots for teams always fill up quick, within a day or two."

UConn encourages high school seniors to come to campus and be a "Husky for a day." Students get to meet people and professors, attend classes and even eat in the dining halls. At the very least, they find out where exactly Storrs, Conn., is—and may very well find themselves returning the following fall.—*Joshua Lotstein*

FYI
If you come to UConn, you'd better bring "an open mind and a fridge to store your alcohol."
What is the typical weekend like? "Friday and Saturday, partying at Celeron, Carriage or some dorm room; Sunday, recovering and doing homework."
If I could change one thing about UConn, I'd "add more parking."
Three things every student should do before graduating from UConn are "go to a men's Basketball game, drink at Carriage or Celeron, play oozeball (volleyball in the mud) during Spring Weekend."

Wesleyan University

Address: Wesleyan, 237 High St, Middletown, CT 06459-0265
Phone: 860-685-3000
E-mail Address: admissions@wesleyan.edu
Web site URL: www.wesleyan.edu
Year Founded: 1831
Private or Public: private
Religious affiliation: none
Location: suburban
Regular Application Deadline: 2-Jan
Number of Applicants: NA
Percent Accepted: 28%
Percent Accepted who enroll: 36%
Number Entering: NA
Number of Transfers Accepted each Year: NA
Mean SAT: 1,390
Mean ACT: 30

Middle 50% SAT range: 1,290–1,380
Middle 50% ACT range: 28–32
Early admission program (EA/ ED/ NA): ED
ED or EA Acceptance Rate: NA
Full time Undergraduate enrollment: 2,805
Total enrollment: 2,805
Percent Male: 50%
Percent Female: 50%
Total Percent Minority: 40%
Percent African-American: 7%
Percent Asian/Pacific Islander: 11%
Percent Hispanic: 8%
Percent Native-American: NA
Percent Other: NA
Percent in-state / out of state: 92% out

Percent from Public HS: 57%
Retention Rate: 95%
Graduation Rate: 84%
Percent in On-campus housing: 98%
Percent affiliated with Greek system: 3%
Percent Varsity or Club Athletes: NA
Number of official organized extracurricular organizations: 220
3 Most popular majors: English, Political Science, Psychology
Student/Faculty ratio: 9:01
Tuition and Fees: NA
Cost for Room and Board: NA
Percent receiving Financial aid, first-year: 44%

The student population at Wesleyan University is so diverse that the school has been dubbed "Diversity University." With a well-rounded student body and a challenging curriculum, Wesleyan attracts many independent and driven individuals. The school is part of the "Little 3 Ivies", as it is involved in intense rivalries with Amherst and Williams. As one student put it, "If you're a person, you'll find a place at Wesleyan."

Academic Rigor

Wesleyan has established itself as an academically rigorous university. However, although the coursework is challenging, students are not competitive. One junior says that "students bend over backwards and genuinely care about increasing the quality of the learning environment." Students here want to learn and are eager to help each other to get to a higher level of education, to have better discussions in class, and to produce a better learning environment. Learning for the sake of learning is a top priority at Wesleyan. "Intellectual curiosity carries on outside the classroom. Because there is so much political activity and passionate discussion outside the classroom, a lot of my education goes on there. Although the idealism sometimes gets to me, the students in general really want to make a significant impact on the world before they even graduate."

While getting into classes can be extremely difficult and at times a "painful experience," there is a wide range of courses offered. During the drop/add period, students are able to attend different classes and adjust their schedules. With over 900 courses offered in 39 departments and 44 major fields of study, students are very motivated to take advantage of the liberal-arts curriculum and are able to dabble in a variety of academic fields. Special academic programs include the College of Social Studies (also known on campus as the "College of Suicidal Sophomores") and the College of Letters.

Wesleyan has very loose curriculum requirements, enabling students to discover their true passions and experiment with a motley array of disciplines; however, Wesleyan does have Gen Ed Expectations which must be completed in order to be eligible for honors. Because of the lack of a solid academic-advising system, Wesleyan students have to be ambitious and take initiative in creating their own schedules. Still, students find that professors are easily accessible and very well-rounded. One student said, "My government professor this past semester was a visiting professor from Yale and was on a first name basis with the [folks at the] White House; [he was] an amazing teacher with our class of 12 people (where his class at Yale was 130), so I couldn't ask for anything more." Wesleyan students thrive in this liberal environment.

Social Life

There is always something happening at Wesleyan, which keeps students on campus most of the time. Wesleyan offers plays, lectures, dances, athletic games, protests, movies and parties to keep its students interested and involved. "I am never bored here and sometimes I find myself not having enough time to do everything I want."

The party scene at Wesleyan is as diverse as the student body. "The parties are open to anyone. Just show up at the door and grab some booze and start dancing." For example, theme houses such as the Out House and International House, as well as students living in In-Town (townhouse-style housing) and wood-frame houses, throw parties that a large proportion of the student body attends on a regular basis. The Naked Party and Wine and Cheese Nights are also popular. Wesleyan holds many festivals such as Zonker Harris Day and Buttstock during the spring. Alcohol is not hard to find on campus, even for freshmen. However, one student pointed out that "life doesn't revolve around drinking and frat parties."

> "It's not uncommon to find a tree-hugging hippie among a bunch of meatheads on a Saturday night in Beta."

"Regarding the relationship scene, there are all different levels. People hook up, are married, or play it loose." The so-called anti-frat, Ecclectic, throws some of the biggest parties of the year, including Queer Prom ("It's the one big night where straight boys make out. Yup. Make out") and the Sex Party ("an intensely wild night, where clothes are basically prohibited"). The Greek scene at Wesleyan is not typical, unlike at larger state universities nearby. Fraternities are not exclusive and are open to the whole campus on the weekends. "It's not uncommon to find a tree-hugging hippie among a bunch of meatheads on a Saturday night in Beta." According to one student, "There is always a party, and you always feel welcome at any party."

Campus Landmarks

The Wesleyan campus is not secluded; it practically extends into downtown Middletown. Recent renovations to the campus include Clark Hall, a freshman dorm; the Freeman Athletic Center; and the Center for Film Studies, which includes a large screening space, making it a popular destination for watching movies on the weekend. Olin Memorial Library, located in the center of campus, is also a favorite place among students to study, although "the first floor is very social" and is known to be a place where students "get it on." A new campus center and the Fauver Residence Complex are under construction. The Fauver Residence Complex will enable more students to live in university-owned housing.

Students rave about the independent living. Freshmen usually live in a one-room double; sophomores live in a single in a dorm; juniors have apartment-style housing; and seniors can live in wood-frame houses with as many as five friends. "Unlike other schools where you live in dorm-style housing for all four years, you become more independent as you progress through college, so real life isn't as much of a shock."

Located in Middletown, Connecticut, only two hours from New York and Boston, Wesleyan is in a convenient location—especially if you can't decide between the urban and small-town college experience. "Middletown's location enables it to attract many talks and performances from highly regarded artists on their way to New York." Students generally take advantage of the concerts on-campus. "Wesleyan has the best ethnomusicology department in the country—people can play in the string quartets, orchestra, jazz bands, or experimental music," one student said.

Although many students complain that Middletown "doesn't provide much entertainment," there is a wide variety of restaurants, among which Thai Gardens, Tuscany Grill, and Japanica II are popular favorites. "Stroll down Main Street; there is free wireless Internet, and classical music discreetly piped in via speakers." Athenian Diner and O'Rourkes are also frequented consistently by students. Both Thai Gardens and O'Rourkes have been written up in the New York Times food section. "You can go to Athenian at 2 a.m. on a weekday and see other people from Wesleyan." Most students live on campus (although it is possible to live off campus) and have cars because the campus is very spread out. In addition to going to New York and Boston, many students also use their cars to go to closer cities such as New Haven and Hartford. Although students complain about the lack of parking around campus and that "public safety is ticket-happy," most students do have cars.

Student Body

There is no typical Wesleyan student. One student said, "I wouldn't characterize students as necessarily crunch or hippy, as much as a large contingent of metropolitan hipsters. There's still a fair share of preppy people, as well as tree huggers, jocks, and artists. That's not to say, however, that you have to be one and not the other. It comes as no surprise when the captain of the lacrosse team is involved in staging a dance performance." Many students get the feeling that the majority of students are from "right outside of New York City or Boston," but Wesleyan has students from all over the country and internationally. Wesleyan is becoming more heterogeneous, "accepting kids who are indeed conservative in contrast to liberal, NPR-listening, Volvo-driving New York-

ers." And unlike at some other schools, the entire student body mixes. One student reports that "cliques don't really exist. It's diverse at all levels—economically, racially and across gender lines."

Wesleyan's diverse population participates in an equally diverse number of clubs and extracurriculars. Many people engage in activities such as a cappella singing, literary magazines, the newspaper, WESU radio, community tutoring, and outdoor activities. If a club doesn't exist to serve a particular interest, it is easy to start up a new one. A number of students also participate in varsity athletics. Although one student flippantly remarked, "I was shocked that Wesleyan even had a football team," Wesleyan does field varsity teams for all major sports, as well as club teams for sports ranging from soccer to inner tube water polo. The school is a member of the New England Small College Athletic Conference (NESCAC), the most competitive DIII conference. If your forte is in academia, sports, or most other creative endeavors, and if you crave a close-knit college experience, Wesleyan is a school that will serve you well.—*Christina Farrell*

FYI

If you come to Wesleyan you better bring "a Pabst Blue Ribbon and a trucker hat."

The typical weekend schedule is: "Weekends start on Wednesday. Wednesday, 'bar night' in Middletown; Thursday, attend a house party; Friday night, chill and see a movie; Saturday, sleep, work, and go to a house party or fraternity party; Sunday, sleep in and work."

If I could change one thing about Wesleyan, "it would be the blind liberalism. For a Democrat, there are no debates to be had except with those in the Green Party."

Three things every student at Wesleyan should do before they graduate are "go to O'Rourkes Diner, go to Spring Fling on Foss Hill, and start a protest."

Yale University

Address: Yale, 38 Hillhouse Avenue, New Haven, CT 06511
Phone: 203-432-9300
E-mail Address: undergraduate.admissions@yale.edu
Web site URL: http://www.yale.edu/
Year Founded: 1701
Private or Public: private
Religious affiliation: none
Location: urban
Regular Application Deadline: 31-Dec
Number of Applicants: NA
Percent Accepted: 9%
Percent Accepted who enroll: 70%
Number Entering: NA
Number of Transfers Accepted each Year: 30
Mean SAT: NA
Mean ACT: NA

Middle 50% SAT range: M:690–780, V:700–780
Middle 50% ACT range: 31–34
Early admission program (EA/ ED/ NA): EA
ED or EA Acceptance Rate: NA
Full time Undergraduate enrollment: 5,349
Total enrollment: 10,237
Percent Male: 51%
Percent Female: 49%
Total Percent Minority: 50%
Percent African-American: 8%
Percent Asian/Pacific Islander: 13%
Percent Hispanic: 8%
Percent Native-American: 1%
Percent Other: 20%
Percent in-state / out of state: NA

Percent from Public HS: 55%
Retention Rate: 99%
Graduation Rate: NA
Percent in On-campus housing: 88%
Percent affiliated with Greek system: NA
Percent Varsity or Club Athletes: NA
Number of official organized extracurricular organizations: 200
3 Most popular majors: Economics, History, Political Science
Student/Faculty ratio: NA
Tuition and Fees: $33,030.00
Cost for Room and Board: $10,020.00
Percent receiving Financial aid, first-year: 100%

No alumni better understand the truism "bright college years go quickly by" than those of Yale University, where the undergraduate experience is defined by its intimate, rich communities and incredible opportunities. Originally founded in 1701 in Connecticut, Yale is one of the oldest universities in the nation, and one of the most dedicated to undergraduates. With an incredible community of scholars young and old, and a supportive atmosphere to boot, Yale offers its students an unrivaled chance to make the most of their "bright college years."

Other Ivys: 32, Yale: 36

With 36 credits required for graduation, versus the Ivy League standard of 32, Yalies have a lot of work to do. This makes for a rigorous academic environment, the intensity of which is only increased by the lack of a fall break and the gray New Haven winters. The positive effects of this dedication to academics, however, include the passionate conversations and debates that continue through every season. Indeed, Yalies chose their school for the invigorating and lively academic scene, and are not disappointed with having to spend a little extra time learning with some of the brightest minds in the world.

Many students describe their professors as being "very, very accessible," while others note that "some professors are approachable, others are frigid—it's a mix. I've had good relationships with profs when I've worked hard at them, others I can't seem to crack."

While some introductory classes at Yale have over 100 students, the majority of classes enroll between 15 and 30 students, with upper-level classes tending to be more selective. For the larger classes, students are divided into "sections" led by Teaching Assistants (TAs). Students report varying quality among their TAs; as one senior reflected, "TAs are a really mixed bag. I would say that 80 percent of my TAs have not been that knowledgeable about the subject they teach . . . a few, one or two, have been wonderful and have helped to shape my academic life."

The first two weeks of every semester are devoted to "shopping period," during which students can attend classes that preliminarily interest them, to see whether the material and professor are a good fit before enrolling. As one student described these two weeks, "the experience to be able to choose your classes based on the content and the professors . . . is really a luxury in academia."

For the 2005–2006 school year, the administration put in place a new set of distributional requirements which, according to many upperclassmen, significantly improve upon the old system. In accordance with these new guidelines, students must complete requirements in both skills and disciplinary areas. A few factors that differentiate this system from the previous one include the greater emphasis on foreign language competence and writing skills. Although these requirements may seem daunting, many students claim that they are easier to satisfy than they seem, as they just give an extra incentive towards pursuing the breadth of study that characterizes a liberal arts education. Many freshmen, however, complain that the new language requirement is too stringent.

Although there are close to 100 distinct majors at Yale, history, economics, political science, psychology and the natural sciences are perennial favorites. Students generally agree that American Studies is the easiest ("joke") major, and that majors in the sciences tend to be the most difficult— perhaps partly due to the fact that students must make daily pilgrimages up "Science Hill," which one chemistry major remarked "is uphill both ways."

What College Are You In?

One of the first questions Yalies ask each other upon meeting for the first time is, "So . . . what college are you in?" This isn't a rhetorical question, but rather an essential one that hits at the core of Yale's undergraduate life. Upon enrolling, students are randomly assigned to one of the 12 residential colleges. Each residential college serves as a microcosm of the University, as the randomness of assignment ensures a diverse and representative collection of students.

Freshmen from 10 of the 12 colleges live on the sprawling Old Campus, and afterwards move into their respective colleges for the remaining three years (while students from the other two larger colleges live in their colleges for all four years). Freshman counselors live with incoming students on Old Campus and function as all-around support resources. In the ensuing years, the master and dean of each college provide stability and direction for students, in both social and academic terms. In addition to living quarters, each college has its own dining hall, common room, library and various other resources (such as printing presses, work-out facilities and pottery studios).

Yale is currently undertaking a massively scaled project to renovate all the residential colleges in turn, a process which will continue into the next couple of years. During each year-long renovation, students from the college being renovated live in "Swing Space," a hotel-style residence hall on the edge of campus that features kitchenettes, in-suite bathrooms and large (if somewhat sanitary-feeling) singles. The colleges aren't the only buildings that are being renovated, however; concurrently, Yale is reconstructing CCL (Cross Campus Library) and segments of the Yale Bowl, while the Yale Art Gallery recently unveiled a newly revamped wing.

From the Quad to the City

Yale's campus is situated in downtown New Haven, Conn., a city that's had its fair share of problems, but is currently receiving a face lift. However, despite the rejuvenation efforts being made by both the University and the city itself, students still report less-than-satisfactory town-gown relations, as evidenced most clearly by the long-term panhandlers on virtually every block. As one disillusioned student said, "It's a sort of safe campus, but feels less and less so, and it's a depressing city to spend four years, no matter what anyone tells you." Citing the dining hall workers' strike in 2003, a senior noted, "it's a very complex relationship between Yale and New Haven . . . and students always get caught in the middle . . . there continue to be socioeconomic tensions between Yale as an institution and the people that make it run."

This "reality check" however, also seems to give Yalies an enhanced incentive to get out and work in the community, producing tangible results. Whether becoming active in Yale's political sphere or volunteering for local organizations, many Yale students seem to stay involved with the outside community. Indeed, one history major commented, "One of my favorite things is that almost everyone does some type of community service in New Haven, and there are lots of ways to become involved somehow and get out of the Yale bubble."

That said, the "bubble" that surrounds the immediate Yale campus is a very enticing place. Besides the distinct grounds of each residential college, the courtyards and buildings of Old Campus and Cross Campus are the heart of Yale College activity, whether they are knee-deep in snow or hosts to sun-bathers. Sterling Memorial Library, described as one of the most beautiful buildings on campus, and Harkness Tower, from which the carillon plays twice daily, both make high marks as well.

Yalies never seem to run out of dining options: each of the 12 residential colleges has its own dining hall, students can swipe at any of the graduate schools, and the grand, communal Commons keeps long hours. On-campus students are required to have a meal plan, and while the prices are somewhat high and the quality not uniform, the dining hall experience of "knowing everyone there and talking for at least an hour" is a treasured one.

Escaping the meal plan, however, appears to be the most widely cited reason to move off campus. One off-campus student noted, "You're better off saving money on the insanely expensive and inflexible meal plan and just moving off-campus and saving a lot and eating healthier and better." There are plenty of other ways to escape the meal plan, as New Haven plays host to dozens of restaurants, many of which are Yalie haunts. Thai, Indian, Ethiopian, Chinese and Japanese eateries abound, giving good reason for one student to say, "The ethnic food is amazing!" For the late nights many Yalies pull, 24-hour snack spots like Gourmet Heaven and A-1 Pizza are sure bets.

A Social Haven

When asked about social stereotypes that are associated with Yale, phrases such as "gay Ivy" and "One in four, maybe more" come to many students' minds. Indeed, Yale is known to have a "vibrant" and "flaming" gay scene—but students seem very comfortable with it. As one freshman counselor commented, "there's a level of comfort that isn't at other colleges or universities . . . people speak about how freeing [Yale] is." The wider world of Yale dating, however, was succinctly summed up by one biomedical engineering major as follows: "It sucks." As on many college campuses, the dating scene at Yale seems to be "either hook-ups or marriage—there's very little casual dating." One student adds, however, that "of course there's also the 'recurring hook-up.' "

Most students agree that there isn't "one Yale student" and that the diversity on-campus is huge and far-reaching. When pressed, however, some students reveal that there may be "a contingent of New York City fast-living coke-using boys and girls" and "a lot of materialism . . . those who wear J. Crew and designer clothing." Clothes seem to be a bigger issue than drugs, however; while students report only seeing marijuana

on occasion ("pot is available if you're interested, but it's no Brown, I suppose . . ."), and very few hard drugs, a well-dressed Yalie is easy to find.

Students at Yale know how to party, too. Besides the weekly parties hosted in the residential college 'party suites,' a fair number of Yalies frequent Toad's Place dance club and frat theme parties, the latter of which occur regularly despite the small Greek population. Many upperclassmen frequent bars or clubs nearby campus, such as favorites Rudy's, Richter's, Café Bottega and Hot Tomato's. Trips into "the City" (NYC) also seem to become more frequent over the college years.

All in all, students praise the University's stance towards alcohol consumption, which "promotes safety over everything else." Instead of cracking down hard on underage drinkers, Yale's administration focuses on providing immediate care without assigning blame, and sponsors awareness programs. As one student said, "It's a great approach to address the issue of underage college drinking." It would, however, be a misconception to say that the social life at Yale revolves around drinking. As one senior noted, "There's a perception that drinking life is dominant in the social scene, but there're a lot of people who don't drink." Going out to eat, taking in a show or a movie, or just hanging out with some friends are also common ways of having a good time.

Regardless of social preferences, virtually all Yalies take part in certain traditional annual festivities, such as those on Halloween weekend (including Liquor-Treating and the Yale Symphony Orchestra midnight concert). Other annual specialties include the Screw-Your-Roommate Dances, Morse & Stiles Casino Night, the Spring Fling concert and barbecue, toasting nights at Mory's, and, of course, the Yale-Harvard football game, which always takes place the day before Thanksgiving break. As one senior gushed, "I love the Yale-Harvard game . . . it's a great excuse to hang out and get drunk with your friends . . . nobody has to go back to do work . . . and we're both so bad at football that it's kind of like a joke." In a generalizing sweep, one anthropology major stated, "Football's just there to serve our social ends. Actually, all Yale athletics are."

So Many Interests

Yalies agree that, in many ways, their sports teams enrich the school's social scene and spirit. At the same time, when asked which teams are most popular, students' responses range from "the one's we're good at" to "volleyball and basketball, and women's squash and soccer" to "Theatre? Debate?" Indeed, students concede that a palpable cultural divide seems to exist between varsity athletes and everyone else. As one chemistry major commented, "Varsity sports are cults—they eat together, lift weights together, party together, even go to class together . . . what part of the day are they not together?" Another student complained, "Many athletes tend to be drunk at Toad's or frats outside my window at three in the morning. It's one form of annoyance upon campus, I suppose, along with people singing really loud in public."

> "Learning alongside all these different people and in all of these different ways makes Yale the best place on earth, next to Disney."

While this divide affects some, many Yalies bridge the gap by becoming involved in club or intramural sports. IMs are extremely popular on campus, with each college competing against each other. In addition, Yale's enormous gym (rumored to be the second largest ever built, next to one that existed in communist Russia) is almost always packed with Yalies of all fitness commitment levels.

The most popular extracurriculars on campus, however, seem to be tied to community service, either independently or through the Dwight Hall social justice network. The wide range of activities to which Yalies commit themselves seems to encompass the entire spectrum, from writing for any number of nationally respected student publications to performing in all types of dance, improv, theater, and singing groups. Of the latter, a cappella is very prominent on campus; with over a dozen groups and an intensive rush process, a cappella at Yale can seem to resemble fraternity scenes at other schools.

Four Bright Years

With such incredible resources and support "in terms of knowledge, life experience, connections, and friends," it is no wonder that an incredibly wide array of people choose to spend their four college years at Yale. With its deeply-rooted traditions and continued enthusiasm for creating new opportunities, Yale has carved out a unique niche for itself in the world of undergraduate institutions. As one senior reflected, Yale has "a reputation for academic rigor but balances that with social life . . . the mental well-being of the students is more emphasized than at other schools." What really differentiates Yale from other highly-regarded academic institutions, however, is the diversity and prevailing attitude of its students. As one senior commented, "Yale's degree of diversity is the best reason to come. And the diversity isn't just in terms of ethnicity; it's also in terms of geographic locale, experiential background, creed, extracurricular interests, and more. Learning alongside all these different people and in all of these different ways makes Yale the best place on earth, next to Disney."—*Elizabeth Dohrmann*

FYI
If you come to Yale, you'd better bring a "car, or know someone with a car, because sometimes you just need to get out of New Haven."
What's the typical weekend schedule? "On Thursdays, Fridays, and Saturdays there's always a show or party to go to; at some point eat out at a Thai restaurant; on Sunday, barely make it to brunch and start studying."
If you could change one thing about Yale, you'd "put it in Jamaica."
Three things every college student at Yale should do before graduating are, "go to the Harvard-Yale Tailgate, drink at Mory's, and take 'Computers and the Law.'"

Delaware

University of Delaware

Address: University of Delaware, 116 Hullihen Hall, Newark DE 19716
Phone: 302-831-8123
E-mail Address: admissions@udelt.edu
Web site URL: http://www.udel.edu/
Year Founded: 1743
Private or Public: public
Religious affiliation: none
Location: suburban
Regular Application Deadline: 16-Jan
Number of Applicants: 21,930
Percent Accepted: 47%
Percent Accepted who enroll: 31%
Number Entering: 3,164
Number of Transfers Accepted each Year: 796
Mean SAT: NA
Mean ACT: NA

Middle 50% SAT range: 1110–1300
Middle 50% ACT range: 24–29
Early admission program (EA/ ED/ NA): NA
ED or EA Acceptance Rate: NA
Full time Undergraduate enrollment: 16,939
Total enrollment: 20,373
Percent Male: 38%
Percent Female: 62%
Total Percent Minority: 17%
Percent African-American: 5%
Percent Asian/Pacific Islander: 4%
Percent Hispanic: 4%
Percent Native-American: 0%
Percent Other: 4%
Percent in-state / out of state: 40%/60%
Percent from Public HS: 80%

Retention Rate: 90%
Graduation Rate: 76%
Percent in On-campus housing: 47%
Percent affiliated with Greek system: 13%
Percent Varsity or Club Athletes: 55%
Number of official organized extracurricular organizations: 200
3 Most popular majors: Education, Psychology
Student/Faculty ratio: 12:01
Tuition and Fees: $18,450.00
In State Tuition and Fees (if different): $7,740.00
Cost for Room and Board: $7,366.00
Percent receiving Financial aid, first-year: 36%

The University of Delaware, 30 miles from Philadelphia, is a large state university with the academic rigor of the most prestigious institutions, and the social atmosphere of the biggest party schools. With an overwhelming amount of school spirit, it is difficult to find anyone dissatisfied with a UD education.

Intense Academics

The University of Delaware has an excellent academic reputation. Well-known for its rigorous academic program, students who graduate from UDel, as the university is affectionately known, are well-prepared for intense and demanding careers. Though general academic requirements are few and easily fulfilled, their number and difficulty vary from major to major. Most students, however, describe them as "challenging, but not impossible." Class size "varies from seven to 300," one student claimed, but

larger classes are broken down into sections, during which time course material is discussed in greater detail by a TA. Though the university has over 20,000 undergraduates, prospective students should not be concerned about losing personal attention. As one junior stated, "I've never had a problem getting extra help when I needed it. Each professor has office hours, and they always take extra time for students who need it." Delaware's course offerings are extensive and varied, including a class on volcanoes and earthquakes, one on the history of rock, and another on ballroom dance.

UD students have over 80 majors from which to choose, from entomology to landscape horticulture. If none are appealing, though, the Dean's Scholar Program allows especially motivated students to design their own major. Of UDel's academic colleges, the business school is the most popular, while the university's physical therapy department is ranked first in the nation. Notoriously difficult is UDel's chemical engineering program, placed among the top in the country, thanks to generous grants from the DuPont Corporation. The biology and nursing programs are, likewise, known as especially challenging among UD students. Students of every major, though, find more than adequate support. A large research university, Delaware offers its students extraordinary facilities, from a 400-acre agricultural complex to its very own apparel design laboratory.

If UDel's standard academic program is not challenging enough, students can apply to the university's competitive Honors College, which boasts smaller class size, better faculty-student interaction, and special dorms. But, if admission to the Honors College is denied, prospective students should have no fear: some classes within the program are still available to non-Honors College students.

Offering some students respite from UDel's challenging academics is Winter Session, a two-month break from mid-December to early February. During that time, some students go home, while others stay on campus to take advantage of the various Winter Session courses offered by the university. Even more students opt to study abroad under one of UDel's extensive study abroad programs. The first university to offer study abroad to undergraduates, students at the University of Delaware have remarkable travel opportunities, including exotic places like Martinique and Fiji.

"We Pregame Harder than you Party"

The social life at UDel, which notoriously revolves around drinking and Greek life, has been described as intense. When asked about the university's reputation as a party school, one undergraduate offered, "Yes, UD is a huge party school. Come over and drink anytime." With a substantial percentage of student involvement, Greek life is very popular at UD, although fraternity parties are always open to non-members. It is important to note, however, that the university's alcohol policy is notably strict. The college's "three strikes and you're out" rule makes partying in the dorms very risky, so most students keep parties off-campus and out of UDel jurisdiction.

For students who choose not to drink, opportunities for fun still abound. With 23 varsity sports and over 200 campus organizations, boredom is not an option at UD. The

university shows many current and older movies, and frequently attracts famous political and pop-culture speakers. The "Hen Zone," located in the Perkins Student Center, offers ping-pong, air hockey, and billiards for every level of gamer. Sports are especially popular among University of Delaware's undergraduate population. The football team, which won a national championship in 2003, has a particularly large following. "Everyone tailgates," one student exclaimed. Thousands of undergraduates flock to every game, supporting UDel and shouting offensive cheers to the opposing team. At UD, football is seen as a great bonding experience. "It's amazing how everyone knows each other here . . . you could never feel lonely at UD," one undergraduate praised.

> **"UD is a huge party school. Come over and drink anytime."**

There are several off-campus hot-spots frequented by UDel hens. The popular Klondike Kate's is always abuzz with UD students, especially on their famous "80s Night." Likewise, "Mug Nights" at the Stone Balloon attracts plenty of partying Hens. For those who prefer to stay on campus, the best frats are rumored to be Pika, Kapa Sigma, and Sigma Chi.

Campus Living

Though students praise the university's social life, they find much at fault with UDel's housing and food. Though the university guarantees housing for all undergraduates, there is a serious dorm shortage, which forces many students to convert doubles to triples and sleep in common rooms. Rodney and Dickinson are infamously known as the "worst frosh housing," and prospective students are warned to stay far from them. The Christiana Towers, though more expensive and slightly farther from central campus, offer apartment-style living, complete with kitchen, bathroom, and living room. If none of the standard dorms appeal to a student, he or she can choose to live in UD's Special Interest Housing, in which students live with others who share common majors or hobbies.

All undergraduates at the University of Delaware are allowed cars with the purchase of a parking pass, though very pricey. Most students don't have cars, though, finding plenty of ways to stay occupied without leaving their fun-filled campus. Those that do bring cars find parking around campus extremely difficult and complain that the Newark police are very strict with tickets; so, if bringing a car to Delaware, be prepared for frequent frustration and heavy fines.

The food, undergraduates complain, is the worst aspect of UD's campus life. Although the university offers several cafeteria options, students assail them as "too expensive" and "not so good." Most students suggest eating in the Trabant student center, while the Perkins student center offers popular chains like Taco Bell and Chick-fil-A. Students can access these chains and other restaurants using UD Flex, a meal plan option for undergraduates. A new off-campus meal plan (OFCMP) was recently instituted, which al-

lows students to purchase meals from several restaurants on Maine Street, a popular off-campus area.

Despite these complaints, students, time and time again describe their campus as "gorgeous" and "pristine." Although some complain that all students come from the same five states (Pennsylvania, New Jersey, Maryland, New York, and Delaware), many describe their classmates as friendly and fun-loving, though not particularly "intellectual." And, although statistics may portray UDel as ethnically homogeneous, the campus has a substantial African American student presence, with a strongly supported and very active Black Student Union. Other minorities, however, are not as well represented.—*Melina Cordero*

FYI

If you come to University of Delaware, you'd better bring "your party face."

The typical weekend schedule includes "Friday night: party; Saturday: afternoon foosball game and Saturday night partying; Sunday: recuperate and get homework done for the week."

If I could change one thing about the University of Delaware, I'd "spend less money on fancy fountains and more on scholarships."

Three things every student at the University of Delaware should do before graduating are "football game with tailgating, Mug Night at the Balloon, and study abroad."

District of Columbia

Address: American, 4400 Massachusetts Avenue, NW Washington, DC 20016-8001
Phone: 202-885-6000
E-mail Address: admissions@american.edu
Web site URL: www.admissions.american.edu
Year Founded: 1893
Private or Public: private
Religious affiliation: United Methodist
Location: urban
Regular Application Deadline: 16-Jan
Number of Applicants: 13,583
Percent Accepted: 53%
Percent Accepted who enroll: 18%
Number Entering: 1,223
Number of Transfers Accepted each Year: 921

Mean SAT: 1,255
Mean ACT: 28
Middle 50% SAT range: 1760–2050
Middle 50% ACT range: 25–30
Early admission program (EA/ ED/ NA): ED
ED or EA Acceptance Rate: 56%
Full time Undergraduate enrollment: 5,962
Total enrollment: 9,702
Percent Male: 34%
Percent Female: 66%
Total Percent Minority: 16%
Percent African-American: 3%
Percent Asian/Pacific Islander: 5%
Percent Hispanic: 4%
Percent Native-American: 1%
Percent Other: 15%
Percent in-state / out of state: 10%/90%

Percent from Public HS: NA
Retention Rate: 87%
Graduation Rate: 70%
Percent in On-campus housing: 75%
Percent affiliated with Greek system: 14%/16%
Percent Varsity or Club Athletes: NA
Number of official organized extracurricular organizations: 128
3 Most popular majors: Social Sciences,Business/ Marketing, Communications/ Journalism
Student/Faculty ratio: 14:01
Tuition and Fees: $29,673.00
Cost for Room and Board: $11,240.00
Percent receiving Financial aid, first-year: 54%

When President George Washington first conceived of a "national university" in the national capital, never did he dream that it would become as prestigious as American University is today. Occupying 84 acres of Ward Circle in Northwest Washington D.C., AU provides students with an intimate yet highly academic experience. Its proximity to downtown Washington D.C. and its connections to the unlimited opportunities the city provides allows each AU student to be exposed to a vibrant and cosmopolitan environment.

Small Setting, Varied Experience

When asked about academics at AU, many students reply that classes vary in difficulty and workload. "You have to work hard in some classes, in others, barely even open a book," notes one student. All AU students are required to fulfill the General Education (GenEd) requirements, which introduce students to five innovative curricular areas: The Creative Arts, Traditions that Shape the Western World, Global and Multicultural Perspectives, Social Institutions and Behavior, and the Natural Sciences. Although some students complain that the total of 30 GenEd credit hours is "too intense," others find it a good way to discover true passions and majors and minors that they had not considered before.

The university is made up of six different schools: College of Arts and Sciences, Kogod School of Business, School of Communication, School of International Service, School of Public Affairs, and Washington College of Law. All schools except the Washington College of Law are open to undergraduate students, the most popular being the College of Arts and Sciences. The Kogod School of Business's Business Administration program is considered one of the top business schools in the country and it houses twice as many undergraduates as graduates.

Personal attention is a key concept at AU and is reflected by its limited number of lecture classes. Most classes are small, discussion based seminars. "I love the smaller class size because it means that I truly get to know my professors and feel connected with the subject," says one student. Other students have commented that the smaller class size allows a sense of camaraderie to develop between classes, particularly between students with the same majors. "People seem to genuinely want to help each other," notes another student. "Nobody is really cut-throat."

> "People seem to genuinely want to help each other. Nobody is really cut-throat."

Students state that what often makes or breaks classes at AU are the professors. AU has a very notable faculty, including former US senators, Nobel Prize winners, and a former reporter for the Los Angeles Times. Despite their high caliber, students laud most of their professors for being "friendly," "approachable,"and "willing to go out of their way to make sure you understand something."

Are you a Northsider or a Southsider?

When asked to describe AU in one word, students often say "diverse."Culturally, AU houses students from over 150 countries and has affiliated campuses on most continents around the world. Promoting international understanding is one of AU's main objectives. A significant portion of students choose a summer internship or a semester abroad program out of the 470 that are offered during their four years at American.

Students comment that AU is also socially diverse. There are two large groups at AU: the "Northsiders" and the "Southsiders."The distinction is not only defined by the physical location on campus but also by the social activities of its denizens. As one student puts it, "Northside is quieter and studious, boring to some; Southside is more outgoing and socially oriented, way too crazy for others. AU has people on both extremes and everyone in between."

One thing common among these groups is the commitment and awareness to political and service activities. 57% of AU undergraduate students participate in significant community service and many participate in campus groups such as the Society of Professional Journalists, College Democrats, and Eco-Sense. It was also recently ranked number eight on the Peace Corps' annual ranking of top participating colleges and universities.

Thursday, Friday, Saturday

Because many students don't have Friday classes, Thursdays mark the beginning of partying at AU. The weekend commences by "going to see a movie" and "dormstorming" in friends' rooms. Fridays are spent studying then going out to one of the clubs or lounges in the DC downtown area. Students find the social and nightlife of DC one of the biggest advantages of AU, offsetting the fact that the campus is technically dry. However, one student notes that, "If you want to drink, you're going to find it."

Saturday nights are often spent at events hosted by fraternities and sororities off campus. AU has 11 fraternities and 11 sororities, and they seem to lead a majority of the social scene. "Greek life is huge," admits one student, "Granted, I am in a sorority, so I'm biased. But you have much better connections to getting to parties and because [AU] is so small, those connections are imperative."

AU also has many other social events that students look forward to. Musical and theatrical performances are regular events, as are nation-wide conferences and rallies held by various student groups. The school hosts big concerts on campus once or twice a year and recent performers have included Ben Folds and Snow Patrol. Although not an official event hosted by the school, "Welcome Week,"the week preceding the year's first classes, is also popular. "So much fun with parties thrown by organizations every night!" exclaims one student.

15 Rooms for Improvement

Residential life on AU campus is "not great, but definitely not bad" says one student. The cafeteria food is known for its great variety—able to satisfy the most outlandish cravings. Everything on campus takes meal swipe cards or eaglebucks (money put on a school account that can be spent at cafeterias or off campus).

The dorm rooms are modern and floors are often divided into interest groups, honors groups, or majors groups. Resident Assistants (RAs) are assigned to students and most students consider them to be "pretty chill," and "just like another person living on the floor." Some RAs do enforce rules strictly but in most cases, students who are caught drinking or using drugs are sent to early morning classes—only in very rare cases are students suspended from dorms.

In order to address the qualms that students have about AU life and in order to improve AU as an undergraduate centered institution, the university has recently established its 15 Points Strategy. Some of the points that the university has come up with include more fundraising efforts to increase its endowment, the implementation of a highly selective interdisciplinary program called University College for freshmen and sophomores, and to increase its reach and operations abroad. Steady steps have been made for the university to reach these 15 goals and there is no doubt that student life in all aspect will see vast changes in the near future.—*Lee Komeda*

FYI
If you come to America, you'd better bring "excitement to see the monuments."
What is the typical weekend schedule? "Hit up many of the bars around the Washington, DC area, take advantage of special lectures at the school, and Sunday is work work work."
If I could change one thing about American, it would be to "allow for a more community atmosphere."
Three things every student at American should do before graduating are "go see the monuments and museums, watch the fireworks on the mall, attend a protest on campus."

Catholic University of America

Address: Catholic University, 620 Michigan Avenue, NE Washington, DC 20064
Phone: 202-319-5305
E-mail Address: cua-admissions@cua.edu
Web site URL: http://www.cua.edu
Year Founded: 1887
Private or Public: private
Religious affiliation: Roman Catholic
Location: urban
Regular Application Deadline: 16-Feb
Number of Applicants: NA
Percent Accepted: 81%
Percent Accepted who enroll: 30%
Number Entering: NA
Number of Transfers Accepted each Year: NA

Mean SAT: NA
Mean ACT: 24
Middle 50% SAT range: 1,040–1,240
Middle 50% ACT range: 22–27
Early admission program (EA/ ED/ NA): NA
ED or EA Acceptance Rate: NA
Full time Undergraduate enrollment: 3,083
Total enrollment: 3,083
Percent Male: 44%
Percent Female: 56%
Total Percent Minority: 15%
Percent African-American: 6%
Percent Asian/Pacific Islander: 3%
Percent Hispanic: 6%
Percent Native-American: 0%
Percent Other: NA

Percent in-state / out of state: 6%/94%
Percent from Public HS: NA
Retention Rate: 81%
Graduation Rate: NA
Percent in On-campus housing: 68%
Percent affiliated with Greek system: 2%
Percent Varsity or Club Athletes: NA
Number of official organized extracurricular organizations: 117
3 Most popular majors: Architecture, Engineering, Political Science
Student/Faculty ratio: 9:01
Tuition and Fees: $27,700.00
Percent receiving Financial aid, first-year: 53%

Don't let the name scare you! Although CUA is a Roman Catholic institution, not everyone goes to church all the time (or at all, for that matter). Most students are "Catholics from New England, Philly and New Jersey," but people of all faiths are not only tolerated but are also encouraged to come. With D.C. as its playground, CUA is a great place to be a student: "You have no reason to be bored!" one senior said.

Not Just for Catholics

Students at CUA are required to complete a number of core courses, including "Intro to Religion," but most people don't mind it. There is a wide variety of difficulty in the course work offered at CUA, ranging from the easier political science major (after all, you are right at the heart of the American political process) to the more challenging engineering and architecture majors that students say "really set CUA apart from other universities." There is also a one-year master's program in engineering for students who completed their undergraduate work at CUA. Students interested in social work should also take note of the opportunities CUA affords in that area—a field placement class takes you outside the classroom and puts you in a social work agency for 16 hours a week. Talk about a hands-on experience! Drama is a popular major at CUA, and the Drama School (for graduate work) is a very well-respected part of the institution. For those with a more scientific mind, the School of Nursing at CUA is an excellent school, consistently ranked in the top 10 nursing schools in the country.

Some of the best classes for undergrads are Dynamics of Christian Spirituality (with Ridgeway Addison), World Religions, Introduction to Peace Studies, and Greek Literature in Translation. For the students not looking to work too hard there are easier classes (like Social Work 101, Anthropology, or Astronomy) but there are definitely opportunities for CUA kids to challenge themselves. Difficult courses like "Fluid Dynamics and Physiology" make people work for their grades more than other classes. Students say that grading "depends on the professor, but it's usually fair." The workload at CUA definitely depends on the student, but many kids work and play sports while still taking a full (or more than full) course-load.

Studying at CUA is a must, and there are plenty of places to work. Some students prefer to stay in the city after work at an off-campus job, working in coffee-shops around D.C., while others enjoy the quiet rooms of Mullin, the main library. If you can't find your books there, have no fear: CUA is a member of the D.C. College Consortium, which also includes Howard, George Washington and American universities. "Pretty much any research material you need, you can find." Furthermore, the largest library in the United States, the Library of Congress, is only a few metro stops away from campus.

Gotta Eat Somewhere . . . Just Not on Campus!

Living arrangements at CUA make other universities look like they came from the Stone Age. Incoming freshmen can look forward to two of the greatest luxuries offered on a college campus—air-conditioning and cable. Furthermore, CUA provides a number of different housing choices for students. The University offers suite-style dorms, apartments, singles, and even trailers (yes, trailers—but only during renovation). There are also typical dorms where students share a bathroom down the hall from their rooms. All of the different styles of living "makes for a great change of pace over the four years," students say. And don't let the seemingly strict administration fool you—CUA kids know how to have a good time, even on campus.

As for food on campus, students at CUA (like at most schools) say it's not worth the money they're paying for it. One senior however, said: "There has been a huge improvement over the four years I've been here. Since our new student center opened up, the dining halls have better hours and more options." There are not always choices available to vegetarian students, and some believe the university could "cater to the more health-conscious eaters better." Students describe food prices on campus as "ridiculous," but there are always other options. Fortunately CUA is so close to downtown D.C. that you can find "any kind of food you want within 10 to 25 minutes . . . ANY kind of food."

Such proximity to a major city might make some parents nervous about their student's safety, but a modern blue-light system coupled with regularly patrolling police make students feel safe. "I've never been scared and walk alone at night without worrying," one girl said. Common sense does, however, always pay off. "I would never walk off campus in the neighborhood alone at night, though." Smart advice for just about anywhere.

It's a Party in the City

"My favorite part of CUA is the student body: they know how to party and have fun, but also how to deal with life!" Despite a reportedly "very closed-minded" administration that "cares more about the 'image' of the school than meeting students' needs," CUA is a great place to spend four years. Located right in the District of Columbia, students take full advantage of city life. There are endless numbers of museums and national monuments to visit in the city, not to mention the exciting social life an urban center provides. Although the school policy is "strict about citing underage drinkers" (there are no kegs allowed), one student pointed out that "it's a big campus." Since the school has its own Metro stop—and D.C. has an extremely well-run public transportation network—students tend to go out in the city rather than on campus. Bars dominate the social scene on party nights (generally Thursday through Saturday). Fado's Irish Pub has "a great local band" on Thursdays, and Brooks and Johnny K's are popular bars for the freshmen to check out. Fortunately, drinking isn't the only thing to do around D.C. "Because we have a big Catholic identity going on, there are actually quite a number of people who don't drink at all," one student notes.

> **"Because we have a big Catholic identity going on, there are actually quite a number of people who don't drink at all."**

Though there isn't a significant Greek presence on campus, students "find their niche pretty easily." People at CUA love that the school is small and say that everyone is "re-ally close," "approachable" and "friendly." One thing that incoming students should definitely know, however, is that CUA is not a place where aspiring athletes thrive. "Don't come here if you want basketball or football games to be the highlight of your weekend," says one student. CUA is a Division III school, but school pride doesn't center on athletics. There are workout facilities for health-conscious students, including a new fitness center for non-athletes. "It has great equipment, but not enough to keep up with the demand on peak-use hours," one student said.

Student life at CUA is busy—many upperclassmen get internships in the city, and student organizations are large. The Campus Ministry "has a lot to offer to one's faith life, including mass, adoration, community service, prayer groups and more," one female student said. Drama is also a popular activity for the student body. With a prestigious Drama School at the University, it's no surprise that CUA attracts aspiring actors and actresses. There are also club sports teams (including Ultimate Frisbee, soccer, and crew) and a Division I rugby team that routinely performs well. All in all there is really something for everyone at CUA. Let's not forget, of course, student-run political groups that attract students from both ends of the spectrum. What else would you expect from a school in D.C.?—*Emily Cleveland*

FYI
If you come to Catholic, you'd better bring "a passion for politics."
What's the typical weekend schedule? "Friday: go clubbing in D.C.; Saturday: spend time with friends and party at night; Sunday: go to church and study."
If I could change one thing about Catholic, I would "make the administration better at dealing with financial issues."
Three things every student at Catholic should do before graduating are "spend a late night at Johnny K's, walk around the monuments at night, and go to a protest."

George Washington University

Address: George Washington, 2121 I Street NW, Washington, DC 20052
Phone: 202-994-6040
E-mail Address: gwadm@gwu.edu
Web site URL: http://www.gwu.edu
Year Founded: 1821
Private or Public: private
Religious affiliation: none
Location: urban
Regular Application Deadline: 16-Jan
Number of Applicants: NA
Percent Accepted: 37%
Percent Accepted who enroll: 34%
Number Entering: 2,413
Number of Transfers Accepted each Year: 793
Mean SAT: 1,240
Mean ACT: 26

Middle 50% SAT range: 590–690V, 590–680M, 640–720W
Middle 50% ACT range: NA
Early admission program (EA/ ED/ NA): ED
ED or EA Acceptance Rate: 58%
Full time Undergraduate enrollment: 10,394
Total enrollment: 10,761
Percent Male: 43%
Percent Female: 57%
Total Percent Minority: 23%
Percent African-American: 6%
Percent Asian/Pacific Islander: 10%
Percent Hispanic: 6%
Percent Native-American: 1%
Percent Other: 76%
Percent in-state / out of state: 1%/99%

Percent from Public HS: 70%
Retention Rate: 92%
Graduation Rate: 79%
Percent in On-campus housing: 67%
Percent affiliated with Greek system: 29%
Percent Varsity or Club Athletes: NA
Number of official organized extracurricular organizations: 220
3 Most popular majors: Socials Sciences, Business/Marketing, Psychology
Student/Faculty ratio: 13:01
Tuition and Fees: $37,820.00
Cost for Room and Board: $11,100.00
Percent receiving Financial aid, first-year: 66%

Going to school in the nation's capital certainly has its advantages. Just a few blocks from the White House, and a mere Metro ride from the National Archives and Capitol Hill, the GW campus is a hub of activity for its students. At GW, lazy afternoons easily turn into historical and political adventures, and even an early morning run has the unique appeal of boasting the Washington Monument and the Jefferson Memorial as backdrops. The Supreme Court is nearby, as is Embassy Row and the Smithsonian Museums. In fact, it's possible to spend four years at GW and not have enough time to explore all of the many options available. Located in the nation's political center and one of the world's most beautiful cities, George Washington University stands out for the opportunities it gives students for learning both inside and beyond the classroom. Whether you're a politics buff or not, it's certainly an exciting place to be.

One Part Academia, One Part Politics

George Washington University is comprised of seven individual schools, each with their own requirements, to which aspiring freshmen apply directly: The Colombian College of Arts and Sciences, The School of Media and Public Affairs, The School of Business and Public Management, The School of Medicine and Health Sciences, The School of Public Health and Health Services, The Elliot School of International Affairs, and the School of Engineering and Applied Sciences. Although the seven schools may seem to have a narrow focus, each student must fulfill general liberal arts requirements, and students are permitted and encouraged to take classes outside of their specific school. (Students warn, however, that it is important to be on top of your own classes and requirements, because it is surprisingly easy to "fall through the cracks" here.) In addition, GW offers a number of specialized programs including an eight-year Integrated Engineering/M.D. program, a seven-year B.A./M.D. program, and an Integrated Engineering and Law Program. The University Honors Program is a smaller, more selective college within the university that allows students a four-year, multidisciplinary, interschool undergraduate experience. Acceptance to the Honors Programs is also sweetened with a significant merit-based scholarship.

The GW faculty and classes receive solid reviews, though students are careful to warn that, "it really varies based on your school, major, and professor." Most students are "happy with the accessibility of the faculty and the quality of the teaching," though students emphasize the need for their peers to make the effort to engage their professors. The workload is described as "pretty average" by most students, with some emphasizing the rigor of first-year/introductory classes. "They try to weed you out," one senior remarked. Grades are "fairly accurate," and there isn't too much "grading on a curve." Double majoring is fairly common, and not too difficult. Class sizes vary, with introductory lectures being the largest. Other classes are usually smaller, with an average of 20 to 50 students. Small discussion groups lead by TAs are a popular way to master the material discussed in larger lectures.

Because of GW's central location, academics tend to go hand-in-hand with taking advantage of the opportunities available in Washington, D.C. Many students are able to intern and work during the school year, with government agencies being a popular job option. "Getting an internship or a job in government or politics may be easier during the school year," one student noted, "because fewer students are here than in the summer, when tons of undergrads want to work and live in D.C." Other advantages of GW's location include the fact that professors will frequently bring notable speakers and politicians in to speak to their classes, and field trips to museums and other attractions are often part of coursework.

A World of Social Possibilities

"Because we're in a city, people spread out a lot on weekends," said one senior. Many students head to bars or dance clubs in D.C., and while they complain about the cover charges, they generally agree that there's little to do on campus at night. "Sometimes freshmen party on campus," said one sophomore. "But as you get older, I think the bars and clubs are more of a draw. You can't really come to GW without a fake ID." That said, partying on campus can be difficult—there is officially no alcohol allowed in campus housing if you are under 21, and students caught three times with alcohol are forced to relinquish their campus housing. Any student found with an illegal substance must move off-campus at the first strike. Community Facilitators (CFs) are GW's answer to residential advisers, and

while many students reported "becoming friends with" their CFs, Community Facilitators are more than willing to write up students on alcohol charges when necessary. Despite this, drinking seems to be a large part of social life at GW. Upperclassmen gravitate toward the bars in Adams Morgan, a notoriously fun part of the city, and bars closer to home, like McFadden's on New Hampshire Ave. The meal plan, called GWorld, can be used at certain local restaurants, which students reported to be a nice feature of GW dining. Students generally say that the meal plan is "good, though nothing to brag about," and are likely to dine out on the weekends, noting the restaurants on Georgetown's M Street and in Dupont Circle as particularly good options.

Drinking may be a big part of social life at GW, but fraternities and sororities are not. Greek life is an option for students that are interested, but many GWers think it unnecessary and a hindrance to enjoying all that Washington, D.C. has to offer. While students report that their peers are "pretty friendly," they also acknowledge that "the university isn't particularly helpful in helping people meet each other." Overall, being in such a great city provides a lot of opportunity, but also causes GW to lack a sense of community spirit. Most students meet their friends through their majors or extracurricular activities, even though few people feel defined by these groups. The administration attempts to foster a greater sense of community spirit by hosting events like Fall Fest and Spring Fest, and increasing the number of formal balls.

Students at GW think of themselves as "fit," and most take part in intramurals and take advantage of the beautiful Washington scenery by frequently running around the city. Nevertheless, GW does not officially recognize contact sports. Non-contact athletic teams are competitive in the Atlantic 10 Conference as well as NCAA Division I tournament play. Students tend to show their (limited) school spirit by attending basketball games, as basketball is by far "the most popular sport on campus." Extracurricular activities are also popular, and most students get involved in at least one organization. "There are tons of options," said one student, "especially in the realm of political and cultural organizations." Students take advantage of their surroundings by joining clubs that take them to the National Gallery of Art and the Capitol, among other locales. Students tend not to feel categorized by the clubs they join, and enjoy the fact that "it always seems like you can meet someone new."

Location, Location, Location

The location of the George Washington University is its greatest draw to students, although particular departments are also very attractive. The main Foggy Bottom Campus (there is a smaller campus in Mount Vernon, VA) is composed of four-by-four square city blocks. "It is definitely an urban, city campus," said one student, "and it is often hard to tell if someone you pass is a GW student or a government employee." While students complain about a lack of grassy space, they are always quick to realize how lucky they are to live in such a beautiful and vibrant city. Students generally feel very safe on campus, though "of course, we're in a major city, so you have to be careful." Security measures have been increased with the threat of terrorism in recent years, and most students seem to feel that the school is doing all it can to protect their well-being.

> "It is often hard to tell if someone you pass is a GW student or a government employee."

Freshmen and sophomores are required to live on campus, and freshmen are usually split between Thurston (affectionately called "the tenements: by residents) and Hobo Hall. Thurston is the largest dorm on campus, and like all on-campus locations, offers apartment-style or suite living (some have kitchens, some do not). Juniors and seniors are not guaranteed on-campus housing, and may take their chances in a lottery that works on the basis of seniority. Mitchell Hall is most sought after, offering the most attractive living conditions: a veranda, and a subway stop. Many upperclassmen opt for apartments in the city (which are "SO EX-PENSIVE!" warns one student) and some choose to live in the suburbs of Maryland or Virginia. For others, sorority and fraternity houses are the way to go.

The Marvin Center—the school's student union—is largely regarded as the center of campus life. The Marvin Center houses the headquarters and offices of student organizations, as well as a few fast-food and chain restaurants. Meals can be eaten in the Marvin Center or in standard dining halls, where food is described as "good but unhealthy." The center is a hub for students, a place where "lots of kids hang out, do their work, and get meals." The center also houses a grocery store and travel agency. The Marvin Center is considered a great convenience, especially for freshmen who don't yet know their way around the city. "If you need something, chances are you can get it there."

Official school statistics show a geographically and racially diverse student population, but students tend to think the school is too dominated by the wealthy. Students complain that people at GW are ostentatious about their wealth. "People here are well-off, and they let you know it." While there are definitely stereotypes about well-dressed, BMW-driving students, others claim that it really depends on where you choose to hang out, and with whom. "A stereotype is just that," said one articulate senior, "it underrepresents the variety of student 'types' on campus."

With a prime location in the hub of the political world, George Washington University provides an education in academics, politics, and real-life, city living. With so much to see, do, and learn, students are more than happy with their choice to come here. "I love GW," said one senior, "and I don't know many people who feel otherwise."—*Erica Ross*

FYI

If you come to GW, you'd better bring "a coffee mug for the Starbucks on every corner in DC!"

What is the typical weekend schedule? "Wake up late, do some work, go out all night, and wake up late again the next day!"

If I could change one thing about GW, I'd "make the administration more accessible to students."

Three things every student at GW should do before graduating are "go to the monuments at night, get a Manuche dog, and party in Georgetown."

Georgetown University

Address: Georgetown, Office of Undergraduate Admissions, Washington, DC 20057-1002

Phone: 202-687-3600

E-mail Address: guadmissions@georgetown.edu

Web site URL: www.georgetown.edu

Year Founded: 1789

Private or Public: private

Religious affiliation: Jesuit

Location: urban

Regular Application Deadline: 10-Jan

Number of Applicants: 15,070

Percent Accepted: 22%

Percent Accepted who enroll: 49%

Number Entering: 1,580

Number of Transfers Accepted each Year: 409

Mean SAT: NA

Mean ACT: NA

Middle 50% SAT range: math: 660–750; verbal: 660–760

Middle 50% ACT range: NA

Early admission program (EA/ ED/ NA): EA

ED or EA Acceptance Rate: 21%

Full time Undergraduate enrollment: 6,152

Total enrollment: 13,345

Percent Male: 48%

Percent Female: 52%

Total Percent Minority: 26%

Percent African-American: 9%

Percent Asian/Pacific Islander: 8%

Percent Hispanic: 8%

Percent Native-American: <1%

Percent Other: 0%

Percent in-state / out of state: NA

Percent from Public HS: NA

Retention Rate: 97%

Graduation Rate: >90%

Percent in On-campus housing: NA

Percent affiliated with Greek system: NA

Percent Varsity or Club Athletes: 25%

Number of official organized extracurricular organizations: 100+

3 Most popular majors: Government, International Relations, Finance

Student/Faculty ratio: 10:01

Tuition and Fees: $34,110.00

Cost for Room and Board: $10,930.00

Percent receiving Financial aid, first-year: 100%

Georgetown makes good use of its resources, as evidenced by the plethora of diplomats who teach at the university and the slew of internships students take advantage of during the school year, as well as during the summer months. While well-known for its proximity to D.C., Hoyas embrace Georgetown's neighborhoody aura, happily sauntering about cobbled stone streets while rubbing shoulders with esteemed Jesuits, professional students and some of this nation's most politically active collegianes.

The ABCs of the CIA

"We have cool classes about the CIA and national security and things like that," boasted one student. And with venerated persons like Madeleine Albright, Donna Brazile and George Tenet teaching at the University, students receive an unparalleled education in national and international affairs. "You can be in class one minute with someone like Albright, and later that night see them on TV being interviewed."

Prospective Georgetown students must send their applications to one of four schools: the College of Arts and Sciences, McDonough School of Business, Walsh School of Foreign Service (SFS), or the School of Nursing and Health Studies. Not only is Georgetown's School of Foreign Service the oldest school of international affairs in the nation, but it is also known to be the most difficult.

Aside from choosing a school to which apply to, students who may wish to look ahead can apply to a variety of inclusive programs offered at Georgetown like a five-year undergrad/MBA, a five-year masters program at SFS, and the Early Assurance Program for medical school to which pre-medical students can apply at the end of their sophomore year. If accepted, candidates are assured of admission to Georgetown Medical School upon satisfactory completion of their junior and senior years, and are exempt from the MCAT.

Although students complain that lectures are big, classes are otherwise typically under 20. "Usually in a big lecture, you'll have a professor and then a TA, and it totally depends on what class, but the TAs can be great or they can be terrible."

One seasoned junior Hoya advised freshmen to get their prerequisites out of the way early on. "It's actually easier to get into those classes as a freshman," she explained.

"You're going to have a problem fulfilling your prereqs senior year because the classes will already be full." The prerequisites—which, for the College of Arts and Sciences, include courses in the following areas: math/science, language, social science, history, philosophy and theology, and humanities and writing—are generally thought to be "annoying," especially the theology requirement, in which "Bible Literature" and "Problem of God" stand out as particularly tedious courses. One student, who referred to the "Problem of God" course as "vague and lame," exclaimed that "everyone who takes it is miserable and wants to die from it." Though the same student admitted that, "the other requirements aren't really that bad."

> "You can be in class one minute with someone like [Madeleine] Albright, and later that night see them on TV being interviewed."

About half of the junior class goes abroad, and Georgetown students generally find the university to be quite supportive of studying overseas. "Georgetown makes it pretty easy to get credit during study abroad," one student explained. "The University offers a ton of programs directly or by affiliation."

Cuisine and the Living Scene

"The coolest thing about my school is probably the surrounding area," said one Hoya. "The downtown area is really cute and the neighborhood I live in is very homey and nice." It should be no surprise that D.C.'s Georgetown neighborhood is voted one of the best college "towns" year after year. With the neighborhood shops and restaurants to satisfy a student's daily urge to splurge or need to feed merely blocks from central campus, a beautiful canal to run along, and downtown D.C. a short drive away, students have the cultural perks of city life and the convenience of a hip, college town, all at the tips of their fingers.

One campus fave for dining out is Tombs, "our underground crew place" that was established as an eating club in 1962 by Richard McCooey. Other top picks include Clyde's for American "tavernish" food, and J.Paul's for burgers and seafood. On-campus dining options are "pretty basic and not the best." Aside from the two dining halls, which students lamented is a rip off: "You're paying

about $13 to go and you never eat 13 bucks worth of food," Georgetown recently opened La Hoya court, which is a conglomeration of "a bunch of fast food places like Taco Bell." Luckily, Georgetown provides flexible meal plans ranging from an all-you-can-eat option to a grab-and-go package where students on the run can pick up pre-ordered and pre-packed meals during the week. "There are a bunch of mid-priced, not super-expensive places to go eat out," one student said. "You don't need to go out for dinner and spend a million dollars, which is cool, because living in Georgetown can get expensive."

The University tries to mitigate the high costs of D.C. living by offering on-campus apartments for upperclassmen. "If you're not in a dorm, you want an on-campus apartment because it's cheaper than living off campus but it's also on campus and it's really convenient." Students agreed that the on-campus apartments are "really nice." Nevertheless, by senior year, "typically everyone lives off campus." This can run students between $800 and $900 a month, but if you're willing to live a bit more out of the way, you can get a place a bit cheaper, "although not much."

Underclassmen, or those who prefer to avoid the burdens of leasing, should be forewarned: "Georgetown has redone some dorms, and left other dorms to rot and die, so you can get either really lucky or unlucky as a freshman." Newer dorms have heat, air-conditioning and are generally considered "clean." And even though the old dorms are "kind of a mess," they do have some perks like individual bathrooms. During freshman and sophomore years, students have the option of residing on the "Living Well" floor or participating in the John Carroll program, which allots a floor for "really study-oriented kids who don't want to be disturbed." Female underclassmen also have the choice to live on an all-girls floor. Georgetown has recently built a new Southwest Quad, but students complained that, "there's still a housing shortage." The school's first performing arts center was recently completed and long-term projects include a separate campus for the Business School, expanded athletic facilities, and a unified sciences center.

Perfectly Preppy

Although not nearly as conservative as its Jesuit roots may suggest, Georgetown is an inarguably preppy school. "We're not very trendy here. . . . Honestly, everyone just wears a lot of Lacoste and Polo." But even if you opt for Georgetown's second-running

Euro-chic look, just be sure to get dressed in the morning. "Some people wear sweatpants to class but it's the exception rather than the norm." But who really cares about what students look like in their clothes? It's what's on the inside that counts . . . right? "I would say that our girls are a lot cuter than our guys," stated one female student. "But then again, I think the guys at our school feel the opposite way." This may be surprising considering that another Hoya characterized the female population as having "a lot of small blonde girls; but think less Paris Hilton, more Kate Bosworth." Still, there is obviously some mutual attraction among students for which to account. "None of my friends had boyfriends freshman and sophomore year and now everyone does," said one junior. "When you're upperclassmen people are getting tired of just hooking up and want to settle down and have someone to stay in and watch a movie with on a Friday night."

And although Georgetown is the nation's oldest Catholic and Jesuit university, its diversity far exceeds its Christian roots. "There are a lot of international kids . . . a lot of diplomats from other countries will send their kids here." Georgetown's strong international presence, as well as its students' diversity of interest, helps to foster students' exchange of information and ideas.

No Frat, No Problem

"If you don't have a good ID, then you're going to have a big problem getting into bars," said one student. Since there is no Greek life at Georgetown, underage freshman will often go to athlete parties—"our pseudo-frats," explained a senior Hoya—or opt to party in the dorms or in on-campus apartments.

For those students of legal drinking age, it's a must to go to Tombs on their 21st birthday. "Everyone goes to Tombs when they turn 21 and they get their heads stamped." Once you've got a real ID, upperclassmen recommended having a drink at Rhino, "a really cool bar that's also really hard to get into," or hitting up Third's on a Thursday night.

Georgetown also hosts some well-attended social activities of its own, like the Holiday Gala, "a big dance" which occurs around Christmas time, and a Homecoming formal that the University just recently started, and students have already heartedly praised as being "a lot of fun." Founded in 1789, it makes sense that Georgetown would also hold a Traditions Day. Started in 2002, the day serves to call attention to Georgetown's rich history.

Although "Georgetown students get ex-tremely lazy in the winter," boredom is never a result of inclement weather. One train ride away and students can dance at the Kennedy Center, visit a host of museums, and eat next to some of the nation's most prominent politicians. Georgetown's student clubs make use of the bustling city—one popular option being tutoring programs that allow for Georgetown students to go downtown in the afternoons to assist elementary and middle school kids with their studies.

Luckily, D.C.'s public transportation makes getting around a breeze. In fact, one student who had her car at school through sophomore year, opted to leave it home for the remainder of her collegiate career. "Cars are more of a hindrance. They're useful to have, yes. . . . It's useful to go to Costco and Safeway, etc. but it's really easy to walk into town." Not to mention that, "parking tickets are horrible to deal with." Students complained that if you don't have a parking spot, it is possible to spend hours each week in search of open spaces

Capitalizing on Opportunities

Georgetown students are just as active as their surrounding neighborhood jaunts. Aside from juggling their academic schedules, students make room for a slew of activities, jobs and semester-long internships. Georgetown recently got a new basketball coach, and the Hoyas are thrilled: "He's slowly turning the team around, which is good, because we love basketball here. Everyone goes to our games against Duke." Men's and women's varsity lacrosse are two of Georgetown's more prominent teams, "but people don't normally go to their games," and track also stands out despite its low publicity.

Some of the more well-known groups on campus include Phantoms, a coed a cappella group and an on-campus student organization called Students of Georgetown, Incorporated, also known as The Corps—the largest student organization in the country. "A lot of my friends work for The Corps. They run the on-campus stores and coffee shops and a bunch of other things, too." *The Hoya*, the student newspaper, is well read and has recently erected an online blog. For those who prefer somewhat less mainstream modes of communication, *The Georgetown Voice*, "our alternative hippy paper," is a weekly magazine with an emphasis on feature stories. Of course, if getting paid for all the extra hours you're logging is a priority, rest assured that Georgetown students are big on the part-time jobs. "A lot of kids work," said one Hoya. "People will waitress or work in stores in Georgetown like Urban Outfitters or any of the small boutiques."

While most college students leave internship stress until the summer months, some Georgetown students pack internships onto their resumes all year long. "A lot of people will intern on Capitol Hill for congressmen," explained one junior. "It's unpaid and you kind of just sit there and fold stuff, but that's just what you do." Financial internships are a close second to political ones. But although there are a ton of internship opportunities, students complained that Georgetown doesn't do an astounding job providing credit for all of them. "You can only get credit for certain internships. For the ones Georgetown permits, you must enroll in a class called Internships and write a short paper. . . . It can get very complicated."—*Dana Schuster*

FYI

If you come to Georgetown, you better bring "a polo shirt . . . sorry, but it's true."

What is the typical weekend schedule? "Thursday: bars; Friday; rent a movie with friends or go out for a big dinner; Saturday: shop around Georgetown or work at your part-time job, go out that night; Sunday: big brunch!"

If I could change one thing about Georgetown, I'd "renovate our gym. It is caught in 1980. We haven't gotten a new machine in a long time . . . like before I was born."

Three things every student at Georgetown should do before graduating are "go to Foxfields, a horse race that students attend every year—you wake up really early and Georgetown rents buses to go to Charlotte, everyone gets dressed up and you drink all day; go to this really cool restaurant called 1789—it is very fancy and one of Bill Clinton's favorites; and spend time in Southeast, D.C."

Howard University

Address: Howard, 2400 Sixth Street NW, Washington, DC 20059
Phone: 202-806-2763
E-mail Address: admission@howard.edu
Web site URL: http://www.howard.edu
Year Founded: 1867
Private or Public: private
Religious affiliation: none
Location: urban
Regular Application Deadline: 15-Feb
Number of Applicants: NA
Percent Accepted: 48%
Percent Accepted who enroll: 37%
Number Entering: NA
Number of Transfers Accepted each Year: NA
Mean SAT: 1,076
Mean ACT: 22

Middle 50% SAT range: 460–690V, 460–680M
Middle 50% ACT range: 20–29
Early admission program (EA/ ED/ NA): NA
ED or EA Acceptance Rate: NA
Full time Undergraduate enrollment: 7,275
Total enrollment: NA
Percent Male: 33%
Percent Female: 67%
Total Percent Minority: 86%
Percent African-American: 84%
Percent Asian/Pacific Islander: 1%
Percent Hispanic: 1%
Percent Native-American: 0%
Percent Other: 14%

Percent in-state / out of state: 23%/77%
Percent from Public HS: 80%
Retention Rate: 85
Graduation Rate: 43%
Percent in On-campus housing: 58%
Percent affiliated with Greek system: 2%
Percent Varsity or Club Athletes: NA
Number of official organized extracurricular organizations: 150
3 Most popular majors: Journalism, Radio & Television
Student/Faculty ratio: 8:01
Tuition and Fees: $12,180.00
Cost for Room and Board: $6,522.00
Percent receiving Financial aid, first-year: 72%

From their very first footstep onto the campus, visitors to Howard University become aware of the strong sense of community that sets Howard apart from other schools across the country. Located in the nation's capital, Howard prides itself on its academic excellence as well as its reputation for turning out strong African-American students who are well-rounded and fully aware of the numerous opportunities that await them after leaving this beautiful, hilly campus situated in the heart of Washington, DC.

Education Beyond the Classroom

In the past, in terms of majors, Howard was always synonymous with either medicine or law. Although these areas are still popular and prestigious aspects of the school, many different colleges have grown significantly in the past few years, including the business school, which has embarked on a campaign to raise $26 million dollars for the renovation of its buildings. Students choose from one of several different colleges to focus on during their time at Howard (Arts and Sciences, Communications, etc). Another distinguishing factor of Howard is that in addition to requiring undergraduates to take a certain number of credits within their own specific concentrations, the school also places a strong emphasis on practical education, manifested in areas such as the required swimming lessons.

Although there are general-education type classes that each student must take, the amount of undergraduates at Howard allows class sizes to stay relatively intimate. A senior mentioned that as she advanced into the higher-level courses within her major, most of her classes had only 15 to 20 students. Because of this, the community enjoys an excellent relationship between students and faculty members. According to another senior, "Because of the small class sizes, teachers develop strong relationships with their students. They are constantly supplying them with opportunities for internships and ways to utilize being in Washington, D.C."

It is because of these great teachers that there are certain "must-take" classes at Howard such as Literature of Love and Pan-Africanism. With readings that vary from Toni Morrison to William Shakespeare, Literature of Love is a class that encourages students to seek to understand human interaction through famous literary works. Well-known professors such as Dr. Gregory Carr and Dr. John Davis are integral parts of life at Howard and are constantly seen at functions all around campus.

On The Hilltop

With a thriving social scene, Howard has opportunities for all different types of people to get involved with student activities. HUSA, Howard University Student Association, is one of the biggest groups on campus. Other students are involved in a wide variety of extracurriculars, including everything from putting on pageants to joining step groups. *The Hilltop*, Howard's award-winning school newspaper, is very highly regarded and has won numerous accolades both nationally and at the yearly HBCU conference. In accordance with the large international student population, the African Student Association and the Caribbean Student Association are also huge forces on campus. Along with chapters of national organizations such as the NAACP and NSCS (National Society of Collegiate Scholars), Howard boasts a unique system of clubs for each of the fifty states. These clubs are known to host activities and gatherings such as the well-attended yearly party thrown by the Louisiana and Texas Clubs. There are other school wide activities such as "Res Fest" where different dormitories divide into teams and compete against other dorms in competitions such as dance contests and sporting events.

Although there are lots of different social scenes around campus, none is more dominant than Greek Life. One student said that "part of the reason the Greek scene here is so prominent is because of its legacy on campus. Greeks have a responsibility that goes beyond partying." Fraternity and sorority members hold positions of power around campus and have a very prominent place at Howard. The groups strive to be more than just social groups, emphasizing both community service and African-American unity.

Growing Up

All Howard students grow and develop in many different ways as their four years go by, and the maturity that comes with age is reflected in the various types of student housing. Freshman students are guaranteed housing and live under relatively strict rules in the dorms, many of which have to do with student safety and the need for constant security on campus due to the high crime rate areas around campus. There are counselors and residential advisors who are there to guide freshmen along their way through the university system. According to older students, when it comes to mealtimes, the freshmen are typically seen eating in the cafeteria, which serves more or less typical college food. For most freshmen, the highlight of the "Caf" menu is Soul Food Thursdays, when the menu includes delicious items such as fried chicken and macaroni.

By the time students are upperclassmen, many are living off-campus in apartments. When talking to students, most said that after a while at school they figure out which areas are safe to go to and which areas to stay away from, in terms of safety issues. Many agreed that there could be improvements in terms of building relationships with the surrounding community and having on-campus security being more attentive while on duty. If upperclassmen are not living off-campus, they are in apartment-style dorms with kitchens, meaning that either they do not have the meal plan or they eat in the newly renovated "Punch-Out," which includes popular fast food places such as Chic-Fil-A. Most students don't have cars, probably due in part to the fact that the DC subway system, the Metro, is a very efficient way to get around the city.

In addition to evolving living situations and eating habits, the social scene, too, changes as students get older. The clubbing scene begins to fade and instead of heading out to clubs like H2O, F.U.R, and Love, as they did as freshman and sophomores, upperclassmen tend to socialize at bars, house parties, and more sophisticated places such as The Diner, which is a coffee-shop-like place to hang out. As the workload increases and the realization that professional life is quickly approaching, many seniors spend weekend time differently than they did their first few years at Howard.

Coming Home to Howard

Probably the most famous event all year at Howard is Homecoming. People from all over the world come to gather together and share in special activities and events that last all week long. From the moment that guests arrive on campus on Sunday, they have the option of attending chapel services, talent shows, concerts, and more. One of the most famous events is the step show that takes place at the yard, where each fraternity has its own section from which to observe the events. Although the weekend is technically centered around sports, the hype is more about the gathering of all different people in a single venue. When asked about Homecoming, one sophomore said, "The fact that you can meet so many people from so many different regions and backgrounds, all with the same goal in mind, is a beautiful thing." For those who doubt the importance of the event: Homecoming was even mentioned in a Ludacris song.

> "The fact that you can meet so many people from so many different regions and backgrounds, all with the same goal in mind, is a beautiful thing."

Besides the events that characterize Homecoming, alumni and other prominent members of the African-American community who return to Howard are reminded of the time they spent at the gorgeous, hilly campus lined with old, New England style buildings. At the highest point of campus is the Yard, where people study and socialize when the weather is nice. In fact, the movie *Stomp the Yard* contains references to this famous area of Howard's campus.

No matter what type of background a person comes from or what activities he or she participates in, Howard is a place where students can build on their potential and grow into future leaders. Students agree that "even with the challenging academic life, Howard provides a unique and rewarding atmosphere for its students by allowing them to face real world problems in a life-like setting."—*Emily St. Jean*

FYI
If you come to Howard University, you'd better bring "a portable chair to stand in lines at the admissions building."
What's the typical weekend schedule? "Go to a house party on Friday night; if it's nice out, relax outside during the day on Saturday; head to Adams Morgan or a bar on Saturday night; and then recover and relax on Sunday, take a shuttle to church in the morning and catch up on work the rest of the day."
If I could change one thing about Howard, I'd "make it so that there was a higher percentage of males on campus."
Three things every student at Howard should do before graduating are "go to Ben's Chili Bowl, get familiar with the city (especially the National Mall area), and attend a homecoming game."

Trinity College

Address: Trinity, 125 Michigan Ave. NE, Washington, DC 20017
Phone: 800-492-6882
E-mail Address: admissions@trinitydc.edu
Web site URL: http://www.trinitydc.edu/admissions/
Year Founded: 1897
Private or Public: private
Religious affiliation: Roman Catholic
Location: urban
Regular Application Deadline: rolling
Number of Applicants: NA
Percent Accepted: 86%
Percent Accepted who enroll: NA
Number Entering: NA
Number of Transfers Accepted each Year: NA
Mean SAT: 820
Mean ACT: 16

Middle 50% SAT range: V:360–482, M:330–480
Middle 50% ACT range: 13–18
Early admission program (EA/ ED/ NA): EA
ED or EA Acceptance Rate: NA
Full time Undergraduate enrollment: NA
Total enrollment: 962
Percent Male: 2%
Percent Female: 98%
Total Percent Minority: 0%
Percent African-American: 68%
Percent Asian/Pacific Islander: 2%
Percent Hispanic: 11%
Percent Native-American: 1%
Percent Other: NA
Percent in-state / out of state: 52%/48%
Percent from Public HS: NA

Retention Rate: 66%
Graduation Rate: 44%
Percent in On-campus housing: 16%
Percent affiliated with Greek system: 0%
Percent Varsity or Club Athletes: NA
Number of official organized extracurricular organizations: 34
3 Most popular majors: Communications Studies/Speech Communications and Rhetoric, Social Psychology
Student/Faculty ratio: 11:01
Tuition and Fees: $17,360
Cost for Room and Board: $7,574
Percent receiving Financial aid, first-year: 93%

Founded by the Sisters of Notre Dame de Namur as one of the nation's first Catholic women's liberal arts colleges in 1897, Trinity has been attracting focused, but fun-loving, women ever since. And after becoming a university in 2004 with the addition of two professional schools, Trinity has even more resources to offer its small female population.

"At Trinity, everything is tradition. It's a very traditional school," one junior said. And indeed, the Trinity campus does abide by deep-seeded social and moral standards. But with its location in the heart of Washington D.C., the campus provides plenty of opportunity to create a mix between old and new, and fun and serious.

A Foundation for Leadership

With only 1,600 students in degree programs, Trinity is a tight-knit community, with many specialized programs to meet the needs of its students. Trinity students complete the Foundation for Leadership Curriculum (FLC), an interdisciplinary program with a professional focus that combines courses from six areas of study: Communication Skills, Cultural Diversity, Knowledge and Beliefs, Tradition and Legacies, Scientific and Mathematical Inquiries, and Individual and Society.

The most popular majors at Trinity are, understandably, politically-focused, with political science as a perennial favorite, trailed by communications, business, psychology, and international affairs. Trinity's political science department has graduated such political stars as California state representative and Democratic Leader of the House of Representatives Nancy Pelosi, Kansas governor Kathleen Sebelius, and several upper-level judges.

Thanks in part to its small size, and also its comfortable all-female dynamic, Trinity fosters an intimacy and a camaraderie in the classroom that students cannot stop raving about. "At Trinity, you're a name, not a social security number," one student said. Another commented, "You definitely walk away with everyone pushing for you."

Students and professors are very close at Trinity, and students say it is not unusual to have a professor's home or cell phone number—or even to have class dinners at the homes of professors during the semester. "The professors at Trinity are amazing," one junior said. "They love teaching and sharing their lives and all that they have learned with their students." Another student put it more succinctly: "Trinity's professors rock!"

On the honor system since 1913, Trinity students are diligent and supportive about their work. Help abounds at Trinity, with both the Academic Support and Career Services (ASCS) offering one-on-one tutoring throughout the four year education and also the Future Focus Program offering help specifically targeted to freshman year.

And while Trinity's academics are sufficient—with classes from Human Sexuality to Political Lives of Women to Civil Rights and Liberties on offer—the University is also part of a Consortium of schools in the D.C. area, allowing students to take classes at any number of other colleges and universities, and also bringing in other students (even men!) to Trinity. Washington D.C. is also the perfect area for professional internships, and Trinity students take advantage of their connections throughout the academic year with internships at anywhere from the White House and the Department of State to the Washington Mystics and the National Zoo.

National Government and Student Government

At Trinity, extracurriculars often take a backseat to academics and internships, but they do play a small part in campus life. A NCAA Division III school, Trinity is a founding member of the Atlantic Women's College conference, and competes at the varsity level in basketball, crew, field hockey, lacrosse, soccer, softball, swimming, tennis, track and field, and volleyball. Students also play a wide variety of intramural sports, but most students seem to spend their time doing individual workouts in Trinity's $20 million state-of-the-art athletic complex, the Trinity Center for Women and Girls in Sports.

Beyond athletics, Trinity extracurriculars run the gamut of usual clubs and organizations, particularly focused on the political and the journalistic. Student government is big at Trinity, as are the College Democrats and the College Republicans. Students run three publications: the literary magazine *The Record*, the yearbook *Trinilogue*, and the newspaper *The Trinity Times*. The Latina American Caribbean Student Association (LACASA) is especially active on campus.

There are no sororities allowed on the Trinity campus, though students are free to join sororities at other schools in the D.C. Consortium. "I think one of the reasons why sororities are not recognized on our campus is that there is not really a need for them. Being an all women's institution necessarily connects us into a sisterhood or community that I can appreciate."

Off-Campus Life

Part of the reason why extracurriculars are not a primary focus of Trinity life is that so many students live off campus. Though the dorms themselves are considered fine, though not by any means spectacular, the University's housing crunch combined with the abundant housing in the D.C. area means that many students commute, especially after freshman year. Trinity is a dry campus, and the dorms are "very restrictive"—"It holds up to all the stereotypes of a private, Catholic women's college," one junior said—so many students also move off campus to get a bit more freedom.

The campus itself, while restrictive, is quite beautiful, sitting on 26 wooded acres. The original Main Building, completed in 1909, contains all administrative offices, most classrooms and faculty offices, the computer center, the post office, the campus bookstore, and a residence hall. In addition to the Main Building, there are two more residence halls—Cuvilly and Kerby—as well as the Science Building, the Sister Helen Sheehan Library, the Trinity Center for Women and Girls in Sports, the award-winning Notre Dame Chapel, and the Alumnae Hall, which houses the campus dining facilities.

Since most students live off campus, they don't rely heavily on the meal plan, though students say Trinity has a "wonderful catering service" which is the same company that contracts for the government and provides food for the House of Representatives and the Senate.

An Emphasis on Diversity

Trinity students' social lives also take place primarily off campus, especially because of Trinity's strict no-alcohol policy and the easy transportation into the city or to surrounding schools. Drinking and drugs are very uncommon on the Trinity campus, with most socializing taking place in D.C. itself—an easy metro ride away. Besides the strict liquor policy, the Trinity lifestyle simply does not lend itself to tons of free time for socializing. "The student organizations fight to create community on campus and have decent success," one student said. "However, Trinity women are typically extremely busy."

The dating scene on campus is, of course, "quite non-existent." Many women, however, date men from area universities and from the D.C. area, and everyone is very enthusiastic about the all-woman atmosphere. "I would say it's comfortable," a junior said. "Many of the distractions that are found on large coed campuses are non-factors at Trinity. I am in college for an education and that is what I get."

> "Many of the distractions that are found on large coed campuses are non-factors at Trinity. I am in college for an education and that is what I get."

But just because only a few men from the Consortium ever enter Trinity's campus does not mean Trinity is not diverse. The school is actually amazingly diverse—less so geographically, but with incredible racial and socioeconomic diversity. Also, because of its continuing education programs, it is not unusual for older women to be in class with the more typical twentysomethings, lending a viewpoint that the younger students appreciate.

Constantly Evolving Traditions

As busy as they are, Trinity women always find the time to participate in Trinity traditions. "We're very into keeping up those traditions." Ultimately, these traditions are not just important to the Trinity experience, but symbolic of it: holding onto the past, but always moving forward into the future.

The many long-standing traditions at Trinity include the First-Year Medal Ceremony, Sophomore Pin Ceremony, Junior Ring Ceremony, Convocation, Cap and Gown Weekend, Founders' Day, Family Weekend, and "Well Sings."

But the most important Trinity tradition, and the one that speaks most to the strong community and legacy that is a Trinity education, is the class colors. The first four graduating classes each chose a color: red, blue, green, and gold. Now, at the end of the year, graduating seniors give their color to the incoming first-year class, to create a common bond between every fourth class. This is what it means to be part of a true sisterhood.—*Claire Stanford*

FYI
If you come to Trinity, you'd better bring "a well-polished resume because you never know who you're going to meet, walking shoes, your own social life."
What's the typical weekend schedule? "Go out on Friday, protest on Saturday, sleep on Sunday."
If you could change one thing about Trinity, I'd "make the school have a bigger budget for more classes."
Three things every student at Trinity should do before graduating are "go on a midnight monument tour, go paddle-boating at the Cherry Blossom festival in the Spring, and see fireworks at the National Mall on the Fourth of July."

Florida

Florida A&M University

Address: Florida A & M, Foote Hilyer Administration Center Suite G9, Tallahassee, Florida 32307
Phone: 850-599-3796
E-mail Address: admissions@famu.edu
Web site URL: www.famu.edu
Year Founded: 1887
Private or Public: public
Religious affiliation: none
Location: urban
Regular Application Deadline: 10-May
Number of Applicants: NA
Percent Accepted: 71%
Percent Accepted who enroll: 60%
Number Entering: NA
Number of Transfers Accepted each Year: NA
Mean SAT: 1074
Mean ACT: 22

Middle 50% SAT range: 440–550V, 440–550M, 520–610CW
Middle 50% ACT range: 19–22
Early admission program (EA/ ED/ NA): NA
ED or EA Acceptance Rate: NA
Full time Undergraduate enrollment: NA
Total enrollment: 9,967
Percent Male: 42%
Percent Female: 58%
Total Percent Minority: 98%
Percent African-American: 95%
Percent Asian/Pacific Islander: 1%
Percent Hispanic: 1%
Percent Native-American: 0%
Percent Other: 2%
Percent in-state / out of state: 95%/5%

Percent from Public HS: 85%
Retention Rate: NA
Graduation Rate: NA
Percent in On-campus housing: 75%
Percent affiliated with Greek system: NA
Percent Varsity or Club Athletes: NA
Number of official organized extracurricular organizations: 10
3 Most popular majors: Business/Marketing, Health Professions, Education
Student/Faculty ratio: 19:01
Tuition and Fees: $14,243.00
In State Tuition and Fees (if different): $3,047.00
Cost for Room and Board: $5,956.00
Percent receiving Financial aid, first-year: 83%

Tallahassee, Florida is known as a great college town. Since the city has two major universities, students who matriculate at Florida A&M (FAMU) can expect that something is always going on. In addition, as the State University System's only historically black university, FAMU has a long tradition of separating itself from the pack and retaining its individuality.

Structured Study

Undergraduates at FAMU have their pick of 103 majors within 62 fields of study in 12 different colleges. Much of the educational activity that goes on at FAMU is geared toward professional or pre-professional studies. In particular, the University's strongest programs are reputed to be in the School of Business and Industry, the College of Education, the School of Architecture, and the College of Pharmacy. The College of Engineering, which is shared with Florida State University, is also popular and well-respected.

Students sometimes complain that the education they receive is a little too structured. "My academic program is way too narrowly defined," one freshman said. "There is little room for personal exploration." On the whole, however, students say the academics are "reasonable" and "manageable" if, like most FAMU students, one enters the school with a clearly defined notion of one's professional goals.

One aspect of FAMU's pedagogical goals that distinguishes the University from its State University System peers is its commitment to undergraduates. While FAMU is trying to expand its graduate program enrollment across disciplines, most of the school's energies are geared toward its undergrads. All classes are taught by professors, who, as a general rule, interact often and individually with their students. TAs are hired only to assist with labs and occasionally to substitute for faculty. This focus on undergraduates has always been a hallmark of the FAMU education.

Chilling at the Set

Housing headaches have long been considered a part of life at FAMU, though this may be changing for the better in the near future. Most students have traditionally lived off campus, but there are residence halls as well. Recently, the University has required all freshmen whose families live 35 or more miles away to live in the dorms. In order to create a more tight-knit community, the University has been trying to make its housing options more attractive to all students. To date, those in the dorms tend to be ambivalent about their living conditions. "[It's] fine—nothing great, nothing awful," one student said. Meal plans are required of those who do live in on-campus housing.

For those who choose their own accommodations, Tallahassee offers a wealth of housing options that cater to college students. Apartments are generally available, and local places to shop and grab a bite to eat (including two malls) are abundant. Clubs and restaurants are also popular destinations. FAMU's campus is very near downtown, which offers not only practical and social advantages but also great educational and professional-development opportunities, given Tallahassee's status as the capital of Florida. FAMU has several established internship programs with local institutions, such as the popular program that places journalism majors at the *Tallahassee Democrat*, the local daily newspaper, for a summer or more.

There is plenty to do on campus as well. One popular hangout is "the Set," which is a common area near the Student Union. It contains the post office, the bookstore, a market and a TV room. Such shared spaces give off-campus residents a great excuse to hang out with on-campus friends. "It is great to have the Set so that off-campus people like myself can still stay connected with the rest of the student body," one sophomore said.

Never a Dull Moment

Popular activities among students include the Student Government Association, fraternities and sororities, musical events, pre-professional societies, journalism, theater, and sporting events. With so much going on, it goes without saying that FAMU students are an active, spirited group.

One of the challenges of the student government has been to keep off-campus students involved in the larger campus life. According to most accounts, they have succeeded admirably. "They do a terrific job," one student said. One popular annual event is "Be-out Day," which brings the student body out to the athletic fields for a day of food, partying and games. Another SGA-run event that "we all look forward to each year" is homecoming.

The Greek system is another big draw for students. According to the Office of Student Union and Activities, all of the national historically black fraternities and sororities have chapters at FAMU. In addition to these more traditional college Greek houses, there are also numerous community-service organizations and honor societies.

Music is also an important part of life at FAMU. The gospel choir is very popular, and the marching band, known as the Marching 100, has achieved an international reputation. In the past 10 years it has been featured in a Bastille Day parade in Paris and played at President Clinton's second inauguration. Several predominantly black high-school bands in North Florida and other areas intentionally imitate the flamboyant, showboating style and discipline of the Marching 100.

> "I love this community, but . . . there is much to be desired in terms of creating a diverse student body."

FAMU Rattler sports are a pretty big deal in Tallahassee, even though they are often in the shadow of the larger and better-known teams of Florida State University. Despite the recent scandals and resulting shakeups in the athletic department, students still show their school spirit by decking themselves in orange and green and attending NCAA Division I sporting events, especially football, which is in Division I-AA. Intramural sports are also popular and are described as "fierce and fun."

A Close Community

With most schools in the country focusing their recruiting efforts on increasing diversity, FAMU has bucked the trend. The school is very proud of its status as Florida's only public historically black university, and has made the recruitment of high-achieving black students its No. 1 priority. At times, FAMU has performed as well as or better than such universities as Harvard, Yale and Stanford in recruiting National Achievement Scholars.

Students say that although they wish there was more diversity on campus, they do appreciate and enjoy the community they have. "I love this community, but . . . there is much to be desired in terms of creating a more diverse student body," one senior said. "I look outside and everyone is so much like me." Of course, the students do have diversity when it comes to their backgrounds and interests (although around 85 percent are from Florida). There is considerable political diversity; but strikingly uniform is the students' take on homosexuality. The small community of gay students isn't organized, and students say they're "not very open-minded when it comes to that."

FAMU has been a traditional top choice for many black students from Florida because of its respected pre-professional and professional academic programs, its warm environment (in more ways than one), and its commitment to undergraduate education. As one senior put it, "I am going out into the real world with not only solid academic training, but a host of life experiences that I won't soon forget."—*Jay Buchanan*

FYI

If you come to FAMU, you'd better bring "some sunglasses, not for the sun, but for all the gold teeth that will hurt your eyes."

What is the typical weekend schedule? "Friday, catch up on sleep; Saturday, go out and party; Sunday, do all the work from the previous week."

If I could change one thing about FAMU, "I'd improve the landscape. There are too many bushes around here."

The three things that every student at FAMU should do before graduating are "chill at the Set, volunteer in Tallahassee and attend Homecoming."

Florida Institute of Technology

Address: Florida Tech, 150 W. University Blvd., Melbourne, FL 32901
Phone: 800-888-4348
E-mail Address: admission@fit.edu
Web site URL: http://www.fit.edu/ugrad/
Year Founded: 1958
Private or Public: private
Religious affiliation: none
Location: urban
Regular Application Deadline: rolling
Number of Applicants: NA
Percent Accepted: 61%
Percent Accepted who enroll: NA
Number Entering: 597
Number of Transfers Accepted each Year: 309
Mean SAT: NA
Mean ACT: 25

Middle 50% SAT range: 500–620V, 550–660M, 570–670CW
Middle 50% ACT range: 22–28
Early admission program (EA/ ED/ NA): NA
ED or EA Acceptance Rate: NA
Full time Undergraduate enrollment: 2,331
Total enrollment: 2,365
Percent Male: 69%
Percent Female: 31%
Total Percent Minority: 45%
Percent African-American: 3%
Percent Asian/Pacific Islander: 3%
Percent Hispanic: 7%
Percent Native-American: 0%
Percent Other: 55%
Percent in-state / out of state: 38%/62%
Percent from Public HS: 70%

Retention Rate: 77%
Graduation Rate: 55%
Percent in On-campus housing: 52%
Percent affiliated with Greek system: 31%
Percent Varsity or Club Athletes: NA
Number of official organized extracurricular organizations: 94
3 Most popular majors: Aerospace Aeronautical and Astronautical Engineering, Aviation/Airway Management and Operations, Mechanical Engineering
Student/Faculty ratio: 13:01
Tuition and Fees: $27,540.00
Cost for Room and Board: $7,400.00
Percent receiving Financial aid, first-year: 90%

Nestled in a tropical, lush environment and boasting a challenging curriculum with unique research opportunities, the Florida Institute of Technology stands apart from other technical universities. Indeed, this small technical school, located five minutes from the beach, offers more than just an education: Florida Tech prepares its students for life.

Challenging Courses

Despite the appeal of relaxing on the beach, students at Florida Tech take academics seriously. Many said they find the academics to be difficult, but rewarding. As one student said, "Classes are challenging. They really put you to the test."

Students say that one of the best aspects of academics at Florida Tech is the small size of a typical class. Since many classes enroll less than 20 people, students have the chance to actively engage in classroom discussions and interact with the professor. As one sophomore said, "You're not just a number. Professors get to know your name, and you get to know a lot about them too. It's a really nice relationship, but they keep it very challenging."

On top of their classes, many students take advantage of the excellent hands-on research opportunities available at Florida Tech. From manatee preservation and beach erosion studies to working at NASA or Lockheed Martin, every student can plug into Florida Tech's extensive research program.

Along with the requirements for each major, most students have to complete core classes, which include Physics I and II, Calculus I and II, Civilization I and II, and Differential Equations and Linear Algebra. Students must also complete various communication classes, including Composition and Rhetoric, Writing about Literature, and Science and Technical Communication.

Although Florida Tech offers numerous majors through its Colleges of Engineering, Science, Aeronautics, Business, and Psychology and Liberal Arts, the two most popular majors are Aerospace Engineering and Marine Biology.

"Everything under the Sun"

Student organizations and clubs exist for "everything under the sun," as one sophomore said. Indeed, with over one hundred registered student organizations on campus, "there's something here for everyone," and students have little trouble finding organizations that interest them. Popular organizations range from bowling and sport fishing to math and skydiving. Many students also get involved with community service. Florida Tech has its own organization for Habitat for Humanity as well as a program for working with local elementary school students.

Students at Florida Tech participate in 15 intercollegiate sports at the Division II level. While Florida Tech may not be known for its varsity athletics, students said that the soccer and basketball teams have recently been particularly successful. One sophomore commented that "Athletic spirit could be better, although it has improved in the last

couple of years." For those not as eager to indulge in athletics at such a high level, Florida Tech also offers many opportunities to get involved with intramural sports.

Social Life

General friendliness seems to abound at Florida Tech. According to one student, "people will bend over backwards to help you." And, because Florida Tech has a small student body, "Everyone really gets a chance to get to know all the students."

On campus, "there's always something going on," as one sophomore said. The student-run Residential Hall Association and the Campus Activities Board set up popular campus events, including comedy shows, concerts and an International Fair, which allows students to explore the traditions of people from different cultures across the world.

Off campus, most students spend their free time hanging out on the beach. While there, people enjoy a range of water activities, including surfing, boating, kayaking or simply relaxing in the sun. Students can also drive less than an hour to get to Disney World.

Greek fraternities and sororities attract a large number of students and are a dominant presence on campus. Some students complain about a lack of on-campus parties, though they acknowledge that parties do take place off campus. Florida Tech tends to have a strict policy against alcohol, although students do not always follow it— "We still drink, of course," one sophomore commented.

Florida Tech's uneven male-female ratio affects social life on campus. Male students joke that, "if you don't find a girlfriend in the first couple of weeks in freshmen year, you won't ever find a girlfriend." However, such sentiment is not pervasive throughout the entire student body. As one male student said, "It doesn't bother me too much. I probably have more female friends on campus than male friends."

Around Campus

Students live in one of seven campus residential halls and two apartment complexes. Campbell and Wood Halls offer housing primarily to freshmen, although their convenient locations draw many upperclassmen to share these residencies as well. Roberts Hall is the largest residence facility on campus and houses only freshmen. Women may choose to live in Shaw Hall, a female-only residence. Outside of the residence halls, students love the Columbia Village Suites and Southgate Apartments. The Southgate Apartments, which come with in-suite amenities and an outdoor pool, are so popular that "people wait outside and sleep in tents for a week to get in," said one student. All freshmen are required to live on campus, while about half of the remaining students choose to live off campus.

> **"It wasn't what I was expecting . . . it was a lot better."**

Residence Halls are watched over by student RAs. One sophomore mentioned, "RAs are pretty strict compared to other schools." Students tend to find the food at Florida Tech to be decent. As one student said, "When I come back from break, I'm excited to eat the food. But after three weeks, I'm kind of tired of it." Students often socialize at "The Rat," an eatery and pub on the lower level of Evans Hall that also features a big screen TV, game room, and computer cluster. Off campus, students enjoy eating at local restaurants such as Carrabba's Italian Grill, City Tropics Bistro and Outback Steakhouse.

Not Typically Techie

Despite its name, Florida Tech offers much more than an education in technology. From the lush botanical gardens on campus to the beautiful beaches just miles from campus, from scuba diving under the water to watching shuttle launches at Kennedy Space Center, from graphs to Greek life, Florida Tech offers the complete college experience. One student put it best, "I wasn't sure what I was getting into. It just blew me away. It wasn't what I was expecting . . . it was a lot better."—*David Flinner*

FYI
If you come to Florida Tech, you'd better bring "a calculator."
What's the typical weekend schedule? "Friday: Get out of class as early as possible and take a nap; Saturday: hang out at the beach; Sunday: Study."
If I could change one thing about Florida Tech, I'd "lower tuition."
Three things every student at Florida Tech should do before graduating are "help out with some community service projects, watch the shuttle lift off, and make many trips to the beach!"

Florida Southern College

Address: 111 Lake Hollingsworth Dr.; Lakeland, FL 33801
Phone: 800-274-4131
E-mail address: fscadm@flsouthern.edu
Web site URL: www.flsouthern.edu
Founded: 1885
Private or Public: private
Religious affiliation: United Methodist
Location: Small city
Undergraduate enrollment: 1,800
Total enrollment: 2,200
Percent Male/Female: 40%/60%
Percent Minority: 10%
Percent African-American: 5%

Percent Asian: 1%
Percent Hispanic: 4%
Percent Native-American: 0%
Percent in-state/out of state: 70%/30%
Percent Pub HS: NA
On-campus housing: 72%
Fraternities: 10%
Sororities: 10%
Number of Applicants: 1,826
Percent Accepted: 71%
Percent Accepted who enroll: 37%
Entering class: 560
Transfers: 150
Early admission program (EA/ED/NA):
Early Decision or Early Action Acceptance Rate: NA

Application Deadline: 1-Apr
Mean SAT: NA
Mean ACT: NA
Middle 50% SAT range: NA
Middle 50% ACT range: NA
Most popular majors: business administration, education, communications
Retention: 84%
Graduation rate: 55%
Tuition and Fees: $19,165
In State Tuition and Fees (if different): NA
Room and Board: $6,800
Financial aid, first-year: 76%
Varsity or Club Athletes: 20%
Library: 200,000 volumes

Shake, rattle and roll for the Water Moccasins of Florida Southern—they'll be sure to show you a good time, with hospitality that keeps with Southern tradition and parties to rival the Greeks. Though Florida Southern itself is small, and nestled into the not-so-large city of Lakeland, students warn that "it's not the country," and one even said, "Parts of it look like New York, in the Old District." The community you'll find at Florida Southern, though, is a little warmer and maybe a little more hospitable. One freshman said, "I only wanted to come to this school because it was close to home, but when I came here, I found out people were so nice and so genuine and so helpful that I decided to stay."

ACE is Wild

Some students complain, "There's really not too much to do around here," but ACE is around to fix that. The Association of Campus Entertainment schedules events every month for students on campus. From concerts to community service activities, ACE keeps commuting students and those who live on campus in touch by bringing them together for some good wholesome fun. Comedians, hypnotists and other entertainers host audiences in the school auditorium or in classrooms, usually at no cost to students. ACE also hosts bands, but don't look for too many weekend events. "They don't put a lot of stuff on the weekends," one student said, "because no one will come. A lot of the students go away on the weekends." Because there aren't too many parties at Florida Southern, many students opt to go to Tampa or Orlando for party weekends, and many commuters spend the weekends at home.

> "I only wanted to come to this school because it was close to home, but when I came here, I found out people were so nice and so genuine and so helpful that I decided to stay."

Intramurals keep Florida Southern students busy, as do trips to local rock-climbing and ice-skating facilities. Even horseback riding trips are offered, and all such trips are free for students. If there isn't enough entertainment to suit your fancy, students recommend just joining ACE. Like any club, ACE is open to non-elected members of the student body, and members are encouraged to develop and bring new events to the campus.

Water Moccasins on a Dry Campus

When Florida Southern does get down and party, students look to their fraternities and sororities to host the shindigs. This is due in part to the Greeks' enthusiastic party publicity. "They're always putting banners up that say everyone's invited," one student said. "They're very welcoming, even if you don't belong to the sorority." Frats and sororities are also the main party source because their houses, while on campus and therefore technically subject to the same rules as all other housing, can sometimes provide alcohol to this dry campus. Under the dry-campus policy, even those of legal drinking age are not allowed to bring alcohol into the dorms. "People are known to go out, and a lot of people drink, because normally dry campuses are like that," one student said. But the school safeguards against excessive drinking when students are away from their campus homes. "If you go out to club and you're drunk," a program called Safe Ride ensures that "the school pays for you to come back to campus," students report.

Livin' La Vida Florida

Freshmen at Florida Southern start out in freshman dorms, which are manned by RAs. A fair number of Florida Southern students are commuters, often because they live nearby and it makes more sense for them to live at home. Students who choose to live on campus get their own dose of parental supervision from their RAs. "My RA is one of my best friends," one student said, "but you can be stuck with a pretty strict one." Other rules include a visitation policy that prohibits visitors past a certain hour, as well as sleepovers with the opposite sex. These regulations are not curfews, but, in combination with the dry-campus policy, they are the administration's attempt to maintain the values of the school's Methodist heritage. But there are benefits: RA-supervised dorm life means the school sponsors pizza parties and movie outings with hallmates.

Freshmen at Florida Southern are required to take a freshman introductory course, worth an hour of credit, for the first half of their first semester. "The Examined Life," or EXL, is the only class at Florida Southern where you can get credit for going on a tour of the college. Other features of the freshman orientation include introductions to faculty members and to the tutoring resources available for students looking for extra help.

The so-called "core" academic requirements then guide undergraduates through their courses of study, requiring that all students take classes in the areas of fitness and wellness, psychology, theater, English, religion and sociology. Students are in favor of the requirements for different reasons. "I think everyone should take a religion class even if you're not that into going to church—it's just something you learn," one student said. Another added, "They want to introduce you into everything the college offers in case you want to change your major."

Students say their "classes are really small, so it's more hands on," and they "get more one-on-one time" because of the intimate learning environment, where "the teachers are very helpful." Still, one student said, "it's nothing like high school."

Moccasins Shed Their Skin

Sometimes commuters have a hard time getting incorporated into on-campus life, so the school administration does a number of things to unite the student body. Off-campus residents are invited to regular lunches in the dining hall to join their campus-dwelling classmates. Convocation is another tradition at Florida Southern. Once a month the entire student body congregates in the auditorium to hear speakers—a professor, a pastor—talk about a given topic. January, for example, focused on the Martin Luther King Jr.

holiday and its value as a human-rights holiday, not as an African-American holiday.

Students take great pride in the diverse and welcoming environment their school fosters. "You'll find all different kinds of people here," one student said. "We have people that are rich, people that are poor, blacks, whites, Hispanics. It's really nice to see all these people. It's really cool to have a college where everyone's welcome." Mr. Moc is a great example of Florida Southern's welcoming arms and warm spirit. Mr. Moc is the unofficial mascot of the school, and, students say, "He's gotta be like 85." A Florida Southern alumnus himself, Mr. Moc heads up traditional cheers at basketball games and joins the most spirited fraternities in dressing up in Florida Southern's colors. "I think he even goes on the road with the basketball team!" one student said. "I think he's pretty representative of the school. You don't have to be a certain race or a certain age. There's people here that I think are professors that are actually students—everyone from 17 to 70."

The diversity extends to religious leanings, too. "It's a Methodist school, but we have students that are Jewish, students that are Muslim." Above all, students comment on the warmth of their classmates. "I love that everyone's so nice here," one freshman said. "Everyone's very friendly to you. That's one of the reasons I'm going here."—*Stephanie Hagan*

FYI
If you come to Florida Southern, you'd better bring "extra money."
What is the typical weekend schedule? "Go to Kau's Thursday night; Friday night, go on a date; Saturday mornings, Habitat for Humanity; and spend the whole day Sunday doing work."
If I could change one thing about Florida Southern, "I'd make it snow."
Three things every student at Florida Southern should do before graduating are "go to Kau's, go to a Convocation, and join a fraternity or a sorority."

F l o r i d a   S t a t e   U n i v e r s i t y

Address: Florida State, Office of Admissions, PO Box 3062400, Tallahassee, FL 32306-2400
Phone: 850-644-6200
E-mail Address: admissions@admin.fsu.edu
Web site URL: www.admissions.fsu.edu
Year Founded: 1851
Private or Public: public
Religious affiliation: none
Location: small city
Regular Application Deadline: 14-Feb
Number of Applicants: 25,593
Percent Accepted: 42%
Percent Accepted who enroll: 38%
Number Entering: 5,672
Number of Transfers Accepted each Year: varies
Mean SAT: NA
Mean ACT: NA

Middle 50% SAT range: 1,120–1,290
Middle 50% ACT range: 24–28
Early admission program (EA/ ED/ NA): NA
ED or EA Acceptance Rate: NA
Full time Undergraduate enrollment: 27,217
Total enrollment: 39,652
Percent Male: 43%
Percent Female: 57%
Total Percent Minority: 26%
Percent African-American: 12%
Percent Asian/Pacific Islander: 3%
Percent Hispanic: 11%
Percent Native-American: 0.3%
Percent Other: 0%
Percent in-state / out of state: 93%/7%

Percent from Public HS: NA
Retention Rate: 87.8%
Graduation Rate: 66.2%
Percent in On-campus housing: 14%
Percent affiliated with Greek system: 28%
Percent Varsity or Club Athletes: NA
Number of official organized extracurricular organizations: 355
3 Most popular majors: Finance, Psychology, Marketing
Student/Faculty ratio: 22:01
Financial Information:, per credit hr
Tuition and Fees: $3,307.00
In State Tuition and Fees (if different): $16,439.00
Cost for Room and Board: $7,078.00
Percent receiving Financial aid, first-year: 52.6%

Students at Florida State University don't hesitate to advertise the fact that their school is known as a party school, but that's not all they're proud of. As one senior stated, "I think what really sets us apart from other schools is the fact that we can balance that kind of social life with hard work in the classroom."

It's Academic

In addition to a vibrant campus nightlife, FSU offers a variety of majors numbering over 200. Most students choose to enroll in the College of Arts and Sciences, but there are other colleges, such as the College of Business, the College of Music and the College of Engineering. Students are expected to choose a major when they apply, but before they can be certified in that major they must complete the university's math and freshman composition requirements and over half of their liberal studies requirements. These mainly consist of two English or literature courses, two math or science courses, and five or six other specific courses, depending on one's major. Along with that, students are also required to take two "x and y" courses in cross-cultural studies and the diversity of Western experience.

The most popular majors at FSU are business, communication, biology, engineering, and psychology. The hardest and most respected major at FSU, as one business major claimed, is "business, of course. I am definitely a little biased, but in all honesty, accounting and finance majors are some of the most respected people on campus." A freshman majoring in exercise physiology has a different opinion: "I think the science majors are definitely the hardest. They always seem to be complaining about their problem set that is due tomorrow."

For students looking for honors programs, FSU boasts a fine one. Students enrolled in this program have their own honors residence hall. For those who are not excited about having to trudge across campus to get to class, the honors halls provide myriad courses within their own walls.

Class sizes vary; introductory courses are notorious for being extremely crowded, but only one course (Biology for Non-Majors) exceeds 1,000 students and the majority (79%) do not exceed 40 students. One senior added, "The profs are very open to the students and want to help. If you are struggling with some material from lecture, most are more than willing to go over it again with you."

"The workload is very manageable," a freshman exercise physiology major said. But a seasoned senior warned, "It only gets harder." There are easy classes at FSU. The same senior commented, "I got three credits for scuba diving and became an advanced certified diver up to 100 feet. It was a really fun class, and the best part was our final exam consisted of a three-day diving trip to the Keys."

In recent years, FSU has made it a top priority to focus more positive attention on its students and academic programs, and to attract more top-quality students. The State of Florida's Bright Futures scholarship program, though controversial, provides up to a full-ride scholarship to highly qualified residents who might otherwise leave the state. These and other excellent students can participate in one of many research opportunities offered by professors. Florida State has begun to establish its reputation as a great place for undergraduates to participate in original research. FSU recently established the Office of National Fellowships, which advises students applying for prestigious grants, such as the Rhodes, Marshall, Truman and Goldwater scholarships. The university has also embarked on a series of goals, known as the Pathways of Excellence Initiative and linked to major investments in faculty development and new facilities for research and creative activities. Within the next five years, 200 new professors will be hired in interdisciplinary clusters centered around common academic themes.

The Seminole Social Scene

Known for its party atmosphere, FSU doesn't lack options when it comes to hanging out with friends. While frats and sororities are prevalent on campus, Greek life by no means dominates the social scene. One sophomore reflected, "The frats can be very cliquey. I rushed and didn't really like it, but now I have multiple groups of friends and have no trouble finding things to do." The influence of Greek life extends off-campus as well. There is a famous bar near campus called PotBellys, but since it is frequently engulfed in Greek socializing it has come to be known as "Frat Bellies."

Greek connections notwithstanding, there's always something fun to do at FSU, any night of the week. One freshman described his weekly activities: "Monday we go to the Plaza, a strip just off campus that has some of the nicer bars in Tallahassee. Tuesday we go to Frat Bellies (Pot Bellies)

or AJ's Sports Bar. Wednesdays are usually sorority or frat socials, general party nights. Thursdays we go to Floyd's Club [Floyd's Music Store]." Friday night students can continue the party options at "country night at Stetson's, or you can just go to the Plaza. Saturday means football after-parties. Then on Sunday I try to get a little work done." One junior cautioned, "Don't try to use fake IDs to get into bars, though; they are usually confiscated—it is much safer to pre-game in someone's room and have a designated driver for the night."

> "We have the best all-around atmosphere. Once you are able to prioritize your life, you get to experience the best of both worlds— excellent academics and a social life."

FSU offers many other options socializing options that do not include alcohol, as well. Movies are shown every couple of days at the Student Life Building, and the Oglesby Union also offers different activities for students. Annual parties at FSU include Homecoming and Parents' Weekend. There are also the pep rallies for the football games, known as the "Downtown Get-Down" and located in the center of Tallahassee. One senior claims, "We have the best all-around atmosphere. Once you are able to prioritize your life, you get to experience the best of both worlds—excellent academics and a social life."

Life as a Seminole

As students look over the FSU campus, they see gorgeous, brick buildings on an extremely well-kept campus. "I was shocked at how clean the campus was when I first saw it. It is really a beautiful place," one student noted. The residence halls on campus are constantly under renovation, but as of fall 2007 renovation of ten of fourteen residence halls will be complete. FSU has a policy on not allowing alcohol in dorms which is strictly enforced. "You just have to keep it [parties] small; we usually just have a couple of friends over before we head out. If you throw a party you will definitely be caught." One senior reflected, "The RAs are pretty strict, but if you can get it [alcohol] past them you are in good shape." FSU students are not daunted by the challenge, and in fact, embrace it. One senior reminisced about how his friends set up a pulley system to transport the beer from ground level outside to their seventh-floor window.

The residence halls are not the only places to live. In fact, most upperclassmen live in apartments in the surrounding area, many of which are designated exclusively for FSU students. Due to many students' off-campus housing, many feel that a car is a must. "If you can't get a car for yourself be sure someone in your group of friends has one. It's a lifeline." Unfortunately, once you do get a car, parking at FSU can be a nightmare. Luckily, the city bus system is free to students and several off campus apartments offer shuttle service.

Students employ a variety of different methods when it comes to getting food. Some are on the meal plan, which is flexible, allowing them to choose the number of meals they get each week. Other options are Garnet Bucks, bought at the beginning of the year, which let students buy whatever they want, at any time, from on-campus eateries. Hungry students, however, are by no means restricted to cafeterias. Favorite places to go when hunger hits are the on-campus Park Avenue Diner ("The service is horrible, but the food is so good") and the off-campus Boston Market ("It may sound strange, but it always reminds me of a nice home-cooked meal").

Seminole Pride and Tradition

Needless to say, the biggest source of FSU pride is football. One student summarized the sentiment: "Football games are some of the most moving experiences you will have here at FSU. As you look out over the sea of [garnet] and gold fans all doing 'the chop,' you can't help but feel a strong sense of pride welling up within you." Every Friday night before a football game, a torch is lit. The following day, the Seminole Indian symbol, Osceola, rides out onto the field, circles to rile up the fans, and then throws a flaming spear into the middle of the field. "It might just be me," commented a sophomore football fan, "but I sure wouldn't want to be the visiting team in an atmosphere like this." Tailgates usually start around 9 a.m., so don't plan on sleeping in Saturday mornings, especially if you have to drive. The campus roads quickly become gridlocked as the rush to the stadium escalates before kickoff.

FSU has a fair number of varsity sports, but, as with other universities, the other main spectator sports are basketball and baseball. It should be noted that the basketball arena recently added a bar that quickly became a favorite hangout for Seminole fans. If you are interested in sports but don't want to make a huge time commitment, FSU has an amazing intramural program. "We have every sport imaginable. It is really an amazing network; for touch football alone, there are over 250 teams registered."

Whether you seek stardom on the IM fields or just want to get in shape, you can do it at the Leach Center. The state-of-the-art gymnasium offers unparalleled fitness opportunities. It has a top-of-the-line weight room, an Olympic-size swimming pool, countless cardio machines, squash courts, three full-size courts open for all students, and more. One freshman says she goes there every day: "It's far and away my favorite spot on campus."

Traditions run deep at FSU. One senior recounted that he has been thrown into the Westcott Fountain on his birthday four times; while this might seem odd to any non-Seminole, it is a common ritual at FSU. There is even a video camera posted on one of the buildings that films all the "swimming" events and is accessible online. Another tradition includes the Tennessee Waltz, also known as the 21st Birthday Waltz. Friends get together on the big day and take you to every bar on Tennessee Street (home to many, many bars). One of the most perplexing rumors around FSU concerns the school symbol. Rumor has it that the famous profile of the Seminole found all over campus is none other than the silhouette of the oldest professor on campus, Tommy Wright, of the College of Music. "I swear it's him," claims one adamant senior, "He has the exact same facial structure [as the design]." Fears that the NCAA might force a mascot change were assuaged by the school's successful appeal in 2005.

The newest official tradition, ironically, may come from the administration's attempt to imbue incoming freshmen with a sense of tradition. The first New Student Convocation, held in 2005, was quite successful and has become yet another source of FSU pride.

Such pride has come to define the FSU experience. The students seem to have great drive in the classroom, and miraculously balance it with a social life that few schools can match. The Seminole spirit, both on the field and in the stands, routinely dwarfs that of opposing teams. While they may seem hostile to opponents, their genuine Southern hospitality makes visitors from the farthest points feel welcome. With its pristine campus and state-of-the-art facilities and technology, Florida State University offers an unparalleled experience for a student seeking a complete, well-rounded college experience.—*Chris Dufek*

FYI

If you come to FSU, you'd better bring "your Rainbows [flip-flops]. You won't see a FSU student without them."

What's the typical weekend schedule? "Friday night: party; Saturday: tailgating, football game, party, maybe throw in some clubs if you're energetic; Sunday: Homework maybe . . ."

If I could change one thing about FSU, "it would be the parking—while it is improving, slowly, it's horrendous."

Three things that every student at FSU should do before graduating are "take a birthday swim in Westcott Fountain, go to as many football games as you possibly can, and do the 21st Birthday (Tennessee) Waltz."

New College of Florida

Address: New College of So. Florida, 5800 Bay Shore Rd, Sarasota, FL 34243-2109
Phone: 941-487-5000
E-mail Address: admissions@ncf.edu
Web site URL: www.ncf.edu
Year Founded: 1960
Private or Public: public
Religious affiliation: none
Location: small city
Regular Application Deadline: 15-Feb
Number of Applicants: 1,266
Percent Accepted: 46%
Percent Accepted who enroll: 36%
Number Entering: 207
Number of Transfers Accepted each Year: 57
Mean SAT: 1,333
Mean ACT: 28
Middle 50% SAT range: 1250–1430

Middle 50% ACT range: 26–30
Early admission program (EA/ ED/ NA): NA
ED or EA Acceptance Rate: NA
Full time Undergraduate enrollment: 746
Total enrollment: 746
Percent Male: 41%
Percent Female: 59%
Total Percent Minority: 16%
Percent African-American: 1.5%
Percent Asian/Pacific Islander: 2.8%
Percent Hispanic: 9.9%
Percent Native-American: 0.5%
Percent Other: NA
Percent in-state / out of state: 82%/18%
Percent from Public HS: 83%

Retention Rate: NA
Graduation Rate: 67%
Percent in On-campus housing: 64.5%
Percent affiliated with Greek system: 0%
Percent Varsity or Club Athletes: NA
Number of official organized extracurricular organizations: 37
3 Most popular majors: Psychology, Evironmental Studies, Economics/History
Student/Faculty ratio: 10:01
Tuition and Fees: $19,964.00
In State Tuition and Fees (if different): $3,734.00
Cost for Room and Board: $6,564.00
Percent receiving Financial aid, first-year: 60%

I magine a college with 750 students, a laid-back atmosphere, a beach-side location, and no grades. This is no cushy finishing school; this is New College of Florida, the state's public honors college. Formerly the honors college of the University of South Florida, New College has only recently been able to stand alone in the State University System as one of Florida's, and the nation's, most unique institutions of higher learning.

Free-Form Academics

One of the most oft-cited facts about New College's academic program is its absence of formal grades. For each class, students receive from their professor a detailed evaluation of their performance that term. A common misconception is that this decreases students' motivation to do their best work. In reality, this system is a great compliment to the culture of self-motivation that is so pervasive at the school. (It's also a great boost to applications to graduate school.)

"The best education demands a joint search for learning by exciting teachers and able students," claims the college's Web site. Though this may sound idealistic, at New College these words are put into practice. "High-caliber" faculty and an eclectic, self-selected group of high-achieving students create for each other the "constructive pressure to succeed," in the words of one sophomore. In elaborating on this 'constructive pressure,' one art major cites not only the close relationships she has developed with the faculty in her department, but also the various student-run art shows that she and her friends have organized. Another student described the typical student-professor relationship: "You'll definitely have professors who know you well—some will probably cook your whole class dinner." Students work especially closely with their professors on their senior thesis, which is a universal graduation requirement.

> "You'll definitely have professors who know you well—some will probably cook your whole class dinner."

In general, the academic requirements are not considered very strict. The distribution requirements are minimal at most, and many students elect to design their own major. There are, however, traditional majors available, with literature, anthropology and the sciences tending to be the most popular. Marine biology is also particularly strong, a fact enhanced by the college's proximity to the Gulf of Mexico.

An Open Atmosphere—Thanks to the 'Walls'

New College has a deserved reputation as being a hotbed of activism. An overwhelming majority of its students consider themselves liberal, and radicalism—including anarchism—tends to be the rule rather than the exception. But rather than identifying themselves based on such labels, students would prefer to be seen as open-minded. Perhaps one student put it best in stating that Novocollegians are better at "theorizing about activism" than practicing it.

But there are certainly other things to do. One of students' favorite New College traditions is "the Walls." These parties are usually held multiple times a week in the school's main courtyard, the Palm Court. Students sign up to host the college-sponsored event, and the whole school is always invited. One sophomore found it hard to describe, other than that the Walls are much more "open and comfortable" than parties at other schools. "If you're not comfortable dancing," she said, "come to New College and you'll soon become a great dancer." Other popular school-wide dance parties include the Palm Court Parties (PCPs), which are more organized and happen on special occasions, such as Valentine's Day and Halloween.

Complementing this open party atmosphere is a widely accepted culture of drugs and alcohol. Marijuana and alcohol are prevalent and widely available, and it is common knowledge that the few law enforcement officials on campus are there to protect students against outsiders, not to break up social gatherings. "Cops look the other way most of the time," one student said. However, most students agree that there is little pressure on those who do not wish to participate in illicit activities.

One aspect of New College's setting that draws complaints is the town of Sarasota. Wealthy retirees are the average residents of this town, which is "a community with aspirations of being cultural and artsy." But the weather gets high marks, as do the tourist attractions: the beach and the Ringling Museum. The latter is gaining more popularity with students because of its efforts to build new student centers and libraries close to campus. And if one is desperate to get out of Sarasota for a while, there's always Tampa, which is less than an hour away by car.

There is plenty to do on campus as well. Many students are involved in such extracurriculars as *The Catalyst*, the weekly student-run newspaper; student government; and activist groups. Sports are admittedly a smaller part of life than at larger universities. New College has no varsity programs, but racquetball and soccer are popular choices for pickup games.

Beds and Bread

Dorm life receives positive reviews from most students. Lucky students are assigned to a Pei dorm or a newer Dort, or Goldstein Hall. The former are apparently the most spacious and best designed overall (originally designed as hotels by I.M. Pei), whereas the latter are more modern in all aspects and have suite-style living arrangements. The Pei dorms are reputedly the most social. "You will see your friends when you enter and leave the building, and hang out outside talking a lot," one resident said. The main drawback is that since New College is working on increasing the size of its student body, many of the rooms that were designed as doubles are suddenly becoming triples.

Campus residents are required to be on the meal plan, which is not considered a bonus. The food leaves something to be desired: "There's a reason we were ranked as the worst college food in the South," one student explained. There is one central cafeteria, but alternatives abound, including the Four Winds, a new student-run cafe.

A One-of-a-Kind Experience

New College is not known to be an incredibly diverse place, as most students are white, middle-class, liberal and suburban. Other aspects of diversity, however, are present on campus. For example, the school has what one sophomore called "gender diversity." The school is very gay-friendly, and all sorts of lifestyles find acceptance at New College.

Overall, the students self-select to a large extent; while this is great for creating and sustaining a unique culture, it has the downside of perpetuating the school's homogeneity.

If you are a Florida resident, you won't find a much better education for the money than New College, as many in-state students are eligible for the state's generous scholarship programs and don't have to pay a dime to go to school. But everyone, both Florida residents and out-of-state students, shares the uniqueness of the New College experience: a noncompetitive, high-quality academic program with laid-back, intelligent students in an ideal campus setting.—*Jay Buchanan*

FYI

If you come to New College, you'd better bring "your stamina and social skills."
What is the typical weekend schedule? "Friday, relax and get ready for the party in Palm Court;
   Saturday, relax and play some sports; Sunday, nothing else but studying."
If I could change one thing about New College, "I'd make the student population more diverse."
Three things that every student should do before graduating are: "go to a Wall or PCP, walk around
   barefoot, and write a thesis."

Rollins College

Address: Rollins, 1000 Holt Avenue, Winter Park, FL 32789-4499	**Middle 50% SAT range:** M:545–630,V:545–630	**Percent from Public HS:** 53%
Phone: 407-646-2161	**Middle 50% ACT range:** 23–27	**Retention Rate:** 84%
E-mail Address: admission@rollins.edu	**Early admission program (EA/ ED/ NA):** ED	**Graduation Rate:** 69%
Web site URL: www.rollins.edu	**ED or EA Acceptance Rate:** 65.2%	**Percent in On-campus housing:** 67%
Year Founded: 1885	**Full time Undergraduate enrollment:** 1,720	**Percent affiliated with Greek system:** 20%/23%
Private or Public: private	**Total enrollment:** 2,454	**Percent Varsity or Club Athletes:** NA
Religious affiliation: none	**Percent Male:** 40%	**Number of official organized extracurricular organizations:** 88
Location: suburban	**Percent Female:** 60%	
Regular Application Deadline: 16-Feb	**Total Percent Minority:** 29%	**3 Most popular majors:** Economics, International business, Psychology
Number of Applicants: 3,036	**Percent African-American:** 5%	
Percent Accepted: 55%	**Percent Asian/Pacific Islander:** 4%	**Student/Faculty ratio:** 10:01
Percent Accepted who enroll: 30%	**Percent Hispanic:** 10%	**Tuition and Fees:** $30,860.00
Number Entering: 501	**Percent Native-American:** 1%	**Cost for Room and Board:** $9,626.00
Number of Transfers Accepted each Year: 123	**Percent Other:** 9%	**Percent receiving Financial aid, first-year:** 85.25%
Mean SAT: 1,194	**Percent in-state / out of state:** 53%/47%	
Mean ACT: 25		

Set in idyllic Winter Park, Florida, Rollins College is "like a vacation every single day." Whether sunning by the outdoor pool, enjoying scenic Lake Virginia, or partying in nearby Orlando, Rollins students know how to have fun, and they do it in style.

Steady Studies

Academics at Rollins are "above average but not too difficult." Students who want to do well can work towards a more intense schedule, but others opt to get by in less demanding majors such as education. Science, business and foreign language majors are "competitive and demanding," required a minimum of several hours work every night, but well worth the professors they feature. "I know a lot of them wrote the text books they teach with . . . several famous politicians graduated from Rollins, too." And since there are no TAs at Rollins, students get the full benefit of their professors' attention.

Rollins students have one complaint in the academic department—thick bureaucracy. It's tough to get into the classes you want, and as one freshman complained, "It's difficult to switch/drop/add classes. I spent two weeks trying to fix my schedule." But such pains are made up for with exceptionally hands-on class options. As one student raved, "Rollins offers a course that allows students to get credit by tutoring elementary kids."

High Class Frats

For the more action-oriented, the party scene at Rollins is packed. "Everyone drinks in the dorm rooms," frat parties are frequent, and Orlando, just 15 minutes away, is packed with bars and clubs. That's a lot to handle in one weekend, especially when combined with a prevalent drug scene. "The drug scene is definitely big," one student said. "Coke is huge."

About half the student body is part of the Greek community. One freshman said that "it isn't hard to rush and I haven't heard of any bad stories. It's expensive, but there are really fun theme parties. Golf Pro's Tennis Hoes was my favorite." ATO and Chi Psi are the "best frats," but "TKE has good parties." Kappa Delta and Kappa Kappa Gamma are the most popular sororities.

Even when they aren't going out, Rollins students dress to impress. "Many people are very preppy," a sophomore commented. "Everyone here owns a Lacoste shirt and many girls wear Lilly Pulitzer dresses and have Gucci and Louis Vuitton bags." Although diversity is lacking at Rollins, beauty is big. One girl said that "the student body is like no other. I've had several friends come and visit and they were all in shock. Everyone wears ridiculously expensive clothing, drives ridiculously nice cars and tries to outdo everyone else." And the old Spanish style campus tends to be as perfectly manicured as the undergrads themselves. The Rollins campus is "absolutely beautiful" and "covered in gorgeous foliage." And it's also a safe haven for students seeking alone time. One student said, "You can always find a place to hide down by the lake" or go running outside at night. "I love that I don't ever have to worry about anything happening."

Dumpy Dorms

For all the good looking people and places in Winter Park, the student dorms don't quite match up. "For the price of Rollins, the dorms are disgusting. They're always filthy and covered in vomit, empty beer cans and cockroaches." "McKean is probably the worse dorm because it's always so dirty. We have a pretty big issue with cockroaches and stray cats right now. It's pretty gross." Air-conditioning is about the only perk. And interestingly enough, Florida law prohibits coed bathrooms. Considering the on-campus housing options, it is no surprise that many students opt to move off. "The apartments and houses in Winter Park are all very adorable so most people want to live close by."

> "Being on a sports team here isn't really a big deal. It's probably better to join a frat or sorority."

Luckily, the food fares a bit better. "The meal plan is great" at Rollins, one undergrad said. Students get $1,700 per semester to use at dining halls and neighborhood restaurants, including Domino's pizza. There is also a deli counter and food store for kids on the run. However, "the dining hall is definitely a social scene," so students try to make time to go there and "talk with friends." When in the mood for a night on the town, Winter Park offers "amazing" restaurants, bars, and shops.

Tars Take it Slow

Extracurricular activities at Rollins "aren't huge" and "not many students work." They're more likely to be found by the pool, one junior commented. Sports aren't very popular either, but as one student pointed out, "the baseball boys have good parties." Baseball games also attract the highest attendance, along with men's soccer (perhaps all its European recruits make it hard for even a Florida girl to resist the accents). Overall, though, "there is little team spirit," which bothers some students, especially since the Tars house a conference-leading men's basketball team.

Those students that choose to participate in extracurricular activities are well respected—particularly the members of the SGA, Rollins' Student Government Association. For theater buffs, the Annie Russell Theater is quite the attraction. One seat is kept empty at all times for the ghost of Annie Russell, said to haunt the building. There are even students who claim to have seen and heard Annie there at night. When students aren't at a practice or in a meeting, they hit the gym. "Many people wakeboard on the lake in their free time," one student said. There is also an outdoor swimming pool and golf course nearby for athletes at heart. "Being on a sports team here isn't really a big deal. It's probably better to join a frat or sorority."—*Lauren Ezell*

FYI

If you come to Rollins, you better bring "a designer handbag, bathing suit and Lilly Pulitzer dress (for girls) and a Lacoste polo shirt, a ton of cash and a BMW (for guys)."

What is a typical weekend schedule? "Party at night, lay by the pool during the day, possibly get some homework done and do it all over again the next night."

If I could change one thing about Rollins, I'd "change the cost of tuition. It's not worth the $42,000 plus."

Three things every student at Rollins should do before graduating are: "Go to Disney World at least once, take a trip to Cocoa Beach and party at Club Paris."

Stetson University

Address: Stetson University, 421 N. Woodland Blvd., DeLand, Florida 32723
Phone: 386-822-7100
E-mail Address: admissions@stetson.edu
Web site URL: www.stetson.edu
Year Founded: 1883
Private or Public: private
Religious affiliation: none
Location: Suburban
Regular Application Deadline: 1-Mar
Number of Applicants: 2,919
Percent Accepted: 65%
Percent Accepted who enroll: 30%
Number Entering: 567
Number of Transfers Accepted each Year: 0
Mean SAT: 1,132
Mean ACT: 24

Middle 50% SAT range: 1,030–1,220
Middle 50% ACT range: 21–27
Early admission program (EA/ ED/ NA): ED
ED or EA Acceptance Rate: 76%
Full time Undergraduate enrollment: 2,185
Total enrollment: 2,705
Percent Male: 42%
Percent Female: 58%
Total Percent Minority: 17.8%
Percent African-American: 4.9%
Percent Asian/Pacific Islander: 1.8%
Percent Hispanic: 8.7%
Percent Native-American: 0.4%
Percent Other: 0.019
Percent in-state / out of state: 80%/20%

Percent from Public HS: 70%
Retention Rate: 80%
Graduation Rate: 0.63%
Percent in On-campus housing: 70%
Percent affiliated with Greek system: 22.5%
Percent Varsity or Club Athletes: 11.7% (varsity)
Number of official organized extracurricular organizations: 124
3 Most popular majors: Business, Education, Psychology
Student/Faculty ratio: 11:01
Tuition and Fees: $27,010.00
Cost for Room and Board: $7,632.00
Percent receiving Financial aid, first-year: 99.8%

It's tough to deny the allure of packing swimsuits and tanning lotion instead of snow pants and boots in preparation for college. But Stetson University, in sunny DeLand, Florida, isn't just any laid-back, rural Florida school. It's known for solid academics—including several well-respected professional programs—and a vibrant campus atmosphere.

Academics

According to *U.S. News and World Report*, Stetson consistently ranks among the best regional schools in the Southeast. There is a lot to choose from when it come to academics: with over 60 major and minor fields available to undergraduates in the College of Arts and Sciences, the School of Business Administration and the School of Music, students can study anything from digital arts (a collaboration between the departments of Art and Computer Science and the School of Music) to chemistry to business law.

In addition to completing the requirements for a major, undergraduates in the College of Arts and Sciences must fulfill a stringent set of distributional requirements, which encompass the areas of "Foundations" (basic courses such as English, math and foreign language), "Breadth of Knowledge" (natural and social science), "Bases of Ethical Decision Making" (ethics courses), and a non-academic requirement, "Cultural Attendance," which entails attending approved cultural events every semester. Some academic requirements can be waived with AP scores, but either way, the fact remains that you will get a well-rounded education at Stetson. "All the requirements can be irritating," one junior said. "But . . . if you're an English major, at least you have the experience of having taken some science."

There are also several programs that encourage Stetson's brightest to go beyond the curricular minimum. The Honors Program, for example, gives students the opportunities to take a Junior Honors Seminar and design their own major, as well as encouraging them to study abroad. Although any entering student may apply, most accepted students have had SAT I scores of 1270 or above and have been in the top fifth of their high-school class.

As one might expect from a school with such a variety of academic disciplines and such a small student body, classes at Stetson are small, and professors are accessible. With relatively few classes within each division, majors often encompass broad areas of study. Students change their majors often, a process that is apparently neither difficult nor stigmatized. But having small class sizes—even in such traditionally impersonal disciplines as business—can make all the difference for some. "You do tend to bond with your professors, whether you like it or not," said one senior, a marketing major. "I have not been in a class with more than 50 students."

Once students have experienced the ease of getting into their desired classes and the delight of having the professor know their names from Day One, there's the actual class work to consider. More difficult subjects are rumored to be biology, chemistry and music. At one point, "Music Theory" had the highest failure rate on campus. Communications and education, according to students, are easier majors.

Dorm life

Since freshmen, sophomores and juniors are all required to live on campus, "dorm life" at Stetson is often synonymous with "campus life." "The dorms aren't particularly nice," one sophomore said, "but they are amazing places to meet people and really learn how to live on your own." Students praised the location of the dorms—they are all within walking distance to central campus.

Other facilities are certainly not lacking. The college gymnasium and pool received high marks. The gym offers classes during the semester, and the pool is "very spacious and a good place to relax," presumably since most of the year is bathing-suit weather.

The dining halls are also decent. The main eating facility is Commons, which is apparently "fair" in terms of food and seating arrangements. Known as a social place, Commons is an area where "you can just pick up a conversation with anyone really." Stetson's flexible dining plan allows students to cash-in unused meals for purchases at other eateries close by, such as the popular grill Hat Rack, Einstein Bros. Bagels, and the nearby smoothie shop.

Campus life

Though Stetson features a variety of clubs and activities for students, the Greeks, with their six fraternities and five sororities, tend to be the biggest force on campus. They often host large parties and events in their mostly off-campus venues. Most of these events are nonexclusive.

Two other prominent groups on campus are the Council for Student Activities (CSA) and the Student Government Association (SGA). They have been responsible in the past couple of years for bringing in such big-name acts as Less Than Jake and Busta Rhymes. In addition, Stetson hosts a variety of speakers every year. "If you want to hear a speaker every week at Stetson, you definitely can," one senior said. There are, of course, a variety of smaller organizations that cater to more specific groups; these, however, tend to be less active.

Athletics are also a big part of campus life. Although the school lacks the draw of having a football team, students report that the other varsity teams' events are well-attended and popular. While the teams themselves "tend to keep together," according to a senior non-athlete, this doesn't keep the rest of the student body from going to games and cheering them on. The basketball and soccer teams receive the most attention. Intramural sports are also popular.

Outside the Bounds of Campus Grounds

The town of DeLand is not generally known as a fun place to hang out, but it has its advocates. This minority says that the town fulfills all "basic needs" with a Wal-Mart and several chain restaurants, that the historic downtown area provides a nice walk, and that "you couldn't ask for a safer place to have a school."

> "You couldn't ask for a safer place to have a school."

But those who seek a setting that includes more than McDonald's, picturesque promenades and a sense of security flock instead to Daytona or Orlando, each of which is less than an hour away. Popular destinations include malls, clubs, bars, theme parks and anything else the rural town just can't provide. To this end, many students do bring cars to campus, but—as with most colleges—the limitations of on-campus parking can make owning a car more of a burden than anything. Many students use their cars to drive home to other Florida cities on a regular basis.

For those who choose to stay on campus or in DeLand, there is certainly not a dearth of things to do. The most popular parties, thrown by the Greeks, are generally held off campus, but there are large on-campus parties as well. These tend to be contained by Public Safety, Stetson's security detail. Drinking is prevalent at all of these parties, but there are alternatives. Many groups, particularly various Christian ones, host dry events on a regular basis. Drug use does occur at Stetson, but it is easy to avoid and by no means popular. According to students, alternatives to "traditional" college partying include bowling, ice skating, going to the movies, and listening to live music.

Conclusion

So why choose Stetson? For many, the appeal is that the college is "a small school close to home." Around 80 percent of the students are Floridians; it's tough for any Florida native to consider going anywhere farther north for school. But the year-round sun is not the only draw: Stetson features high-quality academics on a gorgeous campus. Although it is located in a rural town, Orlando and Daytona are close enough that students don't feel stranded. Add to that the small classes, accessible professors, school spirit and general commitment to excellence, and you've got a school that would be hard for anyone to pass up.—*Jay Buchanan*

FYI

If you come to Stetson, you'd better bring "a bathing suit, because we have a nice pool and people take trips to the beach very often."

What is the typical weekend schedule? "Friday, drive to Daytona; Saturday, spend the afternoon in Daytona and hang out with friends; Sunday, relax in DeLand."

If I could change one thing about Stetson, "I would bring a better selection of food during the weekends."

The three things that everyone should do before graduating from Stetson are "go to all the beaches, join a club or Greek organization and get involved, and enjoy it!"

University of Florida

Address: University of Florida, 201 Criser Hall- Box 114000, Gainesville, FL 32611-4000
Phone: 352-392-1365
E-mail Address: NA
Web site URL: http://www.ufl.edu
Year Founded: 1853
Private or Public: public
Religious affiliation: none
Location: suburban
Regular Application Deadline: 18-Jan
Number of Applicants: 22,093
Percent Accepted: 48%
Percent Accepted who enroll: 63%
Number Entering: 6,702
Number of Transfers Accepted each Year: 2,218
Mean SAT: NA
Mean ACT: NA

Middle 50% SAT range: 1,140–1,360
Middle 50% ACT range: 25–29
Early admission program (EA/ ED/ NA): ED
ED or EA Acceptance Rate: 50.9%
Full time Undergraduate enrollment: 35,110
Total enrollment: 46,549
Percent Male: 46%
Percent Female: 54%
Total Percent Minority: 34%
Percent African-American: 10%
Percent Asian/Pacific Islander: 7%
Percent Hispanic: 13%
Percent Native-American: 0%
Percent Other: 4%
Percent in-state / out of state: 95%/5%
Percent from Public HS: NA

Retention Rate: 94%
Graduation Rate: 79%
Percent in On-campus housing: 22%
Percent affiliated with Greek system: 13%
Percent Varsity or Club Athletes: NA
Number of official organized extracurricular organizations: 500
3 Most popular majors: Business, Finance, Psychology
Student/Faculty ratio: NA
Tuition and Fees: $17,791.00
In State Tuition and Fees (if different): $3,206.00
Cost for Room and Board: $6,590.00
Percent receiving Financial aid, first-year: 36%

G ators are known to be ruthless predators, and that remains true for the Gators at the University of Florida—UF students continue to step up their athletic, academic and overall levels of performance with every coming year. The University of Florida was the flagship school for higher education in Florida, and has grown to be one of the most prestigious schools not only in the state, but also in the country. And who wouldn't want to come to UF? With great weather, national champion sports teams, and an upward climbing academic reputation, students agree that there is not much you could improve about the University of Florida.

The Early Bird Gets the Worm/ Dormancy in a Gator Hole

As the academic standards at UF increase, the acceptance rate keeps dropping. Many students found that applying early helped to ease anxiety about getting in, especially if UF was their first choice. An added incentive to apply early is that the housing application is mailed together with the main application and is handled on a first come, first serve basis. While it is not required, most freshmen live on campus and find it both very convenient and helpful in making fast friends. However, not all the dorms are created equal, and two dormitory buildings even lack air-conditioning, a necessity for most of the sultry Floridian year. There is also not enough on-campus housing for all freshmen, so space fills up fast. No one is required to live on campus at any time, and most upperclassmen move off campus after freshman year if they haven't already. Two sophomores agreed that there are perks to both, and there is "never a better time than freshman year" to live on campus. The dorm rules are relatively strict regarding overnight guests of any gender, but it all depends on the residential assistants who live on each floor. Students can even have small pets of any variety as long as roommate approves. If you do live off campus, like the majority of students at UF, it is "pretty essential" to have a car. However, parking issues are always lurking, and it is considered a rite of passage to get a parking ticket, if not many. One student estimated that there are about three times as many cars as there are parking spots.

If a student does not end up bringing a car, he will probably know someone who did and should take full advantage. Gainesville is located in the center of North Florida, about the same distance from Orlando as from Jacksonville. Tampa and Tallahassee are also within driving distance, which is nice for when the UF-FSU game is at FSU. Another perk of Gainesville's location is its proximity to the beaches, both the Gulf Coast and the Atlantic Ocean are short drives away. One student said he usually takes a trip out of Gainesville about every other weekend, especially when football is in season.

A Winning Combination
It isn't that students want to get out of Gainesville, it's that they are pulled out by tradition. Going to football games, no matter the location or the time of the year, is one of the major traditions that continues every year. Sports are huge at UF, as is the amount of school spirit; everyone claims to "bleed orange and blue." It makes sense, because while they are always top contenders, both the UF football and men's basketball teams won national championships in 2006–2007. As a result of both tradition and the championship titles, one student claimed that "any football or basketball player is basically a god in Gainesville." Since both game tickets and Gator paraphalnalia are always limited, there is a lottery system for tickets but you should bring "something orange to wear to games because everywhere is always sold out."

Southern Comfort
While the varsity athletes get all the glory, there are also many opportunities for less mainstream athletes to compete in either club or intramural leagues on campus. There is everything from rowing to ultimate frisbee to soccer in the club arena. Intramurals at UF are always expanding, and the spring of 2007 saw the first ever rock-paper-scissors intramural tournament. There really is something for everyone, including multiple gym and recreation facilities for both athletes and non-athletes.

> **"Any football or basketball player is basically a god in Gainesville."**

Students also use their free time to work, to volunteer in the community, or to get involved with clubs. Students who work can choose between working a desk job on campus, or working off campus at the Gainesville Mall. The Shands Teaching Hospital provides many opportunities for interested students to volunteer and get hands-on experience in the medical world. There are also groups like GatorTrax, which is a minority engineering program, that cater to a more specific group of students. There are almost as many groups and clubs as you can imagine, but you would be hard pressed to find a student who knew what a capella was.

When asked, UF students claim "there is no stereotypical Gator, we are a very diverse student body," which is a reasonable claim since the student body is more than 40,000 strong. One senior maintained that her fellow students "range from hippies to rednecks to book worms." Although she conceded that many students come from in-state, she listed friends from "England, Saudi Arabia, South Africa, Korea, and most of the states." So while students come from all over the place, there are certain locations on campus where more visible groups can be spotted. A central spot called Plaza of the Americas is a place where "a lot of the hippie-ish people hang out."

Greeks and Gods
While the majority of students are not in fraternities and sororities at UF, Greek life plays a big role in the social scene. There are parties from Thursday night to Saturday night, and the days in between are used to go to clubs like XS on University Avenue. XS has a popular 80s theme night, but if students desire a more laid back atmosphere, there are also many bars on the Avenue such as the Sloppy Gator. Tailgating for games is also big, and the Florida-Georgia game is touted as the "world's largest outdoor cocktail party." As at most universities, drinking is prevalent but students say that it is not the only way students socialize at UF. Many students go bowling or see movies. One junior said that the Blockbuster "is always packed," showing that Gator students have many ways of relaxing.

Variety is the Spice of Life
The reason students need to relax, of course, is school work. UF is not the party school that some may wish it to be. There are many challenging majors, some more popular than others, all of which have serious competition for classes. Some of the most popular majors are business, engineering, building construction and political science. Introductory courses can have as many as 5,000 students enrolled and some are taught online. The financial accounting

class, a requirement for the business degree and known as the "hardest course" at UF, forces some students to change their major. One student found changing majors to be "easy," due to the fact that the university "was very accomodating." She said that her advisors, who are assigned through the students major, are "very helpful." Some students find it easier to declare their major even before the beginning of their freshman year so they can be sure to get in all the requirements. In addition to the specific departmental requirements, UF also has some general education requirements, which can vary depending on one's chosen major. Many students find it beneficial to transfer their AP credits from high school into college credit and many can pass out of some requirements completely. One freshman even upgraded to sophomore standing because she had taken so many AP classes in high school.

Summer school is also an option if you have trouble fitting in all your chosen major's requirements, and Florida legislature actually requires a minimum of six summer school credit hours. Some students find the general education requirements a good way to explore other topics. For example, one student praised the class titled Fruits for Fun and Profit because even if it is not required for a major, "it's interesting and you learn something new you would have never known before. And at the end of every class they give you a bag of fruit to take home."
—*Emily Matykiewicz*

FYI
If you come to the University of Flordia, you'd better bring: "some Tylenol, because there is a lot of screaming that comes along with winning 2 national titles!!! GO GATORS!!!"
If I could change one thing about the University of Flordia, I'd "make it a little smaller."
What's the typical weekend schedule? "Watch the national champion basketball or football team, then head to downtown Gainesville and dance at Whiskey Room, Plasma, or Rue Bar. Maybe catch a movie on Sunday night."
Three things every UF student should do before graduating are: "Experience a Saturday in the Swamp—there is nothing more exciting than cheering the Gators on with 90,000 of your closest friends—study at the new Library West, and go to Lawtey Mud Pit."

The University of Miami

Address: University of Miami, PO Box 248025, Coral Gables, FL 33124
Phone: 305-284-2211
E-mail Address: admission@miami.edu
Web site URL: www.miami.edu
Year Founded: 1925
Private or Public: private
Religious affiliation: none
Location: suburban
Regular Application Deadline: 2-Feb
Number of Applicants: 19,037
Percent Accepted: 40.49%
Percent Accepted who enroll: 26.75%
Number Entering: 2,062
Number of Transfers Accepted each Year: 1,355
Mean SAT: NA

Mean ACT: NA
Middle 50% SAT range: 1,160–1,350
Middle 50% ACT range: 25–30
Early admission program (EA/ ED/ NA): ED/EA
ED or EA Acceptance Rate: 32.97% (ED) / 57.02% (EA)
Full time Undergraduate enrollment: 10,509
Total enrollment: 13,684
Percent Male: 45%
Percent Female: 55%
Total Percent Minority: 37.2%
Percent African-American: 9%
Percent Asian/Pacific Islander: 5%
Percent Hispanic: 23%
Percent Native-American: 0.2%

Percent Other: <1%
Percent in-state / out of state: 55% / 45%
Percent from Public HS: NA
Retention Rate: 87%
Graduation Rate: 71%
Percent in On-campus housing: 42%
Percent affiliated with Greek system: 13.65%
Percent Varsity or Club Athletes: NA
Number of official organized extracurricular organizations: 217
3 Most popular majors: NA
Student/Faculty ratio: 13:01
Tuition and Fees: $31,288.00
Cost for Room and Board: $9,334.00
Percent receiving Financial aid, first-year: 77.33%

We've got some Canes over here! Whoosh! Whoosh!" Loud cheers erupt throughout the Orange Bowl Stadium as thousands of fans gather to witness the annual University of Miami vs. Florida State University football showdown. Clad in orange and green paraphernalia, the enthusiastic spectators show vibrant support for their team. But Hurricane pride is not limited to the athletic field. University of Miami students have a lot to be proud of—top academic programs, a wide array of student activities, and a beautiful campus located in sunny South Florida.

Work Hard, Play Hard

The University of Miami distinguishes itself from other schools in that it focuses heavily on both academics and athletics. What other school can lay claim to both hosting a 2004 Presidential Debate and being home to numerous championship athletic teams? In terms of academics, UM students have over 180 undergraduate programs to choose from, offered through eight colleges: Architecture, Arts and Sciences, Business, Communication, Education, Engineering, Music, and Nursing. Freshmen accepted into the university as "undecided" majors are admitted through the College of Arts and Sciences.

The academic requirements differ depending on your college. Nevertheless, "students have very diverse interests and are encouraged to take classes in other fields and departments," said one psychology major. The most popular majors at UM include Biology, Psychology, and Political Science. Students generally agree that the "hardest majors tend to be in the science and engineering fields," such as biology, neuroscience, biomedical engineering, physics, and genetics. Most students say that introductory courses, which generally contain between 100 and 200 students, are relatively easy. But upper level courses including "Organic Chemistry," "Experimental Psychology," "Ancient Greek," and "Politics of the Middle East" are known for being particularly tough. UM also offers several unique courses, including "Dance Therapy," "Horror Literature" and "Videogame Systems."

The majority of classes are taught by professors, not TAs. One junior notes, "I've had some really amazing professors here who are scarily brilliant and very approachable." Professors tend to be available and "encourage students to take advantage of their office hours."

Extending invitations to only the top 10 percent of the entering class, the University's Honors Program is considered one of the most prestigious academic tracks for incoming freshmen. Students must have a minimum SAT score of 1360 or ACT score of 31 and be ranked in the top 10 percent of their high school graduating class to be admitted. The Honors Program offers over 200 courses and course sections per semester, and classes are generally small seminars that foster intimate class discussion and interactive learning. In addition, the University of Miami has a highly selective Honors Program in Medicine, in which students can earn both a Bachelor of Science and a Doctor of Medicine degree in seven to eight years. Dual Degree Honor Programs in Biomedical Engineering, Marine Geology, Physical Therapy, Latin American Studies and Law are also available. Overall, the academic life is described as "pretty balanced," and "there's room for fun if you break up your time well."

Fun in the Florida Sun

University of Miami students have tons of social options on weekends, both on and off campus. There are frequent activities on campus such as concerts, movie screenings at the free campus cinema, and invited guest comedians and musicians. Frats also regularly sponsor parties where "everyone's welcome." Moreover, club-sponsored socials, such as the Hispanic Heritage Month Gala, are popular weekend options that "cater to everyone." Homecoming is another big event on campus and even includes a parade and fireworks. As one sophomore noted, "now the school is starting to hold more events on campus on Saturdays and Sundays so that people stay more on campus." Drinking is prevalent on campus and the general feeling is that "almost everyone drinks." Nevertheless, students who do not drink say that they do not feel excluded.

Despite the active on-campus social scene, many UM students venture off to enjoy the Miami night life on weekends. As one student put it, "that's the beauty of being in Miami—on any given night there is something to do." Typical weekend hangouts include clubs in Coconut Grove, the Design District, South Beach, and Bayside Marketplace. Usually, the minimum age for admittance into clubs is 21. On Thursdays, however, Coconut Grove has a "College Night," where students 18 and over are allowed to get into its clubs. During the day on weekends, many students catch movies or go shopping at The Shops at Sunset Place, a popular mall near campus. UM students also enjoy hanging out and tanning in South Beach.

> "That's the beauty of being in Miami—on any given night there is something to do."

Although many University of Miami students have cars on campus, the school offers several transportation options to get around Miami. The Hurry Canes shuttle takes students to Coconut Grove and The Shops at Sunset Place, as well as areas on campus. Also, the Metrorail is a convenient way to get to Bayside Marketplace, downtown Miami, and Dadeland, a huge shopping mall.

Living in Paradise
Covered with palm trees and beautiful foliage, the University of Miami is frequently praised for its beauty and described by students as "our own tropical paradise." The buildings on campus are built in modern style, and many, such as Hecht tower, have been recently renovated.

The University of Miami has several central gathering areas for students. One of the most popular campus locations is the University Center (UC), which contains comfortable sofas, an arcade, a café with pool tables, a convenience store, a food court, and the offices of student organizations are located here. The Rathskellar, nicknamed "the Rat" is another popular social area, where students can play pool, watch one of the wide-screen TVs, or sit outside in the tropical warmth at swinging picnic tables. The "Rat" is also a venue for campus entertainment and frequently features live bands and dance parties. Students enjoy hanging out around the pool area to enjoy the Florida sun.

University of Miami students who choose to live on campus are assigned to one of five residential colleges—Eaton, Hecht, Mahoney, Pearson, and Stanford. The dorms are described as "relatively nice" and all are air-conditioned. As freshmen, students are randomly assigned to the dorms. Students have the option of being placed on "quiet floors," where there are stricter rules about noise. Unlike typical college dorms, a faculty master and his or her family live alongside students in each residential college. The residential colleges are also staffed by Residential Coordinators (RCs) and Residential Advisors (RAs). According to students, most RAs are "pretty strict," and

"getting caught drinking or doing drugs will get people in trouble." Alcohol is only allowed in the dorm rooms of students who are 21 and over and if they are drinking, they must keep their door closed.

The University of Miami also has a large number of commuters, some of whom belong to organizations such as the Association for Commuter Students. Upperclassmen generally decide to live off-campus in apartments or houses that rent out to students in the Coral Gables neighborhood. Additionally, UM is constructing University Village, which will consist of "apartments available only to upperclassmen and graduates."

Go Canes!
Students at the University of Miami have incredible school spirit. The University's Division One athletic teams dominate collegiate sports and have won more than twenty national championships. Sports such as football, basketball, and baseball have "a huge presence on campus," and football is generally considered the most popular sport. As one student put it, "football season gets crazy down here . . . tailgates start at least four hours before a game."

Aside from varsity sports, students are encouraged to participate in club and intramural teams. The athletic facilities for both athletes and non-athletes are "amazing." The University's multi-million dollar Wellness Center is a top-notch fitness, recreation, and wellness facility open to all students. The activities offered at the Wellness Center include intramural sports, exercise classes, and wellness programs.

University of Miami students are also passionate about extracurricular activities. Greek life is very popular, with over 1,000 undergraduate members of UM's 29 sororities and fraternities. During Cane Fest, the organization fair at the beginning of fall semester, students are able to choose from a wide variety of clubs. Some popular organizations include Student Government, Council for Democracy, College Democrats, College Republicans, Committee on Student Organizations (COSO), and Hurricane Productions.

There are also a number of honor societies, clubs for specific majors, and community service groups. Moreover, multicultural organizations, such as La Federacion de Estudiantes Cubanos (FEC), are very prominent. Several unique activities exist on campus, such as Salsa Craze, Swing Club, and Adrian Empire, which is a Medieval/

Renaissance Reenactment Group. And as one student remarked, "if there's something you want to do that UM doesn't have, it's pretty easy to start it up." Most students are fairly committed to their extracurricular activities. One sophomore stated, "getting involved . . . has made it so much better because that's how you make friends and gain experience and knowledge that will help you in the future."

'Cane Spirit

Despite a common stereotype that University of Miami students are "rich" and "snobby," most students claim otherwise. Students note that "the majority of people are pretty down-to-earth" and "really friendly." The University also has a great deal of diversity, with students from "all over the world and all around the U.S." A recent graduate described that the prevalent diversity on campus was a "very unique, educational, and rewarding experience."

Students praise the University's commitment to both academics and athletics and attribute the University's growing prestige to President Donna Shalala, who is doing "so many things to get our school's name out there." The tropical climate, beautiful campus, and diverse and nurturing student atmosphere are all factors that draw students to the University of Miami. But what really distinguishes the school for most students is "the fact that people actually really care about their school and are proud to go to UM." Go Canes!—*Eileen Zelek*

FYI

If you come to the University of Miami, you'd better bring "your bathing suit, flip-flops, shorts, and sunscreen."

What is the typical weekend schedule: "For the most part it consists of lots of homework during the day and partying at night. The weekend starts on Thursday with 'College Night' in Coconut Grove and the rest of the time is usually spent tanning or clubbing in South Beach."

If I could change one thing about the University of Miami, "I'd add more parking garages and make the restaurants and dining halls on campus stay open longer."

Three things every student at the University of Miami should do before graduating are "go to a football game at the Orange Bowl, spend time at South Beach, and hang out at the Rat."

Georgia

Agnes Scott College

Address: Agnes Scott, 141 E. College Ave, Decatur, GA 30030
Phone: 800-868-8602
E-mail Address: admission@agnesscott.edu
Web site URL: www.agnesscott.edu
Year Founded: 1889
Private or Public: private
Religious affiliation: Presbyterian
Location: urban
Regular Application Deadline: rolling
Number of Applicants: 1,541
Percent Accepted: 47.5%
Percent Accepted who enroll: 30.2%
Number Entering: 221
Number of Transfers Accepted each Year: varies
Mean SAT: 1,201
Mean ACT: 26

Middle 50% SAT range: 1,110–1,300
Middle 50% ACT range: 24–29
Early admission program (EA/ ED/ NA): ED
ED or EA Acceptance Rate: 17%
Full time Undergraduate enrollment: 833
Total enrollment: 914
Percent Male: 0%
Percent Female: 100%
Total Percent Minority: 34%
Percent African-American: 20%
Percent Asian/Pacific Islander: 5%
Percent Hispanic: 4%
Percent Native-American: 0%
Percent Other: 5%

Percent in-state / out of state: 53%/47%
Percent from Public HS: 71%
Retention Rate: 78%
Graduation Rate: 67%
Percent in On-campus housing: 86%
Percent affiliated with Greek system: NA
Percent Varsity or Club Athletes: 10%
Number of official organized extracurricular organizations: 49
3 Most popular majors: Biology, English, Psychology,
Student/Faculty ratio: 10:01
Tuition and Fees: $25,785.00
Cost for Room and Board: $8,990.00
Percent receiving Financial aid, first-year: 99%

Hollywood, watch out! When it comes to picture-perfect campuses, not even Tinseltown can beat Agnes Scott's storybook setting. The campus, famously featured in the horror flick *Scream 2*, has served as the setting for more than a few movies. This all-female school, tucked away in Decatur, Georgia, attracts studious women as well as movie studios. Agnes Scott offers a strong liberal arts curriculum and a lengthy list of traditions that together form the unique "Agnes Scott experience."

A Peach of a Campus

"Agnes Scott's campus is absolutely beautiful!" exclaimed one junior. Students universally share this sentiment, and maintain that the "gorgeous surroundings" are among the school's best features. The campus, tucked away in a "quiet, mostly residential" neighborhood, overflows with Gothic and Victorian buildings. Several of the administrative buildings are so architecturally noteworthy that they are featured in the National Register of Historic Places and the American Institute of Architects Guide to Atlanta. The campus is built around a grassy expanse known as the Quadrangle, or "Quad." Big brick and stone dorms frame this "green oasis" and provide scenery for those studying and sunbathing on the "always green" lawn. As one sophomore said, "It doesn't take more than five minutes to get anywhere from anywhere else" on this small, centralized campus. Students seem to appreciate the intimacy of their secluded environment, praising the "quiet and solitude" it offers. As one amazed student commented, "You can barely even hear the cars passing by." When seeking even more peace and quiet, students frequent the "Secret Garden," a courtyard within the library.

But as one senior said, "Daydreaming is possible anywhere on this campus. There are so many trees and flowers that it feels like an English country home." Another noted that "the school really prides itself on maintaining this suburban forest—the landscaping budget is through the roof!"

Recent construction and renovations have ensured that Agnes Scott has modern facilities despite its historical status. Students praised the expansion of the McCain Library and the recent opening of new Alston Campus Center, "the most popular place on campus," complete with a bookstore, e-café, and post office. The Science Center is the jewel of Agnes Scott's $120 million building program. This state-of-the-art facility opened in the spring of 2003 and "is a symbol of Agnes Scott College's commitment to putting women in the field of science."

The college lies on the edge of downtown Decatur, Georgia. While Decatur is full of "cute, eclectic shops and great coffee houses, the nearest supermarket is a good 20-minute walk away," moaned one freshman. For this reason, students stress the importance of having access to a car on campus. "While not a necessity, it will make your life a lot more pleasant," said one junior. For those without their own vehicles, borrowing cars is standard practice. Students report that because of Agnes Scott's small-town setting, "safety is simply not an issue on campus." The school police are "everywhere all the time" and "in fact there are more problems with public safety accosting boyfriends and guests than there are of public safety not being present."

Within this self-contained environment, traditions flourish. "There is the sense that you are connected to generations of Agnes Scott women," said one senior. Annual events such as senior investiture, when each senior is capped with an academic mortar board, and the ring ceremony, an evening when every sophomore receives her class ring in the school chapel, create a "strong sense of belonging." Seniors traditionally ring the bell in the tower of Agnes Scott Hall when they are offered a job or get accepted to grad school, and when Agnes Scott women get engaged they are thrown into the pond in the Alumnae Garden. The biggest annual event is Black Cat week, described by one junior as "homecoming minus the football team." Black Cat falls at the beginning of the year and "the entire week is just crazy with competitions between classes." Each class is assigned a color and a mascot and plays elaborate practical jokes on the others. The freshmen

traditionally try to keep their mascot a secret while the sophomores try to guess what it is.

"There is the sense that you are connected to generations of Agnes Scott women."

The week includes a bonfire where each class sings "sister songs," and the Junior Production, an hour-long series of skits satirizing administrators, professors, and the college in general. A formal followed by an awards ceremony marks the end of the festivities.

Scotties' Honor
Another long-held Agnes Scott tradition is the honor system. As one student put it, "The honor system is our defining characteristic." The code applies to all aspects of life at Agnes Scott and creates a level of trust among faculty and students rarely found at other schools. Students take unproctored, self-scheduled exams, "which are probably the best thing that we have here," said one junior. Students are expected to turn themselves in for code violations, and cases go before the student-run Honor Court.

Agnes Scott students take pride in their academic integrity and many students describe classes as "extremely demanding." Professors generally have extremely high expectations, but students enjoy rising to the challenge. "I'm thrilled about being pushed to my limits and exceeding them," said one sophomore. Students also report that professors are "very accessible" and caring. "Agnes Scott professors are awesome. They will do whatever they need to do to help you succeed," raved one freshman. Except for a few foreign language sections, classes are taught exclusively by professors. Class sizes are small, and the average class "never has more than 40 girls. There are usually more like 15 or 20, although English classes can have as few as four or five." While students appreciate the individual attention such small classes allow, "sometimes it would be nice to be anonymous on those days when you didn't finish the reading." Scotties major in a wide variety of areas, although the science and English departments are "standouts."

Students stress that women should major in something that interests them: "a good major would be something that you love to do, because you are going to have to work hard, no matter what you decide." Slackers beware because "to be perfectly honest, there is no such thing as an easy major because the professors here are so demanding." Grade inflation is "a dream;" in reality, "deflation is more likely; the English department is rumored to have a cap on the number of As given per class."

All students must fulfill distributional requirements and take certain required courses in order to graduate. Requirements include an intermediate-level foreign language class, two physical education semester hours, two semesters of science (one with lab), and one semester each of fine arts, literature, history or political science, philosophy, and math. First-year students must also take a first-year seminar and English 101, a composition and literature course. Some wish the requirements were less extensive, but most acknowledged that the expectations went along with their goal of a well-rounded education. As one sophomore said, "I think that the requirements represent a good variety of knowledge that all people need to function in the world; it's a part of the liberal arts education experience." Students also have few complaints about registration, although "freshmen sometimes get stuck with the leftovers," as upperclassmen have priority in class selection. International study is a popular option, and over half the student body goes abroad sometime during their four years. For those looking for new experiences a little closer to campus, Agnes Scott has cross-registration privileges with all Atlanta universities. Students interested in engineering particularly appreciate the opportunity to enroll in a dual degree program with the Georgia Institute of Technology.

Atlanta: Bright Lights, Big City

Agnes Scott students appreciate nearby Atlanta for more than its academic opportunities. With downtown only six miles from campus and easily accessible through MARTA, Atlanta's rapid transit system, Scotties "don't run into that small-town problem of being bored all the time." Agnes Scott has no sororities and there are few parties on campus ("Agnes Scott should be #1 on the Stone Cold Sober College list," remarked one senior), so those who choose to party often explore the "awesome" Atlanta club scene. Attending frat parties at Georgia Tech and Emory is another popular option, especially for those under 21. Those of legal drinking age frequent Atlanta's bars and nightclubs and "some of the better Tech and Emory parties." The administration is "extremely strict" about underage drinking, and all agree that drinking on campus is "all but impossible." Although many leave campus seeking alcohol, as one junior said, "nondrinkers are very welcome on campus. This is not a party school." Upperclassmen stress the importance of getting off campus and note "how easy it is to be consumed by academics." Yet many appreciate the studious atmosphere. As one freshman said, "I came here to get an education and Agnes Scott lets me focus on that goal."

Students do stick around campus to participate in the many clubs and extracurriculars. "It is strongly encouraged for Agnes Scott women to be involved in extracurricular activities and the majority do so," explained one sophomore. The student senate and sports are both reportedly popular, as are more unusual clubs like the handicrafts and origami clubs. Agnes Scott is a Division III school and some athletes lament the minor role of sports: "Is there any team spirit? No. We're lucky if we get 10 people to show up to our soccer games unless the dining hall decides to serve dinner at the field." Many, however, praise the "thriving cultural scene." "Whether it is the African—West Indian Society, the Asian Women Society, the Hispanic Association, the German House, or the Muslim Student Association, there are outlets for all groups to feel comfortable and to share their culture with the campus," said one junior.

Agnes Scott students hail from all over the United States as well as from 31 countries, creating a student body that is "ethnically, geographically, and culturally diverse, especially for a small, Southern women's college." One junior did note that despite the mix of ethnicities, "most everyone it seems is Southern and the Southern mindset can be quite a jolt for us Northerners." Still, "the student body is diverse enough to defy the Agnes Scott stereotypes that we're all either lesbians or stuck-up snobs," said one freshman.

AC and Walk-in Closets: Living the Good Life

No matter where they call home, Agnes Scott students agree that the "palatial" dorms are "downright luxurious." That's a good thing, since all students must live on-campus unless they are married or living at home. Freshmen live together in spacious doubles in either Winship or Walters Hall. The rooms are "bigger then any freshman dorms I have seen at other schools and have walk-in closets, a major perk," said one freshman. Visiting hours for boys, known as parietals, are stricter for first-years than for upperclassmen. Even when parietal restrictions are loosened, bringing boys home can be an awkward experience. Before a boy enters a hall, the Agnes Scott host must shout "man on the hall," at which point "every head in the hall turns and you feel ridiculous for trying to have a guest," lamented one senior. After their first year, students have the choice to either live in one of the traditional dormitories for upperclassmen or move to Avery Glen, a college apartment complex near central campus. Three theme houses offer another option. Themes change annually and are chosen based on student petitions, so "they very much reflect the student body."

Students are reserved in their praise for the dining hall food. They describe Evans, the one central dining hall, as a "fried chicken and collard greens kind of place." Meal variety, or lack thereof, is a common complaint, as are the limited hours. However, Mollie's Grill and the Black Cat Café, both located in the student center, offer later hours and "a welcome break from Evans." Vegetarian options are always available. All students are required to have a meal plan of some sort, ranging from five meals to all 21 meals a week. Eating out in Decatur or Atlanta is popular, but "the dining hall is great for just hanging out with friends or meeting new people." "While there are definitely cliques, they don't mind when you sit with them. Everyone is so nice here," said one sophomore.

Set in the beautiful, verdant town of Decatur just a few minutes away from Atlanta, Agnes Scott offers an excellent education to a motivated and diverse group of women who love their school. While a small, Southern women's college is not right for everyone, those who choose Agnes Scott join a long and special tradition. As one student put it, "being at a small all-girls college isn't what you'd think. This has really been the best experience of my life and I wouldn't trade it for anything."—*Amelia Page*

FYI

If you come to Agnes Scott, you better bring "a fan, an open mind, and an umbrella, because our president rains tears during EVERY speech she gives!"

What is the typical weekend schedule? "Friday, homework and a movie on campus; Saturday, sleep in, study, party at Georgia Tech; Sunday, study, study, break for meals, study some more."

If I could change one thing about Agnes Scott, "I'd leave out the drama. With 900 girls there's a lot of drama."

Three things every student at Agnes Scott should do before graduating are "go to a Tech football game, act in Junior Production, and take advantage of the study abroad programs."

Every fall, former President Jimmy Carter holds an open forum with students at Emory. The Georgia native answers any question a student throws at him, formal or informal, from whether he wears boxers or briefs to his thoughts on the war in Iraq. Unique opportunities like this define the undergraduate experience at Emory, a university that fuses Southern style with challenging academics.

Academics in Atlanta

With 50 majors and 42 minors, Emory offers diverse academic opportunities for its students. The large number of pre-med students makes science majors among the most difficult and competitive. Though the programs are rigorous, one senior who plans to go to dental school said, "If you are pre-med here, you will be very well-prepared. Emory students go to some of the best med schools in the country." The emphasis on science at Emory does not mean that other areas are overlooked; the humanities and liberal arts are also intense and receive high marks from students. According to one junior, "science majors spend more time in labs, but humanities students spend more time reading and writing papers. The

workload evens out in the end, so it just comes down to what you want to spend your time doing."

The Emory College General Education requirements were recently revised for the class of 2009 and beyond. Student must take a set of number of courses in each of the following six groups: Seminars and Writing; Natural and Mathematical Sciences; Social Sciences; Humanities; Historical, Cultural and International Perspectives; and Heath and Physical Education. Some students dislike the requirements for the large number of classes they entail.

Emory also offers a few special programs for undergraduates through its business and nursing schools. Sophomores can apply to The Goizueta Business School, or "B-school" as it is known on campus, to receive a bachelor's in business administration. While students warn that these classes can be the most rigorous on campus, the program's national acclaim makes the challenge worthwhile for many students. There is also a program for students to receive a bachelor's in nursing through Emory's nursing school.

The average class size at Emory is 20 to 50 students, though upper-level seminar classes can be as small as five to 10. TAs usually grade work in large introductory classes, and sometimes even teach them. However, one student pointed out that this is not always a bad thing, as TAs can be more excited about and devoted to the class than professors. In general though, professors draw rave reviews from their students for being "very accessible" and "accommodating." One sophomore appreciated the flexibility of his professors when he had to miss exam period to have surgery. Another senior remembered how one of her professors "stayed up with us until 3 a.m. at a review session the night before the midterm." Professors often have students over for dinner at their homes, and are always willing to schedule extra office hours to meet with undergraduates. One student summed up the teaching philosophy at Emory by saying: "Professors truly want to know students who truly want to learn from them. If you show that you want to learn, they'll give you everything they have to offer."

Frat Parties and Dooley's Ball

Emory's on-campus social scene centers on "Fraternity Row," the street that houses the school's 15 fraternities and nine sororities. Frat houses (or "frat mansions," as one student called them) host parties on a regular basis, while sororities are not permitted to have parties. Statistically, about 30 percent of the student body is Greek, but some say that it can feel more like 80 percent, especially at parties. Still, many non-Greeks maintain they rarely feel left out of the social scene, and that many Greeks are friends with non-Greeks, as well. Rush takes place during second semester to allow freshmen to make friends before joining Greek organizations, and most feel that the rush process is fairly laid-back.

Frat parties usually revolve around drinking. In theory, the frats only serve alcohol to students 21 and older, but these rules are rarely enforced. Police are strict about open-container laws, dissuading students from roaming campus with open alcoholic beverages. Because Emory is located in a residential area, party-throwers must be careful to observe local noise ordinances. One junior commented that the frat scene has "broken down over the last few years because of new regulations against alcohol, noise, and the number of people at parties." Still, frat parties continue to be popular social events on campus.

The Student Programming Council, composed of members of Emory's student body, sponsors other on-campus events throughout the year. The freshman semi-formal dance is always well-attended. The homecoming dance is far less popular, probably because Emory has no football team. The Council also organizes band parties that bring well-known groups like Cake, The Roots, Guster, Ben Folds, and Everclear to campus each semester. Attendance at these events usually depends on the band, but according to one student, "most people usually leave once the free food runs out." Without a doubt, the most popular school-sponsored event of the year is Dooley's Ball, a dance held in honor of Emory's mysterious unofficial mascot. Originally, Dooley was a skeleton in an 1899 biology lab that wrote anonymous articles in the school's newspaper, *The Emory Phoenix*. Nowadays, Dooley takes human form and shows up at special occasions, always accompanied by a group of bodyguards dressed in black. Dooley's identity is carefully guarded, though it's common knowledge on campus that a secret society of students maintains the tradition. Dooley's Ball is at the culmination of Dooley's Week, a celebration featuring theme days, special activities and, of course, parties. The week also includes special visits by Dooley himself, who has the authority to dismiss any class on campus with a mere squirt of his water gun. The Ball, held outdoors on the intramural fields, also features a dramatic entrance by Dooley and his entourage. One student commented that the Dooley phenomenon is "strange and a little scary, but its one of the things that makes Emory really unique. It's also one of the only times that you'll see any school spirit on campus."

Welcome to Atlanta

Most students cite Emory's location just outside of downtown Atlanta as one of the best attributes of the school. Emory Village, the area just outside of campus, offers an assortment of restaurants and convenience stores to serve student needs, but many also make the 15-minute trip to downtown Atlanta to take advantage of the great shopping, eating, attractions such as Centennial Olympic Park, and the city's numerous bars and nightclubs. Off-campus nightlife forms a huge part of the social scene at Emory, and more than one student cautioned, "having a fake ID is key to enjoying Atlanta." If you can get past the bouncers at the doors, there are bars and clubs to suit every partygoer's taste. From the upscale bars in Midtown, to the dance clubs in Buckhead, to the hippy bars in Little Five Points, Atlanta offers students a variety of alternatives to the on-campus social scene. Some clubs also sponsor well-attended Emory nights on the weekends. Being in Atlanta has more serious advantages as well. Aside from its thriving nightlife, the city is a great place for students to find jobs and internships for the summer after graduation.

With so much to do off campus, many students feel that having a car is necessary at Emory. While freshmen aren't allowed to have cars on campus, one junior suggested, "There are ways of sneaking them in." Despite the availability of public transportation and a school-sponsored shuttle service to the supermarket and a nearby mall, some students opt to use a car. However traffic has become an increasing problem that prompts some students to leave their keys at home. "The traffic can make a five-minute drive to class turn into 45 minutes. . . . With that kind of traffic, some people enjoy not having a car," remarked one student.

Preppy, Fit and Motivated

When asked to describe their peers, many Emory students agree that the majority of the student body is wealthy, upper-class, attractive and fit. Some feel that this contributes to a snobby and cliquish atmosphere, while others say that they had no problems getting to know people. One sophomore said, "lots of people here look snobby, but once you get to know them they can be very down to earth." Many students appreciate getting to know people upon arrival at Emory through FAME, Emory's mandatory freshman advisory program, which matches groups of frosh with staff, faculty and upperclassmen. Still, they felt that the social scene gave way too quickly to separate cliques. Students are satisfied with the level of racial diversity, but feel that there is too much self-segregation among students, making it hard to get to know people from different backgrounds. Many also comment that a disproportionate number of their fellow students hail from Long Island and elsewhere in the Northeast.

Students at Emory are highly motivated and intelligent. "The majority of kids here are overachievers," one freshman said. Some feel that this creates a competitive atmosphere, particularly among the pre-med science majors. But it also means that Emory students can be involved and opinionated about their causes. "From Free Tibet to a group that advocates better wages for university workers, to experimental theater, everyone here is in-

volved in something," says one sophomore. However another Emory student described his peers as "extremely apathetic," noting that students rarely commit to causes in large numbers.

Looking good is a priority for many Emory students, producing an attractive and image-conscious student body. One senior related that "there are too many designer purses here for my tastes, but they aren't necessarily a requirement." Students take full advantage of Emory's spacious gym facilities, which were recently renovated, and participate in many intramural and club sports. Though students are "terribly apathetic toward sports," some of Emory's Division III teams in sports like swimming, soccer, volleyball and tennis are fairly competitive. The women's tennis team is a three-time defending national champion, and the men's team has been ranked in the top five for several years in a row. However, many students feel Emory suffers from the lack of a football team. "It makes it difficult for students to really rally some school spirit," one junior said.

Country Club Campus

Students at Emory love their campus, which they describe as "gorgeous" and "very ritzy" with "beautiful Spanish-style architecture." Georgia's mild weather makes for beautiful landscaping, and students spend time outside year-round on Emory's spacious quads. The campus has renovated almost all of its buildings in the last 15 years. Students rave about the updates, which include the installation of computers in the gym and a gorgeous new reading room in the school's main library. Between the brand-new buildings and the well-manicured lawns, students gush that Emory's campus looks "just like a country club."

> "Where else can you get Ivy League academics south of the Mason-Dixon Line? We have better weather, and you still get a great degree."

One senior commented, "Emory has the cleanest, nicest, newest dorms of any school I've ever visited." Ten dorms house first-year students, and each has its own perks and disadvantages. Dobbs has the smallest rooms but the most central location, while Turman offers "enormous rooms" but is further from campus. Freshmen are usually assigned to double rooms, though some singles are available. All dorms are air-conditioned and most have sinks in the rooms. There are also special theme wings or floors for students who want to live with others who share similar interests. While sophomores were to move off campus in years past, they are now required to live in the dorms. Though it initially created some turmoil on campus, the administration is confident that the new rule will ultimately create a strong sense of community. The most coveted dorms are on the Clairmont Campus, a short shuttle ride from Emory's central campus. Available only to upperclassmen, these apartment-style dorms are "drop-dead gorgeous." One resident bemoaned, "I don't want to graduate and move out of here!" Each four-person apartment includes four bedrooms, two full bathrooms, a kitchen, a washer and dryer, a living room, and a dining room. The facilities include four outdoor swimming pools (two of which are Olympic-size) as well as basketball courts, tennis courts, volleyball courts, an indoor gym and a student center called the "SAAC" with lots of study rooms and a grill-style cafeteria. These luxury dorms do come at a higher price than other campus housing, but almost everyone agrees that it is well worth it. Dining options include Dobbs University Center, which has stations for pizza, sandwiches, traditional meals, and international cuisine, as well as Cox Hall, which houses a Burger King, a Chick-fil-A and a Starbucks. Though food options abound, one student remarked that the dining hall is "nothing to brag about."

Great Weather and a Great Degree

Students at Emory seem satisfied with their experiences. Though some bemoan the "snobby attitude" and "competitiveness" of their fellow students, almost all feel that they are getting a great education and that being in Atlanta is a huge asset. As one student observed of Emory's unique atmosphere, "where else can you get Ivy League academics south of the Mason-Dixon Line? We have better weather, and you still get a great degree."—*Jessica Lenox*

FYI
If you come to Emory, you'd better bring a "car and a Prada handbag."
What is the typical weekend schedule? "Thursday night, dancing in Buckhead; Friday night, fraternity party or a bar in Midtown; Saturday night, off-campus party followed by late night at Maggie's; Sunday, brunch and work, work, work!"
If I could change one thing about Emory, I'd "give it a football team!"
Three things every student at Emory should do before graduating are "take a long weekend to Mardi Gras, have lunch with the dean, and lay out at the Clairmont pool instead of studying."

Georgia Institute of Technology

Address: Georgia Tech, Office of Undergraduate Admission, Atlanta, GA 30332-0320
Phone: 404-894-4154
E-mail Address: admission@gatech.edu
Web site URL: www.admission.gatech.edu
Year Founded: 1885
Private or Public: public
Religious affiliation: none
Location: urban
Regular Application Deadline: 16-Jan
Number of Applicants: NA
Percent Accepted: 69%
Percent Accepted who enroll: 44%
Number Entering: 2,837
Number of Transfers Accepted each Year: 518
Mean SAT: 1,302
Mean ACT: 28

Middle 50% SAT range: 590–680V, 640–720M, 650–720W
Middle 50% ACT range: 26–30
Early admission program (EA/ ED/ NA): NA
ED or EA Acceptance Rate: NA
Full time Undergraduate enrollment: 12,361
Total enrollment: 12,103
Percent Male: 69%
Percent Female: 31%
Total Percent Minority: 28%
Percent African-American: 6%
Percent Asian/Pacific Islander: 17%
Percent Hispanic: 4%
Percent Native-American: 1%
Percent Other: 72%
Percent in-state / out of state: 66%/34%

Percent from Public HS: NA
Retention Rate: 92%
Graduation Rate: 77%
Percent in On-campus housing: 51%
Percent affiliated with Greek system: 49%
Percent Varsity or Club Athletes: NA
Number of official organized extracurricular organizations: 357
Most popular majors: Industrial Engineering, Mechanical Engineering
Student/Faculty ratio: 14:01
Tuition and Fees: $20,272.00
In State Tuition and Fees (if different): $4,926.00
Cost for Room and Board: $7,094.00
Percent receiving Financial aid, first-year: 32%

Part of the Public University System of Georgia, the Georgia Institute of Technology is a research-based university that, according to the school's website, is dedicated to "improving the human condition through advanced science and technology." The school is known for the rigors of its science and engineering curricula, its location in the southern metropolitan city of Atlanta, and the vast amount of school spirit among the student body.

Science and Engineering vs. Everything Else

Tech's undergraduate majors are housed under six different departments: the Colleges of Architecture, Engineering, Sciences, Computing, Management, and the Ivan Allen College of Liberal Arts. A bit of a divide exists between Tech's budding engineers, scientists, and architects—those choosing "real" majors, according to one scornful engineer—and its students pursuing a less technically-oriented degree, particularly in management. The latter is known for having a less rigorous curriculum and allowing students to retain more of their most precious commodity: free time. As one engineer asserted, "Tech is not a party school if you have an "E" next to your major." The workload for classes is "challenging" and "time-consuming," and students complain that "a normal sleep schedule isn't possible at Tech." Fortunately, tutoring is available to help students stay ahead, although the undisputed key to success for all majors is "time management."

Georgia Tech is particularly well-known for several of its more specialized engineering majors, including aerospace, biomedical, nuclear and radiological, and polymer and fiber engineering, and while these subjects are notoriously difficult to complete, they are also well respected. In the 2006 edition of the *US News and World Report* college rankings, 9 of the school's undergraduate engineering programs ranked in the national top 10 programs in their respective fields. Students of all majors must satisfy the requirements of the core curriculum, which include at least one introductory calculus class, English Composition I and II, two lab-intensive sciences, and a selection of courses in the humanities, fine arts, and social sciences. These requirements receive mixed reviews from undergraduates, as some prefer to focus on their major subject while others appreciate the breadth of learning. Many of the intro-level science and math courses are known as "weeder" classes that serve to discourage potential majors from pursuing the field. Chemistry I, Physics I, and Calculus II in particular have traditionally lower pass rates than the higher level courses in the same subjects, a fact which makes many students question their true dedication to the subject. Success in these classes depends upon "your high school background and the professor," according to one student.

> **"Tech is not a party school if you have an "E" next to your major."**

Scientific research is a primary focus of Georgia Tech, and the school offers undergraduates plenty of opportunities to dive into the lab. The Undergraduate Research Opportunities Program provides students with a list of available labs for both school-year and summer research and guarantees one-on-one time with professors as well as the chance to practice techniques learned in class in a real-life setting and to make new scientific explorations and discoveries. All students are encouraged to take advantage of the many research opportunities and can work for either course credit or pay.

Another popular program—about 40% of the student body enrolls at some point in their college careers—is the co-op and internship program. Tech's Cooperative Education Program, one of the largest programs of its kind in the nation, allows interested undergrads to follow a five-year course of study in which they alternate semesters of full-time work with semesters of study as a full-time student. Local Atlanta employers in business, industry, education, and government hire these students and provide structured, educational working environments to let them gain working experience in their chosen field as well as earn money for their time. Such industry giants as Coca-Cola, General Electric, and the NASA Johnson Space Center participate as potential employers, and many of these co-ops turn into job offers after graduation, making this experience both valuable and practical.

Nerds and Greeks

Thanks to reduced in-state tuition and the popular state-administered HOPE scholarship, the majority of Tech's student body hails from nearby cities and towns in Georgia. The remaining 35%, however, represent a wide variety of states and countries, including China, India, and South Korea, and help to produce the school's diverse student body. Most freshmen matriculate as prospective engineers, but, as one student articulated, not everyone fits the "nerdy guy with high-waters and glasses" stereotype. There are math aficionados who "tend to stay in their room" and "do talk about calculus in their free time," and happily admit to studying more than twenty hours a week, but there are also equally fun-loving students who pledge Greek and spend much of their time drinking and partying.

A common problem at technical universities tends to be an unequal gender distribution within the student body; at Georgia Tech, this disparity is dubbed "The Ratio." The Ratio, the proportion of male to female students, has hovered slightly below 3:1 for years, distorting the dating scene and inspiring the oft-repeated, tongue-in-cheek maxim of lady Techies: "the odds are good but the goods are odd." However, Tech's proximity to other North Georgia colleges, including Emory University, Georgia State University, Spelman College, and Morehouse College, allows students to mingle with other university populations and helps to offset the gender discrepancy.

The Greek scene dominates social life at Georgia Tech, and about one-fourth of the student body pledges to one of the 42 chapters on campus, usually during freshman year. Although most Tech social events are sponsored by the Greek system, non-pledgers, especially girls, are generally welcome to attend. Various fraternities and sororities sponsor activities such as parties, mixers, sports games, volunteer work, and movie screenings for members and have in the past brought such big-name bands as Sister Hazel on campus to perform.

For those not interested in Greek life, the surrounding city of Atlanta offers many possibilities for entertainment and relaxation. Those interested in more high-brow culture can enjoy an evening listening to the Atlanta Symphony Orchestra, watching a Broadway play at the Fox Theater, or perusing the displays at the High Museum of Art. In contrast, the Midtown clubs and the late-night bars in Buckhead provide an alternative party scene, most of which is easily accessible by MARTA (Metro Atlanta Rapid Transit Authority) for those lacking a car. Many popular eateries are located within walking distance from Tech's campus, including pizza parlors Fellini's and the Mellow Mushroom as well as The Varsity, the world's largest drive-in restaurant that is famous for its hot dogs, french fries, and frosted orange drinks.

Football reigns supreme in the South, and the NCAA Division 1 Yellow Jackets often deliver an exciting time for Tech's spirit-filled spectators. The school's biggest rivalry is with the University of Georgia Bulldogs, and the huge UGA-Georgia Tech game packs tens of thousands of supporters into Tech's Bobby Dodd Stadium in a sea of bee-like yellow and black contrasting against the Bulldogs' competing red and black. Celebrated mascot Buzz works with SWARM, a student-run spirit organization, to pump up the crowd, not only for the football games, but also for the talented Tech basketball and baseball teams.

Located in the heart of Atlanta, Georgia Tech's campus has a distinctly "oasis within the city" feel, as the plethora of green spaces dotting campus help to keep the more urban senses of concrete and overcrowding at bay. However, the two major highways bordering

two sides of the campus prevent students from completely escaping their urban surroundings. The campus is split into two halves—east and west—that each impart their own atmosphere to their respective residents. East campus is older and, with its close-packed dormitory buildings and nearby Greek houses, is more conducive to socializing, while west campus dorms are more spread apart and offer greater peace and solitude. Each side of the campus has its own dining hall and other facilities, although most upperclassmen prefer to cook at home or eat off campus.

In spite of the somewhat eccentric combination of nerds and Greeks, and science and liberal arts majors, Georgia Tech nevertheless boasts a cohesive, spirited student body with great affection for their school. No matter their major, Tech students of all stripes don the traditional Yellow Jacket stripes and support their school teams as well as dedicate themselves to their studies and classes. Tech is known for turning out some of the brightest engineering minds in the country, and its focus on first-class research helps to attract students from all over the world interested in a first-class scientific education.

FYI
If you come to Georgia Tech, you'd better bring "a ruler, a TI-89, and all the other help you can get."
What is the typical weekend schedule? "Friday and Saturday, forget about work and party at the frats; Sunday, face reality and study 'til Monday."
If I could change one thing about Georgia Tech, I'd "equalize The Ratio."
Three things every student at Georgia Tech should do before graduating are "go to the UGA-Georgia Tech football game at Bobby Dodd Stadium, try waffle fries at Chick-fil-A, and spend a night in Buckhead or Midtown."

Morehouse College

Address: Morehouse College, 830 Westview Drive, S.W., Atlanta, GA 30314
Phone: 404-681-2800
E-mail Address: admissions@morehouse.edu
Web site URL: www.morehouse.edu/admissions/index.html
Year Founded: 1867
Private or Public: private
Religious affiliation: none
Location: urban
Regular Application Deadline: 16-Feb
Number of Applicants: 2,544
Percent Accepted: 67%
Percent Accepted who enroll: 46%
Number Entering: 730
Number of Transfers Accepted each Year: NA
Mean SAT: 1,080
Mean ACT: 23

Middle 50% SAT range: 940–1,170
Middle 50% ACT range: 19–24
Early admission program (EA/ ED/ NA): ED
ED or EA Acceptance Rate: NA
Full time Undergraduate enrollment: 2,891
Total enrollment: 2,891
Percent Male: 100%
Percent Female: 0%
Total Percent Minority: 94%
Percent African-American: 94%
Percent Asian/Pacific Islander: 0%
Percent Hispanic: 0%
Percent Native-American: 0%
Percent Other: NA
Percent in-state / out of state: 30%/70%

Percent from Public HS: 80%
Retention Rate: 84%
Graduation Rate: 50%
Percent in On-campus housing: 40%
Percent affiliated with Greek system: 3%/0
Percent Varsity or Club Athletes: NA
Number of official organized extracurricular organizations: 34
3 Most popular majors: Biology, Business Administration/Management, Computer Science
Student/Faculty ratio: 15:01
Tuition and Fees: $14,318
Cost for Room and Board: $8,748.00
Percent receiving Financial aid, first-year: 91%

With such famous alumni as Dr. Martin Luther King, Jr., Morehouse's tradition of brotherhood echoes throughout campus and is absorbed into many aspects of campus life. Undergrads may study engineering or biology in their time at Morehouse, but most importantly, students learn the true meaning and value of the word brotherhood. Many Morehouse students say that graduating from "The House," as it is affectionately known, has changed their lives and allowed them to look at the world differently in order to make an impact.

Traditions and Excellence are Synonymous

The only historically African-American all-male college in the United States, Morehouse prides itself on its traditions of brotherhood, which date back to the college's beginnings in 1867. Spirit Night is a long-standing Morehouse tradition in which underclassmen learn the true ties of brotherhood by playing various games together. As one freshman said, "Spirit Night made me realize how much I could trust my new friends. I'd only known them for a little while, but we all held on, supporting one another like we'd been together forever."

The tradition of brotherhood is also supported by Morehouse's strong academic reputation, reflected today in the extensive General Studies requirements. Before Morehouse students graduate, all must spend over half of their credits fulfilling general education requirements. A one-year course each in composition, literature, history of civilizations (which has a special focus on ancient African civilizations), social science, and physical education are just a few parts of the graduation requirement. Also required is one semester each of art, music, speech, religion, philosophy, physical science, and biological science, and two years of a foreign language. The completion of this rigorous academic program lends truth to the school's unofficial motto: "You can always tell a Morehouse man, but you can never tell him much." Academics are further supplemented with cultural instruction. Students are required to attend the Crown Forum, a weekly address by prominent African-American leaders that many students see as a vital part of the House's social mission. One student commented that, "The speakers at the Crown Forum are one of the most important parts of a Morehouse education. The speakers teach us that knowledge is just knowledge without the ability to make a difference in the real world."

One major benefit of Morehouse's urban Atlanta location is its membership in the Atlanta University Center (AUC), a consortium of five schools including Clark Atlanta, Morris Brown, the Interdenominational Theological Center, and Morehouse's sister school, the all-female Spelman. An advantage to this program is that Morehouse students can enroll in classes at any of the other schools, provided that Morehouse does not offer the same class and that it is pertinent to the student's major.

Competitive but Compassionate

As many Morehouse students eventually seek to attend graduate programs and receive professional degrees, students lean toward majoring in subjects that might lend themselves to pre-professionalism. Biology, business, and engineering are the strongest majors, and for more advanced students, an Honors Program is offered. Additionally, the college offers a "3-2" program in engineering and architecture, in which students can major in both for three years at Morehouse and then transfer to Georgia Tech or the University of Michigan to finish two years of a professional degree.

Morehouse is also notable for its professors. Spike Lee, one alumnus, returns to lecture fairly often. Students describe their relationships with professors as "extremely close." Many students say that it is common for undergrads and teachers to have lunch together, or go to museums and parks outside of class. One student noted that he got invited to dinner at a professor's house on a regular basis. Although some students said that the academics at Morehouse can be very competitive, many declared that the tradition of brotherhood on campus extends into the classroom. "At Morehouse all of your fellow students want you to do well. If you are having trouble, all you have to do is ask the person sitting next to you. People are always tutoring one another," said one student.

Where'd Everybody Go?

One statistic that attests to Morehouse's challenging academic regimen is its low student retention rate. One student declared, "it's definitely a tough school to be successful in—people drop out of here like flies," while another added that his junior class of 600 began as a freshman class of 900. Other academic problems related by undergrads include difficulty with getting into required classes; occasionally, seniors are forced to postpone their graduation because they were shut out of one or two classes. Financial-aid problems, however, are the most commonly cited reasons for leaving Morehouse.

Undergrads report that they spend much of their time studying at one of several libraries in the close vicinity of Morehouse. Woodruff Library, the central library for the five-member institutions of the Atlanta University Center, gets mixed reviews. While some students reported that it is especially good for "social" studying, others declared that the number and variety of students who share the library make resources hard to come by. Students who desire quieter studying travel to the libraries at either Georgia State University or Emory. Hard-core studying takes place in the Frederick Douglass Commons, a student center at Morehouse where students have access to study rooms and materials.

Undergrads can live in seven dorms on campus. Graves Hall, the oldest building on campus, is reportedly the best because it has air-conditioning. Hubert is said to be the least appealing, with no air-conditioning and small rooms. Students can unwind at Kilgore, a dorm that houses pool and Ping-Pong tables, big screen TVs, and a snack shop that stays open until midnight. Dorms have friendly rivalries and are unofficially identified by Greek letters and hand signals. Dorm restrictions include no alcohol and specific visiting hours for women. Undergrads seeking relaxed rules of conduct say the best bet is to move off-campus. Most students say they prefer private apartments on Fair Street to those in the West End, where much of the housing is college-owned. However, residents say that facilities in this area are "run-down" and can get pretty rowdy on the weekends. Students who live on-campus are required to be on a full meal plan that they describe as "below average," but "improving." Those desperate for improved fare eat out at places like Spegal's, a popular pub and restaurant, or fast-food restaurants at West End, a mall close to campus. Athletics also play an important role at Morehouse. The most popular teams, football and basketball, draw dedicated fan support, particularly when Morehouse plays its perennial rivals Howard and Tuskegee. Students say the tennis team is also extremely popular and successful, if "kind of lower profile when compared to basketball."

Reaching Out

Students say they are particularly proud of the extracurricular activities at Morehouse, citing a strong devotion to community service programs, particularly several mentoring programs in which students act as big brothers or academic tutors to inner-city youth. "These programs enable us to teach our code of brotherhood to younger students in Atlanta who are particularly in need of love and respect," one student said. Other organizations, such as the Pre-Law Society, the Health Care Society, and the Business Association, reflect the high aspirations of Morehouse students.

Although some students report that they were skeptical about attending an all-male college at first, many say that Morehouse provides them with the best of both worlds. They feel the all-male environment on campus allows them to cultivate a strong feeling of brotherhood. In fact, undergrads say, the high female-to-male ratio of the AUC provides students with more than adequate opportunities to meet and party with women. Students say that the Morehouse social scene is "perfect for the challenging academic atmosphere." The campus is reportedly calm during the week, to allow for plenty of studying. Over the weekend, however, students can choose from innumerable parties, AUC unity rallies, picnics, concerts, or excursions to local Atlanta nightclubs. Many students say that homecoming is one of the prime social events of the year and is traditionally a time for graduates and their families to return to the House to reminisce. The largest social event of the year, Freaknic, is one that receives much of students' attention. While many students say the annual event is the best party in the entire country, others complain that the large number of visiting students (reportedly 20,000 in recent years) absolutely prevents the students from being able to drive anywhere in downtown Atlanta.

> "What you learn here, they don't teach anywhere else. The overwhelming sense that you are truly a part of something great and that you can accomplish anything you want, simply because you are a Morehouse man."

Students consistently say that the one aspect that makes Morehouse unique is its deeply ingrained sense of tradition and brotherhood. As one student said, "What you learn here, they don't teach anywhere else. The overwhelming sense that you are truly a part of something great and that you can accomplish anything you want, simply because you are a Morehouse man. Even today, when students say they are only attending their college for a diploma and a few connections, being a Morehouse man still means something."—*Nate Puksta*

FYI

If you come to Morehouse, you'd better bring "brotherhood and friendship."

What's the typical weekend schedule? "Friday: Study in the afternoon and chill with friends at night; Saturday: hang out in Atlanta; Sunday: work out and get back to studying."

If I could change one thing about Morehouse, I'd "make the weekdays more social."

The three things that every student must do before graduating from Morehouse are "go to Freaknic, tutor inner-city youth, and go to Spegal's."

Spelman College

Address: Spelman, 350 Spelman Lane S.W., Atlanta, GA 30314-4399
Phone: 800-982-2411
E-mail Address: admiss@spelman.edu
Web site URL: www.spelman.edu
Year Founded: 1881
Private or Public: private
Religious affiliation: none
Location: urban
Regular Application Deadline: 1-Feb
Number of Applicants: 5,248
Percent Accepted: 37%
Percent Accepted who enroll: 11%
Number Entering: 569
Number of Transfers Accepted each Year: 116
Mean SAT: 1,688
Mean ACT: 23

Middle 50% SAT range: 1,560–1,780
Middle 50% ACT range: 20–24
Early admission program (EA/ ED/ NA): ED
ED or EA Acceptance Rate: NA
Student Body Statistics: 1
Full time Undergraduate enrollment: 2,191
Total enrollment: 2,290
Percent Male: 0%
Percent Female: 100%
Total Percent Minority: 100%
Percent African-American: 98%
Percent Asian/Pacific Islander: 0%
Percent Hispanic: 1%
Percent Native-American: 0%
Percent Other: 1%

Percent in-state / out of state: 29%/70%
Percent from Public HS: 84%
Retention Rate: 92%
Graduation Rate: 79%
Percent in On-campus housing: 44%
Percent affiliated with Greek system: NA
Percent Varsity or Club Athletes: NA
Number of official organized extracurricular organizations: 28
3 Most popular majors: Poltical Science, Government, Psychology
Student/Faculty ratio: 11:01
Tuition and Fees: $17,005
Cost for Room and Board: $8,750
Percent receiving Financial aid, first-year: 87%

Founded in 1881, Spelman College is the oldest, and arguably most prestigious, historically black college for women in the United States. The college's unique mission—to instill in its students a profound sense of cultural identity and to prepare them for roles as life-long leaders—has guided the college since its inception and serves to this day as a bulwark for its preeminent reputation. Spelman's storied legacy over the past century, coupled with its ability to grow and evolve in the face of significant obstacles, is an enduring testament to the value of a Spelman education.

Learning with a Purpose

Spelman's core curriculum reflects an emphasis on academic exploration and cultural understanding. All students are required to fulfill broad divisional requirements by taking classes from the humanities, fine arts, social sciences, and natural sciences. They must also complete two specific courses, "African Diaspora and the World" and a course in international or women's studies, to lay the groundwork for the dynamic study of black history that underlies the Spelman experience. Also required are two classes of physical education. Additionally, the college places a strong emphasis on written communication and requires that all students show proficiency in writing, which is normally satisfied by completing the obligatory first-year composition class, English 103. According to one senior, "Most students don't complain about the requirements, because they don't prevent you from taking the classes you really want to take."

Generally speaking, Spelman students take 16 credit hours, or four courses, per semester, and need a minimum of 120 credit hours to graduate. Of that number, approximately 40–48 hours fall within the student's major. Most students declare their major at the end of their sophomore year, although students intending to pursue majors in computer science, mathematics and the natural sciences are strongly encouraged to take the appropriate introductory course during their first year. The work load is "rigorous"; as one student put it, "There is definitely a lot of outside research and studying that goes on here." Professors generally receive positive marks and are said to be "very knowledgeable in their field of study."

In addition to 23 regular majors, Spelman

offers three special degree programs: the Dual Degree Engineering Program (DDEP), a human services major, and an "independent" major. DDEP candidates pursue a liberal arts degree from Spelman, usually completed in three years, and an engineering degree from a cooperating engineering institution—such as Georgia Institute of Technology, California Institute of Technology or Columbia University—for an additional two years. The human services major, another academic program unique to Spelman, offers an interdisciplinary track that prepares students for careers in civil service. Students can also elect the "independent" major option, in which they design their own course of study under the direction of a faculty member.

Small Campus, Big City

The Spelman campus, while feeding off the many amenities of Atlanta, offers an active, independent campus life for its 2,000-plus students. Ten different residential houses—each with its own special characteristics—accommodate over 1,200 students on campus. Most first-year students live in Abby, Howard-Harreld and Manley halls, although some first-year honor students, including Presidential and WISE Scholars, live in the Stewart Living and Learning Center with upper-class students. Other second-, third- and fourth-year students live in MacVicar, McAlpin, Morehouse-James, Laura Spelman, Bessie Strong halls and Living Center II. MacVicar, though conveniently situated above the campus infirmary, and Laura Spelman, a relic from Spelman's early years, generally receive poor marks. Many upper-class students, rather than risk their housing fate on the yearly "selection process," choose to rent apartments off campus, which, according to one senior, "are generally inexpensive and fairly popular among upper-class students due to the small size of the school."

> "Most students don't complain about the requirements, because they don't prevent you from taking the classes you really want to take."

Manley College Center houses the two major dining facilities on campus, with Alma Upshaw Dining Hall, located on the top floor of Manley, functioning as the main dining hall. Students give the dining hall lukewarm reviews; according to one student, the food is just "what you would expect at a college dining hall." Recently, the dining hall has added several restaurant-esque stations—including "Grill Works," "Itza Pizza," and "Salad Garden"—in an effort to improve to the quality and variety of its offerings. The food court occupies the lower level of Manley, offering snacks and meals from recognizable vendors like Freshens, Mrs. Fields and Ben & Jerry's.

Welcome to Atlanta

Apart from its alternative housing options, the city of Atlanta offers a plethora of social and cultural resources to Spelman students. You can amble through the Sweet Auburn district, an area central to the civil rights movement of the 1950s and 1960s that houses the birthplace of Martin Luther King, Jr., as well as several memorials to the Reverend. Lenox Mall and Underground Atlanta offer abundant shopping opportunities, while nightlife thumps in downtown Atlanta clubs like Club Envy and The Library. For dinner in the city, students can choose from a smorgasbord of dining options, ranging from a quick bite at the Three Dollar Café to a traditional southern meal at local favorite John Winan's Chicken and Waffle.

Sisterhood

Another major benefit of Spelman's location in Atlanta is its proximity to other colleges and universities. Morehouse College, Spelman's "brother" institution, is within walking distance from campus. Additionally, Georgia State University, Georgia Institute of Technology, and Clark Atlanta University are all located in downtown Atlanta. Because Spelman heavily emphasizes student decorum, the campus is alcohol-free, and much of the social life gravitates towards parties at Morehouse and other neighboring institutions.

Despite the hum-drum party life, the general campus scene is buzzing with activity. Sororities, which for many epitomize the Spelman ideal of "sisterhood," play a conspicuous role on campus and in the lives of many students. While none of the chapters have actual houses, the sororities at Spelman make their presence felt through on-campus activities and community service projects. Competition for admission into the sorority of one's choice is intense: students must have a 3.0 GPA to take part in the "intake process," Spelman's term for rush, and sorority membership is typically capped at

30 sisters per chapter. Sororities, however, do not dominate the campus scene; one non-Greek remarked that "while there are sororities here, I honestly couldn't tell you how many people are in them. . . . It's just not that big of a deal."

Active Leaders and Athletic Women

Spelman women also tend to be active leaders in school-sponsored clubs and organizations, and such activities are highly encouraged by the administration and considered part of the school's overriding mission. Subject-specific clubs (the Chemistry Club, the Economics Club, etc.), honor societies, and the Spelman Student Government Association (SSGA) are among the organizations that attract widespread membership. For the more musically-inclined, the Spelman College Jazz Ensemble, Glee Club, and the Spelman-Morehouse Players give Spelman students the opportunity to hone their musical and performance skills. Religious clubs, ranging from the Campus Crusade for Christ to the New Life Inspirational Gospel Choir, predominate on campus as well, providing myriad spiritual outlets.

Intercollegiate athletics at Spelman have traditionally taken a back seat to more academic and socially progressive pursuits, although interest in varsity sports teams appears to be growing. The college is currently a provisional NCAA Division III school and a new member of the Great South Conference. Moreover, the Spelman administration has recently begun backing varsity athletics in an effort to visibly promote school spirit, taking the necessary steps to gain admission as a full-fledged member of the NCAA. To date, Spelman students compete against other Division III schools in basketball, cross country, golf, softball, soccer, volleyball and tennis. For those students keen on staying healthy at a lower level of competition, IMs are always a popular option.

The Spelman Mission

Perhaps what truly distinguishes Spelman College is its underlying philosophy. In an effort to empower its students with skills for future success, Spelman requires that all students take a course in public speaking, fulfill a community service requirement, and complete a diverse and culturally probing curriculum. Some schools may espouse high-sounding ideals, but leave them as empty rhetoric; at Spelman, however, the guiding mission and its underlying tenets—sisterhood and leadership—underscore not only the workings of the college but the demeanor and attitudes of its students.—*Kent Garber*

FYI
If you come to Spelman, you'd better bring "both an open mind and a sense of identity."
What is the typical weekend schedule? "Friday, Morehouse parties; Saturday, hit up the city; Sunday, church and work."
If I could change one thing about Spelman, I'd "get rid of the core curriculum."
Three things every student at Spelman should do before graduating are "volunteer in the city, get to know a member of the faculty and use the resources here to expand your awareness as an individual."

University of Georgia

Address: University of Georgia, Terrell Hall, Athens, Georgia 30602
Phone: 706-542-8776
E-mail Address: undergrad@admissions.uga.edu
Web site URL: http://www.uga.edu
Year Founded: 1785
Private or Public: public
Religious affiliation: none
Location: urban
Regular Application Deadline: 16-Jan
Number of Applicants: 15,924
Percent Accepted: 58%
Percent Accepted who enroll: 21%
Number Entering: 5,064
Number of Transfers Accepted each Year: 1,491
Mean SAT: 1,216

Mean ACT: 27
Middle 50% SAT range: 1,130–1,320
Middle 50% ACT range: 24–29
Early admission program (EA/ ED/ NA): EA
ED or EA Acceptance Rate: NA
Full time Undergraduate enrollment: 25,437
Total enrollment: 32,355
Percent Male: 43%
Percent Female: 57%
Total Percent Minority: 17%
Percent African-American: 6%
Percent Asian/Pacific Islander: 6%
Percent Hispanic: 2%
Percent Native-American: 0%
Percent Other: 3%
Percent in-state / out of state: 89%/11%

Percent from Public HS: 81%
Retention Rate: 94%
Graduation Rate: 77%
Percent in On-campus housing: 27%
Percent affiliated with Greek system: 23%
Percent Varsity or Club Athletes: 5%
Number of official organized extracurricular organizations: 352
3 Most popular majors: Psychology, Biology, Business
Student/Faculty ratio: 18:01
Tuition and Fees: $18,040.00
In State Tuition and Fees (if different): $4,964.00
Cost for Room and Board: $6,848.00
Percent receiving Financial aid, first-year: 28%

Located in the ideal college town of Athens, Ga., the University of Georgia is a school that takes its football seriously. The Bulldogs, or "Dawgs" as they are more often called, are proud of their football team and their school as a whole. And why not? UGA, with its approximately 30,000 students, is one of the top state universities in the South. Its size presents a host of extracurriculars, sports and social groups—enough to keep anyone busy for at least four years.

Inside the Hallowed Halls

Most students hail from Georgia (around 90 percent), but natives of other states and countries are not entirely missing from the classroom and social scenes. In fact, students from 127 other nations are enrolled at UGA. The overwhelming number of in-state students is mostly due to the HOPE scholarship program. The vast majority of Georgia students take advantage of the Georgia HOPE, which uses state lottery funds to cover education costs. HOPE provides any student with a B average or better with free tuition and $100 toward books at any public college. Because of this incentive, many top Georgia students study at UGA, which has made UGA much more competitive in recent years. In-state students must now have noticeably higher GPAs and SAT scores in order to be eligible to walk around the famous Georgia "arch." In recent years, UGA has faced criticism for the low percentage of its students drawn from rural parts of Georgia—the majority of in-state students come from big cities like Atlanta.

Some students say that minorities are underrepresented for the size of the school, but efforts have been made to expand minority presence. Politically, however, UGA is fairly diverse. Even though it is "in Georgia, so still extremely Republican," liberal attitudes are more accepted here than at many other Southern schools. While not liberal per se, students appreciate the intellectual diversity found within certain departments like the arts.

As the first state-chartered university in the country (founded in 1785), UGA has a broad range of architecture, both old and new, creating a beautiful campus. The large campus encompasses hundreds of buildings. The emblematic Georgia "arch" on north campus is one of the school's landmarks and symbols, but students are careful not to walk under it until they've graduated, or else, UGA lore cautions, they won't. Sanford Stadium, known as "between the hedges," is located in the heart of campus and is the center of attention during football season. UGA is also continually improving itself and its campus, with, for example, the completion of the brand-new Coverdell Center for Biomedical and Health Sciences.

Once on campus, students have a huge variety of classes to choose from. Many take advantage of the excellent business major or veterinary program. Science majors, as well as psychology, are very popular. However, those who are so inclined can also choose to major in fashion merchandising, turfgrass management or music therapy. The abundance of majors is almost endless. Some students say there is an emphasis on the humanities—"Georgia Tech is the science school!"—but all departments have a "high level of respect for each other."

While some introductory courses are very large (as many as 300), students say that upper-level courses are much smaller and less formal. Professors "tailor the class structure to what students prefer," including discussion, group projects, and case studies. Class participation is key. For overachievers, there is the prestigious honors program. Though their program is time-consuming, honors students are offered classes that are especially known for excellence and small class size, as well as for close contact with faculty.

Play Hard

The weekend at UGA begins on Thursday, and there are parties going on any given night. The Greek scene is ubiquitous—the campus plays host to approximately 40 fraternities and sororities. Most of the events, however, are open to non-Greeks, as well. One student said, "Frats have a great time, but if you're not in one then you hardly know they exist." Although the administration's alcohol policies have become stricter in recent years, almost all parties provide large quantities of alcohol. If the on-campus party scene is not enough, there are a plethora of other options. Some people choose to host parties for their friends, but at the end of the night, "many people end up in downtown Athens to round out the evening."

Athens itself is a thriving city with a buzzing bar scene. The off-campus party scene is "ridiculous," with many students choosing to concentrate their weekend activities there. With something going on every night, Athens is the ultimate college town. One student notes, though, that "it's not just a college town; it's a town with a college." That is, it has a thriving culture apart from

that of UGA. In addition to great nightlife, the music scene is especially notable. Bands such as REM and the B-52s hail from Athens, and this has partly spurred huge diversity in the musical life of the city. Athens's atmosphere, that is at once "artsy and indie and fun and bohemian," is the perfect setting for a school like UGA.

Just as the city of Athens provides a wide array of distractions for students, extracurricular activities are a great way to keep busy and to meet people. The College Republicans are especially popular, as is the Greek system. Student government is another way to become involved. For students who want to give back to the community, Relay for Life and Habitat for Humanity are great options. A more unique service group is the Dance Marathon, which raises money for children's hospitals through a 24-hour dance, feast, and celebration. Religious groups, such as the Baptist Student Union and the Wesley Foundation, are many in number, as well.

The Sport is Football

Like many universities in the South, UGA keeps much of its focus on sports. But at Georgia, fans take their dose of football in over-the-top fashion. The vast majority of UGA students are active Bulldogs fans, attending games both at Sanford Stadium and in "rival territory." On game days, the excitement "encompasses the town and the area around campus." Athens swarms with student and alumni fans ready to cheer for their beloved Dawgs. Tailgating begins 24 hours prior to the kickoff, though many fans head into town as early as Tuesday or Wednesday for a Saturday game, and good tickets are often almost impossible to find by the end of the week. The all-important game against the University of Florida is an annual highlight, as well. Students are devoted to their team, and one student notes that "we bleed red and black here."

"We bleed red and black here."

Other sports are also popular to watch, including basketball, swimming and gymnastics, and a variety of club and intramural sports provide ample opportunities to participate. The Ramsey Student Center for Physical Activities is one of the dominant sites on campus for recreational activities and exercise. At Ramsey, students can keep in shape using the wide variety of amenities this extensive gym provides, such as multiple swimming pools, basketball and volleyball courts, an indoor track, and a weight room.

A Dawg's Pad

Being close to Ramsey and to classes is one reason for living on campus, which is an especially popular option for all freshmen. It is not mandatory that students live in dorms at UGA for any time, although most freshmen take advantage of this option. Dorms are assigned on the bases of seniority, but three high-rises (Brumby, Russell and Creswell Halls) are reserved especially for freshmen. Reed Hall is known for having a great sense of community, while Oglethorpe Hall (known as "O-House") is coveted for its prime location in the middle of campus.

Although "every dorm is a 'party dorm' at UGA," all dorms have a resident assistant (RA). The RAs enforce general rules, but are generally friendly and encourage a sense of community within each hall. Some living quarters have special restrictions, such as all-female dorms or those with no visitation hours, but there are a wide variety of options to suit all interests.

Most students say they enjoy living in the dorms, but few students live on campus past their freshman year, so off-campus housing is widely available. Though the campus borders a residential neighborhood, some off-campus options are more than walking distance away. Almost all students on campus have a car, and even freshmen are allowed to have one. According to students, however, traffic is "annoying" and UGA Parking Services is unhelpful. For those who choose to avoid the parking hassle, UGA has an extensive busing system, as well.

Large enough to satisfy almost anyone's needs, UGA has a place for everyone. A challenging honors program and a rampant party scene exist side by side, making sure that each student can keep busy. Athens, too, provides an outlet for those who grow bored of campus-based activities. Most of all, the pride that the University of Georgia arouses in its students is inspiring: "We're the Georgia BullDawgs! Enough said, in our opinion. Students, faculty and alumni all have a sense of overwhelming pride in the University. It becomes a part of who you are."—*Andrew Beaty*

FYI

If you come to UGA, you'd better bring "a good pair of walking shoes because the campus is huge and hilly."

What's the typical weekend schedule? "Friday: hear a local band downtown; Saturday: tailgate all day until game time, and then watch the Dawgs play; Sunday: church, study then workout at Ramsey."

If you could change one thing about UGA, I'd "make lower-level classes smaller."

Three things every student at UGA should do before graduating are "ring the victory bell behind the chapel, explore the Athens music and bar scene, and go to a Dawgs football game."

Hawaii

University of Hawaii

Address: University of Hawaii, Manoa, 2600 Campus Road, QLCSS Room 001, Honolulu, HI 96822

Phone: 808-956-8975

E-mail Address: ar-info@hawaii.edu

Web site URL: http://www.manoa.hawaii.edu

Year Founded: 1907

Private or Public: public

Religious affiliation: none

Location: urban

Regular Application Deadline: 2-May

Number of Applicants: 6,896

Percent Accepted: 68%

Percent Accepted who enroll: 42%

Number Entering: 2,022

Number of Transfers Accepted each Year: 2,920

Mean SAT: NA

Mean ACT: 23

Middle 50% SAT range: 990–1,190

Middle 50% ACT range: 21–25

Early admission program (EA/ ED/ NA): NA

ED or EA Acceptance Rate: NA

Full time Undergraduate enrollment: 14,037

Total enrollment: 19,716

Percent Male: 45%

Percent Female: 55%

Total Percent Minority: 74%

Percent African-American: 1%

Percent Asian/Pacific Islander: 63%

Percent Hispanic: 2%

Percent Native-American: 1%

Percent Other: 7%

Percent in-state / out of state: 74%/26%

Percent from Public HS: 44%

Retention Rate: 76%

Graduation Rate: 12%

Percent in On-campus housing: 15%

Percent affiliated with Greek system: 1%

Percent Varsity or Club Athletes: NA

Number of official organized extracurricular organizations: 175

Most popular majors: Psychology

Student/Faculty ratio: 12:01

Tuition and Fees: $12,395.00

In State Tuition and Fees (if different): $4,523.00

Cost for Room and Board: $7,185.00

Percent receiving Financial aid, first-year: 32%

While sun, sand, and sea might first come to mind when thinking of this school's exotic location, the University of Hawaii has a whole lot more to offer than gorgeous surroundings. Its proximity to the Asia-Pacific region and unique mix of American, Asian, and Pacific cultures complement the University's academic strengths and friendly environment, making this major research institution a promising place to spend four years.

East Meets West

When asked about the quality of academics, students generally agree that academics are "OK," but reported that several departments are "excellent," such as marine biology, astronomy, geology, and Pacific volcanology. Ethnic studies and Pacific Asian studies were also praised for their high quality. As one student put it, "Pretty much everything is all right, but anything that specifically relates to

Asia is really good." One student lauded the "eminent minds" brought in by the East-West Center, a national center which sponsors scholars from all over the world to examine economic and social issues. Others noted the presence of "renowned professors" and the strong quality of instruction, describing professors as "supportive" and the classroom environment as "progressive."

Regarding the core requirements, however, students offer differing opinions. While most like the "breadth" offered, one student regretted that the focus was primarily on Asia. Mostly, though, students found the core requirements satisfactory and do not have many complaints.

Fun in the Sun

Students rave about the range of social options at the University of Hawaii, noting that "you can pretty much do whatever you want." Most students go clubbing or to parties on Friday and Saturday nights, then recuperate by hanging out at the beach during the day. While the University of Hawaii has a Greek system, fraternities and sororities do not dominate social life. Students described the Greek scene as "not major" and said they feel little pressure to join the Greek scene. Students who dislike partying can choose from a range of other options such as theater, surfing, hiking, or recreational classes such as scuba diving.

Get "Lei-ed"

Occasions to dress up formally at the University of Hawaii are few and far between—guys almost never get to don their tuxedos. The dating scene, however, is alive and well, and it is common for people to go out on dates or have significant others. Random hook-ups "do happen" every once in a while, but, as one student put it, "I've been to some schools that are really promiscuous and this is not one of those." The University of Hawaii also has its fair share of attractive people, with one student raving about the "pretty girls" and their "sexy outfits." Students agreed that interracial dating is very common, but differed on the subject of interracial couples. While some described the attitude toward homosexual couples as "open and non-discriminatory," others insisted that homosexual couples generally tend to "stay low-key" because "this is not a very open climate for them."

Athletic opportunities abound at the University of Hawaii, with the most popular sports being football, volleyball, and surfing. Students are proud of their school's athletics, and there is a general "sporty atmosphere." Even students not affiliated with any of the sports clubs or teams enjoy getting outside and kicking a ball around in their spare time. It is common to see groups of students getting together to play casual sports around campus for recreation, even on weekdays.

Homogenous and Happy

One student described the student stereotype as "people of Asian descent who were brought up in Hawaii." While there were some complaints about the student body being homogeneous, one student emphatically described the student body as "multicultural, diverse, with little segregation." Students dress very casually, with the typical day-to-day wardrobe consisting of "jeans,

shorts, T-shirt." Most are happy with the school's "supportive," "friendly," and "relaxed" atmosphere and say it is easy to make friends. Extra-curriculars are not a significant part of college life at the University of Hawaii, as it is a commuter school and students tend to take on part-time jobs.

Paradise Found

Students describe the campus as "spread out" and like the fact that it's "a campus unto itself." A tropical oasis, the campus consists of a lot of greenery with large lawns and lots of trees. One student enthusiastically described, "The campus is fantastic and really inspiring because it's surrounded by beautiful mountains and if you are on certain parts of campus that are on higher ground, you can look down and see the ocean." The good weather and abundant sunshine also make a good impression on students. In contrast to the beautiful natural surroundings, the buildings get low reviews. Students say the buildings "could be prettier," "could use more funding," and "need to be renovated."

Island Fare

While most students deem the dining hall food just "acceptable," one student said that "the quality is horrible." As cliques do exist, students find that there "is some pressure to always be eating with a group of friends," though it is not uncommon for people to walk into a dining hall and eat by themselves. There are complaints about the lack of great eating establishments near campus; however, "if you go a little further off campus, you can find some really good places, places that I wouldn't mind going to on a date."

> "The campus is fantastic and really inspiring because it's surrounded by beautiful mountains and . . . on certain parts of campus . . . you can look down and see the ocean."

On the whole, most students agree that the beautiful surroundings and friendly people make the University of Hawaii a great place to be. Students insist that they wouldn't trade their experiences here for anything. There is never a lack of things to do or friends to hang out with, and if classes are too stressful, there's always the beach.
—*Wenshan Yeo*

FYI
If you come to the University of Hawaii, you'd better bring "a swimsuit for the beach."
What is the typical weekend schedule? "Friday, go partying; Saturday, go to the beach, more partying; Sunday, watch TV, do homework."
If I could change one thing about the University of Hawaii, I would "renovate the buildings and make them look prettier."
Three things every student at the University of Hawaii should do before graduating are "learn to surf, explore the rest of Hawaii, and learn about the culture and history of Hawaii."

Idaho

Located in the small town of Moscow, Idaho, the University of Idaho offers the complete college experience. Idaho "Vandals" definitely experience the full gamut of classes, extracurriculars, professors, and parties. According to one student, "U of I is a very laid-back place. Moscow is totally a college town, and life here really revolves around the university."

Really Hard or Really Easy

Students at U of I report quite a variety of academic choices. Engineering and business majors are both popular and challenging, while 'slackers' gravitate toward communications and general studies. Just as majors here vary greatly in terms of difficulty, professors vary greatly in terms of quality. "The professors I have experienced range from amazing to straight-up wacko," one student claimed. Professors at U of I go to great lengths to make sure they're acces-

sible to students. They generally keep four to five hours free per week to talk to students, and one student notes that she has "never had a problem getting a hold of a teacher." Class size depends on the course level. Freshman 100-level classes and labs often have many students, and sometimes Teaching Assistants help teach these courses. In other courses, the TAs only grade papers and don't interact with students much. Upper-level classes are generally much smaller than intro-level courses.

The University of Idaho offers the full range of academic opportunities, and then some. "You can take fly-fishing class, archery, scuba diving, ballroom dancing and some other classes that are totally off the beaten track," one student noted. A business major recounted that, "A couple of advertising professors also have their own ad agencies, which I think is really cool because they give us real-world experience."

Greeks, Greeks, Greeks

The social scene at University of Idaho tends to revolve around fraternities and sororities. When asked what they do on a typical night out, students reported that "there are always fraternity parties." When asked whether a lot of students drink, one student did not hesitate, saying, "That is a definite yes." Underage drinking is undoubtedly a common occurrence at U of I. According to students, the Moscow police "love to give drinking tickets," but reportedly "you have to actually get caught with a beer in your hand outside of a party in order to get in trouble." Cliques on campus tend to be based around fraternities and sororities, but dorm cliques do exist and many students who live together in the dorms tend to spend the majority of their time with one another.

There are 19 fraternities and nine sororities at U of I. When asked whether the various fraternities have specific reputations on campus, one female student reported that there are some stereotypes such as the "pretty-boy" house and the "big tough guys who like to fight" house, but added that "for the most part they are pretty diverse." If you're a guy, joining the Greek system isn't too competitive, but word has it that the sororities are "much more selective," and some of them even require a minimum high-school GPA of 3.0. Joining a fraternity or a sorority at U of I does seem to have its perks, as these groups hold a number of exclusive events each year. The Alpha Kappa Lambda fraternity, for instance, hosts a cruise party once a year for brothers and their dates as well as their "Yellow Rose" formal weekend at a hot springs resort in Canada. The Delta Chi fraternity has an annual "Pirate" party where they disguise their house as a pirate ship complete with a moat and the works. In addition, a large part of the dating scene at U of I revolves around group events that take place between fraternities and sororities.

Although frat parties account for the majority of the social life, there are definitely other options for weekend fun-seekers. Those less inclined to pursue the frat party scene enjoy going to basketball games or other sporting events in the evenings, hitting up the bowling alley, or catching a movie at the local cinema. Off-campus hotspots include Gambino's Restaurant and The Corner Club Bar. Looking for something on the wild side? One student noted that "a club called The Beach hosts a once-a-month drag show and other theme parties."

Moscow, Population: 25,000

Yes, Moscow is a *very* small town. There's a cozy feel, yet along with the small-town ambiance comes a very limited number of activities. If you want to have fun in Moscow, the key word is creativity. The party-animal types get creative by experimenting with alcoholic concoctions, while students who prefer more wholesome alternatives use their imagination in other ways. One student noted, "It's generally said that there's not much to do in Moscow other than drink, but I disagree. There are a lot of things to do off-campus if you are creative, active and willing to actually look for things. I have found stuff like hiking and even swing dancing!"

> "There are a lot of things to do off campus if you are creative, active and willing to actually look for things."

Another student enjoys passing time with friends at one of the local coffee shops. Several Vandals say road trips to nearby Spokane (one hour) can be a blast, and ambitious road-trippers sometimes head to Seattle (five hours) when they feel the need for a break. Moscow does offer the basics. A number of restaurants are located nearby (Ale House, La Casa Lopez and Red Door are several solid local spots), as well as some fast-food joints, including the largely popular Pita Pit. Coffee shops include Starbucks and Bucer's. Do you need a car at U of I? As one student explained, "You don't really need one because the town is so small, but it can really come in handy."

Good Times at the Rec Center

Extremely popular among the athletically inclined is the University's new recreation facility. Only a few years old, this beauty boasts an enormous rock-climbing wall, an excellent weight room, an indoor track, a number of basketball courts, and numerous other athletic resources. Other opportunities for athletic competition abound in the intramural sports scene that pits Greek houses against one another as well as independent teams formed by non-Greeks.

In addition to the intramural divisions that separate Greeks and "independents," a physical separation also divides these two populations, because most Greek students tend to live on one side of campus in the fraternity and sorority houses, while the dorms are located on the other side of campus. The nicer dorms include the newly renovated LLC (Living and Learning Community) which consists of apartment-style suites that each house about four students. Dorms to avoid, according to students, include "The Tower" and the "Wallace Complex." Upperclassmen typically receive top priority for dorm choice. One student who experienced both dorm life and fraternity life said, "The best part about the dorms is that you get a little more privacy," but added, "the downside was the lack of parties." Comments regarding the availability of off-campus housing conflict somewhat, and range from "It's totally easy to find" to "I had to live eight miles away because I couldn't get anything closer." The dining options at U of I are also varied. Students who live in the dorms and have a meal plan name "Bob's" as the primary on-campus cafeteria, while fraternities and sororities all have their own cooks who prepare the members' daily fare.

Students seem to agree, however, that the school is lacking in diversity. The vast majority of U of I's student body is white, and students report that the majority of kids are from middle-class backgrounds. Although the school is not demographically diverse, students at U of I do enjoy an extremely wide range of extracurricular groups and campus activities. While the Greek system often divides the campus, one student said that the "Student-Alumni Relations Board is one good extracurricular because there are Greek and non-Greek students there." Students who wish to get very involved with the university can join the ASUI (Associated Students of the University of Idaho), Idaho's student government. A number of Christian groups also draw quite a few students. Community service also represents a large part of extracurricular life at U of I, and fraternities and sororities play a large role in the community-service scene.

Vandalize 'Em

Several sports teams draw large crowds for home games, and football and basketball games are especially well-attended. Vandal spirit pops up occasionally outside of the Kibbie Dome (Idaho's varsity stadium), but most students say that school spirit hits its peak during an exciting sports game. The football team has struggled recently, but the ladies of U of I have made up for it with strong performances from the women's volleyball and basketball teams. In all sports, the rivalry gets fierce between the Idaho Vandals and the Boise State Broncos. Vandal football tailgates for games against the Broncos consist of throngs of beer-guzzling U of I students decked out in their "Buck the Froncos" t-shirts. One student said that at Idaho, "We make t-shirts for practically everything."

What to Expect

High-school seniors often get their first taste of U of I during "Vandal Friday" in the spring. On this day, potential future students have the opportunity to stay on campus for a day or two, get to know the people and the place, and attend skits performed by fraternities and sororities. Those students who decide to attend Idaho receive a welcome extravaganza including a barbecue and a speech or two, and they participate in the freshmen-only tradition called the "Vandal Walk," which is a ceremonial stroll across campus. Some students arrive early to rush fraternities or sororities, while others will settle into the dorm life. Some take calculus, and others take "Western Angling." Whether you join the Greek system at U of I or choose to remain independent, whether you write for the school newspaper or choose to crush the competition in intramural basketball, go crazy at frat parties on the weekend or relax at a coffee shop with friends, you'll definitely get the complete college experience at U of I. Reflecting on her time at University of Idaho, one student concluded, "I have grown as a person here and just love my life overall, I am glad this is where I ended up going to school!"—*Damon Benedict*

FYI
One class every student must take before graduating is " 'Dirty 330' (Psyc 330): Human Sexuality."
The best places to hang out on the weekend are "frat parties, Gambino's and Bucer's Coffeehouse."
If I could change one thing about University of Idaho I would move the "off-campus housing closer to campus."
Three things every student at University of Idaho should do before graduating are "sled down the Delt's Hill on cookie sheets after a snowstorm, take road trips to Seattle, and go hiking or camping somewhere around northern Idaho—it's beautiful!"

Illinois

Address: DePaul, 1 East
Jackson Boulevard, Chicago,
IL 60604-2287
Phone: 312-362-8300
E-mail Address:
admitpu@depaul.edu
Web site URL:
http://www.depaul.edu
Year Founded: 1898
Private or Public: private
Religious affiliation: Roman
Catholic
Location: urban
**Regular Application
Deadline:** rolling
Number of Applicants:
10,414
Percent Accepted: 70%
**Percent Accepted who
enroll:** 35%
Number Entering: 2,537
**Number of Transfers
Accepted each Year:** 1,798
Mean SAT: 1,129

Mean ACT: 24
Middle 50% SAT range:
1,020–1,250
Middle 50% ACT range:
21–26
**Early admission program
(EA/ ED/ NA):** EA
ED or EA Acceptance Rate:
NA
**Full time Undergraduate
enrollment:** 14,227
Total enrollment: 21,969
Percent Male: 41%
Percent Female: 59%
Total Percent Minority: 30%
Percent African-American:
8%
**Percent Asian/Pacific
Islander:** 8%
Percent Hispanic: 13%
Percent Native-American: 1%
Percent Other: 5%
**Percent in-state / out of
state:** 71%/29%

Percent from Public HS: 74%
Retention Rate: 85%
Graduation Rate: 64%
**Percent in On-campus
housing:** 19%
**Percent affiliated with
Greek system:** 5%
**Percent Varsity or Club
Athletes:** NA
**Number of official
organized extracurricular
organizations:** 170
**3 Most popular
majors:** accounting,
communications, finance
Student/Faculty ratio:
16:01
Tuition and Fees:
$22,575.00
Cost for Room and Board:
$10,914.00
**Percent receiving Financial
aid, first-year:** 79%

D ePaul is, at its best, the ideal large urban university. This Catholic-affiliated Chicago university shares all the advantages of a major research university—"huge budget, spending power, name recognition"—but with small classes, caring and attentive professors, an exciting location in the midst of a thriving city, and, most impressively, a campus that feels "close-knit" despite the number of commuters and off-campus residents.

Wine Tasting and the Blues
For many students, DePaul's number-one draw is the strength of its academics: Students appreciate their small classes and professors who are "intelligent, qualified and really care about their students." The faculty teach the vast majority of courses (one sophomore said he has encountered only one teaching assistant in his career so far), and care about not only their undergradu-

ates' academic records but also their personal development and happiness. One music professor even took his class on a field trip—to a blues club.

The most popular option for students entering DePaul is the College of Arts and Sciences, but the University also features undergraduate programs in disciplines from law to commerce, meaning that undergraduates get the chance to interact with peers from various disciplines. Course options are diverse; one class even allows students who are at least 21 years old to sample wines from around the world (for a small fee). For those inclined toward the arts, DePaul's undergraduate theater and music departments are particularly strong, and the communications major is a perennial favorite.

Despite the helpfulness of individual professors, some students report feeling adrift, with little help from a disorganized general administration. "It is the responsibility of the student to monitor class loads, financial aid and any other aspect of the student's life at DePaul," one student said. "There is very little help from advisors."

The student body has its problems, as well. The lack of motivation in some of the student body is reflected in the statistics: only two-thirds of students end up graduating from the school. Being a large university in Chicago has its downsides, says one sophomore: "A lot of students go here because their parents wanted them to go to college. Most people that want to go to DePaul aren't really interested in what they'll study here, but they like that it's in the city."

Happiest in the Nation?
But most students at DePaul love their university, and can't wait to get back on campus after an unusually long winter break (from Thanksgiving until after New Year's). In fact, the DePaul student body has in several surveys been rated the happiest in the nation. Academic advising may leave something to be desired, but the University takes care of its students' recreational needs: A three-story student center features an international food court, game room and lounging areas. Because the center also houses offices for many extracurricular activities, much of the campus finds their way to the center for fun and relaxation.

> "DePaul girls are typically hot, and straight fellas like myself are fortunate for this reason."

DePaul is the largest Catholic-affiliated university in the nation, and, according to its mission statement, tries to integrate "the light of Catholic faith" with "the treasures of knowledge." But although many students are indeed Catholic and attend church regularly, religion does not need to play a role for every student in this diverse community. "The Catholic thing is not a big deal," said one student. "I wouldn't have known this school was Catholic unless someone told me it was; it's not forced on people or anything." The University even requires a set of courses for freshmen that emphasizes the importance of exposure to racial, cultural and religious diversity that DePaul offers, although every student is also required to take two religious studies courses before graduating.

There isn't much dating on campus, but DePaul students say they enjoy a thriving hook-up culture. "DePaul girls are typically hot, and straight fellas like myself are fortunate for this reason," one sophomore said. Thanks to DePaul's sizable gay population and sizable female majority (58 percent), the numbers line up solidly in favor of straight males.

My Kind of Town, Chicago
Universally, DePaul students can't stop singing the praises of their university's hometown. Chicago is "the greatest city in the world, and DePaul is right in the middle of it," one student said. Because far more students live off than on campus, and fraternities are barred from owning on-campus houses, students' socializing occurs almost exclusively off campus, whether at bars, clubs, or apartments. The bar scene in particular is huge: Underage students shell out $300 for fake IDs, which student "experts" examine to let freshmen know which will pass with which bouncers at which bars.

DePaul has an unusually large commuter population: 80 percent of the student body lives off campus; these are either commuters who live in the city of Chicago or its suburbs and travel each day to school, or those who live in nearby off-campus apartments. Even better, apartments are inexpensive and relatively easy to get, students say. The immediate area is the upscale neighborhood of Lincoln Park, which—although it gives DePaul a "residential rather than urban vibe"—offers many attractive housing choices to students. Many choose to rent these off-campus apartments rather than live in dorms that, students say, vary widely in quality from three-story townhouses to lofts and suites.

Extracurriculars often take a backseat to simply hanging out and enjoying all that Chicago has to offer. That said, DePaul's best-known extracurricular activity is basketball—whether actually playing on the team or cheering it on, school spirit centers around the sport. Both the men's and women's teams are strong enough to enjoy a following by fans completely unrelated to the university. The Blue Crew, the athletic department's designated pep team, organizes activities for halftime shows, and distributes souvenirs for sporting events (as well as free "DePaul Athletics" T-shirts) to incoming students each year.

Despite the preponderance of athletes and sports fans, the University offers a diverse enough selection of academics and extracurricular options to satisfy most tastes, said a sophomore who majors in vocal performance and participates in opera outside of class. A weekly student newspaper, *The DePaulia*, is distributed every Friday, and the theater school puts on several shows each year at the professional-level Merle Reskin Theatre. Many students also take on part-time on- and off-campus jobs to help cover the costs of living in an expensive city.

DePaul is unarguably as attractive for its location as for its academics. DePaul students take full advantage of its resources for living and socializing, and many say they wouldn't be at the university if it weren't for the city. But there is more to this university than simply Chicago. Though academics may be uneven and some students may be on campus just to party, the DePaul experience is what one makes of it—if undergraduates seek them out, professors will be more than willing to guide them and help them grow. And if nothing else, DePaul boasts students who are enamored with their school to a degree found at few other institutions. "The only time students are unhappy is because of their own doing—not studying for a test, failing, hating the teacher, hating DePaul," said one student. "Never have I found that students can't find anything to pique their interest here." —*Yotam Barkai*

FYI

If you come to DePaul, you'd better bring "good walking shoes. You'll need them."

What's the typical weekend schedule? "Go to bars, hang out and enjoy the city. Because DePaul is 80 percent commuter students, there is somewhat of a dead campus on the weekends."

If I could change one thing about DePaul, "I'd make more activities that commuter students can participate in—'meet your fellow students' concerts and barbeques at 8 p.m. on a Wednesday isn't the easiest thing for a commuter student to attend."

Three things that every student should do before graduating are "attend the annual Fest concert, talk to at least one homeless person in Chicago (they have a lot to say if someone would listen), and ride on every line of the L."

Illinois State University

Address: Illinois State, Office of Admissions, Campus Box 2200, Normal, IL 61790-2200

Phone: 800-366-2478

E-mail Address: admissions@illinoisstate.edu

Web site URL: www.illinoisstate.edu

Year Founded: 1857

Private or Public: public

Religious affiliation: none

Location: urban

Application and Admissions Information: rolling

Regular Application Deadline: NA

Number of Applicants: 12,000

Percent Accepted: 66%

Percent Accepted who enroll: 39%

Number Entering: 5,000

Number of Transfers Accepted each Year: 3,000

Mean SAT: NA

Mean ACT: NA

Middle 50% SAT range: NA

Middle 50% ACT range: 22–26

Early admission program (EA/ ED/ NA): NA

ED or EA Acceptance Rate: NA

Full time Undergraduate enrollment: 17,842

Total enrollment: 20,261

Percent Male: 42%

Percent Female: 58%

Total Percent Minority: 11%

Percent African-American: 6%

Percent Asian/Pacific Islander: 2%

Percent Hispanic: 3%

Percent Native-American: <1%

Percent Other: 0%

Percent in-state / out of state: 95%/5%

Percent from Public HS: NA

Retention Rate: 84%

Graduation Rate: 63%

Percent in On-campus housing: 40%

Percent affiliated with Greek system: 9%

Percent Varsity or Club Athletes: NA

Number of official organized extracurricular organizations: 300+

3 Most popular majors: Elementary Education, Marketing, Business Administration

Student/Faculty ratio: 1 9:01

Tuition and Fees: $8,039.00

In State Tuition and Fees (if different): $14,730.00

Cost for Room and Board: $6,194.00

Percent receiving Financial aid, first-year: 78%

With over 18,000 undergraduate students, Illinois State fits the profile of a large state school. But students at this Midwestern university are treated as individuals, not just as numbers. Students consistently praise the personal attention they receive from Illinois State's faculty and the quality education they provide. With its diverse curriculum, vibrant student body and highly accessible faculty, students at ISU find a challenging and diverse environment in which to pursue their goal of higher education, nestled among the Illinois cornfields.

The Land of Opportunity . . . and Requirements

ISU offers students the opportunity for a great education, with over 150 fields of study to pursue. The business and nursing programs are very popular, and also known to be the most intense, while the communications major offers a lighter workload. The largest and most renowned program at ISU is its College of Education; the administration estimates that one in seven teachers in Illinois public schools was educated at Illinois State. ISU also has its own very talented faculty who are committed to teaching undergraduate students. One senior said that she could not "imagine an institution where the professors are more approachable or accessible to students than at ISU." Professors receive high marks for their commitment both in and out of the classroom and are always available to help students, whether during office hours or at a late-night study session. One student even commented, "I've seen a few of them out at the bars once in awhile."

Though ISU students reportedly love their professors, the school's general education requirements are less highly praised. Opinions seem to be divided on the topic, as some students think that they are acceptable, while others feel that they prevent them from taking more classes within their majors. Students are required to take one class in each of 15 specified areas, ranging from the natural sciences to United States traditions to the fine arts. Every freshman is required to take the Foundations of Inquiry (FOI) course, a seminar that helps students make the transition from high school to college and prepares them for college-level work. Many students have positive opinions of their experiences in FOI, but others feel that it was an unnecessarily hard course. Classes that fulfill general education requirements tend to be large lectures featuring separate discussion sections led by graduate students. Once students declare a major, however, class size decreases dramatically to between 20 and 30 students. Overall, students say they feel that they are getting a great education at ISU.

Outside of the classroom, some students get involved in some of the over 200 registered organizations (RSOs) on campus. Ranging from the American Marketing Association to the Albino Squirrel Preservation Society, there is a group to suit every student's taste. However, involvement tends to be limited. As one junior said, "Last I heard, only about 10 percent of students are in RSOs." Those who are involved tend to be very focused and devoted to their cause. This lack of involvement can also be seen at the school's sporting events. Though ISU has plenty of talented recruited athletes, students usually only show up "when we're playing the University of Illinois or our big rival, Bradley," according to one junior.

Looking for a Good Time

Though the majority of students at ISU hail from within the state, the student body is far from homogeneous. In fact, as students from the rural parts of the state and those from Chicago and its suburbs come together, they create an interesting and diverse mix. Whatever their origin, students find common ground in their commitment to having a good time. Though alcohol is outlawed in the dorms (except for a few areas, which allow students of age to have alcohol in their rooms), students looking for a party can often find one at a nearby off-campus apartment or fraternity house. "Going out" is a huge part of student social life and a chance for students to strut their stuff. As one senior commented, "People are more relaxed during the day, but at night it's like a competition to see who's hotter!" Parties usually revolve around alcohol, but one student commented that, while hard drugs aren't commonly used, "there are a lot of people here who smoke marijuana." The school does sponsor some alternative social events, and student organizations have brought bands like 311 and Alien Ant Farm to campus. The University Program Board hosts weekly activities that include movies, karaoke and special speakers. Students can also kick back at the BBC—the on-campus billiards and bowling center that offers more relaxed, alcohol-free entertainment. Most large events, like dances and parties, are sponsored by the school's many Greek organizations.

> **"People are more relaxed during the day, but at night it's like a competition to see who's hotter!"**

Due to recent crackdowns on underage drinking by school administration, the social scene is beginning to change. Stringent ID policies and a sign-in, sign-out procedure have cut down on the number and size of parties that fraternities can have. A division of the local police—affectionately dubbed the "Party Police" by students—has been known to break up out-of-control parties, though arrests are rarely made. Upperclassmen prefer to frequent the bars in nearby Bloomington, about a 10-minute drive from campus. Social life is not limited to the weekends, as Wednesday and Thursday are popular nights at the bars which often feature drink specials to attract students. These events are strictly for the over-21 crowd, and students caution against trying to sneak into a bar if you're not of legal age. According to one junior, "Bars can be pretty strict about checking IDs, and the police can come in and shut a place down if they're letting in underage kids."

World-Class Accommodations

Students at ISU rave that their campus is centralized and accessible. With most classroom buildings situated around a large, grassy quad, the campus is easy to navigate and avoids the sprawl of most large state schools. A walkway built over College Road, the main artery of campus, links the quad with the school's library and student center. ISU is in the process of building a number of new campus buildings, including a brand new school of business and several new athletic facilities. One senior commented, "The school looks great. They are really trying to make it new and modern."

With 13 residential buildings on campus, students at ISU have plenty of choice in their housing options. Freshmen and sophomores are required to live on campus, and are usually assigned to double rooms, though some triples and singles are available. Most of the buildings have the same setup, with rooms along a long hallway and large communal bathrooms. Some buildings feature theme areas, which group students with common interests or lifestyles. There are also both single-sex and coed floors available. By

far the most notable residential buildings at ISU are the massive Watterson towers, a 28-floor housing complex that can be seen rising out of the cornfields from miles away. One of the tallest dorms in the world, Watterson's two towers are divided into five "houses" of five floors each, to offer students a greater sense of community within such a large building. While Watterson is definitely the most social dorm, and features the largest rooms, some students prefer the quieter atmosphere of the other, smaller residential buildings. One junior observed: "It's all a matter of preference. I like the smaller buildings, but most of them don't have air-conditioning!"

Each cluster of dorms contains it own dining facilities, but with so many students housed in one place, it is no surprise that Watterson's large dining area features the most variety on campus. One senior raved that the "dining facilities here are amazing!" In addition to the home-cooked fare and salad bars, there are a number of chain restaurants including Sbarro's, Pepe's, Chick-fil-A, and even a Ben and Jerry's in the complex. Each dining facility also has its own Subway franchise that stays open until 2 a.m. and offers student discounts. Students will soon be able to use their meal cards at nearby restaurants in downtown Normal, adding to the already large variety of meal options available to students.

The Normal Life

Most upperclassmen live in off-campus apartments, though one senior says, "They're so close, they might as well be called 'on campus.'" Many students feel satisfied with their off-campus living situations, and appreciate the freedom that comes with escaping the dorms. But finding a suitable apartment can sometimes be difficult; as another senior cautioned, "The landlords are as shady as they come." Many of the sports teams have houses together, and along with the fraternity houses, the sports houses are the usual locations for weekend parties.

Students living off campus can have meal plans, but many choose to explore the bars and restaurants in the Bloomington-Normal area. A popular spot near campus is Avanti's, an affordable Italian restaurant known for its great breads and pastas. A typical assortment of chain restaurants is just a few minutes' drive from campus. While many students do have cars, especially those living off campus, students do not feel that they are a necessity. In fact, the lack of parking on campus can make having a car more trouble than it is worth. Many students take advantage of the free shuttle service that runs from campus to various locations around town.

From the Cornfields to Prime Time

Despite its location among the cornfields of central Illinois, Illinois State University offers an exciting environment with a great academic experience. Most students are overwhelmingly satisfied with their decision to come to ISU. A look at some of ISU's alumni proves that students there are destined for big things; among the notable alumni are actor Sean Hayes, who plays Jack on "Will and Grace," and NBA player Doug Collins. The school's location, solid academic programs and engaged faculty are just some of the reasons it makes for a great college environment. As one senior remarked, "I can honestly say that ISU offers as fine of an education as any public university in the state, or elsewhere for that matter."—*Jessica Lenox*

FYI

If you come to ISU, you'd better bring a "jacket that is warm and waterproof, because the weather can be harsh at times."

What is the typical weekend schedule? "Hanging out with friends, going to a party or out to a bar, homework, and eating pizza."

If I could change one thing about ISU, I'd "have there be more school spirit."

Three things every student at ISU should do before graduating are "join a club, go cosmic bowling at the BBC, and attend a concert at the new performing arts center."

Illinois Wesleyan University

Address: 103 Holmes Hall; 1312 Park Street Bloomington, IL 61701
Phone: 309-556-3031
E-mail address: iwuadmit@iwu.edu
Web site URL: www2.iwu.edu
Founded: 1850
Private or Public: private
Religious affiliation: none
Location: urban
Undergraduate enrollment: 2,140
Total enrollment: 2,140
Percent Male/Female: 43%/57%
Percent Minority: 12%
Percent African-American: 4%
Percent Asian: 3%

Percent Hispanic: 3%
Percent Native-American: 0%
Percent in-state/out of state: 85%/15%
Percent Pub HS: NA
On-campus housing: 75%
Fraternities: 33%
Sororities: 25%
Number of Applicants: 2,770
Percent Accepted: 57%
Percent Accepted who enroll: 36%
Entering class: 564
Transfers: 27
Early admission program (EA/ED/NA):
Early Decision or Early Action Acceptance Rate: NA

Application Deadline: rolling
Mean SAT: NA
Mean ACT: NA
Middle 50% SAT range: 1,190–1,380
Middle 50% ACT range: 26–31
Most popular majors: biology, business administration, psychology
Retention: 92%
Graduation rate: 77%
Tuition and Fees: $29,036
In State Tuition and Fees (if different): NA
Room and Board: $6,714
Financial aid, first-year: 67%
Varsity or Club Athletes: NA
Library: NA

"Everybody here is so nice," one Illinois Wesleyan senior said, and she would probably know. With an enrollment of about 2,000 undergraduates, IWU is smaller than many public high schools, allowing students to quickly form a common identity. Studying in out-of-the-way Bloomington, students reap the rewards of the school's unique academic offerings, including the Gateway Colloquium seminars for first-years, an annual student research conference, and May Term, which allows undergrads to explore non-traditional learning experiences. And if anything can be gleaned from the school's strong record of alumni giving, it is that IWU's unique programs and tight-knit community make a lasting impact on the students who step through its doors.

Challenging and Welcoming Work

Professors are very accessible to IWU students, who often develop meaningful relationships with faculty outside of class. Because the school is almost entirely undergraduates, most students are lavished with attention. Classes range from largish lectures (50–100 people) to very intimate seminars (less than 10 people), and come in varying levels of difficulty. "For the most part," said one sophomore, "the classes are as challenging as you make them."

Certain programs are developing a reputation for particular excellence, with the expectations for students in these majors rising accordingly. Biology and Business are the hot majors, and produce some of the school's top graduates. "A 3.0 in the bio program would translate to a 3.8 almost anywhere else," one Biology major said. Additionally, many science majors cite the value of being able to do research under the guidance of their professors.

The Business program boasts its own unique learning experience. "We have more discussion, more hands on experience," one Business major said. The Business department has a successful record of placing students in summer internships in Bloomington, Chicago, or elsewhere in the country. Despite the recent prevalence of these two programs, IWU still offers strong liberal arts programs true to its founding at 1850.

Today, most upperclassmen agree that the younger classes are smarter and more - interesting every year. "I don't think I would still get in if I had to apply now," noted one senior. First-years who do make the cut benefit from the Gateway Colloquium, a series of small, discussion-oriented classes that focus on writing skills. Students also enjoy the John Wesley Powell Undergraduate Research Conference, a yearly event at which students present their research to the rest of the campus community. "You shouldn't miss it," exhorted a senior female.

Campus Culture and Living Arrangements

If there is a stereotype of IWU students, it centers on their background. "As much as the administration tries to push diversity, everyone comes from the same kind of suburb," said one transfer student. "To some extent, everybody here is a little bit of a nerd," added a physics major.

Stereotypes aside, IWU students are generally hard-working, smart, and from an upper-middle class higher economic back-

ground. "As such," noted one student from the Chicago suburbs, "the students demand a relatively high level of living."

> **"To some extent, everybody here is a little bit of a nerd."**

Integral to the "high life" at IWU is gaming. Video and computer gaming are popular pastimes in the dorms, especially for the guys, with the majority of rooms linked to facilitate multi-player tournaments. "College is the ultimate gaming experience," one male student declared. Intramural sports are also an option, but casual sports, such as Frisbee on the quad, are more prevalent.

Most students applaud the on-campus housing, and though a few live off campus, all are in assigned dorms during freshman year. "I was surprised to have gotten a really cool roommate," one freshman noted. The school has a fairly precise method for putting roommates together, and, according to one sophomore, it "encourages everyone to get to know each other."

A Small Student Body Congregates

The size of the student body doesn't limit its spirit, especially on the few occasions that a large group congregates. All students agree: "Basketball is big." The team is ranked in Division III, and a home basketball game draws more than half of the student body. Other varsity teams are well-regarded, but definitely not as well-supported as basketball. In balancing the athletic experience with his academic load, one varsity swimmer emphasized the accommodation of his professors, "they are very willing to give me make up tests." An athlete could do much worse than the facilities he will be able to use at IWU. The Shirk Center is the large athletic complex and, according to one student, "everything is kept up very well."

The Student Senate also gathers large amounts of attention on campus, as it is the primary liaison between the school administration and the students. "The administration is genuinely receptive to student input," noted one student who worked in the admissions office.

Finally, weekend afternoons and early evenings, much of the student body congregates at the student center, which screens films, brings comedians and other live acts to campus, and acts as a simple meeting point for students before the night's activities.

Food and Drink

"The food is really good," exclaimed one excited sophomore. Still, if the students get tired of "Saga," the main dining hall on campus, they can go to a few on-campus alternatives or take their hunger into Bloomington. Nevertheless, "you have not had the full experience," one sophomore explained, "until you are yelled at by this crazy old lady in the dining hall."

After being chewed out by the elderly, students like to party on the weekends. The fraternities and sororities provide a large majority of the options, though there are invariably other parties on many occasions, if not on every night. Additionally, for those with ID, there are a number of bars in Bloomington that become frequent destinations.

Student opinion regarding the Greeks is mixed. Some think that the parties could be better, while others praise the generally strong social scene given the size of the student body. The truth, however, is that "If you are in the mood for a party, you'll definitely be able to find one."

Extra Opportunities

The experience at IWU would not be complete without "the monkey pit." Beneath a bridge next to the science offices, one can often see students lounging in a space that looks similar to a monkey habitat at a zoo, prompting its nickname.

But the final distinguishing element of the IWU educational experience is May Term. Students finish second semester at the end of April, but almost all continue with a three-week term immediately thereafter called May Term. During May Term, each student takes one class, which meets once a day for a few hours. While it is possible to take normal classes to satisfy major or graduation requirements, most students take advantage of various exciting opportunities.

Students take courses on campus that are offered according to a professor's hobby or special interest. Particularly popular are travel classes. During May term, students can study biology in Costa Rica or Australia, theater in New York City, international politics in the European Union, or classical music in Italy, among other options.

Yet the essence of Illinois Wesleyan remains the opportunities that await students when they leave the school. One senior said, "I feel like I will take the knowledge that I learn here into the real world."—*Peter Johnston*

FYI
If you come to IWU, you'd better bring "Mountain Dew to stay up late."
A typical weekend at Illinois Wesleyan consists of "sleeping late, partying, studying, and playing video games."
If I could change one thing about IWU, I would change "the math department."
Three things every student at IWU should do before graduating are "get yelled at by the crazy old lady at the dining hall, go to a basketball game, and play in the monkey pit."

Knox College

Address: Knox, Knox College Office of Admission, 2 E. South St./Galesburg, IL 61401
Phone: 1-800-678-KNOX
E-mail Address: admission@knox.edu
Web site URL: www.knox.edu
Year Founded: 1837
Private or Public: private
Religious affiliation: none
Location: small city
Regular Application Deadline: 1-Feb
Number of Applicants: 2,086
Percent Accepted: 74%
Percent Accepted who enroll: 27%
Number Entering: 438
Number of Transfers Accepted each Year: 30
Mean SAT: 1,240
Mean ACT: 28
Middle 50% SAT range: 1,120–1,360

Middle 50% ACT range: 25–30
Early admission program (EA/ ED/ NA): NA
ED or EA Acceptance Rate: NA
Full time Undergraduate enrollment: 1,333
Total enrollment: 1,351
Percent Male: 44%
Percent Female: 56%
Total Percent Minority: 15%
Percent African-American: 4%
Percent Asian/Pacific Islander: 6%
Percent Hispanic: 4%
Percent Native-American: 1%
Percent Other: NA
Percent in-state / out of state: 51%/49%
Percent from Public HS: 78%

Retention Rate: 90%
Graduation Rate: 76%
Percent in On-campus housing: 89%
Percent affiliated with Greek system: 17%
Percent Varsity or Club Athletes: 25%
Number of official organized extracurricular organizations: 99
3 Most popular majors: Economics, Anthropology, Political Science
Student/Faculty ratio: 12:01
Tuition and Fees: $27,900.00
Cost for Room and Board: $5,925.00
Percent receiving Financial aid, first-year: 84%

Knox College welcomes students from the minute they set foot on campus. "Other schools just sort of tolerated me when I visited," one current Knox student recalled. "But Knox professors and students alike seemed to take a genuine interest in me." Students come to Knox, located in Galesburg, Illinois, from around the globe to experience the intense academics and the strong community spirit that the college has built. For many, Knox offers the best of both worlds: "Knox students know how to get it done during the week and know how to relax on the weekends."

No Tests in the Bathroom

The academic year at Knox is run on what is commonly known as a "3-3" calendar. Effectively, this breaks the year into three trimesters in which students take three classes at a time in 10-week blocs, leaving a full six weeks for winter break. While this may on paper, appear to be an easy schedule to maintain, students at Knox know better. As one current French and Creative Writing double major asserted, "We'd die if we took any more than three classes at Knox. [Courses] are very intense and fast-paced, since we have to pack in 16 weeks of material." Further-

more, students appreciate the frequent change of classes. As one pointed out, "You never get bored of anything you take."

All freshmen are required to take a course entitled Freshman Preceptorial (according to some, also known as "How To Be A Knox Student 101"). Beyond that, there are a wide variety of directions students can take, depending on their interests. But even the introductory classes at Knox receive rave reviews. "They have a broad scope to begin with," one student explained, "but each professor I've had has created a way for the student to do a project that allows them to work on something they find interesting about the subject." In fact, the popularity of the faculty in general is undeniable. "The staff here is incredible," a current sophomore raved. "It's a great situation to be in and I am absolutely convinced that it is what makes Knox so laid-back."

When classes get really challenging, students tend to form study groups and cooperate rather than compete. "There are so many other things to worry about in college that I'm glad academic competition isn't one of them," one anthropology major said. The unique approach to academics is epitomized in the school's Honor Code. Professors do not proctor exams, so students have their choice of where to take them. In other words, according to one student, "We get to take our tests anywhere we want except for bathrooms and stairwells."

Theme Houses and T-shirts

The unique Knox experience extends beyond the classroom. As one history major who recently spent a spring break working in New Orleans with college funding, explained "Knox realizes that you don't just learn in the classroom . . . you need to experience the real world. And they will assist you in any way to achieve that."

In no way is this point better illustrated than through the study abroad program that Knox offers. In addition to three college-sponsored programs in Buenos Aires, Barcelona, and Besancon, France, Knox students have a wealth of study abroad options to choose from and are strongly encouraged to go. In fact, since a period of "experimental living" (such as study abroad or an internship) is required for graduation, many students find the program to be an integral part of their college experience. And to top it off, the trimester system makes it easy for students to spend a semester abroad and still be back at Knox for two full terms.

Although some students may opt to move off campus, on-campus housing varies. Dorms aside, upperclassmen have a number of different options, including theme houses. Students need to come together as a group to apply for a theme house, explaining both what their theme is and how it could enhance life on the Knox campus. While the types of theme houses vary every year, some current favorites include the Red House (giving its residents a taste in Communist living), and the Do-it-Yourself house.

The food, while every so often drawing predictable student complaints, is reportedly satisfying overall. One of the most popular additions to the dining hall has been stir-fry, with two chefs ready to cook whatever students put together for them. For caffeine and sugar runs on campus, students head for the Gizmo, a coffee house that is open until one in the morning.

But campus life does not end with dorms, houses, and food. In fact, it barely begins there. With more than 100 clubs and activities on campus, Knox has something to offer everyone. Best of all, the community spirit that is fostered on campus encourages many to try something new. One student, for example, came to campus with no musical background and soon found herself taking harp lessons. "Knox is so inclusive. Everyone does all that they can to help people get involved with new things and make them feel comfortable in what they choose to do," she explained.

In terms of nightlife, there are a wide variety of groups—fraternities, sororities, theme houses, and even private suites—that throw parties. And when they do, students tend to get creative. For example, the fraternity TKE hosts "Grafitti Night," during which everyone wears a white t-shirt and sports a washable marker that they are handed at the door. "There are always parties to suit any occasion," a current sophomore noted. And partying at Knox does not necessarily mean getting drunk. "There are a lot of parties that I go to where I just want to dance and not drink and there is no pressure whatsoever," one student explained. "It's definitely a personal choice here and people both acknowledge and respect that."

Pumphandle and Flunk

Among the many campus traditions at Knox, there are two that especially stand out. The first, "Pumphandle Day," occurs on the day before classes start. Everyone who is on campus that day (students, faculty, even family members!) gathers to shake everyone else's hands. As one current senior described, "People dress weird and write strange things on their name tags. It's definitely memorable." This year we had a giant gorilla, a giant banana, a Catwoman and a Superman!" another student noted.

> "[When students] have a paper due, they'll work on the paper for a while and THEN go to the game."

The second can't miss tradition is "Flunk Day," which takes place every spring. When it arrives (the exact date is always kept a secret) the campus is woken up by fog horns in the early morning hours. Classes and meetings are cancelled. In their place, a spring carnival awaits students and faculty alike. And while many students try to describe the various activities of the day, one sophomore asserted, "It's really something you just have to experience. I've never heard a description of Flunk Day that really did it justice."

Both of these events are evidence of Knox's strong school spirit. This pride extends both to the school in general (as one student claimed, "Everyone has at least two things emblazoned with "Knox") and to sports, in particular. "Basketball and football are most popular by far," one current varsity basketball player noted, and most students agree. Even so, many keep academics as their first priority. "[When students] have a paper due, they'll work on the paper for a while and THEN go to the game."

From collaborative efforts in the classroom to dinners at professors' houses, students get to know the people around them in ways that might not be possible at other schools. Looking back, one senior noted that, "I never visited Knox before enrolling, but I felt at home from the moment I stepped on campus." Knox gives students the confidence and comfort they need to enjoy their college experience to the fullest.—*Stephanie Brockman*

FYI

If you come to Knox, you'd better bring: "sweatpants and social skills."
What is the typical weekend schedule? "Lots of work! In general, studying the whole time except for Friday and Saturday night, when there are theme and frat parties, bands, comedians, movies, performances, etc."
If I could change one thing about Knox, I'd "get a few mountains put in nearby . . . The prairie is really hard to get used to!"
Three things every student at Knox should do before graduating are: "Go sledding in the Knox Bowl (our football field), go abroad ANYWHERE, get Roger (our president) to remember your name."

Lake Forest College

Address: Lake Forest, 555 North Sheridan Road, Lake Forest, IL 60045
Phone: 800-828-4751
E-mail Address: admissions@lakeforest.edu
Web site URL: www.lakeforest.edu
Year Founded: 1857
Private or Public: private
Religious affiliation: none
Location: suburban
Regular Application Deadline: 15-Feb
Number of Applicants: 2,198
Percent Accepted: 63%
Percent Accepted who enroll: 29%
Number Entering: 386
Number of Transfers Accepted each Year: 156
Mean SAT: NA
Mean ACT: NA
Middle 50% SAT range: 1,190–1,260

Middle 50% ACT range: 23–28
Early admission program (EA/ ED/ NA): EA&ED
ED or EA Acceptance Rate: ED 75%, EA 42%
Full time Undergraduate enrollment: 1,399
Total enrollment: 1,413
Percent Male: 42%
Percent Female: 58%
Total Percent Minority: 15.5%
Percent African-American: 4%
Percent Asian/Pacific Islander: 5%
Percent Hispanic: 6.5%
Percent Native-American: <1%
Percent Other: 0%
Percent in-state / out of state: 43%/57%
Percent from Public HS: 65%

Retention Rate: 81%
Graduation Rate: 65%
Percent in On-campus housing: 78%
Percent affiliated with Greek system: 13%
Percent Varsity or Club Athletes: 30%
Number of official organized extracurricular organizations: ~100
3 Most popular majors: Communications, Economics, English
Student/Faculty ratio: 12:01
Tuition and Fees: $29,164.00
Cost for Room and Board: $6,960.00
Percent receiving Financial aid, first-year: 99%

Lake Forest College, often referred to as, "Chicago's National Liberal Arts College," is a small school located in the quaint suburban town of Lake Forest, Illinois, 30 miles north of Chicago. With a diverse, spirited, and enthusiastic student body of approximately 1400 students representing 47 states and 54 countries, Lake Forest College promotes a liberal arts education within a cohesive student-faculty environment. As one student put it: "[Lake Forest] is a community of interesting, motivated, and most of all, FUN people!"

Academics

Academic requirements at Lake Forest are not excessively rigorous. One student explained, "Graduation requires a 2.0 and certain 'GEC' requirements as are typical of small liberal arts schools (two math or science class, a culturally diverse class, etc.)." This flexibility allows students to explore multiple programs: "General education requirements are light, so it's easy for people to double major and minor." One disillusioned student complained that although, "Grading is relatively fair," it is somewhat inflated, and the academics are not as challenging as some would like. However, another student pointed out that programs have become increasingly rigorous over the past few years: "Work load is getting heavier because LFC is becoming a better school. It's challenging, but doable."

> **"I can call/email professors whenever! They are very concerned with helping you do well."**

The University offers a variety of very popular majors such as communications, psychology, business, art history, economics, and politics as well as some more challenging majors like education, chemistry, and other math and science oriented subjects. In general, majors in the humanities are considered much easier and more popular, while the science and math departments are more highly accredited and recognized, in particular the economics department. While there is not a large selection of course offerings in these majors, students greatly enjoy the quality of instruction and accessibility of the professors: "I love the fact that the professors who teach at LFC could teach at Northwestern or U of Chicago as well (lots of them used to actually), but they come here because they like teaching to undergrads in a small environment." One student went so far as to say, "I can call/email professors whenever! They are very concerned with helping you do well." Specific professors mentioned were Robert Baade, Carolyn Tuttle, and Robert Lemke in the Economics Department, Les Dlabay in Business, DeJuran Richardson in the Math Department, and Spanish professor Lois Barr. Professor Marquardt's "World Politics" was also noted as a "key class."

Students who apply to Lake Forest College can also seek acceptance into the Richter Program, a competitive freshman research program. Accepted students remain on campus for the summer to pursue research with a professor.

Social Life Title

The social life on campus is heavily dominated by sports teams as well as by fraternities and sororities. Lake Forest College boasts 14 varsity sports teams as well as many intramural and club sports. The most popular sports seem to be hockey, football, and rugby, and a large portion of the student body is involved in sports in some way. The facilities are often described as "inadequate," however, but this doesn't stop the spirited and enthusiastic student body from enjoying them. A student-run organization led by the University's mascot, Boomer, supports the Varsity sports teams. For a small fee, a student can join the, "Athletic Council," or more commonly referred to as the, "Forrest Fanatic," and take advantage of a free fanatic T-shirt, VIP seating at home games, free food at select games, reduced bus fare to away games, behind the scenes updates and highlights, as well as e-mail notifications for upcoming events.

As for Greek Life, there are seven fraternities and sororities (some of which are even international.) One member of Delta Kappa Epsilon said that, "The sororities are strong and fraternities are lacking numbers. However, I have absolutely no regrets about joining a fraternity at Lake Forest College. It has been an amazing experience for me." A member of Delta Delta Delta described the Greek scene as, "relaxed, small, personal and authentic." Another student pointed out that while Greeks tend to be the "most involved" at Lake Forest and often secure top positions in student government, "You don't have to be a Greek to be integrated in the school. Non-Greeks are friends with Greeks."

The social scene in general seems to be heavily campus-based, as Lake Forest itself is not exactly a thriving college town. While most upperclassmen have cars, the majority stay in the area. There are a few campus-wide parties, typically hosted by the fraternities as well as semi-formals for various student organizations. The annual "Mr Casanova Contest," "DKE Rampant Lion March Party," and Winter Ball, held in the botanical garden, are particularly popular. The majority of the campus drinks, although the University has recently become stricter on their alcohol policies. As for drugs one student explained, "They are common but not socially acceptable. They are used behind closed doors (even hidden from other students)," while another stated they are not common at all. As for those who are of drinking age, some venture into the city on the weekends and hit up Chicago's most famous bars. The city of Chicago also offers many alternatives to a typical college social scene such as Navy Pier, museums including the Field Museum, an aquarium and planetarium, two major league baseball teams, a hockey team, and an NFL football team, and Michigan Avenue, a street akin to Fifth Avenue in New York City, which boasts fabulous shopping.

The University takes pride in community service activities. Although, Lake Forest itself doesn't offer many opportunities, Chicago, which is only a 45-minute drive or 1½ hour train ride away, provides many unique community service opportunities. One such group at Lake Forest College is the Big Brothers/Big Sisters program of Lake County. Located in Gurnee, a suburb about 20 minutes north of Lake Forest, this group has been around since 1904. Many Lake Forest College students choose to participate in the program, which focuses primarily on mentoring throughout the Chicago community. Other activities include literary groups such as Collage, as well as political organizations including the League for Environmental Awareness, College Democrats and College Republicans. Art and performance groups include theater and Improv Comedy, and there are a number of religious, cultural, academic and business orientated groups.

Campus Life

Although the social scene is somewhat constrained by the general attitude and environment of the town itself, Lake Forest provides nice on-campus living arrangements. Freshmen are assigned dorms while upperclassmen pick through a random lottery. There is an all girls dorm; one international dorm, four substance free dorms, and the remainder of the dorms are mixed. Gregory is known as the party dorm; although alcohol is allowed in a select number of the dorms and only if the inhabitants of the rooms are 21. One girl explained that, "a large majority of students live on campus, because no one can afford a home in Lake Forest." The town itself is described as, "very high class," "an affluent neighborhood," as well as a, "very safe community—the safest in Illinois." One perk this exclusivity offers is high-paying babysitting jobs. However, one student suggested the homogenizing effect of the school's setting: "The campus looks like a country club, the town is one of the richest in the United States, and this environment tends to influence the students; in some ways I think, the environment 'preppifies' everyone."

There have been a few recent additions to the campus, for example a brand new library as well as a student center and as for on-campus food one girl described it as, "excellent for cafeteria food!" On-campus living includes three meals per day Monday-Friday and two meals per day on the weekend. Miramar, The Lantern, Teddy O's, The Grill, and The Wooden Nickel, are popular local eateries among students.

In general, this small, somewhat secluded university is able to differentiate itself from other universities through its personable professors and enthusiastic social life. One specific reason not to overlook this university; as one student put it, "It is a small liberal arts school close to a big city, it is not located in the middle of nowhere!"—*Caroline Kaufman*

FYI

If you come to Lake Forest, you'd better bring "hat and mittens because it gets cold!"; "an empty stomach because the cafeteria food is AWESOME!"; and "a hard-working positive, attitude because this is the key to your academic success here at LFC."

What's the typical weekend schedule? "After class on Friday take a nap and then get ready to go out . . . South Campus is where the parties are; Sleep in late on Saturday and head to the cafeteria in your pjs, watch movies, and then get ready to go out all over again! Sunday: get your work done . . . Occasionally there are All-Campus Parties that everyone attends . . . they are really fun."

If I could change one thing about Lake Forest, I'd "make the Education Major less difficult! The classes are demanding and tons of work but it is all worth it in the end because they have a history of 100 percent job placement after graduation."

Three things every student at Lake Forest should do before graduating are "Eat at the cafeteria, get involved with on-campus organizations, and study abroad—we have great programs."

Loyola University Chicago

Address: Loyola, 820 North Michigan Avenue, Chicago, IL 60611-9810
Phone: 312-915-6500
E-mail Address: admission@luc.edu
Web site URL: www.luc.edu
Year Founded: 1870
Private or Public: private
Religious affiliation: Jesuit
Location: urban
Regular Application Deadline: rolling
Number of Applicants: NA
Percent Accepted: 77%
Percent Accepted who enroll: 18%
Number Entering: NA
Number of Transfers Accepted each Year: NA
Mean SAT: 1,144
Mean ACT: 25

Middle 50% SAT range: 530–640V, 520–640M
Middle 50% ACT range: 23–28
Early admission program (EA/ ED/ NA): "priority"
ED or EA Acceptance Rate: NA
Full time Undergraduate enrollment: 9,076
Total enrollment: NA
Percent Male: 35%
Percent Female: 65%
Total Percent Minority: 28%
Percent African-American: 6%
Percent Asian/Pacific Islander: 12%
Percent Hispanic: 10%
Percent Native-American: 0%
Percent Other: 11%

Percent in-state / out of state: 68%/32%
Percent from Public HS: 65%
Retention Rate: 84%
Graduation Rate: 61%
Percent in On-campus housing: 36%
Percent affiliated with Greek system: 10%
Percent Varsity or Club Athletes: NA
Number of official organized extracurricular organizations: 175
Most popular majors: nursing, Psychology
Student/Faculty ratio: 13:01
Tuition and Fees: $26,450.00
Cost for Room and Board: $9,930.00
Percent receiving Financial aid, first-year: 74%

Home to approximately 15,000 students, spanning four main campuses, and offering a total of 69 undergraduate majors, Loyola University Chicago is one of the largest Jesuit universities in the nation. Its location in the heart of the Windy City presents students with a myriad of opportunities for jobs, internships, entertainment, and service work, all of which help to make Chicago itself an integral aspect of the university's mission to combine a solid academic curriculum with opportunities outside the classroom in order to provide an extremely well-rounded education.

A Solid Core

The university's goal of educating "the whole person" is demonstrated most visibly—and often most frustratingly—in the high number of credits required for the core curriculum. Each student is expected to take one writing seminar, one art course, one quantitative analysis course, and two courses each of history, literature, philosophy, science, social science, and theology. Said one student, "I haven't heard too much complaining about the core . . . they give you a lot of options in each category." Another student disagreed: "I've thought several times that there are perhaps too many core credits. I

often feel like I'm doing the same thing over and over again." One junior commented that writing is an important factor in nearly all the classes—"I've even heard of people having to write papers in math classes!" The courses are all supposed to fulfill different aspects of a well-rounded education, encouraging students to develop both academically and spiritually. Also manifest in the core curriculum is the Jesuit emphasis on social work, as many classes require service components.

When asked about common majors, students named political science, business, and communications as being among the top choices for many people. Psychology is also a popular major, and there are a large number of students in both the pre-med and the nursing programs. Most classes are small, with the average size ranging between about twenty and thirty students, with only a few classes large enough to fill an auditorium. The workload is "decent," and professors are fair and usually friendly if "you take the time to get to know them." According to one sophomore, "The workload seems relatively light when compared with some other colleges; there is usually a lot of reading to do, but I wouldn't say it's ever unbearable." Another observed, "Since the syllabi are always handed out on the first day, you should know what you're getting yourself into." In terms of specific classes, people agreed that the level of interest and difficulty of classes varied from professor to professor, but that any class related to information systems is usually hated.

In general, students feel that the academics at Loyola are strong and very diverse in their scope and focus. Said one senior, "If you ever have any questions, you can always go to your academic advisor for guidance." Most students have two advisors, one for their major and one for general education requirements, both of whom are often helpful in aspects such as career advice, opportunities for internships, and events, meetings, or talks that might be of interest to their advisees. According to one student, a possible complaint about the school may be its liberal nature, and this aspect of the curriculum may often frustrate conservative students. "Still, you should know that you're going to be talking about social justice, peace, and women's studies in your classes—you *are* going to a liberal arts school, after all."

Cooler By The Lake

One of the most unique aspects of Loyola University Chicago is the division of its campus into four main parts: the Lake Shore Campus, the Water Tower Campus, Maywood Campus, and the Rome Center. The Rome Center, stationed in Italy, is a premiere study abroad location for many students from Loyola and other colleges around the country, and the Maywood Campus is where the medical center is located. Undergraduate students are mostly concentrated at the Lake Shore Campus, which is located next to scenic Lake Michigan, and the Water Tower Campus, which is situated downtown on Michigan Avenue, also known as the Magnificent Mile—Chicago's most famous shopping district. Transportation between the two areas is easy and efficient due to a shuttle service that runs large coach buses for students. All students are supplied with CTA passes that allow for unlimited rides both on the buses and on the "L," the above-ground rapid transit system that runs through the city.

While many upperclassmen live off-campus, freshmen and sophomores are all required to live in the dorms. Previously, dorms were located only on the Lake Shore Campus, but the university just recently has opened new residence buildings downtown, which cost a certain amount more per semester. Said one junior, "When it comes to housing, there are a lot of options and differences in pricing to accommodate all kinds of preferences." Freshman dorms are usually single-room doubles, while sophomores reside in apartment-style housing, often with kitchens and balconies. After the first two years, most students move off-campus, often to nearby Rogers Park, "because it's cheaper and you don't have all those stupid rules. Sometimes living on-campus can be kind of a pain." Regulations in the dormitories, especially freshman year, are strict: in addition to the usual rules about no alcohol and no smoking, there are also rules about the opposite sex not being allowed in dorm rooms late at night, and overnight passes are always required for guests. "The rules are strict, but they're for the safety of the students. And the overnight stuff is a Catholic thing," said one sophomore. Many students did comment on the sketchy nature of the Lake Shore Campus, which is beautiful while on-campus but "not a great scene" just outside. Still, campus and security police are always around to keep everyone safe, and students just need to remember to "use their common sense" as they would in any large city.

Students seem to appreciate both the cosmopolitan nature of the downtown campus as well as the serene beauty at the Lake Shore. Said one freshman, "I like being so urban but still on campus, with places to lay out and sun, cafes to do work in, and wireless internet almost everywhere." Another student said, "Part of the reason why I came here is because it's right on the lake, so there are a lot of great views where you can sit on a bench and face the lake or the beach to the north of campus." The campus architecture is described as "old, but nice," and the university is currently in the process of renovating older structures as well as adding new buildings, such as the new student center, the Sullivan Center. "There are so many renovations going on," said one senior. "I have no idea what the campus will look like ten years from now!"

Nightlife In The Windy City

Students say the social scene, especially for upperclassmen, is focused more on going to house parties off-campus or to clubs and bars in downtown Chicago than to frat parties, since Greek life is apparently not a huge part of weekend festivities. A lot of people go to Hamilton's, a bar near the Lake Shore Campus, or to house parties thrown by students who live in the neighborhood. There are a couple of streets known for their crazy parties three nights a week, where students "try to replicate the idea of a state-school house party where people are doing wild thing like throwing kegs out of the windows," but there are also a lot of commuters and others who avoid that scene in an effort to find weekend activities that are a little more low-key. There is a fair amount of drinking, as at many schools, and also some marijuana use. Drinking regulations in the dorms are strictly enforced, and students caught in the presence of alcohol, even if they aren't partaking, will probably be written up, fined, and perhaps even assigned a certain amount of community service. One junior commented, "I'd say that most people drink, but it's not a problem if you don't . . . It's no different than any other school." There are always alcohol-free campus events, as well, such as films, concerts, and speakers, and there are also all kinds of theatrical shows and musical entertainment in downtown Chicago.

> **"You don't feel ostracized at all if you don't share this belief system."**

Most people met their friends in the freshman dorms, as well as in classes and clubs. Overall, people are "pretty friendly" but "preppy." Students are mostly liberal, although they span a wide range of religious faiths in spite of the school's Jesuit tradition. As one senior explained, "Loyola doesn't force students to go to mass. For those who want that aspect in their lives, they can find it here, but it isn't forced upon them." There are several different religious groups on campus, and students say that the atmosphere is very welcoming. "There's a lot of tolerance," said one sophomore. "You don't feel ostracized at all if you don't share this belief system. It's more about the Jesuit tradition of service, a tradition common in many religions, than it is about the specifics of Catholicism." Many do wish that the school were more diverse, especially in terms of ethnicity. The student and faculty population is largely Caucasian, and even though there are students from all over the country, the majority hails from the Midwest.

Favorite Pastimes

Athletics are not extremely prominent at Loyola; indeed, the university disbanded their football team in the 1940s because they wanted to place more of an emphasis on academics. While the lack of a football team (as well as the spread-out nature of the campus) may lead to less open school spirit than at many other schools, many students don't mind at all. Of course, Loyola still boasts other varsity and intramural sports, as well as other organizations such as cultural groups, religious groups, ethics clubs, and service-oriented clubs like Students Against Sweatshops and Loyola For Chicago, a group that stands for the betterment of the community and the city of Chicago. There are also political organizations, the debate team, the ethics bowl, dance teams, and theatrical societies. Said one student, "You always see flyers around for all kinds of groups, and there are lots to choose from." One complaint was that the arts are not funded enough, and none of the literary magazines are particularly sensational. Still, it is always possible to start a new group and apply for funding from the university. In addition, many students fill their time outside of class by finding jobs downtown in shops, restaurants, or businesses related to their area of interest.

Overall, students say what differentiates their school from others is its welcoming atmosphere, its commitment to service, and the benefits of having a smaller college community within a large city. Because it is a Jesuit school, the idea behind the entire educational system is for students to be engaged in discourse, and to focus on the betterment of the whole person and the whole society instead of zeroing in on only a few particular aspects. Said one senior, "I feel that everyone here is really trying to learn, not just trying to get by, and they're always looking to literature, philosophy, and theology to find answers. A lot of people I've met and become friends with seem dedicated to seeking truth and diversity, and that's just amazing." Asked if she would choose Loyola again if she had to do everything all over again, one student replied, "It's interesting sometimes to think about where paths lead you, and I don't think you should ever regret decisions. I would come here again—I like Loyola, I like the person I have become since I've been here."—*Lindsay Starck*

FYI

If you come to Loyola, you'd better bring "a spirit of compassion."

What's the typical weekend schedule? "Get work out of the way, and go downtown!"

If I could change one thing about Loyola, "I would change the way it's so open to the city. The number of suspicious people walking around is kind of creepy."

Three things every student at Loyola should do before graduating are: "take advantage of the opportunities in Chicago, have a picnic at the beach along Lake Michigan, and join an extra-curricular activity."

Northwestern University

Address: Northwestern, 633 Clark Street, Evanston, IL 60208

Phone: NA

E-mail Address: ug-admission@northwestern.edu

Web site URL: http://www.northwestern.edu

Year Founded: 1851

Private or Public: private

Religious affiliation: none

Location: suburban

Regular Application Deadline: 2-Jan

Number of Applicants: 15,637

Percent Accepted: 30%

Percent Accepted who enroll: 38%

Number Entering: 1,915

Number of Transfers Accepted each Year: NA

Mean SAT: 1,401

Mean ACT: 31

Middle 50% SAT range: 1,320–1,500

Middle 50% ACT range: 29–33

Early admission program (EA/ ED/ NA): ED

ED or EA Acceptance Rate: NA

Full time Undergraduate enrollment: 8,060

Total enrollment: NA

Percent Male: 47%

Percent Female: 53%

Total Percent Minority: 39%

Percent African-American: 6%

Percent Asian/Pacific Islander: 16%

Percent Hispanic: 6%

Percent Native-American: 0%

Percent Other: NA

Percent in-state / out of state: 25%/75%

Percent from Public HS: 73%

Retention Rate: 97%

Graduation Rate: NA

Percent in On-campus housing: 65%

Percent affiliated with Greek system: 32%/38%

Percent Varsity or Club Athletes: NA

Number of official organized extracurricular organizations: 415

3 Most popular majors: Economics, engineering, journalism

Student/Faculty ratio: 7:01

Tuition and Fees: $33,408.00

Cost for Room and Board: $10,266.00

Percent receiving Financial aid, first-year: 42%

Prestigious academics, a small town located conveniently near a big city, and a huge party named after an armadillo—Northwestern University has it all. Located in Evanston, Illinois, only a short train ride away from Chicago, Northwestern provides a stimulating academic environment and some of the greatest opportunities for a memorable four years—cold weather notwithstanding.

Please, Not Another Exam!

Academic requirements at Northwestern are not too stressful—as one sophomore put it, there is "a good balance of what you need and what you want." Northwestern itself consists of six separate schools: Arts and Sciences, Communications, Education and Social Policy, Engineering and Applied Science, Journalism, and Music. Within these different schools, everyone has to take two classes in six different distributional areas. Students, however, have many choices for the specific classes they wish to take in each area. In addition to the famous journalism and communications schools, students list economics and political science as the most popular majors on campus. The university runs on a quarter system, which consists of three quarters during the "typical" school year, plus a summer quarter. The students describe their relationship with the quarter system as "love-hate." The coursework ends up being fast paced and intensive, with exams every three weeks. However, the system allows Northwestern students to take a larger variety of classes, which come to an end that much quicker.

When it comes to classes themselves, there are a variety of sizes and levels of difficulty to choose from. The intro classes are rather large lectures of about 300 to 500 with smaller, T.A.-led discussion sections; upper level classes range from 20 to 50, and language classes are always capped at 20. Many students describe the coursework as very reading intensive but manageable. As for grades, one student summed it up by explaining that, "It's hard to get an A, but it's also hard to get a C." Organic chemistry is unanimously proclaimed as the most difficult of all courses. On the other end of the spectrum, Introduction to Sociology is commonly labeled as a very easy and extremely interesting class, thanks to Charles Moskos, a legendary professor on campus, whose impressive resume includes the position of aide to President Clinton. The students find it helpful to use the University-provided online evaluation system to screen their classes; honest feedback from students who previously had taken the courses proves to be a gold mine and an irreplaceable tool for building that perfect schedule.

In terms of forging relationships with professors, one student maintained that, "if you want, it is easy to blend in." But most describe their professors as accessible, with regular office hours and willing to help out and talk. One junior even recalled a (rare) example of one economy professor who made an effort to learn the names of all of the 300 people in her lecture class.

Ugg Thugs and Greeks who Chug
The student population, as described by one student, breaks down into "one third who study all the time, one third who have too much fun and are overcommitted, and one third who manage to find some sort of a balance." Freshman year is important in terms of making friends, and the freshman dorm is overwhelmingly the primary center of social activity. After the first year, "people are not as accepting," and it becomes more difficult to meet people. Some students even complained of a clique problem. The stereotypical student as described by most is an upper-middle-class prep, complete with Uggs and North Face-clad exteriors. Students also pointed out that there is a division between the athletes and the non-athletes, and a certain degree of self-segregation occurs among ethnic groups. Diversity still abounds on campus, however, and in general, the environment is described as competitive but definitely friendly.

The social scene for underclassmen is dominated by Greek life; about 40% of the student body belongs to either a sorority or a fraternity. Upperclassmen often party at off-campus apartments, and many also travel to Chicago on the weekends to go bar-hopping. In Evanston itself, the college bar scene includes Monday nights at The Keg, and Thursdays at The Duce (officially the Mark II Lounge). The most highly anticipated day on campus, however, is Dillo Day (short for Armadillo Day), which takes place on the first day of reading week of the third quarter. All students gather outside for concerts and enjoy the freely flowing alcohol all day long. Yet, despite the apparent prominence of alcohol and Greek life on campus, students insisted that those who prefer not to participate in either activity could still manage to find their own ways to have fun.

North vs. South
The Northwestern campus is picturesque and beautiful. It has a mix of architecture ranging from ivy-covered old buildings to concrete boxes. As one student explained, "You can find the ugliest and the prettiest building here next to each other." As described by one sophomore, the shape of the campus is "long and skinny," polarizing the North from the South. The north side, which houses mainly athletes, Greeks, and science majors, is known for its numerous parties. The south side, which houses mainly theater and communication majors, has a quieter and calmer atmosphere. All dorms are patrolled by community assistants (CAs), that are responsible for monitoring compliance with dorm rules. The campus is technically a dry campus. No alcohol is allowed in rooms where an underage person is present. Whether this policy is actually followed, students said, depends on the type of CA who has to make the decision.

Living options include freshman-only dorms, different size co-ed dorms, and small and intimate residential colleges. Each class goes through its own lottery system, which generally works out so that most students actually get their first choices. Many of the dorms have stereotypes attached to them: Jones houses theater people, Elder has freshman athletes, and Bobb is the party dorm. While all freshmen are required to live on campus, starting sophomore year people begin to move into off-campus apartments, and very few juniors and seniors remain in dorms. Parking is rather difficult to come by, so not many students bring cars—which is not a problem, since most people insist that everything is within walking distance.

When tired of dining hall food, which most describe rather unenthusiastically as "acceptable," Northwestern students take refuge in Evanston, universally proclaimed the "dining capital of the North Shore." Choices include a wide variety of ethnic foods, chain restaurants, and cafés. There is also a newly opened crepe restaurant, and, of course, the indispensable 24-hour Burger King for those late night cravings.

Make it Glow Purple

Varsity sports at Northwestern receive a rather lukewarm response on campus. Football games are the only sporting event that boasts consistently good attendance. However, intramural sports, the most popular of which are volleyball and ultimate Frisbee, more than make up for the lack of varsity spirit. Athletics aside, extracurricular activities extend far and wide. Some of the many organizations on campus include the Dance Marathon, which involves planning and participating in an all-night dance for charity, Associated Government, and the *Northwestern Daily*. The school also offers a cappella and countless culture and service-oriented groups. As for some quirkier traditions, Northwestern has a rock in a central campus location where students paint announcements. The catch? You have to guard the rock for 24 hours before you can paint it, and it can only be painted when the sun is down.

> "I was exposed to so many new things here and tried so many things I normally wouldn't!"

All of these traditions combine to help give Northwestern students a memorable and meaningful college experience. One junior said, "I was exposed to so many new things here and tried so many things I normally wouldn't." By constantly challenging its students and providing countless opportunities for something new, Northwestern breaks people out of their comfort zones and provides an environment in which students thrive and make memories to last a lifetime.—*Dorota Poplowska*

FYI

If you come to Northwestern, you'd better bring: "A warm jacket, or two, or three, or four."

What is the typical weekend schedule? "Friday go out to dinner, relax, drink, and sleep. Saturday you do it all over again, except in football season you attend a football game in the morning. Sunday intramurals happen and you do work."

If I could change one thing about Northwestern, I'd: "change how big of a role the Greek life plays."

Three things every student at Northwestern should do before graduating are: "paint the rock and guard it for 24 hours, go to Dillo Day, and spend a night on the Lakefill (a hang out place at Lake Michigan)."

Principia College

Address: Principia, 1 Maybeck Place, Elsah, IL 62028
Phone: 618-374-4000
E-mail Address: NA
Web site URL: www.prin.edu/college
Year Founded: 1898
Private or Public: private
Religious affiliation: Christian Scientist
Location: rural
Regular Application Deadline: 1-Mar
Percent Accepted: 87%
Percent Accepted who enroll: 61%
Number Entering: NA
Number of Transfers Accepted each Year: NA
Mean SAT: 1,177
Mean ACT: 25

Middle 50% SAT range: V:510–650, M:500–620
Middle 50% ACT range: 21–30
Early admission program (EA/ ED/ NA): EA
ED or EA Acceptance Rate: NA
Full time Undergraduate enrollment: 542
Total enrollment: NA
Percent Male: 48%
Percent Female: 52%
Total Percent Minority: 19%
Percent African-American: 1%
Percent Asian/Pacific Islander: 1%
Percent Hispanic: 1%
Percent Native-American: NA
Percent Other: 16%

Percent in-state / out of state: 12%/88%
Percent from Public HS: 61%
Retention Rate: 79%
Graduation Rate: 85%
Percent in On-campus housing: 99%
Percent affiliated with Greek system: 0%
Percent Varsity or Club Athletes: NA
Number of official organized extracurricular organizations: 29
3 Most popular majors: Business Administration, Art, Communications
Student/Faculty ratio: 8:01
Tuition and Fees: $21,150.00

As the only exclusively Christian Scientist college in the world, Principia College attracts followers of its faith from all over the globe. Located high above the bluffs in Elsah, Illinois over the Mississippi River, the small liberal arts school affectionately known as Prin, is a small, tight-knit community dedicated to both academic excellence and devotion to the Christian Scientist faith.

An Academic Haven

Since Principia's founding in 1898, its academic mission has evolved, placing an increased emphasis on developing students' analytical thinking, problem solving, and communication skills. In order to address the specific academic needs of freshmen, Principia instituted its First-Year Experience (FYE) program in 1998. Upon arrival, each freshman enrolls in FYE, which consists of two or three courses to be taken during one's freshman year. Each program of courses has a unique theme and incorporates several classes from different departments, and the variety of programs allows freshmen to choose a theme that appeals to their personal academic interests. After FYE, students choose from 32 majors and four minors, or they may design and petition for a special major not already offered by the school.

No matter what they major in, Prin students will have a hard time skipping class or dozing off during lectures. As one junior explained, "Most of the classes are 20 students or less, and attendance is a part of the grade in most classes." The upside is that the small classroom size and campus environment makes professors very accessible. "Most of them list their home phone or cell phone numbers on the course syllabus," one student said of the Prin professors.

Live by the Code

Outside the classroom, Principia students are held to an additional standard of integrity known as the honor code. The school's honor code is based on the principles set forth by Mary Baker Eddy, the Discoverer and Founder of Christian Science, and by Mary Kimball Morgan, who founded Principia. While most secular liberal arts school have some sort of general honor code loosely regulating the basics—i.e. no plagiarism and no stealing—Principia's code addresses its students' more personal and spiritual activities. It outlines specific requirements for social conduct, academic integrity and performance, financial integrity, and spiritual reliance. In following the code, students agree to abstain from alcohol, tobacco, drugs, and premarital sex, as well as rely exclusively on Christian Science for healing. Principia's administration finds that following these guidelines is vital in fulfilling

Principia's original mission and keeping in line with the Christian Scientist faith. Enforcement of the code is taken very seriously.

Party, Prin Style

Do not be fooled by Principia's claim to be a "small" liberal arts college—its campus spans 2,600 acres. Since the nearest town is 20 minutes away, Prin has its own social committee that "provides a wide range of activities both on and off campus for the students and ways to get to them." Special events include live music courtesy of on and off-campus bands, weekly movies screened on a large movie screen, and regular parties hosted by dorms. In fact, there's so much going on at Prin that people often forget that the bustling city of St. Louis, with its restaurants, sports teams, and famous zoo, is a mere 40 minute drive from campus. Although students admit that, "there is some drinking that goes on, both on campus and off," it's definitely against the code, and undergrads caught drinking can get suspended.

Feels Like Home

Nearly all students live on campus in one of 10 house-like residences, many of which were designed by the renowned architect Bernard Maybeck. In fact, Principia was designated a National Historic Landmark to honor Maybeck's exceptional architecture. All new freshmen live on campus in two dorms: Anderson Hall and Rackham Court. Each freshman dorm houses eight upperclassmen who serve as resident assistants (RAs). And the living ain't shabby. One Principia student even went so far as to say that "... Anderson House is enormous and beyond beautiful ... we are all spoiled. I could not have asked for a better place to live my first year in college."

> "I could not have asked for a better place to live my first year in college."

After freshman year, almost all students move to another house where they will reside their sophomore, junior and senior years. Some students, referred to as nontraditional students, or "non-trads (generally those students older than traditional college age), live in Hitchcock, one of three "cottages" designed by Maybeck, or in off-campus housing. Yet, most Prin students reside on campus and enjoy Maybeck's architecture along with its great facilities. All residences are equipped with computer labs, laundry rooms, and kitchens—and there are Christian Science and academic study rooms available in each building that are open at all times. Students agreed that houses serve as smaller communities where people can make friends and become involved in extracurricular activities. Each house has its own student government and board members who plan social functions, coordinate intramural athletics, and lead student orientations. Aside from planning activities within the house, the board members coordinate annual campus-wide activities in each residence. Rackam house kicks off the first weekend of the fall with an annual toga party, and Ferguson has a popular haunted house during Halloween. Later in winter the Sylvester house holds an 80s dance in their rec room. Members of each residence come together each year to throw some fun cohouse parties, and everyone on campus gets to enjoy activities planned by all of the other houses throughout the year, which, as one junior put it, is "not a bad deal!"

Get Involved!

The combination of Principia's small and motivated student body and the college's vast resources makes it a great place to cultivate leadership roles in extracurricular activities. In terms of sports, Principia is a Division III school and has 10 varsity sports teams for men and women, not to mention a variety of IMs. There are multiple opportunities to get involved in theatre and musical groups as well, including the winter dance production and the spring play. Prin students can write for the campus newspaper, edit the yearbook, host a radio show on Principia's FM-radio station (WTPC), or even help to coordinate the annual Public Affairs Conference (PAC), which tackles questions like, "Is Democracy the Global Solution?" Getting back to basics, the Christian Science Organization (CSO) offers undergraduates a chance to further the study of their common faith. In short, Principia offers a multitude of activities and opportunities for its students, while still furthering its mission to instill the values of the Christian Scientist Church.— *Suzanne Salgado*

FYI

If you come to Principia, you'd better bring "an open mind."

What's a typical weekend schedule? "Football, volleyball, or basketball game Saturday afternoon, a movie or trip into town Saturday night, church Sunday morning and homework Sunday afternoon."

If I could change one thing about Principia, I'd "change the strictness . . . Prin is fairly reasonable for why it has the rules it does, but some of them seem a bit ridiculous."

Three things everyone should do before graduating Principia are: "travel abroad, be part of a dance or theater production, and go to the City Museum with all your buds!"

Southern Illinois University / Carbondale

Address: So. Illinois, Carbondale, 425 Clocktower Dr, Carbondale, IL 62901
Phone: 618-536-4405
E-mail Address: joinsiuc@siu.edu
Web site URL: www.siuc.edu
Year Founded: 1869
Private or Public: public
Religious affiliation: No Affiliation
Location: rural
Regular Application Deadline: rolling
Number of Applicants: NA
Percent Accepted: 71%
Percent Accepted who enroll: 37%
Number Entering: NA
Number of Transfers Accepted each Year: NA
Mean SAT: NA
Mean ACT: 22

Middle 50% SAT range: 1,440–1,860
Middle 50% ACT range: 19–24
Early admission program (EA/ ED/ NA): NA
ED or EA Acceptance Rate: NA
Full time Undergraduate enrollment: 16,697
Total enrollment: 21,441
Percent Male: 57.2%
Percent Female: 42.8%
Total Percent Minority: 31.1%
Percent African-American: 15%
Percent Asian/Pacific Islander: 2%
Percent Hispanic: 3.2%
Percent Native-American: NA
Percent Other: 10.8%
Percent in-state / out of state: 86%/14%

Percent from Public HS: NA
Retention Rate: 67%
Graduation Rate: 42%
Percent in On-campus housing: 28%
Percent affiliated with Greek system: 10%
Percent Varsity or Club Athletes: NA
Number of official organized extracurricular organizations: 402
3 Most popular majors: Workforce Education and Development, Health Care Management, Engineering
Student/Faculty ratio: 16:01
Tuition and Fees: $13,276
In State Tuition and Fees (if different): $6,831
Cost for Room and Board: $5,582
Percent receiving Financial aid, first-year: NA

Southern Illinois University at Carbondale, among its claims to fame, boasts one of the most unusual mascots of any American university—the Saluki, an Egyptian hunting dog. Although the connection between the Saluki and SIU (originally a small teacher's college founded in 1869 with a mere 143 students enrolled) remains mysterious. Nevertheless, Salukis take pride in their mascot and love their school, which has grown from humble beginnings into one of the largest and most affordable universities in the country—not to mention one of the most famous party schools in the Midwest.

Southern Illinois, Southern Hospitality

Approximately three fourths of SIU students come from Illinois, and as many students explained, there is a common misconception that all Salukis are just "southern Illinois hicks." But despite an apparent lack of geographic diversity, the student body is composed of individuals with a variety of backgrounds and interests. One student noted, "There are students here of all ages, varying from the traditional fresh-out-of-high school student to the parent of three trying to get a better job. People here come from all different backgrounds and tend to mesh together very well." The large number of students at SIU—21,000 total—make it easy to make friends. "There are all sorts of opportunities to meet people," explained one student. "For the most part, everyone on campus is friendly. Whether you meet them in class or out at the bars, chances are you'll be friends on Facebook before the day is over."

Home Sweet Home

With such a large student body, SIU provides four main undergraduate housing areas: University Park, Brush Towers, Thompson Point, and University Hall. Each housing area has its own laundry facility and dining hall. Students are only required to live on campus during their freshman year. Salukis typically describe the on-campus housing as "pretty nice . . . besides the cinder block walls." University Park has the smallest rooms, but is located in a picturesque, wooded part of campus. Students who live in Brush Towers enjoy it particularly because of its private bathrooms and small suite-shared kitchenettes, but some say that it can be chaotic living in a large complex of apartment-like towers. Thompson Point, said to be the "prettiest," is located on nearby Thompson Lake. University Hall is a bit further away from the other three, but it offers the same amenities. All of the residential facilities have RAs. Students say that usually RAs are easy to talk to and helpful with problems, although some can reportedly be strict disciplinary figures. Most juniors and seniors at SIU choose to live off campus, which is where most of the famed SIU partying takes place.

> "For the most part, everyone on campus is friendly. Whether you meet them in class or out at the bars, chances are you'll be friends on Facebook before the day is over."

There are three meal plans to choose from at SIU, and they can be used at any of the four on-campus dining halls. The meal plan is based on a points system, and any unused points at the end of the week can be used to purchase snacks and other food and drink items from the on-campus market. Unfortunately, despite the variety of options offered by the meal plan, the food at SIU is not something students brag about. Descriptions of SIU food ranged from, "it is disgusting" to "it sucks!" Luckily, there are many restaurants near campus. Some student favorites are Buffalo Wild Wings, Applebees, Lonestar Steakhouse and Quatros.

Work Hard . . .

At such a large research university, plenty of academic opportunities abound at SIUC. And most Salukis tend to agree that having a variety of resources allows them lots of opportunity for hands-on work, whether on a farm for agricultural studies majors or in a broadcast station for radio and TV majors. The university has a core liberal arts curriculum that must be completed by all students before graduation. Although core classes tend to be the largest, students say that even the professors in the big lecture classes are accessible, and there are plenty of opportunities to take small classes or seminars. SIUC students' general opinion with regards to the university's professors is that they are relatively easy. As one student said, "The grading scale varies from teacher to teacher, but is generally pretty lenient." Another added, "All of my professors are really easy."

In terms of majors, different ones require different workloads. In particular, science classes like engineering and aviation prove to be especially challenging. The most popular major at SIU is Workforce Education and Development, followed by Healthcare Management and Engineering Technology. Students are asked to declare a major when they are admitted to SIU, but if they are unsure of what they want to do, they are admitted to the pre-major program with a pre-major advisor. Salukis in the pre-major program must declare a major before the end of their sophomore year.

Most students at SIU are satisfied with their overall academic experience and try to take advantage of the university's resources. "Academically we are a great school," stated one sophomore. "Departments and professors provide very hands-on learning and are willing to work with students to see that we all succeed."

. . . Play Hard

Not only is it easy to make friends at SIU, but Salukis agree that it is easy to have a good time. SIU lives up to its reputation as being a party school, but many students say that the stereotype is blown way out of proportion. One male student explained that, "underage drinking is definitely an issue here, but just as it is everywhere else." Most students agree that the drinking at SIUC seems about comparable to that of any other state school, but admit that the social scene does revolve around alcohol. People go out Wednesday through Saturday nights, but "there is a party somewhere every night if you want one." Bars on "the strip" in Carbondale are popular, and although the legal drinking age is 21, it is not hard to obtain drinks if you're underage. Furthermore, the SIU administration is relatively easygoing about alcohol monitoring. They "try to look the other way," one student explained.

Saluki Spirit

Without doubt, SIU students are definitely proud of their Division I sports teams. Among the plethora of varsity sports, football and basketball are among the most popular. Students say that club sports are competitive, especially softball, but that they're all fun to play. There is a large Rec Center at SIU, where Salukis can enjoy basketball and racquetball courts, as well as an Olympic-sized swimming pool. The Rec Center also rents out sports equipment and camping supplies to students. Non-athletes will be glad to know that there are about 500 clubs and RSOs (Registered Student Organizations) on campus in which students can become involved. Students say the most popular RSO is "definitely the sky-diving club." For some fun closer to the ground,

The Student Programming Committee plans student events like dances, concerts, and movies. Greek life at SIU is relatively small, with four sororities and 21 fraternities. Some students complain that, "people here do not really understand [Greek life] because it is so small" while others say that they enjoy the minimal Greek presence on campus. Whatever their preference, Salukis can always find an organization to become a part of during their time at SIU.

Most Salukis say they feel relatively safe on campus and very welcomed by the residents of Carbondale. Many even hail Carbondale as "the perfect college town." The majority of students live on campus and do not have cars. But a lack of wheels doesn't prevent Salukis from taking advantage of a vast amount of resources and Carbondale's collegiate charm. Salukis just know how to have fun while keeping busy.
—*Becky Bicks*

FYI

If you come to SIU, you'd better bring: "Clothes for all seasons—the weather changes every five minutes."

What's the typical weekend schedule? "Sleeping in, drinking at night, and working on homework."

Three things every Southern student should do before graduating are "Join an RSO, Go to Saluki football and basketball games, and have LOTS and LOTS of fun."

One thing I'd change about SIU, I'd "Improve the parking policy and build another lot or two without unfair regulations.

University of Chicago

Address: University of Chicago, 1101 E 58th Street, Rosenwald Hall Suite 105, Chicago, IL 60637

Phone: 773-702-8650

E-mail Address: college admissions@uchicago.edu

Web site URL: http://www.uchicago.edu

Year Founded: 1890

Private or Public: private

Religious affiliation: none

Location: urban

Regular Application Deadline: 3-Jan

Number of Applicants: 9,538

Percent Accepted: 38%

Percent Accepted who enroll: 34%

Number Entering: 1,259

Number of Transfers Accepted each Year: 157

Mean SAT: NA

Mean ACT: 31

Middle 50% SAT range: 1,320–1,530

Middle 50% ACT range: 28–33

Early admission program (EA/ ED/ NA): EA

ED or EA Acceptance Rate: 48%

Full time Undergraduate enrollment: 4,807

Total enrollment: 10,880

Percent Male: 50%

Percent Female: 50%

Total Percent Minority: 52%

Percent African-American: 4%

Percent Asian/Pacific Islander: 13%

Percent Hispanic: 8%

Percent Native-American: 0%

Percent Other: 25%

Percent in-state / out of state: 17%/83%

Percent from Public HS: 63%

Retention Rate: 98%

Graduation Rate: 89%

Percent in On-campus housing: 56%

Percent affiliated with Greek system: NA

Percent Varsity or Club Athletes: 14%

Number of official organized extracurricular organizations: 400

Most popular majors: Economics, English

Student/Faculty ratio: 6:01

Tuition and Fees: $34,005.00

Cost for Room and Board: $10,608.00

Percent receiving Financial aid, first-year: 48%

Above all, the University of Chicago is known for its dedication to academia mania. How many schools can boast about CIA agents looking for a student who had made a nuclear reactor in a dorm room? The nuclear reactor was a project for UChicago's annual Scavenger Hunt, an event organized by the University in which students compete to fulfill tasks off of a master list. Such tasks can include everything from building a nuclear reactor to downing a shot of sweat, getting circumcised (apparently some used creativity and forged medical records), placing a kick-me sign on a Scav Hunt Judge and creating a Lake Michigan nude beach. From the funny to the bizarre, the Scav Hunt embodies the "madness" that is a defining part of one of the best schools in the nation.

"Where Fun Comes To Die"

While this unofficial but well-known student motto is an example of UChicago students' facetious air about their extremely demanding and intense academics, UChicago students are proud of their academics. Seventy-eight Nobel Laureates, more than any other college in the United States, have been faculty members, students or researchers at UChicago. Run on the quarter system, classes last 10 weeks, but cover generally the same amount of material as others school do in a semester, making life hectic. As one student put it, academics are a "love/hate relationship—there's just so much work to be done, but the atmosphere here is very academic, and everyone here is proud to be nerd." Most students describe the work load as tough. A junior explained she had "about four hours of work for each class for each time it meets a week," but all students accept the heavy load as a fact of life.

All students are required to fulfill the Common Core, general education requirements that are meant to provide a "true liberal arts education." The common core is composed of six courses in the humanities and civilization studies (at least two in "Hum," pronounced "hume;" two in civilization studies; and one in the fine arts), six in the natural and mathematical sciences (at least two biological, two physical and one mathematical science), three social sciences, a foreign language requirement, a physical education requirement, and a swimming test. "Most students would normally end up taking classes that fulfill the Core anyway," one student commented, "it just reflects the type of

students here, students who want to know everything and anything."

Since the Core includes such a large number of requirements, few classes are limited to freshmen only, as juniors and seniors are still trying to fulfill the Core. The main two requirements that almost all students take freshmen year are math and Hum. "There are no easy calculus classes here," one student lamented, so most students try to fulfill the requirement while still fresh from high school. Most students take Hum courses early on to improve their writing (Chicago has a nationally renowned writing program). While in the natural sciences there are a few easy classes for non-majors, other requirements, like math, can be satisfied by only the typically rigorous classes. However, there is a large selection of classes to choose from to satisfy the Core. Two of the most popular Hum classes are "Human Being and Citizen" and "Greek Thought in Literature;" "they've been around for ages, tried and true."

As for concentrations at UChicago—what UChicago calls majors—the two most popular are Economics and Biology. The Economics Department is supposedly the best in the nation and is the most famous department of UChicago, home to Steven Levitt (author of "Freakonomics"). While the quality of the school (and number of students) is really divided evenly between the sciences and humanities, "everything tends to be very theoretical." Concentrations at UChicago vary from biochemistry, which has 37 required classes, to Big Problems, in which an individual focuses on all the global aspects (political, social, economic, religious, etc.) that constitute a "big problem." UChicago does not offer an engineering major.

Where the Living is Easy

At UChicago, students live in one of 10 residential halls. With the exception of two dorms, residential halls are mixed with students of all years. Blackstone is meant for transfers and upperclassmen only, while 5700 Stony Island is an apartment building for upperclassmen only. Residence Halls are broken down into "Houses," each composed of about 77 students, usually sharing a floor or two of the building. Each House also has a resident head (or heads), who coordinate everything from study breaks to intramurals while also offering academic and personal advice.

Each dorm and house is known for having its own social characteristics and traditions. Max Palevsky, the most recently built residence hall, is pink and still forming its traditions. Max-P is the most highly sought-after residence hall, as it boasts most modern features like air-conditioning, close proximity to campus and a meal plan with Bartlett Dining Commons, which is known for its great food. Because Max-P is in such hot demand and about half of the rooms are reserved for freshmen, students have no guarantee that they will be placed into the same house or same residence hall the next year. Residence Halls at UChicago tend to be a trade-off between space and distance to campus. The farthest away, Shoreland, was once a luxury hotel where Al Capone stayed. Now the residence hall offers students spacious rooms. Pierce, on the other hand, has "tiny rooms" but is closest to campus.

People tend to make very close friendships with the people that are in their house. During O-Week (Orientation week) and the week after, houses are required to eat together at House Tables in their designated dining commons. Houses are also a great way for freshmen to integrate and meet upperclassmen. Filled with pride, spirit, and traditions, Houses often grow very close, even forming Scav Hunt teams together. But while most students like the house system, many students tend to move off campus senior year into apartments in Hyde Park. Of all students on campus, the only students who might want a car are those who live off campus and need to go grocery shopping; otherwise, "cars are extraneous and a bother."

While UChicago doesn't have a Student Union, the Reynolds Club attempts to fill the void, offering several different small shops and eateries thrown together. One student explained that "all students go to the Reynolds Club, whether to eat or study, but mainly to check and see what's happening." Some students come to Reynolds to eat or to meet up with a friend, and, in addition, several student organizations have offices at the Reynolds club (such as the UChicago radio station and Chicago Weekly news "Wednesdays [at the Reynolds Club] are not to be missed," raved one student, "because it is dollar shake days in the C-Shop." Reynolds Club is also where the Reynolds' seal is, and rumor is that anyone who steps on the seal will not graduate in four years.

Dining is broken down into three different places, Burton and Pierce, which offer all-you-can-eat fares, and Bartlett. Burton is known for its popular "Wok," and Pierce is known for its great pizza. At Bartlett, students who have dining points can swipe out food a la carte. Because "the school needs to keep people out of Bartlett" and to foster House relations, students are given certain meal plans (the Bartlett plan and the non-Bartlett plan) that limit where students can eat according to their residence halls. All residence halls are closed for Saturday dinners so that students go out and eat in the surrounding neighborhood. The Snail, a Thai restaurant, is known for having cheap and good food, and the other popular place to eat is Ragin' Cajun, but "there are so many good restaurants to try in Hyde Park and Chicago, and Chinatown is close by."

Nerds Who Can Have Fun
Most students know what they are getting into when they go to UChicago. The student body is very diverse, but all the students seem to have "one thing in common—a passion for academics." While the common perception of students is that they are either pent up in their room studying or "wearing a black turtleneck sweater sitting in some coffee shop, listening to jazz," students come from all different backgrounds, with all sorts of varying interests. "While we aren't known for throwing wild parties like other schools, we know how to have fun as well," one student mentioned. Frat parties (about 10 percent of the undergrads are part of the Greek life) are still a popular social scene, frequented by students who want that social party atmosphere. Parties also occur in the dorms which have a relaxed drinking policy (you can drink in your room but no open alcohol in the hallway), allowing for a safe drinking environment, with resident advisers (juniors or seniors) who live in the dorms. Upperclassmen tend to party either in clubs or in their apartments, as most seniors live in apartments off campus.

A large portion of the student population doesn't drink, and there are lots of things to do for non-drinkers too. "One of the greatest resources that we have at our disposal is the great city of Chicago," one student explained. "It's so easy to go into the city, and there's always a cultural event going on, a show or play to go watch, a movie to see." Because the majority of the students take Friday and Saturday night to go into the city, students always have many options on what to do for fun.

Not that the campus doesn't provide parties as well. Large parties tend to be the ones thrown by cultural groups, but the big party attended by all on campus is "Summer Breeze," which occurs in late spring and involves parties all over campus with big-name acts. Summer Breeze is one of the three main traditions of UChicago. Kuviasungerk/ Kangeiko, which happens in the middle of winter, is a week in January where students can get up at 6 a.m. to do a combination of yoga, Pilates and other physical activity, enticed by the offer of a free T-shirt if they go every day. "In my house," one student says, "it's such a big tradition that upperclassmen wake everyone up and drag the students kicking and screaming to Kuvia." On the last day, students get up early to do the physical activity in the snow at the Point, on Lake Michigan. The big climax is the Polar Bear Run, where students run in their skivvies and sometimes less in the cold weather. Explaining the popularity of the Polar Bear Run, one student explained that "you don't need to run if you don't want to, but you can always show up to support the runners." The Scav Hunt, as described earlier, is another big campus tradition.

Life—UChicago Style

"We aren't known for our sports," one student frankly stated. As one student put it, "Even though we may go out in the city and maybe visit some coffee shops, more often than not you'll end up arguing Marx with an-other student, or something like that." Nonetheless, extracurriculars also play a big part of the daily life of a UChicago student. Intramural sports are popular, and clubs on campus range from Model UN of the University of Chicago to cultural organizations and community service groups; people are always organizing events that everybody can take a part in.

> "Even though we may go out in the city and maybe visit some coffee shops, more often than not you'll end up arguing Marx with another student, or something like that."

UChicago students are critical of their school by nature. "We make fun of ourselves, but we know and love the way we are, and accept it." UChicago is not your typical school of football, frats and beer. But with the combination of famous faculty, an intensely academic atmosphere and a quirky student body, UChicago offers students a distinct and high-caliber education.—*Jesse Dong*

FYI
If you come to UChicago, you'd better bring "a sense of humor."
What's the typical weekend schedule? "Party Friday night, sleep in Saturday, do work Saturday afternoon, go out for dinner Saturday and into the city, and do work all Sunday."
If I could change one thing about UChicago I would "make all the doors uniform—as the stories go, you need to pull some, push others, wiggle and turn yourself around for the rest."
The three things every student should do before graduating are "do yoga on the point during Kuvia at 6 a.m., be part of a Scav Hunt team, and watch people avoid stepping on the seal in front of Reynolds."

University of Illinois / Chicago

Address: University of Illinois, Chicago, 601 S. Morgan St., Chicago, IL 60607
Phone: 312-996-7000
E-mail Address: uicadmit@uic.edu
Web site URL: www.uic.edu
Year Founded: 1965
Private or Public: public
Religious affiliation: none
Location: urban
Regular Application Deadline: 16-Jan
Number of Applicants: 13,000
Percent Accepted: 58.15%
Percent Accepted who enroll: 37.73%
Number Entering: 2,852
Number of Transfers Accepted each Year: 2,074
Mean SAT: NA
Mean ACT: 23
Middle 50% SAT range: NA

Middle 50% ACT range: 21–26
Early admission program (EA/ ED/ NA): NA
ED or EA Acceptance Rate: NA
Full time Undergraduate enrollment: 15,006
Total enrollment: 22,320
Percent Male: 45%
Percent Female: 55%
Total Percent Minority: 50%
Percent African-American: 9%
Percent Asian/Pacific Islander: 24%
Percent Hispanic: 16%
Percent Native-American: 0.3%
Percent Other: <1%
Percent in-state / out of state: 96% / 4%
Percent from Public HS: 79%

Retention Rate: 79%
Graduation Rate: 36%
Percent in On-campus housing: 12%
Percent affiliated with Greek system: 1%
Percent Varsity or Club Athletes: NA
Number of official organized extracurricular organizations: 200
3 Most popular majors: Biology, Information Science, Psychology
Student/Faculty ratio: 14:01
Tuition and Fees: $22,138.00
In State Tuition and Fees (if different): $9,748.00
Cost for Room and Board: $8,100.00
Percent receiving Financial aid, first-year: 72.56%

Founded in 1963, the University of Illinois at Chicago (UIC) is one of the youngest campuses in the Illinois public university system. Located in one of America's most vibrant metropolitan areas, UIC is known for its strong ties with the city and its energetic atmosphere. If you dream of going to a school in the middle of a large city filled with extracurricular distractions, you should definitely consider UIC as a potential college choice.

The Blessing of Chicago

All students live on or nearby the two UIC campuses (East and South) in the heart of a city known to some as one of the premier business, cultural, and entertainment centers of America. "The great thing about UIC is that you are so close to the city," explains one student. Although the school itself offers a relatively quiet learning environment, there are plenty of activities just outside the confines of its walls because of the prime location. Despite the fact that there are few activities organized by the college during the weekends, it is obvious that UIC students are never bored. Since UIC has one of the lowest tuition cost for four-year universities, students can afford to spend more

money than many other college students in the country on recreational activities.

UIC and Chicago are closely connected as evidenced by UIC students frequenting the countless eateries, stores, theaters, bars, and malls around the campus as many residents of the city visit the campus to "take a tour and experience the college life" as one student noted. On the downside, being so close to the city also means a greater exposure to the city's crime, making student safety a concern.

Understated Academia

Of all the University of Illinois schools, the campus at Chicago is one of the least well-known. However, it does not mean the school offers little in terms of academics. "Despite what other people say, people come here to study," said one senior student.

One strong feature of UIC is its science departments. "Our science departments are very hard. Classes are generally very competitive," said another student. The humanities and social science classes are also known for their rigor. Most students agree that UIC has excellent faculty in a variety of fields. Classes are based on semester hours. Most classes are four hours per week, and the students need 120 semester hours to graduate; therefore, people generally take four to five classes per semester.

> **"The great thing about UIC is that you are so close to the city."**

One of the distinctive elements of UIC is that it has graduation requirements in almost all subjects offered in the school in order to help students "achieve a more rounded education." There are requirements in humanities, natural sciences, and social sciences, an English composition requirement, and a "cultural diversity" requirement that allows students to "study the culture, social and political institutions, and value systems of social groups, regions, or nations different from those present in the dominant American culture." Students are also required to take a few of the many seminar courses offered in a variety of disciplines to supplement the large lecture courses that make up the bulk of their schedules.

The students at UIC choose their major among the 88 different bachelor's degrees ranging from Movement Science to Social Work. The most popular majors at UIC are business management, engineering, and psychology. Students can also make their own major if they can justify having their own course of study with faculty approval and supervision.

The course load is described as challenging by UIC students. According to one student, "UIC has one of the largest work loads for any class whether it be sciences, social sciences, humanities etc. All areas are challenging and UIC encourages their students to try them all."

Living in the City

It is often very difficult for UIC students to connect with their professors because of UIC's tendency to have mainly large lecture classes. The average class size of 29 is misleading because the classes tend to be extremely large or extremely small, and it is often very difficult to get into the tiny seminars. "The only professor I actually got to know in person is my psychology seminar. I don't think my other professors even know my name," one female student complained. Even though most professors have office hours, some students still complain about the lack of opportunities to interact with professors.

The majority of UIC students don't live in dorms. 75% of the students live in the greater Chicago area and commute to class everyday from home or off-campus in apartments. Those students that do live on campus describe their housing as being more like apartments than the typical idea of a dorm. Since many students immediately leave campus after class and Chicago is so dynamic, on-campus activities are described as limited. Fraternities and sororities do not have a heavy influence at all on the social scene. Instead, students prefer to party off-campus in Chicago's bars and clubs. One student remarked, "Going to parties is a chance to mingle with the locals and students from other colleges in the area." Many report that some bars and clubs are lenient about letting in underage students, making alcohol an important factor in UIC social life.

UIC is ranked in the top five of America's most diverse colleges. Minorities combined to make 51% of the college population, with 30% of the total population being non-native speakers of English. Also, 56% of UIC population is female, a situation very different from many other University of Illinois campuses.

Overall, students have a good opinion about their school. UIC students love their city, their fellow students, and are for the most part, satisfied with the education they are receiving.—*Xiaochen Su*

FYI
If you come to UIC, you'd better bring "wind-resistant clothing."
What is the typical weekend schedule? "Go shopping and party at clubs in the city."
If I could change one thing about UIC, I'd "lower the noise level around campus."
Three things every student at UIC should do before graduating are "go to downtown Chicago, go watch a White Sox or Cubs baseball game, and take a few seminar classes."

University of Illinois/ Urbana-Champaign

Address: Univ of Illinois, Urbana-Champaign, 901 West Illinois Street, Urbana, IL 61801
Phone: 217-333-0302
E-mail Address: ugradadmissions@uiuc.edu
Web site URL: http://www.uiuc.edu
Year Founded: 1867
Private or Public: public
Religious affiliation: none
Location: urban
Regular Application Deadline: 3-Jan
Number of Applicants: 22,300
Percent Accepted: 65%
Percent Accepted who enroll: 50%
Number Entering: 7,172
Number of Transfers Accepted each Year: 1,356
Mean SAT: 600V/680M
Mean ACT: 28

Middle 50% SAT range: 1,200–1,399
Middle 50% ACT range: 27–31
Early admission program (EA/ ED/ NA): NA
ED or EA Acceptance Rate: NA
Full time Undergraduate enrollment: 31,472
Total enrollment: 42,728
Percent Male: 53%
Percent Female: 47%
Total Percent Minority: 33%
Percent African-American: 6.1%
Percent Asian/Pacific Islander: 10.68%
Percent Hispanic: 5.9%
Percent Native-American: 0.29%
Percent Other: 10.03%
Percent in-state / out of state: 88%/12%
Percent from Public HS: 75%

Retention Rate: 93%
Graduation Rate: 82%
Percent in On-campus housing: 50%
Percent affiliated with Greek system: 22%
Percent Varsity or Club Athletes: NA
Number of official organized extracurricular organizations: 1,000
3 Most popular majors: Cellular and Molecular Biology, Political Science, Psychology
Student/Faculty ratio: 17:01
Tuition and Fees: $21,128.00
In State Tuition and Fees (if different): $7,042.00
Cost for Room and Board: $7,716.00
Percent receiving Financial aid, first-year: 40%

I magine a sea of orange, a dancing Indian chief, and thousands of fans cheering I-L-L-I-N-I. Anyone who has ever been to a sporting event at the University of Illinois can tell you how much pride students have for their school "in the cornfields." The University of Illinois in Urbana-Champaign has grown from its agricultural roots in 1867 into one of the nation's elite public research universities. U of I has something for everyone with a wide variety of majors ranging from "crops" in the College of Agricultural, Consumer, and Environmental Sciences to the relatively new bioengineering major in the world-renowned College of Engineering. As home of the first homecoming football game, supercomputer, the country's largest Greek scene, and the nation's oldest marching band, the University of Illinois offers its 31,000 undergraduates plenty of academic, extracurricular and social action. Everyone can find a niche even if you aren't an Illinoisan (the s is silent).

Shooting for the Sky

The University of Illinois offers an array of undergraduate academic options. Freshmen apply to one of eight colleges: the College of Agricultural, Consumer, and Environmental Sciences, College of Applied Life Sciences, College of Business, College of Communications, College of Education, College of Engineering, College of Fine and Applied Arts, College of Liberal Arts and Sciences and the Institute of Aviation. Each college has its own set of requirements and a distinct personality. The Colleges of Engineering and Business are top-notch: the Engineering program recently placed fourth in a ranking of public engineering colleges. The College of Liberal Arts and Sciences, commonly referred to as LAS, is by far the most popular college with 15,000 undergraduate students. Because of the amount of red tape involved, transferring from one college to another can be challenging.

Most students don't view the general education requirements as too challenging; one freshman commented that any student could "make [a course load] as hard as they want." One student laments classes are "a lot different from high school" in that they are "pretty demanding" and more reliant on computers. The student estimates that for every hour spent in class he must prepare two and a half hours of homework. However, assignments vary by college. An undergraduate in the College of Business said students spend about two hours a night on homework but added that they rarely read to prepare for class. Another said that "lots of us shoot for the sky;" there aren't many slackers. Of those students going out each night, most finish school work before heading to the bars.

> "Lots of us shoot for the sky."

Students at Illinois find that their class sizes are as diverse as their academic opportunities. A student may have a sociology lecture with 750 people and a Spanish course with 15 classmates. Not all students dislike the large lectures, and one student commented that they "could still see what was going on and could meet people more easily." Professors teach the lectures but some students complain about TAs who "have no idea what they are talking about." Students are pleased to find that some of their professors teach from their own textbooks, like Fred Gottheil in the economics department. Another special attraction is the grandson of Gandhi (Rajmohan Gandhi) who teaches in the Global Studies Program; one excited undergraduate commented, "He asked me what my name was!" Overall, the academics at U of I has something for everyone; as one student put it: "classes are challenging, but a degree from the U of I pays off in the end."

Social Illini

While many students at Illinois are content to stick around campus with their choice clubs and interests or even spend their weeknight hours roaming Green Street trying to find cheap Chinese food, it cannot go unacknowledged that like the social scene at many large state universities, Illini chill at the local bars and campus frat houses.

With the largest Greek system in the country, many freshmen decide to rush. For girls, rushing is a formal affair with elaborate dinners and scheduled events. For guys, rushing is more informal and consists of meeting the brothers and eating with them as a way to get acquainted. The intensity of rush depends on the individual frats and one male pledge said that rush lasted 12 weeks, but his fraternity has the longest rush period of all

the frats. Students don't need to join a fraternity or sorority to make friends, and many students meet some of their closest friends on their dorm floors. Students don't even have to join in on the Greek system to party. Bars in Champaign-Urbana (aka Chambana) are open to 19 year olds, and "once you get in it's easy to drink if you want to." The University is generally relaxed in its alcohol policy as long as "you don't die" but local cops do frequently raid bars and pass out drinking tickets.

Many people limit their weekends to Thursday through Saturday nights, but there are designated hang-out places for every night of the week. One student said that Mondays at the local bar Gully's were not to be missed. Sporting events are always popular, especially football at Memorial Stadium and basketball at the Assembly Hall. Just like its academics, social and extracurricular life at the University of Illinois has a lot to offer. You don't have to drink to have fun; there is something for everyone.

Popped Collars

There is no typical U of I student; to the question on the school's level of "preppy-ness" one student responded that there are "not many popped collars." The University's level of diversity doesn't only apply to popped collars. U of I is third in the Big Ten Conference for minority student enrollment and has the tenth highest international student enrollment in the United States. Caucasians make up most of the student population, about 74 percent, but there are also a large amount of other ethnic students on campus. There are many cultural activities and groups on campus. The Casa Cultural Latina is one the oldest university culture centers in the nation, and the newly-built Japan House features rock gardens, a stroll, and a place to drink tea. While the student body at the University of Illinois is diverse, many students expressed that "cliquiness" tends to be a problem.

Illinois Livin'

First year students are required to live in a University residence hall, university-certified housing, or a sorority or fraternity house. About three-quarters of the incoming freshmen live in a University residence hall, and the other quarter lives in universally certified housing (students choose where they live before they come, and students who decide to rush and to live in a fraternity or sorority do so after school has already begun). Dorms at the university are "stereotypical college dorms." Most consist of two people living together in a small room that is "big enough." Some dorms such as the Six Pack have special reputations (the Six Pack refers to more than just six buildings). The class of 2009 had an especially hard time finding dorms because the freshmen class was the largest in the university's history. Some students opt to pay extra to live in university-certified housing which offers special amenities, like the air-conditioning and carpet found in Bromley or Illini Tower. Some dorms are nicer and bigger than others, according to a girl in an all-girls dorm who said "corner rooms are ridiculously big."

There is no consensus on the dining hall food. Meal plans are different for each student—some have 10 meals a week and others have more; students can also add points to their account to eat at other places besides their dorms. Green Street is a popular street frequented by students for fun and satisfying cuisine with places to eat like Za's, an Italian restaurant with good pasta and sandwiches, and Garcia's, for pizza. Most upperclassmen move off campus into apartments, but those who stay around get first choice of dorms. Officially, alcohol is not allowed in dorms, but enforcement usually depends on the strictness of RAs; "they usually don't go looking for stuff."

The University of Illinois's campus generally consists of buildings that "look old, have columns, and have a lot of marble." Most buildings are of the Georgian style with brick and white columns. New buildings are constantly being built or remodeled especially for the Colleges of Engineering and Business.

Morrow Plots is an experimental field first used by the College of Agriculture in the 1800s. The main freshmen library—the Undergraduate Library—was built underground, beneath the field, so it didn't block sunlight from reaching the corn. U of I's library system is the third largest in the nation and consists of 43 libraries across campus. The Undergraduate Library is situated at one end of the expansive Quad. The Quad is large, flat, and green (when it is not covered by the snow that is common during Illinois winters), and is a fun place to hang out. One student characterizes the Quad as the "typical image of college" with students playing Frisbee, sunbathing, and studying. Opposite of the library is the Illini Union (at most schools it would be called the "Student Union"—but hey, school spirit is high). The Union includes a hotel, meeting rooms, a bookstore, a recreation room with bowling and billiards, an art gallery, and multiple eating options (Cactus Grill, Sushi San, McDonald's, and others). Assembly Hall, the giant dome-looking structure on campus, had one of only two-edged supported domes in the world when it opened in the 1960s. The stadium is the second largest in Illinois, and when it is not host to an Illini basketball game, major bands perform (recent bands have included Yellowcard, Kanye West, and the Dave Matthews Band).

Lots to Do

Extracurricular activities form an integral part of life at U of I. "There is a club for everyone." One student added that "anything you can think of has a club version at U of I." There is even a "Medieval Fighting Club." Everyone seems to be committed and has something they do. The Ultimate Frisbee Club is popular along with an array of academic clubs. Illini Pride is a popular organization that sets up social events and participates in community service. They also make up the famous "Orange Crush" at basketball games—a group of highly-dedicated, orange-wearing fans. Intramural sports are also an important extracurricular activity, and almost anyone can make their own league. Football games and basketball games are always popular—Illinois plays other Big Ten schools such as Indiana and Purdue and competition can get pretty intense. Two years ago, the Fighting Illini basketball team won second place in the NCAA tournament. Football games are popular social events on Saturday—many people get up early to tailgate. Most people don't have jobs, but those who want them can find them. While some opt to work in the library or dining halls, others find employment in bars as "shot girls."

Forever an Illini

Overall, the University of Illinois is a top-notch public institution. The typical student is the type of person that is motivated to get their homework done but can also go out afterwards. U of I is a large university that offers the academic, social, and extracurricular opportunities to match its size. A student at the University of Illinois can "become anything they want to become," but they will always be an Illini at heart.—*Josh Blair*

FYI
If you come to Illinois you'd better bring "a pair of good walking shoes."
What is the typical weekend schedule? "Go out at about 10:30 on a Friday night; on Saturday, sleep
   in and relax, then go to the gym or play an intramural sport before going out later. On Sunday, do
   homework."
If I could change one thing about Illinois, I'd "want there to be less walking."
Three things every student at Illinois should do before graduating are "go to Moonstruck Cafe for
   chocolate, go to a sporting event, and see Chief Illiniwick dance."

Wheaton College

Address: Wheaton, 501 College Avenue, Wheaton, Illinois 60187
Phone: 800-222-2419
E-mail Address: admissions@wheaton.edu
Web site URL: www.wheaton.edu
Year Founded: 1860
Private or Public: private
Religious affiliation: interdenominational Christian
Location: suburban
Regular Application Deadline: 11-Jan
Number of Applicants: NA
Percent Accepted: 56%
Percent Accepted who enroll: NA
Number Entering: NA
Number of Transfers Accepted each Year: 102
Mean SAT: 1,299

Mean ACT: 29
Middle 50% SAT range: 1,220–1,460
Middle 50% ACT range: 27–31
Early admission program (EA/ ED/ NA): EA
ED or EA Acceptance Rate: NA
Full time Undergraduate enrollment: 2,365
Total enrollment: NA
Percent Male: 49%
Percent Female: 51%
Total Percent Minority: 15%
Percent African-American: 2%
Percent Asian/Pacific Islander: 7%
Percent Hispanic: 3%
Percent Native-American: NA
Percent Other: NA
Percent in-state / out of state: 79% out

Percent from Public HS: 61%
Retention Rate: 94%
Graduation Rate: 77%
Percent in On-campus housing: 90%
Percent affiliated with Greek system: NA
Percent Varsity or Club Athletes: NA
Number of official organized extracurricular organizations: 75
3 Most popular majors: Economics, English, Psychology
Student/Faculty ratio: 12:01
Tuition and Fees: $22,540.00
Cost for Room and Board: $7,040.00
Percent receiving Financial aid, first-year: 46%

As one of the premiere Christian colleges in the United States, Wheaton College stands apart from secular institutions of higher learning with its motto, "Christo Et Regno Ejus"—"For Christ and His Kingdom." Indeed, this moderate-sized liberal arts college, located in the western suburbs of Chicago, not only provides an excellent education, but also "prepares people to better the kingdom of God," as one student noted. Wheaton College changes lives for those who seek its top-notch academics and community committed to the Christian faith.

In the Christian Classroom

As a liberal arts college, Wheaton requires all students to fulfill a general education requirement in competencies and learning courses. Competencies include foreign language, quantitative skills, oral communication, writing, and Biblical content, while learning courses include studies of faith and reason, philosophy, studies in society, studies in nature, and literature and the arts. In addition, all students must take one course in both the Old and New Testament. Yet, even with the requirements, students do not feel pressured to enroll in classes that they do not enjoy. "There are a lot of options to meet the requirements," said one sophomore.

As a Christian college, Wheaton offers a number of majors that integrate faith and learning along with the more traditional majors. Among the majors distinctive to Wheaton are Biblical and theological studies, Christian education, and various ministry-related music majors. Students report that Biblical studies and Christian education are particularly strong. In general, the high caliber of academics at Wheaton means that no single major stands out as much easier than the others. However, students say that the sciences are the hardest majors at Wheaton. Wheaton also has an excellent Conservatory of Music.

Most students agree that the faculty enhance the challenging curriculum. "The professors are engaging and really passionate about what they teach," said one student. All professors at Wheaton are Christian, and many bring their faith to the classroom. Professors tend to open class with a devotional or thought of the day. Sometimes the devotional relates to class, but "sometimes they just share what's in their hearts." In class and out, the professors "really love interacting with the students." Many students take advantage of special programs that allow students to travel to third world countries to complete service projects, such as building wells or medical clinics.

The Wheaton Covenant

Each semester, students sign an official statement of responsibility and promise to uphold certain Christian values. By signing the Wheaton Covenant, students agree to refrain from smoking, drinking alcohol, and premarital sex. Most students find that the covenant offers more benefits than restrictions. "It helps us know what we stand for," one student commented. Another student added, "I've been really surprised about how true people at Wheaton stay to the whole 'For Christ' thing. It permeates the entire atmosphere." Most students follow the covenant on the major points, but students do acknowledge that everyone does not always live up to its standards. "Obviously, no one's perfect, but in terms of the major things it's generally followed."

> "I've been really surprised about how true people at Wheaton stay to the whole 'For Christ' thing. It permeates the entire atmosphere."

In addition to the covenant, Wheaton students must attend mandatory chapel services three times a week with up to nine excused absences per semester. Although Wheaton requires students to attend chapel, most people enjoy attending the services. According to one student, "At first I thought I wasn't going to like it at all, but we get pretty good speakers like government officials, famous theologians, and authors to come. Chapel is really good."

Social Creativity Required

When asked about the social life at Wheaton, one student responded, "It needs work." Some students feel that they have limited options to socialize at Wheaton, however this is not a pervasive belief. According to some students, "Social life at Wheaton is what you make of it." The campus is dry and there are no fraternities or sororities. Students feel the absence of a traditional frat party lifestyle allows for a more creative social atmosphere. The college hosts events for students such as bringing in popular Christian bands for concerts. Recent concerts have included performances by Jars of Clay and Caedmon's Call. To supplement these more current concerts, students at the Conservatory of Music offer classical performances of their own, which are quite popular among the student body.

Freshmen are not allowed to have cars, but upperclassmen enjoy making quick escapes to local restaurants, bookstores and a giant movie theater complex. One of the bonus features of Wheaton is its proximity to the city of Chicago. Students can walk from the campus to the train station and arrive in downtown Chicago in less than an hour. Students take advantage of the train to shop, catch a baseball game, or to relax on the beautiful Lake Michigan beaches.

Campus Living

Students describe Wheaton's campus as "beautiful" and an "overall really good location for a college." Safety on campus is not an issue for most students at Wheaton. As one student put it, "Wheaton's pretty much one of the safest places you can find." Around campus, students enjoy playing Frisbee outside and hanging out in the recently completed Beamer Center where they can grab a quick bite from the eatery, play pool in the game room, or enjoy a quiet respite in the study rooms or prayer chapel.

All undergraduates live on campus for the first three years. Freshmen live in one of three dorms: Fischer, Traber or Smith. Most freshmen live in Fischer, which is known as the liveliest dorm on campus. In contrast to Fischer, Smith is known as a very studious place. Attached to the side of Smith, Traber houses many of the male athletes. While Wheaton has coed dorms, all floors are single sex. If you want to visit a member of the opposite sex, all dorms are open from seven to midnight on Wednesdays and Fridays, and coed lobbies located in each dorm stay open all the time for people to socialize. Students seem to like the floor rules; "There are always places you can go to hang out with people. It makes the dorms better if you need to do work." Besides the dormitories, some upperclassmen choose to live in college owned apartments.

Some students feel frustrated with Internet access at Wheaton. According to one freshman, "A lot of times it's really super slow." Wheaton also filters their networks for questionable material. Currently only major student centers like the Beamer Center have access to wireless Internet connections.

Finally, Wheaton tends to lack ethnic diversity, but has recently made an effort to increase it. What it lacks in ethnic diversity, it makes up for in Christian diversity within the different denominations. Wheaton attracts believers of all denominations and a considerable amount of international students from missionary families.

Ring by Spring

Many Wheaton students find their spouse by the time they graduate. When a couple gets engaged at Wheaton, tradition dictates they climb the tower at Wheaton and ring the bell. After they ring the bell, the couple leaves a token of their visit in the tower that will stay there forever. One couple left a life-size statue of Amy Grant.

Many students feel that dating at Wheaton is a bit forced. According to one freshman, "There is this idea that if you have dinner with a girl, you're automatically going to get married." However, not all dating need be so serious. Blind dates among different floors allow students to have fun and get to know each other.

Wheaton recently changed its longstanding policy of prohibiting social dancing. Now, the college hosts several dances throughout the year including a swing dance, square dance, and salsa dance. A few days before each dance, the college provides lessons for students who do not know the dances. Wheaton's decision comes with much approval from the student body: "A lot of people go to the dances. They're really fun."

Getting Involved

Athletics play a major role in the extracurricular life at Wheaton. As a NCAA Division III school, Wheaton participates in 21 different sports and competes against other institutions of higher learning in Illinois and Wisconsin. While many students compete in varsity athletics, a majority of the campus participates in intramural activities. These sports run the gamut from inner tube water polo and dodgeball to bowling and sand volleyball.

Wheaton offers a variety of other extracurricular activities. Among many options, some students participate in student government, write for *The Record* (Wheaton's student newspaper), join an improv group, or sing in a choir. Most students also get involved with community service and ministry outreach in the surrounding communities.

A Personal Choice

Wheaton College is not for everyone, but people who choose to go there have, "a really strong connection to the school," as one student said. "You feel that you are connected to something bigger." Indeed, the fusion of excellent academics and devotion to faith at Wheaton College prepares its students to do big things, "For Christ and His Kingdom."—*David Flinner*

FYI

If you come to Wheaton College, you'd better bring: a Bible, time management, and warm clothes.

What's the typical weekend schedule? "Friday night: watch a movie; Saturday afternoon: go to the football game; Saturday night: visit Chicago; Sunday morning: attend church; Sunday night: study"

If I could change one thing about Wheaton College, I'd "give students more control over the Internet."

Three things every student at Wheaton College should do before graduating are "visit Chicago; take Intro to Christian Education with Dr. Root; play an intramural sport."

Indiana

DePauw University

Address: DePauw, 101 E. Seminary St., Greencastle, IN 46135
Phone: 800-447-2495
E-mail Address: admission@depauw.edu
Web site URL: www.depauw.edu
Year Founded: 1837
Private or Public: private
Religious affiliation: United Methodist
Location: rural
Regular Application Deadline: 2-Feb
Number of Applicants: 4,074
Percent Accepted: 68%
Percent Accepted who enroll: 22%
Number Entering: 596
Number of Transfers Accepted each Year: 28
Mean SAT: NA
Mean ACT: NA

Middle 50% SAT range: 1,130–1,330
Middle 50% ACT range: 25–29
Early admission program (EA/ ED/ NA): both
ED or EA Acceptance Rate: ED: 82 EA: 79%
Full time Undergraduate enrollment: 2,276
Total enrollment: 2,326
Percent Male: 44%
Percent Female: 56%
Total Percent Minority: 15%
Percent African-American: 6%
Percent Asian/Pacific Islander: 3%
Percent Hispanic: 5%
Percent Native-American: 1%
Percent Other: 2%
Percent in-state / out of state: 57%/43%
Percent from Public HS: 83%

Retention Rate: 92%
Graduation Rate: 81%
Percent in On-campus housing: 99%
Percent affiliated with Greek system: 75%
Percent Varsity or Club Athletes: NA
Number of official organized extracurricular organizations: 119
3 Most popular majors: economics, English, communications
Student/Faculty ratio: 10:01
Tuition and Fees: $27,780.00
Cost for Room and Board: $7,800.00
Percent receiving Financial aid, first-year: 73%

In the months before the brutal cold of Midwestern winter hits Greencastle, Indiana, students at DePauw University often spend their time playing Campus Golf, "the biggest thing ever." This "uniquely DePauw" sport uses golf clubs and tennis balls on student-created courses all over campus—and occasionally even through buildings! Though probably not what the Methodist Church had in mind when it founded DePauw in 1837, campus golf is characteristic of the fun-loving and friendly student body that DePauw attracts.

An Academic Adventure

Life at DePauw is not all fun, games, and campus golf; rigorous academics are par for the course. Students are required to take a total of 31 course credits drawn from six categories: social and behavioral sciences; natural science and mathematics; foreign language; historical and philosophical understanding; literature and the arts; and self-expression. Students speak highly of the freedom provided by the broad requirements. "I've never been forced to take a math class!" raved one senior. A sophomore agreed, "I'm paying the University and I should be able to decide for myself which classes I want to take." The loose course groupings help "keep students open to new options." Another facet of DePauw's flexible, adventurous approach to learning is Winter Term, held during January. Winter Term is an opportunity for students to take one class intensively for a month with a diminished focus on grades. Students can also use this time to take advantage of off-campus internship opportunities.

DePaul is recognized for being one of the most "connected" campuses in the country. Wireless technology throughout the college allows professors to hold virtual office hours and give exams over the Internet. Fittingly, all incoming freshmen are required to bring laptop computers to school. Under its "361°" initiatives, the University focuses on using new technology to enhance teaching and learning at DePauw.

DePauw has competitive and well-respected honors programs: management fellows focus on pre-business study, media fellows work in print and broadcast media, and science research fellows undertake independent lab research. These programs help ambitious students to foster specific interests, and frequently provide unusual opportunities for their participants. One media fellow said that her class had speaking time with an embedded journalist during the 2003 war in Iraq: "We could hear the tanks in the background. It was amazing."

Classes are widely acknowledged as "challenging but not impossible." Many DePauw students "could have gone to Ivy League schools, but for whatever reason, chose not to," and the intense academic atmosphere means that most are "notoriously over-committed" and "involved in a little bit of everything." This well-roundedness can tend to "hamper [our] ability to do one or a couple of things really well," but students love being able to pursue their many interests.

You Can Run but You Can't Hide

Almost every class at DePauw is small and personal. "I've never been in a class with more than 32 people!" exclaimed a sophomore. Students say that professors are known for developing relationships with students that extend beyond the classroom. "My professors have me over to their houses for dessert, ask me to babysit their kids, and would do anything for me," said a senior. Students admit that the small setting does have some downsides: "You will never be able to remain anonymous, take a nap, or skip class without it being noticed." Another student's biggest complaint was about the comfort of the classrooms: "Some of the desks are really uncomfortable. They kill my back."

Several students commented on the "interesting dynamic" that exists between the "very liberal" professors and the politically "moderate to conservative" student body but agree that there "is a lot of mutual respect" that extends beyond political lean-

ings. Overall, students agree that they "love most of the professors" and that "they are good teachers." Some students complain that professors have become increasingly reliant on technology for homework assignments and grading. Professors reportedly "overuse" the online homework system and "take a lot of liberties with the e-mail system and expect us to check our computers every 10 minutes." However, most students believe that professors will tailor their use to student feedback in the future.

Greencastle Goes Greek

At DePauw, "the party scene is the Greek scene." Students speak highly of the Greek system, and over 70 percent of the student body belongs to one of the 14 fraternities and 11 sororities. Most agree that Greek life at DePauw is different from the Greek scene at other colleges simply because "it's not a cut-throat thing." Since almost everyone rushes, "it's really laid back. If you want to be in the Greek system, you can be in the Greek system." Most students look at it as "a tradition and a place to live." One sorority girl raved, "I love it. I live with 60 great girls in a beautiful house." Though most Greeks drink on the weekends, students say that non-drinkers are "never pressured" to participate in that aspect of Greek life.

> **"The party scene is the Greek scene."**

For "independents," students who choose not to join a Greek house, life at DePauw is markedly different. Being a "God-Damned Independent (GDI) does carry a stigma, and you can become ostracized as an arrogant elitist pretty easily. You have to try harder not to become antisocial," said a junior. Still, the average DePauw student, Greek and non-Greek alike, is friendly and outgoing, so that "once you go out and make connections, people come to accept that you're not just that weirdo who prefers dancing to AC/DC in front of his mirror" over hanging out in a frat house. Many students agree that another problem with the Greek system is that it "encourages and perpetuates an attitude of casual intimacy and stamps out the possibility of serious, and even not so serious, dating" said a student. Students say that, when they do occur, relationships tend to be long-term and with students outside of DePauw.

Some students stress that it is possible to have fun at DePauw outside the Greek scene. As one sophomore put it, "I would argue with the naysayers who insist that there is nothing to do. Any time you have a group of students, you can think of something fun to do. Having a good time in Greencastle just requires a little creativity." Besides, "all you really need for fun is Wal-Mart, anyway, and we have one of those," according to another. There is also a plethora of college-sponsored activities like movie nights, get-togethers, and music jams hosted by various organizations.

The college certainly adds some spice to the otherwise "pretty dull" rural town vibe in Greencastle. Still, a few popular restaurants bring students into town. Students frequent Marvin's, a "greasy spoon" famous for the garlic cheeseburger students have nicknamed the "GCB;" "cute" coffee shops like Gathering Grounds; and bars like the Fluttering Duck, Topper's, and Third Degree. Many students are fond of taking short road trips to nearby Indianapolis, or "Indy." Because many of DePauw's students are from in-state, upper-middle class families, cars are never difficult to come by and freshmen are allowed to have them on campus. Several students mentioned that this allows DePauw students "a sense of independence" which makes Greencastle a little less claustrophobic.

Life Is Beautiful at DePauw

What DePauw lacks in urban excitement, it makes up for in the rural charm of "small town America": namely, safety, physical beauty, and comfort. Students report that the campus is a place "where you never have to lock your doors." "I leave my stuff all over school and I never worry that it will be taken," claimed a freshman. Greencastle itself is mostly farmland and the campus "is always green and gorgeous." When the weather is nice, students gather around the pond at Bowman Park for "concerts, movies, and hanging out." The "picturesque" buildings receive high praise from students, particularly East College, one of DePauw's oldest structures. The University prohibits off-campus living, so students either live in the dorms or with their fraternity or sorority. Freshmen are required to live in the dorms, which are "very nice, though a little small." Most dorm floors are coed and

the bathrooms are communal. Apartment-style dorm housing is open to upperclassmen. Many students choose to live in their Greek house after sophomore year because "it's basically like living in a mansion." The food at DePauw is decent but unexciting. One junior advised, "Cereal is always a good backup." Most Greeks take meals in their houses, which students agree is generally more entertaining and less costly than eating in the dining halls.

Athletics and "the Game"

The DePauw student body is athletic and fit, even though the school's teams compete in Division III and do not offer athletic scholarships. Many students compete in intramurals, which provide a more relaxed forum to "continue the sports they played in high school." Golf, women's soccer, and women's tennis are among the most successful varsity teams, though students say that few go to watch the games. Students insist that this is not from a lack of DePauw pride but rather an unfortunate consequence of the hectic schedules most students create for themselves.

There is one notable exception to the lack of athletic spirit at DePauw. The Monon Bell game, often simply known as "the Game," is as clear an indication as any of the fierce love and pride DePauw students have for their school. The Game, against nearby rival Wabash College, is one of the oldest football rivalries west of the Appalachian Mountains. Despite the fact that "we're both these tiny schools," the Game is "a really big deal. Alumni pay a huge amount of money for tickets." Each year, the victorious school keeps the Monon Bell, which is "bolted into a glass case" when it is at DePauw. This tight security was imposed after a group of Wabash students tried to steal the bell from DePauw a few years ago. The near disaster amplified the rivalry to an unprecedented and enjoyable intensity.

Homogeny and Acceptance

Students say that DePauw's reputation does not seem to extend far beyond the Midwest, and that the student body reflects this homogeneity. However, administrators are working to recruit minority students and students from areas beyond the Midwestern states. With such a friendly, outgoing, accepting student body, students say it is only a matter of time before DePauw's population better reflects the makeup of the country. Students "always say hi to each other" and "you can meet people as you walk to class."

There are social "pockets that are a bit more eclectic or extreme" than the rest of the population and there is a visible, widely accepted gay, lesbian, bisexual, and transgender organization. "A casual atmosphere" is DePauw's most pervasive characteristic,

and it's not uncommon to see things like a "woman in sweatpants, a baseball hat, and a T-shirt sitting next to her friend who is wearing high heels, a skirt, and a sweater." "Everyone has their own style and everyone can find a niche," and for the most part, people "will accept you for who you are."— *Claire Gagne*

FYI

If you come to DePauw, you'd better bring a "a car, or a friend with a car" and "a cell phone, but make sure it gets reception in Greencastle."

What is a typical weekend schedule? "Friday and Saturday, take a nap, study, scrounge for food, hang out with friends, go to a Greek party; Sunday, study, work, hang out, work."

If I could change one thing about DePauw, I would "make it more diverse. We need more unusual, artistic, ethnic, and diverse people."

Three things every student at DePauw should do before graduating are "eat a GCB or Veggie GCB, do a Boulder Run (even if you're in your undies), and make lasting friendships with the people here."

Earlham College

Address: Earlham, 801 National Road West, Richmond, IN 47374
Phone: 765-983-1200
E-mail Address: admissions@earlham.edu
Web site URL: www.earlham.edu
Year Founded: 1847
Private or Public: private
Religious affiliation: Seminonery, Society of Friends (Quaker)
Location: suburban
Regular Application Deadline: 16-Feb
Number of Applicants: 1,554
Percent Accepted: 68%
Percent Accepted who enroll: 27%
Number Entering: 314
Number of Transfers Accepted each Year: 49
Mean SAT: 1,200

Mean ACT: 26
Middle 50% SAT range: 1,100–1,350
Middle 50% ACT range: 24–29
Early admission program (EA/ ED/ NA): both
ED or EA Acceptance Rate: ED: 95 EA: 79%
Full time Undergraduate enrollment: 1,206
Total enrollment: 1,345
Percent Male: 47%
Percent Female: 53%
Total Percent Minority: 10%
Percent African-American: 7%
Percent Asian/Pacific Islander: 2%
Percent Hispanic: 1%
Percent Native-American: 0%
Percent Other: 10%
Percent in-state / out of state: 32%/68%

Percent from Public HS: 68%
Retention Rate: 82%
Graduation Rate: 70%
Percent in On-campus housing: 87%
Percent affiliated with Greek system: 0%
Percent Varsity or Club Athletes: NA
Number of official organized extracurricular organizations: 70
Most popular majors: History, Psychology
Student/Faculty ratio: 12:01
Tuition and Fees: $29,320.00
Cost for Room and Board: $6,200.00
Percent receiving Financial aid, first-year: 84%

Earlham College, located in the heart of Middle America, is a Quaker school, a fact that colors every aspect of campus life. Even the sports teams are called the Quakers. Advisory committees, comprised of both students and faculty, make the decisions that govern both the current state and future direction of the college—all reached by consensus, of course. Everyone is referred to by his or her first name—the current president is affectionately referred to as "Dougie B."

The school's Quaker heritage contributes to its overall emphasis on fostering individual growth. As one third year explained, "The education here is geared towards individual learning, and if you expect to be spoon fed a degree and then feel accomplished, you'll be sadly mistaken."

From India to Indiana

Through different study abroad programs, to numerous small classes and seminars taught by professors who are actively interested in their students, Earlham offers countless academic opportunities that are there for the taking. All freshmen (or first years, as they are called at Earlham) must take two reading and writing intensive seminars. The topics of each class vary from year to year, but they often are, as one student put it, "whatever the professor is passionate about." And with class size capped at 15, there is plenty of room for professors to pass this enthusiasm onto their students. "You leave the class and everyone's still discussing the topic," recalls one second year. With subjects such as the History of Sexuality in the Nineteenth and Twentieth Centuries to Religion: For or Against the Common Good, these courses work to provide first years with an introduction to the ins and outs of Earlham academic life.

Another defining emphasis of an Earlham education is its international focus. Earlham not only attracts a large number of international students, but the college also boasts a great number of its own programs run by Earlham professors in countries around the globe. The travel opportunities offered by such programs (some remain in one city, while others take students on guided tours throughout specific areas) in conjunction with the expertise of professors, largely accounts for the popularity of studying abroad for Earlhamites.

> "[Professors] are always available to answer questions individually and personally connect with students. I don't even know what a T.A. is."

Whether they are in India or in Indiana, Earlham professors are always more than willing to work and learn with their students. "They are always available to answer questions individually and personally connect with students. I don't even know what a T.A. is," one senior asserted. Through their "enlightening discussion-based classes," professors are able to work closely with their students. "I came planning to be a journalist and pretty quickly changed to politics mostly because of my professor . . . many professors here are inspiring and completely change the direction people go," one student said.

Hymnals and "Hash"

Outside the classroom, Earlham students can immerse themselves in a variety of extracurricular activities and sports. And if there is a part of campus life or the Earlham administration that does not satisfy students they can join a committee that addresses that particular issue. One popular committee is the Admissions and Financial Aid Advisory Committee, which recently redrafted the Earlham application. Another popular student group is the International Education Committee, which focuses on revising and expanding Earlham's international focus. As members with positions equal to the faculty that also serve on these committees, students have a great impact in creating their own college experience.

Earlham is, in the words of one student "not a jock school." But even though "our teams suck, we are still really proud of them." Soccer, for example, never fails to draw a crowd of enthusiastic Earlhamites who sing "uproaringly funny fight songs at sports games." More often than not, students (lovingly) poke fun at their school through these cheers. In fact, the cheers themselves have been printed into a "hymnal," so that generations after generations can use them to reflect their own quirky sense of school spirit.

Although students at Earlham seem to be more than content with their choice of school, one common complaint concerns the surrounding town of Richmond. But as one student put it, "Indiana is what you make of it." Luckily, there are a number of cities within driving distance that can keep students entertained when not on busy on campus.

In fact, the on-campus activities at Earlham often make students reluctant to leave, even when they have the chance. And with few other alternatives, there is a high turnout for many of the larger events sponsored by Earlham. "This makes for a good sense of campus cohesion," one senior noted. "Everyone gets to know everyone." Furthermore, the creativity of students, when it comes to finding ways to entertain themselves, is second to none. Many rave about the "quirky theme parties" that are thrown on the weekends, with some past favorites including, "Come As Your Favorite Lesbian" and "Seventh Grade."

Even though Earlham is a dry campus, one junior claimed that, "Earlham tacitly accepts and does not punish many of the known drinking gatherings that occur on a regular basis." One of the most popular of these events is an off-campus party known as "the Hash." "People gather together at two or three on a Saturday afternoon . . . they [sing] a little song while holding hands," a freshman explained. After that, students follow a long and winding flour path around campus that eventually ends at the keg provided somewhere in the 600-acre "back campus." This unconventional approach to partying is undoubtedly characteristic of the adventurous nature of the Earlham student body.

Home Away From Home

Earlham housing offers a variety of options from which students can choose. All first years live in dorms, but after that, students can choose to stay in the dorms, or move into on-campus houses (usually theme houses dedicated to a particular culture or concept). For the truly adventurous, there is an opportunity to live and work on Earlham's Miller Farm. "It has a three story treehouse with a fire pole!" one junior exclaimed.

And for those who are thinking about venturing to off-campus housing (the majority of which is owned by Earlham itself), be wary. Many students have suffered from a small sense of regret. As one student explained, "As mushy as it is to say, we have a wonderful campus community . . . I often feel that I miss out on some of that by being off campus."

Earlham's international focus, combined with the creativity of its students and its Quaker roots, enable the college to offer an unforgettable educational experience, in and out of the classroom. "In the residence halls, classes, dining halls and everywhere else on campus, I am constantly engaged," one senior said. "I am challenged in my assumptions and beliefs almost everywhere I go."—*Stephanie Brockman*

FYI

If you come to Earlham, you'd better bring a "Sense of independence and willingness to find things out for yourself."

What is the typical weekend schedule? "A concert, dirt-cheap beer, a theme party, reading, and papers."

If I could change one thing about Earlham, I'd "Put it closer to a big city, or have more things of interest in a closer radius."

Three things every student at Earlham should do before graduating are "go off campus for a semester, take a random class outside of your major and interest area and serve on Earlham Student Government in some way."

Indiana University

Address: Indiana University, Bloomington, 300 North Jordan Avenue, Bloomington, IN 47405
Phone: 812-855-0661
E-mail Address: iuadmit@indiana.edu
Web site URL: www.iub.edu
Year Founded: 1820
Private or Public: public
Religious affiliation: none
Location: urban
Regular Application Deadline: NA
Number of Applicants: NA
Percent Accepted: 80%
Percent Accepted who enroll: 38%
Number Entering: NA
Number of Transfers Accepted each Year: NA
Mean SAT: 1,121
Mean ACT: 25

Middle 50% SAT range: 490–610V, 510–630M
Middle 50% ACT range: 22–27
Early admission program (EA/ ED/ NA): 4/1 ("priority")
ED or EA Acceptance Rate: NA
Full time Undergraduate enrollment: 29,258
Total enrollment: NA
Percent Male: 48%
Percent Female: 52%
Total Percent Minority: 12%
Percent African-American: 5%
Percent Asian/Pacific Islander: 4%
Percent Hispanic: 2%
Percent Native-American: 0%
Percent Other: 4%
Percent in-state / out of state: 70%/30%

Percent from Public HS: NA
Retention Rate: 88%
Graduation Rate: 50%
Percent in On-campus housing: 36%
Percent affiliated with Greek system: NA
Percent Varsity or Club Athletes: NA
Number of official organized extracurricular organizations: NA
3 Most popular majors: marketing
Student/Faculty ratio: 18:01
Tuition and Fees: $18,498
In State Tuition and Fees (if different): $5,507
Cost for Room and Board: $6,352.00
Percent receiving Financial aid, first-year: 56%

Recently highlighted in the film *Kinsey*, Indiana University may be best known for its powerhouse basketball team. Yet while it's true that the Hoosiers "live for IU basketball," Indiana has much to offer in many areas, and students are bound to find many things that meet their interests.

Lots of Choices

There are many different schools within IU in which undergraduates can enroll, including the prestigious business and music schools as well as the College of Arts and Sciences. Basic requirements for the College of Arts and Sciences are split into three groups: "fundamental skills" that include studying a foreign language for four semesters; "distribution requirements" that encompass humanities and sciences courses; and the credits required for one's major. As one student said, "you definitely leave here being a well-rounded student whether you like it or not."

As might be expected from a large school such as IU, there are many enormous lecture courses. These are split up into sections led by TAs, however, and there are also plenty of courses available that have far fewer people in them. Students are informed of the projected class size when they register for a class, so it's possible to avoid big or small classes, depending on your fancy.

Though sometimes tough to deal with, IU's size makes a wide variety of classes possible. There is also an Honors College that offers special classes for those looking for that extra challenge, though some students cite the regular departments as being challenging enough. Students tend to consider the English department tough to earn an A from, as well as the PE department, strangely enough. (The PE department formally ensures its classes are challenging enough to deter anyone looking for an easy A.)

Additionally, "some math classes can be almost impossible because many of the associate instructors don't speak English very well so it makes math hard, even when it's not." But, notes one student, "there's really something here for everyone academic-wise. If you are an idiot and you just want to get in and party and get out, there's a class for you. If you are a genius and want to be challenged in every class, then that can also be arranged. So really it all works out."

Big and Beautiful

On-campus living at IU is comparable to most colleges. As one student puts it, "dorms suck—I think that's a universal thing." Yet there are many options available, and most students are generally happy with their living situation. While the majority of the people living on campus are freshmen, there are many different dormitories, most of which contain students of all years. Upon enrollment, students can choose whether they want to spend their first year in residential communities designated for different undergrad schools and the honors program. Residence Halls are divided into three distinct "neighborhoods"—Northwest, Central, and Southeast. Most dorms are coed by floor, and each floor has an RA, who is there "just in case." Students seem content with their RAs, who do not have a reputation of being too strict. Despite this, however, most people do leave campus after their freshman year. Those who do continue with University housing often opt for on-campus apartments.

The campus itself is, according to student after student, beautiful. Says one: "Trying to get around can be difficult because it's just so beautiful here. There are so many trees." Water runs through the campus in several places, and willow trees adorn the streams. "The only problem," warns one student, "is the allergies. The school is in BLOOMINGton."

Not only beautiful, students describe a very comfortable existence with the surrounding town, probably because, as one put it, "the school is the town." Bloomington offers everything the typical college town should, including several vintage clothing stores and lots of music places, trendy shops and tons of great places to eat. As another student describes, "the downtown area is very charming . . . we had a large art festival two weekends ago, and a world music festival here last weekend."

A stark contrast to bustling small-town Bloomington is its surroundings. Outside the town limits are endless cornfields, and the city of Indianapolis is 45 minutes away. Students often take road trips there or to Chicago and St. Louis to find the excitement of big cities. Because the school and surrounding town are so intimate, the police presence seems "unnecessary," but is there to ensure safety at all times.

There are several dining halls around

campus that are set up food-court style, with food priced per item. The Edmondson Dining Hall at Collins offers a home-style buffet, but at a fixed price per meal. Meal plans are basically meal points put onto student ID cards, which then work like a debit card. One student complains, "The dining hall food is dining hall food. It's not bad but it's not great. It just gets old, and the food is very overpriced." Other Hoosiers find comfort in the fact that, "you can always find hamburgers or pizza."

In addition, students often frequent the many restaurants around town. IU is also home to the nation's largest student center, a huge building that houses restaurants, a bookstore, a bowling alley, pool tables, a movie theater and a four-star hotel.

Greek Mansions

The social life at IU is varied, and can be limited if you are not yet 21 (or not equipped with a fake ID). One student humorously remarks that "there is a saying in Bloomington—'Bloomington: a drinking town with a basketball problem.' " There are a lot of bars around and a lot of bands that come and play 21+ shows, but "if you aren't 21 yet those suck." Alcohol does not seem to rule the social scene, however. "Not everyone drinks and that's fine, nobody really cares whether you drink or not," explains one student. Policemen on campus do bust parties, so watch out. Alcohol rules are reportedly sometimes taken seriously.

> **"People smile as they walk by and a lot of people will even say hi, whether they know you or not."**

Other than the bars, most things in town close relatively early. Perhaps partly for this reason, the Greek system exerts a certain amount of influence on campus. One student remarks, "the Greek houses are amazing. They look like mansions." For the most part, however, no one cares if you are Greek or not and IU is a very comfortable place to be overall. "People here are very friendly, that's something I noticed the first time I was on campus. People smile as they walk by and a lot of people will even say hi, whether they know you or not." Students also describe IU as being a diverse environment where everyone feels like they fit in

and have a place to go. To help support diversity efforts, the school recently established a Center on Diversity.

The biggest social event at IU is unquestionably the "Little 500," an enormous bike race, immortalized in the film *Breaking Away*, where clubs, organizations and everyone else on campus participate. The entire week is filled with parties and fun, and the event unites the whole campus.

Hoosier Hysteria

The IU basketball team, formerly coached by Bobby Knight, is known throughout the country, and the students at IU rally behind their team in a way only they can. School spirit peaks during March Madness, which is known on campus as "Hoosier Hysteria." Student turnout at the games is excellent, and tickets are easily attainable. One student describes the basketball atmosphere: "I love sports and I've been to many pro and college events, but NOTHING compares to the experience and the rush you get at an IU basketball game." School spirit extends to more than just the basketball team. As one student explains, "IU is a Big Ten school, so we try to compete." The football team "is worse than bad but they try and it's fun to go to those games anyway. A lot of people tailgate before the game and never make it in; either way it's fun." For varsity athletes and everyone else, the sports facilities on campus are "awesome," including a nice basketball court, a new football field, and a recreational gym. Many students play intramurals, including serious athletes and those who just want a break from homework.

In addition to sports, students also devote time to other extracurriculars. There are hundreds of student organizations, and "people are pretty committed to what they do." A lot of students also hold jobs at places like the mall, local restaurants, the movie theater, on campus, or at the food courts.

Though IU's large size can be somewhat overwhelming, it makes a lot possible. Consequently, there is something for everyone at IU, whether you're looking for a school devoted to its teams, an academic challenge or a specific organization. The beautiful surroundings and a school spirit that inspires Hollywood can't hurt either.
—*Kevin Davis*

Purdue University

Address: Purdue, Schleman Hall of Student Services, West Lafayette, IN 47907-2050
Phone: 765-494-1776
E-mail Address: admissions@purdue.edu
Web site URL: www.purdue.edu
Year Founded: 1869
Private or Public: public
Religious affiliation: none
Location: small city
Application and Admissions Information: rolling
Regular Application Deadline: NA
Number of Applicants: NA
Percent Accepted: NA
Percent Accepted who enroll: NA
Number Entering: NA

Number of Transfers Accepted each Year: NA
Mean SAT: 1,129
Mean ACT: 25
Middle 50% SAT range: NA
Middle 50% ACT range: NA
Early admission program (EA/ ED/ NA): NA
ED or EA Acceptance Rate: NA
Full time Undergraduate enrollment: 30,545
Total enrollment: 39,228
Percent Male: 59%
Percent Female: 41%
Total Percent Minority: 13%
Percent African-American: NA
Percent Asian/Pacific Islander: NA
Percent Hispanic: NA
Percent Native-American: NA
Percent Other: NA

Percent in-state / out of state: NA
Percent from Public HS: NA
Retention Rate: NA
Graduation Rate: NA
Percent in On-campus housing: NA
Percent affiliated with Greek system: NA
Percent Varsity or Club Athletes: NA
Number of official organized extracurricular organizations: NA
3 Most popular majors: NA
Student/Faculty ratio: NA
Tuition and Fees: $20,870.00
In State Tuition and Fees (if different): $6,700.00

Purdue University boasts about being one of the best engineering and physics schools in the nation. After all, one of Purdue's most famous alumni is astronaut Neil Armstrong. Purdue offers students a wide variety of excellent academic programs, along with a longstanding legacy of superior athletics, all in a lively and safe environment.

While Purdue University's main campus is in West Lafayette, Indiana, the University also has a number of campuses (some in conjunction with Indiana University) that are mainly commuter schools, although some offer housing. Whether or not students choose to transfer from these schools to the West Lafayette campus, they receive diplomas with the powerful Purdue name.

Engineering, Physics and . . .

Purdue is best known for its top-ranked engineering, computer science and physics programs, but it also offers particularly well-respected opportunities in the pharmaceutical sciences, business management, and veterinarian sciences. In these three subjects (on both the undergraduate and graduate level) Purdue consistently ranks among the top 15 in the nation. Despite the large number of strong programs, statistics reveal that about one-fifth of all undergraduates thought about, attempted to, or did major in engineering at Purdue.

Engineering majors do not have much space for electives in their schedules, but Purdue offers incredible diversity for students pursuing other programs. The over 200 available majors attract many students seeking a wide range of options. Popular courses include glass blowing in the chemistry department, flower arranging in the horticulture department and "wine appreciation" in the food science department. The wine appreciation class is an example of the interesting and unexpected academics found at Purdue University. The recently retired professor who taught the class for 15 years has a world-renowned reputation that helped make Purdue (and the state of Indiana) the chosen host for many wineries and international wine tasting events.

At a school this size, popular and introductory classes are bound to be big. Indeed, intro-level classes range anywhere from 200 to 450 plus. But as students progress and take higher level courses, class size decreases. While the large size of some classes may seem daunting at first, most students say that it does not significantly detract from the quality of the class, as most teachers use equipment that makes it easy for the entire class to see and hear the teacher.

As for grades, one engineer said that Purdue "does not have grade inflation, nor should you expect it to." However, liberal arts, interior design and elementary education are generally considered easier.

The Social Situation

Greek organizations on campus play a major role in the social scene. In previous years, hazing and alcohol violations by various fraternities and sororities have caused some concern. However, hazing is now practically non-existent on campus (except for the few horror stories) because of a strict no-hazing policy supported both by Purdue and by the Greek houses themselves. This change occurred recently after several fraternities had their licenses suspended for hazing activities. Of course, some mild hazing still goes on, but most students accept it as part of the rush process. In fact some students even think that the campus cracks down on hazing too much, because "hazing that just involves the rushees doing push-ups is fine." Despite the campus's strict policy on alcohol, many Greeks have continued to party and drink. Police visits, though few in number, have often ended with disputes in court.

While the freshmen and sophomores flock to the frat parties, upperclassmen tend to hang out in the local bars. The bars nearby are concentrated in one area, and the popular local bars are Where Else, the Cactus, the Wabash Yacht Club and Harry's Chocolate Shop. Harry's Chocolate Shop was once a chocolate shop and soda fountain, but was renovated into a bar. Where Else is extremely popular on Wednesday nights for its beer pong contest. During the second to last week of classes in the spring semester, the Grand Prix (a go-cart racing tournament) calls for a week of partying on campus. Luckily, Purdue's campus is generally considered extremely safe, even late at night. As one student said, "it's one of the benefits of living in the middle of nowhere."

For those seeking a tamer scene, there are plenty of alternatives to parties, including campus movie theaters with nine screens each, restaurants such as Triple XXX (Indiana's first drive-in restaurant, named after Triple XXX root beer), and local malls. Triple XXX is especially known for its biscuits, gravy and Duane Purvis All-American, a hamburger with peanut butter. Students are known to frequent Triple XXX at all times during the day—including the morning—since it's open 24 hours a day, six days a week.

> "While there is still a lot of interaction between all groups of people, finding your niche will help tremendously."

While there is a great deal of interaction between students of all backgrounds, social groups are often formed along racial and ethnic lines—perhaps due to the intimidating size of the school. As one student said, "In the end, finding your group of friends is very important. While there is still a lot of interaction between all groups of people, finding your niche will help tremendously."

The Train, Purdue Pete and Rowdy

While most schools have only one or mascot, Purdue boasts three, though only one is official. The train, known as the "Boilermaker Special IV", is a Victorian conception aiming to exemplify the tradition and excellence of engineering. Purdue Pete, the notable fiberglass head and hard hat, with hammer in hand, is a tradition from the '60s. Last but not least is Rowdy, Pete's younger brother, who one day hopes to be a Boilermaker.

School spirit at Purdue is strong, especially when it comes to athletics. Purdue enjoys its status as part of the Big Ten and boasts such a strong football program that football games become an event in themselves. Tailgating, both before and after the game, allows for great parties and barbecues during the weekends, and the marching band entertains the devoted fans. The strong school spirit also carries over to both the men's and women's basketball teams. Tickets for games at Mackey Arena (for basketball) sell out quickly, and the showing at every football game is quite strong.

Football at Purdue has several long standing traditions. One of them is the annual game against Indiana University, where the winner keeps the Old Oaken Bucket, a traveling trophy that signifies the schools' strong rivalry. The other is the "Breakfast Club" a longstanding tradition (if you are 21 and over) which is like "Halloween every Saturday." Seniors dress up in costumes, hit local bars in the morning to drink, and then head to the football game to cheer for the team in their costumes. Of course, if you can't wake up before the game (we are talking about college students), you can still go to the bars after the game to join in the tradition.

Even students who are not on varsity teams still seem to be heavily involved with sports on campus, especially in intramurals. The huge sports complex, Co-Rec as its called, has everything you could possibly want from the expected weights, basketball, handball, and squash courts, to a 50-meter indoor pool, a diving well with a 10-meter platform, and a "ridiculous" number of tennis courts.

While sports are certainly a big part of Purdue, no tuition money goes directly into the sports program. Instead, sports programs at Purdue are funded solely by individual contribution. In this sense, football and men's and women's basketball are unique programs in that they actually generate revenue.

The *Flat* Campus

Purdue's campus stretches over a wide, flat terrain about one mile long, and dormitories are all together in one location relatively far away from central campus. For those who live on campus, cars are a "necessity if you would like to do something other than study." A popular alternative to cars is the Lafayette-West Lafayette bus system, which is free to students, but less popular. The central campus is relatively compact, making it easy to get around by foot. Sophomores and freshmen typically choose to live in frat houses or dorms, and end up occupying almost all of the available on-campus housing. First-year students are housed in doubles in a mainly freshman dorm. While it is not recommended for freshmen to bring cars, cars become a necessity for the upperclassmen who decide to move away from central campus. Upperclassmen private apartments are mostly located closer to the bars and stadiums, and the campus apartments offered by the school are also pretty far from central campus. One student said that the apartments "are so far away that I don't see why anybody would live there.". Parking is a big problem on campus—not only is it difficult to find legal parking spaces, but the police are strict about enforcing the time limits.

Purdue is in the middle of renovating its dining halls. The renovated dining halls are described as "pretty good," and they've even been nationally recognized, but the old ones are "less preferable" since they only serve "standard fare." The meal plan at Purdue consists of a weekly number of meal swipes and supplementary dining dollars, which can be used at on-campus mini-marts and grills. Dining dollars allow for flexibility in the plan and PDQ (Purdue Dining Quickly) allows students to use swipes on the go.

"All of the campus buildings are red brick and square," one student complained. Except for the Rawls Hall and Kannert building, which are made of limestone, all of the campus is built in classic red brick. Legend has it that John Purdue required that all of the campus buildings be made of red brick or all of his inheritance would go to his heirs. While Rawls Hall and Kannert Hall are both evidence that the legend is false, each has included red brick as part of its foundation to keep up with the tradition.

Diversity and the "Strategic Plan"

For a public university, Purdue enrolls a large percentage of international and minority students: international students comprise about 12 percent of the student body, while American minorities make up an additional 12 percent.. While this figure cannot rival the percentage at top private universities, it has been increasing as a result of a new plan. Since 2001, Purdue has been implementing its "Strategic Plan," which aims to expand diversity on campus, as well as decrease the student-faculty ratio, increase interdisciplinary research opportunities, and make a stand for new innovations in technology facilities and economic development

Full of Surprises

In general, Purdue really surprises its students; it even has a nuclear reactor. While the University has its roots in agriculture and engineering, and continues to be one of the premier schools in engineering, Purdue's friendly atmosphere, variety of strong academics, lively social scene and abundant school spirit make a Boilermaker education great for engineers and non-engineers alike.—*Jesse Dong*

FYI

If you come to Purdue, you'd better bring "both a fan and winter gear—the winters are too cold, and during the hot weeks of summer, air conditioners are not allowed."

What is the typical weekend schedule? "Spend Friday and Saturday involved with sports and/or club activities. Then party on Friday and Saturday night. Sunday (and sometimes Saturday) you do the all of your last-minute homework."

If I could change one thing about Purdue, I'd "add more arts and live entertainment venues and events here."

Three things every student at Purdue should do before graduating are "join the Breakfast Club, run through all the water fountains, and stand underneath the bell tower."

Rose-Hulman Institute of Technology

Address: Rose-Hulman, 5500 Wabash Avenue, Terre Haute, IN 47803
Phone: 800-248-7448
E-mail Address: admissions@rose-hulman.edu
Web site URL: www.rose-hulman.edu
Year Founded: 1874
Private or Public: private
Religious affiliation: none
Location: suburban
Regular Application Deadline: 1-Mar
Number of Applicants: 3,059
Percent Accepted: 70%
Percent Accepted who enroll: 25%
Number Entering: 500
Number of Transfers Accepted each Year: 40
Mean SAT: NA
Mean ACT: NA

Middle 50% SAT range: 1,250–1,400
Middle 50% ACT range: 28–32
Early admission program (EA/ ED/ NA): NA
ED or EA Acceptance Rate: NA
Full time Undergraduate enrollment: 1,900
Total enrollment: 1,975
Percent Male: 79%
Percent Female: 21%
Total Percent Minority: 8%
Percent African-American: 2%
Percent Asian/Pacific Islander: 1%
Percent Hispanic: 2%
Percent Native-American: 0%
Percent Other: 3%
Percent in-state / out of state: 40%/60%

Percent from Public HS: 74%
Retention Rate: 92%
Graduation Rate: 82%
Percent in On-campus housing: 60%
Percent affiliated with Greek system: 40%
Percent Varsity or Club Athletes: 25%
Number of official organized extracurricular organizations: 61
Most popular majors: Mechanical Engineering
Student/Faculty ratio: 12:01
Tuition and Fees: $29,040.00
Cost for Room and Board: $7,950.00
Percent receiving Financial aid, first-year: 91%

Rose-Hulman Institute of Technology is a small technology/specialty school of about 2,000 students located amidst trees and rolling hills on the fringes of Terre Haute, Indiana. Rose is a utopia for those students who value a quality education over a name-brand university. It offers a more relaxed environment than its rivals, as cutthroat competition is unheard of. Because of this balance between rigor and relaxation, students are genuinely happy to be at Rose-Hulman.

Tough as Nails

Most Rose students were accustomed to getting As in high school, but things quickly change for them at Rose, where Bs are only feasible for those who work hard. Indeed, students don't exaggerate the work load when they claim "straight As are really rare." On the other hand, if the rumors are true, no student who attends every class has ever failed a course either.

There are few easy routes to a diploma, though students agree that certain majors such as civil engineering aren't as demanding as others. The most popular majors are "anything engineering," such as mechanical engineering, electrical engineering, chemical engineering, or computer engineering. Regardless of a student's major, one sure bet is that "most students are lucky if they get five hours of sleep a night because they are doing homework all night." Despite Rose students' work ethic, "students here don't tend to compete with each other. We work cooperatively. Rose really stresses group projects and practical experience."

The first two years are considered the most difficult, but luckily, the work load improves after that. The sophomore curriculum is known to be brutal because it consists of classes that teach the basics for all the disciplines. Students can count on help from their professors, since they have "very good relationships." Professors often give students their home phone numbers in case they ever need help outside of office hours and professors "will help students with work for other classes as well." They are clearly "willing to put in extra hours to help students and [they] make an effort to get to know the students, and really care about us," says one student. One notorious professor, Dr. Rickert, "can solve two different math problems at the same time on the board—solving one with each hand. This is true." He also races against the computer math program, Maple, and wins sometimes. Moreover, all classes at Rose are taught by professors, though TAs are also available to help students with questions.

In spite of the work load, students are truly happy and say that the school is all they expected. One student says, "The teachers are nice, the work is challenging, and I have made a lot of new friends." Also impressive is Rose's record of nearly 100-percent job placement rate for graduating seniors and its rank in *U.S. News & World Report* as the top college in math, science, and engineering for the last seven years running, proving that the hard work is definitely worth the trouble. As one student puts it, "Rose-Hulman has given me opportunities that I could never have found anywhere else. Its supportive environment has helped me grow to become the person I am today."

When They Aren't Studying

Rose-Hulman has over 60 clubs and organizations, and students are encouraged to create a club if they can't find one that suits their needs. Apparently, "The Gun Club" has a high membership, though students are "not sure if that's to relieve stress or what." Drama, WMHD radio, Student government, the student newspaper, yearbook, and other major-related clubs are also very popular, and people are dedicated to their organizations "but class work comes first."

Intramurals are also competitive; students compete in tennis, Ultimate Frisbee, indoor soccer, and flag football—regardless of their skill level. Since Rose is a Division III school, it can't give athletic scholarships and this enhances the all-around feeling that classes take precedence in life at Rose. Varsity football and basketball games, however, still manage to draw fairly big crowds. Rose is also not without its own traditions. Each year during homecoming the freshmen build a huge bonfire and guard it all week from the sophomores who try to knock it down. In past years, the bonfire has been enormous and required air-traffic monitors, but the fire department has started enforcing stricter rules.

Beautiful, Safe Campus Living

Half of Rose's buildings have been built in the last 15 years, so it has a pretty modern feel: "the campus is cozy and pretty, with two little ponds in the center, some woods and lots of deer and squirrels." Rose has a small campus and everything is within walking distance. Those students less concerned about their appearance can roll out of bed 10 minutes before class and still make it there on time. Students are described as "geeky—few people make time to dress up, and some people wear pajamas to morning classes."

The campus is generally considered beautiful, and is improving everyday. Recent renovations include the multimillion-dollar Sports and Recreation Center, the observatory, the technology center, and new residence halls. "The school is always building something new, and our SEC [Sports and Recreation Center] is amazing and a great place to relieve stress." 2004 heralded the opening of the new apartments, affectionately called "Sammy Suites" by students, which provide apartment-style living for upperclassmen.

Rose is described as "very safe since there is zero crime on campus." The campus is far enough away from the city of Terre Haute that safety isn't much of an issue. To further deter crime, emergency phones are located all over campus. Despite these efforts, most students feel comfortable enough to leave their dorm doors open all the time and say they "have never felt threatened on campus."

Dorm Life

Students have few complaints about the dorm system at Rose. Freshmen have normal dorm rooms, sophomores have suite-style ones, and juniors and seniors on-campus have apartment-style dorms. The dorms are big, come with nice oak furniture, and most are air-conditioned. While freshman floors are segregated by sex, the halls are not, and upperclassmen can live on coed floors. Rooms improve each year, and dorms help foster unity among the students, especially during freshman year. "The facilities themselves are pretty good, but it's the atmosphere and staff that make them great. RAs and sophomore advisors (SAs) are really great people and help make the transition to college pretty seamless," claims one student. Each freshman has one RA and two SAs, and "you can ask anyone on campus and they see their RA as a friend more than a rule enforcer." This advising system is quite unique to Rose.

> "One of the janitors took about 45 minutes to give me a tour of the buildings, show me classrooms, and explain how to keep from getting lost."

Another perk of Rose's on-campus living is that a housekeeper cleans the rooms once a week. The garbage is taken out, beds are made with fresh sheets, and the floors are vacuumed. "The housekeeping ladies are wonderfully motherly and the building janitors all take a lot of pride in their work and show good feelings toward the student body." Students say that the people who work for Rose are treated well and as a result are happy and helpful. One student describes how, during her freshman orientation, she was wandering through the academic buildings trying to find classes, and "one of the janitors took about 45 minutes to give me a tour of the buildings, show me classrooms, and explain how to keep from getting lost. He still says hi to me in the halls." Clearly, Rose has an all-together friendly atmosphere among its students, faculty, and staff.

Engineered Food

Rose-Hulman has one dining hall, and food can be found on-campus until midnight. The food is described as "edible," but students warn, "don't come here for the food." The campus has recently added a Subway, which has spurred improvement in the dining services: "either Subway will take over campus or the cafeteria food will have to get better."

In addition to the main dining hall and Subway, "The Worx" in the basement serves burgers, chicken nuggets, French fries, and salads after dining hall hours. There are also restaurants off-campus such as Moggers, which serves sandwiches, an Italian restaurant, Mexican restaurants, and lots of steakhouses and chains. As one can see, "Terre Haute is packed with restaurants."

Nerds Have Fun Too

Terre Haute is not exactly an amusement mecca; Rose students must be adventurous in creating their own fun. On campus are eight fraternities and two sororities, and the school is small enough that Greek life dominates the social scene. Approximately half of the student body are involved. There is a frat on-campus for every type of person, but "we are not the stereotypical Greeks because we are all nerds underneath." Rushing is a six-week dry process. It is a great way to meet people and is described as very non-committal. "We say that fraternities rush you because they take guys out to eat, have lots of events at their houses, and generally drop a lot of money on rush."

Since there aren't a lot of women at Rose-Hulman, guys tend to hang out with girls from Indiana State University, which is right down the road. As one student said, "Coming in I figured it would be a bunch of nerds in their rooms on weekends, but it's definitely not like that." Each fraternity has their own annual parties and students typically go out on weekends and Tuesday nights (if they don't have a lab due the next day). Each year the annual Camp Out party transforms a frat house into the wilderness, completely filled with leaves and a 25-foot tall tree.

Diversity?

Rose-Hulman might not offer an ideal setting for those students wanting culture and diversity, since most of the student body are described as white, upper-middle-class males from the Midwest. However, while there's limited diversity, there's definitely no discrimination. "People who aren't Caucasian stick out. There is also a strong gender imbalance, but I don't think people are intolerant."

Rose has only been co-ed since 1995, and this attributes to the huge imbalance of male to female ratio. Rose is about 80 percent male and 20 percent female, but one girl said that instead of feeling part of the minority, "I feel appreciated for being a girl, which is a nice feeling." Along with Indiana State University, Rose men also look for girls at nearby St. Mary-of-the-Woods College to counteract the imbalance. Despite this imbalance, Rose-Hulman offers an incredible undergraduate education that is quite balanced when it comes to working hard, as students here still maintain a strong sense of fun and relaxation.—*Terren O'Reilly*

FYI

If you come to Rose-Hulman, you'd better bring "an eagerness to learn in an educational yet relaxed environment."

What's the typical weekend schedule? "A trip to Indiana State University or St. Mary-of-the-Woods College if you're a guy (not enough women at Rose-Hulman Institute of Technology, suck it up if you're a girl.)"

If I could change one thing about Rose-Hulman, I would "find lots more girls or make it easier."

Three things every student at Rose-Hulman should do before graduating are "hours of homework on a Friday night, go through rush/recruitment, and get to know everybody (at least in your major)."

Saint Mary's College

Address: St. Mary's, 122 Le Mans Hall, Notre Dame, IN 46556

Phone: 800-551-7621

E-mail Address: admission@saintmarys.edu

Web site URL: www.saintmarys.edu

Year Founded: 1844

Private or Public: Private

Religious affiliation: Catholic

Location: suburban

Regular Application Deadline: 15-Feb

Number of Applicants: 1,181

Percent Accepted: 80%

Percent Accepted who enroll: 45%

Number Entering: 427

Number of Transfers Accepted each Year: 30–40

Mean SAT: 1,130

Mean ACT: 25

Middle 50% SAT range: 1,040–1,230

Middle 50% ACT range: 23–27

Early admission program (EA/ ED/ NA): ED

ED or EA Acceptance Rate: 82%

Full time Undergraduate enrollment: 1,501

Total enrollment: 1,633

Percent Male: 0%

Percent Female: 100%

Total Percent Minority: 10%

Percent African-American: 2%

Percent Asian/Pacific Islander: 3%

Percent Hispanic: 5%

Percent Native-American: 0%

Percent Other: 0%

Percent in-state / out of state: 28%/72%

Percent from Public HS: 57%

Retention Rate: 86–88% of class

Graduation Rate: 74–76%

Percent in On-campus housing: 83–86%

Percent affiliated with Greek system: 0%

Percent Varsity or Club Athletes: 25–40%

Number of official organized extracurricular organizations: 75+

Most popular majors: Nursing

Student/Faculty ratio: 10:01

Tuition and Fees: $26,872.00

Cost for Room and Board: $8,678.00

Percent receiving Financial aid, first-year: 60%

Nestled in South Bend, Indiana, minutes from the University of Notre Dame, is one of the nation's best-kept secrets in women's colleges. In addition to offering top-notch academic programs, Saint Mary's College provides a "welcoming" environment for women with ambition, individuality, and faith. While "it isn't the school for everyone," current students, or 'Belles,' sing the college's praises—when asked if she could go through the application process again, one student gushed "I would choose Saint Mary's 20 times over." Though many are not familiar with the small women's college in South Bend, those seeking strong academic programs, as well as a focus on spirituality and self-expression, might want to give Saint Mary's a second glance.

Getting the W

Saint Mary's strong academic programs are a key draw for applicants. The school offers a liberal arts education, and students are required to take a wide range of courses in areas such as the sciences, religion, and literature to satisfy their General Education requirements. Most students do not consider the requirements a hindrance, and some are even grateful for the requirements—one mathematics and economics major stressed the benefit of the liberal arts background they provide. But the same student also recommends spreading out the GEs over four years, to avoid being stuck with a semester full of classes in one discipline as an upperclassman. Those seeking a wider range of options to choose from can pursue a co-exchange program with Notre Dame, which involves taking two classes a semester at the campus across the street.

In addition to fulfilling their GEs, students must satisfy an extensive writing requirement by getting their 'W's. General writing proficiency must be achieved as a first-year and again within the major as a junior and a senior—but students describe the requirement as a plus. "I feel more confident writing papers now that I have the W," one sophomore said. Writing portfolios are graded by professors from all departments, and include work done in disciplines other than English. In combination with the typical course load, the writing requirement ensures that "you learn how to write and how to communicate your ideas" during your four years at Saint Mary's.

Academics at Saint Mary's are not for the weak-willed—the workload is described as "heavy" and "intimidating" but "definitely manageable." Students take around five courses, or 16–18 credits, a semester. Those seeking a laid-back academic atmosphere be warned—there is a decent amount of competition for honor societies and internship opportunities. "The college is small, all the students are women, and women can be really competitive," as one student explains. However, another described the atmosphere as encouraging rather than cutthroat: "We're all helping each other out, but we're all pushing each other at the same time." While all areas of study are demanding, some say communications majors enjoy a bit less work than others. Strong advising systems established through the Academic Affairs and First Year Studies office help students chart out their academic plans.

Benefits of the college's small size—there are only about 1500 undergraduates on campus—include intimate class settings and tight relationships with professors. The average class size is 16, and upperclassmen report that they have had few classes with more than 20 students. Art students call instructors by their first names, and math students share Memorial Day picnics with professors and their families. Professors typically list their home and cell phone numbers on syllabi, and students have known to dial them as late as 1 a.m. with questions on the homework. This one-on-one attention also means professors are more than willing to provide career guidance, research opportunities, and valuable graduate school recommendations for their students.

A Packed Social Calendar

While Saint Mary's students devote themselves tirelessly to their studies, they also find time to unwind. The Student Activities Board keeps Belles busy with a host of campus activities. Two of the biggest events are the SMC Tostal and the Twilight Tailgate; others include Jamaica Shaka (a freshman orientation mixer with Notre Dame students), pumpkin carving, and Sundaes on Sundays. Dalloway's, a student-run coffee house, is a popular venue for those seeking a diversion from their studies. The organization offers karaoke, bands, dating games, and other activities throughout the week.

Weekends at SMC are described as fairly low-key; students often stay in to watch movies with their friends or catch up on work. One of the benefits of SMC's proximity to the University of Notre Dame is the extra set of activities the school offers. Notre Dame's film screenings draw large crowds from Saint Mary's, as do school-sponsored activities such as laser tag. While Saint Mary's permits dorm parties for those over 21, many head across the street for a more lively night life. "We go to Notre Dame if we want to go to a party," said one SMC student. A non-drinking club between the two schools, Flipside, hosts at least one activity each weekend for those who prefer to abstain. *The Observer*, a publication that serves Saint Mary's, Notre Dame, and the College of the Holy Cross, keeps students on all three campuses up-to-date on what's happening each weekend. As one student said, "Within this five mile sphere, there is never a dull moment!"

The University of Notre Dame also provides a nice outlet from the same-sex environment at SMC. "You don't realize you're missing men in classes, but on the weekends, you do," confessed one student. A trolley runs back and forth between the two colleges, making intercollegiate dating a definite possibility.

Those seeking a break from the on-campus night life gravitate toward nearby bars and restaurants but one student confessed that "South Bend is sort of rundown, not the kind of place you want to hang out." Liquor locales in the surrounding area include Bookmakers, Fever, The Linebacker, and Rum Runners. Trips to Chicago are also popular for those seeking respite from campus life. For those lacking a car, the school sponsors a few bus trips to the city each year.

The Facts of Life

Freshmen are placed within one of the four residence halls on campus: Le Mans, Holy Cross, Regina, and McCandless. LeMans Hall, designed by a Notre Dame architecture student, is one of the more sought after dormitories. Once a building for both classrooms and dorms, it features marble in the bathrooms and chalkboards in some of the bedrooms. In general, students are pleased with the size of the rooms: "You don't feel like you're getting the shaft." Suites in McCandless even include a separate carrel for studying, because "Saint Mary's believes you should separate study from sleep."

Roommates are assigned freshman year. If the relationship becomes less than idyllic, students can seek mediation at the Counseling Center, which offers help for everything from roommate troubles to stress management to depression. Resident Advisors serve on hall floors or sections to provide guidance for underclassmen. There are also Hall Directors, who tend to be recent college graduates. While many upperclassmen opt to move off campus, "really beautiful" senior apartments opened in 2004—and that just may be enough to reel students back to campus grounds.

SMC recently revamped both the student center and the dining hall. Students cite a significant improvement in the food since the reopening. In addition to soup, salad, and cereal, students can choose from six food stations which offer pizza, hamburgers, Asian, vegetarian, and home-style options. While some say the meals are "really, really good," they are also eager for more options. "I've never eaten anything that's bad, I just sometimes wish there would be more variety," said one student. Praise for the dining hall manager abounds; students who request certain goodies or recipes from home find their cravings answered within a few weeks. Some meal plans include "munch money," which can be used at the convenience store,

Dalloway's, the Cyber Café, or on-campus restaurants.

Saint Mary's was founded by the Sisters of the Holy Cross in 1844, and is still sponsored by the organization today. The GE requirements include two courses in religion, but the focus on religion extends beyond the classroom. Prayer groups and intercultural groups are common. Overall, students describe their peers as open-minded when it comes to religion on campus, so students who don't practice Catholicism should not be deterred from applying. "It's not looked down upon if you don't go [to church]," explained one student. However, those who do attend services can expect to see a large number of their fellow classmates in the pews, especially on Sunday nights. "It's like a social event to go to church," said one sophomore.

While students said they were more than pleased by most facets of the St. Mary's experience, they were unanimous in their concern for the lack of diversity on campus. In particular, they emphasized the lack of racial diversity on campus: "We need more diversity—the majority of Saint Mary's is Caucasian," said one junior. The school has made a concerted effort in recent years to address the issue, but, as one student pointed out, recruitment can be difficult given the current student body makeup: "It's kind of intimidating because you have this white, conservative, catholic student body."

Despite the lack of visual diversity on campus, a broad range of socioeconomic backgrounds are represented. A large portion of the student body receives financial aid. In addition, women come to SMC from across the country—at least 48 states are represented in a typical class.

A League of Their Own

Tight relationships exist both inside and outside the classroom at Saint Mary's. Students describe their peers as "welcoming" and "friendly," which can help ease the transition freshman year. There are no sororities on campus but that may be because they aren't needed—a running joke is that the whole school is a sorority. Annual T-shirts supporting "ΣMC" say "no rush required" and "the most exclusive sorority." Indeed students are quick to describe the sense of sisterhood that develops among women at the college.

Overall, SMC students don't seem to lament the dearth of Y chromosomes on campus. While some freshmen list the same-sex atmosphere as one of their least favorites things about Saint Mary's, upperclassmen often report just the opposite. The guy-free environment has been known to bring out the more assertive sides of some students, and women can find themselves pursuing positions and activities they wouldn't have considered in a coed environment.

> **"It is just a very empowering environment to be immersed in as a female college student."**

Saint Mary's offers students an exceptional academic experience on a campus brimming with a "strong sense of community and pride." As one transfer student said, "I was completely caught off guard. . . . I fell in love with the school, the professors, classes, and student body immediately." Women hesitant to embrace four years without men should not be deterred from applying to Saint Mary's; the Notre Dame campus sits less than a mile away, and a same-sex learning environment does offer a host of benefits. As one SMC senior said, "all the leadership positions are held by women, our president is a woman . . . it is just a very empowering environment to be immersed in as a female college student."—*Christen Martosella*

FYI

If you come to Saint Mary's, you'd better bring "something that reminds you of your faith, your family, your friends."

What's the typical weekend schedule? "Friday: stay in for girls night and watch a movie; Saturday: work during the day, go to Notre Dame for a film screening or party at night; Sunday: go to brunch, study, go to church."

If I could change on thing about Saint Mary's I'd "increase diversity."

Three things every student should do before graduating are: "Learn how to ask questions, go through the haunted tunnels, and participate in midnight madness (a series of competitions between classes held in athletic facility, followed by a huge all-night blow-out party)."

University of Notre Dame

Address: University of Notre Dame, 220 Main Building— Admissions, Notre Dame, IN 46556

Phone: 574-631-7505

E-mail Address: admissions@nd.edu

Web site URL: http://www.nd.edu

Year Founded: 1842

Private or Public: private

Religious affiliation: Roman Catholic

Location: suburban

Regular Application Deadline: 31-Dec

Number of Applicants: 11,316

Percent Accepted: 32%

Percent Accepted who enroll: 58%

Number Entering: 1,995

Number of Transfers Accepted each Year: ~150

Mean SAT: 1,379

Mean ACT: 31

Middle 50% SAT range: NA

Middle 50% ACT range: NA

Early admission program (EA/ ED/ NA): NA

ED or EA Acceptance Rate: NA

Full time Undergraduate enrollment: 8,260

Total enrollment: 11,417

Percent Male: 53%

Percent Female: 47%

Total Percent Minority: 19.1%

Percent African-American: 3.7%

Percent Asian/Pacific Islander: 6.1%

Percent Hispanic: 8.5%

Percent Native-American: 0.8%

Percent Other: 3.4%

Percent in-state / out of state: 9%/ 91%

Percent from Public HS: 50%

Retention Rate: 98%

Graduation Rate: 96%

Percent in On-campus housing: 77%

Percent affiliated with Greek system: 0%

Percent Varsity or Club Athletes: NA

Number of official organized extracurricular organizations: 260

3 Most popular majors: Political Science, Psychology, English

Student/Faculty ratio: 11:01

Tuition and Fees: $33,407.00

Cost for Room and Board: $8,730.00

Percent receiving Financial aid, first-year: 78%

At the University of Notre Dame, academics, athletics and faith blend together in a rural setting. But what truly distinguishes Notre Dame is the passion its students feel for their school. It is a passion that is evident in their spectacular displays of school pride at sporting events, in their commitment to their studies, and in their attendance at mass every week.

Academic Enlightenment

Notre Dame's rigorous curriculum motivates students with its wide variety of choices and prepares them well for the future. All freshmen enter the First Year of Studies School, where they can adjust to college life while they determine which curriculum they will study for the next three years: Arts and Letters (the most popular), Engineering, Business or Science. An array of over 50 majors is available. While there is a lot of freedom within each major in fulfilling requirements, once the first year requirements have been fulfilled, each college has their own requirements which must be fulfilled in the sophomore year before a major can be declared.

Notre Dame students enjoy small classes. With the exception of large intro classes, most have fewer than 40 students and many have less than 20. The University prides itself on its focus on undergraduates, which students commend, especially when it comes to attention from professors. Some professors hold dinners at their houses or pull crazy stunts in class to attract students' attention. One student said her finance professor would "dump a glass of water on his head because he wanted people to pay more attention." Professors are also able to eat in the dining halls for free so that classroom discussions can continue outside of class during meals. Students receive several hours of homework every night, but the university provides tutors in every subject for those who need additional help. Despite the demanding academics, most at Notre Dame are willing to embrace the challenges their education requires.

A Longstanding Reputation

There are few people who are unaware that Notre Dame is a Catholic institution. Does that mean the entire student body is Catholic? Not necessarily. Approximately 85% of Notre Dame students are Catholic, although not all of them practice. Many students feel that religion is not overbearing on campus but it is pervasive all the same. Unsurprisingly, theology is one of the requirements for all students, although it does not have to be Catholic theology.

Each dorm has a chapel in which mass is held every day except Saturday. Many students attend, but those who don't say there is no pressure. Some students feel that faith is a unifying factor on campus, furthering community values and lending a sense of family to the undergraduate community.

Crucifixes in classrooms and residence halls serve as a reminder of the University's Catholic affiliation. Another reminder is the single-sex dorms and the "parietals," rules for when the opposite sex can enter residence halls. To compensate for the stringency of the policy, the university does provide several 24 hour lounges where both sexes are free to socialize. Despite the unpopularity of parietals, most students agree that Notre Dame is worth the inconvenience.

Another common complaint is the lack of diversity among the student body. The minority situation was described by one student to be "perhaps the most disheartening aspect of this campus . . . non-white and non-Catholic is a definite minority." The relative homogeneity among the student body and religious faith practiced by many result in a conservative environment in the political, sexual, and social spheres. Despite the conservative leanings of the student body, progressive proposals—such as the official recognition of the Gay-Straight Alliance—all come from the students.

Life Off the Field

At Notre Dame, students know how to do more than study. Depending on their schedules, many start their weekends on Thursdays, when they go to local bars and clubs like Corby's, the Linebacker, and Fever. Attendance, however, is limited to those over 21 as all the bars scan IDs and many have been known to confiscate fake IDs. Parties also can be found on-campus, but many head to off-campus venues for a livelier scene. The police have been cracking down on underage drinking recently, forcing students to change their usual social routine. On campus, the drinking policy is "beer-only." Hard alcohol is banned and punishments can be severe.

There is plenty of beer to be found, however, throughout weekends in the fall, as tailgaters gather for the football game, an amazing show of athleticism and school spirit. Almost every student buys season tickets and "the shirt," whose color changes every year, making the student section immediately recognizable. As one student put it, "there is nothing in the world like a Notre Dame football game." One Fighting Irish fan claims that words could not do it justice. On Friday nights before home games, there is a pep rally that most of the school attends, bag pipes at midnight and Saturday morning, and the entire campus is abuzz with energy and activity before students, faculty, alumni and fans alike pack into the stadium to cheer on their team. Students stand for the entire game. Enthusiasts are usually tired after a full day on Saturdays, which tends to be a more relaxed night for parties.

> **"There is nothing in the world like a Notre Dame football game."**

Although many social events tend to be centered on sports and involve alcohol, other options do exist. A student explained that "there is other stuff to do—hang out with friends, go to a show, go to a movie. There is an organization called Flip Side that puts on a lot of non-drinking fun activities on the weekends." In addition, every dorm has its own formal, which is often themed.

An Athletic Campus

Besides football, athletic pride and spirit is pervasive on campus. The student body is also very athletic. Most work out regularly in the excellent training facilities and almost everyone participates in dorm sports. As one student put it, "Dorm sports are HUGE. Everyone I know plays." In fact, Notre Dame is the only university with fully padded recreational footballs teams.

Apart from sports, students keep busy with other activities and community service. There are myriad of student-run clubs and organizations on campus for all tastes and interests. The arts and theatre scene puts on a student film festival every year, along with numerous plays. There is Battle of the Bands in the spring and the school has been working to bring high-profile names to campus, including Third Eye Blind and Ben Folds. Guest speakers are also common, including George W. Bush and the president of

Ireland, both of whom have come to speak at graduation.

Out and About in South Bend

Living in South Bend, Indiana may not be the most exciting part of the undergraduate experience at Notre Dame, but it does offer the Morris Performing Arts center, the Coveleski Stadium, and a downtown area which is undergoing major renovation. A new strip mall is being built close to campus with student-friendly stores like J.Crew and Urban Outfitters. Restaurants including Chipotle and Buffalo Wild Wings, are also new to campus.

The Notre Dame campus is closed off to traffic, making it completely self-contained. The campus landscape is beautiful, but many students complain about the weather, especially the "endless winter" when it is always "cold, or raining or snowing." Except for occasional bike thefts, campus crime is practically nonexistent. Once they are situated in a dorm, students are expected to live there for the next four years, though many move off-campus in their senior year. In the absence of Greek life, the dorms tend to foster close-friendships; roommates are randomly assigned to "foster community and lifelong friendships." Students take great pride in their dorms, especially since each dorm has a distinct identity, with its own mascot, hall government and reputation. The dorms are also well-equipped. Just this year, the University added cable and wireless to every room. And construction on two new dorms is about to begin in 2007 to accommodate an increasing student population. New cell phone towers were also added to improve reception.

Food options receive praise from students on campus. There are two central dining halls, North and South, and students are polled on their food preferences. Many students go to South because "it looks like Hogwarts from Harry Potter." Outside of the dining halls, students enjoy Burger King, Subway and Starbucks at the bustling LaFortune, the equivalent of a Student Union. Students can also head over to Recker's, a local sandwich shop on campus. Dining out is popular as well, since many students have cars on campus.

From football to religion to academics, Notre Dame is rife with rich traditions. With those traditions comes responsibility, but for most at Notre Dame, they cannot imagine it any other way.

FYI
If you come to Notre Dame, you'd better bring "boots and a North Face coat or parka."
What's the typical weekend schedule: Thursday go to Fever; Friday go to pep rallies and campus
parties or bars, depending on age; Saturdays tailgate and go to the football game and maybe to a
party; Sundays recover and study."
If I could change one thing about Notre Dame, I'd "move campus closer to a city."
Three things every student at Notre Dame should do before graduating are "rush the football field,
go to the Grotto/attend mass at the Basilica and play in the intramurals."

Valparaiso University

Address: Valparaiso, Kretzmann Hall, 1700 Chapel Drive, Valparaiso, IN 46383-6493

Phone: 219-464-5011

E-mail Address: undergrad.admissions@valpo.edu

Web site URL: www.valpo.edu

Year Founded: 1859

Private or Public: private

Religious affiliation: Lutheran Church

Location: suburban

Regular Application Deadline: 16-Aug

Number of Applicants: 3,785

Percent Accepted: 89%

Percent Accepted who enroll: 23%

Number Entering: 762

Number of Transfers Accepted each Year: 160

Mean SAT: 1,131

Mean ACT: 35

Middle 50% SAT range: 1,020–1,270

Middle 50% ACT range: 22–28

Early admission program (EA/ ED/ NA): EA

ED or EA Acceptance Rate: 93.74%

Full time Undergraduate enrollment: 2,904

Total enrollment: 3,352

Percent Male: 48%

Percent Female: 52%

Total Percent Minority: 9%

Percent African-American: 4%

Percent Asian/Pacific Islander: 2%

Percent Hispanic: 3%

Percent Native-American: 0%

Percent Other: NA

Percent in-state / out of state: 36%/64%

Percent from Public HS: NA

Retention Rate: 81%

Graduation Rate: 76%

Percent in On-campus housing: 64%

Percent affiliated with Greek system: 23%

Percent Varsity or Club Athletes: NA

Number of official organized extracurricular organizations: 83

3 Most popular majors: Atomosphere Sciences and Meteorology, General; Nursing—Registered Nurse Training (RN, ASN, BSN, MSN); Psychology, General

Student/Faculty ratio: 12:01

Tuition and Fees: $23,200

Cost for Room and Board: $6,640

Percent receiving Financial aid, first-year: 71%

N ot far from the windy city of Chicago lies Valparaiso University, a small private Lutheran school in northwest Indiana, where students enjoy nationally recognized academic programs, an active social scene, a variety of popular extracurricular activities, and, of course, a great basketball team.

"The Human Experience"

When freshmen arrive at Valparaiso (affectionately nicknamed Valpo), they are automatically enrolled in the "Valpo Core." Also known as "The Human Experience," the core covers themes such as creation, citizenship, coming of age, vocation and love, through a year-long course that not only includes lectures and readings, but for-credit basketball game attendances and pasta gatherings in professors' homes. Most Valpo students value their core experiences. As one psychology major said, "At first I thought I would hate taking the required core. I thought it would be really boring since every freshman has to take it. Now that I've taken the courses, though, I really feel like core gave me a great background that I've built my entire Valpo education on top of."

Students who choose to enter "Christ College," the honors college at Valpo, substitute "Texts and Contexts: Traditions of Human Thought" for core credit; the class focuses on critical reading, writing, and discussion of great works of literature. This two-semester course includes a fall play written and performed by the students, and a spring debate before the campus community.

> "Now that I've taken the courses, though, I really feel like core gave me a great background that I've built my entire Valpo education on top of."

Aside from core, students can take classes in four other colleges at VU: Arts and Sciences, Nursing, Engineering, or Business Administration. The meteorology program in the College of Arts and Sciences is a popular yet demanding major. Classes outside of the core and other general education requirements are usually small, and Valpo prides itself on the absence of TAs. Most students find their work loads manageable. As one student says, "It just depends on what you do. Like at any other college, you can make Valpo what you want it to be. If you try to do everything at once, the workload's going to seem a lot bigger."

Always Something to Do . . .
Despite the fact that Valpo is a dry campus with a zero-tolerance policy on underage drinking, students at VU find many different options when it comes to the social scene. Some students have dorm parties, while others visit the fraternity houses around campus or head up to the bars and nightclubs of Chicago. While the majority of Valpo students do drink, non-drinkers rarely feel left out. The Union Board at Valpo is extremely active, constantly arranging movies, lectures, concerts and diversity events for the entire campus.

The Greek scene at Valpo is thriving, with close to half of the students involved in the 15 fraternities and sororities. While fraternities may have houses off campus, sorority members find themselves in on-campus dorms, separated into their respective sororities by wing. The reason? As one engineering student explains, "If you have six or more girls living together in one house in Indiana, it's considered a brothel. Not that I would complain, but I think Valpo would rather avoid having all their sororities labeled as brothels. Plus, the girls probably wouldn't like it either."

Most Valpo students find it easy to meet people and make friends, especially within the student dorms, where your floor is often the source of your closest friends. Students are rarely labeled by their activities or interests, so cliques are rare at VU. Almost every student at Valpo would agree with one theology major, however, that "there is NO diversity! Everyone you meet here is white, Christian, and upper-middle-class. Practically everyone is from the Midwest, too."

From Christian Crusades to Basketball
Most students at VU are actively involved in some kind of extracurricular activity. As one student says, "Everybody has at least one thing that they do that is really theirs. Some people may do a lot of different stuff too, but everyone has got their own activity that they are really committed to." Intramural sports are very popular at Valpo, and most students are involved in community service projects; and the Campus Crusade for Christ and the Voodoo Comedy Club are always fun organizations. Students interested in journalism can get involved with *The Torch*, Valpo's weekly newspaper.

While many Valpo students show their school spirit and make their way out to football games in the fall, the real source of school pride is the Valparaiso basketball team. One of the most well-attended school events of the year is Midnight Madness, when the entire school turns up to watch the first basketball practice session of the year. The players are introduced to the student body one by one and a huge pep rally led by the VU Crew is held until the players begin their first practice at midnight.

Living at Valpo
Most students at Valpo live on campus, in dorms that are single-sex by floor. Students enjoy comforts such as pullout futon beds, big windows, and sinks within their bedrooms. However, the university-regulated curfew is extremely unpopular. Members of the opposite sex must be off one another's floors after 1:00 a.m. on weekdays and after 2:00 a.m. on weekends. Drinking and smoking are prohibited in the dorms as well. RAs can be found in all dorms, but they are generally friendly and welcoming, and are seen more as companions than authority figures.

There are four main cafeterias on campus. The largest is located in the student center, where, as one student says, "You come, you eat, you leave." There are three other, smaller cafeterias, which are located in three of the dorms; their residential nature means students can often be found studying or relaxing. In addition to eating on campus, Jimmy John's and various off-campus pizza restaurants are popular dining options for students. The campus at Valparaiso is home to the second-largest university chapel in the country; its size makes it the focus of the green, gently hilly campus. Situated about an hour from Chicago and in the town of Valparaiso, Valpo creates a home for its students unlike any other. As one sociology student says, "I just love the fact that this is where I wake up every morning."

Students at VU are quickly able to find their own niches in the Valpo community and make the small Lutheran school their new home. As one Valpo student proudly boasts, "Whatever you want in a college, Valpo's got it. If you want to be in a small town community, that's Valpo. If you need the excitement of the city, Chicago's less than an hour away. If you want a lot of extracurricular activities, Valpo's got everything. If you're more concerned with the academic aspects of a college, Valpo's classes and professors are amazing. And last of all, who wouldn't want to root for our basketball team?"—*Sarah Newman*

FYI

If you come to Valparaiso, you'd better bring "a jacket, gloves and a fan."

What's the typical weekend schedule? "Party hard on Friday night; sleep in late Saturday morning; go to the basketball game Saturday night and party with friends; go to church Sunday morning; and then study, study, study all day on Sunday."

If I could change one thing about Valparaiso, I would "make our student body more diverse."

Three things every student at Valparaiso should do before graduating are "go to El Amigos, ring the Victory Bell, and do crowd push-ups at a volleyball game."

Wabash College

Address: Wabash, PO Box 352, Crawfordsville, IN 47933
Phone: 765-361-6225
E-mail Address: admissions@wabash.edu
Web site URL: www.wabash.edu
Year Founded: 1832
Private or Public: private
Religious affiliation: none
Location: suburban
Regular Application Deadline: Rolling
Number of Applicants: 1,319
Percent Accepted: 51%
Percent Accepted who enroll: 40%
Number Entering: 268
Number of Transfers Accepted each Year: 9
Mean SAT: 1,161
Mean ACT: 25

Middle 50% SAT range: 1,070–1,273
Middle 50% ACT range: 22–28
Early admission program (EA/ ED/ NA): EA and ED
ED or EA Acceptance Rate: ED: 74.47%
Full time Undergraduate enrollment: 874
Total enrollment: 874
Percent Male: 100%
Percent Female: 0%
Total Percent Minority: 12%
Percent African-American: 5%
Percent Asian/Pacific Islander: 2%
Percent Hispanic: 5%
Percent Native-American: 0%
Percent Other: NA
Percent in-state / out of state: 74%/26%

Percent from Public HS: 93%
Retention Rate: 87%
Graduation Rate: 72%
Percent in On-campus housing: 90%
Percent affiliated with Greek system: 54%
Percent Varsity or Club Athletes: NA
Number of official organized extracurricular organizations: 52
3 Most popular majors: English Language and Literature, General; History, General; Psychology, General
Student/Faculty ratio: 10:01
Tuition and Fees: $24,342
Cost for Room and Board: $7,064
Percent receiving Financial aid, first-year: 82%

As one of America's few remaining all-male institutions, Wabash College students benefit from the school's rich tradition of excellence, impressive endowment, small class sizes and academic rigor. From the long-held football rivalries to the major Greek presence on campus, Wabash offers a unique college experience for highly focused young men.

Small Classes, Personal Experience

Class sizes at Wabash tend to be much smaller than at competing institutions. "The largest size I have ever heard of for a class at Wabash is around 35," reported one student. When classes attract larger volumes, the school generally responds by offering several sections, rather than limiting those who can enroll. The intimate classroom environment provides students with the opportunity to foster relationships with professors, who students say "encourage individual thought and contribution in class" and are "almost uniformly excellent." After completing courses, students frequently visit and maintain lasting relationships with professors. One senior noted, "Students can build strong relations with their professors here at Wabash, and these contacts will later be valuable resources for recommendations and help in finding a career." All this personal attention seems to pay strong dividends to Wabash's graduates. In the years after graduation, approximately 75 percent of students attend graduate or professional school, and a remarkable 80-plus percent of premed students are accepted to medical school, a percentage much higher than the national average.

> "Students can build strong relations with their professors here at Wabash, who will later be valuable resources for recommendations and help in finding a career."

The academic standards at Wabash are high. Wabash requires all freshmen to participate in the Freshman Tutorial program. This set of introductory courses concentrates on everything from sculpture to nanotechnology, providing freshmen with the opportunity to critically interpret and discuss topics of interest. Many enjoy the tutorials and find them to be a great way to "get freshmen used to the college way of thinking." Another requirement, somewhat less heralded than its freshman-year counterpart, is the year-long course entitled "Cultures and Traditions," a world humanities survey offered for sophomores. Students are also required to demonstrate proficiency in writing and a foreign language. To graduate, seniors must complete "comps." These comprehensive exams, taken over the course of a week, cover every course taken in the student's given major. Some at Wabash compare this period of extensive examination to graduate school defense boards.

Life at Wabash

Wabash students generally find living without women fairly easy to get used to; however, some feel that the academic and social scenes are lacking without members of the opposite sex. One student explains the college's obligation to remain all-male: "Unfortunately (or not, depending on how you look at it), Wabash relies on alumni for our proportionally gigantic endowment, and none of the alumni want to see 'Wabash tradition' destroyed by going coed." Despite the occasional complaints about the lack of female presence, many say they feel less pressure to conform to fashion trends and are able to avoid relationship-related drama.

In terms of social life, the Greek system dominates at Wabash, with 10 nationally recognized chapters and approximately 70 percent of students choosing to live in frat houses. Incoming freshmen often move into fraternities prior to the start of classes, and pledge different frats after having lived with the brothers. Alternatives to this unorthodox Greek system are, however, plentiful. Other housing options include living on campus in Martindale, College, Morris or Wolcott halls, as well as in college-owned off-campus housing.

Every fall, near the end of September, the fraternity pledges compete against one another in singing—or what has become screaming—the Wabash school song, "Old Wabash," at an event dubbed "Chapel Sing." The freshmen are judged by the Sphinx Club, an upperclassmen leadership group with fraternity-affiliated members. These seniors ultimately decide the winning house. In recent years, the students have been required to tone down this tradition as many were adversely affected by the yelling. One student described the administration's reasoning behind regulating the festivities, "[Chapel Sing] had sort of degenerated over the years into a big screaming mass of hoarse, painted, shirtless men. And we're talking bleeding-throat, can't-talk-for-a-week-screaming."

Most students complain that the social offerings of Crawfordsville, the small town of about 15,000 that's near to Wabash, aren't exactly thrilling. One student described it as a "Nowhereville along the side of I-74." Commercial outlets are few and far between, with little beyond a Wendy's, Wal-Mart, a bowling alley and a theater. For most students, however, the limitations of Crawfordsville don't stand in the way of a good time. With regular parties and activities on campus, most deem venturing into town unnecessary. On weekends, many students also elect to travel to Indianapolis, only an hour away by car, or Lafayette, hometown of Purdue, to "sample the real college-town atmosphere." In addition, juniors and seniors have made a tradition of frequenting the Cactus Bar, a Lafayette establishment.

While students are generally "pretty satisfied—not complaining too loud" with housing and the social scene, they are less than thrilled with the food selection. As is the case at almost every college and university, the food at Wabash can be less than stellar, especially considering its high cost. Dining options at the Sparks Center have been described as "really scandalously bad." The food prepared by fraternity-hired cooks tends to be of a similarly mediocre quality, negating the perceived advantage of "living in-frat."

Athletics but No Cheerleaders

One student describes the athletic presence on campus as "pretty huge." One student reported that "Wabash has a top-notch athletics facility and is very focused on athletics, even though it is a Division III college." For 112 years Wabash has taken on DePauw University in one of the Midwest's longest-standing football rivalries: the Monon Bell Game. The winning team is awarded possession of the Monon Bell, a former fixture on the regular train running between Greencastle, home of DePauw, and Crawfordsville, and hold onto it until the following meeting. This prize has historically been highly prized, with students from both schools making repeated theft attempts over the years. While Wabash places a major emphasis on football, many other athletic programs on campus are also quite popular. Wabash track and field coach Robert Johnson offered world-class athletes his expertise as an assistant coach at the 2000 Summer Olympics held in Sydney, Australia; he was the first Division III coach ever to work in that capacity. Wabash students take advantage of the great athletic resources available to them, with 40 percent of students participating in one of 10 varsity sports, and nearly 75 percent partaking in one of 23 intramural activities ranging from canoe racing to volleyball. Whether it's on the athletic field or in seminar, Wabash men are determined to get the most out of the college experience.
—*Natalie Hale*

FYI
If you come to Wabash, you'd better bring "a car for all the weekend travel you'll want to do."
What's the typical weekend schedule? "Hang out with friends at frats and dorms at night, and work out or do laundry during the day."
If I could change one thing about Wabash, I would "change the town; it's boring here."
Three things every student at Wabash should do before graduating are "hang out at the Silver Dollar Bar, attend the Wabash/DePauw game, and branch out and go to a social event at a neighboring school."

Iowa

Address: Cornell College, 600 1st St. SW, Mt. Vernon, IA 52314
Phone: 319-895-4000
E-mail Address: communications@cc.edu
Web site URL: http://www.cornellcollege.edu
Year Founded: 1853
Private or Public: private
Religious affiliation: Methodist
Location: small city
Regular Application Deadline: 1-Mar
Number of Applicants: 1,791
Percent Accepted: 362.9%
Percent Accepted who enroll: 29.5%
Number Entering: 319
Number of Transfers Accepted each Year: 39
Mean SAT: 1,244

Mean ACT: 26
Middle 50% SAT range: 1,130–1,340
Middle 50% ACT range: 24–29
Early admission program (EA/ ED/ NA): EA&ED
ED or EA Acceptance Rate: 72%
Full time Undergraduate enrollment: 1,166
Total enrollment: 1,179
Percent Male: 45%
Percent Female: 55%
Total Percent Minority: 13%
Percent African-American: 4%
Percent Asian/Pacific Islander: 1%
Percent Hispanic: 3%
Percent Native-American: 1%
Percent Other: 4%

Percent in-state / out of state: 30% / 70%
Percent from Public HS: NA
Retention Rate: 85%
Graduation Rate: 68%
Percent in On-campus housing: 92%
Percent affiliated with Greek system: 24%
Percent Varsity or Club Athletes: 25%
Number of official organized extracurricular organizations: 127
3 Most popular majors: Psychology, Education, Economics / Business
Student/Faculty ratio: 11:01
Tuition and Fees: $24,800.00
Cost for Room and Board: $6,760.00
Percent receiving Financial aid, first-year: 70%

N o, Cornell College is not an Ivy-League university in Ithaca. Despite its small size and rural setting, however, it does attract some top talent from across the country—and it was founded 12 years earlier than that other Cornell in upstate New York. At Cornell College in Mount Vernon, Iowa, students have the opportunity to enroll in only one course at a time, join "social groups," and participate in one of the country's few college steel drum ensembles.

One-Course-At-A-Time

For students who prefer concentrating on only one subject as opposed to juggling four or five per semester, Cornell's unique One-Course-At-A-Time, or OCAAT, scheduling system is a big attraction. All courses are scheduled in blocks, with each year consisting of nine, three-and-a-half week blocks. Most courses meet for morning and afternoon sessions every day of the week, with courses requiring labs often running longer

sessions than other courses. Overall students tend to give OCAAT very positive reviews. As one student described, "it allows students to focus, and also to be more intense."

Additionally, students said they appreciate OCAAT for the strong student-faculty relationships it fosters as well as for the flexibility it provides. Because professors, too, have only one course at a time to focus on, they can devote all their energy and resources to the students of that particular course. Students described their professors as "awesome" and "totally dedicated" to teaching and advising. And, since so many professors live right in the small town of Mount Vernon, casual meetings outside of the classroom are very common.

Furthermore, class sizes tend to be fairly small, since all are capped at 25 students (some are even capped at 18), including introductory-level courses. The combination of small classes and block scheduling thus gives students more opportunities to attend field trips, take advantage of their own classrooms—which are not shared during the block period, and get one-on-one attention from professors.

Of course, as any student will tell you, OCAAT has its drawbacks, too—aside from the fact that taking an uninteresting course will only be that much worse when one has to go to it every day for a month. Students also acknowledged that while OCAAT works well for most classes, it can be problematic for certain areas of study. For example, it might be difficult to cram certain technical- or memorization-intensive courses, such as an introductory language course or mathematics class, into such a short period of time. But students also said Cornell is in the process of trying to adjust OCAAT slightly to better accommodate these differences. Possibilities include combining harder courses into two-block courses, or grouping some classes for interdisciplinary purposes.

Cornell also allows for a decent amount of academic flexibility. Students said they appreciated OCAAT because it allows them to take a "vacation block" if they so desire. During that time, they might decide to go on a trip, do some community service, relax, or get an early start on a summer internship. The college also makes it relatively easy for students to double major, or to add a minor to their major. One student, who had planned on majoring in biomedical engineering before coming to Cornell, said she decided to take advantage of the school's flexibility and create her own tailor-made biophysics major. "There's a big emphasis on independence," she explained.

Not Just Another Cornfield in Iowa

Due in part to Cornell's unique academic offerings, students said the school is surprisingly not as homogenous as one would expect. "For being a small school in the middle of a cornfield in Iowa, it's really diverse," noted one junior. Although racial diversity is perhaps not as strong as in some other colleges—"it's predominantly white middle-class"—Cornell's 1,100 students do hail from all over the country, with only about 30 percent coming from Iowa. Students also said that while the campus is often described as "very liberal," voices from a broad political spectrum are heard as well. "We lean to the left, but there's room for discussion and there's a lot of it that goes on," remarked one student.

In addition to OCAAT, Cornell's diverse base of students might also be attracted to the school for its beautiful campus and lively atmosphere. "I know a lot of people who made their decision to come here solely based on the campus—we're located on a hill, one of the few in Iowa," one student joked. The architecture, too, is noteworthy. Mt. Vernon, a town of just over 4,000 boasts three National Historic Districts. "The campus is often described as a 'slice of New England hilltop in the Midwest,'" noted one student, "and I think it's kind of corny but also kind of true." Though many of the buildings on and around campus do tend to be old, they are also well-preserved and often newly-renovated.

The 87 percent of students who live on campus also tend to live in older buildings, although one newly built senior dorm features a more modern suite-style setup. While the dorms may not be "as lavish as some other places," they do the trick and suit students "just fine."

Unfortunately, the quality of the food is not quite as impressive as the campus scenery and architecture. Students are required to purchase meal plans, with either 14 or 20 meals per week, and even students living off campus must still purchase a partial meal plan of seven meals a week. Although students said the quality of the food and the setup of the college's single cafeteria were "improving," they also said having a meal plan can get tiresome. "We're a 'Tier II' school when it comes to food," noted one senior, "there's even worse and I can't imagine what that would be."

Getting Involved

Cornell students also take advantage of the many extracurricular organizations available. About 100 different student organizations exist, but if there's not a group that strikes a student's fancy, he or she is easily able to start one independently. The Student Senate is in charge of doling out funds to the various organizations, which range from the Medieval Renaissance Club to the Union of Progressive Students to *The Cornellian*, the college newspaper. One of the more popular activities at Cornell is Pandemonium, a steel drums ensemble comprised of about 20 people performing a wide variety of traditional and contemporary music on four different kinds of drums.

Athletics are also very popular at Cornell, with several intramural activities offered during each block period. Though traditional sports, like basketball and volleyball, tend to be the most popular, students also participate in intramural watermelon seed spitting contests, indoor whiffleball games, and dodgeball tournaments. While many also participate in varsity sports, students noted that there's definitely an athletic and non-athletic crowd on campus. Interest in athletics is "not campus wide," but games for football, as well as for basketball and volleyball, tend to get "pretty decent" turnouts, particularly for such a small college. Wrestling also tends to be popular, as Cornell is in one of the toughest Division III wrestling conferences in the country.

Going Social

Unlike at larger institutions, much of the social interaction at Cornell tends to take place on a smaller scale—a characteristic many students said they appreciated. "It's a small town so it's a much smaller scene, but I'm the type of person who's okay with that," explained one senior. Another noted that "because we're so small and isolated, it really pulls our campus together." The Performing Arts and Activities Council at Cornell also hosts a number of popular activities, brining popular comedians, bands or speakers to campus for all to enjoy on the weekends.

> **"Because we're so small and isolated, it really pulls our campus together."**

However, Cornell students are still able to enjoy large campus-wide parties, with "social groups" frequently hosting some of the larger off-campus gatherings. Social groups act similarly to fraternities and sororities elsewhere—but while they have Greek names, they are not nationally-affiliated and so are unique to Cornell. Some of the groups are service-based, like the Taus and Rhozes, and others are more "party-oriented," like the Delts, Owls and Phi-Os. About half of all students are members of a social group, but parties are often open to the entire university. Although events including the Delts' St. Patty's Day party and the Gamma's pig roast are popular, the social groups also host formals and semi-formals every year, too.

If the pub scene is more fitting to a party-goer's interest, there are several bars within Mount Vernon, "each of which usually has a different crowd on a given weekend night." For a wider array of entertainment options, a lot of students also travel to Cedar Rapids or Iowa City (where the University of Iowa is located), both of which are a mere 20 minute car ride away. Students said that while alcohol is popular and easily accessible, there is "no more or less of a problem than at any other college."

Testing Out the Waters

Students suggested that potential Cornell applicants might consider spending a night or going to classes for a day or two to feel out the One-Course-At-A-Time schedule. "You either love it or hate it," remarked one student, adding that a fair number of students realize upon entering Cornell that one course at a time may not suit them as well as they thought. Regardless, incoming freshman should look forward to taking advantage of small class sizes and professor accessibility. "Professors are here because they like to teach, and the interactions we can have with them are just priceless." And, of course, they might also want to check out Cornell's social groups, scenery and historic landmarks. Said one student, "If you're looking for a good time here, you'll find it."—*Kendra Locke*

FYI

If you come to Cornell College, you'd better bring "a lot of warm clothing, because it gets pretty windy here."

What is the typical weekend schedule? "Go to social group parties, bars, or Iowa City or Cedar Rapids on Friday and Saturday nights, and relax with friends or study on Sunday."

If I could change one thing about Cornell College, I'd "put it somewhere warmer, maybe by a beach somewhere."

Three things every student should do before graduating are: "Go sledding down Pres Hill in downtown, go camping at Palisades-Kepler State Park, and take a block off and spend it however you want."

Grinnell College

Address: Grinnell, 1103 Park Street-2nd Floor, Grinnell, IA 50112

Phone: 800-2470113

E-mail Address: askgrin@grinnell.edu

Web site URL: www.grinnell.edu/admission

Year Founded: 1846

Private or Public: private

Religious affiliation: none

Location: rural

Regular Application Deadline: 20-Jan

Number of Applicants: 3891

Percent Accepted: 37.1%

Percent Accepted who enroll: 29.7%

Number Entering: 429

Number of Transfers Accepted each Year: varies

Mean SAT: NA

Mean ACT: NA

Middle 50% SAT range: math: 640–730; 640–750 verbal

Middle 50% ACT range: NA

Early admission program (EA/ ED/ NA): ED

ED or EA Acceptance Rate: 72%

Full time Undergraduate enrollment: 1,546

Total enrollment: 1,577

Percent Male: 45.3%

Percent Female: 54.7%

Total Percent Minority: 14.6%

Percent African-American: 4.2%

Percent Asian/Pacific Islander: 5.6%

Percent Hispanic: 4.4%

Percent Native-American: 0.4%

Percent Other: 0%

Percent in-state / out of state: 11%/78%

Percent from Public HS: NA

Retention Rate: 92%

Graduation Rate: 87%

Percent in On-campus housing: 87%

Percent affiliated with Greek system: NA

Percent Varsity or Club Athletes: NA

Number of official organized extracurricular organizations: 178

3 Most popular majors: English, Biology, Economics

Student/Faculty ratio: 9:01

Tuition and Fees: $29,030.00

Cost for Room and Board: $7,700.00

Percent receiving Financial aid, first-year: 76%

Grinnell College offers an idyllic setting—the small rural town of Grinnell (one of the 25 "Best Small Towns in America"). Founded in 1846, the college lies between baseball's "Field of Dreams" and the bridges of Madison County. The town's 9,105 local residents and Grinnell College's 1,500 students, hailing from all the states and 50 other countries, give the school a quaint cosmopolitan feel, which helped it win the title of "Best All-Around College" in *Newsweek*'s "Hot Schools of 2004" list. However, students choose this private liberal arts college not only because of its national rankings, but also for its combination of challenging academics, unconventional opportunities, and active social life.

Hitting the Books

Grinnell students boast about their week-long fall break, but are quick to point out that they earn this extra break through "pretty extreme" workloads. Some classes demand more than 100 pages of nightly reading from academic journals or literary masterpieces. Students who don't want to read volumes can always become sociology majors, since students nominate it as "the only easy major." It's generally considered

less demanding than most disciplines, while chemistry, physics, and neuroscience are said to be the most difficult.

Grinnell students enjoy small classes throughout their college careers. Average class enrollments range from two to 25 students. The only graduation requirement at Grinnell is the freshman tutorial, in which groups of 12 students practice their writing and analytical skills in classes with surveyed topics, such as "Inside Star Trek" and "UFOs in American Society." A very wide variety of topics are represented, and students can select tutorials focused on historical events or intellectual property, among other areas.

Also popular among Grinnell students is the opportunity to create their own courses through the MAP (Mentored Advanced Project). The Grinnell Web site describes the Mentored Advanced Project as "a chance to work closely with a faculty member on scholarly research or the creation of a work of art."

Class size remains fairly small after the freshman tutorial, and there are "rarely above 20 students" in a class. "A class with 30 students feels stiflingly large to the average Grinnellian." As one student put it, "A class of more than 30 students? I can't think of any." Competition for classes is minimal, but the Intro Biology class is popular and quite competitive, and linguistic classes are tough to get into because of the department's small number of professors. "Some of the more interesting 200-levels go pretty quickly," one student conceded. However, the school has developed a new system for regulating enrollment that has been fairly successful. This is a welcome development, as the old enrollment system ran on a first-come-first-serve basis and often spurred students to "stay overnight in the classrooms" to secure spots in a class. "Grinnellians are geeky enough to actually stay overnight to get the classes of their choice, and yet they're quirky enough to bring crochet needles and yarn with them so they have something to do in line."

> "A class with 30 students feels stiflingly large to the average Grinnellian."

Small class sizes, a rural setting, and the overall "awesome" relationships between students and their professors make Grinnell a close-knit academic community. The faculty is regarded as "approachable and reasonable," and it is not uncommon for students to have dinner at professors' houses. Many students share the sense that "there is a big connection" between themselves and their professors. And, most students agree "professors are really friendly as are people in the town and on campus." There are no TAs—graduate students that help with classes—so Grinnell professors rely on undergrad "mentors" who have previously taken the class to assist with grading and tutoring. All lectures or class discussions are led by full-time faculty, "all of whom emphasize teaching over scholarship." Although Grinnell professors are dedicated to educating students, Grinnell is one of the few liberal arts colleges that actually insist on maintaining high levels of faculty scholarship.

Grinnell further fosters an enjoyable learning environment by offering ExCo classes for non-credit. ExCo, which stands for "Experimental College," are unconventional educational forums that allow townspeople, students, and college staff to collectively pursue shared interests. ExCo classes are usually taught by students, they're adaptive and experimental to the needs of everyone in it, and unlike regular classes, ExCo classes lack fixed curriculums, attendance, or participation requirements. Typical ExCo classes include Star Gazing, Belly Dancing, Vegetarian Cooking, the X-Files, Auto Mechanics, and Swing Dancing.

Relaxing Grinnell-Style

Since Grinnellians need to hit the books hard, the Burling Library provides a welcome, quiet place for studying. Students report that some release pent-up energy in the library by contributing to the graffiti on the basement's bathroom walls. Other students prefer the two student centers, Harris Center and the Forum; the latter has a popular grill, providing just one of many ways to procrastinate (students can peruse the art gallery, play the grand piano, or visit the student government offices.) Harris also has its share of recreational facilities, including a concert hall for parties and bands, a TV lounge, and a game room with pool and foosball tables.

Grinnell's campus is very diverse architecturally, as the school's large endowment allows for continuous renovations and developments. The campus has a mix of "old Ivy-League brick buildings," modern buildings, and four new dorms. Grinnell's gym, PEC, was recently torn down and replaced by a completely new facility. A new student center, "the Joe," was constructed to serve as the new dining hall for all of campus. The Joe includes a new post office, student government offices, and a place for students to get food after hours.

Although off-campus housing is conveniently close to campus and generally more affordable than on-campus housing, most students choose to live on campus. The campus is divided into three main areas: North, South and East Campuses. "North campus is more athletes and south campus is more tree-huggers," explains one student. Students choose to live on the new East Campus "for the new feel of elevators in every dorm, new furniture, and air-conditioning." Bob's Underground Café, an enclosed terrace and dining hall, is situated between the North and South Campuses. Grinnell's main dining hall has been expanded to include a wider selection; meals now include cuisines from a variety of countries and U.S. regions, and the dining halls offer vegetarian and vegan options at every meal. Popular off-campus restaurants include AJ's Steakhouse, La Cabana, the Main Squeeze, Café Phoenix, Pizza Hut, and Pag's.

Partying Like Pioneers

Grinnell students are given a large amount of freedom under the school's "self-governance" policy, which is labeled a "don't ask, don't tell" system by some. Self-governance is a philosophy that allows students to have greater control over their lives. The administration encourages the students to act responsibly and work out their problems without administration intervention. This is not to say, however, that campus security and other disciplinary bodies don't get involved; rather, the administration looks to students to act first. When asked if they are allowed to drink in dorms, one student replied, "Of course!" Grinnell reportedly allows students the freedom to "basically take care of yourself, and try to work out conflicts on your own, so for the most part there's no campus security walking around." There are no RAs (resident advisers), but Grinnell does have SAs (student advisers) who aren't paid by the college, so they have a perspective similar to that of the students. Of SAs one student remarked, "I've never met a strict one—they're just there to make sure people on the floor get to know each other."

Free from the watchful policing of RAs, Grinnellians can drink in the dorms and it is common to see students partying in dorm lounges or attending house parties. Despite the demanding course load, Grinnell students usually find time to party on Friday, Saturday, and, as one student explained, "Wednesday is a huge night. Students try to plan their schedules so that they get Thursdays off."

Students also rave about the annual theme parties, such as the Waltz (the semester formal), Disco (the yearly disco dance), Mary B. James (the annual cross-dressing party), and Alice in Wonderland (a music festival with live bands), among others. Almost all students attend these galas, as they "give everyone a reason to dress up and take away from the stress of the week." Also popular is the yearly party on 10/10—the day students get their first paychecks for the academic year. During this celebration, students start partying on the north end of campus and progressively move to the south end. Grinnell offers many other free-time activities, thanks to the yearly "activity fee" that funds free plays, concerts, and on-campus movies.

Involved and Ambitious

Grinnell students put just as much effort into their extracurricular activities as they do into their studying and partying. Participation rates are very high, therefore, among organizations, sports teams, and volunteer groups. Among others, Grinnell offers conventional extracurriculars, such as community service, comic and literary magazines, a weekly paper, and a symphonic band. In keeping with Grinnell's eccentricity, however, students can also join the Beard & Moustache Society (to enlighten the campus about beards and moustaches), Chips 'N Dip (to provide late-night social gatherings, based on eating chips and dip), and Dagorhir (to safely pursue the art and sport of medieval combat)—though one student described the latter group as "just nerds who hit each other with Styrofoam all day."

Grinnell students are stereotypically liberal, in stark contrast to their conservative neighbors in town. The Campus Democrats is a popular club at Grinnell due to the passionate liberalism among students.

Although Grinnell can boast to being the host and winner of the first intercollegiate football and baseball games west of the Mississippi, sports at Grinnell don't draw huge crowds anymore. The men's basketball team has "an unorthodox style but is successful," and won the Midwest Conference championships in 2001 and 2003. The sports teams on a whole aren't always great, but they give every student a chance to play regardless of skill level. The varsity-level teams are competitive, though, so some students opt to join the more toned-down intramural teams. Popular IM teams include football, Ultimate Frisbee, and rugby. Indeed, when asked if sports are big at Grinnell, one student responded, "Umm . . . does Ultimate Frisbee count?"

Located in a picturesque Midwest town and drawing students from all over, Grinnell is "a melting pot from all over the nation, which makes for a good combo." Grinnell College fosters intensity in all areas of its students' lives, whether through demanding course loads, extracurricular involvement, political activism, or simply partying on the weekends. In all aspects of life, Grinnell, therefore, offers an educational experience of the utmost quality.—*Terren O'Reilly*

FYI

If you come to Grinnell, you'd better bring "a hookah and a coat."

What's the typical weekend schedule? "Going to a movie, or watching a movie in someone's room, then drinking for a while in someone's room, or on a loggia if its warm, then going to a Harris party or some other party, then going to the forum or Bob's, then going back to where you started drinking."

If I could change one thing about Grinnell, I'd "add 200 people."

Three things that every student at Grinnell should do before graduating are "contribute to the graffiti in Burling Library, explore the steam tunnels, and go the Mary B. James cross-dressing dance."

Iowa State University

Address: Iowa State, 100 Alumni Hall, Ames, IA 50011	**Middle 50% SAT range:** 510–640V, 540–690M	**Retention Rate:** 83%
Phone: 800-262-3810	**Middle 50% ACT range:** 22–27	**Graduation Rate:** 31%
E-mail Address: admissions@iastate.edu	**Early admission program (EA/ ED/ NA):** NA	**Percent in On-campus housing:** 37%
Web site URL: http://www.iastate.edu	**ED or EA Acceptance Rate:** NA	**Percent affiliated with Greek system:** 31%
Year Founded: 1858	**Full time Undergraduate enrollment:** 20,035	**Percent Varsity or Club Athletes:** NA
Private or Public: Public	**Total enrollment:** NA	**Number of official organized extracurricular organizations:** 690
Religious affiliation: none	**Percent Male:** 56%	
Location: Urban	**Percent Female:** 44%	**3 Most popular majors:** finance, marketing, mechanical engineering
Regular Application Deadline: 1-Jul	**Total Percent Minority:** 8%	
Number of Applicants: NA	**Percent African-American:** 3%	**Student/Faculty ratio:** 15:01
Percent Accepted: 90%	**Percent Asian/Pacific Islander:** 3%	
Percent Accepted who enroll: 46%	**Percent Hispanic:** 2%	**Tuition and Fees:** $16,110
Number Entering: NA	**Percent Native-American:** 0%	**In State Tuition and Fees (if different):** $5,352
Number of Transfers Accepted each Year: NA	**Percent Other:** 8%	**Cost for Room and Board:** $6,445.00
Mean SAT: 1,180	**Percent in-state / out of state:** 79%/21%	**Percent receiving Financial aid, first-year:** 54%
Mean ACT: 25	**Percent from Public HS:** 93%	

Sir Lancelot and Elaine swim on placid Lake Laverne next to the Memorial Union. The royal swan pair is the pet darling of Iowa State, second only to the official mascot, the Cyclone. Add the sculpture of Dutch artist Christian Petersen, Iowa State alum, to this idyllic scene and you've got Iowa State University's campus.

Upperclassmen say they can tell freshmen from returning students as they cross the campus because they're dressed up and raring to go. Upperclassmen who've been at Iowa State for a little while are all "running behind, still wearing their pajamas, and haven't combed their hair." This picture of Iowa State was pegged as "not extremely diverse." Another student put it more severely: "Since we're in the middle of Iowa, it

tends to be mostly white people . . . that's what's in Iowa." Minority attendance is encouraged by a growing number of scholarships and cultural information sessions and parties, but students say the school has a difficult time retaining minority students because they're so outnumbered in the University's vast student population.

Cracking the Books

Iowa's original six colleges have multiplied to include offerings such as business, education, design, and liberal arts and science. Students enter Iowa State in one of these colleges, sorted according to their major. Those who enroll as undecided are automatically placed in the College of Liberal Arts and Sciences (LAS), and then they "take a bunch of classes that are designed to help you try and find what you like to do best." One student cited the difficulty of the engineering college as "really grueling, I think the first or second in the nation" but offered business as a kinder, gentler alternative. "The joke here is it's kind of the place engineers go to die," he said. "If they fail out of engineering they go to business."

> **"The joke here is [Iowa State]'s kind of the place engineers go to die."**

Some students complained about large class sizes that made individual attention hard to get. Class size varies depending on your college, but be reassured: students say they've gotten individual help from professors "just by going into their office and talking to them or asking questions." Really large classes have TA sections that break them down into more manageable groups. Students complain that TAs "usually don't know what they're doing," or "know their area, but can't teach their area." The only classes you'll find you have to tolerate, TA or not, is English. Two English credits are required for students in all colleges to graduate.

One benefit on the school's large size is the vast array of academic options. Liberal Arts and Sciences with 22 departments and over 50 majors ranging from botany, to journalism, to criminology and criminal justice, a new major being starting fall 2006. For those itching to get out of Iowa for a semester or two, LAS offers study abroad programs across the globe. Options include Belize, Florence, India, and even Antarctica.

No Place Like Home

Students often start to find their niche at Iowa State by living in the dorms, and find they get a warm reception from their peers: "The doors are almost always open to everyone's rooms, and people just stop by and say hi." Resident advisors "go out of their way to make you feel part of the community." Another student added, "Up here it's pretty easy to make a small circle of friends. It's kind of hard to get lost in a crowd." The downside of the dorms is that they're none too new, though many dorm facilities are being renovated, and others are going up to replace the old buildings.

After living on campus for a year or two, most students move out of the University's old dorms. New university-owned apartments are hailed as "really really nice." There are also plenty of apartments available in surrounding Ames. While it may mean a longer walk to classes in the Iowa winter, most students choose some form of off-campus housing.

What's Doin' In Iowa

While some students complain that there's nothing to do in the corn state, they say "it's not that bad," even though you "have to be creative." The area surrounding Iowa State University is growing to meet college students' demand for fun. Welch Avenue, the street that separates one dorm from main campus, is lined with bars. When you're out not painting the town red, consider paintballing (a new paintballing facility is in the works), go-carting, or hanging out on the university's Frisbee-golf course nearby.

Most students have cars so they can go anywhere in the city, though you won't need one on Iowa's centralized campus. The city's bus system offers another option for getting around. Wherever you are on the weekends, you can call the Moonlight Express (or, as some students have named it, "the drunk bus") to ensure a safe journey.

If you want to stay on campus for a low-key weekend, the Memorial Union has a hotel on its top floor, big halls for dances and performances, eating areas with a number of vendors, a bar, a library, and a university bookstore. On the lower level you can shoot pool or even go bowling. There's no shortage of possibilities, because "there are so many people" at Iowa State who "do so many different things." Beware of Memorial Union after dark, though. An entranceway in the building that commemorates World War II and Vietnam veterans is said to be haunted by some of the wars' nurses.

Beneath the Campanile

Iowa State's oldest and most-loved tradition is campaniling. On the Friday of homecoming, students gather under the big clock tower on campus, called the campanile. "When it strikes midnight you're supposed to kiss your significant other. That's called campaniling." Homecoming also means the height of Greek life, including a construction contest. Fraternity or sorority lawns sport such original creations as the set for Pee Wee's playhouse or re-creations of Cy, Iowa State's yellow-headed avian mascot.

The other big event of the year is VEISHA, an annual celebration during basketball season put together by a board of student volunteers. VEISHA's initials represent the six original colleges at Iowa State, including veterinary medicine, engineering, industrial science, home economics, and agriculture. Events of the festival include a parade and Olympic-style competitions between teams of students. It's also a chance to reach out to the community. "They shut down a couple of the streets and they set up booths and stuff for kids and families to come," one VEISHA fan said.

Ice, Ice, Baby

For a school whose football and basketball teams "aren't too good this year," Iowa State offers a number of exciting intramural sports, which are recommended by students as "just too much fun" to pass up. Students pick their own teams and compete in sports such as broomball, an Iowa State tradition. "You take a ball to the ice rink where the hockey team plays," one senior explained, "and you just get a broom and you hit it to your goals." While billed as a low-contact sport, broomball can get pretty risky for those who don't slide around too well in tennis shoes. For those who are less athletically or icily inclined, intramurals also offers competitions like chess and quiz bowl. Students can also compete against their professors once a year when their colleges are celebrated for a week. Business Week, for example, honors the business college, and students and teachers go up against each other in games and contests "just to get to know each other better" and have a good time.—*Stephanie Hagan*

FYI

If you come to Iowa State, you'd better bring "a beer bong."

What is the typical weekend schedule? "Friday night everybody gets dressed up, makes themselves look nice, then goes out and parties pretty much all night. Get up around noon on Saturday, sit around and watch football or study for the rest of the afternoon, and party all night. Get up at noon again on Sunday, and spend the day studying."

If I could change one thing about Iowa State, I'd "have the size of classes be smaller."

Three things every student at Iowa State should do before graduating are "go campaniling, go to VEISHA, and party—that's just gotta happen."

University of Iowa

Address: University of Iowa, 107 Calvin Hall, The University of Iowa, Iowa City, IA 52242
Phone: 800-553-4692
E-mail Address: admissions@uiowa.edu
Web site URL: www.uiowa.edu
Year Founded: 1847
Private or Public: public
Religious affiliation: none
Location: urban
Regular Application Deadline: 2-Apr
Number of Applicants: 14,350
Percent Accepted: 82.79%
Percent Accepted who enroll: 36.1%
Number Entering: 4,289
Number of Transfers Accepted each Year: 2,097
Mean SAT: NA
Mean ACT: NA

Middle 50% SAT range: 1,060–1,320
Middle 50% ACT range: 23–27
Early admission program (EA/ ED/ NA): NA
ED or EA Acceptance Rate: NA
Full time Undergraduate enrollment: 20,300
Total enrollment: 26,385
Percent Male: 47%
Percent Female: 53%
Total Percent Minority: 9.5%
Percent African-American: 2%
Percent Asian/Pacific Islander: 4%
Percent Hispanic: 3%
Percent Native-American: 0.5%
Percent Other: <1%
Percent in-state / out of state: 63% / 37%

Percent from Public HS: NA
Retention Rate: 84%
Graduation Rate: 66%
Percent in On-campus housing: 30%
Percent affiliated with Greek system: 9.65%
Percent Varsity or Club Athletes: NA
Number of official organized extracurricular organizations: 400
3 Most popular majors: Communications, English, Psychology
Student/Faculty ratio: 15:01
Tuition and Fees: $19,465.00
In State Tuition and Fees (if different): $6,293.00
Cost for Room and Board: $7,250.00
Percent receiving Financial aid, first-year: 57.93%

Only one university in the Midwest can claim to have the nation's finest creative writing program. Besides this distinction, however, the University of Iowa also offers its students a picturesque campus, a thriving social scene, and the excitement of its Big Ten athletic teams. Through this atmosphere of academic stimulation and routine partying, most U of I students find themselves very satisfied with their college experience.

Hawkeye Academia

To many, the most distinctive features of the University of Iowa, both academically and culturally, are its world-renowned writing programs. The U of I was the first university in the United States to offer a graduate program in creative writing, and today the program continues to lead the field. Tennessee Williams and John Irving are just two of the well-known authors and graduates of the program, and notables such as Louise Gluck, Adam Haslett, and Ian McEwan are among the list of current teachers and visiting faculty. The most prominent of the graduate programs are "The Writer's Workshop," "The International Writing Program," and "The Center for the Book," each sponsoring similar programs designed for undergraduates. In fact, quite a few undergraduates choose the U of I because of these opportunities to become a part of "the hub of the literary world."

The academic rigor at the University of Iowa is considered by most to be challenging but manageable. The general education requirements for graduation are described as "reasonable," and include a rhetoric or speaking/writing course (depending on AP placement), one semester's competency in a foreign language, and classes from the disciplines of interpretive literature, historic perspectives, humanities, the natural sciences, the social sciences, and quantitative or formal reasoning. Most undergraduates come in undeclared—called "open majors"—and there is no deadline by which one must choose a major. Students have 100 different areas of study to choose from, with the work load varying from major to major. Business is considered by some to be "the biggest blowoff major ever," while premed and prenursing require much more focus. Not surprisingly, the English, creative writing and music composition departments are considered excellent.

Classes at U of I are usually smaller than 50 students, and those in large lectures are put into 20-person discussion sessions with TAs. Sometimes, however, undergraduates find a lack of personal attention, as one student noticed when she was handed back an original composition that was graded but had no comments. On the whole, though, students at the U of I find that if they do their research on classes, they can find and pick ones that are pleasing to them in both rigor and instruction.

Not Just Bars

Moving beyond its writing programs, a lesser-known jewel of the University of Iowa is its art museum, which houses a famous Jackson Pollock work titled "Mural," as well as works by artists such as Léger, Matisse, Picasso and Franz Marc. Noticing the museum's dirty carpets and handwritten captions, however, one student expressed the general conception that the art scene at U of I "has great potential, but hasn't yet found full support and funding."

Support definitely does exist for U of I sports, though. As one freshman noted, "Iowa's known for the wrestling and the writing." Socially, football and men's basketball games provide many opportunities for one of the favorite activities of U of I students: tailgating. During football season tailgating "becomes a really big thing—people start drinking at eight in the morning and by three they're slammed." Drinking, parties, random hookups and sports typically dominate the social scene, and Iowa City's many bars (such as The Union Bar, Gabe's Oasis, and The Green Room) are big party spots that advertise "You Call it $1.00's." The administration is aware of the heavy drinking scene and has tried to curb it, demanding strict action by the university police officers. In spite of this, to some students it seems like "security attempts to follow the rules of the administration, but it's really one big joke."

> "Iowa's known for the wrestling and the writing."

Most U of I students agree that there are a good number of socializing options for those who are non-drinkers. People often frequent coffeehouses (there are almost as many coffeehouses as bars), go to movies, and attend musical concerts. On a regular basis the university hosts speakers, and in the "Saturday Scholars" speaker series students can hear lectures on a wide variety of disciplines and issues. In addition, traditional events such the Homecoming Parade and the Dance Gala always draw a big crowd.

A Hill Amidst the Corn

There are actually no cornfields on the U of I campus, but according to one student, "to get anywhere you need to go up and down a hill." The center of campus is the Pentacrest, where the old Iowa State Capital is located. The campus itself is separated into east and west, the west being newer and closer to the medical school and hospital (which is the third largest teaching hospital in the nation). A variety of architectural styles are represented in the U of I buildings, and in between them all, right through the heart of campus, runs a river. Downtown Iowa City is very much an extension of the campus, as the bars, coffee shops, restaurants, and other businesses there all cater to the students. Outside of those venues, however, some students say that there is "not a lot going on."

Got to Eat and Sleep

There are two dining halls at U of I: one on the west side of campus in the Hillcrest dorm, and the other on the east side in a dorm called Burge. The widespread opinion is that Hillcrest has a much better cafeteria, but it's a 15-minute walk for those who live on the east side of campus. The food is generally described as "OK," but on weekdays a service called "Grab 'N Go," which allows students to make to-go lunches, is very popular. The Iowa Memorial Union, which has recently undergone a renovation, offers a food court and a host of dining options.

Students often eat with the people they live with, and through the University's housing system, people with similar interests can live together. There are several "learning communities" (Honors, International Crossroads, Performing Arts, and Women in Science and Engineering) in which students can opt to be placed. Those who don't choose learning communities select a specific dormitory, each of which has its own character. Hillcrest is considered the jock dorm, while Burge, the "party dorm," is rumored jokingly to have "the highest STD rate of any dorm in the country."

Though most juniors and a fair percentage of the student body choose to live in off-campus apartments, the dorms are very clean and nicely sized. The RAs pay attention to what's going on, but are more "like friends." The dorm is, according to one composition major, a place where "a lot of crazy things go on, and I think it's all very interesting."

From Illinois to Greeks

Interestingly enough, the University of Iowa draws people mainly from two places: "Everyone you ask is either from a small town in Iowa or suburban Chicago—it really is like 'The University of Illinois at Iowa.' " Though racial diversity is lacking, there is a supportive atmosphere that accepts interracial dating and various sexual orientations. In the end, though, most students—no matter what their socioeconomic levels, interests or orientations—merge into a unified student body that often wears jeans and University of Iowa sweatshirts.

The varying interests of U of I students are exemplified in their many extracurricular activities. There are over 360 student-run organizations, including ones that focus on equal justice, fine arts, engineering, community service, and even free bikes (the "Free Ride Bike Association" began in 2002). Over 20 of the extracurricular organizations are fraternities and sororities; about 13 percent of the campus is involved in Greek life. The rush season is described as intense, with the first day being "hell" and the last "the most awesome night." Fraternities and sororities engage in many social activities among themselves, but the university's social scene is not seen as being dominated by them.

A scene that does draw all U of I students is the Big Ten sports scene. Whether tailgating, playing intramurals, or watching the wrestling team bring home another title, students share their enthusiasm for a school that is the happy home to many.—*Elizabeth Dohrmann*

FYI
If you come to the University of Iowa, you'd better bring a "fleece pullover."
What is the typical weekend schedule? "Go to a bar, get drunk, take someone back to your room, get laid, sleep late, eat, get dressed, go to a bar, get drunk, take someone back to your room . . ."
What one thing would you change about the U of I? "Make the food on our [east] side of the river better."
Three things every student at the U of I should do before graduating are "go to a poetry reading, lose your virginity, and go to the Dance Gala."

Kansas

Kansas State University

Address: Kansas State, Office of Admissions, 119 Anderson Hall, Manhattan, KS 66506
Phone: 800-432-8270
E-mail Address: k-state@k-state.edu
Web site URL: consider.k-state.edu
Year Founded: 1863
Private or Public: public
Religious affiliation: none
Location: suburban
Application and Admissions Information: rolling
Regular Application Deadline: NA
Number of Applicants: 7,705
Percent Accepted: 62.1%
Percent Accepted who enroll: 69.1%
Number Entering: 5,034
Number of Transfers Accepted each Year: 1,631
Mean SAT: NA

Mean ACT: 23.7
Middle 50% SAT range: NA
Middle 50% ACT range: NA
Early admission program (EA/ ED/ NA): NA
ED or EA Acceptance Rate: NA
Full time Undergraduate enrollment: 16,680
Total enrollment: 23,151
Percent Male: 51.1%
Percent Female: 48.9%
Total Percent Minority: NA
Percent African-American: NA
Percent Asian/Pacific Islander: NA
Percent Hispanic: NA
Percent Native-American: NA
Percent Other: NA
Percent in-state / out of state: NA
Percent from Public HS: 44%

Retention Rate: 81%
Graduation Rate: 59.3%
Percent in On-campus housing: 29.8%
Percent affiliated with Greek system: 22%
Percent Varsity or Club Athletes: NA
Number of official organized extracurricular organizations: 380
3 Most popular majors: Jounalism, Mechanical Engineering, Animal Science and Industry
Student/Faculty ratio: 15:01
Tuition and Fees: $4,744.00
In State Tuition and Fees (if different): $13,136.00
Cost for Room and Board: $5,912.00
Percent receiving Financial aid, first-year: 63%

As one of the nation's first land-grant schools, Kansas State University has always been known for its top-notch agriculture programs. However, it also boasts several of the leading academic departments in the nation. Four of its nine colleges are ranked in the top ten in the United States, including the College of Agriculture, College of Human Ecology, College of Architecture and College of Veterinary Medicine. Among the state's high school seniors and community college transfers, K-state is ranked as the No. 1 choice of universities. One reason might but its outstanding Honors Program: over the past 20 years, the University has produced more Rhodes, Truman, Marshall, Goldwater and Udall scholars than any other public school in the country.

Real-World Preparation

Students have the opportunity to begin taking courses in their college of choice as early as freshman year. As the backbone of the University, the College of Arts and Sciences has the largest student enrollment, with about 7,000 undergraduates. But with more than 250 majors available and 50 minors to choose from, many students tend to mix degree programs to match their specific interests. For example, K-State has the largest Leadership Studies program in the country, with over 1,200 students earning a minor in that program.

Each department has its own general education requirements that students must meet before graduation. The requirements vary from college to college, but they can include English, math, foreign language and even public speaking courses. Though some students complain that requirements are a nuisance, others recognize that such courses help provide a "broad, well-rounded education," even though they may not be related at all to one's major.

Each student is assigned a faculty member who serves as their academic adviser at the beginning of freshman year. Students said advisors have been known to be helpful not only for providing academic assistance, but for providing "real-world" guidance as well, such as finding part-time jobs or internships in a student's field of interest. According to one student, the K-State faculty is committed to "instructing students so that we walk away with the traits needed to be successful."

Students noted that the relationship between students and professors at K-State is "pretty good," and that professors on the whole are perhaps more receptive and dedicated to the undergraduate's education than at other similarly large research universities. One sophomore remarked that the faculty has "been good as far as making undergraduates feel like they're important." He said the majority of professors are interested in interacting with their students, and receptive to speaking with anyone during designated visiting hours. While introductory classes tend to be quite large—often enrolling several hundred students at a time—upper level courses tend to be much smaller, sometimes with as few as 10 students in the more advanced ones.

K-State also provides its students with a good learning environment. All of the University's general classrooms are currently being renovated to serve state-of-the art technology, and in 2006, the campus became completely wireless. Students described their buildings as "very beautiful," with fairly uniform architecture throughout, accented by limestone and ivy.

An At-Home Atmosphere

Despite the fact that K-State boasts nearly 23,000 undergraduates, it "has the sort of atmosphere that makes everyone feel comfortable." In fact, many students enjoy studying at K-State because it has "such a friendly campus." One student noted that the administration "bends over backwards to help you out," adding that such guidance was one of the main reasons she decided to attend the University in the first place. While the majority of students are from Kansas, the quality of academic programs and the school's out-of-state affordability also make it an attractive place for students from all over. All 50 states are represented in the student population, but most out-of-staters come from Missouri, Nebraska, Texas and Colorado.

Students agreed that most people feel very comfortable on-campus, no matter what their background is. Others, however, noted that Kansas is a conservative state and characterized the University, too, as somewhat of a "closed and conservative place." One foreign student remarked that even though the majority of people on campus and in the surrounding town are "very nice to outsiders," sometimes he got the sense that many are "just not used to dealing with people from different cultures." Still, students at K-State tend to be more moderate in their political views than one might expect, and overall the campus is "very receptive" to different opinions and backgrounds.

The Little Apple

One hundred and twenty-five miles west of Kansas City and populated by just under 50,000 residents, Manhattan, Kansas is definitely known as a college town. Yet it is also home to Fort Riley, a large military base, so its residents are accustomed and welcoming to large amounts of people moving in and out of town.

> "[K-State] has the sort of atmosphere that makes everyone feel comfortable."

Students agreed that the University's relationship with Manhattan is a very good one—the community is involved in university activities, and students are also involved in the community. For example, the student government sends liaisons to attend all city commission meetings and some have even been elected to the city commission, so that a line of communication is maintained between the city and the student body, while the town's residents often attend many of the athletic and cultural events held on campus. Students said that residents are "generally really supportive" of the University, beyond the standard occasional complaints about things like parking, traffic congestion and noise during large events.

Some K-State students complain of a lack of activity and shopping options in Manhattan, since it's primarily a college town. However, they also noted that it is an extremely affordable place to live, and in the words of one student, "you can concentrate here pretty well." Furthermore, residents on the whole are very "nice and kind" to students who are new to the area. Some even noted that Manhattan is experiencing quite a bit of positive growth, and that several new retail and housing opportunities are being developed as well.

Housing provided by the University is separated from the city, but most students do decide to live off campus. While freshmen are not required to live on campus, it is highly encouraged and about 90 percent choose to do so. By sophomore year, students begin moving into apartment buildings, town homes or houses, and by junior year the majority of students choose to live away from campus. The University is currently in the process of completing a $100 million housing project that will include more townhouses and apartments to complement the existing suites and residence halls.

Kicking Back in Aggieville

Despite its location in the "Little Apple," K-State campus and surrounding area provide plenty of options for students looking to have a good time. Aggieville, an approximately four-block district of bars, cafes, restaurants and nightclubs within walking distance of campus, is a popular place for crowds to gather both during the week and on the weekends. While it may not be filled with tons of "trendy, hip lounges" for students to hang out in, students said the bar scene is "great," and that there are plenty of fun places to meet up with friends.

With a fairly sizable portion of the student body deciding to join fraternities or sororities, some students considered K-State to be a "huge Greek school." As one student noted, "If you decide to go to the Greek system, your life pretty much revolves around that stuff." Though drinking is a big part of the social scene, particularly for students in the Greek system, "there's still a lot of stuff to do if you don't drink." And for students not involved in fraternity or sorority life, there's also a fairly sizable house party system.

One student described the social scene at K-State as an "at-home atmosphere that's really laidback and accented by great nightlife." Yet for those not as interested in the bar or frat scene, there are plenty of other options as well. A union programming council coordinates activities several nights each week, while other student groups spon-

sor their own events. The student union, for example, puts on concerts, free movies and poker nights, among other programs.

Rooting for the Wildcats

As a member of the Big 12 Athletic Conference, K-State boasts championship football and basketball teams. Football games in the fall are an extremely popular activity with students and the Manhattan community alike, who also enjoy attending away games every once in a while. The school has big rivalries with the state's other big public school, the University of Kansas, but also competes heavily with Nebraska and Oklahoma. The Homecoming game is a fairly strong tradition at K-State, during which fraternities, sororities and other student groups create giant floats and parade around town with the marching band.

Beyond the Wildcats, students have the opportunity to participate in over 400 student clubs and organizations on campus encompassing a broad range of interests, including academics, politics and religion. Groups like the Future Financial Planners, Entrepreneurs Club and Pre-Veterinary Medicine Club also emphasize career interests. Club sports are popular as well, and include water polo, lacrosse, softball and even skydiving teams. Students said campus involvement is a strong tradition at K-State, and one added that the University does a "pretty good job of getting students interested and active in student organizations."

Students recommended that incoming freshmen get involved in some sort of student organization when they arrive on campus. Many agreed that they developed a strong sense of camaraderie working with their peers in various organizations, and that they tended also to interact socially with their groups on the weekends as well. Athletics, in particular, are a good way for students to get to know the University a little better—whether it is joining a club team, playing an intramural sport or just cheering on the Wildcats at a football game. The large number of clubs is also conducive to helping students develop leadership skills, which is something that K-State emphasizes heavily. As one student commented, "the University really empowers students to do great things if they come with an open mind and a positive attitude."
—*Kendra Locke*

FYI
If you come to K-State, you'd better bring "school spirit and a love of football!"
What's the typical weekend schedule? "The bar scene is big on Thursday nights, students go out
  with friends on Fridays and Saturdays, and relax around town or study in the library on Sundays."
If I could change one thing about K-State, I'd "improve the transportation situation by adding some
  parking garages and developing a mass-transit system."
Three things every student should do before graduation are "go to an away football game, spend a
  summer in Manhattan to get to know the town a little better when there aren't so many students
  around, and check out the outdoor opportunities in the Konza Prairie Preserve, which is owned by
  the University."

University of Kansas

Address: University of Kansas, 1502 Iowa Street, Lawrence, KS 66045
Phone: 785-864-3911
E-mail Address: adm@ku.edu
Web site URL: www.ku.edu
Year Founded: 1866
Private or Public: public
Religious affiliation: NA
Location: small city
Regular Application Deadline: 1-Apr
Number of Applicants: 10,000
Percent Accepted: 75%
Percent Accepted who enroll: 57%
Number Entering: 4,153
Number of Transfers Accepted each Year: 2,000
Mean SAT: NA
Mean ACT: 24.6
Middle 50% SAT range: NA

Middle 50% ACT range: 22–28
Early admission program (EA/ ED/ NA): NA
ED or EA Acceptance Rate: NA
Full time Undergraduate enrollment: 21,353
Total enrollment: 29,613
Percent Male: 48.5%
Percent Female: 51.5%
Total Percent Minority: 12.2%
Percent African-American: 3.4%
Percent Asian/Pacific Islander: 4.2%
Percent Hispanic: 3.3%
Percent Native-American: 1.3%
Percent Other: 87.8%
Percent in-state / out of state: 69%/31%
Percent from Public HS: NA

Retention Rate: 80.5%
Graduation Rate: 59.3%
Percent in On-campus housing: 18%
Percent affiliated with Greek system: 12%
Percent Varsity or Club Athletes: NA
Number of official organized extracurricular organizations: 400+
3 Most popular majors: Biological Sciences, Business, Psychology
Student/Faculty ratio: 19.8:1
Tuition and Fees: $6,153.00
In State Tuition and Fees (if different): $6,153.00
Cost for Room and Board: $5,747.00
Percent receiving Financial aid, first-year: 47%

Located atop Mount Oread in Lawrence, Kansas, "KU" boasts gorgeous hillside scenery and a warm, friendly student body. There is something for everyone here with the large student body and the sheer range of activities it fosters.

Plenty of Choices

The University of Kansas offers 11 undergraduate schools. Freshmen can enter directly into the School of Engineering, the School of Architecture and Urban Design, the School of Fine Arts, or pursue a more broad-based curriculum in the College of Liberal Arts. Everyone enrolled in the College of Liberal Arts is required to meet a core group of requirements, which includes classes in the history of Western and modern civilizations. The Western civilization

classes include the study of classical thinkers like Plato and Aristotle, and the modern civilization classes focus on more recent developments and current events. While students were generally enthusiastic and deemed the course content as interesting, one student complained about the "immense amount of reading that was really demanding" and argued that "it should be pared down." Within the different programs of study, the core requirements vary greatly, and, while most students found them "helpful," one junior commented that "it would be better if the core requirements were more major-specific."

The Honors College offers a select group of students small seminar classes known for their better student-to-faculty ratio and excellent instruction. Students not in the honors program, however, found nothing to complain about, even if they are unable to get into the smaller classes. One sophomore raved that even the largest classes at KU were "still awesome" because of the first-rate teaching staff. Students were especially enthusiastic about the broad scope of classes and agreed that, while getting into classes was not a problem, "unless you're in the honors program, it can be hard for freshmen and sophomores to get into certain science classes." The same student noted "the professors are great and really know their stuff," and that one of his favorite classes at KU was, in fact, a large lecture class. Most students found the work load sufficiently demanding without being overwhelming, though one student noted that the architectural engineering program was particularly rigorous. In particular, Dennis Dailey's class on human sexuality was described as "notoriously controversial" and always attracts large numbers of curious students.

Mt. Oread or Mt. Olympus?
The Greek scene is large and active at University of Kansas, and parties are never in short supply. Most of the Greek parties are open to the entire student body, though there are certain formal events hosted and attended only by Greeks. One student commented that "While the Greek system is fairly popular, it's not 'the thing,' so there's not much pressure to join." With the generally friendly atmosphere, students report that "it is pretty easy to make friends," saying that "you can just talk to people in classes and they will warm up to you." Students also maintain that most of their friends come from their dorms or halls. Furthermore, "there are not very many cliques" and no particular groups dominate student life. In terms of dating, students say that people tend to couple up, with one student noting that the majority of people have significant others. One single (and hopeful) student commented, "Even though there are lots of couples around, if you're single you can still find somebody to hook up with." And chances are the hookup will be a good one, according to one student who praised the "good selection" and "fair number of attractive people" at the University. Students described the number of homosexual couples and interracial couples as few, but did acknowledge their presence on campus.

Cute and Preppy
Most students agreed that there was no dominant student stereotype at KU. In the words of one student, "There are 27,000 kids, and it makes me happy that there's every type of student here." However, one student noted the lack of geographic and socio-economic diversity, stating that "there are a lot of affluent kids who come from Johnson County and drive SUVs." Another student said that the campus is "mainly Caucasian, and there's a lack of diversity that way, but [it] has improved recently." Students report a good mix of preppy and casual clothing on campus, and were happy to note that fashion at KU is "pretty much up to you—you don't have to dress up for class if you don't want to."

> **"The professors are great and really know their stuff."**

One student observed that the dressing style often develops as the day progresses, noting that "at 7 a.m. most people look like they've just rolled out of bed and are wearing jeans and pullovers, but by noon people start looking cute and preppy."

On or Off?
Students generally were satisfied and found dorms at KU ranging from "comfortable-sized" to "very nice." One student raved about the "great" facilities in the three newly renovated dorms, but described the older dorms as "basically just a 12' by 12' cubicle which two people share, unless you request a single, in which case you get the 12' by 12' cubicle to yourself." There are single-sex dorms on campus, though most of the housing is coed. However, it is important to note that at KU mainly freshmen and sophomores stay in the dorms, with most juniors and seniors opting to live off campus in apartments or houses for lease. Options for off-campus housing are plentiful with cheap rents and close proximity to campus, making it an attractive prospect for upperclassmen looking to escape the cubicles and save some money. Dining hall food is generally praised by students for its good quality; they report that there is a decent range of options, including salad bars, dessert bars, and grill food. One student said that the food was relatively reliable because "the pizzas and hamburgers are pretty decent" and agreed that "you can always find something to eat." Another student, however, complained that while food quality was satisfactory, "it can be repetitive when they keep hashing the same thing." Students were happy to report that menus are posted on the

Internet, making it easy to check the day's selections before setting foot in a dining hall. Most upperclassmen eat off campus, and for those students and hungry underclassmen as well, Kansas City is a popular destination "if you want to get really good food."

Picture Perfect

Students raved about the "gorgeous" campus, with its picturesque landscaping full of "trees, flowers and hilly contours." The presence of "big red roofs, beautiful stone architecture, old buildings, and bustling people" completes the idyllic scene and one student happily noted "it feels like you're in a huge park." The scenery comes at a price, though, and one student felt that the hilly landscape was a problem because it makes you develop "huge calves from walking up the hill." Because of the somewhat exhausting terrain, students generally take the bus to campus and are very happy with the efficiency of the transportation system. A female student mentioned that although "security on campus has improved recently with better lighting," she still does not feel comfortable walking alone at night and argued that improvements still were needed.

Jayhawk Rock

KU students are extremely active, as seen through the popularity of varsity sports and the prevalence of extracurricular activities. Students take great pride in their athletics. The school's basketball team is particularly strong, and basketball games are described as "always very packed—sometimes so packed that you can't get in." But while old-time favorites such as basketball and football pack the bleachers, intramural sports, community service, the law society, and the medical society were also noted as being popular. Students are happy to note that the intramurals are now free, whereas in the past a small fee was charged in order to participate. At KU, new groups and activities are formed every day; as one student commented, "This semester there are at least four or five new clubs that I've personally seen start up."

Given the strong school spirit, the active social life, and vibrant extracurriculars, the University of Kansas is definitely an exciting place to be. Add to that the gorgeous campus, strong academics, and warm and friendly people, and this school is guaranteed to provide an enjoyable college experience.—*Wenshan Yeo*

FYI

If you come to the University of Kansas, you'd better bring "an open mind, because you'll meet all kinds of people here."

What's the typical weekend schedule? "Party on Friday and Saturday nights; procrastinate and do homework on Sunday."

If I could change one thing about the University of Kansas, I would "make it less hilly."

Three things every student at the University of Kansas should do before graduating are "go to a basketball game, walk through the Campanile when graduating, and enjoy a leisurely walk around the gorgeous campus."

Kentucky

Nested in the middle of Danville, a small town of 18,000, Centre College provides its 1,130 students with a unique education that includes going to the ballet or to see a musical for credit, a guaranteed internship and semester abroad, and over 200 years of history

Centre Commitment

Centre promises every student that he or she will graduate in four years, receive an internship, and study abroad for a semester or Centre will pay for one additional year's tuition. This promise is known as the Centre Commitment. And thanks to its small size, Centre can afford to make such promises.

All students must fulfill a General Education requirement, which includes a broad distribution of classes outside one's major, including a foreign language requirement, two health (and human performance) classes, and convocation credit. Convocations are events that "help a student become cultured." Such events range from the Nutcracker ballet, to a Martin Luther King, Jr. celebration. "Where else can I get credit for *The Nutcracker*, *Menopause the Musical*, and a lecture on crime in America?" boasted one student. Every year, about 40 events are designated convocation credits, and students who attend 12 in an academic year receive one course hour of an A on their transcript. As for unusual academic classes, Stephen Rolfe Powell, a famous glass artist offers glass blowing classes that are very popular with students. Despite the enormous variety of unconventional courses, the top three most popular majors at Centre are anything but unexpected: English, history and government.

Classes generally range from 10 to 15 in size, but the largest classes don't exceed 35 students. Competition for courses is virtually non-existent, and for smaller classes that cap at 20, professors tend to be flexible. Although "grading is pretty hard," students agree that "it varies a lot from professor to professor." Luckily, most students receive a considerable amount of individual attention from their professors. "I routinely talk to my professors outside of class. For example, one professor and I argue about college football all the time," one student said. "Professors at Centre are wonderful. Professors are more than willing to meet up with students outside of class, and are concerned for students' academic and non-academic well-being. Where else will the college president know every student by their first name?"

At Centre, not only is fulfilling your General Education requirements a breeze, but fulfilling major requirements is so easy (not to say that the classes are), that many students can fit in a double major, as well as study abroad. Centre works on a 4-1-4 semester schedule, so that students have three weeks in the month of January, known as CentreTerm, to go abroad or take unusual classes outside of their major like the course Basketball as Religion. Popular CentreTerm classes abroad include studying volcanoes in New Zealand, primates in Barbados and history in Vietnam. About 86 percent of the student population studies abroad, and most study abroad programs are Centre college programs.

On Campus Life (Like It Or Not)

Unlike many other colleges, most of Centre's students live on campus—a whopping 96 percent. Freshmen all live together in single-sex dorms, but recently a housing squeeze allowed for one of the freshman dorms to be co-ed, although it is still gender-segregated by floor. Centre is embarking on building a new, larger dorm for freshmen that should be ready in 2009 that will feature suite housing, as opposed to current doubles only system.

Except for the Independent Thought theme house, almost all dorms are single-sex. Not only is housing segregated by gender, but students at Centre also have a three week (previously six weeks) rule where students cannot be found in any of the opposite genders dorms for the first three weeks of school, and even after the three weeks, there are curfews for visitors of the opposite sex. Housing offered to students varies. Centre owns dorms, as well as houses that it breaks down into apartments for rent, a popular option with upperclassmen who "want a kitchenette but still the convenience of campus housing." The upperclassmen women's dorm, Breckenridge, is supposedly haunted by dead confederate soldiers from when the dorm was used as a military hospital during the civil war.

There are three on-campus facilities in which to eat: the Dining Commons, the Warehouse (a grill), and Jazzman's (a café). Because there is only one Dining Commons, students can generally see most of the student population at a meal. Meal plans involve different combinations of "flex dollars" and meals at the Dining Commons, as both the Warehouse and Jazzman's are à la carte. Popular places to eat off campus include Guadalajara's, Freddie's and Burke's Bakery, though most places tend to be fast food joints, national like McDonald's, or local, like the "fantastic" Mexican taco stand called La Hacienda.

Polishing Up The Greek Alphabet

Greek Row is a popular place to be. Almost all parties are thrown by the fraternities and sororities. That's not to say that they are exclusive or anything. "Everyone is welcome to any frat party, and indeed, everyone shows up, Greek or not." Some of the big annual parties include the Rave Party thrown by Phi Delta Theta, and Phi Kappa Tau's Air Guitar talent show. There a few non-Greek parties like Holiday Ball and the Beach Ball, but most parties, especially the big ones, reside in the fraternity houses. The big non-Greek event thrown every year is the Carnival, a week full of games and fun sponsored by the Student Activities Council.

Fraternities and sororities are different at Centre. More than half of the student body is in a fraternity or a sorority, but since the Greek houses can only fit about ten students, most members live on campus. Fraternities at Centre tend not to be the stereotypical party-hearty fraternities, though most frats are "jock heavy." The frats do very little hazing, but any hazing by a sorority member merits being kicked out of the sorority. "I would never have joined a sorority if I hadn't come to Centre," one student said, "It's just a different atmosphere here."

Most frat parties have a BYOB (bring your own beer) policy, especially since alcohol cannot be bought in Danville county at night, students have to go on a beer run to the next county over, about a 30 minute trip by car. While alcohol and pot are prevalent on campus, but there is no pressure to drink, and many choose not to. In fact, many events are required to be dry, like the Holiday Ball. Sororities also have rules against upperclassmen women giving alcohol to freshmen, which is a severe recruiting infraction.

There are many alternatives to the Greek

party scene, such as the free Midnight Movies (on campus or off) that the Student Activities Committee offers, or the many musical performances that Centre brings. Pop culture artists tend not to count for Convocation credit, but national tour groups often stop in Centre to perform in the Norton Center for Arts or the theater in the newly built Crounse Hall. Participation in community service activities have increased over the past few years, and organizations like the Bonner program give students a chance to give back to the community. Other organized service activities include the likes of the Freshmen Plunge, a day of service for freshmen to get involved with the community.

The Division III soccer games are popular, as are most of the homecoming football and basketball games. "Because we are in Kentucky, and half of the people are from in state, football is a big thing." Everyone at Centre talks about the "formula for football success, "C6H0," referring to the time when Centre College beat Harvard 6-0 in 1921. That year, not only did Centre upset Harvard's then-undefeated team, but Harvard had also won the NCAA Division I championship the year before. Intramurals, on the other hand, are not quite as big of a deal, although the recently built Sutcliffe Hall, which boasts newer and bigger athletic facilities, may soon influence IM participation.

Gender relations at Centre are an interesting phenomenon. As one student mused, "Sociologists have done studies on why the two different genders don't interact well here outside of parties. In the dining commons, a guy and a girl sitting with each other is subject for gossip." That's not to say that intermingling of the different genders is not improving. The move from a six week preliminary period before co-ed genders can mix to a three week preliminary period, heralds change in the school policy. "Hopefully all dorms will be co-ed, at least by floor, with one half male and the other half female, like the freshman dorm this year," one sophomore said. Some students believe that the cause for the awkward tension between male and female undergrads is simply because most students are too busy studying to have time to casually date, and therefore gender relations are already somewhat strained.

Centre and Danville: Too Close for Comfort?

Danville is a very quaint "Norman Rockwell" town in southern Kentucky. "While there will be a few rednecks who may stare at you, everyone is actually very friendly and helpful." The Centre bookstore is in town, but most students don't leave the "Centre bubble" for Danville, unless it's to eat.

Students complain that there isn't really too much to do in Danville and are generally pretty happy that a lot happens on campus. When students want to get away, most pile into a car and drive to Louisville or Lexington. Even though Danville is such a small town, most students need a car to get around off campus whether it's to go to Lexington or to go on a beer run.

Danville isn't the only small thing about Louisville. "At Centre, everyone knows everyone's business, but you will also meet everyone and get to know them like your neighbor." Most people meet their close friends in class and extracurricular activities, but feel as though they know "most of the people" on campus pretty well.

Traditions, Histories, and . . . Streakers

With over 200 years of history, Centre College has built up a treasure chest of stories to share. In addition to the haunting of Breckenridge and "C6H0," Centre is truly rich in myths and legends.

Take another interesting tradition involving former Supreme Court Chief Justice Fred Vinson, who was born in Louisa, Kentucky. A brother of Phi Delta Theta at Centre, he kept close ties with Centre after he graduated, including attending as many home games as he could. After his death in 1953, the brothers of Phi Delta decided that there was no reason that he should miss the games that he had so loved to attend. The Phi Delta brothers bring a portrait of him to almost every home sporting event, affectionately referring to the portrait as "Dead Fred." When Centre hosted the vice-presidential debates of 2000, "Dead Fred" was the first to be seated.

> **"We are the Harvard of the South."**

As for romantic tales, myth has it that if students kiss on the brass college seal at midnight in front of Old Campus, the oldest building on campus, they will end up marrying each other. With the alumni magazine reporting that two out of three Centre students end up marrying another Centre alum, it seems that there might be some truth to the myth. "My RA's boyfriend proposed to her right after kissing her on the seal [at midnight]," one student noted.

The other really popular tradition involves the Flame, a sculpture donated by an alumnus meaning for it to represent the lamp of knowledge on Centre's seal. For current students, "running the flame" has become a mythical tradition. To participate, students start out from a stairwell near Crounse Hall, strip down naked, run to and around the flame, and run back to where they started from, all while avoiding being fined $100. This late night tradition can be witnessed every once in a while, especially during the rush season for fraternities, and after sports victories.

While the percentage of minorities at Centre falls less than 5 percent, about half of the student population is from out of state, and Centre draws for a diverse socioeconomic pool. Centre's great academics (as one student noted "We are the Harvard of the South"), its commitment to its students through both the Centre commitment and its professors, as well as its two centuries worth of history and tradition make Centre college an appealing choice for many students.— *Jesse Dong*

FYI

If you come to Centre, you'd better bring "a car and directions to Lexington and Louisville."
What is the typical weekend schedule? "Go out for Friday dinner, then go see a musical performance or play, then go to a Greek party. Saturday, sleep in, work during the afternoon, meet up with friends for dinner, go out again and probably end up at a Greek party. Sunday sleep in till brunch where you see everyone on campus, attend an athletic function, then lock yourself in the library."
If I could change one thing about Centre, I'd "improve the gender relations."
Three things ever student should do before graduating from Centre are: "run the flame, make a night beer run, hang out with a professor outside of class."

University of Kentucky

Address: University of Kentucky, 101 Main Building, Lexington, KY 40506-0029
Phone: 859-257-2000
E-mail Address: admisso@uky.edu
Web site URL: www.uky.edu
Year Founded: 1865
Private or Public: public
Religious affiliation: none
Location: urban
Regular Application Deadline: 16-Feb
Number of Applicants: 10,508
Percent Accepted: 82.32%
Percent Accepted who enroll: 44.34%
Number Entering: 3,835
Number of Transfers Accepted each Year: 1,614
Mean SAT: 1,134
Mean ACT: 24

Middle 50% SAT range: 1,030–1,270
Middle 50% ACT range: 22–27
Early admission program (EA/ ED/ NA): NA
ED or EA Acceptance Rate: NA
Full time Undergraduate enrollment: 18,702
Total enrollment: 24,187
Percent Male: 47%
Percent Female: 53%
Total Percent Minority: 8.1%
Percent African-American: 5%
Percent Asian/Pacific Islander: 2%
Percent Hispanic: 1%
Percent Native-American: 0.1%
Percent Other: <1%

Percent in-state / out of state: 83% / 17%
Percent from Public HS: NA
Retention Rate: 79%
Graduation Rate: 60%
Percent in On-campus housing: 19%
Percent affiliated with Greek system: 16.12%
Percent Varsity or Club Athletes: NA
Number of official organized extracurricular organizations: 348
3 Most popular majors: NA
Student/Faculty ratio: 17:01
Tuition and Fees: $13,970.00
In State Tuition and Fees (if different): $6,510.00
Cost for Room and Board: $7,262.00
Percent receiving Financial aid, first-year: 63.64%

If Wildcat basketball comes to mind when you think of the University of Kentucky, you're on the right track. The thousands of students that call this campus home all come together in support of their famed team. But the excitement doesn't end there; many students at UK find themselves satisfied with the academics, busy with all the opportunities and ecstatic with school spirit.

Kentucky Academia

When students apply to UK, they apply to one of the University's 16 colleges, which include Agriculture, Engineering, Architecture, Arts and Sciences, Business and Economics, Communications, and five Medical colleges. No matter which college students attend, however, all must complete a core curriculum, called the "General Studies Program." Before graduation, students take courses in speaking, cross-cultural studies, humanities, and the social sciences. Additional math, English, and science class requirements depend on the individual college.

On the whole, students find that they "aren't that inspired" by core classes, as the classes are easy to let slide. But once students latch onto the department of their major, the academics are described as "pretty good." The science-oriented classes are cited as the most difficult, along with classes in the College of Architecture, where students can be working on projects "from 2 a.m. to 2 p.m., four days a week." Pharmacy and nursing are very popular areas of study, and the campus is "surrounded by hospitals, which makes for a lot of opportunities."

People choose to study many different things at UK, but most agree that "though lots come to party, those who do work find UK equally good in the humanities and the sciences." Many students receive scholarships or financial aid from the university. A good number of students also apply for the Honors Program. Once accepted into the program, students take one Honors course each semester, with the course usually focused on the humanities. All undergrads at UK have an advisor from their college and an adviser in their major, and Honors students have an additional advisor from the program.

> **"Though lots come to party, those who do work find UK equally good in the humanities and the sciences."**

For all students, registering for classes can be an ordeal. Though Honors students get to register first, almost everyone finds that it can be hard to get into classes. Introductory classes are often very large; one freshman commented that UK "accepts every AP credit (with a score 3 or above) to get people out of 100-level classes . . . you're lucky if you get a chair." Labs and sections for these huge classes are taught by TAs—many of whom don't speak English well. One biology major related a story of her first day in a calculus class. While students were filing into the classroom, one girl announced that the class wasn't on calculus, but a foreign language. A few minutes later, the teacher, who had a heavy Chinese accent, came out to tell the students that it really was their calculus class after all.

Despite some language barriers, many students say that they are very happy with the teachers they have had. Most adopt the ritual of asking around to find out who the best professors for each class are, and are usually not disappointed. One freshman claimed: "I've been really pleased with the faculty. They have a strong background and are interested in getting the students to do their best." Many professors encourage students to come to their office hours, and this personal attention—especially noticed in the smaller-sized Agricultural College—makes UK students feel "less like a number."

Bring Out the Bourbon

Outside of academics, most Wildcats lead a very active social life. The most dominating social force is the Greek system, which provides the central scene for partying at UK. Though the fraternities and sororities are officially dry, per the school's no-alcohol policy, students often rent off-campus spaces to take their festivities outside of regulated grounds. More drinking seems to go on at UK than hard drugs; after all, "Kentucky grows tobacco and makes bourbon." Students frequent drive-thru liquor stores, and upperclassmen often go to clubs or bars.

Students say that "there're definitely the sorority-girl and fraternity-boy stereotypes" at UK. Most of the undergrads are white and middle-class, and many of the girls frequent tanning beds. A freshman noted that "there's not as much diversity as I expected," especially in reference to blacks and gays.

However, though "it can feel a little cliquey," those who aren't into the Greek scene find other ways to enjoy themselves. Sometimes "a lot of people who don't drink go home on the weekends," but often friends watch movies and go to coffeehouses, such as Starbuck's, Common Grounds and Coffee Time. In addition, the University often puts on-campus events such as concerts, street parties, and pep rallies. The popular pep rallies are also sponsored by the student government, which puts on a Halloween party every year, as well.

On the dating front, people tend to lean towards hook-ups, but dating and steady relationships also exist. There are not many interracial or gay couples; one student said that she "doesn't see much of it" and "doesn't hear much about it."

How the Wildcats Live

The University of Kentucky is located in Lexington, where its red-brick buildings stand in green lawns full of trees. The campus is divided into three sections: North Campus, home to six dorms; Central Campus, with classroom buildings, the new library, and two dormitories; and South Campus, which has low-rise dormitory towers. Students select which dorms they want to live in on a first-come, first-serve basis. Patterson and Boyd Halls (the Honors dorms) are located on North Campus, as is Jewell Hall (the international dorm), and Blazer and Holmes Halls (all-female, all-male dorms, respectively). Also on North Campus is the Wildcat Lodge, the unofficial dorm for the basketball players, who are "treated like royalty."

On Central Campus is the "gorgeous and fairly easy to navigate" William T. Young Library. Nearby are the all-male Haggin Hall and the all-female Donovan Hall (said to be the hardest dorm to get into, because of the nice rooms). South Campus has Kirwan and Blanding Towers, along with several low-rises. The new, $5 million athletic complex, called the Johnson Center, is also located on South Campus. While this facility is greatly enjoyed by most, some students wish the money had been spent on "getting more teachers and more parking."

When not sleeping, partying, working out, or studying, there's a good chance that students are eating. There are three dining halls around campus, one in each campus section. Blazer Hall is on North Campus, the Student Center serves meals on Central Campus, and The Commons caters to South Campus. The library also has a highly praised café called Ovid's. Though vegetarians complain about not having many options, students can charge their meal account at on-campus eateries, such as Starbucks. Also popular are fast-food restaurants like McDonald's and KFC; but for a change, there's Joe Bologna's (a small Italian restaurant) and nearby restaurants like the Macaroni Grill. Tolley-Ho's, however, is the most popular off-campus restaurant. UK students have been eating and hanging out there for years, making it a real campus tradition.

We Come Together

But the biggest tradition at the University of Kentucky revolves around extracurriculars. Besides the fraternities and sororities—some of which do community outreach—students get involved in campus ministries, student boards, intramurals, the *Kentucky Kernel* (the daily newspaper), and organizations like the Green Thumb Club. As one student said, "Anything that you want to be involved in they have, or they encourage you to start yourself."

But nothing can compare to something that began a long while ago—the UK Wildcats basketball team. The men's team plays in the Rupp Arena, which now has a student section appropriately called "The Eruption Zone." Erupting is exactly what students do when they get together for a game: The "crowd is crazy" and enthusiasm skyrockets. Fireworks are set off before every home game, and afterwards the cheerleaders and band always play and sing "My Old Kentucky Home."

No matter which UK college students are in, or what their different interests are, almost everyone comes out to support their team. Students cite this common spirit that "brings so many students and groups together" as the force that really makes their university unique. With everyone cheering their Wildcats on, it makes UK, a large research university full of opportunities, "seem so much smaller."—*Elizabeth Dohrmann*

FYI

If you come to the University of Kentucky, you'd better bring "a valid ID and something blue."

What is the typical weekend schedule? "Friday: The bar of your choice with a late-night food stop at Tolly-Ho. Saturday: Football/Soccer/Basketball/Baseball game with tailgating before and hopefully a celebration afterwards. Sunday: Sleep followed by cramming. Excellent Exceptions: All weekend activities in April and October revolve around tailgating and betting on horse races at the beautiful Keeneland Race Course."

If I could change one thing about UK, I'd "make the campus wet again."

Three things every UK student should do before graduating are "make an early rise and go to the Saturday morning brunch and practice runs at Keeneland in April (starts at 7:00 am), sit lower level for a CATS game at Rupp Arena, and read *The Bluegrass Conspiracy* (it makes you look at all of your surroundings in a totally different light)."

Louisiana

Louisiana State University

Address: Louisiana State, 110 Thomas Boyd Hall, Baton Rouge, LA 70803
Phone: 225-578-1175
E-mail Address: admissions@lsu.edu
Web site URL: www.lsu.edu
Year Founded: 1860
Private or Public: public
Religious affiliation: none
Location: urban
Regular Application Deadline: 15-Apr
Number of Applicants: NA
Percent Accepted: 73%
Percent Accepted who enroll: 63%
Number Entering: NA
Number of Transfers Accepted each Year: NA
Mean SAT: 1,160
Mean ACT: 25

Middle 50% SAT range: 520–630V, 540–660M
Middle 50% ACT range: 22–27
Early admission program (EA/ ED/ NA): "priority"
ED or EA Acceptance Rate: NA
Full time Undergraduate enrollment: 25,301
Total enrollment: NA
Percent Male: 48%
Percent Female: 52%
Total Percent Minority: 15%
Percent African-American: 9%
Percent Asian/Pacific Islander: 3%
Percent Hispanic: 3%
Percent Native-American: 0%
Percent Other: 4%
Percent in-state / out of state: 87%/13%

Percent from Public HS: 55%
Retention Rate: 83%
Graduation Rate: 27%
Percent in On-campus housing: 23%
Percent affiliated with Greek system: 27%
Percent Varsity or Club Athletes: NA
Number of official organized extracurricular organizations: 300
Most popular major: Psychology
Student/Faculty ratio: 22:01
Tuition and Fees: $11,281.00
In State Tuition and Fees (if different): $2,981
Cost for Room and Board: $6,498.00
Percent receiving Financial aid, first-year: 47%

It's a sunny Saturday afternoon, and the crowd at Louisiana State's Tiger Stadium is going wild in a sea of purple and gold. During football season, Baton Rouge, La., turns into Football Town, USA. As one senior raved, "It gets pretty rambunctious at the games, but that's life. You plan your week around who we play in the game. Saturday at Tiger Stadium, it's not a date . . . it's an event!"

It Never Rains in Death Valley

The fans bleed purple and gold in Baton Rouge. The school's unofficial color seems to be orange, though—the color of Mike the Tiger, LSU's beloved mascot. Fans often try to get the tiger to roar before games for good luck; one such student admitted, "The other day I was walking by his cage and I heard a huge roar. I thought to myself, 'It's going to be a good day!'"

Tigers go crazy for the pigskin at LSU. "Students come from out of state, specifically Texas, to attend the LSU football games. Football's a huge deal," said one sophomore. Everyone parks cars and trucks around campus the Friday night before the Saturday game. The fun begins with catered tailgates where students and visitors alike consume vast quantities of alcohol around the barbecue. Out-of-state fans often arrive in their purple-and-gold painted RVs on Thursday night, completely filling the two huge commuter parking lots by the stadium. These tailgates are elaborate affairs; one year, someone even towed along a swimming pool to the parking lot to splash around in before the game. Tiger Stadium has been nicknamed "Death Valley," where the mantra is that it never rains. Mere drizzles, however, could never keep these fans from the stands.

Students sit in a section called the N-Zone. The demand for tickets in the Zone is so high that students often squish in, standing room only. As one girl said, "If you don't live on-campus, you'd better get there by 7 in the morning on Saturday if you want any chance of getting in." To say the least, "school spirit is definitely a big deal here." Fans also come to cheer the marching band, called Golden Band from Tiger Land, as well as the popular Golden Girls dancers who lead cheers from the sidelines. The fans have many traditions; for instance, students claim they cheer "Geaux Tigers!" instead of "Go Tigers," as a nod to the area's Cajun-French culture. One junior explained, "It's a Southern thing!" Football games are more than just fun sporting events at LSU, they also serve as a bonding experience for the students. Cheering Tigers often wear T-shirts that read, "Saturday night in Tiger Stadium is the best time spent with 92,600 of your closest friends." Many students claim, "We're like a family. It's so big here so you can't say you know everyone, but we're a football school. So that's our common ground."

Life Beyond the Stadium

Of course, not all students at LSU consider football games the highlight of their college experience. As one sophomore said with a laugh, "LSU wastes all its money on sports." Luckily for others like her, there's a wide variety of activities both on campus and in the Baton Rouge area. Greek life is a huge social force at LSU. According to one senior, over 900 girls rush sororities each year. This student commented, "Greek life is a big deal here. There are always exchanges, socials, intermixing of fraternities and sororities, as well as different bar nights and themed parties where you can bring a date."

For those who don't want to join the Greek scene, there is still plenty to do. Many musical artists, such as Pat Green, give concerts on-campus, and the Pete Maravich Assembly Center hosts a variety of theatrical performances and lectures. Students are also regulars at nearby movie theatres and can choose from over 625 restaurants of Baton Rouge. The bar scene is another popular social option at LSU. There are at least 30 bars and clubs, though freshmen seem particularly fond of Tigerland, a strip of six bars where you only have to be 18 to enter, though you still must be 21 to drink. A "Drunk Bus" shuttles back and forth between Tigerland and campus every 15 minutes to pick up inebriated students and drop them off at their dorms. Other services like the campus transit also help to lower the rate of drunk driving, which until a few years ago was a big problem since mostly everyone on-campus owns a car.

Alcohol is not hard to find on campus either. Students report that the administration is generally relaxed about enforcing alcohol policies. On-campus parties where alcohol will be served do have to be approved, though. If the watchful eye of campus security catches alcohol at a party that hasn't been pre-approved, the party hosts can get into a lot of trouble. Though alcohol is prevalent at LSU, many sober students "like to go out even though [they] don't drink and have no problems going to parties where alcohol is being served." Other students, however, go "wild because there's so much freedom. I wouldn't call it peer pressure, more like trying out a new lifestyle, doing things you've never done before. At home you were sheltered, but here you are responsible for yourself."

A Breeding Ground for Scholars?

While some hard-working students maintain that LSU is not as much a party school as it is reputed to be, others say that academics are not their first priority. Most undergraduates enter LSU with a major already declared. Those who aren't sure what they want to do, stay in a general studies program for a year or two until they make up their minds. Switching majors can be a pain, as most credits don't transfer between programs. Dealing with registration can also be a draining and frustrating experience. One sophomore suggested that "it helps if you know your major, since getting into classes becomes a lot easier." Students agree that the science classes, particularly biology, are among LSU's toughest courses. As one freshman put it, "The biology courses weed out a lot of people." Library science is well-known as the easiest class LSU offers, and it is considered a "one-hour easy A." Class size varies greatly depending on the subject. Many English classes have only 15 to 30 students, while some popular biology and music lectures have to be held in the gym to accommodate the over 1,000 students that enroll in them. The average lecture class size hovers around 150 students, however.

LSU professors and TAs are generally responsive to student needs. They are good about returning student e-mails and setting up appointments. One senior was impressed that when he ran into one of his professors at the grocery store, as she not only greeted him by name, but even had a conversation with him. LSU also offers a variety of free tutoring services. A center for freshmen is also available for academic counseling and for setting students up with the appropriate upperclassmen tutors. One student was particularly fond of the writing center, where students can get all their papers proofread. A common academic complaint, however, is that many of the foreign professors are extremely difficult to understand—so difficult, in fact, that many students drop classes because they simply cannot understand the professors. Generally the workload is decent, though the most diligent students report studying 20–30 hours weekly. Undergraduates who want to graduate within four years have to take at least 15 credit hours per semester. Often students will take lighter schedules than this, and stick around for summer school to make up the extra credits.

Beautiful Creatures in Their Natural Habitat

When one sophomore girl was asked if she thought that LSU students were on the whole an attractive bunch, she exclaimed, "My freshman year I didn't see any cute people at all, but this year I see all kinds of hot people!" A similar response came from an upperclassman, who said, "The girls are way hotter here. . . . There's a tremendous amount of gorgeous girls and a lot of guys lacking style." Needless to say, random hookups are not rare phenomena. However, the administration "strongly frowns upon shackin' up," so guys are required to sign in and out of the girls' dorms.

The students are beautiful, and "the campus is gorgeous," as well. The school invests a lot of resources to remodel buildings and to maintain the grounds. All the dorm rooms are air-conditioned, though the freshman rooms are "like closets with beds" and dorm life often involves sharing a bathroom with an entire floor of people. Many people move into off-campus apartments by sophomore year, though most agree that LSU students should try dorm life for at least one year. About 700 people

live in each dorm, Herget being one of the most sought-after of the coed freshman dorms and Kirby Smith being one of the least desirable.

While classes are never more than a mile apart, most students opt to drive to class. The abundance of cars on campus can present a problem where parking is involved. As one frustrated sophomore confided, "There are never any parking spaces! Then the ticket people get ticket-happy and we get random parking tickets." LSU offers a great bus system that transports students from their dorms and off-campus apartments right to lecture halls, though few students actually use this service.

> "We're like a family. It's so big here so you can't say you know everyone, but we're a football school. So that's our common ground."

Despite the annoyance of parking problems, LSU students love Baton Rouge and their school. They particularly enjoy the fun atmosphere and the warm and friendly people. Most students agree that "everyone's really nice" and that "LSU is not a superficial campus." However, there seems to be conflicting views regarding diversity on-campus. While one senior mentioned that "LSU is not a very diverse campus right now, the majority of students being Caucasian, and the faculty being also mostly white," several others maintained that LSU is a very diverse place where there are many international students and an impressive mix of black and white students.

LSU offers a bit of something for everyone. Regardless of whether you're looking for a place to party hardy, to attend the finest football games on this side of the bayou, or to enjoy the benefits of a large university with friendly professors, LSU is definitely worth checking out. By the time you leave, you too will be bleeding purple and gold.
—*Jenny Zhang*

FYI
If you come to LSU, you'd better bring "a party cup" and "a pair of walking shoes."
What is the typical weekend schedule? "Go out until the wee hours, go to the football game, and recuperate on Sunday from the strenuous weekend."
If I could change one thing about LSU, I'd "have smaller classes."
Three things every student at LSU should do before graduating are "attend a football game, roll down Indian Mound, and go to a foam party."

Tulane University

Address: Tulane, 6823 St. Charles Ave., New Orleans, LA 70118
Phone: 800-873-9283
E-mail Address: undergrad.admission@tulane.edu
Web site URL: www.tulane.edu
Year Founded: 1884
Private or Public: private
Religious affiliation: none
Location: urban
Regular Application Deadline: 16-Jan
Number of Applicants: NA
Percent Accepted: 45%
Percent Accepted who enroll: 21%
Number Entering: NA
Number of Transfers Accepted each Year: NA
Mean SAT: 1,320
Mean ACT: 30

Middle 50% SAT range: V:628–725, M:603–700
Middle 50% ACT range: 28–32
Early admission program (EA/ ED/ NA): ED and EA
ED or EA Acceptance Rate: NA
Full time Undergraduate enrollment: NA
Total enrollment: 7,952
Percent Male: 47%
Percent Female: 53%
Total Percent Minority: 0%
Percent African-American: 8%
Percent Asian/Pacific Islander: 3%
Percent Hispanic: 3%
Percent Native-American: 0%
Percent Other: NA
Percent in-state / out of state: 30%/70%

Percent from Public HS: NA
Retention Rate: 88%
Graduation Rate: 73%
Percent in On-campus housing: 65%
Percent affiliated with Greek system: 68%
Percent Varsity or Club Athletes: NA
Number of official organized extracurricular organizations: 250
3 Most popular majors: Business/Commerce, Engineering, Social Sciences
Student/Faculty ratio: NA
Tuition and Fees: $31,210
Cost for Room and Board: $7,925
Percent receiving Financial aid, first-year: 11%

In August of 2005, the winds of Hurricane Katrina sent Tulane students scattering to their homes and to other universities around the country. The losses for Tulane were phenomenal. The human loss of faculty members, workers and friends was devastating, and the University's recovery costs were approximately $200 million. Students entering Tulane in fall of 2006 saw a very different university from the ones who matriculated in fall of 2005, and time will only tell where the future will take Tulane University.

Academic Overhaul

The University's "Survival to Renewal" plan aims to move the University forward after the hurricane. The program will expand Tulane's community involvement, but other programs are to be reduced to accommodate for the financial constraints created by the hurricane recovery costs. According to the University's official report, "The University will focus its undergraduate, professional and doctoral programs and research in areas where it has attained, or has the potential to achieve, world-class excellence. It will suspend admission to those programs that do not meet these criteria."

Effective in the fall semester of 2006, the undergraduate academic experience became a completely different one from previous years. Whereas previously, undergraduates were divided in Tulane and Newcomb colleges, a system that one student called "cumbersome and confusing," the new system unites all undergraduates in the Undergraduate College. After matriculation, students share a core curriculum of writing, language, science, culture, public service, interdisciplinary studies (through the TIDES seminar), and the capstone experience (an individual project). In addition to these requirements, students will also complete the requirements of their individual majors and will graduate with degrees from the School of Liberal Arts, the School of Science & Engineering, the School of Architecture, the School of Business, or the School of Public Health & Tropical Medicine. One exciting change is that all undergraduate courses are taught by full-time faculty, instead of the previous practice of using adjunct or part-time faculty.

So how do the students feel about all these changes? Right now, it's difficult to tell, but students seem positive about what's ahead. According to one student, "Some people have been saying that the administration used Katrina as an excuse for its own overhaul agenda, but I still think most people agree that these are great changes, and that everyone will benefit from this streamlined system." But these changes were not good news for everyone: "I feel really bad for the students whose programs got cut—they just have to leave."

Hard Times in the Big Easy

The hurricane forced Tulane to reconsider its role in the community, and as a result, the University has established programs to improve community involvement. The Center for Public Service will provide students a more centralized community service network, and the Partnership for the Transformation of Urban Communities, will sponsor educational programs, research initiatives and other activities to connect the university to New Orleans and the Gulf Coast region. Also, the newly established Institute for the Study of Race and Poverty will tackle the difficult race-based questions of the day, through a consortium of Tulane, Loyola, Dillard and Xavier universities. The new Institute for the Transformation of Pre-K-12 Education will advocate for urban public school reform.

The administration seems to be really hopeful about the partnership, and students seem to mirror those sentiments: "I'm really excited to see what these new programs can do. It should be really great for the community." "New Orleans really needs it, so it's great to see Tulane reaching out."

Life at Tulane

Tulane seems to be a match for lots of different types of people. "I know that every school says it's open to people of all different lifestyles, but at Tulane it's really true," one student said. "Tulane is a really accepting place, and I think all these new initiatives will really make it even more inclusive," another said. According to another, "all sorts of minorities can find a home at Tulane," and in 2006, Hillel ranked Tulane one of the top 10 private universities for Jewish life.

For the athletes, Katrina has seriously affected their opportunities. Students interested in playing varsity sports should be aware that the athletic program post-Katrina has been pared down to only eight sports—football, baseball, men's and women's basketball, volleyball, and women's indoor and outdoor track and cross-country. This may be bad news for some, but according to one student "Tulane students aren't that school-spirited in terms of sports anyway."

> **"Tulane kids really like to party, and no hurricane could change that."**

For the social butterflies, have no fear. "Tulane kids really like to party, and no hurricane could change that." While the hurricane definitely put a damper on students' social lives for a time, overall, Tulane students seem resilient. While one student said that "being in New Orleans is really depressing," another stressed that "hurricane or no hurricane, New Orleans is one of the best parts about being at Tulane." According to one student, "For people whose weekends revolved around going into the city, Katrina really hurt their social lives, but for people who liked to stay on campus it hasn't changed that much." What most students are in agreement about, though, is that the city and the University are on the upswing. "Things are getting better all the time," and never fear, for "we will always find a party, no matter what."—*Susanna Moore*

FYI
If you come to Tulane, you'd better bring "a work-hard, party-hard attitude."
What is the typical weekend schedule? "Party on Friday, chill out and do something fun with your friends on Saturday, party again Saturday night, and sleep late and do homework on Sunday."
If I could change one thing about Tulane, I'd "make it so that Katrina never happened."
Three things every student at Tulane should do before graduating are "party hard at Mardi Gras, eat in one of the amazing New Orleans restaurants, and listen to some real jazz music."

Maine

Bates College

Address: Bates, 23 Campus Avenue, Lewiston, ME 04240
Phone: 207-786-6000
E-mail Address: admissions@bates.edu
Web site URL: www.bates.edu
Year Founded: 1855
Private or Public: private
Religious affiliation: none
Location: small city
Regular Application Deadline: 1-Jan
Number of Applicants: 4,356
Percent Accepted: 29.2%
Percent Accepted who enroll: 38.5%
Number Entering: 510
Number of Transfers Accepted each Year: 20
Mean SAT: NA
Mean ACT: NA
Middle 50% SAT range:
  V: 630–700, M: 640–700

Middle 50% ACT range: NA
Early admission program (EA/ ED/ NA): ED
ED or EA Acceptance Rate: 38%
Full time Undergraduate enrollment: 1,684
Total enrollment: 1,684
Percent Male: 49.2%
Percent Female: 50.8%
Total Percent Minority: 12.5%
Percent African-American: 2.6%
Percent Asian/Pacific Islander: 4.3%
Percent Hispanic: 2.4%
Percent Native-American: 0.4%
Percent Other: 2.8%
Percent in-state / out of state: 11%

Percent from Public HS: 52.4%
Retention Rate: 94.2%
Graduation Rate: 88.9%
Percent in On-campus housing: 93%
Percent affiliated with Greek system: 0%
Percent Varsity or Club Athletes: 62%
Number of official organized extracurricular organizations: 101
3 Most popular majors: Economics, Political Science, English
Student/Faculty ratio: 10:01
Tuition and Fees: $44,350.00
Percent receiving Financial aid, first-year: (76%)100%

Bates College, a small liberal arts school generally grouped with other Maine colleges such as Bowdoin and Colby, is located in Lewiston, ME, a town whose claim to fame, as one student pointed out, is that "Mohammed Ali fought here." However, this middle-of-nowhere school proudly boasts such a fun-loving, tight-knit college community that students overwhelmingly proclaim that they could not imagine themselves elsewhere.

More Professors than Students?

Students at Bates know they are getting a first-class education; national surveys consistently rank Bates among the top liberal arts colleges in the nation. Though small liberal arts colleges often do not have the resources to offer the wide array of subject areas and depth of study that universities can provide, students at Bates almost universally cite the small class size as something that sets Bates apart from other colleges. A large number of classes have 25 students or less, and even larger lecture classes usually don't have many more than 75 students. The Bates website cites the student-to-professor ratio as 10 to 1 and stresses the college's focus on small group learning in settings such as seminars and laboratories. According to one freshman, "The great thing about Bates is that the classes are pretty small. You are not merely considered a number in the classroom, but instead you become an active participant whom the professor really gets to know." Professors are also easily approachable outside the classroom and are extremely receptive to student interest; another student commented, "In my experience, professors are very happy to talk outside of class about their research, any problems you may be having in the class, concerns, or just life in general. I've also realized that professors are happy to talk to students who aren't in their classes if they show an interest in the professor's field." Though a small college, Bates offers the diversity of a liberal arts education and does have distributional requirements, including a three science class requirement that "for non-science people is just too much!"

> The great thing about Bates is that the classes are pretty small. You are not merely considered a number in the classroom, but instead you become an active participant whom the professor really gets to know.

Bates is a very good school, and in terms of workload there is "a LOT of reading." According to a freshman girl, "the work load can be intense when midterms and finals come around, but normally it is manageable if you learn how to organize your time." Despite the workload, students observe very little competition both in and out of the classroom.

Small School, Big Parties

Bates, located in tiny Lewiston, Maine, does not boast a thriving metropolis as one of its attractions. However, students don't seem to mind; there are enough parties, events and activities on campus to keep most students from having to leave at all. According to one student, "Because there's not a lot to do in Lewiston, people stay on campus and party in the dorms and houses." Students cite dorm parties, concerts, comedy shows, dances, and off-campus parties as just some of the wide array of activities offered within the confines of Bates. The small nature of the school is conducive to creating a cohesive community, and students are generally extremely happy with their on-campus social life; as one girl commented, "Students generally don't want to leave campus because there's too much going on and they don't want to miss it. I can't imagine missing a weekend here!"

There are no fraternities or sororities at Bates; however, this is generally considered an advantage rather than a disadvantage. One freshman commented, "There is no Greek life at Bates, which I think most of the students appreciate. The social scene is much more open because of the lack of a Greek system." The students make up for this with huge annual parties, such as the 80s dance, Halloween dance, and foam dance, which are "well-attended, and everyone goes all-out and gets really into them."

In terms of drinking, the school has a relatively strict hard-liquor policy; students are subject to a three-strike rule applying to hard liquor that lasts all four years. The three strike rule requires anyone seen in a room with hard liquor to be given a strike; students with three strikes must meet with the dean. However, this rule applies only to hard liquor and drugs; the school is much more lenient in regards to wine and beer. According to students, "A lot of students do drink, but it is definitely not something you need to do to have fun here, and I know a lot of people who go out each weekend and never drink." Bates also offers a wide array of extracurricular activities, unrelated to partying, that are enjoyed by many. Athletics are popular, and students can participate on the varsity, club, or intramural level. In addition, there are four competitive a cappella groups that are extremely popular. One student exclaimed, "The Deansmen and the Manic Optimists are all male groups, the Merimanders are all women, and the Crosstones are co-ed. They are all amazing! They have concerts every once in a while and they are always packed!"

For those few students who have cars and want to get off campus, Lewiston is located relatively close to Freeport, a shopping hub, and Portland, which boasts great restaurants, a bustling city life, and a wide array of ski slopes. However, the center of Bates is clearly the campus itself, and students see this is as one of Bates' major attractions. Another student commented, "Every once in a while people will drive out to dinner on the weekends, or those who have cars will drive to ski resorts, but most of the time students stay on campus." As campus parties span three or four-day weekends, starting on Thursday and continuing to Sunday, students don't want to miss out on anything that goes on!

Close quarters = Close friends

Students overwhelmingly describe the Bates population as extremely friendly, welcoming and accepting. One student proclaimed, "If there's one reason to come to Bates, it's the people." Several students explained that, possibly due to the fact that there are two all-freshman dorms to foster a sense of family among the members of the class, their best friends have generally been people they lived with freshman year. In addition, pre-orientation programs are offered to give freshman additional chances to make friends and become comfortable in an environment away from home. Students describe the Bates campus as extremely welcoming, in part due to its small size. One student commented, "It is very easy to meet people because on the weekends you go out with friends from your floor and you end up meeting people from different dorms and classes. The students at Bates are so friendly!" Another student agreed: "It's incredibly easy to meet people because the campus is so small, and everyone's looking for new friends."

Generally, students who go to Bates are perceived as well-off, and, though the school has been making efforts to diversify the campus, the campus is primarily white, with a majority of students coming from the New England area. However, the environment at Bates is relatively laid-back; as one student commented, "When walking around campus, you wouldn't necessarily know that the students come from families with money—students really don't flaunt it. The 'dress-code' is very laid-back, which is great. People wear sweatpants everywhere, and that's completely accepted. While some people do get more dressed up on the weekends, it's certainly not fancy at all; I wore heels one night and felt completely out of place."

Family Away from Home

At Bates, the relatively small campus is designed to foster a sense of community among the students. Most freshmen are placed in one of two freshman dorms, Smith and Hedge, though Hedge will be turning into offices in the coming year. Hedge is currently smaller, consisting of 60 students who generally become so close that they are referred to as the "Hedge Cult." Smith is much bigger and contains rooms set up in quads. Upperclassmen often move off campus to nearby houses or, according to one student, "an area called the village, which is made up of apartment-like buildings with suites inside."

One unique thing about Bates is that there is only one dining hall, which was created in response to a request from the students to create an even more closely-knit community. Commons, the dining hall, is "the hot spot on campus." The students describe the food as "surprisingly good" and describe Commons as the perfect place to hang out, chat, and people watch. It's a good thing that the food in Commons is good; students explain that there are not many restaurants near campus, and other dining options are somewhat limited.

In terms of favorite hangouts, there is also Pgill (full name: Pettengill), a building open 24 hours a day and containing classrooms, lounges, professors' offices, and "really comfortable couches." Pgill is described by one freshman girl as "a much more relaxed study space than the library, and it's nice to have another place to go to work. It also has a wall of windows that overlooks the pond, so it's absolutely gorgeous."

Bates is known for being in the middle of nowhere, and it does not shy away from this reputation. However, the tightly-knit community created by the students provides a second family for many, and this is almost everyone's favorite thing about Bates. In the midst of impressive academics and a beautiful landscape, this home-away-from-home hosts some of the happiest students around.—Michelle Katz

FYI

If you come to Bates, you'd better bring "a big winter coat and slippers from LL Bean."

What's the typical weekend schedule? "Go out on Friday night, sports or homework on Saturdays and then out, work on Sundays. Weekend mornings are usually dedicated to long brunches at Commons."

If I could change one thing about Bates, "I'd create an underground tunnel for students to get to Commons and other buildings without having to freeze!"

Three things every student at Bates should do before graduating are "do the puddle jump (jump in the pond in the middle of January as part of Winter Carnival), go to Commons drunk, and spend a full night in Pgill."

Bowdoin College

Address: Bowdoin, 5000 College Station, Brunswick, ME 04011-8441
Phone: 207-725-3100
E-mail Address: admissions@bowdoin.edu
Web site URL: www.bowdoin.edu
Year Founded: 1794
Private or Public: private
Religious affiliation: none
Location: suburban
Regular Application Deadline: 1-Jan
Number of Applicants: 5,401
Percent Accepted: 21.6%
Percent Accepted who enroll: 40.6%
Number Entering: 483

Number of Transfers Accepted each Year: ~15
Mean SAT: NA
Mean ACT: NA
Middle 50% SAT range: NA
Middle 50% ACT range: NA
Early admission program (EA/ ED/ NA): NA
ED or EA Acceptance Rate: NA
Full time Undergraduate enrollment: 1,666
Total enrollment: 1,666
Percent Male: NA
Percent Female: NA
Total Percent Minority: 30%
Percent African-American: 6%
Percent Asian/Pacific Islander: 12%
Percent Hispanic: 6%

Percent Native-American: 1%
Percent Other: NA
Percent in-state / out of state: NA
Percent from Public HS: NA
Retention Rate: NA
Graduation Rate: NA
Percent in On-campus housing: NA
Percent affiliated with Greek system: NA
Percent Varsity or Club Athletes: NA
Number of official organized extracurricular organizations: NA
3 Most popular majors: Political Science, Economics, English
Student/Faculty ratio: NA
Tuition and Fees: $34,280

D oes the thought of cold winters and snow banks scare you? Fear not, Bowdoin's warm community and charming campus is enough to make the ice melt! Bowdoin attracts an active student body that is ready to take advantage of all that Brunswick, Maine has to offer, from its cute restaurants to the ski-slopes nearby.

Edgy Academia

While Bowdoin does require its students to complete eight core requirements, freshmen seminars and small writing intensive workshops, one junior explained that, "although these requirements sound so stereotypically 'liberal artsy' they are also totally valid and encompass a wide range of courses the colleges offers." Bowdoin offers 42 majors and 38 minors. The faculty is also very accommodating of students wishing to create their own major. Those looking for a lighter route, are advised to sign up for the government major (with an American studies concentration), which also happens to be the most popular major at Bowdoin (coincidence? I think not). Other popular majors include economics and history. Bowdoin also boasts a fabulous science department that even has its own neuroscience program—an impressive inclusion for such a small school.

Bowdoin puts a large emphasis on student research, and pushes service learning in particular. One junior worked with a group to create their own charter school as part of a class entitled "Anarchy, Nationalism and Fundamentalism." Getting into classes is generally quite easy, and class sizes are flexible to meet demand although the average class size is kept small, about 35 in a lecture and 16 in seminar. Students are taught by professors rather than TAs, and professors are known to be friendly and welcome post-class discussions over coffee. The workload can be significant, and potential students should expect about three to four hours of homework a night. Grade inflation, like at most American colleges, is prevalent; however physics majors seem to have the toughest time of it. They have the lowest overall GPA of all the majors.

The Simple Life

While their mascot is a polar bear, and the winters can get a bit nippy, students at Bowdoin love living in Brunswick. One student described Brunswick as "wicked cute," borrowing a phrase from the local vernacular. Brunswick is filled with lots of great restaurants, ranging from Scarlet B's to the Sea Dog Brewery. For those looking for a break Portland is not too far away (although it does require a car). Students head to Portland when in need of a really good meal or a minor-league baseball game. Freeport is a bit closer and offers great retail therapy. And of course, one of the big perks about living in Maine, is that great skiing is only a two-hour drive away.

Of course, the campus isn't half bad either. Bowdoin combines charming New England red brick and ivy with modern architecture, resulting in an aesthetic that is not only easy on the eyes, but also practical and comfortable. As far as dorms go, freshmen have it best. All freshman dorms were rebuilt in the past two years and feature two doubles with a spacious common room. "My frosh room was like a palace and that was pretty universal." Freshmen are well taken care of by their RAs and proctors. Each freshman dorm is assigned a proctor who tends to be much more hands on than the RAs who live on each floor. Freshmen develop close relationships with their proctors, who are there to help them out rather than report them. "I love my first-year proctor group that lived on my floor and the floor below me and loved the relationship with our proctor, an upper-class res-life student who basically took care of us," one student said. After freshman year, the living options are a bit more limited, although housing is guaranteed for all students. Sophomores tend to live in the social houses, while juniors and seniors chose between the 16-story Cole tower, campus-owned apartments, social houses, and off-campus houses, although few opt for off-campus. Bowdoin students are very happy with their housing options, and even more so with the food. One student raved, "Bowdoin dining is number one according to *Princeton Review* and it totally stands up to its reputation. I am a junior and still eat at least two meals a day in the dining hall."

"Home of the Original Patagucci-Prep"

One may ask, what is a Patagucci-Prep? One need go no further than this little Maine college to find the answer dressed in head to toe JCrew, Patagonia outerwear and snow boots (although Uggs are frowned upon). The dress code is preppy-conservative, although come Halloween, all bets are off—it's time to get risqué! And the look is au-natural, so leave your hair pomade and curlers at home. Students agree that the campus is "pretty homogenous," with most students coming from upper-

middle class backgrounds. While it certainly has no shortage of prep school grads, Bowdoin is not the place for snobbery. Describing the general atmosphere as "like a family," Bowdoin students are proud of their tight knight community and their "Bowdoin hello." (Note: those too awkward to say a friendly "Bowdoin Hello" to those they pass on the sidewalk need not apply.) With a student body of just 1,727 it is easy to get know a large portion of people, an aspect of college life here that many students love.

Life of the Party

Greek life was phased out in 2000 but that certainly hasn't put a damper on the Bowdoin social scene and for the most part students seem glad to be rid of the Greek system. "Thank god we don't have frats or sororities . . . and I think 99 percent of students would agree with me" one student said. Instead of the Greek life, Bowdoin boasts all-inclusive social houses, which are where most of the sophomores and some of the juniors live. The administration gives the social houses money to throw parties (often themed) every weekend.

> "Thank god we don't have frats or sororities . . . and I think 99 percent of students would agree with me."

What about the freshmen? All freshmen dorms are affiliated with one of the social houses, and freshmen tend to be the main attraction at these shindigs. "No worries if you aren't 21; you just get an "X" on your hand at the door," one junior assured. "This means that if security comes, you need to put down your keg cup and look mildly sober."

Upperclassmen however, tend to move away from the social houses and off campus where the place to be is the "Crackhouse." "Senior Lax Daddies reside in this classy establishment where lots of beer pong is played, there is a "Boom Boom Room" for dance parties (black lights and 80s music included) and a keg that never seems to get kicked," one "Senior Lax Daddy" explained. The scene at the "Crackhouse" varies from year to year, but one constant that never seems to go out of style is the Pub, the local Thursday hot spot located in the student center. Students rave about the yearly Junior/Senior Ball, a senior event held in the spring (think, Prom with lots of alcohol) and the "IVIES," which includes a fun-filled weekend of drinking, cookouts, and bands. "Everyone loves Ivies, even though no one seems to ever remember it."

So what about the non-boozers out there? As is quite true on most college campuses, non-boozers are a bit more limited in their choice of weekend activities. However, the administration does make a valiant effort. "Non-drinkers are not ostracized by any means. There are not a lot of 'social' events for the non-drinking set," including a fair number of "chem-free" social houses. The weekends are also packed with opportunities to go to lectures, movies, and dance classes. The Bowdoin Film Society puts out a number of great films, some old, some new, every weekend. And the student center and the Union, which includes a gym, café, convenient store, and pub, are always booming.

All this talk about parties is definitely setting the mood! Love is in the air at Bowdoin, or for some at least. One junior reported that the love life at Bowdoin consists of people who either start dating freshman year and stay together for the four years, or a series of random hookups. But beware! Random hook-ups on such a small campus can get quite awkward! One student warned, "Bowdoin is politically pretty left, but suddenly becomes a bunch of gossipy moralists if people are hooking up with many different people on a semi regular basis. And when I say many, I mean more than one person per weekend or more than a couple people a month." And while the gay scene may not be prevalent, it certainly does exist, with a number of gay-couples happily out in the open.

Bowdoin College is a little gem tucked away in Maine with a cozy tight knight community, where one can enjoy the great outdoors, a flexible class schedule and a great social life. Bowdoin leaves students saying, "I love Bowdoin and would love to be able to do it all again."—*Victoria Wild*

FYI

If you come to Bowdoin, you better bring "a Patagonia Parka, huge boots (preferably not Uggs) and your drinking shoes."

What is the typical weekend schedule? "Watching or playing in a weekend game, going to some sort of party and a trip to Freeport, Portland or dinner in Brunswick."

If I could change one thing about Bowdoin I "wouldn't change a thing!"

Three things every student at Bowdoin should do before graduating are "Explore downtown Brunswick, drive to the ocean and attend as many guest lectures as possible, particularly those during Common Hour."

Colby College

Address: Colby, 4800 Mayflower St., Waterville, ME 04901
Phone: 1-800-723-3032
E-mail Address: admissions@colby.edu
Web site URL: www.colby.edu/admissions
Year Founded: 1813
Private or Public: private
Religious affiliation: none
Location: small city
Regular Application Deadline: 1-Jan
Number of Applicants: 3,874
Percent Accepted: 167.8%
Percent Accepted who enroll: 35.1%
Number Entering: 511
Number of Transfers Accepted each Year: 10
Mean SAT: 1,352
Mean ACT: 29

Middle 50% SAT range: 1,305–1,420
Middle 50% ACT range: 27–31
Early admission program (EA/ ED/ NA): ED
ED or EA Acceptance Rate: 40%
Full time Undergraduate enrollment: 1,871
Total enrollment: 1,871
Percent Male: 46.5%
Percent Female: 53.5%
Total Percent Minority: 10.6%
Percent African-American: 1.8%
Percent Asian/Pacific Islander: 5.7%
Percent Hispanic: 2.6%
Percent Native-American: 0.5%
Percent Other: N/A

Percent in-state / out of state: 11%/89%
Percent from Public HS: 55.7%
Retention Rate: 93.7%
Graduation Rate: 88%
Percent in On-campus housing: 94.1%
Percent affiliated with Greek system: 0%
Percent Varsity or Club Athletes: 74%
Number of official organized extracurricular organizations: 106
3 Most popular majors: Economics, Biology, English
Student/Faculty ratio: 10:01
Tuition and Fees: $44,080.00
Percent receiving Financial aid, first-year: 42%

Academic, athletic, intimate and environmentally aware, Colby College offers the best of many worlds for especially talented students. Located in Waterville, Maine, this selective liberal arts college boasts everything from rigorous academics to great food, wacky traditions and an enthusiasm for the rugged outdoors.

Academics: In the Classroom and Beyond

Chartered in 1813, Colby College is the 12th-oldest independent liberal arts college in the nation, and the depth and breadth of its current academic offerings clearly reflect such a longstanding tradition of excellence. With 53 majors and 31 minors, Colby aims to give its students an opportunity for unique intellectual exploration. Most students appreciate these offerings, but admit that "it's a lot of work."

Priding itself on giving students a truly diverse liberal arts education, Colby College has a rather hefty set of graduation requirements, in addition to those classes required for one's particular major. Students must take a foreign language, one English composition class, one literature class, two natural sciences, one course in

the social sciences, one in the arts, one in Historical Studies, one in quantitative reasoning, and two courses that deal with diversity issues. While most students do not outright dislike these requirements, some find them more burdensome than others do. As one senior said, "It's a lot of requirements, and people have complained about it." On the other hand, another student pointed out, "I think it's important that you at least have some diversity in your education. You're going to a liberal arts school. . . . It makes sense."

Of course, as at most schools, Colby students have found ways to fulfill certain requirements they find particularly distasteful with the token "gut" classes. Students not so math- and science-oriented, for example, may take "Math as a Liberal Art" or "Rocks for Jocks."

One student pointed out that science majors tend to have more work. "The sciences are very challenging. They have a lot of core requirements, but the more liberal arts majors have a lot more room to take other courses." Popular majors include Government, Economics, English, History and Biology.

Perhaps what makes academic life at

Colby most appealing, though, is the January Program, affectionately dubbed "Jan Plan" by the students. This plan allows students in the month of January (between semesters) to broaden their academic horizons by doing something different. This can involve taking less traditional classes on Colby's campus, such as African drumming, participating in a Colby-organized program abroad, or even coming up with a project of your own. Freshmen are generally required to stay on campus. One senior noted that she spent the month driving around the East Coast in order to write her own travel guide. "It's pretty lenient," she said. "You can get credit for a lot of stuff."

Finally, academics at Colby stand out because of the small class sizes and potential for close student-teacher relationships. Introductory classes are the biggest, but even in these classes, one student said that there are never more than 100 people. Moreover, teachers are known for looking at the class roster (which includes pictures) before class and thus being able to call students by name on the second day.

Nonetheless, some students emphasize that there is a bit of a myth that at any small school students are close with teachers. "Just because you're at a small college doesn't mean that automatically you'll have these great relations with teachers," one student cautioned. "You have to search for it." The opportunity, though, is undeniably there.

Maine Campus: Living in the Great Outdoors

As one student put it, "Colby is pretty small, and it's just absolutely beautiful. All the buildings match; you just want to have it in a little snow globe." Indeed, nestled in Maine not too far from Acadia National Park, Colby College lives up to the stereotypical quaint and rugged Maine image, with an ice-skating pond of its own and a dedication to environmental awareness and sustainability. "It's beautiful. There are trees everywhere. The grass is always very green."

As one student explained, there is definitely a "big outdoor culture." The college president recently traded in his SUV for a more environmentally friendly Prius, and "If you walk around in the winter, you'll see everyone in their Patagonia parkas."

But while students appreciate the natural beauty of the campus, they seem more disillusioned with the housing system. Most generally, students are guaranteed housing all four years, though approximately 100 people (mostly seniors) live off campus each year. Dorms are not segregated by class but rather must include a certain number of students from each class, as well as a certain number of males and females. Dorms have co-ed floors.

Upper class students are assigned rooms based on a lottery system, but many complain that the current system (with the class quotas per dorm) actually discriminates against seniors who want to live together. As one student said, the system "works really well in some ways for making every dorm a diverse place age-wise, but it can really screw over juniors and seniors." One student was more blunt: "The housing is pretty sub-par. That's Colby's biggest downfall, probably."

For students who live off campus, the closest town is the city of Waterville. While Waterville is not generally considered a college town—"Waterville is not bad, it's not great"—it is only a short distance from campus. Students can bike, drive (many have cars), or even take an inexpensive taxi. The town also has a few bars and restaurants, but town-gown relations have become increasingly strained, with Waterville police becoming, according to Colby students, more eager to crack down on underage drinking and partying.

If students complain about Colby housing, though, they certainly do not complain about Colby food. Colby has three dining halls, including options for vegetarians and vegans, and "the food is great!" One student even mentioned how you can get lunch to go—not just by making a sandwich, wrapping it in napkins, and stuffing it in your backpack, but rather by picking up an actual pre-made bag lunch.

Preppy Partiers

With no fraternities or sororities and no major urban attractions, Colby students admit that there is a lot of heavy drinking. While the cops have been trying to crack down on underage drinking, students generally find ways to party both in the dorms and off campus. Since the dorms house students in all years, there is no strict ban on alcohol, and the HRs (head residents) are generally there more to keep students safe than to get them in trouble.

Also, Colby College itself sometimes organizes social evening activities, and a pub in the student center, Cotter Union, is popular among the students. The pub is also known to be pretty strict about carding, creating what one student described as a "more controlled environment."

> "People really like the school . . . and it's shown by how people are really involved in stuff on campus."

The social scene is also dominated, many students say, by an athletic crowd. But beyond being an athletic campus, Colby has also earned itself other reputations. One student said the "typical" Colby student "lives 20 minutes outside of Boston, went to prep school, drives a Jeep, has a house on the Cape, and wears brand-name clothing." Indeed, "It's very white. There's no getting around that."

Where Everyone Does Something

If Colby is not very ethnically diverse, it is very diverse in terms of varying student interests and passions. "Everybody here is very unique and very different and ac-

cepted," one student said. "People really like the school . . . and it's shown by how people are really involved in stuff on campus."

More specifically, Colby boasts over 100 active clubs and organizations, including everything from the skateboarding club to the Movement for Social Justice. Many students are involved in volunteer work with the surrounding communities, and many also are involved with athletics.

Colby is also known for its school spirit. The Colby-Bowdoin hockey game is particularly popular and always sells out, and, in general, sports seem to have an intense presence. Moreover, while one student admits that not everyone goes to the football games, school spirit manifests itself in other ways (even beyond athletics) as well. Every year, for example, students make boats out of non-boat materials (including everything from gardening pipes to balloons and bicycles) and then race the contraptions in a regatta across the pond on campus, Johnson Pond.

In general, most students at Colby seem to adore their school. "The people at Colby are really great. I've loved the friends I've made."—*Jen Sabin*

FYI
If you come to Colby, you'd better bring "a warm jacket and a pair of skis."
What is the typical weekend schedule? "Thursday night: go out to a bar in Waterville; Friday night: hang out with friends, go to a smaller party; Saturday: get up at noon, sit around, work out, go to a big party off campus or a school-organized dance."
If I could change one thing about Colby "I'd lessen the sports culture."
Three things every student at Colby should do before graduating are "climb Mt. Katahdin, slide down the president's half-pipe, take a walk in the arboretum."

College of the Atlantic

Address: College of the Atlantic, 105 Eden Street, Bar Harbor, ME 04609
Phone: 800-528-0025
E-mail Address: inquiry@coa.edu
Web site URL: www.coa.edu
Year Founded: 1969
Private or Public: private
Religious affiliation: none
Location: rural
Regular Application Deadline: 15-Feb
Number of Applicants: 301
Percent Accepted: 66.4%
Percent Accepted who enroll: 37%
Number Entering: 98
Number of Transfers Accepted each Year: varies
Mean SAT: 1,210
Mean ACT: 28

Middle 50% SAT range: NA
Middle 50% ACT range: NA
Early admission program (EA/ ED/ NA): ED
ED or EA Acceptance Rate: 14%
Full time Undergraduate enrollment: 320
Total enrollment: 336
Percent Male: 34%
Percent Female: 66%
Total Percent Minority: 6.5%
Percent African-American: <1%
Percent Asian/Pacific Islander: 1.5%
Percent Hispanic: 2%
Percent Native-American: <1%
Percent Other: 0%
Percent in-state / out of state: 65% /35%

Percent from Public HS: NA
Retention Rate: 90%
Graduation Rate: 64%
Percent in On-campus housing: 33%
Percent affiliated with Greek system: 0%
Percent Varsity or Club Athletes: N/A
Number of official organized extracurricular organizations: 3
Most popular major: Human Ecology
Student/Faculty ratio: 10:01
Tuition and Fees: $27,850.00
Cost for Room and Board: $7,710.00
Percent receiving Financial aid, first-year: 70%

I n 1969 a bunch of Harvard grads got together and decided that people would benefit by learning to understand the importance of how humans interact with their social and natural environments. The interdisciplinary approach they drew up boiled everything down to what they called Human Ecology. They chose the picturesque little seaside town of Bar Harbor, Maine, as the site for their project. Soon enough, they had created a small school of extraordinary opportunities that challenged students to rethink their roles in the world.

And the Meaning of Life Is . . .

Before graduation, every College of the Atlantic (COA) student is required to produce a thesis that answers the question "What is human ecology?" Human Ecology, the sole major at COA, introduces students to an interdisciplinary approach to defining the relationship between humans and the natural environment. Yes, it's a big topic to tackle, but when you are taking classes like "Landscapes of Power," "The Aesthetics of Violence," and "Use and Abuse of our Public Lands," somehow the answer tends to work itself out.

The degree requirements are extensive, but reveal COA's unique learning philosophy. To graduate, students must engage in community service, pursue an internship of at least one term, create a final project, and write a Human Ecology essay discussing their development as a human ecologist.

Although some struggle to find their area of focus, most say that COA "doesn't box you in with a major." Students can switch their focuses within the Human Ecology major. One senior reported that she had switched her focus from environmental law to Latin American studies to a preveterinary school track. However, with a student body of approximately 275 and faculty of approximately 30, COA is a "hard place to specialize when there is one professor who is the math department and another who is the philosophy department," according to one third-year student. The 55 classes offered per trimester also quickly fill up to their average limit of 18. Some students find it frustrating that the small school may not offer classes within their particular interest.

In turn, COA encourages students to pursue independent studies. One student explained, "If you're motivated, good, if not, you might have a hard time here. For example, most of my work in the last year and a half has been independent, outside of class. I did an internship, then a group study, followed by a residency (the equivalent of three interconnected independent studies), and when I get back from Yucatan I'm going to do my senior project." Graduation requirements also call for students to take time off from campus to do an internship.

On average, students take three classes per trimester—"four can be a lot." The work load focuses on class presentations and "intense" papers, as opposed to exams. A 10:1 student-faculty ratio means that students get individual attention and know their professors well—everyone is on a first-name basis!

Classes also make use of research resources that include Mt. Desert Rock and Great Duck Island Lighthouse, Mt. Desert Island Biological Laboratory, Jackson Laboratory, a weather station, and a Global Monitoring System. "We may, for example, dissect whales or seals found on the coast and determine the cause of death," explains one student.

Housing: Converted Mansions, but Limited Space

COA guarantees housing, usually singles, for first-years only. The three-level horse-shoe-shaped Blair-Tyson dorm houses about 40 students. Around six to eight students share a kitchen and a bathroom, which features recycled toilet paper and no stalls! Seafox, a converted mansion, is "supposedly" substance-free, but really just a more quiet dorm of 12 students with spectacular views of the ocean. RAs are pretty easygoing about marijuana and alcohol and even bring their first-years to off-campus parties to bond with upperclassmen. One RA admitted, "I'm pretty loose about it. Although if someone is having a problem, I'd certainly confront him about it."

Most upperclassmen envy the first-years who get to stay on campus. "I had a blast!" claimed a former Blair-Tyson dweller. "But there's not enough room for us, which is a bummer." Upperclassmen find apartments in town about five minutes away or in more remote locations reached by bike or car.

The Grub—A Vegan's Paradise

The environmentally-conscious student body enjoys top-ranked cooking at its sole dining hall Take-a-Break, or TAB in local lingo. In 2002, PETA (People for the Ethical Treatment of Animals) ranked TAB first out of 1,200 college dining halls for its vegetarian and vegan fare and gave it the privileged title of "Veggie Valedictorian." "The worst thing about the dining hall is its dining hours: dinner between 5:30 and 6:30 is kind of ridiculous," complained one student.

Also, no meals are served on the weekends, so students make use of the many on-campus kitchens.

The food is all organic and mostly from local farms, including the COA's own Beech Hill Farm where students can participate in the work-study program or volunteer. All waste is disposed of in the school's compost garden. Being on the ocean, TAB features a lot of fresh seafood. "Basically, it's not McDonald's, so don't come looking for it," affirmed one senior.

The Weekend Chill

The illegal substance of choice is reportedly marijuana, "unsurprising" for the "chill" school that enrolls many "hippied-out" students. As opposed to hard liquor, beer is the choice beverage. "My buddies and I might throw back a couple of beers, but we don't often get rip-roaring drunk," reported a third-year student. Another student warned, "There are no crazy discos or mad party places, so if that's what you're looking for you might have a hard time here. It is Maine, after all." Students claim that hard drugs are pretty rare.

Because there are no Wednesday classes (due to Student Government meetings), "there are two weekends, Tuesday nights and Friday and Saturday nights." The scene starts, according to one student, "ridiculously early! Things get started around 8:00 and end by 11:30 or 12:00." Parties are held mainly at upperclassmen residences. The Thirsty Whale, Little Anthony's, and Nakorn Thai are popular town bars. "Only really good IDs work," complained one student about the strict drinking policy.

As for the dating scene, news travels fast. One senior lamented her days as a first-year, when she "may have made one too many 'mistakes' that I couldn't escape. I saw them around nearly every day." Some students admit COA is a hard place to date because there are not a lot of new people to meet around. But the small size "makes random hookups a lot less random." COA is also very tolerant and accepting of homosexual relationships. Reportedly, "lesbians are usually more open than gay males."

Students Take Charge

The Student Government at COA is a remarkably powerful body. It has significant say in all major decisions of the school. Students even attend Trustee meetings. Classes do not meet on Wednesdays to accommodate Student Government committee meetings in which most students participate. Additionally, at 1 p.m. every Wednesday an All College Meeting to which all student organizations and committees report takes place. One student complains however, "It's always the same people that show up and, for the most part, say the same things, so reaching common decisions has less to do with compromise and more with tiring your opponent."

The Student Activities Committee, a branch of the Student Government, brings about two or three bands per term to perform in TAB. The committee also sponsors coffeehouses, weekly Open Mike nights, the Winter Carnival, and Earth Day.

For the Outdoorsman in You

COA sports teams are completely nonexistent. But students are serious about outdoor activities, rain or shine. First-years pile all the essentials—boots, bikes, backpacks, cross-country skis, you name it—into the family car when they first arrive. With Acadia National Park in COA's backyard, students can be found scaling the island's mountains (at least ten!) on weekends and have often tackled them all by graduation. Students have free passes to the local YMCA, can explore the miles of bike trails, catch a free whale-watching ride with the Allied Whale (a program for sea-mammal study and saving), or sit on the dock with their toes in the water and watch the sailboats float by.

Winter term is known as the trimester for hard work because sub-zero temperatures supposedly keep people inside. This hibernation is overstated, claimed one student. Even when Bar Harbor shuts down at the end of tourist season, COA students are still recreating outdoors with cross-country skiing, snowshoeing, Broomball, and even midnight dips in the ocean. With all these activities, TV is reportedly "*not* a big pastime." At COA, something like the campus tree swing is a big attraction.

Who You'll Meet

Students at COA report that Earth Day is "the only day that we actually get off." Naturally a place like this is going to attract a certain kind of student. One student described the typical student as "someone who smells like tea-tree oil, has dreadlocks, wears Birkenstocks, and is environmentally-aware, politically-conscious, outdoorsy, pretty athletic, and earthy." Oh, and liberal. "There are maybe three Republicans here," warned one student, "I would not come here if I were a Republican." Although the school is often stereotyped, many students admit surprise at the diversity of opinion. One third-year student remarks, "I wasn't expecting anyone to challenge me." Another student determined the "dirty hippie" population to be less than a quarter of the school.

> **"I would not come here if I were a Republican."**

Students are generally from an upper-middle class socioeconomic background, and though a substantial portion of the student body hails from Maine, students come from all over the United States. For such a small school, COA boasts a significant number of international students who are attracted by the special full scholarship package as well as the uniqueness of the school. In one student's words, "COA students usually have really strong beliefs about a lot of things, and like to voice them. I guess another way to look at it is that if you took the staple "weird kids" from any high school, most of them would fit in just fine at COA."—*Baily Blair*

FYI
If you come to COA you'd better bring "a Nalgene, a backpack, and long johns."
What is a typical weekend schedule? "Go for a hike, do some reading, chill with friends, and lay low."
If I could change one thing about COA, I'd "move it to the tropics or a big city."
Three things every student should do before graduating are "join the Yucatan Program, go for a swim at Sand Beach on a night in January, and summit all the mountains on the island."

University of Maine / Orono

Address: University of Maine, Orono, 5713 Chadbourne Hall, Orono, ME 04469
Phone: 207-581-1561
E-mail Address: um-admit@maine.edu
Web site URL: www.umaine.edu
Year Founded: 1862
Private or Public: public
Religious affiliation: none
Location: rural
Regular Application Deadline: Rolling
Number of Applicants: 5,702
Percent Accepted: 80.32%
Percent Accepted who enroll: 38.28%
Number Entering: 1,753
Number of Transfers Accepted each Year: 678
Mean SAT: 1,086
Mean ACT: 23
Middle 50% SAT range: 1,030–1,240

Middle 50% ACT range: 20–25
Early admission program (EA/ ED/ NA): EA
ED or EA Acceptance Rate: NA
Full time Undergraduate enrollment: 9,179
Total enrollment: 11,435
Percent Male: 48%
Percent Female: 52%
Total Percent Minority: 4.8%
Percent African-American: 1%
Percent Asian/Pacific Islander: 1%
Percent Hispanic: 0.8%
Percent Native-American: 2%
Percent Other: <1%
Percent in-state / out of state: 87% / 13%
Percent from Public HS: NA
Retention Rate: 79%

Graduation Rate: 53%
Percent in On-campus housing: 43%
Percent affiliated with Greek system: NA
Percent Varsity or Club Athletes: NA
Number of official organized extracurricular organizations: 224
3 Most popular majors: Business, Education, Engineering
Student/Faculty ratio: 16:01
Tuition and Fees: $18,414.00
In State Tuition and Fees (if different): $7,464.00
Cost for Room and Board: $7,125.00
Percent receiving Financial aid, first-year: NA

I t is cold during the winter in Maine. But the arctic temperatures don't seem to bother the students at the University of Maine in Orono. In fact, they actively seek it out. Whether they are braving the chill outside by walking through the campus's extensive, forested grounds, or perhaps frosting their breath while screaming for their beloved hockey team in the Alfond Arena, UMO students know how to have fun ... while wearing ski jackets.

"Maine" Focus = Academics

UMO students are adamant in proclaiming "this isn't the party school everyone thinks it is." In fact, UMO offers an extensive and rewarding honors program and actively seeks matriculation from the brightest high school students in the state. Students applying to University of Maine must choose between its five colleges: liberal arts and sciences, engineering, education and human development, and the natural sciences: forestry and agriculture. An early concentration on career-based majors demands both important decisions and hard work from the student body. Each school maintains its own specific requirements, but there is a set of university-wide core requirements including

basic courses in English and math. Engineering is "by far the hardest school" many students reported, whereas the classes in the education department are rumored to be less demanding. Entering freshmen have the opportunity to enroll in the Academic and Career Exploration Program (ACE) instead of one of the baccalaureate degree colleges at the University. ACE allows students to explore the entire system for one year before narrowing their area of focus. ACE kids are also, as one student noted, "more likely to have a close relationship with their academic advisor." This same student lamented the fact that regular, department-based advisors at UMO are "distant" and "basically there to sign your schedule."

Of the general classes, "Human Sexuality" is known as the "go-to class" and is one of the biggest classes, with a head count of about 350. Other than large general requirement classes, class size at University of Maine is reported to be small—"about 35 kids per class," reported one student. The professors enjoy a good reputation, and one student stressed that one must "try to develop relationships with the professors, not only as teacher to student, but as friend to friend. It is possible here but professors don't usually seek students out." While the professors receive passing grades from the students (and hopefully vice versa), the system for registering classes is reported to be stressful for many students, especially freshmen. Upperclassmen receive priority in signing up for classes through either an online server or over the phone, and one freshman reported he "stay[ed] up all night to try to get the classes that [he] wanted. It was really frustrating and I feel that freshmen are left with little choice."

Grin and Bear It

The hockey team, the Black Bears, is a source of campus and state pride for all those who attend the games. With two national championships under their belts (in '93 and '99), and number one rank in the nation by *USAToday/USA Hockey Magazine*, it is no wonder that UMO students keep coming to the rink in droves. The mischievous mascot Bananas the Bear is an adoring fan present at all UMO games and, to present an odd couple, so is the "Master of Horror" Stephen King. While they are physically in separate spheres at the games, King in his private box and Bananas on the sidelines egging on the massive crowd, both are in fact subject of popular legends. King is perhaps the University's most illustrious alumnus, having graduated with a degree in English from UMO in 1970 (just three years before the publication of Carrie made him famous). He remains a visible presence on campus often giving lectures or donating money to various school and area organizations.

> **"Your own community is here, but it's up to you to find it."**

Bananas the Bear, although not a bestselling author, is famous in his own right. A popular legend states that the original mascot was a live black bear cub kept in one of the fraternity houses' basements when not making appearances at sporting events. The live bear, though, had to be replaced by a costumed performer after attacking the University of Connecticut husky at a basketball game.

Though hockey by far has the most loyal fan base, the entire athletic department at UMO is very strong. Basketball is extremely popular, and the football team has improved greatly in the last couple of years. But UMO students don't spend all their time cheering

from the sidelines. Whether it is intramural sports, music, drama, or even animation, UMO students are passionate about what they do outside the classroom. As one student said, "Your own community is here, but it's up to you to find it." There are clubs and organizations to foster the interests of any and all students. Students are also known to take their own initiative and start their own interest groups. "Cinefi" hosts weekly screenings of independent and foreign films and plans collaborations with various cultural groups in order to "unify students" using this particular medium. Likewise, there are sporting clubs, political organizations, religious groups, and, in true Maine fashion, even a "Woodsmen Team."

No Parking Anytime

UMO students come from all over . . . all over the state of Maine, that is. An overwhelming majority of students come from within the state, and they bring their cars and pick-up trucks with them. The campus is fairly large and spread out, as is the town of Orono. Bangor, a neighboring city, about a 10-minute drive away, is often a destination for students seeking escape from the isolated yet idyllic campus. Many students use their cars to work in various stores, restaurants, and bars in Bangor, or to simply go home for the weekend. Add up all these factors and consider the roughly 11,000 students who attend the University and you have a big problem with a capital "P": Parking. Public Safety is notorious for giving out parking tickets, and many students complain that there is simply not enough room for the multitude of cars around the campus. Public Safety at UMO can be rest-assured that all those scowls are simply for the tickets, as many students praise them on other, perhaps more important, facets of their jobs. The campus, once regarded as dangerous, has been greatly improved in terms of safety in recent years. Improvements include better lighting along pathways and also a walking escort service for students, though apprehensions remain as one female student confessed that she "wouldn't walk anywhere alone at night."

A New Union

The campus itself boasts a large number of facilities designed to enhance the student experience. Most of the 18 residences are said to be in "fair condition" and ones located on "the hill top," equipped with private bathrooms, are rumored to be the best. Recently, a new student union was built that houses recreational rooms, computer clusters, study areas, and a post office. Dining halls, known as "Commons," are rumored to be social centers—and the students gathered aren't even complaining about the food! While the cafeteria food is said to be "just plain cafeteria food" with "lots of cereal," students praise the dining options they are able to entertain. Students are able to purchase food from small stores located around campus, cafes, and even local restaurants and delivery services by using a "Maine Card" through which all expenses are charged to your account. Students praise the "Maine Card" yet seasoned delivery-fans warn of hidden costs demanded by local restaurants. Local eateries such as the Market Café, locally famous Pat's Pizza, and Margarita's (which doubles as a watering-hole) welcome students and compete with popular chains located in Bangor such as Olive Garden and, for those on a typical student budget, Taco Bell and Pizza Hut.

"Fill the Steins to Dear Old Maine"

Any school that references beer in its fight song has got to be a good time. UMO students would agree and indeed fill their beer mugs at frat parties and off-campus gatherings alike. The Greek system at UMO is quite strong, with frats such as SAE and Sigma Nu ruling the on-campus scene. Off-campus entertain-ment is also an enticing option for students, and clubs such as Ushuia's in Orono and various bars and pubs in Bangor draw many UMO students out on the weekends. While alcohol runs freely in the minds of UMO students, it does not run as freely on campus. Public Safety has been "really cracking down on underage drinking," one student noted.

UMO students enjoy the reputation of being a "relaxed and friendly community." While many students stated that they wished for a more diverse student body, others admitted that the campus was "pretty much as diverse as it gets in rural Maine." Due to its large and spread out student body (as many upperclassmen opt to live in off-campus housing after freshman year), one UMO student stated that he "could go for a day without seeing anyone [he] knew and got lonely," only to "see all my friends all over the place the next day."

UMO students have succeeded in creating an esteemed place of learning and living where individuals are excited to be a part of a club, a class, or simply a cheering crowd. Students, while happy with many aspects of the beautiful campus and strong classes, constantly strive to make UMO personally challenging and fulfilling all at once. The sense of community is reinforced by the actions of the bright, committed student body. One only has to attend a Black Bears game to view the enthusiasm of this strong community.—*Marisa Benoit*

FYI
If you come to the University of Maine, you better bring "a truck."
What is the typical weekend schedule? "Friday night, stay out doing bad things. Saturday, get up at 2 p.m. and go out again. Then on Sunday, you better sleep."
If I could change one thing about University of Maine I would "make it closer to the ocean and to Acadia National Park."
Three things every student at University of Maine should do before graduating are "go to a UMO vs. UNH (University of New Hampshire) hockey game, eat Pat's Pizza, and live in the dorms."

Maryland

Goucher College

Address: Goucher, 1021 Dulaney Valley Rd., Baltimore, MD 21204-2794

Phone: 410-337-6100

E-mail Address: admissions@goucher.edu

Web site URL: www.goucher.edu

Year Founded: 1885

Private or Public: private

Religious affiliation: none

Location: suburban

Regular Application Deadline: 2-Feb

Number of Applicants: NA

Percent Accepted: 70%

Percent Accepted who enroll: 20%

Number Entering: 451

Number of Transfers Accepted each Year: 85

Mean SAT: NA

Mean ACT: 26

Middle 50% SAT range: 560–670V, 530–630M, 620–700W

Middle 50% ACT range: 23–27

Early admission program (EA/ ED/ NA): EA

ED or EA Acceptance Rate: 78%

Full time Undergraduate enrollment: 1,446

Total enrollment: 1,414

Percent Male: 33%

Percent Female: 67%

Total Percent Minority: 11%

Percent African-American: 5%

Percent Asian/Pacific Islander: 2%

Percent Hispanic: 3%

Percent Native-American: 1%

Percent Other: 17%

Percent in-state / out of state: 24%/76%

Percent from Public HS: 67%

Retention Rate: 82%

Graduation Rate: 70%

Percent in On-campus housing: 86%

Percent affiliated with Greek system: 0%

Percent Varsity or Club Athletes: NA

Number of official organized extracurricular organizations: 70

3 Most popular majors: English Language and Literature, Mass Communications/Media Studies, Psychology

Student/Faculty ratio: 9:01

Tuition and Fees: $29,325.00

Cost for Room and Board: $9,225.00

Percent receiving Financial aid, first-year: 73%

Before there was Goucher, there was a beautiful landscape: 287 acres of wooded forest, just north of Baltimore. Then there was the Women's College of Baltimore. No longer just land or WCB, Goucher has become a haven for its small, open-minded student population. Since 1885, it has been a thriving liberal arts college geared primarily for those looking to major in the natural sciences. Yet, no matter what major Goucher students pursue, they find endless possibilities. With a picturesque campus and a great location, most students are able to find exactly what they want from the college experience. From sports to study, city to country, party to peace and quiet, there are ample opportunities for just about everyone to have a good time at Goucher College.

Educational Opportunities

One of the key factors that differentiates Goucher from other schools is class size. The college consists of only 1,310 students. This allows students to form close relationships with the staff and fosters an agreeable educational environment for both students and professors. Indeed, it is not surprise that the student to professor ratio is 12:1. Although you might expect to find a more limited class selection here than at a larger school, Goucher finds a way to keep the educational program flexible and comprehensive, allowing students to pursue whatever they want however they want. The Goucher administration is so eager to please that it will often help students find ways to take classes even if those classes don't pertain to their majors.

Many students come to Goucher to study natural sciences. Indeed, Goucher is also known for its post-baccalaureate program in which people come to take pre-med classes after already graduating from other colleges or universities. Common majors at

Goucher include physics, math, biology, chemistry and psychology. And, even with the great flexibility of classes, some students find a need to search outside of Goucher for specific courses. Fortunately, Goucher's central location and strong relationships with neighboring universities makes this easy to do. Baltimore is home to 20 universities and caters to over 100,000 students. Johns Hopkins University, for example, is just 15 minutes down the road from Goucher and has a special program (the "3/2 Program") that allows students to earn a double major by studying at Goucher for three years and at Johns Hopkins for two. In this program, the students earn a Goucher Bachelor of Science degree in either mathematics or physics after three years, and then receive a second BS from Johns Hopkins after two years of studying mechanical engineering, electrical engineering, or computer science.

Goucher's open-mindedness makes it a great home college for study abroad. The school doesn't just encourage international study; the completion of at least one international study program or domestic internship is required to graduate. Students have the opportunity to study political science in London, science in Madrid, philosophy in China, or pursue virtually any other discipline in places ranging from Germany to India. Students who decide to intern also have ample opportunities, finding internships in Baltimore, D.C. or other locations within the community.

The Sporting Scene

In the last few years, Goucher has been actively supporting its sports teams both on and off the field. A new $3 million outdoor stadium was recently erected for the men's and women's lacrosse and soccer teams. This new stadium has drawn a new wave of top recruits, foreshadowing years of Goucher improvement. If neither of these sports appeals to you, there is also a strong equestrian culture. The two most obvious voids in the varsity scene, however, are of football and baseball teams. The basketball and the swim teams, as well as volleyball, field hockey, cross country and tennis, all have their plates covered. For non-varsity athletes, Goucher also has many club teams, including Ultimate Frisbee, Frisbee golf, a ski team, bowling and dance.

Life at Goucher

With all its academic, athletic, and personal growth opportunities, Goucher is perfectly outfitted for people of various tastes. One Goucher student put it best by saying that the social life is "up to you." Two major on-campus events are the Spring Gala, a formal dance, and Getting Into Goucher (GIG) day, which features an all-day party. Though the campus is located right outside the city of Towson, remnants of that 287-acre forest shield the campus from the hustle of this university town, which is also home to Towson University. When students wish to venture into the heart of city life, however, Baltimore is just 20 minutes away, with restaurants, a zoo, an aquarium and many museums waiting to be explored. In order to do this, however, you need a car. Thus, many students have cars on campus to get out every so often, and those who don't have cars "should always be able to find someone with a car" to give them a lift.

> **"Your social life is up to you."**

Although the administration has banned both kegs and a Greek system from Goucher, the students still know how to have fun. Goucher males have an easy time finding dates thanks to the extraordinarily high percentage of females (70 percent). Security on campus is mostly relegated to the gates of the college, but campus security also patrols the grounds to a certain extent. Student dorms are seldom patrolled and are leniently monitored by RAs. Of the 17 residential housing units, one is designated for most of the freshmen. Seniority snags students the best rooms, and virtually all students live on campus.

Secluded in a gorgeous wood but close enough to Baltimore to offer innumerable urban opportunities, Goucher offers its students a wonderful education and an enriching four years nestled between the best of both worlds.—*Benjamin Dzialo*

FYI
If you come to Goucher, you'd better bring a "a car!"
What's the typical weekend schedule? "Thursday night is hanging out with friends at parties, Fridays and Saturdays are the same type of thing, but Saturday is always big for those who have a car and go to other colleges or head to Fell's Point."
If I could change one thing about Goucher, I'd "add other places to eat."
Three things every student at Goucher should do before graduating are "go to midnight madness, take a trip to downtown Baltimore, and take a class off campus."

Johns Hopkins University

Address: Johns Hopkins, 3400 N. Charles St., Baltimore, MD 21218
Phone: 410-516-8000
E-mail Address: NA
Web site URL: www.jhu.edu
Year Founded: 1876
Private or Public: Private
Religious affiliation: NA
Location: Urban
Regular Application Deadline: 2-Jan
Number of Applicants: 13,900
Percent Accepted: 27%
Percent Accepted who enroll: 32%
Number Entering: 1,207
Number of Transfers Accepted each Year: ~100
Mean SAT: NA
Mean ACT: NA
Middle 50% SAT range: 1,290–1,490

Middle 50% ACT range: 28–32
Early admission program (EA/ ED/ NA): ED
ED or EA Acceptance Rate: 51%
Full time Undergraduate enrollment: 4,419
Total enrollment: 6,124
Percent Male: 53%
Percent Female: 47%
Total Percent Minority: 36%
Percent African-American: 5.7%
Percent Asian/Pacific Islander: 21.8%
Percent Hispanic: 6.1%
Percent Native-American: 0.6%
Percent Other: 0%
Percent in-state / out of state: 14%/86%
Percent from Public HS: NA
Retention Rate: 97%

Graduation Rate: 93%
Percent in On-campus housing: 61%
Percent affiliated with Greek system: 21%
Percent Varsity or Club Athletes: NA
Number of official organized extracurricular organizations: 300+
3 Most popular majors: Biomedical Engineering, Chemical & Biomolecular engineering, International studies
Student/Faculty ratio: 9:01
Tuition and Fees: $33,900.00
Cost for Room and Board: $10,622.00
Percent receiving Financial aid, first-year: 75%

Want a top-notch education without selling your soul to an Ivy League college? If so, Johns Hopkins is an ideal school for you. Though you will work hard, you will play hard too, and at the end of your four years at Johns Hopkins, you will be prepared to take on just about anything.

Hard Work Pays Off

Johns Hopkins is known as a challenging school that focuses mainly on the sciences, and therefore is crowded with premeds and engineers. Most undergrads enroll in either the Krieger School of Arts and Sciences or the Whiting School of Engineering, and though many students are pre-med, biology or biomedical engineering majors, Hopkins' academic strengths are not limited to the sciences. The International Relations pro-

gram, for example, is an extremely popular and considered one of the strongest in the nation.

There is no "core" curriculum; students are required to fulfill distributional requirements, which students describe as relatively easy to complete. Pre-meds and engineers are known to have considerable workloads; however, almost everyone works hard at Hopkins, and grading is generally considered difficult, with "no grade inflation here at all." Hopkins offers the opportunity, however, for first-semester freshmen to have "covered" grades, meaning that as long as freshmen maintain a 2.0 GPA, they pass and their grades are never revealed in their records. "Your grades will never be uncovered, and I think that's probably one of the ways they try to lessen competition among the students," one freshman stated. "It takes off the stress of trying to adapt to your new surroundings in a really nice way," another freshman said. Competition is somewhat prevalent at Hopkins, especially among premeds; however, covered grading is helpful in shielding new students from this competitive atmosphere.

In terms of class size, the introductory classes are generally large and offer very little teacher/student interaction, though there are teaching assistants who provide extra help if necessary. However, as students reach upper-level classes, especially in the sciences, the class size drops dramatically, offering students the chance to foster close relationships with professors.

Out of the Library, onto the Playing Field

Though Hopkins students work hard, they also know how to let off steam—many students are involved in extracurriculars, including sports, a cappella, volunteering and clubs for just about everything. Hopkins showcases its school spirit best, however, in its students' support for the school's athletic teams. The men's lacrosse team won the NCAA championship in 2005, and fans turn out in large numbers at lacrosse, soccer, football and rugby games, among others. Another significant extracurricular presence is that of Greek Life. There are 11 frats and four sororities, and many of the fraternities are arranged according to sports teams. SAE, WaWa and Pike are the most popular frats, and sororities, though they do not have houses, provide a good way to get into the social scene and meet people. The Greek scene also plays a role in the nightlife at Johns Hopkins, though it is more popular with freshmen than upperclassmen: "Frats are crowded and hot, so they're not a great place to hang out with people and get to know them, but they're a great place to meet people initially." On Thursdays, several fraternities host Game Night, which consists of drinking games that are open to anyone interested in playing.

A Night on the Town

At Hopkins, "There are two types of students: those, predominantly in engineering and the sciences, who study a lot and keep to themselves, and then the other half who go out." Though weekdays (except Thursday) are generally times for serious study, a significant part of the Hopkins pop-

ulation balances their hard work with partying hard on the weekends. "There are lots of people who are serious and study and don't go out, but there are plenty of premeds that go out and have fun—it's a stereotype that is true for some people but not true for others."

> "There are lots of people who are serious and study and don't go out, but there are plenty of pre-meds that go out and have fun—it's a stereotype that is true for some people but not true for others."

Drinking exists as a popular option; however, there is a population that chooses not to drink. Though the freshman social scene is mainly on campus (because of a lack of transportation and ID), and therefore revolves around frats, the upperclassmen often frequent the bars immediately around Johns Hopkins. Two bars, PJ's and Charles Village Pub (CVP), are located directly across from campus and are popular with upperclassmen, often becoming late-night hot spots due to their close proximity to campus. In addition, Baltimore is a short, albeit expensive, cab ride away, and Baltimore's Inner Harbor boasts an area called Power Plant, which houses several clubs and offers College Night every Thursday.

In terms of safety, the administration at Hopkins has stepped up the numbers of "Hop Cops" patrolling the area in and immediately surrounding Hopkins as a result of increased violence in recent years. The campus itself is well-patrolled and safe, with restrictions on dorm access that make them secure "almost to the point of being annoying." A few blocks from campus, the area becomes less safe, but the presence of Hop Cops can be felt as far as several blocks from the center of the school.

Home Sweet Hopkins

In terms of student living, the options run the gamut from dorm living, required of all freshmen, to school-provided apartments for upperclassmen, which feature private kitchens and bathrooms. Freshmen live on three main areas of campus, and each has its own unique reputation. Alumni Memorial Residences (AMR) are very social, but don't have nearly as many amenities as the other two dorms (i.e., there's no air-conditioning, and the bathrooms are on the halls); however, this style of living gives these dorms their extremely social nature. Buildings A and B, on the second main area of campus, offer suite-style living with bathrooms in each suite, and are socially conducive, though not at the same level as the AMRs. Finally, Wolman and McCoy, freshman dorms that also house some sophomores, are the nicest of the three groups' buildings, as they contain suites with kitchens. However, these dorms are also the quietest and least social, as many people keep to themselves. In addition, Hopkins offers its students the unique opportunity to become involved in dorm life by joining the Residential Advisory Board, which "has a lot of different committees and is just another way for students to express what they like and don't like about living on campus."

Juniors and seniors are currently required to find housing off campus; however, Hopkins recently opened a new upperclassman dorm, Charles Commons. In addition, there are several apartments and row houses located extremely close to campus, making off-campus housing relatively easy to find.

Though the food options offered at Hopkins are not stellar, only freshmen are required to eat on the meal plan, and though the cafeteria style dining isn't great, Hopkins also offers a food court, which is significantly better. Upperclassmen generally have kitchens, so they elect not to eat on the meal plan. And for everyone, Pete's Grill is a popular dining alternative.

On campus, a popular hangout is The Beach, a big grassy area located directly in front of the library where people sunbathe, read and play Frisbee—a picturesque example of the college experience at Hopkins. This scene also showcases a student body that is more diverse than one would expect. "The stereotype is that Hopkins is just a bunch of pre-meds, but the truth is there's a lot of diversity here in terms of nationality, race and socioeconomics. There are a lot of kids here on scholarship and in work-study programs." This diversity, coupled with the incredible academic opportunities, makes Hopkins one of the most respected academic institutions in the country.—*Michelle Katz*

FYI

If you come to Johns Hopkins, you'd better bring "a lacrosse stick."

What's the typical weekend schedule? "Go to a sporting event (football, lax, soccer), go out to eat, get ready, go to two or three frats (frat-hop), stop at University Mini Mart (Uni Mini) to get food before you go home."

If I could change one thing about Johns Hopkins, I'd "make the food better, because you have to eat it freshman year."

Three things every student at Johns Hopkins should do before graduating are "go to the inner harbor on College Night, eat at Pete's Grill, and attend the night lacrosse game."

St. John's College

Address: St. John's, Admissions Office, PO Box 2899, Annapolis, MD 21404
Phone: 800-727-9238
E-mail Address: admissions@sjca.edu
Web site URL: www.stjohnscollege.edu
Year Founded: 1784
Private or Public: private
Religious affiliation: none
Location: small city
Application and Admissions Information: rolling
Regular Application Deadline: NA
Number of Applicants: 494
Percent Accepted: 76%
Percent Accepted who enroll: 40%
Number Entering: 150
Number of Transfers Accepted each Year: 15–20
Mean SAT: 0

Mean ACT: NA
Middle 50% SAT range: V: 660–760; M: 590–680
Middle 50% ACT range: NA
Early admission program (EA/ ED/ NA): NA
ED or EA Acceptance Rate: NA
Full time Undergraduate enrollment: 479
Total enrollment: 573
Percent Male: 0.53%
Percent Female: 47%
Total Percent Minority: 8%
Percent African-American: 1%
Percent Asian/Pacific Islander: 3%
Percent Hispanic: 3%
Percent Native-American: 1%
Percent Other: 0%
Percent in-state / out of state: 13%/87%

Percent from Public HS: 60%
Retention Rate: 81%
Graduation Rate: 0.68%
Percent in On-campus housing: 80%
Percent affiliated with Greek system: 0%
Percent Varsity or Club Athletes: 2%
Number of official organized extracurricular organizations: 20
3 Most popular majors: No majors—all liberal arts
Student/Faculty ratio: 8:01
Tuition and Fees: $34,306.00
Cost for Room and Board: $8,270.00
Percent receiving Financial aid, first-year: 49%

Higher education underwent a drastic change after World War II. The focus of education shifted away from the liberal arts as the technological revolution increased the need for specialization. Before then, the curricula of most schools consisted primarily in the liberal arts with a heavy emphasis on reading the Western canon. Although many colleges today offer a modern liberal arts education with a choice of concentration, St. John's College offers a true liberal arts education in this classical humanist tradition. The curriculum, often touted as the Great Books Program, consists of many the great works from Western Civilization, from Classical Greece to the Modern Era.

The Great Books Program

The most striking feature of St. John's College is indubitably its strict curriculum. All the students take the same classes and read the same books. The foundation of a St. John's education lies in the Great Books of the Western Canon. The reading list, which for the most part has not changed since the program was started, is a daunting list of some of the greatest minds in history: Aristotle, Anselm, Kant and Nietzche for philos-

ophy; Homer, Vergil, Cervantes and Milton for literature; Euclid for geometry; Newton for physics. There is a huge emphasis on reading primary sources, and learning the great ideas from the original authors. Readings are discussed in seminars of about 20 students, with two tutors. Tutors would be the equivalent of professors, but the spirit of St. John's is that "the actual teachers are the program authors themselves: Plato, Newton, Appolonius, Hegel etc." The seminars are described as "long conversations" among the students. The tutors serve merely to "start the discussion and help bring it back when it gets off track." The heart of St. John's lies in the seminars, which meet two hours two nights a week. The spirit of discussion that is fostered through the seminars is diffused throughout the college. Students admit that "out-of-class hours are greatly used as a more casual discussion of the program readings." There is a mysticism surrounding the seminar that students find difficult to describe. "There's something about actually being around the seminar table, being part of the discussion, that's impossible to describe the experience to anyone on the outside."

It is a common misconception that the only classes are seminars. Along with four required years of seminar, all students must fulfill four years of math, three years of laboratory science, one year of music, and four years of language—two years of French and two years of ancient Greek. Language, math and music are taught in tutorials, in which the focus is learning facts instead of discussing themes. The curriculum may seem unyieldingly strict, which it is, but juniors and seniors do have a small selection of electives which explore in more depth authors that the seminars would have just briefly passed over. Because the nature of the curriculum is to cover everything, it is difficult to explore any of the texts to great depth. Many of the works, especially in philosophy, aren't even read completely. It is a joke among the students that the curriculum is the "Great Excerpts Program." But students also praise the architects of the program for an "excellent job" choosing excerpts, and there is still "an amazing continuity" among the readings. And it is this continuity that students most appreciate about the program; one girl sums up her St. John's experience in one moment when she "saw a deep parallel between the Conics of Apollonius and Dante's Divine Comedy—the epiphany . . . that was a Johnnie moment."

Taking Tutors out to Lunch

Students stress the relationships they have with their tutors. The tutors serve as guides, and they are treated with somewhat less formal respect than they would elsewhere. They are referred to as Mr. and Ms., just as are all the students, which provides for a very egalitarian atmosphere around the seminar table. It is not uncommon to see students and tutors discussing coursework outside of class. The college has a program for students to take their tutors out to lunch at the main dining hall. There is one minor complaint about the tutors, that they "aren't held responsible for standards." Each tutor grades his or her class differently, weighting class participation, progress and papers in various ways. So the grades are unpredictable, influenced greatly by the student's strengths and the preferences of the tutor. But, the school does not emphasize grades, and many students do not check their grades until they graduate.

It is important to emphasize that the program is not for everyone. It suits a very special kind of student that is inquisitive, hard-working, and talkative. The workload is intense, with three and a half hours of class a day and up to six hours of studying a day. Furthermore, there are about two papers per non-seminar class each semester, and a yearly essay that can be on any work covered in the year. But, more importantly, one needs to have the right character. It is a challenge adjusting to such a "personal and individually based program." One girl who transferred after her freshman year said, "it's a great school for people who like to read and talk, especially people who like to argue." Many have difficult adjusting, and a considerable number end up dropping out. But, for those hardcore "Johnnies" who stick it through, the experience is "very satisfying."

> "The actual teachers are the program authors themselves: Plato, Newton, Appolonius, Hegel etc."

St. John's has "a distinct lack of minorities," but that has been changing over the past years as the college is now actively recruiting a more diverse student body instead of relying on word-of-mouth publicity. The student body is "predominately white males," but there is some economic diversity, which "adds a flavor to the college." Despite the lack of diversity, the student body is very welcoming. The traits that make a good Johnnie "cross all ethnic and cultural lines." As long as a student has the qualities of a Johnnie, he will fit in. There is a deep camaraderie among Johnnies, because they all take the same classes, read the same books, and have the same thirst for knowledge and understanding.

Reality outside the Great Books

For being such a small school—the student body numbers from 450 to 475—the social situation is "not as bad as one would assume." One student described how there are three different types of parties: waltz parties, dorm parties and Reality parties. Reality parties—"standard college parties, with lots of dancing and free beer"—are very popular. Reality is a group of juniors that plan events and host parties, and receives money from the College. Essentially, "the school pays for beer." Besides parties, there are plenty of other things to do. On Wednesdays, popcorn and apple cider are given out at "firesiders" at the on-campus coffee shop. Every Friday night, there is a lecture for the community—people from outside the college come, too—that brings "educated, intelligent speakers."

Because it is a small liberal arts school, St. John's does not offer much for varsity sports. There are only two intercollegiate sports, crew and croquet. Only the croquet team is competitive, and in the past has been the national champions—albeit, out of five teams. Every year, the school gathers for the most important croquet match of the year, the Annapolis Cup against the United States Naval Academy. A lot of alumni come, and the Johnnies dress "super-preppy" for the event. There is also a popular intramural sports program. The entire campus is divided into five teams of students, tutors, and staff. The games are very casual, and both the "dorkiest [and the] most athletic guys have a great time." Students are allocated randomly freshman year, and there is a draft sophomore year.

The college has recently built two new dorms, which has relieved a moderate housing crunch that had been a problem. Everyone who wants to live on campus usually can, and freshmen are guaranteed housing. The dorms are described as "bigger than most," and because the buildings have been built anywhere from 1830 to 2005, "they all have their quirks." Most upperclassmen have either singles or live off campus. The food is "really good for Parents' Weekend," but otherwise does not receive high marks. There is a decent selection; there is always a vegetarian option. As one student said, "they meet the standards of health, but the taste and quality are crappy." Also, there is only one dining hall, Randall, which "helps to nurture the feeling of community," since everyone eats there.

Centuries of Tradition

St. John's, which has not changed its curriculum in centuries, naturally has a lot of traditions. There are still waltz parties on one or two Saturdays every month, although now they are "really more swing dances."Lessons are offered for those who do not know how to dance. At the Collegium, the student body gathers to sing, dance and read poetry. During Dead Week, the last week of classes, where the students only meet for seminars, the campus gathers together for Spartan Madball, which is a "brutish, rugby type of game where the only rules are no shoes or cars on the field." Also, there is the annual Senior Prank, which is planned throughout the year. It usually involves the seniors disrupting the seminars in some way. One year, they played a movie during the seminar and passed out Jello shots. Another part of the prank is a skit performed in front of the whole student body, in which the seniors usually poke fun of the junior class. Lastly, as soon as the students turn in their final papers, they get to ring a big bell near campus.

The campus is located in historic Annapolis, right across the street from the United States Naval Academy. There is not a lot of interaction between the schools, as they are starkly different institutions. The harbor is within walking distance, and there are a lot of "boat people" in the area. In October, Annapolis hosts an annual boat show that's "great to see." The area is quite vibrant, with "a few nice coffee shops and restaurants that students enjoy." For students who prefer the outdoors, St. John's College also has a campus in Santa Fe, N.M. Because the Program is the same at both schools, it is easy for students to transfer. Although the academics are the same, "they do have different feels." The Annapolis campus is more traditional, a perfect atmosphere to foster its very traditional and unique academic program.—*Ryan Galisewski*

FYI

If you come to St. John's College, you'd better bring: "a lighter, unbearable pretenses, and an open mind."

What's the typical weekend schedule: "Friday—Go to Friday night lecture, then to a little party. Saturday—Sleep in, go to an intramural sports game, and at night go to a waltz party. Sunday—Grab an omelet at Randall and read the rest of the day."

If I could change one thing about St. John's College, I'd "improve public transportation to BW/ Baltimore/Washington."

Three things every student at St. John's College should do before graduating are "play croquet, take a tutor out to lunch, go sculling on College Creek."

The United States Naval Academy

Address: U.S. Naval Academy, 117 Decatur Road, Annapolis, MD 21402-5018
Phone: 410-293-4361
E-mail Address: NA
Web site URL: http://www.usna.edu/Admissions/
Year Founded: 1846
Private or Public: public
Religious affiliation: none
Location: urban
Regular Application Deadline: 1-Feb
Number of Applicants: 14,426
Percent Accepted: 14%
Percent Accepted who enroll: 81%
Number Entering: 1,244
Number of Transfers Accepted each Year: NA
Mean SAT: 1,295
Mean ACT: NA

Middle 50% SAT range: 1,120–1,370
Middle 50% ACT range: NA
Early admission program (EA/ ED/ NA): NA
ED or EA Acceptance Rate: NA
Full time Undergraduate enrollment: 4,479
Total enrollment: 4,479
Percent Male: 81%
Percent Female: 19%
Total Percent Minority: 24%
Percent African-American: 6%
Percent Asian/Pacific Islander: 5%
Percent Hispanic: 9%
Percent Native-American: 2%
Percent Other: NA
Percent in-state / out of state: 95%/5%

Percent from Public HS: 60%
Retention Rate: 96%
Graduation Rate: 87%
Percent in On-campus housing: 100%
Percent affiliated with Greek system: 0%
Percent Varsity or Club Athletes: NA
Number of official organized extracurricular organizations: 70
3 Most popular majors: Economics, Political Science, and government
Student/Faculty ratio: 8:01
Tuition and Fees: NA
Cost for Room and Board: NA
Percent receiving Financial aid, first-year: NA

The United States Naval Academy is situated in Annapolis, MD. Founded in 1845 by the Secretary of the Navy, George Bancroft, the historic academy is responsible for the training of future officers of the Navy or Marine Corps. Despite its strict regiment, and array of rules and hazing rites of passage that range from the silly to the unbearable, the camaraderie that develops among the midshipmen is incomparable. Students praise the institution not only for its training, but for the faculty's dedication in doing everything in their power to see their students succeed.

Fit Mind and Body

The Naval Academy stresses academia, resulting in what some students consider a "much heavier course load than that of other schools." Students are not allowed to take fewer than 15 credits a semester. As one student explained, "You don't have the option to take longer than four years. If you are on that path then you get kicked out before graduation time." Of course, the faculty's dedication to its students undoubtedly pays off in USNA's small classes, which have "between 15 and 25 students, and "no

graduate students" teaching. All professors have PhDs and "they're really available," one student said. Aside from its emphasis on a class hierarchy, the Naval Academy at times tends to resemble high school in other ways—"a strict high school," that is. "It's hard to do bad here because the professors are always on you." Engineering is the most popular major at USNA, perhaps due in part to the Academy's recent quota that enables "only 30 percent of the students" to be humanities majors. Balancing a heavy course load is only encumbered by fulfillment of one's military requirements. "Your final GPA is a combination of your academic grades, military grades, and physical fitness grades."

Love Hurts

"The upperclassmen run the school and they can punish you." Unfortunately, unlike high school, there's no running to the administration to escape initiation traditions or seniors with paddles, a la *Fast Times at Ridgemont High*. "The first year is basically being initiated into a superfraternity." The Academy is particularly rough with its freshmen, as that first year is key for weeding out the dedicated for the not-so much. One student exclaimed that, "only 75 percent of the initial class size graduates." Those 25 percent might have failed following the simplest of rules, such as the one that prohibits freshmen from touching their beds from 6:30 a.m. to 10:30 p.m. Frosh regulations are severe. Plebes, first-year students, "only get to leave campus from 10 to 10 on Saturday" and, in a fraternity pledge mentality, must "run in the hallway." And newcomers ought to remember to put all DVDs away. Freshmen are prohibited from listening to music or watching movies. Of course, in addition to the strict restraints on daily activities, plebes lament that "there's a lot of bullshit knowledge you have to know" upon an upperclassmen's request, such as three current newspaper articles in advance or how many days until Thanksgiving break. Although "it's a hard system," many of the rules are relinquished in one's sophomore year. In addition to a few overnights, students agree, "the biggest thing you get as a sophomore is that you get to sleep during the day."

> "The party scene here is in the weight room."

The Crisco of Camaraderie

One of the Academy's most memorable traditions occurs upon completion of freshman year, when the students climb Herndon, a 21-foot high monument shaped like the Washington Monument. "There's a freshman cover (hat) that's replaced with a midshipment cover," a student explained. "Before you climb it, they put grease, Crisco all around it." The inch-thick fat lining results in tedious hours during which thousands of students attempt to climb the slippery monument. Other traditions include painting the statue in the center of campus before every football game. And the easiest way Naval Academy students can guarantee a goodnight peck? It's USNA tradition that if a girl puts on a guy's cover, she owes him a kiss. "A regular girl," one student clarified, "not a Naval Academy girl."

Party in the Weight Room

"The party scene here is in the weight room." Although the Annapolis scene is "great if you're 21," since drinking is not allowed on campus and students are only allowed out during certain hours on the weekends, students find that "most people honestly do work, run, workout, and go out to eat on the weekends." Plebes are not allowed to drink, even if they are 21. Most people abide to the rigorously enforced rules, especially since "underage drinking is punished severely" and there are random weekend breathalyzers for the underage. On the other hand, seniors are allowed to buy beer at the school restaurant or drink at the officer's club, as long as they don't come back belligerent. Perhaps the slew of rules and punishments account for why intramural sports, although mandatory, provide the social aspect that is sometimes hindered by USNA's strict policies. Football is huge at the Naval Academy, with pep rallies and mandatory attendance at the games greatly promoting school spirit. While such camaraderie is prevalent throughout the school, it is stronger within each company—the 140 people or so with whom a student lives and interacts. There are 30 companies in total.

No Kissing, No Asking, No Telling

You're not allowed to show affection in any form at the Academy. There is no kissing and while PDAs are often in poor etiquette anyways, USNA makes sure to enforce Emily Post's seduction guidelines. "Girls are allowed in guys' rooms, although the door must remain open and there must be no physical contact." Students agreed that such seriousness is understandable in light of sexual harassment cases, especially the Air Force Academy scandal. "Although females are only 19 percent of the school, I feel that the administration has done an excellent job making everything equal and not tolerating any discriminative practices—no matter how mild," praised one student. Despite the female-friendly environment, one male student claimed that, "Most females here tend to have a chip on their shoulder due to the male environment." Of course, despite the rule-infused school, the Naval Academy isn't a completely hands-off boys club. "We have dances and you're allowed to bring dates to those." The dances are "a pretty big deal." One of the biggest events is the Ring Dance at the end of the year. "It's kind of like prom, that type of big, and you get your ring, and you get it in the water from the seven seas and your date is supposed to put it on you." Of course, dancing or lifting weights, "homosexuality is definitely very taboo." Students said it is "not accepted at all, but then again, nobody expects it to be in the military." Most cite the "very conservative student body" as one of the main reasons for the "don't ask, don't tell" mentality that is prevalent on campus.—*Dana Schuster*

FYI

If you come to USNA, you'd better bring a "a sense of humor and long-term perspective. The only way you will be able to survive this place is by being able to laugh it off when you get yelled at and laugh at yourself when you screw up, because both will happen . . . a lot."

What is the typical weekend schedule? "For Freshman: Start with SMT (Saturday Morning Training) around 0630. Then eat, clean, organize, do homework before liberty commences, unless there is a football game. There isn't a lot to do out in town so most either go out to eat, watch a movie, or stay back in the hall and study. Sunday: Sleep until 1:00pm or go to church services. After 1:00pm, be ready to take an exam on information you are supposed to learn about the Navy, Marine Corps, and other services. After the test, prepare for the following days classes and study!"

If I could change one thing about USNA, I'd ". . . I wouldn't change a thing . . . The bad things and hard times, which are quite frequent, are as much a part of the experience as the good times and the opportunities are."

Three things every student should do before graduating are "sneak through the Ho Chi Min trail, join the Salsa club, and mess with Master Chief Quiblin's office."

University of Maryland / College Park

Address: University of Maryland, College Pk, Mitchell Building, College Park, MD 20742
Phone: 301-405-1000
E-mail Address: um-admit@uga.umd.edu
Web site URL: www.umd.edu
Year Founded: 1856
Private or Public: public
Religious affiliation: none
Location: suburban
Regular Application Deadline: 21-Jan
Number of Applicants: 22,428
Percent Accepted: 49.05%
Percent Accepted who enroll: 38.27%
Number Entering: 4,211
Number of Transfers Accepted each Year: 3,545
Mean SAT: NA
Mean ACT: NA

Middle 50% SAT range: 1,170–1,390
Middle 50% ACT range: NA
Early admission program (EA/ ED/ NA): EA
ED or EA Acceptance Rate: NA
Full time Undergraduate enrollment: 25,104
Total enrollment: 34,937
Percent Male: 51%
Percent Female: 49%
Total Percent Minority: 33.3%
Percent African-American: 13%
Percent Asian/Pacific Islander: 14%
Percent Hispanic: 6%
Percent Native-American: 0.3%
Percent Other: <1%
Percent in-state / out of state: 78%/22%

Percent from Public HS: NA
Retention Rate: 92%
Graduation Rate: 79%
Percent in On-campus housing: 42%
Percent affiliated with Greek system: NA
Percent Varsity or Club Athletes: NA
Number of official organized extracurricular organizations: 527
3 Most popular majors: Criminology, Economics, Political Science
Student/Faculty ratio: 18:01
Tuition and Fees: $21,345.00
In State Tuition and Fees (if different): $7,906.00
Cost for Room and Board: $8,562.00
Percent receiving Financial aid, first-year: 48.39%

With an undergraduate enrollment of over 25,000 in 2006, the University of Maryland, College Park, may seem at first blush intimidatingly large. Yet on this unique campus, uniting the resources and opportunities of a large research institution with the academic rigor of one of the nation's most prestigious schools and the athletic excellence and spirit of a big state university, students of every race, creed and passion can find a niche for themselves. The diversity of the student body creates an open and welcoming environment, while the fierce pride and school spirit demonstrated by everyone on campus creates a sense of unity rivaling that of any smaller institution.

Academics: Large in Every Sense

As a large, academically prestigious research university, UMD includes an impressive array of academic departments, courses and possible majors: "They offer a wide variety of subjects, so you can take classes in whatever you may be interested in." All undergraduates are required to fulfill the requirements of the CORE program, including nine course credits in the humanities, ten in math and science, nine in the social sciences and history, and three in Emerging Issues, in addition to more specific English writing and math requirements. CORE also requires students to take six credits at the advanced (300–400) level in one or more fields outside their major. Students say the CORE program does a good job of "[covering] pretty much everything, from science and math to English and diversity"—and though the number of stipulated CORE classes may seem demanding to some, the sheer number of courses offered by the university creates a "large availability to fulfill requirements."

Undergrads must be enrolled in at least 12 credits per semester in order to be considered full-time students, and at least 120 are needed to graduate; further academic requirements vary depending on your major of choice. Among the most popular majors cited by students are Business, Engineering, Journalism, Architecture, Education, Criminology, Government & Politics, Computer Science and Psychology. UMD does not permit students to minor, though multiple majors are both allowed and encouraged. The university also offers several special academic programs, including College Park Scholars, the University Honors Program, Honors Humanities and Gemstone. Benefits range from the opportunity to design and engage in independent scientific research projects together with a team of selected students (in the case of Gemstone, a four-year multidisciplinary research program) to the chance to attend special seminars and enroll in smaller classes (through the two-year University Honors Program).

At a large university like this one, the variety of classes tends to be correspondingly large—in UMD's case, including everything from introductory calculus to the perennially popular "History of Rock and Roll"—but so does their size. Students say popular introductory classes can be as large as 200 to 300 people, though "as you move higher [in course level], class sizes become smaller." Another student pointed out a further drawback in some classes, especially introductory courses with a large number of students: "Some of the more popular majors have classes with large amounts of people, so those classes tend to rely on Power Point presentations for notes, which are generally posted online. . . . I don't very much like classes where I feel like I don't need to go." To remedy some of the issues caused by large classes, many lectures with a high enrollment are split up into smaller weekly discussion sections of about 20 to 30 people, usually led by a graduate student teaching assistant. Nevertheless, students describe professors as generally "accessible and approachable" if you make the effort to interact with them, though one sophomore adds that "when you're in a very large class at times it's easier to just talk with the TAs."

Overall, students say they feel both satisfied with and challenged by UMD's strong academic programs. As one student states, "Like most universities, it's largely independent, which works for me. No one holds your hand. That can be a pro or a con, depending on your study style."

Work Hard, Play Harder

The excellence and rigor of the university's academics aside, however, College Park students are hardly all work and no play. "We are, after all, one of the Top 20 party schools!" The university boasts a thriving social scene, where fraternities and sororities "are very popular, but at the same time, there are a lot of people who don't partake, and no one is ridiculed for either." Thursday, Friday and Saturday nights are a time for many students to go out and have fun with friends; some choose to stay on campus and attend sporting events or shows (the university regularly hosts concerts by artists like Ben Folds and Dashboard Confessional) or see a movie at the Hoff Theater, while others take the Metro into nearby Washington, D.C. in search of a good time. Says one student, "The most popular student hangouts are the Comcast Center for basketball games or Byrd Stadium for football games, but when those aren't options, most students go to restaurants or bars on Route 1, the main road in front of campus." Alcohol and, to some extent, drug use (particularly pot smoking) has a large presence on UMD's campus; university policy does not allow drinking in dorms, "but unless you're being really rowdy about it, it doesn't tend to be a problem." Students also add that "the good thing about a big campus is that you can find people who want to drink every night until they get sick or people that drink occasionally. Even if you don't drink at all, there are still plenty of things to do and people to hang out with."

Students have high praise for the friendliness and openness of the social scene in general: "It is easy to make friends at UMD if you are outgoing enough, and especially so if you live in the dorms." Between residence halls, extracurricular activities, jobs and classes, there are plenty of places to meet people and plenty of people to meet. Students also say that honors programs help them to make friends: one sophomore cites the Gemstone program as the place where she met many of her friends, "since most of us lived in the same dorm freshmen year, and had some of the same classes."

Above all, students praise the diversity of the university's student body: "Our school is extremely diverse, and people are very tolerant and accepting." Students come from all over the globe and from all walks of life. When asked to describe the "typical" UMD student, all agreed that it was "impossible," as "there's really no stereotypical UMD student"—in fact, the one common trait students could agree on was diversity. Geographically speaking, like many state schools, UMD includes a large percentage of students from the area as well as a fairly high number of commuters—overall, according to a student, "about 95% of the school comes from MD, NJ or NY (particularly Long Island), and that about 70% of the school comes from MD alone." Nevertheless, the campus is very ethnically, economically and culturally diverse, ensuring that students can always find their niche.

Living it up in College Park

On a campus where finding friends often begins with your dorm, it is no surprise that many students, especially underclassmen, prefer to live on campus. In fact, as enrollment expands, the demand for on-campus housing usually exceeds the supply (with preference given to entering freshmen). The university is seeking to remedy the situation by constructing more on-campus housing, but in the mean time, many upperclassmen and transfer students must settle for apartments or other housing off campus.

Freshmen and students who do get lucky in the housing draw are placed in one of UMD's 34 residence halls or, in the case of some upperclassmen, in an on-campus apartment complex owned by the university. Freshmen are housed in separate dorms from upperclassmen and usually get the short end of the stick as far as amenities; students say freshman dorms are typically "fairly plain and don't have air conditioning, and are not usually given the best of locations." On the upside, students in these dorms do tend to make more of an effort to interact with their neighbors. Students enrolled in honors programs like Gemstone and Honors Humanities live in separate dorms.

The surrounding town of College Park, though described as "a little bit on the seedy side" and not a place to walk out alone at night, offers students a wide array of opportunities to dine, shop or hang out. On weekends, many students frequent bars, shops and restaurants on the aforementioned Route 1. Popular dining choices in the area include Chipotle, Mama Lucia's, DP Dough and the Hard Times Cafe, which one student termed "the best place in the world for wings."

But students don't need to venture out into College Park to find good places to chill, eat or study. The beautiful brick architecture of UMD's campus affords plenty of places to spend time. One favorite student hangout is Stamp Student Union, which features a "very nice restaurant," Adele's, that serves as an alternative to dining hall food for students on the meal plan; the Union also boasts a pool hall, arcade and bowling alley, along with the Hoff Theater, which screens movies daily for as little as $3. Many of the university's buildings are new or recently renovated, including the Clarice Smith Performing Arts Center, the Jeong H. Kim Engineering Building and the Robert H. Smith School of Business.

"Go Terps!"

When you come to UMD, be prepared to cheer long and loud—if there's one uniting factor on this campus, it's school spirit: "Everyone has school spirit and, despite it being large, it feels very close-knit." Sports have a "HUGE presence on campus," most prominently football and basketball, and the intensity of the crowd that packs the stadium to cheer on the Terrapins (or "Terps") borders on fanaticism. So popular are Terps games that the university has instituted a lottery system for student tickets to football and basketball games, "where you earn points for each game you attend and students with more points are more likely to get tickets."

> "Everyone has school spirit and, despite it being large, it feels very close-knit."

You don't have to be a star athlete to play sports at Maryland, however. UMD has a thriving intramurals program, offering sports ranging from soccer to flag football at two levels of competition, A ("competitive") and B ("just for fun, though it gets pretty competitive as well"). The Eppley Recreation Center, "well-known for its excellent facilities," provides students with excellent athletic facilities and is only one of several gyms on campus.

And the extracurricular opportunities at UMD go far beyond sports. The wide array of campus organizations offer something for everyone, and students find extracurriculars a good way to make friends at a school that can seem intimidatingly large. From service groups to ethnic organizations to a cappella to even a skydiving club, chances are that no matter what your interest, there will be an organization for you. Many undergraduates also hold jobs during their time at UMD; the university offers plenty of on-campus jobs at locations like the gym, "a good opportunity for students who want to work but don't want to make a huge commitment out of it."

There is really no easy way to sum up the University of Maryland, College Park. The diversity of its student body and the sheer number of opportunities, courses and activities it offers ensure that no matter what your personality or interests, you will fit in here. What really unites the students is a fierce pride in their university: "Everyone is so passionate about this school, and everyone has a genuine love for it."—*Amy Koenig*

FYI

If you come to UMD, College Park, you'd better bring "a red UMD shirt, for all the sporting events you're going to go to."

What is the typical weekend schedule? "Very laidback. People sleep in, watch TV, hang out in their rooms. Lots of people go out Friday and Saturday nights. However, if it's a football game weekend, tailgating starts early, and most students are up and out hours before the game. Usually people study on Sundays or just hang out."

If I could change one thing about UMD, I'd "make the buildings closer together (it's exhausting going from class to class)."

Three things every UMD student should do before graduating are "go to a Maryland/Duke basketball game, eat a DP Dough calzone, and make sure never to step on the intersection of the lines that used to point to the campus' buildings that burned down in 1912, because if you do, you won't graduate in four years!"

Massachusetts

Amherst College

Address: Amherst, Box 5000, Amherst College, Amherst, MA 01002-5000

Phone: 413-542-2328

E-mail Address: admission@amherst.edu

Web site URL: www.amherst.edu

Year Founded: 1821

Private or Public: private

Religious affiliation: none

Location: rural

Regular Application Deadline: 1-Jan

Number of Applicants: 6,142

Percent Accepted: 19%

Percent Accepted who enroll: 38%

Number Entering: 433

Number of Transfers Accepted each Year: NA

Mean SAT: 1,443

Mean ACT: 31

Middle 50% SAT range: V:670–770, M:660–760

Middle 50% ACT range: 28–33

Early admission program (EA/ ED/ NA): ED

ED or EA Acceptance Rate: NA

Full time Undergraduate enrollment: 1,648

Total enrollment: 1,648

Percent Male: 50%

Percent Female: 50%

Total Percent Minority: 55%

Percent African-American: 9%

Percent Asian/Pacific Islander: 13%

Percent Hispanic: 7%

Percent Native-American: 0%

Percent Other: 26%

Percent in-state / out of state: 12%/88%

Percent from Public HS: 59%

Retention Rate: 98%

Graduation Rate: 96%

Percent in On-campus housing: 98%

Percent affiliated with Greek system: 0%

Percent Varsity or Club Athletes: NA

Number of official organized extracurricular organizations: 100

3 Most popular majors: Economics, English, Political Science

Student/Faculty ratio: 8:01

Tuition and Fees: $34,280.00

Cost for Room and Board: $9,080.00

Percent receiving Financial aid, first-year: 81.3%

The "College" in Amherst's name says it all: the anonymous and overwhelming aspects of a large university are nowhere to be found at Amherst College, where 85 percent of classes have less than 18 students and professors frequently invite their students to dinner at their homes. Yet Amherst manages to foster a supportive community without sacrificing academic rigor or the spirit of competition—and with the other four members of the Five College Consortium nearby, it's easy for Amherst students to feel like a part of a greater campus as well.

Competitive, not Cutthroat

Many students say that "one of the most fabulous things about Amherst" is the school's lack of core requirements, which affords students a significant amount of freedom when it comes to choosing classes. Freshmen are required to take a seminar in their first semester at the college, but students agree that with so many options, finding one in your area of interest is easy. "The only purpose of the seminars is to have some sort of writing intensive class when you begin college," said one sophomore. Students can enroll in seminars whose topics range from music or theater to science, philosophy or English.

Students are required to declare a major by the end of their second year, and generally must complete eight to ten courses in that major. Students said that this continues to give Amherst scholars a real chance to explore classes that interest them. "The great thing about having so few requirements is that the students that take a certain class take it because they really want to be in that class. They aren't just there to get a requirement filled," said one sophomore. The only tricky part to registering for classes, pointed out one student, is that several courses taught by Amherst's "superstar professors"—including political science professor Austin Sarat and philosophy professor Thomas P. Smith—can be difficult to get into.

Academic enthusiasm is fundamental to the typical classroom environment at the college; with an average class size of 15, Amherst students are left with very little wiggle room when it comes to showing up to class prepared and ready to participate. "It's hard to hide," said one sophomore. Still, another student cited the school's consistently small class sizes as the best part of her academic experience thus far. The somewhat pressured environment produced by such small classes is more than offset, students say, by the close student-professor relationships that form.

One student cited the school's lack of teaching assistants as yet another perk of attending a college rather than a large university, saying, "The professors are conscious that they're there to work with the students, and you don't have to worry that they'll be preoccupied with researched or focused on their graduate students." Amherst even works to foster friendships between students and their teachers, sponsoring a program known as TYPO, or Take Your Professor Out, whereby the college pays for small groups of students to take their professors out to dinner.

Despite the prevailing work ethic on-campus, Amherst students insist that they are not known for being holed up in the library seven days a week. One student observed that many students, while "on the books" from Sunday to Wednesday, are equally devoted to their athletic or artistic pursuits. As another student said, "This is such a cliché, but Amherst kids really are work hard, play hard."

In keeping with their "well-rounded" reputations, Amherst students most frequently choose to be English, political science, economics, psychology, or biology majors. One sophomore who recently declared her double major of biology and theater/dance said that while the school is generally known for its offerings in the liberal arts, the professors and facilities she has encountered in her science courses have all been top-notch. "I think the science department is really an undiscovered gem at our school," she said.

While Amherst students attend a school where academic excellence is prized ("it's not the kind of place where people look down on you if you say that you think chemistry is really interesting") one of the college's most valuable components is its atmosphere of friendly rather than malicious competition. "Everyone really supports each other," said one sophomore. "It's not a competitive or cutthroat environment at all. Everyone here works hard, and they work together."

AED? ÓËÖ Try TAP

While Amherst does not have any Greek life, students report that both a relatively permissive alcohol policy and the close proximity of "something like 30,000 other college students" make for a lively party scene on the weekends. With an overwhelming majority of students opting to live in on-campus housing, the main part of the social life occurs in dorms on campus. Amherst also hosts a monthly TAP ("The Amherst Party") with a different theme each month—perennial favorites include Luau, Endless Summer and "the most famous one, the Madonna TAP."

Students seem to agree that drinking is a large part of Amherst's social scene, but one sophomore girl maintained that "the good thing is that the college isn't ignorant to that." Consequently, incoming freshmen have the ability to request substance-free housing. This idea continues with "health and wellness dorms" for upperclassmen. Even while offering these options, Amherst remains a school with a less-than-strict approach to on-campus drinking. "I mean, if you have a keg at a party, you have to register the keg," said one sophomore. "Sometimes if a party's too loud the police will come bust it up. But they can't go into your room and search for alcohol, so it's really not hard to drink."

While it's relatively rare for most students to venture to any of the other four schools for parties, one student said that "the girls from Mount Holyoke and Smith are definitely looking for a social life outside of their schools" and said that it was more common to see them—dubbed "Mo-Hos and Smithies" by Amherst girls—at Amherst parties. "I don't think Amherst girls are that excited by their presence on campus," she said. "The guys . . . that might be another story." Students said that outside of this, the majority of their social interaction with students at other schools occurs in town at bars. Still, in the words of one student, "It can be nice to get off campus and meet other people. Amherst can definitely become its own little bubble after awhile."

The Amherst Bubble

One thing all Amherst students—regardless of their own personal interests—agree on is that their school is full of athletes. One varsity athlete estimated that a third of the school played a varsity sport and that almost two-thirds played either varsity or intramural sports, but she maintained that due to the fact that athletes live in the same dorms as their less athletic counterparts, "everyone is out every weekend to support their friends and teammates. It's not a jocks vs. non-jocks situation." Another sophomore stated that while the environment at Amherst is relatively true to its advertisement as "super-diverse as far as liberal arts colleges go," the school was also true to its stereotypical classification as a place with "a lot of preppy athletes."

Jocks or not, students uniformly classify Amherst's physical campus—particularly the "insanely beautiful view from Memorial Hill that overlooks the Mount Holyoke range"—as "absolutely gorgeous." One praised "the beautiful New England feel of the entire place" and another described Amherst as "a school that seems like a perfect, philosophical place to go to college—this idyllic setting is what you imagined college would be like when you were a little girl, you know? Sitting in a coffee shop reading a book, or lying out on the grass studying in the spring." In the colder months, students often take advantage of snow by "stealing trays from our dining hall, Valentine, and going down Memorial Hill on them."

> "This idyllic setting is what you imagined college would be like when you were a little girl."

In the end, whether they are seeking out courses in specialized subjects at one of the nearby colleges, driving to Hampshire to see a dance show, playing for the Jeffs in a varsity game or going apple-picking or hiking, Amherst students pursue their goals and passions with drive and enthusiasm. One sophomore summed up the typical Amherst coed like this: "Generally, it's just that everything we do, we work really hard at."
—*Angelica Baker*

FYI
If you come to Amherst, you'd better bring "a popped collar, some purple clothing, and money for food from town—the stuff at Valentine isn't that great."
What's the typical weekend schedule? "Wake up late, try to make it to Valentine before lunch closes, do some homework, see a sports game and go to a great party on Saturday night."
If I could change one thing about Amherst, I'd "change its location—it's definitely not rural, but we don't trek out to Boston every afternoon either.
Three things you have to do before you graduate are: "Take a class at one of the other four colleges, swim in Puffer's Pond, and climb one of the academic buildings."

Babson College

Address: Babson, 231 Forest Street, Babson Park, MA 02457-0310
Phone: 781-239-5522
E-mail Address: ugradadmission@babson.edu
Web site URL: www.babson.edu
Year Founded: 1919
Private or Public: private
Religious affiliation: none
Location: suburban
Regular Application Deadline: 16-Jan
Number of Applicants: 3,436
Percent Accepted: 37%
Percent Accepted who enroll: 35%
Number Entering: 443
Number of Transfers Accepted each Year: 81
Mean SAT: NA
Mean ACT: NA

Middle 50% SAT range: 1,690–1,960
Middle 50% ACT range: 25–29
Early admission program (EA/ ED/ NA): ED/EA
ED or EA Acceptance Rate: 51%
Full time Undergraduate enrollment: 1,776
Total enrollment: 3,359
Percent Male: 59%
Percent Female: 41%
Total Percent Minority: 31%
Percent African-American: 3%
Percent Asian/Pacific Islander: 11%
Percent Hispanic: NA
Percent Native-American: <1%
Percent Other: 16%
Percent in-state / out of state: NA

Percent from Public HS: NA
Retention Rate: 95%
Graduation Rate: 87%
Percent in On-campus housing: 81%
Percent affiliated with Greek system: 10%/12%
Percent Varsity or Club Athletes: NA
Number of official organized extracurricular organizations: 64
3 Most popular majors: Business, Management, Marketing
Student/Faculty ratio: 14:01
Tuition and Fees: $32,256.00
Cost for Room and Board: $11,222.00
Percent receiving Financial aid, first-year: 96%

At Babson College, located in the affluent Boston suburb of Wellesley, Massachusetts, a concentration in some field of business management is mandatory. This is not a school for the unmotivated or unfocused. In fact, one student described his peers as a "cult of mavericks each ready to gun for millions" upon graduation, an exaggerated stereotype that nonetheless gives an accurate impression of the intensity with which Babson students approach their educations.

Future CEOs of the World

From the moment freshmen arrive on campus, they enter a structured academic program geared towards their particular business interests. Freshmen must enroll in Foundation Management Experience (FME). This program, which introduces students to concepts in accounting, marketing, and business and information systems, feeds into Intermediate Management Core (IMC), of which students must take three semesters into their junior year. IMC demands that students study the practical workings of a real-life company of their choice and prepare a presentation on their findings. While Babson takes care to expose students to the liberal arts, only 50 percent of classes fall

outside the realm of business-related fields. Though, as one student noted, "not everyone here is an aspiring entrepreneur," students understand that an intense business education is central to the Babson experience. What's more, students choose not from a variety of majors but rather from various concentrations in entrepreneurship. Among these, marketing and finance are most popular.

Class size averages roughly 30 students, and Babsonians appreciate the personal contact with professors that this small size affords. Students give their professors rave reviews, suggesting that perhaps professors deserve more credit than they are often given. One student referred to his professors as "war heroes," alluding to the experience in business management that members of the distinguished faculty bring to campus.

Professors include the founder of Jiffy Lube and former CEOs of Digital Equip and Pizza Hut. The emphasis in the classroom is on the dynamics of teamwork and the relevance of working knowledge in any given field. TAs have no place at Babson; instead, upperclassmen "peer mentors" give freshmen support in the requisite introductory classes. Students complain about the heavy workload that often makes a Monday-through-Friday workweek necessary. Other students take issue with the curved grading system. Because grades are scaled down to meet a pre-determined average, the prevalent sense is that "anywhere else, it would have been an A."

Parties: Taking Advantage of Boston

Freshmen and upperclassmen at Babson do not tend to segregate when the weekend finally does roll around. Together, Babsonians of all years seek out the best parties, usually found in either suites or fraternities. About 20 percent of the student body identifies with a Greek organization, although Greek parties are also open to the greater college population. Although students estimate that alcohol and drug use are less prevalent here than at schools of comparable size, the party scene does play a large role in the social plans of students. The administration takes a by-the-book approach to policing alcohol offenses, a stance which aggravates students who would prefer a more lax approach. Once a student accumulates three "strikes"—that is, three documented instances of violation of the alcohol policy—the student is no longer allowed to live on campus. As an alternative to alcohol-centered parties, the college hosts various theme parties throughout the year: fall weekend, Oktoberfest, Harvest, and the president's black-tie ball are among the most popular. The black-tie ball is not the only chance for students to dress up during the school year. On the contrary, professors regularly ask that students wear business suits to class in an attempt to give them a taste of a professional atmosphere.

Despite the vibrant party scene, many students complain that random hookups are not as common as at other colleges. Perhaps for this reason, students often venture to Boston University or Boston College in search of a more diverse social environment. Students also seek out bars both around Wellesley and in the city. Although Boston is easily accessible via the T (Boston's subway system) and other means of public transportation, students find the hours of public transportation relatively inconvenient, thereby making cars the dominant mode of transportation. Parking, however, creates another problem, especially for freshmen, whose location on Lower Campus distances them from the parking lots available to students.

Common Breeds

Students come to Babson in hopes that the combination of hard work and the college's program of study will make for a successful—and prosperous—future. Social concerns are of less importance. Indeed, one student described Babsonians as "hardworking, rich geeks." The student body is racially homogenous and politically and socially conservative. Students do not only segregate themselves by ethnicity; athletes, Greeks, international students, and those who live together freshman year often withdraw into their own cliques. The relatively high male-to-female ratio plays another important factor in student relations at Babson. Though the college has made an effort in recent years to correct this inequality, having approximately two guys on campus for every girl only increases the homogenous profile of Babson.

A Campus That Mimics Its Location

The Boston suburb of Wellesley, Massachusetts, houses the Babson campus. Students appreciate the safety and beauty afforded by this affluent town but complain that the area immediately surrounding their campus all but closes down by 9 p.m. The campus itself, like the student body, is small, with an architecturally distinct set of buildings. Students congregate at the Campus Center or Pub Reynolds for socializing; the library is better suited for serious studying. Of the dorms on campus, three in particular—Pietz, Vanwinkle, and Coleman—are consistently lauded as the most sought-after. While almost all freshmen live on Lower Campus, seniors have first choice in the room draw and often end up with singles and suites. Students seem, on the whole, happy with their living arrangements. An RA system is in place for all students to further ensure their comfort.

> **"The standard-issue vehicle is pick-a-number-series BMW."**

The quality of dorms, coupled with the high cost of off-campus apartments, accounts for the fact that 81 percent of students live on campus. For these students, a meal plan is required. Although dining on campus is met with student approval for both its taste and variety, the required meal plan for those living on campus frustrates those who would prefer to take advantage of the many Boston-area restaurants.

The Beaver Stays Home

At Babson, few organized activities outside of the classroom ever gain much popularity. Participation in community service, for example, is low. In spite of the fully equipped PepsiCo Pavilion Gym, athletics draw relatively small followings and do not elicit much school spirit for "the Beaver," Babson's mascot. Ethnic organizations and in-tramural sports, however, do draw in a relatively high percentage of students.

Students often come to Babson with lofty career goals in mind and, thanks in part to the school's efforts to distinguish itself as a top business school, they are not disappointed with the rigorous curriculum. Here, there is little evidence of diversity in ideals or background; as one student commented, the "standard-issue vehicle is pick-a-number-series BMW." For many, it is this common path that makes the Babson experience worthwhile.—*Greg Hamm*

FYI
If you come to Babson, you'd better bring a "business suit, a coffee maker, and an alarm clock."
A typical weekend at Babson consists of "Thursday night Pub Night, Friday exams and presentations, Saturday in Boston, Sunday studying and homework."
If I could change one thing about Babson, I'd "increase the school's overall population."
Three things every student at Babson should do before graduating are "attend a Knight Party, start at least one business, and intern at a company."

Boston College

Address: Boston College, 160 Commonwealth Ave, Chestnut Hill, MA 02467	**Mean ACT:** NA	**Retention Rate:** NA
	Middle 50% SAT range: NA	**Graduation Rate:** NA
	Middle 50% ACT range: NA	**Percent in On-campus housing:** NA
Phone: 617-552-3100	**Early admission program (EA/ ED/ NA):** EA	**Percent affiliated with Greek system:** NA
E-mail Address: ugadmis@bc.edu	**ED or EA Acceptance Rate:** NA	
Web site URL: www.bc.edu		**Percent Varsity or Club Athletes:** 16%
Year Founded: 1863	**Full time Undergraduate enrollment:** 9,000	**Number of official organized extracurricular organizations:** 212
Private or Public: private	**Total enrollment:** 14,500	
Religious affiliation: Roman Catholic	**Percent Male:** 48%	**3 Most popular majors:** Communications, Finance, English
Location: suburban	**Percent Female:** 52%	
Regular Application Deadline: 2-Jan	**Total Percent Minority:** 24%	**Student/Faculty ratio:** 13:01
Number of Applicants: 26,584	**Percent African-American:** NA	**Tuition and Fees:** $33,506.00
Percent Accepted: 29%	**Percent Asian/Pacific Islander:** NA	
Percent Accepted who enroll: 30%	**Percent Hispanic:** NA	**Cost for Room and Board:** $11,438.00
Number Entering: 2,284	**Percent Native-American:** NA	
Number of Transfers Accepted each Year: 75	**Percent Other:** NA	**Percent receiving Financial aid, first-year:** 40%
Mean SAT: NA	**Percent in-state / out of state:** NA	
	Percent from Public HS: NA	

Imagine waking up on a Saturday morning and seeing gold-clad army walking across campus. No, it's not your mind playing tricks on you. It's the fervent Boston College Superfans marching over to Alumni Stadium to root on the Eagles football team. With their maroon-and-gold Superfans T-shirts, the students enthusiastically cheers on their team, creating a formidable presence for visiting teams. While the Superfans are an extreme example of school spirit, no matter who you are, it is easy to get swept up by the excitement and energy of being an Eagle.

For those who want the city life without the nuisance of city noise and traffic, Boston College is located six miles outside of downtown Boston. A Jesuit school, BC provides its students with a balanced mix of academics and parties.

Striking a Balance: Academics

Undergraduates have the choice of enrolling in one of four schools: the College of Arts and Sciences, the Wallace E. Carroll School of Management, the Lynch School of Education, and the School of Nursing. While students must enroll in one school, they have the option of switching to another school via a not-so-rigorous application process. Students have the option of taking courses in other schools, but some are restricted to students in the school. Most students have selected a school by the end of sophomore year.

Each school has a core curriculum that explores a diverse range of subjects. These fields include history, literature, arts, mathematics, philosophy, social sciences, natural sciences, and theology among others. BC also requires all freshmen to take a writing course. Though the requirements are many, students are able to find a balance between both core courses and elective courses. One student commented that the core curriculum "gives you a good, solid education and a level playing field." Within each core group requirement, there is a wide variety of classes to choose from that satisfy the core such as "History of Dinosaurs" and "History of Rock and Roll." Pre-med is one of the hardest majors where students feel that the intro classes try to weed out students. Theology and philosophy also rank amongst the hardest, while communications and history rank among the most popular majors.

In the larger introductory and lecture courses, students find it much harder to interact with professors, but in the more advanced courses, professors are a great resource of knowledge and everyday experience. While understandably there are some bad eggs in the mix, many of the professors seek out friendships with students and have the desire to see that the student grows and succeeds during their college years. "They try to help you out and will refer you to places for internships and jobs," one student said.

Housing: A System of Chance

BC guarantees its students three years of housing without differentiating between those with financial aid and those without. Freshmen are split between either Upper Campus or Newton Campus. While there are those that find living on Newton a pain, as going to class involves waiting for the shuttle in the cold, some of Newton's residents say that it's a great experience. A former Newton inhabitant commented, "Everyone's basically in the same boat, and you get to know each other better." For those on Upper Campus, class is just a short walk from the dorms. With mainly freshmen living there, the newcomers are closer to the action and social scene.

After the first year, students are entered into a lottery system for the next year's rooming. Sophomores aspire to live on Lower Campus where the weekend parties happen and where the majority of upperclassmen reside. Here, students can draw apartment-style rooms with kitchens and private bathrooms. However, some get the short end of the deal and are forced to live on Upper, where the rooms are similar to the freshmen dorms. Juniors typically move off-campus into apartments in order to guarantee housing for senior year. There is a bus line available for transportation to and from off-campus housing vicinities. After living a year off-campus or abroad, seniors return to campus in order to get a chance at living in the modulars or mods, which are located in the middle of the university. Every weekend, seniors often throw parties and hold barbeques outside these small townhouses.

On each campus, there is one large dining hall. Of these three, the Lower Campus dining hall, Lower Live, is the most popular by far, as it is the largest and closest to the majority of the student body. Most students find the dining-hall food to be decent, but the Lyons Dining Hall—nicknamed "The Rat"—receives rave reviews. The Rat offers fried foods and other grilled products for lunch during the weekdays. Also, the Café at McElroy on Upper Campus features a Chocolate Bar where students have access to chocolate fondue and other confectionary treats. The dining halls often offer special themed meals throughout the year. BC operates on a debit system where students have dining bucks to purchase whatever food they want from any of the dining locations. However, some students remark that BC overcharges on food and that they find themselves running out of dollars before the semester is over.

Maroon and Gold (And Very White)

Students who come to BC are often shocked at first by the lack of diversity. A very large majority of the student population is white. One student typified BC's racial make-up as "being like high school where people of the same group tend to stick together, like the black or Asian table." Another who came from a similarly homogeneous neighborhood found it surprising that at BC "race seemed like a bigger factor, and I usually hang out with a less diverse group than in high school."

> "While racial lines appear to be more distinct during the first year, upperclassmen remark that as students advance in class, the distinctions become less noticeable."

Despite the small minority population, there are many ethnic groups that support those of different ethnicities. The African-American, Hispanic, Asian, and Native American (AHANA) assists and oversees organizations for minority students. These groups provide students with career services, besides creating a close group of friends. The annual dance competition, named "The Showdown," highlights the cultures of the many ethnicities and is one of the most popular events on campus. While racial lines appear to be more distinct during the first year, upperclassmen remark that as students advance in class, the distinctions become less noticeable.

Athletics: A Proud Tradition

With historic moments such as Heisman winner Doug Flutie's Hail Mary pass for a touchdown with no time left to beat the University of Miami on national television, it is no wonder that BC fans take pride in their sports teams. Football is huge at BC, with the team perennially ranked amongst the nation's best. Whenever BC plays Notre Dame, thousands crowd into Alumni Stadium to cheer on the Eagles in this heated rivalry. Students describe tailgates as "awesome" and as being some of the best. However, a new tailgating policy has been put into place

to ensure that students actually make it into the stadium. In addition, the mods often hold barbeques before the games and generally, students, parents, and alumni all make an appearance.

Every winter, sports fever erupts as the men's basketball and hockey teams take the stage. Since the Eagles basketball team is a contender for the national championship, the Conte Forum is regularly filled with fans. The hockey team is also a perennial contender, playing games in Kelley Rink and the Fleet Center.

While the varsity athletic facilities are newly refurbished and feature up-to-date technology, the gym for non-athletes is lightly under par. The Flynn Recreation Complex features elliptical trainers, treadmills, bikes, basketball courts, a swimming pool, an indoor track, and squash courts. Students complain, however, that there aren't many free weights for use and that the equipment available can be very shabby. Long waits for machines are frequent.

No Animal House, But the Party Still Goes On

Even though BC is a Catholic school, much partying occurs throughout the year. BC maintains a strict zero-tolerance alcohol policy, and the BC Police Department reinforces the regulations. In the dorms, RAs watch out for violations and will not hesitate to write up offenders. Freshmen are not allowed to have alcohol in the dorms, while for upperclassmen, there are certain dorms that allow the possession of alcohol. Despite the numerous restrictions, students with a thirst for Jungle Juice will be able to find it.

Since BC has no Greek system, most of the partying occurs either in the mods or off-campus. The mods have a consistent crowd, as they are located in the central part of campus. However, it is more common for students to head off-campus where the juniors live, since the bus line is so convenient. Partying starts on Thursday and continues on through the whole of the weekend. Freshmen come in with a disadvantage though. Because they live on either Newton or Upper Campus, it is hard to get to know upperclassmen and get an idea of where to go. One student stated, "Everyone had this Animal House impression of college, but when I got there, I was just sitting in my room trying to find stuff to do."

For those who are of legal age, there is

the option of traveling to Boston, where bars and clubs run aplenty. One of the more popular watering holes for juniors and seniors is Mary Ann's, where the rounds are cheap and the atmosphere is very relaxed. Boston also offers plentiful shopping opportunities, movies, concerts, professional sporting events, and other excursions for those looking to get away from campus.

Every spring, BC holds the ever-popular Middlemarch dance. However, this dance is not for everyone. Invitations are limited, and students must go through a lengthy process to acquire one. Students have to be able to find out the location of the secret meeting where they unveil the details of the upcoming dance and begin the scavenger hunt for a ticket. Running around campus to answer clues, students who succeed in the hunt are then entered into a raffle for one of the coveted tickets.

Catholicism 101?

Students say they can feel the Jesuit presence at BC but do not find it imposing. Some of the faculty members are Jesuits and contribute to a strong Theology program at BC, and the surroundings are dotted with beautiful churches. In addition, the school offers several religious retreats throughout the year that are quite popular. While Catholics find themselves at home at BC, even non-Catholic students feel welcome and believe that the Jesuit-based education is a positive influence on their lives.

The Jesuit tradition at BC places a large emphasis on helping out the community and public service. There are many prominent community service groups on campus. 4Boston is one of the biggest groups on campus where members go into Boston and spend about four hours a week performing services for the city. During spring break, many forgo a vacation to the beach in favor of going on the Appalachia trip, where students help build homes for the poor. The experience typically has a big draw, making a waiting list necessary. As one student claimed, "BC molds you as a person and makes you realize what you need to do for society."—*Thomas Hsieh*

FYI

If you come to BC, you'd better bring a "fake ID to get into places."

What is the typical weekend schedule? "Thursdays: go to bars and clubs. Fridays: go to class and then at night to parties on and off campus. Saturdays: tailgate, take a nap, wake up, drink some more. Sundays: watch football and then do work."

If I could change one thing about BC, I'd "change the whole setup of housing so freshmen don't have to live far away and so sophomores don't get screwed in the lottery and have to live up on Upper Campus."

Three things every student should do before graduating from BC are, "going on the Appalachia trip, going to see the Red Sox at Fenway Park, and attend the speeches of the famous speakers that come to BC."

Boston University

Address: Boston University, One Sherborn St., Boston, MA 02115
Phone: 617-353-2300
E-mail Address: NA
Web site URL: www.bu.edu
Year Founded: 1839
Private or Public: private
Religious affiliation: none
Location: urban
Regular Application Deadline: 2-Jan
Number of Applicants: 31,851
Percent Accepted: 58%
Percent Accepted who enroll: 22%
Number Entering: 2,124
Number of Transfers Accepted each Year: 653
Mean SAT: 1,276
Mean ACT: 27
Middle 50% SAT range: 1,770–2,060

Middle 50% ACT range: 25–29
Early admission program (EA/ ED/ NA): ED
ED or EA Acceptance Rate: 39%
Full time Undergraduate enrollment: 18,521
Total enrollment: 29,491
Percent Male: 38%
Percent Female: 62%
Total Percent Minority: 44%
Percent African-American: 3%
Percent Asian/Pacific Islander: 14%
Percent Hispanic: 7%
Percent Native-American: <1%
Percent Other: 19%
Percent in-state / out of state: 19%/81%
Percent from Public HS: 70%
Retention Rate: 91%

Graduation Rate: 81%
Percent in On-campus housing: 66%
Percent affiliated with Greek system: 3%/5%
Percent Varsity or Club Athletes: NA
Number of official organized extracurricular organizations: 400
3 Most popular majors: Social Sciences, Business/Marketing, Communications/ Journalism
Student/Faculty ratio: 12:01
Tuition and Fees: $33,792.00
Cost for Room and Board: $10,480.00
Percent receiving Financial aid, first-year: 88%

Located conveniently in the heart of Boston, Boston University presents its students with solid academics, friendly people, and a famous hockey team. And, if you're looking for off-campus adventures, the Boston T will take you anywhere you like in one of the most exciting and historic cities in the country.

What Do You Make of It?

Among BU's 18 graduate and undergraduate schools and 250 degree programs, there is plenty of room to maneuver. Still, as one sophomore commented, "it seems like everyone is either a pre-med or pre-law." Other popular majors include international relations, psychology, and management. The university curriculum also offers a challenging honors program for ambitious freshmen and sophomores. Like most universities, BU holds large lectures for most introductory courses with smaller discussion sections attached. Upper-level classes shrink significantly to as low as 10 or even five students. Surprisingly, competition for those classes is not really a problem, and undergrad's chances only improve with seniority. And if lady luck is not on your side, "there are so many options, you can always find something else you will enjoy," like a class taught by Elie Wiesel, Nobel Peace Prize winner and one of the most popular professors at BU.

Rumors about grade deflation at BU is universally acknowledged to be based on "a misconception," according one sophomore, "no one has ever been able to prove its existence." At BU, students praise their professors for being accessible; as one student stated, the experience is "what you make of it."

No ID, No Way

Despite the strictly enforced policies against drinking, alcohol still finds its way into the lives of most BU students. Student social life is diverse in terms of locale; many undergraduates center their weekends around parties at off-campus apartments or the few off-campus frats (not funded or recognized by the university). The nearby colleges such as MIT and Harvard also offer viable party options. One student said that the Boston scene "opens up many social lives for those over 21 (or those with a really good fake ID)" and upperclassmen flock to the numerous bars and clubs in the area, such as Jillian's and The Dugout. Without an ID, students are out of luck, as Boston recently passed a law prohibiting any underage clubs, causing many undergrads to simply take their chances in the RA monitored dorms (although some say that that is a riskier option). BU weekends typically start on Thursday for those resourceful enough to avoid the Friday classes. If you prefer your weekends dry, never fear—there are still vibrant options for a social life outside of drinking activities, many of which take place in Boston, a city that provides endless restaurants, theaters, and shopping along Newbury Street.

From Jail to Hotel

The dorms at BU vary from great apartment-style dorms to small closet-like rooms. Competition is stiff for the recently built student village apartments, as well as two other residences that were former hotels on Commonwealth Avenue. Yet, getting a good dorm is a matter of luck of the draw. One student warned that some of the dorms "have been designed by an architect who used to designed jails." Warren Towers, the freshman dorm, has some of the least desirable rooms; however it makes up for it by having its own vibrant and close-knit social community. Students describe the campus, which is divided into East and West, as "long and skinny." The West campus is the more lively side, since it tends to house more athletes and parties. Moreover, many students move off campus after their sophomore years. The primary complaints from all students concerns BU's old fashioned guest policy: coed sleepovers are prohibited. And although students realize that the policy is meant to ensure safety on campus, it is commonly referred to as "outdated."

Fortunately, food rates pretty well at BU. There are five dining halls on campus and endless restaurants, some favorites of which include T. Anthony's pizza restaurant or anything in the North End. For those on the run, there are fallback options such as the George Sherman Union and numerous small convenience stores along the campus.

BU students generally do not bring cars to campus, and as anyone who has ever driven in Boston will tell you, it is not a good idea to have a car. Besides the nightmarish parking, students agree that Boston's one-way streets will significantly impede even the most experienced of navigators. The extensive subway system known as the T, however, more than makes up for the lack of personal transportation.

East Coast Style

This ultimate East Coast university has a generally friendly atmosphere. Students say that it is easiest to meet people through dorms and extracurriculars, although sometimes smaller classes foster friendships too. Students admit that BU could be more diverse, but they assert that the stereotype of a white, middle-class student body is only partly true.

> "There are so many options, you can always find something else you will enjoy."

Some of the most popular clubs at Boston University are student governments and programming council. The campus is also home to many cultural clubs like the Indian Club, which is one of the biggest organizations on campus. Students report that many, if not most, of their peers have jobs. Many work on campus in dining halls through work-study programs. Others find that Boston has plentiful job opportunities, including waiting tables or being cashiers.

Skates Are Required

When asked about school traditions, students responded the same way: there aren't any. Most undergrads agree that very little school spirit exists at BU. And, since the school does not have a football team, what spirit exists is entirely poured into the hockey team; hockey games are some of the most crowded and energetic events at BU, with the pep rallies against BU rival, Boston College, being widely attended. In fact, the BU versus BC hockey game is one of the most entertaining and well-attended events on campus.

For those who have no interest in hockey, Boston provides more than enough sports teams to root for including the Celtics, the Red Sox, and the New England Patriots. For those hoping for an active life of their own, the University has many popular intramural teams as well as a three floor Fitness and Recreation Center.

Boston University may not have the packed football stadiums of other schools, but BU students have pride in their school. And with Boston as the students' backyard playground, who could say no to that?
—Dorota Poplawska

FYI

If you come to BU, you'd better bring "money."

What is the typical weekend schedule? "Wake up late, gym, dinner and desserts at North End, party."

If I could change one thing about BU, I'd "improve the guest policy to something less strict."

Three things every student at BU should do before graduating are "Go to a baseball game at Fenway Park, attend a BU versus BC hockey game, and attend an Elie Wiesel lecture."

Brandeis University

Address: Brandeis, 415 South St M5003, Waltham, MA 02454-9110

Phone: 781-736-3500

E-mail Address: sendinfo@brandeis.edu

Web site URL: www.brandeis.edu

Year Founded: 1948

Private or Public: private

Religious affiliation: none

Location: suburban

Regular Application Deadline: 16-Jan

Number of Applicants: NA

Percent Accepted: 36%

Percent Accepted who enroll: 28%

Number Entering: NA

Number of Transfers Accepted each Year: NA

Mean SAT: NA

Mean ACT: NA

Middle 50% SAT range: 1,260–1,460

Middle 50% ACT range: 27–32

Early admission program (EA/ ED/ NA): NA

ED or EA Acceptance Rate: NA

Full time Undergraduate enrollment: 3,257

Total enrollment: 4,774

Percent Male: 44%

Percent Female: 56%

Total Percent Minority: 15%

Percent African-American: 3%

Percent Asian/Pacific Islander: 8%

Percent Hispanic: 4%

Percent Native-American: 0%

Percent Other: NA

Percent in-state / out of state: NA

Percent from Public HS: 70%

Retention Rate: 96%

Graduation Rate: 84% in four years, 86% in six

Percent in On-campus housing: 79%

Percent affiliated with Greek system: NA

Percent Varsity or Club Athletes: NA

Number of official organized extracurricular organizations: 246

3 Most popular majors: Economics, Psychology, Biology

Student/Faculty ratio: 8:01

Tuition and Fees: $31,951.00

Percent receiving Financial aid, first-year: 48%

Brandeis mailed hats arrived to the first 500 prospective Brandeis applicants last year. This effort to woo potential students shows how Brandeis has attempted to expand its application pool and move beyond the stereotype as an all-Jewish university. Located 15 minutes outside of Boston, Waltham is home to the only nonsectarian Jewish-sponsored college or university in the country. Although the majority of students are Jewish, Brandeis' population is growing more diverse every year. The University, named after Supreme Court Justice Louis Brandeis and founded in 1948, is a national research university that offers the intimate feel of a small liberal arts college.

Freedom to Mix and Match

Brandeis provides opportunities for students to study many different subjects and potentially double or even triple major. Popular majors include economics, psychol-ogy and history. If none of the school's 41 majors are appealing, however, students have the option of creating their own. Freshmen need not fear the wide range of academic offerings. Every first-year student is provided with a faculty advisor that stays with him for his first two years. Freshmen also participate in the much-praised University Seminars in Humanistic Inquiries. One freshman said of her "Creating the Theatrical Essay" seminar, "It is great. All I do is write about myself."

Brandeis' academic requirements are extremely broad and allow to students to get their "hands in different departments." One student lauded the requirements because "You are getting a little bit of everything." Brandeis also offers several special programs, such as one that leads to early acceptance at Tufts University School of Medicine. Yet one student warned that pre-med students "really need a lot of willpower" because of the rigorous requirements. A lot of effort is also required for theater majors due to the large number of courses required to fulfill the major. The Brandeis workload is generally considered difficult, but manageable. One freshman noted that school is "a lot of work, but I still can sleep at night."

Introductory courses aside, classes are small in size. Students are able to interact closely with even the most highly acclaimed professors such as 2005 Pulitzer Prize winning historian David Hackett Fischer and Robert Reich, who served as Secretary of Labor under Bill Clinton. These are in addition to the notable people who have taught at Brandeis, such as Eleanor Roosevelt.

Thursday Through Saturday, Hit Up Boston

After a long week of classes, students often try to get off campus and into Boston. Dance clubs, bars, and Harvard Square are some of the most frequented locations. A good fake ID and a car are considered crucial to fully take advantage of Beantown. Since freshmen are prohibited from having cars on campus, they are forced to bum rides off upperclassmen or use Brandeis-sponsored transportation. While students without IDs still can find things to do, on-campus parties are plagued by "good intentions, bad results." Nevertheless, Mela, a campus-wide party hosted by the South Asian Society, and "Madfest" are must attend social events. Fraternities and sororities, located off campus, play a limited role in the Brandeis social scene. The Greek life system is not endorsed by the University in accordance with the school's policy of not supporting any type of exclusion. Be warned: "the frat scene is kind of sketchy!" Freshmen live in "dry quads," but one upperclassman noted "since my freshman year, I have never had trouble getting alcohol."

> "The on-campus parties are plagued by 'good intentions, bad results.' "

One female student was quick to comment on the attractiveness of the campus-population: "On a scale of 1 to 10, the attractiveness is -1." Despite this critical view, a hook-up culture exists, though it is "positively correlated" with drinking. Weed is the most predominant drug on campus. One senior recalls a "distinctive smell coming from the sophomore dorms," adding that

anything harder than pot is much less prevalent.

Solid Infrastructure

Brandeis dorms are "just pretty OK." On-campus housing is not guaranteed after freshman year; nevertheless, roughly 80 percent of Brandeis students choose to live on campus. The nicer dorms reserved for upperclassmen receive lots of praise. One of Brandeis' original buildings, "Castle," and the modern-looking "Village," are two of the most sought-after options.

The Division III Brandeis Judges compete in the Eastern College Athletic Conference. The most well-attended varsity athletic event is women's basketball, which over the past few years has evolved into a "powerhouse." The school's mascot, Ollie the Owl, can be seen along the sidelines attempting to get crowds into the game. The Judges lack a football team, except on the intramural flag football level. Indeed, IMs are popular, while many students flock to Gossman Gym to pump iron or just try and stay in shape. The recent addition of a new soccer field equipped with lighting greatly improved the sports facilities.

Widespread Social Justice

The school was founded on the principles of social justice and tolerance, which are exemplified by the student body's lack of cliques and socially restrictive groups. Political activisms in all forms compose a major part of campus life. The political climate is considered "very, very liberal." There is a sense on campus that one must "pay it forward;" students recognize that they are privileged to be at the University and for the most part are "do-gooders."

At Brandeis, "there are a lot of Jews, but it is easy to be anything you want here." Students get off for major Jewish holidays and kosher food is widely available. But despite its predominantly Jewish student body, the school is far from homogeneous and "diversity does exist." The population is continuously becoming more and more varied. Brandeis students think very highly of their gregarious peers. One student went as far to say, "Even the strange people are nice here."

In general, Brandeis students seem to love their school. In spite of the most common misconception, Brandeis brings together a decent blend of people from different backgrounds to Waltham. The best part: they might even send you a hat just for applying.—*Harry Etra*

FYI

If you come to Brandeis, you'd better bring a "Hebrew accent."

What is the typical weekend schedule? "Attend a large student event on campus or go into Boston."

If I could change one thing about Brandeis, I'd "change the ridiculous weather conditions."

The three things that every student do before graduating from Brandeis are "take a class with David Fischer, 'Sherman-shop,' go to Friday night services at Chabad."

Clark University

Address: Clark University, 950 Main Street, Worcester, MA 01610-1477

Phone: 508-793-7431

E-mail Address: admissions@clarku.edu

Web site URL: http://www.clarku.edu

Year Founded: 1887

Private or Public: Private

Religious affiliation: none

Location: urban

Regular Application Deadline: 15-Jan

Number of Applicants: 4,463

Percent Accepted: 62%

Percent Accepted who enroll: 20%

Number Entering: 599

Number of Transfers Accepted each Year: ~50

Mean SAT: NA

Mean ACT: NA

Middle 50% SAT range: 1,100–1,310

Middle 50% ACT range: 24–28

Early admission program (EA/ ED/ NA): ED

ED or EA Acceptance Rate: 85%

Full time Undergraduate enrollment: 2,052

Total enrollment: 3,118

Percent Male: 40%

Percent Female: 60%

Total Percent Minority: 12%

Percent African-American: 3%

Percent Asian/Pacific Islander: 4%

Percent Hispanic: 3%

Percent Native-American: 0%

Percent Other: 2%

Percent in-state / out of state: 64%/36%

Percent from Public HS: 68%

Retention Rate: 86%

Graduation Rate: 70%

Percent in On-campus housing: 77%

Percent affiliated with Greek system: 0%

Percent Varsity or Club Athletes: 20%

Number of official organized extracurricular organizations: 85

3 Most popular majors: Psychology, Government, Biology

Student/Faculty ratio: 10:01

Tuition and Fees: $31,200.00

Cost for Room and Board: $5,900.00

Percent receiving Financial aid, first-year: 54%

Nestled in the middle of a post-industrial town in central Massachu-setts is an intellectual oasis called Clark University. Perhaps best known as the only American university where Sigmund Freud lectured and as Jerry Garcia's favorite place to trip, Clark is more than a novelty stopping point for international celebrities—it is a close community of creative thinkers.

The Academy

Founded in 1887, Clark's graduate school is the oldest in the country. Although the University's literature is quick to point this out, Clark's focus is decidedly on the under-graduate student. Roughly 2,000 under-grads inhabit the small red-brick campus. From Red Square, the center of the cam-pus, most buildings are no more than five minutes away by foot. Journeys from dorm to classroom are mercifully short in the brutal New England winter, which drops an average of 67 inches of snow on "Clarkies" every year.

Clark offers 28 different majors, of which the most popular are psychology, govern-ment and international relations, business management, and communications and culture. With a student/faculty ratio of 10 to 1 and an average class size of 19, many Clarkies find their classes smaller in college than they were in high school.

All faculty members teach undergraduate courses, and all undergraduate courses are taught by faculty. This means no TA-taught classes and no grad-school-only professors. As far as the quality of individual teachers, students say they range from mediocre to brilliant.

Students agree that the workload is fairly light; however, they also say that it's easy to create a rigorous and rewarding academic program. It's all about how much effort you put in. In-class conversations are generally stimulating because almost everybody brings something unique to the table. "Clark's environment is much more intellectual than the college rankings would indicate," one sophomore says.

Extracurriculars

Clark offers the usual cornucopia of extracurricular activities—everything from a cappella groups to written publications to community service. Of the roughly 70 student organizations at Clark, there are a few perennial main attractions. Clark's biweekly newspaper, *The Scarlet*, satisfies journalistic cravings. Other publications, such as the Wheatbread literary magazine, showcase Clark's creative writers. The all-female Counterpoints and the coed Clark Bars lead Clark's a cappella scene. Though religious groups are not as popular as at other schools, the Clark Christian Fellowship and Hillel offer students some faith-based activities. Theatrical groups include The Clark University Players' Society and Clark on Drama, while a comedy troupe called the Peapod Squad is a campus favorite. The Clark University Film Society offers 30 free film screenings per year, and the Bisexual, Lesbian, and Gay Association (BILAGA) is also big on campus.

> "Clark's environment is much more intellectual than the college rankings would indicate."

Clark offers many community service opportunities—most notably through the Massachusetts Public Interest Research Group (MassPIRG), an environmental and consumer advocacy group. MassPIRG is a statewide organization with branches in major cities across the state. Worcester's head organizer works with Clarkies on all types of causes. "Our goal is to involve students in research, service, and environmental campaigns," he said. "We want to inspire students to become good citizens and good leaders by working on these projects. It's all about fighting for what's right for the little guy."

As far as sports go, Clark is not exactly a powerhouse. An NCAA Division III school, Clark recruits athletes but does not offer athletic scholarships. Men's basketball and women's soccer are fairly popular on cam-

pus, but most of the school's 17 varsity sports are only paid attention by other athletes. Intramurals usually get a solid turnout, however, and one can always find a couple Clarkies tossing a Frisbee around the quad if the temperatures are above freezing.

Grungies, Dudebros, and Party Life

Like most Northeastern liberal arts colleges, Clark prides itself on diversity even though students say it isn't really that diverse. The student body is 7 percent international, and 9 percent Asian-, Latino-, African-, and Native-American. The majority of students fall into the category of alternative or "dude-bro," the nickname given to jocks on campus because of their tendency to use the words "dude" and "bro" at least twice in every sentence. However, Clark is a decidedly alternative campus. Converse is the shoe of choice; Urban Outfitters is the wardrobe for most, while Salvation Army clothes the hardcore. The Nike-and-Polo uniform of the jocks is fairly rare. "You look at them sometimes and you're like, 'What the hell are you doing here?'" one sophomore observed. "But there are definitely more jocks at Clark than you would think."

At the same time, sports often serve as a unifying force on campus. Not the sparsely attended Clark sports, mind you, but pro sports—especially baseball. Worcester is located less than 50 miles from Boston, the capital of Red Sox nation, and the 65 percent of students who aren't from Massachusetts quickly get swept up in pennant fever. When the Red Sox came back from a 3-0 series deficit to defeat the Yankees in the 2004 ALCS, Clarkies stormed the president's house and demanded he cancel classes the next day. Though he refused this accommodation, the president placated his students by inviting them into his house for cider and cookies.

Clark's administration is more conservative than its students, but there is still a healthy party scene. Kegs are banned on campus, but ambitious Clarkies get fake IDs or attend off-campus parties. Many say they smoke pot instead; both alcohol and marijuana are reportedly fairly easy to obtain. Students describe the school's alcohol and drug policy as "tough, but not out to get you." Resident Advisors (RAs) try to act as friends, but they often write Clarkies up for violating substance abuse policies. Students say that it all depends on your RA. One girl claimed that an RA reported her to the campus police for having a glass bottle and a lighter in her common room because that suggested drug use. Other Clarkies report that RAs will issue two or three warnings before writing students up.

There is at least one annual gigantic blowout party at Clark—Spree Day. Once a year during the spring, on a date kept secret from the majority of students until the morning it happens, school is cancelled and Spree Day, 24 hours of partying and relaxation, is instituted in its place. Spree Day is announced early in the morning by roving bands of upperclassmen, and upon awakening, Clarkies are treated to concerts, snacks, and general revelry. It's no wonder that Spree Day is Clark's most beloved tradition.

Waffle Ceilings and Culinary Mediocrity

Housing at Clark ranges from smallish to spacious. Most dorms are set up in the typical collegiate arrangement—floors of doubles and singles. Some lucky Clarkies live in roomy suites of five or six, complete with a common room and private bathroom. But the first thing one notices in a Clark dorm room is the ceiling. Almost all of the residential ceilings are made of the same waffle-like cement grid.

The cafeteria, or "The Caf," as Clarkies call it, is average at best. Despite the charming ambiance created by the cafeteria's previous function as a gym, the cafeteria gets weak reviews from students. "Some nights there's nothing you want to touch, but usually there are some finds," observed one student. There are, however, other dining options available to those who just can't stomach The Caf. On campus, the Bistro and the Moonlight Café get decent reviews from Clarkies, and both establishments accept student flex dollars. For the free spender, Worcester offers a number of tasty eating establishments, from House of India to Tortilla Sam's. Fast food, especially Wendy's, is also a popular alternative to cafeteria fare.

It's Pronounced "Wuh-stah"

Though Worcester is frequently derided as dangerous, boring, or hard to pronounce, it offers Clark students a solid selection of activities. Massachusetts' third-biggest city hosts everything from monster-truck rallies to Eminem concerts. The city has its share of dilapidated areas, but some students actually enjoy this. "Some parts of the city are pretty run-down," one sophomore said. "But in a way, that's what gives Worcester its character. Everybody is trying to make a living, so there are all sorts of cool shops and cheap restaurants. My favorite is the 35-cent donut place."

For those lucky enough to have a car on campus, trips to Boston are a great antidote to the Worcester blues. Clarkies also journey to the many nearby nature trails and ski areas in their spare time. Despite having to deal with the mediocrity of Worcester and the occasional ennui of small college life, Clarkies generally enjoy their college experience. Though Spree Day only comes once a year, students agree that Clark is a great place to spend four wonderful years of their lives.—*Zack O'Malley Greenburg*

FYI
If you come to Clark, you'd better bring "an accepting outlook to take in all our diversity."
What is the typical weekend schedule? "Check out local bars and chill with friends, catch up on sleep and work."
If I could change one thing about Clark, I'd "up the school spirit and lose Worcester."
Three things every student at Clark should do before graduating are "get something pierced, eat at Wendy's Clark Brunch, and take a nap on the green."

Emerson College

Address: 120 Boylston St.;
   Boston, MA 02116-4624
Phone: 617-824-8500
E-mail address:
   admission@emerson
   .edu
Web site URL:
   www.emerson.edu
Founded: 1880
Private or Public: private
Religious affiliation: none
Location: urban
Application Deadline:
   1-Jan
Number of Applicants:
   4,321
Percent Accepted:
   48%
**Percent Accepted who
   enroll:** 34%
Entering class: 701

Transfers: 51
**Early admission program
   (EA/ED/NA):** NA
**Early Decision or Early
   Action Acceptance Rate:**
   NA
Undergraduate enrollment:
   3,401
Total enrollment: NA
Percent Male/Female:
   43%/57%
Percent Minority: 11%
Percent African-American: 2%
Percent Asian: 5%
Percent Hispanic: 4%
Percent Native-American:
   0%
**Percent in-state/out of
   state:** 35%/65%
Percent Pub HS: NA
On-campus housing: 45%

Fraternities: NA
Sororities: NA
Mean SAT: NA
Mean ACT: NA
Middle 50% SAT range:
   1,150–1,320
Middle 50% ACT range:
   25–29
Most popular majors:
   communications,
   journalism, media studies
Retention: 83%
Graduation rate: NA
Tuition and Fees: $24,064
**In State Tuition and Fees
   (if different):**
Room and Board: $10,420
Financial aid, first-year:
   65%
Varsity or Club Athletes: NA
Library: 175,000 volumes

For those looking for a creative and unique learning experience in the heart of Boston, Emerson is the school for you. As one of the premier colleges dedicated to communications and the arts, Emerson makes sure to ground its focus within a liberal arts context. Budding creators and performers are sure to flourish on Emerson's supportive campus.

More Than Just Arts

Emerson is far from your typical college. It uniquely combines a pre-professional art curriculum with a more traditional liberal arts experience and prides itself on striking a balance between the two. Emerson students are encouraged to cultivate their creativity and passion while building upon a traditional foundation.

Upon arrival, Emerson students have a variety of requirements to fulfill both their freshmen year and over the course of four years. Freshmen are required to take two writing courses, which draw some complaints for being sub-standard. In keeping with Emerson's liberal arts base, students must take courses in history, non-western civilization, psychology or philosophy, and research and expository writing. The required curriculum also includes aesthetics, fine arts, and performing arts. One student

comments that at times "the school definitely focuses more on its job-specific courses and many of the liberal arts courses tend to go by the wayside as far as strong teachers go," but students generally seem to find the requirements more helpful than not. One senior reflects that, "All students appreciate the exposure to other disciplines."

Emerson students choose between two schools, the School of the Arts and the School of Communications, when declaring their major. The School of the Arts includes the performing arts, visual and media arts, and writing while the School of Communications encompasses communication sciences, journalism, and marketing. Many students declare their major, and in effect their school, after their freshman year, but as one freshman notes, "When students are unsure of their major, they often declare it as media studies," presumably with the option of changing at a later date. Although students are technically divided by their choice of school, many students laud the benefits of having both schools under one roof. There is a great deal of involvement between the two because students are required to take classes from both, as well because of the interdisciplinary nature inherent in many of Emerson's courses. One student remarks that the existence of both schools encourages both professors and students to look at their subject in the context of other disciplines. For example, within a writing course, a professor may reference a film or television show, giving students a broader prospective.

Study abroad is a very popular option among Emerson students. Most students participate in one, if not more, of the three programs run by Emerson. Castle Well in the Netherlands is one popular destination that opens up all of Europe to students. The Los Angeles programs sends students to California for a semester to take advantage of internship opportunities and networking with the entertainment industry. The Prague Summer Film Festival is the third, very popular abroad opportunity.

Emerson students show creativity even when picking their majors. It is extremely popular to double major, minor or even create your own major. Some have been known to both double major and double minor. Students often pick unrelated subjects to study, reflecting their varied interests. Some of the more popular majors include marketing and film. Theater is known as a difficult major, as is communication disorders. Writing is another particularly rigorous major. Emerson boasts some very interesting courses, including History of Burlesque. One common complaint centers on the length of classes. Emerson classes last from between an hour and fifteen minutes to almost two hours. On the upside, classes are generally small and average to about twenty students, with the largest classes rarely topping one hundred students. TAs are rare and one senior claims, "I have never had a TA or even heard of one at Emerson." The consensus among students is that the workload is what you make. And, on top of the normal paper writing and reading, Emerson students "come to act, produce films, write poetry, and create art."

Student Body

Emerson prides itself on representing a diverse range of opinions and people. Students are practically required to arrive on campus with an open mind and according to one student, "I found kids I could get along with and relate to, and I think even if something isn't your style, you can still fit in." This attitude aside, there are some stereotypes for the student body, including "white, rich, gay" and crazy liberal. Many are very politically active on campus. Stu-

dents laughingly joke that all incoming guys will be "gay by May," but this is offset by an extremely accepting atmosphere on campus. This does mean dating can be tough for girls on campus. Students often look to other colleges in Boston for dating opportunities. One large complaint heard among students is that Emerson is not racially or economically diverse. But the overwhelming atmosphere is one of creativity, diversity and enthusiasm.

> "I found kids I could get along with and relate to, and I think even if something isn't your style, you can still fit in."

This creativity is directly channeled into the variety of activities Emerson students take on. Many of these directly relate to majors, especially with fields such as film studies. Emerson provides the means and equipment to support creative endeavors. There are student publications, theatre groups, one of the most popular college radio stations, as well as opportunities all over Boston. Emerson recently renovated the Cutler Majestic Theatre, a former opera house, as a venue for student productions, as well as visiting artists.

Not Your Average Campus

For students, "Emerson IS Boston." The school and the city are well integrated and inseparable as an experience. Weekends are jam packed because of all the bars, theatres, and events Boston offers, but that does not mean there is a lack of things to do on campus. From shows to parties, there is something to satisfy everyone. Upperclassmen often gather on campus for parties. According to one senior, "Emerson students really like to dress up for each other and spend money. It wouldn't be strange to go to a semi-formal cocktail mixer." Greek life exists, but is far from a defining social force.

Emerson students are guaranteed housing for their first two years and these are not two years of suffering. Descriptions of housing have included "awesome" and "like hotels." Some students live in standard doubles off a hall in the Little Building, while Piano Row boasts newer suite-type rooms. Upperclassmen tend to move off campus into apartments. On campus, there are RAs and strict alcohol regulations in the dorms, but those over twenty-one are allowed to drink. Food on campus is described as "fine, but can get old." There are cafes and convenience stores in the dorm, but there are also thousands of cheap food options all around Boston. On-campus facilities also boast a library that caters to communication majors, a new gym and soccer field, and a new performing arts theatre that was featured in the Martin Scorsese film, *The Departed*.

Emerson boasts a world-class location in the heart of the theatre district of Boston. Emerson's students are just as familiar with the city around them as they are with the campus. Combined with the diversity and interdisciplinary academic and art focus, Emerson is a truly unique and exciting experience for students looking to make the most of their four years at college.—*Janet Yang*

FYI

If you come to Emerson you better bring "a Mac, knowledge of art and film, and big sunglasses."
The typical weekend schedule is "dinner at a trendy restaurant in Boston, seeing an Emerson show, going to a cast party, film shoot wrap party or cocktail party."
If I could change one thing it would be "the scarcity of straight men."
Three things every student should do before graduation are "see a show in the Majestic, study abroad, go to the EVVY awards."

College of the Holy Cross

Address: Holy Cross, 1 College Street, 105 Fenwick Hall, Worcester, MA 01610-2395
Phone: 800-442-2421
E-mail Address: admissions@holycross.edu
Web site URL: www.holycross.edu
Year Founded: 1843
Private or Public: private
Religious affiliation: Roman Catholic
Location: suburban
Regular Application Deadline: 15-Jan
Number of Applicants: 6,705
Percent Accepted: 34%
Percent Accepted who enroll: 33%
Number Entering: 739
Number of Transfers Accepted each Year: 16
Mean SAT: NA
Mean ACT: NA

Middle 50% SAT range: 1,200–1,320
Middle 50% ACT range: NA
Early admission program (EA/ ED/ NA): ED
ED or EA Acceptance Rate: 28%
Full time Undergraduate enrollment: 2,788
Total enrollment: 2,816
Percent Male: 45%
Percent Female: 55%
Total Percent Minority: 13%
Percent African-American: 4%
Percent Asian/Pacific Islander: 4%
Percent Hispanic: 5%
Percent Native-American: 0%
Percent Other: 0%
Percent in-state / out of state: 37%/63%

Percent from Public HS: 51%
Retention Rate: 97%
Graduation Rate: 91%
Percent in On-campus housing: 88%
Percent affiliated with Greek system: 0%
Percent Varsity or Club Athletes: 25%
Number of official organized extracurricular organizations: 102
3 Most popular majors: Economics, Political Science, History
Student/Faculty ratio: 11:01
Tuition and Fees: $33,313.00
Cost for Room and Board: $9,580.00
Percent receiving Financial aid, first-year: 72%

In the bustling college town of Worcester, Massachusetts lays a small liberal arts school with strong Jesuit ties. Surrounded by other colleges in a "consortium," students at Holy Cross are able to get the close community feel and at the same time expand their horizons to a dozen other schools nearby.

Strong Core

The academic program at Holy Cross is meant to provide students a well-rounded liberal arts foundation. To this end, there is a core curriculum. In order to graduate, students must take one class in several departments including history, philosophy, religion, literature, art, math, and science as well as two classes in the social science department. Although the students inevitably find that "some of the requirements are worthless", most students at the end of their four years do not see it as an obligation, but rather as a chance to leave college with a strong foundation in many different arenas. The wide variety of classes offered by each department allows students to select courses that are interesting to them, so that no one is too far out of his or her academic comfort zone. For example, a student interested in biology may take a course in bioethics to satisfy the philosophy requirement. Outside of the requirements, there are a number of unique courses for students to pick from, including the Irish American Experience and History of Rock.

Once students specialize, there are many fields that they may enter. One popular major is history. Many students choose a double major in economics and accounting. This is a difficult course of study, but the consensus suggests that the most demanding program at Holy Cross is biology with the pre-med concentration. As one student in the program explained, "There are so many requirements for pre-med students, so it is challenging to manage your schedule when it comes time to take some required classes." The biological/pre-medical concentration is set apart by the fact that it requires about seven hours of lab work per week. At the other end of the spectrum, some social science majors, including sociology and psychology, are generally considered easy. This does not mean they are "slacker majors," though. A junior lamented, "If only Holy Cross had a slacker major!"

Academics at Holy Cross are challenging, and there is definitely a sense of competition among students. On average, students do about 25 to 35 hours of work outside of class per week. Again, science majors bear a slightly heavier load and 40 hours of work per week is not out of the ordinary. The work is not easy. "I would say that the academics are very challenging at Holy Cross," added a sophomore. "There aren't many 'easy A' classes if we have any at all." Though rigorous, the learning environment is tailored to the students. Many classes are discussion-oriented and small in size. In addition, professors are accessible outside of class for students who want extra help. All professors have office hours and almost always give out their home phone numbers so students can reach them while working on a project or studying for a test.

On and Off Campus

Socially speaking, Holy Cross offers something for everyone. Options include school-sponsored social events, parties, and even opportunities to take advantage of the not-too-distant Boston shopping and nightlife scene. Weekends allow students a chance to get slightly farther away from campus. Boston, a 45-minute drive or train trip, has much to offer, and the University conveniently provides a free shuttle on Friday and Saturday to Boston, Providence, The Shoppes at Blackstone Valley, Price Chopper supermarket, and Solomon Pond Mall, a nearby shopping center with a great movie theater.

Closer to campus, Worcester may not be the thriving metropolis one would hope, but there are several nice restaurants nearby that cater to nights out with friends. Worcester also has museums and the Centrum Centre, a concert venue. The bar scene in Worcester is popular among upperclassmen and accessible to those with cars. On Wednesdays for example, Irish Times Pub draws a crowd. While the bar scene is limited for underclassmen, there are plenty of parties in the dorms to keep everyone occupied. There are also a large number of off-campus parties at the residences that border the campus. The sports teams dominate many facets of life at Holy Cross, and the social scene is no exception. Many parties are hosted by members of teams at locales such as the Football House and the Hockey House.

Holy Cross makes a great effort to provide entertainment with a bevy of on-campus activities. There are concerts and traditional annual parties. Spring Weekend is a campus wide party complete with carnival and concert. St. Patrick's Day is another good "excuse to go to class drunk and make a mess of the dining hall." Freshmen attend the Opportunity Knocks dance in the fall. As a student who has attended in the past recounted, "It's a little different than your normal dance in that your roommate has to set you up with someone by calling his or her roommate, so the people going to Opp-Knocks together don't know until a day or two before the dance."

Holy Cross has a strict drinking policy and limits the number of people who can assemble in a room. Noise violations also lead to infractions. However, while the University is dedicated to maintaining a safe and alcohol-free environment for minors, and

Worcester police are tough on underage drinkers and fake IDs, students claim that the overall atmosphere is fairly tolerant. "RA attitudes only relax more as you move into upperclassmen housing."

One of the best features of Holy Cross is the ability to easily meet people and make friends. There is no Greek System, which makes the entire student body relatively cohesive. Still, there are cliques and small social groups. The best way to meet people is still through classes or in the dorms.

> **"Holy Cross kids handle academics by drinking heavily Wednesday through Saturday and working like hell Sunday through Tuesday."**

In short, the social scene at Holy Cross, while more open to those with transportation and those who can legally drink, is hardly boring. Holy Cross students play as hard as they work and according to one senior, "Holy Cross kids handle academics by drinking heavily Wednesday through Saturday and working like hell Sunday through Tuesday." There is something for everybody, both during the day and evening, and while some are initially put off by the lack of a dating scene, the ease of forming friendships and social circles seems to make up for the absence.

The Holy Cross Lifestyle

Holy Cross is a small campus built on Mount Saint James. It is very traditional, with redbrick buildings and ornate architecture that gives the campus an older feel. In the fall, the campus is covered with vibrant foliage that enhances the atmosphere. By contrast, Worcester, or "Wootown," leaves a lot to be desired. The majority of central Worcester seems run-down and unattractive. Few students venture out regularly, but those who do choose Shrewsbury Street (Exit 15 off East 290) for the selection of restaurants and its convenience to campus.

Campus life is extremely full at Holy Cross, and this may be attributed, at least in part, to the impressive amenities that the campus boasts. The facilities on campus provide opportunities for research and creative enjoyment. The science facilities are excellent and soon to be renovated. The libraries are also well regarded and the art resources, too often overlooked, are notable. There are two gyms, one for varsity athletes and another, with an indoor track, for the general student body.

At Holy Cross, sports are king, though there are no historic rivalries. Basketball is the most popular, and school spirit pervades the entire campus during the season. "There is so much school spirit," says one student. "The games are so much fun and they're always so packed." Purple Pride Day, announced only a day in advance, is a campus-wide celebration of Holy Cross spirit. Although students often spend Thursday and Saturday nights partying, many reserve Fridays for supporting their teams at games. With so many people living on campus, the dining halls are also always busy social scenes. Students especially enjoy the themed dinners thrown on Halloween, Thanksgiving, Easter, and other holidays. Kimball, the main dining hall, is buffet style, and most students can find something there. In addition, Lower Kimball, or "Lower," which is located below the main dining hall, offers quicker and more varied lunch options. Lower Kimball has a deli bar, a grill, ready-made meals, and Chinese food. Upperclassmen often opt to eat in Crossroads, a grill-style eatery with a wider selection.

Beyond the essentials and their weekend partying, many students pursue their interests through extracurricular activities. The largest organization on campus is the Student Government Association (SGA). The SGA provides a variety of services such as buses to Boston, a movie rental store, and a supermarket shuttle. Campus Activities Board (CAB) is another large group on campus that organizes social events such as Opp-Knocks and brings in guest speakers and comedians. Clubs on campus help foster the sense of community at this school. "Getting out there and trying your hand at any number of activities is really the easiest way to make friends," noted one sophomore. Living together also helps cement this bond and very few students move off campus, especially now that new senior apartments have been constructed.

The unity at Holy Cross is definitely felt through the closeness of the community and school spirit, but also through religion. The student body is somewhat homogenous and is mostly white, upper middleclass, Catholic and northeastern. Conservatism may pervade the steeples of Holy Cross, but so do the long-lasting traditions of education, liberal arts, and spiritual unity.—*Mita Nester*

If you come to Holy Cross, you'd better bring "a Northface fleece and all your family members who also went to HC."

What is the typical weekend schedule? "Thursday, bar; Friday, athletic event, comedian, movie; Saturday, study and go to a party; Sunday, recover, study hard, and for the Catholics, attend 'Last Chance Mass' at 10pm."

If I could change one thing about Holy Cross, I'd "make the student body more liberal."

Three things every student at Holy Cross should do before graduating are "slap Jesus's hand at the monument on the front steps of the main library, play stickball on Wheeler Beach, and go to the corned beef and cabbage dinner on St. Patrick's Day."

Hampshire College

Address: Hampshire, 893 West Street, Amherst, MA 01002
Phone: 877-937-4267
E-mail Address: admissions@hampshire.edu
Web site URL: www.hampshire.edu
Year Founded: 1965
Private or Public: private
Religious affiliation: none
Location: rural
Regular Application Deadline: 16-Jan
Number of Applicants: NA
Percent Accepted: 56%
Percent Accepted who enroll: 29%
Number Entering: 392
Number of Transfers Accepted each Year: 103
Mean SAT: NA
Mean ACT: 27

Middle 50% SAT range: 610–700V, 540–660M, 600–690W
Middle 50% ACT range: 26–29
Early admission program (EA/ ED/ NA): ED, EA
ED or EA Acceptance Rate: 69%
Full time Undergraduate enrollment: 1,434
Total enrollment: 1,434
Percent Male: 38%
Percent Female: 62%
Total Percent Minority: 14%
Percent African-American: 4%
Percent Asian/Pacific Islander: 2%
Percent Hispanic: 7%
Percent Native-American: 1%
Percent Other: 86%
Percent in-state / out of state: 15%/85%

Percent from Public HS: 49%
Retention Rate: 79%
Graduation Rate: 61%
Percent in On-campus housing: 91%
Percent affiliated with Greek system: 0%
Percent Varsity or Club Athletes: NA
Number of official organized extracurricular organizations: 114
3 Most popular majors: English Language and Literature, Social Sciences, Visual and Performing Arts
Student/Faculty ratio: 12:01
Tuition and Fees: $34,605.00
Cost for Room and Board: $9,030.00
Percent receiving Financial aid, first-year: NA

Deep in the Pioneer Valley, nestled in the quaint serenity of New England, lies a radical college devoted to inflaming the passions of its highly individualistic and motivated student body. This college was founded in the '70s by the other four colleges of the current Five College Consortium—Amherst, Smith, Mt. Holyoke, and UMass-Amherst—as an experiment in education. There are no majors at Hampshire. Every student must design his own course of study, and there is a heavy emphasis on individually driven project-based work. Hampshire College attracts a wide range of talented and self-motivated students to an energetic and liberal setting.

The Hampshire Curriculum: Div-ying up Academic Freedom

The most striking feature of Hampshire College is its "experimenting" academic program. Students must advance their way through three different divisions, called Div I, Div II and Div III. "First-years" must start their journey in Div I, which consists of taking eight classes, and at least one in each of the five Schools of thought: Humanities Arts and Cultural Studies, Interdisciplinary Arts, Social Science, Cognitive Science, and Natural Science. They must also take a tutorial class and complete some Learning Goals, which are meant to develop important academic skills. In the third "limbo semester," students complete their Div I requirements and start soliciting professors for their Div II work. Each student has a committee of two or three professors that helps him to create a unique course of study that concentrates his interests in preparation for the culminating Div III project. Once a student completes his Div III project and is reviewed by a committee of five professors, he can triumphantly ring the Div III Bell in the center of campus and declare himself "Div-Free." Because of all the committees involved in preparing one's course of study, there is a lot of paperwork. Hampshire suffers from a complex and sometimes frustrating bureaucracy. But, that is the price the students pay for an unprecedented amount of academic freedom available at no other college.

Another striking feature of Hampshire is the absence of grades. Instead, a student receives a written evaluation at the completion of a course. The students have high praises for the evaluations, which are "more telling than grades" because "they specifically relate to what [the student] can do better." Since there are no grades, the students do not feel obligated to do work that they feel isn't meaningful. That is not to say that Hampshire students are slackers. There is "a lot of outside work"—one student estimated as many as three hours of outside work for one hour of class time. Working with professors, it is not uncommon for students to rewrite a paper multiple times. Since the focus is on critical evaluation and personal improvement, many students feel it is "easy to get a good rapport [with professors] because of interaction."

There has been a movement in recent years to reform the Div I program to incorporate more individual work. This Re-Radicalization (or Re-Rad, for short) has "overwhelming" student support and is a "well-established student group." In the spring of 2004, a group of Re-Rad revolutionaries occupied the president's office in order to draw attention to their cause. This year, a Re-Rad pilot program began pairing third-semester students with Div III students for "mentored independent study."

Hampshire boasts strong programs in film, photography, and creative writing. It also created the first undergraduate interdisciplinary cognitive science program in the country. But, Hampshire is a small college and does not have the resources of a greater institution. Also, many of its classes are "narrowly focused," which hinders students who want to make a broad inquiry

into a subject. Whenever a student wants a course that Hampshire does not offer, he can go to one of the other schools in the Five College Consortium. As one student succinctly said, "The Five College Consortium makes Hampshire possible." The other colleges are an invaluable academic resource, and most students take classes elsewhere, especially during Div II when they need specific courses for their concentration. The Pioneer Valley Transit Authority runs buses between all the Five College schools throughout the day and most of the night.

"Spacey" Singles and "Revolutionary" Mods

Most first-year Hampshire students live in one of two dorms—Dakin or Merrill. Ninety percent of the rooms are singles, and the students seem very happy about that fact. Although "most of the rooms are relatively small," the students say it is nice to have quiet space for oneself. During a housing crunch this year, some students were living in lounges, but the problem was solved as students dropped out. There is a "fair amount of socializing" in the dorms, and most people become good friends with their hallmates.

Starting their second year, most students move into the mods, which receive high praise. A mod is essentially an on-campus apartment, in which four to 10 students share a common living space. All mods contain a kitchen, and many students go on a half-meal plan and cook meals in the mod. For this, students can buy a food share and receive inexpensive fresh vegetables year-round through the farm center and the community supported agriculture (CSA) program. There are three different mod sections—Prescott, Greenwich, and Enfield—each with its own personality and building style. The quality of the mods varies; some have been recently renovated and are dearly sought after. The housing lottery, which occurs in the spring, is "high-strung and dramatic." It takes place in a barn, where all the students mass and compete to get a good mod. Mod selections are based on seniority, so older students usually get the better housing. Most are satisfied and "the minority are horrified by the result."

There are a surprising number of options for social activity at Hampshire. There is always something happening on campus, especially in the mods. The social scene is very laid-back; one student described how most people "hang out, drink, do drugs, talk, play music, or any combination of the above." Although drugs are prevalent on campus, there seems to be a consensus that there is "no pressure to do anything." The college provides lots of events for the students, such as movie nights and speakers. Local and college bands play around campus, in any space that's available. Even if something is not happening on campus, there is always the option of going to one of the other of the Five Colleges, which also have vibrant social scenes and countless activities. The "liberal, arts-friendly town" of Northhampton, lined with coffee shops and bookstores, is also a popular hangout place.

Hampshire, for such a young college, already has some famous traditions. Hampshire Halloween, once called "Trip or Treat," is the biggest event of the year, a "fashion show on acid." People take their costumes very seriously, and the college plans events the whole evening. At the end of the night, the professors serve students breakfast in the dining hall. In the spring there are the Drag Ball and the Easter Keg Hunt, during which student organizations set up kegs in the woods and students bring their own cups in search of free beer. Another favorite event is the Spring Jam, a "big music festival with inflatables."

The Hampshire World: Nerds, Hipsters, Hippies and "Earthy Types"

Hampshire admittedly suffers from a stereotype of being a haven for scruffy, pot-smoking hippies, but the students thoroughly dismiss this idea. Although there are a "fair number of hippies," that is not the only type of person on campus. Indeed, one of the greatest things about Hampshire is that there is a "niche for everyone." When students are asked to describe the typical Hampshire student, they say he is "passionate," "committed" and "not competitive." It is not uncommon for students to talk at length about their academic work. The students are very friendly, and "everybody's always discussing something, out on the quad, on the bus." Furthermore, Hampshire students have a wide range of interests and have a "greater acceptance of nontraditional things." Granted, there are a few areas in which Hampshire lacks diversity. The campus is "predominately white upper-middle class" and ideologically "very left of

center." Still, the student body is quirky and interesting. For example, a number of students dressed up as pirates on Sept. 19 to celebrate International Talk Like a Pirate Day.

> "[Hampshire] did its job well; I learned how to educate myself and go after the things I want."

No matter what kind of person comes to Hampshire, he will be able to find a place. There are various groups on campus, covering all variety of interests. Hampshire Theater and its theater board, all run by students, elect student-run productions to be put on show, and host an annual play festival. Excalibur, the science fiction and fantasy fan club, one of the biggest groups on campus, hosts weekly movie screenings. Once a semester, Excalibur hosts Death Fest, a night-long role-playing-game tournament. A Circus Group was just created, where students can learn to juggle and do acrobatics. For aspiring writers, *The Hampshire Free Press* will fund periodical or book projects. Publications come and go, but the current ones are: *The Climax*, a newspaper that comes out every few weeks; *The Reader*, an annual literary arts magazine; and *The Omen*, a free-speech publication. *The Omen* is the longest-running paper at Hampshire and has been at the head of much controversy for publishing almost anything unedited. "[They're] so free speech, they won't correct your spelling." Like much of Hampshire, the writing scene suffers from "a lot of disorganization" but is "pregnant with opportunity." That is, although there are very few structures in place, if one takes the initiative, he can achieve a lot through his own effort.

SAGA and the Vegan Conspiracy

The only dining hall at Hampshire is SAGA (it's spelled in all capitals, but no one knows why). One student summed up the student opinion quite nicely when he said, "The food's fine. People complain about it because it's fun to complain about it, but it's not as bad as the complaining makes it seem." The dining hall offers a lot of options apart from the standard meal, including a salad bar, a sandwich bar, and a waffle station. It is also "very very vegetarian- and vegan-friendly." Their vegan desserts are said to be much better than the normal desserts, prompting the idea that there is a vast vegan conspiracy trying to convert the non-vegans. If SAGA is closed or a student wants something else to eat, the other places to get food on campus are the Tavern and the Bridge Café.

Hampshire was built in the '70s, and it shows. One student described the architecture of the buildings as "brutalist concrete and brick, squat, and ugly." The same student described the rest of the campus as "f—ing beautiful." Although the buildings on campus are "cramped," the rest of campus is very open. The campus is criss-crossed with "woodsy paths," and many students say they enjoy taking leisurely walks around campus. The Yellow Bike program takes care of communal bikes for use by the students. When the weather is better, spontaneous drum circles overtake the campus's grassy fields. In the fall, students can pick apples all over campus. The Cultural Village is the site of the Yiddish Book Museum and the Eric Carle Children's Book Art Museum, where one can make his own children's picture book in the studio. Another popular spot is the Lemelson Design Center, where students can take lessons in blacksmithing.

Hampshire may be the most radically unique college in the nation. But it is not for everyone. It is not, as some Saturday Night Live skits might suggest, a "weird slacker school." A serious caveat to anyone looking at Hampshire: It takes a certain kind of student to profit from a Hampshire education. Many come to Hampshire and find they cannot function without structure, or find the level of work too difficult. Consequently, Hampshire has a relatively high dropout rate. But, for those who are self-motivated and have a passion for learning, a Hampshire education will do great things. One recent alum said, "[Hampshire] did its job well; I learned how to educate myself and go after the things I want." In a way, a Hampshire education is empowering, in that it frees the students from the constraints of a structured academic system. The high level of individual work and inquiry-based projects gives Hampshire the reputation of being the "graduate school for undergraduates." Hampshire prepares students well for future academic work, and graduates enjoy one of the highest grad school acceptance rates in the country.
—*Ryan Galisewski*

FYI

If you come to Hampshire College, you'd better bring "a Frisbee, hippie drums, and a pirate costume."

What's the typical weekend schedule? "Wake up Saturday morning, go on a crazy adventure, and then wake up realizing it's Monday."

If I could change one thing about Hampshire College, I'd "make money grow on the Hampshire tree."

Three things every student at Hampshire College should do before graduating are "occupy a building, take a class with Lynn 'don't f—ing call me Mr.' Miller, and buy a farm share."

Harvard University

Address: Harvard, 86 Brattle Street, Cambridge, MA 02138
Phone: 617-495-1551
E-mail Address: college@fas.harvard.edu
Web site URL: www.admissions.college.harvard.edu
Year Founded: 1636
Private or Public: private
Religious affiliation: none
Location: urban
Regular Application Deadline: 1-Jan
Number of Applicants: 22,754
Percent Accepted: 28.6%
Percent Accepted who enroll: NA
Number Entering: NA
Number of Transfers Accepted each Year: NA

Mean SAT: NA
Mean ACT: NA
Middle 50% SAT range: NA
Middle 50% ACT range: NA
Early admission program (EA/ ED/ NA): NA
ED or EA Acceptance Rate: NA
Full time Undergraduate enrollment: 6,613
Total enrollment: 19,849
Percent Male: 51%
Percent Female: 49%
Total Percent Minority: 43%
Percent African-American: 8%
Percent Asian/Pacific Islander: 18%
Percent Hispanic: 8%
Percent Native-American: 1%
Percent Other: 8%

Percent in-state / out of state: NA
Percent from Public HS: HA
Retention Rate: 97%
Graduation Rate: 97%
Percent in On-campus housing: 97%
Percent affiliated with Greek system: NA
Percent Varsity or Club Athletes: >75%
Number of official organized extracurricular organizations: 300+
3 Most popular majors: NA
Student/Faculty ratio: 8:01
Tuition and Fees: $33,709.00
Cost for Room and Board: $9,946.00
Percent receiving Financial aid, first-year: 70%

H arvard University. The name may call to mind a few stereotypes: arrogant, intellectual students, discussing philosophy in pompous New England accents. Yet, while it maintains that time-honored reputation for academic excellence, Harvard is also an extraordinary place in which talented, creative minds can flourish and form friendships that last beyond their four years.

Beyond the Core

One of the biggest draws to Harvard is certainly its strong academic community. Harvard brings in some of the biggest professors and talented graduate students in their fields, giving students incredible opportunities to learn. The school is famous for its Core Curriculum, which requires freshmen to take eight specific classes in 11 different disciplines that broadly cover disciplines like the humanities, languages, and sciences. Students report that the Core is actually undergoing a revamping process, which will open up the requirements and allow students to declare their concentration at the beginning of their sophomore year, rather than the end of their freshman year. While the major complaints about the Core have to do with the large lectures that students must attend, overall, as one student

put it, "I really liked the Core . . . at times it can feel restrictive, but it . . . helps you learn to study in different areas and put society in a historical perspective." Another senior agreed that, "At the time, my Core classes were kind of annoying, but looking back, it seemed to be really helpful."

In terms of concentrations, economics and government are universally recognized as the most popular, with psychology coming in a close second. However, as one student said, "in these departments, people often complain that they feel like a number, and in the smaller, quirkier departments, you can be closer to faculty." These "quirkier" departments include Folklore and Mythology and Obstructing Social Space. "Someone just sat in a box in the middle of the science center, to see how it affected people. So there's room for all kinds of projects here." Harvard's unique schedule, with a "shopping week" in the beginning of the semester and a reading week towards the end, gives students room to develop their own projects and to space out their workloads.

Regardless of concentration, professors at Harvard are always accessible. "They are always around to help," one student said. "They will even go out to lunch or dinner with you." While many lower-level lectures, especially in the science departments, are taught and graded by teaching fellows (TFs), students insist that "there are always opportunities" to find smaller classes and seminars and that class size truly depends on your concentration and course of study. When asked about grade inflation at Harvard, most students gave similar answers, saying that, "It's hard to get an A, or even a B, but it's also hard to get a D" and that "most people are just competing for that narrow band of grades in between."

Finals Clubs and the French Revolution

Outside of the classroom, Harvard students are just as talented and excited about their social lives. "I am always pretty impressed by the creativity of the student body," one junior said. "They are generally open and allow you to be yourself." One student even asserted that, "The best thing about Harvard is the people. Learning from each other and having conversations allow you to learn a whole lot of new things, from new people. They're absolutely amazing." Although there is a whole host of ethnic, cultural, and geographic diversity, one student admitted that, "There are many Type A personalities here . . . sometimes, I just let other people do things like calculate tip, because eventually, it'll get done." When Harvard students channel that energy into planning their weekends, the sky's the limit. "When a bunch of smart people get into a room and start planning a party, they come up with some pretty cool stuff." In terms of partying, the options are small, but they are there. "If you want to go drink on Wednesday at 3 a.m., it might be harder. And our weekends definitely don't start on Thursdays. But, on the weekends, if you're looking for it, it's there." Another student countered that, "Getting absurdly drunk . . . is not really a part of daily life here, not even on the weekends. It's just more relaxed."

While Harvard has fraternities, they are not sponsored by the university and make up a fairly small part of the social life. Instead, there are finals clubs, which are exclusive societies that own houses and throw parties on the weekends. The clubs, most of which are all-male, are a kind of throwback to Harvard's good-old-boy reputation and are fairly controversial. As one student put it, "If people really want to party, that is an option, but some people don't like the 'old-boys-club' aspect—and, if you're a woman, it's pretty unfair." Instead,

Harvard students get a bit quirkier with their parties. "One of my favorite memories is of the 'Revolution Party.' Each room represented a different revolution, from the French Revolution to the Sexual Revolution. And the last room was Dance Dance Revolution. It was great."

For those looking to leave their rooms and frat houses to have fun, Harvard Square offers a whole host of great bars and restaurants. Some popular ones include John Harvard's and the Kong, which is "the closest thing to a sketchy bar that we have." In terms of underage drinking, students report that "it is hard to drink as a frosh, but overall, the Harvard police are pretty lenient." The more adventurous can hop on the T and head to Boston itself or to the many other nearby schools. But, as one student explained, "We have a bit of a 'Crimson Bubble' here. People can plan to go to Boston on the weekends, but you have to be a bit more pro-active."

Harvard Housing

Harvard is divided into a community of 12 residential houses, each of which has its own special characteristics and defining features. While all freshmen start from the same place, the dorms on Harvard Yard, they enter the housing lottery in groups (a process called "blocking") and become affiliated with a respective house starting their sophomore year. While the river houses are often thought to be the most desirable (including Eliot, Adams, and Leverett) because they are closer to the main areas of campus, the houses on the quad are not nearly as bad as their reputations would have them seem. "Some people dread being quaded, because they don't want to be cut off," one student said, "but everyone seems to enjoy living there, they have their own party and social atmosphere."

Each house has its own dining hall and facilities, its own housing council, and its own unique campus-wide parties. Some examples include the annual Eliot House party, which is invitation-only, and the Mather Lather, a giant foam party. Proctors in the freshman dorms and tutors in the upperclassmen houses "serve mostly as advisors and don't really care" about being disciplinarians. Since the housing system does make the entire school decentralized, there is no student center, but each house has its own social spaces for parties, dances, and just plain hanging out. The dining halls are all split by house as well, although one student claims that, "Hillel [the Jewish student center] has the best food on campus. Seriously!" Overall, as one student put it, "Everyone tries to pretend that their houses are better . . . there are differences between the houses, but really it's so random, and most of the amenities are the same." And off-campus life is basically non-existent. As one student described, "I've met two people who live off campus . . . it's difficult."

Cheering on the Crimson

When it comes to extracurriculars, Harvard has something in which everyone can be involved. There are classic Harvard mainstays, like the daily newspaper the *Crimson*, the humorous *Lampoon*, and a myriad of a cappella groups. However, there are also community service organizations, performing arts groups, and even a Chinese yo-yo club. In terms of sports, one student summed it up: "We have more varsity sports teams than any other school in the country. Whether we're any good at them is another story." Football is probably the biggest varsity draw (and the Harvard-Yale game the most popular sporting event of the year), but, as one student wryly observed, "You'll catch people reading during the football games, even if they do go." One student asserted that, "A lot of people are athletes, even though we don't have a whole 'sports pride' mentality. People will go to sports events to support their friends."

If you're not up to varsity competition, there are a whole lot of accessible and fun intramural sports to keep students occupied, the most popular of which are volleyball, Ultimate Frisbee, soccer, and basketball. Those who really get into it can join the intra-house competition for the Straus cup. And, if you're looking for something more than your house gym, the campus-wide sports facilities are being renovated, making it even more accessible for non-athletes.

> "You'll catch people reading during the football games, even if they do go."

Harvard offers a combination of academic stimulation, social opportunities, and a traditional New England college setting that genuinely cannot be found anywhere else. Though one senior admitted that, "It is very easy to get wrapped up in this culture of intensity, to burn out and forget about the outside world," he also countered by saying that, "My stereotypes about this place were shattered when I got here. You just have to come here and experience it for yourself." If you're up to the challenge, it just may be the place for you.
—*Alexandra Bicks*

FYI
If you come to Harvard, you'd better bring "your favorite book."
What's a typical weekend schedule? "Thursday nights, there are karaoke nights or trivia nights in the houses; Friday nights, stay in or go out to dinner, maybe a party; Saturday nights are bigger, more parties, concerts, plays; Sundays, brunch, homework . . . of course, no one will judge if you just want to stay in."
If I could change one thing about Harvard, I'd "change the schedule. It's really annoying to have finals after December break."
Three things every student should do before graduating are "the famous three: hook up in the library, pee on the John Harvard statue, and run Primal Scream."

Massachusetts Institute of Technology

Address: MIT, 77 Massachusetts Ave, Cambridge, MA 02139
Phone: 617-253-1000
E-mail Address: NA
Web site URL: http://web.mit.edu/
Year Founded: 1861
Private or Public: Private
Religious affiliation: None
Location: Urban
Regular Application Deadline: 1-Jan
Number of Applicants: 11,374
Percent Accepted: 13%
Percent Accepted who enroll: 66%
Number Entering: 1,002
Number of Transfers Accepted each Year: 17
Mean SAT: NA
Mean ACT: NA

Middle 50% SAT range: V: 660–760, M: 720–800
Middle 50% ACT range: ACT Composite: 30–34
Early admission program (EA/ ED/ NA): EA
ED or EA Acceptance Rate: 12%
Full time Undergraduate enrollment: 4,068
Total enrollment: 10,253
Percent Male: 56%
Percent Female: 44%
Total Percent Minority: 46%
Percent African-American: 6%
Percent Asian/Pacific Islander: 26%
Percent Hispanic: 12%
Percent Native-American: 1%
Percent Other: 54%
Percent in-state / out of state: 9%/91%

Percent from Public HS: NA
Retention Rate: 98%
Graduation Rate: 93%
Percent in On-campus housing: 91%
Percent affiliated with Greek system: 52%
Percent Varsity or Club Athletes: NA
Number of official organized extracurricular organizations: 350+
3 Most popular majors: Mechanical Engineering, Electrical Engineering and Computer Science, Management Science
Student/Faculty ratio: 7.4:1
Tuition and Fees: $33,600.00
Cost for Room and Board: $9,950.00
Percent receiving Financial aid, first-year: NA

Just a few T stops away from Harvard, some of the most talented college students in the country are working hard in labs, graphing calculators in hand. The Massachusetts Institute of Technology certainly has a reputation for churning out brilliant engineers and physicists, and for making them slave away in the process. Yet, while students admit that some stereotypes about people being "nerdy" are true, it is the friendliness of the MIT community that makes the school one of the most unique and exciting places to spend four years or more. As one junior puts it, "People are not only motivated and ambitious, but fun and creative—which creates an air of excitement I have not felt in any other place."

Nobel Prize Winners in Training

The first semester of freshman year, during which all classes are taken pass/fail, is a bit more relaxed, but things start to get intense during second semester. The school has a few core requirements, which most students try to get out the way by the end of their freshman year. These GIRs, or General Institute Requirements, include courses in physics, chemistry, and calculus, with a lab requirement mixed in too. But don't think that the science overload prevents MIT kids from getting enough exposure to the humanities—eight classes in the humanities, social sciences and arts are also part of the core. Two of these have to be "communication intensive," or involve significant amounts of writing. There is even a requirement for four quarters of physical education, but it's easy enough to fulfill, as one student explains, "Varsity sports actually count for two quarters. It's not too hard."

The humanities classes themselves elicit mixed reviews, since they do prevent some students from devoting that time to fulfilling the requirements of their major. Most people who concentrate in the humanities end up minoring or double-majoring rather than making it the focus of their academic program at MIT. On the outset, the humanities seem easier than the science requirements, as one male student explains, "The 'joke' is that if you want to boost your GPA, take a humanities class at Harvard, because it's easier there!" However, most people say that "the quality of teaching in humanities classes is excellent," since most classes are taught directly by professors, many of whom are foremost in their field and have the Pulitzer or Nebula to show for it. Despite the stereotypes, the humanities and communication requirements are essential components of the MIT education, since they, as one student puts it, "make sure students are ready for the adjustments of the real world."

> **"People are not only motivated and ambitious, but fun and creative—which creates an air of excitement I have not felt in any other place."**

After getting through the large introductory-level classes, which can have up to 400 students, most classes shrink in size, ending up with anywhere from 10 to 80 students. For freshmen who are interested in more specialized classes, there are five specific programs of study open only to freshmen, including the most well-known, the Experimental Study Group (ESG). Open to only 50 freshmen, ESG teaches students in small seminar or tutorial style groups and allows for direct interaction with professors and grad students.

The most popular majors are electrical and mechanical engineering. Management courses are considered one of the easiest and quickest paths to graduation. Aerospace/aeronautical engineering is almost unanimously touted as the hardest major, but, despite the work, "aero" remains one of the most popular majors on campus. Even management, sometimes called the "easy" major, still requires its students to demonstrate proficiency in programming and multivariable calculus. And, unlike at many other top-notch schools, grade inflation has not made it to the ranks of MIT. As one junior stated, "As far as grading goes, don't expect A's. A's are reserved for geniuses."

One of the biggest draws of MIT academics is its distinguished faculty. Out of the school's current 992 professors, seven are Nobel Prize winners, not to mention the various other distinguished names who might end up being your physics tutor or English professor. Yet, far from being intimidating or aloof, professors are generally "accessible and personable," and make themselves available for students who need extra help.

One student even relates, "One night last year I was in the lab at 1:30 a.m. when I e-mailed my professor with a question on the homework. Not five minutes later, he came down from his office and was sitting by my side helping me work it out."

One of the most unique ways in which students and professors at MIT come together is the Undergraduate Research Opportunities Program (UROP). Students can work on UROP projects as volunteers or for either course credit or pay, and they learn to apply their classroom knowledge to the real world of changing technological developments. As one excited student put it, UROP offers "a priceless opportunity to form relationships with faculty while learning in an innovative environment."

Despite all the good MIT has to offer, if you're in need of a change of scenery, MIT students can cross-register to take classes at Harvard or Wellesley, giving them a great opportunity to meet and interact with other students in the Boston area as they learn.

Greek Life, Glassblowing and the Great Dome

Of course, there is much more to life at MIT than its stellar academics. Despite the stereotypes, the intramural sports scene is incredibly popular and varied, and about 20 percent of students participate in some kind of varsity sport. Students insist that "lots of people are athletic" at MIT, with IM Frisbee and hockey being some of the favorite choices of sports. While its varsity teams are Division III and compete mostly against other New England Colleges, MIT has the largest number of NCAA-sponsored programs in the country. The campus facilities, like the new Zesiger Sports and Fitness Center, are also top-notch and open to everyone, since, as one student says, "MIT really puts an emphasis on health, both physical and mental." Unfortunately, the fan base for varsity sports is a little lacking—one junior explains, "the joke is that the visiting football team usually has more fans here than we do."

As for other extracurricular activities, MIT has over 350 clubs and organizations. From more traditional extracurriculars like a cappella groups to the quirkier Glassblowing and Skydiving Clubs, there is something at MIT for everyone to be involved in; one female student even commented that "what I love about MIT is how friendly everyone is and how animated they are about their activities!" One of the most unique ways that MIT students enjoy demonstrating their creativity and sense of fun is the campus tradition of "hacking," or pulling "harmless yet ingenious pranks" that are continually topped by different student groups every year. Most hacks involve the "Great Dome," the large classical dome atop Building 10 that is a central campus landmark and, therefore, a perfect target for determined hackers. Famous hacks of the past have included constructing an exact replica of an MIT police cruiser (complete with dummy policeman inside) on top of the Dome, as well as building a model of the Wright Brothers' plane in 2003 to commemorate the anniversary of their flight.

The social scene at MIT is one of the most notorious in the country, as one student proudly states, "MIT frats and dorms throw more parties than any school in Boston." While Greek life does play a huge part in MIT social life, with six sororities and 26 fraternities hosting parties at least once a week, students are quick to say that social life doesn't revolve around the frat scene. MIT's drinking policy is quite lax, which gives students lots of opportunities to party without fear of disciplinary action—one student clarifies, "as long as you don't disrupt others, your party will be fine." MIT students also take advantage of the club and bar scene both on campus and off—MIT's own Thirsty Ear pub and the Crossroads Irish Pub in Boston are both a "10 minute walk from campus," and there are lots of clubs where MIT students can dance and mingle with students from all of the other nearby schools.

The Ultimate College Town

If you prefer your weekends dry, never fear—non-drinkers can find all kinds of social alternatives to the party scene in Boston or Cambridge. Host to a huge number of colleges, Boston has a reputation for being "full of life—the ultimate college town." The Boston public transportation system, otherwise known as the T, and the "easy biking distance" between most locations in Boston allow MIT students to take advantage of its many museums, coffee shops and movie theaters. The Museum of Fine Arts is always a popular spot to visit, and the more upscale restaurants and shops along Newbury Street give students a chance to take full advantage of their famous surroundings. Some favorite off-campus restaurants include John

Harvard's in Cambridge ("great burgers and beer") and Bertucci's, a popular Italian chain. Even without leaving campus, students take advantage of the variety of restaurants around them by ordering in, as one student jokingly explained, "MIT students love to have food delivered to them."

Safety is also an important concern for MIT students, as one junior points out, "We do live in a big city which, along with the benefits, does come with some inherent dangers." The college's SafeRide system, which runs campus buses to off-campus living areas and frat houses, provides an alternative to walking around campus alone at night, and while Central Square between Harvard and MIT is "a little bit less safe," most of the areas surrounding MIT, like Boston's Back Bay, are generally fairly friendly and town-gown relations are "great—there's no conflict with Cambridge."

Pi and Pie

MIT housing consists of a variety of dorms and houses, each with its own unique character that "provides a great way to meet a diversity of people and get involved in different activities." Like all buildings on the MIT campus, dorms are assigned numbers—even though most people refer to them by name. While all freshmen must live in dorms, they are first placed in temporary orientation housing, during which they get a chance to attend various dorm parties and rush events to figure out where they want to live. The result of this process is that most people end up finding a living situation that works for them, whether through a computerized lottery that matches you with your first choice of dorms or joining a sorority or cultural house. Baker and Simmons are also architectural standouts on MIT's campus, which is characterized mostly by "mostly drab '60s and '70s concrete." Baker is a wave-shaped dorm designed to maximize river views, and Simmons is a new example of modernist architecture about which one student admits, "I think it looks like Swiss cheese, but it's a neat landmark to have on campus." Finally, every dorm floor has an RA, who are "more like surrogate parents than rule enforcers."

The food on campus is described as "tasty but expensive," and the student meal plan serves as an added benefit to choosing to live on campus, since food is often "a pain to get" without the MIT ID card, which can also work at certain local businesses.

While classes don't officially start back at

MIT until February, most MIT students return in January to participate in the Independent Activities Period, or IAP. During these four weeks, faculty and fellow students offer a mind-boggling amount of fun classes and activities for the whole community to participate in, from juggling to figure skating. IAP is an optional program, yet most students come back on campus to relax and enjoy the chance to show off their passions and talents in a low-stress, laid-back environment that one student calls "the most fun time I've had in college."

It is this combination of genuine love of learning and creative intensity that makes MIT one of the standout schools in the country. Coming to MIT means, as one junior said, "making a commitment to yourself . . . to take advantage of the opportunities available here." If you're up to the challenge, it may just be the perfect place for you. —*Alexandra Bicks*

FYI

If you come to MIT, you'd better bring "a cell phone and a flask."

The typical weekend schedule at MIT "combines work, partying and catch-up sleep . . . we're truly a 'work hard/party hard' school."

If I could change one thing about MIT, I would "move it someplace warm!"

The three things every MIT student should do before graduating are "take advantage of IAP, party at other schools, and take an upper-level class within the Humanities Department."

Mount Holyoke College

Address: Mount Holyoke, 50 College Street, South Hadley, MA 01075
Phone: 413-538-2023
E-mail Address: admission@mtholyoke.edu
Web site URL: http://www.mtholyoke.edu
Year Founded: 1837
Private or Public: Private
Religious affiliation: none
Location: Suburban
Regular Application Deadline: 16-Jan
Number of Applicants: 2,912
Percent Accepted: 53%
Percent Accepted who enroll: NA
Number Entering: 572
Number of Transfers Accepted each Year: NA
Mean SAT: 1,270
Mean ACT: 28

Middle 50% SAT range: 1,210–1,390
Middle 50% ACT range: 27–30
Early admission program (EA/ ED/ NA): ED
ED or EA Acceptance Rate: NA
Full time Undergraduate enrollment: 2,134
Total enrollment: 2,134
Percent Male: 0%
Percent Female: 100%
Total Percent Minority: 48%
Percent African-American: 4%
Percent Asian/Pacific Islander: 11%
Percent Hispanic: 6%
Percent Native-American: 1%
Percent Other: NA

Percent in-state / out of state: 25%/75%
Percent from Public HS: 62%
Retention Rate: 92%
Graduation Rate: 82%
Percent in On-campus housing: 93%
Percent affiliated with Greek system: NA
Percent Varsity or Club Athletes: NA
Number of official organized extracurricular organizations: 150
3 Most popular majors: English, International relations, Psychology
Student/Faculty ratio: 10:01
Tuition and Fees: $34,090
Cost for Room and Board: $10,040
Percent receiving Financial aid, first-year: 52%

Located in the quiet town of South Hadley, Massachusetts, Mount Holyoke is a small women's college with a big impact. The idyllic campus helps to foster strong bonds among the women of Mount Holyoke. As a member of the Five College Consortium, Mount Holyoke's resources are shared with those of Smith College, University of Massachusetts at Amherst, Amherst College and Hampshire College. Students are able to reap the benefits of individualized attention and support, while drawing from a wide range of academic and social opportunities.

Small, But Intense

The academic expectations at Mount Holyoke are almost universally described as "intense." Students face a variety of distribution requirements, including three courses in the humanities, two courses in math and sciences, and two courses in social sciences. They are also required to fulfill a multicultural credit, foreign language requirement and physical education credits. While these courses can take up a lot of time, most students seem to find them "reasonable" and flexible enough to be a positive aspect of their academic experience. Students not only need a major, but also either a minor or one of a variety of Five College certificate programs. Some of the more popular majors at Mount Holyoke include biology, English and psychology. Those not afraid of logging extra time in the library can find themselves majoring in international relations, math, or one of the sciences. Students looking for an easier four years, on the other hand, tend to gravitate toward psychology or art history. While some introductory level courses can be larger in size, most classes have enrollments of less than 25, allowing for closer student-professor interaction. Professors are known for giving a sizable workload in general, with intensive assignments and reading due weekly, often to prepare for difficult exams. According to one student, "I do feel a little jealous of my friends at other schools because I feel they have more time for fun than I do." But, students agree that the quality of the professors often compensates for the sky-high expectations. Among the more well known professors are Chris Pyle, who specializes in politics, Joe Ellis of the History Department, and Bill Quillian, a well-regarded James Joyce scholar. There are also a variety of unique classes available such as Zen and the Art of Meditation, a cryptology seminar, and horseback riding for physical education credit.

> **"This is definitely not a party school."**

Mount Holyoke boasts some unique academic features. J-term is a period during the normal winter break when students can stay on campus to take extra, often nontraditional courses or try out a short internship. Students are also encouraged to take advantage of the Five College Consortium. There is a free busing system among the different campuses that allows students to enroll in courses offered by other schools. This widens the course offerings available and lets students get off campus should they feel the need.

It's On (Campus) All the Way

Students rave about the beauty of Mount Holyoke's campus through all four seasons. The school's small size also contributes to its general appeal as a peaceful and friendly haven. Students agreed that South Hadley, as a town, does not contribute much to life on campus or really cater to the college. Luckily, the nearby presence of Amherst and Northampton alleviate that problem.

Over ninety percent of students live on campus, thanks to both the lack of appropriate housing in the surrounding residential areas, and the close-knit nature of the student body. Dorms vary in size and layout. The older buildings tend to have larger rooms, but dorms overall garner positive reviews. Most students live in singles by the time they are upperclassmen. There are Student Advisers on every floor and Hall Presidents for each dorm. Both groups generally make an effort to get to know the students they live with and they "usually get more worked up about noise than alcohol." There are mandatory quiet hours each night set by the halls, and these are most strictly enforced during finals. Open alcohol isn't allowed in hallways, but students generally find very few problems with this regulation.

The food on campus is rated highly by students and was even praised by one as being "great!" There are dining halls attached to each dorm, as well as one in the campus center. The school goes to great lengths to offer a variety of options for those with restricted or special diets, including vegetarian, vegan, kosher and halal.

Sisterhood of the Traveling Party

The social life at Mount Holyoke is very much characterized by the fact that it is a women's college. Life on campus is more toned down than at your average coed institution and as one student put it, "This is definitely not a party school." Drinking is mostly confined to weekends or special occasions. A capella groups are a popular social outlet and sports teams are most likely to hold parties in dorms. Once a year, the school hosts Las Vegas Night, an immensely popular party that includes dancing and gambling and attracts students from other colleges. Students spend time hanging out with friends and going to movies, but they tend to gravitate off campus if they are looking for a party or members of the opposite sex. Many Mount Holyokers will leave during the weekend to visit boyfriends elsewhere. UMass and Amherst are popular destinations for fraternity parties, especially TAP, which are huge parties held at Amherst on Thursday and Saturday nights. The busing system makes the nearby colleges and bars very easily accessible.

Students participate avidly in a variety of extracurricular activities. Sports play an increasingly large role on campus, with girls participating on all levels from varsity to club. Rugby is a particularly popular and eagerly cheered on sport. Other strong programs include crew, field hockey, and lacrosse. Mount Holyoke's main rival is Smith and varsity games between the two schools are well attended. Extensive athletic facilities are also available to students, with the equestrian center often hailed as one of the shining stars. As for non-athletic activities, student government plays a large and vocal role on campus and Holyokers agreed that "the group makes sure to keep the student population well informed of its happenings." Those musically inclined can choose among a capella groups, glee club and various instrumental ensembles. No matter what one's passions are, most students find that they can discover or create a niche for whatever their particular interests may be.

Living Among Women

As a women's college, students reached a general consent that Mount Holyoke is, in many ways, not the typical college experience. According to one student, "Women's colleges certainly are not fit for everyone, but it seems that students at Mount Holyoke really considered their decision before enrolling and are ultimately very satisfied."

Although students have to work a little harder if they desire contact with the opposite sex or wish to experience the typical college party, the all-female environment more than makes up for such voids with its own unique benefits. The campus is characterized as being very friendly and students are easy to get to know, as many students interviewed found that being among all women makes for a more comfortable, accepting atmosphere on the whole, both in and out of class. The campus is also incredibly diverse on all ethnic and socioeconomic levels, and although cliques do emerge, there is always a good level of interaction among the collective student body. Mount Holyokers are also "fairly open" to all sexual orientations and relationships.

Ultimately, the majority of students seem to adapt well to the all-female environment, but like at any school, at times "there are days when people are sick of Mount Holyoke" and committing to four years of being surrounded entirely by women involves particular and personal considerations for each individual. As one student expressed, "If Mount Holyoke works for you, it's a great place to be."—*Janet Yang*

FYI

If you come to Mount Holyoke you better bring "a heavy coat for those harsh New England winters."
What's the typical weekend schedule? "Sleep late, do work, go out by either taking a bus to
  Amherst or staying on campus and hanging out, come back late."
If I could change one thing about Mount Holyoke, "it would be to have some students lighten up and
  go out and have more fun."
Three things every student should do before graduating are "take a class off campus, climb Mount
  Holyoke on Mountain Day to get free ice cream, and eat a Chef Jeff cookie."

Northeastern University

Address: Northeastern, 360 Huntington Avenue, Boston, MA 02115
Phone: 617-373-2200
E-mail Address: admissions@neu.edu
Web site URL: http://www.northeastern.edu/
Year Founded: 1898
Private or Public: private
Religious affiliation: none
Location: urban
Regular Application Deadline: 16-Jan
Number of Applicants: 24,436
Percent Accepted: 45%
Percent Accepted who enroll: 24%
Number Entering: 2,778
Number of Transfers Accepted each Year: NA
Mean SAT: 1,230
Mean ACT: 26

Middle 50% SAT range: 1,150–1,330
Middle 50% ACT range: 24–28
Early admission program (EA/ ED/ NA): EA
ED or EA Acceptance Rate: NA
Full time Undergraduate enrollment: 15,195
Total enrollment: 15,195
Percent Male: 50%
Percent Female: 50%
Total Percent Minority: 37%
Percent African-American: 6%
Percent Asian/Pacific Islander: 7%
Percent Hispanic: 5%
Percent Native-American: 0%
Percent Other: NA
Percent in-state / out of state: 35%/65%

Percent from Public HS: NA
Retention Rate: 90%
Graduation Rate: NA
Percent in On-campus housing: 49%
Percent affiliated with Greek system: 4%/4%
Percent Varsity or Club Athletes: NA
Number of official organized extracurricular organizations: 225
3 Most popular majors: Business/commerce, engineering, health services
Student/Faculty ratio: 16:01
Tuition and Fees: $29,910.00
Cost for Room and Board: $10,970.00
Percent receiving Financial aid, first-year: 62%

Interested in gaining the advantage of real-life work experience during your college years? If so, Northeastern and its unique co-op program might be for you. Northeaster University (NU) places a distinct emphasis on pre-professional training as well as education and offers its students a co-op internship program that places them with various companies during the academic year.

One Step Ahead: the Co-op Program

At Northeastern, students alternate between classroom study and periods of paid, professional experience. Each period is six months, which means, as one student says, "You don't really have summers that much." It also means that the majority of students go to school for five years, rather than the typical four at other schools.

At the same time, though, students who participate in the co-op program gain a distinct advantage in the "real world." "You come out of college with a stacked resume; you know how to interview, and you know how to be professional. You just have an edge on everybody." The real-life experience also allows a student to "get a good sense of whether you're in the right field."

This means, of course, that even though you don't officially select a major until sophomore year, many students applying to NU have a clear idea of what career they wish to pursue. For those who do know where they would like to end up after college, this program not only gives them a lot of resume-building experience, but it also connects them with potential employers and business opportunities. Upon graduating, many students are offered jobs at the companies they worked at in the co-op program. As one student working for an inventing company in New Hampshire declared, "I'm learning more by working than [I am] in classes."

Approximately 90% of NU's student body participates in the co-op program. In fact, it seems that "most kids that come to NU come for the co-op program." Students who choose to start the co-op freshman year take an orientation class and begin work sophomore year. Co-op classes are required and can focus on job-relevant skills such as interviewing or writing resumes. Students are also assigned co-op faculty coordinators who help them find opportunities that match their goals and interests. While these resources are available, however, it is up to the student to schedule and prepare for interviews as well as perform well on the job. Even then, NU cannot guarantee that each student will have a job during the co-op term. Also, if students accept positions outside the Boston area, they are responsible for finding their own housing and transportation in the area they choose. But if a student plans to accept a local position, he or she may continue living in the NU residence hall.

> "You come out of college with a stacked resume; you know how to interview, and you know how to be professional. You just have an edge on everybody."

The hard work seems to be well worth it: students graduate from college and can move straight into the work force. Another appealing incentive is the pay: students who opt to enroll in the co-op program can earn a lot of money during their 6-month work periods.

The Penthouse Suite

Most students feel that the on-campus freshman housing at Northeastern is "basically like any other school"—neither exceptional nor terrible. Quality does vary, since some buildings have been renovated in recent years while others have not, but overall the freshman housing is generally described as "decent." Upperclassmen housing, on the other hand, is "*so* nice." "From sophomore year on, the housing is either relatively new or has been renovated within the last decade." Many residential halls, such as the West Village halls or Davenport Commons, have units that can include 2 to 3 bedrooms, 2 bathrooms, a "huge" living room, and a kitchen. Other amenities include cable TV, air-conditioning, and high-speed Internet. West Village E is particularly famous—made completely of glass, it is what's known as the penthouse suite, with two glass walls that overlook a stunning view of downtown Boston. Such luxury, though, comes with a price. "It's really expensive," one student complains, so much so that "it's actually much cheaper to live off campus"—a bold statement when weighed against the difficulty of finding affordable housing in Boston.

For those who do choose to live on campus, buildings are divided into single-sex wings, and NU offers special-interest housing,

such as a "wellness" dorm (the alcohol, drug, and smoke-free Coe Hall), an honors dorm, and an international dorm. Each residential section is assigned an Resident Assistant (RA). Some students claim that their RAs have been lax about alcohol policies, provided that students respect the rules and property. One admitted, though, that this was the exception more than the rule. "I had an RA who was really relaxed about alcohol, but a lot of the RAs in other dorms were very strict and kids were always getting into trouble."

Students seem to be impressed with the campus facilities because "everything on campus is really well-maintained." This may be because the administration is "very responsive to student suggestions, and if there is a complaint, "everything gets fixed pretty quickly." Some of the facilities available to students are the Marino Recreation Center, where students, athlete and non-athlete alike, can work out, and the Matthews Arena, the oldest indoor arena in the world. This is where the hockey teams play, and games attract an enthusiastic following, outside the University as well as within. Every year, for example, the city holds the Bean Pot, a tournament in which Northeastern, Boston University, Boston College, and Harvard compete for bragging rights as the best hockey team in the city. It's held at the TD North Bank Garden arena and attracts quite a crowd. The University also maintains common areas stocked with pool tables and lounge chairs. Some of the most popular hang-out areas are the Curry Student Center and the Cyber Café in Snell Library.

Students have several options when it comes to dining. Along with its three dining halls, there are several restaurants on campus, including Taco Bell, Starbucks, Pizza Hut, Wendy's, and Qdoba. The University offers several meal-plan options, one of which includes putting money on a Husky Card, which can also be used at local eateries off campus. This conveniently allows students to take advantage of NU's advantageous location in the hustle and bustle of Boston. There are several good eateries near campus, and one particular favorite is Chicken Lou's, a "little shack" at which you'll have "probably the best food you will ever eat— you would stand in line in the Massachusetts cold for that food."

So Much to Do, So Much to See

As for extracurricular activities, students at NU have a variety of choices. "The administration is very lenient with on-campus organizations," and the student government, in charge of approving clubs, distributes a hefty allocation of money to these student groups. One of the most popular clubs—and also the largest with over 600 members—is NUCALLs. Members of this organization are students fluent in other languages, and they offer peers interested in learning that language tutoring sessions for free. Intramural sports are also a popular pastime, one of the most popular sports being broom-ball. "Broom-ball is huge around campus," and students sign up for teams in the spring and fall to play a carefully organized series of games that culminate in that semester's play-offs. Other organizations include typical college organizations, such as a Student Government Association and daily newspapers, as well as unique ones, such as *The NU Times New Roman*, a humor newspaper. Greek life is present on campus, but not a driving force. Only about 8% of the total student body joins fraternities or sororities, and although they throw occasional parties, no one seems to be in any hurry to rush them.

Party City: Boston, the College Town

The social scene at Northeastern comes alive each weekend. Drinking is prevalent, but there is a significant percent of the student population that opts not to drink as well. For those who do, however, alcohol is relatively easy to come by, as are parties. Some of the most popular events on campus are SpringFest, Midnight Madness, and International Carnevale. Partying on-campus has its downside, though, because the university has strict rules about drinking. "The school is looking to get you into trouble," according to one student.

However, being in a city like Boston, NU's social scene is not limited to on-campus events. It lies in the midst of several other universities—"it's a 5-minute walk to Boston University, a 15-minute train ride to Boston College, and a 20-minute train ride to MIT or Harvard"—which means students at NU have several opportunities to meet students from other schools. It also gives students a wide variety of parties to choose from on weekends. "There are just so many options; I know there are always hundreds of things going on in the city." Another student said, "I can party anywhere—at a house, apartment, fraternity, or bars, clubs, concerts, and other schools."

Clubbing used to be a popular weekend activity for many NU students, but in light of new legislation, clubs are no longer 18 and up. What's more, fakes are not a good idea when partying in the city because "all the cops are out to get you." While many students enjoy spending time at bars or clubs on the weekend, these establishments tend to be extremely strict when it comes to IDs. "Every liquor store scans IDs, and several bars black light them." If a student is 21 or older, popular clubs include Avalon, Roxy, and Matrix; the most popular bar is Punter's.

The Sum Total

Overall, Northeastern students take advantage of the opportunities the school provides. The urban campus provides an endless stream of events and activities, and students actively participate in campus life, joining groups and enjoying their college years to the fullest. While enjoying the NU social scene, students simultaneously gain work experience in the co-op program, which distinguishes Northeastern from other universities. The expertise gained in real job experience gives graduating students a considerable edge post-college and is perfect for motivated, career-oriented students. All of this, combined with a respectable faculty, diverse student body, and fast-paced Boston environment, offers Northeastern students a unique and fruitful experience.—*Caroline Garner*

FYI
If you come to Northeastern, you'd better bring "skis or snowboards, to take advantage of all the ski trips the school organizes."
What's the typical weekend schedule? "Drink when and where you can, or go clubbing. Fit in a little work."
If I could change one thing about Northeastern, it would be "the proportion of students from certain regions; most are from the New England area."
Three things every student at Northeastern should do before graduating are "do the co-op program, go to a Red Sox or Patriot game, and explore what the city has to offer."

Simmons College

Address: Simmons, 300 The Fenway, Boston, MA 02115

Phone: 800-345-8468

E-mail Address: ugadm@simmons.edu

Web site URL: www.simmons.edu

Year Founded: 1899

Private or Public: private

Religious affiliation: none

Location: urban

Regular Application Deadline: 1-Feb

Number of Applicants: 2,537

Percent Accepted: 59%

Percent Accepted who enroll: 29%

Number Entering: 436

Number of Transfers Accepted each Year: 201

Mean SAT: 1,106

Mean ACT: 24

Middle 50% SAT range: 1,010–1,200 (510–610 V/ CR, 500–590 Math)

Middle 50% ACT range: 22–27

Early admission program (EA/ ED/ NA): EA

ED or EA Acceptance Rate: 59%

Full time Undergraduate enrollment: 2,001

Total enrollment: 4,466 (includes graduate students)

Percent Male: 0%

Percent Female: 100%

Total Percent Minority: 20%

Percent African-American: 7%

Percent Asian/Pacific Islander: 7%

Percent Hispanic: 3%

Percent Native-American: 0%

Percent Other: 2%

Percent in-state / out of state: 30%/70%

Percent from Public HS: NA

Retention Rate: 83%

Graduation Rate: 75%

Percent in On-campus housing: NA

Percent affiliated with Greek system: N/A

Percent Varsity or Club Athletes: NA

Number of official organized extracurricular organizations: 50+

3 Most popular majors: NA

Student/Faculty ratio: 12:01

Tuition and Fees: $26,708.00

In State Tuition and Fees (if different): $26,708.00

Cost for Room and Board: $10,710.00

Percent receiving Financial aid, first-year: over 90%

Nestled in the bustling city of Boston rests the tranquil oasis of Simmons College. Roughly 1,800 young women attend Simmons for its liberal arts with a special focus on science. Students rave about the close-knit student body and excellent, approachable professors, which combine to form a welcoming and laid-back atmosphere.

Science Anyone?

Simmons College offers a liberal arts education with special career preparation opportunities. The nursing program feeds student internships in the city, while the physical therapy major has a six-year doctorate program. Science at Simmons is especially strong. Nursing, biology, and chemistry are considered the most difficult majors, while communications and psychology are "not as demanding, but still difficult," according to one student. Class size is small, making it easy to enroll in most classes and enabling students to take a more active role in the classroom. Students rave about their professors. One student explained, "[The professors] give you their e-mail, cell phone number, home number, office number and office hours. They want you to come and talk to them. They are interested in helping their students."

Students must fulfill academic distributional requirements in six "modes of inquiry": Creative and Performing Arts; Language, Literature, and Culture; Quantitative Analysis and Reasoning; Scientific Inquiry; Social and Historical Perspectives; Psychological and Ethical Development. In the process, students become more well-rounded and prepared for life after college. The requirements are surprisingly unrestrictive, though, and one student commented, "I found that I was able to experiment more during my freshman year than my friends at other schools."

An Escape from Beantown

The Simmons campus receives high marks from its students. Its peaceful green quadrangle in the middle of a busy Boston neighborhood serves as a quiet haven. One student exclaimed, "Our campus is beautiful. Most people come onto campus and forget they are in a city. When you walk through the gates, it feels very much unlike a city and a lot more like home." The campus is divided into an academic portion and a residential portion separated by one city block. The residential campus consists of a picturesque quadrangle bounded by the college's residence halls and Bartol Dining Hall. Also located on the residential campus is the Holmes Sports Center, boasting an eight-lane swimming pool, suspended track, weight room, sauna, basketball court, dance studio and squash courts. Next door is the Simmons Health Center, which offers its comprehensive services to students.

> "[The professors] give you their e-mail, cell phone number, home number, office number and office hours. They want you to come and talk to them. They are interested in helping their students."

Approximately five minutes' walk from the residential campus is the main campus. Here the college's main classrooms are located in the Main College Building (affectionately referred to as the "MCB") and the Park Science Building, where all science courses are taught. The main campus also hosts the Beatley Library and the newly constructed and unusually named One Palace Road Building. One Palace Road provides a number of student resources such as career services and counseling, as well as two graduate school departments.

Standard of Living at Simmons

The quality of dorm rooms differs at Simmons depending on renovations and specific buildings. Most freshmen live in doubles in Mesick, Morse or Simmons Hall, but there are a few triples. There is an RA on every floor, and one student said, "They're just there to help out, and are not too strict." Students are very pleased with their living situation. Recently renovated Evans Hall and Arnold Hall are "really nice and the only ones with elevators on campus," one student reported. Praise is not as free-flowing, though, when students are asked about the food at Simmons. Bartol Dining Hall is Simmons' main dining hall and students label the food as "fair." Luckily for hungry Simmons students, the best of Boston's restaurants, with its first-class seafood and ethnic

fare, lie just outside the college's gates. Other dining options available to students on campus include the Quadside Café, serving as a snack bar and grocery, The Fens, with a deli and grill, and Java City (Simmons' Coffee Kiosk), which doles out coffee and snacks.

Livin' It Up in Beantown

One student put it best by saying, "Basically, Boston becomes your campus." For this group of young women, the possibilities of the city are boundless. Students are able to take advantage of the city's many fabulous restaurants, go shopping on Newbury Street, attend a Boston Red Sox game, and go to a concert at the Orpheum Theater. Boston offers anything and everything under the sun . . . and under the moon as well, as Simmons girls take advantage of the city's exciting nightlife.

Simmons is a dry campus, and because of alcohol and noise restrictions students often go out to Boston clubs or to frat parties at BU and MIT for a more festive atmosphere. One student comments that because of this situation, "Simmons' girls have a lot of random hookups because they really don't know when the next chance will be." These meetings often develop into something more substantial, however, and students note that many of their peers are involved in serious relationships—both heterosexual and homosexual.

From Tea to Tennis

Students describe the student body as "intelligent" and "friendly." The small class size promotes unity and school spirit. According to one student, a tradition that has been going on for a few years now is the Friday Hall Teas, where all the girls from each hall come together to "have tea or snack on goodies and just hang out and have fun."

Many Simmons students take part in sports and other extracurricular activities. The campus is described by one "as very active and involved." Simmons is home to eight Division III varsity sports, and one student described Simmons sports as "not awful"— basketball and soccer seemed to be the most popular sports among students. Other student organizations such as Simmons College Outreach, a student-run community service organization, and the Student Government Organization are just two of the many student activities and clubs in which students take part.

When John Simmons founded this college in 1899, his mission was to allow women to earn the "livelihood" they deserved and to create a new generation of well-educated women. Today his mission continues to be realized, as Simmons produces well-prepared, independent women ready to enter the world. —*Kieran Locke*

FYI

If you come to Simmons College, you'd better bring a "Boston Red Sox hat."

What's the typical weekend schedule? "Hanging out, shopping, and eating in Harvard Square or on Newbury Street and going to an occasional party at a fraternity from a neighboring college."

If I could change one thing about Simmons, I would change "the dining-hall food."

Three things every student at Simmons should do before graduating are "visit the Isabella Stuart Gardner Museum, eat Ankara Frozen Yogurt, and go on the Swan Boats in Boston Commons."

Smith College

Address: Smith, 7 College Lane, Northampton, MA 01063
Phone: 413-585-2500
E-mail Address: admission@smith.edu
Web site URL: http://www.smith.edu
Year Founded: 1871
Private or Public: private
Religious affiliation: No Affiliation
Location: rural
Regular Application Deadline: 15-Jan
Number of Applicants: NA
Percent Accepted: 53%
Percent Accepted who enroll: NA
Number Entering: 650
Number of Transfers Accepted each Year: 100
Mean SAT: 1,974
Mean ACT: 27

Middle 50% SAT range: 1,720–2,060
Middle 50% ACT range: 25–29
Early admission program (EA/ ED/ NA): ED
ED or EA Acceptance Rate: NA
Full time Undergraduate enrollment: 2,600
Total enrollment: 2,600
Percent Male: 0%
Percent Female: 100%
Total Percent Minority: 50%
Percent African-American: 7%
Percent Asian/Pacific Islander: 12%
Percent Hispanic: 7%
Percent Native-American: 1%
Percent Other: NA

Percent in-state / out of state: 22%/78%
Percent from Public HS: 67%
Retention Rate: 91%
Graduation Rate: 85%
Percent in On-campus housing: 88%
Percent affiliated with Greek system: NA
Percent Varsity or Club Athletes: NA
Number of official organized extracurricular organizations: 133
3 Most popular majors: Political Science, Psychology, Visual and Performing Arts
Student/Faculty ratio: 9:01
Tuition and Fees: $32,320
Cost for Room and Board: $10,880
Percent receiving Financial aid, first-year: 65%

Walking around the Smith campus one night, you see students covered in duct tape and tissue paper, and some are covered in very little at all. When you ask one of the students, apparently the strange attire is a tradition for one of their famous parties known as the "Convocation Party." Convocation is just one of the interesting and bizarre traditions that make Smith such a unique liberal arts college. Students can explore more than just the typical types of courses offered by liberal arts colleges within an all-female population that most students find empowering.

The Smith Education

While students certainly have interest in entertaining traditions like Convocation and House Teas, academics are clearly the first priority for Smith women. The general expectation is that a large portion of the week is allocated to studying, as opposed to the obligatory "Sunday Afternoon Crunch" found at other schools. For most students, the work they encountered at Smith was harder than they expected, and there was more of it. And while one student felt that the academic environment was somewhat overwhelming, both because of the amount of work and the intensity of other students, another thought that since "you can choose your classes, you look forward to doing work and it's not a chore to study." Despite the intensity of the workload, most of the students felt it was an academically safe environment.

Smith students certainly do have a lot of choice when it comes to academics. There are no general education classes, and other than a writing requirement which must be completed in freshman year, students are free to take classes in whatever field interests them. Students must have a broad curriculum, because only half of the classes taken can be in a student's major. There are no other requirements than these unless a student wishes to graduate with Latin Honors. In this case, the student must complete courses in each of the seven major fields of knowledge: Literature, Historical Studies, Social Science, Natural Science, Mathematics and Analytic Philosophy, the Arts, and Foreign Language. Most of the classes are pretty small, with the smallest under 20 and the larger classes generally under 30. There are a few larger-sized intro classes, but these are still generally kept under 50 students.

All classes at Smith are taught by professors (TA's only help grade), leading to closer relationships between students and professors than those normally found at other schools. Some of the more popular professors are Floyd Chung in the English department, Sam Intrator, and Susan Etheredge. Don't expect these classes, while interesting, to be undemanding, or even easy to get into. According to students, some of the more popular classes (such as "The Amerian Teacher" with Intrator), are difficult to get into, and do have a high level of competition within the class. Despite the difficulty of some of the classes, students tended to find the academic experience at Smith very rewarding. "There are a lot of different dimensions to learning at Smith," said one student. "You encounter many intellectuals with a lot of different perspectives."

For those not quite ready to leap into an entire course schedule full of intense classes, there are certainly easier ways to rack up credits. Students can take tai-chi, yoga, pilates, and scuba diving for credit. In addition, performance classes are a good way to get all your credits needed for a year. To complete the class, all you have to do is "show up," according to one student.

So what's the real difference between the education received at Smith at that received at another school? "Gung-ho, outspoken women," claimed one student, and she seems to be correct. While it seems as if most women at Smith would major in more typical liberal arts areas, such as English or art history, Smith women defy these stereotypes, and have just as many majors in the sciences as in the humanities. And while English, art history, and women's studies are popular, many students are biology, pre-med, or engineering majors. The Picker Engineering Program is able to provide a first-class engineering program within a liberal arts education, and is the only engineering program at any all-women college.

Yet another one of the reasons Smith's academic programs are so strong is because of their place in the Pioneer Valley's Five College Consortium. Smith women can take classes at Amherst, U-Mass Amherst, Mount Holyoke, and Hampshire colleges.

No Bass, But Lots of Activity

A capella is one of the major extracurriculars on campus, with groups like the Smithereens, the Smiffenpoofs, and the Vibe. Sports are also fairly popular, with soccer, basketball, crew, and rugby generally seen as some of the more popular sports. In addition, there are intramurals in which many students participate. And while some students said that people don't really attend the games, others said that attending sports events was relatively popular. "Lots of people go to the games," said one student. "There's lots of spirit, and people go to cheer on their friends."

Perhaps the largest organization at Smith is SOS, Service Organizations at Smith. There are many different organizations within this broader group, including the Smith Democrats and Republicans and the Smith College Feminists, as well as many non-political organizations. According to one student, "almost everyone is involved in at least one SOS organization." In addition, some students choose to work on the Smith radio channel WOZQ, or participate in student-run religious groups or student government groups. "Everyone's involved in at least one or two things," remarked one student.

There are no sororities on campus, although students can join the ones at U-Mass

Amherst. However, sororities don't seem to be particularly popular anyway. Said one student, "there just not really that big of a deal." Students don't seem to miss the Greek scene, according to many students. This seems most to do with the housing situation at Smith, one that is truly unique to the college.

Living and Working in Mansions

At Smith, housing is much nicer than you would find at many other colleges. Instead of living in dorms, students live in renovated mansions housing 90–100 people. Students live in their houses for four years, although there is certainly the ability to transfer. "It's a lot more homey, because the dorms aren't really separated," said one student.

The dorms all have different personalities, although freshman year the housing is assigned randomly. Houses on the Quad tend to be really loud and party more, while houses on Green Street tend to be more quiet and studious. The mansions all have different styles, and many once belonged to the founding families of North Hampton.

Students generally live in singles or doubles freshman year and occasionally have doubles sophomore year, but all upper classmen have singles. All houses have living rooms, TV rooms, and laundry rooms. Most have dining halls located within the house, and some of the houses even have cleaning services. "The rooms are actually huge," said one student. "Every single room has amazing views, and we all have our own closets. The doubles are huge, and the singles are really big too, especially for juniors and seniors. They're probably bigger than the doubles in most other colleges."

Not only do students have the advantage of living in these mansions, they have the advantage of running them too. There are no faculty living in the houses, and the houses are run by two seniors, one who acts as House President, and another who acts as House Resident. There is an adult in charge of every five or six houses, but they're not involved in the day-to-day affairs of the students. "It just seems like at Smith there is so much trust," remarked one student. "They trust us to run the houses, and to be responsible for the most part." People usually stay on campus all four years because of the quality of the housing, although there are some co-op apartments.

Each house serves a tea Friday at four p.m. It's the responsibility of four of the freshman to set up and clean up. Students serve tea, chips, sandwiches, and a variety of different snacks, and students request the snacks for the different tea's. "It's just a nice opportunity to talk to people," said one student. The food at Smith seems to be just as impressive as the housing. According to many students the food is very good. The students have a lot of choice in what they want to eat, because many of the dining halls have different themes, such as kosher, Mediterranean, and vegetarian/vegan.

Girls Know How to Have Fun

Although there is a lack of men at Smith, there is no lack of partying. Friday and Saturday are the biggest nights to party, and Thursday is also "pretty rowdy," according to one student. Most of the parties occur in the houses, although students can also choose to go to parties at any of the other four colleges in the Five College Consortium.

Students say that there is no pressure to drink, but if you do decide to it is harder to get alcohol if you are under 21. Alcohol can generally be found by most in smaller room parties, though. There is a no-drinking policy for students under 21, but it is not strongly enforced, as the administration generally doesn't search the rooms. Although there is certainly some drinking, other drugs are not particularly prevalent on campus.

> "Women who go to Smith are proud to be in an environment with so many other empowered and intelligent women."

The most popular parties to go to on campus include the Immorality Party, Halloween, and Convocation Night. For Convocation, the students of each house dress up in a particular theme. Some have had to make their costumes out of aluminum foil, or have had a theme of wearing as little as possible.

While there certainly seem to be enough on-campus activities in which to become involved, students also make regular trips into town. Northampton is only a five or ten-minute walk from campus, and students enjoy going to town for coffee and food in cafés like Haymarket, the Woodmarket, and Thorn's. "Downtown is always nice," said one student. "It's close by, and there's a lot of stuff to do. Although there's always a lot of stuff going on ever day on campus, and sometimes there were weeks where I didn't go at all.

It's A Girl Thing

Smithies talk about the friendliness of the student body, and the openness with which new students are accepted. There is a general trend of acceptance at the school, including an openness with lesbianism and sexuality that is not always seen elsewhere. As for having all women, all the time, most students say that they don't notice it after the first few weeks. "I was kind of scared about the all-women's thing, but I really forgot about it after I got to," said one student. "I only remember when people ask about it." Some students said that not having boys was not a problem, since they could meet that at other colleges in the consortium. However, others lamented that there weren't enough boys at parties or on campus. Women who go to Smith are proud to be in an environment with so many other empowered and intelligent women. Like the motto on some of their shirts, the women seem to believe that Smith is "not a girls' school without men— it's a women's school without boys."—*Ariel Shepherd-Oppenheim*

FYI

If you come to Smith, you'd better bring "lots of CD's for house parties, rain boots, and weird things to dress up with for Convocation."

What's the typical weekend schedule? "It consists of tea on Friday, staying on campus for a concert Friday night, going to North Hampton Saturday night, and studying Sunday."

If I could change one thing about Smith I'd "want there to be more boys at parties."

Three things every student should do before graduating are: "go to Immorality, take a class at another college, and jump in the pond."

Tufts University

Address: Tufts, Bendetson Hall, Medford, MA 02155
Phone: 617-628-5000
E-mail Address: NA
Web site URL: www.tufts.edu
Year Founded: 1852
Private or Public: private
Religious affiliation: none
Location: suburban
Regular Application Deadline: 2-Jan
Number of Applicants: NA
Percent Accepted: 27
Percent Accepted who enroll: 31
Number Entering: NA
Number of Transfers Accepted each Year: NA
Mean SAT: NA
Mean ACT: NA
Middle 50% SAT range: 1,340–1,480

Middle 50% ACT range: 29–32
Early admission program (EA/ ED/ NA): ED
ED or EA Acceptance Rate: NA
Full time Undergraduate enrollment: 4,982
Total enrollment: 9,693
Percent Male: 49%
Percent Female: 51%
Total Percent Minority: 0%
Percent African-American: 6%
Percent Asian/Pacific Islander: 13%
Percent Hispanic: 6%
Percent Native-American: 0%
Percent Other: NA
Percent in-state / out of state: 25%/75%

Percent from Public HS: 60%
Retention Rate: 95%
Graduation Rate: 92%
Percent in On-campus housing: 75%
Percent affiliated with Greek system: 19%
Percent Varsity or Club Athletes: NA
Number of official organized extracurricular organizations: 160
3 Most popular majors: Economics, English language and Literature, International Relations and Affairs
Student/Faculty ratio: 7:01
Tuition and Fees: $34,730
Cost for Room and Board: $9,770
Percent receiving Financial aid, first-year: 38%

A small New England school most notably characterized by a huge hill which students lovingly trek up each and every day, Tufts is a bit like high school (the hook-up web is all too easy to trace here), but with less catty, smarter kids and famous professors who make going to class anything but daily drudgery. Keeping true to their Jumbo elephant mascot, Tufts provides big opportunities for a diverse group of students (Tufts has one of the highest rates of international student enrollment) who blow off steam from their rigorous schoolwork in any of the various social and shopping meccas surrounding the Bedford town.

Academics

The distribution requirements at Tufts are "quite rigorous," with the six-semester language requirement standing out as students' biggest grievance. But despite being an easy target for disgruntled undergraduates, fulfilling the language requirement isn't all that burdensome. Especially since "three of them can be filled with culture classes," like former Tufts provost Sol Gittleman's Introduction to Yiddish Literature, "instead of classes in the actual language." Gittleman's "grandfather-like mannerisms and stories are priceless," praised one student. In fact, most students end up finding the obligatory courses to be quite fulfilling in the long run. As one junior explained, "By taking classes I otherwise would never have considered, I learned a lot about new subjects and myself."

No matter how one goes about fulfilling his or her distribution requirements, students generally concede that the workload is "consistent and demanding, but not overly consuming." Of course, a few majors like pre-med, engineering and international relations stand out for being especially competitive. "Engineers are constantly in the library studying for tests and doing problem sets, and IR students are known for having endless pages of reading and very long papers." For those interested in IR, but not so interested in camping out in the library for nights at end, undergrads advise majoring in political science if you wish to "gain the same education experience, without so many requirements." And as if the pre-med, major weren't competitive enough, those students craving a little extra push can apply to Tufts Medical School during their sophomore year, without even taking "the killer MCATs." Tufts' small size makes getting into the

classes of your choice relatively easy, although registration can be frustrating. "As long as you show the professor that you really want to take a course they will usually let you in even if it is full." Classes range from five to 200, but most classes cap at about 25 people, which explains why TAs aren't really a big thing at Tufts. "Most of the teachers know your name and are always available for help outside of class or just to talk." Alas, small classes do have their pitfalls. "The attendance policy is a little rough. Participation usually counts towards your final grade," which some students find to be "annoying."

Frat Attack

Clearly, one of Tufts' main allures is its proximity to Boston, whether students opt to spend a sunny Saturday afternoon shopping on Newbury or to spend a bundle of money snagging a table at Aria or Avalon. Luckily, for those individuals who would rather not bump heads with bossy bouncers, the University's frequent club-sponsored events for students 18 and over, make getting in downtown a whole lot easier (Tufts even provides the transportation!). However, the truth is, most students don't regularly head to the city for nights out on the town until their senior year. "Upperclassmen usually go to bars in the Medford/Somerville area until they are 21, because bars in Boston have a reputation for being hard on fake IDs," a student explained. Not to mention cold-weather-induced laziness, which tends to keep students close to home when the chill hits their bones.

No ID? No problem. There are plenty of on-campus partying options available, although one wise upperclassman explained that "It takes a semester or two to realize there are options besides the frats," like a wide range of off-campus parties at students' apartments and houses. Still, most Tufts students agree the frat parties, which host such themed fiestas as the traditional toga bash to "Secs and Execs," can be "fun" even if a bit overcrowded. A student lamented that you sometimes have to wait in line just to get in the fraternity door. But students are happy that some fraternities can still even open their doors. Recently, the Tufts administration has become noticeably stricter with their alcohol policy, after a handful of the University's fraternities and sororities have been put on probation for serving alcohol to minors. Although such restrictions include the prohibition of kegs, students agree that, "what they don't know or see won't hurt them!" Nevertheless, Tufts police have been making an effort to make their presence known. "It has become quite common for the cops to break up a party, whether it be at a frat house or off campus, at 12:30." "Make no mistake," a student advised, "Tufts is not a party school!"

Kinda like High School All Over Again

Although Tufts' small size is great for classes, it's not so great when you've made out with half the people in your class. "The social scene at Tufts is small enough that you usually know of at least one other person who hooked up with the same person you hooked up with," one student said. This might explain why STDs are not a common problem at the New England college (although Health Services is a visible presence on campus). Sure, hooking up is the way to go at Tufts. But once students hit junior year, "it seems as though people begin to settle down with a partner." Even then, "going on dates is not common practice."

Students are described at Tufts as being generally friendly, although "pretty cliquey." One student stated that "many people know your business and most cliques have some type of reputation." Still, students maintain the view that "it is possible for almost any type of person to fit in here," even if some characterize the student body as being from "upper-middle class families." It ought to be noted, however, that Tufts has one of the highest rates of international students of any college. Additionally, students collectively agree that friendships are constantly evolving, and your freshman-year friends are "not necessarily the people you will hang out with all the time for the next four years." In any case, students appreciate the small-campus feel. "I love walking around campus and recognizing everyone."

> "It is possible for almost any type of person to fit in here."

Despite the fact that Tufts' Greek scene is far from prominent (especially with the fraternities under careful watch), one junior girl nevertheless praised rushing a sorority as a great way to step out and meet new people. "In the end, whether you decide to pledge a house or not, rush is a great way to meet new people freshman year. Plus, the parties are fun. . . . You get to dress up in themes costumes, eat good food, listen to a bunch of girls sing songs for you and basically just soak up the attention."

At the Top of the Hill

Other than the Homecoming football game, athletics don't really play a large role at Tufts. Since it is a Division III school, recruiting does happen, but no scholarship money is given for athletics. In fact, intramural sports often draw more spectators than that actual Tufts teams do. However, in the spring, people do venture to the rugby games, although "it's more about the socializing than it is about the sport." Luckily, despite Tufts' "state-of-the-art" gym, most students get enough of a workout trekking up the campus hill. Campus is informally divided into "uphill" and "downhill," with the upper area housing most of the academic buildings and the lower area boasting the student center. "Although it is good for your quads, it does get tiring," one student said.

Aside from putting a strain on students' muscles, the difference of living uphill or downhill is huge and may dictate who your friends are for the rest of your college experience. "The uphill kids tend to eat in the uphill dining hall, while the downhill kids stick to theirs," a student explained. Regardless, students don't seem to mind Tufts' on-campus policy, which requires all students to live in campus housing for a minimum of two years (although sophomore year, a student can live in a dorm room or in one of the various interest houses on campus).

There are two all-freshmen dorms at Tufts, although freshmen are also scattered throughout all the other dorms. Each dorm has its own way of separating genders, either on a room-to-room basis or by female/male-designated floors. In either case, the bathrooms are always single-sexed. Right now, Tufts is in the process of building a new upperclassman dorm. Currently, South Hall is the newest and most modern dorm, and even though the "rooms are very small," "each bathroom has a single shower and a single toilet." Meanwhile, West Hall is known as the party dorm. Appropriately, that's where Tufts' annual Naked Quad Run takes place. The Naked Quad run is a notorious Tufts tradition. During finals in the winter, students lose their clothes (and their frustrations) and run around the academic quad. During this campuswide event, the West Hall "is one big party." "The cops actually relax for a change and allow people to drink without saying anything," a senior said.

Some of aforementioned on campus houses are themed, like the Rainbow House, the International House and La Casa (the Spanish House). "These houses promote the campus's self-segregation," one student complained, "but they are fine for people who feel the need to live with people who are all identical to them." Wherever you decide to live, just be prepared for the campus housing lottery system, which can be "very frustrating and very competitive." Of course, you can bypass the trials and tribulations of the lottery by moving off-campus, which most upperclassmen choose to do since "rent is not expensive" and all the houses are "within a five-minute walking distance to school." Even though a lot of upperclassmen have cars, "it is definitely not necessary." No need for frosh to worry about whether to bug Mom and Dad to let you bring their Volvo to school—freshmen are not allowed to have cars on campus.

Dine, Wine and Busta Rhymes

Tufts is known for its great food, but students admit to being reminded of how decent their college cuisine is only "when students from other school come to visit and rave about it." Luckily, freshmen will have snacks to share since they are required to have an "all you can eat" meal plan, which some students complained "ends up being excessive."

But as long as you've got the pre-paid dining bucks, might as well sit down and enjoy yourself. The dining halls are "definitely a hang out spot." Tufts students claim that they are "never empty" and "you really can sit all day and chat, do work, or watch the world go by (both dining halls have huge floor to ceiling windows)." Unfortunately (or not), you won't be passing the time alone. "At busy times, it is hard to find an empty table, so you often have to sit with people you don't know," although a student promised that "it's not awkward." There are two main dining halls on-campus and one take out place, as well as two restaurants in the campus center which serve made to order sandwiches, pizza and hot dishes.

Not in the mood for a taste of Tufts? Walk to Davis square or Boston Avenue (or take the Tufts shuttle if you're truly lazy) for nearby restaurant like True Grounds for sandwiches and bagels, and an amazing ice cream parlor. And on the weekend, roll out of bed and head to "the best restaurant in the world," Soundbites, within five minutes of Tufts. "Soundbites is the place to be on Saturday and Sunday mornings after a rough night out. The line around the corner is well worth the wait for eggs, home fries, and healthier options such a granola and fresh fruit."

Vibing Well and Good

Even though Tufts is a relatively small school, it knows how to go out big. Take, for example, the "kick-ass" student-run Tufts Concert Board, which decides on Tufts' Spring Fling lineups. "It is such a fun event because almost the entire student body congregates on the President's Lawn for the all-day event." Past Spring Flings' main stages have been occupied by the likes of Busta Rhymes and the Roots. In the fall, students likewise congregate on the President's lawn for last-minute sunbathing and premature sledding (oh, New England weather!). "As the leaves change color, you feel like you could be in a movie," a freshman stated, later citing the library roof as a prime place to hang out on a Sunday and catch "an amazing view of Boston."

Nature's free pleasures are only compounded by Tufts' complimentary events. Students regularly attend free on-campus screenings of relatively new movies and free lectures. Past years' lecturers have included Sen. Hillary Clinton and Morgan Spurlock. Just make sure to act quickly, because "seating is limited." "The environment at Tufts is awesome," one student raved. "When I'm there, I never want to leave and when I'm home, I'm counting down the days till I can go back!"—*Dana Schuster*

FYI

If you come to Tufts, you'd better bring "a hoodie, Uggs and sunglasses."

What is a typical weekend schedule? "Go to one of the Medford/Somerville bars on Tuesday night as long as you don't have too much work. Go to either a Medford/Somerville bar, or to an on campus party on Thursday night. Have a chill movie night on Friday, or maybe go out to dinner and have a few drinks. Wake up Saturday morning, have breakfast at Soundbites, hang out with friends, go to bar in Boston or frat party on campus. Sleep in on Sunday, go to the library and do some work, order in dinner and watch TV."

If I could change one thing about Tufts, "I'd make more parking spaces and I'd want the 'easy' classes to actually be easy."

Three things every student at Tufts should do before graduating are "make out on the library roof, go on a duck tour of Boston, and go abroad."

University of Massachusetts / Amherst

Address: U Mass Amherst, Whitmore, 181 President's Drive, Amherst, MA 01003-9313
Phone: 413-545-0222
E-mail Address: mail@admissions.umass.edu
Web site URL: http://www.umass.edu
Year Founded: 1863
Private or Public: public
Religious affiliation: none
Location: suburban
Regular Application Deadline: 16-Jan
Number of Applicants: 20,205
Percent Accepted: 71%
Percent Accepted who enroll: 26%
Number Entering: 4,486
Number of Transfers Accepted each Year: 1,939
Mean SAT: 1,143
Mean ACT: NA

Middle 50% SAT range: 1,040–1,260
Middle 50% ACT range: NA
Early admission program (EA/ ED/ NA): EA
ED or EA Acceptance Rate: 22%
Full time Undergraduate enrollment: 19,394
Total enrollment: 25,164
Percent Male: 50%
Percent Female: 50%
Total Percent Minority: 2%
Percent African-American: 1%
Percent Asian/Pacific Islander: 1%
Percent Hispanic: 0%
Percent Native-American: 0%
Percent Other: NA
Percent in-state / out of state: 77%/23%
Percent from Public HS: 90%
Retention Rate: 83%
Graduation Rate: 65%

Percent in On-campus housing: 61%
Percent affiliated with Greek system: 8%
Percent Varsity or Club Athletes: NA
Number of official organized extracurricular organizations: 200
3 Most popular majors: Biological and Physical Sciences, Communications Studies/Speech Communication and Rhetoric, Psychology
Student/Faculty ratio: 17:01
Tuition and Fees: $9,937.00
In State Tuition and Fees (if different): $1,714.00
Cost for Room and Board: $6,989.00
Percent receiving Financial aid, first-year: 50%

U Mass academics are hard," a student said, surprised. For those who remember UMass's party school reputation, they'll be amazed to find that parties now mainly happen off campus, or on a much smaller scale. Through recent renovations, new buildings, and academic reviews, UMass has recast its image as a college whose athletics and academics are its main appeal.

Academic Overhaul

Amidst the formation of UMass's new public image, the university has been working to redefine itself physically, as well as academically. Within the last few years, the Renaissance Center (one of six in North America), Computer Science Building, the Child Care building and the Engineering Lab II have all been constructed, with a new Studio Art building on the way. Current facilities, including the WEB Dubois Library which boasts over 26 floors, are said by students to be "world class."

No matter where one's interests may lie, UMass academics will likely have an appropriate program. "I don't see any reason why you shouldn't be interested in what you're majoring here," one senior said. "We've got everything and anything to study." Majors range from Building Materials and Wood Technology to Marketing to Communication Disorders, or you could even create your own major courtesy of the Bachelor's Degree Individual Concentration (BDIC). Not interested enough to major in it? Many majors can also be minors, or you can build a unique minor that may fulfill a more esoteric interest (UMass offer minors from Entomology to Military Leadership). While best known for its management and linguistics programs, UMass is strong in both liberal arts and the sciences, too.

If students can't find a class they wish to take at UMass, they are able to cross-enroll in classes at any of the other Five-College Consortium, an intercollegiate academic program that includes Smith, Mount Holyoke, Amherst, Hampshire College and UMass. Whether it's merely to try out something new, or just to taste a new learning environment, many students seize this opportunity.

However, despite such leeway, all students enrolled at UMass must fulfill their General Education requirements, which are aimed at increasing the width of each student's education. The writing requirement consists of a freshman college writing class and a junior year writing requirement (mandatory for every major). Six "Social World" courses must be taken, one course in each section: literature, arts, history, and social and behavioral sciences, another social and behavioral science, and another course in any section. Math and sciences require that you fulfill three natural science courses (one biological and one physical), one basic math skills and one analytical reasoning course. Finally, there must also be one interdisciplinary course. On top of that, the university requires that students take two classes on diversity, one on U.S. diversity, and another on global diversity. Surprisingly, most students stated that they "had no problem fulfilling the requirements."

Classes tend to start large in the beginning and get smaller in one's junior and senior years. "Unless you are taking a course required for a couple majors, like intro biology, you can keep your classes to under 30," an engineering major noted. One complaint was that UMass was too research oriented. Not all classes are taught by professors. Instead, PhD students, who many undergraduates felt are less comprehensive than professors, teach some smaller classes.

For those who are interested in more academically rigorous courses, the honors program, Commonwealth College, provides roughly 2,000 students with smaller class sizes and more challenging workloads. Commonwealth College ("ComCol") promotes strong faculty and student ties through events like "Pizza and Prof. Night" on Thursdays. ComCol also emphasizes different aspects of the college life, like required Dean's book seminar class, an individual "capstone experience" (a six-credit project), and community service.

Living at Amherst

Amherst, a college town in the historic Pioneer Valley of Western Massachusetts, is "a great place to go, especially to be off-campus." The bus system, free to UMass students, can take you everywhere—to the four other consortium colleges, around campus, into town, and even to the mall. Security isn't a top problem either. "I feel safe walking all alone at three in the morning," one female student said. "That's how safe it is

here." Despite the lack of crime concerns, the school is still cautious, installing security cameras on the entrances, exits and the exteriors of the residential buildings, hiring a very large security detail, and having a bus that circles the large campus every 15 minutes.

There are six different residential sections of campus: North, Northeast, Central, Southwest, Orchard Hill and Sylvan. According to the students, each has its own distinct personality. For example, Sylvan is known to be quiet, while Southwest is where most of the parties are. Orchard Hill has a lot of ComCol students, Central is very hippie, Northeast has a large Asian presence. North, opened for the first time in Fall 2006, has apartments, an attractive detail to many upperclassmen.

Special residential arrangements at Amherst include the Talent Advancement Program in which students are grouped by major, and the Residential Advancement Programs, in which students are grouped by class selection. These programs are formed to promote interaction among students with similar interests, and to facilitate easier transition into college life for freshmen. However, these special arrangements, and student selection of residential halls closest to their department buildings (for example, Northeast is closest to Engineering) often causes students to complain that "most students end up segregating themselves by major, and there is very little interaction between students of different interests."

Students eat in one of five Dining Commons (DC's) by swiping their UCARD. Students can choose their meal plans, so that they can have between 112 swipes a semester (7 swipes a week) to unlimited. Depending on one's meal plan, swipes can also be used at retail locations, like cafés around campus to buy food. Berkshire DC underwent renovation in Spring 2006 and students love the food there. "Berkshire offers a variety of delicious food," one student raved. "I hope they renovate all the other DC's too." Students can also eat at any of the nearby restaurants, like the popular Pasta E Basta and Antonio's Pizza. They also hang out in the fair trade convenience store and bagel shop People's Market, as well as a vegan/vegetarian eatery Earthfoods Café at the Student Union. But the main central hub of campus remains the Campus Center. The Campus Center offers the Blue Wall eatery and a fair trade coffee stand, and it also supplies copies of the *Daily Collegian*, UMass's daily newspaper.

There are two free athletic facilities, Boyden and Totman Gym. Those who wish to work out closer to the dorm can use the wellness facilities housed in certain residential halls. These are generally available with workout equipment, which students may use after paying a fee. Student recreational athletic facilities are separate from those used by athletes, but the campus has announced that it plans to renovate the two gyms, as well as possibly construct a new athletic facility.

Bringing down the House

While parties used to be big on campus, in recent years several fraternities have been demolished or bought out by the university. The reason for this trend can be attributed to fact that the university wants to smarten up its image. "Parties are almost always shut down by the campus police," one senior complained. "When I was a freshman, they had no problems with these parties." Neighbors complain as well about the noise level, drunken disorderly conduct, and trash left on the grounds after a party. Still, parties do occur, especially during big weekends like Orchard Hill Bowl Weekend, the Spring Concert, and after sports victories. Most of these parties take place in Southwest and Puffton, an area where the majority students live off-campus. After the Red Sox won the World Series, there was even a party so large that campus security had to be called in to shut down the "riot." Still, some students who are not content with the party scene on campus head to other schools for big parties, like the Halloween Party at Smith College. Popular local bars and clubs include McMurphy's, Monkey Bar and Sky Bar, which on Thursday nights allows students above 18 years of age.

For those who may not want to drink and party every or any night, performances and other events can almost always be found, both on and off campus. UMass has very large performance venues that constantly showcasing various productions and concerts. UMass also offers a movie theater that shows first release films on Friday and Saturday nights.

> **"I would never have expected to see so many different kinds of people at UMass."**

Sports play a big role on the Division I campus. "Everyone attends the hockey games," one student said. "Where else are we going to shout at the BU students 'BC Rejects!'?" Immense school spirit is highlighted at the Mullin Center, which doubles for the arena for both hockey games and basketball games. Football games are also extremely popular, and boast a significant alumni presence. Even the UMass marching band has its own share of celebrity, having won numerous national honors.

"I would never have expected to see so many different kinds of people at UMass," one student commented. "People come from all backgrounds, all ethnicities, and all over the nation and the globe with all different types of interests." And with access to four other well-respected colleges, UMass is on the way to spreading its academic wings.—*Jesse Dong*

FYI
If you come to UMass at Amherst, you'd better bring "a better pad for your mattress."
What is the typical weekend schedule? "Attend a hockey game Friday night, go off campus on Saturday afternoon, party with friends Saturday night, and spend all of Sunday doing homework."
If I could change one thing about UMass at Amherst, I'd "renovate all the DC's."
Three things ever student should do before graduating from UMass at Amherst are: "go to Bowl Weekend, attend a hockey game and go to a frat."

Wellesley College

Address: Wellesley, 106 Central Street, Wellesley, MA 02481-8203
Phone: 781-283-2270
E-mail Address: admission@wellesley.edu
Web site URL: http://www.wellesley.edu
Year Founded: 1870
Private or Public: private
Religious affiliation: none
Location: suburban
Regular Application Deadline: 16-Jan
Number of Applicants: 3,974
Percent Accepted: 36%
Percent Accepted who enroll: 25%
Number Entering: 586
Number of Transfers Accepted each Year: 49
Mean SAT: 1,383
Mean ACT: 30

Middle 50% SAT range: 1,310–1,470
Middle 50% ACT range: 29–31
Early admission program (EA/ ED/ NA): ED
ED or EA Acceptance Rate: 47%
Full time Undergraduate enrollment: 2,224
Total enrollment: 2,330
Percent Male: 2%
Percent Female: 98%
Total Percent Minority: 39%
Percent African-American: 6%
Percent Asian/Pacific Islander: 26%
Percent Hispanic: 7%
Percent Native-American: 0%
Percent Other: NA
Percent in-state / out of state: 12%/88%

Percent from Public HS: 64%
Retention Rate: 95%
Graduation Rate: 87%
Percent in On-campus housing: 97%
Percent affiliated with Greek system: 0%
Percent Varsity or Club Athletes: NA
Number of official organized extracurricular organizations: 160
3 Most popular majors: Economics, General; English Language and Literature, General; Psychology, General
Student/Faculty ratio: 9:01
Tuition and Fees: $32,384
Cost for Room and Board: $10,216
Percent receiving Financial aid, first-year: 56%

The Wellesley woman is quick to boast about her college choice, supporting her claim with the school's strong reputation for turning women with potential into women with opportunities. Well-known and accomplished Wellesley alumnae include the likes of former Secretary of State Madeleine Albright, Senator Hillary Rodham Clinton and broadcast journalist Diane Sawyer. One student said less famous alumnae in her hometown impacted her decision to apply: "They have all chosen intelligent direction and things to do that are meaningful in their lives and careers." Wellesley College is a small but united family, and for its size, boasts an impressive 1000 classes and 53-plus majors. By promoting a common consciousness of honor and a tradition of excellence among its students during their four-year stay on campus, Wellesley gives a student much more than a single-sex classroom. The Wellesley experience prepares students for a distinguished way of life after graduation.

Classrooms for Speaking Up

The Wellesley classroom is not for the faint of heart or mind. "Most everyone who comes here was the valedictorian of her high school,

or in the top 10 percent. I think you learn so much from your peers that it will sometimes almost eclipse your professors." One premed student said that for the most part, students' competitive attitudes had not reared their heads until the administration instituted a new grade-inflation policy two years ago. "They were noticing that class averages were an 'A,' so now mandatory class averages are set at B+." Another student said the competitive spirit is "mostly self-imposed."

With a 9:1 student to faculty ratio, many classes are taught in seminar-style settings that provide a space where it's easy for all to know each other so that "everyone contributes." However, participation in bigger classes is sometimes lacking because "younger students are much more hesitant to participate," one junior said. Also, in lectures—which often max out in a size ranging from 50 to 60 students—three or four older girls sometimes steal the show, but this atmosphere is mostly exclusive to larger, introductory lectures.

No one gets off easy at Wellesley. Thirty-two credits (four per semester) complete with distributional requirements, as well as the obligatory Writing 125, demands effort from all Wellesley women. "The reading load is obscene, of course," one student admitted. Academic advising is available to students during their first year but like at many universities, it's hard for professors to guide students who have not yet found their own direction. "Eventually you have to pursue [advising] for yourself. You must take the initiative, make appointments and develop the relationship so they can learn the nature of what you're doing." While there may be some self-initiative required by students to find the advice they're hoping for, professors never hide from students at Wellesley. "I've never found a professor to not make themselves available to me. If there's been any lack of support, it's because I've been reluctant to go see them or haven't taken it upon myself to do it." While another student says, "we're not notable for professors who baby students," a junior points out that all professors "know how hard students work and how ambitious they are. When there may be a problem, they give you the benefit of the doubt."

For the most part, class sizes are very small and once in the classroom, "professors make an effort to get to know students as individuals." One student said that many professors have mandatory office hours, "so you have to talk to them about the paper that's assigned, the news, or golf. 'Just come in to see me,' they'll say. Professors don't like you because you get good grades. They like you because you're a good person. They're human, in other words." Students identify with professors in the fact that "they've been here before. Even a lot of the female professors here are Wellesley alumnae, and that's a nice connection to have and one of the things I like best about the classroom experience."

> "Professors don't like you because you get good grades. They like you because you're a good person. They're human, in other words."

Double-majoring is a new and growing trend at Wellesley. "For a lot of people who go abroad, it becomes very easy because you fulfill requirements in the language and culture of that area you travel to while abroad." Students not only choose to study abroad but may also join off-campus study pro-

grams. By participating in the Twelve College Exchange Program, women have the option to spend a semester at Amherst, Bowdoin, Connecticut College, Dartmouth, Mount Holyoke, Smith, Trinity, Vassar, Wesleyan, Wheaton, or Williams. Students may also cross-register for courses at MIT or even work toward a MIT-Wellesley double-degree.

Honor and Tradition

A unique trait of the Wellesley academic and social community is the unwritten honor code. "It's unwritten because it's supposed to be on the inside. You must feel that an action is wrong." The honor code is taken so seriously that students self-schedule their finals. "We take an exam on our own time and the professor is not there." The honor code even stretches to instances when one should "steer clear of another's tasty leftovers in the fridge."

If you visit Wellesley in late May, you may see one lucky woman thrown in to the scenic Lake Waban after having taken part in Hoop Rolling, when each senior rolls a wooden hoop across campus in a race to the lake. Historically, the first woman to the lake would be deemed first to marry. Now, however, the winner is most likely to become first CEO in the class. Lake Day once tempted students to skip class for carnival festivities by the lake, but according to one student, part of the tradition has died since "people never skip school here." Something not to miss is the annual Junior Show when the junior class performs a parody of Wellesley life and its students. At the Junior Show put on by the Class of 2007, the biggest party girl on campus received the "Shaken, Not Stirred Award" after being nominated and voted on by the entire college community. First-year students participate in Flower Sunday, held annually in early September. The younger students are chosen by upperclasswomen, who act as "big" sisters. The "big" sister gives the "little" sister a flower at Houghton Memorial Chapel. The event serves as a celebration meant to ease the transition from home to college. Also look for one of the main party events of the year: Dyke Ball, "a prom that lesbians would be comfortable taking their girlfriends to."

Manicured Living

Wellesley is a walking campus. "They made it so women would be strong in body, mind and heart, so there are hills all over." One student said Wellesley spends a ton of money on landscaping—"for the trees, the leaf pickup"—that coordinates with the gothic, brick and stone buildings. The extra effort to keep the green space in shape "helps a lot when you're working really hard. You can always enjoy your surroundings here."

First-year students join 10 or more students living in their dorm to be mentored by the same upperclassman RA. After spending the first weeks at school together, the girls create a "first group of friends." One student calls the first-year group a "good starting block." Whether or not the experience is positive or negative varies and is circumstantial. "It depends on whether or not you get a charismatic mentor or an upperclassman who wants to act only as an RA."

Each dorm includes a living room with a fireplace where many social gatherings occur. Every floor has a kitchen and an attached living room space. Floors host events. One student said, "Last week, my floor had bowling. We used coke cans." One student said the College President is adamant that students spend time making connections with others instead of sitting in front of television sets. "But if that's her motive, she should ban our laptops!"

The brand new Wang Campus Center is a "huge" modern building made of copper and glass which makes it "weirdly inviting," one student said. It houses a new dining area and coffee bar, a café and pub—both student run—and space for student organizations, performances and social functions. Students use $200 worth of flex points—part of the meal plan—to buy tasty food in the student center, which is a "nice place to go and relax." Students "definitely" study there in the cozy corners made for reading.

"You can't really live off campus because we're in an affluent neighborhood so it'd be like trying to find an apartment in Beverly Hills." Students do, however, venture into the town of Wellesley, called the "Ville," for a meal at Amarin, a popular spot offering affordable Thai cuisine, or at Blue Ginger, a pricier student favorite. Women also make the short drive to town for coffee at one of the "cute cafes." Because of the college's suburban surroundings, the campus is especially safe. However, "it is unsafe to make a politically incorrect statement" at Wellesley.

Renaissance Women

How does one define extracurricular activities at Wellesley? "It's a competition of whose plate is the fullest." While most students take four classes, "some take five and they have six or seven different clubs they're in and sports and volunteering in Boston, too." It's a good thing Wellesley students are so busy, "because we're a way out here with a 20 minute drive to Boston and if there's nothing to do, we're going to kill time hitting the books, doing good for the community or getting stuff done."

All students are required to fulfill a physical education requirement but "it's easy to get rid of with any yoga or pilates class or sailing if you're not sports inclined. As a student involved in Division I athletics at Wellesley "you're involved in the most extreme sense and your entire existence is devoted to it." But "if you have an athletic interest but you're not good enough or not willing to make the varsity commitment, there's plenty to do," like joining the equestrian team or the popular dorm crew teams. Club rugby and ultimate Frisbee are the "unofficial varsity sports" with an intense social scene that comes along with team membership. According to one student, for a lot of people, "if they're about to come out of the closet or are looking for other girls, they'll join the team."

The Social Hitch: Not Just Boys

"Sometimes I forget that there are not boys here. It doesn't hit me until I see one." A student who spent a summer studying in a coed classroom at another liberal arts college said she now believes more than ever that "women can be much more mature and respectful and easier to discuss things with in a classroom setting. I didn't always think there was any difference." If you don't mind men's absence from the classroom but do mind their absence from your social life, do not fear. One student confirms that "once your friend has a boyfriend and you meet his friends, then you can have a guy-friend." A junior student offers this perspective: "Sometimes the divide can be abrasive or jarring, because if you come to Wellesley your first year and don't like what you find at frat parties, you wonder what you got yourself into." But when you find those guy friends some students hope for, "you have to make an effort to see each other so the ones you actually see are your close friends."

Wellesley students represent more ethnic and socioeconomic diversity than most expect to see in a student body at a small liberal arts college. According to one student, online forums help students who feel the most isolated in their backgrounds to gain exposure by seeking others who might feel less like the norm in some sense, but a variety of ethnic and cultural groups at the College allow many students to find a desired community.

Stereotypes about the Wellesley woman aren't always true. "We're sometimes characterized as lesbians who stay home and do homework" but "probably the percentage of lesbians at Wellesley is a little bit higher than at coed colleges, and the reason they stand out is they have a lot of support here. There are a lot of gay-straight alliance groups. It's supposed to be a safe space." There's also the label of the "Wellesley girl who does everything." One student said that the majority of people are "your Renaissance woman who is in many clubs. Every person I know is an extremely hard worker."

Students may choose to join campus societies, which are "sororities with an academic spin;" each highlights an interest in an area like art and music or literature. Members do not live in a society's house, but the houses are used to host guest lectures, other speakers, and parties. While many friends are found within the dorms, one student admitted she wanted to extend her social circle and "decided to join a society so I could meet upperclasswomen who weren't nerds."

Students apply to societies after their first semester in a "pretty intense" application process including projects and essays as well as required participation in three-hour long teas.

Boston is a popular destination for students on the weekends. Frosh are not allowed to have cars so when searching for a social scene they hop on the Senate Bus (the name of the single mode of transportation bringing Wellesley women back and forth from the Boston/Cambridge area) to visit frat row at MIT or to attend parties at Harvard. Nearby Babson is also a place to hang out. Some students feel that they must leave campus every weekend "in order to maintain a level of normalcy" while others stay at home, and "it can depend a lot on how you were in high school."

The Wellesley experience is nothing less than challenging, but well-worth it, according to many current students. "Ultimately, you survive Wellesley together. Most people I know were unhappy during their first year here. But now, most people love it and can't imagine going any where else. It forces people out of their comfort zone." If you hope to participate in a demanding four years at a place where you will reap rewards for your intellectual and social investments, Wellesley might be the school for you.—*Bess Hinson*

FYI

If you come to Wellesley, you'd better bring "your backbone. You can be shy at Wellesley, but you need a spine so you don't get pushed around. Likewise, bring your voice, not only for speaking up, but so you LEARN that you can be heard."

What's the typical weekend schedule? "Using the extra days to do everything you've denied during the week—be it sleep, play, exercise, relaxation or study."

If I could change one thing about Wellesley, I'd "give some girls some manners. Female empowerment does not have to include discarding your femininity."

Three things every student at Wellesley should do before graduating are "not go to class for a day, just to see what it feels like, and take a class at a coed university to realize how happy you are to be at Wellesley."

Wheaton College

Address: Wheaton, 26 East
Main Street, Norton, MA
02766
Phone: 508-286-8251
E-mail Address:
admission@wheatoncollege
.edu
Web site URL:
www.wheatoncollege.edu
Year Founded: 1834
Private or Public: private
Religious affiliation: none
Location: suburban
**Regular Application
Deadline:** 15-Jan
Number of Applicants: 3,614
Percent Accepted: 41%
**Percent Accepted who
enroll:** 28%
Number Entering: 434
**Number of Transfers
Accepted each Year:** ~50
Mean SAT: NA
Mean ACT: NA

Middle 50% SAT range:
1,180–1,350
Middle 50% ACT range:
25–28
**Early admission program
(EA/ ED/ NA):** ED
ED or EA Acceptance Rate:
42%
**Full time Undergraduate
enrollment:** 1,548
Total enrollment: 1,561
Percent Male: 38%
Percent Female: 62%
Total Percent Minority:
17%
Percent African-American:
4%
**Percent Asian/Pacific
Islander:** 4%
Percent Hispanic: 4%
Percent Native-American:
<1%
Percent Other: 4%
**Percent in-state / out of
state:** 33%/67%

Percent from Public HS:
63%
Retention Rate: 86%
Graduation Rate: 75%
**Percent in On-campus
housing:** 96%
**Percent affiliated with
Greek system:** NA
**Percent Varsity or Club
Athletes:** 51%
**Number of official
organized extracurricular
organizations:** 60+
3 Most popular majors:
English, Psychology,
Economics
Student/Faculty ratio: 12:01
Tuition and Fees:
$34,610.00
Cost for Room and Board:
$8,150.00
**Percent receiving
Financial aid, first-year:**
55%

Wheaton is a small liberal arts school located in the sleepy town of Norton, Massachusetts. It boasts a challenging and varied academic program where students can take classes in everything from dreams to globalization. The Wheaton community is a close-knit group where even the RAs just want to be your friend. Wheaton students have a thriving extracurricular and social scene that is greatly benefited by the campus's location between Providence and Boston, two cities just begging to be utilized by car-owning and train-hopping Wheaties.

The Right Balance

Most Wheaton students are very happy with the academic environment of their campus. "The academics are just right," says one freshman, "I'm not overstressed, but I'm being challenged. And here we have the ability to do well in school and be involved in other activities, too." Popular majors include English and education. Education, along with the natural sciences, is said to be one of the hardest majors because the program involves student teaching and requires that students double major. Wheaton is thought of as more of a humanities school, but the administration is beginning an increased focus on science. They have implemented a plan to rebuild all the science buildings on campus by 2014 and are seen as being very encouraging of students pursuing science majors.

Classes are small, usually 15 to 20 students, except in some introductory lectures. Students say that professors are very committed to getting to know them and being a part of their intellectual growth. "One of my professors gave us extra credit just for coming to her office hours so she could get to know us," said on Wheatie. There are no TAs at Wheaton, further enhancing the personalized touch. Though the professors are friendly and helpful, they are tough. Students don't think there is much grade inflation at all at Wheaton and also report relatively few curves. They stress that one must work hard to do well.

Wheaton students say their distribution requirements, called "foundation courses" are reasonable and they have an interesting array of classes in which to fill them. Foundation courses include a first-year seminar, English 101, a math course, two semesters of a foreign language, and one semester of "Beyond the West," ie a class that deals with a culture outside of Western society. In first-year seminars, groups of 20 freshmen become acclimated to Wheaton academic life in a laid back atmosphere while studying topics that vary from "Surgeons and Shamans" to "The Rituals of Dinner." Wheaton also has a program called Connections, where students are able to choose a set of related courses that interest them. Examples of Connections include "Human Biology and Movement," "Modern Italy, and Music: the Medium and the Message." Students say that the Connections courses are an interesting way to fulfill requirements. Wheaties also take advantage of the fact that their college is a part of the 12-college consortium that includes among others, Amherst, Bowdoin, Wellesley, and Dartmouth. Wheaton students can attend a college in the consortium for a semester or a year. Wheaton also offers numerous and very popular opportunities for study abroad.

A Perfect New England Family

Nearly every student has high praises for the sense of community at Wheaton. "One of the things I noticed at accepted students' day that I didn't notice at others schools was how friendly everyone was," one freshman said. Wheaton upperclassmen are especially enthusiastic about making sure new students feel welcome and are aware of the importance of not making novice Wheatie mistakes. During freshmen orientation, upperclassmen herd confused freshmen into the chapel where they begin to chant the incoming class's graduation year. After the chanting, an upperclassman runs through the chapel and squirts water on an unsuspecting frosh who automatically inherits this illustrious job. Besides being simply funny, this tradition emphasizes Wheaton's fun and family-like atmosphere. The fact that Wheaton's student body numbers less than 1600 seems to be an important reason for this. "I like that it is a small school because I can get to know a lot of people well, but still see a few new faces every day," reported one girl. Additionally, "the importance of acceptance and friendship are stressed at Wheaton," says one Wheatie.

Most likely a testament to their widespread acceptance of difference, students are quick to say that there is no "typical" Wheaton student. When pressed, they will admit that most students are middle or upper class and from Massachusetts, Maine,

Connecticut, and surprisingly, California. "For some reason, lots of people in California know about Wheaton. I guess they like small liberal arts schools," explained one Wheatie. Another trait that bonds Wheaton students together is being physically fit. A large segment of students is involved in athletic endeavors that vary from varsity sports to the equestrian team to intramurals. There are no sororities and fraternities at Wheaton, and many say that the a capella groups function as a more positive version of the Greek system. A capella is very popular at Wheaton, as are a wide range of other extracurricular activities, especially community service ones. "Wheaton has a lot to offer, there's always something to join," explains one Wheatie.

Though they don't like to be typecast, Wheaton students as a whole can be summed up as both studious and typical preppy New England kids. They seem particularly fond of The North Face fleeces, colorful rain boots, and for the female students, designer purses. Wheaton students admit that their campus is not incredibly diverse, though the administration is working hard to change that. Wheaton boasts a thriving cultural center, the Marshall Multicultural Center, and is involved in a scholarship program called the Posse Program. New York City minority students receive scholarships to Wheaton in groups called posses, which helps them feel less isolated while increasing Wheaton's racial diversity.

Road Trippers

On any given weekend, a large contingent of the Wheaton student body can be found in Boston, which is 40 minutes away, or Providence about 20. Transportation couldn't be easier since many students have cars and the school offers a shuttle that runs every 30 minutes to a nearby train station. Wheaties love hitting the restaurants, theaters, and club scenes of these two New England cities. The administration encourages their students to take advantage of what their excellent location has to offer. Through the Boston and Providence Connections programs, students pay just five dollars for dinner and a concert or play on select nights. A premium outlet mall is very close to campus, giving Wheaton fashionistas yet another attractive weekend option.

Wheaton students' obvious devotion to Boston and Providence trips shouldn't be seen as a sign that there is nothing to do at

Wheaton. Some students admitted that some weekends on campus are a little slow, but there are usually a wide variety of on campus activity to choose from. The Balfour-Hood Student Center hosts well-attended theme parties in its large lobby, called the Atrium. Wheaton often hosts concerts as well. Recently, students were surprised when a subsidized concert by a Persian pop star, which they wrote off as random and amusing, was packed with outsiders who happily shelled out 40 dollars a ticket.

> "I know that this might seem pretty lame, but Wheaton really would not function in the same way without the common bond and sense of belonging that the students and professors share."

Wheaton has a campus bar, the Loft, where students can get burgers, pizza, and alcohol "if you're over 21 or have an ID that says you are." Wheaton's 11 theme houses also throw popular parties. The Lyon's Den is the campus coffee shop, and serves as a popular hangout and a more laid back alternative to the Loft. Though many social events seem to revolve around alcohol, students report not feeling much pressure either way. The administration is fairly lax on students who do drink, and Wheaties are very accepting of students who don't.

Endless Food, and Not Just Wheaties

Most students have good things to say about Wheaton's dining system. They have unlimited access to the two dining hall, one of which stays open until midnight. Pizza and ice cream seem to be available at all times, though there are more nutritious, family style options available as well. Unlimited access makes some students grow weary of the selection. "I like the food, but sometimes I get tired of it," said one girl. When this happens, students head to the nearby town of Mansfield to eat at chains like Subway.

The campus is pretty, secluded, and very Ivy League-esque with ivy-covered brick and a quaint pond that surrounds the Chase Dining Hall. The campus is not very big, which only adds to the community atmosphere and also simply helps Wheaties easily get where they need to go. Students like their dorms when there are a proper number of people living in them. Some freshmen find themselves in forced triples on Lower Campus. Upperclassmen, on the other hand, often live on Upper Campus in newly renovated dorms that "are like hotels," said one envious freshman.

Wheaton students are overwhelmingly very pleased with their college. "I know that this might seem pretty lame, but Wheaton really would not function in the same way without the common bond and sense of belonging that the students and professors share," said one Wheatie. The combination of Wheaton's strong sense of community, challenging, but manageable academics, and prime location make it a great place to spend four years.—*Keneisha Sinclair*

FYI

If you come to Wheaton, you'd better bring "rain boots and a DVD player because there's no cable."
What is the typical weekend schedule? "Napping after last class on Friday, trips to Boston and Providence, dances at the Theme Houses and concerts at the Loft, playing in or going to see a game, and lots of homework on Sunday."
If I could change one thing about Wheaton, I'd "make Norton more exciting."
Three things every student at Wheaton should do before graduating are "jump in the pond, study abroad or do a college exchange, and get really involved in a Wheaton extracurricular activity."

Williams College

Address: Williams, 33 Stetson Ct., Williamstown, MA 01267
Phone: 413-597-2211
E-mail Address: admission@williams.edu
Web site URL: www.williams.edu
Year Founded: 1793
Private or Public: private
Religious affiliation: none
Location: rural
Regular Application Deadline: 1-Jan
Number of Applicants: 6,002
Percent Accepted: 18%
Percent Accepted who enroll: 48%
Number Entering: 540
Number of Transfers Accepted each Year: 6-Mar
Mean SAT: NA
Mean ACT: NA
Middle 50% SAT range: V: 660–760, M:665–760

Middle 50% ACT range: 29–33
Early admission program (EA/ ED/ NA): ED
ED or EA Acceptance Rate: 40%
Full time Undergraduate enrollment: 2,100
Total enrollment: 2,150
Percent Male: 48%
Percent Female: 52%
Total Percent Minority: 29%
Percent African-American: 10%
Percent Asian/Pacific Islander: 10%
Percent Hispanic: 8%
Percent Native-American: 1%
Percent Other: 0%
Percent in-state / out of state: 10%/90%
Percent from Public HS: NA

Retention Rate: 98%
Graduation Rate: 96%
Percent in On-campus housing: 97%
Percent affiliated with Greek system: 0%
Percent Varsity or Club Athletes: 55%
Number of official organized extracurricular organizations: 150+
3 Most popular majors: Psychology, English, Economics
Student/Faculty ratio: 8:01
Tuition and Fees: $31,760.00
Cost for Room and Board: $8,550.00
Percent receiving Financial aid, first-year: 49%

O n the first Friday morning in October, Williams students celebrate "Mountain Day." Bells ring to cancel class, and Ephs (named for school founder Colonel Ephraim Williams) hike up nearby Mt. Greylock to drink hot chocolate, sing songs, and enjoy the gorgeous view. Situated in the Berkshire Mountains in the corner of Massachusetts, Williams boasts a "close-knit" community of fewer than 2,000 students and "a really good environment to gain an education—very peaceful."

All in a Hard Day's Work

While the surroundings may be peaceful, the education at Williams is rigorous. According to one senior, "there's definitely a consensus on campus that the amount of work is greater than friends have at other institutions—even Ivy League schools." One student attributed this to "the pain of having more attention. I think that it can be really tough, just because so many of the courses are small—if there's a lot of reading for a class with four people, it's going to be pretty obvious that you didn't do it."

The flip side of such small classes is an education that is extremely personal. "You're not a number in a class of 500," said one senior. "You're a person with a personality; the professor knows who you are." Professors teach all classes and labs at Williams and often invite students over for dinner or coffee. They also encourage collaboration "ad nauseum," making for an environment that is "not at all cutthroat or competitive."

The intimate classroom environment is epitomized by Williams' unique tutorial system. Starting spring semester freshman year, students can choose to take one tutorial course per semester, where two to three students meet with a professor to present and debate their weekly papers (or, in math and science tutorials, review problem sets). Despite the heavy workload, students describe tutorials as "really good, awesome—an amazing experience."

Students are also pleased with Williams' 4-1-4 schedule: four-month fall and spring semesters, with a one-month Winter Study period in between. During Winter Study, students choose from a vast array of unusual classes such as "Lego Mindstorms Robotics" and "Victorian Monsters," or submit their own proposal for a Winter Study project. Freshmen are required to stay on campus, but many upperclassmen take travel classes as varied as working at Nicaraguan eye care clinics or investigating traditional culture in Bali. Winter Study also features the Free University program, which lets students teach and take non-credit mini courses including origami, bartending, and Rubik's Cube. Because students take only one class, "there's lots of time to do other stuff—recreation, parties, skiing."

Williams requires students to take three courses in each of three divisions: Languages and the Arts, Social Studies, and Science and Mathematics. Students must also take one course relating to Peoples and Cultures, one involving Quantitative Reasoning, and two classified as Writing Intensive. In addition, students must complete four quarters of physical education, which many fulfill by playing sports at some level, while others take courses ranging from Badminton to Yoga. Generally, students "don't have a problem" fulfilling these requirements.

> "You're not a number in a class of 500. You're a person with a personality; the professor knows who you are."

Popular majors include English, psychology, economics, history, biology, and art. In particular, the art history department at Williams is "world-renowned," featuring several art museums a short walk from campus and one of Williams' two graduate programs (the other is in development economics). Even non-art majors agree that art history lectures are "just unbelievable." Despite Williams' strength in the liberal arts, science majors do benefit from "a plethora of opportunities to do research as early as freshman year."

Williams students can also opt to study abroad, or they may choose Williams in New York or Williams-Mystic Program for maritime studies in Mystic, Connecticut, two programs which combine varied fieldwork with academic coursework in a new location.

Williams has a lot to offer academically, and students are eager to rise to the occasion. As one high school valedictorian put it, "every single person I meet here I feel is very smart—in different ways, but all capable of having a very intelligent conversation—not just in the super-nerdy sense."

Ephs of All Breeds

"It's hard to group people at Williams," said one junior. "There's no one stereotype that fits everyone." The campus is "quite diverse" economically and geographically, and ethnic diversity is increasing. In terms of style, "Williams kids just throw on whatever they have," reported one student, though another claimed that "preppy kids are quite visible, though by no means the majority."

Despite their differences, students share one characteristic: friendliness. "The campus has a really friendly feel," marveled a freshman. "If you're walking around, there's going to be someone smiling at you and saying hello."

Ephs are involved in a wide range of activities outside the classroom. "The extracurricular involvement is unparalleled," said one student. "It continues to amaze me how people are able to juggle school with all their other activities. It really enables and encourages you to do a lot." About 40 percent of students play intercollegiate sports, and Williams has ranked as the top Division III school for the past seven years. Intramurals are also "very big, though you don't have to be that athletic to play in them." All students can also benefit from the school's top-notch pool, field, track, squash courts, and golf course, but the weight room "is mediocre—it has what you need, but could definitely be upgraded."

Even non-athletes enjoy attending games, especially those against rival Amherst. As one student emphasized, "Physical activity is very popular at Williams—whether playing broomball with your entry freshman year or playing a sport—but you don't have to be an athlete to love Williams. The strength of other extracurriculars is enough that if sports is not your interest, you shouldn't feel that Williams isn't the place for you."

Popular activities include the student newspaper, a capella groups, and Cap and Bells—the oldest student theater company in the nation, which enjoys a recently-opened theater and dance center. Also big is the Williams Outing Club, which organizes and rents equipment for hiking, kayaking, rock climbing, and winter sports. More offbeat groups include the Chocolate Lovers Association, Waffle Club, and Origami Club. Although there "isn't much political back-and-forth," students remain highly aware of current events and are "very proactive in helping out," rallying together to raise money and serve the community in times of need. Additionally, campus jobs—whether tour guiding, working in the admissions office, or working at the library—are not uncommon.

Living and Chilling on Campus

Overall, housing at Williams receives pretty high marks. Freshmen live on either Frosh Quad or the Berkshire Quad, and are divided into groups of 25 called "entries." Students in an entry live in the same building, along with two Junior Advisors (JAs), who organize events like weekly study breaks and trips to New York. JAs are generally well-liked, and exist to make sure their entries have fun and stay safe, not to police students' behavior.

"I really like the entry system," raved one freshman. "From the beginning, just to have 20 people to be able to go to dinner with or sit around your common room with put me at ease." Almost 50 percent of freshmen get singles, and upperclassmen, who pick housing in groups of up to four, "have the option of a double, but are pretty much guaranteed a single."

In the fall of 2006, Williams initiated a "cluster house" system, in which students are affiliated with a cluster of dorms in an effort to foster a sense of attachment similar to that provided by residential houses at other universities. The vast majority of students live on campus, though up to 100 seniors may live off-campus or in Williams-owned "co-op" housing.

With four dining halls to choose from, students enjoy a wide variety of food, which they describe as "really good." That's important, because "going into town involves walking across the street and walking down Spring Street—a quaint little street with a few shops, restaurants, a bar, and a bank," leaving students with few options beyond the dining halls. As one student added, "If you want a bar scene, if you want to go do cultural things in New York City, Williams is not for you. You have to acknowledge that you're choosing a school on the outskirts of rural Massachusetts, not in a big city."

The lack of nightlife in Williamstown "promotes more hanging out with your friends and socializing." Since there are no frats, students choose from parties in dorm rooms or off-campus houses, known for throwing "your typical college party with kegs, people drinking and playing beer pong." Though "alcohol is readily available at every party, it's never uncomfortable—nobody imposes or expects you to drink." All Campus Entertainment (ACE) also holds many well attended theme parties, as well as events like homecoming, Winter Carnival and Spring Fling (which recently featured Wyclef Jean). ACE even holds a weekly "Stress-Busters" event, where students can get free massages.

Cars are unnecessary for getting around, and Williams offers a shuttle on the weekends, enabling students to visit a shopping mall, supermarket, or even Wal-Mart. Getting to the airport, New York City, or Boston usually involves catching a ride with friends, but Williams also provides shuttle buses near the end of the semester or holidays.

Students applaud the college's effort to bring the outside world to campus. "Honestly, the three years I've been here I've gone to Boston once and NYC once," said a junior. "Williams always tries to have people from outside come to campus—speakers, entertainment, that kind of stuff. There's always something to do here."—*Sameer Jain*

FYI
If you come to Williams, you'd better bring "a warm jacket and a dislike for Amherst."
What's the typical weekend schedule? "Watch or play in a sporting event, party, and then work."
If I could change one thing about Williams, I'd "speed up construction on the new student center so it opens before 2007. The temporary student center, Goodrich Hall, isn't doing its job very well."
The three things every student at Williams should do before graduating are "hike up a mountain," "take a tutorial," and "either take or audit Art History 101 and 102."

Worcester Polytechnic Institute

Address: Worcester Polytechnic Institute, 100 Institute Road, Worcester, MA 01609
Phone: 508-831-5286
E-mail Address: admissions@wpi.edu
Web site URL: www.wpi.edu
Year Founded: 1865
Private or Public: private
Religious affiliation: none
Location: suburban
Regular Application Deadline: Feb. 1
Number of Applicants: 4,931
Percent Accepted: 66%
Percent Accepted who enroll: 24%
Number Entering: 777
Number of Transfers Accepted each Year: 99
Mean SAT: 1,888
Mean ACT: 27

Middle 50% SAT range: 1,750–2,030
Middle 50% ACT range: 25–30
Early admission program (EA/ ED/ NA): EA
ED or EA Acceptance Rate: 74%
Full time Undergraduate enrollment: 2,816
Total enrollment: 3,903
Percent Male: 74%
Percent Female: 26%
Total Percent Minority: 14%
Percent African-American: 2%
Percent Asian/Pacific Islander: 6%
Percent Hispanic: 4%
Percent Native-American: 0%
Percent Other: 2%
Percent in-state / out of state: 50%/50%

Percent from Public HS: 66%
Retention Rate: 90%
Graduation Rate: 75%
Percent in On-campus housing: 59%
Percent affiliated with Greek system: 30%
Percent Varsity or Club Athletes: 39%
Number of official organized extracurricular organizations: 200
3 Most popular majors: Mechanical Engineering, Electrical & Computer Engineering, Computer Science
Student/Faculty ratio: 13:01
Tuition and Fees: $33,318.00
Cost for Room and Board: $9,960.00
Percent receiving Financial aid, first-year: 86%

Worcester Polytechnic Institute may be the third oldest engineering college in the country, but students are always amazed at how up-to-date it seems. Set in Worcester, Massachusetts, WPI, as it is universally called, manages to combine the latest in engineering and technology with the area's best college social life.

Engineering as Life

WPI is on the quarter system, which means the academic year is divided into four seven-week terms. Students usually take three or four classes per term, most of them meeting at least four times per week. "This is perfectly suited for engineering courses," says one student, noting how the unique academic plan allows one to heavily concentrate on one subject area. Advisors and administrators warn, however, that students must be organized and ready for the fast pace, because "some professors hand out midterm exams after only three weeks." Students also complain that the quarter system, while ideal for engineering classes, is not suited for humanities and high-level math classes. "I had to read nine Shakespeare plays in six weeks," reported one student, a mechanical engineering major.

The quarter system also enables students to quickly make strong academic relationships with faculty and other students. In fact, WPI was ranked #1 by the National Survey of Student Engagement for student/faculty interaction. "Even when I was in larger classes, like the general chem and physics classes, I could still get to know the professors on a personal basis," reports one student. WPI professors are their own breed, and although sometimes zany, they love nothing more than making someone as interesting in their field of study as they are. One student simply states that "they are there to teach their students, and make that their entire effort as professors." Students who stop by to ask a simple question during office hours find themselves leaving hours later, in love with topics they had never even considered. Students almost always have stories about just how accessible the professors are; one student reports sending an email at 3:00 AM and getting a reply minutes later.

Life in the Projects

Close student/faculty relationships are almost required for a WPI degree because every student must complete three independent projects. The Interactive Qualifying Project (IQP) forces students to connect technology to everyday life. The projects take students from the labs of WPI to London, Thailand, Namibia or Puerto Rico, along with many more, with the Global Perspectives Program, a competitive program involving a third of WPI students. The best IQP projects awards get the President's Award, in which the student and the faculty advisor are commended for superb research and presentation. Past award winners include "The Development of an Irrigation System in the Village Of Nong Din Dam" and "Development of Communal Washing Facilities for the Northwest Settlements of Windhoek, Namibia."

A more work-intensive project is the Major Qualifying Project (MQP), a research project done with the standards and scope of professional scientists and engineers. Students receive full access to WPI facilities and also work in industrial laboratories, through an innovative program conducted by WPI Projects & Registrar's Office. Students typically work within one department, "so it is basically impossible not to know the entire department." Although students decide how much they work on their own projects, in almost every case these projects take hundreds, if not thousands of hours. Like the IQP, the MQP also offers students the opportunity to complete their work in places like Budapest or on Wall Street. Most students, however, complete their project on or around campus. As this project is the hallmark achievement of a WPI student, the school spares almost nothing in helping them find whatever resources they need.

The Humanities Sufficiency Project requires students to take five courses in one area of the humanities. Although WPI offers courses in English, history, philosophy, and foreign languages, to name a few, the school and faculty recognize that no one goes to WPI to studies humanities. Students can also complete this project abroad, with a specially designed program in London. WPI is lacking in comparison to similarly sized schools in the breadth and depth of its humanities courses, especially in foreign languages where it offers only Spanish and German.

Students can take courses at other schools within the Worcester-based Consortium, including at liberal-arts based schools like Holy Cross and Clark University, but most students do not even consider this prospect. All 13 other schools in the Consortium are not on the quarter-system and have schedules that do not fit WPI's. "I don't think I know anyone who has ever taken a course at another school," reports a student. WPI students often do, however, access materials at other colleges' libraries, and in some cases, the books are brought directly to WPI.

Engineering is one of the most sought after fields in education, and few places teach engineering better than WPI. The Career Fair usually held in the fall, hosts dozens of firms, each searching for qualified engineers. Although students in some fields, such as mathematics and biology, find it necessary to go on to grad school, students generally have no problem finding jobs. WPI offers a fully staffed Career Development Center, and was recently ranked ninth by the *Princeton Review* in "best career prospects." WPI holds long term relationships with many companies, including BOSE and Grace. In the winter of 2007, WPI a Biomedical and Life Sciences Building in Gateway Park three blocks from the main campus, which will also house local entrepreneurs and small start-up companies.

The Fraternal Calling

Worcester, Massachusetts may not be perceived as the typical college town, but why not? There are, after all, 13 colleges in and around Worcester, with over 30,000 students. Although the other schools do have party scenes, WPI is the only school in Worcester with fraternities and sororities. WPI has 11 fraternities and 2 sororities, and both of these numbers are set to increase. WPI social life revolves around the Greek system, and there are parties every weekend during the school year, and even some during the summer, reflecting many WPI students' willingness to stay in Worcester. Students from all around Worcester attend the WPI parties, especially from nearby Becker and Assumption. Although the male-female ratio at WPI hovers around 3:1, there are often more girls than guys at WPI parties.

The WPI and Worcester police generally leave campus partiers alone. "The police know that they have other things in Worcester to worry about," said one self-described partier. Although Worcester, a city of 170,000, has its fair share of crime, the area around the WPI campus is generally safe. A large fire in a fraternity in August 2005 left no students hurt, but almost 20 without a place to live. Students might want to be wary of the police's over-aggressiveness in handing out parking tickets—commuting students joke about the sheer number of parking tickets they receive on a regular basis.

Although Worcester is the third largest city in New England, it is fairly spread out. WPI is not within walking distance of a movie theater, mall, or any shopping center except for a large, 24-hour supermarket. Although WPI brags about Highland Street., it only has a few restaurants, one café, and two convenience stores. Most WPI upperclassmen (and many underclassmen) have cars, which only contributes to a very dire parking situation on Worcester's narrow streets. In the winter, "it's impossible even to find an *illegal* parking space," reported one student.

WPI's rising number of applications in recent years, especially among women, has not been without problems. For the last few years, WPI has been forced to cram students into already-overcrowded dorms because of a higher than expected student yield. "Forced triples" have become standard in some dorms. Due to the lack of space, and because of Worcester's relatively cheap housing (for urban New England, at least), most students live off-campus as upperclassmen.

WPI offers dozens of sports on intramural, club, and varsity levels (NCAA Div. III), competing throughout New England. It also offers numerous clubs, honor societies, and service organizations serving Worcester and beyond. Science and engineering clubs, such as FIRST Robotics, are especially popular. Music groups also are renowned, and often travel to locations such as Puerto Rico and Europe for tours. Although humanities organizations tend to have low turnout, there is no difficulty, for example, in writing as much as one wants about almost any topic in *Tech News*, the school newspaper. "To put it kindly, some of the articles are interesting," says one student. The university also offers a radio station, writing center, and even a nuclear reactor (with intensive faculty cooperation) for use by students and faculty.

Many students report that WPI offers some of the best food in the country. "For a small college, the options are endless: pizza, burgers, wraps, grill food, a la carte, Burger King, Dunkin Donuts and multiple entrees— every day!" commented one visitor. Although most students live off-campus, many continue to eat at WPI, "because of the quality of the food."

> "A prospective student really needs to get a good understanding of the term system also, because it is quite different from other schools."

WPI presents itself as a school with many old traditions, including the competition between classes to find Gompei, a bronze goat head. According to custom, the class that ends up in possession of Gompei at the end of spring gets its year engraved onto the figure. But according to one student, "[Not] that many students really are interested in WPI traditions like that." One alumnus even reported that "the admissions tours are essentially the same as when I applied, and I started here in 1968." WPI students are much more intent on keeping up with the modern age—like boasting one of the country's "Top 100 Most Wired Campuses," according to Yahoo.

Thinking of Applying?

Students recommend that interested applicants attend classes for at least one day at WPI, as well as spend a night on campus. Every student has a favorite professor, so take the opportunity to meet one of them. High school students are no oddity at WPI, because the university hosts many camps and programs. In the only program of its kind in the state of Massachusetts, the public high school Massachusetts Academy of Math and Science, located three blocks from WPI's campus, sends its entire senior class to take all of their senior year classes at the university. In addition to sampling the food and the social life, one student said, "a prospective student really needs to get a good understanding of the term system also, because it is quite different from other schools." If you are prepared to work hard and devote yourself to science, math, and engineering, WPI is a perfect place to prosper.—*Eric Purington*

FYI

If you come to WPI, you'd better bring "a graphing calculator and laptop suitable for computer programming."

What is the typical weekend schedule? "Going to frat and apartment parties on Friday, relaxing on Saturday with some easy problem sets, partying harder on Saturday, and finishing up those problem sets on Sunday."

If I could change one thing about WPI, I'd "add more women."

Three things every student at WPI should do before graduating are "paint the rocks at Institute Park the color of your club or fraternity, eat at all the restaurants on Highland St. after 1 a.m., and play the WPI game, which entails driving around, asking if people go to WPI, and then partying with them."

Michigan

Address: Albion, 611
E. Porter, Albion, MI 49224
Phone: 800-858-6770
E-mail Address:
admissions@albion.edu
Web site URL:
http://www.albion.edu
Year Founded: 1835
Private or Public: private
Religious affiliation:
Methodist
Location: suburban
**Regular Application
Deadline:** 2-Mar
Number of Applicants: 1,972
Percent Accepted: 82%
**Percent Accepted who
enroll:** 36%
Number Entering: 480
**Number of Transfers
Accepted each Year:** 48
Mean SAT: 1,180
Mean ACT: 25

Middle 50% SAT range:
1,060–1,315 (writing not
included)
Middle 50% ACT range:
22–27
**Early admission program
(EA/ ED/ NA):** EA
ED or EA Acceptance Rate:
NA
**Full time Undergraduate
enrollment:** 1,979
Total enrollment: 1,979
Percent Male: 44%
Percent Female: 56%
Total Percent Minority: 10%
Percent African-American:
4%
**Percent Asian/Pacific
Islander:** 3%
Percent Hispanic: 1%
Percent Native-American:
1%
Percent Other: 3%
**Percent in-state / out of
state:** 90%/10%

**Percent from Public
HS:** 75%
Retention Rate: 86%
Graduation Rate: 72%
**Percent in On-campus
housing:** 88%
**Percent affiliated with
Greek system:** 32%
**Percent Varsity or Club
Athletes:** NA
**Number of official
organized extracurricular
organizations:** 122
3 Most popular majors:
Social Sciences,
Psychology, Biology
Student/Faculty ratio:
13:01
Tuition and Fees:
$26,122.00
Cost for Room and Board:
$7,408.00
**Percent receiving
Financial aid, first-year:**
95%

Envision approximately 2,000 students crammed into beautiful, but overpopulated, Gothic buildings. Everything is surrounded by large trees. This is Albion College, set within the small city of Albion, Michigan. With its newly renovated science complex, a comprehensive First-year Experience program, and a recurring place on *U.S. News & World Report*'s list of the 40 "Best Value" colleges, this midwestern school provides students a strong liberal arts education with all the benefits of a small college.

No Nonsense Academics

One student boldly remarked, "Albion is a no nonsense school." Most students stick to standard majors such as economics, psychology, pre-med and chemistry. The majority of the atypical classes are religious, one of the more popular of which is called "Death and Dying." The classes are also competitive, in particular the math and science classes—to do well in physical or organic chemistry, you should expect at least 25 hours of studying a week.

In the Albion system, you need 32 credits to graduate, including major and more general liberal arts requirements. Instead of simply creating distributional requirements, each class at Albion is assigned a "mode" and a "category." "Modes"—or the approach to the subject—include Artistic Creation and Analysis, Historical and Cultural Analysis and Textual Analysis. "Categories"—or the actual subject the class falls under—include Environmental Studies, Gender Studies, and Global Studies. In addition, all freshmen participate in the First-Year Experience, designed to ease students' academic and social transition into college. The program includes Orientation, Common Reading Experience, as well as a set of seminars on topics ranging from "Art in the Environment" to "Vietnam: Then and Now."

Albion also has a few more specific academic programs. One of the best known programs at Albion, the Carl A. Gerstacker Institute for Professional Management, is an honors business program which involves 10 semesters in four years—seven semesters of on-campus study, one summer term after sophomore year, and two internships during the fall term of junior year and the summer after junior year. Many choices for these internships are located in Europe. For students interested in political science, education, law, or community service, Albion also offers the Gerald R. Ford Institute for Public Policy and Service. Founded by the former president, the Institute allows students to pursue a major of their choice while taking classes in fields such as ethics, public policy, and government.

Fight for Your Right to Party

Historically, Albion has been known for a large party scene. But recently Albion officials have been trying to crack down on the party scene in the college, doling out $500 fines to underage drinkers. There have been problems of overdrinking in the past mainly because a small group of students overdo it and, as one Albion student said, "screwed it up for the rest of us." With its isolated location, life at Albion can get monotonous, leading to occasional problems with drug use. Sometimes, though, the isolation can pay off: During the annual "Senior Week" event at the end of the year, Albion students compete in a drinking Olympics in a barn out of town—not your typical end-of-year venue.

> **"Albion is a no nonsense school."**

Other than the occasional novel event, one of the drawbacks of the remote campus is that many students have a difficult time finding interesting activities. But with the city of Jackson nearby and Ann Arbor less than an hour away, there are plenty of options for the many students who decide to keep cars on campus.

Fraternity parties epitomize the social scene at Albion. Since the student population is generally friendly and outgoing, the frat scene is more open than at other schools, including everyone and allowing everyone at the parties. However, the Greek life at Albion has recently felt the impact of the crackdown on parties, with some students and officials citing the fraternities and sororities as a major source of drinking. But other students are reluctant to call for the elimination of fraternities because many age-old traditions unique to Albion are connected to the Greek system. At least one student expressed a fear about the effect on social life in general, saying that the party scene revolves around the fraternity houses.

Living in Style

Living arrangements are standard for all four years at Albion, with most students living in the dormitories the whole time. The dorm rooms are assigned by seniority, though juniors and seniors sometimes move off campus into neighboring apartments. Freshmen are housed in either Wesley Hall or Seaton Hall; RAs live in all dormitories, and alcohol is prohibited to those who are underage. It just goes by chance, however, how strict an RA will be—some supervisors have been known to be lax about the rules.

The dorms are definitely not the only buildings that will catch your eye at Albion. The multimillion-dollar science complex, newly finished in 2006, is an impressive addition to the campus. Another more noticeable feature of Albion is the quad—located between all the class buildings, the quad is a great place to hang around during the warmer months. The Nature Center is also worth noting for its beautiful landscape; thought to be the most beautiful spot on campus by many of the students, it is an "unspoiled habitat where anything can be seen."

The dining halls are famed for their relatively good cuisine and easy-to-deal-with meal plans allowing students to pick how many meals they want per week. But be warned that you will have to maintain regular eating patterns, with limited hours. Since the school is relatively small, the only times the dining halls stay open late is during finals. Also, one unique rule is that off-campus residents are not allowed in the dining halls, but with many good restaurants in the town, students have other options when they want to eat out. However when students do venture off campus, they usually try to be back before dark since the surrounding area is not particularly safe.

Extra Awesome Extracurricular

Albion College hosts extracurricular fun for everyone in all sorts of forms. Although it is a Division III school, sports are very popular—one student estimated that "half of the campus plays a sport." Basketball and football are the most popular spectator events, but students are known for being fickle fans: at times, they rally in full force for Albion, while other times they skip homecoming games entirely to watch other local rivalries such as the University of Michigan versus Michigan State football game. Intramural sports, including soccer, basketball, volleyball, dodgeball, hockey, and tennis, are a must at this school. The IM fields are given great care and the games are known to get very competitive.

There are also some non-athletic clubs that are very popular. The most recognized are Break the Silence (the Gay and Lesbian Awareness Group) and the Medieval Club, which puts on mock sword fights and archery competitions.

Overall, Albion is a small school filled with friendly students. Despite the school's isolation, the campus is a beautiful and safe place where students easily become very personal with their professors and become well prepared for life outside of college. Ultimately, Albion is a great place for students who want to have fun but at the same time are willing to work hard.—*Benjamin Dzialo*

FYI

If you come to Albion, you'd better bring "a friendly, outgoing attitude."

What's the typical weekend schedule? "Friday: No class, or class finishes early. Workout, nap, or do nothing with your friends until you start drinking which will last all night (or you study). Saturday: Maybe get some work done, typically don't do anything; partying at night. Sunday: Cram day. Wake up late, study all day if need be."

If I could change one thing about Albion, I'd "fix the town—people wouldn't drink so much if the town wasn't falling apart, and there was more to do."

Three things every student at Albion should do before graduating are "attend a talk by at least one of the great speakers Albion brings in, walk in the Whitehouse Nature Center in the winter, and talk with a professor outside of class."

Alma College

Address: Alma, 614 W. Superior Street, Alma, MI 48801-1599
Phone: 800-321-2562
E-mail Address: admissions@alma.edu
Web site URL: http://www.alma.edu
Year Founded: 1886
Private or Public: private
Religious affiliation: Presbyterian
Location: rural
Regular Application Deadline: Rolling
Number of Applicants: 1,878
Percent Accepted: 70%
Percent Accepted who enroll: 24%
Number Entering: 313
Number of Transfers Accepted each Year: 51
Mean SAT: NA
Mean ACT: 24

Middle 50% SAT range: 1,480–1,830
Middle 50% ACT range: 21–26
Early admission program (EA/ ED/ NA): NA
ED or EA Acceptance Rate: NA
Full time Undergraduate enrollment: 1,215
Total enrollment: 1,215
Percent Male: 45%
Percent Female: 55%
Total Percent Minority: 7%
Percent African-American: 1%
Percent Asian/Pacific Islander: 1%
Percent Hispanic: 2%
Percent Native-American: 1%
Percent Other: 2%
Percent in-state / out of state: 96%/4%
Percent from Public HS: 90%

Retention Rate: 80%
Graduation Rate: 70%
Percent in On-campus housing: 86%
Percent affiliated with Greek system: 17%/30%
Percent Varsity or Club Athletes: NA
Number of official organized extracurricular organizations: 93
3 Most popular majors: Business Administration/Management, Education, General, Kinesiology and Exercise Science
Student/Faculty ratio: 12:01
Tuition and Fees: $22,380.00
Cost for Room and Board: $7,774.00
Percent receiving Financial aid, first-year: 78%

The comfortable campus of Alma College can feel isolated at times, but students report that the remote location often helps them more fully assimilate into "the college experience." Characterized by its small size and convivial atmosphere, Alma provides students with the opportunity to receive a well-rounded education and prepares them to venture into the professional world.

A Liberal Arts Tradition

One Alma student describes her school's philosophy as "a little bit of everything;" in keeping with the liberal arts philosophy, there are significant general education requirements needed to complete a bachelor's degree. Students must pass composition, math, and foreign language classes, as well as distribution requirements including humanities, literature, history, social, natural, and physical sciences, the arts, and more. Though one student said "It is a little hard to fit [all the requirements] in," most agree that they are necessary components of a college education.

To graduate with a bachelor's degree, students are required to take a total of 136 credits. They also must complete two spring terms of enrollment. The spring term is a month from April to May when students are able to take classes in more creative and hands-on areas. One of these courses must be an "S" course, which draws on an international, interdisciplinary perspective and often includes travel.

The most popular majors at Alma are also some of its strongest, including business administration, biology, and those in the health professions. All of these prepare students very well for graduate school in medicine or law, or for professional work right out of college, and are consequently accompanied by a significant amount of homework. The curricular options for fine and performing arts are very strong, especially for a school of Alma's size. Students appreciate the training though—as one said of the classes, "They are very challenging, but in a good way." Though work is difficult, they also report a low level of competition, and believe that the on-campus atmosphere is generally conducive to doing well.

Students appreciate that the small size of their school keeps class size down and allows for a lot more interaction with their professors, who are highly attentive and devoted to teaching. One student said she appreciated simply "being able to go see your professor and having them know who you are." Several professors also write their own textbooks, and students agree that because of the intimate atmosphere, science demonstrations are especially "cool." One biology professor routinely "throws balls representing molecules around the room to illustrate a point." A town the size of Alma also means that professors make up a large proportion of the population. "My professor for calculus, Nyman, is the mayor of Alma," said one student, "and he cracks a lot of jokes—while still getting enough information through to my brain that it hurts after class."

Inventive Activities

Although the small size of both the college and the surrounding town leaves students without a huge number of options for the weekends, most agree that those who are inventive will find plenty to occupy them. The student body mixes and freely associates amongst itself. With approximately 1,300 students, in general it is "super easy to meet people—everyone is very friendly. Groups form but they are always open to new people." Although many students join fraternities or sororities, students agree that these "don't control social life," and the parties are attended by a variety of different people. However, the frats are limited by the administration to only one alcoholic beverage party per month, and kegs are officially barred from the campus. The President is actively trying to abolish the Greek system, but one student said that "if that ever happened, I think a lot of people would leave Alma, because of the fact that there would then be NOTHING to do." Students note that in general there is a lot of hooking up, but a lack of outing destinations makes dating somewhat rarer.

In the rest of their free time, Alma students can see live shows at the Heritage Center, go shopping, and check out the restaurants in Mt. Pleasant (15 minutes away). Some students also choose to attend larger parties at nearby Central Michigan and Michigan State University. Students work out and play sports at the newly refurbished recreation center. And as one student noted, "Going to Wal-Mart is always an option."

Extracurricular groups and clubs also inspire devotion among the students, and many students come to be identified with the things they do outside of class. One student estimates that she spends 15 hours a week with her dance company. Musical and dramatic groups are equally rigorous, and students extol the "consistently fabulous" performances. The choirs at Alma are particularly popular, with nearly 15% of the student body participating in the Women's Glee Club, the College Chorale, or the Alma Choir. Community service is a common activity as well. Some students work on-campus jobs, but a few work in the surrounding community.

The Alma Scots' sports teams are strong for a small school, although not usually a central part of student life. The volleyball team is especially good, and recently won a state championship. Football, soccer, and golf also fare well, and games are "decently attended." Many students take full advantage of the recreation center, and both varsity and non-varsity athletes play on the "tons" of intramural sports teams.

Living Cozily

Alma's pleasant brick campus makes its students feel "cozy." Although the buildings are not particularly unique architecturally, they are well maintained and the facilities are good. The campus' central location means that students often take full advantage of its proximity to neighboring cities and other schools. However, one student answers the question of whether there are enough things to do nearby the campus with a resounding "NO!"

Many students live in the dorms all four years—only upperclassmen may move off campus, and their ability to do so is regulated by a lottery system. Some dorms are co-ed, some are not—"however you want it to be," said one student—and though "the underclassmen dorms are kind of old, that's not to say they're not spacious." Freshmen have residential advisors, who are "pretty good about handling things." Some students opt to live in themed dorms (athletic, band, etc.) and there is a service house, as well as Greek housing.

The dining options are cited as adequate, though some students have issues with the fact that they have to apply to different meal plans and can end up being denied. However, there are opportunities throughout the day for unused meal credits to be reclaimed. Vegetarian options are plentiful and the dining halls are clean and well-supplied. Some seating arrangements are fairly established but Alma's amiable nature means that no tensions result from this stability. As one student described, "Sororities and athletic teams usually sit in the same spot, but they'd gladly move if you were there—or sit with you." For dates, students often go to restaurants in Mt. Pleasant, followed by bowling or ice skating.

> **"[It's] the perfect place for me. I didn't expect how much I'd not miss home."**

Alma tends to attract a vast majority of its students from Michigan, many from the suburbs of Detroit or Grand Rapids. Although many fit the bill of "the general stereotype of a middle-class white kid," this doesn't mean that everyone brings the same viewpoint. As one student said, "Though Alma isn't very culturally diverse, it is very diverse in personality." Students also believe that "there is a lot of mixing" among different social groups, and social marginalization or isolation is rare. One student noted, "[It's] super easy to meet people, everyone is very friendly. Groups form but they are always welcoming towards new people."

Overall, Alma students are at school there because it offers what they want from college academics, as well as a social and congenial student body. One student said that it was "the perfect place for me. I didn't expect how much I'd not miss home." Isolated though it may be, Alma offers students the chance to live and participate fully in the collegiate environment, and to learn skills that directly enhance their futures.—*David Carpman*

FYI
If you come to Alma, you'd better bring "a car."
What is the typical weekend schedule? "Sleep until brunch at 11:30, rock climb, work, study, watch movies, play video games, party, and go to sleep around 2 a.m."
If I could change one thing about Alma, "I'd move it to a city where there are more things to do."
Three things every student at Alma should do before graduating are "go to Bar Night, go to a percussion performance, climb the rock wall."

Hope College

Address: Hope College, 69 E. 10th St., PO Box 9000, Holland, MI 49423

Phone: 616-395-7850

E-mail Address: admissions@hope.edu

Web site URL: www.hope.edu/admissions

Year Founded: 1847

Private or Public: private

Religious affiliation: Reformed Church in America

Location: small city

Regular Application Deadline: rolling

Number of Applicants: 2,665

Percent Accepted: 80%

Percent Accepted who enroll: 35%

Number Entering: 834

Number of Transfers Accepted each Year: 110–120

Mean SAT: NA

Mean ACT: NA

Middle 50% SAT range: 1,080–1,310

Middle 50% ACT range: 23–28

Early admission program (EA/ ED/ NA): NA

ED or EA Acceptance Rate: NA

Full time Undergraduate enrollment: 3,029

Total enrollment: 3,141

Percent Male: 40%

Percent Female: 60%

Total Percent Minority: 9%

Percent African-American: 2%

Percent Asian/Pacific Islander: 2%

Percent Hispanic: 2%

Percent Native-American: >1%

Percent Other: 2%

Percent in-state / out of state: 72%/28%

Percent from Public HS: 86%

Retention Rate: 80%

Graduation Rate: 72% (4 years)

Percent in On-campus housing: 80%

Percent affiliated with Greek system: 6% Fraternities, 15% sororities

Percent Varsity or Club Athletes: NA

Number of official organized extracurricular organizations: 67

3 Most popular majors: Management, Psychology, Political Science

Student/Faculty ratio: 13:01

Tuition and Fees: $22,570.00

Cost for Room and Board: $6,982.00

Percent receiving Financial aid, first-year: 75%

Students at Hope College come together for many reasons. In the bleachers and on the sidelines, they all cheer on their remarkably successful athletic teams. Walking across their pine tree-lined campus, they live up to their reputation of Midwestern friendliness by saying "hi" to everyone they meet. And in chapel on Sundays, many students at this Christian Reformed college come together to celebrate their common religious values. Located near the shores of Lake Michigan in the heart of pretty downtown Holland, Hope College provides its students with solid academic programs, the personal attention only possible at a small school, and a warm social atmosphere, all structured around a core of Christian values.

Common Values

Spirituality is important to students at Hope, and religion influences nearly every aspect of campus life to some degree. Still, students maintain that nonreligious students are not pressured to participate in religious activities, which are all optional. As one junior said, "At Hope you can be as strong or as loose in your faith as you want." One of the most popular religious events on campus is the Sunday night "singing-and-celebration" service called the "Gathering." Such a great number of students pack the chapel for the Gathering that all the seats fill up, and late-arrivers are left to sit in the aisles or stand in the back of the building. The Gathering is just one of the times when religion unites the student body. Groups of Hope students travel all over the world every spring break on mission trips; one junior who spent last spring break building homes for a deaf community in Jamaica described it as one of the best experiences of his life. A soccer player said his coach sometimes uses faith in his coaching style. Religion even makes its way into the classroom; according to one senior, "Some professors do incorporate [religion] in their classes." While non-religious students are definitely in the minority at Hope, they are not excluded from campus life. A non-religious student commented that most students come from a Christian background and are "open and not afraid to profess their opinions. However, they are usually not that overbearing."

Students say that the typical Hope student is Christian, usually conservative and often from Michigan or the greater Midwest. One student said she liked that Hope students are "generally well-rounded and geared toward future goals." The student body is predominantly white. However, Hope, in addition to its Dutch population, also has a substantial Hispanic segment. Attempts have been made to increase the school's diversity, and a senior said she was "surprised at how many students are from out of the state and even the country." However, a sophomore expressed frustration that because so many students have similar, religiously conservative backgrounds, they tend to "generate the same old boring views and stances on subjects." Despite this, he said that there are still a substantial number of "more open-minded" people on campus.

Hitting the Books

Students at Hope universally agree that the best parts of their academic experience are the close relationships they build with the professors, who teach all their classes. One sophomore praised how "available and flexible" they are to student needs. Professors at Hope frequently go to sporting events to cheer on their students, and often invite their classes to their homes at the end of the semester for dinner parties. Many students become so close with their professors that they keep in contact even after their classes are over.

Part of the reason students and teachers are able to form such close bonds centers on the small size of classes at Hope. The average class has 20 to 25 students in it. Many upper-level classes are even smaller, allowing students to get personal attention and sometimes even giving them the opportunity to get involved with their professor's research. One junior said he liked Hope's small classes because they gave him the confidence to "be more bold to ask questions" of the professor in front of the group. The small class size does cause some problems, however, since it often becomes difficult for students to get into popular classes that quickly fill up. Students in popular majors sometimes have difficulty getting into courses necessary for graduation and end up needing to either plead to the dean for class admission, or to stay on campus for a summer term in order to graduate on time.

Popular majors at Hope include biology and education, and both of these departments have excellent programs. Students majoring in education get to start doing fieldwork in local classrooms as early as their freshman year. One sophomore said that Hope "prides itself on its sciences," and the humanities majors are often less intense. Hope recently renovated its science buildings, and the premed program has a reputation for getting its students into selective medical schools. Biology is considered one of Hope's most challenging majors, as is religion. Students interested in studying religion benefit from the Western Theological Seminary—right next to Hope—and in fact, every year several students enroll in this seminary after graduation. A junior estimated that Hope students study about three hours a day; students in difficult majors put in a few more hours. Students who want a less intense academic experience typically major in communications, although there is also substantial interest in broadcast journalism, public relations and advertising. Academic requirements at Hope include taking several credits of religion, completing at least a 200-level foreign-language class, a class on cultural diversity and a class called "Health Dynamics," which one athlete said "is a joke. It's basically gym class, and even if you play a varsity sport, you still have to take it." Still, most students agree that the annoyance created by some of their distributional requirements and unsuccessful class registration is a small price to pay for the excellent education they receive at Hope.

Kicking Back

When they're not studying, students at Hope enjoy a wide range of social activities. Only a third to a half of the campus drinks, so while a more traditional "party scene" exists for those students who want it, non-drinkers have plenty of social options. The Student Activity Committee (SAC) sponsors $2 movie nights at Graves Hall, and brings in comedians, magicians and bands to give performances open to the student body. The campus itself is dry, so technically no alcohol is allowed in the dorms. One junior said that while RAs (resident advisers) can be "pretty strict" about this rule at times, people can generally get away with drinking in their dorms as long as everything stays quiet and hidden. A significant proportion of the student body is Greek, although there are few national frats or sororities on campus.

Most of the Greek organizations are branches of smaller, local fraternities. They often hold theme parties, but not all of these are open to the whole student body—many are open only to other Greeks. Parties are often also held in some of the off-campus houses, especially those where members of the soccer and football teams live. Upperclassmen who want to enjoy a beer in a slightly classier atmosphere favor the New Holland Brewery, especially on Wednesday "Stein Nights," when students who bring their own beer stein can get it filled up at a discounted price.

> **"The legend goes that you'll find your soul mate at Hope."**

Walking around campus on the average Saturday night, you'll probably see a lot of good-looking people. Hope students are an attractive bunch on the whole. As one student said, "Whenever my friends come to visit from other schools they always say how hot the girls here are." Since Hope students are over two-thirds female, this seems like pretty good odds for the guys. But Hope isn't a school for someone looking for a lot of random hookups; many students are involved in serious relationships. "The legend goes that you'll find your soul mate at Hope," said one junior in a committed relationship, and reportedly a lot of Hope students end up marrying others from their school. Students say that Hope is a friendly place. "You could go up to anyone and say hello," according to one student. Partly because of the school's small size, there aren't many cliques, and people tend to have a lot of friends of different ages.

Housing in Holland

Hope students typically live in dorms for their freshman and sophomore years. Students live in double rooms on single-sex hallways and share common bathrooms. "The dorms are overall well-kept and comfortable," said one sophomore, although all the buildings have different reputations. In addition to the coed buildings, there is one all-male dorm and three all-female dorms, including Dykstra, "where all the guys go to scope for women," according to one male student. Kollen Hall is the most social dorm; "It's the party dorm, the loudest and craziest," said one former resident. Voorhees Hall

houses "a lot of artsy types," while international students tend to cluster in Scott. By junior year, most Hope students move into the "cottages." These are small houses on the perimeter of campus where groups of about six students live; they are still considered "on-campus housing" and have RAs, but they have their own kitchens and living rooms. The cottages are "a fun alternative to big-school living," according to one upperclassman. Seniors often move off campus, either to houses or to apartments in downtown Holland. In total, there are 11 residence halls, 15 apartment buildings, and 72 cottages.

Hope's campus is small. "You can walk all the way around it in 15 minutes," a junior said. Most academic buildings are in the center of the pine-tree-filled campus, while the dorms and the cottages are around the perimeter. Many of the historic buildings are red-brick, while some of the newer buildings, like the recently constructed science center, are more modern. One senior raved that the campus is "so cute! Hope is big on preserving the old buildings it does have, but also on adding new buildings as the college expands."

Dining hall food is "pretty good" according to most students. Freshmen often eat in Phelps Hall, which supposedly has the worst food on campus; but upperclassmen enjoy eating the much tastier food in Cook Hall, which typically serves a choice of several entrees every night, including vegetarian options. When students get bored of the dining halls, downtown Holland has a variety of unique restaurants less than a five-minute walk from campus. Windmill's is a favorite for breakfast, and students also enjoy relaxing and studying in coffee shops such as Java Joe's (which has a stage where bands perform) and Lemonjello's (pronounced le-MON-jel-lo's by those in the know).

Sports and Spirit

Students leave campus and go into Holland for more than food and coffee, however. Faith-based community service is extremely popular at the school. One junior said there are "a ton of opportunities to work in church soup kitchens or tutor kids or anything like that." Many students also spend their free time playing intramural sports ranging from inner-tube water polo to Ultimate Frisbee. When the weather is warm, students make the short trip down to the shores of beautiful Lake Michigan to hang out on the beach. Hope's Division III varsity athletic teams have had excellent records in the past few years. Both men's and women's basketball and soccer teams are extremely competitive, and draw massive support both from students and from members of the community who come out to watch, as well.

The crowds are in large part due to the high level of school spirit at Hope. A combination of factors, including the small size of the student body and the shared core of Christian values, bind students closely to their school. "If I could do it all over again I would definitely, definitely choose Hope," one junior said. "It's been a place where I can get a great education while strengthening my faith. I've gotten to meet some really great people, and made friendships I think are going to last for a long time."— *Katherine Kirby Smith*

FYI

If you come to Hope College, you'd better bring "a Nalgene bottle—everybody has one here."

What's a typical weekend schedule? "Friday, hang out with friends or go to a house party at night; Saturday, sleep until noon, study, go see a sporting event, then do something social or go to another party; Sunday, get up early and go to church, eat downtown at the Windmill, study, and go to the Gathering at night."

If I could change one thing about Hope College, I'd "loosen up the housing policy and make it easier to register for classes."

Three things every student at Hope College should do before they graduate are "attend Gathering, go on a mission trip for spring break and go streaking on a Chapel Run."

Kalamazoo College

Address: Kalamazoo, 1200 Academy Street, Kalamazoo, MI 49006

Phone: 800-253-3602

E-mail Address: admission@kzoo.edu

Web site URL: http://www.kzoo.edu

Year Founded: 1833

Private or Public: private

Religious affiliation: none

Location: urban

Regular Application Deadline: 15-Feb

Number of Applicants: 1,800

Percent Accepted: 69%

Percent Accepted who enroll: 31%

Number Entering: 381

Number of Transfers Accepted each Year: 14

Mean SAT: NA

Mean ACT: NA

Middle 50% SAT range: math: 600–690; verbal; 610–710

Middle 50% ACT range: 26–31

Early admission program (EA/ ED/ NA): EA&ED

ED or EA Acceptance Rate: 86%

Full time Undergraduate enrollment: 1,263

Total enrollment: 1,263

Percent Male: 47%

Percent Female: 53%

Total Percent Minority: 20%

Percent African-American: 3%

Percent Asian/Pacific Islander: 5%

Percent Hispanic: 3%

Percent Native-American: 0%

Percent Other: 9%

Percent in-state / out of state: 70%/30%

Percent from Public HS: 83%

Retention Rate: 87%

Graduation Rate: 77%

Percent in On-campus housing: 75%

Percent affiliated with Greek system: 0%

Percent Varsity or Club Athletes: 25%

Number of official organized extracurricular organizations: 52

3 Most popular majors: Psychology, Business and Economics, Biology

Student/Faculty ratio: 12:01

Tuition and Fees: $27,054.00

Cost for Room and Board: $6,915.00

Percent receiving Financial aid, first-year: 72%

W hen asked to describe their campus, Kalamazoo College students joking refer to their administration's description of "K" having an "idyllic setting on an Arcadian quad." There is some truth to this poetic description. Nestled on a wooded hill near downtown Kalamazoo, Michigan, the beautiful campus provides an ideal environment for students looking to combine experiential learning and foreign study with an academically rigorous liberal arts education in a small, close-knit community.

Life in the 'Zoo

K students often refer to the "K-bubble," which is characterized by the feeling that their on-campus lives are cut-off from the rest of life in Kalamazoo, Michigan. Entering Kalamazoo College truly feels a bit like entering a separate world. Nearly everything, from the streets to the dorms to the academic buildings, is made of red brick, giving the campus a sense of unity and consistency. The focal point of campus is the Quad, a large, sloping, rectangular courtyard surrounded by academic and administration buildings, dorms, the student center, and Stetson Chapel. In warmer months, K students can be found on the Quad reading, socializing, or playing one of Kalamazoo's favorite past-times: Frisbee golf. During the snowy Michigan winter afternoons, students grab their sleds and head for the steep hill. In all seasons, groups of students can be seen running naked across the Quad. "Streaking the Quad is one of those things almost everyone does at least once here," explained one junior. "It's kind of what we're known for."

Most dorms are located either at the top or the bottom of the Quad, forcing most students to walk up and down the hill several times a day to attend classes and visit friends. One senior said that while the hill is pretty, "I have friends who won't come visit me because I live at the top of [it] and they live at the bottom, and they say the walk is too far." Regardless, its hillside setting makes Kalamazoo's campus aesthetically pleasing, though for students with physical disabilities the campus can be challenging to navigate.

All K College students are required to live on campus for their first three years. Though Severn and Chrissey Halls are generally considered the nicest, and Hoben Hall is cited as slightly more run-down, on the whole one sophomore raved, "The dorms are awesome!" Most freshmen are randomly assigned to live in a suite with five other first-year students. These suites generally consist of two doubles, two singles, a common lounge, and a bathroom. In all buildings the suites are single-sex, and floors are coed. After freshman year, students enter a lottery for housing, and though one junior commented, "Rising juniors get the worst rooms while rising sophomores get the best," even those juniors get to choose between living in suites or in more standard double rooms.

Living-Learning Housing Units are one of Kalamazoo's most unique features. An option for students after their freshman year, these "experiential learning centers" are freestanding, on-campus houses in which eight to ten students with an expressed common interest apply to live. In the past, themes for these houses have included the Service Learning House, the Women in Professional Fields House, the Wellness House, and the Men's Issues House. Other perks of "LLHU's," according to one junior, include "getting away from RAs (Resident Advisers), and getting off the meal plan." Though one senior joked, "the major 'Men's Issue' seems to be beer," these houses are designed to allow students to surround themselves with people who share one of their main interests. Furthermore, this unique living structure serves as a resource for the college as a whole, via the campus-wide educational themed events each house is required to hold throughout the year.

Many seniors choose to live off campus in one of the nearby student neighborhoods. Off-campus housing reportedly proves much cheaper than living in the dorms, and often includes kitchens where seniors can cook for themselves. All students can purchase various meal plans, some of which allow students to transfer money to the Quad Stop, the on-campus grill and snack bar. Kalamazoo's one dining hall features many options, including a grill line, a vegetarian line, and an a la carte option. Though most students grumble about the quality of dining hall food, one sophomore admits, "We think the food is pretty bad here, but when friends visit from other colleges they think our food is really good."

Where Did All the Juniors Go?

Though students can't move off campus until their senior year, freshmen and sophomores predominantly populate the dorms. Juniors are conspicuously absent on campus at K, because nearly 85 percent of students at Kalamazoo spend at least part of their third year abroad, pursuing foreign study. Kalamazoo College's foreign study program was named best in the nation by *U.S. News & World Report* in 2003, and many students cite the emphasis on travel as one of the best things about K. The college sponsors 26 different programs on six continents, allowing students to spend three to nine months anywhere from Ecuador to Thailand. A special endowment fund pays for students' overseas airfare, and this perk is very appreciated. Programs exist for students with a range of language skills, and because credits from foreign study easily transfer into K credits, even students in rigorous programs like premed are able to study elsewhere. A sophomore mentioned that Spain and Australia are "probably the easiest, and the biggest 'party places'" to study, but more adventurous students can live with families in Nairobi or Beijing. Another sophomore said that while it may seem strange that there are few juniors on campus at K, "it's normal to us because almost everyone here goes on foreign study."

A Studious Campus
Foreign study is just one aspect of Kalamazoo's unique academic philosophy, called the K-Plan. In addition to junior year study abroad, the K-Plan includes a liberal arts curriculum; career development internships in which nearly 80 percent of students participate after their sophomore year; the Senior Individualized Project, or "SIP," which is a one or two credit final project in the subject of one's major; and an electronic portfolio or online resume. To graduate, seniors must take comprehensive exams, or "comps," in their major, which according to one student are "very stressful, and everyone dreads them." In addition to fulfilling requirements for their major, students must satisfy a variety of liberal arts requirements, including those in written expression, oral expression, quantitative reasoning, computer literacy, and creative expression, as well as five terms of physical education. Most students enjoy this last requirement, since possible PE classes include bowling and indoor rock climbing, while one student complained that all the academic requirements "took up a lot of time I could have spent taking classes I would have enjoyed more." All freshmen are required to take a first-year writing seminar. These seminars have a diverse range of subjects, focusing on anything from the literature of King Arthur to road trips to science writing. One computer science major commented that he "liked the fact that there were freshmen seminars catered to non-humanities majors." Students also have to complete 25 LAC (language arts colloquium) credits by attending musical and dramatic performances, or by listening to on-campus speakers.

Kalamazoo operates on the trimester system, meaning that students start school in late September, have three 10-week terms during of three classes each, and get out of school in mid-June. Because each class only lasts for 10 weeks, "we move very quickly through the material," said one sophomore, "and it can get very stressful." Another student observed, "We are a very studious campus." Students at K report spending hours a day keeping up with reading and other work. The workload at K is reportedly heaviest in biology and chemistry, two of the school's exceptionally strong programs, although subjects such as English and economics are also popular. "The science facilities are so nice," one senior said. "They get all the money!" The Dow Science building has indeed recently been renovated to update and improve laboratories and classrooms. The Light Fine Arts building has also had a major "facelift" in the past few years, and the Upjohn Library has undergone a multi-million-dollar renovation.

Regardless of their major, students agreed that the small class sizes and close relationships with professors are the best parts of a K education. "I've never been in a class with more than 20 students," said one junior. Some introductory classes enroll up to 70 students, but as K students start taking more advanced classes in their major, they often find themselves in classes with fewer than 10 students. "Because the classes are so small, you can really go in and talk to your professors when you need help," said one sophomore, "and the professors definitely love it when you do." Overall, students at Kalamazoo College enjoy the challenge and the opportunity presented by their academic environment.

After Class
Students at Kalamazoo College don't spend all their time on schoolwork. Despite the school's small size, a wide variety of social and extracurricular options are available at K. Though one junior reported, "about half the students go out and party, and the others stay in and study all the time," to the half who venture out, alcohol is readily available both on- and off-campus. Though technically alcohol is not allowed in underage students' rooms, the penalty for being caught drinking is "a slap on the wrist, and maybe some community service," according to one senior. Although a sophomore warned that "RAs can be pretty strict, and if you get caught drunk too many times you can get kicked out of school," this doesn't seem to deter most K students from partying on the weekends.

Dorm parties are infrequent and Kalamazoo does not have a Greek system, so most large weekend gatherings take place at seniors' off-campus houses, which one student says get "really packed because there are usually only a few parties a weekend." In addition to alcohol, one senior mentioned that there's "a lot of pot" at K, but that most students tend to avoid harder drugs. The school sponsors some large parties, such as Monte Carlo night, and the Crystal Ball, where students traditionally dress in drag, but most social gatherings are more informal. Non-drinkers typically hang out in the dorms with friends on the weekends, watching movies or playing games, or they attend one of the many cultural functions that take place regularly on campus.

> "My favorite part about K is that I can walk down the street and see so many of my friends."

Of the many extracurricular options available on campus, sports are by far the most popular. Students say that almost everyone plays either a varsity or an IM sport. Though some varsity teams—such as soccer, tennis and swimming—are extremely successful, athletic participation doesn't seem to translate into athletic spirit because, as one sophomore commented, "there isn't as much enthusiasm for watching sports here as there is at other schools."

Frelon, Kalamazoo's dance company, is the school's largest extracurricular organization. "You don't have to have any previous dancing experience to be in it, and it's pretty fun," one group member said. Also popular is K's improv comedy group, Monkapult. "The shows are usually packed," one sophomore said. Kalamazoo College also has an active Habitat for Humanity chapter and many cultural organizations. "You can pretty much find a group for whatever you want here," one student said.

Homogenous but Open-Minded

The typical K student, according to many, is white, upper-middle-class, and from a Detroit suburb. While it's true that there's little ethnic or economic diversity at Kalamazoo College, and that most students are from Michigan, one sophomore observed, "even though we are not very racially diverse, I feel we are open-minded." The students at this traditionally liberal institution are a close-knit group. "My favorite part about K is that I can walk down the street and see so many of my friends," said one student. Unified by a unique educational experience, students at Kalamazoo College learn to make the most of the resources of their school, their community, and the world.—*Katherine Kirby Smith*

FYI

If you come to Kalamazoo, you'd better bring "a water filter because the water in the dorms tastes terrible."

What is the typical weekend schedule? "Sleep till noon, do schoolwork in the afternoon, go to a party or watch movies with friends at night."

If I could change one thing about Kalamazoo, "I'd change the amount of academic stress put on students."

Three things every Kalamazoo student should do before graduating are "streak the Quad, go on study abroad, and steal something from the dining hall."

Michigan State University

Address: Michigan State, 250
Hannah Administration
Building, East Lansing, MI
48824-0590
Phone: 517-432-6642
E-mail Address:
admis@msu.edu
Web site URL:
www.admissions.msu.edu
Year Founded: 1855
Private or Public: public
Religious affiliation: none
Location: suburban
**Application and Admissions
Information:** rolling
**Regular Application
Deadline:** NA
Number of Applicants:
23,229
Percent Accepted: 73%
**Percent Accepted who
enroll:** 30%
Number Entering: 7,175
**Number of Transfers
Accepted each Year:** 2,054
Mean SAT: NA

Mean ACT: NA
Middle 50% SAT range:
1,040–1,270
Middle 50% ACT range:
22–27
**Early admission program
(EA/ ED/ NA):** NA
ED or EA Acceptance Rate:
NA
**Full time Undergraduate
enrollment:** 35,678
Total enrollment: 45,166
Percent Male: 46%
Percent Female: 54%
Total Percent Minority:
18%
Percent African-American:
9%
**Percent Asian/Pacific
Islander:** 6%
Percent Hispanic: 3%
Percent Native-American: NA
Percent Other: 0.1%
**Percent in-state / out of
state:** 90%/10%
Percent from Public HS: NA

Retention Rate: 90%
Graduation Rate: 69%
**Percent in On-campus
housing:** NA
**Percent affiliated with
Greek system:** NA
**Percent Varsity or Club
Athletes:** NA
**Number of official
organized extracurricular
organizations:** 550
3 Most popular majors:
Finance, Accounting,
Marketing
Student/Faculty ratio:
20:01
Tuition and Fees:
$8,893.00
**In State Tuition and Fees
(if different):** $21,538.00
Cost for Room and Board:
$6,044.00
**Percent receiving
Financial aid, first-year:**
NA

The fight song for MSU begins "On the banks of the Red Cedar . . ." for a reason. Amidst a vast plain of farms and the concrete "jungles" of Central Michigan lies an oasis of beautiful green trees surrounding a river called the Red Cedar. People come to this collegiate haven to learn just about anything they please, from agriculture to political science. In their free time these same MSU students participate in sports teams and clubs; they party and cheer their fellow Spartans on; or they just enjoy some downtime. The students here are diverse, but share at least one trait: their love for green and white.

With Big Campus Comes Big Opportunity

There are a lot of choices at Michigan State. With over 40,000 students, more than 5,000 acres of land, and over 600 buildings, MSU offers unmatched opportunities. There are 14 colleges for undergraduates, including the College of Engineering, College of Education, and the College of Social Sciences. The university is best known, however, for its first college, the College of Agriculture and Natural Resources. MSU's close prox-

imity to local farms and wildlife is a key factor in why it became the first agricultural college in the USA in 1855. MSU is also known for its fine College of Veterinary Medicine and James Madison College, which is dedicated to political science and international relations. For those who are undecided, there is always the College of Arts and Letters, which follows a liberal arts curriculum.

The size of classes at MSU varies dramatically. There are classes with as few as 30 people or large lectures with as many as 500 people. Most of the larger and harder classes, however, also have what is called a weekly "recitation," during which a small section of the class gets together to work over what was learned in lecture. One downside to the immense size of MSU is the difficulty of forming working relationships with the professors. In some of the larger classes, students don't even get to meet their professors. However, as one student points out, "there is always plenty of help offered in any course," as there is an abundance of teachers' assistants who are willing to assist the students.

Recently, Michigan State made an effort to become more internationally involved. Consequently, more than 4,000 international students and scholars come to Michigan State every year. There are also many opportunities for students to study abroad. Indeed, there are over 180 programs in 57 different countries from which to choose. Most students who go abroad consider it to be an important life experience in which they learn how to live and study in a new culture alongside other MSU students. Study-abroad courses are usually fairly easy with an intense concentration on hands-on learning.

The Loveable Sparty

Located in MSU's "IM Circle" is a bronze statue of Sparty, the "copper"-toned warrior ready for battle. This statue is sacred to the students of Michigan State and is vigilantly protected during the week of the football game against cross-state rival, the University of Michigan. Sparty is protected from toilet-papering, paint, and even drive-by paintball attacks. Despite a fair amount of turnover in Spartan coaches, the MSU versus U of M football game is always close and intense. Of the many reliable fans at the big game, the most obvious is Sparty. He makes his appearance not as a bronze statue, but as a student dressed up in colorful foam that brings to mind a Japanese anime cartoon more than a Greek warrior. Fans pack into the stadium after going to one of the most popular tailgates in the country. Here, kegs and beer-pong tables are lined up in long rows, and people from all over the country come to visit their friends and fellow alums. The stadium has just been renovated to add seating and suites to accommodate all these visitors.

If you think MSU gets excited about football, just wait till basketball season. The basketball teams are hailed as a group of demigods and tickets for home games in the Breslin Center are nearly impossible to get. Doing well by its fans, the Michigan State teams have been a top competitor for the national title for the past decade. In 2000 they claimed this title, and they they've won many Big Ten Championships and a few trips to the Final Four as well. For this, the students love Coach Izzo and many consider him a hero. In addition, many other MSU sports teams thrive in the Big Ten conference; for instance, men's golf recently won two Big Ten titles.

Living Situations

Michigan State has modest living arrangements for undergraduates in dorms. All freshmen are required to live in dorms to help encourage the meeting of new people. The most popular dorm for freshmen is Brody, although James Madison students live in Case Hall. Most rooms are doubles, but singles are an option if you are willing to pay a little more. The two most popular setups are large doubles with community bathrooms or smaller doubles that share a bathroom. Alcohol is banned in all rooms except those that house 21 year-olds and older, and the RAs do reportedly enforce this rule.

The dorms are conveniently located near classrooms and dining halls. Each dining hall offers just about the same food as any other. As one MSU student remarked, the dining hall food "SUCKS." Others disagree, saying the cafeterias are just as good as at any others. Brody's cafeteria boasts being the largest non-military cafeteria in the nation. For those who do not like the cafeterias, there are many other options. East Lansing offers some popular eatery chains that are rare on other college campuses. Pancheros is a favorite for any student who is a fan of burritos, and Mongolian Barbeque is also popular. Georgios is considered a must not only because it is a favorite for eating on weekends, but also because the varsity athletes are known to frequent this restaurant. Students flock to two other favorites during the late hours of the night: Bell's Pizza and Jimmy Johns. The normal selection of chain restaurants are also represented nearby.

North of campus are many houses and apartment buildings for people who want to live off-campus. Most upperclassmen opt out of living in dorms all four years and rent a house or apartment in groups. Most of these houses are relatively close to campus, though the distance can still be considerable when taking the campus's size into account. Other people decide to live in fraternity or sorority houses. Greek life is a predominant presence on-campus and many parties are held at fraternities. There is no need to be affiliated to enjoy the social life and parties provided, however.

Parties and Other Extracurricular Activities

Michigan State has historically been one of the top five party schools in the nation. Recent security efforts made by the administration and authorities have caused this national ranking to drop, but that hasn't greatly affected MSU students. One student explains that, "MSU students have a reputation for being wild and most try their best to live up to that." As a way to ensure this, the weekend "usually starts on Thursday but sometimes on Wednesday." Parties are mostly split between Frat parties and house parties. However, the pervasive social scene allows for most everyone to find a group they are comfortable with. Though many students party, they mostly stick to alcohol. One student said she has never seen anyone using drugs.

> "[Broomball is] a game some say was invented by the heavens as a gift to man."

You don't have to drink to have fun during the weekend, as the college itself offers many alternatives to drinking. Recreation buildings are open every day until midnight, and Wells Hall is open to all students free of charge to watch new movies on the big screen. During the beginning half of the week, students also enjoy the many IM sports available at MSU. These include traditional and nontraditional sports such volleyball, softball, kickball, flag football, inner-tube water polo, and broom-ball. There is a lot of participation and support for all the IMs. When asked about broomball—where two teams face each other on the ice rink trying to knock a ball into a goal using a broom—one student responded by poetically calling it "a game some say was invented by the heavens as a gift to man."

Enough about the College, What about the People?

Most agree that Michigan State has a diverse student population. "People are different ethnically, racially, economically, culturally, and geographically," says one student. Other students are a little more cynical, citing the fact that most people are white and come from the suburbs of Detroit. The great number of people at MSU, however, sometimes overwhelms students from nearby towns, preventing them from making new friends, because it is so much easier to just hang out with old high-school buddies. The setup in the dorms discourages this, however, motivating students to meet a broad range of people and not just their roommates. By the end of their undergraduate career, most students at MSU have long since branched out from their high school friends and have enjoyed personal development both socially and academically.—*Benjamin Dzialo*

FYI

If you come to Michigan State, you'd better bring "comfortable shoes. Walks to and from class are perhaps the longest among all college campuses in the country."

What's the typical weekend schedule? "There are always tons of parties going on at the frats. Some people go to the Campus Center for movies and other activiites. Others just catch up on sleep."

If I could change one thing about Michigan State, I would "[implement] better cafeteria hours and better transportation during the weekend."

Three things every student at Michigan State should do before graduating are "study abroad," "go to a tailgate," and "walk on the Spartan stadium field."

Michigan Technological University

Address: Michigan Tech, 1400 Townsend Drive, Houghton, 49931
Phone: 906-487-2335
E-mail Address: NA
Web site URL: www.mtu.edu
Year Founded: 1885
Private or Public: public
Religious affiliation: NA
Location: suburban
Regular Application Deadline: rolling
Number of Applicants: NA
Percent Accepted: 82%
Percent Accepted who enroll: 38%
Number Entering: NA
Number of Transfers Accepted each Year: NA
Mean SAT: 1,152
Mean ACT: 25
Middle 50% SAT range: NA

Middle 50% ACT range: NA
Early admission program (EA/ ED/ NA): NA
ED or EA Acceptance Rate: NA
Full time Undergraduate enrollment: 5,534
Total enrollment: 6,544
Percent Male: 77%
Percent Female: 23%
Total Percent Minority: 13%
Percent African-American: 2%
Percent Asian/Pacific Islander: 1%
Percent Hispanic: 1%
Percent Native-American: 1%
Percent Other: NA
Percent in-state / out of state: 74%/26%
Percent from Public HS: NA

Retention Rate: 81%
Graduation Rate: 61%
Percent in On-campus housing: 41%
Percent affiliated with Greek system: 7%/11%
Percent Varsity or Club Athletes: NA
Number of official organized extracurricular organizations: 197
3 Most popular majors: Civil engineering, electrical engineering, mechanical engineering
Student/Faculty ratio: 12:01
Tuition and Fees: NA
Cost for Room and Board: NA
Percent receiving Financial aid, first-year: 53%

Originally established in 1885 to train mining engineers, Michigan Tech has evolved into a widely renowned institution with a vast array of opportunities for engineers and non-engineers alike. Located in the upper region of Michigan in the town of Houghton, this mid-sized college boasts a beautiful campus surrounded by snow-covered mountains, woods, and trails. But don't be fooled by the calm and quiet surroundings—Michigan Tech is one of the busiest places to spend one's college years.

Not Just For Engineers

Although Michigan Tech emphasizes its diversity of academic opportunities, offering over 120 majors, it is most famous for the College of Engineering. The engineering school, regularly ranked in the top 25 in the country, offers a slew of hands-on research projects, and co-op and internship programs. Most of the 6,000 students at the University are engineers, followed in second by science majors. Nevertheless, non-engineers are still able to find a niche at Michigan Tech. And one student joked, "I'm personally not an engineer, but I love having them around. Mechanical [engineers] can fix my car, electrical [engineers] can fix my circuits, etc."

Michigan Tech prides itself on its abundant research opportunities, especially its prized Enterprise Program. The program provides hands-on work with outfits like NASA, DaimlerChrysler, SBC Ameritec and the EPA. Teams of 20 to 30 students solve real-world engineering and manufacturing problems submitted by Michigan Tech's industry, business, and corporate partners. The field of research for each group varies, including, but not limited to aerospace, alternative fuels, robotic systems, and wireless communication.

Whether you're doing engineering research or not, chances are you'll be working hard at Michigan Tech. As one student said, "Most people here are very into their schooling, so I am able to keep on track as well." The school's atmosphere is intensely preprofessional; undergraduates are often taking career goals into account as they work. One student explained, "Classes are very tough, but our job placement is very high. For pre-med majors, there is an 80 percent for med school, while the national average is 40 percent." This type of education guarantees that Michigan Tech students are prepared for the real world.

Small Town Snow Sports

Houghton, Michigan is a very cold place, so you better bring some snow boots. The campus is covered with snow, water, woods and trails, and the University even owns its own ski and snowboarding mountains with discounted season passes for students. The powder-covered mountains and serene hills create a calm, safe campus environment. So safe, in fact, that many people claim Houghton to be the safest town in Michigan.

> "The people here are very laid back . . . I like the whole 'small town' feel."

But safe definitely doesn't mean boring. With over 150 student groups on campus, there is certainly no shortage of things to do. "[There is] almost too much to do, there are many things I want to do that I just don't have time for . . . and most people think there is nothing to do up here because we're in the middle of nowhere," one student noted. With about 6,000 undergraduates, Michigan Tech is large enough that each activity attracts a substantial group of students. Yet, it is small enough that students can hold leadership positions without feeling too stressed out about their extracurriculars. As one student explained "The people here are very laid back . . . I like the whole 'small town' feel."

Life in the Winter Wonderland

In terms of housing, all freshmen are required to live in one of three fully-equipped residential halls, encouraging class bonding and facilitating the integration of the "frosh" into the campus scene. After that, students can choose whether or not to stay on campus for their next three years. To keep themselves entertained, Michigan Tech students take advantage of the many concerts and performances staged around campus—some recent performers have included Mary Chapin Carpenter and Tap Dogs Rebooted. Greek life, in spite of its small numbers, has a substantial influence on the campus' social scene. Greeks coordinate several parties every semester for everyone's enjoyment. One of the biggest events of the year is the annual Winter Carnival held in February. Human dogsled races, ice bowling, snow volleyball, and fireworks are all part of the extravaganza that is Winter Carnival. Groups on campus spend weeks preparing, creating statues, snow sculptures, and teams to compete in the various races. The event is so popular that it attracts tourists from all over Michigan.

Diversity is a bit lacking at Michigan Tech—the school is about 85–90 percent Caucasian. Yet, students said that there is a growing international and minority presence, and all undergraduates have the option of participating in exchange programs or study abroad. The gender ratio is also unbalanced. Like most tech schools, the male majority leaves the lucky ladies with ample choices. "The dating scene is more competitive here . . . and the women tend to use that to their advantage," one student explained. Overall, students agreed that Michigan Tech "is very accepting" of all types and is working to improve its reputation and racial and gender diversity.

Hockey, Skiing, and . . . Broomball?

With a Division I Men's Hockey team, a dozen DII teams, and many intramural teams, it is no surprise that many students choose to stay active. In fact, nearly 90 percent of students partake in intramurals. "A lot of people like to get involved with sports up here . . . [it is a] great way to stay in shape and meet a lot of people," one intramural athlete noted. The cold weather encourages sports unique to snow and ice. Aside from the usual skiing and ice hockey, students use the icy conditions to play a school favorite: broomball. One student explained the glories of their prized sport: "Broomball is huge up here. It is like hockey played on ice but you wear street shoes and use brooms as hockey sticks . . . you have to wear kneepads or else you will get very bruised . . . Everybody gets really into it, everybody!" Students can be found playing broomball whenever possible—during intramural games, pickup games, and, of course, during Winter Carnival.

It is this mix of academic seriousness and fun-loving athletic spirit that continues to draw students to Michigan Tech year after year. And if you are excited by its combination of intellectual and athletic rigor, it just might be the place for you. Just don't forget your kneepads.—*Suzanne Salgado*

FYI
If you come to MTU, you'd better bring "snow shoes and a shovel."
What's the typical weekend schedule? "Days are spent at meetings or in the library, nights are for
  going out with friends, and Sundays especially are for homework."
If I could change one thing about MTU it would be "to have more parking—I have to get up early to
  get a good parking spot."
Three things every student at MTU should do before graduating are: "Go cliff jumping, explore
  the copper country, and learn to ski/snowboard (and if you know how to ski or snowboard, go to
  Mt. Bohemia)."

University of Michigan

Address: University of
  Michigan, 515 E. Jefferson
  St., 1220 SAB, Ann Arbor, MI
  48109-1316
Phone: 734-764-7433
E-mail Address: NA
Web site URL:
  www.admissions.umich
  .edu
Year Founded: 1817
Private or Public: public
Religious affiliation: none
Location: urban
**Regular Application
  Deadline:** 1-Feb
Number of Applicants:
  25,733
Percent Accepted: 47%
**Percent Accepted who
  enroll:** 45%
Number Entering: 6,092
**Number of Transfers
  Accepted each Year:**
  912
Mean SAT: NA
Mean ACT: NA

Middle 50% SAT range:
  1,900–2,160
Middle 50% ACT range:
  27–31
**Early admission program
  (EA/ ED/ NA):** NA
ED or EA Acceptance Rate:
  NA
**Full time Undergraduate
  enrollment:** 25,467
Total enrollment: 39,933
Percent Male: 49%
Percent Female: 51%
Total Percent Minority:
  32%
Percent African-American:
  8%
**Percent Asian/Pacific
  Islander:** 13%
Percent Hispanic: 5%
Percent Native-American:
  1%
Percent Other: 5%
**Percent in-state / out of
  state:** 63%/37%
Percent from Public HS:
  NA

Retention Rate: 96%
Graduation Rate: 85%
**Percent in On-campus
  housing:** 37%
**Percent affiliated with
  Greek system:** 15%
**Percent Varsity or Club
  Athletes:** NA
**Number of official
  organized extracurricular
  organizations:** 1,000+
3 Most popular majors:
  Psychology, Political
  Science, Economics
Student/Faculty ratio:
  15:01
Tuition and Fees:
  $9,724.00
**In State Tuition and
  Fees (if different):**
  $29,132.00
Cost for Room and Board:
  $7,838.00
**Percent receiving
  Financial aid, first-year:**
  88%

As one of the country's most notable public institutions, the University of Michigan is wrought with history. Not only was it home to Jonas Salk's laboratory when the polio vaccine was discovered in 1955, but it was here that John F. Kennedy first proposed the Peace Corps during his presidential campaign of 1960. Yet, despite its imposing legacy, and the fact that Michigan boasts the benefits of a public institution, with "millions of things to do," the University of Michigan still maintains a distinct "homey" Midwestern feel.

M is for Majors . . . and Minors
With nearly 25,000 students, over 200 acade-

mic departments in 11 undergraduate schools and colleges, the academic opportunities at Michigan are endless. In fact, many students cite this variety as their favorite aspect of the school. The choices begin with the application process—students may apply directly to one of eleven undergraduate schools. Though most first year students enroll in the College of Literature, Arts, and Sciences (LSA), several other colleges are also open to freshmen, including the College of Engineering and the Art School.

Freshmen also have the option of enrolling in a number of special academic programs. The four-year honors program, for example, is offered through LSA and select students are offered admission to the program after being accepted into the college. During their first two years, students in the honors program are offered unique advising and research programs, and can enroll in special courses not offered to the general undergraduate population. The honors program even boasts its own housing option.

Students may also opt for the Residential College (RC), a four-year interdisciplinary liberal arts program within LSA. With 900 students, and over 50 professors, RC is described as a "living-learning community." Students who choose to enroll in the program take classes and live together n the East Quadrangle Residence Hall. Another unique academic living environment is available through the Residential Programs, which are sorted through specific interests such as writing, art, women in science and engineering. According to one freshman, "They are great ways to make this huge school feel smaller and more personal."

Regardless of major, every student in LSA must fulfill natural science, humanities, social science, and "the dreaded language requirement," among others. But most students do not consider the requirements too demanding. In fact, one freshman was told by her advisor not to worry about them, "because if I just take a full course load every semester, I'll probably fulfill my requirements anyway."

The variety of classes and departments at Michigan results in an academic environment that can invariably suit each student's individual needs. "Whether you want a class that requires five hours of studying per week, or five hours for the entire semester, you can find one," explained one student. Class size varies dramatically as well. Lower-level classes and lectures can range from 50 to 500, but most classes split into 20 to 30 student discussion sections led by Graduate Student Instructors (GSIs).

One option to keep class sizes manageable is the First Year Seminars, which are offered on a number of topics, ranging from hippies to Slavic countries, from sex to theology. Since they are led exclusively by professors, students recommend taking as many of these seminars as possible during one's first year in order to form relationships with professors early on. There is no

general rule as to accessibility of the instructors. "It depends on the professor," one student remarked. "Most are very approachable but I have come across a a couple who could care less about the students." Another student said that close relationships with professors are "one of those things that you kind of give up by going to a big school," but most agree that if you make an effort most professors won't turn you away. "Professors want their students to succeed," said one undergrad, "they are invested in the success of their students even if it means being flexible about their office hours, or spending a little extra time on this, and cutting back on that." Another commented that, "It's easy to get to know the professors if you are interested in doing that, and it's easy to be another face in the crowd if you don't want to be noticed."

The classes at Michigan also vary in their level of competitiveness. According to one student, "my microeconomics class is a prerequisite for the business school," which inherently means it is populated by competitive students. Others note that such competition is present among architecture and pre-med students as well. But, in contrast, one student from New York City claims that she has "seen no competition whatsoever." Not only has she found that students rarely talk about their grades, but "people here in the Midwest are always willing to help one another out." This "warm and welcoming community" is for many "one of the great qualities of this school."

So does Michigan's huge academic curriculum possess any shortcomings? One undergraduate complained that Michigan has, "the weakest study abroad offerings I have come across for a school of this size." Although the university claims to feature numerous specialized study abroad programs, such as the Engineering International Program, as well as study abroad scholarships, students admit they are disappointed by the offerings, especially those that don't require a foreign language.

The Animal House Way of Life

"Straight out of the movies," is how one enthusiastic freshman characterized Michigan's dominating Greek scene. With nearly 60 chapters, many students "don't know many people that aren't in frats," and for those who haven't gone Greek, the lifestyle may at times seem overwhelming and exclusive. For example, the Office of Greek Life recently instituted a new policy that only allows those in frats and sororities to attend frat parties unless the student can somehow get his or her name on the guest-list beforehand.

But for many students, Greek life is just another way to make a huge school more manageable. One freshman noted that joining a sorority allowed her to "make a place for [herself] in such a huge community." Furthermore, because nearly 65 percent of students are Michigan natives, the out-of-state students often find fraternities and sororities an integral part of meeting new people. For girls, sorority rush is "a ten day-long process in the fall, involving dress codes, lining up alphabetically, and a lot of fake smiling," while rush for fraternities is much more informal. Neither involves hazing, as it is strictly prohibited.

While many underclassmen join fraternities and sororities and/or attend frat parties every weekend, for those who are of age, the bar scene and house parties are common weekend activities. Some notable bars include Studio 4, Scorekeepers (aka Skeeps), Touchdowns, Necto, and Rick's. The most popular nights to go out are Thursday, Friday, and Saturday, although Tuesdays are also popular bar nights.

So how do underage students manage? Although there are alcohol regulations both legally and within the Greek system, drinking ages and policies are not strictly enforced. According to one student, in terms of the Greek rules, "No one really pays attention until they've been on social probation." Similarly, an underage student is not too likely to find him or herself in trouble for drinking. "The cops are pretty strict," one freshman admitted, "but as long as you don't act like an idiot and you remain in control of yourself it isn't a problem." One sophomore agreed, stating that, "For the most part, the only way to get in trouble by the police is to be obnoxious."

Not surprisingly, alcohol is extremely prevalent among the Michigan undergrad populations, and "soft drugs," such as marijuana, are fairly common among those who choose to partake. In fact, while alcohol possession by a minor will most likely result in a court appearance, marijuana possession is only a civil infraction and a violation merely results in a small fine. Though hard drugs are much harder to come by, rumor has it that cocaine use at Michigan is on the steady rise.

Regardless of their particular interests, Michigan students generally agree that finding friends is not difficult. "In such a big school, everyone is trying to find their own little niche," remarked one student, "so everyone is really friendly and enthusiastic about meeting people." The student body at Michigan is also characterized as being extremely diverse. This does not prevent self-segregation from occurring, but one student noted that diversity has become "a huge topic of interest lately since the state banned affirmative action programs in the 2006 election."

Home is Where Ann Arbor Is

"[As a freshman] you can live in a single or a double. You can live in apartment style dorms, or in dorm style dorms. There are suites and there are halls. They have everything you can imagine!"

"The Hill" is composed of five dorms and is "basically the place to live if you're a freshman." Some students, as a means of ensuring that they will live in this popular area, apply to one of the residential programs that houses its students on The Hill. Dorms on The Hill include Stockwell, an all-girls dorm, Lloyd Hall, (nicknamed Lloyd Island, due to the numerous Long Islanders that live there), Couzens, which is rumored to have once been a mental institution, Mosher-Jordan (aka MoJo), which is currently being remodeled, and Markley, the "social dorm with small rooms."

> "At Michigan, bigger is better."

Another common freshman housing area is South quad, which is home to the optional honors student housing and also the athletes' dorm—rumored to have the best food on campus. Students in the RC live and take classes on East Campus, while North Campus, a 15 minute bus ride away from the central campus, is home to many of the architecture, theater, and engineering students. One of North Campus' most notable dorms is Bursely, the third biggest dorm building in the country. According to one student, "Generally, the smaller the dorm, the worse its reputation is. At Michigan, bigger is better."

All freshman halls have RAs, and there is plenty of debate about their roles. "They make sure there isn't any drinking in the dorms and handle problems with roommates," one sophomore explained. "They also punish you if they find you drunk." But in the words of another student, the primary job of the RAs is to "decorate the bulletin boards and let you into your room if you get locked out."

Most students only have to deal with RAs during their freshman year, though, since the majority of Michigan sophomores move off campus. Some move into fraternity or sorority houses, while others move into co-ops where "people do chores for the house so the rent is cheap." There are also many apartment buildings and houses surrounding campus comprised mainly of students.

With ten different dining halls on campus, "there is always something to eat." While the food might not be great, every dining hall features a salad bar, sandwich bar, pasta, and several other "staples." One student noted that, "UMich food has been rated some of the best campus food in the country!" But some students disagree. As at many colleges and universities, "You can get lucky or you can eat cereal." But as one student admitted, "It's better than cooking my own food."

Other than the lack of dining hall food, it is often hard for off-campus students to tell that they are not on university property. "The off-campus neighborhoods just feel like an extension of the campus." Students often find themselves spending their free time on Main Street, which is not only full of shops and restaurants, but also Ann Arbor residents. According to one student, other than on Main Street "I only see college kids." But she added, "There *are* 25,000 of them."

One of the favorite student hangouts on campus, especially on warmer days, is The Diag, the main quad that is surrounded by classroom buildings. It is called The Diag because of the many crossing paths throughout. In the middle is a huge gold "M", source of the oldest campus legend. It is rumored that if you walk over the "M" you will fail your first blue book exam. The curse can only be broken if someone runs naked from the Diag to the clock tower when it chimes at midnight, but since the city council banned the clock from chiming past 11 p.m., "the curse is here to stay." According to one freshman, "I decided I wanted to come to Michigan when I was on The Diag."

For outdoorsy students, Nicholas' Arboretum is a perfect "getaway" from campus. "It's just a million miles of nature. It's beautiful, clean, and fun to hike and walk around in."

Beer Bottles and Footballs

Although it may seem outrageous, some students actually choose University of Michigan just for the football team, and for many, it's the highlight of their college experience. "I have never been so excited to be a Michigan student as I was when I walked to my first football game," exclaimed one freshman. "The streets are filled with students all in Maize and Blue." Getting to the stadium is not a problem, as the main drag to "The Big House" is packed with fans on all sides of the stadium. "Walking down State Street is an amazing experience. You walk with 100,000 other fans to Michigan stadium to watch football."

In spite of the fact that sports such as men's basketball and hockey always draw a crowd to their games, football rules at Michigan. As one student admitted, "If the football team loses, don't expect a great night out," and another added, "If you don't like beer and football, you will when you get here!"

Regardless of athletic or extracurricular interests, all students agree that one of the best aspects of the Michigan student body is its undying spirit. "You know you're at Michigan, even in the middle of winter, when everyone is bundled in their winter jackets, because Michigan hats and scarves and mittens are everywhere." And no matter where you are on campus, if you listen carefully, you will probably hear the distant chants of "It's great! To be! A Michigan Wolverine!"—*Jessica Rubin*

FYI

If you come to Michigan, you'd better bring "Tolerance for everything that goes on here. If you don't, you won't make it past welcome week."

What's the typical weekend schedule? " Party, party, party, party . . . okay and maybe you can sleep, eat, and work a little too!"

If I could change one thing about Michigan, I'd "Move it to a warmer, sunnier place."

Three things every student at Michigan should do before graduating are "Go to a football game against Ohio State, run the naked mile, stop and listen to one of the crazy men ranting in the middle of the Diag. You may learn something."

Minnesota

Carleton College

Address: Carleton, 100 S. College Street, Northfield, MN 55057
Phone: 507-646-4190
E-mail Address: admissions@carleton.edu
Web site URL: www.carleton.edu
Year Founded: 1866
Private or Public: private
Religious affiliation: none
Location: rural
Regular Application Deadline: 15-Jan
Number of Applicants: 4,465
Percent Accepted: 32%
Percent Accepted who enroll: 36%
Number Entering: 504
Number of Transfers Accepted each Year: 5–15
Mean SAT: N/A
Mean ACT: N/A
Middle 50% SAT range: 1,320–1,500

Middle 50% ACT range: 28–32
Early admission program (EA/ ED/ NA): ED
ED or EA Acceptance Rate: 50%
Full time Undergraduate enrollment: 1,936
Total enrollment: 1,936
Percent Male: 48%
Percent Female: 52%
Total Percent Minority: 21%
Percent African-American: 6%
Percent Asian/Pacific Islander: 10%
Percent Hispanic: 5%
Percent Native-American: 0.7%
Percent Other: N/A
Percent in-state / out of state: 78%/22%
Percent from Public HS: 73%

Retention Rate: 96.7%
Graduation Rate: 87%
Percent in On-campus housing: 85%
Percent affiliated with Greek system: 0%
Percent Varsity or Club Athletes: 50%
Number of official organized extracurricular organizations: 140
3 Most popular majors: Political Science/IR, Biology, Economics
Student/Faculty ratio: 9:01
Tuition and Fees: $34,272.00
Cost for Room and Board: $8,379.00
Percent receiving Financial aid, first-year: 55%

At the northern reaches of Northfield, Minnesota sits the highly respected liberal arts school Carleton College. Besides being very small and very cold, Carleton prides itself on combining a top-notch, highly personal academic experience with a demeanor that refuses to take itself too seriously. Intramural sports, artistic interest groups, and political activism provide social outlets and break up academic rigors.

Hitting the Books

Carleton is known for its intensive but exhilarating academic program. The year is divided into trimesters, giving students more opportunities to choose new courses. Trimesters also make it easier for students to fulfill distribution requirements, which call for a minimum number of classes in four groups: arts and literature, math and science, social sciences, and humanities. For the most part students tend to appreciate the breadth of courses this program urges them to take. Regarding the distribution requirements, one junior said, "It makes you think more about your major rather than assuming that your high school ambitions are still what you want to do with your life." The most popular majors are biology, economics, political science, and American studies. Nearly all majors offer study abroad programs which are highly encouraged and widely taken advantage of, particularly during junior year. In the senior year, all students must complete an intense program called "comps" in order to cap off the major. The nature of the project varies by major, as students can choose to do anything from taking exams to traveling the world.

In addition, Carleton students seem to share a love of their professors. "Professors are very accessible and generally really interesting and cool," said a senior. "I've only had one professor in my three years here who didn't insist on being called by his first name," added a junior. Due to the small classes, students get to know their professors and often meet them outside of class. One student cited a professor who required everyone in the class to go out for coffee as part of "social credit," worth 5 percent of the grade.

Dorm Living

One of the benefits of a very small school is that everything is highly accessible no matter where you live. The dining hall is very close to the dorms, as are all the classroom buildings. The dorms themselves tend to be fairly large and comfortable. A unique aspect of the Carleton dorm system is that students of all graduating classes share the same floors. This lack of segregation creates a social environment with very little class hierarchy; freshmen are not hazed, but rather helped out by their upperclassmen floormates.

> "I've only had one professor in my three years here who didn't insist on being called by his first name."

Usually floormates form close-knit groups of friends. Floors compete against each other for intramural sports and there is an ongoing rivalry among floors in everything they do. The floors are also co-ed and some of them have co-ed bathrooms. One freshman felt wary about the dorms at first but soon warmed up to the idea: "I wasn't used to living with girls and sharing a bathroom. But I guess it's a good time to start and I've made a lot of friends in the process." The few complaints from students regarding dorm life center on noise pollution from the hyperactive radiators in the winter.

The food tends to be a bit more of an issue. Most Carleton students have a tremendous amount of school spirit and are reluctant to reveal any information that might reflect poorly on the school.

However, when they do mention a drawback, it often involves the food. One junior remarked, "Well . . . It's not as bad as some. . . . They do have a decent salad bar and soup if all else fails." While the food receives lukewarm reviews, students rave about the brand new academic and dining building referred to as "linguistics and linguini."

Fun . . . Not in Class, Not in the Sun

Carleton students tend to keep busy despite the long winter. Division III varsity sports are a part of campus life, but the only boast made about the football team is that they have the highest GPA in the conference. The biggest sport at Carleton is Ultimate Frisbee and games are always well attended. Intramural sports are taken surprisingly seriously (in good fun, of course). They are organized by floor and include floor hockey, tennis, sailing, softball, and broomball. As one student mentioned, "IMs are a really big deal. Championship teams win T-shirts that go a long way towards winning the respect of their peers."

When students are not sporting, they are often getting involved in their community through clubs and organizations on campus. The outdoor enthusiast club (known as CANOE) is one of the biggest groups, and political clubs, which tend to be left-leaning, are quite popular. There are four a cappella groups on campus who perform regularly, along with various theater groups who offer several plays each term.

Carleton also has fun with its traditions. One of the more notable traditional activities is the annual softball game with as many innings as years that Carleton has been in existence. Usually beer accompanies the 130-inning softball game, and more times than not a naked inning is played. A slightly more heart-warming tradition is the Dacie Moses house. Dacie left her house to the university when she died, on the condition that there would always be ingredients to bake cookies. "Any time I want, day or night, I can go to Dacie's and bake cookies with my friends. It's really fantastic," said an enthusiastic student.

Social Life

The nightlife at Carleton is not raging . . . but that's not to say it does not exist. Carleton is not a state school, and it doesn't have fraternities. Nonetheless, Carleton students cannot be stopped from having a good time. Without a Greek system the student body is very open, without defined cliques. One junior girl explains that this means, "No more jocks! No more losers! And the wonderful thing about Carleton is we're all dorks!" The closest things to defined social entities on campus are the special-interest houses. These include the Farm House, the Culinary House, the Yoga House, the Canoe House, the Green House, and a variety of cultural houses. The buildings usually only house about 10 people, but they are not considered clique-forming, as they are required to put on regular campus-wide events.

Drinking on campus is very prevalent, but students note a lack of pressure to participate. One sophomore commented that drinking is considered a "social choice, neither condemned nor romanticized." Parties are very casual, and it would not be uncommon to see party-goers sporting sweatpants and T-shirts. If students are not in the mood to party, they may instead attend Friday night convocations with a wide variety of outside speakers.

Northfield is a quaint town with restaurants and cafes. The Contended Cow is a popular pub with good music where students go when they want to get off campus. When students want to get farther away, a weekend trip to the Twin Cities is always an option. But for the most part there is a lot of activity on campus and students don't feel the need to leave. Indeed, many do not want to leave, as they find the small Carleton community cozy, supportive, and stimulating. If you value a snug environment, proximity to the fresh, frigid outdoors, and a challenging, personalized education, then you will surely be happy at Carleton.—*Quinn Fitzgerald*

Revised by Lindsay Starck

FYI

If you come to Carleton, you'd better bring "a sense of humor" and "a hat—Minnesota is cold."
What is the typical weekend schedule? "Procrastination, partying, and, inevitably, homework."
If I could change one thing about Carleton, I'd "change the cold weather."
Three things every student at Carleton should do before graduating are "go streaking, go traying (sliding on the snow with trays), and go out to coffee with a professor."

Gustavus Adolphus College

Address: Gustavus Adolphus, 800 West College Avenue; St. Peter, MN 56082, NA
Phone: 507-933-7676
E-mail Address: admission@gustavus.edu
Web site URL: www.gustavus.edu
Year Founded: 1862
Private or Public: private
Religious affiliation: Lutheran
Location: suburban
Regular Application Deadline: 4/1 Rolling
Number of Applicants: NA
Percent Accepted: 79%
Percent Accepted who enroll: 33%
Number Entering: 685
Number of Transfers Accepted each Year: 72
Mean SAT: 1,210
Mean ACT: 26

Middle 50% SAT range: 520–670V, 540–670M, 600–650W
Middle 50% ACT range: 23–28
Early admission program (EA/ ED/ NA): NA
ED or EA Acceptance Rate: NA
Full time Undergraduate enrollment: 2,603
Total enrollment: 2,603
Percent Male: 42%
Percent Female: 58%
Total Percent Minority: 9%
Percent African-American: 2%
Percent Asian/Pacific Islander: 5%
Percent Hispanic: 2%
Percent Native-American: 1%
Percent Other: 91%
Percent in-state / out of state: 80%/20%
Percent from Public HS: 92%

Retention Rate: 89%
Graduation Rate: 82%
Percent in On-campus housing: 78%
Percent affiliated with Greek system: 18%
Percent Varsity or Club Athletes: NA
Number of official organized extracurricular organizations: 120
3 Most popular majors: Business Administration/Management, Communications, Psychology
Student/Faculty ratio: 12:01
Tuition and Fees: $26,700.00
Cost for Room and Board: $6,400.00
Percent receiving Financial aid, first-year: 67%

The Gustavus Adolphus campus, which is seated upon 350 hilltop acres, is the center of the small town of St. Peter. The college is completely self-contained, abutted by a delightful arboretum dense with trees from Minnesota and Sweden. The modern face of the "Gustie" campus owes a lot to the 1998 tornado that nearly shut down the school and after which the college "invested quite a bit in remodeling." According to students, there are "several very new buildings on campus, mixed in with older ones." These new buildings include a new 200-resident dormitory that offers a mix of regular dorm rooms available to students of all years and apartment-style living for upperclassmen. Also newly renovated are the fitness facilities at the Lund Center, and Old Main, the oldest building on campus.

Living on the Hill

With such a high percentage of Gusties residing on campus—including all first- and second-year students—housing options are very important. Norelius Hall, known to students as "Coed," houses 400 freshmen and is located at the northern end of the campus. The building set-up includes "sections" of 11 rooms with a common area at the center. The arrangement facilitates interactions and friendships among first-years; one junior reported that even after two years, all of her best friends lived in her "section" in Coed. The remaining freshmen, as well as the rest of the on-campus students, reside in various other mixed-year dormitories. Students of all classes may apply to live in the International Center, where both American and international students reside and participate in programs that foster cultural awareness. The Collegiate Fellow (CF) on every floor is responsible for enforcing dormitory regulations, and while "it totally depends on the CF," many will be strict only "when they have to be," such as issuing citations for underage possession of alcohol in the dorm or excessive noise in the hallways. Those with junior or senior standing may apply for permission to reside off-campus in St. Peter.

On-campus residents take meals at the highly acclaimed cafeteria, The Caf, which has "great food" and a good selection. In addition to a "grille, rotisserie and sandwich counter," students may select from "fire-oven baked pizza, pasta, vegetarian selections, ethnic cuisine, a salad bar and desserts." Meals are offered on a declining balance system; students opt for one of several sized plans and are charged for the exact amount of food they take by a swipe of their Three Crowns Card. The cafeteria is open daily from 7 a.m. until 11 p.m., although the best selection of food is available at the "usual" eating times. While students may also use meal plan dollars at the campus center coffee bar, there are no off-campus meal options available.

Not Just a Number

Gustavus Adolphus runs on the semester system, with four-month fall and spring terms sandwiched around a January "J-term" that offers an opportunity for intensive exploration. Each course counts for one credit, and students must complete 34 credits—including three J-term courses—over their four years. Despite the "pretty extensive list of general education requirements" that forms the basis of the college's liberal arts philosophy, many students find space in their schedules to double-major; one even reported two majors and a minor. Beginning with the class of 2009, two semesters of foreign language study are included in the general education requirements.

Biology is reportedly the most popular major, with communication studies quickly gaining sway. Many students also choose to study management. Biology and physics classes are known to be difficult, and one senior called Bio 101 "the true weeding-out class for pre-med students." While introductory lecture courses may enroll many dozens of students, higher-level classes taken for the major often have fewer than ten people. Registration for classes is online, and students with more credits register first. While getting excluded from capped classes is sometimes a problem for underclassmen, nobody reported trouble enrolling in a class for the major.

> "It's a nice feeling not to be just a number in the crowd of students. No one really falls into the masses here."

In addition to attending some larger lecture classes, every freshman enrolls in a First Term Seminar (FTS), chosen from a wide variety of disciplines. The FTS serves both as an introduction to college writing (a much appreciated writing credit for the general education requirements) and an opportunity to develop a relationship with a faculty member who will serve as the student's adviser until the declaration of a major.

In addition to the formal relationship with their FTS instructors and major advisers, students report the high availability of all of their professors as a great strength of the college. "I've never had a problem catching a professor," said one sophomore, who added that in addition to posting and holding regular office hours, most instructors are available by appointment or for meals. "Even the president of the college eats in The Caf!" According to another student, "when you start to get into your major, the classes get really small, and your professors will see you on campus and know your name. It's a nice feeling not to be just a number in the crowd of students. No one really falls into the masses here."

The Gustie Life

"Gusties" involve themselves in a wide variety of activities, including the *Gustavian Weekly* (the student newspaper), the student senate, College Democrats and Republicans, choir, theater, Queers and Allies, and even the "Gaming Group," which spends its early mornings fencing with foam swords while wearing capes. Because Gustavus Adolphus is a Lutheran college, "there is a huge focus on faith on campus," and there are several Christian student groups. One popular group, Proclaim, is particularly notable for its Tuesday evening contemporary worship service. The high level of participation in extracurricular organizations, religious or otherwise, makes such activities popular ways for Gusties to meet each other.

Fraternities and sororities are moderately popular, with about a quarter of the campus involved in Greek life. The two-week pledge period takes place at the beginning of sophomore year, with pre-rush events held at the end of the first year. Greek organizations are not allowed to have houses, but many have "unofficial houses," which are best known for their weekend parties. Even so, one sister reports that Greeks are "required to be pro-active on campus and do educationals and activities for the rest of campus and for the St. Peter community."

In addition to attending parties at off-campus houses, many freshmen pass their Friday nights at "The Dive," Gustavus Adolphus' campus dance club. One sophomore describes the scene at The Dive as "drunk, sweaty freshmen dancing close together." Having exhausted the limited social options of St. Peter, upperclassmen tend to take their cars to Mankato, about ten minutes away from campus and the home of Minnesota State-Mankato, or to the Twin Cities of St. Paul and Minneapolis, about an hour's drive. The availability of on-campus parking for less than $100 per year makes it possible for the majority of upperclassmen bring their cars. Gusties usually take trips to Mankato "to shop, go to the bars or eat out." In addition to the traditional party nights of Friday and Saturday, many students spend Wednesday nights out because few have Thursday classes.

Gustie athletic events are another social outlet for many students, especially when the highly ranked Division III program is enjoying success on the field, court or rink. Soccer, football, basketball and hockey ("It's Minnesota!" one student reminds us) are all favorites. At the game, in the classroom, or on campus, there will always be people wearing Gustavus apparel. As one student notes, "if you're a Gustie, you're proud of it."

Despite the variety of activities in which Gustavus Adolphus students involve themselves, many cite the same complaint about the college: a lack of diversity. Gusties acknowledge that the recruitment of minority students is a "genuine" institutional priority, but that the school has difficulty drawing students from outside of "Minnesota, Wisconsin, Iowa and the Dakotas," as one student put it. The college has increased its recruitment of international students, but according to one student, the campus is still "more of a 'tossed salad' than a 'melting pot,' " with minority students befriending other minority students or spending time at the Diversity Center.

A Community of Scholars

Despite Gusties' brief lamentation over the things that their campus lacks, most describe the Gustavus Adolphus experience as an overwhelmingly positive one. Many look forward to the annual Nobel conference in October, when the campus hosts Nobel laureates and other renowned scholars. Previous conference topics have included "Genetics in the New Millennium," "Unveiling the Solar System: 30 Years of Exploration," and "Nature out of Balance: Unlocking the New Ecology." Other major events include the May Day Conference, held every May 1 on topics of peace, and Christmas in Christ Chapel, an annual Christmas program involving "the entire choir and dance departments."

Most of all, Gustavus Adolphus students appreciate the sense of community that the college fosters. One junior said, "I love the idea that I am able to walk around on campus and pretty much have a general sense of who people are, but still be able to meet new people. Because the campus has enough students to do that, I meet someone new practically every day!" Gusties enjoy themselves while taking advantage of the college's myriad opportunities, and many echo this simple sentiment of one senior: "I love this little campus on the hill."—*Douglas London*

FYI

If you come to Gustavus Adolphus, you'd better bring "a snowsuit, mittens, a hat, a facemask, a HUGE jacket, and a strong will to be outside in these subzero temperatures!"

What's the typical weekend schedule? "Depends on who you are. Some drink, some do homework, but it is a guaranteed good time at Gustavus!"

If I could change one thing about Gustavus Adolphus, "I would increase diversity and cultural awareness."

Three things that every student at Gustavus Adolphus should do before graduating are "go 'traying' down Old Main Hill after the first snow, spend a starry night in the Arboretum, and have a 4 a.m. breakfast at Oodles after pulling an all-nighter."

Macalester College

Address: Macalester, 1600 Grand Avenue, St. Paul, MN 55105
Phone: 651-696-6357
E-mail Address: admissions@macalester.edu
Web site URL: http://www.macalester.edu
Year Founded: 1,874
Private or Public: Private
Religious affiliation: Presbyterian (historic affiliation)
Location: Urban
Regular Application Deadline: 15-Jan
Number of Applicants: 4,826
Percent Accepted: 39%
Percent Accepted who enroll: 27%
Number Entering: 523
Number of Transfers Accepted each Year: varies
Mean SAT: NA
Mean ACT: NA

Middle 50% SAT range: math: 630–710; verbal: 630–740
Middle 50% ACT range: 27–32
Early admission program (EA/ ED/ NA): ED
ED or EA Acceptance Rate: 50%
Full time Undergraduate enrollment: 1,884
Total enrollment: 1,918
Percent Male: 42%
Percent Female: 58%
Total Percent Minority: 17%
Percent African-American: 4%
Percent Asian/Pacific Islander: 8%
Percent Hispanic: 4%
Percent Native-American: 1%
Percent Other: 0%
Percent in-state / out of state: NA

Percent from Public HS: 68%
Retention Rate: 93%
Graduation Rate: 86%
Percent in On-campus housing: 66%
Percent affiliated with Greek system: 0%
Percent Varsity or Club Athletes: 35%
Number of official organized extracurricular organizations: 80
3 Most popular majors: Economics, Political Science, English
Student/Faculty ratio: 11:01
Tuition and Fees: $31,038.00
Cost for Room and Board: $7,982.00
Percent receiving Financial aid, first-year: 93%

Want to learn how to play the bagpipes for free? Or to express your political beliefs on a large rock? At Macalester, you're in luck. Bagpipe lessons and "painting the rock" are only two of the many opportunities that Mac offers its quirky, passionate students. "Everyone at Macalester is a dork about something," one sophomore remarked. "Everybody has their thing that they're totally into and totally not ashamed of, whether that's music or geology or obscure Asian countries." At Macalester, students have the opportunity to explore these interests—and develop new ones along the way.

Academics: The Difficult and the 'Trippy'

Popular majors include International Studies and Political Science, though one senior adds that Mac students "have pretty random minors" due to the diversity of their interests. To fulfill distribution requirements, many non-science majors flock to classes such as

"Contemporary Concepts" (better known as "Physics for Poets"), which one student describes as "sort of trippy." And while another student compared his astronomy class to a "PBS kid's show," academic life at Macalester is certainly not easy. "Professors won't hand you anything on a platter. . . . Classes can be hard, and they should be," remarked one sophomore. Students contend that grade inflation is minimal, but department policies differ. Chemistry and Economics, for example, rank amongst the most difficult subjects to get A's in.

Students rave about the availability of professors, most of whom are addressed by first name. "They are your friends, advisers and devil's advocate in discussion. . . . You get tons of personal attention," said one political science major. From their first days on campus, students have a chance to interact closely with their professors. Every freshman enrolls in a "first-year course," which is capped at 16 students. The professor serves as the adviser for everyone in the class. Roughly half of these are "residential courses" in which students live on the same floor as the rest of their class. One current senior fondly recalls his own time spent writing papers late into the night with his floor, and the "comfortable feeling of coming home" that such a community engenders. His first year course, four years later, still has reunions.

Coming Home

Freshmen and sophomores are required to live on campus. Three residence halls—Turck, Dupre, and Doty—are reserved for freshmen. Dupre, with its "castle-slit windows, cinder block walls, and a generally retro decor" is acknowledged as having the worst rooms. But, as one sophomore notes, "It was truly dorm living. Everyone had their doors open all the time and it was a great way to get to know people." On the other end of the spectrum is Turck, which was renovated in the summer of 2004.

After freshman year, housing is assigned by lottery, in a process aided by "staff people and colorful maps," which one student affirms is "actually rather civil." Students are impressed by "amazingly spacious sophomore housing," which may boast extras such as walk-in closets and alcoves. Upperclassmen can choose to live in the "gender-blind" suites of George Draper Dayton (GDD), where anything goes as long as there are no male/female pairs sharing a double. On campus housing also includes the Veggie Co-op, language houses, and the cultural house, which also provides meeting space for campus multicultural organizations.

Those who chose to venture off campus are supported by ResLife, which maintains a database of available housing in the area. However, students typically find housing through friends or word of mouth instead. In either case, students generally agree that off-campus housing is both convenient and not impossible to find. "The neighborhood is packed with Mac kids," observes one junior. For those living off-campus, a car is not necessary—the public transportation system is described as "pretty incredible," and most housing is within an easy bike ride of classes.

In and Out of the Bubble

"It does get cold here . . . but we get most of January off, and that really, really helps," remarks a sophomore from California. Aside from the winters that "toughen you up," Macalester's location in St. Paul, Minn., is ideal. Students are able to take advantage of the easy access to both the rest of St. Paul and nearby Minneapolis both in and out of the classroom. One geography major reflected on his experiences in Urban Geography, a class requiring extensive exploration of St. Paul. "It gave me a good understanding of the discipline of geography and a real appreciation for the city of St. Paul and American cities beyond New York," he asserts. Others take advantage of the many cultural events, internships and volunteer opportunities that the Twin Cities provide, giving students a chance "to explore the real world instead of being stuck in a college bubble."

The Macalester campus itself also has much to offer. Two of the busiest buildings on campus are Old Main and Campus Center. Old Main is the oldest building on campus and is described as "cheerful . . . like something out of Harry Potter." It houses several academic departments and classrooms. It is also connected to the campus library, a much appreciated convenience during the long Minnesota winters. Known as the "Link," the space is used 24 hours a day as a study room. Meanwhile, the relatively new Campus Center houses everything from the post office to a lounge with a large TV and comfortable couches to the one cafeteria on campus—Café Mac.

Whether they're meat-lovers, vegans, or somewhere in-between, students seem satisfied with the offerings of Café Mac. One freshman raved about the wood-fire baked pizza, "so many varieties and ALL so good!" Others have a soft spot for grilled cheese and tomato soup, and still another relies on "the old faithful option: rice with four different and alternating types of curry". The café also functions as a social center of campus. "My social life revolves around seeing people there (well, and in the library)," one junior remarked.

"Running Boy"
Both volunteerism and social justice are important focuses of campus life at Macalester. Students engage in a variety of community service projects, with focuses on everything from local refugee populations to conservation to the public school system. "We do tend to get ahead of ourselves," laughed one sophomore, in recognition of the strong presence of politically active students. "I thought I was WAY liberal before coming here. Now I think I'm more middle of the road," another student remarks. "Mac is defined by people's willingness to listen to a variety of ideas."

The college is also defined by a strong international presence on campus. Macalester boasts an impressive number—between 14 percent and 18 percent—of foreign students, depending on whether or not those with dual citizenship are counted. A plethora of on-campus groups showcase and celebrate this diversity, and the cultural house serves as an important venue for some of these functions. Some complain, however, that these students tend to be cliquish. As one sophomore remarked, "One on one, the international students are great. But when they're gathered together I don't really feel comfortable around them." Upperclassmen find that this trend fades as students become older.

> "People look and dress and act however they want and it's all OK. As long as you're not a Republican."

The student body is described by one member as "small-but not too small." Its size allows the entire student body to at least recognize each other, while some of the quirkier members become pseudo celebrities. Standouts include "Running Boy," a student who wears cargo shorts year round and runs through the cold, "Che," a student fond of channeling Che Guevera's look, and the recently graduated "Pirate Guy." For most, however, campus style is casual bordering on effortless. "There's just very little pressure here," said one student. "People look and dress and act however they want and it's all OK. As long as you're not a Republican."

Entertainment on campus abounds, and social life is almost as diverse as the student body itself. While the surrounding Twin Cities offer their own fair share of attractions, there's enough happening on campus to more than satisfy Mac students. Some students choose to drink, but report feeling no pressure to do so. "The baseball and football parties are the closest thing we have to frat parties, and they're still pretty far away from that label," says a current senior. However, this is certainly not the only weekend option. "There are the clusters of students watching movies, playing guitar, gaming, organizing alcohol-free dances in the basement of the freshman dorm, or hanging out at the cafés half a block away. Oh yeah, or swing dancing in the Campus Center," reports one student.

Introducing . . . Mac the Scottie
Students may participate in varsity, junior varsity, club, or intramural sports at Macalester. Intramurals are casual—for some team members, the games serve as their first exposure to a sport! Club sports vary in terms of time commitments. Women's crew, for example, rows for more than two hours a day. Women's club rugby, recently revived by Macalester students, demands about six hours a week from its members. In sum, student athletes who do not wish to compete on the varsity level have a decent amount of options to chose from.

In the words of a current sophomore, "People don't come here hoping it will be a rah-rah football school." Indeed, one student said the football team "just plain sucks." Soccer games, however, are relatively popular events. Macalester boasts "the most creative and outlandish fans anywhere." who enjoy supporting their team with shouts of "drink blood, smoke crack, worship Satan, go Mac!" (ironically, Macalester is officially Presbyterian). Furthermore, efforts to improve school spirit have included the introduction of a new mascot, Mac the Scottie.

"There's a big sense of community at Mac. We're very proud to be a school that values internationalism, multiculturalism, and diversity so highly," remarks one student. Indeed, the opportunities at Macalester are so vast that its reach spans the globe. As one Tanzanian student asserts, "Coming from many miles away the social and academic environment has been fulfilling. . . . I think that is the most important investment anybody can make in their life."—*Stephanie Brockman*

FYI

If you come to Macalester, you'd better bring "a socially conscious cause to fight for" and "an atlas."

What's the typical weekend schedule? "Friday night: party hopping at upperclassmen's houses off campus. Saturday: sleep in, brunch at the dining hall, homework in the afternoon. Saturday night: a cultural show or a play and then just casually hanging out with some friends, maybe go to an on campus dance, maybe have a few beers. Sunday: work."

If I could change one thing about Macalester, I'd "add a few more fiery conservatives to the student body."

Three things every student at Macalester should do before graduating are "go to a soccer game and realize that we have school spirit, walk out on the rocks by the Mississippi River because it's really cool and the Minneapolis skyline is pretty, and have a 3 a.m. meal at Mickey's Diner to see the kind of people who hang out late at night in Downtown St. Paul."

St. John's University / College of St. Benedict

Address: St. John's/St. Benedict, PO Box 7155, Collegeville, MN 56321-7155

Phone: 320-363-2196

E-mail Address: admissions@csbsju.edu

Web site URL: www.csbsju.edu

Year Founded: 1857

Private or Public: private

Religious affiliation: Roman Catholic

Location: rural

Application and Admissions Information: rolling

Regular Application Deadline: NA

Number of Applicants: 2,651

Percent Accepted: 86%

Percent Accepted who enroll: 46%

Number Entering: 1,133

Number of Transfers Accepted each Year: 87

Mean SAT: 0

Mean ACT: NA

Middle 50% SAT range: 1,060–1,290

Middle 50% ACT range: 23–27

Early admission program (EA/ ED/ NA): NA

ED or EA Acceptance Rate: NA

Full time Undergraduate enrollment: 3,904

Total enrollment: 4,103

Percent Male: 48%

Percent Female: 52%

Total Percent Minority: 10%

Percent African-American: 1%

Percent Asian/Pacific Islander: 2%

Percent Hispanic: 1%

Percent Native-American: 1%

Percent Other: 5%

Percent in-state / out of state: 81%/19%

Percent from Public HS: 72%

Retention Rate: 90%

Graduation Rate: 80%

Percent in On-campus housing: 82%

Percent affiliated with Greek system: 0%

Percent Varsity or Club Athletes: NA

Number of official organized extracurricular organizations: 89

3 Most popular majors: Management, Biology, Psychology

Student/Faculty ratio: 13:01

Tuition and Fees: $24,924.00

Cost for Room and Board: $6,697.00

Percent receiving Financial aid, first-year: 99%

The "Bennies" and "Johnnies" of College of St. Benedict/St. John's University know they attend a unique institution. Forget, for a moment, the on-campus abbey and monastery, which house some of the schools' professors. CSB/SJU, one of the top Catholic liberal arts schools in the country, is actually two schools in one: College of St. Benedict, an all-women's school, and St. John's University, an all-men's school. Each boasts its own administration, athletic program, library, bookstore and dining halls. Yet at the same time, students from both schools interact with each other on a daily basis, both in and out of the classroom. Only late at night, when everyone is (theoretically) asleep, are the two campuses single sex.

Not only do CSB/SJU students know their campus is unique, they also know it is gorgeous. The campus is surrounded by woods and filled with trails that offer tons of opportunities for exploration and recreation. Some students, for example, enjoy the "chapel walk," a trail which leads to the Stella Maris Chapel on the SJU campus. Legend has it that if two people walk it together, they will get married.

Two of Everything

Because the institution is really two different schools, students benefit from access to facilities on both the St. Ben's and St. John's campuses. When it comes time to study they may head to either one of two libraries. According to students, the CSB library often turns into "a social gathering," but also features a café where they can grab some caffeine to fuel late-night studying. Meanwhile, the SJU library offers a quieter atmosphere. While its basement, nicknamed 'The Dungeon,' is "creepy" for some students, it offers others the silence they need. One junior summed up the difference by stating that he studies "in St. John's library when I want to get things done and St. Ben's library when I don't . . ."

Classrooms are also split between the two campuses. But the half hour between classes gives students plenty of time to commute from one side to the other by taking 'The Link,' a free shuttle bus service. The Link operates day and night to allow students to travel between St. John's and St. Ben's not only for academic purposes, but also to visit friends and participate in extracurricular activities.

Throughout their four years on campus, CSB/SJU students have the opportunity to develop strong relationships with their professors. Even at the introductory level, students may work closely with their professors because class sizes are so small. Additionally, all first-year students participate in a symposium, a seminar capped at 18 students. The professor of the symposium class serves as the academic advisor for his or her students, and students say everyone gets to know each other extremely well. And while they do take academics seriously, students say they still maintain a deep sense of community on campus. "People get really competitive, but in a good way," one freshman observed. "It is not like they are ready to kill each other, but they really give their best to be on top."

Bennies and Johnnies have many opportunities to explore their academic options. "I switched majors more times than I can count," admits a current double major in communication and Spanish, ". . . and I was even able to study abroad for seven months." The sheer diversity of classes offered and opportunities extended to students is also impressive. In particular, study abroad is a very popular option for students on both campuses. One Bennie pointed out, "You ask your friends 'where are you going to study abroad,' not 'are you going to study abroad.' " CSB/SJU offers 17 different semester-long programs in several countries. In many of these programs, students participate with other Bennies and Johnnies and are taught by local professors. Academic advisors are "very helpful" in working with students to include study abroad credits in their academic schedule while still completing required classes and the requirements of their major(s).

Eating and Sleeping

Students are more than satisfied with the housing at both St. Ben's and St. John's, especially with the apartment-style residences available for juniors and seniors. Luetmer, an on-campus apartment complex for CSB seniors, offers each resident his or her own bedroom and includes a washer and dryer within every apartment. Either a community advisor (CA) in upperclassmen apartments or a resident advisors (RA) in the residence halls will act "as a program planner, conflict solver, therapist, rule enforcer, etc." Furthermore, in accordance with the Benedictine Values, students at SJU adhere to a tradition of keeping the doors to their rooms open when they are in the room. "This allows other students the opportunity to stop in, say hi, and meet new people," pointed out a current sophomore.

Students give campus food mixed reviews. While one student asserted that "it's not that good and it's overpriced," another felt "the food is really good on both campuses." Regardless how they feel about the food itself, however, students do appreciate the variety of options offered. A popular eating destination is the Refectory, or "the Reef," the dining hall at St. John's.

St. John's and St. Ben's prohibit underage students from drinking on campus, a policy which is strictly enforced. However, on weekends, one freshman observed, "everybody or almost everybody is drinking." Adds a current junior, "if people choose not to drink they are questioned as to why they made that decision—it seems abnormal." But another student countered, "I get [pressured to drink] more at home with my friends there. I like to have a good time, and am pretty crazy without the alcohol, so I seem to fit in just fine." Students over 21 can obtain permits to have parties in their rooms on campus, and St. John's University has its own on-campus pub. Otherwise, students may head to St. Joseph, the town in which College of St. Benedict is located. The small town boasts numerous "party houses" with names such as "Chubbie," "Dingleberry," and "The Chicken Shack."

But weekends at CSB/SJU are about more than just partying. There are frequent opportunities to see movies on campus, attend cultural events such as the Festival of Cultures and the Asian New Year, or even venture into nearby St. Cloud for shopping, dining, or just hanging out. Of course, students also have the option of participating in one of the many extracurricular activities at CSB/SJU. Community service is "a huge thing on campus," and additional opportunities range from writing for the school newspaper to participating in Companions on a Journey, a faith group, or campus ministry. And of course, there are the football games.

Alumni Gone Wild

Football games are some of the most important student events of the year. "People go crazy!" exclaimed one Bennie. Alumni turn out for the home games with "their spouses, kids, grandkids . . . you name it, they are there." One CSB senior bragged that "there is a lot of pride in being a 'Bennie' or a 'Johnnie'." As a social event and as a display of school spirit, football games are "definitely a big deal," boasting the "highest attendance for football games among Division III sports." And with a 2003 NCAA Division III championship under their belts as well consistently successful seasons, the football games' popularity is well deserved. Students also pointed to hockey and Bennie basketball as other popular sports to attend.

Of course, students have ample opportunities to participate in sports as well. A former varsity swimmer cited his athletic experience on campus as a positive one, stressing that "my coaches were really understanding that my academics come first." Student athletes, who also enjoy a large banquet and dance at the end of the year, note that sports are a great opportunity to meet others. But if the time commitment of a varsity sport is too demanding, participation in intramural sports is always an option. "There is simply no question that the best intramural sport on campus is softball," asserted one Johnnie, who added that large numbers of Bennies and Johnnies turn out every year for the sport.

Feeling Comfortable on Campus

Campus traditions are numerous. Many rave, for example, about the CSB/SJU Thanksgiving dinner. "Students are dressed formal and served as a table. Somebody from the table has to get up and carve the turkey and then all the food is served family style," one current senior said, adding, "It's really fun." Other traditions range from a large snowball fight on the first snowfall of every year to Pinestock, an annual event in which a "big name band" comes to campus to put on a day-long music festival. "So many students look forward to April!" one Johnnie explained.

> "Both campuses are very welcoming and the students are very friendly."

Time and again, Bennie and Johnnies point out the feeling of community that truly defines their college experience. "Both campuses are very welcoming and the students are very friendly," noted one junior. Another pointed to the role of Benedictine Values, a set of 12 Christian guidelines practiced in everyday campus life. Although students may not know them by heart, they nevertheless "play a pretty big role here . . . Students are helpful and very respectful of one another." Remarked one Johnnie, "I wouldn't change my college for all the money in the world."—*Stephanie Brockman*

FYI
If you come to CSB/SJU, you'd better bring "a smile...fitting in means being friendly!" What is the typical weekend schedule? "Finish classes, have some fun, do a little homework, have some fun, finish the homework you didn't do yet, go to church (time permitting)."
If I could change one thing about CSB/SJU, I'd "have more diversity on campus."
Three things that every student at CSB/SJU should do before graduating are "take the Chapel Walk, study abroad, and go to the annual Thanksgiving dinner."

St. Olaf College

Address: St. Olaf, 1520 St. Olaf Avenue, Northfield, MN 55057

Phone: 507-646-3025

E-mail Address: admissions@stolaf.edu

Web site URL: http://www.stolaf.edu

Year Founded: 1874

Private or Public: Private

Religious affiliation: Lutheran

Location: Rural

Regular Application Deadline: rolling

Number of Applicants: 3,437

Percent Accepted: 66%

Percent Accepted who enroll: 35%

Number Entering: 792

Number of Transfers Accepted each Year: NA

Mean SAT: 1,920

Mean ACT: 28

Middle 50% SAT range: 1,810–2,120

Middle 50% ACT range: 25–30

Early admission program (EA/ ED/ NA): ED / EA

ED or EA Acceptance Rate: NA

Full time Undergraduate enrollment: 2,993

Total enrollment: 2,993

Percent Male: 55%

Percent Female: 45%

Total Percent Minority: 10%

Percent African-American: 1%

Percent Asian/Pacific Islander: 5%

Percent Hispanic: 2%

Percent Native-American: 0%

Percent Other: 2%

Percent in-state / out of state: 58%/42%

Percent from Public HS: 84%

Retention Rate: 93%

Graduation Rate: 85%

Percent in On-campus housing: 96%

Percent affiliated with Greek system: 0%

Percent Varsity or Club Athletes: NA

Number of official organized extracurricular organizations: 139

3 Most popular majors: English Language and Literature, Mathematics

Student/Faculty ratio: 13:01

Tuition and Fees: $28,200

Cost for Room and Board: $7,400

Percent receiving Financial aid, first-year: 81%

A belief in the value of a strong and cohesive community suffuses St. Olaf's idyllic Northfield, Minnesota campus. Boasting a freethinking, committed student body, diverse academic programs (especially strong in the arts), and a good relationship with the town, St. Olaf offers every student "a chance to really fulfill your own potential."

Keeping Busy in the Cold

One of the realities of going to school in rural Minnesota is that the winters are, quite simply, freezing. Though the students don't seem to mind this—activities such as an extravagant Christmas Fest and traditions such as sliding down Old Main Hill on a dining hall tray necessitate winter weather—it is a defining characteristic of the campus life. However, there are plenty of distractions from the chilly environment, and on a compact campus like St. Olaf, it isn't difficult to find them.

The hilltop campus, comprised mostly of limestone buildings "built to look like Norway," is called "gorgeous" and "an absolute utopia" by students. One remarked, "Our campus is even more beautiful than the pamphlets." Another added, "The gorgeous natural lands around the campus are great for taking a walk or a run." Student groups, faculty and staff all work together to protect the natural ecology with an active agenda of environmental awareness and conservation. The fall brings spectacular color to the trees, and the winter a significant amount of snow. In good weather, "Oles" congregate on the lawns to socialize or study; in the winter, they gather in the library or in the Fireside Lounge. One academic building, Holland Hall, is said to look like Hogwarts. In addition, the University has recently built a number of new facilities, including the Tostrud Athletic Center and the Dittmann Center for Visual Arts and Dance.

Students are actively involved in the surrounding town, as many organizations branch out into the community and a lot of students attend church off campus. The "Love Bus" is the convenient, popular mode of transportation to get into town on the weekends. One particular aspect of St. Olaf's location that several students mentioned is its proximity to Carleton College, as the Oles enjoy a healthy rivalry with that other student body.

St. Olaf is internationally known for its

arts programs, most notably in music. Both inside and outside of the popular formal music major, a musical influence pervades the campus. One student says that although it seems that "everyone is in Ole choir (we have a nationally broadcasted concert every Christmas) it's not true. There actually are people here who are not musical." Many students come to St. Olaf for the excellent (though notoriously challenging) music performance, theory and education curriculum. There are also a plethora of concerts held by all different kinds of student groups on campus.

Students say that other extracurricular opportunities are strong and varied, with large numbers participating in political groups, social organizations and religious groups, of which the Fellowship of Christian Athletes is "the biggest." Other popular clubs are Frisbee, tennis, golf, ballroom dancing and swing dancing. There are more unique organizations as well, such as the American Sign Language Club and Musiko Nova, a group for student composers and anyone interested in contemporary music. Many students work on campus jobs, which one student said is "a great way to make friends." Another student noted that "entrepreneurship is highly valued at St. Olaf," and there is a special fund set up to give students money to produce CDs or buy equipment for a fledgling business. Students are encouraged to start their own clubs, and they often participate in organizing activities such as the Nobel Peace Prize Forum, which features a Nobel Laureate as the keynote speaker and draws a national audience.

Varsity athletic programs at Division III St. Olaf are strong, especially in cross-country (the women's team consistently wins their conference), swimming and baseball. One student noted that the hockey team is also popular, and "a lot of people go to football games, but the team isn't actually all that good." In general, Oles turn out to support their teammates. "There's a fair amount of spirit," a junior said. "Since it's such a small school, it's just being faithful to your friends." Intramurals are extremely popular, and the on-campus sports facilities are well-kept. The newly constructed Tostrud Building houses an indoor track, weight rooms, and a climbing wall.

A Strong Foundation

In general, academics at St. Olaf are what one would expect from a school its size—small classes, lots of personal attention, and interesting professors. "I've been extremely pleased with all of my professors," said one senior, noting "their approachability and their genuine concern for my life as an academic and as a developing adult." One student recalled a professor who sent students in and out of the revolving doors of the student center as a way of demonstrating protein transport across cell membranes; another had an art class where the professor "jumped up on the table and started screaming profanities." Physics professor Rober Jacobel recently had a glacier in Antarctica named after him.

Although academics are strong across the board, students agree that the St. Olaf atmosphere is more focused on the humanities. The strongest and most competitive major is music, while English also gets positive reviews. Some students say economics and psychology are weaker, though psychology is improving. The hard sciences are strong, but as one student said, "don't take organic chemistry unless it is absolutely necessary. If you do, be prepared to seek counseling for a loss in self-worth." In addition to all the usual majors, the school also offers a program through its Center for Integrative Studies where students can design their own majors. According to one student, "This is a unique opportunity for students to work one-on-one with various faculty members and other experts in an interdisciplinary or highly specialized academic focus that may not otherwise be offered at the undergraduate level."

Students at St. Olaf are required to complete 35 full courses (each one worth approximately four semester credits) to receive their degree. They also must complete the general education distributional requirements, which are made up of three different areas. "Foundation studies" includes basic skills in writing, language, math, and a physical education requirement. "Core studies" covers more diverse areas, emphasizing history, literature and natural science, which includes two courses on biblical and theological study. The third component is an "integrative ethics" course in which students pick from a variety of offerings. According to the course catalog, this course area addresses "the questions of justice, morality, rights, and responsibilities, often in the context of a student's major." One student deemed the general education requirements "very reasonable," but another believed that they "change a little too often" and can be difficult to keep track of.

Every class at St. Olaf is taught by a full professor, and students report few problems getting into classes, especially after freshman year. The logistics of keeping classes small can be difficult—as one student said, "Registration is a nightmare, but class size is great, usually about 20 to 30 students." There is also a well-connected and widely used study abroad program. One student called the school "very serious" about enabling students to spend a term or more in another country.

Music and Revelry

St. Olaf's campus is officially dry, which can mean different things to different students. While they generally agree that alcohol is easily obtainable, it also means that there are lots of alternatives, and the social scene is diverse. One student said, "I would compare it to high school. People do drugs here; some people do a lot. While drinking is common, one never needs to feel left out. There are always people who aren't drinking." Another added, "When people are bored, they get creative. Sledding is a good example." Buntrock Commons, the student center, is the home of "The Pause," a completely student-run hangout that features pool tables, movies, concerts, and dances. Some students will also go into town to places such as the American Legion Club for live music, or to unique local bars such as the Contented Cow or Froggy Bottoms. The biggest off-campus parties happen either at the Legion or at the Grand, an old theater converted into a dance hall and bar.

The casual dating scene at St. Olaf is rather non-existent, which one student attributed to the intimacy of the campus in general. "Casual dating is hard because if you go *anywhere* with someone, people who know you see you and ask about it later," she said. "So people tend to not date around at all or to be in very long term relationships. There's not a very active middle ground . . . sadly."

The musical tradition of St. Olaf means that there are also many concerts happening all the time. The most famous is the annual Christmas Festival, when 12,000 people descend on Northfield to hear, among other things, five St. Olaf choirs and the school's top orchestra. The Pause hosts weekly musical performances given by students (such as the Limestones, the famous all-male a

cappella group), faculty, or guest musicians. In addition, theater and improvisational comedy groups are active and well supported.

Students live in coed buildings on single-sex floors, and the lack and price of nearby housing means that over 90 percent of students live on campus all four years. First year students have JCs (Junior Counselors) and everyone has RAs (Resident Assistants) who "can bust you for having alcohol" but who are also "pretty cool." Older students have the option of living in "honor houses." Some of these houses are themed, such as the French House, but a senior reported that "generally people will come up with a year-long service project and they will get a house." One student calls the main dining hall "a mecca for conversation and people watching," and the food is cited as "practically gourmet," with a large number of options for vegans and vegetarians. One student boasted, "We also have an awesome dessert selection. Try the white chocolate chip cookies!" In addition to the dining hall, there is a café called The Cage for snack foods and drinks.

St. Olaf was founded as a Lutheran college, and its official history declares that since its founding, "our Lutheran Christian perspective has remained at the very core of our identity." There are certainly non-Lutheran students at St. Olaf, but its religious spirit strongly influences the campus atmosphere. While some non-Christian students report feeling uncomfortable at times, others say they appreciate the general respect for spirituality on campus, and people don't feel like religion is being forced upon them.

> "The sense of community and honesty and trust here are really the core ingredients of this school."

As one might expect from a Lutheran college in Minnesota, the student body tends towards homogeneity. Many are of Scandinavian descent, and a large number come from Minnesota and Wisconsin. As one student pointed out, "We swim in a sea of Norwegian sweaters." However, a senior extolled the "huge international perspective. Oles have traveled the world and bring their experiences into their everyday lives. People are aware of the world, and in that sense we are diverse." Another added, "St. Olaf is not your typical small, overwhelmingly liberal college. There is a great diversity of political beliefs and a lot of (usually) respectful discussion and debate."

In general, Oles love the tight-knit community and close relationships their college provides. As one student put it, "The sense of community and honesty and trust here are really the core ingredients of this school." He went on to add, "We don't have locks on our mailboxes, kids just leave their schoolbags unattended outside of the dining hall when we eat, everyone smiles and waves even at people they don't know in passing." One senior commented that since "we live in a beautiful area with everything we could want, sometimes the real world is a shock when we graduate," but even so, students' experiences at St. Olaf are something that they would never trade. One student's final remark was, "Despite its idiosyncrasies, St. Olaf is truly an idyllic place full of thoughtful people with a passion for pursuing knowledge for the sake of improving life not only for themselves, but those people whose lives they will touch. I treasure the time I spent there."—*David Carpman*

FYI

If you come to St. Olaf, you'd better bring a "a Nalgene bottle, a musical instrument and a heavy winter coat."

What is the typical weekend schedule? "Friday night, a little studying before the dances start; Saturday, going on little trips to the cities, or the apple orchard, or a coffee shop, then parties in the houses on Ole Ave; Sunday, church and then homework."

If I could change one thing about St. Olaf, I would "diversify the campus."

Three things every student at St. Olaf should do before graduating are "go to Christmas Fest, have lunch with your favorite professor, and try the lutefisk."

University of Minnesota

Address: University of Minnesota, 240 Williamson Hall, 231 Pillsbury Dr. SE, Minneapolis, MN 55455
Phone: 800-752-1000
E-mail Address: NA
Web site URL: admissions.umn.edu
Year Founded: 1851
Private or Public: public
Religious affiliation: none
Location: urban
Regular Application Deadline: 15-Dec
Number of Applicants: 20,614
Percent Accepted: 71%
Percent Accepted who enroll: 36%
Number Entering: 7,187
Number of Transfers Accepted each Year: 2,900
Mean SAT: NA
Mean ACT: NA

Middle 50% SAT range: 1,110–1,350
Middle 50% ACT range: 23–28
Early admission program (EA/ ED/ NA): NA
ED or EA Acceptance Rate: NA
Full time Undergraduate enrollment: 26,957
Total enrollment: 51,175
Percent Male: 47%
Percent Female: 53%
Total Percent Minority: 22%
Percent African-American: 4%
Percent Asian/Pacific Islander: 9%
Percent Hispanic: 2%
Percent Native-American: 1%
Percent Other: 5%
Percent in-state / out of state: 74%/26%

Percent from Public HS: NA
Retention Rate: 87%
Graduation Rate: 61%
Percent in On-campus housing: 22%
Percent affiliated with Greek system: NA
Percent Varsity or Club Athletes: NA
Number of official organized extracurricular organizations: NA
3 Most popular majors: Social Sciences, Engineering, Business/Marketing
Student/Faculty ratio: 15:01
Tuition and Fees: $9,410.00
In State Tuition and Fees (if different): $21,040.00
Cost for Room and Board: $6,824.00
Percent receiving Financial aid, first-year: 61%

D o you want to become part of a tradition of groundbreaking innovation and crowd-shaking victory? Students at the University of Minnesota attest to the variety of opportunities available at their college both inside and outside the classroom.

Go-pher it!

How does the University of Minnesota offer so many choices, opportunities and possibilities? One answer to this question is the size of the university itself. With four campuses—the Twin Cities campus standing as the largest—the University spans broadly across the center of Minneapolis. The urban setting of the university is one of its best aspects, says one freshman. It allows students to take hold of many metropolitan advantages, such as a major national center for business and the performing arts where many conventions, symposiums and exhibitions occur monthly. Also, students can attend the home games of many professional sports teams, including the Vikings, the Twins and the Timberwolves. According to one student, "Easy access to downtown Minneapolis is a huge plus. We go downtown all the time to shop, watch movies, eat dinner, and go to shows and concerts."

When one has enough of the busy activities in and around the University, one student reported that she goes to one of the national parks or lakes nearby to find some solitude and enjoy some time with nature. A frequently visited location around the University is an area known as Dinkytown, which is full of coffee shops, restaurants and clothing stores. One particularly popular restaurant is Annie's Parlour, an American food restaurant famous for its delicious ice cream. On campus, the University offers over 600 organizations, all of which give students yet another way to manifest their interests and find their own particular place within their large environment.

Many students enjoy the areas around the University so much that they decide to move off campus to relatively cheap housing nearby. Some consider joining the Greek life at the University, encouraged by sororities and fraternities that constitute a large part of the social scene. Even though the majority of students do not become members of the Greek system, a large portion of the student body attests to having attended several Greek parties before they graduate. "Frat parties are the thing to do, especially freshman year," says one sophomore.

For freshmen, dorm housing is guaranteed with the submission of a timely application. The University has eight residence halls and three apartment complexes, all of which provide suitable accommodations and locations proximal to classes. Many freshmen are housed in the "super block," an area with four dorms that one sophomore described as "pretty loud and rowdy," Other dorms, such as the Riverbend Commons, are quieter and can seem more like apartments than dormitories. To make the walk to class more comfortable and to shield students from cold or precipitation, the University of Minnesota is equipped with underground tunnels for student travel between the major university buildings. Rumor has it that the University of Minnesota adopted the Gopher as its mascot because it is symbolic of the burrowing done by students in the tunnels everyday. Another easy way to get around is the convenient bus system known as the Campus Connector, which students use to move between the East and West banks especially during the winter season.

The University's mission is threefold: research and discovery; teaching and learning; and outreach and public service. With so many things being offered, what else could you need at a place like this? Students say some warmer weather would be a major plus at the university campus, but then again, that's why the Gophers have their tunnels.

A Tradition of Accomplishment

The University of Minnesota, founded in 1851, has hosted the inventions of the first heart pacemaker, the retractable seat belt for automobiles, the heart-lung machine, and the black box for aircraft. As the only major research facility in the state, with the campus boasting a total of 14 libraries and award-winning faculty members, the University enjoys many federal grants for its hundreds of thrilling research projects. With a legacy of research achievements, the university particularly appeals to science-driven individuals. However, the University of Minnesota has much more to offer its incoming students than just science-based curricula. "The opportunities at the University of Minnesota run as rampant as the student spirit of the Gophers themselves!" says one freshman.

> **"The opportunities at the University of Minnesota run as rampant as the student spirit of the Gophers themselves!"**

The University includes several undergraduate colleges: the College of Food, Agricultural and Natural Resource Sciences; the College of Biological Sciences; the College of Education and Human Development; the College of Liberal Arts; the Carlson School of Management; the Institute of Technology; the College of Design, the College of Education and Human Development; and the College of Continuing Education. Each college offers a multitude of prestigious programs, fascinating lectures and hands-on opportunities, as well as a grand total of more than 145 majors. The offered areas of study satisfy a wide range of interests that spans from agricultural education to computer science to finance to sport studies. Whether a student wants to study forestry during a study-abroad program in Chile or take an online course to enhance his self-discipline and study skills at home, he can find a multitude of possibilities wherever he turns. One senior reports, "At first I was overwhelmed by the choices, but now I appreciate the freedom I have to choose." Many students choose a program that includes both a major and minor.

Maroon and Bold
The University of Minnesota boasts an impressive sporting legacy. These days, basketball and hockey take the lead in most fan attraction. One student reported that "Sporting events are always fun; hockey games are great, and so is basketball, for both men and women." Basketball certainly brings an added dimension of excitement for the University of Minnesota student body as it grows in strength and success from season to season. The teams continue to attain thrilling victories, providing students with great entertainment on the weekends. Men's basketball at the University of Minnesota has had a history of turning players into NBA stars. Most recent graduates that have since played in the NBA include Bobby Jackson, Quincy Lewis and Voshon Lenard. Women's basketball, likewise, has been an impressive squad for the Gophers, remaining a contender in the top 10 for many seasons.

The Mariucci Hockey Arena is also no stranger to huge crowds of rowdy, student fans. But the fans are not the only ones cheering loudly at the rink. In fact, the University of Minnesota is the birthplace of cheerleading. The first spirit squad was formed in 1898 by Johnny Campbell, a student disgruntled from three straight football losses for his team; today the cheerleading program at Minnesota is just yet another athletic legacy that proudly shows the school's colors of maroon and gold. Many fans enjoy the sporting tradition of their university by watching a basketball game, fencing competition, or gymnastics. They sometimes engage in the tradition rally cry, "Minnesota Rouser," as they support their classmates and friends. "Minnesota, hats off to thee! To thy colors, true we shall ever be" run the first two lines of the time-honored chant. Not all University of Minnesota undergraduates actively participate in sport playing or sport watching, but the sporting legacy at the university adds a sense of unity and pride for all.

Finding Your Niche
Because the University of Minnesota is so huge, a lot of prospective students worry about getting lost amid all the bustling activity that takes place on campus. One sophomore said reassuringly, "I thought that I would get lost in a big school but really I have found a nice niche for myself here. It may seem surprising, but you do see people you know all over campus." Most students seem to agree that although the campus is big, it will seem a lot more manageable to freshmen as soon as they start joining clubs and meeting people. There are groups and organizations "to fit the needs of pretty much every student on campus," including fraternities and sororities, athletic clubs, cultural groups, volunteer organizations, and political groups, among others. For those interested in the fine arts, there are a number of concerts put on by musical ensembles that students can either perform in or simply attend. Although the University isn't as diverse as it could be (most of the population is Caucasian), "there are student groups for many different ethnicities that allow students of a common background to come together."

Even though students may at first feel overwhelmed by the size and scope of the campus, and perhaps even bewildered by the vast array of classes and activities to choose from, current students say that "it mostly depends on you. It is important for students to realize that they can make the campus smaller by themselves." In addition, the University makes an active effort to make things seem smaller by "offering freshman seminars, tons of clubs and activities, and honors classes. You develop a personal network of friends and faculty fairly quickly, which makes the University seem less overwhelming."

In general, most students leave Minnesota happy with their college experience. One student echoed the sentiments of many when she said, "I love it here. I would definitely choose Minnesota again in a heartbeat."—*Aleksandra Kopec*

FYI

If you come to the University of Minnesota, you'd better bring "a bike."

What is the typical weekend schedule? "There's usually a sporting event to attend. The Superblock, a group of four dorms adjacent to one another, is also a great hangout for freshmen on the weekends."

If I could change one thing about the University of Minnesota, I "would make the campus smaller."

Three things every student at the University of Minnesota should do before graduating are "walk the bridge, sleep in the quad at the Superblock, and go to the state fair."

Mississippi

Millsaps College

Address: Millsaps, 1701 N. State Street, Jackson, MS 39210-0001

Phone: NA

E-mail Address: admissions@milsaps.edu

Web site URL: www.milsaps.edu

Year Founded: 1890

Private or Public: private

Religious affiliation: United Methodist

Location: urban

Application and Admissions Information: rolling

Regular Application Deadline: NA

Number of Applicants: 5,778

Percent Accepted: 69%

Percent Accepted who enroll: 50%

Number Entering: NA

Number of Transfers Accepted each Year: 1,966

Mean SAT: NA

Mean ACT: 24

Middle 50% SAT range: NA

Middle 50% ACT range: NA

Early admission program (EA/ ED/ NA): NA

ED or EA Acceptance Rate: NA

Full time Undergraduate enrollment: 12,555

Total enrollment: 16,101

Percent Male: 52%

Percent Female: 48%

Total Percent Minority: 27%

Percent African-American: 24%

Percent Asian/Pacific Islander: 1%

Percent Hispanic: 1%

Percent Native-American: 1%

Percent Other: NA

Percent in-state / out of state: 82%/18%

Percent from Public HS: NA

Retention Rate: 80%

Graduation Rate: 56%

Percent in On-campus housing: 30%

Percent affiliated with Greek system: 18%

Percent Varsity or Club Athletes: NA

Number of official organized extracurricular organizations: 300+

3 Most popular majors: Business Marketing, Education, Engineering

Student/Faculty ratio: 14:01

Tuition and Fees: $4,596.00

In State Tuition and Fees (if different): $10,552.00

Cost for Room and Board: $6,331.00

Percent receiving Financial aid, first-year: NA

Though largely unknown outside of Mississippi, Millsaps College is highly respected throughout the area as a school that offers a well-rounded liberal education at a competitive price. Though Millsaps majors may seem to have lackluster school spirit when it comes to supporting their athletic teams, most students enjoy life at Millsaps.

Work Hard

Millsaps was the first school in Mississippi to have a chapter of the academic honor society Phi Beta Kappa, and the school generally ranks high both for its academics and for its relatively low tuition. Millsaps offers 28 majors, and though the requirements vary by major, each student must complete 10 core courses, offered in topics ranging from history to science to mathematics. Students must also take a course in the fine arts.

A major selling point for many students is the small size of the classes at Millsaps. The average class size is 16 people, and the student/faculty ratio is 12:1. This class size fosters open discussion, as well as closes relationships between professors and students. According to one student, "the classes are very engaging, very discussion-oriented." Students say that their professors "really do care about their students" and several admitted that they considered the relationships formed with their professors the most valuable part of their college experiences. "I consider some of these professors my friends." While students definitely note that the academic life is very "strenuous," most say they were fulfilled in their academic lives. "I feel like I learn so much."

Party Hard

The social life at Millsaps seems to revolve pretty much exclusively around the Greek system. There are six fraternities and six sororities governed by the Panhellenic Council and the Interfraternity Council. While students say that it is not essential to be in a fraternity or sorority—"it's not like if you aren't Greek you're going to have an awful time"—it seems pretty hard to escape the fact that the Greek scene is *the* scene at Millsaps. This is highlighted in particular by the fact that non-Greeks are referred to as "independents." Though it is perfectly acceptable to be an independent, an independent who won't set foot in a fraternity house might have a hard time finding a party, particularly during freshman and sophomore years. As students get older, however, "they tend to drift off campus more." Many upperclassmen enjoy local spots Hal & Mal's or Schimmels for drinks, music or just hanging out with their friends. According to one student, "A lot of times you can find your professors at Fenian's."

> **"I consider some of these professors my friends"**

Drinking rules on campus seem to be pretty sensible. Though rowdy behavior in the dormitories is prohibited, students appreciated the fact that "the RAs treat us like adults." The two large campus-wide events every year are the homecoming football game in the fall and Major Madness in the spring. At Major Madness, students gather on "The Bowl"—the large, grassy area in the middle of campus—and play games, eat, drink, and listen to music. Though the musicians are rarely big-name stars—bands have included Better Than Ezra, Stroke Nine, and the North Mississippi All Stars—"it's definitely stuff you can dance to, sing to and drink to."

With the exception of the homecoming game, Millsaps students in general don't get extremely excited about sports. "It's definitely not like an SEC school, so if people come to Millsaps expecting that, then they're not going to get it." Instead, supporting athletic teams is more of a matter of supporting your friends who happen to be on those teams than a statement of school pride.

On Campus—Where it's At

Approximately 87 percent of Millsaps students live on campus. Most choose to live in the dormitories for all four years, though some upperclassmen move off campus. The housing is divided up by the North Side and the South Side. Freshman year, everyone lives on the North Side. After freshman year, students pick their rooms based on a room draw, which functions on a point system. Each student entering the room draw receives points based on his or her class year and GPA. Students then combine with their roommates and vie for the best dorms. The residence hall rooms are all double-occupancy, and the halls feature traditional double rooms, apartment-style and suite-style rooms. Though the students admit that the dormitories aren't by any means luxurious, "they do their best to make it pleasant." "My friends who are from other colleges always talk about how nice our dorms are here."

For most students, more important than the dorms themselves is the fact that the dorms provide a social outlet as well. "It's really cool when all your friends live on campus." This social atmosphere is also extended to the main cafeteria, also known as "The Caf'". The Caf' is one of two dining options on campus, the other being the Kava House, which provides quick meals to go. At The Caf', students select from a menu of salads, soups, sandwiches and daily hot meals. Students generally seem to be quite pleased with the quality of the food, though opinions differ about the variety of food choices. While one senior said that she was "really going to miss [the food] next year," another complained that the food choices were repetitive.

The Center of the State

Students seem to have mixed feelings about being in the city of Jackson itself. In one 2004 ranking, Jackson was ranked the nation's 17th most dangerous city. For this reason, students say they must exercise caution while out on campus, but they don't feel that the crime level in Jackson is detrimental to their college experience. Students are very well aware that "Jackson isn't the safest of cities." While one student said that she generally feels "safe on campus," she was sure to note that she "wouldn't walk around alone in the dark."

One advantage of being in the city of Jackson—which has a population of just under 180,000 people—is the city's position as the capital of the state, and thus the center of state politics. Particularly for students with an interest in politics or governments, Millsaps is a good place to get a taste of the political arena. Students say it is very easy to get internships in the state or local government, and that state officials will sometimes teach classes at Millsaps as adjunct professors.

Though the city of Jackson is very much a political city, students say that campus life is "not too hard-core politically" and that the student body as a whole does not lean very heavily left or right politically. Both "the Millsaps Young Democrats and the Republicans are very well-represented and well-spoken for." Students say that Millsaps is a place for political expression, but that there are also many students who abstain from political discussion altogether.

Diversity?

New students to Millsaps may be surprised by the lack of geographic and racial diversity. Over 50 percent of the students are from the state of Mississippi, and the 2005–2006 freshman class at Millsaps was comprised of only 17 percent minority students. While some students lamented that fact—"I'd like it to be more diverse than it is"—students across the board were impressed by the openness of students to new ideas and to different types of people. "Millsaps is very diverse if you look at the big picture, not just at race." Another said, "What makes up for [the lack of racial diversity] is the diversity of ideas and of opinions." Though there is little racial diversity on campus, student organizations like the Black Student Association provide minority students with a sense of community.

For many students, the mere size of Millsaps contributes to this openness for different types of students. With just over a thousand undergraduates, "I feel like I've met everyone on campus one way or another," one senior said. Another student chalked up the open-minded atmosphere at Millsaps to the philosophy of education at the school. "They really teach you to be warm-hearted and open to everything and not close-minded at all."—*Susanna Moore*

FYI

If you come to Millsaps, you'd better bring "a willingness to work hard and party hard."

What is the typical weekend schedule? "Friday—go to dinner and to the fraternity houses, Saturday—watch football all day or go to the football game, eat dinner, pre-party, and go to the fraternity houses, Sunday—wake up late and do your homework."

If I could change one thing about Millsaps, I'd "make it farther from home."

Three things every student at Millsaps should do before graduating are "swim in the fountains, Bowl-sit, really get to know a professor."

Mississippi State University

Address: Mississippi
State, The Office of
Admissions and
Scholarships. PO Box 6334,
MSU, MS 39762
Phone: 662-325-2224
E-mail Address:
admit@msstate.edu
Web site URL:
admissions.msstate.edu
Year Founded: 1878
Private or Public: public
Religious affiliation: none
Location: rural
**Regular Application
Deadline:** rolling
Number of Applicants: 5,245
Percent Accepted: 70%
**Percent Accepted who
enroll:** 54%
Number Entering: NA
**Number of Transfers
Accepted each Year:** NA
Mean SAT: NA
Mean ACT: 23

Middle 50% SAT range: NA
Middle 50% ACT range:
20–27
**Early admission program
(EA/ ED/ NA):** NA
ED or EA Acceptance Rate:
NA
**Full time Undergraduate
enrollment:** 11,321
Total enrollment: 15,934
Percent Male: 52%
Percent Female: 48%
Total Percent Minority: 23%
Percent African-American:
9%
**Percent Asian/Pacific
Islander:** 1%
Percent Hispanic: 1%
Percent Native-American:
0%
Percent Other: NA
**Percent in-state / out of
state:** 83%/17%
Percent from Public HS: NA
Retention Rate: 82%

Graduation Rate: 57%
**Percent in On-campus
housing:** 14%
**Percent affiliated with
Greek system:** 11%/14%
**Percent Varsity or Club
Athletes:** NA
**Number of official
organized extracurricular
organizations:** 313
3 Most popular majors:
Business administration/
management, elementary
education/teaching,
geology/earth science
Student/Faculty ratio: 14:01
Tuition and Fees: $9,772.00
**In State Tuition and Fees
(if different):** $4,312.00
Cost for Room and Board:
$5,859.00
**Percent receiving
Financial aid, first-year:**
59%

T he college-bound student seeking a
friendly environment should take a
look at Mississippi State University.
MSU is an increasingly challenging university that attracts students from within the
state of Mississippi and across the nation.
It's a school built on unity, friendliness, and,
of course, education. Tucked away from the
hustle and bustle of city life in quiet Mississippi State, Mississippi, students at MSU
take great pride in their school and its athletic teams.

Bulldogs and Textbooks
MSU is divided into eight different colleges
of undergraduate studies, ranging from the
College of Education to the liberal arts-
oriented College of Arts and Sciences. MSU
also offers a variety of programs in agricultural, engineering, and forestry studies. At
the College of Agriculture and Life Sciences,
a student can major in anything from human
sciences with an emphasis in interior design
to food safety with an emphasis on management and production. MSU offers a wide
range of pre-professional programs ranging
from premed to poultry science, but freshmen are preoccupied with a core curriculum

that covers a writing course, courses in the
humanities, social and physical sciences, as
well as computer literacy. In addition, MSU
has a unique and highly rated Golf and
Sports Turf Management Program, as well
as a Landscape Architecture program (separate from the College of Architecture).
Some freshmen, especially those going into
the architecture field, find that they have
much more work than other students. "I
have 23 hours of work a week, models to
build, but that's what happens at the best architecture program in the South," said one
freshman majoring in architecture. Another
freshman agreed, "The architecture program is great here. But, it is a little too demanding sometimes, although I love making
all the models." MSU students note that the
architecture, engineering, and biology majors provide the most challenging courses
on campus. A sophomore noted that "architecture and engineering, hands down" are
the most time-consuming. No matter what
they major in, all MSU students are required
to study a foreign language. A sophomore
majoring in international business explained that it is "really a double major; business and a foreign language." A psychology

major said that his foreign language requirement of four credits is "not that bad; at least I get to learn French."

Athletics Are the Weekend

MSU students feel Bulldog love flowing through their veins. The school is united by the common desire for the success of their athletic teams, particularly football, baseball, and basketball. "You have to be there if there is a game going on; it's what this place is all about," said a freshman. "We usually all go to the stadium, and if the game is going well, we will all stay until the end. Lately, the wins have been difficult to come by, but it will turn around," said a hopeful MSU senior. Since most of MSU's students are from within the state, many even go home if there's no athletic event to attend that weekend.

The biggest football game of the year is the Egg Bowl, which is usually on or around Thanksgiving Day. It pits MSU against archrival Ole Miss. "The Egg Bowl is something that I always look forward to. It is so much fun, and everybody comes out and shows some school spirit," said a sophomore. No one's quite sure how the Thanksgiving-season matchup got its name, but according to one freshman, "it doesn't matter what it's called, what matters is that we beat Ole Miss, and that's all." According to legend, many years ago a cow walked onto the field during the Egg Bowl, and MSU proceeded to win the game. Ever since, MSU students proudly ring cowbells at the game for good luck. One junior said that the administration has been trying to ban the cowbells because they're considered artificial noisemakers, but "we still find a way to sneak them in. I can't wait to do it this Thanksgiving."

Greek life dominates the MSU party scene. On football weekends and other big occasions, the fraternities always "make sure that there is a party to attend." Around 20 percent of the student population is involved in the fraternity and sorority system. One sophomore observed that Greek life is a "pretty big deal here, especially if you want to party. You have to know someone in the frat if you want to drink." But a freshman who did not rush a fraternity because of his workload reassured, "I still party every weekend, and I can go to a frat if I want to. It is not frowned upon to not be a brother, or even if you don't want to drink. It's really great." Another non-drinking junior agreed that "people are friendly to you, regardless."

Most MSU students are quick to note that there is very little drug use on campus. "We are very lucky to not have problems with extreme drug use or STDs or any of that other stuff that happens at other schools," according to one freshman. Students who drink admit that it is easy to get around the policy, and that if you "are just careful, you aren't going to get busted," although the strictness of enforcement "totally depends on your RA (Resident Advisors)."

> "That is the best thing about going to MSU: the people and the friendliness."

MSU students are known for their Southern hospitality. One sophomore raved "that's part of the magic here, everybody says hello to each other." A freshman commented that it's easy to make friends at MSU, and that "you find your niche faster than at any other school, it is awesome." Another freshman similarly said "that is the best thing about going to MSU, the people and the friendliness."

Southern Charm

Students love that their campus feels so "homey and cozy" and that people are "friendly wherever you go." The campus is literally the only thing in town; the borders of the school make up the borders of the city of Mississippi State, Mississippi, which borders the small town of Starkville. "It's so flat, so spread out, but everything feels so close together as time passes by," said one sophomore. Because of the campus's large size, however, many students feel that they "cannot make it here without a car." Though the school's administration has tried to introduce alternate transportation options, students often jump in their cars to get to far-away classes. "Most people just bring their cars to school, especially the people that live within driving distance. It is just something you need here," said one junior. Another reason for having a car is that most students go home for the weekend if there is "nothing going on." Cars are also helpful for the three-quarters of upperclassmen who choose to live off campus. "By the time you're a sophomore, you want to get together with your friends and move to an apartment," one junior said. There are plenty of apartment complexes in Starkville, but only a handful located within walking distance of the main part of campus.

For those students who do live in dorms, the facilities are in the process of being upgraded. The current standard freshman dorm "could be a lot worse," according to one freshman. All freshmen live in double rooms equipped with a sink and a refrigerator. Most freshman dorms are single-sex, and the coed dorms still segregate the sexes by hallway. As stated, MSU has been engaging in a major dorm renovation, demolishing three of the oldest existing dorms and building three new ones: the Roy H. Ruby Residence Hall, the S. Bryce Griffis Residence Hall and Hurst Hall. An additional residence hall is slated to open in 2007. These new dorms feature private baths, wireless internet, and cable television. Upperclassmen who decide to stay on campus usually live in suites, "which are a little ratty." One junior who lives on campus says that upperclassmen live in lackluster dorms because the "school has already made a good impression on the freshmen, and most people don't usually stay on campus for the rest of their years." Upperclass suites usually have four single bedrooms and a connected bathroom.

At MSU, students feel like they are gaining more than a higher education. Not only are students learning, they feel "it is just so great here." They are quick to say that the best part about MSU is the friendliness of the student body and the faculty. One freshman said that "folks here are just good people—it is just that simple." As one senior put it, "it's just the good ol' South here, with good ol' people. I will be a Bulldog until the day I die."—*Alberto Masliah*

FYI

If you come to MSU, you'd better bring "a car. Things are all spread out."

What is the typical weekend schedule? "Wake up, study, visit friends, party, go to the game, party again."

If I could change anything about MSU, I would "make the buildings more attractive."

Three things every student should do at MSU before graduating are "go to the Egg Bowl with a cowbell, go to at least one game of every sport, get involved in an organization."

University of Mississippi

Address: University of Mississippi, PO Box 1848, University, MS 38677-1848

Phone: 662-915-7226

E-mail Address: admissions@olemiss.edu

Web site URL: www.olemiss.edu

Year Founded: 1844

Private or Public: public

Religious affiliation: none

Location: urban

Regular Application Deadline: 21-Jul

Number of Applicants: 7,849

Percent Accepted: 84%

Percent Accepted who enroll: 39%

Number Entering: 2,570

Number of Transfers Accepted each Year: NA

Mean SAT: NA

Mean ACT: NA

Middle 50% SAT range: 920–1,170

Middle 50% ACT range: 20–26

Early admission program (EA/ ED/ NA): NA

ED or EA Acceptance Rate: NA

Full time Undergraduate enrollment: 12,661

Total enrollment: 14,554

Percent Male: 47%

Percent Female: 53%

Total Percent Minority: 15%

Percent African-American: 13%

Percent Asian/Pacific Islander: 1%

Percent Hispanic: 0.90%

Percent Native-American: 0.30%

Percent Other: <1%

Percent in-state / out of state: 67%/33%

Percent from Public HS: NA

Retention Rate: 80%

Graduation Rate: NA

Percent in On-campus housing: NA

Percent affiliated with Greek system: 33%

Percent Varsity or Club Athletes: NA

Number of official organized extracurricular organizations: 250

3 Most popular majors: Accounting, Education, Marketing

Student/Faculty ratio: 19:01

Tuition and Fees: $10,560.00

In State Tuition and Fees (if different): $4,603.00

Cost for Room and Board: $4,524.00

Percent receiving Financial aid, first-year: 56%

Students of the University of Mississippi affectionately call their school Ole Miss, reflecting how dear to their hearts this 158-year-old school has become. Indeed, Ole Miss quickly grows on a student, with its friendly atmosphere and traditional Southern feel. Yet at the same time, students find themselves immersed in an internationally aware institution, one that is quickly expanding not only physically but academically as well.

Academically Balanced

Students describe Ole Miss as academically well-balanced. The University offers seven undergraduate schools: the College of Liberal Arts and the Schools of Accountancy, Applied Sciences, Business Administration, Education, Engineering and Pharmacy. The College of Liberal Arts and the School of Business Administration have the largest enrollments from the University's nearly 9,000 students. Students say that the Schools of Pharmacy and Engineering offer the most rigorous programs, while the School of Education is probably Ole Miss' biggest academic weakness.

At Ole Miss, as at any state school, class size is a concern. Indeed, although one student said that most classes are generally anywhere from 18 to 25 students, freshman core courses can get quite large and one history lecture course that she took had 175 students. The sophomore student insisted that she "never felt like a number, though" and that, despite the state school atmosphere, it's hard to feel anonymous at Ole Miss. Moreover, Ole Miss offers several special programs tailored to provide closer attention for more specific, individualized needs. The University houses the McDonnell Barksdale Honors College, an integral part of the University. Admitting just 120 freshmen in 2001, the Honors College selects students of higher caliber, with an average SAT score of 1350 and an ACT of 31.5. In addition, Ole Miss boasts an elite program known as the Croft Institute for International Studies that admits only 40 students and prepares them for international leadership. Ole Miss also offers several courses to all students from its Center for the Study of Southern Culture, which analyzes the less-studied yet "invaluable" tradition of the South. All freshmen are required to take what is called University Studies. University Studies is designed to help freshmen make a smoother transition from high school to college and occupies an hour credit for the first

half of the first semester. "It really is a big help," said one sophomore, "especially because it is a great way to meet fellow freshmen."

The Good Ole Life at Ole Miss

Students at Ole Miss describe their dorms with a bit of ambivalence. As one student wryly said, "It's not the nicest place, but it's not the worst." The University is in a process of improving and modernizing its housing; students attribute the renovation of the dorms to the dramatic increase in enrollment in the past two years. For better or worse, the University adheres to a state law that forbids any form of coed housing. As a result, undergraduates live in single-sex dormitories; the main freshman buildings are Martin for women and Stockard for men.

Ole Miss students also must abide by strict rules. Guests must check in at a designated front desk and be accompanied by a host throughout the residential halls at all times. Moreover, Ole Miss dorms generally have rigid visitation hours: 11 a.m. to 11 p.m. on the weekdays, with late-night extensions to 1 a.m. on the weekends. The students of each dormitory, however, may vote to extend visitation hours during the first week of each semester.

The Mighty Greeks

When questioned about social life at Ole Miss, one marketing and communications major preferred to sum it up with statistics: "Thirty-three percent of our students are involved in Greek life—the largest percentage, I think, of any public university." Enough said. Indeed, fraternities and sororities play a prominent role in life at the University of Mississippi. While hazing is strictly forbidden on campus, Greek traditions are highly visible. During rush week in the fall, freshmen perform silly but otherwise innocuous stunts like standing outside in the cold without a T-shirt and inventing creative chants in order to gain admittance to the Greek organization of their choice. Such activities can require the complete dedication of each rushee, and one freshman described rush as bringing the University to a halt, noting that "a lot of classes have been dismissed or canceled."

Students insist, contrary to popular misconceptions, that the campus on the whole does not revolve around Greek life. "[Fraternities and sororities] aren't [all] we have to offer." Off campus, there are bars for the 21-and-up crowd, and some are even open to all kids 18 and older. There is a student-run shuttle called the Rebel Ride that runs back and forth between the square (where the bars are located) and campus on Thursday, Friday and Saturday nights, giving students the option of getting off campus if they want a change from the weekend frat scene. In addition, in terms of extracurriculars, students participate in numerous organizations beyond the Greek scene: religious organizations and special interest groups are popular, and students find these a nice alternative, or addition, to frat and sorority events on campus.

Belles of the Ball

Nonetheless, fraternity parties remain a popular choice on weekend nights. During football season, fraternities host live bands on weekend nights, and these bands range in genre from country to '80s covers. The exclusivity of these events depends largely on where they are held and which organizations are holding them. "Girls can get into any party," one undergraduate said, "but boys have to know someone in the fraternity to go." Yet even male students who don't get into these parties won't have trouble meeting beautiful people. "We have the finest women in the South . . . they're unbelievable," said one male student. Even a female student concurred, "Ole Miss is supposed to be known for having really pretty girls, which I personally don't notice."

> **"We have the finest women in the South . . . they're unbelievable."**

At Ole Miss, dating is common, although often not in the conventional sense. Dates are often set up around football games, arranged specifically for having a companion to the Saturday event, and successful dates span from the night before a game to the night after. "You get a date for the football game," one student related. "They take you out for dinner, you go to a fraternity party together, and then you go to the football game." As odd a combination as dating and football may be, football's influence on Ole Miss life extends far beyond the social and dating scenes.

Getting into the Grove

When interviewed, one student simply captured the spirit of Ole Miss by proclaiming, "We're a football school." Football games of-

ten become a focal point of life at Ole Miss, although one student conceded that the same applies at any school in the Southeastern Conference. Undergraduates at Ole Miss are especially given to watching games with passion and reacting to results explosively. One student remembered a traumatic loss: "We really wanted to beat Texas Tech. A lot of people were disappointed because we were ahead. There was a lot of crying, a lot of throwing things."

Ole Miss prides itself not only on the games themselves, but on the social events that stem from them. Tailgating at the Grove, a 10-acre grassy knoll at the center of campus, is a favorite pastime at Ole Miss. Students invest plenty of time and energy into making tailgating an elaborate festival; one student was quick to point out, "[There's] no actual tailgating, you don't stand next to your truck." Rather, she described the tailgate as an almost formal experience: "People bring in these nice tables, delicious food, they hang chandeliers, they bring candles and flowers, and sometimes they'll bring their good silverware." Students often come to football games and tailgates dressed up— it isn't uncommon to see boys in slacks and collared shirts and girls in sundresses. While intense, the amount of attention and planning that goes into these football events allows for many social opportunities. "You talk to people, you go from tent to tent, and you can eat everybody's food." Whether a football game is scheduled or not, Ole Miss students spend plenty of time at the Grove in general. Students laud the University and the student programming board for scheduling a variety of on-campus events, many of which occur at the Grove. Concert on the Grove is a favorite series, bringing artists like the Nappy Roots, Pat Green and local bands to Ole Miss.

Controversy in Costume

Ole Miss's history is undeniably entwined in racial issues, and although the Civil Rights movement lies decades in the past, vestiges of that dark time in the school's history still remain. At the foremost is the Ole Miss mascot, Colonel Rebel, which was banned from the football sidelines in the 2003 season but is still an official trademark of the University. The mascot is controversial because, according to one African-American student, he resembles an old plantation owner. To some, Colonel Rebel is a reminder of Ole Miss's infamous past as a segregated university. Several students cited the historic integration case of 1962, in which Ole Miss's first African-American student, James Meredith, needed to be escorted by the U.S. military into the University's halls. Addressing the mascot controversy as a manifestation of the University's racial history, one student commented, "Our chancellor says it isn't a racial issue, but if you look at the big picture, you know it is." One student applauded the steps the administration has taken toward replacing the mascot, saying "Our current chancellor is really working hard to get over the stereotypes." The administration and the athletics program have decided to change Colonel Reb to a more positive image, but the transformation has been slow. In fact, the process has dragged on so long that a student movement to retain Colonel Rebel as the symbol of the school has gained momentum.

Ole Miss thus continues to tread the line between preserving tradition and identity, and accommodating the demands of a changing world. Students at the University of Mississippi find a school with a rich (albeit controversial) tradition, but one that's slowly changing in its policy, its physical plant and in its people.—*Christopher Lapinig*

FYI

If you come to Ole Miss, you better bring a "rolling cooler for tailgating on the Grove."

What is the typical weekend schedule? "Stop by a fraternity party on Friday; wake up on Saturday, go to the Grove, go to a football game, come back to the Grove, and then go to the bar Library; and then rest all day Sunday."

If I could change one thing about Ole Miss, "I'd rewrite the negative history of segregation we have had."

The three things that every student at Ole Miss should do before graduating are "work on your tan at Sardis Lake, eat chicken-on-the-stick at 3 a.m., and road trip to Graceland Too."

Missouri

University of Missouri / Columbia

Address: University of Missouri, Columbia, Office of Admissions, 230 Jesse Hall, Columbia, MO 65211

Phone: 573-882-7786

E-mail Address: MU4U@missouri.edu

Web site URL: http://admissions.missouri.edu

Year Founded: 1839

Private or Public: public

Religious affiliation: none

Location: small city

Regular Application Deadline: 1-May

Number of Applicants: 13,102

Percent Accepted: 78%

Percent Accepted who enroll: 47%

Number Entering: 5,792

Number of Transfers Accepted each Year: varies

Mean SAT: NA

Mean ACT: NA

Middle 50% SAT range: NA

Middle 50% ACT range: 23–28

Early admission program (EA/ ED/ NA): NA

ED or EA Acceptance Rate: NA

Full time Undergraduate enrollment: 20,238

Total enrollment: 28,253

Percent Male: 49%

Percent Female: 51%

Total Percent Minority: 12%

Percent African-American: 5%

Percent Asian/Pacific Islander: 3%

Percent Hispanic: 2%

Percent Native-American: 1%

Percent Other: 0.5%

Percent in-state / out of state: 86%/14%

Percent from Public HS: NA

Retention Rate: 85%

Graduation Rate: 69%

Percent in On-campus housing: 37%

Percent affiliated with Greek system: 22%

Percent Varsity or Club Athletes: 2.4%

Number of official organized extracurricular organizations: 480

3 Most popular majors: Business Administration, Journalism, Psychology

Student/Faculty ratio: 18:01

Tuition and Fees: $7,308.00

In State Tuition and Fees (if different): $16,890.00

Cost for Room and Board: $7,000.00

Percent receiving Financial aid, first-year: 45%

From its very beginnings in 1839 as the first public university west of the Mississippi River, the University of Missouri-Columbia has endeavored to provide a wide variety of opportunities for its students both during and after their time at the University. The possibilities also extend outside the classroom as the student body of over 21,000 students mixes with the welcoming town of Columbia. As one student put it, "Mizzou offers you the chance to go anywhere, whether it's to New York City or back to the farm, while at the same time preparing you to be successful in any field you choose."

Academic Opportunities

Fondly called "Mizzou" by nearly everyone who has visited the campus, the University provides a wide range of academic options for its students. By providing over 270 majors ranging from Animal Science to Business Administration to Textile and Apparel Management, Mizzou hopes to fulfill the vision of public education where students from anywhere can learn just about anything. All the 270 majors fall within one of nine colleges and schools including the colleges of Agriculture, Arts and Sciences, Business, Education, Engineering, Human Sciences, and the schools of Health Professions, Journalism and Nursing. Furthermore, nearly every major has many different emphases which allow further specialization to fit the desire of the student. Some of the most popular majors include Elementary Education and Hotel and Restaurant Management.

Professors receive mixed reviews at Mizzou. Although a few are "so dead-set in their ways that if you ask them about a grade they take it as if you're questioning their authority" most professors are regarded as "accommodating and helpful" and certainly more accessible and approachable in the smaller departments. Many professors, including Dr. James Spain of the College of Agriculture, Food and Natural Resources, offer the opportunity for students to learn from experts in their field who truly care about each of their students. Despite the size of the student body, students feel that the academic life at Mizzou helps to encourage them to take the initiative and can "definitely help to set the course for a future career."

The Social Scene

The social life at the University of Missouri revolves around, well, basically anything that a student wants it to revolve around. The University's size ensures that everyone can find their niche. Even though over 20 percent of the campus is involved in a fraternity or sorority, it "isn't the end all and be all of everyone's social life." In fact, the four major parties that the independent students throw every year are some of, if not the biggest parties on campus. The Greek system does provide good communities for students who seek the Greek life. Hazing is discouraged if not downright outlawed by most fraternities, and the wide range of houses on campus gives everyone who is interested in the Greek life many different options.

> "Mizzou offers you the chance to go anywhere, whether it's to New York City or back to the farm, while at the same time preparing you to be successful in any field you choose."

Smack-dab in the middle of the Midwest, most students would characterize Mizzou as a friendly place and they say that meeting people is "very, very easy" and "the more you get involved with activities on campus, the easier it becomes." Extracurricular groups are very appealing to most all students. Prominent groups include Missouri Students Association, Chancellor's Leadership Ambassadors, Tour Team and Campus Crusade for Christ. Students at Mizzou aren't the type to do extracurricular activities "in a half-hearted way." Many people are involved in some group on campus and "organizations are the second most time consuming activities on campus next to studying." However, this does not mean that Mizzou students don't know how to have fun.

Going Out

When asked where student go on the weekends, nearly everyone answers, "downtown," which fortunately for students is located right next to campus. Whether it's clubs like The Big 12 and The Fieldhouse, restaurants like Shakespeare's Pizza and The Heidelberg, or hangouts like Harpo's that are steeped in tradition, downtown Columbia serves as a decent area of town to go on the weekends. Thursdays, Fridays and Saturdays are the big nights when students go out, and most of Sunday is spent either relaxing or more often getting the homework done for Monday.

Students can't talk about the weekend, at least in the fall, without mentioning Missouri Tigers home football games. Even if there's an early game, much of the campus turns out to tailgate and cheer on the Tigers, especially when they're going to (and winning) bowl games. The same school spirit carries over into men's basketball and also up-and-coming sports like volleyball and gymnastics. Sports play a critical role in the Mizzou college experience, and there is no lack of Tiger pride for the school or the sports teams.

Not Just Livin' On a Prayer

In regards to students' living situation, Mizzou takes great strides to ensure that student living buildings are not dorms but rather residence halls, because "a dorm is only where you sleep, while a residence hall is where you live." Many freshmen are placed in residence halls according to their prospective majors or their Freshman Interest Groups (FIGs) which help incoming students meet other freshmen with similar interests. The FIGs are yet another way to make the campus a little smaller for each student and provide familiar faces during the first two semesters at the University. Although most students only live in the residence halls during their freshman and sophomore years—after which they move into off-campus apartments—the majority of students are very satisfied with their "comfortable and friendly" living arrangements and especially the dining halls. The "pretty darn good" residential food receives such high marks that many upperclassmen—who move off campus after their freshmen or sophomore year—often keep their meal plans. The only complaint stems from the point system, which inadvertently causes some students to make meals, especially lunch and dinner, bigger than normal. Not only do students have access to better-than-average food, but they also have a membership to what Sports Illustrated calls the best college rec center in the nation. The "MizzouRec" boasts nearly a dozen basketball courts, a 50-meter pool and 10-meter diving well, not to mention the plasma TVs, sauna and whirlpools that were designed after houses on MTV's "Cribs." Altogether, not a bad combination for campus living.

Yeah, I Guess It is a Big School

Although many students are originally hesitant to go to a college with over 20,000 students, they often find that it isn't nearly as big as they thought. One student commented, "I thought I would be overwhelmed, that I wouldn't really matter, but everyone here is much more caring than I thought and they want you to enjoy your experience." Many also believe, "Mizzou is as big as you want to make it." The school spirit, the quality professors, the friendly atmosphere and many ways to make the campus much smaller make Mizzou a place where many students want to spend their college years.—*Mark Godfrey*

FYI

If you come to Mizzou, make sure to bring "a Mizzou hooded sweatshirt. Everyone has one and you don't want to spend $60 at the bookstore and you don't want to be left out."

What's the typical weekend schedule? "Go out on Friday, sleep late Saturday (if there's not a home football game), do laundry Saturday afternoon, go out. Sunday is for homework."

If I could change one thing about Mizzou I'd "make it smaller."

Three things every student at Mizzou should do before graduating are "walk through columns at one of the ceremonies, experience football game on Saturday, swim in the Tiger Plaza fountain."

University of Missouri / Kansas City

Address: University of Missouri, Kansas City, 5100 Rockhill Road, Kansas City, MO 64110

Phone: 816-235-1111

E-mail Address: admit@umkc.edu

Web site URL: www.umkc.edu

Year Founded: 1929

Private or Public: public

Religious affiliation: none

Location: urban

Regular Application Deadline: Rolling

Number of Applicants: 3,228

Percent Accepted: 71.03%

Percent Accepted who enroll: 29%

Number Entering: 956

Number of Transfers Accepted each Year: 2,078

Mean SAT: NA

Mean ACT: 24

Middle 50% SAT range: 1,040–1,350

Middle 50% ACT range: 20–27

Early admission program (EA/ ED/ NA): NA

ED or EA Acceptance Rate: NA

Full time Undergraduate enrollment: 9,383

Total enrollment: 12,704

Percent Male: 41%

Percent Female: 59%

Total Percent Minority: 25%

Percent African-American: 15%

Percent Asian/Pacific Islander: 6%

Percent Hispanic: 4%

Percent Native-American: 0.60%

Percent Other: <1%

Percent in-state / out of state: 77% / 23%

Percent from Public HS: NA

Retention Rate: 73%

Graduation Rate: 76%

Percent in On-campus housing: 10%

Percent affiliated with Greek system: 4%

Percent Varsity or Club Athletes: NA

Number of official organized extracurricular organizations: 200

3 Most popular majors: Business/Management, Liberal Arts and Sciences/Studies, Psychology

Student/Faculty ratio: 9:01

Tuition and Fees: $17,925.00

In State Tuition and Fees (if different): $7,659.00

Cost for Room and Board: $7,308.00

Percent receiving Financial aid, first-year: 67%

Over 80 percent of University of Missouri Kansas City students live off campus, but that doesn't prevent them from having a full college experience. Those UMKC students with a little bit of initiative enjoy rich academic, extracurricular, and social lives throughout their years at school. With a quickly increasing enrollment and strong focus on research, the University offers a vast range of experiences on an exciting campus.

Small Classes, Big Pride

UMKC students are required to complete 120 credit hours to graduate. If they are pursuing a B.A., they must also take three consecutive semesters of the same foreign language. One popular track of study is a six-year medical program, after which graduates receive an M.D. Students may earn a bachelor's degree in over 40 concentrations in the arts, sciences, humanities, social sciences, music, and nursing; UMKC's mission calls for a focus on "visual and performing arts, health sciences, and urban affairs." In addition, one sophomore communications major reported an extracurricular club for almost every area of study.

Students are proud of UMKC's standing relative to its peer institutions, saying "its research is excellent and so are its teachers." While there can be "a lot of competition for classes," a first-year student reported that "most of my classes have 25 people" or fewer, and upper-level courses tend to be smaller than the required general education classes. Undergraduate commonly interact with the faculty "online through discussion boards." Though one junior mentioned eating meals with her professors "all the time," another such close interaction occurs more often even in graduate programs or the Conservatory of Music, ranked one of the top in the nations. Other unique programs include the six-year medical program, as well as the reputable Bloch School of Business and Public affairs and the School of Law. The school boasts the only pharmacy and dental schools in the state. The University recently launched a major building project for Health Science 1, to provide more research space and classrooms for the health and life science departments.

Students noted the sizable population of older students and graduate students, making for a less-traditional college setting. As a result, said one undergrad, "UMKC is a great place for self-sufficient scholarly students, who are interested in hitting the books."

Double Your Dorms

In the fall of 2004, UMKC opened Oak Street Hall, approximately doubling the number of students that can live on campus. Despite the high cost, the hall receives praise for the quality of housing it offers. With the leveling of Twin Oaks, the University is planning to construct a residence with town-style apartments. Nevertheless, both campus culture and economics often push students to the houses around campus, with one student noting after one year that it was "much cheaper . . . to rent a house near campus." Dorms, then, are a popular option for students arriving from outside of Kansas City only until they form a group of friends with whom they can move off campus.

One student described the University's location in the heart of Kansas City as "fantastic." Students spend much of their free time in the Country Club Plaza area of Kansas City, which offers "luxury shopping" and food options to break up the day. One freshman described this spot, along with the Westport area, as the "dominant social scene," since most students do not spend much time on campus while they aren't in class. For those on campus at meal times, the University of Missouri Kansas City offers food at its dining hall on a debit system, with students loading their cards at the beginning of the semester and spending down until the balance is zero. One student critical of the dining hall compared the food to that of her "high school cafeteria." Another agreed, saying that the cafeteria is "widely criticized." Students not invested in a semester-long meal plan tend not to spend much time in the dining hall because "food is expensive to purchase with cash."

Outside the Classroom and Off the Campus

Since most UMKC students live off campus, they do much of their socializing there. There are, however, many opportunities for students to get involved with university-sponsored activities, as well. In addition to academically oriented groups and the Student Government Association, there are plenty of opportunities for community service in the Kansas City metro area. Ethnic organizations and academic-focused groups were noted as particular active. Also, the University boasts six fraternities and seven sororities. Many students, including those from outside the Kansas City area, make friends "by joining organizations," though one senior found that because so many students leave campus after class, some "organizations are begging for members."

> **"Everyone drinks, except for the really religious types."**

The campus is dry, but that is no stumbling block to the off-campus consumption of alcohol. According to a senior, "everyone drinks, except for the really religious types." Even so, a female junior reported no pressure as the only non-drinker in her group of friends. Fridays and Saturdays are the most popular nights out, with venues ranging from small gatherings in houses to Westport, "the largest collection of bars in the Great Plains." Most students have "at least one job," at "Starbucks, in retail, work-study," and a variety of other part-time placements. Those who are employed tend to work off campus, or have an off-campus job to augment their work-study.

Typical Kangaroo?

One freshman recommended dressing up as the UMKC mascot, Kasey the Kangaroo, at least once during college. Given the make up of the student body, though, the odds are that you will find a different type of student wearing the costume at every game! "You can't really say that we have one particular stereotypical student," said one junior. "Young and old, different cultures, and different attitudes" are all represented at UMKC, even though many students are from small towns in-state. The strongest representation may be of "middle-class white" backgrounds, but students do note the diversity on campus.

To further expose students to a variety of worldviews, UMKC runs an International Academic Programs office, offering students guidance in applying for fellowships and study abroad programs. The University of Missouri Kansas City currently has programs with schools in 21 countries in Europe and Asia, as well as ones in Mexico, Australia, and New Zealand. The office also works with students to transfer financial aid packages to study abroad programs. On campus, the school boasts an international population of around 10 percent.

UMKC competes athletically in the Mid-Continent Conference of the NCAA's Division I. The University sponsors a variety of sports, ranging from basketball and volleyball to golf, tennis, softball, and rifle, but for most of the student body, the UMKC-Valparaiso basketball game is the biggest athletic event of the year. For those not inclined to commit to Division I athletics, the Swinney Recreation Center offers fitness facilities and a swimming pool to the university community.

The University of Missouri Kansas City is a school with many opportunities for academic, extracurricular, and social growth, but it requires some initiative from its somewhat scattered student body. According to those who have taken that extra step, seeking out a professor for lunch or joining a campus political organization can make for a fulfilling college experience, taking advantage of the "good education" that UMKC can provide.—*Douglas London*

FYI
If you come to UMKC, you'd better bring "a sense of humor."
The best places to hang out on the weekend are "Friday and Saturday, go to bars or go out to eat, and sleep in on Sunday."
If I could change one thing about the UMKC, "I would make parking free and plentiful."
Three things that every UMKC student should do before graduating are "go on an internship out of state or country, join a club, and live in a dorm."

Washington University in St. Louis

Address: Washington Univ St. Louis, Campus Box 1089, One Brookings Drive, St. Louis, MO 63130-4899
Phone: 314-935-6000
E-mail Address: admissions@wustl.edu
Web site URL: www.wustl.edu
Year Founded: 1853
Private or Public: private
Religious affiliation: none
Location: suburban
Regular Application Deadline: 15-Jan
Number of Applicants: 21,515
Percent Accepted: 19%
Percent Accepted who enroll: 34%
Number Entering: 1,535
Number of Transfers Accepted each Year: NA

Mean SAT: NA
Mean ACT: NA
Middle 50% SAT range: M: 690–770, V: 670–750
Middle 50% ACT range: 30–33
Early admission program (EA/ ED/ NA): ED
ED or EA Acceptance Rate: NA
Full time Undergraduate enrollment: 6,169
Total enrollment: 13,383
Percent Male: 50%
Percent Female: 50%
Total Percent Minority: 23%
Percent African-American: 9%
Percent Asian/Pacific Islander: 10%
Percent Hispanic: 3%

Percent Native-American: <1%
Percent Other: 0%
Percent in-state / out of state: 12%/88%
Percent from Public HS: 63%
Retention Rate: 96%
Graduation Rate: 91%
Percent in On-campus housing: 65%
Percent affiliated with Greek system: 25%
Percent Varsity or Club Athletes: NA
Number of official organized extracurricular organizations: 200
3 Most popular majors: Arts and Scinces, Engineering, Business
Student/Faculty ratio: 7:01
Tuition and Fees: NA

Even if you didn't already know that it is in St. Louis, chances are high that you have heard some wonderful things about Washington University. Wash U. (or WUSTL, as many have dubbed it) is a school that has been on a steady upward move through the college rankings in recent years, putting this dynamic Midwestern hot spot in a position to compete with top universities across the country. Offering generous financial aid packages, Washington University has attracted some of the nation's most talented students. As one junior commented, "I know plenty of people who turned down Ivy League institutions once they visited Washington and felt its great atmosphere." Both interest and attendance have swelled in response to this newfound popularity, as more and more students discover just what this university has to offer. There is an incredible energy in the air, as students seize every opportunity to explore city life from the safe haven of their St. Louis campus. Like the city that hosts the college, Wash U. is a lively, stimulating place that combines friendly Midwestern values with vivacious intellectual curiosity.

Weeding Out the Pre-Meds

According to one student, "about 60 percent of incoming students claim that they are pre-med." However, this number (actually closer to 25 percent, according to the administration) quickly drops after students discover the "intense" and "cutthroat" atmosphere of Wash U's pre-med (biological sciences) program. Students who remain on the pre-med track acknowledge that science classes are definitely tough, but are quick to point out that Wash U. is a very challenging school—no matter what your major is.

To graduate, students must complete 120 hours of class credit and must fulfill the requirements of the school's "cluster system," which aims to expose students to a variety of disciplines and fields before they graduate. Though students feel that the system can be a good way to learn about the different departments, many find it incredibly frustrating. As one junior claimed, "Most undergrads don't even understand the details of the requirements." Thankfully, Wash U. provides its students with an extensive support system of faculty and peer advisers. One sophomore said, "I have at least three different advisers at all times." Students can also seek guidance from their easily accessible professors, who receive rave reviews for their dedication in the classroom and out. Professors teach all classes with the exception of the Freshman Writing Class, for which graduate students lead sections. One student said, "Not only do you learn a lot from the professors here, but you also get the sense that you have a personal relationship with them and that they care about your learning."

The flexibility of Wash U.'s academic departments seems to be the most cherished aspect of students' academic experiences. It is not uncommon for undergrads to double or triple major in such diverse fields as biology and art history, or to have a major in one field and a minor in another. Wash U. offers five undergraduate colleges: The College of Arts and Sciences, The School of Engineering and Applied Science, The College of Art, The College of Architecture, and the John M. Olin School of Business. The School of Business, which is affectionately known as the "B School pre-school," is said to be easier than that other schools, while students in the School of Engineering and Applied Sciences and the College of Architecture reportedly "never sleep." Despite the apparent disparity in workload, students say that all of the schools are incredibly flexible when it comes to meeting student interests, and many students are able to craft their own majors by combining existing disciplines. One senior reported that the "opportunities and facilities continually amaze me and everyone's enthusiasm is so encouraging, you want to do well for more than just a grade."

The Overachiever Complex

"I think you'd be hard-pressed to find a student who is not involved in at least one extracurricular," one student claimed. With hundreds of clubs and student organizations ranging from skydiving to chess, Wash U. students are overwhelmed with opportunities to get involved, leading to what one student called the "overachiever complex." In fact, freshmen must quickly learn how to say no because, according to one student, "if you did a tenth of everything that you could possibly do here, you'd never sleep!"

The most popular activities include intramural sports ("a huge pastime here"), Campus Y (the community service organization), a cappella and improv comedy groups, and the Congress of the South 40 (the student governing body). Each major has its own student government body as does each class, offering plenty of opportunities for political involvement on campus. Also popular are the College Democrat and Republican organizations, which got their 15 minutes of fame when one of the 2004 presidential debates was held on Wash U.'s campus. The city of St. Louis also provides many opportunities for internships and work. In such an energetic environment, the "possibilities are endless."

Work Hard, Play (Really) Hard

At Wash U., the old adage really is true. Described as "very wet on weekends and dry as a bone on weeknights," Washington University is the quintessential work-hard, play-hard environment, as its students are quick to point out. Though some feel that the administration has tried to crack down on drinking in recent years, parties are still a huge part of the social scene and can be found in the dorms or on frat row every Friday and Saturday night. RAs (Resident Advisers) are known to be fairly lenient, and one student observed that "The University really treats you as an adult; as long as you're not seriously disturbing the peace, you can do whatever you want." Given their proximity to the headquarters of Anheuser Busch, Wash U. students claim a fondness for a certain golden brew and report no difficulty in obtaining alcohol at any age. However, they are also quick to defend the right to abstain and say that "there isn't really any pressure on those who don't want to drink."

Many upperclassmen explore the bars and clubs of the surrounding area once they are of legal age, but for freshmen and sophomores the social scene revolves primarily around fraternity events. Sororities do not have houses on campus, so frats are responsible for showing the campus a good time. At a school where about 25 percent of the student body belongs to one of the 12 fraternities or the six sororities, Wash U. maintains a fun environment that is both open and inviting. Deferred rush gives students the chance to relax into Greek life before joining, and one underclassman praised the sororities' inclusiveness: "They are great! They don't haze at all and have a genuine philanthropic focus—unlike so many other schools I know."

Off frat row, popular parties on campus include W.I.L.D., Walk-In Lay Down, a campuswide party held on the first and last Friday of the year featuring both local and nationally recognized bands. Ben Folds, Sister Hazel,

Nappy Roots, Live, and Talib Kwali have been recent performers. Considering almost nobody on campus takes any interest in school sports events ("Our homecoming is a joke," one student said), W.I.L.D. is one of "the few times almost all student socialize together for an extended period of time." Still, Wash U. students praise the fun, social atmosphere of the school and appreciate having a balance of work and play.

You Go to School Where?

Once students get over the fact that Washington University is in Missouri, not tucked away in the Pacific Northwest, they learn to love the city of St. Louis. One student raved, "It's great—you can be at the arch in a 10-minute drive!" The clubs, bars and music of downtown lure students who own cars, but even those who depend on public transportation find St. Louis incredibly accessible and appealing. A 15-minute walk from campus, "The Loop" is known for its inexpensive shops and restaurants, and as an "off-beat, college-town" section of St. Louis. Students also cite the City Museum as a favorite downtown destination. Described as a "huge jungle-gym for adults," this indoor playground stays open until 1 a.m. and is a great place for students seeking to reconnect with their inner child.

Getting people to leave Wash U.'s campus tends to be a problem, however. Known as the "most beautiful campus anywhere," and "the only school that actually looks like its brochure," Wash U. students love the look of their campus. As one junior put it, "Students love going to school in sparkly pink castles." The Gothic architecture provides the perfect backdrop to a vibrant collegiate experience, and the "incredible quadrangles" are ideal for enjoying the mild St. Louis weather.

Old Dorms vs. New Dorms

Because of its increasing popularity over the last few years, Wash U. has built a number of new dorm buildings on the South 40 (the main residential area on campus, named for the 40 acres of land it occupies). These new buildings are popular with students, but are considered by some to be "more hotel-like than a college should be." with their carpeted floors. Some students caution that the walls of the new dorm buildings are too thin to provide much privacy from one's neighbors. For freshmen, rooms in the new dorms are arranged as suites with two double rooms sharing a common bathroom. Students who are assigned to the older dorm buildings

reside in a more traditional dorm arrangement, with double rooms assembled along a coed hall with a large common bathroom at either end. Students at Wash U. tend to bond strongly with others on their freshman floor and are quick to defend the building that they lived in freshman year. According to one junior, "People who lived in old buildings will tell you that they are the best—more fun and more social. People who lived in the new buildings will tell you about how great it is to have a private bathroom." Whether you live in an old or a new building, dorm life is central to the social setting at Wash U. and provides a great way to meet other people and form lasting friendships.

> **"I know plenty of people who turned down Ivy League institutions once they visited Washington."**

After freshman year, Wash U. students often live in suites of four to six students, with singles clustered around a common room. A smaller residential area called the Village offers apartment-style and themed housing for upperclassmen, and is said to be a great option for people who are "getting sick of dorm life." Other juniors and seniors opt for a unit in one of three university-owned apartment complexes or an off-campus apartment in one of the surrounding neighborhoods. One student living off campus commented, "The off-campus apartments are definitely the cheapest, but make sure you check out the area before you commit. Some of the neighborhoods are not the safest."

Wash U.'s dining system draws high marks from nearly all students, with one sophomore commenting, "I wouldn't be surprised if we got the award for best food on a college campus." A mix of cafeteria-style and grab-and-go eating is available at campus centers near the South 40 and the village. All students, even those living off campus, are required to purchase a campus meal plan based on a point system in which one point corresponds roughly to one dollar. Some students feel that the food can be somewhat overpriced, while others bemoan the attempts to make the food "too fancy." One student expressed such a complaint, saying, "A prepackaged turkey sandwich will often contain the fancy and generally disliked basil and roasted red pepper, instead of the standard and universally liked lettuce and tomato." Whatever your food preferences may be, Wash U. has enough dining options to satisfy most tastes. There are also a number of restaurants, cafes, and coffee shops surrounding campus where students often eat on weekends or grab a bite between classes.

The Wash U. Bubble

Wash U. students call themselves a "moderate to very attractive student body." Wash U. prides itself on having well-dressed students, but some feel that there is "a bit too much Abercrombie and Fitch on campus." Although a sizable portion of the population hails from the upper middle class, Wash U. is too big to be defined by one stereotype, and students genuinely appreciate the diversity on campus. There are a number of students from metropolitan areas like Chicago and New York, but Wash U. also attracts students from other parts of the county and the world—creating an extremely diverse, sophisticated atmosphere. "The people" are universally hailed as what makes Wash U. so special. Surprising to many students, "everyone is involved in everything and incredibly energetic about what they're doing." Students, faculty and neighbors are all "so unbelievably friendly" that even with its other strengths, most students believe that Wash U.'s greatest asset is its Midwestern charm.—*Emily Barton and Jessica Lenox*

FYI

If you come to Wash U., you'd better bring "an open mind and a day planner because you will meet so many different types of people from so many places."

What's the typical weekend schedule? "Most people go out either Friday or Saturday night, and go to Frat Row or in to St. Louis' Central West End or to the clubs downtown. During the day, we study or go shopping or just hang out with friends."

If I could change one thing about Wash U., it would be "either the name or the lack of school spirit and traditions."

Three things every student at Wash U. should do before graduating are "go up in the St. Louis arch, find out how to get on the roof of a campus building, and eat Ted Drewes frozen custard (a St. Louis tradition!)."

Montana

Surrounded by mountains and adjacent to the Clark Fork River, its no wonder University of Montana students call themselves Grizzlies. "You can literally walk off campus into a wilderness area," raved one freshman. "It's definitely the most beautiful campus I've seen—and I was all over the West Coast looking at schools." Add to that a wide variety of academic options and the thriving small-city nightlife of Missoula, and you get a "really neat place to go to school."

Hitting the Books

UM has programs in the arts and sciences, forestry and conservation, technology, business, education, pharmacy, journalism, and fine arts, offering students a wide variety of majors, from Anthropology to Zoology and everything in between. Entering freshmen apply to the University of Montana at large; students apply to a specific major later, before the end of junior year. The most popular majors include psychology, forestry, and marketing, which is known for being relatively easy.

Regardless of major, all Grizzlies must take 120 course credits to graduate (an average courseload is 15–18 credits, or 3–5 classes, per semester), at least 39 of which must be in upper-division courses. In addition, students must fulfill an English requirement, Mathematical Literacy requirement, and a Foreign Language or Symbolic Systems requirement. Also, each student must take a total of 27 credits in the following six "perspectives," with at least 2 credits from each: Expressive Arts, Literary and Artistic Studies, Historical and Cultural Studies, Social Sciences, Ethical and Human Values, and Natural Sciences. To some students, the number of requirements seems like "overkill," though they're "good for someone who doesn't have a major in mind because you can figure out what you want to do." In any case, said one junior, "There's usually enough of a selection that you can find something you'll like—there's so many different choices that if you can't find something you can at least deal with, you're not trying very hard." Indeed, at least some requirements can be met with "easy and interesting" classes like History of Rock and Roll, Use and Abuse of Drugs, Human Sexuality, and Intro to Anthropology.

> "It's definitely the most beautiful campus I've seen—and I was all over the West Coast looking at schools."

Unfortunately, with over 11,000 undergrads, getting the classes you want can be "pretty hard." "Classes go really fast" in online registration, said one freshman. This leaves some students "stuck with classes at really weird times," but teachers will often sign an override slip if you talk to them in person. Students can also sign up for the Four Bear program, where they plan out a tentative four-year schedule ahead of time with an advisor, and get to pick classes before everyone else.

While competition to get into classes is tough, competition within classes is almost nonexistent. "I really would not call UM cutthroat," said one junior. "While it attracts all types, people are generally pretty laid back here." Class sizes range from 20–30 person upper-division seminars to intro lecture classes with over 400 students. Professors teach the majority of classes, though TAs (who are generally "pretty good") teach basic introductory English and Math classes, in addition to leading lab sections. Even in large lecture classes, "there's a lot of access to your professor," said a junior biology major. "If you can't make it to their office hours, they'll go out of their way to meet with you," echoed a freshman. Most students are "pretty happy" with their professors, who, in addition to being "really approachable," are also "extremely knowledgeable" and "enjoy teaching."

Students seeking a more intense education can apply to the Davidson Honors College at the same time they apply to UM. Honors classes are similar in subject matter to non-honors courses, but average 22 students per class. That means "more work—because it's a smaller class, it's not as easy to sit back and tune out," but also "a lot more discussion, a much better learning environment." Non-honors students can also take honors classes, but honors students get priority, and must take at least 7 honors courses, including a senior project, to graduate. UM also has a "really strong" study abroad program, which offers the opportunity to study in 38 different countries, including Australia, Canada, Chile, China, France, Morocco, and Thailand.

A Grizzly's Den

Dorms at UM get mixed reviews. All are located "close to the core of campus," no more than a 10-minute walk from classes, and have laundry facilities, game rooms, and lounges. However, they vary in style and quality. Jesse and Aber, the high-rise dorms, are "housing projects designed to pack in as many people as possible," while Craig and Duniway have bigger rooms, and Miller, renovated in 1996, offers singles. Knowles houses honors and international students, Elrod is male-only, and Turner houses only women. Students can also choose substance-free floors or quiet floors if they so desire.

All students who live in the dorms must purchase a meal plan, which allows students to eat at the Food Zoo (the main cafeteria), as well as at an on-campus food court or coffee shops. The Zoo offers "pretty good variety," and the food is "good for mass production," especially with its new Farm to College program, which brings in fresh meat and vegetables from local farms.

Freshmen, who are required to live on campus, are distributed throughout the various dorms. Events like the weekly "Floor Snack" and monthly trips to a bowling alley or pizza place make it easy to meet new people. These events are organized by upperclassmen RAs, who live on each floor and range from "real well-trained" to "horrible. [They'll] write you up if you're overly loud, drinking, doing anything that's slightly weird." Overall, said one freshman, "They're good at what they do—they keep the place running really smoothly—but they definitely stick to the rules." Even though the newest dorm, Pantzer, is reserved for upperclassmen, most students move off campus by junior year; however, many claim that "finding something that's affordable close to campus gets difficult."

Unfortunately, "parking on campus is absolutely insane—it's impossible to get a spot," and "public transportation isn't real great," so many students are forced to leave their cars in Park and Ride lots. Luckily, "it's really easy to get around" with a bike, said one Grizzly. Bike lanes are ubiquitous in Missoula, and "everything is really close—I can ride my bike to the mall, Target, and back to campus in like half an hour."

Here Come the MIP's

UM certainly lives up to its reputation as "a really big party school." Every spring, Grizzlies "dress up country style" to attend the Foresters' Ball, in which the forestry department turns the gym into a logging camp, complete with a saloon and "hitching post" where students can get "married." Other popular annual parties include Maggotfest, when rugby teams come from across the nation to compete in the spring tournament, and then have a "giant party with an absurd number of kegs and people pouring beer all over each other."

Although frats throw "their fair share of parties," Greek life is "not very big," which makes the Greek scene a "really tight-knit community," but "not a large part of the social network." Alcohol is generally "pretty easy to get," but drinking is "definitely more of an off-campus thing," since RAs zealously report underage drinking in the dorms. Even off campus, however, police "are more than eager" to cite students for "a DUI, BUI (biking under the influence), or MIP (minors in possession)."

On most weekends, students frequent house parties or head into the "very active downtown," which includes a variety of restaurants, pool halls, and "a ton of bars that are always packed." Students report that "bars are pretty easy to get into if you know people that know people," even if you're not 21. Non-drinkers enjoy a variety of options as well. Popular with both students and locals is the Elks Lodge, an 18-and-up club in Missoula which invites musical performers every night. On campus, there are "Nite Kourt" events, where university organizations bring in "hypnotists, comedians, all kinds of stuff."

Grizzlies at Play

When they're not partying or studying, UM students are involved in a plethora of extracurricular activities. As one junior put it, "There's pretty much a club for any-

thing you want." The diversity of clubs reflects a diversity of students: although racial diversity is limited (the student body is "very, very white"), students hail from all over the country, and even as far away as Japan, Korea, Hong Kong, Australia, Germany, and Tajikistan. Organizations include the popular ASUM (student government), which organizes many events on campus, and *Kaimin*, the student newspaper, as well as unusual clubs like the "Footbag Alliance," devoted to hacky sack. As Missoula is the most liberal part of Montana (though not as liberal as some universities in other parts of the country), activism is also big. "There are a lot of causes to rally around," said a junior. "There is always something for people who want to get involved socially or politically." Jobs are also fairly common, though many students complain that the minimum wage in Montana is a paltry $5.30.

But the biggest draw is the great outdoors. Students enjoy fly-fishing in the Clark Fork River right off campus, as well as hiking up to the concrete "M" on Mt. Sentinel. There are also many outdoor clubs, which organize weekend camping and backpacking trips to nearby Glacier National Park (two and a half hours away), Yellowstone (three hours), or Hot Springs (less than half an hour). Moreover, the Recreation Center, a recently renovated on-campus facility, rents whitewater rafts, ski equipment, backpacking gear, and kayaks at reduced prices.

The rec center is also "absolutely awesome" during the winter, containing an indoor track, weight machines, exercise rooms, swimming pool, and climbing wall. Students looking for more competitive activities can play intramural sports, the most popular of which are Ultimate Frisbee, soccer, softball, and basketball; and for those students who are particularly athletically inclined, UM also offers 14 Division I varsity sports.

According to most students, there is a lot of school spirit. Students and Missoula residents regularly sell out the 23,000-seat stadium for football games, which feature skydivers jumping onto the field at halftime. Before games, "people go nuts about tailgates—they pull up in motor homes painted with the Montana colors." Whether they come for the exciting party scene, academic choices, or "gorgeous" location, students agree: "UM is a cool place to be."—*Sameer Jain*

FYI

If you come to UM, you'd better bring "Chaco sandals, a warm jacket, and a sense of adventure."

What's the Typical Weekend Schedule? "Thursday: head out to a party. Friday: go to a pool hall or bar downtown, maybe a party. Saturday: tailgate, football game, nap in the afternoon, party at night. Sunday: homework, laundry, recovery. Or head to Glacier National Park or the Hot Springs for the whole weekend."

If I could change one thing about UM, I'd "increase racial diversity—I've seen literally 4 black people the 3 months I've been here."

Three things every student should do before graduating are "go to a football game, go to the Foresters' Ball, and hike to the M (a huge white concrete M about a 1000 feet up Mt. Sentinel which people hike to all the time)."

Nebraska

Creighton University

Address: Creighton, 2700 California Plaza, Omaha, NE 68178
Phone: 402-280-2703 or 800-282-5835
E-mail Address: admissions@creighton.edu
Web site URL: http://admissions.creighton.edu/
Year Founded: 1878
Private or Public: private
Religious affiliation: Roman Catholic
Location: urban
Regular Application Deadline: rolling
Number of Applicants: 3,435
Percent Accepted: 87%
Percent Accepted who enroll: 28%
Number Entering: 1,078
Number of Transfers Accepted each Year: 170
Mean SAT: 1,200

Mean ACT: 26
Middle 50% SAT range: 1,090–1,310
Middle 50% ACT range: 24–29
Early admission program (EA/ ED/ NA): NA
ED or EA Acceptance Rate: NA
Full time Undergraduate enrollment: 3,731
Total enrollment: 6,791
Percent Male: 43%
Percent Female: 57%
Total Percent Minority: 18%
Percent African-American: 3%
Percent Asian/Pacific Islander: 7%
Percent Hispanic: 4%
Percent Native-American: 1%
Percent Other: NA

Percent in-state / out of state: 40%/60%
Percent from Public HS: 54%
Retention Rate: 92%
Graduation Rate: 74%
Percent in On-campus housing: 61%
Percent affiliated with Greek system: 24%
Percent Varsity or Club Athletes: NA
Number of official organized extracurricular organizations: 180
3 Most popular majors: Psychology, Marketing, Biology
Student/Faculty ratio: 12:01
Tuition and Fees: $25,136.00
Cost for Room and Board: $7,842.00
Percent receiving Financial aid, first-year: 85%

O maha may be the largest city in Nebraska, but students at Creighton University feel like they are members of a small community of familiar faces. Creighton students love the fact that their education consists of small class sizes and lots of personal attention. Students agree that "faculty involvement with students and interest in their education" sets Creighton apart from other colleges.

"The Professor Knows My Name!"

Students at Creighton all rave about the same thing: small class sizes and a personal education. With a relatively small enrollment of about 3,500 total undergraduates, even introductory classes like basic chemistry and psychology have a maximum of 50 students. One student comments, "Most classes are small and very personable. I've had classes with anywhere from five to 25-

plus students. What's great is that the professors teach all of the classes." Not only are classes more interactive, professors are dedicated to giving personal attention to students as individuals. The availability of professors also leads to increased research opportunities; Creighton is known as a great place for undergraduates to conduct original research.

While selecting the perfect schedule for the semester, students in the College of Arts & Sciences at Creighton need to consider the required core curriculum. Out of a total 128 required credit hours, half of those are core requirements. This demanding guideline strives to expose students to all aspects of a liberal arts education, including six classes in theology, philosophy, and ethics; six in culture, ideas, and civilizations; two in natural science; two in social science; and three in skills (English, math and communications). The college also has a foreign-language requirement—students must either take one year of intro-level classes in a new language, or one higher-level class for a continued language study. The core curriculum irks some students, who feel that "the core classes are stupid. They give a good overall view of every major, but for those people that already know what they want to major in, it is quite pointless." Not all students agree, however; others feel these core classes contribute to the "whole-person education."

Many Creighton students home in on pre-medical, pre-dental and pre-law studies, since Creighton has well-rounded professional graduate schools; also popular pre-professional tracks are pharmacy, occupational therapy and physical therapy. Business, biology, nursing and psychology are by far the most popular majors. The College of Business is considered to be more slack by those in the College of Arts & Sciences, but business students feel this misrepresents such difficult majors as accounting and finance. There is lots of support for students who are interested in the health profession and many find it exciting to be surrounded by others with the same interests. Even though many students are science-geared, Creighton offers wonderful programs in modern and classical languages and fine arts; the largest non-science major is journalism and mass communications.

While academics are not competitive in a cutthroat way, Creighton is challenging. When asked about the workload, one student responded: "Being in a school recognized for its academics, most students are overachievers. I'd say anywhere from 15 to 17 credit hours per semester is about average." Students warn prospectives against expecting gut classes in the sciences and to be prepared for many papers in other concentrations.

Comfortable Living

All freshmen and sophomores must live on-campus. Of the five dorms, three are freshman dorms and two are for sophomores. Each dorm is unique; Kiewit Hall is known as the freshman party dorm and a popular freshman hangout. Accommodations are fairly nice: Swanson, for example, consists of suites with two double bedrooms connected by a private bathroom. Each floor also has its own study room, kitchen and lounges. For juniors and seniors, who are not required to live on campus, new apartment-style housing is available—a new building was recently constructed in August 2006. Although housing is available for all four years, about 60 percent of students live on campus.

Freshmen and sophomores must buy a meal plan, which they can use at the two main dining halls or the Student Center; the plans also include bonus dollars that can be redeemed at the four retail food stores on campus. The Student Center can satisfy all cravings for fast food, such as Blimpie's sub sandwiches, Godfather's pizza or the American Grill. With these options, some off-campus students feel that Creighton could "make the campus friendlier to those who don't have meal plans [by making] the other dining options more affordable to a college student."

Even though it is situated at the heart of a large metropolitan center, students at Creighton are confident in their school's security. With 24-hour foot and vehicle patrols and transport and escort services available at all hours of the night, students consistently report feeling very safe. The city of Omaha gives ambitious and eager students the opportunity to get involved in the world outside of Creighton with a host of internships and summer opportunities. For those who enjoy the outdoors, wildlife refuges and state parks abound in the surrounding area. Students also love hanging out at the Old Market, a hotbed for "incredible restaurants and a great place for a date."

The Social Scene

Despite these attractions, many students still feel that Omaha can be "boring" and say the social scene on weekends centers around friends' rooms for house and frat parties. Greek life is pretty dominant in the social scene, as about a third of the undergrads at Creighton are in a fraternity or sorority. While this may seem like a large number, most students feel that being in a fraternity or sorority is not necessary to be in the social circuit. One student remarks: "There are also many social alternatives. Everyone will find one or many social niches."

These niches include numerous student organizations on campus. With groups ranging from the Ultimate Frisbee Organization to the Health Administration and Policy Student Group to the Hui O Hawaii Club, students can usually find a group with their same interests. Many students are involved in community service, especially through Habitat for Humanity. Students interested in journalism can write for the *Creightonian* or work for JTV, the student-run television station. There's also a Creighton tradition of holding a candlelight mass at historic St. John's Church in the middle of campus. "Hundreds of students take a study break at 10 p.m. every Sunday night to attend a non-traditional mass celebrated almost entirely by candlelight."

> **"You can always recognize and chat with a friend on the way to class. The beautiful campus is an oasis surrounded by a modern urban landscape."**

Athletics at Creighton centers almost exclusively on the Division I men's basketball team. Bluejay basketball games are always well attended, especially against Southern Illinois and Drake University. Spirited students cheer from the rowdy "Birdcage," the student section of the arena. Intramurals are huge at Creighton, with great turnouts for volleyball, baseball and soccer. This athletic spirit is complemented by a large on-campus gym featuring five basketball courts, four racquetball courts, a weight room, a swimming pool and hot tub, and an indoor track.

In reference to the makeup of the student body, many undergrads do feel that Creighton is not as diverse as other schools. However, many students notice that Creighton is "making an effort to recruit more diversity." There is a growing number of Hawaiian students on campus, and the percent of out-of-state and international students is also growing. In addition, Creighton is seeking to aesthetically improve the campus by renovating and reconstructing out-of-date buildings. Students report feeling that there is always some kind of construction going on, with new facilities popping up every year; among the university's current projects is a $50 million "Living-Learning Center," intended to integrate student services with academic support, classrooms, study areas and recreational spaces. Getting out of the dorm room, students can study beside "peaceful fountains, beautiful gardens and many neatly landscaped areas." One enthusiastic student notes, "You can always recognize and chat with a friend on the way to class. The beautiful campus is an oasis surrounded by a modern urban landscape." But still, when asked what they like best about their school, students at Creighton stress the academic acclaim and personal attention they receive in the classroom.—*Karen Chen*

FYI
If you come to Creighton, you'd better bring "a willingness to be challenged."
The typical weekend schedule is "hanging out with friends, catching up on sleep and laundry, some partying, and homework on Sunday."
If I could change one thing about Creighton, I'd " put a bar on campus."
Three things that every student at Creighton should do before graduating are "cheer on the Bluejays as part of the rowdy "Birdcage" student section, discover yourself and others on a retreat at Creighton's rural retreat center, and take a course with Dr. Gardener in Irish literature and drama."

University of Nebraska

Address: University of
  Nebraska, Lincoln, 313
  N 13th St, Lincoln, NE
  68588-0256
Phone: 800-742-8800
E-mail Address:
  admissions@unl.edu
Web site URL:
  http://admissions.unl.edu/
Year Founded: 1869
Private or Public: public
Religious affiliation: none
Location: urban
**Regular Application
  Deadline:** 2-May
Number of Applicants: 7,993
Percent Accepted: 73%
**Percent Accepted who
  enroll:** 65%
Number Entering: 3,849
**Number of Transfers
  Accepted each Year:** 1,288
Mean SAT: NA
Mean ACT: 25

Middle 50% SAT range:
  1,040–1,320
Middle 50% ACT range:
  22–28
**Early admission program
  (EA/ ED/ NA):** NA
ED or EA Acceptance Rate:
  NA
**Full time Undergraduate
  enrollment:** 17,371
Total enrollment: 21,707
Percent Male: 54%
Percent Female: 46%
Total Percent Minority:
  8.8%
Percent African-American:
  2%
**Percent Asian/Pacific
  Islander:** 3%
Percent Hispanic: 3%
Percent Native-American:
  0.8%
Percent Other: <1%
**Percent in-state / out of
  state:** 86% / 14%

**Percent from Public
  HS:** NA
Retention Rate: 84%
Graduation Rate: 62%
**Percent in On-campus
  housing:** 45%
**Percent affiliated with
  Greek system:** 16%
**Percent Varsity or Club
  Athletes:** NA
**Number of official
  organized extracurricular
  organizations:** 335
Most popular majors:
  Business, Psychology
Student/Faculty ratio:
  19:01
Tuition and Fees:
  $15,317.00
**In State Tuition and Fees
  (if different):** $5,867.00
Cost for Room and Board:
  $6,183.00
**Percent receiving Financial
  aid, first-year:** 63%

A t the University of Nebraska, football comes right after a warm winter coat on the list of biological necessities. "You can't go two minutes on this campus without hearing someone mention the football team or seeing a sweatshirt branded with Cornhusker paraphernalia," a junior declared. With five National Championships to their name and arguably the most devoted throng of fans, Cornhusker spirit runs deep in this part of the country, with the university's Memorial Stadium holding the all-time record for 220 consecutive sold-out games. As a freshman summed it up proficiently, "We don't mess around when it comes to football."

Making the Grade

While students don't always speak with the same vitality about studying as they do about last Saturday's football game, they seem to be satisfied with the academic program. The University offers a total of 149 majors, creating a niche for just about everyone in the academic domain. The majors are divided between 10 academic colleges: the College of Agricultural Sciences & Natural Resources, the College of Architecture, the College of Arts & Sciences, the College of Business Administration, the College of Education and Human Sciences, the College of Engineering & Technology, the College of Fine & Performing Arts, the College of Graduate Studies, the College of Journalism & Mass Communication, and the College of Law. Workload varies tremendously depending on the major, class, and number of credit hours taken per term. One student summarized, "Basically, if you take a lot of science classes, your workload will be more difficult." Organic Chemistry and Genetics were noted as two of the most grueling classes. The toughest majors and academic programs are Pre-Law, Pre-Med, Anthropology, "and almost any science."

For students seeking a challenging academic schedule, UNL offers the University Honors Program. Students are accepted to the program before freshman year based on high school academic records and standardized test scores. They have access to some of the University's best professors, smaller classes, and honors computer centers, and live in special housing in Neihardt Hall. For those willing to reserve most of their energy for the football games, "Generally, most people here are pretty laid-back, and I'd say business majors and English majors are the least difficult," a sophomore explained.

Most classes take place in lecture halls and cater to around 150 students. However, if you're not big on standard lecture classes, "English classes and others similar to that are usually smaller, with about 30 people in them," an English major commented. No matter the number of students enrolled, however, professors are friendly and willing to work with students' schedules to set up out-of-class meetings. TAs generally serve as helpful guides through complex subject matter. Although one student warned, "You can't count on the TAs in the science department to speak English very well, so while they're always willing to help, sometimes they just don't understand your question."

Living and Eating: the Good, the Bad and the . . .

Students are required to live on campus freshman year, and while many live off campus after that, they generally view the requirement as beneficial to their college experience. "You meet a lot of people that you might otherwise never get to know, some of whom become your best friends." All of the dorms are coed, although bathrooms are single-sex. Cather and Pound are two upperclassmen dorms that offer their residents laundry facilities and computer clusters on every floor. UNL also now offers two dorms that have apartment-style living for students.

> "You can't go two minutes on this campus without hearing someone mention the football team or seeing a sweatshirt branded with Cornhusker paraphernalia."

All of the first year dorm rooms are fairly similar. Most are doubles and have a basic set of two beds, desks, shelves and closets, as well as a high speed Internet connection and cable. The rooms are air-conditioned, too, which is a major plus on those humid Nebraska days. Freshman dorms are staffed by upperclassmen RAs (Residential Advisors) to keep the dorms a place conducive to studying and sleeping as well. UNL is a dry campus, and one of the RA's major responsibilities is to help enforce the policy, taken quite seriously by the administration. A sophomore clarified the conditions, "There is no alcohol allowed on campus at all, and

the administration has really been cracking down on offenders in the last two years." At a place where, "weekends start of Thursday," and the primary social options are sorority and fraternity parties or the bars on 'O' Street, drinking is a focal point. While a typical Nebraska student may be a pre- and post-gamer (football games are other drinking fests), the administration's position on alcohol makes socializing without booze more fun and feasible for those Huskers who aren't hardy partying types.

Most of the students move off campus after freshman year due to both the dry campus policy and the abundant availability of inexpensive housing near campus. "Rent is about $250–$350 per person and most people really like the idea of finding a group of friends to live with and setting up their own place." Other common housing options are fraternity and sorority houses. While students insist that there is no stereotype for the sort of person who thrives at UNL, one student observed that, "Greek men and women seem to hold more leadership positions on campus." Statistically, the average Greek GPA is higher than the overall University average, as well.

The dining halls are very clean and never too crowded. Speaking to the food's quality, a student commented, "It's decent. Most people complain, but it's a buffet and you can always find soup, salad and sandwich stuff." On the up side, meal plans allow students to eat in any of the dining halls, and their ID cards also serve as charge cards to pick up snacks and meals on the run.

The Layout

The Husker's campus is divided into two sections, City Campus and East Campus. Students agree, "It would be quite a walk between the two, but it's only about a five minute drive." Shuttle buses run between the sections for students without cars. City Campus houses most departments, while the home economics and agriculture schools are on East Campus. As for the favorite buildings on campus, some agree that the Nebraska Union, the campus's social center, is top of the list, while others call for Memorial Stadium, standing for the Husker's passion for football. The Nebraska Union houses the University Bookstore, a convenience store, auditorium, copy shop, game room, food-court and big-screen television lounge. Memorial Stadium also recently underwent renovations in 1999 when $40 million was invested in the addition of new skyboxes. In addition, the stadium, weight room, indoor practice facilities, and weight rooms are currently undergoing a massive renovation.

Something for Everyone

Other UNL teams boast impressive records in addition to football. Some notables are the men's gymnastics team with eight national titles, women's indoor track and field with three, and the women's volleyball team, which won the national championship in 1995 and 2000. Intramural sports are the most popular extracurricular activity, offering students an outlet for physical activity as well as a great way to meet new people. Most popular events are flag football and softball. Active students also take full advantage of the Lee Sapp Recreational Center, housing two indoor tracks, a climbing wall, basketball and racquetball courts, and a weight room.

Outside of academics and athletics, students keep busy with an array of other activities including community outreach volunteer programs, various on-campus publications such as the Daily Nebraskan, and the performing arts. 'Scarlet and Cream', a men and women's singing and dance group, is among the most prestigious of the performing groups. Many UNL students add a job to their busy schedules, as well. One student predicted that, "about 70 percent of the student body works at least a few hours a week to make extra spending money."

The Greek houses are known for throwing some of the best parties of the year. If you like to get dressed up, each frat and sorority has two formals a year. Every house has theme parties, too. Some recent themes were the '70s, cowboys, disco, doctors and nurses, beach party, and Catholic school. "You name it, and we've done it," a student declared.

Other places to spend evenings out are the bars on 'O' Street, frequented by many upperclassmen. The city of Lincoln offers university students more than just a place to bar hop though. There are some great places to catch dinner with a group of friends such as Lazlos, Old Chicago, Ruby Tuesdays, and Applebee's. The Haymarket, a quaint section of town near campus, is a popular place to go on dates, and if you're into movies, there are several theaters down town.

Home football games are all-day events not to be missed. A typical game day begins at the tailgate, reaches its crescendo with students painted red from head to toe, trickling into the evening as students make their way back home to catch a televised game before heading out for some more partying in the evening. The University of Nebraska, with its celebrated football tradition, array of academic opportunities, laid-back atmosphere and enthusiastic student body presents Huskers with the chance to have some the best four years of their lives.—*Susanne Kenagy*

FYI

If you come to the U of Nebraska, you better bring "a warm winter coat, you usually have to walk a little ways to class and it can get very cold."

What's the typical weekend schedule? "Go to a frat party on Thursday and Friday nights, prime before the football game on Saturday, get pizza after, wake up late on Sunday and do homework in the afternoon."

If I could change one thing about the U of Nebraska, "I'd get rid of the train tracks that run through campus. You have to wait on your way to class while trains pass."

Three things every student should do at the U of Nebraska before graduating are "swim in the fountain in front of the Union, pass library class, and go to a football game."

Nevada

University of Nevada / Reno

Address: University of Nevada, Reno, 1664 North Virginia Street, Reno, NV 89557-0042
Phone: 866-2NEVADA
E-mail Address: asknevada@unr.edu
Web site URL: www.unr.edu/
Year Founded: 1864
Private or Public: public
Religious affiliation: none
Location: urban
Regular Application Deadline: Rolling
Number of Applicants: 4,838
Percent Accepted: 86%
Percent Accepted who enroll: 57%
Number Entering: 2,357
Number of Transfers Accepted each Year: 1,541
Mean SAT: NA
Mean ACT: NA
Middle 50% SAT range: 920–1,160

Middle 50% ACT range: 20–25
Early admission program (EA/ ED/ NA): EA
ED or EA Acceptance Rate: NA
Full time Undergraduate enrollment: 13,134
Total enrollment: 16,446
Percent Male: 45%
Percent Female: 55%
Total Percent Minority: 18%
Percent African-American: 3%
Percent Asian/Pacific Islander: 7%
Percent Hispanic: 7%
Percent Native-American: 1%
Percent Other: <1%
Percent in-state / out of state: 82% / 18%
Percent from Public HS: NA
Retention Rate: 75%

Graduation Rate: NA
Percent in On-campus housing: 14%
Percent affiliated with Greek system: 6%
Percent Varsity or Club Athletes: NA
Number of official organized extracurricular organizations: NA
3 Most popular majors: Business/Marketing, Education, Social Sciences
Student/Faculty ratio: 19:01
Tuition and Fees: $13,595.00
In State Tuition and Fees (if different): $3,684.00
Cost for Room and Board: $8,199.00
Percent receiving Financial aid, first-year: 59%

At the heart of the "Biggest Little City in the World" and the base of the Sierra Nevada mountain range lies the University of Nevada, Reno. Home to renowned academic facilities, experienced faculty members, a variety of extracurricular activities, and an active social scene, UNR offers its students "a state university where you can get an Ivy League education."

From Shake Tables to Western Traditions

The undergraduate academic programs at UNR find their homes in the College of Agriculture, Biotechnology, and Natural Resources; the College of Liberal Arts; the College of Business Administration; the College of Education; the College of Science; the School of Medicine; the College of Engineering, the College of Health and Human Services; the Mackay School of Earth Sciences and Engineering, and the Reynolds School of Journalism. Of the 12 total schools and colleges, the Mackay School of Mines is internationally recognized, the School of Engineering houses the second-largest shake table in the country (used to test roadside structures under earthquake conditions), and the Reynolds School of Journalism boasts Pulitzer Prize-winning professors and alumni.

The smaller class sizes available at UNR allow students to develop personal relationships with the school's talented faculty members. Aside from getting to know the reigning experts in areas from terrorism to Chinese studies, one journalism student says, "I can call my Pulitzer Prize-winning professor's home phone number with a question when I'm copy editing for the *Sagebrush* [UNR's student newspaper]."

The UNR honors program draws raves from students. "You're in smaller classes and you get to register early so you can get into any class at any time," says one freshman in the honors program. The only drawback, according to one student, is that "the whole point of the honors program is to get into really good classes your freshman and sophomore years, because after that there aren't any honors classes offered in most majors." Another student agreed, saying, "It's one of those school secrets that everybody knows about."

Students find the workload at UNR manageable, though most agree with the opinion of one senior: "The workload's what you make it. The more priorities you have and the more things you're involved in, the harder the workload seems." Many students find engineering courses to be among the hardest, although many find Western Traditions (WT), part of the core curriculum requirements at UNR, to be difficult as well. Completing the WT requirements—which include philosophy, literature, and history—"includes a lot of reading from primary sources, a lot of writing, and a lot of lectures."

High School All Over Again

Nearly 85 percent of all UNR students come from their home state, Nevada. Of these, 60 percent come from high schools in and around Reno. Like one freshman student, many feel as though "UNR is like an extension of high school. Most of the people I see are either from my high school or from another high school in Reno."

For many native Nevadans, the biggest draw of UNR is the Nevada Millennium Scholarship, which provides generous financial aid to students who meet certain eligibility requirements and graduated from a Nevada high school. As one UNR student said, "How could I turn down the Millennium Scholarship? I'm basically getting paid to go to school here." Some of the out-of-state students and those without the Millennium Scholarship express feelings of resentment toward the "Reno kids going to school for free," but on the whole, the local students and those from outside Nevada find that "it's an easy place to meet people and make friends quickly."

It's All Greek to Me

The majority of UNR's social scene takes place at the fraternity and sorority houses surrounding the campus. Although the fraternity constitutions were recently amended so that they are no longer allowed to serve alcohol, as one students says, "UNR's like any other college campus—there's definitely alcohol here, and people definitely have no trouble finding it if they're looking." Of the 11 fraternities and eight sororities found at UNR, Sigma Nu reportedly throws the best parties and Delta Delta Delta is the most popular sorority. While many students choose to rush fraternities or sororities, those who aren't involved usually agree that they are always welcome at Greek parties.

Students can also find house parties in nearby areas, whether thrown by the intramural rugby team or partiers living off campus. For students 21 and over (or those with fake IDs), downtown Reno offers drinking and gambling at infamous casinos, nightclubs, and bars like The Wall and Beer Barrel.

While some UNR students reportedly use drugs, one student assures that "there's no pressure to do anything you don't want to do." Another student agrees, saying, "Everyone is just here to have a good time and have some fun. If you don't drink or do drugs, you'll find the people who don't do that either. If you do drink or use drugs, you'll find people that do the same." Most students agree that marijuana is the most widely used drug.

Something for Everyone

Many UNR students are involved in some type of extracurricular activity. Student Orientation Staff, a group in charge of welcoming incoming freshman to UNR, is one of the largest groups on-campus, while the Campus Greens, a liberal organization, and the Feminist Majority Leadership Alliance are also popular clubs. The campus newspaper, the *Sagebrush*, is written and produced entirely by students, and intramural sports are a common way for students to participate in athletics at a less competitive level than varsity sports.

In addition, the student government organization and the student union bring in cultural events and entertainment for UNR students. From concerts to lectures to movie showings, students rarely find themselves with nothing to do on campus. If students are up for an hour-long drive north of Reno, they can even get involved with the U.S. Wolf Refuge, home to 14 wolf-hybrids and run by University employee Diana Chamberlain.

Battle for the Cannon

Football games are always well attended by UNR students, alumni, and much of the Reno community, but no game can compare with the annual "Battle for the Cannon." Each year the football teams from the University of Nevada, Reno and the University of Nevada, Las Vegas compete for possession of the coveted Fremont Cannon. The game is held at UNR every other year, when students from both universities pack into Mackay Stadium proudly wearing their respective "FUNR" and "FUNLV" shirts.

While football remains the favorite sport on campus, other sports are growing in popularity as well. Volleyball draws a consistent devoted crowd, while soccer and softball are consistently gaining more and more viewers.

Students of All Ages

About 85 percent of UNR students live off campus and commute to and from school every day. For these students, most agree with one engineering major that "a car is an absolute necessity." Many of these students are older; they hold proper jobs and sustain families. Although not your typical college scene, these older students pepper classes with their life experiences and anecdotes. There is something to be said about age-old wisdom, and younger students actually enjoy the companionship of the older students.

Those who choose to live on campus find themselves in Manzanita, White Pine, Lincoln, Canada, Juniper, Nye, Argenta or New Hall. While Nye Hall is the oldest and generally has smaller rooms, it is considered to be the most social dorm on campus. Incoming students hope to find themselves in Argenta Hall, which was completed most recently. As one student describes it, "Argenta Hall has huge, luxurious dorms with vaulted ceilings and private bathrooms in each dorm room."

Most halls are coed and RAs (Resident Advisors) live with freshman in the halls to ensure that rules are enforced and to provide support for the transition from high school to college. Visitors must sign in and out at the entrance to each hall, and alcohol is prohibited unless all residents are over 21.

> "At first I was only interested in the Millennium, but now, given the choice, I'd choose UNR again even without the scholarship money."

Argenta isn't the only new building that has popped up on campus, nor is it the most acclaimed. In fact, the 2005 Architectural Portfolio—a national publication released by the American School & University magazine—featured four UNR projects in its headlines, including the Pack Village, the Crossroads dining facility, the Nell J. Redfield student building, and the campus Master Plan. With such nationally-acclaimed university structures, a new generation of UNR students will be able to enjoy easy access to enhanced resources.

Whether for its exciting social scene, its renowned academic departments and programs, its reasonable tuition, or its extracurriculars and athletics, UNR's reputation is growing. More and more out-of-state students find themselves at UNR, while local students continue to enjoy the benefits of the Millennium Scholarship and being able to live at home. As one student said, "At first I was only interested in the Millennium, but now, given the choice, I'd choose UNR again even without the scholarship money. I love it here!"—*Sarah Newman*

FYI
If you come to UNR, you'd better bring "good luck in case you decide to try the casinos."
What is the typical weekend schedule? "Try to do something fun on Friday night; head to an extracurricular meeting Saturday morning; go to a football game Saturday night; and try to get some work done on Sunday."
If I could change one thing about UNR, I would "make the campus level instead of on that hill."
Three things every student at UNR should do before graduating are "watch UNLV lose the Cannon, go to a frat party, and figure out what you're really interested in."

New Hampshire

I t is a clear, cold night in October, and the natives are restless. The glow of the 70-tier bonfire lights up the dark sky and the sound of cheers, singing, and laughter punctuate the stillness of the New Hampshire night. Bare-chested young men and face-painted young women dash around the crackling, blazing behemoth while the Hanover village elders—community members, alumni, even some startled parents—cheer on the running masses. Unusual? Yes. Chemically-enhanced? Probably. But this is just one of the many traditions Dartmouth students hold near and dear to their hearts. Welcome to Homecoming "Big Green-style" and to the wild, fun, and sometimes down-right feral world of Dartmouth College.

"But a Small School. . . ."

"It is but a small school, sir, and yet there are those who love it," explained Dartmouth alumnus Daniel Webster in the famous Dartmouth College Case brought before the Supreme Court in 1819. Some things haven't changed in almost 200 years, and students continue to rave about the small classes and individual academic attention Dartmouth provides. While classes range from large lectures to small seminars, students insist that, at Dartmouth, "You are never completely anonymous, unless you try to be, and even then it's pretty tough." Courses are generally regarded as intense and fast-paced, a necessity when terms only meet for 10 weeks. All classes are taught by professors, and TAs are few and far between, mostly appearing to correct papers and facilitate study groups. As one junior stated, "The classes at Dartmouth are wonderful because you get such close interaction with outstanding professors . . . all the perks of the Ivy League without the hassles of overcrowding."

Dartmouth's respected faculty and rigorous academic programs are spread evenly across its varied curriculum. Strong in its liberal-arts approach to education, top majors range from government, economics, and English to chemistry and engineering. While legendary professors Peter Saccio and Rogers Elliot remain old favorites on the faculty, students also laud professors David Lagomarsino and Jane Carroll for their classes in history and art history, respectively, and speak highly of Allan Stam's government classes. Education 20: Educational Issues in Contemporary Society is longstanding in its reputation as one of Dartmouth's most popular classes, each year drawing over 200 students and a waiting list for enrollment. Students describe Professor Andrew Garrod's class as "changing the way you view the education system and the social inequities that exist," and as responsible for attracting many Dartmouth graduates to programs such as Teach for America.

Digging the D-Plan

The unique academic schedule known as the Dartmouth Plan is one of the most unusual, sometimes confusing, and ultimately prized elements of a Dartmouth education. The school year is divided into fall, winter, spring, and summer terms, with each academic term lasting about ten weeks. Students are required to remain on campus their freshman and senior years, but otherwise are able to supplement their education with time spent studying abroad and completing one "off-term." The off-term, spent in a place and discipline of the student's choosing, is designed in part to give Dartmouth students internship and/or job opportunities during times less competitive than the summer, and students take full advantage of their unusual schedule. To the bewilderment of high school friends everywhere, all Dartmouth students must stay on campus during the summer after sophomore year. Promoted by the administration as a time to "build bonds with faculty and grow as a class," "Sophomore Summer" in fact is regarded by many students as "by far the best term at Dartmouth." Also popular are the numerous LSA (Language Study Abroad) and FSP (Foreign Study Program) options offered through a number of academic departments. With programs such as Coral Reef Ecology in Costa Rica and Language and Culture in Russia, Dartmouth recently ranked at the top of the Ivy League in study abroad options, with about 55 percent of students taking the opportunity to study, work, and live in foreign countries while enrolled. Students were quick to mention

the darker side of the D-plan, though, citing difficulties in relationships, activity participation, and living arrangements due to the fluidity of the system. One sophomore stated that she wished "she knew how difficult it is to deal with the D-plan, though in retrospect it was a positive learning experience and I'm better off having survived the transition."

The Mighty Greeks

At Dartmouth, there is a fair amount of what some students might call "frattitude." On a campus that infamously inspired the 1978 film Animal House, Greek organizations still "clearly rule the social scene." While the administration is trying hard to change the social dynamic, the Greeks maintain a reputation that would make Bluto and Otter proud. Houses retain their own flavor and often draw their members from certain sports teams or social groups. Traditional sorority and fraternity organizations are supplemented by "coed" houses such as Tabard (famous for their "Disco Inferno" party) and Phi Tau. In adherence to the administration's regulations, students are not allowed to rush until the fall of their sophomore year, and the process can also be complicated by the D-plan schedule. Despite the restrictions, freshmen and seniors alike crowd into the steamy basements of the numerous houses for a little drinking, a little dancing, and a whole lot of "pong." Oh, and for those of you who think you know what beer pong is, you may be wrong. At Dartmouth, there's no messing around with throwing Ping-Pong balls into cups of beer. From "shrub" to "tree" to the ultimate "black forest" tournaments, it doesn't count if it doesn't involve actual paddles, house rules, and copious amounts of beer. From SAE's annual Beach Party, when they bring in ten tons of sand to create a realistic atmosphere, to the dance hits emanating from Chi Gam, weekends are ruled by the Greeks, for, as one student explained, "you just can't beat free beer and themed parties."

> **"There's a lot of drinking at Dartmouth. 4,000 kids in the woods, what do you think is going to happen?"**

Needless to say, "There's a lot of drinking at Dartmouth. 4,000 kids in the woods, what do you think is going to happen?" summed up one student. The stereotype was even celebrated in recent years with the controversial introduction of "Keggy," the unofficial school mascot who made his first appearance at the 2003 Homecoming game and appeared the following year on ESPN. The anthropomorphic keg now makes special appearances at sporting and social events, dancing in the stands and giving students the opportunity to "pump his head for good luck." The "work hard, play harder" reputation of Dartmouth is something that the administration is currently evaluating and hoping to change. A few years ago, the administration launched the Student Life Initiative. A large part of the program focused on a crackdown of the Greek system and brought into being the increasingly strict drug and alcohol policies now in effect. Efforts to shift attention away from the Greeks has spurred new housing plans and the building and organization of "clusters," groups of dorms connected by common rooms, in order to foster a sense of community while students live on campus. The administration also organizes and funds events such as concerts and movies at the "Hop" (Hopkins Center), comedy acts, and even runs a dance club, FUEL, in the basement of the Collis student center. In addition, a weekly on-campus event called "Friday Night Rock" features student bands playing live music in Collis.

"D" is for Diversity

While students report the population as being "predominantly white and from the East Coast" in fact many different cultures, nationalities and ethnicities are represented on campus. Recent efforts have involved recruiting more Native American and international students, but cultural houses and organizations take a prominent role both in the educational and physical landscape of Dartmouth. However, though this diversity may exist, students tend to self-segregate, as many nationality groups have their own "cultural affinity houses." Students describe the typical Dartmouth student as being "a cross between a Polo and a Patagonia ad—relatively preppy with an outdoorsy edge." Regarded by many as being the most attractive student body of the Ivy League, Dartmouth students waste no time in exploring the Great Outdoors and each other. Students report that there are "a lot of random hookups" on campus, though others claim that "long and meaningful relationships are possible." One senior credited the D-plan and the Greek social scene with complicating dating strategies, but mentioned that "all of my friends now have significant others."

"A Voice Crying in the Wilderness"

Ok, so you've done it. You successfully hit it off with that girl/guy in the depths of the crowded frat basement, even "blitzed" (Dartmouth version of e-mail) them to meet up at a later date. Now what? Where do Dartmouth kids go for a good time in Hanover, New Hampshire? "Take to the woods," suggest many students when asked about their extracurricular and off-campus activities. The area abounds with hiking trails, fresh water ponds, a beautiful golf course, and even its own ski mountain. The DOC (Dartmouth Outing Club) takes full advantage of these natural gifts and it is the largest student organization on campus, taking up to 80 percent of the student population on whitewater rafting trips, skiing, or even fly-fishing. "I love the serenity and beauty of New Hampshire," one student noted, "I think it is a good contrast from the craziness of college in many ways." Favorite romantic rendezvous spots around campus include Bartlett Tower, the Robert Frost statue, the Ledyard Canoe Club, Collis Porch, BEMA (Big Empty Meeting Area), and "Occom Pond in the winter."

The town of Hanover itself is often regarded as the picture of serenity, though some students express frustration with its small size and somewhat limited entertainment options. Students love local restaurants Boloco, Molly's and Murphy's when dining-hall fare gets tedious, and the new Canoe Club is reportedly the hot spot for a night on the town. Late-night staple EBA's (Everything But Anchovies) supplies necessities such as pizza and mozzarella sticks and will deliver until 2:15 a.m. The town also hosts a small movie theater (the Nugget) and college-town essentials such as a bookstore, Co-op, Gap, and Ben and Jerry's.

It IS Easy Being Green

Dartmouth students keep themselves quite busy on campus, however, with a range of athletic, social and cultural activities to participate in, cheer on, or simply sit back and enjoy. While some disagree with the "jocks with brains" stereotypes that thrive on campus, many students marvel at the high degree of athleticism amongst their peers. IM sports abound and varsity sports events are well-attended. While Dartmouth football has been less than successful in years past, the men's hockey and lacrosse teams are always competitively ranked and draw large crowds of fans. Club Rugby is also popular and attracts large turnouts at games. Likewise, women's hockey (both field and ice) always fare well in their leagues, and the sailing team is one of the best collegiate racing teams in the country. The Kresge Fitness Center was recently renovated, and is now three times larger and very modern.

Green with Ivy

"It is so inspiring to study in such an amazing place," raved one female student when asked about the aesthetics of the Dartmouth campus. "It is classic in its beauty— lots of white clapboards and red brick, surrounded by lush green." Sound idyllic? Dartmouth students would agree and most rave about their living, studying and partying environments. The magnificent Baker Library, situated on the expansive green, dominates the center of campus. New additions to campus include the Berry Library, "doubled in its capacity of library space," and students also report that new dorms are "always being built"; in fact, the David T. McLaughlin Cluster on Maynard Street, which will contain six residence halls and a student commons, is currently under construction. Students are generally quite happy with the dorms themselves. While most continue to live on campus for four years, some move "off" to either Greek houses or into apartments and houses "in town." Students agree that "the River and the Choates" take the dubious award for worst housing on campus, due to their small doubles, ugly facades and distance from the center of campus. "Mass Row" garnered the most praise

for on-campus living, and students raved about its "pretty spacious rooms, old-fashioned style" and the fact that it is "so close to Food Court."

Contrary to just about every article that's ever been written about college dining fare, students had absolutely nothing bad to say about Dartmouth's selections. "I love the food here, probably too much" gushed one sophomore. While students do agree that "it's a bit pricey," the quality of food, breadth of choice and general convenience all make for pleasant dining at Dartmouth. Students appreciate that "some dining hall somewhere" is open from "7 a.m. to 1 a.m. every day" and mentioned the convenience of having four dining halls spread across campus. The healthy choices at Homeplate and Collis Café garnered particular praise.

Oh the Places You'll Go

Such were the words of yet another, slightly younger, man who spent four happy years at Dartmouth. Theodore Geisel went on to become a doctor (Dr. Seuss, that is) after graduating Dartmouth in 1925. Other famous alums include poet Robert Frost, former Vice President Nelson Rockefeller, and U.S. Surgeon General C. Everett Koop. Even Fred Rogers once called Hanover home. The real secret behind Dartmouth's storied past and promising future lies in the happiness and confidence of having a top-notch education and a first-rate college experience . . . with a pump of Keggy's head for good luck.
—*Marisa Benoit*

FYI
If you come to Dartmouth, you'd better bring " a warm quilt."
What's the typical weekend schedule? "Going to classless frat parties, watching TV, going to classless frat parties."
If I could change one thing about Dartmouth, I'd "put it closer to a big city. Sometimes Hanover gets lonely."
Three things every student at Dartmouth must do before graduating are "take Valentino's Gov 5 (international relations) class, climb Mt. Moosilauke, play a game of pong (water or other beverage . . .)."

University of New Hampshire

Address: University of New Hampshire, 4 Garrison Avenue, Durham, NH 03824
Phone: 603-862-1360
E-mail Address: admissions@unh.edu
Web site URL: http://admissions.unh.edu/
Year Founded: 1866
Private or Public: Public
Religious affiliation: none
Location: rural
Regular Application Deadline: 2-Feb
Number of Applicants: 13,991
Percent Accepted: 66%
Percent Accepted who enroll: 32%
Number Entering: 3,079
Number of Transfers Accepted each Year: 764
Mean SAT: 550CR/550M
Mean ACT: NA
Middle 50% SAT range: 1,000–1,180

Middle 50% ACT range: NA
Early admission program (EA/ ED/ NA): EA
ED or EA Acceptance Rate: 74%
Full time Undergraduate enrollment: 11,388
Total enrollment: 14,848
Percent Male: 44%
Percent Female: 56%
Total Percent Minority: 6%
Percent African-American: 1%
Percent Asian/Pacific Islander: 2%
Percent Hispanic: 2%
Percent Native-American: <1%
Percent Other: 11%
Percent in-state / out of state: 57%/43%
Percent from Public HS: 81%
Retention Rate: 86%
Graduation Rate: 69%

Percent in On-campus housing: First Year, 96%, Sophomores 70%, Juniors 37%, Seniors 23%
Percent affiliated with Greek system: 8%
Percent Varsity or Club Athletes: 5% (Varsity)
Number of official organized extracurricular organizations: 197
3 Most popular majors: Business Administration, Psychology, English
Student/Faculty ratio: 17:01
Tuition and Fees: $22,851.00
In State Tuition and Fees (if different): $10,401.00
Cost for Room and Board: $7,584.00
Percent receiving Financial aid, first-year: 70%

In many ways, the University of New Hampshire serves as an exemplar of balance. Located halfway between the major cities of Boston, MA and Portland, ME—and a stone's throw away from the White Mountains—the university's establishment in rural Durham provides its own unique environment. Additionally, the university's designation as a land-grant, sea-grant, and space-grant institution by Congress demonstrates its comprehensive commitment to cutting-edge research in these fields. However, students must take the initiative to find their own equilibrium in this sea of opportunities, because there are hundreds of ways to get involved in the UNH community.

Individual Initiative

Though UNH gives enough academic guidance through its various programs, in the end, students must choose the most suitable path for themselves according to their own interests and goals. UNH comprises seven colleges in the following areas: Engineering and Physical Sciences (CEPS), Liberal Arts (COLA), Life Sciences and Agriculture (COLSA), Health and Human Services (SHHS), Thompson School of Applied Science (TSAS), University of New Hampshire at Manchester (UNHM), Whittemore School of Business and Economics (WSBE). WSBE is generally known to be a strong program and—maybe not coincidentally—its Business Administration major is far and away the most popular major at UNH. Perhaps this is one reason why The Princeton Review and Forbes.com named UNH one of the nation's most entrepreneurial campuses. Other interesting majors include Justice Studies, Kinesiology, and Horticultural Technology.

At the heart of a UNH education is the General Education Program, which requires students to take one course in each of eight major areas in order to learn the "fundamental skills" that allow them to make intellectual progress. While at first glance the Gen Ed requirements may look heavy, one student mentioned that it is not as harsh as it seems; aside from First Year Writing—which every freshman must take—each of the categories includes a diverse array of courses to choose from. For example, the "Historical Perspectives" category alone has almost 50 possible course options.

> **"People take IM sports seriously. I ended up in the penalty box for one of the broomball games."**

Perhaps what differentiates UNH from other comparable institutions is the number of ways in which students can take advantage of the university's unique location in pristine New England. For example, since UNH was originally incorporated as a college of agriculture and mechanical arts, and because its chief benefactor was a farmer and businessman named Benjamin Thompson, the university has always emphasized agriculture. Making use of the university's resources, students majoring in Dairy Management—in addition to learning the skills necessary for the "successful management of a dairy enterprise"—can apply their classroom knowledge by tending real herds on the rural campus farms.

Furthermore, many programs take advantage of the outdoors, such as the 3,000+ acres of university-owned forestland, White Mountains National Forest, or the aquatic ecosystems of the Lakes Region of New Hampshire. In other words, the theoretical knowledge of students can be applied to real-world settings, allowing for a more balanced learning experience.

The classroom experience itself can vary in many ways. Though the intro-level courses may be dauntingly large, almost all upper-level seminars involve discussions around a circular table. In terms of workload, one student believed that the difficulty of a course was proportionate to the amount of reading: "if you don't do the reading, you can't participate in class at all." On the whole, students are encouraged to realize their potential and develop study habits that work well for them.

Friendly Folks
Sports and Greek life constitute a significant proportion of the UNH social scene. According to one student, Greek life is "a really big part of the weekend activities at UNH." This is because many students rush the dozen or

so fraternities and sororities, and also because such organizations each year host a number of the bigger parties on campus. "Frat parties here are the way to go," stated one student.

Like most other colleges, most students at UNH drink lots of alcohol. Though the official alcohol policies seem strict, it really depends on the enforcement by RAs on each floor of the dorms. The general policy is that one open container is permitted in a room for each person over 21 years old. However, if one's RA is easy-going, disciplinary action for alcohol abuse is unlikely. On the other hand, students mentioned that "not everyone drinks" and that many people find other activities to occupy their time when the weekend rolls around.

Meeting students at UNH is "quite easy." One student mentioned the importance of the all-freshman dorm as a way to form new friendships early on. Because "everyone is in the same boat", this student said, it was really easy to approach new people. Sports also provide another avenue for making new friends. The common bond amongst students rooting for the hockey team and playing on the IM fields is "conducive to meeting new people", said one student. Regarding the character of the typical student, one student commented that "UNH students are wicked friendly."

Brilliant Brick Buildings
Most students live in dorms provided by the university for at least two years. While some eventually choose to move off-campus into apartments, one student said that the upper class dorms are "really nice." For those students trying to find others with similar interests, UNH offers themed housing such as the study-oriented ("Making the Grade"), substance-free ("Chem Free"), computers and technology ("Wired"), and intramural sports ("The Clubhouse") houses. As part of UNH's master campus plan, construction is underway for a set of residence halls to be opened in the southeast campus in fall 2007.

The campus prides itself on the "Old Brick" look of its architecture. The primary building is Thompson Hall, built in honor of the eponymous benefactor to the university, which currently houses the administration. Because the Dimond Library is a member of the Boston Library Consortium, students have access to a large catalog of books through the interlibrary loan system. The building that is closest to the hearts of most UNH students, however, is the Memorial

Union Building (also known as the "MUB"), which—with an "award-winning" and "excellent" dining hall, Holloway Commons—serves as the center of UNH's campus life. MUB is the hub; it houses an expansive food court, an entertainment center, a game room, multiple movie theaters, the Wildcat's Den (for dances and performances), and many multipurpose lecture rooms.

Hockey is Holy

Outside of classrooms and labs, UNH offers the full spectrum of activities. Again, the school's location in rural New England offers oudoorsy individuals an infinite number of pastimes. Because of the university's prime location, the Outing Club—"the oldest and largest club on campus"—normally offers 2–5 trips to various areas each weekend, from Nordic skiing to extreme sledding to ice climbing. Another popular on-campus activity is working for the student newspaper, *The New Hampshire*. Other prominent activities include the university radio station, WUNH, and various a cappella groups such as the all-male *Not Too Sharp*. Finally, the intramural sports program is very popular and, according to one student, "very competitive." With over 28 sports and tournaments, students have plenty to choose from. Broomball (on ice), flag football, ice hockey, and indoor/outdoor soccer are among the favorite IM sports.

In a world of its own, though, is UNH hockey, which stands as the athletic face of the university. The UNH Wildcats men's and women's hockey programs are consistently title-contenders for the NCAA and Hockey East. As a result of their successes, students zealously rally around the teams during each game. One tradition that demonstrates the unifying nature of the hockey team is the "White out the Whitt" ("Whitt" is short for the Whittimore Center), where, during crucial games, everyone wears white in support of UNH. Another interesting tradition is that of the brothers of the Zeta Chi fraternity, who ceremoniously toss a fish onto the ice after UNH scores its first goal of a game. The hockey games are such a central part of the school that obtaining tickets has become a feat of its own. One student described the ticket-purchasing process: "I sat in line from 6 in the morning. When the game came, I sat in line for another 3 hours just to get a good seat!" Additionally, past alums always make appearances at the hockey games to cheer their alma mater on to continued success.

Fertile Futures

In the end, the University of New Hampshire is a committed state university that constantly strives to improve itself. Its entrepreneurial spirit is supported by the Land, Sea, and Space Grant programs, and it was the only public institution in New England to rank in the Top 10 in its number of Fulbright Scholars. Having produced astronauts, NHL hockey players, and acclaimed writers, UNH is just as fruitful as the farmland around it when it comes to producing outstanding alums. There are no boundaries at UNH. Students are encouraged to take their classroom knowledge and apply it directly to the real, outside world. Ultimately, though, it is up to the UNH student to take advantage of all that the University of New Hampshire has to offer.—*Wookie Kim*

FYI
If you come to UNH, you'd better bring "your game face, walking shoes (the campus is hilly), and a North Face jacket."
What's the typical weekend schedule? "Thursday: classes, late-night parties; Friday: classes, sports game, party; Saturday: sleep, sports game, recover, party; Sunday: study."
If I could change one thing about UNH, I'd "offer more specialized courses in specific subjects."
Three things every student at the University of New Hampshire should do before graduating are "go to the UNH/Maine hockey game, play intramural sports, study abroad."

New Jersey

The College of New Jersey

Address: The College of NJ, Paul Loser Hall, Room 228; 2000 Pennington Road, P.O. Box 7718, Ewing, NJ 08628-0718
Phone: 800-624-0967
E-mail Address: breese@tcnj.edu
Web site URL: http://www.tcnj.edu/~admiss/
Year Founded: 1855
Private or Public: public
Religious affiliation: none
Location: suburban
Regular Application Deadline: 16-Feb
Number of Applicants: NA
Percent Accepted: 44%
Percent Accepted who enroll: 36%
Number Entering: NA
Number of Transfers Accepted each Year: NA
Mean SAT: 1,261
Mean ACT: NA

Middle 50% SAT range: V:570–670, M:590–700
Middle 50% ACT range: NA
Early admission program (EA/ ED/ NA): ED
ED or EA Acceptance Rate: NA
Full time Undergraduate enrollment: NA
Total enrollment: 6,037
Percent Male: 42%
Percent Female: 58%
Total Percent Minority: 0%
Percent African-American: 6%
Percent Asian/Pacific Islander: 7%
Percent Hispanic: 8%
Percent Native-American: 0%
Percent Other: NA
Percent in-state / out of state: 95%/5%
Percent from Public HS: 85%
Retention Rate: 95%

Graduation Rate: 86%
Percent in On-campus housing: 60%
Percent affiliated with Greek system: 26%
Percent Varsity or Club Athletes: NA
Number of official organized extracurricular organizations: 186
3 Most popular majors: Biology, Elementary Education and Teaching, English Language and Literature
Student/Faculty ratio: 13:01
Tuition and Fees: $17,099
In State Tuition and Fees (if different): $10,553
Cost for Room and Board: $8,843
Percent receiving Financial aid, first-year: 46%

Hidden in the Garden State is The College of New Jersey, also known as TCNJ—a gem of the public education system. TCNJ boasts a world-class education combined with a rarely matched level of affordability. Having evolved from its origins as the New Jersey Teachers' College, TCNJ is now one of the best educational deals available to students both in and out of state.

Hit the Books

TCNJ's highly selective nature means that its students are prepared to take on the highly rigorous academic schedule. The school redesigned its core curriculum in 2004 to provide for fewer, but more intense courses, while making sure to preserve the option of interdisciplinary study. This Liberal Learning program works to provide students with a solid foundation through its three platform elements: Intellectual and Scholarly Growth, Civil Responsibility, and Human Inquiry. Although the requirements can be onerous, most students find the requirements generally "worthwhile." One junior reflected that while some classes were "very pointless, others were very interesting." One of these more "interesting" options is the freshman seminar, "Athens to New York"—an intense cultural study of the city. By the end of their four years, TCNJ students have all added writing, public speaking, humanities, natural sciences and cultural studies into their academic experiences.

TCNJ has branched out from its roots as a teachers' college, but education still remains one of the most popular majors, in addition to business and biology. Students looking to log as much time in the library as possible generally find themselves majoring in the sciences. But, for those on the other side of the spectrum—the lazy, tired, or mere lovers of life—would be wiser to choose majors like communication, health and exercise science or law and justice. Whatever the major, each department has its share of both interesting and feared courses and professors, like a campus favorite professor Rabbi Joel Chernickoff, who teaches a variety of religion courses. TCNJ students are known for being particularly obsessive with checking up on certain courses on virtualratings.com to see what they are getting themselves into.

Class sizes are generally small and range from 10 to 20 students. Such personalized learning contributes to the school's reputation as being focused on the undergraduate experience. Students are able to gain a feeling of camaraderie within their small classes and have intimate contact with their professors. Additionally, within all disciplines, TCNJers are offered the option of an honors program. Students generally agree that their peers are motivated and hardworking and that the school has its share of both overachievers and slackers. One point of complaint, however, is the online registration system. Students describe the system as "freak out" inducing, when it slows during high traffic times, making it difficult to secure places in desired classes. Luckily, most individuals manage to weed through the process and come out with a schedule that pleases them.

To Stay or Not to Stay

The weekend party scene is thriving at TCNJ. Friday and Saturday are always popular nights to go out. Since students often don't have classes on Wednesday, Tuesday is also a big party night. The party scene covers a wide spectrum: fraternities and sports houses, dorms, and bars, although underclassmen tend to stick to the former. Parties in dorms are common, but alcohol is not officially allowed, so regulations can be strict. Fortunately, most students hold that as long as "common sense is used, it's generally OK." Those over 21 will hit nearby bars such as Firkin Tavern which boasts a game room complete with foosball and pool tables. Since many upperclassmen bring cars to campus and Trenton is only a short drive away, students will hit up popular hangouts like Katmandu. Philadelphia is another popular option within driving distance.

That's not to discount some of the school-sponsored events like Homecoming weekend, however, when the college brings in a variety of popular musical groups, or the school-hosted formals and semi-formals that take place throughout the year. Although drinking generally makes up a large portion of the weekend scene, one student explained that, "While drinking is a part of any college, you don't have to drink to have fun here." Even though the weekends are pretty packed on campus, the school still retains somewhat of a "suitcase" school mentality. Many students take off for home in various parts of NJ for the weekend and even those who generally stay, will at times tire of the scene and go elsewhere.

Campus Life

TCNJ guarantees housing for a student's first two years, and the majority of freshmen and sophomores take the school up on that offer. Underclassmen are housed in Travers and Wolfe or Cromwell Hall. Travers and Wolfe are high-rise towers with double rooms, while Cromwell is arranged in more of a suite style. Students characterize dorms at TCNJ as "generally nice," stating that, "nothing is unbearable."

Perhaps such good spirits are partly abetted by a wide support system put into place for freshmen. Not only do Resident Assistants live on their floors, but Community Assistants also live on floors to act as hall organizers, and Peer Advisors are readily available to foster a feeling of community. Students generally agree that their freshmen floor friends play a huge role in their four years, and become many of their best friends.

Upperclassmen who don't receive housing in one of the townhouses—"beautiful residences" for about 10 people, organized by gender-specified floors—generally move off campus to locations varying in distance from school (since many students have cars, distance is less of an issue than for students at other colleges). Greeks have unofficial houses off campus, too, which are generally just a group from the same fraternity living together. TCNJ is currently in the process of knocking down some of the older buildings to make room for upperclassmen apartments.

Food at TCNJ is far from gourmet. One student went so far as to characterize it as "terrible." Recent changes have been made to the main dining hall, but unfortunately many students were not thrilled by the new developments. Vegetarians are often hard-pressed to find options from which they can pick, and there are no facilities open after 8 p.m. Freshmen eat carte blanche at the main dining hall, Eickhoff. Additional food points can be used at the Student Center, Travers and Wolfe after 6 p.m. or the Rathskellar, a popular upperclassmen dining joint because it serves beer.

In general, students give TCNJ's campus mixed reviews. On the positive note, layout is fairly easy to navigate, as basically everything is within a 10-minute walk. The colonial red brick architecture, complete with white columns, lends an air of grace to the campus. And there has been a variety of new construction, including the addition of a new and popular library. Many of the science buildings have also received renovations. Meanwhile, older buildings such as Kendall Hall, the music center that is reputed to be haunted, retain their charm amidst the new developments.

Computer labs are available in almost every building on campus, although Holman is especially popular with art majors because it is equipped entirely with Macs. The Browser Student Center houses the bookstore and student activities office and also contains the Rathskellar, or "The Rat," which boasts a bar that acts as a venue for various local acts.

Many students complain that Ewing lacks the feel of a college town. It is a small, residential neighborhood and students are forced to look farther abroad toward Trenton, Philadelphia, or New York for entertainment. Philadelphia is about half an hour away and New York is an hour long, ten-dollar train ride away. Students also go to nearby Princeton, and New Hope, Pennsylvania for shopping on nice days.

Something for Everyone

The student body at TCNJ is fairly homogenous—the stereotype repeated by students is: "middleclass white kids from N.J." Despite the fact that the campus lacks in diversity, the administration has been making an effort to change that. In recent years, ethnic student organizations such as the Asian American Association, Black Student Union and Jewish Student Union have risen in popularity and on-campus activism.

> "If you don't put effort toward getting involved, nothing will jump right out at you."

Although not dominant by any means, sports maintain a strong presence on campus. TCNJ's Division III athletics are very competitive, with field hockey, soccer and baseball ranking among the most popular sports. Club sports also get a large following—in particular, lacrosse and rugby—and some even have off-campus houses. For those a bit less adept at athletics, feel free to try your hand at intramurals and makes use of the on-campus athletic facilities—there are gyms scattered throughout campus.

At TCNJ, while it is very easy to get involved, there is an element of being proactive. One student put it this way: "If you don't put effort toward getting involved, nothing will jump right out at you." This might explain why TCNJers, although described as very friendly, collectively noted that "it gets harder to meet people after freshman year." Just as much effort needs to go into students' social and extracurricular lives, as their academic ones.—*Janet Yang*

FYI
If you come to The College of New Jersey, you'd better bring "ramen noodles and a big fan because the freshmen dorms aren't air-conditioned."
What's the typical weekend schedule? "Party, party, homework."
If I could change one thing about TCNJ I'd "change the food on campus."
Three things every student should do before graduating are "get picked up with all the freshmen for a party, order from Cluck U Chicken, go to a toga party."

Drew University

Address: Drew, 36 Madison Avenue, Madison, NJ 07940
Phone: 973-408-DREW
E-mail Address: CADM@DREW.EDU
Web site URL: http://depts.drew.edu/claadmis/
Year Founded: 1867
Private or Public: private
Religious affiliation: Methodist
Location: suburban
Regular Application Deadline: 16-Feb
Number of Applicants: 4,532
Percent Accepted: 64%
Percent Accepted who enroll: 17%
Number Entering: 481
Number of Transfers Accepted each Year: 78
Mean SAT: 1,190
Mean ACT: 26

Middle 50% SAT range: 1,060–1,280
Middle 50% ACT range: 24–28
Early admission program (EA/ ED/ NA): ED
ED or EA Acceptance Rate: 61%
Full time Undergraduate enrollment: 1,608
Total enrollment: 2,420
Percent Male: 34%
Percent Female: 66%
Total Percent Minority: 24%
Percent African-American: 10%
Percent Asian/Pacific Islander: 5%
Percent Hispanic: 8%
Percent Native-American: 1%
Percent Other: 13%
Percent in-state / out of state: 59%/41%

Percent from Public HS: 61%
Retention Rate: 83%
Graduation Rate: 73%
Percent in On-campus housing: 87%
Percent affiliated with Greek system: 0%
Percent Varsity or Club Athletes: NA
Number of official organized extracurricular organizations: 80
3 Most popular majors: economics, political science, psychology
Student/Faculty ratio: 11:01
Tuition and Fees: $33,054.00
Cost for Room and Board: $9,001.00
Percent receiving Financial aid, first-year: 69%

With 1,600 undergraduates, Drew is smaller than many high schools. But what the liberal arts school lacks in size it makes up for in multiple ways, from its first-rate faculty to its beautiful campus. Belying most Garden State stereotypes, Drew is located on 200 wooded acres in northern New Jersey. New York City is also just 30 miles away, so students can experience the best of both city and country living while receiving a well-rounded education.

Friendly Faculty

Drew requires that students complete a major and a minor. But with 29 majors to pick from and even more options for minors, including traditional disciplinary minors and 18 interdisciplinary minors, there is no shortage of options. Students can also design their own majors and minors that focus on topics of their choosing—as long as they are approved. More popular concentrations include theater studies and English though one student said that in general "it is pretty spread out between arts, economics, biology, political science and behavioral sciences."

Drew has several special programs, too, such as the dual-degree medical program, dual-degree programs in engineering and applied science as well as pre-law, pre-medicine, and pre-business programs.

Drew prides itself on its intimate academic setting. Classes are generally small, most with between 15 and 20 students, allowing students to interact with their classmates and professors. In 2002, the Princeton Review ranked Drew third among colleges where "Classroom discussion is encouraged."

Students said that one of the best parts about Drew is the accessibility of the professors. Unlike at larger universities, professors teach most of the courses at Drew and make themselves available to students. "Professors are extremely easy to talk to if you need them, and they always know your name," said one student. Only first-year writing classes are taught by teaching assistants.

Drew also offers a plethora of off-campus study opportunities, giving undergraduates a chance to experience other parts of the country and the world while earning credits toward their degree. Programs range in length and location. Students can spend a semester taking classes in London, Eritrea or New York or a summer soaking the language and culture in Barcelona, China and Venice. Student can also take classes at nearby schools such as Fairleigh Dickinson and St. Elizabeth's.

Cribs and Grub

Housing at Drew is guaranteed for all four years. Dorms consist of single, doubles or suites and students have the option of living on single-sex or coed floors. To keep an eye on things, every floor has a residential adviser. "RAs are strict in the freshman dorms," one student said. "Everywhere else is pretty relaxed as long as you are smart about things." Another student agreed, "In order to get in trouble, you really need to do something wrong."

Because on-campus housing is so habitable and housing in Madison is expensive and hard to find, most students never move off campus. The result is a close-knit community. "Though Drew is a small campus you still see new faces everyday. Everyone is so friendly here and it really is home to me," one junior said. Foreign language and other themed buildings—such as La Casa, a Hispanic-American dorm, and the Earth House, an especially environmentally-friendly hall—are also available to upperclassmen.

Drew only has one dining hall, but students said the food is good. Plans come with 10, 14 or 19 meals a week as well as points that may be used at the school "snack bar."

Work Hard, Play Hard

Small, quiet and quaint, Madison is not exactly the prototypical college town. Come the weekend, some students head home while others go into Manhattan, which is less than an hour's ride by train or bus. The train station is within walking distance of campus and buses to New York are available from the main gate of the campus.

Most students, however, stick around for the weekend. Though there are no fraternities or sororities, Drew has its fair share of parties. Many take place at The Suites, a dorm for upperclassmen, where a lot of athletes usually live. For junior, seniors and ride-bumming underclassmen—freshmen and sophomores are not allowed to have cars on campus—Morristown is just a five-minute drive away.

Drugs are not prevalent on campus, but drinking is. "Everyone I know [drinks], but you don't have to if you don't want to," said one senior, who added, "If you are caught underage drinking, which is easy to avoid, you are put on probation and possible alcohol classes." One student summed up the social scene by saying that Drew "can be a party school for some people or completely quiet and reserved for others depending on where you go and what you're looking for."

> "Drew can be a party school for some people or completely quiet and reserved for others depending on where you go and what you're looking for."

There are several special events over the course of the year, including Winter Ball, a formal dance; Festival of Lights, a holiday celebration; and 99 Nights, a party for seniors. Every year at the end of spring semester, Drew also throws the First Annual Picnic, a huge blowout where "bands play and they hold kegs for those of age." Last year the musical act was Howie Day.

Something for Everyone

When they are not studying or partying, students are very involved in extracurricular activities. Whether singing in an a capella group, writing for *The Acorn* or building homes with Habitat for Humanity, they take full advantage of the dozens of clubs and organizations on campus as well as one of the top-ranked theater departments in the country. Student-acted and directed productions are put on throughout the year, often attracting bigger crowds than sports events: "Going to see shows in our theatre are a big thing." Many students additionally have jobs on or around campus. As one student said, "Everyone on campus is extremely involved and I find that every student is passionate in at least one thing."

Drew, a member of Division III, has over 15 varsity teams. Most compete in the Middle Atlantic States Conference along with teams from other schools in the New Jersey and Pennsylvania area like Delaware Valley College, Wilkes University and the University of Scranton. According to one varsity lacrosse player, sports are "not overly important but a big part of the social gatherings." He added that soccer is the big sport on campus but "all sports get respect."

Drew also has clubs teams in rugby, ultimate Frisbee, volleyball and dance, which travel throughout the country to compete. For the less athletically inclined, intramural sports provide a fun, and commitment-free way to get away from the books and relieve some stress. Offerings include flag football, tennis, billiards, squash, ping pong, dodge ball, racquetball, basketball, softball, and wiffle ball. Students can also lift weights, run on a treadmill, or take a yoga class at the state-of-the-art Simon Forum and Athletic Center.

Though most students are from the tri-state area, others come from throughout the nation and the world—39 states and 10 countries to be exact. What draws them to Drew are the small classes, the great professors, the outstanding accommodations and, yes, New Jersey.—*Josh Lotstein*

FYI

If you come to Drew, you'd better bring "an open-mind, a sled, a fan, a tool set."

What is the typical weekend schedule? "Very loud suite parties, sometimes theme parties, free movies every weekend, performances at the Space and TOE, and a capella concerts."

If I could change one thing about Drew, I'd "make the dorms closer to the classes and the library."

Three things every student at Drew should do before graduating are "swim in Tipple Pond in the rain when it fills up, take a walk in the Arboretum and go to the Shakespeare Theatre."

Princeton University

Address: Princeton, 110 West College, Box 430, Princeton, NJ 08544-0430
Phone: 609-258-3060
E-mail Address: uaoffice@princeton.edu
Web site URL: www.princeton.edu/main/prospective/
Year Founded: 1746
Private or Public: private
Religious affiliation: none
Location: suburban
Regular Application Deadline: 2-Jan
Number of Applicants: NA
Percent Accepted: 10%
Percent Accepted who enroll: 69%
Number Entering: NA
Number of Transfers Accepted each Year: NA
Mean SAT: 1,450
Mean ACT: NA

Middle 50% SAT range: 1,370–1,590
Middle 50% ACT range: 30–34
Early admission program (EA/ ED/ NA): ED
ED or EA Acceptance Rate: NA
Full time Undergraduate enrollment: 4,775
Total enrollment: 6,785
Percent Male: 54%
Percent Female: 46%
Total Percent Minority: 31%
Percent African-American: 9%
Percent Asian/Pacific Islander: 14%
Percent Hispanic: 7%
Percent Native-American: 1%
Percent Other: NA

Percent in-state / out of state: 16%/84%
Percent from Public HS: NA
Retention Rate: 98%
Graduation Rate: 96%
Percent in On-campus housing: 98%
Percent affiliated with Greek system: NA
Percent Varsity or Club Athletes: NA
Number of official organized extracurricular organizations: 250
3 Most popular majors: Political Science, Economics, History
Student/Faculty ratio: 5:01
Tuition and Fees: $33,000.00
Cost for Room and Board: $10,980.00
Percent receiving Financial aid, first-year: 51%

Work hard, play hard and look good while doing it. Such is the life of students at Princeton. Couple beautiful Gothic architecture with intellectual rigor, locate it in an upper-class suburban town, add a unique but incredibly lively social scene, and you've got Princeton University.

Room, Board, and Company

Located halfway between New York City and Philadelphia, Princeton is home to approximately 4,800 undergraduates representing each of the 50 states and more than 45 countries worldwide. Upon arrival freshman year, students are randomly assigned to one of five residential colleges—Mathey,

Rockefeller, Butler, Wilson or Forbes (each of which has several different dorms). Each college is equipped with its own dining hall, library, and computing facilities, and students remain in the same residential college for the first two years. The University is currently in the process of restructuring its residential college system. Whitman is being built as a sixth residential college. The University is planning to increase its student body by 500 students by 2012 and convert the system into three four-year colleges and three two-year colleges. Thus each student will be linked to one of the four-year residential colleges regardless of whether or not they live there and the underclassmen will also be linked to the corresponding two year college.

Academic advising for these years (for Bachelor of Arts students) is coordinated through the residential colleges, though students pursuing a Bachelor of Science are advised by faculty members in the School of Engineering and Applied Science. Another form of advising is provided by juniors and seniors who live in the dorms and act as academic and personal mentors.

After sophomore year, students—either individually or with a group of friends—enter the housing lottery and are scattered in various dormitories across campus. The new residential college system beginning fall of 2007 will allow more upperclassmen and graduate students to live in the residential colleges and open the dining halls to upperclassmen which were previously for the sole use of underclassmen. Students of course still can choose to join one of the school's 10 "Eating Clubs,"or else opt to cook for themselves in cooperative or independent residences. Of course, many students also grab food from the student center, Frist, or take out from an eatery in town (Hoagie Haven, T. Sweet, and the Bent Spoon are particularly popular).

Some students complain, though, that, by senior year Princeton can begin to feel quite stifling. Whether it's the upscale nature of the town—"it's not a college town"—or the more limited social options on campus, one student said "There is an honest Princeton bubble," which seems to shield those at Princeton from the outside world. Other students, however, value the college isolation. As one student put it, "You're free of all concerns when you're here."

Moreover, although the campus does not actually have a smaller minority rate than most of the other elite institutions in its league, students agree that in terms of diversity Princeton has a "long way to go." One student said that there is "some validity" to the preppy stereotype and added that a typical Princeton student may indeed fall into the category of "popped collar" for guys and "pearl necklace" for girls. Yet, as one student pointed out in Princeton's defense, "Diversity at Princeton is not different shades of blonde."

Eating Clubs—Old School Style

Established in the 19th century after the banning of Greek fraternities and in an effort to provide adequate dining options for an expanding student population, eating clubs at Princeton now serve not only as dining halls but also as the hub of the social scene. Located on Prospect Street, known most commonly as simply "The Street," these turn of the century mansions are technically eating halls, but many also boast fully equipped tap rooms, libraries, pool rooms and residential quarters for the club's officers. Meals are generally prepared by chefs, and the food is thought to be particularly tasty. Some of the more exclusive clubs, namely Ivy, even have waiters.

The 10 eating clubs are classified as either "bicker" or sign-in, and approximately half fall into either category. For those who do decide to become a part of the eating club scene, there is the option of joining a non-exclusive sign-up club or else going through the "bicker" process, one generally reminiscent of fraternity and sorority pledging. Each club, therefore, is generally thought to have its own reputation. While Tiger Inn (or TI) has an "alcoholic, fraternity" vibe, Cap and Gown is supposedly more athletic, Cottage is more "southern," and Ivy is more northern elite. The bicker process can involve anything from swallowing a goldfish to dancing on a bar to going through a series of interviews.

"There is an honest Princeton bubble."

Some students also point out that while the university does not officially recognize any fraternities or sororities, these groups do have a presence on campus and sometimes act as "feeders" for certain eating clubs. These organizations do not have houses and are generally more active with underclassmen, but it is rather understood that, for example, SAE feeds into Ivy and Tiger Inn, and Kappa Alpha feeds into Cottage.

While some students find the eating club system exclusive and snobby, others enjoy the sense of community it fosters and its guaranteed social atmosphere. Indeed, even those clubs which do have a bicker process are most often open to everyone for weekend parties, and members can invite their friends to meals. As one senior put it, "It's not like your social life is ruined if you don't get in."

Hitting the Books—Hard

There is no doubt about it. Princeton students work hard. One senior reported reading up to 1,000 pages a week, and a final thesis (at least for Bachelor of Arts candidates) is mandatory. Moreover, with relatively short semesters (12 weeks each), one student said a tremendous amount of work is crammed into a smaller period of time, which makes the time itself more stressful. Most students agree, though, that while there is some level of healthy competition, it is not overly competitive or bothersome. One student even described the academic scene as "comfortable" and "laid back."

In terms of requirements, Princeton students pursuing a B.A. must take 31 classes before graduation, and students pursuing a B.S. must take 36. Other requirements, for B.A. candidates, include a writing seminar, a foreign language, a junior essay, a senior thesis (there is a heavy emphasis on writing), and a distribution of courses in Epistemology and Cognition, Ethical Thought and Moral Values, Historical Values, Literature and the Arts, Social Analysis, Quantitative Reasoning, and Science and Technology, including two mandatory lab courses. Most students, however, do not find these requirements particularly burdensome, especially due to the fact that up to four out of the 32 classes may be taken "PDF" or pass/d/fail. The two lab classes, though, do seem to generate the most bitterness.

Classes at Princeton are numerous and diverse. With options ranging from freshman seminars on the Chemistry of Chocolate, to famous courses taught by "hard hitters" such as Cornell West, Peter Singer or Toni Morrison, and finally to notoriously easier classes dubbed with affectionate names like "Rocks for Jocks" (a geology class) or "Physics for Poets," students are able to exercise much choice in their schedules. Courses also vary greatly in size. While smaller majors such as Art History tend to have many smaller classes, other more popular majors (such as Economics and History) have more large classes, which are then divided into smaller groups called "precepts" taught either by the professor or by a graduate student. Of course, even these larger majors offer smaller seminars as well, though generally for upperclassmen.

Most students agree that it is very easy for students to get to know their professors. Every professor is required to have open office hours during which time any student can come to ask a question or simply to discuss a topic of interest. Finally, as one senior put it, there is definitely a welcome intellectual atmosphere at Princeton. While students are undoubtedly able to forget about their classes while partying on the weekends, in class, students are genuinely enthusiastic and engaged.

Sports and Extracurriculars

Princeton is a NCAA Division 1 school that boasts 38 varsity sports and nearly 40 club teams. While most students said that there is not a tremendous amount of school spirit and games are not particularly well attended, one student said he and his friends do attend the football games on the weekends (and the tailgates). Intramural sports, with teams from various residential colleges and eating clubs, are also extremely popular.

Beyond athletics, though, Princeton students are extremely active in scores of other activities and organizations as well. At some schools, students say "everyone does something." But, according to one senior, "at Princeton, everyone does two things." Opportunities abound for participation in the arts, journalism, student government, debate and community service. There are also some clubs labeled "special interest" clubs, which run the gamut from the Epicurious Gourmet Cooking Club to the Aeromodeling Club.

Baby When the Lights Go Out . . .

However hard Princeton students may work, they party just as hard. From Thursday through Saturday, with Friday being more of a "chill" night, students meet up with friends, "pre-game" in their rooms and head ultimately to The Street. Since the town of Princeton does not offer much by way of bars or clubs, The Street really is the place to see and be seen.

Once at The Street, students can wonder in and at of the clubs and are basically bound to bump into almost everyone. Different clubs have "theme nights," and one special weekend, known as "weekend of the house parties," involves a semiformal, a formal and a day of lawn parties. For the lawn parties, students tend to sport their best pastels and enjoy the (hopefully) nice weather as they listen to various bands and enjoy much food and drink.

While most students agree that Princeton does not have a large drug culture, drinking is very apparent. "It's a drinking scene," one student said. "There's a lot, a lot of heavy drinking." Students are allowed to keep alcohol in their rooms, and the role of resident advisers for freshmen is not supposed to be authoritative nor punitive.

Nonetheless, students also report that there is not necessarily any real pressure to drink, since drinks are generally separate in the eating clubs (the tap rooms are downstairs while the dance floors are upstairs), and the bicker process is actually supposed to be dry. Some students, though, will take advantage of the different social options which abound, such as improv comedy shows, a cappella concerts, and theatrical events. Some even venture to nearby New York City or Philadelphia.

Although some students complain about New Jersey, and others lament a lack of school spirit, students at Princeton seem quite happy in general. They appreciate the top-notch academics and the genuine intellectual curiosity which students bring to class; and at the same time they revel in the chaos of the eating clubs and thrive on Princeton traditions. As one senior said, "Everyone who is at Princeton loves Princeton."—*Jennifer Sabin*

FYI

If you come to Princeton, you'd better bring "seersuckers."

What is the typical weekend schedule? "Thursday night: pre-game, Street; Friday: wake up at 1, start work at 5, chill night; Saturday; tailgate, nap, pre-game, fraternity activities, Street; Sunday: brunch, work."

If I could change one thing about Princeton, "It wouldn't be in New Jersey."

Three things every student should do before graduating from Princeton are "swim naked in the Woody Woo (Woodrow Wilson School) fountain, take a class with Cornel West, and have a debate with someone who has strong controversial opinions and who is willing to discuss them with you."

Rutgers / The State University of New Jersey

Address: Rutgers, Office of University Undergraduate Admissions Room 202; 65 Davidson Road, Piscataway, New Jersey 08854-8097
Phone: 732-932-INFO
E-mail Address: NA
Web site URL: http://admissions.rutgers.edu/
Year Founded: 1766
Private or Public: public
Religious affiliation: none
Location: suburban
Regular Application Deadline: Rolling
Number of Applicants: 27,560
Percent Accepted: 58%
Percent Accepted who enroll: 33%
Number Entering: 5,274
Number of Transfers Accepted each Year: 2,250

Mean SAT: 1,210
Mean ACT: NA
Middle 50% SAT range: M:570–680,V:530–640
Middle 50% ACT range: NA
Early admission program (EA/ ED/ NA): NA
ED or EA Acceptance Rate: NA
Full time Undergraduate enrollment: 26,286
Total enrollment: 33,943
Percent Male: 50%
Percent Female: 50%
Total Percent Minority: 47%
Percent African-American: 9%
Percent Asian/Pacific Islander: 24%
Percent Hispanic: 8%
Percent Native-American: 0%
Percent Other: 6%
Percent in-state / out of state: 93%/7%

Percent from Public HS: NA
Retention Rate: 89%
Graduation Rate: NA
Percent in On-campus housing: 49%
Percent affiliated with Greek system: NA
Percent Varsity or Club Athletes: NA
Number of official organized extracurricular organizations: 400
3 Most popular majors: Business, Engineering, Psychology
Student/Faculty ratio: 16:01
Tuition and Fees: $18,463.00
In State Tuition and Fees (if different): $9,958.00
Cost for Room and Board: $9,312.00
Percent receiving Financial aid, first-year: 67%

While the name Rutgers refers to one university, it also translates to an enormous range of experiences. More a system of schools than just one institution itself, Rutgers University, New Jersey's public university, is comprised of three campuses across the Garden State—the oldest and largest at New Brunswick and two smaller locations at Newark and Camden—as well as schools within these campuses. While many Rutgers students grew up in New Jersey, the university is known for its diversity and its wide offering of majors and organizations.

Each campus and school offers a unique academic, social, and extracurricular experience of its own. Rutgers is a university of commuters and dorm-dwellers, of hardworking academics and tireless partygoers. Indeed, you can sample every flavor of college lifestyle and take advantage of a vast selection of exciting opportunities at such an expansive state school—as long as you're willing to brave the nuisances of Rutgers life.

Cows and the City

With over 50,000 students spread across New Jersey, Rutgers is a behemoth of a university. The University spans three separate campuses: Camden in South Jersey, Newark in North Jersey, and the largest, New Brunswick-Piscataway, which is the physical and figurative center of the Rutgers. In addition to this, each location houses several subordinate colleges. While Camden houses the College of Arts and Sciences, Newark is home to its own liberal arts college and schools of business, nursing, and criminal justice. As home to over half of the Rutgers population, the New Brunswick campus offers ten outstanding undergraduate colleges: Cook College for Agricultural and Environmental Studies (which is located quite far from the downtown New Brunswick Campus); Douglass College, the Women's College at Rutgers; Livingston College (a "progressive and contemporary" school that offers socially relevant programs); Rutgers College (New Brunswick's oldest and largest liberal arts college); the

Edward J. Bloustein School of Planning and Public Policy; the Ernest Mario School of Pharmacy; the Mason Gross School of the Arts; the Rutgers Business School; the School of Communication, Information, and Library Studies; and the School of Engineering. All three campuses offer university programs for older and working students.

Each school has its own academic focus, and, fittingly, its own personality and look. One Cook College student proudly extolled the beauty of her campus. "Cook Campus is probably one of the nicest campuses—very green, many open spaces, but plenty of trees and lots of squirrels. We have an outdoor roller rink and volleyball sand pits, and barbecue grills everywhere. And a swing set." Nonetheless, students agree that the buildings around campus leave much to be desired. "The architecture is not overly impressive. Most of it is utilitarian and brick, built 30 years ago or so," one freshman said.

Between the urban streets of Newark and the more suburban area of New Brunswick-Piscataway, Rutgers University boasts both rural and urban campuses. One freshman said that one of the defining features of the Cook campus is "the smell on a rainy fall afternoon. We have horse stables next to the freshman dorms, cows further down the road, and a 'piggery.'" Meanwhile, Newark students enjoy a "campus" integrated into New Jersey's largest city with all the trappings of a cosmopolitan cultural center. Although Rutgers students enjoy the both the city feel of the Newark campus and the suburban feel in New Brunswick, many noted one major source or irritation: the bus system. With classes on different campuses, and they have to rely on the bus system, for which they can wait as long as 30 minutes on weekdays and up to an hour on weekends. Nevertheless, this disadvantage is outweighed by Newark resources such as the recently completed New Jersey Performing Arts Center.

Despite the marked schism between the urban landscape of Newark versus the quieter areas of Camden and New Brunswick, one issue—campus safety—concerns Rutgers students university-wide. "Outside of campus, it can get pretty dangerous," one Newark student said. "Inside the campus it's pretty safe. There are police cars all over the place." New Brunswick students expressed a similar concern, despite their campus' more suburban location. In the past year, the New Brunswick police station moved into a more dangerous area, but it is still close to campus. One tall, male senior who lives off campus in New Brunswick has admitted he often feels unsafe walking back from the library to his off campus house at night. But he was quick to add that "once you get past the dangerous part of town, there is a decent downtown area."

Excruciating "Expos"

According to Rutgers students, the academic requirements do force some people to take classes that they might never have considered before. "Just like most other colleges, you have to take some sciences if you're a fine arts major and dance if you're a bio-tech major," one sophomore said. "All that we are missing is mandated physical education classes." Students insist, however, that fulfilling these requirements is not very troublesome. "Everyone tries to cover all areas by choosing classes that overlap like 'Writing Papers in the Biological Sciences' to cover an English and a science course."

> "Rutgers is both the only university to reject its Ivy League invitation to receive state funding and the only state university that is not named after the state."

There is one dreadful gauntlet of a course that all freshmen are forced to endure. "Expository Writing," not-so-affectionately known as "Expos," is universally hated among Rutgers students. "Basically, they choose two readings and tell you to make some kind of connection," one junior recalled. "You would have to analyze the two readings thoroughly and try to find some common ground between them, like one reading on potatoes and another on military groups. You would have to B.S. a lot, but it would have to make sense." Students profess that the class is a lot of work and not very gratifying. "I used to stay up all night writing my papers," said one student.

With so many schools under its canopy, Rutgers offers academics that cover the spectrum of difficulty. Each college and campus has its own personality: Livingston, for example, is widely considered the easiest to get into and graduate from, while the School of Pharmacy, though prestigious, is renowned for being rigorous. The Business School on the New Brunswick-Piscataway campus is known to be the most difficult.

Unlike other colleges within Rutgers, the Business School requires students to have above a 3.3 GPA to get into the program.

Dealing with Numbers

Rutgers offers several unique programs that prepare students for less popular, yet fruitful careers in fields such as veterinary medicine and pharmacy. The School of Pharmacy, in fact, offers a well-respected 2+4 Program. Students spend two years at either the Camden or Newark campuses and upon completing that "preprofessional" phase move on to study for four "professional" years at the New Brunswick practice. This accelerated program allows students to receive their Pharmacy diplomas within six years, yet it does so at a cost. "You really have to love pharmacy in order to stick with the program," one student said.

Students say that large class sizes and poor TAs are significant problems at Rutgers. One freshman commented, "The worst thing is the size of Rutgers as a whole, because it means enormous classes, like 3,000 biology students in eight classes or getting stuck with recitation grad students who can barely speak English or don't know what they're doing." A Cook College student, however, insisted that these problems vary from college to college. "Cook College is relatively small, so we receive a good deal of individual attention in certain classes and with academic advisors." However, the same student concluded, "It's hard to go from a close-knit high school to being just a number."

Making the Connection

For ninety percent of Rutgers-Newark College of Arts & Science students, college life does not involve a dorm. While convenient for some who live in the area, complaints about the commuter lifestyle are common among Newark students. "It's really hectic because you have to get up early and go to class early, and if you have lecture you have to get to class early to get a good seat," said

one student. Moreover, students say that, especially in a school as large as Rutgers, commuting makes it hard to meet people. "If you drive to school, you don't get as much interaction with people, so I guess you miss out in a way."

Even on the New Brunswick campus, people find themselves off campus often. "Since it is a state school, a significant fraction of people go home on the weekends," said one New Brunswick freshman. For people who do stay on campus for the weekend, though, students say there's plenty to do. Greek life, especially on the mainly residential New Brunswick campus, offers the majority of the parties, where "lots of people go to party and drink." However, one student insisted, "If you're not interested in frat parties, there are also many clubs you can join. In fact, Rutgers offers clubs including a Polish Club, a Medieval Club, and a Ping Pong Club." One student said of the Medieval Club, "They tried to recruit my friend as a member, asking if she knew how to sing, dance, or sew because they have no women in their club. No wonder they have no women."

Come Together, Right Now

Although the prospect of attending such a densely packed university may seem overwhelming, students insist that meeting people often comes naturally. One New Brunswick sophomore said, "My hallmate would be friends with some guy I met online a long time ago—it's just a lot of connection everywhere." According to students, Rutgers can help your love life, too. "People from all over New Jersey come here, and it's good to get to know people from the South when you're from the North," said one student. "My boyfriend is from Lebanon, New Jersey, and I'm from Jersey City. I never would have met him if I didn't come to Rutgers." Indeed, as one sophomore happily concluded, "Rutgers brings people together."—*Christine Geiser* and *Christopher Lapinig*

FYI

If you come to Rutgers, you'd better bring a comfortable pair of shoes because classes are spread out.

What is the typical weekend schedule? "Party on Thursday; hangover Friday morning; go out with friends Friday night; sleep in until noon on Saturday; party and hit the bars on Saturday night; and then catch up on readings on Sunday."

If I could change one thing about Rutgers, I'd improve the transportation on campus, especially buses and parking.

Three things every student at Rutgers should do before graduating are "eat Grease Trucks, a fatty but delicious sandwich made with chicken fingers, mozzarella sticks, Philly cheese steak, French fries and marinara sauce; get kicked out of the strict club, Knight Club; and take 'Theatre Appreciation' before you graduate."

Seton Hall University

Address: Seton Hall, 400 South Orange Ave., South Orange, NJ 07079
Phone: 800-THE-HALL
E-mail Address: admissions@shu.edu
Web site URL: www.shu.edu
Year Founded: 1856
Private or Public: private
Religious affiliation: Jesuit
Location: suburban
Application and Admissions Information: rolling
Regular Application Deadline: NA
Number of Applicants: 5,100
Percent Accepted: 70%
Percent Accepted who enroll: NA
Number Entering: 319
Number of Transfers Accepted each Year: 613
Mean SAT: 1,096
Mean ACT: NA

Middle 50% SAT range: NA
Middle 50% ACT range: NA
Early admission program (EA/ ED/ NA): NA
ED or EA Acceptance Rate: NA
Full time Undergraduate enrollment: 5,200
Total enrollment: 9,700
Percent Male: 52%
Percent Female: 48%
Total Percent Minority: 46%
Percent African-American: 11%
Percent Asian/Pacific Islander: 6%
Percent Hispanic: 9%
Percent Native-American: 0%
Percent Other: 20%
Percent in-state / out of state: 68%/32%
Percent from Public HS: NA

Retention Rate: 82%
Graduation Rate: 0.57%
Percent in On-campus housing: NA
Percent affiliated with Greek system: NA
Percent Varsity or Club Athletes: NA
Number of official organized extracurricular organizations: 100+
3 Most popular majors: Communication, Finance, Criminal Justice
Student/Faculty ratio: 15:01
Tuition and Fees: $25,779.00
Cost for Room and Board: $9,358.00
Percent receiving Financial aid, first-year: 90%

Enroll at Seton Hall University, and you will experience two dichotomous worlds: It has a strong Catholic tradition on one hand, but enormous diversity on the other; it is isolated in a quiet Northern New Jersey suburb, but is also less than 20 minutes from the most exciting city in the world; it is overflowing with athletic fervor, but also boasts some of the country's most renowned undergraduate programs in diplomacy and business; it is thought of to be unchallenging by some, but it actually is dominated by many career-driven students in search of double and even triple majors. This pattern even applies to the student body makeup, which is split almost equally between commuters from neighboring New Jersey communities and on-campus residents. Both of these highly diverse groups enjoy Seton Hall's world-renowned professors, super-charged basketball and soccer games, and thriving community service organizations and Greek life.

Heavy, but Rewarding Work

Though a high acceptance rate has contributed to a perception of Seton Hall as not very selective, students say the workload is intense and requirements are heavy, but that "intelligent and supportive" teachers "who will do anything to help you" make the experience worth the stress. Undergraduates at Seton Hall apply to one of six schools: the College of Arts and Sciences, the Stillman School of Business, the College of Education and Human Services, the College of Nursing, the School of Theology, or the School of Diplomacy and International Relations. Within the largest division, the College of Arts and Sciences, many students take advantage of an innovative Communications major, fostered by Seton Hall's state-of-the-art environment, offering concentrations in media, performance, and graphics. Other popular majors include business, criminal justice, and the social sciences. Unusual majors include sports management and diplomacy. "Girls are mostly education majors here," one student said, "and guys are usually business or diplomacy majors."

The strongest point of Seton Hall academics may be that "there are the most amazing professors here, many of whom come from Ivy League schools," as one student said. "I've learned so much from them that I don't think I could have gotten a better education at a higher-ranked school." Jim McCartin's history class, and the history department in general, is a favorite among students. Many of the top professors are found in the "internationally renowned" School of Diplomacy and International Relations, a school formed in 1997 in a partnership with the United Nations. The school regularly features prominent speakers including U.N. Secretary-General Kofi Annan, former Secretary of State Henry Kissinger, and the President of Iran, Mohammad Khatami.

However, many students said they were extremely burdened by core requirements, which sometimes force students into "a five-year contract with the University." Students are limited in the number of classes they can take per semester by 18 credits, but still must fulfill close to 60 credits on top of majors, second majors, and minors depending on their program. One diplomacy student said, "There's just an absurd amount of requirements. It allows you no leeway to take an additional or extra course that may be outside your major, but within the realm of your field." However, another student said the core curriculum made her "very well-rounded, even though it's a pain. I know I complain a lot, but I've learned so much in my core classes."

> **"There are the most amazing professors here."**

Whether a class is a core fulfillment, introductory lecture, or advanced seminar, size is small across the board. According to one student, "it's not surprising if they close out a class after 30 people"—Seton Hall has no TAs—and so it is important to avoid "late registration." Must-take classes include "Catholic Church of the United States," which fulfills one of three required theology—not necessarily Christian-based—electives and "Scuba Diving." When choosing these classes, advising may be hard to find, with advice coming predominantly from a "university class" that one student called "a subpar method of creating an interaction between advisors and new freshman." But another student said she "met most of her friends in that first encounter" with her freshman advising group.

Technology is central to Seton Hall's innovative academic program. Soon after *Yahoo Internet Life* ranked Seton Hall in the top 20 of "wired" universities, it quickly became one of the most "wireless," too. Nearly all of Seton Hall's South Orange, N.J., campus is wireless, and is complete with a private cellular network. Free laptops are provided to every student upon matriculation, and technology is integrated in the classroom.

Ethnic and Location Diversity

Just as Seton Hall features state-of-the-art academics, the University also represents a cross-section of modern culture. "Everyone's different here, and that's what makes people get along," one student said. "I think that pretty much sums up Seton Hall." The student body consists of almost 40 percent minority students. At the same time, Seton Hall is like "going to a larger high school that's not really small, but not big either . . . and a lot more fun."

The diversity of Seton Hall extends to its location, which is sandwiched between serene suburban communities and cities like Newark, which "students generally avoid" to ensure safety. Location is one of Seton Hall's major pulls, with most students, especially commuters, coming to the university from the Northeast's Tri-State Area. Though South Orange currently includes Starbucks, Cold Stone Creamery, and several bars, the town is in the process of a build-up effort that may bring a movie theatre and new restaurants. According to one student, "it's not a college town—a lot of places close early, and there isn't really much to do." But for many students, Friday nights mean a 20-minute ride to New York City that provides excitement and gives the University its "edge over other smaller colleges farther from bustling cities."

An Ever-Improving Campus

Though Boland Hall is notorious for a fatal dormitory fire that broke out in 2000, Boland and every other dorm are now equipped with "like 10 sprinklers per room" and are now among the safest rooms in the country. For those who reside on campus, options also include Aquinas Hall and Xavier Hall. In spite of the small rooms, Aquinas dorms foster a sense of community, and according to one resident, "provide a great experience, because everyone gets together and is very friendly to one another." But a freshman said his Aquinas Hall dorm looks more like "the jail on Rikers Island" than his home. Xavier Hall, with suites and painted walls, is reportedly Seton Hall's best living option, which one student said, "feels like living in a hotel." Farther from campus is the Ora Manor apartment "complex" which provide rooms smaller than those on central campus. However, a significant number of students live off-campus in Greek housing since the university doesn't allow Greek life on-campus.

When students are not inside studying, they stroll Seton Hall's small campus, described by one student as a "strange hodgepodge of old and new." Contemporary Jubilee Hall, featuring marble, glass windows and a planetarium on top, is balanced by Duffy Hall, which "looks like it's straight out of the '70s." However, there have been recent upgrades to the campus, and a new 35 million dollar Science and Technology Center, which in its early stages already looks "absolutely amazing," will become one of the largest science centers in New Jersey. The Bishop Dougherty University Center is the social, nutritional, and activity hub of Seton Hall, featuring the Pirate's Cove, "a nice place to have lunch or coffee, but depressing in its magenta and turquoise color scheme," student organization meeting rooms, and televisions where students gather to "watch football games."

Due to the heavy workload, students spend a great deal of time at the Walsh Library, now opened 24/7. One junior described the building as "outside looking nice, but ugly inside with carpet falling off in some areas." Another student said the library does not carry enough books. "I just had to borrow a basic book from another college," she said. "It was embarrassing that we didn't carry it."

Students have mixed reactions to the campus food options. One freshman complained, "the food is an on-and-off thing; you usually end up having pizza and salad bar every night." However, take-out options are plentiful: Students order from Cluck-U Chicken, a "very good" sub sandwich shop, and the surrounding Italian-heavy neighborhood's numerous pizzeria options. The South Orange Alliance for Redevelopment promises to bring even more eateries to the community in coming years.

Service and Social Bonding
Even commuters become involved in some of the over 100 Seton Hall activities offered, which range from politically-charged to fundriven. Popular organizations include the Student Government Association; Pirate TV, the renowned campus radio station; the weekly student newspaper, *The Setonian*, which covers the extremely popular intramural sports program; a gospel choir; and the pep band. A satirical newspaper called *The Rampage*, which "no one knows the editor of or who writes for it," provides weekly entertainment for students.

But the prevalent ethnic and service groups on campus distinguish Seton Hall most. These include six African-American student associations; nearly 10 other ethnic clubs for Filipino, Italian, Indian, Arabic, Asian and international students; a popular Habitat for Humanity chapter; and an award-winning chapter of the National Society of Collegiate Scholars established for top students to engage in community service. Campus events sponsored by various groups have included a concert by Third Eye Blind for the University's 150th Anniversary and the annual University Day in October for which families are invited to a festive carnival. One student recalled, "I've never seen the campus so alive before."

Sports and the SHU Experience
Although Seton Hall's once indomitable Division I men's basketball team has waned over the past several years, enthusiasm for sports has not decreased, especially when the nationally ranked men's soccer team stole the limelight. Though Seton Hall has no football team, "basically everyone's into sports here," one junior said. "Students get really into it when we win, and very sad when we lose." At the Midnight Madness pep rally, there are games like "shootouts for thousand dollar prizes" and the chance to see the men and women basketball teams in action. But one student complained, "The culture here is dominated by sports as opposed to academia."

The social culture is also dominated by Greek life. Fraternities and sororities range from service-centered to purely social to academic. Drinking on campus is "surprisingly not prevalent," but when it does take place, it is mostly "in group settings, especially at frat parties." One student said that after a while, "Seton Hall may seem like a glorified high school, but you are comfortable because you often see people you know." But another said, "If you don't live here, you may not get the full experience of it all." That experience—a cross between academic rigor and athletic excitement, religious bonding and exploration of differences, and South Orange serenity and New York City bustle—may be ideal, as one junior suggested, for "someone who likes diversity, a great education, not being too far from home, and absolutely awesome professors."—*Andrew M. Mangino*

FYI

If you come to Seton Hall, you'd better bring "a surge protector because they take fire safety very seriously here."

What's the typical weekend schedule? "Thursday night—come home from an internship and party; Friday night—sleep in and then take a bus to New York City or the Short Hills Mall; Saturday—see a soccer or basketball game and have a date at night; Sunday—time to study."

If I could change one thing about Seton Hall, I'd "lower the percentage of commuters, because if more people lived on campus, then it would be even more alive."

Three things every student at Seton Hall should do before graduating are "Go to Cryn's, an Irish pub in South Orange, as soon as you turn 21 as a rite of passage, explore New York City, and see a Pirates basketball game."

Stevens Institute of Technology

Address: Stevens, Wesley J. Howe Center, 8th Floor, One Castlepoint on Hundson, Hoboken, NJ 07030

Phone: 800-458-5323

E-mail Address: admissions@stevens.edu

Web site URL: www.stevens.edu/undergrad

Year Founded: 1870

Private or Public: private

Religious affiliation: none

Location: urban

Regular Application Deadline: 15-Feb

Number of Applicants: 2,418

Percent Accepted: 47%

Percent Accepted who enroll: 43%

Number Entering: 518

Number of Transfers Accepted each Year: varies

Mean SAT: NA

Mean ACT: NA

Middle 50% SAT range: 1,180–1,370

Middle 50% ACT range: NA

Early admission program (EA/ ED/ NA): ED

ED or EA Acceptance Rate: 32%

Full time Undergraduate enrollment: 1,788

Total enrollment: 4,689

Percent Male: 75%

Percent Female: 25%

Total Percent Minority: 31%

Percent African-American: 5%

Percent Asian/Pacific Islander: 9%

Percent Hispanic: 11%

Percent Native-American: 0%

Percent Other: 0.06%

Percent in-state / out of state: 61%/39%

Percent from Public HS: NA

Retention Rate: 88%

Graduation Rate: 72%

Percent in On-campus housing: 75%

Percent affiliated with Greek system: 33%

Percent Varsity or Club Athletes: 25%

Number of official organized extracurricular organizations: 85

3 Most popular majors: Mechanical Engineering, Computer Engineering, Business

Student/Faculty ratio: NA

Tuition and Fees: $31,750.00

Cost for Room and Board: $10,150.00

Percent receiving Financial aid, first-year: 68%

What makes Stevens different from other schools? "Laptops," said one student. "Freshmen get their own laptops for free." Other perks? Internship programs, a happening Greek frat scene, and frequent trips to New York City are high up on the list and make it clear that Stevens Institute of Technology offers a diverse, stimulating environment for students with a strong interest in the sciences. Because of its relatively small undergraduate population and its location just across the Hudson River from Manhattan, Stevens provides the atmosphere of a small college with the resources of the nation's liveliest city.

Work at the Core

Academics at Stevens are both rigorous and thorough. Depending on the major, schedules are determined by a preset course track that students follow from the start of freshman year. As the school name suggests, students do not come to Stevens to major in English. "We see the same 30 students every day in all our classes," one student said. "We travel around together." But some students find that the course track is "very annoying, because we have to take a lot of classes we don't need."

The most popular major at Stevens is engineering, even though the core for engineering is "much harder" than that of science majors. Some other popular majors are computer science and chemical biology. Like every school, Stevens also has a major for the so-called "slackers"—business technology. However, students at Stevens hesitate to call any of their peers by that name. "There really are no slackers here; everyone has to work hard. But the course load for biz tech compared to engineering is very, very light." "Biz Tech" includes a "watered-down version" of calculus and a lighter core.

Stevens' professors are knowledgeable, but many students have trouble following them in class. As one student stated, they "know a lot, but can't teach, and you end up having to teach yourself." However, another student said, "The professors are always there, there's always someone to contact if you don't understand something." There're also mixed opinions about the TAs. One student said, "The TAs are not always helpful, because many have limited English experience," while another said, "Some of the TAs can't really speak English, but, overall, they are good."

Because students must take 19 to 21 credit hours a year, which is an "abnormally high number for a regular college," they usually end up doing work "deep into the night," as one student said. "If you can't work on your own, you won't survive," warned one student. "You have to have independent study habits. If you know how to study, you'll do fine." "We have too many classes," one student complained. "They are quite a bit of work," another student agreed. "It was an academic shock."

Stevens has several special programs: the seven-year doctorate program, the seven-year medical or dentistry program, the "co-op" program, and the Reduced Load program. The Reduced Load program allows students to graduate in five years with a tuition-free fifth year, allowing students an easier time with their classes. The Co-op program offers students a five year plan in which they pick three out of the ten semesters to work at a company instead of taking classes. Companies such as Johnson and Johnson, Colgate, Merck, and Lucent come on-campus and conduct interviews, and students are paid about $7,000 a year for the internship. Most students enjoy their experience, but some students complain that their job consists solely of "running errands." Other students, however, are able to conduct chemical experiments during their internships. "It's really great because you al-ternate between working and going to class. What you learn in the classroom you bring to your internship and what you learn during your internship you bring to the classroom," one student said.

Going Greek

The Greeks are "involved with every organization on campus," one student stated, making them a ubiquitous presence at Stevens. They also hold get-togethers such as the popular Halloween weekend party, Christmas parties, and weekend parties. To the chagrin of many students, recent years have been declared "dry periods," during which any frats or sororities caught serving alcohol to underage students were forced to shut down. At parties, girls generally have their choice of dance partners—the guy-to-girl ratio at Stevens is a staggering 7:2. As one student said, "Girls are treated like queens." One female student said, "It's a lot easier to meet guys here—the majority of my friends are guys."

> **"Girls are treated like queens."**

As most students are from New Jersey, many freshmen go home on weekends . . . but those who stick around on campus have plenty to do. As one frosh said, "There's lots to do, you just have to be motivated to do it." For the non-partier, the largest lecture rooms in Buchard Building, which are converted into movie theaters on weekends, offer an attractive alternative. Jacobus Hall, the student lounge, is equipped with couches, a large-screen TV, billiards table, and climbing wall, and popular clubs such as Exit, Hammerstein Ballroom, Bahama Mamas, and Planet are right around the corner in Hoboken and New York City. Hoboken, according to one student, has "more bars per square mile than any other city in the world." Being underage is an inconvenience, but not a big problem because of all the other activities students can take part in. Another popular location is Washington Street, which is described as being the "main hangout," complete with "everything you need—clothes, restaurants, food, groceries, and ATM machines."

Typical Stevens Students

The self-described stereotype of Stevens students is "nerdy," "dorky and always sitting in front of the computer," or "very math-oriented." But is this stereotype really accurate? Some students agree: "For the most part it's true; if you go here, you're gaining a lot of math background. People spend a lot of time in their rooms in front of the computer." But other students disagree. As one student said, "Most people aren't really like that; people like to have a good time here."

Stevens students tend to form cliques according to ethnicity, Greek affiliation, or which sport they play. "People tend to self-segregate here," one student said. Another said, "I'd like to see a little bit more diversity—Stevens is very lacking in that respect."

Students spend a fair amount of time on extracurricular activities at Stevens, "between five and seven hours a week." And "if people hold office in the Greek organizations, they are much more active," one student said. Some of the most popular activities include ethnic groups like the Chinese Student Association, Black Student Union, and Latin American Association; the co-ed service fraternity, Alpha Phi Omega; and the weekly newspaper *The Stute*. About 80 percent of the students at Stevens are part of the work-study program.

As a Division III school, athletics at Stevens generate much enthusiasm within the athlete population. For instance, it is common for volleyball players to watch soccer matches, and for lacrosse players to rally behind the volleyball team. However, team spirit is distinctly lacking within the "non-jock" population. Although there is no football team, both men's and women's lacrosse teams, as well as the women's soccer team, have performed very well in the past. For those who do not want to play varsity sports but still wish to keep in shape, the recently-renovated Charles V. Schaefer Jr. Athletic Center offers a gym and a pool, as well as basketball, squash, and tennis courts. Intramurals are very popular, as are spontaneous games of ultimate Frisbee, volleyball, and lacrosse on the spacious lawns.

Setting and Sustenance at Stevens

Freshmen are guaranteed housing—men live in Davis Hall and women in Humphrey Hall. Although there is no air-conditioning, the double rooms are "livable" and no more than five to ten minutes away from classes. With all the freshmen living together, groups form pretty quickly. "Most people meet their closest friends in the hall they live in," one student said. After freshman year, there's a "big fight" for the best dorm rooms. Seniors and juniors get first pick for a room in one of the five dorms on-campus. The most expensive residences are Castle Point Apartments, which have rooms equipped with a kitchen, bathroom, and two 'living' rooms.

The campus itself is "beautiful. It's right on the waterfront; the location is extremely good." Said one student: "There's lots of grass, lots of trees, you have the city right next to you and when you look across the river, you see Manhattan." Parking is a problem, even though freshmen and sophomores are not allowed to park their cars at Stevens unless they commute. According to one student, "The security is not that great, but you don't really need it. People think Hoboken is ghetto, but nothing's going to happen to you."

One student said bluntly, "The food really sucks, but they're trying to make it better." A recent effort to "make it better" was renovating Pierce Dining Hall, the main eatery on-campus. "They added more types of food, like Asian and Italian; it's roomier, more convenient, and everything looks a little more appetizing," a student said. Besides Pierce, there are fast-food joints and late-night cafés around campus.

A Degree with a Good Reputation

When asked whether they would return to Stevens if given a second chance, most students were thoughtful but generally answered affirmatively. "I'd probably choose the school again because it's close to home and it's small," one student said.

So what kind of person is right for Stevens? As one student put it, "If you're looking for the typical college experience, our campus life isn't rich enough. If you're not sure about what you want to do, don't come here. But if you're looking for good engineering experience and a degree with a good reputation, this is the school for you."—*Frances Cheng*

FYI

If you come to Stevens, you better bring "a jacket, because the school's a wind tunnel."

What is the typical weekend schedule? "The weekend doesn't start until Friday night, and most frosh go home, but some students go to the city, hang out with friends, or eat in Hoboken. Sunday is saved for studying."

If I could change one thing about Stevens, "I'd improve campus life quality."

Three things every student at Stevens should do before graduating are "enjoy the fireworks displays from Castle Point, go bar-hopping on Washington Street, and get internship experience."

New Mexico

Address: New Mexico State, PO Box 30001 MSC3A, Las Cruces, NM 88003

Phone: 800-662-NMSU

E-mail Address: admissions@nmsu.edu

Web site URL: www.nmsu.edu

Year Founded: 1888

Private or Public: public

Religious affiliation: none

Location: small city

Regular Application Deadline: 1-Mar

Number of Applicants: 5,377

Percent Accepted: 88%

Percent Accepted who enroll: 47%

Number Entering: 2,760

Number of Transfers Accepted each Year: 500

Mean SAT: NA

Mean ACT: 21

Middle 50% SAT range: NA

Middle 50% ACT range: NA

Early admission program (EA/ ED/ NA): NA

ED or EA Acceptance Rate: NA

Full time Undergraduate enrollment: 11,800

Total enrollment: 16,072

Percent Male: 44%

Percent Female: 56%

Total Percent Minority: 56%

Percent African-American: 3%

Percent Asian/Pacific Islander: 1%

Percent Hispanic: 42%

Percent Native-American: 3%

Percent Other: 7%

Percent in-state / out of state: 78%/22%

Percent from Public HS: NA

Retention Rate: NA

Graduation Rate: NA

Percent in On-campus housing: 15%

Percent affiliated with Greek system: NA

Percent Varsity or Club Athletes: NA

Number of official organized extracurricular organizations: 276

3 Most popular majors: Business Administration, Elementary Education, Mechanical Engineering

Student/Faculty ratio: 19:01

Financial Information: per semester

Tuition and Fees: $2,115.00

In State Tuition and Fees (if different): $6,905.00

Cost for Room and Board: $2,788.00

Percent receiving Financial aid, first-year: NA

Less than an hour north of Mexico, in the middle of the desert, lies the oasis of New Mexico State University. The town of Las Cruces charms most with its Southwestern Navajo style and hospitable feel. With its strong agricultural and applied sciences programs, a spacious campus, a varied and lively social scene, and its abundance of cultural diversity, NMSU is the place for those looking for a quality education with a relaxed atmosphere.

Viewing a Wider World

New Mexico State University students enjoy a wide variety of majors incorporated in the six undergraduate colleges of Business Administration and Economics, Education, Health and Social Services, Arts and Sciences, Agriculture and Home Economics, and Engineering. While some majors, like communication studies or family and child science, are considered easier than others, most students agree that "the workload is challenging, but rewarding at the same time."

Many students rave about the "Viewing a Wider World" program, in which students are required to take six credits in two departments other than the one in which they are majoring. In the words of one communication studies major, "You really find out a lot about other areas that you otherwise wouldn't have even thought about learning about."

All NMSU students seem to be able to agree on the accessibility and helpfulness of the faculty. One student offered, "All of the professors I've had here have been really approachable and willing to help in any way they can. Most of them are always asking students to come to their office hours, even if it's just to talk to them for a little while."

From El Paso to Mexico

NMSU students enjoy a social setting as diverse as their student body. The large university is home to an active and popular Greek system, not to mention that El Paso is less than an hour away with its restaurants, movies, theater, and other entertainment. The college often sponsors activities, such as the well-attended homecoming bonfire and a variety of cultural events. Meanwhile, the local night clubs sometimes sponsor college nights for students of all ages, and, of course, in the words of one student, "There's a lot of partying going on." Many underage students, particularly freshman, prefer to cross the border into Mexico to party, where it's more difficult to get into trouble for underage drinking. Greek life does exist, and although frats only attract a small percentage of the student body, they do throw parties almost every weekend.

While its students love NMSU for different reasons, an overwhelming majority agree that the school's diversity is one of its best features. As one Family and Child Science major puts it, "Our student body is really amazingly diverse. I had expected a lot of Caucasian or Latino students, but now I've got friends from Japan, Kuwait, and Thailand." In addition to student appreciation for all the different cultures represented at NMSU, the school administration and the Union Program Council (UPC) host regular cultural events to celebrate the different customs of all the students.

The dating scene at New Mexico State University is variable as well. In the words of one student, "There are definitely random hookups. There's definitely dating. There are some homosexual couples and definitely some interracial couples. Some people find their future husband or wife here. It's such a big system that there's a lot of everything going on."

Most agree that dining out is superior to the meal plan at school, which the majority forego. In the words of one senior, "I think they've made some improvements in the food here since my freshman year, but back then, even the people who paid for their meal plans wouldn't eat that stuff." Instead, students prefer a number of on-campus restaurants that serve everything from Mexican to Chinese to pizza.

"The Horseshoe"

New Mexico State University is one of the nation's largest campuses. Much of the space comes from the school's renowned Agriculture Department, but all NMSU students can enjoy their wide, spread-out campus. Some of the favorite spots on campus include "The Horseshoe," a wide ring of buildings spread out in the shape of its name. There, students can find everything from athletic facilities and ROTC practice fields to student services and the financial aid office. One senior, however, enjoys the Horseshoe for one of its less well-known features, "I love the duck pond! It's my favorite place on-campus." What's more, the Horseshoe is just outside of the student dorms, making it a convenient place for students to visit.

> "I'd choose to come here again without a doubt, and, in fact, I only wish I'd known about it earlier."

Whether it is New Mexico State University's highly regarded academic programs, the great cultural diversity, the warm and sunny weather, or just the duck pond that strikes your interest, NMSU students would agree with the advice of one communication studies major, "This is a really great place to go to school. I'd choose to come here again without a doubt, and, in fact, I only wish I'd known about it earlier."—*Sarah Newman*

FYI
If you come to New Mexico State University, you'd better bring "a pair of sandals."
What is the typical weekend schedule? "Do some sort of on-campus activity, hang with friends, get some sleep in, and do some work."
If I could change one thing about New Mexico State University, I'd "stop raising the tuition fees."
Three things every student at New Mexico State University should do before graduating are "go to El Paso, go see the mariachis, and visit the duck pond."

University of New Mexico

Address: University of New Mexico, Office of Recruitment Services, Student Services Center, Rm 180, Albuquerque, NM 87131
Phone: 800-CALLUNM
E-mail Address: apply@unm.edu
Web site URL: www.unm.edu
Year Founded: 1889
Private or Public: public
Religious affiliation: none
Location: urban
Regular Application Deadline: 16-Jun
Number of Applicants: 7,134
Percent Accepted: 73.65%
Percent Accepted who enroll: 59%
Number Entering: 3,091
Number of Transfers Accepted each Year: NA
Mean SAT: 1,070
Mean ACT: 22

Middle 50% SAT range: 860–1,130
Middle 50% ACT range: 19–25
Early admission program (EA/ ED/ NA): NA
ED or EA Acceptance Rate: NA
Full time Undergraduate enrollment: 18,725
Total enrollment: NA
Percent Male: 42%
Percent Female: 58%
Total Percent Minority: 47%
Percent African-American: 3%
Percent Asian/Pacific Islander: 3%
Percent Hispanic: 35%
Percent Native-American: 6%
Percent Other: NA
Percent in-state / out of state: 79%/21%

Percent from Public HS: NA
Retention Rate: NA
Graduation Rate: NA
Percent in On-campus housing: 8%
Percent affiliated with Greek system: 6%
Percent Varsity or Club Athletes: NA
Number of official organized extracurricular organizations: 363
3 Most popular majors: Psychology, Business, Management
Student/Faculty ratio: 20:01
Tuition and Fees: $14,258.00
In State Tuition and Fees (if different): $4,361.00
Cost for Room and Board: $6,680.00
Percent receiving Financial aid, first-year: NA

C omprised of sprawling green lawns and adobe buildings in Albuquerque, N.M., the University of New Mexico is a college that gives students the opportunity to be what they want to be. Among its 30,000 enrollees are recent high school graduates, preprofessionals and continuing-education students returning to college. This diversity offers undergraduates a unique college experience in the heart of a Southwestern city.

Academics: Lost Among Many, but Not Lost in Life

Many students enter UNM with a good idea of their career paths. Thus, although there are a significant number of students in pursuit of their bachelor's degrees in the liberal arts, many opt to take the preprofessional route. "Everyone is pre-something," one student said, "and the premedical and prenursing tracks are huge because UNM is a great medical school." According to students, this can make the environment "very competitive," especially in the larger "weed-out" introductory science courses. Some students report that because of the high number of students, getting into classes can sometimes be tricky, especially for undergrads who want to take graduate-level courses. Students having trouble with the material can, however, seek help from the free tutoring program offered by the library.

Despite the dominance of preprofessional programs, students also noted that the geology and photography departments are quite good. UNM also boasts a good Fine Arts school, which gives students who are undecided about their future plans a good opportunity to try out different tracks and find the one that best suits them. Classes are largely taught lecture-style at UNM and sometimes number 300-plus students, with the smaller math and English courses numbering 20 to 30. Some students complain about the large class size, but note that if a student is motivated, closer, fulfilling professor-student relationships are easy to come by. Academic facilities are outstanding, with six libraries, and a number of good study and social centers, including the Student Union Building (SUB) and the Cellar. In addition, UNM is fast becoming one of the Southwest's premier research institutions, as the University just received a large amount of money for research facilities and lab upgrades.

Looking for a Party?

A portion of the UNM party scene is dominated by fraternities and sororities. According to students, the more popular fraternities are Pi Kappa Alpha and Sigma Alpha Epsilon and the most notable sororities are Kappa Kappa Gamma and Alpha Chi Omega. However, because of the dry status required of fraternities by the UNM administration, the popularity and frequency of fraternity parties has dropped off in recent years.

> "Everyone is pre-something. . . . The premedical and prenursing tracks are huge."

The widely diverse of the student body at UNM, which boasts an average age of 27, means the Greek scene does not account for all of the social life by any stretch. Older students say they prefer the "nicer" 21-and-over clubs downtown. Although UNM is officially a dry campus, most students agreed that alcohol was "easy to find," even for those underage. Several described the campus community as very "tightly knit," saying that "everyone knows everyone through someone else." Most agreed that it is relatively easy to meet new people at parties and other extracurricular gatherings.

UNM also sponsors a number of concerts and social events. Toward the beginning of the year, there is a "Welcome Back Night," where students are invited to watch a movie screened in the school's sports facility, Johnson Field. Another notable event is the "Balloon Fiesta," at which hot air balloons are launched from a nearby park built by the city a few years ago. The balloons are released every morning for a week in October, and this event attracts not only students but visitors from all over the world. UNM also attracts a number of headlining bands throughout the academic year. One recent event featured indie rock band The Donnas.

Off Campus and Off Hours

The city of Albuquerque offers UNM students a "fun and interesting place to live." A famous local restaurant called Frontier is a popular local hangout—"everyone is there at two in the morning on Friday nights," one sophomore said. Another favorite is the Student Union Building, the SUB, which reopened after renovation this fall, and contains a number of restaurants and a computer center.

For students with cars, there are numerous recreational opportunities in the area. Several malls in the nearby area offer shopping, and many students leave campus on weekends to explore the greater Albuquerque area. Parking, however, is described as "very difficult," and campus parking has been alleged to overfill its lots.

Dwelling and Dining

There is a lot of variation in the quality and pricing of on-campus housing. Students apply for a particular building and are later placed according to their ranked preferences. The dorms are a social place, and a good way to make friends, especially for incoming freshmen. Many attested to the superior accommodations found in the Student Residence Centers, which consist of suites of six bedrooms connected by a common kitchen and living room area. An alternative housing option is Coronado, which has been described both as the worst of the spectrum with "a billion rooms sharing just one bathroom," and the best: "a great place to party because there are so many people in it."

The residence halls have an RA (Resident Advisors) system, which can be "a pain if your RA is strict." Despite the fact that housing is available all four years, most students choose to move off campus after freshman year. Housing is easy to find in the surrounding area, especially because "many students are from nearby." Students still advise living on campus at least one year, however, because it is a good way to meet people.

Students living on campus are automatically placed on a meal plan. Meals can be redeemed at the cafeteria, which stacks three floors of cafeteria-style options and is open continuously between 7 a.m. and 7 p.m. Several students affirmed that the cafeteria food was extremely unpopular. For those who can't stomach the cafeteria option, meal plan "point" alternatives are redeemable at the SUB, the bookstore and the on-campus Pizza Hut stand.

What Makes a Lobo

While a couple of students complained about a lack of campus cohesion and student involvement, UNM boasts several hundred undergraduate organizations that one student noted "include almost anything you could think of to do." Club and intramural sports are also "very popular," and it is "typical" to find students working out in the

Johnson Center, the athletics center, late into the evening.

Varsity sports events, particularly football and basketball games, are well attended. The annual football game against New Mexico State University draws a large crowd, and festivities include a pre-game bonfire and lots of tailgating. The school's mascot, Louie Lobo, and his female counterpart, Lucy Lobo, are the inspirations for the signature cheer, in which fans scowl at opponents before basketball games.

Students offer that the above lack of cohesion was due to the incredible diversity of the student body at UNM, which attracts a wide variety of students in various stages of their lives. They describe the student body as mostly middle-class, and "very culturally diverse." UNM is also remarkably ethnically diverse, and many report the feeling that white students are more of a minority on campus than ever before. There is a support network for minority students, which includes a number of student centers and the school's dedication to bilingual education. While there are student jobs aplenty, obtaining on-campus employment involves meeting a financial aid requirement; consequentially, many students hold part-time jobs in the surrounding area, which are reportedly easy to find in the commercial districts. Along with this student diversity comes an atmosphere of political freedom and protests, and though one student described the campus as "so liberal that it hurts," he maintains that liberals and conservatives alike can enjoy the activism that pervades the campus.

As one student put it, your experience at University of New Mexico is what you make of it. In a university of 30,000 students, it is possible to get lost in a sea of preprofessionals, but it is also possible to take advantage of unmatched diversity and resources. Students who understand this principle and are prepared to optimize their college experiences for themselves will find an outstanding value at the University of New Mexico and an extensive wealth of educational opportunities.—*Stephanie Teng*

FYI

If you come to University of New Mexico, you'd better bring "your old school notes, your skis, and an attitude to work."

What is the typical weekend schedule? "Friday, frat parties, clubs, or bars downtown; Saturday, sleeping in or leaving campus, finding a party or concert at night; Sunday, doing homework or going to work."

If I could change one thing about University of New Mexico, I would "improve the food."

Three things every student at University of New Mexico should do before they graduate are "try to meet a lot of new people, attend the pre-NMSU bonfire, and join a student organization."

New York

Adelphi University

Address: Adelphi, Levermore Hall, Room 110, 1 South Avenue, P.O. Box 701, Garden City, NY 11530-0701
Phone: 516-877-3050
E-mail Address: admissions@adelphi.edu
Web site URL: http://admissions.adelphi.edu/UGrad/
Year Founded: 1896
Private or Public: private
Religious affiliation: none
Location: urban
Regular Application Deadline: Rolling
Number of Applicants: 5,496
Percent Accepted: 68%
Percent Accepted who enroll: 23%
Number Entering: 839
Number of Transfers Accepted each Year: 1,183
Mean SAT: 1,119
Mean ACT: 24

Middle 50% SAT range: V:480–580; M:490–590
Middle 50% ACT range: 20–25
Early admission program (EA/ ED/ NA): EA
ED or EA Acceptance Rate: 78%
Full time Undergraduate enrollment: 4,930
Total enrollment: 8,053
Percent Male: 27%
Percent Female: 73%
Total Percent Minority: 28%
Percent African-American: 14%
Percent Asian/Pacific Islander: 6%
Percent Hispanic: 8%
Percent Native-American: 0%
Percent Other: 0%
Percent in-state / out of state: 92%/8%

Percent from Public HS: 75%
Retention Rate: 78%
Graduation Rate: 61%
Percent in On-campus housing: 23%
Percent affiliated with Greek system: 5%/4%
Percent Varsity or Club Athletes: NA
Number of official organized extracurricular organizations: 79
3 Most popular majors: Business Administration/ Management, Education, General, Nursing
Student/Faculty ratio: 11:01
Tuition and Fees: $20,900.00
Cost for Room and Board: $9,500.00
Percent receiving Financial aid, first-year: 28%

Tucked away in the middle of an affluent Long Island residential district, the Adelphi campus setting attracts students who reside in nearby communities. If you live on Long Island and are considering commuting to college, you'll find yourself among friends at Adelphi. Although the student body may be comprised of a large commuter population, the University successfully creates an intimate college experience both socially and academically. Adelphi not only provides students with a solid base in academics, it also offers students pre-professional tracks so they may immediately pursue their passions. If you are a student who looks to branch out of your home community without really leaving it, Adelphi can offer the best of both worlds. While one student cautions, "Adelphi isn't for everyone—the commuter-school aspect sets it apart," its tradition of strong programs and commitment to developing career opportunities make it worth a closer look.

A Variety of Options

Students interested in Adelphi have the option of applying to the College of Arts and Sciences, the Derner Institute of Advanced Psychological Studies, the Honors College, the School of Business, the School of Education, the School of Nursing or the School of Social Work. The schools each have different requirements, but students in the popular College of Arts and Sciences must take General Education courses that, while "fairly numerous," are "pretty easy as long as you show up." These courses include a freshman orientation experience, an English composition seminar, a freshman seminar and at least six credits in each of four areas: arts, humanities and languages, natural sciences and math, and the social sciences. One student complained that of those courses there were "a handful I haven't liked." Freshmen also say the required seminar and orientation course are "a necessary annoyance."

Students cite the nursing and business programs as particularly strong. One girl raved, "My experiences working in a hospital a few times a week really prepared me for a career in nursing." However, the quality of the experience is very dependent on the teacher you get, a problem that students in various programs and majors mentioned. A communications major said that his professors' personalities had ranged from very enthusiastic about the subject to simply uninspired and "big assigners of busy work."

Many qualified students choose to enroll in the Honors Program, especially because of the generous scholarships Adelphi offers. They live, attend classes and study in this exclusive academic and living arrangement, which is "almost its own separate community." However, "you should visit the campus before you just accept the scholarship," warns one student, "because it is a pretty different college experience." For the rest of the population, one of the most common grievances is the difficulty in enrolling in classes. One student complains that "I've been trying to get into this one class for two years and haven't been able to." But once you get into courses, the atmosphere is "very tight-knit, with a close student-faculty relationship," because of the school's small size. Students even mention going into the city for performances and then to bars with their professors.

Adelphi's humanities courses are "much better and more popular" than math and science, and students "wouldn't recommend the school for pre-med." But many professors really "make you think outside the box." Overall, students classified their schoolwork at Adelphi as "definitely not too hard," and "grading is fair and lenient."

Seeking Out the Scene

Adelphi's status as largely a commuter school situated in a wealthy Long Island suburb is one of the main obstacles to a really active social life. So many students go home on the weekends that "the campus can be pretty dead by Thursday night," and surrounding Garden City is such a sheltered community that there isn't much night life nearby. In fact, when the campus recently hosted a Roots concert, it was shut down early because neighbors complained of the noise. The school also hosts many other events in the University Center. Recent speakers include

Daniel Liebeskind, the architect in charge of rebuilding the World Trade Center.

Those students who live on or near campus find a reasonable social scene at a few local bars and clubs, where Adelphi's seven fraternities and sororities often host gatherings for the student body. There are "quite a few" students in Greek organizations, and some "really make themselves known through advertising and recruiting," but because of the Garden City rule that "classifies more than six unrelated girls in a house as a brothel," the sororities don't have their own housing.

Students called Adelphi "more of a drinking school," saying that most people pregame in their rooms before heading out to bars and clubs, but since the dorms are dry, "it's hard to tell how many people drink because they have to keep it pretty quiet." Overall, it's very self-controlled, and drugs "can be hard to find," although "pot is available if you want it" and "a lot of people smoke."

One student said that if you want to get socially involved at Adelphi, "you have to actively seek out the scene," whether by attending weekly comedy shows, sampling the popular theater program, or heading out to New York City. The train station is on the edge of campus, just a few blocks away, and the trip takes about 45 minutes. Students really feel that the city is the redeeming factor in the otherwise quiet environment of Garden City—there are just so many opportunities for entertainment, from plays and museums to well-attended bars and clubs.

Most people meet their friends based on their living situations, whether in the dorms or off campus, but the small class sizes make it easy to meet people who share your academic interests. Students characterize the stereotypical Adelphi students as "very Long Islandish: girls get really dressed up to go to class, and boys can be very fashionable and wealthy too." However, others say that there is a lot of diversity at Adelphi, particularly because it attracts many international students. One senior explained, "There is more diversity of culture than of race, because within the largely white population, many nations are represented."

One girl said that one of the most surprising aspects of Adelphi is that its student population is predominantly female. "There are a lot of hookups because guys who are hot and straight are usually taken, and you have to be quick," she admitted. The school does have an overall accepting attitude towards the gay population, which is sizable—in fact, a senior estimated that "half the males are probably gay." In the spring, the Lesbian-Gay-Bisexual-Transsexual-Queer (LGBTQ) organization puts on mock "weddings" just to show the community's support for gay couples.

People Do Live Here

Adelphi's campus is described as "truly beautiful," and students estimate that the university spends a sizable amount of money just on landscaping. The effect is a picturesque campus with spacious lawns and well-kept foliage. While many Adelphi students choose to live at home and commute to school, there is a lot of competition for housing on or near campus. Students who live in the dorms have the choice of air conditioning, which is more expensive, or just the standard housing, but students say that "it's pretty cool in Garden City, so the lack of AC isn't a big deal." If you want housing and are new to the school, you are entered in a lottery to try to get a room in the full dorms, but if you have already been living there a semester, you have "squatter's rights" and can keep your room. One student explained, "You'll most likely get housing if you want it, but you have to be on top of the deadlines." All of the rooms are doubles and triples, and some doubles used to be triples, so "they're pretty big." The honors dorms have suites, which include a living room and two doubles.

There is an RA on each floor and a Residential Health Director in each building, and while they do enforce the strict no-alcohol policy of the dorms, they are usually "nice and will work with you in other areas." However, "you will get in trouble and your alcohol will be confiscated if you're going to be dumb about it." New Hall is the newest dorm and is thought to be the nicest, while Earle Hall is known for housing a lot of theater majors.

Off-campus housing is apparently more difficult to find, since there are "few apartments for college students" due to the rich residential neighborhood around the campus. When they do find housing, it is usually pretty expensive as well. Students say that pricey off-campus housing is the reason why so many choose to live at home.

Downtown Garden City, a mile away, offers some shopping, including a popular mall, movies, and the nearest grocery store. A shuttle bus takes students to and from the downtown district, but "it can be unreliable or not frequent enough." It's a good idea to bring a car so you can get out of the area, but "the traffic gets pretty bad" and "one of the biggest problems on campus right now is the lack of parking available." However, the university is working to construct a new parking facility.

Students who live on campus are required to purchase a meal plan, however, many do so unwillingly. The food is reportedly "absolutely terrible," but there are other on-campus options, like at Post Hall, which houses a Sbarro's, the Panther Grill and a convenience store, where students can use their meal cards like credit cards. Overall, though, there "isn't much variety and the food is of dubious quality" in the two dining halls. Students say they order takeout from local restaurants a couple times a week and sometimes go out to eat on the weekends. The nearby Chinese and Italian restaurants are "especially good," but "if you drive you can find a lot more options."

Getting Involved

One problem that many students pointed out about student involvement on campus is that it seems very low and apathetic. A senior said that she feels like "people just want to sit around and complain about how there's nothing to do instead of taking advantage of campus events." However, Adelphi does boast a number of organizations that attract loyal followings, such as the Theater Club, the NAACP, Circle K and its student newspaper, the *Delphian*. Many students also get involved in the Student Government Association, which allows them to voice their opinions about the Adelphi community and lobby for change.

> **"You won't get lost in the crowd at Adelphi."**

Adelphi is the home of a men's Division I soccer team, and all its other teams are Division II. Students say that "it's not a big athletic school, but a lot of people are interested in going to the games and supporting the Panthers." In fact, one of Adelphi's most fun annual traditions is Midnight Madness, when the men and women's basketball teams are announced at midnight at the beginning of the season, and the school's hip-hop team performs. One guy said, "It's one of the few events that almost everyone goes to and shows their school pride." For those who want to get more involved, intramural sports "always have flyers up" and can even get "intensely competitive."

Many students have jobs, whether working for the school on-campus or in the surrounding community. One popular off-campus option is working in the downtown mall. However, a particularly exciting aspect of attending Adelphi is the opportunity to participate in internships in New York City. Many students take advantage of this unique privilege and spend time learning more about their fields of interests.

While Adelphi may not be the typical college experience, it offers a variety of opportunities, from the excitement and internationalism of nearby New York City to renowned professional programs truly dedicated to preparing students for careers. While the school is ideal for many who are looking for a good school close to home, others may want to consider the additional advantages it holds. Even with the lack of an on-campus community, life at Adelphi is close-knit and friendly. As one student put it, "You won't get lost in the crowd at Adelphi."—*Kimberly Chow*

FYI

If you come to Adelphi, you'd better bring "a willingness to involve yourself in campus activities, because the school needs more participation."

What's the typical weekend schedule? "Hanging out with friends and having dinner on Friday, going to the City on Saturday, going to bars and clubs at night, or just going home for the weekend."

If I could change one thing about Adelphi, "I would increase communication between the administration and students, because sometimes I feel like I'm on my own when planning my studies."

Three things every student at Adelphi should do before graduating are "attend the Erotic Student Film Festival, participate in the Student Government Association, and sneak onto the roof of the science building for the great view."

Alfred University

Address: Alfred, Alumni Hall, 1 Saxon Drive, Alfred, NY 14802

Phone: 607-871-2115

E-mail Address: admwww@alfred.edu

Web site URL: www.alfred.edu/admissions/

Year Founded: 1836

Private or Public: private

Religious affiliation: none

Location: rural

Regular Application Deadline: Rolling

Number of Applicants: 2,134

Percent Accepted: 78%

Percent Accepted who enroll: 31%

Number Entering: 429

Number of Transfers Accepted each Year: 183

Mean SAT: 1,137

Mean ACT: 24

Middle 50% SAT range: 1,020–1,240 (writing not included)

Middle 50% ACT range: 21–27

Early admission program (EA/ ED/ NA): ED

ED or EA Acceptance Rate: 74%

Full time Undergraduate enrollment: 1,991

Total enrollment: 2,310

Percent Male: 48%

Percent Female: 52%

Total Percent Minority: 29%

Percent African-American: 6%

Percent Asian/Pacific Islander: 1%

Percent Hispanic: 3%

Percent Native-American: <1%

Percent Other: 18%

Percent in-state / out of state: 65%/35%

Percent from Public HS: NA

Retention Rate: 80%

Graduation Rate: 69%

Percent in On-campus housing: 67%

Percent affiliated with Greek system: NA

Percent Varsity or Club Athletes: NA

Number of official organized extracurricular organizations: 90

3 Most popular majors: Business Administration/ Management, Ceramic Sciences and Engineering, Fine/Studio Arts

Student/Faculty ratio: 12:01

Tuition and Fees: $22,100.00

Cost for Room and Board: $10,040.00

Percent receiving Financial aid, first-year: 90%

Set in a quaint and historic village in upstate New York, Alfred University is far from the frenetic pulse of Manhattan. But what the campus lacks in big-city glamour, it makes up for in small-town charm and rustic beauty. Alfred is described as a "welcoming" and "very liberal" school, with a "gorgeous campus" to boot. And don't let the University's small size fool you—with four separate schools, students can be sure to find a course of study that interests them. Home to a world-renowned ceramic engineering program, Alfred offers a plethora of academic opportunities for everyone from painters to engineers to aspiring CEOs.

An Academic Buffet

Incoming freshmen can apply to one of four schools: the College of Business, the School of Engineering, the School of Art and Design, or the College of Liberal Arts & Sciences. For those interested in entering the College of Business, Alfred offers degrees in accounting, business administration, finance and marketing. While all the schools are considered challenging, the School of Engineering is considered particularly work-intensive. Students also point out the internationally known School of Art & Design as offering a challenging but well-respected program. In the academic realm, Alfred is perhaps best known for its School of Ceramic Engineering. Boasting an international reputation, this "super-selective" school is the only center in the United States that offers a Ph.D. program in the field. As one student said, "Ceramics is definitely a big thing at Alfred." However, Ceramic Engineering's eminence also comes with a heavy workload—according to one student, "those people . . . never sleep."

Those seeking a more generalized course of study can enroll in the College of Liberal Arts and Sciences, which includes a First-Year Experience (FYE) Program. FYE aims to expand students' horizons by exploring issues of race, ethnicity and gender. The General Education Requirements also ensure that Liberal Arts students are exposed to a variety of topics. The requirements are divided into three "Basic Competencies": Writing, Foreign Language, and Quantitative Reasoning, as well as six "Areas of Knowledge": Literature, Philosophy or Religion, the Arts, Historical Studies, Natural Sciences, and Social Sciences. Students in all schools must take a course in physical education—"I guess they want us all to be fit," one student said.

Students who want to study the arts while still enjoying the breadth of a liberal arts education can participate in BAFA, a unique program which allows fine arts scholars to gain a Bachelor of Arts degree. Unlike those seeking entrance to the School of Art & Design, BAFA applicants don't need to submit a portfolio. However, the program does require that students meet all General Education requirements. Students say these differences prompt a light-hearted rivalry between Art School and BAFA students: "They just kind of rag on each other," said one student.

Alfred also has an honors program, which currently enrolls about 120 students. The program is known for offering seminars on unusual and intriguing topics. Recent course titles include "T'ai Chi," "Theory/Practice of Time Travel," and "Nip, Tuck, Perm, Pierce, and Tattoo: Adventures with Embodied Culture." In addition to enjoying classes on offbeat topics, program participants benefit from mentorship and thesis funding.

One benefit of attending a small university such as Alfred is small class size—most courses enroll fewer than 20 students and even large lectures remain below 100. Intimate class settings are a key attribute of the Alfred academic experience: "You're not just a number," one junior said. Not surprisingly, Alfred students form close bonds with their instructors that extend outside of the classroom: "We see them all over town." As a whole, professors at this liberal university are described as "accepting," "very accessible" and "easy to talk to."

The Daily Grind

Incoming students are housed in one of the many all-freshman dorms, which are corridor-style and coed. Among these halls, the newly renovated Barresi receives high marks, while the other freshman dorms are "not so nice." Openhym, one of the largest halls, includes large lounges on each floor and a late-night study area. Resident Advisors live with the freshmen. Students say they vary in strictness—some write up students frequently, while others are more laid-back. Upperclassmen dorms include Kruson, Bartlett and the Brick. The Brick, used as an infirmary during World War II, houses mostly junior and seniors. As the building is a coveted residence among upperclassmen, students say, one must get lucky in the housing lottery to claim a room there.

Alfred recently switched to a new dining service, and now features stations for stir fry, pizza, and grilled food. Students are generally pleased with the results. While the dining halls are still "working out the kinks," there are now a plethora of vegetarian options to choose from. However one student noted that the meal plan, required for those living on campus, is "ridiculously expensive." Students who tire of the dining hall can use their "dining dollars" as a debit card at two cafes on campus. Popular off-campus spots include the Terra Cotta Coffee House;

Old West; the Japanese café Nana's; and Café Za, a restaurant and bar.

Set in the foothills of the Allegheny Mountains, the University boasts a "gorgeous" and "very safe" campus. Historical brick architecture blends with the work of Alfred art students to create a "beautiful setting." One student noted that her favorite place on campus was the Bandstand, a huge gazebo beside the campus creek where students can be found playing drums on the weekends. The Powell Campus Center, which houses a radio station and most club meetings, is another popular hangout.

While the campus may be idyllic, town-gown relations aren't always as peaceful. "Our campus is super liberal, but as soon as you go across the street, it's super conservative," one student said. Tensions can arise with the local authorities. "The police hate us!" one sophomore said. In support of this claim, a student cited the $50 "disorderly conduct" fine she received from local police for skateboarding across campus at night. That said, students feel extremely safe on campus. The school provides security phones and an escort service for those walking home at night.

Sports fanatics be warned: At Alfred, arts easily trump athletics. As one student said, "If you want to be into sports, don't go to Alfred." Despite the more artistic vibe on campus, football and lacrosse games do attract fans. Intramural sports are popular, and the newly-renovated gym boasts a complete fitness center and nightly open swim. Popular extracurricular groups on campus include Pirate Theater, Spectrum (the gay, lesbian, bisexual and transgendered alliance) and the radio stations.

Seeking a Scene

When asked to describe her peers, one junior expressed her appreciation for the variety of "types" on campus. Indeed, the broad range of academic programs available at Alfred helps to ensure a diverse student body. Business students sporting "preppy collared shirts" intermingle with "artists wearing hippie clothes" and "normal liberal arts students wearing jeans and a sweater." However another student noted the prevalence of students from upstate New York who have "face-piercings and crazy hair" and "wear thrift store clothes, or sew their own clothes out of thrift store clothes." One student also noted the well-known clique of undergrads known as "Art Stars." "They make really weird art and then say you aren't as intellec-tually in tune with art as they are if you don't understand it."

Given Alfred's diverse student body and unique academic programs, it's no surprise that nightlife options aren't your typical university fare. Alfred abolished Greek organizations in 2002, following the fraternity-related death of a student. While those still yearning for the traditional frat party can head to nearby Alfred State, most students remain on campus. Instead of frequenting frat row, they gravitate toward off-campus get-togethers and art house parties featuring rock bands. The Student Activities Board also brings musicians and comedians to campus on a regular basis. Popular annual events include the Winter Blues Bash, Glam Slam and Hot Dog Day, a weekend of activities held in conjunction with Alfred State to raise money for charities. The weekend is marked by performances, a parade through town, street vendors selling hand-made pottery, and the mud Olympics. During the spring event, "alcohol runs freely through the streets," and students get a welcome break from their studies.

An Eye-Opening Education

Not only has the lack of Greek activity not hindered Alfred's night life, but it may contribute to the freethinking atmosphere that characterizes the school. "The campus has gotten really liberal since they've gotten rid of the frats and sororities," one student said. "Tolerance has definitely gone up a lot." Another cited the support among students and administration alike for Spectrum's "Gay? Fine by Me" T-shirt campaign as testament of the open-minded atmosphere that pervades campus.

> "The campus has gotten really liberal since they've gotten rid of the frats and sororities."

For those looking to study art, ceramic engineering, business or the liberal arts, Alfred University offers stellar academic programs in a quaint, picturesque village. The small-town surroundings and tight-knit campus make it easy for students to form fast friendships. But what students emphasize most about Alfred is its liberal, open-minded atmosphere. One previously "sheltered" student described her experience at Alfred as a "real eye-opener."—*Chrissy Levine*

FYI

If you come to Alfred, you'd better bring: "an open mind—if not, people won't even talk to you. And a really heavy coat."

What's the typical weekend schedule? "Friday: go to Nevan's theater on campus to watch a movie; Saturday: sleep in, brunch, basketball game, go dancing with your friends; Sunday: sleep in, wake up at noon, study all day."

If I could change one thing about Alfred, I'd "change the hills. It's beautiful, but it's a pain in the butt to walk everywhere."

Three things every student at Alfred should do before graduating are: "Participate in Mud Olympics, go dumpster diving, and get a radio station."

Bard College

Address: Bard, 30 Campus Road, Box 5000, Annandale-on-Hudson, NY 12504-5000

Phone: 845-758-7472

E-mail Address: admission@bard.edu

Web site URL: www.bard.edu/admission/

Year Founded: 1860

Private or Public: private

Religious affiliation: Episcopal Church

Location: rural

Regular Application Deadline: 16-Jan

Number of Applicants: 4,828

Percent Accepted: 29%

Percent Accepted who enroll: 36%

Number Entering: 498

Number of Transfers Accepted each Year: 21

Mean SAT: 1,330

Mean ACT: NA

Middle 50% SAT range: 1,320–1,430 (reading not included)

Middle 50% ACT range: NA

Early admission program (EA/ ED/ NA): EA

ED or EA Acceptance Rate: 60%

Full time Undergraduate enrollment: 1,735

Total enrollment: 2,012

Percent Male: 47%

Percent Female: 53%

Total Percent Minority: 32%

Percent African-American: 3%

Percent Asian/Pacific Islander: 3%

Percent Hispanic: 3%

Percent Native-American: 1%

Percent Other: 22%

Percent in-state / out of state: 27%/73%

Percent from Public HS: 64%

Retention Rate: 87%

Graduation Rate: 74%

Percent in On-campus housing: 77%

Percent affiliated with Greek system: NA

Percent Varsity or Club Athletes: NA

Number of official organized extracurricular organizations: 70

3 Most popular majors: Visual and Performing Arts, Social Sciences, English

Student/Faculty ratio: 9:01

Tuition and Fees: $34,782.00

Cost for Room and Board: $9,850.00

Percent receiving Financial aid, first-year: 86%

Small classes, no core curriculum, and clubs like "The Surrealist Circus"—all of these are typical of Bard College. Located in upstate New York, Bard provides interested students with a very unique type of liberal arts education and the opportunity to explore all kinds of enjoyable activities during their four years—even if they involve juggling.

Academics of Choice

At Bard, students are required to design their own course of study based on what admissions materials term as a "series of active choices." This decidedly active role in shaping one's own curriculum allows students to focus in on the area they most want to explore. But this doesn't mean there are no distributional requirements. Although the requirements include, for example, a laboratory science course, such classes can thankfully be fulfilled by the likes of "Acoustics"—though one junior claimed he had to remain on a "wait list for two or three semesters before getting a chance to take it." Despite the fact that at first glance, the requirements seem to be easy, they can often be neglected by students in favor of a more major-intensive curriculum. "My advisors are brilliant professors, but maybe not as helpful as they could have been," explained one student who realized in the middle of his junior year that he was missing five distributional requirements. He also emphasized, however, that professors are "very accessible . . . and give a lot of individualized attention," even personal comments on student transcripts.

The most popular majors at Bard include film and music, which are also extremely competitive. "There is a cold-calloused filtering system . . . professors in the film department won't take you seriously until you actually declare that you're a film major," one student warned. Other difficult majors include economics and political science. Students claim that the least popular major at Bard is "probably Business Skills . . . considering the strong distaste for capitalism here." Others complained, however, that few business-related classes are offered at Bard.

A Change of Party Scenery

Bard was once known as one of the biggest party schools in the U.S. In the last couple of years, however, there has been a "massive fragmentation" of the traditional party scene at Bard, forcing students to find other options for the building known as the "Old Gym," which once housed famous events such as "drag races." At present, a few years after the Old Gym's closure to social events, no good candidates for a new location have been found. "There's some controversy over the newer options," one student explained. And although many mourn the drastic change in the party scene at Bard, others say it is still "not as bad as other schools . . . we still live up to [our reputation], though it's much tamer than we used to be."

Political Un-Diversity

Bard is notorious for being one of the most liberal schools in America. "Politically, Bard is not diverse at all," one student explained. "Ethnically there's some diversity, but mostly the student body is composed of wealthy, white, moneyed Americans." The students, however, are known to be extremely friendly and open-minded and, as one student put it, there is "no place where it's cooler to be gay than Bard." Putnam County, where Bard is located, is a well-known right-wing stronghold, but students claim there is no tension between the community and the more conservative college affiliates.

Tranquil, Beautiful, Isolated

Bard is located next to the Hudson River, and has some remarkable views of the Catskill Mountains. The natural surroundings, however, aren't all that Bard has to offer. Its architecture is greatly varied and noteworthy, too. The Blithewood Manor, home to the Levy Economics Institute, is frequented by students in warmer weather to hang out in the gardens. "We'll go and watch the sunset . . . the views are really beautiful." Also, the new Fisher Center for the Performing Arts, designed by Frank Gehry, is extremely popular with both tourists and students.

As for dorms, there exists a fair amount of variety. Students can choose from a Vegan co-op, the hotel-like Robbins house, or the ecologically sound Village Dorms (among many others). The Upper College Village Dorms, designed in conjunction with Bard students, are constructed from non-virgin timber sources, and are heated through a geothermal heat exchange system. About half of the dorms have singles, and most of them are co-ed. Students who live on campus are required to have a meal plan, which caters to vegans, vegetarians, and non-vegetarians. The food is in general pretty good, but one student warned that, "the fish and pork should definitely be avoided."

Clubs and Circuses

There are approximately 60 student organizations at Bard. One of the most well-known clubs on campus is the Surrealist Circus made up of some of the "most creative and boldest people here, in a place where there are many creative and bold people." Bard also boasts several model student civic groups, such as the Bard New Orleans Project, which sent 150 student-volunteers to help repair some of the flood damage incurred by Hurricane Katrina. There is a general lack of enthusiasm for sports at Bard, but that doesn't mean that there aren't any. Soccer is probably the most popular sport on campus, due in part to the lavish facilities donated by an heir to the Ferrari fortune. There are several varsity and club sports for those who wish to get their athleticism on.

> "I fell in love with this place and have no desire to leave."

Although the Bard College experience requires dedication and foresight on the behalf of the students, studying at Bard is incredibly rewarding. As one student put it, "On my first visit to Bard I thought it was a wondrous institution, and so far I have not been proven wrong. I fell in love with this place and have no desire to leave."
—Melissa-Victoria King

FYI

If you come to Bard, you'd better bring "a bike."

What's a typical weekend schedule? "There is no typical anything here. There are many exceptions to week rules."

If I could change one thing about Bard, I'd "Give athletes the ability to pre-register for morning classes, so they don't interfere with practice and games."

Three things every student at Bard should do before graduating Bard are "Attend an American symphony orchestra performance or theatrical production at the Fisher center, see the Surrealist circus perform in the spring, and attend one of the infamous *Moderator* magazine release parties.

Barnard College

Address: Barnard, 3009 Broadway, New York, NY 10027

Phone: 212-854-2014

E-mail Address: admissions@barnard.edu

Web site URL: www.barnard.edu/admiss/

Year Founded: 1889

Private or Public: private

Religious affiliation: none

Location: urban

Regular Application Deadline: 2-Jan

Number of Applicants: 4,599

Percent Accepted: 26%

Percent Accepted who enroll: NA

Number Entering: 556

Number of Transfers Accepted each Year: 119

Mean SAT: 1,355

Mean ACT: 30

Middle 50% SAT range: 1,920–2,190

Middle 50% ACT range: 29–31

Early admission program (EA/ ED/ NA): ED

ED or EA Acceptance Rate: 38%

Full time Undergraduate enrollment: 2,350

Total enrollment: 2350

Percent Male: 0%

Percent Female: 100%

Total Percent Minority: 34%

Percent African-American: 3%

Percent Asian/Pacific Islander: 18%

Percent Hispanic: 9%

Percent Native-American: <1%

Percent Other: 3%

Percent in-state / out of state: 34%/66%

Percent from Public HS: 64%

Retention Rate: 96%

Graduation Rate: 87%

Percent in On-campus housing: 91%

Percent affiliated with Greek system: NA

Percent Varsity or Club Athletes: NA

Number of official organized extracurricular organizations: 100

3 Most popular majors: Public Administration and Social Services, Psychology, English

Student/Faculty ratio: 10:01

Tuition and Fees: $33,078.00

Cost for Room and Board: $11,392.00

Percent receiving Financial aid, first-year: 100%

A supportive all-women's college located in the greatest city in the world with access to caring, famous professors and an Ivy University across the street? Yep, that's Barnard for you. Located in the neighborhood of Morningside Heights in New York City, Barnard has been educating women for more than a century. With a top-notch curriculum and a diverse student body, Barnard continues to educate modern women for the 21st century.

Core Curriculum with a Barnard Twist

Academics at Barnard are taken seriously. As one student said, "if you are a slacker, you don't really go here. Or you do and leave." As an independent affiliate of Columbia University and as a liberal arts school with a hefty core curriculum, students are fully aware of their academic responsibilities. The core requirements, more individualized and woman-oriented than Columbia's, introduce students to a variety of topics, aiming to create well-versed women who can tackle a math problem as well as remark on the fine details of a Rembrandt painting. The core includes an interdisciplinary First-Year Seminar, First-Year English, physical education, and courses fulfilling the nine "Ways of Knowing," which includes topics such as historical studies, languages, and visual & performing arts, as well as laboratory sciences and quantitative & deductive reasoning. Students have varied opinions on the core classes. Some wish the requirements did not exist, while others are thankful for the opportunity to take "classes which you might otherwise shy away from. Frequently, you end up finding your major in one of those requirements you wouldn't have otherwise taken."

The reported hard majors at Barnard are natural sciences, economics, and political science. Film and art are difficult time-wise, and women's studies, dance, and English receive high marks. Class sizes vary and can consist of 20 to 200 people depending on the subject and type of class (lectures versus seminars and colloquiuma). One fact that students are very enthusiastic about is that "TAs simply don't exist." One side effect of keeping class sizes small and TAs out of the picture, however, is that students report some difficulty trying to get into popular classes. One Barnard student described "waiting in line for hours just to get your name on a list for class is somewhat hopeless," but well worth it if the effort succeeds.

> "It's all women who care about the world and care about succeeding in even the most male-dominated professions. It's very empowering."

An added benefit of belonging to Barnard College is that one can go across the street and take classes at Columbia College, as Barnard is technically called Barnard College *at* Columbia University. Barnard students can take classes at Columbia and vice versa, both of which are frequently done. However, one junior did admit that "being a Barnard student in a joint class that happens to meet at Columbia can be difficult" due to the fact that "some Columbia students are not comfortable with the idea of Barnard girls in their classes. After all, they applied to Columbia, and we did not." However, alternatively, many students found that Columbia students had no problem taking class with them, especially because many of them take classes at Barnard themselves. While the workload can be whatever you choose to make it, students say that academics are competitive and most people do a lot of work, but that's what college is supposed to be about. The academics can be described in three sentences. As one student said, "It's Barnard. It's top-notch. It's great."

Social Life

For a college student, New York City is a great backyard. On the weekends students gravitate toward downtown for shows, museums, and club and bar hopping. "Most places here or downtown don't card," said a student. Favorite haunts for Barnard students include Starbucks, the West End, the Abbey, the Heights, 1020 and Mona. Nondrinkers, however, do not feel left out of the social scene. In fact, one student says, "One-third of students don't ever drink."

Women at Barnard do go out on dates and attend semi-formals a few times a year, as guys can be found at any one of the numerous colleges around town including Columbia, Julliard, Fordham, Marymount College and the Manhattan School of Music. Also, according to one junior, "Most of my friends meet guys off campus just randomly, which is the beauty of New York City—you're not restricted to your campus." However, according to one senior, students mostly go out in groups as opposed to dating. A student center helps create a centralized place of interaction for students where they can go to the snack bar, lounge, student store, and music practice rooms. There is a very small Greek population at Barnard, but those who are in it seem to enjoy it immensely. While not absent, students report that alcohol and drugs on campus do not seem to be a problem. Many Barnard women are active in clubs, sports teams and artistic endeavors, and they report that most of their good friends come from these outside activities.

Living on the Edge

More than 90 percent of Barnard students live on campus because of the exorbitant rents for Manhattan abodes off campus. Students can choose to live in a Barnard/Columbia dorm, off-campus, or in Barnard's dorms. Living off-campus isn't something students suggest. One said, "20 and alone in a big city? Harlem? No." Students complain that the dorms are very small, especially on the Quad, where most freshmen live and where one is required to have a meal plan. One aspect of on-campus living that Barnard students enjoy, however, is the special housing options available. "You can find a house for basically whatever your heart desires, or you can make your own and get special interest housing with your friends," one student said. Students warn that rooms should be kept "very, very clean" due to pest problems in New York City buildings. However, as one student assured, "exterminators are easily reachable." As far as counseling goes, an RA (Resident Advisers) system allows students to get advice and guidance. Students report that the RAs are not strict and want to be friends as opposed to authority figures.

Students speak highly of Barnard's four-acre campus. Barnard's beautiful architecture, steps, and green space in the middle of a bustling city are a welcome change from the usual city high-rises. In fact, one student mentioned that "the main walk through campus is called 'College Walk.' It was 116th street . . . and is this gorgeous brick walk now lined with tall trees." Students report that they feel safe at Barnard, "more so than elsewhere," one student commented, "even though there have been some instances of sexual assault in the campus area."

Where to Chow Down and Chill Out

Students have no major complaints about the dining hall food, besides the fact that there are only a limited number of places to eat, including two dining halls on campus and one at Columbia. Vegan and kosher options are readily available, and students boast of the abundance of ethnic food offered. Many people, though, cook in their apartments or out to eat at local restaurants—Le Monde for French food, the West End for Burgers, Tomo for Japanese and Sophia's for Italian.

While people are very dedicated to community service and extracurriculars at Barnard, sports do not seem to draw such a large crowd. There are intramurals that people can participate in, but students report that there is not not much interest in sports because "all Barnard athletes compete on Columbia's teams . . . but Columbia's teams in general are really bad, so it's a touchy issue," said one student.

The Skinny

Students report that one of the greatest aspects about the school is that it's all female. "It's all women who care about the world and care about succeeding in even the most male-dominated professions. It's very empowering," one senior said. At Barnard, students obtain the tools to continue changing the world, while the world of New York City continues to change around them as well. As one junior commented, "What happened here? American Revolution. Manhattan Project. Riots of '68. What didn't happen here?"—*Lisa Siciliano*

FYI
If you come to Barnard, you'd better bring "black pants and a MetroCard."
What is the typical weekend schedule? "Fridays are usually filled with labs if you're premed, sections, office hours, or are used for recovering from Thursday night. On weekend nights, most people go out around campus or head downtown to have fun. But pretty much you can find people working all the time."
If I could change one thing about Barnard, I'd "change housing and the way the administration communicates with the students about it."
Three things every student at Barnard should do before graduating are "go to midnight breakfast where the deans serve breakfast in the gym the night before finals start, learn the school song, and have a debate with a Columbia student on why Barnard is better."

City University of New York System

The City University of New York (CUNY-pronounced "kyoony") has been undergoing ground-breaking changes that its Chancellor Matthew Goldstein hopes will "redefine and substantially broaden the view of the role and promise of a public urban university." CUNY's 2004–2008 Master Plan Amendment, approved by New York State, proposes a number of high-reaching goals, such as enhancing research opportunities, expanding academic support for students, and increasing full-time faculty instruction to 70 percent. In 2006, the Chancellor called upon the state to provide further support for CUNY and fully restore the Tuition Assistance Program, which helps New York residents finance their education. These efforts ensure that CUNY will continue to improve its academic image, strengthen its offerings, and yield a high retention rate of its students in the years to come.

Variety and Different Focus
CUNY is one of the largest university systems in the world with more than 220,000 students on 23 campuses throughout the five boroughs of New York. The system includes 11 undergraduate colleges, six community colleges, one technical school, and five graduate schools; the Graduate School of Journalism, led by former *Business Week* Editor-in-Chief Stephen Shepard, opened in Fall 2006. An additional 230,000 part-time and continuing-education adult students attend a CUNY school. The school's student body reflects the city's ethnic diversity: 30 percent of students are black, 28 percent white, 27 percent Hispanic and 16 percent Asian. Although the differences among colleges are immense, nearly all the students interviewed mentioned the word "bureaucratic." As one student said, the colleges are "run by the city of New York, so basically . . . anyone you deal with at the administrative level gives you the same attitude you would expect at the Department of Motor Vehicles."

A Good Deal
Yet despite the dissatisfaction with the administration, most CUNY students feel they're getting a good education and a good deal. The huge variety of night courses attracts a large population of students who work during the day. All of this is available at a price made more reasonable by the fact that most students are from New York and can live at home, which is "a big reason" many students choose CUNY schools. According to one undergrad, "Most students I know here work and are from families where that's necessary." Understandably, most students take up to six years to graduate and the graduation rate is low.

Each school has its individual strengths. "[Each college] has different concentrations," one student said. "Hunter has a big nursing school; at Queens, it's English; at Baruch, it's business; and The City College covers the technical areas: engineering and computer science." According to students, these individual strengths help them decide which school to attend. "If a student lives in Brooklyn, and wants to be an English major, it's not that big a commute—he'll go to Queens," one student explained.

Grab Bag
Campus environments vary as well. Students describe the colleges in Manhattan as more fast-paced and urban than those in the other boroughs; they are also considered "more liberal" and "free." According to one undergrad, some students from suburban Long Island "come to Queens and are in awe of it—if they went to Manhattan, they'd have a heart attack. The culture is different in Long Island: you really don't see anyone with a shaved head and nose ring walking around the other campuses." Students in Manhattan say, "It's Manhattan"—in the middle of everything, creating an extremely diverse and exciting environment.

Admissions criteria depend on the individual school. Spaces in the community colleges are guaranteed to New York students who have earned a high school diploma, while the four-year schools maintain more selective admissions policies. Overall, students praise the faculty as one of the CUNY system's greatest assets. "We have a lot of really fine teachers here," one student said. Others described their professors as "gifted people as well as gentle and giving teachers," and "excellent, and nationally renowned."

New York City serves as both CUNY's campus and its source of extracurricular activities; a CUNY ID can get a student discounts at many museums, galleries, and theaters around town. One student even claimed that "if you make arrangements, there's hardly a museum in the city that won't let you in for free." However, this does not prevent some CUNY schools from having strong extracurriculars, including newspapers, clubs, and student government.

Students generally agree that the CUNY system provides a solid education for people of all ages, interests, schedules, and backgrounds. General Colin Powell and Jerry Seinfeld are two of many distinguished alumni of the CUNY system, as is the current Chancellor Goldstein. The colleges are reportedly "malleable to the individual student's ambitions" and meet the changing needs of a remarkably diverse population. According to one student, "Overall, the administration is pretty unpopular, but the teaching is informative if you choose the right courses—it's a good education."—*Seung Lee and Staff*

City University of New York / City College

Address: 160 Convent Avenue; New York, NY 10031	**Percent Asian:** 22%	**Early Decision or Early Action Acceptance Rate:** NA
Phone: 212-650-6977	**Percent Hispanic:** 36%	
	Percent Native-American: 0%	**Application Deadline:** rolling
E-mail address: admissions@ccny.cuny.edu	**Percent in-state/out of state:** 97%/3%	**Mean SAT:** NA
		Mean ACT: NA
Web site URL: www.ccny.cuny.edu	**Percent Pub HS:** NA	**Middle 50% SAT range:** 830–1,100%
	On-campus housing: 0%	
Founded: 1847	**Fraternities:** NA	**Middle 50% ACT range:** NA
Private or Public: public	**Sororities:** NA	**Most popular majors:** social sciences, engineering, biology
Religious affiliation: NA	**Number of Applicants:** 6,584	
Location: urban	**Percent Accepted:** 35%	**Retention:** 78%
Undergraduate enrollment: 9,117		**Graduation rate:** 29%
	Percent Accepted who enroll: 5%	**Tuition and Fees:** $10,979
Total enrollment: 12,108	**Entering class:** 1,171	**In State Tuition and Fees (if different):** $4,179
Percent Male/Female: 49%/51%	**Transfers:** 1	**Room and Board:** NA
Percent Minority: 87%	**Early admission program (EA/ED/NA):** NA	**Financial aid, first-year:** NA
Percent African-American: 29%		**Varsity or Club Athletes:** NA
		Library: 1,413,641 volumes

What's it like to go to college in the heart of Harlem? Just ask the students of City College of New York (CCNY). About 10 street blocks in length and two avenues wide, the campus of CCNY is at the center of a vibrant neighborhood. Everything from local restaurants to annual festivities projects the community's diversity and invites exploration by CCNY's eager and adventurous students.

A Cultural Hotbed

At CCNY, "everyone's different and has their distinct personalities," said one freshman, who was amazed by the diversity of the student body and its active involvement on campus and in the Harlem community. Located in the heart of one of the most diverse cities in the world, CCNY attracts students who are open to learning about others: "There's a mixing of cultures here; you won't see a black table or an Asian table in the cafeteria." CCNY students are, as a rule, very involved in extracurriculars. "There are so many clubs, and people are always outside the cafeteria encouraging people to join," commented one student. These clubs can be both serious in focus, like the AIDS- and cancer-awareness organizations, or more recreational in nature, like the Jackass Club, which gets together to perform "stupid stunts," or the Game Club, "for dweebs who get together to play the latest video games." Community service activities are among the most popular, as students frequent local soup kitchens and help out with toy drives. While most agree that there isn't a stereotypical CCNY student, all seem to share the ability to multi-task. Most students work part-time and attend classes full-time. For example, one particularly busy student attended classes full-time, worked in the student government, helped with the History Club, was very involved with his church, tutored children two days a week, and helped coach a youth football team.

> **"There's a mixing of cultures here."**

Students enjoy the resources in the city around them and the "awesome variety of food and cultures in Harlem." According to one junior, "the culture is so rich in Harlem, you can easily find food from every culture from West Indian to Asian." Currently, New York City is investing a large amount of money in the area to build shopping centers and draw public attention to the neighborhood's rich history. As another junior noted, "Harlem is going to be one of the premier shopping districts in New York City. People who once looked to midtown [Manhattan] as the place to shop will soon discover Harlem."

Making the Rent
CCNY is distinctive because, unlike most colleges, there are no dormitories for students. The school does own The Towers, an apartment style building, where around 600 students are housed first come first serve. These are charged much like normal apartments, only included in financial aid. Without much on-campus housing, most opt to live at home or rent apartments near campus. One student who lives at home reported that most CCNY students come from the five boroughs of New York City, though a few commute in from the surrounding suburbs. A convenient CCNY bus picks students up every 15 minutes from the nearest subway station and drops them off at campus. Another freshman reported that while he takes three subways to get to school each day, "the difficult commute is not really a problem, since the subway is right by the college."

To help with accommodations, a campus agency does provide some assistance in the search for affordable housing. However, one sophomore expressed frustration with the service. "A lot of people apply for housing, but most are still waiting," he said. A freshman warned, "I'm telling you, it's not cheap." Harlem's economic resurgence, while great for the neighborhood and for the overall City College experience, is driving up real-estate prices in the area. Students reported paying no less than $1,000 a month for small, one-bedroom or studio apartments in nearby brownstones. To help pay for the rent, many CCNY students take part-time jobs after classes and on the weekends. The work-study program offers students great opportunities to learn and make some money at the same time. According to one student, "It's not a problem to find work. I always see students working in the library and various offices."

Not Exactly Social Butterflies
Without dorms to structure campus living, the weekend experience at CCNY is different than at most schools. Since most students head home after their classes and extracurricular commitments are finished and stay off-campus for the weekends, CCNY "is not too big on social life." The school does sponsor a Kick-Off party at the beginning of each semester, and another party every month, usually held in Shepherd Hall or in the gym. Turnouts for these events vary; the first party of the semester reportedly had so many people that it was shut down, while in other cases students admitted being "too lazy to go back to campus for the parties." At CCNY, according to one junior, "weekends usually don't revolve around the school, except for doing school-work."

Despite the mostly non-existent party scene, there is a plethora of daytime on-campus activities to enrich the City College experience. The school organizes many free concerts and has hosted a number of motivational speakers. Recently, concert pianist Jeni Slotchiver visited and entertained students from CCNY and other area colleges with several pieces. Luncheons and dinners with well-recognized authors, poets, and other speakers also draw large crowds. Last year, Walter Cronkite, who used to teach at CCNY, came and spoke, and currently students are eagerly awaiting the visit of ex-Secretary of State (and alumnus) Colin Powell. Other notable speakers have included Russell Simmons, the producer of Def Jam Records, as well as Senator Charles Schumer and Governor George Pataki.

Students agree that there is a strong sense of school spirit. According to one junior, "because of City College's 150-year history, everyone feels proud of the school." Walking around New York City, you'll see people wearing their City College sweatshirts, and the sense of community and camaraderie is nothing new—this is "the way the college has always been."

Climbing the Educational Ladder

The self-proclaimed "best of CUNY," City College students are generally very satisfied with the education they receive. According to one history major, the toughest major offered is "without a doubt electrical engineering, though biochem is also rough." Although it is difficult, the strongest program at CCNY is engineering, and in recent years this and the other science programs have grown quickly. CCNY also offers a variety of special premedical options, including the Sophie Davis program, a seven-year track that partners with the State University of New York's Downstate Medical Center. For those students who don't want to struggle through years of hard classes, CCNY students report that there is one easy major: psychology. "[It's] the prettiest major to have. Everyone ends up with a high grade."

In order to smooth the transition to college life, a block system was recently instituted for CCNY freshmen. In this system, 20 to 30 first-year students are grouped together and attend the same classes with the same professors their first semester. One block participant raved that this is a "great way for freshmen to get to know some faces and gives them a set schedule for their first semester, so that they'll be ready to pick their own classes second semester." Students are placed in blocks based on their intended major, but most of the block classes are in the liberal arts. By pairing three liberal-arts courses with one course for their major, the block system gives freshmen "a fuller view of what the school has to offer" and what another student calls "a community feel." In ad-

dition, all freshmen have to take a "freshman seminar," which teaches time-management and study skills, encourages them to explore the city, and offers general counseling services. While students receive no credit for the freshman seminar, most are glad to have it. As one freshman noted: "In high school you're stressed [by teachers] about doing this and doing that; here it's up to you. You can go to class or not—you decide whether to take the education for granted. They don't take attendance here, so you're really responsible for yourself."

CCNY professors recognize that learning takes place both in and out of the classroom. Art and music professors in particular like to send their students to the Metropolitan Museum of Art and to the Museum of Natural History for projects. At CCNY, all grades given are whole letters; there are no pluses or minuses to be found. According to one junior, this motivates students to work harder, as they will not be complacent and settle for what would usually be a B+ when they could put in a little more work and earn that A.

And there are certainly a number of good places to work or to hang out on-campus. Many CCNY students bring their laptops to the library and cafeteria, where they can work and eat at the same time. The cafeteria offers deli sandwiches, rice and beans, and other fast food at a reasonable price. Students will often kick off their sneakers and take a little nap, and "occasionally you'll hear a little snore" in between classes. Students also named Shepherd Hall and the Game Room as good places to unwind— "you see a lot of guys in the Game Room, so if you're a single female, that's definitely where you want to go."

For anyone looking for a good education in an urban setting—at a fair price, no less— City College is definitely worth checking out. The students are friendly, active, and as diverse as the Harlem area itself. CCNY students don't miss having "a cute little dorm room," because they have a whole city to explore.—*Jenny Zhang*

FYI
If you come to City College, you'd better bring a "planner to keep up with all the things going on" and "a cell phone, because you'll get a lot of numbers from all the cute girls."
What is the typical weekend schedule? "Sleep in on Friday, work, then party on Saturday, and work and sleep on Sunday."
If I could change one thing about City College, I'd "add dorms."
Three things every student at City College should do before graduating are "visit every building, go to a jazz concert, and do something dramatic."

City University of New York / Hunter College

Address: CUNY—Hunter, 695 Park Avenue, Room 100 North Bldg., New York, NY 10021
Phone: 212-772-4490
E-mail Address: admissions@hunter.cuny.edu
Web site URL: http://admissions.hunter.cuny.edu/
Year Founded: 1870
Private or Public: public
Religious affiliation: none
Location: urban
Regular Application Deadline: 15-Mar
Number of Applicants: NA
Percent Accepted: 34%
Percent Accepted who enroll: 25%
Number Entering: NA
Number of Transfers Accepted each Year: NA
Mean SAT: 1,076

Mean ACT: NA
Middle 50% SAT range: 490–580V, 500–600M
Middle 50% ACT range: NA
Early admission program (EA/ ED/ NA): NA
ED or EA Acceptance Rate: NA
Full time Undergraduate enrollment: 14,434
Total enrollment: NA
Percent Male: 32%
Percent Female: 68%
Total Percent Minority: 50%
Percent African-American: 14%
Percent Asian/Pacific Islander: 17%
Percent Hispanic: 10%
Percent Native-American: 0%
Percent Other: 11%
Percent in-state / out of state: 96%/4%

Percent from Public HS: 70%
Retention Rate: 82%
Graduation Rate: 11%
Percent in On-campus housing: 4%
Percent affiliated with Greek system: 2%
Percent Varsity or Club Athletes: NA
Number of official organized extracurricular organizations: 130
3 Most popular majors: Accounting, English language, Psychology
Student/Faculty ratio: 16:01
Tuition and Fees: NA
In State Tuition and Fees (if different): $4,000.00
Percent receiving Financial aid, first-year: 67%

L ocated in the heart of a great cultural center, Hunter College in New York City has an extremely diverse undergraduate community, dedicated professors at the top of their fields and solid educational opportunities. Dubbed a "mini-NYC" by students and boasting an academic program offering independent-minded undergrads plenty of freedom, Hunter is a place rich in both diversity and opportunity for those who choose to attend it.

Academic Opportunities

Students cite nursing, education and the performing arts as the best departments at Hunter, with English and communications also garnering high praise. The honors program offers interdisciplinary courses to qualified students, which allows them to devote less attention to core requirements and more to their majors. Hunter also offers study-abroad programs in Europe, Africa, Asia, South America and the Caribbean, with Europe being the most popular destination.

The college's distribution requirements include lab science; several courses in the hu-

manities; music, sociology or economics; and four semesters of a language. Few students complain about these requirements. Classes can be as large as 300 in the sciences and introductory lectures, and as small as 10 in the upper-division and honors classes. Evening sessions are popular at Hunter, especially among the many students holding day jobs.

Students say professors are supportive and "treat us as human beings." At least 50 percent of the staff is adjunct professors, whom students say are outstanding. Students don't have as much access to these professors, however, because adjuncts have neither on-campus phone numbers nor offices. For the most part, students say they must make appointments to see their professors. "The professors are there but students have to make the effort to get help," claimed one undergraduate. TAs do not lead sections or teach classes.

Commuter School

Hunter's main academic buildings are uptown, on East 68th Street, but the only dorm is on 25th Street. A shuttle bus runs from the dorm to the campus every hour, and public transportation is abundant. First- and second-year students generally remain at the school for the whole day. Between classes, they hang out or study in the cafeterias, hallways, lounges, or club offices. Although Hunter is primarily a commuter school, students say it's easier to meet classmates and become involved in campus life if they live in the dorm, which houses about 400 people. Most of the dorm residents are in the nursing, physical therapy, athletics or honors programs. With no meal plan, students are forced to dine in the neighborhood's numerous eateries or, as most prefer, prepare food for themselves in the kitchens located on every dorm floor. Each dorm room has the added convenience of a sink. Many undergrads go to Hunter's library to study. As one sophomore put it, the silence is "like a cemetery." Commuter students generally opt to study at home.

New York City provides students with countless options for entertainment including, but hardly limited to, world-famous theaters, restaurants, and museums. Campus parties are rare, and students say drinking is rare as well. Sororities and fraternities play a minor role in campus life, occupying no houses and performing charity work as their main activity. Cultural clubs organize some social events such as dances and rallies. RAs (Resident Advisors) on each floor of the dorm sponsor activities each month, ranging from a papier-mâché night to game nights.

Politically Active

The fact that most Hunter students hail from New York, New Jersey or Connecticut does not at all imply a homogeneous student body. According to one student, "It's incredible; everyone's completely different, yet they live together in harmony." Another student called Hunter a "mini-NYC." Many students are politically active, especially concerning issues of racism, feminism, abortion rights, the environment, gay and lesbian rights, and AIDS. The student branch of New York Public Interest Resource Group (PIRG) gets students involved in both environmental and campus issues. The active student senate represents academic departments, school interest, and students at large. One student said anyone can join the senate, although not everyone gets to vote. The teachers involved are said to be "top-notch."

Although sports are not a big priority oncampus, both basketball games and wrestling matches are well attended. Intramurals like volleyball are also quite popular. Hunter's athletic facilities receive positive reviews despite the complaint that, as one student put it, "they're hidden in the basement." Students read the *Hunter Envoy*, a biweekly newspaper, as well as other student publications. Ethnic organizations (such as the Asian-American, Caribbean, Greek, Puerto Rican and African-American clubs) are very popular, as are dance groups, choir, jazz band, and theater clubs. The student-run Shakespeare Society also produces a full play and a collection of scenes once a semester. No classes are held during Dean's Hours every Tuesday from 2 to 3 p.m. and Wednesday from 1 to 3 p.m., so that student clubs and organizations can hold meetings.

The City

The Hunter campus is truly part of the city. According to one student, "At times it's good because you're involved with the real world, but you also miss out on the things a private university in the city can offer, like a campus and unity." One undergraduate said there's "not really a campus, just some buildings together, and the dorm is by itself." Many students work full-time and consider school a "part-time thing." The city provides easy access to work and job openings.

> **"It's incredible; everyone's completely different, yet they live together in harmony."**

"The school is involved with the community, and the community is involved with the school," one student said. The area around Hunter is a commercial district, so it's busy, and students assert that they "blend in." The school has taken measures to ensure student safety, including emergency phones and guards that "roam around a lot." Each dorm resident is generally allowed no more than two guests at a time.

According to one student, "The teachers are at the top of their fields and really want to teach, but they're not teaching under the best conditions." Students are managing all the same, however. As one undergraduate pointed out, "It is a city school, and the tuition is still low."

One student warned incoming freshmen to "make sure you're on top of your education and getting what you want. No one's going to help you unless you ask for help." Another student suggested that if you're looking for a structured program and lots of guidance, Hunter might not be the best choice. But

Hunter students seem satisfied. "We get a much richer experience because of the huge diversity in terms of nationality and also in terms of age," one said. "This diversity gives a unique flavor to Hunter College." In fact, many undergrads see Hunter as a working model of the real world.—*Andrew Hamilton*

FYI

If you come to Hunter, you'd better bring "a map—the city and buildings can be confusing."

What is the typical weekend schedule? "A lot of people participate in student government and political activities on the weekend. Also, many like to go downtown or to midtown. The options are endless in the city."

If I could change one thing about Hunter, I'd "change the career adviser system. It is very impersonalized now and things can get overwhelming."

Three things every student at Hunter should do before graduating are "see a student drama production, eat from a street vendor, and walk across the third-floor bridge from the outside (all the buildings are connected by bridges)."

City University of New York / Queens College

Address: Queens College, Jefferson Hall Lobby, 65-30 Kissena Boulevard, Flushing, NY 11367
Phone: 718-997-5600
E-mail Address: NA
Web site URL: www.qc.cuny.edu/admissions/
Year Founded: 1937
Private or Public: public
Religious affiliation: none
Location: urban
Application and Admissions Information: rolling
Regular Application Deadline: NA
Number of Applicants: NA
Percent Accepted: NA
Percent Accepted who enroll: NA

Number Entering: NA
Number of Transfers Accepted each Year: NA
Mean SAT: NA
Mean ACT: NA
Middle 50% SAT range: NA
Middle 50% ACT range: NA
Early admission program (EA/ ED/ NA): NA
ED or EA Acceptance Rate: NA
Full time Undergraduate enrollment: 12,991
Total enrollment: 17,000
Percent Male: NA
Percent Female: NA
Total Percent Minority: NA
Percent African-American: NA
Percent Asian/Pacific Islander: NA

Percent Hispanic: NA
Percent Native-American: NA
Percent Other: NA
Percent in-state / out of state: NA
Percent from Public HS: NA
Retention Rate: NA
Graduation Rate: NA
Percent in On-campus housing: NA
Percent affiliated with Greek system: NA
Percent Varsity or Club Athletes: NA
Number of official organized extracurricular organizations: NA
3 Most popular majors: NA
Student/Faculty ratio: 17:01
Tuition and Fees: NA

Sprawled over 77 acres in the residential neighborhood of Flushing, NY, just a 30-minute drive from midtown Manhattan, Queens College offers "an incredibly beautiful view of the city skyline" and a convenient location for thousands of New York City students. Less apparent, but just as spectacular, are the vast array of academic, social, and extracurricular opportunities this commuter college provides.

An Amazing Academic Assortment

Queens College offers a variety of academic options to meet the needs of a diverse group of students. The college offers 63 majors, of which the most popular are accounting, sociology, business administration, and psychology (known as a "joke major" for its relative ease). There is also "a good load of people in the sciences," which are reportedly "incredibly tough"—"much harder" than other majors.

Whatever their major, all students are required to take at least 120 credits (each class is worth three to five credits, depending on difficulty), a Freshman English Course, and three additional writing intensive courses. They also must demonstrate competency in mathematics and a foreign language and complete Liberal Arts and Science Area Requirements (LASAR) in seven areas. The requirements are "somewhat inconvenient if you have a major that has lots of requirements in itself," but "it's actually not too bad to fulfill them—you just happen to end up taking them," and students averse to math and science can take "fake math and science classes" like statistics or psychology instead, while Urban Studies 101 is known as an easy way to fulfill the social science requirement. Freshmen get help planning their schedule during a mandatory advising session, and all students can consult the Advising Center on a drop-in basis, through email, or by appointment.

Unfortunately, with an undergraduate population of over 13,000 (there are also about 4,600 graduate students), many students find that registering for classes (online or in person) can be "really frustrating," especially for smaller, upper-level seminars. Students taking classes for their major get first choice, followed by seniors, juniors, sophomores, and freshmen. As a result, "class registration can sometimes take a very long time, and in that time you can get closed out of classes." However, according to one senior, "if you go directly to the department or appeal to the professor, you can almost always get in."

Given its large student body, Queens College offers a surprising level of personal attention. While large introductory lectures have up to 200 students, upper level seminars, recitation sections, and labs rarely exceed 20 students. Although sections and labs are often led by graduate student TA's, all seminars and lectures are taught by professors, who are, in the words of one senior, "the normal mix—some good, some not so great." Other students noted that "professors are very available and very enthusiastic, even in large lecture classes," so that "even if you're sitting in a class with 100 other people, you can get to know the professor if you want to."

While some professors are tougher than others, the workload is generally "not too much, but definitely not a walk in the park." As one sophomore put it, "You can get by

taking the easiest classes, and there are definitely classes where if you're half awake you'll do fine, but you can also have an academically challenging college experience."

Students looking to take their education to a higher level can take advantage of plentiful undergraduate research opportunities or study abroad in 30 countries (popular destinations include Israel, England, Australia, the Galapagos Islands, and Florence, Italy). They can also take honors track classes, which are small, rigorous classes taught by top professors.

While honors track classes are open to all students, Queens College admits only 40 exceptionally talented and motivated students per year to Honors College, a program where students take classes on the Queens College campus, but receive fully-paid tuition, funding for internships and study abroad, an academic stipend, a free laptop, and free access to museums across New York City. Honors College students must take 4 Honors College seminars in addition to taking regular Queens College classes. According to one enthusiastic sophomore who had considered several Ivy League schools, these seminars offer "academically challenging, small classes" and "really amazing" professors, making for an experience comparable to that of a top small liberal-arts institution.

Queens College also features the SEEK program—which provides low-income, first-generation college students free tuition and additional guidance—as well as weekend classes, night classes, a program for adults 25 years and older, and even the Center for Unlimited Enrichment, which lets senior citizens take classes at reduced cost. The college is also home to the renowned Aaron Copland School of Music, to which students apply separately.

This vast array of academic choices attracts students of all ages, races, and income levels. "You have an enormous variety," raved one sophomore. "People who are 45, and people who are 18. People who are interested in politics, and people who are interested in music. The people in my medical anthropology class last semester had such varied life experiences, and the conversation took such interesting turns. It makes the education so much more enriching."

Campus Life for Commuters

Like most of the other CUNY colleges, Queens College is a commuter school. There are no dorms, and most students live at home with their parents, though a few rent apartments near campus. Students either take a public bus or drive to school, though the amount of on-campus parking, assigned by a lottery system, is "not necessarily adequate."

Because they live off campus, many students spend little time on campus outside of class. "You go to class and go home," said one sophomore. "You don't really chill there for the heck of it." Some students say this makes it difficult to get to know their classmates. Still, students report that their peers are "friendly," and for those who want to get involved on campus, plenty of opportunities are available.

Freshmen can enroll in the Freshman Year Initiative program, where students take three of their classes with the same 40 students, giving them a chance to build strong relationships. Another common way to meet people is through extracurricular clubs and organizations. The most popular clubs are cultural groups such as Hillel and Latin American Club, the weekly *Knight News*, and student government; but with 140 organizations to choose from, "if you can think of it, it's there." Most clubs have offices in the Student Union, which also has game rooms and big-screen TVs, making it a popular hangout during lunch.

On-campus dining includes a main cafeteria (which ranges from "not very appetizing" to "repetitive but pretty good"), a kosher cafeteria, a Chinese restaurant, and several cafés. There are also several small restaurants right across from campus on Main St., including the popular Gino's pizzeria.

In addition to lunchtime, students have "free hours" twice a week during which no classes are held, providing a convenient time for students to hang out, hold club meetings, or, "during the not-so-freezing days of summer and spring," play pickup football or Frisbee on the quad.

Although Queens is the only CUNY college to have Division II sports, there is no football team, and sports play a small role in the lives of most students. Most teams "aren't bad," but attending games is "hardly popular," though tennis and volleyball matches do draw some spectators. The on-campus gym, pool, weight room, and tennis courts are free of charge to all students, but "no one really takes advantage of them" unless they are taking classes in sports or physical education. There is also a small intramural program for students who are interested.

> "It's a little bit more difficult because it's a commuter campus, but it's really what you make of it. There are definitely opportunities to have a campus life."

Because so many students live far from campus, few stick around for nighttime activities. As a result, "there is little to no drug/alcohol presence on campus. People who want to indulge in either tend to hang out off campus." There are a handful of fraternities and sororities, but since none of them have houses, they are a minor presence. However, clubs and associations will often sponsor on-campus parties, which are usually on the weekends, and "fairly well-attended." Throughout the week, students can also attend frequent lectures, concerts, and plays on campus, often held at the Colden Center for the Performing Arts.

A sophomore summed up life at Queens College with the following words: "It's a little bit more difficult because it's a commuter campus, but it's really what you make of it. There are definitely opportunities to have a campus life."—*Sameer Jain*

FYI

If you come to Queens College, you'd better bring: "passion for something—anything," "an apartment," and "a laptop."

What's the typical weekend schedule? "Go to a part-time job, internship, or use the time to study." "At night, go into the city."

If I could change one thing about Queens College, I'd change "being part of a city bureaucracy. It's really awful—getting things done means many, many forms in triplicate, and many meetings, and many hurdles in terms of protocol."

Three things every student at Queens College should do before graduating are "play a game of pick-up Frisbee on the main quad," "visit the on-campus museums—the art gallery in the library, all three of the galleries in Klapper Hall, the Louis Armstrong archives in Rosenthal Library, and the geology exhibits," and "study abroad (huge selection, and the cost is equivalent to CUNY credit tuition)."

Clarkson University

Address: Clarkson, Holcroft House, PO Box 5605, Potsdam, NY 13699-5605
Phone: 800-527-6577
E-mail Address: admission@clarkson.edu
Web site URL: www.clarkson.edu
Year Founded: 1896
Private or Public: private
Religious affiliation: none
Location: rural
Regular Application Deadline: 16-Jan
Number of Applicants: 2,428
Percent Accepted: 84%
Percent Accepted who enroll: 32%
Number Entering: 646
Number of Transfers Accepted each Year: 148
Mean SAT: 1,172
Mean ACT: 25

Middle 50% SAT range: 1,080–1,280
Middle 50% ACT range: 22–28
Early admission program (EA/ ED/ NA): ED
ED or EA Acceptance Rate: 95%
Full time Undergraduate enrollment: 2,515
Total enrollment: 2,515
Percent Male: 74%
Percent Female: 26%
Total Percent Minority: 10%
Percent African-American: 2%
Percent Asian/Pacific Islander: 2%
Percent Hispanic: 2%
Percent Native-American: 1%
Percent Other: 2%
Percent in-state / out of state: 74%/26%

Percent from Public HS: 85%
Retention Rate: 84%
Graduation Rate: 74%
Percent in On-campus housing: 83%
Percent affiliated with Greek system: 30%
Percent Varsity or Club Athletes: NA
Number of official organized extracurricular organizations: 45
3 Most popular majors: Business, Civil Engineering, Mechanical Engineering
Student/Faculty ratio: 16:01
Tuition and Fees: $27,090.00
Cost for Room and Board: $9,648.00
Percent receiving Financial aid, first-year: 88%

N estled in the small college town of Potsdam, New York, Clarkson is a thriving undergraduate university primarily dedicated to the teaching of engineering and business. With approximately 2700 undergraduate students, and with class sizes averaging only 20 students per class, Clarkson is a closely knit community where students and professors come together to solve real-world problems in a hands-on manner.

And You Thought the SATs Were Hard . . .

One thing that all students at Clarkson can attest to is the rigorous and demanding workload. As one senior put it, "Clarkson is a fast-paced school where professors have high expectations." However, few students find their workload unmanageable, with most students agreeing that what they gain from their courses is well worth the work they put in. Some of the things that students liked best about classes at Clarkson include the emphasis on interdisciplinary learning and team-based approaches to problem solving. Although the workload might be hard at Clarkson, most students agree that their "professors are great." Not only do

most professors have flexible office hours, some even make the effort to visit students or hold study sessions in student residence halls. In addition to academic interactions however, some professors also interact with students socially through intramural sports or other extracurricular activities. It seems that the only negative thing students had to say about teaching at Clarkson was the inevitable presence of TAs and professors with strong accents.

Since Clarkson is mainly an engineering and business school, most students major in those two areas, although majors in the sciences, humanities, and liberal arts are available as well. Popular majors at Clarkson include mechanical engineering, interdisciplinary engineering and management, and e-business. Regardless of what the major is, however, each student at Clarkson must complete a common set of distributional requirements. These include courses in the humanities, social sciences, natural sciences, engineering, computers, and math. Clarkson is renowned for its strong emphasis on "learning by doing" in which students are encouraged to apply the skills that they gain in classrooms to solving practical, everyday problems. For example, a program called Venture Moore House allows a group of sophomores to design and market a new product while living together. Indeed, this is representative of the Clarkson academics atmosphere where "rather than being a competitive environment, Clarkson is more of a cooperative learning environment in which students are encouraged to work in collaborative group projects."

Living and Dining

All freshmen at Clarkson live in well-furnished doubles with "good heating." For freshmen, these rooms are located in a cluster of residence buildings (the Quad) that house approximately 60 students per floor. After freshmen year, students can also choose to live in themed houses, Greek houses, or townhouses, which one junior considered "the cream of the crop." Last year, Clark took an unconventional approach to student housing by allowing students to define their on-campus living experience. Through a special application process, Clarkies choose a group of friends with whom they want to live and propose a theme with related student-designed programs. Nineteen groups were selected to set up themed houses on campus last year with themes ranging from art, environmental sustainability, philosophy and the Western frontier to sexYOUality, cooking and knitting and relaxation. Most students at Clarkson live on-campus for all four years and permission must be obtained to live off campus. However, off-campus housing is not too difficult to come by and is usually available within a ten-minute walk from campus. An RA (Resident Advisor) system does exist in the Clarkson dorms, although for the most part, RAs are generally viewed as fair. As one RA put it, "Just don't be stupid and you'll be fine, but if you feel the need to be stupid, at least be nice to the RA who catches you."

Food at Clarkson received mixed reviews. As one student summed it up, "the food used to be bad, but it has really improved in the past few years. For the most part they have something for everyone, and if they do not, they are more than willing to work with you on the issue." For the occasions when dining hall food simply will not do, Potsdam offers many great restaurants serving different national and international cuisines. Some of the more notable spots include The Cantina, Lobster House, and Little Italy, any of which would be "great spots for a nice date."

Filling up Free Time

Although Clarkson is not a dry campus, partying in residence halls are forbidden, so most of the alcohol-related activities occur in either the various fraternity houses on and off-campus or the local bars. A typical freshman weekend generally includes at least one such party and most students agree that being underage does not pose a large problem. However, one student complained that "these parties serve just beer" and that "only a few themed parties each semester serve something besides beer." Just how freely does the beer flow at these parties? When asked if drinking ever gets out of hand, one student thought that Clarkson "has a problem of not being harsh enough" about alcohol and that "problems [occur] every weekend." Another thought that most people were "very responsible" about their drinking. For students not into the party scene, Clarkson organizes movies, guest speakers, and other events for students each week.

> "Clarkson is a fast-paced school where professors have high expectations."

Other extracurricular activities also play a large part of life at Clarkson. Some of the more popular activities include the Outing Club, Clarkson TV, Clarkson Radio, and the Clarkson Senate. Devotion to extracurricular activities varies. While some students are "involved in way too many things," others concentrate just on a few. Overall, extracurriculars are "pretty much what you choose to make of them."

Golden (K)nights

The Greek scene at Clarkson, consisting of 10 recognized fraternities and two recognized sororities, plays a large role in the lives of many students. There is delayed rush at Clarkson, which is "great because you get to know other students well before you pledge, so you don't end up picking the wrong house." Fraternities and sororities live together in recognized Greek houses that offer their own optional meal plans. Apart from throwing the various weekend parties mentioned above, fraternities and sororities play an important role in the Potsdam community by raising money for charities and performing countless hours of community service. It is interesting to note that Clarkson recently held the honor of having the highest fraternity and sorority average GPA in the Northeast.

But what do students do on Saturday nights, before the kegs are tapped at the frats? Why, go watch a hockey game, of course. At Clarkson "Hockey is #1." As the only Division I teams on-campus, the men and women's hockey teams are extremely important to school spirit—games against arch-rival and neighbor St. Lawrence University always sell out quickly. In order to maintain the level of their hockey team, Clarkson actively recruits players from around the country. This practice has created some resentment among students, one of whom disliked "the money wasted on athletics when many parts of the campus need fixing."

Not a varsity athlete? No problem. "If you want to play a sport but not on a school team, there are over 100 intramural teams to play on." Furthermore, Clarkson boasts a top-notch indoor recreation center that houses a long list of facilities including a gym, a pool, a weight room, and several basketball courts.

In and Around Campus

Clarkson students come from predominantly Northeast middle-class families. Ethnically, the student body is largely white, though as one student said, "a proud black community" exists on-campus. Unfortunately, as one female student noted, because Clarkson is an engineering school, "the guy to girl ratio is so off that there are a lot of single guys out here."

The Clarkson campus is situated on 460 wooded acres and consists of 49 buildings. Although many of the buildings on-campus house state-of-the-art facilities, most students find Clarkson's buildings aesthetically "boring." What Clarkson lacks in architectural beauty, it makes up for in natural beauty, especially during the fall. However, don't forget your boots—being buried under snow for four months of each year is yet another endearing characteristic of the university.

Potsdam is a typical college town that bustles during the school year and hibernates during academic breaks. It is not unusual to hear some students complain "there is nothing to do in Potsdam." One junior countered that such people "need to get out of their rooms more, and see what [Potsdam] has to offer. [The city] may not be a metropolis but there are definitely things to do, and places to see."

When the need to get away from Potsdam arises, many options exist, most of which are within a few hours' drive from campus. These include Syracuse and Albany in New York, as well as Cornwall, Ottawa, and Montreal in Canada. Montreal, one of the renowned party cities of North America, is especially popular. Many students, however, are satisfied with the campus life at Clarkson and the small (but promising!) local community of Potsdam. Watch some hockey, play in the snow, and you'll be fine.—*Anthony Xu*

FYI
If you come to Clarkson University, you'd better bring a "warm coat" and a "computer."
What is the typical weekend schedule? "Saturday, sleep in, have brunch with friends, go watch the Men's Hockey game, and then party; Sunday, sleep in, do homework all afternoon, and then catch up on TV with friends."
If I could change one thing about Clarkson University, I'd change "the male to female ratio and the fact that it snows all year long!"
The three things every student at Clarkson should do before graduating are "cheering on you Golden Knights to victory, making 'creative' snow sculptures at night, and going clubbing in Canada."

Colgate University

Address: Colgate, Office of
  Admission, 13 Oak Drive,
  Hamilton, NY 13346
Phone: 315-228-7401
E-mail Address:
  admission@mail.colgate.edu
Web site URL:
  www.colgate.edu
Year Founded: 1819
Private or Public: private
Religious affiliation: none
Location: rural
**Regular Application
  Deadline:** 16-Jan
Number of Applicants: 7,873
Percent Accepted: 28%
**Percent Accepted who
  enroll:** 34%
Number Entering: 750
**Number of Transfers
  Accepted each Year:** 45–50
Mean SAT: NA
Mean ACT: NA
Middle 50% SAT range:
  1,310–1,480

Middle 50% ACT range:
  29–33
**Early admission program
  (EA/ ED/ NA):** ED
ED or EA Acceptance Rate:
  44%
**Full time Undergraduate
  enrollment:** 2,743
Total enrollment: 2,779
Percent Male: 49%
Percent Female: 51%
Total Percent Minority:
  15%
Percent African-American:
  4%
**Percent Asian/Pacific
  Islander:** 6%
Percent Hispanic: 4%
Percent Native-American:
  <1%
Percent Other: 4%
**Percent in-state / out of
  state:** 29%/71%
Percent from Public HS:
  68.0%

Retention Rate: 94%
Graduation Rate: 87%
**Percent in On-campus
  housing:** 91%
**Percent affiliated with
  Greek system:** 31%
**Percent Varsity or Club
  Athletes:** NA
**Number of official
  organized extracurricular
  organizations:** 120
3 Most popular majors:
  English, Political Science,
  Economics
Student/Faculty ratio:
  10:01
Tuition and Fees:
  $35,030.00
Cost for Room and Board:
  $8,530.00
**Percent receiving
  Financial aid, first-year:**
  39%

1 3 dollars, 13 prayers, and 13 articles." That is the beginning of Colgate University. In 1817, 13 men met in Hamilton and founded the Baptist Education Society. Almost two centuries later, Colgate is considered one of the country's top liberal arts universities. With a student population of about 2,750, Colgate seemingly combines the best of both worlds—the intimacy of a liberal arts college and the strong athletics program of a big university.

Nuts for Nature!

Like many of its peers in the world of liberal arts universities, Colgate is located in a small, serene location. Hamilton, NY, a village of around 3,000 people, is nestled right in the middle of New York State, about an hour drive from Syracuse. It is also two hours away from Cornell University, Colgate's biggest rival in sports.

Quaint Hamilton is almost the same size of Colgate, which leads to good town-gown relationships. Even though it celebrated its bicentennial in 1996, the village, originally called "Payne's Settlement," has changed very little. Some students do feel that Colgate's location is an significant shortcoming

of the university, given the fact that "there is really not much to do outside of the campus." "Everything in Hamilton revolves around Colgate," added another student, "There is really nothing for entertainment around here."

Nevertheless, students agree that the campus is beautiful. Gorgeous architecture is an important aspect of the university, especially Memorial Chapel's golden steeple, the most recognizable feature on campus. Its pristine location in upstate New York is also a prime attraction for nature lovers. "Colgate is perfect for people who enjoy the beauty of nature," one student said. Taylor Lake and Payne Creek both sit inside Colgate's campus and provide a relaxing backdrop to an otherwise hectic campus. To make use of all of its surroundings, Colgate's outdoor education program provides a fully equipped Base Camp right on campus, so students can take out rentals for snowshoeing, skiing, backpacking, and even camping. Colgate even maintains a camp in Upper Saranac Lake in the Adirondacks for the exclusive use of its faculty and students.

Despite any perceived shortcomings of the town, Colgate maintains a good relationship with Hamilton, where most of the Colgate faculty and staff live. In fact, about 85 percent of the faculty lives within 10 miles of the university. Another contributor to the goodwill between Hamilton and Colgate? As one student pointed out, "most locals go on vacation over Spring Party Weekend."

The Colgate Core

Colgate's admission process might not be as competitive as the Ivies, but it remains a highly selective school with admissions rate below 30 percent. The average SAT scores are between 1310 and 1480, and more than 83 percent of its students are in the top 10 percent of their high schools. The average GPA for class of 2010 was 3.71. "Given the admission standards," said a student, "the people here are generally smart and willing to work hard."

Colgate is a challenging school. Students need to work hard to get good grades, and several introductory classes are particularly difficult. As one student pointed out, "The intro classes are designed to cull the weak." Nevertheless, most students are happy with their classes, which are generally very small, giving students the opportunity to closely interact with their professors.

Undergrads can choose between 51 different concentrations. There is a core requirement that expects students to take four special seminars by the end of their sophomore year. Two of these courses teach students about the Western civilization and their contemporary challenges. The two other courses are designed to give students a better understanding of a specific culture in the non-Western world and the effects of science and technology.

Colgaters have to take a minimum of 32 classes to graduate, including six classes for distributional requirements in humanities, social sciences, and natural sciences and four physical education credits, a specialty of Colgate. Most students are fine with the requirements. According to a student, "the required Core classes are easy but usually involve a lot of reading." The gym classes, however, have mixed reviews. While some love the idea of going outdoors to learn about hiking and survival skills, many others do not think that they should be part of the college curriculum. "I appreciate the goals of the gym classes, but I just don't think that they should still be here at the college level. We have so many intramural sports anyway, and half of the students participate in them," said a student.

Weekends That Never End

People work hard at Colgate because of the vigorous academic standards, but they also party hard. Undergrads agree that most Colgate students have a solid sense of self-discipline that allows them to do well academically, while enjoying the nightlife.

Since a great majority of Colgate students stay on campus, there is no shortage of things to do. There are always parties going on throughout the week, not just during the weekends. Fraternity parties are probably the most prominent social scene on campus, although the sports teams are also frequent fiesta hosts. Teams often have townhouses or apartments where students go for partying and dancing. For those who grow tired of the Greek system, the Jug is the most frequented bar for Colgate students, who generally agree that everyone should go there before graduating.

> **"Another contributor to the goodwill between Hamilton and Colgate? As one student pointed out, 'most locals go on vacation over Spring Party Weekend.'"**

With all the partying, most students drink significant amount of alcohol. Nonetheless, as many students have pointed out, drinking is not a particular problem on campus. Nevertheless, although there are also social opportunities for those who stay away from the parties, students agree that they are generally limited. After all, given the number of parties available, it becomes hard for students not to take advantage of them. Plus, since dating is "not the norm" at Colgate, parties seem to facilitate the more prominent random hook-up scene.

Dorms and Diversity

Students at Colgate are generally happy with their freshman housing, which is fortunate because 92 percent of *all* Colgate students live in residence halls and university-owned houses. Freshmen are required to live in residence halls, but as they move up, they are free to choose between a wide array of options, including townhouses, apartments and suites. Another way in which Colgate differs from most colleges is that fraternities and sororities must live in university-own houses. But most students see no problems with on-campus living. "The residences are great," said a student. "There are a nice theme houses for upperclassmen."

Colgate is often seen as a relatively rich, upper-class school, and the minority population is still very small, only around 15 percent of the entire student population. Nonetheless, the school is currently trying to attract a more diverse student body, both ethnically and financially. "Colgate is filled with rich, upper-class kids," one student admitted. "But it definitely isn't as preppy as it is made out to be. People are generally laid back and looking for a good time."

And who wouldn't be laid back with the serene backdrop of upstate New York and a motivated and fun-loving student body? As one student said, "Colgate is one of those schools that find the right balance between partying and studying. That's why it is so great." When the men of the Baptist Education Society met in 1819, who knew that they would make 13 such a lucky number for 2,750 undergraduates?—*Xiaohang Liu*

FYI

If you come to Colgate, you'd better bring "a worn-in hoodie."

What is the typical weekend schedule? "Friday: happy that it's Friday. Saturday: party time. Sunday: freak out at the amount of work and spend the whole day in library."

If I could change one thing about Colgate, I'd "move campus to a warmer climate."

Three things every student at Colgate should do before graduating are "go to the Jug, sled around the campus, and hit some balls at the driving range overlooking campus."

Columbia University

Address: Columbia, 212 Hamilton Hall, New York, NY 10027
Phone: 212-854-2522
E-mail Address: ugrad-admiss@columbia.edu
Web site URL: www.columbia.edu
Year Founded: 1754
Private or Public: private
Religious affiliation: none
Location: urban
Regular Application Deadline: 7-Jan
Number of Applicants: 17,151
Percent Accepted: 12%
Percent Accepted who enroll: 58%
Number Entering: 1,022
Number of Transfers Accepted each Year: 78
Mean SAT: 1,432
Mean ACT: 30

Middle 50% SAT range: 1,350–1,540
Middle 50% ACT range: 28–33
Early admission program (EA/ ED/ NA): ED
ED or EA Acceptance Rate: 23%
Full time Undergraduate enrollment: 4,184
Total enrollment: 5,593
Percent Male: 48%
Percent Female: 52%
Total Percent Minority: 39%
Percent African-American: 11%
Percent Asian/Pacific Islander: 14%
Percent Hispanic: 13%
Percent Native-American: 1%
Percent Other: 11%
Percent in-state / out of state: 26%/74%

Percent from Public HS: 49%
Retention Rate: 98%
Graduation Rate: 94%
Percent in On-campus housing: 94%
Percent affiliated with Greek system: 25%
Percent Varsity or Club Athletes: NA
Number of official organized extracurricular organizations: 300
3 Most popular majors: social sciences, history, English
Student/Faculty ratio: 5:01
Tuition and Fees: $35,166.00
Cost for Room and Board: $9,648.00
Percent receiving Financial aid, first-year: 81%

An "island in the middle of New York City," Columbia University offers its students a collegiate experience that few other schools can: a combination of one of the nation's top academic programs and the immense wealth of resources of the Big Apple. Despite the fact that Columbia is planted in the midst of one of the world's richest and most crowded gardens, the university and its diverse student body are marked by a defined sense of community.

Tunnel Vision

Columbia's backdrop is one of the most diverse cities in the country, and it boasts an extremely diverse student body, with a third of students from minority backgrounds. "There is an impressive mix of opinions and interests on campus." While the student body is statistically diverse, one student joked, "It does sometimes seem like everyone here is Jewish and that all the guys are gay." While students feel that all ethnic and racial backgrounds are accepted and valued in the community, differing political views are not as well-tolerated. "Basically, conservatives are not welcome here." A liberal spirit pervades campus, and the Columbia Democrats remain one of the most popular and largest organizations on campus.

Though Columbia is often accused of being "light on tradition," several students mentioned the myth of the Columbia tunnels, a system of tunnels that apparently lie underneath the campus and which used to be available until 1968. "I've heard all sorts of rumors about the rooms that the tunnels connect to," one sophomore said. "I've heard there's a swimming pool in one room and one place just full of trampolines." The marching band is also a cultural institution, performing funny half-time shows at sporting events and other events throughout the year.

While most agree that the food at the campus' main dining hall—John Jay—is "edible," one student put it bluntly: "I wouldn't take anyone there." While there are other places to eat on campus, many students choose to eat in one of the many dining options that the city offers. Upperclassmen housing often includes kitchens, allowing students to cook their own food as a money-saving option. There are four different meal plans to accommodate the desires of most students. "Columbia Points" is a debit account system which allows students to purchase a la carte food and beverages at 12 different retail locations on campus.

Students to the Core

"Academics are the strongest aspect of the school," one sophomore said. One of the attributes of Columbia that differentiates it most from its peer institutions is "the Core," a core curriculum of classes that all students must take to graduate. Most students like the Core as it provides each Columbia graduate with "a common set of knowledge." One complained, though, that "it goes way too quickly to cover the great works in a satisfactory way." While students laud the small class size and top-notch professors of the Core classes, there are a few complaints

about the Core. For some students, Core classes add significantly to their work loads in addition to the classes they are taking in their major. Other students complained about the "misguided" Frontiers of Science class, the newest addition to the Core curriculum.

Columbia is also unique in that students are not required to declare a major, though most students still eventually decide to focus their studies on one area. Due to the Core, Columbia attracts more Humanities types, as opposed to science enthusiasts. The humanities majors tend to be the most popular, though one sophomore said, "It sometimes seems like everyone here is a political science or econ major." Several students pointed out the science and math classes do tend to be "slightly weak." Students in the School of Engineering post a lower average GPA and more hours of class per week than those in Columbia College. "It's definitely a harder curriculum," one junior in the School of Engineering said, "We're probably unhappier in general."

Many courses take advantage of the New York City setting, as teachers bring their students into the museums, buildings and parks to add a new dimension to lessons taught in the classroom. Other classes, such as Jeffrey Sachs' course in sustainable management, are the sort of unique offerings that make Columbia stand out.

Students said that while it is definitely possible to become close with faculty, students have to be proactive. Nevertheless, a few students complained about the increasing number of TAs teaching Core classes and TAs who cannot speak English well. But the bond between students and faculty can become so strong that some students mentioned teachers who would take them out drinking on the weekends. Despite occasionally boozing it up with professors, it's no secret that Columbia students work hard. "Some kids are just in the library 24/7," one student observed.

Stay on Campus at Your Own Social Risk

"Among the people who come to Columbia and end up not liking it, the primary reasons tend to be social," one senior said. The majority of Columbia students tend to spend at least one night per weekend off campus. "It's just hard to form communities because people are leaving so often." While Columbia does have fraternities, on campus parties are rare and often not very well attended. "No one takes the frats seriously." One sophomore said that freshman year at Columbia was especially difficult because it was overwhelming to adjust to a community in which people were not often on campus during their downtime.

The nightlife at Columbia—reflecting the evening scene of New York City—is focused on the clubs and bars, making a fake ID a student's best friend. "When you come to Columbia, you're 17 and you suddenly become 21," one junior said. Even so, many students concurred that drinking does not have to be the central component of the Columbia experience. "There have been times when I've been at a bar every weekend, and then month-long periods when I don't go at all," one sophomore said. "It's all what you're in the mood for." The local bars in Morningside Heights, such as the West End, are popular joints for students.

> **"When you come to Columbia, you're 17 and you suddenly become 21."**

Not everyone believes that the Columbia social scene is as unexciting as it is made out to be. One student pointed out that the student council and other organizations are attempting to create more events on campus, such as the annual "Glasshouse Rocks" dance held in the (glass-paneled) student center. Other popular on-campus events include Orgo Night, when—the night before the Organic Chemistry final—the marching band plays a full concert in the library in a performance marked by "a funny script and borderline offensive jokes" to a packed crowd of frantic students.

A Plethora of Options

As at most Ivy League schools, "everyone here has a club or organization that he is deeply involved in—it's New York; everyone is constantly running around and pressured." With over 200 clubs and organizations offered, there really is something for everyone to get involved in.

The Columbia Spectator, the school's newspaper, is one of the most popular extracurricular activities on campus. Theater and acting groups are also extremely popular, as is a cappella for budding singing talents. Columbia's athletics programs are notoriously underappreciated on campus. While one student did note that homecoming is always well-attended, almost all students

agreed that attending sports games is just not a major part of people's social lives on campus. A recent decision by the administration to ban the presence of alcohol at sporting events has also had a negative affect on the attendance at games. While there are definitely teams that perform well—such as fencing, tennis and swimming—there really is not a lot of "athletic school spirit." As one sophomore said, "The scene can become pretty artsy."

Your Own Private Manhattan

One of the best features for students attending the university is that housing—a major problem in New York City—is guaranteed on campus for all four years. Columbia's campus is in Morningside Heights, a neighborhood located between 110th Street and 125th Street. Because finding housing in the Big Apple is so strenuous, over 90 percent of the student body remains on campus for all four years—there are 15 different residence halls on campus.

From the Pantheon-like Lerner Library to the lawns in the central quad to the modern glass walls of Lerner Hall, the architecture on campus is lauded for its intricacy. "The architecture is one of the main reasons I came here," one sophomore said. "I visited some pretty ugly colleges." In general, students approve of the on-campus housing options: "the dorms are perfectly comfortable, if not always luxurious." Freshmen housing is unanimously praised for the quality of the rooms and the location. The freshmen dorms are located on the quad, creating a physical grouping of freshmen in an attempt to forge bonds between the underclassmen. There are some disparities within the dorms, however, as one freshman noted that her dorm had air conditioning, whereas other freshmen dorms did not. Sophomore and junior housing can be hit or miss, as some rooms have kitchens and ample space that others lack. Seniors can live in actual townhouses. ("When else do you get the chance to live in a townhouse in the Upper West Side for $600?" one student asked.) RAs live on each floor of all campus dormitories for all four years, though RAs at Columbia are not necessarily harsh disciplinarians. "My RA has tried really hard to bond with all of the kids on the floor," a freshman said, "Every week, we have study break parties in a different room on the floor." All freshmen floors are dry, though students admit that even if an RA catches a student in the act, that student will rarely be written up. All students living in residence halls live in either singles (35 percent) or doubles (65 percent).

While parents may worry about their children attending college in the chaotic city, most students said they feel entirely safe. "Our neighborhood is really one of the safest areas in the city," one senior said. Of course, another pointed out, "You still have to be smart about what you're doing." Another student said that the increasing gentrification of Morningside Heights has led to a safer feel on campus: "When you're in New York City, there are people all around you, but when you're just walking around Morningside Heights, it's suddenly as if you're in Small College Town U.S.A."—*Josh Duboff*

FYI

If you come to Columbia, you'd better bring "a fake ID, a good pair of workout clothes, and Daddy's credit card—New York City ain't cheap!"

What is the typical weekend schedule? "There's no such thing as a typical weekend schedule here, just as there's no such thing as a typical day in New York City."

If I could change one thing about Columbia, I'd "change the real attitude problem on campus. There is a real disconnect, an impression that the University doesn't care about the students."

Three things every Columbia student should do before graduating are "attend Orgo Night, explore the tunnels, and drink 40s on the steps outside the library."

The Cooper Union for the Advancement of Science and Art

Address: Cooper Union, 30 Cooper Square, 3rd Floor, New York, NY 10003
Phone: 212-353-4120
E-mail Address: admission@cooper.edu
Web site URL: www.cooper.edu
Year Founded: 1859
Private or Public: private
Religious affiliation: none
Location: urban
Regular Application Deadline: 1-Jan
Number of Applicants: 2,586
Percent Accepted: 10%
Percent Accepted who enroll: 79%
Number Entering: 235
Number of Transfers Accepted each Year: 30–35
Mean SAT: NA
Mean ACT: NA

Middle 50% SAT range: 1,300–1,500
Middle 50% ACT range: NA
Early admission program (EA/ ED/ NA): ED
ED or EA Acceptance Rate: ~30%
Full time Undergraduate enrollment: 949
Total enrollment: 1,005
Percent Male: 65%
Percent Female: 35%
Total Percent Minority: 35%
Percent African-American: 5%
Percent Asian/Pacific Islander: 20%
Percent Hispanic: 9%
Percent Native-American: 0.5%
Percent Other: 0%
Percent in-state / out of state: 4%/96%

Percent from Public HS: 60%
Retention Rate: 97%
Graduation Rate: 82%
Percent in On-campus housing: 20%
Percent affiliated with Greek system: 5–10%
Percent Varsity or Club Athletes: 10–15%
Number of official organized extracurricular organizations: 95
3 Most popular majors: Fine Arts, Architecture, Engineering
Student/Faculty ratio: 7:01
Tuition and Fees: $1,500.00
Cost for Room and Board: $13,180.00
Percent receiving Financial aid, first-year: 87%

Located in the heart of the big apple, The Cooper Union for the Advancement of Science and Art consists of five buildings and about 900 students residing in Manhattan's Cooper Square. Founded by philanthropist Peter Cooper in 1859, the institution is unique among its peers in that every admitted student is granted a $30,000 full tuition scholarship.

Known for its highly selective admission standards and tightly knit community, Cooper Union offers students a challenging and fun time in a diverse environment. Though only about 40 percent of students are female, and over half of the student population is from New York State, one student remarked, "Overall, Cooper is probably the most diverse school in the country.

It is truly a reflection of New York City," she said. "I think at least 75 percent of the people here speak another language fluently."

A School of Polar Opposites

Cooper Union is composed of three different schools: The school of architecture, the school of art, and the highly-ranked school of engineering. According to the admissions office, the average freshman class includes about 210 students—35 in architecture, 65 in art and 110 in engineering.

> "Overall, Cooper is probably the most diverse school in the country—it is truly a reflection of New York City. I think at least 75 percent of the people here speak another language fluently."

Students in each of the three schools at Cooper Union have the majority of their course schedule planned for them when they enroll. In addition to the classes relevant to a student's specialty, every student must take general academic requirements within the first two years in order to fulfill his or her degree requirements. These requirements primarily include seminars in literature, history and government as well as other areas of the humanities and the social sciences. Art and architecture students must also take several natural science classes. Students do not have much flexibility in course selection until junior and senior years when they can more freely choose from a variety of electives.

Some students feel that the engineering, art, and architecture students naturally divide themselves into different social circles. A recent chemical engineering graduate commented on the engineering school's intimidating reputation, "Cooper is very hard. I did not give it the time it deserved in order to excel. So, I graduated with a GPA which still haunts me to this day."

Despite the academic rigor of the engineering programs, the student added that attending Cooper Union was "the best" choice he had made in his life. "Yes, it takes work, but the more of yourself you put into something, the more you get out." Another student expressed the strength of the small community that the school fosters, exclaiming, "I absolutely love it. It's a ton of work, but it's great."

A Test with No Solutions

Cooper prides itself on its selection process, especially for Art and Architecture School applicants. At the annual open-house and portfolio days every fall, prospective art and architecture students can meet with professors who comprise the selection committee and receive feedback on their portfolio. Talent—rather than SAT scores or GPA—is key in getting into Cooper.

The emphasis on evaluating and developing talent is part of the philosophy behind the institution's "home test." The home test is a relatively abstract assignment which enables the admissions committee to assess a student's talents and creativity in a standardized manner. There is a different "home test" for the architecture and art programs. Each one consists of a number of artistic projects to be completed within one month and returned to Cooper Union for review.

Once accepted students enroll, they can request gallery access to design an exhibition of their work. Several galleries around campus are available to exhibit the work of students and outside artists in solo and group shows. The annual student exhibition prior to commencement each year celebrates the work of art and architecture students at all levels.

Living On Your Own

Cooper Union's student residences are located across the street from the Engineering School. Suites vary in size from three to five people with most housing arrangements being two bedroom units shared by four people. Each unit contains a bedroom, bathroom and kitchenette and each apartment building contains a study, laundry room and common room. "The living area is usually much smaller than the bedrooms, so you will end up spending most of your time in the bedrooms," one student remarked. "However, the bedrooms are huge compared to what you would normally get in a New York City apartment for the price, and you will have, at most, one roommate."

On the top floor of the student residences are rooms affectionately known as lofts. The lofts are, in the words of one student, "very tall rooms that do not have separate sleeping areas and living areas." Artists in particular tend to like the lofts because they offer a lot of space to hang artwork, as well as providing different views of the city.

Student residence housing is only available for 182 students, and Cooper does not guarantee housing past the first year. Students who cannot secure a place in the student residence are faced with the responsibility of finding a residence in the city. While many students enjoy this challenge and freedom, others find it to be a deterring obstacle.

One plus of living off campus is that instead of eating campus food, the vast majority of students eats at local restaurants or cooks their own meals. "There're so many options to choose from," one student said, adding that "the food here is some of the best (food) anywhere."

Extracurricular Activities

Each school at Cooper Union has its own student council, each with its own unique constitution. The three councils also combine into the joint student council to discuss issues that affect the entire student body. Students also run a newspaper, though circulation and regular publication is difficult due, in part, to the fact that all upperclassmen live off campus. Cooper also sponsors a variety of cultural, ethnic and religious organizations, as well as community service clubs, art and drama clubs, and clubs that are more geared toward improving the social atmosphere on campus. While each club attracts its own aficionados, very few boast large numbers or a dedicated membership.

Campus athletics is virtually nonexistent at Cooper. There is very little commitment to intramural sports. Some students complain that the minimal athletic facilities of Cooper Union are in poor condition. Greek life also has a very limited presence on campus. Only 10 percent of male students are part of one of the two national fraternities on campus, and only 5 percent of female students are members of the local sorority.

Engineering and architecture students face particularly rigorous curriculums, so many regularly forego their social opportunities to spend time on class work. Art students often have more mobility to experience the New York City nightlife, visiting several clubs and checking out the museums and Broadway shows on the weekends. Overall, all students say they love the New York atmosphere.

An Incubator for Social Progress and Creativity

Cooper Union has long been a source of many social and progressive movements. Within a year of its inception the Great Hall at Cooper Union was the site of a passionate debate between Abraham Lincoln and Stephen Douglass. Since then, the Hall has featured American Presidents Grant, Cleveland, Taft, Theodore Roosevelt, Wilson and Clinton. Today the Great Hall remains a host for prominent performances and lectures.

The NAACP and the Red Cross were both initially organized at Cooper Union, and Susan B. Anthony located her offices there. Cooper has also been host to some of the more creative and optimistic people in the 20th century. Supreme Court Justice and ACLU founding member Felix Frankfurter attended Cooper Union and Thomas Edison enrolled in class there. Mark Twain, Samuel Gompers, and Betty Friedan are also among the many influential and progressive individuals to speak at Cooper Union.

Bruce Degen the illustrator for the best-selling "Magic School Bus" children's series is a more recent alum of Cooper Union, and he calls Cooper Union "something that changed my life."—*Mark Schneider*

FYI
If you come to Cooper Union, you'd better bring "extra spending money for weekend activities, art supplies, and textbooks. Living in New York is expensive!"
What's the typical weekend schedule? "Eating out for dinner and studying (or painting) on Thursdays and/or Fridays, a concert, museum, movie, Broadway show, sporting event, night club or road trip on Saturdays, and hanging out and catching up on work on Sunday."
If I could change one thing about Cooper Union, "I'd expand the housing options to accommodate more students who have difficulty finding a place to live for the semester."
Three things every student at Cooper Union should do before graduating are "experience New York, get to know your professors and classmates well, and display your work in a student exhibition if you're an art student or compete in the annual egg-drop contest if you're an engineering student."

Cornell University

Address: Cornell University, 410 Thurston Avenue, Ithaca, NY 14850-2488
Phone: 607-255-5241
E-mail Address: NA
Web site URL: http://admissions.cornell.edu/
Year Founded: 1865
Private or Public: private
Religious affiliation: none
Location: rural
Regular Application Deadline: 2-Jan
Number of Applicants: 28,098
Percent Accepted: 25%
Percent Accepted who enroll: 47%
Number Entering: 3,188
Number of Transfers Accepted each Year: 669

Mean SAT: NA
Mean ACT: NA
Middle 50% SAT range: 1,280–1,490
Middle 50% ACT range: 28–32
Early admission program (EA/ ED/ NA): ED
ED or EA Acceptance Rate: 39%
Full time Undergraduate enrollment: 13,523
Total enrollment: 18,704
Percent Male: 52%
Percent Female: 48%
Total Percent Minority: 29%
Percent African-American: 6%
Percent Asian/Pacific Islander: 16%
Percent Hispanic: 6%
Percent Native-American: 1%
Percent Other: 17%

Percent in-state / out of state: 34%/66%
Percent from Public HS: NA
Retention Rate: 96%
Graduation Rate: 92%
Percent in On-campus housing: 46%
Percent affiliated with Greek system: 50%
Percent Varsity or Club Athletes: NA
Number of official organized extracurricular organizations: 823
3 Most popular majors: engineering, business, agriculture
Student/Faculty ratio: 9:01
Tuition and Fees: $32,981.00
Cost for Room and Board: $10,726.00

N estled in the beautiful Finger Lakes region of upstate New York, Cornell is a member of the prestigious Ivy League and one of the nation's most preeminent institutions of higher learning. It was founded in 1865 by Ezra Cornell and Andrew Dickson White, and was immediately distinguished from the rest of the Ivy League by its status as both a private and a federal land-grant institution. To this day, Cornell still exists as both a private and a public university.

"Any Study"

Cornell is the only Ivy League school with an English motto: "I would found an institution where any person can find instruction in any study." These were the words of Ezra Cornell, and today, his vision comes true in the shape of 70 undergraduate majors and seven undergraduate colleges. Since Cornell is both private and public, the state funds schools like the College of Agriculture and Life Sciences and the College of Human Ecology, while the private sector includes the colleges of Engineering and Arts & Sciences. Which meansthat students can major in anything from Crop and Soil Sciences to Hotel Administration to Textiles and Apparel. If students still cannot find what they want to study, there is always the choice of the independent major.

Cornell is a big school, with some 13,500 undergraduates. The private Arts and Sciences is by far the largest, followed by the public Agriculture and Life Sciences. This means that a huge breadth of classes is offered—more than 4,000 in a given year. As one junior said, "The thing about Cornell is that it's a really big school, so every class you can possibly want is offered. For example, one of our biggest classes is Introduction to Wines—it's really popular among seniors." Another extremely popular class is Introductory Psychology with Professor James B. Maas, who "has been teaching that class forever!" Incidentally, it was Professor Maas who first developed the term "power nap."

Even though most of the courses are composed of less than 20 students each, current students do say that freshman introduction classes tend to be very large. "The largest classes I've ever had had about 500 to 700 students," one student remembered. However, the class size doesn't necessarily mean that students will not get the individualized attention they need—for better or for worse. For some lectures, students are assigned seats, and teaching assistants will mark down absences based on empty seats. Still some students complain about the lack of attention to undergraduate teaching by some professors and the bureaucratic red tape that comes with being in such a large university.

Nevertheless, the breadth of classes that are available to students is one of Cornell's greatest resources. Said one engineering student, "If I can give any advice to incoming freshmen, it's to take advantage of all the academic opportunities that are available to you. Although it's really competitive here, the flexibility and diversity of the classes really makes up for it."

Frats, Fun and . . . Fish?

Cornell students' weekend schedules are as diverse as the classes that they take, but students tend to agree that Friday and Saturday are the big party nights. Greek life is a big part of the social scene at Cornell, especially during the fall, when fraternities and sororities jockey for freshman bids. "There is always something to do, whether it be a school sponsored event or a party outside of school," one student said. "When you're a freshman you tend to go to a lot of frat parties, but in your later years you tend to go other places." Other students agreed. "Freshmen go with their entire halls to frat parties. Upperclassmen tend to go to house parties. I mean, by then you have a lot of friends, so it's pretty rare for a weekend to go by without anyone having a house party." For those who do not partake in drinking, Cornell also has a "CU2Nite" program that helps groups organize alcohol-free events.

Students agree that Ithaca does have some bars and clubs, but they're usually pretty strict on the age limit and fake IDs. On campus, though, the alcohol policy is pretty lenient. Students will get referred to a Judicial Administrator (JA) if they are caught drinking underage, but usually dorm parties do not get broken up unless there is a lot of noise and disturbance. Also, North Campus students tend to get caught more often, since it is a freshman-only residence area, but on West Campus, "the RAs don't know who's 21 and who's not, so it's easier to get away with stuff." Another student estimated that the great majority of Cornell students do drink every weekend.

Of course, Cornell has no lack of interesting extracurricular activities that don't involve chugging beers. "If you want to do it, get some friends together and you can have a club," one student said. From Jello-tossing and unicycling to Darfur and Democracy Matters, there is something for everyone. Another student cited this diversity of organizations as one of Cornell's most winning attributes: "There's always so much to do on campus, and funding is really easy to get."

Which is good, because Cornell students are passionate about their causes. "The most activist groups are those with a political and social change in mind," one biological sciences major said. "We once had a sit-in by environmentalist students in the president's office in order to save Red Bud Woods from being turned into a parking lot. They were later arrested due to their refusal to leave the office."

> **"If you come to Cornell, bring an open mind . . . a friendly attitude doesn't hurt either!"**

Even though Cornell does have a Division I-A football team, hockey is the sport to watch here. Dedicated hockey fans even have a special name for their team—the Icers. "You have to go to at least one game before you graduate," one junior enthused. The biggest athletic event of the year is the Harvard-Cornell game, for which students would camp out for 24 hours in order to get tickets. The rules for ticket buying have since changed, but nevertheless, hockey gives Cornell "a great, vibrant atmosphere on Friday and Saturday nights." It's also been a Cornell tradition to throw fish onto the ice—legend is that it began as retaliation for the Harvard team tying a live chicken to the Cornell goal.

Cornell is Gorges

Living at Cornell has its perks, such as the great natural resources of being in upstate New York. Cornell is actually big enough to have its own zip code, and it sits atop the Cayuga Lake, the largest of the Finger Lakes. Two sides of the campus are surrounded by gorges, so even in the rush of day, students can hear the sound of falling water as they walk to class.

All freshmen live in North Campus, in one of the four halls, where they get to know each other as a class. Freshmen can choose from among the traditional dorm settings, the Townhouse Community, themed houses, and single-sex dorms. Singles are plentiful even during this first year; said one student. "I actually asked for a double and ended up with a single." Most sophomores do live on-campus, but they usually move off campus as juniors and seniors. Upperclassmen who stay on campus are housed in Collegetown and West Campus, the latter of which is currently seeing old dorms in the process of being torn down and rebuilt. Cornell aims to have five brand new dorms on West Campus in the near future.

To complement the residential overhaul, there are now a whopping 31 dining locations on campus, with eight all-you-can-eat buffets. In fact, Cornell was recently ranked as having one of the best-quality dining services in the United States. From early in the morning to the wee hours of the night, Cornell students can choose from buffets, à la carte locations, and convenience stores. However, there are discrepancies between dining locations. "The food on North Campus is definitely better," one junior said. And of course, there's always Cornell's famous dairy farm, which provides award-winning ice cream that creates legends and traditions all onto itself.

Whenever students are bored of campus food (which is "very possible," a student admitted) there is always Ithaca. Off campus, there are plenty of ethnic eateries in Collegetown. One student gushed, "Every kind of cuisine you can think of, you can find in Collegetown." Another was equally effusive: "If you come to Cornell, you should definitely try new foods that you've never had before. There's such a good variety of cultural cuisine nearby—Thai, Greek, Indian, Mediterranean, Japanese, Korean, you name it."

The Big Red Life

As a university with a long and illustrious tradition, Cornell has its share of tradition. "If a virgin walks across the Arts Quad at midnight, the statues of Andrew White and Ezra Cornell are supposed to get up, walk to the middle of the quad, and shake each others hands," one sophomore explained. "The senior class paints the footsteps across the quad each year." There is also the 173-foot McGraw clock tower, which was the home of the famous pumpkin, a stunt now referred to as The Pumpkin. Once, a 60-kg pumpkin was placed on top of the tower, which fueled many articles in *The Cornell Daily Sun* about how it got there. To this day, students still do not know how strange objects find their way to the top of the tower.

Dragon Day is a famous Cornell tradition in which Architecture students construct a huge dragon and parade it down to Arts-Quad, where they light it on fire. Dragon Day was said to have been the brainchild of a 1901 student named William Straight who believed that the School of Architecture should have its own celebratory day. Throughout the last century, Dragon Day has been through various reincarnations, resulting in the current tradition, which is to construct different animals to chase after the dragon.

Perhaps one of the most indicative Cornell traditions is the Primal Scream, in which students open their windows just before finals and scream out all of their frustrations. Cornell's academic atmosphere is not made for the cowardly. "The academic atmosphere at Cornell is extremely competitive. Every student is trying to be the best they can be, so it's difficult." Another student agreed. "A lot of kids here were number one in high school, but it's really, really hard to be number one in Cornell . . . I sleep a lot more than most of my friends and I get about six hours a night." As to whether that may be the reason for Cornell's famously high suicide rate, students point out that Cornell's gorges, while beautiful, naturally attract daring people who have untimely accidents.

From Janet Reno to Bill Nye to E.B. White and William Strunk, Cornell has never suffered for influential alumni and faculty. Indeed, it has a lot to offer. With its strikingly beautiful campus, quirky traditions and active student life, it is hardly any wonder that so many choose Cornell to be their alma mater.—*Janet Xu*

FYI
If you come to Cornell, you'd better bring "an umbrella that's small enough to fit in your bag."
What is the typical weekend schedule? "Go to parties on Friday and Saturday nights, do stuff for clubs in the day, go back to the library on Sunday."
If I could change one thing about Cornell, I'd "make it a less competitive environment in order to relieve a little stress for all students."
Three things ever student should do before graduating from Cornell is: "Climb to the top of the clock tower to see the view, go gorge-jumping or swimming, and make the Walk of Shame—there's more to life than classes!"

Eastman School of Music

Address: Eastman School of
Music, 26 Gibbs Street,
Rochester, NY 14604-2599
Phone: 800-388-9695
E-mail Address:
admissions@esm.rochester
.edu
Web site URL:
www.esm.rochester.edu/
apply/
Year Founded: 1921
Private or Public: private
Religious affiliation: none
Location: suburban
**Regular Application
Deadline:** rolling
Number of Applicants: 2,000
Percent Accepted: 29%
**Percent Accepted who
enroll:** 47%
Number Entering: 135
**Number of Transfers
Accepted each Year:** 0

Mean SAT: 1,250
Mean ACT: NA
Middle 50% SAT range:
1,010–1,300
Middle 50% ACT range:
22–28
**Early admission program
(EA/ ED/ NA):** NA
ED or EA Acceptance Rate:
NA
**Full time Undergraduate
enrollment:** 503
Total enrollment: 503
Percent Male: 45%
Percent Female: 55%
Total Percent Minority: 29%
Percent African-American:
3%
**Percent Asian/Pacific
Islander:** 6%
Percent Hispanic: 2%
Percent Native-American:
0%

Percent Other: 18%
**Percent in-state / out of
state:** 17%/83%
Percent from Public HS:
80%
Retention Rate: 89%
Graduation Rate: 86%
**Percent in On-campus
housing:** 73%
**Percent affiliated with
Greek system:** 31%
**Percent Varsity or Club
Athletes:** NA
**Number of official
organized extracurricular
organizations:** 8
Most popular majors:
Performing arts, Education
Student/Faculty ratio: 4:01
Tuition and Fees:
$29,172.00
Cost for Room and Board:
$10,552.00

D o you love music? Not just as a
hobby, but as your life? Do you love
music enough to practice until you
get calluses from playing your instrument
for so long? Enough to sing not just in the
shower, but for hours at a time? If you do,
you probably already know about this world-
renowned music school. At the Eastman
School of Music, serious musicians can immerse themselves in an environment where
everyone thinks about, listens to, or plays
music 24 hours a day.

Learning About Music
Eastman provides its students with a rigorous and thorough musical education as well
as a solid humanities background. Most students are performance majors (the technical name is "applied music"). The next most
popular majors are music education, composition, and theory. The performance major requires three years of theory, two years
of music history, covering everything from
Gregorian chants to contemporary music,
and, of course, weekly lessons. Performance majors must be competent piano
players regardless of their chosen instrument. All performance majors must take
Piano 101 and 102, or test out of this require-

ment. Eastman also has a humanities requirement, which can be filled with a new
one-semester Freshman Writing Seminar,
courses in literature, history, languages, philosophy, or a combination of these. Eastman
students are serious about their humanities
classes as well as their music, and classes
are not easy. As one undergrad explained, "It
seems like either you do really well or you
completely fail." By senior year, most of
Eastman's requirements are out of the way,
and students have more flexible schedules
that allow them to audition for jobs or graduate school.

Students interested in a 50:50 type course-
load between their liberal arts or science
studies and their music concentration can
pursue a BA or BS program at Eastman. Following this track, students take 40–60 percent of their courses in their music
concentration of choice, compared to 80–90
percent for those pursuing a Bachelor of
Music.

Because Eastman is part of the University
of Rochester, students have access to the
University's libraries and other facilities.
Some of the humanities classes are held on
the U of R campus, although as one student
said, "You can make it all four years without

leaving this campus." The reason many like to stay on the Eastman campus is the 15- to 20-minute bus ride to the U of R.

Students who apply to Eastman can ask to work with a particular professor, and many apply to the school primarily to do just that. One student, for example, said he met his cello teacher at a summer music camp and decided to go to Eastman so he could continue to study with her. Some popular professors include clarinetist Kenneth Grant, pianist Barry Snyder, and flautist Bonita Boyd. The members of the Cleveland String Quartet also teach at Eastman and attract many to their classes and concerts. Students have substantial contact with faculty members, both in lessons and in other contexts like chamber groups.

Living and Breathing Music

Everything at Eastman revolves around music. The musical motif on campus is inescapable; the snack bar is called the Orchestra Pit and the newspaper is called Clef Notes. Students rave about their "access to music on hand anytime." They can go to concerts every night if they want to; Eastman's calendar is filled with student and faculty performances by soloists and groups in the Eastman Theater, concerts every other week by the Rochester Philharmonic Orchestra (Eastman students get free tickets), and limitless other performances. Eastman's Sibley Library also has an enormous music collection (the second-largest in the nation), including books, manuscripts, and recordings of "just about everything," one student said. Whenever undergrads want to listen to music but just can't find a concert to go to, they can always listen to their favorite symphony or opera at the library. Students who want to participate in athletics, student government, and other nonmusical extracurricular activities can journey over to the University of Rochester campus.

For those with the energy to play for more than the three to six hours they're expected to practice each day, there are plenty of opportunities to perform. Some students give several recitals a year, while others only do one in their four years at school. Many undergrads participate in chamber orchestras, quartets, or other small ensembles, either for credit or for fun. Jazz bands and string quartets are in constant demand at local restaurants and bars. Traveling Broadway shows that come to

Rochester sometimes need a player to fill in and look to Eastman students for help. Students also have many chances to play at church services, weddings, and other special events.

Few Distractions

The Eastman campus is small, with just three buildings located in the heart of downtown Rochester: Eastman Commons, a classroom building, and Sibley Library. The food at the cafeteria is "pretty normal," according to one student. "You know, it's got a salad and pasta bar, burgers and fries, and a frozen yogurt machine." In the dorm, freshmen live in doubles, and all upperclassmen have singles. Moving off campus is a popular option for juniors and seniors, but freshmen and sophomores are required to live on campus. Many students prefer the dorm because the surrounding neighborhood reportedly "isn't the greatest." Dorm life exposes students to an environment where everyone knows everyone else and has the same interests, so life can get a little boring. For those who need to get away, popular options include the Rochester Club, which features jazz every Friday night, and the Spaghetti Warehouse. Students also like to hang out and "go crazy" at nearby dance clubs in downtown Rochester.

> "It's not like a big old party school."

Campus social life is somewhat limited. As one student explained, "It's not like a big old party school." For those who favor the Greek scene, there is one all-male fraternity, one sorority, and one coed fraternity. The all-male and all-female groups each have a floor of the 14-story Eastman Commons to themselves. The all-male fraternity sponsors most of the parties, while the other Greek groups focus on community service work. Eastman has two annual formals, one in the fall and one in the spring. Small parties in the dorm are common; one student remarked that the delivery truck from a local liquor store is frequently spotted outside the dorm. Students don't seem to mind the low-key social scene; as one sophomore pointed out, "The fewer distractions, the easier it is to concentrate on practicing—which is good, I guess."

Freshmen typically arrive at Eastman from all corners of the world with visions of their names in lights. Each dreams of being the next great viola player, soprano soloist, or jazz pianist. These dreams become transformed over the next few years into more realistic aspirations. One junior explained that

it doesn't matter to her whether she ends up as the soloist with a major symphony or a player in a community orchestra: "As long as I'm playing, that's cool with me."—*Susanna Chu*

FYI

If you come to Eastman, you'd better bring, "a lamp, because the dorms don't have overhead lighting."

What is the typical weekend schedule? "Practice and go to concerts."

If I could change one thing about Eastman, I would "change the weather!"

Three things every student at Eastman should do before graduating are "attend a seminar by a world-famous musician, play every instrument once, and go see Niagara Falls."

Eugene Lang College

Address: Eugene Lang College/ New School, 65 West 11th Street, New York, NY 10011

Phone: 212-229-5665

E-mail Address: lang@newschool.edu

Web site URL: www.lang.newschool.edu

Year Founded: 1919

Private or Public: private

Religious affiliation: none

Location: urban

Regular Application Deadline: 2-Feb

Number of Applicants: NA

Percent Accepted: 66%

Percent Accepted who enroll: 29%

Number Entering: 283

Number of Transfers Accepted each Year: 203

Mean SAT: NA

Mean ACT: NA

Middle 50% SAT range: 560–670V, 500–620M, 560–670CW

Middle 50% ACT range: 22–28

Early admission program (EA/ ED/ NA): ED

ED or EA Acceptance Rate: NA

Full time Undergraduate enrollment: 1,147

Total enrollment: 1,164

Percent Male: 29%

Percent Female: 71%

Total Percent Minority: 21%

Percent African-American: 4%

Percent Asian/Pacific Islander: 7%

Percent Hispanic: 9%

Percent Native-American: 1%

Percent Other: 79%

Percent in-state / out of state: 24%/76%

Percent from Public HS: 26%

Retention Rate: 66%

Graduation Rate: 53%

Percent in On-campus housing: 30%

Percent affiliated with Greek system: 0%

Percent Varsity or Club Athletes: NA

Number of official organized extracurricular organizations: 7

3 Most popular majors: Area Ethnic Cultural and Gender Studies, Creative Writing, Social Sciences (General)

Student/Faculty ratio: 22:01

Tuition and Fees: $29,210

Cost for Room and Board: $11,750.00

Percent receiving Financial aid, first-year: 79%

Students at Eugene Lang College know that theirs is not the typical college experience. They wouldn't have it any other way. "There was nowhere else I could see myself going," said one student. "I had to come to Eugene Lang." Eugene Lang College, also known as The New School for Liberal Arts, is one of eight colleges that comprise The New School, located in New York City's Greenwich Village. Founded in 1919 by a small group of intellectuals, The New School began as a forum for discussion, inviting the public to its lectures and encouraging dissent. Over the next 70 years, The New School founded

seven other divisions, or colleges, including a design school and a program in jazz and contemporary music. Students apply to one of The New School's eight branches, but they reap the benefits of the close partnership of the divisions. Depending on their program of study, students are allowed to take a certain number of classes at other divisions of The New School. Students also report a great deal of "non-academic interaction" between students in different divisions, as residence halls are not divided by college, and school-sponsored events bring New School students together.

An Engaging Environment

Students agree that the school's philosophy of learning distinguishes it from other colleges. Classes at Eugene Lang are virtually all seminars, though recently a two-lecture requirement was instituted for all students. Still, at Eugene Lang, the focus is on small classes and intense discussion. Students praised the richness of the classroom environment: "Students bring so many different arenas of thought into the classes, which make the classes deep and meaningful." The curriculum at Lang is highly interdisciplinary, with such programs as Arts in Context—the study of fine or performing arts in the context of the liberal arts—and Cultural Studies and Media. Furthermore, Eugene Lang is committed to developing exceptional writers. Writing is one of the most popular concentrations at Lang (which does not have "majors"), and one student pointed out that "even if you're not in the writing program, classes at Lang are writing-intensive." All freshmen are required to take a year-long writing class, about which students had mixed opinions. One student found the first semester of the class, on essay-writing, to be unhelpful, but she raved about the class's second semester, which surveyed methods of research. In general, however, students had nothing but praise for the academic experience at Eugene Lang. The small seminars allow for a high level of engagement with the material, students claim, and Lang's interdisciplinary approach fosters an uncommon academic experience. "People think hard about what they are reading and how it applies to their lives," one student said.

To Dorm or Not to Dorm?

Lang freshmen are guaranteed housing, and most choose to live on-campus. Students reflected positively on their experience in dorms, pointing out that dorm life introduced them to the Lang community and often helped establish lasting relationships. Students from different divisions of The New School live together in the dorms, and one student praised this integration as a means of "bringing different people together to share their experiences, which is what The New School is all about." Loeb Hall is particularly coveted, since University Health Services are located there. The New School's dorms include many rooms with in-suite kitchens, making on-campus living an attractive alternative to finding an apartment in the city. What's more, with the ex-

ception of two, all dorms are located close to campus, while off-campus students must pay more to live close by, or, more often, live in Brooklyn and endure the hassle of commuting to school.

> "Students bring so many different arenas of thought into the classes, which make the classes deep and meaningful."

Regardless, most students choose to live off campus after their freshman year. One upperclassman claimed that choosing to live on-campus as an upperclassman was "a bad decision, because you're over the freshman thing—yelling in the dorms and going out a lot—but you're living with freshmen."

Because of the popularity of off-campus living, most Lang students have moderate or minimal interaction with the school's food service. Students who live on campus must purchase a meal plan, though depending on the dorm they live in, students may be able to choose a less inclusive plan. One student maintained that "you can get better food around the city for the same price," though he did point out that the cafeterias are conveniently located.

Student Politics and Bizarre Bars

Students at Eugene Lang are involved in both the campus community and the city community. Students claim that there is "a lot of programming for people looking for a college community," including frequent, sponsored events such as conferences, lectures, and readings. But students also point out that many Lang students are more interested in exploring New York City than becoming involved in the Lang community. One student admitted that Lang is "infamous for not having much community" but added that this is "a superficial judgment." Indeed, many students enjoy off-campus parties that are "packed with Lang students." In conclusion, most students enjoy the opportunity to immerse oneself in the culture of New York and "make friends all over the city" while having the chance to "make of the Lang community what you want to make of it." Students point out that the interaction between Eugene Lang and the city is essential to the college's mission to integrate the arts and ideas of the city into the learning process. For example, many classes send students out into the city to study its religious culture or art.

One group of students, however, is committed to building community at Lang. The Lang Student Union, which is a consensus-based rather than representative body, meets regularly and is open to all Lang students. Student Union facilitators present proposals, which a single student has the power to block. Students speak highly of the consensus system, claiming that "it's rare that a compromise can't be reached" through negotiation. One Student Union facilitator highlighted a difficulty of the consensus system, however, pointing out that at a school as diverse as Lang, it's often difficult for students to agree on what they want.

Lang students are busy off campus as well. Many students work in the city, often as event promoters or party planners. As a result, many Lang students have ins at exclusive New York clubs. Otherwise, the weekend finds Lang students at apartment parties or nearby bars and clubs such as French Roast (a combination restaurant, bar, and café), Cooper 35 (a freshman hangout), and the Bulgarian Culture Club. One student described Lang haunts as "weird places, with cheap drinks, that are on the verge of being incredibly bizarre."

One thing Lang students don't experience on the weekend is the college football game. There are no varsity sports teams at Lang, and there are a few IMs coordinated through the local YMCA, but students say that they are not popular. Lang does offer less traditional physical activities, such as Capoeira, yoga, salsa dancing, and meditation. One student recalled an epic dodgeball game, organized by a Cultural Studies professor, with particular fondness. But those looking for a traditional sports scene should look elsewhere.

To be sure, Eugene Lang is not your typical college. As students point out, taking the road less traveled is in Lang's nature: "The courses at Lang encourage you to think about things in different ways," said one student. "You piece together your own history."
—*Kathleen Reeves*

FYI

If you come to Eugene Lang, you'd better bring "Said's *On Orientalism* and Foucault's *Discipline and Punish*, which are central to Eugene Lang's canon."

What's the typical weekend schedule? "The weekend starts on Thursday night, Friday is free for jobs, sleeping in, or museum visits, and Friday and Saturday nights, we head to bars, coffee shops or apartment parties or visit friends at other schools around the city."

If you could change one thing about Eugene Lang, it'd be "the bureaucracy. Communication between the administration and the student body is often mediocre, and it's hard to get things changed or implement new programs."

Three things every student at Eugene Lang should do before graduating are "attend a reading by professors in the Writing Concentration, or read your own at an open mic event; read *The Weekly Observer*, an online publication, to find out about the many school-sponsored events, such as Air America tapings or a social justice conference; and attend a Student Union meeting.

Fordham University

Address: Fordham, 441 E. Fordham Road, Bronx, NY 10458
Phone: 800-FORDHAM
E-mail Address: enroll@fordham.edu
Web site URL: www.fordham.edu
Year Founded: 1841
Private or Public: private
Religious affiliation: Jesuit
Location: urban
Regular Application Deadline: 16-Jan
Number of Applicants: NA
Percent Accepted: 47%
Percent Accepted who enroll: NA
Number Entering: 1,722
Number of Transfers Accepted each Year: 554
Mean SAT: 1,186
Mean ACT: 26

Middle 50% SAT range: 550–650V, 550–640M, 620–690CW
Middle 50% ACT range: 24–24
Early admission program (EA/ ED/ NA): EA
ED or EA Acceptance Rate: NA
Full time Undergraduate enrollment: 7,451
Total enrollment: 7,701
Percent Male: 49%
Percent Female: 61%
Total Percent Minority: 23%
Percent African-American: 5%
Percent Asian/Pacific Islander: 6%
Percent Hispanic: 12%
Percent Native-American: 0%
Percent Other: 76%
Percent in-state / out of state: 50%/50%
Percent from Public HS: 47%

Retention Rate: 90%
Graduation Rate: 78%
Percent in On-campus housing: 56%
Percent affiliated with Greek system: 0%
Percent Varsity or Club Athletes: NA
Number of official organized extracurricular organizations: 133
3 Most popular majors: Business Administration/ Management, Communications, Social Sciences
Student/Faculty ratio: 13:01
Tuition and Fees: $30,265.00
Cost for Room and Board: $11,630.00
Percent receiving Financial aid, first-year: 77%

With a whiff of the countryside, a hint of suburbia, and a dash of metropolis, the three campuses of Fordham University combine the best of what New York City and its bordering communities have to offer. If you're seeking a mix of academics with cultural and outdoor opportunities, Fordham might just be for you.

A Boom, No Bust

Recent changes at Fordham have taken place so rapidly that, to many, it seems like a whole new school, and most agree that the new version is much better than the old.

The $230 million endowment which, according to one student, is "approaching half the GDP of Sierra Leone" has made many major renovations at Fordham's Lincoln Center campus in Manhattan possible. During the summer of 2003, the Fordham administration dedicated funds to a video production facility, a new computer lab, a general facelift in Quinn Library, a new White Box Theater, the expansion of the Pushpin Gallery, a gallery for student work, on-campus wireless Internet capabilities, and several new classrooms and faculty offices. A music professor at the Rose Hill campus discussed long-term plans to build a new performance space dedicated solely to the arts, as now the only sufficiently large space available is at the adjacent Fordham High School.

One junior cites major improvements in the Lincoln Center campus dining hall: "the Fordham Cafeteria has gone out of its way to reinvent itself," now serving grilled chicken wraps and fresh smoothies. Despite their low ranking as one of the worst college dining halls less than five years ago, a Rose Hill campus senior agrees that the cafeteria has "gotten much better" and offers "more options." The 1998 merger of the all-women's Marymount College with Fordham University added exciting new elements to Fordham academics, social life, and resources.

Three Are Better Than One

Fordham's eleven undergraduate and graduate schools are divided into three campuses: Rose Hill in the Bronx, Lincoln Center in midtown Manhattan, and Marymount, 25 miles north of the city in Tarrytown, New York. Each campus has its own unique vibe, so students can choose which best meets their liking while benefiting from the diverse resources of three distinct campuses. Students apply for admission to one, but often cross-register and can transfer once they matriculate. One student claims that the Rose Hill campus was voted "the greenest" location in all of New York City. "In addition to the very picturesque gardens and trees that you can sit under while reading," she says, "there's this huge field in the middle of campus (Eddie's Parade), that's perfect for playing on. Some people break out the soccer ball or softball gloves or lacrosse sticks; I prefer Frisbee." Rose Hill focuses on a classic liberal arts education and includes an undergraduate College of Business Administration. In the spirit of healthy rivalry, one student insists that Rose Hill is the "much cooler campus" compared to Lincoln Center—"except for being in Manhattan." And being in Manhattan is key. Known for its excellence in art, media, and the performing arts, the Lincoln Center campus provides students ideal access to the city's thousands of cultural resources.

More than 70 percent of Fordham students live on-campus in traditional college residential halls. Some dorms offer special features, like kitchens in a senior dorm and Queens Court, which holds daily debates and public speaking events, as well as other cultural events and dinners with faculty. While the "dorms are pretty nice," with fitness centers, 24-hour security, and apartment suites for two or three, many upperclassmen choose to live off-campus.

For typical extracurricular opportunities other than those in the performing arts, Lincoln Center students go to the Rose Hill campus and participate in activities and club sports. In turn, Rose Hill students visit Lincoln Center for its cultural events and use it as a "starting-off point" for a night out on the town. The Ram Van comes regularly to take students from campus to campus for free, which is about a half-hour ride.

While the bulk of activity may seem to be in full force at its original campus locations, the all-women's Marymount campus in Tarrytown, New York, clearly holds its own. Female students looking for more of a sense of family with smaller, more intimate classes choose the Marymount campus. Marymount students experience all the benefits of an empowering women's college, while associating with a larger, co-ed community.

A Three-Headed Academic Beast

Fordham is increasingly becoming more selective and competitive. Students commend small class size and award-winning professors as integral to the excellence of a Fordham education. Except for the biology department, there are no teaching assistants,

which means that professors themselves lead discussion groups. Professors reportedly make themselves available to talk with students and are approachable.

Fordham features a true liberal arts education, requiring its students to take classes in literature, philosophy, theology, history, math, natural science, social science, fine arts, and a foreign language. Students commence their Fordham careers with a freshman seminar and complete it with a senior seminar in Values and Moral Choices. Students must also take classes that fulfill their global studies and American pluralism (which focuses on issues of ethnicity, race, and class) requirements. The extensive core curriculum is not especially popular among freshmen daunted by "seemingly endless" requirements, but seniors "appreciate" the core curriculum for exposing them to fields of study that they otherwise would have overlooked.

Your Roommate

When asked what the typical Fordham student is like, one student responded, "white, from Long Island and a communications major." Many are Catholic and "over-privileged," coming from private schools in the tri-state area (New York, New Jersey, Connecticut), Massachusetts, and Ohio. As a result, many students complain about the lack of diversity in ethnicity, religion, and geography.

Commuter students make up a large percentage of the student body (at the Lincoln Center campus, it's a 1:1 ratio of residential to commuter students). One student says that commuters are stereotypically "total metrosexuals" from Westchester who are "always dressed up" and "all drive BMWs."

Out and About

The bar scene typifies Fordham nightlife. Rose Hill students can be found flooding the bars on Arthur Avenue of the Bronx's Little Italy. Lincoln Center students scatter among bars and nightclubs all over Manhattan, though many frequent nearby favorites. Because of the hassle of registering parties and the requirement that all suitemates hosting a party must be at least 21, on-campus nightlife generates little support. One student wishes Fordham held "more events, more concerts" and would "like to see a bar on-campus" in order to generate a sense of community.

The bar-scene social life means alcohol is the substance of choice for most students and contributes to the fact that there are reportedly more drunken random hookups than relationships. But the influence of the school's Jesuit tradition attempts to mitigate these facts. The student organization Prevention PARty hosts alternatives to alcohol-infiltrated social events. Moreover, there's the co-habitation policy, which is sometimes a point of contention. Fordham enforces a 3:30 a.m. curfew for students visiting members of the opposite sex. One incensed student declares, "How arbitrary. One can visit but not spend the night. A 3:30 curfew, however, allows individuals plenty of time and room to engage in behavior the church would find shameful."

Fordham sports aren't anything to go crazy about. Athletic teams are "okay to good," but "Fordham doesn't usually have great school spirit." Rose Hill has decent facilities, including a "typical university fieldhouse." But the Lincoln Center campus has only a fitness center and doesn't support any teams. Fordham's strong ties to religion are expressed in a well-developed Campus Ministry, though one student reported, "Nobody complains about the theology requirements." For all the talk about Catholicism, students insist that Fordham is open to people of all religious traditions.

The City That Never Sleeps

And what do you think college kids smack-dab in the center of the world would do for fun? With restaurants, museums, nightlife, cultural events, and little nooks and crannies just waiting for discovery, New York City defines the Fordham experience. Exploring New York is a "major part of the Lincoln Center campus," reports one senior. Among one Lincoln Center student's favorite activities are hanging out in Central Park, people-watching along Mulberry Street in Little Italy, celebrity-watching at key restaurants, and going to talk shows, like David Letterman, for free.

> **"[Fordham has] eight million opportunities to open new horizons."**

With summer internship opportunities sometimes literally just across the street, the city provides unbelievable resources. Internship programs at major corporations and media outlets attract many Fordham students. The Lincoln Center campus also offers a Bachelor of Fine Arts in dance through its joint program with the Alvin Ailey Dance Center only a few blocks away. With its "eight million opportunities to open new horizons," New York City offers Fordham students an invaluable resource. As one student put it, "It's why I'm here."—*Baily Blair*

FYI
If you come to Fordham you'd better bring "a Frisbee!"
What is the typical weekend schedule? "Wake up at 3 p.m., do nothing until dinner at 8 p.m., and go out again at 1 a.m. to party."
If I could change one thing about Fordham, I would "make it more diverse."
Three things every student should do before graduating are "go to Alumni Court at least once, go see a show in New York City, and be at school for Spring Weekend."

Hamilton College

Address: Hamilton, 198 College Hill Road, Clinton, NY 13323
Phone: 315-859-4421
E-mail Address: admissions@hamilton.edu
Web site URL: www.hamilton.edu
Year Founded: 1812
Private or Public: private
Religious affiliation: none
Location: rural
Regular Application Deadline: 2-Jan
Number of Applicants: NA
Percent Accepted: 36%
Percent Accepted who enroll: 33%
Number Entering: 501
Number of Transfers Accepted each Year: 4
Mean SAT: 1,343
Mean ACT: NA

Middle 50% SAT range: 630–720V, 640–720M, 670–740W
Middle 50% ACT range: NA
Early admission program (EA/ ED/ NA): ED
ED or EA Acceptance Rate: 48%
Full time Undergraduate enrollment: 1,801
Total enrollment: 1,821
Percent Male: 47%
Percent Female: 53%
Total Percent Minority: 18%
Percent African-American: 5%
Percent Asian/Pacific Islander: 8%
Percent Hispanic: 4%
Percent Native-American: 1%
Percent Other: 82%
Percent in-state / out of state: 33%/67%
Percent from Public HS: 60%

Retention Rate: 93%
Graduation Rate: 88%
Percent in On-campus housing: 98%
Percent affiliated with Greek system: 48%
Percent Varsity or Club Athletes: NA
Number of official organized extracurricular organizations: 80
3 Most popular majors: Economics, Political Science and Government, Psychology
Student/Faculty ratio: 10:01
Tuition and Fees: $34,980.00
Cost for Room and Board: $8,910.00
Percent receiving Financial aid, first-year: 80%

Looking for a beautiful campus, a close community of spirited, involved and just-plain-nice people with small classes that are only taught by professors? Hamilton College, located in the picturesque Adirondack area of Clinton, N.Y., might be just the school for you. Having witnessed numerous changes over recent years—including physical improvements, major changes in the curriculum, and a new president—Hamilton is an exciting and welcoming place to be.

The Curriculum: New and Improved

As of last year, Hamilton did away with distributional requirements in an effort to encourage students to design their own curriculum. Still essential to a Hamilton education, however, is the writing requirement, which requires that students take three writing-intensive classes in any subject by the end of their sophomore year. While this may prove difficult if you don't plan your schedule well—"last semester was pretty bad because I took all writing classes, so it got a bit monotonous, always writing papers," bemoaned one freshman—Hamiltonians undoubtedly graduate with a strong foundation in writing skills. "My writing has definitely improved since I was a freshman; I thought that I had learned to write well enough in high school, but there is always room to grow in that area," a junior commented.

It's no surprise, then, that Hamilton's English department is very strong, and that English 150, a survey of Western literature, is the most popular class among freshmen. There is also a writing center where other students are available to edit papers and hash-out ideas. Other popular majors include government, economics and psychology, while the language departments are considered weaker. Hamilton's academic offerings are strengthened across the board by the great amount of tutorial support. Such aid is not limited to the liberal arts at the writing center—if you need some help with math, you can always head over to the Q-Lit center to meet with a tutor.

Classes run small at Hamilton, ranging from around 40 in freshmen classes to six in some upperclassmen courses. This can make some classes very difficult to get into, but if you make your case to the professor or if you are a major in that subject, your chances are greatly improved. Students praise the interaction with their professors, who are "very personable," and feel that small classes allow for a wealth of intellectual opportunities. "The professors are incredible and so willing to meet with and help you. Almost every professor I've had has extended office hours if needed and given us his or her home telephone number," a junior gushed. Of course, some popular departments, such as government, tend to have bigger classes, even in the upper-division major courses. In terms of Hamilton's workload, it depends on what classes you take, but one junior says that "most students are very focused throughout the year, and it gets a little more hectic during finals."

Sports, Greeks and . . . the Dog Pound?

While there is no pressure to drink, alcohol is important to the social life for many— "you're in the middle of nowhere; what else is there to do?" one student pointed out. Hamiltonians generally drink one to four nights a week, though there aren't many "four-nighters." This past year, however, with the arrival of the new president, Hamilton has been enforcing its alcohol policy and underage drinking has reportedly decreased a little. "There are ways around the strictness, but it's not really worth it," said a freshman. "However, if you want something you can get it." With or without alcohol, Hamiltonians are not lacking in opportunities for fun. About 30 to 35 percent of students go Greek, so fraternities and sororities contribute greatly to the party scene by hosting most of the on-campus parties. Everyone is invited to their themed parties that are reputedly always well-themed, from '80s night to "farm party." Societies sometimes host parties off campus, but those are often invite-only because partygoers must be shuttled.

If you're not into the frats, there are other options. Non-Greek activities, like frequenting acoustic coffee-houses, are common, but as one sorority member pointed out, "It's hard to attract athletic and Greek types to stuff like that," and at Hamilton that's a large percentage of the student body. Groups like the Campus Activity Board (CAB) and the Inter-Society Council, however, try to provide a variety of gatherings that unite the student body, such as Alexander Hamilton weekend, during which there are relay races and a carnival day.

Sports are undoubtedly a big part of the social scene—Friday nights are pretty dull, for example, because athletes don't go out in preparation for Saturday games. Even though all of Hamilton's sports are Division III and academics always come first, students love their teams. "School spirit has increased since I came here," one junior claimed. Sporting events are popular, and Hamilton has great hockey, basketball and lacrosse teams. The football team is not too fantastic, but Hamiltonians still come out to cheer, especially since the basketball fans' tradition of the "Dog Pound" has spread to other sporting events. This tradition consists of a group of exceptionally fanatical guys dressed up in costumes cheering and going crazy in a roped-off area of the field or gymnasium.

Play a Sport or Wreak Some HAVOC

Hamilton's extracurriculars are dominated by sports, and if you're on a team, that obviously takes up a lot of your free time. The less intense types play intramurals, which are very popular. Beyond the playing field, a lot of Hamiltonians are involved in HAVOC (a student-run community-service organization), yearbook, and the Hamilton Outing Club, from which you can rent just about any outdoors equipment. While extracurriculars are not as popular here as at other institutions, "after freshman year, when you don't do too much, you start wanting to get more involved," an upperclassman noted.

The Campus: Old, New and Improving

Hamilton was once made up of two colleges: Hamilton College for men and Kirkland for women. Now it's one, but Hamilton, the north side, and Kirkland, the south side, have very distinctive architectural tones. The north side's buildings are old and "feel very New-England, very prestigious," while Kirkland, built in the '60s, has "imposing" and "cold-looking" modern architecture. The two campuses are close and small enough that commuting between the two is not a problem. While there isn't a whole lot around the campus, "it's less isolated than I thought it would be when I came here," a freshman said. You need a car to get anywhere, and though freshmen cannot own cars, there is a jitney service that runs to nearby malls and to various places on campus. Clinton itself "is a beautiful town, and there are no issues with locals coming on campus—it's an open campus," one student noted. Hamilton has two main dining halls, as well as a diner and a pub that are part of the meal plan. As at any college, it's easy to get sick of the food, but there are a variety of options offered, from sushi to pizza. As a part of the college's dedication to its physical plant, Hamilton's science buildings are now undergoing major renovation: there will be a new part added, and all the labs will be brought up to date.

Hamilton's dorm options are recently renovated and well liked, especially since Greek houses were taken away and made into dorms for upperclassmen in 1996. "While a lot of frat members were very upset about that," a junior said, "I love it. I'm around so many different people. It's a great way to meet people by not having them segregated by societies in different houses." There is a lottery system for all students except freshmen, who live among upperclassmen. Other options are available in terms of housing; you can opt for a single-sex floor or for a substance-free dorm that is located in Root Dormitory. Off-campus housing is available to only a small number of seniors, and the administration is trying to eliminate it completely.

A Typical Hamiltonian . . .

Hamilton is not known for its ethnic diversity; most students will probably tell you that a diverse campus was not their priority when they chose their school. The student body is quite homogeneous, "it's pretty much white kids from Connecticut who wear J. Crew," and there is considerable self-segregation, from races to fraternities, the latter of which are generally divided by sports. Despite the modicum of diversity that the lack of Greek houses fosters, upperclassmen often room with members of their own society or sports team. "The administration is trying to pass a rule that will bar students in societies from living together, but that is a long way from happening," said a freshman. There is a definite conservative political presence on campus: "Hamilton's academics are liberal, but the student body is quite conservative. I thought that I would find more liberals here because of the academics," a junior noted.

According to one junior, "the dating scene is so weird." There are a lot of random hookups, and then couples who are all but married. Certain drugs also prevail on campus—Hamilton has a zero-tolerance policy for narcotics like cocaine, but "study drugs" like Ritalin are present. The small student population has its curses and its blessings. News travels fast in such a small institution: "Everything gets passed around so quickly and you sort of know everyone's name or face. Sometimes it can feel a bit like high school, but in a good way," a freshman said.

> "People just hang out and spend a lot of time together, and they don't really leave on the weekends. When I got here, it felt like camp."

Hamilton's close-knit community is, in fact, what students really love about it. Its small size especially allows freshmen to feel at home from the start: "All the upperclassmen are really nice and welcoming," lauded a freshman. "I was very attracted to the small, intimate campus," one student said. "And it sounds cliché, but everyone here is so friendly. People just hang out and spend a lot of time together, and they don't really leave on the weekends. When I got here, it felt like camp." Hamilton may be small, but Hamiltonians' love of their campus, their professors and their community is immense.
—*Samantha Wilson*

FYI
If you come to Hamilton, you'd better bring "a warm jacket for the winter."
What is the typical weekend schedule? "Friday, hang out, dinner and a movie; Saturday, party, then to the bar (which is "downtown", i.e. down the hill); Sunday, homework all day.
If I could change one thing about Hamilton, I would "put it in San Diego. Everyone's so much happier when it's nice out."
Three things that every student at Hamilton should do before graduating are: "go to a Bundy party, go for a walk in the Root Glen, and dance at the diner late-night."

Hobart and William Smith Colleges

Address: Hobart and William Smith, 629 S. Main St., Geneva, NY 14456
Phone: 800-852-2256
E-mail Address: admissions@hws.edu
Web site URL: www.hws.edu/admissions
Year Founded: 1822
Private or Public: private
Religious affiliation: none
Location: small city
Regular Application Deadline: 1-Feb
Number of Applicants: 3,266
Percent Accepted: 63%
Percent Accepted who enroll: 23%
Number Entering: NA
Number of Transfers Accepted each Year: NA
Mean SAT: 1,175
Mean ACT: NA

Middle 50% SAT range: 540–620V, 545–640M
Middle 50% ACT range: 24–27
Early admission program (EA/ ED/ NA): ED
ED or EA Acceptance Rate: 79%
Full time Undergraduate enrollment: 1,825
Total enrollment: 1,825
Percent Male: 46%
Percent Female: 54%
Total Percent Minority: 12%
Percent African-American: 4%
Percent Asian/Pacific Islander: 2%
Percent Hispanic: 4%
Percent Native-American: 2%
Percent Other: 1%
Percent in-state / out of state: 47%/53%

Percent from Public HS: 65%
Retention Rate: 85%
Graduation Rate: NA
Percent in On-campus housing: 90%
Percent affiliated with Greek system: 15%
Percent Varsity or Club Athletes: NA
Number of official organized extracurricular organizations: 77
3 Most popular majors: Economics, English, History
Student/Faculty ratio: 11:01
Tuition and Fees: $31,850.00
Cost for Room and Board: $8,386.00
Percent receiving Financial aid, first-year: 59%

Nestled in upstate New York next to Seneca Lake is the gorgeous campus of Hobart and William Smith Colleges. HWS is actually a combination of two schools, Hobart, the men's college, and William Smith, the women's college. Each has its own masters, deans, athletic teams, and student governments, but they share the same campus and classes. HWS offers its students the full package with an intimate academic setting, as well as a comfortable lifestyle.

Two Colleges, One Campus

Hobart and William Smith's "coordinate system" of two colleges sharing one campus and one academic experience can sometimes catch first year students off guard. But most come to praise the unique setup. Although the schools have separate administrations, most daily happenings are coed—there are just a larger number of same-sex dorms than there would be at different college. The majority of freshmen are placed into same-sex dorms, but students have the choice of living in coed housing after their first year. Even given that choice, many girls find that "living with all girls as a start to

college can be nice . . . it's an easier transition into college." Not to mention that, "girls' floors are much cleaner and nicer!" Nevertheless, female students did remark that living in separate dorms made "it slightly more difficult to find a consistent group of guy friends."

Wine Tasting Makes the Grade

Hobart's academics emphasize an interdisciplinary approach to liberal arts within a very intimate setting. The academic calendar is organized into semesters. Students are expected to take four classes each semester. Class sizes range from as tiny as seven people to around 30 at most. According to one student, "Professors have been really interested in getting to know me as a person in and outside of the classroom. I've had gourmet dinners at my professors' homes and they have come to extracurricular activities that I'm involved in."

Students are required to complete the requirements for an academic major, as well as a minor or second major. Some of the more popular majors include psychology and economics. Hobart and William Smith is also strong in political science, English, women's studies, and biology. Of course, the sciences are cited as majors for those who "don't mind spending more of their time in the library." For students hoping to exist on the opposite end of the work-intensive spectrum, dance is one of the easier majors at HWS.

Freshmen are given a variety of multidisciplinary seminar options ranging from Music of the Harlem Renaissance to Theories of Masculinity. An extremely popular course for those of legal drinking age is the wine tasting class, which takes advantage of the numerous wineries in the area. The majority of Hobart students go abroad at some point during their four years and the school offers programs in an impressive number of locations around the world. HWS students run the gamut from extremely intellectual to those less focused on academics, but in general students manage to get their work done well and also enjoy campus life.

A Lakeside View
Hobart and William Smith students are required to live on campus for all four years, with very few exceptions granted to seniors. Students generally agree that the, "dorms are really nice compared to other schools." There are housing options ranging from traditional doubles on a hall to apartments and condos to theme houses such as the Community Service House or Music Appreciation House. The Greek houses situated along the lake are prime property, not only because of their location, but also for being "large and beautiful." Students are required to be on a school meal plan and there are two dining halls and a café on campus. The food is generally satisfactory and the school provides a variety of choices everyday. Unfortunately, budget cuts in the last year have caused a noticeable decline in the food quality.

Students agree that their campus is picturesque. In the words of one student: "I doubt there has been one person to walk onto our campus and not find it beautiful." Seneca Lake also adds an element to campus life, providing a variety of year-round activities such as boating, tubing and sailing. As one student put it, "Everyone loves the lake when it's nice out." The campus itself is well maintained, and thanks to the lakefront location, HWS is a gem to behold. In the past decade, the school has put a great deal of money into updating science, lab and athletic facilities, as well as into wiring the school and improving the library,

which includes building the Melly Academic Center.

> **"I doubt there has been one person to walk onto our campus and not find it beautiful."**

Although Geneva is not a college town, a number of area venues cater to the school. Geneva boasts numerous pizza places, bars, and dance clubs. And students should familiarize themselves with the yearly line-up at The Smith Opera House, a performance center where artists such as Bruce Springstein and Garth Fagan's dance company have performed. The town is within walking distance and the school provides free shuttles, making it not only a popular destination, but also a convenient one at that!

Herons in the Holiday Spirit
The social scene at Hobart provides something for every interest. Greeks do not dominate in any sense, but there are a few frats who supply the occasional late night or party, such as Delta's annual beach party. The fraternity brothers fill the house with sand and bring in a band and open bar. Dorm regulations are loose and games of Beirut and flip cup commonly start up in rooms as pre-games. Once midnight hits on weekends, everyone flocks downtown to either Holiday, a favorite college bar, or one of the other bars or dance clubs. The typical nights to go out are Wednesdays, Fridays and Saturdays. One of the larger school-sponsored events is the annual Spring Fling.

HWS students are involved in a variety of extracurriculars. Athletics have a huge presence. Lacrosse is particularly strong, and according to one enthusiastic Heron, "The Syracuse versus Hobart Division I lacrosse game is a can't miss!" Koshare, the student run dance club, is also incredibly popular and a cappella always draws a large crowd. ORAP, the outdoors club, sponsors many widely attended trips such as white water rafting and overnight hikes.

Hobart and William Smith students are characterized as "friendly and easy to meet," but are not necessarily the most diverse group. The student body seems to pull mainly from the tri-state and mid-Atlantic region. A description of the average student is a "J.Crew-wearing, white, middle class, preppy kid." Despite a conspicuous lack of diversity, those who differ from the norm also do not feel pressure to conform. Minorities make up around 20 percent of the student population and the small gay and lesbian community is well accepted with the help of organizations like the Gay, Lesbian, Bisexual Friends network.

Hobart and William Smith attracts motivated and well-balanced students by way of a beautiful campus and an excellent academic setting. The merging of the men and women's colleges makes for a good fit and students are generally thrilled to be there.— *Janet Yang*

FYI

If you come to HWS, you'd better bring "warm clothes!"

What's the typical weekend schedule? "Friday and Saturday nights involve pre-gaming in a dorm room, hitting some bars, going back to a frat's late night and grabbing pizza before heading home. Saturday afternoons are spent enjoying the weekend and Sundays are devoted to work."

If I could change one thing about HWS, it would be "uniting Hobart and William Smith and giving one common diploma."

Three things every student at Hobart and William Smith should do before graduating are "hike in Watkins Glen, go sailing on Seneca Lake, and eat at Water Street Café."

Hofstra University

Address: Hofstra, 100 Hofstra University, Hempstead, NY 11549-1000

Phone: 800-HOFSTRA

E-mail Address: admitme@hofstra.edu

Web site URL: www.hofstra.edu

Year Founded: 1935

Private or Public: private

Religious affiliation: none

Location: suburban

Application and Admissions Information: rolling

Regular Application Deadline: NA

Number of Applicants: 13,493

Percent Accepted: 62%

Percent Accepted who enroll: 21%

Number Entering: 2,383

Number of Transfers Accepted each Year: 1,601

Mean SAT: NA

Mean ACT: NA

Middle 50% SAT range: 1,100–1,230

Middle 50% ACT range: 22–26

Early admission program (EA/ ED/ NA): EA

ED or EA Acceptance Rate: 25%

Full time Undergraduate enrollment: 7,762

Total enrollment: 12,550

Percent Male: 47%

Percent Female: 53%

Total Percent Minority: 14%

Percent African-American: 10%

Percent Asian/Pacific Islander: 5%

Percent Hispanic: 8%

Percent Native-American: <1%

Percent Other: 0%

Percent in-state / out of state: 68%/32%

Percent from Public HS: NA

Retention Rate: 77%

Graduation Rate: 56%

Percent in On-campus housing: 46%

Percent affiliated with Greek system: ~7%

Percent Varsity or Club Athletes: 7%

Number of official organized extracurricular organizations: 150

3 Most popular majors: Psychology, Accounting, Marketing

Student/Faculty ratio: 14:01

Tuition and Fees: $23,230.00

Cost for Room and Board: $9,800.00

Percent receiving Financial aid, first-year: 69%

If you enjoy the peace and quiet of suburbia, the bustling and hectic life of New York City, and have a car, then Hofstra may be the place for you. Whether you plan on commuting or living on campus, the best of both worlds is easily accessible at Hofstra, a small, affordable academic sanctuary just a short train ride away from the city.

Progressive Learning

Academics at Hofstra cover a broad spectrum of topics, with 2,150 classes and 140 programs and majors to choose from. The college even offers a couple programs that lead directly to a graduate degree, namely LEAP (a BA/JD program) and a BBA/MBA program. Majors are often chosen based on how much one is willing to put into one's studies. For example, a chemistry major will have a far different workload than a physical education major. One student said that Hofstra's academics are "not very challenging," yet diverse in the sense that they give opportunities for exploration into new subjects.

Despite common core requirements in math, social studies, natural science, humanities, foreign language and cross-cultural studies, most students are able to create unique schedules from the many classes offered. The diversity of Hofstra's offerings is reflected in the various schools that make up the college: the Hofstra College of Liberal Arts and Science, the Saturday School, the New College of Hofstra, Zarb School of Business, the Honors College and more.

The progressive style of learning found at Hofstra, and especially in the New College and the Honors College, gives students flexibility in their schedules. However, it also requires students to take on the responsibility of making wise choices about their education. Many students enthusiastically say that a great advantage to Hofstra is its small class sizes. The largest class size is 65 students, while the average class has 25 or fewer. "Professors help incite our curiosity in different subjects by giving us a lot of personal attention," one economics major said. Another student said: "They really respect everyone's needs and limitations. Sometimes a prof will let you into a capped class if you show interest and motivation."

Traditional Minds
One of the biggest strengths of the Hofstra experience is its wide variety of options for people of all interests, which Hofstra calls its "progressive" style. In some ways, however, the student body does not seem to reflect Hofstra's progressive view on education. Although socioeconomic and racial diversity is reflected in the statistics, students comment that the undergraduate population can seem homogeneous—"rich preppy kids from Long Island," as one student put it. Another commented that "everyone goes overdressed to class—like they're going to a nightclub," though another added that he certainly doesn't mind that so many female students look their best for early morning classes.

Intramural, club and varsity sports are definitely popular on campus, but they are not necessarily community events. The most popular sports include football, lacrosse and basketball. Many student athletes, however, travel on weekends with their teams and many go home. One student described a Hofstra game as "an empty stadium with potential."

> "Everyone goes overdressed to class—like they're going to a nightclub."

Student organizations are another one of the many things to do outside of the classroom at Hofstra. For journalists, there is *The Chronicle* and *Nonsense Magazine;* for the politically minded, there are opportunities to become involved in student government; and for performers there are various theater and music groups. Moreover, a new state-of-the-art black box theater is being opened on campus to serve the needs of the growing drama department, and add other functional spaces such as those for music rehearsals. A frequently used resource is the Hofstra Recreational Center, which has sports facilities such as ball courts, a track, a pool and space for the many gym classes offered.

Free Spirits
Hofstra's social scene boasts lots of free spirits. The school's active Greek life, composed of 13 sororities and 17 fraternities, provides a strong party scene at which students can let loose on weekends. Bar hopping is also popular. Some of the annual campus parties include the Freak Formal, put on every Halloween, and Homecoming. "The Freak Formal is one of those things you have to go to at least once," one student said.

The University also makes an effort to bring popular music groups to campus for student enjoyment. Student-produced plays, theater events and movie specials are also frequent at Hofstra. Although those students who commute usually go home for the weekends, the campus isn't dead at all. Some people complain, however, that they have a hard time meeting people and making friends, and that it's easier to meet people off campus than on campus. Others say that they fit right in, indicating that perhaps Hofstra is a place for specific people with similar interests.

Ins and Outs
The influx and outflux of students at Hofstra varies by the hour, as commuter students rush to class, chill at cafés, hit the books at Axinn Library, and go home once again. Half of the student body commutes, as most live in the near vicinity. Many students who decide

to live on campus also often go home on weekends. Despite the mass exodus, Hofstra students tend to be satisfied on campus. Residential life is characterized by dorms that are "OK" with "average RAs [who] don't really do anything." The setting has lots of "trees and statues and squirrels." Most agree that Hofstra has an exceptionally beautiful campus, which one student described as not only gorgeous, but "conveniently divided into classes, sports and dorms facilities."

The area around Hempstead, however, is considered to be a little rough—"it's ghetto," one student said. Safety is not a major concern for those on foot, but most students erring on the side of safety learn to walk in pairs, drive or take public transportation at night. The town of Hempstead isn't, apparently, the hippest place to be, but it nonetheless houses enough shopping establishments and restaurants to attract many students. Like at so many colleges, however, those who drive complain that parking "can be an absolute nightmare."

More than a few students express dissatisfaction with the food on campus, which they deem expensive and bland: "It should be better for the price we pay." Most students eat at the Student Center, where wraps are very popular. It is easy, however, to escape the blandness of the campus eateries by frequenting nearby restaurants. The most popular establishments for students include Bits n' Bytes or Kate and Willie's.

For the more outgoing student, more excitement can be found only a short drive or train ride away in New York City. Students rave that Hofstra's second best asset after the intense personal attention from the school is the school's proximity to New York City. "It makes up for Hempstead and definitely sets Hofstra apart from other schools," one student said. All in all, students at Hofstra extol their school, appreciate their liberal and flexible education, and definitely enjoy their college experience.
—*Carolina Galvao*

FYI

If you come to Hofstra, you'd better bring "cash and a fake ID."

What is the typical weekend schedule? "Study all weekend long . . . yeah right! Go home, sleep, chill with friends, go into New York, and wait for the night to start up to go to bars and parties."

If I could change one thing about Hofstra, "I would [keep] a dining place open 24/7, providing coffee."

Three things every student at Hofstra should do before graduating are: "Eat at Sbarros at least 100 times, and regret each time saying 'OK, this was the last time,' and suffer from three fire alarms a day!"

Ithaca College

Address: 100 Job Hall; Ithaca, NY 14850-7020

Phone: 800-429-4274

E-mail address: admission@ithaca .edu

Web site URL: www.ithaca.edu

Founded: 1892

Private or Public: private

Religious affiliation: none

Location: rural

Undergraduate enrollment: 6,098

Total enrollment: 6,412

Percent Male/Female: 44%/56%

Percent Minority: 13%

Percent African-American: 3%

Percent Asian: 3%

Percent Hispanic: 3%

Percent Native-American: 0%

Percent in-state/out of state: 47%/53%

Percent Pub HS: NA

On-campus housing: 70%

Fraternities: 1%

Sororities: 1%

Number of Applicants: 11,100

Percent Accepted: 75%

Percent Accepted who enroll: 21%

Entering class: 1,680

Transfers: 171

Early admission program (EA/ED/NA): ED

Early Decision or Early Action Acceptance Rate: 74%

Application Deadline: 1-Feb

Mean SAT: NA

Mean ACT: NA

Middle 50% SAT range: 1,080–1,280

Middle 50% ACT range: NA

Most popular majors: Business, Communications, Visual and Performing Arts

Retention: 86%

Graduation rate: 64%

Tuition and Fees: $25,194

In State Tuition and Fees (if different): NA

Room and Board: $9,950

Financial aid, first-year: NA

Varsity or Club Athletes: NA

Library: NA

Ithaca College may have started out as a conservatory of music in downtown Ithaca, but it now offers strong academics in addition to a world-class music program. Though many students may look at Ithaca and see only Cornell, Ithaca College offers students a smaller, tightly-knit community combined with a great education.

"We're Equipped with the Biggest . . . Radio Tower"

Out of Ithaca College's six undergraduate schools—including Communications, Health Sciences, Humanities and Science, the Music School, Interdisciplinary and International Studies, and the Business School—Communications, along with Health Sciences and the Music School, are the three most popular.

Most of The Park School of Communications students (or "Parkies" as they're called) end up winning national honors from the top professional organizations and are often offered great opportunities both on campus and off campus. IC also has two radio stations. IC's radio tower is the biggest thing on Ithaca's skyline. The Music School is considered to be the hardest school, both in terms of admittance and academic rigor. The students at this school are also the ones who "do their own thing," effectively separated from the rest of the college. As one senior music student said, "Music majors don't have a lot

of free time, with recital attendances, ensemble requirements, practices, etc."

The Health Science and Human Performance School have mainly two types of majors, the Physical Therapy majors (PT's) and the Physical Education majors (PE's). Due to the physical component of the two majors, it is not surprising, said one student, that the "PT's are a bunch of jocks." The program offers several combined bachelors and masters five year programs, many of which also provide professional certification.

While there is a General Education requirement and most departments push for students to take courses outside their school, students end up really "staying within their schools." A very popular course, however, that many students across the schools end up taking is "Anatomy and Physiology," mainly because it is a requirement for many majors, and it fulfills a common science requirement.

The academics at IC "aren't necessarily hard" but they do give "a substantial amount of homework, about four-five hours worth a night," said one student, though students at all the schools seemed to agree. Teachers are "really open and willing to talk, especially outside of class" and they're "genuinely interested in helping you in the class." IC isn't considered to be to be of the same academic caliber as its neighbor Cornell University, but that doesn't mean the teaching quality suffers. "I was surprised," one student noted, "that almost all the professors here are well-known in their fields." Due to the college's relatively small size, only intro classes are large, and most classes have only 20–30 students. "Make a good impression early," one student recommended. "IC is small enough that by the time junior and senior year comes around, you'll have a rep, and you'll want it to be a good one." Another student agreed that the smaller campus required student interaction. "Ithaca College is definitely not the place to go if you want to stay in the background."

Division III Contenders and Other Extracurriculars

The large amount of jocks from the Health Science School translates into a great athletic program and great athletic teams. Ithaca College has one of the strongest athletic programs in the NCAA's Division III. School spirit is fierce at Ithaca College, which generates not only great games, but also great attendance. The IC Bombers are well known for their football team and women's crew team, and "everyone and their mom attend the football games." The big football game of the year is the Cortaca Jug, against the SUNY Cortland Red Dragons, "which you must go to" to cheer on the team, though admittedly it's also "an excuse to get drunk." Other particularly popular sports include baseball, softball, and women's lacrosse. If you don't have the time for varsity sports, there are also club sports and recreational (intramurals) sports. Students can be competitive and aggressive on the field, but they are all there "just to have fun." Despite the heavy athletic programs, the athletic facilities are still "pretty accessible."

> **"Ithaca College is definitely not the place to go if you want to stay in the background."**

Of course, if sports aren't your thing, there are numerous extracurricular clubs and community service opportunities. Specifically, there are a large number of performing opportunities and performances to attend. But be forewarned: "If you're not a music major, it's really hard to get lessons because they're in great demand." A lot of clubs on campus "fall in with the Ithaca atmosphere and end up being about human rights, animal rights, or union rights." Everyone can get a job on campus, but finding a job off campus is a lot harder because, as one

student said, "we have to compete with all those people at Cornell."

White Bread

The stereotype of the students is that they are "white bread, mainly white upper middle class students from the Northeast" who can afford the hefty tag attached to an IC education. When asked whether there is a lot of ethnic diversity on campus, students commented "not really, unless you're in the music school." However, "the gay and lesbian population is well-sized."

The common stereotype is that IC students are either artsy, due to the strong Music School and Theatre departments, or jocks, because of the Health Science School. "Parkies are a mix—half jocks (marketing, television and radio) and half artists (visual arts and cinematography)." Most students agree that the stereotype is mainly true, but "there are enough exceptions to make life interesting."

Staying on (or off) Campus

Residential housing, one freshman said, is "nice but not that great." According to several upperclassmen, "The buildings aren't ugly, and the rooms are small but adequate." While IC offers a large variety of halls to live in (some coed, others single sex), the majority of students cite residential life as "not a strength of IC." Most students move off campus senior year, but are required to live on campus the first three years. The Towers (two large towers that are dorms) are the most prominent features of Ithaca College. Visible from almost anywhere in Ithaca, they are famous for both the fact that they sometimes have parties (one of two places to party on campus) and that on New Year's eve, the lights in the building change year numbers (i.e., from 06 to 07). The Terraces are the only dorms that offer suites, and most seniors either live in the Garden apartments, the recently built Circle apartments, or move off campus to live on Prospect Street. Almost all of the halls (except the apartments) house freshmen, but the Upper and Lower quads have a larger concentration of underclassmen.

"Ithaca College really makes an effort to help freshmen transition," said one student. In addition to the three residential halls the school offers to freshmen only (with twice as many RAs), the college also hosts events, technically open to all undergraduates but specifically targeting freshmen, as an alternative to drinking. With concerts, comedians and dances, IC makes an effort to help students feel comfortable on campus. "The school really tries to limit the amount of underage drinking on campus." Drinking still occurs, just not on campus. Most parties are held off campus, specifically on Prospect Street, known as "the college town of IC." On Friday and Saturday nights, people can expect parties on Prospect Street and in the Circle apartments. However most of the partying by Ithaca College students doesn't occur there either. In fact, most partying doesn't even happen on the Ithaca College side of Ithaca. "If you want to party, go to a Cornell frat party." That's right, IC students go to Cornell frat parties, mainly because "alcohol is a lot less controlled there. And as it turns out, they aren't nerds after all."

In terms of the drug scene, IC is becoming more and more a non-smoking campus (at least in the Residence Halls), but most people at IC who smoke, smoke pot. Greek life isn't all that big on the IC campus except for a few small music fraternities and sororities. Finally, students are not thrilled with the food options on campus. "The food here isn't all that great either, unless you go to Terrace, which is pretty good." Rated between the three dining halls, Terrace is the best, Campus Center is the worst, and Towers is somewhere in-between. Terrace is described as "beautiful, because it has fountains in the dining hall, and offers a great variety of food." Meal plans are required for those who live on-campus, and they all cost the same, although different combination plans are offered with the possibility of "Bonus Bucks" that can be used for food elsewhere. "Bonus bucks make life so much simpler since I'm freed from having to eat on campus and can eat at random times."

"Ithaca is Gorges"
Ithaca is a great, "but small," community to live in, which is "very open." "Most people take enough advantage of Ithaca" but in order to do so "you *need* a car." In fact most upperclassmen have cars, though freshmen find it harder to have a car on campus because they have to pay more for student parking. "People feel the need to get off campus sometimes, and cars are the way to do it." The other source of transportation is Ithaca's bus service TCAT, a "wonderful resource, especially if you don't want to drive during Ithaca's winters." Two of the most popular clubs among Ithaca College students are the Haunt and the Octopus downtown, known for their live (and most of the time, local) music. Popular bars are Micawbers, Moonshadow, and Blue Stone, but like most bars in Ithaca, "don't expect the bars to fill up until after 11."

If partying is not your thing, the town of Ithaca offers an assortment of other things to do. The many waterfalls and state parks near Ithaca make it one of the most beautiful places to live. Right near the campus is Six Mile Creek, a "wonderful place to go skinny dipping." Another popular activity is gorge jumping (a word of caution, clear the rocks!). If it's "Ithacating—any form of precipitation with a cloudy sky"—you can always go to one of the two independent movie theaters in town, or hang around the Ithaca Commons.

A Word on the Weather
If there is one thing upon which all students agree it is this: Ithaca is cold. Yet, IC students understand that they live in Ithaca, and thus must live with Ithaca's weather. Ithaca is known for not only its freezing winters, cloudy and rainy springs and falls, but also for the erratic changes from one to another. "Only in Ithaca could you experience all the seasons in one day." It starts to snow in late October and early November, and despite the spring thaws, it's possible for it to snow in May.—*Jesse Dong*

FYI
If you come to Ithaca College, you'd better bring "good winter boots and an appreciation for sports and music."
What is the typical weekend schedule? "Party at a Cornell frat party Friday night, Cheer on the IC Bombers, attend a performance, party some more at Cornell and hit up a few bars, spend all of Sunday doing homework."
If I could change one thing about Ithaca College, I'd "make it more handicapped accessible."
Three things every student should do before graduating from Ithaca College are "jump in the fountain, go to a Cornell frat party, and attend the Cortaca Jug."

The Juilliard School

Address: Juilliard, 60 Lincoln Center Plaza, New York, NY 10023-6588
Phone: 212-799-5000, ext. 223
E-mail Address: admissions@juilliard.edu
Web site URL: www.juilliard.edu
Year Founded: 1905
Private or Public: private
Religious affiliation: none
Location: urban
Regular Application Deadline: 1-Dec
Number of Applicants: NA
Percent Accepted: 7%
Percent Accepted who enroll: 71%
Number Entering: NA
Number of Transfers Accepted each Year: NA

Mean SAT: NA
Mean ACT: NA
Middle 50% SAT range: NA
Middle 50% ACT range: NA
Early admission program (EA/ ED/ NA): "priority"
ED or EA Acceptance Rate: NA
Full time Undergraduate enrollment: 482
Total enrollment: NA
Percent Male: 52%
Percent Female: 48%
Total Percent Minority: 20%
Percent African-American: 10%
Percent Asian/Pacific Islander: 15%
Percent Hispanic: 5%
Percent Native-American: 0%
Percent Other: 30%
Percent in-state / out of state: 15%/85%

Percent from Public HS: NA
Retention Rate: 94%
Graduation Rate: NA
Percent in On-campus housing: 50%
Percent affiliated with Greek system: 0%
Percent Varsity or Club Athletes: NA
Number of official organized extracurricular organizations: 5
3 Most popular majors: Piano, Stringed Instruments, Voice
Student/Faculty ratio: NA
Tuition and Fees: NA
Cost for Room and Board: NA
Percent receiving Financial aid, first-year: 67%

Centrally located in the heart of New York City, Juilliard is the serious young artist's ultimate opportunity. Not only are students immersed in the school's rigorous training programs in dance, music, and acting, but they are also constantly influenced and inspired by the cultural and artistic happenings in the hub of the creative world.

Pinnacle of Performance Arts

With an only 7% acceptance rate, Juilliard is one of the most competitive programs in the world for young aspiring actors, musicians, and dancers. Along with a standard application evaluation, potential Juilliard students must also undergo a rigorous audition process, in which the entire faculty of a specific department determines an applicant's admission. Unlike most universities, where SAT scores and transcripts weigh most heavily on a student's chance of admission, at Juilliard, the audition process is by far the most important piece of the application. Grades and scores are taken into account, but the student must, first and foremost, prove their musical, dance, or theatrical abilities and potential.

Although the program is a challenging one to get into, most students are happily surprised that the workload isn't too intense academically. One sophomore Juilliard student, initially intimidated by Juilliard's extremely serious artistic training was actually "pleasantly surprised to find the atmosphere much less intense and competitive than what I expected, and the classes challenging without being overwhelming." In this small, close-knit community of less than 800 undergraduates, students receive tons of individual attention. With only 90 students in both the drama and dance departments, students are under constant pressure to perform and learn at the highest, most superior level. Along with group classes focusing on their particular creative major, each student within the drama, dance, or music divisions are assigned to private, individual master classes to advance their talents.

Being a part of a group with such highly skilled actors, musicians, and dancers is stressful, but most of the kids at Juilliard have been training for years, and know exactly what they're getting themselves into. It seems too, for most Juilliard students, being around their classmates does not intimidate them or make them shy away from their artistic endeavors, but it actually motivates them: "some people might think that students would burn out after going through such intensive artistic training, but at Juilliard, it's just the opposite. Being surrounded by such incredible creativity in dance, music, and theater constantly re-inspires me each day."

Ping Pong and the City

Some concerns with the programs at Juilliard come from worries that students feel they won't be trained to succeed professionally outside of their artistic pursuits: "sometimes I'm concerned that I won't be able to do anything else with my life other than music, which is natural, but a lot of times I do wish I had gone to a school that offers more pre-professional opportunities." There also are not a ton of extra-curricular activities outside of the music, dance, and theater scene: "There aren't many organized groups—no sports teams at all (not even organized ping pong!)—though we have an art centered service club called ArtReach that meets regularly and plans activities and projects and two Christian groups." But between masters classes, performances, auditions, and academics, many students wouldn't have time for extracurriculars, and if need be, always one of the most desirable places in the world, New York City, at their fingertips.

> "Being surrounded by such incredible creativity in dance, music, and theater constantly re-inspires me each day."

All freshmen and first-year students live on-campus in double bedrooms and suite-style rooms, with three bathrooms and a common living room area. There are computer labs, a gym, a cafeteria located on the lobby level, all available to students living within the dormitory. However, housing is not guaranteed for all four years of school, and many students move off-campus after their first year: "Most of my friends have moved off-campus because they're so eager to get into the New York social scene, but living on-campus my freshman year definitely helped me meet a lot of cool kids." First-time college students are always assigned to a double room, and singles become available as a second year student.

Dominant social scenes are informal student groups- the dancers, the actors, people in the same year or some instrument studio, occasionally inter-disciplinary "cliques" just hanging out. There are not many academically inclined groups. One student noticed that her friends at Juilliard are "so focused on their individual art and fitting practice time into their day that many don't get excited about their academic classes, however, one notable exception is those students, mostly musicians, who take classes at Columbia College in addition to their music classes here."

Best of All Worlds

Overall, students at Juilliard seem to love their experience in such a rigorous dance, music, and theater environment, but they also seem to know what they'll be getting themselves into. Students here understand that their lifestyles will include composing and practicing music, rehearsing scenes, and choreography. At Juilliard, if students are willing to sacrifice the typical college experience and to endure this competitive environment, they have the opportunity to succeed to unprecedented heights and take in some skills of the most tenured dancers, musicians, and actors in the world. Its ideal environment located in a mecca of creativity provides inspiration and motivation for its students, and an outlet and experience unlike any other. "In one weekend I can walk over to the Lincoln Center, see an opera at the Metropolitan, or see a ballet. You just can't get that anywhere else in the world."—*Catherine Reibel*

FYI

If you come to Juilliard, you'd better bring "a lot of energy to practice dance, practice piano, or rehearse for theater!"

What's the typical weekend schedule? "A lot of time is either spent working on performance pieces or actually participating in shows. If one doesn't have a show one weekend, time is spent seeing your friends' shows! Bar-hopping is always fun on less busy weekends, however they're aren't a lot of large campus parties or anything."

If I could change one thing about Juilliard, I'd "make it a little bigger. I wish there were more people to meet. Sometimes it feels like a high school environment."

Three things every student at Juilliard should do before graduating are "visit a school where they can have a "real college experience" (only to realize that Frat parties suck), get to know New York City as well as possible, and embrace the fact that we have so many awesome performers and artists as resources to connect with."

Manhattanville College

Address: Manhattanville College, 2900 Purchase Street, Purchase, NY 10577
Phone: 914-694-2200
E-mail Address: admissions@mville.edu
Web site URL: www.mville.edu
Year Founded: 1841
Private or Public: Private
Religious affiliation: none
Location: Suburban
Regular Application Deadline: 2-Mar
Number of Applicants: 3,464
Percent Accepted: 52.77%
Percent Accepted who enroll: 27.84%
Number Entering: 509
Number of Transfers Accepted each Year: 120
Mean SAT: 1,100
Mean ACT: 23

Middle 50% SAT range: 1,400–1,680
Middle 50% ACT range: 20–24
Early admission program (EA/ ED/ NA): ED
ED or EA Acceptance Rate: 70%
Full time Undergraduate enrollment: 1,705
Total enrollment: 2,975
Percent Male: 34%
Percent Female: 66%
Total Percent Minority: 31%
Percent African-American: 7.37%
Percent Asian/Pacific Islander: 2.73%
Percent Hispanic: 14.91%
Percent Native-American: 0.71%
Percent Other: 74.28%

Percent in-state / out of state: 64%/36%
Percent from Public HS: NA
Retention Rate: 74%
Graduation Rate: 65%
Percent in On-campus housing: 80%
Percent affiliated with Greek system: NA
Percent Varsity or Club Athletes: NA
Number of official organized extracurricular organizations: 55
3 Most popular majors: Management, Psychology, Finance
Student/Faculty ratio: 12:01
Tuition and Fees: $28,540
Cost for Room and Board: $12,240
Percent receiving Financial aid, first-year: 90%

In the small town of Purchase, New York, close student-teacher relationships are the most valuable selling point of Manhattanville College. Personal attention is received by all students, who study hard to acquire a well-rounded liberal-arts education. Located on a 100-acre campus a half-hour away from New York City, Manhattanville offers students a spacious sanctuary of learning as well as the chance to explore the resources of a metropolitan city.

Subject Matter

Manhattanville College may be small in size, but it has a relatively large scope of majors and programs from which to choose. Students report that its strengths lie in the humanities and social sciences, and according to one student, "the journalism program is awesome and amazing." Reportedly, its weaker programs are in the sciences, and students even mention sometimes finding difficulty in taking science classes. There are also a significant amount of distributional requirements to fulfill. Students must take six credits from four of the five main areas: mathematics and science, social sciences, humanities, languages, and fine arts. In addition, all students take a mandatory writing intensive course, and all freshmen take a year-long preceptorial class, which encompasses many different types of world literature. One student claimed the requirements "got in the way of classes I would rather have taken." However, the general sentiment is that everyone suffers together.

Following the general trend of "smallness," class size is usually limited to 20 students, with review and help sessions led by student instructors (SIs). This creates a tight bond between students and professors, who are all easily approachable and available. Professors are also instrumental in finding and writing recommendations for internships, which many students apply for at nearby companies such as IBM and Pepsi. Many others study abroad for a semester—especially language majors—in one of the college's overseas programs. However, as one student commented, "it's difficult to go away for a term with all the requirements. Most people who go abroad graduate late."

The "portfolio" system is another manner in which personal attention is given at Manhattanville. In this system, students meet with academic advisors at the beginning of their freshman year to form a tentative list of courses to put in their portfolio. They then meet again every spring to see how closely they are following or deviating from their plans; they also submit a sample of their work from that year, along with a written self-examination. Portfolios are then reviewed by a board of faculty to assure that students are succeeding academically.

Only a Hop and a Skip Away

Manhattanville is like an island: a small, self-contained and comfortable community. However, only a short distance away is one of the grandest and most energetic cities in the world—New York. Manhattanville's size and its proximity to New York City are two more reasons most students attend. While campus is essentially a bubble, isolating students from the everyday hassle of cities, frequent trips to New York allow students a chance to get away from the small-town feel of this school. Besides the ability to take trips into the city, many students live in the tri-state area and go home frequently. According to one student, "I like that I live close enough that I can go home when campus gets too stifling."

For those who'd like to experience the city for more than just weekends, Manhattanville offers Semester in New York City. Participants live in Brooklyn Heights and pursue internships in range of industries, in addition to taking classes.

The Bubble

While this small environment is conducive to close relationships with faculty and staff, it is somewhat isolated from the outer community. True, students frequently hang out in New York City, but, said a senior, "we sort of forget about interacting with our own community and almost avoid it." Indicative of this is the low participation in community service or outreach activities. Furthermore, most students either commute or live on campus.

There are four dorms, all of which are said to be comfortable and homey. Spellman is a dry hall that houses freshmen, while Tenney is a multicultural dorm. Both have been recently renovated. Also, to the surprise (and delight) of many, floors and suites are all

coed. As for dorm food, students generally regard the food on campus as decent. There is one main dining hall that one student commented "tries hard to serve variety," and The Café @ Benzinger, which serves "junk food and coffee," is open late.

Since a large portion of the student body comes from nearby areas, some commute and many go home on weekends. This reportedly damages the prospects for exciting on-campus social events on weekends, though students make an effort, particularly through the Clubs Council, to make do. The Council organizes weekend events such as the Spring and Fall Formals, the Quad Jam, movie marathons, and performances. In-suite parties are common, but difficult to organize because of strict administrative rules: alcohol policies are less than lax and prohibit kegs on campus. The Pavilion is the name of the student center and serves as a popular hangout spot. It hosts the traditional Monday Night Football screenings where students can "eat, drink, and be merry," one student joked. Other popular weekend options are hitting the city or checking out nearby pubs.

> **"The personal attention we get here is amazing."**

During the week, students engage in extracurricular activities. There are about 50 clubs on campus, and intramural and club sports are popular, as is writing for school publications, such as the newspaper, *The Touchstone*.

With all their activities, students are often overwhelmed by opportunities and things to do. Ultimately, said one senior, "the personal attention we get here is amazing, more than I ever expected in college. It's been great to be able to get so close to my professors and make such good friends along the way."
—*Carolina Galvao*

FYI
If you come to Manhattanville, you'd better bring "a word processor and a spirit willing to be shared."
What is the typical weekend schedule? "Depends, either go home or hang out on campus and party or go into the city."
If I could change one thing about Manhattanville, I'd "make more people stay on campus over the weekends."
Three things every student at Manhattanville should do before graduating are "go to Monday Nights at the Pavilion, spend time in New York with friends, and break one of the administration's strict rules!"

New York University

Address: NYU, 22 Washington Sq North, New York NY 10011
Phone: 212-998-4500
E-mail Address: admissions@nyu.edu
Web site URL: www.nyu.edu/admissions
Year Founded: 1861
Private or Public: private
Religious affiliation: none
Location: urban
Regular Application Deadline: 16-Jan
Number of Applicants: 34,944
Percent Accepted: 28.4%
Percent Accepted who enroll: 37%
Number Entering: NA
Number of Transfers Accepted each Year: 1,702
Mean SAT: 1,306
Mean ACT: 29

Middle 50% SAT range: 1,310–1,440
Middle 50% ACT range: 29–31
Early admission program (EA/ ED/ NA): ED
ED or EA Acceptance Rate: 33%
Full time Undergraduate enrollment: 20,604
Total enrollment: 50,917
Percent Male: 38%
Percent Female: 62%
Total Percent Minority: 33.6%
Percent African-American: 3.2%
Percent Asian/Pacific Islander: 23.2%
Percent Hispanic: 6.7%
Percent Native-American: 0.30%
Percent Other: 3.2%
Percent in-state / out of state: 28%/72%

Percent from Public HS: NA
Retention Rate: 92%
Graduation Rate: 80%
Percent in On-campus housing: 51%
Percent affiliated with Greek system: 2%
Percent Varsity or Club Athletes: NA
Number of official organized extracurricular organizations: 350
3 Most popular majors: Drama and dramatics/theater arts, Finance, Liberal Arts and Sciences
Student/Faculty ratio: 13:01
Tuition and Fees: $33,740.00
Cost for Room and Board: $11,730.00
Percent receiving Financial aid, first-year: 52%

Mainly situated in the heart of Greenwich Village, New York University enables its undergraduates to explore the vast array of opportunities available not only through its location, but also courtesy of its curriculum, extracurricular, and internship opportunities. The bustling university grounds provide students with a plethora of activities, and while the university doesn't necessarily have a central campus, students of NYU have no problem with having New York City as their playground.

Academics in the City

Of course, at such a large university, getting lost in a sea of classes could be a plausible fear. However, one student reassures that although "NYU seems like one big university, at the end of the day it really breaks down into the individual schools." NYU is made up of 14 separate schools, seven of which are devoted to undergraduates. Some of the more well-known schools include the Stern School of Business (which ranks among the top 15 nationally), the Gallatin School of Individualized Study and the Tisch School of the Arts. Of course, their formidable reputations increase the difficulty of getting accepted into any of them.

Each of the schools has it's own unique assets. Aside from outstanding professors in Tisch's arts programs, two of the largest student organizations at NYU are based at Tisch: the Tisch Talent Guild, a student run talent agency, and the Stern-Tisch Entertainment Business Association. Meanwhile, the Gallatin School is one of NYU's unique programs, enabling students to devise one-a-kind academic careers that are tailored to meet one's academic needs, professional ambitions and creative interests. Some NYU students, however, think that Gallatin's relaxed mentality may really just be hiding a lighter workload: "Everyone wants to be in Gallatin so they can do nothing," laments one student, "but they're making Gallatin a lot harder now, so it's becoming more legitimate." Of course, both Gallatin students and Arts and Science students can supplement their college experience with New York City internships ranging from the Lincoln Center for the Performing Arts to *Newsweek* magazine or the United Nations.

One of Gallatin's biggest draws is its small classes. Although NYU's general liberal arts "seminars are pretty small—20 kids or less" students are "more likely to have large lectures that break down into recitation one to three times a week." Science lectures can hold in the upwards of 400 students. While NYU does offer a breadth of classes (over 2,500 classes in all), students often find the core requirements "annoying," especially the "Writing the Essay" course that is required of all freshmen. Students complain that "it's very repetitive and very unnecessary," but they grudgingly accept that "you're always required to take a writing course to practice your writing skills some more."

> **"You will not find the preppy jock population at NYU."**

Nonetheless, students praise NYU's innate ability to integrate the school's location into lessons. One student who took a "Lyrics on Lockdown" class about the prison industrial complex raved about New York's magnetic academic pull: "It was an activism course, and being in New York, it was just a great opportunity to open your eyes up to things."

Urban Nightlife

"Going to NYU is kind of really like living in the city and going to class at NYU," explains one sophomore. And while most students who attend NYU arrive to school acknowledging the importance of an independent spirit, many are nevertheless put off by the school's lack of cohesion. "If you go to NYU sports game there will be more fans from the away team than there are from NYU," one student said. Aside from a lack of athletic pride, the lack of unity may have something to do with the relatively non-existent Greek scene at the university. "About 2 percent are Greek here," a student said. Another added: "It's very hard to find everyone going to the same party. There's no Greek life, therefore there's no organized party for Saturday night." Of course, "Anybody who knows what to do or knows how to have fun goes to bars." Although this is a common understanding, a common bar for all NYU students to congregate in can be a little less easy to come by, thanks to the thousands of lounges, pubs and clubs New York has to offer to those over 21 (or to the underage who report being blessed with indestructible fake IDs or wads of $20s to slip the bouncer). Thank God for Josie Woods— deemed a "classic" by the NYU collegiates. "It's just a sports bar—dart boards, cheap drinks," explains a student, but somehow this relatively nondescript place has staked claim as one of the main NYU hangouts. "There are class boundaries by bars," students note. "Underclassmen go to 3rd Avenue bars and upperclassmen go more uptown." And in a city full of temptation, it is no surprise that, "Everyone smokes pot," according to one student. "It's hard to find anyone who doesn't."

Converse, Art, Lattes, Oh My!

"You will not find the preppy jock population at NYU," notes an NYU student. "A lot of kids choose NYU because of their interest in art or music, so there are a lot of artsy people." Of course, what better place to culminate and craft one's artistic aspirations than at a coffee shop? Although the non-chain variety would seem more befitting of the NYU mentality, with a Starbucks (or two!) on every street corner it's hard not to be mainstream— especially when one of the most popular student lounges is a Starbucks that is actually owned by NYU. This half-coffee shop, half-lounge is "always packed" exclaimed an NYU student, with kids "typing away and studying." Although the artsy crowd is definitely a dominant group at NYU, some students are nonetheless shocked by the lack of diversity at the university. One student has noticed that, "More and more students tend to be rich, wealthy kids from L.A., Long Island or New Jersey." And although she points to a large Asian population, students are still disappointed by the lack of collegiate diversity in such a diverse city.

Hey Big Spender

It's a widely known that "the best freshman dorms are Brittany and Weinestein." But even if you luck out with a prime living space, be wary of the NYU resident assistants. Some students claim that "they're all on a power trip," although others praise the tight campus dorm security system for easing any parental "My child is living alone in Manhattan" nightmares. RA issues often subside quickly because of the high percentage of upperclassmen who live off-campus. "A lot of kids decide not to live in dorms because you can find cheaper apartments in the city." Staying on budget in a city where it can cost $10 to "cab it" 10 blocks is key for students who want to have money left over to enjoy the concrete jungle of pleasure. When not apartment bargain-hunting, students venture to Mamouns, a New York staple for 30 years, for $2 falafels. Of course, despite the slew of thrifty finds in New York, many students (and parents alike) feel the city pinch. Whether students compensate by waitressing, clerking or modeling, a job is key. "Most people I know hold a job, and some people even hold two," one student said. "But there are so many great opportunities in New York City that plenty of music majors, for example, are happy making money in the music industry through internships."—*Dana Schuster*

FYI
If you come to NYU, you'd better bring "an iPod."
What's the typical weekend schedule? "Go out on Thursday, (usually no classes on Friday), hang out with friends on Friday night in the dorms, out again on Saturday night, usually to a bar or an apartment party."
If I could change one thing about NYU, "it'd be to be able to meet people more easily, especially in the dorms."
Three things every NYU student should do before graduating are "visit the MoMa, go to the Comedy Cellar, and eat at Mamoun's."

Parsons School of Design

Address: Parsons, 65 Fifth Avenue, Ground Floor, New York, NY 10003
Phone: 212-229-8910
E-mail Address: parsadm@newschool.edu
Web site URL: www.parsons.edu
Year Founded: 1896
Private or Public: private
Religious affiliation: none
Location: urban
Regular Application Deadline: 2-Mar
Number of Applicants: NA
Percent Accepted: 47%
Percent Accepted who enroll: 45%
Number Entering: NA
Number of Transfers Accepted each Year: 1,248
Mean SAT: 1,096
Mean ACT: 24

Middle 50% SAT range: 940–1,210
Middle 50% ACT range: 19–26
Early admission program (EA/ ED/ NA): NA
ED or EA Acceptance Rate: NA
Full time Undergraduate enrollment: 3,180
Total enrollment: 3,610
Percent Male: 21%
Percent Female: 79%
Total Percent Minority: 26%
Percent African-American: 3%
Percent Asian/Pacific Islander: 17%
Percent Hispanic: 6%
Percent Native-American: less than 1%
Percent Other: NA
Percent in-state / out of state: 43%/57%

Percent from Public HS: NA
Retention Rate: 85%
Graduation Rate: 72%
Percent in On-campus housing: 24%
Percent affiliated with Greek system: NA
Percent Varsity or Club Athletes: NA
Number of official organized extracurricular organizations: 3
3 Most popular majors: Design and Visual Communications, Fashion/Apparel Design, Illustration
Student/Faculty ratio: NA
Tuition and Fees: $30,270.00
Cost for Room and Board: $11,750.00
Percent receiving Financial aid, first-year: 47%

Ever fantasized about a curriculum that includes courses like "Cell Phone Design" or "Children's Book Illustration?" Ever wished your homework was to sketch a fashionable taxicab or concoct a cast of video game characters? Then Parsons School of Design may be the Big Apple campus of your art nerd dreams.

Revered as one of the largest and most prestigious colleges of design in the nation, the school isn't suffering from delusions of grandeur when its Web site boasts, "Parsons virtually invented the modern concept of design in America." In fact, it did, and its students continue pushing the envelope today, imagining everything from cotton-candy evening gowns to trendy voting booths. As one sophomore promises, "Parsons students are some of the wackiest, wittiest, most hard-working design students on the planet, and they tend to actually have a social conscience."

Who Needs a Campus?

Located in the heart of New York City, it's little wonder that Parsons undergrads don't waste a lot of time lamenting their scattered and rather unimpressive campus. With one of the world's most dynamic cities directly at their feet, who needs a dinky college coffee shop or even a comfy student lounge? If you're looking for school spirit, turn elsewhere; because artsy students flock to Parsons for the thrill of exploring fast-paced city life and delving into intense coursework, most don't seem to miss the fact that there is no central hang-out spot beyond the cafeteria or the 54,000-volume Gimbel Library.

> "Parsons students are some of the wackiest, wittiest, most hard-working design students on the planet, and they tend to actually have a social conscience."

Parsons' two main campuses are situated in Greenwich Village and Midtown Manhattan, both areas that are every bit as exciting as they are expensive. Freshmen tend to live in Loeb Residence Hall, a building that provides access to an art studio, a reading room, a lounge and a laundry room. The other two residence halls, the Marlton House and Union Square, offer singles, doubles and occasional suites to students above 19 years of age. The vast majority of students opt to move off campus eventually, confronting the Herculean task of finding reasonably priced housing in a city where closet-sized lofts can boast castle-sized price tags.

Future Fashion Divas, Unite!

Although Parsons offers an impressive menu of undergraduate areas of study—33, to be exact—many say that "Fashion Design" still reigns supreme as the school's most well-known and highly esteemed degree. Following in the footsteps of glamorous alumni like Donna Karan, Tom Ford and Narciso Rodriguez, Parsons' fashion students have ample justification for their reputation as the snub-nosed divas of the design world. While they receive some of the best professional guidance and internship opportunities in the country and lay claims to a famous annual fashion show, these distinctions come at a cost. "The fashion kids don't sleep, don't eat, don't even seem to live," claims one student in the Illustration program. "They're so competitive

and snobby that girls actually run out of the classroom crying from time to time."

Don't let the cutthroat fashion department deter you, say many students in Parsons' other excellent areas of study, ranging from Animation to Industrial Design to Robotics. Graphic Design, Product Design and Photography have received rave reviews from students, but all three areas of study entail a substantial workload—a burden that seems to loom large over most Parsons students regardless of what degree program they choose to pursue.

Parsons provides three four-year undergraduate art and design degree options: BFA, the Bachelor of Fine Arts; BBA, the Bachelor of Business Administration; and the five-year BA/BFA degree. The five-year dual degree offers students a complete studio art or design major along with a liberal arts education. Parsons also hosts graduate programs in areas such as Photography and Architecture, not to mention esoteric lines of study such as "History of Decorative Arts & Design," thus adding more resources, intellectual juice and creative energy to the Parsons milieu.

Students whose needs aren't met by the undergraduate or graduate curricula can theoretically pursue electives at the New School University, since Parsons has been a partner of the New School since the late 1960s. However, many students complain that this option works better in theory than in reality. "The practical separation between the New School and Parsons can get frustrating," says one junior. "There's so much our University has to offer that we're not really allowed access to!"

Freaking Out at Foundations

Most freshmen don't seem to share this frustration, since they're too busy slaving away at the rigorous "Foundation Courses" that comprise the first year's curriculum. Focused on the basics of drawing and design, the Foundation program is formulated to immerse (or drown?) students in the broader skills and critical practices of art and design through a combination of courses, workshops and lectures. Although the grueling program is known for weeding out slackers, it also has its perks: field trips and on-site visits take students to professional design offices and show them the ropes of New York City's art scene.

Students who survive the Foundation program immediately choose their majors and begin focusing on their future trajectories, since Parsons tends to be "a very career-minded school." This careerist orientation is also reflected in the biographies of the professors, who are almost exclusively "working professionals" at the top of their fields, rather than armchair academics. While this means that most profs have their fingers to the pulse of current design trends and are infinitely hipper than the average Ivy League lecturer, it also means that they aren't often readily available for extra help outside the classroom.

The career focus of Parsons is also mirrored in the substance of much of the coursework, which emphasizes the practical applications of art and design over its loftier, let's-contemplate-the-nature-of-beauty components. Students remark that Parsons is a "School of Design" rather than a "School of Art," meaning that the focus tends to be on marketing one's designs and making money, rather than on pontificating about the fine arts or learning specific crafts. To be fair, the curriculum is peppered with its share of more theoretical courses, many of which don't receive particularly stellar reviews (be forewarned: " 'Global Issues' sucks"). For those who hanker after the staples of a liberal arts education, the Critical Studies Department offers several worthwhile options, and for the occasional soul who craves a taste of the sciences, there are even a few artsy-sounding natural science courses with titles like "The Biology of Beauty, Sex and Death" and "Cosmic Mysteries."

Urban Immersion

Just as the treasure trove of New York makes up for Parsons' lackluster campus with its endless galleries (for art students), advertising agencies (for communications students), textile manufacturers (for fashion design students) and more, the bustling nightlife of the city compensates for Parsons' dearth of a homegrown social scene. While there may be no theater collective, no Greek life and no vibrant dorm party scene, there is certainly no shortage of things to do on a Friday or Saturday evening. Most students take to clubbing and drinking, although being underage can present a predictable (if surmountable) obstacle. Others connect with social circles at local universities like NYU, or tap into the city's endless array of trendy scenes for music, social activism, theater and passions of every stripe. "Boredom," explains one student, "would be inexcusable."

Parsons students tend to be "very funky, individualistic and fast-paced." For this reason, the school gels best with students who already have a strong sense of who they are and what they want. The campus has developed a substantial gay/queer community, and some joke that it's much harder for straight students to find a date than it is for their non-straight counterparts.

It's a Small World After All

The spirit of internationalism infuses Parsons at every level, from the curriculum to the student body. More than one-fourth of the undergrad population is comprised of minorities, a good percentage of whom hail from far-away nations and diverse ethnic backgrounds. "Right now, I'm in a class of 14 students that includes someone from Sweden, Spain, Colombia and a whole bunch of random states. Diversity is huge here."

This global ethic is also evident in the curriculum, through which professors try to instill an international perspective on design while emphasizing the ethical and social dimensions of artistic production. Students who can't get enough of this approach or who eventually grow tired of New York's hustle and bustle can take off for one of Parsons' four popular affiliate schools in Paris, France; Kanazawa, Japan; Seoul, South Korea; or Altos de Chavon, Dominican Republic. The Paris campus is particularly well-regarded, with its sky-lit studios, romantic central courtyard, intimate class sizes, and dreamy location near the Eiffel Tower. Study abroad programs in Israel, the Netherlands, Great Britain and Sweden also rank highly with many students.

Luckily, going abroad is a luxury, rather than a necessity. Many students note that Parsons has everything the young designer could ask for: a diverse and passionate student body; connections to top industry professionals in the classroom and beyond; and internship opportunities with hot designers and companies like Ralph Lauren, MTV, PETA, and Fossil. Just make sure you're ready for a big workload and an even bigger budget in a big, big city.—*Sarah Stillman*

FYI

If you come to Parsons, you'd better bring "career-mindedness, plenty of money, and an appetite for big city life."

What's the typical weekend schedule? "Work all day, club all night . . . Sleep, repeat. Maybe add a museum or two."

If I could change one thing about Parsons, I'd "make the New School's resources more open to Parsons students and tell the fashion snobs to chill out."

Three things every student at Parsons should do before graduating are "dedicate yourself to marathon museum-hopping, spend time abroad (do France!), and make connections with cool teachers who work in your field."

Rensselaer Polytechnic Institute

Address: 110 8th Street; Troy, NY 12180-3590
Phone: 518-276-6216
E-mail address: admissions@rpi.edu
Web site URL: admissions.rpi.edu
Founded: 1824
Private or Public: private
Religious affiliation: NA
Location: suburban
Undergraduate enrollment: 4,894
Total enrollment: 4,929
Percent Male/Female: 75%/25%
Percent Minority: 21%
Percent African-American: 4%
Percent Asian: 12%
Percent Hispanic: 5%
Percent Native-American: 0%

Percent in-state/out of state: 51%/50%
Percent Pub HS: NA
On-campus housing: 56%
Fraternities: 39%
Sororities: 18%
Number of Applicants: 5,406
Percent Accepted: 75%
Percent Accepted who enroll: 27%
Entering class: 1,079
Transfers: NA
Early admission program (EA/ED/NA): ED
Early Decision or Early Action Acceptance Rate: 74%
Application Deadline: 31-Dec
Mean SAT: NA
Mean ACT: NA
Middle 50% SAT range: 1,220–1,420

Middle 50% ACT range: 24–28
Most popular majors: Engineering, Computer and Information Sciences and Support Services, Business, Management, Marketing, and Related Support Services
Retention: 92%
Graduation rate: 80%
Tuition and Fees: $31,857
In State Tuition and Fees (if different): NA
Room and Board: $9,506
Financial aid, first-year: 72%
Varsity or Club Athletes: NA
Library: 494,493 volumes

Located in upstate New York, Rensselaer Polytechnic Institute is known for churning out Noble Prize-bound engineers and NHL-bound hockey pros. Though the heavy workload and brutal winter weather can be intimidating, RPI's strong programs and cutting-edge facilities make it a mecca for engineers, architects, and hockey fans alike.

A (Metric) Ton of Work

When asked why he chose RPI, one student simply said: "It sets you apart in the engineering world." RPI's stellar reputation and top-notch academic programs make it an appealing option for students interested in engineering and a host of other fields. Students can apply to one of five schools within the University: Science, Architecture, Engineering, Humanities and Social Sciences, or Management and Technology. The architecture program is praised for its professors and its small size—while the University enrolls over 5,000 undergraduates, the prestigious architecture school enrolls 60–70 freshmen per year. Those who make the cut gain access to RPI's lighting research center, one of the best in the country. While RPI is predominantly known as an engineering school, the school is working to further develop its programs in other areas. The new EMPAC (Experimental Media Performing Arts Center) will mix cutting-edge technology with the arts, a reflection of the growing diversification of academic options.

Slackers beware: RPI academics are intense. As one engineering student said: "it's definitely a lot harder than I thought it'd be. They say it's hard, but it really is. They're not lying." It's common knowledge that students must spend at least 30 hours a week outside of class "to even have a chance in hell of getting by." Most people devote much time than that, setting aside an entire day (9 a.m. to midnight) each week to catch up on work. At least the professors believe in curving. Though students' final grades are determined by how well they perform in comparison to their peers, competition is not cutthroat. While it does exist, some say "It's us against the teacher more than us against ourselves." Furthermore, the combination of a rigorous program and RPI's good name means that graduates are well-prepared for the working world. Students praise the career center and the University as a whole for its focus on landing students enviable jobs after graduation.

All students in the engineering program must take a set of core classes, usually during their first three or four semesters. While students say that the relevance between these core classes and their specific major can seem doubtful at first, professors aim to make the courses applicable to all programs. "You might not know what it relates to when you take it, but longer down the road you get it," said one junior.

With rigorous programs and a large student body, RPI undergrads are encouraged take a pro-active stance in their education. "If you don't put out the effort, you're a number," said one student. Extensive class preparation is required, and students must learn a number of things on their own from the textbook. Students say it "goes both ways" in terms of professor accessibility—some are always available while others are constantly traveling the world. The University is known for offering undergraduates an abundance of research opportunities.

Bricks & Bread

Campus buildings boast the best of both worlds: on the outside, the gothic structures have a "traditional, collegiate look," while on the inside they offer cutting-edge technology. The majority of campus is wireless, and every classroom is set up so that students can plug in their laptops. The University even provides incoming freshmen with a personal laptop and wireless card.

The Quad, RPI's largest residence area, sits on the main campus. It houses upperclassmen in single, double, or triple rooms. There are also 10 residence halls, including five freshman dorms, surrounding the Commons Dining Hall. Upperclassmen looking to escape traditional dorm life can live in the recently-renovated apartments, which are complete with a kitchen and dining area.

While only first-year students are promised on-campus housing, upper-class students say they don't have any difficulty finding residences to their liking.

The dining hall receives lukewarm ratings in terms of quality—it's "hit or miss." At least "[it] doesn't cause any problems internally and tastes decent," as one content diner reported. There are six styles of food to choose from each night, so "you can always find something that you like." And for those fearing the Freshman 15—"there are lots of healthy options." Students are generally pleased with the flexible meal plans. "In theory you can go to the dining hall 15 times a day."

Most upperclassmen don't have meal plans, so they cook their own food or purchase meals at the student union. The student-run Rensselaer Union, renovated in 2000 to incorporate campus-wide technology, is a popular student hang-out. It features two floors of food courts, including a Starbucks and café. The U-shaped quad is another destination for those seeking a place to chill. But the academic rigors don't leave many stretches of time for ambitious RPI students to just lay low. "Honestly, you're going to find most people in the student union center or on their computers," said one student.

A Social Scavenger Hunt

Students agree that the low-key nightlife at RPI demands a "pro-active attitude" from those seeking a quality party. "There's stuff to do," said one student, "but it's not the University of Miami." Fraternities and sororities have a big presence on campus, with more than a quarter of the University involved, and current students encourage incoming freshmen to consider rushing. However, the RPI administration has been tightening the reins on underage drinking in recent years, making fraternities hesitant to throw full-scale parties, and leaving the nightlife-starved student body even hungrier for a full social calendar. "Our school is trying to deal with underage drinking. They feel they should be changing policies for the entire United States," said one frustrated Greek member. Outside of the Greek system, popular annual parties include the Big Red Freak-Out, to support the hockey team, and Grand Marshal week, when the elections for student representatives take place. GM week is full of games, and students enjoy time off from classes. In general, students point to the academic intensity as the reason behind the tame party scene. "People are so busy—you don't have time to party until the weekend."

While some students complain that the surrounding town of Troy is, to put it bluntly, "pretty crappy," as well as a bit unsafe, others indicate the recent renewal effort that the city has been experiencing. Its art community in particular has made Troy more attractive. For those so inclined, students of drinking age point out worthwhile destinations like Club Lime, a rugby bar called The Ruck, and O'Learys for food. Troy and Albany also host occasional concerts. While most upperclassmen have a car on campus, few venture outside of the Troy area on a regular basis. Many students choose to hang out with friends made through activities, rather than just those from within the major.

"The Odds are Good but the Goods are Odd"

RPI students are known for their book smarts, but some confess that their peers' social skills could use a little fine-tuning. "The standard issue RPI kid is probably a big computer nerd," admitted one junior, echoing a common view on campus. One student painted the caricature of an RPI student as someone who "walks around in a black trenchcoat, doesn't speak any - English, and stays in his room to play videogames or download porn." Indeed, the high-tech atmosphere can have a downside: it's not uncommon for some students to stay glued to their laptop through the weekend. "They're very computer-oriented students," explained one undergrad; "[they] make my college look bad!" However, many RPI students are witty, outgoing, and have a great sense of humor; they assure that the caricature is not the norm and that "there is plenty of social interaction on campus." Overall, undergrads are described as friendly, laidback, and into outdoor activities. One junior summed up the situation by saying that there are two kinds of smarts—book smarts and wit—and every RPI student has at least one in the bag.

> "The standard issue RPI kid is probably a big computer nerd."

There are few complaints about ethnic diversity at RPI—the strong academic programs draw students from across the world.

But students tend to be less enthusiastic about the gender ratio and dating prospects. The skewed male-female ratio of 3:1 can definitely put a kink in a guy's game. As one Greek brother said: "There are 30 fraternities and four sororities—just by that fact you can kind of figure it out." Not surprisingly, long-term relationships tend to prevail over random hook-ups: "If a guy finds a girl he usually hangs on to her." Guys sometimes complain of RIBS ("ratio-induced bitch syndrome") among the minority sex, as "very pretty girls get hit on all the time, so they think they're the greatest thing in the world." Female students have their own set of troubles, though. "The guys always complain about the fact that there are no girls, but a lot of the guys are the ones who sit in the rooms and play videogames," one female explained. "Girls also have difficulty."

Puck Pros

Hockey is huge at RPI. "Going to a hockey game is like going to a professional game," explained one student. In fact some players do head straight from RPI to the NHL, including such notable alumni as Joe Juneau and Adam Oates. Men's and women's hockey are the only Division I sports at the University, but football also attracts large crowds. RPI is planning to construct the new East Campus Athletic Village, which will include a new football field, gym, 50-meter pool, and tennis courts. Whether it's on the varsity, club, or recreational level, many students participate in some sort of athletic activity of campus. Undergrads can often be found skateboarding, riding bikes, or in the midst of a snowball fight.

Making the Most of It

While the stereotype of the RPI computer nerd seems to have some truth behind it, students have a sense of humor about it and prove that social interaction doesn't have to be limited to study sessions and videogame marathons. Facing a massive workload and large introductory classes, students are urged to shape their own paths at RPI, and to make time for fun. "You're going to go crazy if you don't take control of what you're doing," said one student. Another RPI undergrad offered this piece of advice to incoming freshmen: "Bring a willingness to do everything you can. The work is going to be really hard, but you're not going to be able to make it without friends."—*Christen Martosella*

FYI

If you come to RPI, you'd better bring "a work ethic."

What's the typical weekend schedule? "Friday: go to O'Leary's for chicken wings, pizza, beer; after that, go to a frat house or wherever to party; Saturday morning: lounge around for bunch, maybe go to an RPI football game or Greek event; Saturday night: bar or house party; Sunday: do work."

If I could change one thing about RPI, I'd "make people more socially involved."

Three things every student should do before graduating are "look into joining Greek life," "go to a hockey game—preferably the big game against Clarkson in February" and "plan your own schedule. Make sure that your senior year you can take one semester that's not crazy."

Rochester Institute of Technology

Address: Rochester Tech, Bausch & Lomb Center, 60 Lomb Memorial Drive, Rochester, New York 14623-5604

Phone: 585-475-6631

E-mail Address: admissions@rit.edu

Web site URL: www.rit.edu

Year Founded: 1829

Private or Public: private

Religious affiliation: none

Location: urban

Regular Application Deadline: 2-Feb

Number of Applicants: 10,219

Percent Accepted: 65%

Percent Accepted who enroll: 36%

Number Entering: 2,374

Number of Transfers Accepted each Year: 1,196

Mean SAT: NA

Mean ACT: NA

Middle 50% SAT range: M:570–670, V:530–630

Middle 50% ACT range: 23–28

Early admission program (EA/ ED/ NA): ED

ED or EA Acceptance Rate: 73.8%

Full time Undergraduate enrollment: 12,532

Total enrollment: 15,557

Percent Male: 69%

Percent Female: 31%

Total Percent Minority: 26%

Percent African-American: 4%

Percent Asian/Pacific Islander: 6%

Percent Hispanic: 4%

Percent Native-American: >1%

Percent Other: 11%

Percent in-state / out of state: 55%/45%

Percent from Public HS: 85%

Retention Rate: 89%

Graduation Rate: 63%

Percent in On-campus housing: 65%

Percent affiliated with Greek system: 5%

Percent Varsity or Club Athletes: NA

Number of official organized extracurricular organizations: 170

3 Most popular majors: Business Administration/ Management, Information Technology, Photography

Student/Faculty ratio: 14:01

Tuition and Fees: $25,011.00

Cost for Room and Board: $8,748.00

Percent receiving Financial aid, first-year: 83.25%

Every fall, the president of the Rochester Institute of Technology (RIT) plays a softball game with students. He also bets that no one can hit a home run off his pitch. The close relationship between the faculty and students reflect the practical learning that goes on at this career-oriented university, as RIT brings technical expertise together with a liberal arts curriculum.

Real-World Academics

While many students at RIT come interested in engineering and the sciences, they often end up taking modern-day interpretative dance, pottery making, or the history of the French Revolution. The foundation of the school still lies upon a liberal arts curriculum, with core classes that cover the humanities, social sciences, and sciences.

But be warned, RIT academics are not for the faint of heart. The school year runs on the quarter system so there are 10-week classes followed by a final in the fall, winter, and spring. Within each quarter, students typically take three to five classes. This all comes down to 40 percent more credit than other schools. Freshmen usually have relatively bad schedules since they have last pick in class registration.

With eight colleges ranging from business to the National Technical Institute for the Deaf, RIT has plenty to offer. Yet its best known feature is the co-op program. "One of the oldest in the country, the RIT co-op experience often turn into full-time jobs," a student said. Some majors require students to do a co-op, which consists of taking a certain number of academic quarters off to work at a company.

For instance, the engineering major actually takes five years to complete because of five quarters of required co-op experience. Other majors don't require a single co-op. But many students jump on co-ops because of the real-world experience and tangible rewards, like cash!

RIT also makes it easy to match you up with the type of work you would be interested in, from designing computer chips to designing fabrics for the spring fashion line. The campus career center and co-op office run year-round to match up the thousands of students with hundreds of top companies.

How to Build a Racecar

Students at RIT don't just build race cars, they swing dance! The swing dance club teaches newcomers the fine art and also competes at various dancing showoffs. For those more interested in things that may explode, many engineering majors every year have designed, built, and raced F1-like cars in competitions. If these two clubs don't whet your appetite, there are 168 others to choose from.

The photography department and art programs at RIT are very well respected. There are countless dance companies, jazz assembles, and theater troupes on campus. Each year, three or four plays are produced, and many concerts are held.

The WITR is RIT's unique noncommercial and student-run radio station that reaches the greater Rochester region, a great outlet for students interested in everything from management to political commentary. *The Reporter* is RIT's undergraduate magazine, published weekly with the collaboration of writers, managers, photographers, and editors. At the ESPN Sports Zone, RIT students actually tape the show, *Sports Break*, which airs on ESPN 2.

Of course, if you don't find a club that exactly matches your niche, just start your own. It's very easy at RIT, and many fledgling organizations receive funding from the Student Government, which is the perfect place for the politically-oriented.

Engineers, Photographers, and Hockey Players

The first thing a student displaced from Hurricane Katrina noticed when she set foot on campus was the diversity of the student body. "Everyone's pretty well rounded," another student said. Although RIT may seem like a very technical school given its name, "there are photographers and artsy people, not just engineers," she said. However, there are more guys than girls at RIT, thus the saying around campus, "the odds are good but the goods are odd." RIT is also home to the largest population of deaf students, who are well integrated into the general student body but mostly take specially designed classes with accommodations.

> **"The odds are good but the goods are odd."**

"There are still students who play computer games in their rooms all day," one student admits. This stereotype of RIT certainly doesn't explain the facts that over half the students play in intramurals. Nonetheless, recruited athletes remain a minority on campus. All sports are Division III but hockey recently became Division I, huge news for a school that schedules homecoming around the hockey season. The lack of a football team makes hockey, as well as basketball, popular social outlets on the weekends.

Bricks, Bricks, and More Bricks

"On the outside, the campus may look bland because everything's covered in brick," one student said. But "it looks much nicer on the inside where you can enjoy the landscaping, since the buildings are roughly in a circle." The campus is medium-size in a relatively rural area. Yet RIT is also only minutes from Rochester, a booming metropolis for weekend partiers.

"A whole new college town is being developed, with an outside amphitheater, and new stores and shops," a student eagerly revealed. Because RIT owns a lot of land, the school has been on a spending and developing spree of late, growing to keep up with their rise in popularity.

Freshmen have to live in dorms, but this gives them a chance to meet each other. The campus housing consists mainly of singles, doubles, and triples, with a few suites available. But the housing assignments are completely random. Some upperclassmen live in one of five campus apartments, while others find housing off-campus; since RIT is relatively tucked away, housing is pretty affordable. Still others go off to live in fraternities. But 60 percent of students still choose to live on campus.

Food Cornucopia

"I eat on campus every day," one student said. "The food is good." The new cafeteria, situated on the freshman campus, attracts students at all times of the day. This main dining hall has a student run pizza parlor and various fast food options.

While some tout the dining options, another student said that the food is horrible, and that students deserve better food for the relatively high cost of going to RIT. For those dissatisfied with on-campus dining options, nearby restaurants offer a welcome escape. Five to ten minutes down Jefferson Road, a major traveling route, students find plenty of places to satisfy their hunger for Mexican, Chinese, Italian, steak, and good old home cooking.

On their breaks, RIT students enjoy relaxing at the coffee shops scattered around campus. The College Grind, open seven days a week, is the perfect meeting place and serves a mean espresso that will surely pick you up on those late-night study sessions. Many points along the underground halls between buildings also sell snack foods, like RITchie's, complete with the latest arcade games and big screen TV.

"Going to Wegmans at three in the morning is an awesome experience," said one upperclassman. This institutional icon is a 24-hour grocery store that's perfect for students working through the night.

Beyond the Co-op

There's always something going on along the "Quarter Mile," the busy walkway that cuts through the campus. Of course, to relax, you could go to the gym and take fencing lessons. There's also a student-run nightclub along the way. But the busiest building by far at RIT is the Union, the center of the social scene. There's a 500-seat theater that screens films, a Ben & Jerry's ice cream parlor, and various game rooms. The Union also has the unique ESPN SportsCenter desk, where you can tape your dreams of being a sports broadcaster.

Some students find having a car very useful, particularly for shopping in the surrounding areas. The Marketplace Mall is a quick drive and distraction from the busy campus. But transportation is very convenient, with free shuttles that go off-campus.

The social life on the weekends truly spans the spectrum. RIT lives by the motto, "study hard, play hard." For those into the party scene, the best places are off-campus in apartments and frats, although room parties still exist. There are 19 fraternities on campus, and 10 sororities, which undoubtedly serve as key social centers during the weekend. One student commented on the general lack of campus-wide parties, partly due to the relatively strict alcohol policy. But one weekend always alive with festivities is Brick City Homecoming, which boasts more planned events than one could ever attend and appearances by Jon Stewart and Rudy Giuliani.—*Jerry Guo*

FYI
If you come to RIT, you'd better bring "a laptop and a winter coat."
What is the typical weekend schedule? "Procrastinate, procrastinate, and procrastinate. See a drive-in movie on Thursday night, go to Friday Night at the Ritz, do a little work on Saturday, and study on Sunday."
If I could change on thing about RIT, I'd "put more hours in a day and make more students get involved in extracurricular activities."
Three things every student at RIT should do before graduating are "make a difference in the community, play Frisbee in the snow, and walk the nature trails."

Sarah Lawrence College

Address: Sarah Lawrence, 1
Mead Way, Bronxville, NY
10708-5999
Phone: 800-888-2858
E-mail Address:
slcadmit@sarahlawrence.edu
Web site URL: www.slc.edu
Year Founded: 1926
Private or Public: private
Religious affiliation: No
Affiliation
Location: suburban
**Regular Application
Deadline:** 1-Jan
Number of Applicants: 2,720
Percent Accepted: 46%
**Percent Accepted who
enroll:** 30%
Number Entering: 307
**Number of Transfers
Accepted each Year:** NA
Mean SAT: NA

Mean ACT: NA
Middle 50% SAT range: NA
Middle 50% ACT range: NA
**Early admission program
(EA/ ED/ NA):** ED
ED or EA Acceptance Rate:
NA
**Full time Undergraduate
enrollment:** 1,339
Total enrollment: 1,662
Percent Male: 26%
Percent Female: 74%
Total Percent Minority:
18%
Percent African-American:
6%
**Percent Asian/Pacific
Islander:** 5%
Percent Hispanic: 5%
Percent Native-American:
1%
Percent Other: NA

**Percent in-state / out of
state:** 33%/77%
Percent from Public HS:
54%
Retention Rate: 81%
Graduation Rate: 0.79%
**Percent in On-campus
housing:** 85%
**Percent affiliated with
Greek system:** NA
**Percent Varsity or Club
Athletes:** NA
**Number of official organized
extracurricular
organizations:** 56
3 Most popular majors: NA
Student/Faculty ratio: 6:01
Tuition and Fees: $35,280
Cost for Room and Board:
$12,152
**Percent receiving Financial
aid, first-year:** 59%

Located in a quiet suburb of New York City, Sarah Lawrence provides an individualized education for the atypical student, and gives students the opportunity to meet a wide variety of students. The school emphasizes a liberal arts education, while also encouraging students to apply classroom knowledge while acquiring professional experience through internships in New York City.

Where School is Tailored to You

Sarah Lawrence has few requirements, requiring only that students take one course in three out of four disciplines, which include creative arts, social sciences and history, natural sciences and math, and creative arts. To ensure some breadth, the school also places a limit on how many credits can be taken in each discipline, with individual caps being 50 of the total 120 needed to graduate. Typically, students take three classes a semester. The advising system provides students with a personalized education. During freshman year, students are assigned a "don" in the field of their choice. A student's don serves as a general academic advisor as well as an aid while the student selects classes. As one sophomore said, "It is really nice having an advocate. Your don takes care of any issue you need." In addition, bi-weekly meetings with professors "ensure that you are not

just another number." The consensus was that the professors have great respect for the students and do not treat them as their inferiors. "Professors are here because they want to be. They want to closely advise students." The most popular majors (known as "concentrations" at Sarah Lawrence) are writing and the humanities. Science is not as popular, but students say the science concentrations still have "a presence" on campus.

Instead of final exams, students must complete Conference Projects in their humanities classes. Conference Projects range from creative group projects to research papers designed by the student under the guidance of a professor. One student commented that "conference projects, while a lot of work, teach you how to write in a way most people can't." The method of choosing classes was also described as one of Sarah Lawrence's strengths. Before a student is enrolled in a course, the student and professor interview each other to see if the class will be an appropriate match for the student. One sophomore noted, "Because it is a two-way system, I feel like I am respected by my professors and that I am not just another number in a big lecture hall." This is further reinforced by the small class size, as most courses are taught as seminars limited to 15 students. "Class size is why I chose Sarah Lawrence and what makes Sarah Lawrence

Sarah Lawrence," said one senior. The workload can be challenging and "time management is key," said one student, but according to another, the environment is not competitive. "People are not cut throat because you are in competition with yourself." To supplement material learned in the classroom, many students hold internships in New York City because of its close proximity.

> **"Professors are here because they want to be. They want to closely advise students."**

Grading and advising are also unique. Sarah Lawrence gives detailed comments instead of grades. Further, grades are less a result of performance measures such as tests, but rather on effort and knowledge of the course material as perceived by the professor. One senior added that you are "graded not on your performance on a test, but on what they think you have learned. Grades/comments here are about doing the best job you can, not being in the top percentage of your class."

Overall, students like the academics at Sarah Lawrence. One senior commented that "Sarah Lawrence prepares you more broadly. SLC prepares you really well to write, understand, and do work." One complaint, however, was that not all concentrations receive the same amount of resources from the college. As one senior griped, "A few departments are nonexistent, and I would like to see more equal distribution around the college."

In Between Two Cities

Located on the border of Yonkers and Bronxville in a quiet suburb of New York City, SLC does not have much of a positive relationship with the locals. Those from Yonkers ignore the students, and according to students, there has been some hostility between the students and those from Bronxville. Generally, the campus is self-contained as most students live on campus, especially freshmen and sophomore. The quality of the dorms varies, with freshman dorms described as small, and senior dorms described as "quite spacious and nice." Those who do move off campus move to Yonkers as it is less expensive than Bronxville. Freshmen are prohibited from having cars, but they are popular among Sarah Lawrence's upperclassmen.

Freshmen have a mandatory meal plan and tend to congregate at Bates Dining Hall. The meal plans are rather expensive, so upperclassmen tend to cook or get takeout. Moreover, many of the dorms have kitchens that are quite popular. During the day many students go to the on-campus pub that serves fast food, and although students acknowledge the dining halls "could use some work," many agree that they are "fine overall."

Finding Your Place at SLC

According to students, Sarah Lawrence can be socially isolating at times. The campus is often somewhat deserted during weekends because many students go to New York City. In addition, there are many types of people at SLC, and "finding your group can be difficult sometimes." It takes someone "socially outgoing to appreciate the social life." Consequently, New York is one of SLC's strengths, as it gives students the opportunity to get off campus. Shuttles as well as the train make transportation easy. "SLC attracts the type of student that will use New York for all that it has to offer."

Still, diversity can be an issue; while the campus is socially diverse, it is not ethnically. Students say the University is making efforts to change this, with days devoted to promoting education about diversity and financial issues. Financial aid remains a problem at Sarah Lawrence. One senior said that "the University is eager to use its money for financial aid. The only problem is that our endowment is not that large. They are doing great with what they have, but it is still not enough." Identity-based groups are quite popular on campus. For example, Coming Out month is quite popular and well received, and students say the gay population is "quite large and well accepted." The female to male ratio is higher than average, which probably attributable to the fact that SLC was an all girls' school until 1968. In terms of finding relationships, "one must look for the dating scene, but it is there."

The drug an alcohol policy is "fairly standard." Drugs are never allowed; however, students say that marijuana and alcohol are treated less severely. If caught, a student is ticketed and then has a meeting with "student affairs." "The college has a pretty good sense of its priorities" said one sophomore; if a student does have a problem with drugs and alcohol, the university focuses on helping the student, rather than punishing him. Still, due to the restrictions against substances, parties tend to be small and moved off campus.

Sports are not overwhelming on campus, but "are a part" of campus life. While the students interviewed could not name all of the teams, they could name many of the school's major varsity athletics. SLC has atypical school spirit. One student commented, "You won't see a bevy of college sweatshirts walking around campus, but there is a sense of pride and tradition." One senior described it as a "very strong sense of tradition. The tradition is to be different from most colleges. It's a pretty wonderful place."

In general, the only complaints students had were about the occasional professor that he or she did not really enjoy, although one student commented that career services could improve their contacts and do a better job of helping students. Sarah Lawrence is a great school for those who fit the non-mold. Sarah Lawrence is full of "self-motivated students looking for a great education in a non cookie-cutter form." SLC fosters academic growth while exposing students to many things both in and out of the classroom, and provides the opportunity for an individualized college experience unmatched by most other schools.—*Hilary Cohen*

FYI

If you come to SLC you'd better bring "an open mind and a bookshelf for all of the reading you will do."

What is the typical weekend schedule? "Thursday: Party, or leave for New York City, Friday: registered parties from a student organization. Alcohol is there but only for people of age. The rest of the weekend: schoolwork."

If you could change one thing about SLC, "it would be the size of the endowment and the amount of money available to undergraduates."

Three things you should do before you graduate are "run around naked on campus, go to a senate meeting, have at least one conference paper done on time."

Skidmore College

Address: Skidmore, 815 North Broadway, Saratoga Springs, NY 12866

Phone: 800-867-6007

E-mail Address: admissions@skidmore.edu

Web site URL: www.skidmore.edu/admissions/index.htm

Year Founded: 1903

Private or Public: private

Religious affiliation: No Affiliation

Location: suburban

Regular Application Deadline: 15-Jan

Number of Applicants: 6,650

Percent Accepted: 39%

Percent Accepted who enroll: 26%

Number Entering: 610

Number of Transfers Accepted each Year: NA

Mean SAT: 1,980

Mean ACT: 27

Middle 50% SAT range: 1,790–2,030

Middle 50% ACT range: 25–28

Early admission program (EA/ ED/ NA): ED

ED or EA Acceptance Rate: NA

Full time Undergraduate enrollment: 2,300

Total enrollment: 2,300

Percent Male: 40%

Percent Female: 60%

Total Percent Minority: 15%

Percent African-American: 3%

Percent Asian/Pacific Islander: 6%

Percent Hispanic: 4%

Percent Native-American: 1%

Percent Other: NA

Percent in-state / out of state: 30%/70%

Percent from Public HS: 61%

Retention Rate: 92%

Graduation Rate: 0.78%

Percent in On-campus housing: 74%

Percent affiliated with Greek system: 0%

Percent Varsity or Club Athletes: NA

Number of official organized extracurricular organizations: 80

3 Most popular majors: Business Administration, English, Fine Arts

Student/Faculty ratio: 9:01

Tuition and Fees: $34,224

Cost for Room and Board: $9,556

Percent receiving Financial aid, first-year: 55%

S tudents looking for a close-knit college experience are well advised to take a good look at Skidmore. Located in Saratoga Springs, New York, Skidmore offers a strong liberal arts focus, a small and supportive environment, and a great time all around. If students can handle the winter snow, Skidmore is a great place to get the whole package.

Living and Learning

Students give Skidmore's small size high marks in the classroom. The small student to teacher ratio means that students have "small classes with a lot of individual attention and the opportunity to have their voices heard." Regarding the curriculum, the much-maligned LS1 and LS2 programs for freshmen and sophomores has been replaced with the First Year Experience. The anchors of this program are the Scribner Seminars. Freshmen are required to choose from many interesting options, including Gender Benders, Chinese Wisdom and Queens, Italian Cinema and Psych Out the Stock Market. These well-reviewed courses are also integrated into the living experience by placing students in the same seminar within close proximity in the dorms to encourage and facilitate a learning environment that extends out of the classroom. As far as other requirements, a senior reflects that, "If taken before you declare a major, the required courses can be helpful, but if you find yourself a senior and needing to fulfill courses unrelated to your major, they're a pain."

Skidmore students find that the classes run the gamut from "classes that require a tremendous amount of work" and those that "do not require significant effort to get by." Among the majors, Business, Government, and Art are the most popular, while Economics, the sciences, and Studio Art are generally known as the majors requiring the most work. Both in and out of their majors, students can find a variety of creative and interesting courses. One of the most popular courses is MB 107, an introductory business class that draws crowds every year. Some of the more unusual courses include West African Drumming, Dance for the Child, and a course on The Beatles.

> **"You can handle everything here at your own pace and that is the benefit of being at a small school."**

Students have almost only positive comments on their professors and classes. Classes are described as "personal" with the normal size hovering between 15 and 20 students. "Professors for the most part are extremely qualified and genuinely enjoy their interactions with students." Professors take advantage of their proximity to students by having fun with their classes. One professor is known for occasionally bringing a banjo or guitar to class. Another advantage of the small size of the school according to students is that, "if a professor isn't good, you'll definitely hear about it from another student."

Skidmore students are self-described as having a "wide range of approaches to academics." While some study around the clock, others do the least that is required. And, although certain students admit they would sometimes like to see more out of their peers, the majority seems to agree with one student's comment that, "Everyone seems to come out fine. I like it because there is no pressure to be a certain way in terms of academics. You can handle everything here at your own pace and that is the benefit of being at a small school."

Play Time

When not hitting the books, Skidmore students look to have a great time. Students are regularly out all weekend starting on Thursday night, and during the week, Tuesday nights are popular. While there is no Greek presence on campus, there are still a variety of different social groups and scenes to encompass every interest. Sports teams and former athletes, for example, dominate certain aspects of the social life. At the same time, the small size of the school encourages different groups and classes to be inclusive and socialize together. As one student expresses, "Parties that my friends throw tend to be larger because we try to incorporate all social groups." This atmosphere of camaraderie makes it easy for freshmen to meet people. Drinking plays a large role within the social scene, especially during the snowy months that keep students indoors. While the campus has recently made an effort to become dry, certain living areas, such as the Northwood apartments, still maintain a reputation for fun. Off-campus housing, such as Stables, also serves as a focal point for weekend partying. Saratoga boasts a large bar scene that has expanded from being not only a key destination for upperclassmen, but also underclassmen. Popular destinations in downtown Saratoga include Tin and Lint, a classic college bar, and Peabody's, a restaurant and club. Saratoga is described as "a great college town" and students rarely run out of things to do.

While drinking appears to be the dominant factor in Skidmore social life, one student explains, "Drinking is not essential, just easy to find if you want. The school does a fairly good job of making sure there are alternatives to drinking every weekend." These activities include movie nights, theatrical productions, and outdoor pursuits such as hiking and skiing. A few of the most popular annual events include the Junior Ring dance, a semiformal affair, Spring Fling in April, and Fun Day in May. Lake George, Saratoga Park, and Yaddo, an artist and writer's colony with botanical gardens, are also a draw for students.

Campus Life

Skidmore's administration has been putting an effort toward bringing upperclassmen back into on-campus housing. Dorms are generally rated either "not notably good or bad" or "not great," with the new apartments in Northwoods Village standing out as the best among the options. Many sophomores live in Scribner Village, which features on-campus townhouses. Starting junior year, students often move off campus, largely due to crackdowns on the social life on campus. The move to bring upperclassmen back into dorms is fairly unpopular among students, especially in light of a general feeling that overcrowding needs to be alleviated. There is a new dining hall on campus, although the food is described as "average" and "mediocre." While there are few food alternatives on campus, there are a number of restaurants within minutes of campus and many delivery options. Some popular restaurants in Saratoga include Scallions, Sperry's, and Lillian's.

The Skidmore campus benefits from its beautiful location in upstate New York surrounded by the Adirondacks and the Vermont mountains. Saratoga Springs also serves as a draw because of its appeal as a college town. On campus, notable facilities include the Tang Museum and Art Gallery, the new dining hall, and Wieking Hall, a relatively new dorm. Scribner Library also draws positive reviews, as does the newly expanded gym.

Skidmore boasts a large number of student activities and groups on campus, enough to provide a niche for every interest. Some of the more prominent and popular groups include the Wombats, an ultimate Frisbee team, student government, and SkidTV. Outdoors activities are understandably popular in light of Skidmore's location and the great skiing, lakes and hiking opportunities in the area. Skidmore athletics do not play a huge role on campus, and many students lament the lack of school spirit. According to a former athlete, "One of the main reasons I stopped playing was due to the fact that nobody on campus cared about all the hard work we were doing to represent our school." Despite this occasional apathy, students are given a world of resources on campus to pursue whatever their interests may be.

Skidmore students agree that they are a welcoming and friendly bunch. As one senior expresses, "There are the stereotypical student groups, but they are all usually nice, friendly kids" who are easy to meet. One issue the school faces is a lack of diversity on campus as most of the students tend to be white and upper middleclass. There is also a large contingent of students from the Northeast, although there are a number of international students. The school seems to be working on its diversity issue, and students find that "there is intermixing between groups and people are accepting of kids regardless of race or orientation." Generally the campus leads toward the liberal, and even hippy, side, but there is something here for everyone.

Skidmore students may differ in their interests and activities, but they all agree that they love their school and Saratoga Springs. The cold winters are no barrier to this hard working and fun loving group.—*Janet Yang*

FYI
If you come to Skidmore you better bring "warm clothing, a lighter, and a car for weekend escapes."
Three things every student should do before graduation are "go to the racetrack, go skiing on a weekend, and experience a summer in Saratoga."
The typical weekend schedule is "go out to an off-campus house party, then downtown to the bars, sleep in late or go skiing, then go out some more."
If I could change one thing it would be "making the school's administration more relaxed and less likely to punish students for minor problems."

St. Lawrence University

Address: St. Lawrence, 23 Romoda Drive, Canton, NY 13617
Phone: 800-285-1856
E-mail Address: admissions@stlawu.edu
Web site URL: www.stlawu.edu
Year Founded: 1856
Private or Public: private
Religious affiliation: none
Location: rural
Regular Application Deadline: 15-Feb
Number of Applicants: 3,192
Percent Accepted: 59.2%
Percent Accepted who enroll: 35.0%
Number Entering: 614
Number of Transfers Accepted each Year: 30–40
Mean SAT: 0
Mean ACT: NA
Middle 50% SAT range: NA

Middle 50% ACT range: NA
Early admission program (EA/ ED/ NA): ED
ED or EA Acceptance Rate: 23%
Full time Undergraduate enrollment: 2,111
Total enrollment: 2,264
Percent Male: 48%
Percent Female: 52%
Total Percent Minority: 12%
Percent African-American: 2.1%
Percent Asian/Pacific Islander: 2%
Percent Hispanic: 2.4%
Percent Native-American: 0.6%
Percent Other: 4.6%
Percent in-state / out of state: 45%/55%
Percent from Public HS: 71.4%

Retention Rate: 90%
Graduation Rate: 71.4% (4 years)
Percent in On-campus housing: 98%
Percent affiliated with Greek system: 14%
Percent Varsity or Club Athletes: 32%
Number of official organized extracurricular organizations: 122
3 Most popular majors: English, Psychology, Government
Student/Faculty ratio: 11:01
Tuition and Fees: $33,690.00
Cost for Room and Board: $8,630.00
Percent receiving Financial aid, first-year: 90%

Tucked into a corner of the Adirondacks, in a small town in New York near the Canadian border, sits St. Lawrence University—just small enough to fit into the little town, but big enough for its students to call it home. The relatively small size of SLU allows the formation of a close-knit community, both within the student body and between the students and faculty. The rural location affords opportunities for outdoor activities and gives the campus its beautiful backdrop, the pride of many an SLU student. Even though many students complain about the huge piles of snow in the cold winter months, most agree that the warmth of the friendly people around them more than makes up for the weather.

Studying at SLU

Academics at St. Lawrence are described as difficult at times, but, as one student said, "you don't have to be doing work ALL the time." Some of the most popular departments include economics, psychology and biology. Because of the small size of SLU, students benefit from small class sizes and they enjoy close contact with professors right from the start of their freshman year. Many professors provide student with their home phone numbers and encourage students to contact them with questions or problems. Students reported that essentially all classes enroll no more than 25 students (the average is 16), are taught exclusively by professors, and have a TA or two to give extra help to students who need it. Small class size rarely results in students being shut out of classes they want to take, though. Registration now takes place online, and involves meeting with an advisor to gain a PIN that is then used to select classes.

St. Lawrence's academic program includes a fair number of requirements. Undergraduates must take a class in each of the following areas: "Arts or Expression," humanities, math and social science. They also must fulfill a natural science requirement, which must include one course with a lab. Opinions of these requirements vary from "a hassle" to "a good way to get us to start exploring different departments." In addition, freshmen participate in the First Year Program, a semester-long course devoted to developing oral and written communication skills, taken with other students from the same dorm. While many students acknowledge the benefits of FYP, others complain about how the course often conflicts with other desired courses.

When students at St. Lawrence want to study, they often head for Owen D. Young library, the main library on campus. ODY is a fairly modern building; although its aesthetic merits are often debated, most agree that the recent renovation has made the atmosphere on the inside cheerful and stimulating. However, the lively atmosphere also frequently inspires conversation, and many students describe ODY as more of a social place than a studious one. For hard-core studying, Madill, the science library, is your best bet.

Living and Eating

Housing at SLU is mainly in dorms, although there are also off-campus options such as Greek and theme housing and athletic suites. The dorms are mostly set up in traditional singles and doubles, and are coed, but some dorms also offer the option of suites with kitchens, mostly for upperclassmen. Students cite Sykes as one of the best dorms, with Whitman as the best dorm for freshmen. On the other hand, Lee and Rebert halls are said to be the worst, although even in those less desirable dorms, rooms are reportedly spacious and nicely furnished. Almost universally, students praise their dorms, whether they live in the best or worst location, for the sense of community fostered there.

> **"You don't have to be doing work ALL the time."**

As upperclassmen, students at St. Lawrence have more housing options, although finding an apartment in Canton isn't one of them; the University requires that undergraduates reside on campus. However, many upperclassmen choose to live in Greek houses, which lie just at the edge of campus; one student living in her sorority house described her experience by saying it is "very home-like, and there is always something to do." Theme housing is another alternative to dorms available after freshman year, and such houses include a house for environmentalists, for people who enjoy outdoor activities, and for cultural groups and international students. Seniors can also apply to live in on-campus townhouses.

SLU students tend to give their meal plan and dining options high ratings. There are three on-campus eating establishments: Dana Dining Hall (a traditional cafeteria), the Time Out Café and the Northstar Café in the New Student Center. The café has more of a

relaxed atmosphere where students go to hang out and relax, and the food there is considered the best of the options on campus, particularly the chicken wrap sandwiches. There are two meal plans available to students, the 21-meal plan, which is only accepted at Dana, and a declining-balance plan which is accepted at all three on-campus locations. While students favor the declining-balance plan because of its flexibility, most agree that it is impossible not to run out of money before the end of the semester, and so that plan is better for students who are not eating all of their meals on campus.

When students get tired of the places to eat on campus, or just want to treat themselves, they look to the restaurants in the town of Canton. For quick meals, there are the standard chains: McDonald's, Burger King and Pizza Hut, and also A-1 Oriental Kitchen, which is a popular delivery choice. Other restaurants in Canton include Sergi's Pizza, which has pizza and Italian food, Jerek Subs, Josie's and Phoebe's; the Cactus Grill, a Mexican restaurant located in nearby Potsdam, is also frequented by many St. Lawrence students. During Family Weekend, students often take their parents to McCarthy's.

Life After Studying

Students at St. Lawrence spend a lot of time on extracurricular activities, and there is "always something to get involved in." One of the most active groups on campus seems to be the Outing Club, which goes on lots of trips and does other activities together. A recently founded karate club, which is student-run and student-taught, is growing rapidly, an example of the ample opportunity to start new organizations if you are interested. Many students also spend their time working for *The Hill News*, the main weekly publication of St. Lawrence.

Sports are also an option at St. Lawrence, both for fans and athletes. Varsity soccer and hockey are the most popular, with rugby and lacrosse games also drawing crowds. School spirit peaks at the time of the Clarkson-SLU hockey game, and the long-time rivalry draws huge crowds. Students say that you have to get tickets at least a week in advance if you don't want to stand up to watch the game, but that it is one of the highlights of the year that cannot be missed. Sports are not limited only to varsity athletes, though, as St. Lawrence has a wide variety of intramural teams, which allow people of all levels the opportunity to play. In addition, the athletic facilities are described as "great, and always available to everybody." All of the sports facilities have been recently renovated and according to one student athlete, "facilities at SLU are in tip-top shape." SLU is also currently working on a drastic multimillion-dollar expansion of its arts facilities, and a state-of-the art, environmentally friendly Science Center is scheduled to open in the fall of 2007.

Unfortunately, the social life and weekend plans are definitely limited by the small student body and the school's rural locale. Some things that students do when they are hanging out or partying include shooting pool, going to see a movie (free on campus), going to see a band playing at Java House or going to a frat party. However, students complain that campus security and Canton police strongly frown upon student alcohol use. On top of that, on-campus and off-campus parties alike tend to get shut down soon after they begin. Thus, most students say that they spend a lot of time hanging out

in bars in Canton with their friends, or taking trips on the weekend to Ottawa, the capital of Canada, or to Syracuse, both of which are within a few hours' driving distance.

Even though there may be downsides to living in a remote, rural town, students at St. Lawrence agree that the beauty of their campus and the surrounding area is worth it. The architecture of the university, a mixture of old and modern buildings, the quaintness of the town of Canton, and the beauty of the mountains and forests make St. Lawrence a scenic and pleasant place. If you are looking for a school with a fast-paced, urban environment and a restaurant and club for every night of the week, SLU may not be for you; however, if you want a school with a tight-knit community of professors and students, set in a beautiful landscape offering a place to hike or just sit and contemplate, St. Lawrence University could be the one.—*Lisa Smith*

FYI

If you come to St. Lawrence, you'd better bring "a jacket. It's really cold out."

What is the typical weekend schedule? "There are two groups on campus. For one group, the weekend starts on Thursday nights ['Thirsty Thursday'], and they go to bars. The other group is the outdoorsy group. They go to the Adirondack Mountains to go hiking, backpacking, skiing and kayaking."

If I could change one thing about St. Lawrence, I would "make it so that the clubs could be completely student-run."

Three things every student at St. Lawrence should do before graduating are "streak the Candlelight Freshman Experience,""ring the bells in the chapel," and "attend a Laurentian Singers Concert."

State University of New York System

The State University of New York System is one of the largest state university programs in the United States, consisting of 64 individual campuses and over 418,000 students. SUNY offers a variety of degrees, ranging from the one-year certificate programs at the system's 30 community colleges, which are designed to prepare students for specific employment, to the advanced doctorate degrees offered at the 13 university locations. The centers of the system lie in Binghamton, Buffalo, Stoneybrook, and Albany. Other campuses are scattered around New York, and are represented in Brockport, Brooklyn, Canton, Clinton, Erie, Farmingdale, New Paltz, Old Westbury, Onondaga, and Syracuse. Aside

from the community colleges and the university center programs, the remaining SUNY schools are divided into schools focused on cultivating different specific academic interests, including technology, veterinary medicine and forestry studies.

To simplify the process of applying to such a diversity of schools, prospective students may apply to up to eight campuses at once. Forty-nine of the 64 SUNY schools accept this common application.

Like many state university programs, the SUNY system is almost completely comprised of in-state students. Almost 90 percent of SUNY's enrollment comes from New York, and these students pay a heavily discounted price for their education. Although this makes college significantly more affordable, when combined with the increasing number of students the SUNY system admits each year, students say it also creates large lectures and low levels of attention for undergraduates.

Many SUNY students agree that the SUNY system is not one to pamper its students. In order to get involved on campus or find direction either academically or with extracurricular activities, a student must be self-motivated. According to one student, the isolated locations of most SUNY campuses make it difficult to maintain a social life and get off-campus.

Despite these challenges, however, the SUNY system boasts a wealth of opportunities at a very affordable price. With over 7,669 degree and certificate programs available and a niche for any student willing to make an effort to find it, SUNY provides a magnitude of resources only made possible by such a broad range of campuses and students. Following are articles about the SUNY campuses located in Albany, Buffalo, Binghamton and Stonybrook.—*Stephanie Teng*

State University of New York / Albany

Address: SUNY Albany, University Administration Building 101, 1400 Washington Avenue, Albany, NY 12222
Phone: 518-442-5435
E-mail Address: ugadmissions@albany.edu
Web site URL: www.albany.edu
Year Founded: 1844
Private or Public: public
Religious affiliation: none
Location: suburban
Regular Application Deadline: 1-Mar
Number of Applicants: 16,700
Percent Accepted: 62%
Percent Accepted who enroll: 23%
Number Entering: 2,350
Number of Transfers Accepted each Year: NA
Mean SAT: NA
Mean ACT: NA

Middle 50% SAT range: 1,560–1,830
Middle 50% ACT range: 21–26
Early admission program (EA/ ED/ NA): EA
ED or EA Acceptance Rate: NA
Full time Undergraduate enrollment: 11,400
Total enrollment: 16,400
Percent Male: 50%
Percent Female: 50%
Total Percent Minority: 29%
Percent African-American: 8%
Percent Asian/Pacific Islander: 6%
Percent Hispanic: 7%
Percent Native-American: 0%
Percent Other: NA
Percent in-state / out of state: 95%/5%
Percent from Public HS: NA

Retention Rate: 84%
Graduation Rate: 62%
Percent in On-campus housing: 61%
Percent affiliated with Greek system: 17%
Percent Varsity or Club Athletes: NA
Number of official organized extracurricular organizations: 177
3 Most popular majors: Business Administration, English, Psychology
Student/Faculty ratio: 19:01
Tuition and Fees: $10,610
In State Tuition and Fees (if different): $4,350
Cost for Room and Board: $10,194
Percent receiving Financial aid, first-year: 62%

The State University of New York (SUNY) system is one of the best public college networks in the nation. Founded in 1844, Albany is one of the more highly regarded SUNY schools. Though it has a bit of a party school reputation, Albany offers impressive academic resources—and less impressive guidance systems—to its body of 12,457 undergrads and 5,000 grad students, a diverse bunch who range from nerdy bookworms to seven-days-a-week boozehounds.

A Feast of Academic Options

As one of the more prominent SUNY campuses, Albany is known for its plethora of academic resources. But as is the case in many state-run institutions, help is hard to come by. Undergraduate advisors are notoriously unhelpful. As a result, much of a student's experience at Albany depends on his or her major and ability to figure things out alone. "The thing about Albany's academics is that it can really vary from student to student as to what their experience will be," one student commented. "Some people breeze right through doing practically nothing, while other students work ridiculously hard all the time."

Albany has particularly strong programs in political science, psychology, sociology, business and physics, to name a few. Lately, the University has gained attention for its writing program after the founding of The Writers' Institute in 1984 by novelist William Kennedy. The Institute has boosted Albany's curriculum by beefing up the writing-related offerings and bringing famous authors to speak on campus. Biology is another strong department at Albany. Students interested in messing around with lab rats can check out the Mutant Mouse Regional Resource Center, a bank of specimens with "unique phenotypes" on campus. Students in the public service sector often take advantage of the internship opportunities afforded by Albany's location. Albany also offers 40 different BA/MA combination degree tracks.

Albany has a comprehensive core curriculum called the General Education Program. According to the school's Web site, the program "proposes a set of knowledge areas, perspectives, and competencies considered by the University to be central to the intellectual development of every undergraduate." Students must demonstrate proficiency in disciplinary perspectives, cultural and historical perspectives, mathematics and statistics, communication and reasoning, and foreign language. Although these classes are not very difficult, some students complain that it is very hard to fulfill Gen Ed requirements. "It is almost impossible to get into Gen Ed course classes," one junior said. "[Albany] seems to be accepting more and more students, but not really opening up more classes."

A New York State of Mind

Located in upstate New York in the state capital, Albany's picturesque autumns quickly turn into brutal winters, though this is par for the course in the Northeast. Still, trekking across the frozen tundra between Albany's three campus centers is often a trying affair. While walking, students can admire the architecture of Edward Durrell Stone, designer of Lincoln Center, though they may tire of this pastime when they realize that many buildings are reproduced almost identically throughout the campus.

About 93 percent of Albany's students hail from the Empire State. The freshman facebook reads like the Long Island-Westchester Yellow Pages—and with good reason. New Yorkers pay about $6,000 tuition per semester, or half what out-of-state students pay, plus roughly $8,000 for room and board.

The campus is divided into two main locations—uptown and downtown. On Uptown Campus, students live in four symmetrical quads named Indian, Dutch, Colonial and State—after New York's four historical periods. Students also live in the apartment-style Freedom and Empire dorms, as well as the Alumni quad downtown. The dorms are generally described as average. Most are low-rise buildings surrounding a central tower, and consist of suites with two to three rooms with a common area.

Getting good housing can be competitive, especially when it comes to Empire, one of the nicest dorms on campus. An Empire suite consists of four singles and two bathrooms, and comes pre-furnished with couches and dressers, a full kitchen, plus a washing machine and a dryer. "It definitely beats collecting quarters and lugging your laundry to a basement," said one junior. "[Empire] is more expensive but it's worth it." Dorms such as Wellness Hall, Math Hall, and Substance-Free Hall offer themed housing for those with special interests and recently the University announced three new themed living communities for upperclassmen: Beyond Hollywood and Bollywood, China House, and Francophone.

The number one complaint of Albany students is the weather, but food is a close second. The University's dining system is about as popular as MC Hammer—and Albany food didn't even experience a brief burst of popularity in the early 1990s. Students often chose to eat downtown instead of testing the mush dished out by university cooks.

Perhaps the dining situation has an impact on school spirit—Albany students are lukewarm when it comes to representing their university. According to one student, "Sports at Albany are horrible . . . there is very little school spirit and events are not well-attended. The school has tried to change that recently, but it has not been very successful yet."

Albany offers standard extracurricular fare, including intramurals, student government, performance organizations, frats and sororities. In November 2005, Albany's Earth Tones (all-male) and Serendipity (all-female) finished second and third at the collegiate a cappella Northeast Quarterfinals and are big attractions on campus. The Albany Student Press publishes a newspaper two days a week, and the Student Association governs student affairs and plans campus events.

Party Time

Though Albany no longer shows up on Top 10 Party School lists as it did throughout much of the 1990s, it is hardly a dry campus. Fraternities and sororities are not recognized by the school, but they do exist. However, it is the bar scene that dominates campus party life. "Bring enough money to drink," one student said. "That's the main source of entertainment here at Albany . . . if you wanna make it a relaxing night, you know exactly what to buy from your local provider." Famous festivities include Fountain Day, a celebration of the return of water to the campus fountain at the end of winter; Kegs and Eggs, a springtime drunkfest; and Party in the Park, a year-end party featuring live music and plenty of eats.

Despite its reputation, Albany has fairly strict rules on underage drinking: two strikes and you're kicked out of housing. But the regulations are rarely enforced. "It really depends on your RAs," one student said. "I always drank in my dorm room and never gotten in trouble for it . . . As long as you're not really loud it'll be fine."

Albany students report that partying is more frequent for underclassmen, and some freshmen and sophomores go out almost every night of the week. Upperclassmen don't go out as much as they start to buckle down and focus on their studies. "The freshman-sophomore party experience is nuts, but so much fun," one junior remarked. "I wouldn't trade those years for anything."

> **"The freshman-sophomore party experience is nuts, but so much fun."**

SUNY Albany is a big school with big resources, but it's not too big a drain on the pocketbook. For most, Albany is what you make of it. Students just have to make sure they don't get lost in the shuffle, and most seem to make it a productive and enjoyable time in the capital of the Empire State.—*Zack O'Malley Greenburg*

FYI

If you come to SUNY Albany, you'd better bring "an umbrella, a warm jacket, beer money, and food to keep in your room."

What is the typical weekend schedule? "Starts on Thursday, which is mainly a bar night—you won't really find parties around. Friday: hit up happy hour around four o'clock (Paulie's is the cheapest) then maybe go to some parties. Saturday morning: recover, enjoy the fine cuisine that is Chartwell's brunch omelets made to order. Saturday night: go out to the bars, unless a good friend is throwing a party. Older crowd is further downtown. Sunday: sleep in and watch movies on HBO."

If I could change one thing about SUNY Albany, I'd "change the food, it really is just bad. Except the cookies . . . they're good."

Three things every student at SUNY Albany should do before graduating are "experience a warm Fountain Day, attend Kegs and Eggs, and go to class drunk."

State University of New York Binghamton

Address: SUNY Binghamton, PO Box 6001, Binghamton, NY 13902

Phone: 607-777-2171

E-mail Address: admit@binghamton.edu

Web site URL: http://admissions .binghamton.edu/

Year Founded: 1946

Private or Public: public

Religious affiliation: none

Location: suburban

Regular Application Deadline: rolling

Number of Applicants: 22,853

Percent Accepted: 43%

Percent Accepted who enroll: 24%

Number Entering: 2,319

Number of Transfers Accepted each Year: 783

Mean SAT: NA

Mean ACT: 27

Middle 50% SAT range: 1,800–2,030

Middle 50% ACT range: 25–29

Early admission program (EA/ ED/ NA): EA

ED or EA Acceptance Rate: NA

Full time Undergraduate enrollment: 11,523

Total enrollment: 14,373

Percent Male: 52%

Percent Female: 48%

Total Percent Minority: 45%

Percent African-American: 7%

Percent Asian/Pacific Islander: 19%

Percent Hispanic: 10%

Percent Native-American: 1%

Percent Other: 0.08%

Percent in-state / out of state: 91%/9%

Percent from Public HS: 87%

Retention Rate: 90.4%

Graduation Rate: 77%

Percent in On-campus housing: 56%

Percent affiliated with Greek system: 8%

Percent Varsity or Club Athletes: NA

Number of official organized extracurricular organizations: 172

3 Most popular majors: Business Administration, English, Psychology

Student/Faculty ratio: 20:01

Tuition and Fees: $10,610

In State Tuition and Fees (if different): $4,350

Cost for Room and Board: $8,540

Percent receiving Financial aid, first-year: NA

Students at SUNY Binghamton know a good thing when they see it: most of them decided to go to Binghamton because of the "excellent value for the money," and many have found that the "middle of nowhere" can be a wonderful place to enjoy college. While several students complained about the monotony—campus life is "typical" and students easily fall into "daily routines"—all were generally happy about their choice to attend. Most agreed that freshman year adjustment was tough, but the majority of students echoed the sentiment that once you're at Binghamton, you're bound to love it.

The Ivy of the SUNYs

Binghamton is widely recognized as the most academically competitive SUNY, attracting many of New York's best with its affordable quality education. In fact, 87 percent of the entering class was in the top 25 percent of their high school classes. With an eye toward attracting the best students, the University is comprised of five undergraduate schools catering to a wide range of interests: the Harper College of Arts and Sciences, the Decker School of Nursing, the School of Management, the School of Education and Human Development, and the Thomas J. Watson School of Engineering and Applied Science.

Graduation requirements vary within each school and program. Most majors have to fulfill at least one course credit in each of five core areas: language and communication; global interdependencies and pluralism in the US; laboratory sciences, social sciences, and mathematics; aesthetics and humanities; and physical education/wellness. All students must earn two physical education credits and satisfy a writing requirement. Views on the requirements are mixed. While one junior said "there are tons of classes that fulfill the requirements, so you don't have to take anything you don't like," a senior stated that they're "easy enough to achieve, but kind of a waste of time."

Wasting time is not something Binghamton students take lightly—as one senior explained, "Even if it was easy enough to get into Binghamton, it can be really hard to stay in. You have to budget your time—a lot." Students of all majors claim to grapple with "substantial" workloads, but engineering, management and science (especially pre-med) majors seem to suffer the most. Human development is widely considered the easiest major, though one senior said, "it can be challenging if you pick the tougher courses." Almost everyone agreed that "there is no grade inflation here!"

Class sizes at Binghamton follow traditional college patterns—huge introductory courses of up to several hundred students with numbers usually shrinking as classes become more specialized in the upper levels. Teaching is generally rated as average. "I've had professors that made me love the subject, and I've also had profs that put me to sleep. It varies a lot here." TAs often co-teach and lead discussion sections for lower-level courses. Students were generally happy with the student-faculty interaction, though one explained that the "students are responsible for making it happen."

Collegiates at Binghamton register for classes via computer, a process that seems to be rather popular. Because class availability follows a pecking order dictated by seniority and major, freshmen sometimes have difficulty getting into the classes they want. But, according to one senior "you'll get into every class you want, eventually. You just have to be patient." Students are generally happy with the variety of classes offered, noting that, "there's something for everyone here."

Despite the academic excellence of Binghamton and the variety of courses offered, students complained that some majors cannot be taken as minors. Another popular qualm was the difficulty of taking courses in other schools. Students must get the permission of the dean to take courses in schools in which they're not enrolled. "You can get into another school's course if it's cross-listed, but otherwise it's a pain," one senior explained. "It limits you a little bit."

Community Living

Modeled on the collegiate structure of Oxford University, Binghamton has seven distinct residential complexes: five residential communities and two apartment complexes, which are not open to freshmen. Each of the five communities contains several residence halls and a dining hall. While none offer freshman-only housing—the University thinks it's better for students of all years to "live and learn together"—each has coed dorms and options for substance-free living. With few exceptions, freshmen are required to live in the dorms. Before arriving

at Binghamton, freshmen can rank their preferences for residential communities, and usually receive their first or second choice. At the end of freshman year, students may choose to stay in their community, switch to another one (or an apartment complex), or move off campus. Most sophomores opt to remain on campus, while juniors and seniors tend to move off.

In addition to fostering a sense of community, the residential complexes offer great variety. Each has its own personality, distinctive character, and stereotype. For the most part, Newing College is the Greek-dominated party dorm. Hinman is quieter, catering to the more studious. Dickinson is racially and ethnically diverse, and College-in-the Woods (CIW) is more of a "hippy scene." Mountainview is the newest of the five communities—known for a high population of athletes. Regardless of freshmen's assigned community, they tend to enjoy living on campus and being fully immersed in Binghamton. As one senior said, "I loved living on campus! It was a great way to meet people." While the residential communities are very much about socializing, they also play a role in students' academic lives. Most communities have libraries where students may work, and common rooms often play host to study groups. The main Bartle Library is one of the most popular study spots. Late-night studiers seeking a quiet atmosphere can find it in the "tombs," a popular nickname for a scary tomb-like section of Bartle's lobby.

After a couple of years on campus, most Binghamton students move into apartments. They're generally "cheap and easy to find," but students without cars may find transportation to be a problem. This doesn't weigh too heavily though, as most upperclassmen have cars. After freshman year, "if you don't bring a car, it's likely that one of your roommates will," said a junior. "After all, we are in the middle of nowhere."

Things That Make You Go mmm . . .

Binghamton students study like they're in the Ivy League, and they need plenty of late-night chow to keep them going. After study sessions, students gravitate toward Snax or the Night Owl, late-night feeding spots respectively open until midnight and 1 a.m. Best of all, students can charge purchases at either place to their meal plans. Thanks, mom.

For meals, students have the option to eat

in the community dining halls, which are generally considered to be "average, at best." While students complain that the choices—salad bar, some hot entrees, sandwiches, etc.—are "edible, but get rather repetitive," they speak highly of the newest dining hall at Mountainview. Students may also eat at the New Union, which sells typical food-court fare like Taco Bell, smoothies, pizza, pasta, and grill. The New Union is a "social scene popular with Greeks."

Students looking to escape dining hall fare can scope out Binghamton's main throughway, Vestal Parkway. Dozens of eateries ranging from dirt-cheap grease to pricier four-star cuisine dot this strip. Popular options include T.G.I. Friday's, Olive Garden, and IHOP—good food at good prices. Number 5 is a favorite date spot (and popular Parents Weekend option), and Fuji San got rave reviews for its sushi and hibachi. But what's food without a bit of drink? Binghamton lures students with its sports bars and handful of clubs. Students favor Sportsbar and The Rat, popular downtown bars for Thursday and Saturday nights—collectively agreed to be the most popular nights to hit up the town.

The Self-Contained Brain

Seen from the air, the Binghamton campus is arranged in a circle, which students have affectionately dubbed "the Brain." Wooded mountains enclose the campus, creating a valley of sorts. Unfortunately, this valley tends to keep clouds in above school grounds, which results in lots of rain and snow. "Bring an umbrella and a North Face," advised one student. "You'll get used to the rain after a year or two."

Just a short walk from campus is a nature preserve spanning 117 acres. "It's a great place to take a date" said a male undergrad. In the past, students flocked to the nature preserve to escape the loud renovations going on all over campus. Now, those renovations are almost complete, and Binghamton boasts a new student union, new dorms, and a sparkling event center to keep students busy. (The event center played host in 2006 to the NCAA Easter Conference Championships for the second year in a row.)

Because Binghamton's campus is so isolated, most students agree that cars are necessary for off-campus treks. While a "majority" of students bring cars to campus (not including freshmen, who are not permitted to do so), parking can be a problem, as parking spaces are limited and lots are

inconveniently located. As a result, many students wait until they move off campus to bring a car. Cars are also great for weekend getaways: Although New York City, a three-hour drive, is a bit far for a quick trip, Syracuse and Ithaca, both major college towns under an hour away, are ideal destinations.

The Social Scene

Sports, extracurricular activities, and Greek life tend to dominate the social scene at Binghamton. Though most agreed with one junior who said sports are "only a big deal if that's your thing," there were only few complaints of a lack of school spirit. In fact, certain teams, like men's basketball, have quite a following. Intramural teams are also popular—and somewhat competitive—though not as intense as intercollegiate sports. Binghamton students tend to be very committed to their extracurricular activities, which one student described as "a nice break from your daily sleep and study routine."

In terms of social life, most students agree that partying off campus is the way to go here. "While campus isn't 'dry,' you have much more freedom if you party off campus," a male undergrad explained. On campus, the Greek scene dominates: Binghamton has eleven fraternities and six sororities, which are free from racial or academic distinction. The frats regularly throw weekend parties, where alcohol flows freely for a $3 cover charge. While drinking and random hook-ups are common, drugs seem to be less so. "You can get drugs if you want them," remarked one sorority sister, "but they're not that popular." Impressions of Greek life vary, supporting one sophomore's claim that "if you join a fraternity, you can make it as much or as little of your life as you'd like."

> "Because we're in the middle of nowhere, there's a strong sense of community here."

The frat party and drinking scene is popular with underclassmen, while juniors and seniors often break into smaller groups, hang out at an apartment, or hit the bars. Dating, although less common than the ubiquitous random college hook-up, does happen. The University also offers social options sans drinking. Movies, student productions, guest lectures and dances are just a few of the alternatives to the frat lifestyle.

The campus pub is also a fun hangout, complete with a bowling alley, arcade and billiards.

Diversity, Close to Home

Binghamton's absence of a football team does not entirely void the student body of school spirit. Intramurals or "co-recs" are pretty popular, especially soccer and rugby. The University athletic facilities are divided between the East Gymnasium and FitSpace Center. In addition, many students are involved in extracurricular groups. The Student Association, Binghamton's student government, is popular. And cultural organizations also have impressively high student participation. The best and the brightest at Binghamton have a variety of interests, whether it be writing for a campus publication or singing in a school musical group. "There's definitely a place for everyone here."

For a school predominantly consisting of New Yorkers, Binghamton's population is surprisingly diverse. While students complained that certain regions—Long Island, Westchester, and New York City—are overrepresented in the student body, they also expressed enthusiasm for the religious, ethnic, and socioeconomic diversity of their campus. "Going to a public school provides a lot of diversity," said one senior. "I'm still amazed at how many new and interesting people I meet." Another student echoed these views: "I expected Binghamton to be flooded with Long Islanders, but the first guys I met freshman year were from Scotland!" In fact, the only complaint about diversity here was that "sometimes, it's stressed too much. We forget how similar we all are, too."

One similarity is definitely how overwhelmingly friendly Binghamton students are. "Everyone on campus is really nice," said one new student. "Because we're in the middle of nowhere, there's a strong sense of community here. It made coming to college very easy."—*Erica Ross*

FYI

If you come to Binghamton, you better bring "a smile and an umbrella."

What is your typical weekend schedule? "Thursday nights are big—watch the OC, pregame with friends, and go out to parties or the bars downtown. Fridays are quieter, and upperclassmen often stay in and hang out, or get work done. Saturday nights are a lot of fun, and Sundays are spent doing all the work you thought you'd have done by now."

If I could change on thing about Binghamton, "I'd make it stop raining!"

Three things every student at Binghamton should do before graduating are "Eat at Pepe's, have a Scorpion bowl at The Rat, and see the leaves change colors at the nature preserve—it's incredible!"

State University of New York / Buffalo

Address: SUNY Buffalo, 17 Capen Hall, Buffalo, New York 14260-1660
Phone: 888-UB-ADMIT
E-mail Address: ubadmit@buffalo.edu
Web site URL: www.buffalo.edu
Year Founded: 1846
Private or Public: public
Religious affiliation: none
Location: suburban
Regular Application Deadline: rolling
Number of Applicants: 19,351
Percent Accepted: 55%
Percent Accepted who enroll: 31%
Number Entering: NA
Number of Transfers Accepted each Year: NA
Mean SAT: NA
Mean ACT: NA

Middle 50% SAT range: V:530–620, M:570–670
Middle 50% ACT range: 24–29
Early admission program (EA/ ED/ NA): ED
ED or EA Acceptance Rate: NA
Full time Undergraduate enrollment: 18,165
Total enrollment: 27,220
Percent Male: NA
Percent Female: NA
Total Percent Minority: NA
Percent African-American: NA
Percent Asian/Pacific Islander: NA
Percent Hispanic: NA
Percent Native-American: NA
Percent Other: NA
Percent in-state / out of state: 93%/7%

Percent from Public HS: NA
Retention Rate: NA
Graduation Rate: NA
Percent in On-campus housing: NA
Percent affiliated with Greek system: NA
Percent Varsity or Club Athletes: NA
Number of official organized extracurricular organizations: 260
3 Most popular majors: NA
Student/Faculty ratio: 15:01
Tuition and Fees: $12,389
In State Tuition and Fees (if different): $6,129.00
Cost for Room and Board: $7,526.00
Percent receiving Financial aid, first-year: 70%

In 1846, the University at Buffalo was a private medical school consisting of a few lecture rooms in an old church. As the years went by, the University steadily expanded by adding a school of pharmacy, a law school, a dental school, a school of arts and sciences, a school of management and numerous other offerings. After becoming part of the SUNY system in 1962, the school grew rapidly and split into a North Campus and South Campus and became the largest public university in the entire Northeast. With their school offering the largest faculty in the SUNY system and the greatest number of degree programs, students at SUNY-Buffalo can be found exploring a wide variety of studies and interests.

Options, Options and More Options

"This school has just about every single major you can think of." Buffalo offers a wide variety of majors to meet the tastes of its large student body, but if you can't decide on one there's always the option of double-majoring, or of minoring in another subject. According to one student, "You would be amazed by the number of students who choose to take on a second major or minor." Those who do not wish to follow a traditional major program have the freedom of designing their own major, but students agreed that this is rarely necessary and that "it is hard enough just trying to decide on which major to choose amongst all of the ones that are already there."

When asked about the academic environment at Buffalo, one student said, "It is a big science and engineering school." The engineering and pharmacy departments in particular are highly regarded and rank among the best in the SUNY system. Students agreed that science, engineering and computer science courses, as well as pre-med classes, tend to be on the difficult side. However, the campus is by no means dominated by science lovers. Although generally considered easier than the sciences, communications is a strong and popular major. When asked about pre-med courses at Buffalo, one communications major said, "I don't see the pre-med students often. . . . I think they spend most of their time studying in the health and science library." The general feeling among undergraduates is that "your workload depends on which classes you take," and that it is possible to challenge yourself to whatever extent you are motivated.

Registration is probably the biggest source of complaints with respect to academics at Buffalo. The large student body can make it "extremely hard to get the classes you want." Students use an online registration system, but classes fill up quickly, and that is when the trouble begins. One junior said "getting closed out of two classes isn't uncommon," and this means waiting on the end of a telephone in an attempt to get into classes. One glimmer of hope is for students to appeal to their advisors, who can occasionally get them into a class.

Buffalo does require students to take certain core classes their freshman year. These classes range from math to social studies, and according to one student, "nobody wants to take them." You can expect these and other introductory classes to have as many as 300 to 400 students in them. Although developing a relationship with a professor is harder in such lecture classes, students can get to know them by visiting during weekly office hours, which every teacher holds. Students can also receive help by attending the smaller recitations led by graduate student TAs. Students are happy with the majority of their professors; however, "sometimes you will come across a teacher or TA [who is] difficult to understand or doesn't know English all that well—especially in the math department." Regarding the overall academic environment, one student said, "I hate work, but I love to learn."

Social Life

When the week of classes is over, students have fun by doing almost whatever they want. The bars on Main Street are some of the most popular destinations for a night out and according to one student, "You could show them a library card and you would get in." Only about 10 percent of students are involved in Greek life, but the fraternities and sororities make up a large part of the social scene. Parties in dorms are also popular among students. There are plenty of other options, such as the movie theater, the symphony orchestra, concerts, or just hanging out with friends. After a hard week, friends never hesitate to "just stay in and watch a movie or some TV."

Buffalo's big social events each year are Fall Fest and Spring Fest, when popular bands perform at North Campus for the students. Students can easily attend local Buf-falo Bills or Sabres games or travel about 20 minutes north to Canada. As one student said, "There is always something to do, but it's up to you to take advantage of it."

The large student body at Buffalo makes it possible for almost anyone to find a group of friends that shares his or her interests. A sophomore member of a sorority spoke not only of her close ties with her sisters, but also of having met some of her best friends in classes and in her dorm. Students agreed that it is very easy to meet people in all different parts of the campus. One negative aspect of the size of UB is that people must make a conscious effort to keep up contacts. With so many students, "groups form right away but can change in an instant."

Never Go Outside

Since UB is part of the SUNY system, nearly all of the students are New York state residents. The school has a reputation for having a large number of middle-class students from Long Island and Rochester, but students agreed that you are still "able to meet all kinds of different people from very different parts of the state."

> **"You can do pretty much anything you want in the dorms, but there are some limits."**

Buffalo is the only SUNY school that does not require freshmen to live on campus, but the majority of underclassmen choose to do so, while upperclassmen tend to move off campus. Said one student, "The rent is decent, and the proximity is not bad either." Those who live on campus get to take advantage of the University's underground walkway system that allows students on North Campus to get to most dorms and classes without ever stepping outside to brave the harsh, snowy winters of Buffalo. "I don't think I would ever make it to class in the winter if it weren't for those tunnels," one student said. Some students are also lucky enough to live in the Hadley Village Undergraduate Apartments or the newer South Lake Village Apartments, which come furnished and are considered to be very nice. There are RAs for everyone living in dorms regardless of year. When asked about their level of strictness, one student offered, "You can do pretty much anything you want in the dorms, but there are some limits."

For the most part, students feel safe while on Buffalo's large campus, but some girls said that they were not crazy about parts of South Campus and certain other areas around campus. Although there were mixed opinions about needing a car, there was a general consensus that having wheels is helpful. Most freshmen tend not to have cars, but many decide to bring them when they return sophomore year. As one student said, "there's everything here, but you have to be able to get to it."

I'm Getting Very Hungry

Buffalo students enjoy eating out once in a while and can pick from a large number of choices, including a nearby Olive Garden and Red Lobster. Said one student, "There are lots of really good lesser-known restaurants around, but you need a car and someone who knows how to get there." There are plenty of fast-food options close to campus as well, which always make for "quick meals or great late-night snacks." Of course, Buffalo wings are a favorite among many UB students. As multiple students said, "It's Buffalo. How can you not eat Buffalo wings? They're just that good!"

While eating on the University's meal plan, students have several places where they can enjoy all-you-can-eat dining-hall food. There are plenty of vegetarian options available and the meal plan is flexible, allowing hungry students to use credit at other locations. The new food court on North Campus is said to have great chow and a lot of options. The dining halls and food court are more than just a place to grab a quick bite. Students can often be found chatting in noticeable cliques long after they have finished their meals.

Taking Sports into Their Own Hands

Basketball and football are big sports at UB. Even though the Division I-A football team does not have a winning reputation, one spirited student remarked, "I don't miss a home game." On campus, there is much more to sports than the varsity teams. Each year, over 9,000 UB students take a break from their work and participate in club sports or intramurals. The athletic facilities are good and mostly open to all students. "There are all the gym facilities you could [ask for];" the football stadium is only a few years old, and the natatorium has hosted the World University Games and the Empire State Games in the past.

The city of Buffalo has much to offer to the University and its students. The size of the school allows people to choose their own education and have a great time along the way. When approached with the idea of going back and choosing a college again, one undergraduate enthusiastically replied, "I would definitely choose UB. I love it!"—*Brett Youngerman*

FYI
If you come to SUNY Buffalo, you'd better bring "a heavy winter jacket."
What is the typical weekend schedule? "Watch some movies and hang out in the dorms with friends by day; go out to the bars or a party by night."
If I could change one thing about SUNY Buffalo, I'd "move it to Florida, where it is warm."
Three things every student at SUNY Buffalo should do before graduating are "go to the Steer, eat wings at the Anchor Bar, and go to Canada."

State University of New York / Stony Brook

Address: SUNY Stony Brook, Office of Undergraduate Admissions, Stony Brook, NY 11794-1904

Phone: 631-632-6868

E-mail Address: enroll@stonybrook.edu

Web site URL: www.stonybrook.edu

Year Founded: NA

Private or Public: public

Religious affiliation: none

Location: suburban

Application and Admissions Information: rolling

Regular Application Deadline: NA

Number of Applicants: 21,292

Percent Accepted: 47%

Percent Accepted who enroll: 27%

Number Entering: 4,080

Number of Transfers Accepted each Year: 3,672

Mean SAT: 1,215

Mean ACT: NA

Middle 50% SAT range: M: 590–680, V: 540–620, W: 520–620

Middle 50% ACT range: 25–29

Early admission program (EA/ ED/ NA): EA

ED or EA Acceptance Rate: 9%

Full time Undergraduate enrollment: 13,738

Total enrollment: 22,527

Percent Male: 49.5%

Percent Female: 50.5%

Total Percent Minority: 39.7%

Percent African-American: 8.8%

Percent Asian/Pacific Islander: 21.9%

Percent Hispanic: 8.8%

Percent Native-American: 0.2%

Percent Other: 0%

Percent in-state / out of state: 91%/9%

Percent from Public HS: NA

Retention Rate: 89%

Graduation Rate: 59%

Percent in On-campus housing: 57%

Percent affiliated with Greek system: NA

Percent Varsity or Club Athletes: NA

Number of official organized extracurricular organizations: ~300

3 Most popular majors: Psychology, Health Science, Business

Student/Faculty ratio: 16:01

Tuition and Fees: $5,631.00

In State Tuition and Fees (if different): $11,891.00

Cost for Room and Board: $8,450.00

Percent receiving Financial aid, first-year: NA

L ooking for a belly-dancing club? Sweatshop protests? A vegan club? SUNY's Stonybrook campus has enticing offerings for every kind of student. Just east up Long Island, close to Port Jefferson, the actual city of Stonybrook is two hours by train, far away from the clean, tree-covered suburban campus. While the city of Stonybrook might be "far from everything," as one student complained, its proximity to Manhattan is a major selling point for students who like to get into the city for its cultural, artistic, culinary, and entertainment options.

Location, Location, Location

One undergraduate said life at Stonybrook means having "the best of both worlds," because the town is "pretty clean, you're out in the 'burbs kind of thing—but it's not that rural." The train station on campus lets students pop over to New York whenever they want. Few students stay on campus over the weekend because the city features so many things to do. The majority of students who hail from Long Island make a mass homeward exodus weekly. Some even live at home, though others choose to live in university housing. For the first year, this means being doubled or tripled (two or three students to a bedroom), but upperclassmen get nicer room arrangements in suites of four to six with a common room and a shared bathroom. One freshman said being tripled can be really trying, but "if you tough it out for the first year it [housing] can get pretty good afterwards." Stonybrook also has a brand new apartment complex for its undergraduates, and off-campus apartments are always an option.

On DEC

All Stonybrook students have course requirements known as "DEC requirements," short for Diversified Education Curriculum. These requirements, falling in categories A through K, are "classes assigned in order to make you a more well-rounded student." They include courses in writing, history, engineering, and a foreign language. While one student found DEC requirements "kind of annoying" because they "make you learn a lot of stuff not really [relevant] to your major," others say DEC requirements are helpful. One senior attested, "I came into Stonybrook thinking I wanted to be a chemistry major, but then I changed my mind. As I went through my DEC classes, I found out what I wanted to do."

Big Pond, Lots of Fish

Students say class size at Stonybrook can be a problem, especially in introductory classes. Professors split large classes up into TA sections, but students say TAs can be difficult to track down and somewhat unresponsive to student needs. "It's really hard to get help, because it's a big school. You have to educate yourself." Some of the teachers are not that helpful and classes are too big." Going to professors' office hours and getting to know your department advisor helps individual students stand out among a sea of faces.

> "It's like you have lots of little worlds going on, because you have people who are into this and people who are into that."

One student said that upon first arriving at Stonybrook, she "felt like I was all by myself." To get out of the slump, Stonybrook mans its dorms with Resident Advisers (RAs), who are there to give advice and bring some college experience to the table. The RAs are "cool," and "if you have problems they'll help you out," advisees say. Part of the RAs' job, as always, is discipline, but students say, "They're not there to prevent you from having fun; they're just there to make sure everything stays in check. It's not prison-ish." Students also recommend living with other students in your area of study, so that you get to know others with similar interests. Another great way to meet people and distinguish yourself from the others around you is to be part of a club or organization. With an array of extracurriculars ranging from belly-dancing to political protest groups, everyone is sure to find a niche. "This is a very diverse campus, so there's not one look or one way" to be, dress or act. Joining a sorority or fraternity "definitely makes you active in stuff on campus," one upperclassman said, "but it's not the only way to get involved." The unique thing about Greek life is it's something you can only get in college. If going Greek is for you, don't hold back. But don't feel pressured if that's not your style. One non-Greek said "the school is so big you can get away from" being Greek, and it's "not as rowdy as it seems on TV." Greek life is just one of many other pos-

sibilities at Stonybrook, there for the taking. Students say they appreciate that they have "people who are into this and people who are into that. It's like you have lots of little worlds going on."

That's Delivery

While one freshman said that food options at Stonybrook were great, offering variety and flexibility, upperclassmen were less enchanted. Stonybrook's campus is divided into four quads, each of which offers its own meal options, including buffet and homestyle dining as well as restaurants and fast-food chains like Taco Bell and Pizza Hut. If the offerings are less than delectable, students say they "must give them props for having a lot of different options." "They have delivery too!" one student added, saying that the ever-popular college staples of Chinese and pizza were available among the delivery options. First-year students are required to have a meal plan—hardly an inconvenience when even delivery is paid for this way—but after that year students are welcome to fend for themselves. One deli in the student union offers not only meals, but also a grocery store. Every dorm on campus has a kitchen on each floor, though there are no in-suite kitchens. There is also a cooking building for students who plan on making all their own meals.

There are other ways of getting fed at Stonybrook that offer educational and cultural experiences on the side. Many groups, like the popular Caribbean Student Organization (CSO), throw parties and host workshops and lectures for their fellow students. Students come to learn about international relations and cultural differences, and for the chow. Don't look for alcohol at these gatherings and parties, though. Students say the administration is strict about keeping alcohol off campus and unavailable to those under 21.

Who Reigns in the Parade?

Homecoming week brings out the spirit of Stonybrook's Sea Wolves in full force. The Friday parade features floats built by student teams who represent their quads and organizations. Students make banners and enter them in competitions, and every building on campus decorates a bulletin board. As if that weren't enough, Stonybrookers also make boats every year for the Roth Regatta. So named for the quad on which the Stonybrook pond is located, the event brings out all Stonybrook's would-be boat makers and has them race their boats on the pond. Spirit

Week, an event much like Homecoming, takes place every spring. Residence halls compete in trivia and Olympic-style competitions in the gym to win glory for the Stonybrook name.

When Stonybrook students aren't competing for spirited titles, you might find them at the Wang Center, a new Asian center at the University where students can find sushi and a whole lot of information about Asian history. The Staller Center, another cultural location on campus, offers workshops and art in its theaters and galleries, or you can stop by on a Friday night to see chic in action at one of Stonybrook's fashion shows.—*Stephanie Hagan*

FYI

If you come to Stonybrook, you'd better bring "a laptop."

What is the typical weekend schedule? "Thursday's a big party night at clubs like Rumba Skies; Friday night, go to a movie on campus or take the train, go into the city, and hang out with friends; Sunday, go to the library and study."

If I could change one thing about Stonybrook, I'd "change the dorms. Some of them are really old!"

Three things every Stonybrook student should do before graduating are "realize that Manhattan is so close and actually go do something in the city, join an organization, and go to the Staller Center."

Syracuse University

Address: Syracuse, 100 Crouse-Hinds Hall, Syracuse, NY 13244
Phone: 315-443-1870
E-mail Address: orange@syr.edu
Web site URL: www.syr.edu
Year Founded: 1870
Private or Public: private
Religious affiliation: none
Location: Urban
Regular Application Deadline: 2-Jan
Number of Applicants: 19,744
Percent Accepted: 51%
Percent Accepted who enroll: 30.1%
Number Entering: 3,054
Number of Transfers Accepted each Year: 257
Mean SAT: NA
Mean ACT: NA

Middle 50% SAT range: 1,130–1,310
Middle 50% ACT range: NA
Early admission program (EA/ ED/ NA): ED
ED or EA Acceptance Rate: 65%
Full time Undergraduate enrollment: 11,546
Total enrollment: 18,815
Percent Male: 44%
Percent Female: 56%
Total Percent Minority: 20%
Percent African-American: 6.4%
Percent Asian/Pacific Islander: 7.4%
Percent Hispanic: 5.3%
Percent Native-American: 0.6%
Percent Other: 10.7%
Percent in-state / out of state: 43%/57%

Percent from Public HS: 80%
Retention Rate: 92%
Graduation Rate: 79%
Percent in On-campus housing: 75%
Percent affiliated with Greek system: 20%
Percent Varsity or Club Athletes: NA
Number of official organized extracurricular organizations: 300
3 Most popular majors: Psychology, Political Science, Architecture
Student/Faculty ratio: 12:01
Tuition and Fees: $29,595.00
Cost for Room and Board: $10,420.00
Percent receiving Financial aid, first-year: 72%

Everything about Syracuse University, it seems, is big. In addition to the large student body (roughly 12,000 undergraduates and 5,000 graduates attend), the University boasts 9 undergraduate colleges as well as the gigantic 50,000-seat Carrier Dome. Even the weather—with a winter season that begins in November and extends into March and April—speaks to the larger-than-life quality of this nationally recognized research institution. For students who can navigate their way through all that Syracuse has to offer, though, the experience can be unparalleled.

Choosing Early

Where students applying to other schools often need not declare their majors, students who intend to come to Syracuse must apply to one of the 9 undergraduate colleges: architecture, arts and sciences, education, engineering and computer science, human services and health professions, information studies, management, public communications, and visual and performing arts. Although they do have the option of applying to a plurality of colleges at the time of application, students must choose one upon matriculation. In order to encourage a diverse course of study, the administration allows students to sample courses outside their colleges. For those students who prefer grounding in a liberal arts education, the College of Arts and Sciences offers a more interdisciplinary, less pre-professional, program of study. Freshmen in this college receive an introduction to their school through Freshman Forum, a seminar-style class that pairs a small group of undergrads with a professor in an intimate setting. Among the other colleges, the S.I. Newhouse School of Public Communications enjoys the most national renown among peer institutions. Admission to the communications school tends to be more competitive and selective. Yet some on campus question the quality of education offered at Newhouse, arguing that the courses demand little of students. The schools of architecture and management consistently top the list of Syracuse's most rigorous schools.

> **"[The social scene] is the only thing that gets us out in the winter."**

Appropriately, class sizes and academic requirements vary by college. Popular classes—macroeconomics, for example—and general educations classes ("gen eds") typically draw upwards of 200 students, though classes tend to get smaller, and, as one student notes, "more comfortable," each year. Students deem the workload "time consuming, but nothing too difficult," and report spending "three hours a night" studying on average. Although they give their professors favorable marks for knowledge, lecture presentation, and accessibility, students are more divided with regard to teaching assistants, who lead outside-of-class "recitations." While some acknowledge that TAs are helpful because of the experience they bring to their particular field, others cast them off as "useless."

Frats and Bars

Students do not deny that theirs is a party school—on the contrary, they are proud of the balance of academics and busy social calendars. Given the cold weather for which their school is notorious, the social scene "is the only thing that gets us out in the winter." Syracuse is home to a large Greek system, and the many fraternities and sororities take advantage of their influence and presence on campus to host well-attended keg parties and the occasional formal. Those in the drinking crowd who tire of frat parties often take a walk down Marshall Street to check out the bar scene or seek out the house parties around campus. Students find that the party scene becomes more manageable each year; as one student put it, "freshmen look for parties, upperclassmen are rocking the parties." The only problem in all this, it seems, is overcrowding at parties, which has the effect of detracting from the experience. Apart from alcohol, pot is prevalent, though "nothing is forced on anyone." In an effort to crack down on the amount of underage drinking, the University maintains a three-points-and-you're-out policy, strictly forbidding alcohol in underage rooms. The University also sponsors events that aim to draw students away from parties. Despite these efforts, students easily circumvent the administration's policies.

Big and Small

In spite of Syracuse's large size, stereotypes persist. One student characterized the typical student as "rich, drunk, and NorthFace-wearing." Nonetheless, students are quick to defend the heterogeneity of their school and add that, at Syracuse, it is easy to make friends, "especially in the first few weeks or so" before cliques begin to form, generating a feeling of community within the greater student body. Considerations of diversity aside, students rally around their nationally ranked basketball team and their mascot, Otto the Orange, named by MasterCard as one of the nation's best mascots. The Carrier Dome, located on campus, regularly draws capacity crowds for football and basketball games; it has also attracted big-name acts such as Elton John and U2 to Syracuse. Because only a small portion of students actively participate in sports, many students take advantage of intramurals, which offer everything from basketball to broomball. Many extracurricular activities are also widely popular, among them learning-based service programs, the student newspaper (*The Daily Orange*), and campus radio and TV stations. University Union, commonly known as UU, hosts comedians, concerts and speakers as well as annual events like the Juice Jam Music Festival.

Syracuse: City and Campus

Syracuse University is set on a hill overlooking the city of Syracuse, giving students the unique opportunity to experience campus and city life simultaneously. It is rumored that if two students share a kiss on a particular bench on campus, they will marry. Such is the charm of the campus. Students appreciate the mix of modern and classical buildings that surround them, particularly on the Quad, which serves as the geographic center of campus. Although the various colleges have their own buildings, no walk across campus takes more than 15 minutes. The 120-step climb from the Quad to the Mount (home to several frosh dorms), on the other hand, requires a little more stamina, especially in the icier months. Dorms, especially during freshman year, provide the formative social experiences that allow students to develop close relationships that last into senior year. But don't expect to live in palaces—as one student said, "the dorms in bad shape." While one of the major dorms

has been recently renovated, the others are described as "small" and "poorly equipped." Most freshmen live in either open or split doubles. Less than regal dorms and a city with a low cost of living make off-campus housing an attractive option for upperclassmen. The food at Syracuse draws so-so reviews in terms of quality and variety, although dining halls vary considerably across campus. To get away from the monotony of the meal plan, students venture into the city to such original restaurants as the Pita Pit, Acropolis Pizza, and Dinosaur BBQ. Another diversion is the huge Carousel Mall, although Syracuse offers little else in the way of entertainment and culture. Nor does it have a completely clean safety record, and robberies are not unheard of. Back on campus, though, blue lights everywhere assure students that their administration does not take a passive approach to policing the area.

Thanks to its size, Syracuse University is in a unique position to offer its undergraduates a richly diverse academic and social experience even as it asserts its position as a premier research institution. And just in case they become too wrapped up in college life, the town of Syracuse, located at the foot of the college, offers an appropriate dose of the "real world."—*Greg Hamm*

FYI

If you come to Syracuse, you'd better bring a "Gore-Tex jacket, because you'll need it by the end of October."

What's the typical weekend schedule? "Up at 2 p.m., bum around until night, out at 10, back at 3. And do it all over again."

If I could change one thing about Syracuse, I'd "increase the average daily temperature and create a better city."

Three things every student at Syracuse should do before graduating are "rush the court/field at the Dome, sled down one of the streets during a blizzard, and enjoy all the opportunities to meet people and hear interesting speakers."

Union College

Address: Union, 807 Union St., Schenectady, NY 12308
Phone: 888-843-6688
E-mail Address: admissions@union.edu
Web site URL: www.union.edu
Year Founded: 1795
Private or Public: private
Religious affiliation: none
Location: urban
Regular Application Deadline: NA
Number of Applicants: 4,373
Percent Accepted: 43%
Percent Accepted who enroll: 30%
Number Entering: 676
Number of Transfers Accepted each Year: varies
Mean SAT: NA
Mean ACT: NA
Middle 50% SAT range: 1,130–1,320

Middle 50% ACT range: 24–29
Early admission program (EA/ ED/ NA): ED
ED or EA Acceptance Rate: 77%
Full time Undergraduate enrollment: 2,178
Total enrollment: 2,212
Percent Male: 53%
Percent Female: 47%
Total Percent Minority: 13%
Percent African-American: 3%
Percent Asian/Pacific Islander: 6%
Percent Hispanic: 4%
Percent Native-American: 0%
Percent Other: 0%
Percent in-state / out of state: 42%/58%

Percent from Public HS: 65%
Retention Rate: 93%
Graduation Rate: 86%
Percent in On-campus housing: 89%
Percent affiliated with Greek system: 29%
Percent Varsity or Club Athletes: ~30%
Number of official organized extracurricular organizations: 90
3 Most popular majors: Political Science, Psychology, Economics
Student/Faculty ratio: 11:01
Tuition and Fees: $43,043.00
Percent receiving Financial aid, first-year: 87%

At the small liberal arts institution called Union College in Schenectady, New York, graduation means more than wading through the general curriculum and completing the twelve trimesters. Union's uniqueness is captured in the "unofficial" graduation requirements: the "campus crawl," which involves having a beer at each of the fraternities all in one night; painting the Idol, a stone statue on campus; running naked around the Nott Memorial; and throwing oranges onto the ice following Union's first hockey goal against RPI.

General Education

Regardless of one's major, all students at Union college must satisfy core curriculum requirements. Freshmen take two history, two science, one math, one social science, and two literature/civilization classes, as well as the Freshmen Preceptorial, a class that includes a lot of reading, and "basically teaches you how to write." Students give a positive rating to this system; those that come to the school undecided will be exposed to a wide range of subjects, while those already declared will graduate with a well-rounded education. The class sizes are small, with approximately 40 students in introductory courses and 10 in upper-level classes. "Professors are extremely accessi-

ble and even in large classes, you get to know your professors very well," said one student, who also praised Union for its "near-perfect balance between a rigorous workload, low average class size, and professor accessibility." Students enjoy their classes, for the most part. "A seminar professor took our entire class out to dinner at a great Indian restaurant, and then to a movie," said one student.

Union runs on a trimester system, giving students three distinct segments of study as opposed to two in the traditional semester system. School starts two weeks later than most schools in the fall, and includes a Christmas break of over six weeks, though school does not finish until the middle of June.

Students often take three classes per semester, many of which meet only on Monday, Wednesday, and Friday. The trimester system, however, means that there are only 10 weeks to complete a course that usually requires 15 weeks, which makes these weeks quite intense. In total, students must complete 36 courses in 12 terms. The course load is generally tough, with upper-level courses expecting around five to seven hours of homework or reading per week. One course, Congressional Politics, has reputedly over 24 hours of work per week.

Students identify the most popular majors as being political science, biology, and economics; the hardest majors are said to be chemistry and any of the engineering sciences. Some reportedly 'slacker' majors are political science, English, and history.

There are many opportunities for studying abroad. Students can study in England, through a program sponsored by the English department, as well as in Vienna, where one student's favorite class consisted of walking around the city, touring museums: "It was in Vienna, had no homework, and was very hands-on."

Greeks and Alcohol

Greek life and alcohol seem to dominate the social life at Union. With 13 frats and three sororities, Union is "the mother of the fraternities," in the words of one student. However, Union recently enacted a plan that may result in some Greek organizations losing their traditional houses. Social life is centered on the fraternities, as they provide the entertainment and alcohol for the students. "If you like to drink and party, Union is the place for you," said one student. "If you don't like to drink, you could be bored." Students agree that the school tries to be strict on their alcohol policy, but many underage drinkers still manage to find alcohol easily. Frat parties are usually free and open to all, which prevents non-Greeks from feeling excluded. The dating scene consists almost exclusively of hook-ups; no one seems to date. One student put the number at "five hook-ups a year."

Students often feel that the social life is centered on how much money each student has. "The parking lots are filled with BMW's, Land Rovers, Mercedes, etc," one student noted. Some profess feeling as if they have stepped into a J. Crew catalog, as dress is important to the student body. Many students come from wealthy Northeastern backgrounds (New York and Massachusetts are well represented). Few students come from outside the Mid-Atlantic and New England states, and even fewer are internationals. Union can be difficult for students on financial aid since most packages do not cover the expenses of academic materials, which can be expensive at the school.

You Come to Schenectady for Union

An admissions staff member once said to a student, "You don't come to Union for Schenectady, you come to Schenectady for Union." The campus is very beautiful and well-kept. "The students take great pride in the gardens, the buildings, and the overall atmosphere," said one student. "The compact nature of the campus keeps everything within easy reach and view . . . the gardens are a miraculous and wonderful place to spend a spring afternoon." The off-campus area has improved over the last few years, but students often choose not to leave the campus on foot at night. The school has a trolley service, which students find very accessible and useful. Although freshman may not have cars on-campus, over 80 percent of upperclassmen have their own vehicles in order to take advantage of the surrounding areas, according to students. Albany is a half-hour drive from Union, and home to many bars, clubs, and a great deal of shopping.

> "You don't come to Union for Schenectady, you come to Schenectady for Union."

Students find the dorms to be satisfactory. "Generally, the conditions are good. There are few complaints." Union is constantly improving the living conditions through renovations, though there are many other options available. Some students live in apartments that Union leases right across the street from campus. Some buildings, West, Fox, and Davidson have the reputation as party dorms. Other dorms that provide calmer living arrangements include Webster, the co-ed, substance-free dorm and Richmond, which is co-ed by floor. Members of Greek societies can choose to live in their respective houses. Others may choose to live in a theme house, where students share similar interests. Housing is guaranteed only through junior year, spurring some students to utilize the nearby apartments.

Students generally have no complaints about the food. There are two dining halls on-campus, which offer a wide variety of foods. The "Rathskellar" sells greasy foods, but not much else. Students agreed that, even though some may not care for the dish of the day, there is such a wide variety that most everyone is content. Most students eat on-campus in the main dining halls.

Choice of Activities

Union students have the choice of over 70 clubs to participate in, including ballroom dancing, a capella singing groups,

Concordiensis (the weekly newspaper), the *Idol* (a literary magazine), the Minerva Committee (bringing speakers to campus), and many more. Drama students may choose to join the Mountebanks, a popular theater troupe.

Hockey and football are the school's biggest sports. Each home hockey game attracts at least a quarter of the undergraduates. Pre-game parties are often well attended, and "pride runs high for hockey in particular." Union's biggest rival is RPI, both in hockey and football. Although turnout may be high, few students care to wear Union clothing. "There is not a whole lot of shouting unless people are drunk," said one student. "There is cheering but it comes mostly from the alumni and faculty. Union kids are very apathetic."

Students are proud that their school is set apart from others both by the small size of the student body and the beautiful campus, "which is just amazingly picturesque and unique." "I am extremely happy here," said one student. "The people are friendly, the profs are amazing and really nice, always willing to help, and I love the area."
—*Andrew Hamilton*

FYI

If you come to Union, you'd better bring "a warm hat and gloves."

What is the typical weekend schedule? "Parties both Friday and Saturday nights. Otherwise, hockey games (winter) or time outside (spring and fall) with work Sunday evenings are popular pastimes."

If I could change one thing about Union, "I'd build a new gym and fieldhouse."

Three things that every student at Union should do before graduating are "paint the Idol, take a term abroad, and try something new."

United States Military Academy

Address: U.S. Military Academy, Building 2101—5th floor, West Point, NY 10996

Phone: 845-938-4328

E-mail Address: diane.mckiernan@usma.edu

Web site URL: www.usma.edu

Year Founded: 1802

Private or Public: public

Religious affiliation: none

Location: rural

Regular Application Deadline: NA

Number of Applicants: 10,226

Percent Accepted: 6.4%

Percent Accepted who enroll: 15%

Number Entering: 1,309

Number of Transfers Accepted each Year: 0

Mean SAT: NA

Mean ACT: NA

Middle 50% SAT range: V:570–680, M:590–680

Middle 50% ACT range: 25–29

Early admission program (EA/ ED/ NA): NA

ED or EA Acceptance Rate: NA

Full time Undergraduate enrollment: 4,347

Total enrollment: 4,347

Percent Male: 83%

Percent Female: 17%

Total Percent Minority: 21.5%

Percent African-American: 6.3%

Percent Asian/Pacific Islander: 7%

Percent Hispanic: 7.2%

Percent Native-American: 1%

Percent Other: 1.3%

Percent in-state / out of state: 4%/96%

Percent from Public HS: 95%

Retention Rate: 78.6%

Graduation Rate: 78.6%

Percent in On-campus housing: 100%

Percent affiliated with Greek system: 0%

Percent Varsity or Club Athletes: 100%

Number of official organized extracurricular organizations: 100+

3 Most popular majors: Civil Engineering, Systems Engineering, Mechanical Engineering

Student/Faculty ratio: 7:01

Tuition and Fees: See Sheet 3

Cost for Room and Board: 0

Percent receiving Financial aid, first-year: none

If your picture of college life includes sleeping in, veggin' in front of the TV while eating midnight pizza and enjoying a beer, binge drinking till you blackout at a frat party, or finding your trophy wife or husband, the United States Military Academy is not for you. West Point emphasizes leadership, service, and challenge. Discipline permeates every aspect of life here for the Plebes (freshmen), the Yuks (sophomores), the Cows (juniors) and the Firsties (seniors). "Freshman Orientation" is fittingly called "The Beast" and consists of six weeks of rigorous training, including target practice and long hikes (not the scenic kind). After this intense welcome session, students prepare themselves for four years of embracing the four pillars of cadet life: Academic, Physical, Moral-Ethical, and Military Development.

Hardcore Curriculum

Class size is very small, ranging from five to 20 students. As one student stated, "Class sizes are perfect, no more than 15." And despite the fact that "people are very competitive," it is "rarely at the cost of others' performance." Students have mixed responses regarding teamwork and competition. However, it is generally agreed upon that while there are those who believe in cooperation and the group spirit, some students prefer to "do it for themselves" and achieve high grades on their own.

The following core curriculum classes are required for all students: English, History, Leadership, Philosophy/Ethics, Foreign Language, Social Sciences, Law, Math, Chemistry, Physical Geography, Information Technology, Physics, Engineering/Science Design, Military Design, and Physical Education. The first two years at the Academy are spent fulfilling these core curriculum requirements. Courses for specific majors are not taken until junior and senior year. Although one student claims, "a Harvard 'A' is a West Point 'C'," most agree that although academics are rigorous, grading is fair. One student explained: "West Point teaches problem solving, critical thinking, and effective communication. You're incredibly productive every day here."

Originally founded as an engineering school, West Point's engineering programs remain the most popular among students. Stereotypes regarding certain majors definitely exist. "People who major in Leadership just don't want to work on anything academic," and "the Nuclear Engineering major is ridiculously hard." Another student said that, "Engineering majors are geeks, Law and Management majors are slackers," while his peer claimed that, "People are always like, 'I want Foreign Language because it's easy.'" Even a Foreign Language major agreed, clarifying that, "Foreign languages, other than Chinese and Arabic, are easy."

Because Active Duty professors are on rotation and class syllabi are standardized, very few students can name "favorite" professors, though all will agree that instructors are dedicated. One female West Point student explained that, "Besides getting up every morning at 6, having two mandatory meals a day with formation, and having military training on Saturdays and the summers, what really sets West Point apart from other schools is the instructors . . . They are fully committed." Most students agreed that instructors are very accessible, often providing their home phone numbers for students to call with questions. "I appreciate the amount of time professors are willing to spend with whoever needs it."

Only Firsties Get Thirsty.

Freshmen, Sophomores, Juniors, and Seniors are respectively referred to as Plebes, Yuks, Cows, and Firsties. Aside from the unique names, Class/Year distinction is made very clear, especially for freshmen. "Plebes have a look on their face like a dog who just shat the carpet and got caught . . . that is to say, they look scared," explained one Cow. Plebes must walk around with their hands "at position of attention" (in a fist), do not wear rank on their uniforms, and are required to greet all upperclassmen with appropriate greetings, such as "Go Buffaloes, Sir" or "Beat Navy, Sergeant." In addition to this, perhaps the most noticeable difference between Plebes and freshmen at other schools is the strict enforcement of underage drinking violations. Freshmen can expect to be served with a brigade board, which includes 100 hours of marching around a square in the middle of campus, 60 days of room restriction, and enrollment in an alcohol course if they are found with alcohol.

The rule for alcohol is "No alcohol until you're a Cow on post." Juniors (a.k.a. Cows) who are 21 are allowed to drink at clubs on campus (a.k.a. Post) that are only open Thursday through Saturday nights. With periodic drug and alcohol tests, the substance policy is taken very seriously. Only seniors are allowed to drink Monday through Saturday nights.

"Perhaps the most coveted place on the Academy grounds is known as Firstie Club, or the First Class Club," longingly explained one Plebe. The lucky few that enter the club come to enjoy $5.50 pitchers of Yuengling and Killians beer. The club is decked out in black and white snap shots of cadets over the last 100 years in "undisciplined poses" that you won't find in the Academy's yearbooks. But don't expect to be making plans for heading anywhere after Firstie Club—with taps check, all cadets must be back in their rooms by 11:30. A mass exodus of drunken cadets leave Firstie Club and head back to the barracks. With punctuality being key, there is no time for drunken stumbling around here. Hordes of underclassmen will often stand outside of the barrack windows cheering for the seniors attempting to sprint back on time.

Checking out the 'Racks:

Cadets are housed in barracks that are assigned by company. Each company has approximately 135 people, and some students claim that each company has a stereotype. "First regiment is known as 'West Point University' because it's really chill. Fourth regiment is known for doing well militarily. Third regiment is the one with the most rules and the one that is hardest on the Plebes." When asked about whether alcohol use was permitted in the barracks, one student replied, "Yea, if you want a Brigade Board."

Barracks are immaculate on the inside. Daily room inspections require that the garbage can be empty, and that closet doors are open at a 90 degree angle, revealing evenly spaced clothes hangers. Failure to do otherwise results in incantations that "you won't survive."

In Good Company

The opening days of the Beast require people to "get pretty close pretty fast." Most students are closest with the members of their company or their sports teams. Because the entire student population is in extremely good physical shape and playing a sport is required, sports play a large role in everyday life. "Sports dominate the social scene, especially football games. If you come here, you will attend most of the home football games, if not all." Some weekends are actually designated "Football Weekend," more commonly referred to as "F weekend," where cadets have an optional Saturday breakfast and then attend a football game before being released to continue the weekend. (The other two types of weekend are: 1) A/C Weekend, which includes a mandatory breakfast and military training for 4-5 hour before being released, and 2) B weekend, which is the "free weekend" and cadets are released after class on Friday and do not have to return until an assigned time on Sunday.)

While there are significantly fewer women than men (women comprise only 14 percent of the student population), most West Point women do not feel that this is an issue. Likewise, ethnic diversity is very good, as one student praised the fact that, "students come from many countries and all walks of life."

Annual events include a Christmas/Holiday dinner where the Plebes decorate dinner tables and buy all the upperclassmen cigars. Everyone goes out to the Apron, an open area around the marching plain, and smokes it. "Even if you don't smoke, it's fun to go and stand with everyone and take part in one of the oldest traditions," explains one student. Each class also has a special event each year. The Plebes have Plebe Parent Weekend, the Yuks have Camp Illumination and Yearling Winter Weekend, the Cows have 500th night (celebrating 500 nights from graduation), and the Firsties have Ring Weekend, Branch Night, and 100th Night.

Cup o' G.I. Joe, and Spirit Missions

While one student claimed that, "our life is very unpleasant," no alcohol simply means sober fun for the freshmen. While students at other colleges may find themselves having alcoholic tendencies, at West Point, "most cadets have a caffeine addiction," explained one Yuk. And where do they get their fix? Most cadets opt for Grant Hall, "an ornate, intricately decorated student union of sorts with a bunch of generals' portraits mounted on the walls and a big screen TV blaring ESPN or *The Simpsons*."

> "This is not just a school—it is a choice of lifestyle for the next nine years of life (at least) after high school."

Once one gets his or her caffeine fix, going on a spirit mission is a must for every cadet. Spirit missions are missions that occur after lights out, and include pranks on another company or cadets from the Naval and Air Force Academies. Cadets also put on a 100th Night Show, a parody of the Firstie experience in the form of a musical that is performed 100 nights from graduation. "Almost nothing is off limits. It makes fun of officers, events, cadets, etc. There are so many inside jokes, cadets always have to explain everything to their dates that they have invited."

A Choice of Lifestyle

"This is not just a school—it is a choice of lifestyle for the next nine years of life (at least) after high school," commented one senior. West Point cadets understand that much higher levels of mental agility, physical readiness, and discipline are required. Living a more atypical college life is, quite simply, different. But in the end, as one cadet explained, "There's nothing I'd change about West Point. It's a military school, you know what you're getting into when you sign the dotted line."—*Christine Lin*

FYI

If you come to West Point, you'd better bring: "EXCEPTIONAL PHYSICAL SHAPE. It makes everything that much easier, is one less thing to worry about while getting yelled at about everything else, and first impressions here are mainly that first day at 0520 in the morning."

What's the typical weekend schedule? "They typical weekend starts Friday night, and Saturdays will either be military training days, football games, or free use. Each cadet has a number of passes to use to travel off post. When they run out, you must return to the barracks at night.

If I could change one thing about West Point, I'd "get more time off."

Three things every cadet should do before graduating are "blow post once, drink at the Firstie Club, and survive."

University of Rochester

Address: University of Rochester, Wilson Blvd, Rochester, NY 14627
Phone: (585) 275-2121
E-mail Address: admit@admissions.rochester.edu
Web site URL: http://www.rochester.edu
Year Founded: 1850
Private or Public: private
Religious affiliation: none
Location: suburban
Regular Application Deadline: 16-Jan
Number of Applicants: 11,314
Percent Accepted: 45%
Percent Accepted who enroll: 21.4%
Number Entering: 1,102
Number of Transfers Accepted each Year: 197
Mean SAT: NA
Mean ACT: NA

Middle 50% SAT range: V: 610–710; M: 630–710
Middle 50% ACT range: 27–30
Early admission program (EA/ ED/ NA): ED
ED or EA Acceptance Rate: 42%
Full time Undergraduate enrollment: 3,858
Total enrollment: 7,254
Percent Male: 54%
Percent Female: 46%
Total Percent Minority: 24%
Percent African-American: 5%
Percent Asian/Pacific Islander: 13%
Percent Hispanic: 5%
Percent Native-American: 1%
Percent Other: NA
Percent in-state / out of state: 46%/54%

Percent from Public HS: NA
Retention Rate: 95%
Graduation Rate: 80%
Percent in On-campus housing: 86%
Percent affiliated with Greek system: 20%
Percent Varsity or Club Athletes: 15%
Number of official organized extracurricular organizations: 200
3 Most popular majors: Clinical & Social Psychology, Engineering, Biological Sciences
Student/Faculty ratio: 9:01
Tuition and Fees: $32,650.00
Cost for Room and Board: $10,192.00
Percent receiving Financial aid, first-year: 75%

Yes, the University of Rochester is cold and it gets its fair share of snow. And no, despite global warming, this will not change. Located on the Genesse River near Rochester, N.Y., the University of Rochester, also called UR, U of R, URoch and Roch by its students, has some of the harshest weather in the country, but the sizzling academic culture of U of R is only getting hotter. Both the college at large and its engineering program are ranked in the top 50 in the country. The esteemed science programs are some of the best college students have to choose from, while the humanities are hardly lacking. Students at Rochester also have access to the Eastman School of Music, which is one of the best places to study music in the world. While it is hard to ignore the weather in upstate New York, undergraduates often forget the cold because they are immersed in a fine academic environment.

Unique Academics at U-Roch

The University of Rochester and its undergraduates always speak of how Rochester, and especially its curriculum, differs from those of other universities. The University of Rochester states that "excellence requires freedom," and in order to promote this freedom, Rochester offers the Rochester Curriculum. The Rochester Curriculum does not include any required classes, instead requiring Clusters in areas of learning outside the major. Clusters are a group of 12 interrelated credits (usually three classes) in humanities, social sciences or natural sciences. Each student must complete a Cluster in the two areas of studies that are not included within their major. Most students are indifferent toward the Rochester curriculum. One said, "I would rather just have free electives, but I didn't really find it a burden." Although Clusters are usually defined by the University, students are welcome to suggest new groupings. Many of the Clusters are like actual majors, such as applied economics, while others are more concentrated than majors, such as "Mind-Body Somatics." With the Rochester Curriculum, students are able to study almost any subject area as either a major, minor or Cluster.

The Rochester education would not be complete without a tight bond with faculty members, who teach 95 percent of all classes. The faculty, of whom 99 percent have the highest degree available in their fields, includes multiple Nobel Prize laureates. Unlike many universities, top professors teach undergraduates, oftentimes in lower-level classes. "If you make an effort, you can get to know your professors real well," one Mechanical Engineering major said. In fact, professors who concentrate on teaching rank 12th in the United States for their sheer research productivity. Many students engage in their own research at some point in their UR careers, which builds close contact with members of UR science faculty and laboratory assistants.

> **"There is no slacking off at URoch."**

Despite having a student body of about 4,000, which is about the size of many small liberal arts colleges, Rochester offers one of the strongest science programs in the country. The most popular science majors are biology, computer engineering and chemistry. All areas of studies in the natural sciences, from mechanical engineering to pre-med, are very strong. Although Rochester has a reputation of being difficult, one engineering major said, "It's not *too* hard." That said, students majoring in the sciences require more work than other majors. Students generally have to put just as much time and effort into humanities and social science classes as they do for classes in the natural sciences. "There is no slacking off at URoch," an economics major said. While UR is not a campus known for political action, political science is the most popular major overall.

Although Rochester does not offer a general pre-med program, its chemistry, biology and mathematics programs are sufficient to fulfill medical school requirements. The Rochester Early Medical Scholars Program, or REMS, is one of the most rigorous and highly ranked in the country. It consists of an eight-year undergraduate and medical school program. "REMS students are really some of the best students in the country, but you never see them because there are so few and they always have to study," a sophomore said. Participants have exclusive access to some of the top faculty in the medical and dental school. Getting in, however, is not easy. Of the 600 applicants, 40 are interviewed, and only 10 are accepted per year. For qualified students, though, there are few better options out there. This program is, as one student reports, "way better than the Ivies." Students often report that they practically live in the library. They do, however, find the opportunity to participate in everything from varsity sports to drama and music.

Outside the Library

Rochester combats its reputation as a nerd school by offering an incredible variety of extra-curricular actives. University of Rochester students write a number of exceptional publications, from *The Campus Times*, Rochester's daily newspaper, to *The Rochester Review*, a magazine that covers events and issues in both the U of R campus and in the wider world. Students can also receive the *Current Digest*, an electronic forum that keeps the entire university up-to-date on each day's happenings. "It's never a problem to figure out what is happening," a junior said. Another popular online forum is *The Buzz*, which constantly connects students' events on the Genesse River campus and in greater Rochester because it is updated at least three times per day.

Although the University of Rochester is not known for athletic prowess, the university has been an active participant in intercollegiate athletics since the 19th century. A member of the Division III Liberty League and University Athletic Association (the conference affiliation depends on the sport), Rochester competes against many other academically minded schools like Brandeis and the University of Chicago. One male athlete noted, "It's not like we're in the Big Ten, but we have fun." While the football team has been a middle of the pack team in recent years, other teams, such as men's tennis and field hockey, have been strong. The men's tennis team in particular has managed to recruit many top athletes from around the world. The Athletic Department also offers intramural sports in basketball, floor hockey, football, flag football, soccer, volleyball and ultimate Frisbee, as well as club sports, such as crew, skiing and rugby.

It is no surprise that the University of Rochester has some amazing musicians because of its proximity and close relationship with the Eastman School of Music. Although Eastman is a completely different college from the College of Arts and Sciences, it is under the umbrella of the University, allowing students to seamlessly enroll in courses there. "If you ever want to be blown away by pure musical talent, take a class at Eastman," remarks a freshman. There are over 20 music groups on the River Campus. University Symphony and the Symphonic Wind Ensemble play both traditional and untraditional composed instrumental music, and URoch also boasts a cappella groups like the Yellowjackets, Slingshot!? and After Hours, many of which record annual CDs. Drama, too, has a following on the UR campus, where students perform three to four productions a month in Todd Theater, UR's prime performance area for drama; offerings include the annual One Act New-Play Festival, as well as full-length productions.

Living it Up

Drama students have the opportunity to live in the Drama House, which is across the street from the Todd Theater. Other "theme housing" options, called Special Interest Housing (SIH), include the Tiernan Project (community service), Foreign Language Floor, Community Learning Center (community service and education), Music Interest Floor, Health & Home Program and Computer Interest Floor. Freshmen live in one of six halls, which consist mostly of doubles. "The rooms are probably pretty average for college dorm rooms," a student said. Upperclassmen live in a different area of the campus, and their room layout tends to be more varied. UR also has "affinity housing," which provides the option to live on a chemical-free hall, or with

students who like to keep noise levels down.

Eighty-five percent of students live in University Housing (including all freshmen and sophomores, who are required to do so), although off-campus housing is becoming more popular. Rochester's relatively low real estate prices give students the flexibility to live off-campus, though most choose to spend their four years at the River Campus. Although around 25 percent of men and 20 percent of women participate in Greek life, many do not live off-campus because fraternities and sororities are often housed on floors of dorms, or in other university-owned buildings.

Although the University figures state that roughly a quarter of the student body is involved in the 16 fraternities and sororities, Greek life has a far greater influence on the social scene. Many frat houses host parties every weekend, and there is often some sort of special event, such as a formal or cocktail party, at one of the Greek houses.

UR's well-earned academic reputation does not keep its students from having a good time. There are parties almost every night of the week, thrown both by fraternities and by students in their own rooms. On Tuesdays, in fact, students throw some of the best parties, known as Crazy Tuesday Parties. Students do have fun, but "kids make sure other kids are not getting out of control." Although most students take a break on Wednesdays, the parties begin on Thursday and don't end until the early hours of Sunday. Although Rochester provides restaurants and cafés, as well as the opportunity to hang out with other college students at RIT and Nazareth, most students just stay on campus. "There's too much to do here," one freshman said.

Fun in the (Upstate NY) Sun

Students who do not feel like partying five days a week can always hang out at the Wilson Center, an I.M. Pei-designed building, built to resemble a pinball machine. It is one of the better student centers in the country, with lounges, game rooms, and restaurants, and is one of the focal points of campus. Every year, Yellowjacket day in the fall and Dandelion Day, also known as D-Day, in the spring bring carnival games and food to the lawn around the Wilson Center. "This is the best time of the year!" a junior said. During the year, there is also Wilson Day, on which all the freshmen participate in a community service project, and the Boar's Head Dinner, in which students, faculty and administrators don medieval-style clothing for a banquet that happens just before winter break. There is also Meloria Weekend, on which Homecoming, Reunion, Family Weekend and the Stonehurst Capital Regatta all take place.

Who Should Apply?
Students, especially those with an interest in the sciences, should take a hard look at the University of Rochester. The REMS program has few peers, and even students not in that program receive one of the best medical preparations in the country. Unlike many science-minded schools, UR also has a strong humanities and social sciences program and a vibrant social scene. Students who take a special interest in music, but do not want to major in it, also could find UR a special match because of its integration with the Eastman School of Music. Few come to the University of Rochester for the weather; instead, they come for the invigorating combination of academics, athletics, social life and people.—*Eric Purington*

FYI

If you come to University of Rochester, you'd better bring "a graphing [calculator] tested in sub-zero conditions."

What is the typical weekend schedule? "Do homework, go to a frat party, hang out with friends, and then repeat."

If I could change one thing about the University of Rochester, I'd "make it more integrated with the city of Rochester."

Three things every student should do before graduating are "become a champion snowball fighter, wake up early and party for D-Day, and waste time in the Wilson Center."

Vassar College

Address: Vassar, 124 Raymond Avenue, Box 10, Poughkeepsie, NY 12604
Phone: 845-437-7300
E-mail Address: admissions@vassar.edu
Web site URL: www.vassar.edu
Year Founded: 1861
Private or Public: private
Religious affiliation: none
Location: small city
Regular Application Deadline: 2-Jan
Number of Applicants: 6,075
Percent Accepted: 30%
Percent Accepted who enroll: 37%
Number Entering: 670
Number of Transfers Accepted each Year: 25
Mean SAT: 1,385
Mean ACT: 31

Middle 50% SAT range: 1,340–1,440
Middle 50% ACT range: 28–32
Early admission program (EA/ ED/ NA): ED
ED or EA Acceptance Rate: 43.0%
Full time Undergraduate enrollment: 2,380
Total enrollment: 2,380
Percent Male: 40%
Percent Female: 60%
Total Percent Minority: 24%
Percent African-American: 6%
Percent Asian/Pacific Islander: 12%
Percent Hispanic: 6%
Percent Native-American: <1%
Percent Other: <1%
Percent in-state / out of state: 25%/75%

Percent from Public HS: 65%
Retention Rate: 96%
Graduation Rate: 90%
Percent in On-campus housing: 98%
Percent affiliated with Greek system: 0%
Percent Varsity or Club Athletes: 25%
Number of official organized extracurricular organizations: 100
3 Most popular majors: English, Political Science, Psychology
Student/Faculty ratio: 9:01
Tuition and Fees: $36,030
Cost for Room and Board: $8,130
Percent receiving Financial aid, first-year: 100%

Nestled in the Hudson River Valley, Vassar College looks a little bit like paradise. The campus is designated as an arboretum, and besides the various, well-preserved trees that grace the campus, students lounge on grassy quads, walk or run on wooded paths, and read by Sunset Lake. For Vassar students already enjoying a top-notch education, this beautiful setting is the icing on the cake.

Small Classes . . . and a Library Like a Castle

Students were overwhelmingly positive about academics at Vassar. One recent graduate praised the education he received at Vassar, giving it "the highest rating." Vassar's small classes and enthusiastic professors contribute to an academic experience unmatched at many other colleges. Students point out that most of the "large" intro classes at Vassar contain 25 to 30 students, while many higher-level seminars contain 10 students or less.

In such an intimate setting, students get to know their professors very well. One student said she even calls her professors by their first names—while this level of familiarity is not necessarily the norm at Vassar, she explained, it does point to a greater trend of accessibility and friendliness among professors. "The professors here really like to teach," said one student. In addition to the personal environment of the classroom, professors encourage one-on-one meetings throughout the semester. Fellow students are friendly as well. As one student put it, "The work is not easy, but it's not competitive either. The stress level is self-created."

Most students at Vassar pursue studies in the humanities. English, psychology, and political science are common majors at Vassar, and interdisciplinary majors, like American Culture or Africana Studies, attract a lot of students as well. Students may also choose to create their own multidisciplinary majors. Furthermore, the arts are well-represented in Vassar's curriculum. Drama and film classes are popular, and one of Vassar's most famous classes is "Introduction to Art History"—which, at about 200 students, is the one of the school's largest classes. Yet students who choose to pursue science at Vassar are not disappointed, either. One pre-med student, for example, pointed to the University library's impressive collection of bound periodicals in the sciences.

In general, students had nothing but praise for Vassar's Thompson Library. Beautifully Gothic yet recently renovated, spacious yet intimate, the library combines aesthetic grandeur with user-friendliness. A magnificent stained-glass window graces the West Wing of the library, but students pointed out that the library does not feel like a cathedral. One student characterized the library's atmosphere as "very, very friendly" and emphasized that she feels at home there. Students may borrow laptops at the front desk and obtain keys to "study rooms" to guarantee uninterrupted work. Indeed, the library is one of the jewels of the Vassar campus.

Close Communities, and a Vegan Co-op

Virtually every Vassar student lives on campus. Students were enthusiastic about dorm life, claiming that the dorms create strong communities. Each dorm has a House Team, composed of student officers, which works to enhance dorm life. The House Teams are a part of Vassar's student government, and they receive budgets to host study breaks and plan large-scale dorm events. Freshmen are welcomed into their dorm communities by Student Fellows, Vassar's version of RAs. Student Fellows, usually sophomores, guide freshmen through orientation and provide help or counsel whenever they are requested. They have no disciplinary power, which students applauded. "You can go to them with any problem because you know they're not going to get you in trouble," one student said. Another student pointed out that Student Fellows have a rigorous application process, so they are generally excellent.

Students said that each dorm at Vassar "has its own feel." Strong, an all-women's dorm, is unpopular with some because not all of its inhabitants requested to live in a single-sex dorm. It is, however, clean and quiet. Lathrop House, on the other hand, is known as the "party dorm." Jewett House was recently renovated, and while some students say that it feels "sterile," others appreciate the renovation. Other dorms at Vassar have yet to be renovated, and sometimes, according to students, it shows. Furthermore, most people agreed that Noyes is the undesirable dorm at Vassar, as it is, in the words of one student, "an architectural nightmare." But students were generally enthusiastic about their dorms, claiming to feel a connection to the people and the place.

One of the highlights of residential life at Vassar is senior housing. Almost all seniors live in the Townhouses, Terrace Apartments, or South Commons, all of which provide apartment-style living, including kitchens, for groups of four or five students. Furthermore, students can apply to live in Ferry House, a Co-op whose aim is sustainable living. The Co-op cooks only vegetarian and vegan food, although students do not have to be vegetarians to live there.

Students were divided on the quality of food at Vassar. Some students claim the food has improved in the past few years, while others say that it has gone downhill.

Most agreed that the food is fine, but complained that the offerings don't change much. "After your fifth quesadilla of the week, it gets old," one student pointed out. The meal plans at Vassar work on a point system, and students must redeem most of their points at the All Campus Dining Center, or ACDC, the hub of Vassar dining services. While students commended the smoothie station and the stir-fry station at ACDC, most claimed to prefer the food at the Retreat. The Retreat, located in the College Center in Main Building, is open later than ACDC and serves a limited menu, including various packaged foods. Students also recommended UpCDC, a snack bar located above ACDC. Serving legendary milkshakes, UpCDC is also a place for students to congregate and do homework. With wireless internet and an appealing ambience ("quiet bands" sometimes play there), UpCDC is a favorite of Vassar students.

Artistically Inclined and Athletically Apathetic

Vassar students are passionate about extracurricular activities. With over 100 organizations to choose from, it's hard not to get involved in something, students say. In the unlikely event that students don't find a group that interests them, they may start their own. For example, Vassar's Student Government recently recognized a Pagan Study group. Students also cited the Queer Coalition and various animal rights groups as some of the more prominent groups on the extracurricular scene.

Students agree that sports do not receive much attention at Vassar. Vassar's lack of a football team is a vestige of its days as a women's college, but also, perhaps, an indication of student apathy towards athletics. "Most Vassar students are uninterested in sports," one student said. However, one student pointed out that some teams "are actually really good," such as men's and women's rugby, women's volleyball, and baseball. Members of the baseball and basketball teams, which, according to students, are the more heavily-recruited teams at Vassar, tend to "stick to themselves."

Intramural sports, on the other hand, are popular at Vassar. Students enjoy the "relaxed system" of IMs, which allows them to participate in sports without the commitment of a varsity sport. "It's a fun thing to do with your friends," said one student. Vassar also has an active club sports scene—Ultimate Frisbee is particularly popular.

The arts, especially drama, are also strong at Vassar. Many Vassar students take part in drama and music at Vassar (a cappella is popular), and those who don't take part enjoy frequent performances. "There's at least one concert every night," said one student. Furthermore, art lovers enjoy the Frances Lehman Loeb Art Center, which houses an extensive collection in an impressive, eye-catching building.

Where's the Party?

Vassar students enjoy less-refined diversions, as well. Plenty of partying goes on on campus, students say, though not all students characterized this partying in the same way. Some students claimed that there are parties "everywhere," especially in senior housing, while others said there are not many big parties at Vassar, but rather, small ones "that you don't go to unless you know someone there." The biggest parties, at the Senior Housing complexes, take place outside, and therefore only happen when the weather is warm.

Students agreed that on a Friday or Saturday night, all roads lead to the Mug. Matthew's Mug is a bar in the basement of Main Building where students claim you'll find many familiar faces at the end of the night. "Everyone gets drunk and dances like idiots," one student said. Other than the Mug, Vassar doesn't have a bar scene to speak of. With the exception of The Dutch, a popular spot on Thursdays, students don't tend to sample Poughkeepsie's nightlife—or much else in Poughkeepsie, for that matter. Town-gown relations are "strained," students say, because of "mutual distrust." One student pointed out that most of Poughkeepsie is not accessible without a car, although the streets around Vassar are gradually becoming more college-oriented.

Some students say that the administration has recently cracked down on partying. While parties at Senior Housing are usually undisturbed, Campus Security often breaks up dorm parties. Security may also enter students' rooms and administer citations for drinking or drug use. One student said that "it seems, for the first time, like Security is out to get you." Other students disagreed, however, claiming that Campus Security doesn't interfere as long as students are safe and "things aren't getting out of hand."

The biggest party of the year is Founder's Day, a day in the beginning of May when the student government provides "carnival-type rides," including a Ferris wheel and a bounce house, and live music. "Everyone goes, and everyone has a great time," said one student. "Even last year, when it rained all day, everyone was in high spirits."

Leaning to the Left

According to students, Vassar lives up to its reputation as a haven of liberalism. However, students argued that the school is not a haven for dissenting ideas. Many students pointed to a contradiction in Vassar's political climate. "Vassar is into being politically correct," said one student. "But conservative views are the one thing they're not tolerant of." Another student said that many Vassar students, while ostensibly open-minded, are in fact closed-minded because they do not give credence to non-liberal perspectives. One student pointed out that Vassar doesn't even have a chapter of College Republicans. "People don't mind that there are conservatives here," said one student, but added that if a student expressed conservative views in a conversation, "it would get awkward."

> **"Vassar is into being politically correct."**

Despite the tendency toward political homogeneity, Vassar students praised the environment of the college. With close-knit dorm communities, strong relationships with professors and a dizzying array of extracurricular offerings, Vassar students have it all.—*Kathleen Reeves*

FYI

If you come to Vassar, you'd better bring "Birkenstocks, because you'll do a ton of walking."

What's the typical weekend schedule? "If it's warm, go to a party at Senior Housing; if it's not, hang out in the dorm, listen to music, and then hit the Mug."

If I could change one thing about Vassar, "I would like to see more intellectual and political diversity at Vassar, and I wish they hadn't modernized a lot of the interiors of the buildings. They tried to make parts of campus look not as old as they are."

Three things every Vassar student should do before graduating are "sit in the Quiet Room of the library [The Quiet Room is a room, with a beautiful view, reserved for quiet contemplation], dance by yourself on the dance-floor of the Mug, and go to Sunset Lake at night."

Wells College

Address: Wells, 170 Main Street, Aurora, NY 13026
Phone: 315-364-3264
E-mail Address: admissions@wells.edu
Web site URL: http://www.wells.edu
Year Founded: 1868
Private or Public: private
Religious affiliation: none
Location: rural
Regular Application Deadline: 2-Mar
Number of Applicants: 1,075
Percent Accepted: 71%
Percent Accepted who enroll: 23%
Number Entering: 167
Number of Transfers Accepted each Year: 82
Mean SAT: 1,100
Mean ACT: 23
Middle 50% SAT range: 1,000–1,200

Middle 50% ACT range: 20–26
Early admission program (EA/ ED/ NA): EA and ED
ED or EA Acceptance Rate: EA: 79.2%, ED:73.3%
Full time Undergraduate enrollment: 469
Total enrollment: 469
Percent Male: 16%
Percent Female: 84%
Total Percent Minority: 13%
Percent African-American: 6%
Percent Asian/Pacific Islander: 2%
Percent Hispanic: 4%
Percent Native-American: 1%
Percent Other: NA
Percent in-state / out of state: 68%/32%
Percent from Public HS: 97%
Retention Rate: 72%

Graduation Rate: 50%
Percent in On-campus housing: 87%
Percent affiliated with Greek system: 0%
Percent Varsity or Club Athletes: NA
Number of official organized extracurricular organizations: 35
3 Most popular majors: English Language and Literature, General; Psychology, General; Visual and Performing Arts, General
Student/Faculty ratio: 8:01
Tuition and Fees: $15,580
Cost for Room and Board: $7,800
Percent receiving Financial aid, first-year: 83%

Pick a tradition, any tradition. Wells has more than enough to go around. Yet despite their overwhelming popularity amongst students, one of the school's most significant traditions has recently been broken. Wells, formerly an all-girls school, admitted its first coed class in the fall of 2005. The close community spirit engendered by such a small campus, however, ensured a smooth change. "For the most part I have had no problems at all", remarked one male freshman. "I feel very at home and the people here are very nice." Indeed, at Wells, community and tradition blend to create the "relaxed and laid-back campus" students value.

One on One

Within the framework of a small student body, students have considerable access to their professors. "The one-on-one time that students at Wells get is priceless," remarked one Public Affairs major. The quality of Wells professors makes this accessibility especially appealing. "Many of my professors are literally brilliant," exclaimed one freshman. And while the grading may be tough, "you learn quite a bit."

One of the more interesting courses offered at Wells is Book Arts, in which students study the processes of book binding and book restoration, and even learn how to use a printing press. "It's really neat," remarked one junior, who also commented on the uniqueness of the college's Book Arts center. Wells also has much to offer to those interested in education. An elementary school, Peachtown, is located on campus and Wells students are greatly involved in its activities.

Science and math majors are a minority. One math major did complain about the lack of incentive to enter her field. "To give copious awards for sports or writing doesn't really encourage others to major in math," she noted. Still, she praised the department itself. "I enjoy it and find it challenging, especially the upper level courses, which is what I wanted when I came here."

'Breathtaking' Beauty

Most students are content living on campus. "The campus is absolutely breathtaking. I mean it is really, really beautiful," one freshman explained. However, the process of determining where to live on campus can be slightly more involved. Weld "has the best kitchen and individual bathrooms" while Glenn Park, the former home of Wells' founder, boasts spiral staircases and numerous lounges. Main, the biggest residence hall, also hosts the dining hall and is effectively the center of campus. In addition, the fourth floor serves as the Healthy Lifestyles floor, which offers a living environment in which "people don't come up drunk or create havoc." While Leach "is crazy," students tend to avoid Dodge because "the style is a bit . . . retro" and it is further than the other dorms from academic buildings.

No matter where students end up, the natural beauty of Wells' campus is available for everyone to enjoy. Students have access to the nearby lake for everything from science classes to skinny dipping, and many enjoy spending time on the docks. "There are trees everywhere—I came here because of the trees," one student asserted, adding that "the town of Aurora is also incredibly picturesque".

Just as students agree on the beauty of campus, they also agree on the quality of the food. Unfortunately, the consensus is not a positive one. "The dining hall is awful," complained one junior. "It's so bad," explained a sophomore, "that I *lost* 15 pounds freshman year." Still, there are a few who have good things to say about the food served on campus, so not all is lost. One senior praised "Dean Green's macaroni and cheese at soul food/home cooking night," explaining that "the administration actually comes and serves food sometimes." Furthermore, each residence hall has its own kitchen, so students always have the option of cooking for themselves.

On and Off Campus

The close relationship between the administration and students is not limited simply to the dining hall. "Wells has a ton of committees where students go right to the administration," said one Performing Arts major. "We have committees for everything from the dining hall to student diversity that meet with the senior staff on a regular basis." Aside from such committees, students have a wide range of opportunities for involvement on campus. Since Wells is strictly an undergraduate institution, Wells women and men have the opportunity to work as TAs in different subjects. Others spend their time in activities ranging from choirs, to the Japanese Culture Club, to groups such as Q&A (Queers and Allies).

Despite the abundance of extracurricular activities on campus, Wells students usually head to nearby Cornell or Ithaca College for parties. And while drinking on campus does exist, "it is usually pretty discrete in dorms.

People are fairly mellow." As one junior explained, "people come to Wells to study . . . not party." Still, many students enjoy the social activities centered at Wells. One senior pointed to Sex Collective and the Women's Resource Center as one of her favorites, crediting them with "The Erotic Ball" and "The BDP" (Big Dyke Party).

> "People come to Wells to study . . . not party."

Whether or not they choose to party in Ithaca, Wells women and men tend to agree that having a car on campus is very convenient. Though Wells offers shuttle van services to a variety of locations, one sophomore points out that they "don't go to too many places and the times at which you're allowed to take the van are set by the Transportation Department." Cars offer students the freedom of movement that shuttles simply cannot provide.

Above All, Tradition
Students love the great variety of traditions on campus, citing them as a large part of what makes Wells unique. The role of traditions is deeply ingrained in campus life, and begins every year with the Senior Champagne Breakfast and Opening Convocations. "We [the entire school] all make a huge circle in front of Macmillian and . . .

light candles," described a current freshman. After convocation, seniors jump into the lake wearing their lingerie.

"Moving Up Day" is also a monumental event at Wells, officially marking the transition as students move from one year to the next or from student to alum. "The fire alarms are pulled around 6 or 7 a.m. and everyone gathers in front of Main building," one student recounted. "We 'circle up' and do the classes song . . . After singing the seniors race to get in line to kiss the feet of the statue of Minerva." Traditions marking the end of the school year include dancing around the sycamore tree on the last day of classes.

No matter which tradition they chose as their favorite, students are enthusiastic about the atmosphere such customs create. "I think it's special; I've never heard of these traditions anywhere else," noted one sophomore.

Wells has much to offer its undergraduates, and students find that their experiences more than exceed expectations. As one senior reflected, "the minute I stepped on campus I fell in love with it. It's exactly the place I knew I had to be and there has never been a moment . . . that I second guessed my decision." She added, "It has helped me grow as a person and challenged me in ways that I'm not sure I would have been at other schools. I love Wells and everything it has done for me."—*Stephanie Brockman*

FYI
If you come to Wells, you'd better bring "a car."
What is the typical weekend schedule? "Sleep, study, then head to Cornell."
If I could change one thing about Wells, I'd "move it closer to a city."
Three things that every student at Wells should do before graduating are "participate in all the traditions they can, skinny dip in the lake, be in a theatre or dance production."

Yeshiva University

Address: Yeshiva, 500 W. 185th Street, New York, NY 10033
Phone: 212-960-5277
E-mail Address: yuadmit@yu.edu
Web site URL: www.yu.edu
Year Founded: 1886
Private or Public: private
Religious affiliation: none
Location: urban
Regular Application Deadline: 1-Feb
Percent Accepted: 78%
Percent Accepted who enroll: NA
Number Entering: NA
Number of Transfers Accepted each Year: NA
Mean SAT: NA
Mean ACT: NA
Middle 50% SAT range: V:550–660, M:550–680

Middle 50% ACT range: NA
Early admission program (EA/ ED/ NA): NA
ED or EA Acceptance Rate: NA
Full time Undergraduate enrollment: 2,927
Total enrollment: 4,575
Percent Male: NA
Percent Female: NA
Total Percent Minority: 5%
Percent African-American: 0%
Percent Asian/Pacific Islander: <1%
Percent Hispanic: 0%
Percent Native-American: 0%
Percent Other: 5%
Percent in-state / out of state: NA
Percent from Public HS: NA
Retention Rate: NA

Graduation Rate: NA
Percent in On-campus housing: NA
Percent affiliated with Greek system: NA
Percent Varsity or Club Athletes: NA
Number of official organized extracurricular organizations: NA
3 Most popular majors: Business, Psychology, Liberal Arts
Student/Faculty ratio: NA
Tuition and Fees: $28,700.00
Cost for Room and Board: $8,670.00
Percent receiving Financial aid, first-year: NA

Yeshiva University, a prominent Jewish University, offers its students the unique opportunity to spend their freshman year on the other side of the Atlantic. With 40 yeshivas and institutions located throughout Israel to choose from, YU students can earn a year's worth of credits and enter YU with sophomore standing. All credits earned are transferable from Israel to YU in New York.

Two in One Curriculum

Yeshiva University emphasizes both secular and religious studies. Undergraduates' double curriculum encompasses the Judaic areas such as Halacha (Jewish law), the Bible, and the Talmud, as well as the liberal arts and sciences. YU is made up of Yeshiva College for Men and Stern College for women. The two gender-segregated campuses are located in Upper Manhattan and Midtown Manhattan, respectively. Students may also enroll in special schools such as the Belz School of Music and the Sy Syms School of Buisness. In order to fulfill the Judaic studies requirement, Yeshiva College students choose from variety of classes offered at James Striar School of General Jewish Study, the Isaac Breuer College of Hebraic Studies, the Irving I. Stone Beit Midrash pro-

gram and the Yeshiva Program/Mazer School of Talmudic. Students generally take Judaic courses in the morning, while reserving their afternoons for secular studies. One student described the graduation requirements as "doable" and "not burdensome." Many undergrads also take advantage of the opportunity to spend their freshman year in Israel through the S. Daniel Abraham Program.

Rewarding Academics

With over 30 majors to choose from, YU also offers a plethora of joint degree program in engineering, dentistry, optometry, podiatry, Jewish studies, social work, nursing, and psychology. The S. Daniel Abraham Honors Program at Stern College and the Jay and Jeanie Schottenstein Honors Program at Yeshiva College allow students with high SAT scores to enhance the rigor of their studies.

Students seem to find their classes "rewarding." One commented that "the teachers are of a sound quality" while another said that "the professors are reachable, making it not intimidating to ask a question." Some of the more popular majors are business and sociology. One sociology major said, "it is a pretty easy major" compared to the "harder majors" in the sciences. YU will also help in the job search after college. One student felt strongly that "they will hook you up with a pretty good job right after you get out." Despite the greater number of hours YU students spend in the classroom, students enjoy their dual curriculum.

Competitive Out of the Classroom

Although Yeshiva University is "sometimes lacking school spirit," the men's basketball team is the big draw of the school's varsity sports program. Last season, the Maccabees—or Macs for short—finished with a 14-11 record that included a program-record eight game winning streak. For the less athletically gifted, there is a wide range of ways to compete at YU in a non-varsity setting. YU has developed a strong, completely student-run intramural sports program that offers everything from bumper pool to an Iron Man competition. But do not be fooled by the intramural sports label, IMs "tend to be very competitive." Other popular ways to stay in shape are at the well-liked Furst Gymnasium and the Gottesman Swimming Pool.

The Western Capital of the Jewish World

Like many New York City schools, one of YU's greatest assets is its location. A Jewish university situated in the "Western Capital of the Jewish World," boasting the greatest Jewish population outside of Israel, provides religious students easy access to kosher dining and synagogues. Yeshiva college students love that they can get on the subway from their Upper Manhattan campus and take advantage of the Big Apple's many diversions. Stern girls find themselves in Midtown with convenient access to Times Square. Very few students have cars, so the average YU student relies on New York's public transportation system.

There are not many bars located around Yeshiva College. Thursday nights and Saturday nights are the big going out nights. One junior remarked that while "the more religious crowd tends to hang out at restaurants downtown . . . some YU kids actually experience the real NYC nightlife." This can vary from bars and restaurants to trendy clubs. The on-campus party scene is limited. There are currently no fraternities, but there is an effort being made to establish a chapter of AEPi, a national Jewish fraternity.

Basic Accommodations

The majority of those attending YU live within a three block radius of campus. Underclassmen generally live in school operated dorms while upperclassmen usually move into apartments. Some students who live in the New York-New Jersey area commute to school. There are three main dorms. "The Rubin Dorm is located on top of a cafeteria and athletic center. The MUSS Dorm, considered to be the least nice of the three, is situated above the main Beit Midrash. Morge is the largest dorm and is found in the center of campus. One freshman said his dorm room "is depressing, but it gets the job done." Every floor has its own RA, who usually is "friendly and not strict." The Wilf campus, where the Yeshiva College for Men is set, spans three blocks and all the housing options lie within easy walking distance. The Stern College for Women, located at the Beren campus in Midtown Manhattan, offers independent housing in addition to three residence halls: 36th Street, Brookdale, and Schottenstein. All of these options are just a few blocks away from the Stern Campus Main Building at 34th and Lexington.

> "There are no real traditions at YU, except for the Torah."

Students must sign up for the school-run meal program. All the food is kosher and "it is not terrible." However, one sophomore complained, "I feel like I am paying 15 dollars for a tuna sandwich." Along with the perks of being in the NYC, including great restaurants, there are drawbacks. In the past, there have been reported muggings on or near campus. The school takes security very seriously and places 24-hour security guards on campus street corners to protect students.

The Last Word

Yeshiva University is a religious Jewish institution and as such there is little religious diversity on campus. One sophomore stressed that the typical YU student is an upper middle class, Jewish and white. But YU is filled with Jewish students from outside of the United States. The University draws students from Canada, France, Israel, and South America, among other places. Since a large portion of students spend their freshman year studying in Israel, many arrive on campus with already established friendships. The general vibe on campus is "real friendly." There is a lot of camaraderie between students of all years. Underclassmen are often in the same classes as upperclassmen, and "they tend to know each other from the same neighborhoods, high schools, or yeshivas in Israel." A religious university without much of a party scene, YU is in many ways a unique school. As one student put it, "There are no real traditions at YU, except for the Torah."—*Harry Etra*

FYI
If you come Yeshiva University, you'd better bring "a yarmulke."
What is the typical weekend schedule? "Hang out with friends on Thursday (no class on Friday), go away for Shabbat, and back to chilling on Saturday night."
If I could change one thing about Yeshiva, I'd "make it more competitive to get in."
Three things every student at Yeshiva should do before graduating are "go to a Yankees game, spend a Shabbat on campus, play in the dirty snow."

North Carolina

Davidson College

Address: Davidson, Box 7156, Davidson, NC 28035-7156
Phone: 704-894-2230
E-mail Address: Admission@Davidson.edu
Web site URL: www.Davidson.edu
Year Founded: 1837
Private or Public: private
Religious affiliation: Presbyterian
Location: suburban
Regular Application Deadline: 1-Jan
Number of Applicants: 4,258
Percent Accepted: 30%
Percent Accepted who enroll: 40%
Number Entering: 460
Number of Transfers Accepted each Year: varies
Mean SAT: 1,360
Mean ACT: 29%

Middle 50% SAT range: NA
Middle 50% ACT range: NA
Early admission program (EA/ ED/ NA): ED
ED or EA Acceptance Rate: NA
Full time Undergraduate enrollment: 1,683
Total enrollment: 1,683
Percent Male: 49%
Percent Female: 51%
Total Percent Minority: NA
Percent African-American: 6%
Percent Asian/Pacific Islander: 2%
Percent Hispanic: 4%
Percent Native-American: 1%
Percent Other: 6%
Percent in-state / out of state: 18%/82%
Percent from Public HS: 48%

Retention Rate: 96%
Graduation Rate: 87%
Percent in On-campus housing: 91%
Percent affiliated with Greek system: 40%
Percent Varsity or Club Athletes: 23%
Number of official organized extracurricular organizations: 185
3 Most popular majors: History, English, Biology
Student/Faculty ratio: 10:01
Tuition and Fees: $30,194.00
In State Tuition and Fees (if different): $30,194.00
Cost for Room and Board: $8,590.00
Percent receiving Financial aid, first-year: 34%

A long with a reputation for conservatism, Davidson College boasts a reputation for excellence. Since its founding by Presbyterians in 1837, the 1,600-student residential haven has made itself known by leaving its mark on several noteworthy individuals who have passed through its grassy courtyards and majestic colonial halls. As one student noted, "Woodrow Wilson went to school here for two years then left and went to Princeton because it was too hard."

A Core that's No Bore

The crux of the Davidson education is undoubtedly its adherence to the liberal arts philosophy of expanding the mind through exposure to multiple disciplines. The core curriculum demands ten courses in six general categories: literature, fine arts, history, religion and philosophy, natural sciences/math and social sciences. If that isn't enough structure, Davidson also requires its students to take three semesters or the equivalent of a foreign language, four physical education courses, one composition credit in the first year to establish skills in college-level writing, and a cultural diversity course focusing on a non-western region. Academically claustrophobic individuals can be rest assured that Davidson's rigid core program is broadened by a unique set of in-class opportunities. One student explained, "For a composition course, 'Trial of Jesus,' my group created a newspaper meant to depict the way Jesus' execution might have been reported in the ancient Roman Empire."

Students reported that although fulfilling requirements may seem a daunting task at first, doing so is actually rather easy. Four AP credits are accepted and may be used to eliminate introductory requirements and accelerate within a discipline. What shocks incoming freshmen is the general academic rigor from which President Wilson reportedly shied away. Grade inflation is a distant myth. According to one student, "People lament that if they had gone elsewhere they would have had higher GPAs." Another student noted that, "A papers are now B or B— papers." The tougher majors are generally agreed to be those in the sciences, including Chemistry, Biology and the notorious Premed track, while majors such as Psychology, English and Anthropology are in most cases a bit easier to digest.

> "People lament that if they had gone elsewhere they would have had higher GPAs."

While there's certainly no dearth of challenges, Davidson offers an impressive set of resources in all areas of academic life. Compassionate student-professor relationship stories are commonplace—and its no surprise in a place with a student-faculty ratio of 11 to one. The largest classes are capped at 35 in the humanities and 32 in the sciences, but "as soon as you move into upper level courses the cap drops drastically to 20, 15, 10, eight, even five students," says one student. Classes are not difficult to get into, but if there are problems, many a solution has been reached by emailing the reputedly accommodating professors. TAs are better known as ATs and are primarily available for hour-long language sessions during which students meet in a group and speak a particular language. The CIS, or Center for Interdisciplinary Study, is the undecided, jack-of-all-trades student's academic heaven. Faculty in CIS is available to work with students who wish to construct a major Davidson does not offer. One student reported that "recent majors have ranged from neuroscience to choral conducting to international politics to medical ethics." Apparently, the sky is the limit.

Charming or Claustrophobic?
Davidson College's campus is composed of regal Georgian architecture, miles of grassy hills, a set of cross country trails that "snake through the woods next to campus," consistently temperate weather that "never seems to be overcast," the idyllic scenery of Lake Norman, and a notoriously charming wishing well. A responsible, active police force contributes to the general feeling of safety that students experience while on campus. However, the sense of intimacy that for some enhances the beauty of their "small but charming" home is a bit oppressive for others. According to one student, "Campus can get very claustrophobic after a while, [so] it is great to have your own car."

Though a convenient asset, and a means for getting to a mall (one feature that Davidson lacks), a car isn't necessary for experiencing the various charms and treats that the quaint town of Davidson has to offer. Most students report that they go off campus a few times a week, and although Davidson is only about 20 miles north of Charlotte, most tend to stick to their small-town surroundings. However, one student stated that, "if you want to go shopping, you go somewhere else." The town does have a CVS and a few small, rather expensive boutiques, but its strengths are undoubtedly its culinary highlights, which include a restaurant that is famous for its sumptuous chocolate milkshakes and Summit, an excellent coffee shop that is frequented by many Davidson Wildcats.

The majority of students live on campus and have few complaints in terms of housing and dining. All freshmen are placed in doubles according to the Myers-Briggs Personality Test, which is also applied in the arrangement of each freshman hall. Two Hall Counselors, upperclassmen in charge of enforcing rules and serving as role models and sources of advice for their corresponding freshmen, are assigned to each fresh floor. Doubles and singles are available after the first year, and most seniors live in an apartment with four or five roommates. Floors are single-sex with the exception of Belk. Freshmen start with the largest meal plan, known as "the 19," which can be reduced or eliminated as desired. The student ID can be used at multiple locations on campus and even at a few local restaurants. The dining hall, along with being aesthetically pleasing and offering a plethora of options, is not segmented by cliques and is "great for people-watching," one student noted.

Tradition Meets Innovation
The focal points of Davidson's diverse social life illustrate the clash between convention and ingenuity, habit and experiment. The Union, the group responsible for organizing campus-wide events, works to provide students with a number of stimulating pursuits, whether through lectures and talks, or more leisurely movie nights and free pottery painting sessions. The student center, which was dubbed by one student as the "hub of all

campus activity," houses the campus P.O. boxes, as well as a café, and is open at all hours for casual socializing, group projects, or those notorious late-night cramming sessions.

The Union also strives to offer "social alternatives to the Patterson Court Scene." Patterson Court is the formal name for the eight international fraternities, four female eating houses and one coed eating house that compose Davidson's active Greek scene. The eating houses came about when Davidson began enrolling women. Female students rush for spots in the eating houses and about 70 percent of Davidson's female students hold membership. Half of the men participate in a fraternity. Though the Greek scene is rather dominant on campus, parties are open to all and generally adopt themes ranging from toga to boy-band or tacky parties.

Students admit that although the school's policy is strict when it comes to alcohol, it is definitely available to those who want it. In fact, each incoming freshman is assigned an upperclassman "sibling" of the opposite sex who is officially supposed to help the student meet upperclassmen, but who unofficially is there to "mainly just buy you alcohol."

Students generally agree that random hook-ups are significantly more common than official dates, for as one student noted, the campus is almost too "excluded" for a romantic night out on the town. But despite all this arbitrary "messing around," students report that STDs are not rampant. In regards to alcohol, the administration makes efforts to involve itself through Davidson's 101 courses, which basically teach students how to act responsibly when engaging in potentially dangerous activities, such as sex and drinking. "Davidson 101 courses present sexual activity as a normal activity for college students. However, I know of many who disagree and feel targeted for not being sexually active," one student revealed.

Pearls and Polos

Davidson certainly manages to attract to its campus a "quiet, hard-working, respectful" student body, but this convention is accepted a bit more easily than the one that involves, as one student termed it, the "stereotype of the rich, snobby white kids who wear sundresses and polos to class every day." Many students emphasize the above as simply an exaggerated generalization. But according to one student, "Most people dress VERY preppy. Collared polos, khaki shorts, loafers, and pearl earrings are the standards. Most are fairly wealthy, as can be seen by their clothes, cell phones, vacations, houses, cars, and dorm rooms." Students also express dissatisfaction with the lack of international diversity and the fact that international students are housed separately. On the other hand, while, as one student noted, "most people are similar and come from similar backgrounds," another commented that, "the school is really working on diversifying the student body." Additionally, groups do not tend to self-segregate, so that the level of diversity that does exist is enhanced by a willingness to interact with various types of people.

Surely there is a general mold for the typical Davidson student's background. But this cast tends to disintegrate in the face of the manifold extracurricular opportunities that are available to every student. Sports range from the more popular football and Division I basketball to the less widely acclaimed flickerball. Students report that community service and activism groups are the most popular on campus. And there always exists the opportunity to translate a novel idea into a new club for those to whom the more conventional organizations do not appeal. According to one student on the possibility for redefinition in such a diverse extracurricular community, "I feel free to participate in what I want to here without feeling like I will get dissolved irrecoverably into a certain group or clique."—*Juliann Rowe*

FYI

If you come to Davidson, you'd better bring: "a futon, flip-flops, and plenty of suits/dresses."
What's the typical weekend schedule? "Wake up around 11 or 12, have brunch, study for a while, go out to eat, and head down to the Court/Union/or watch a movie."
If I could change one thing about Davidson, I'd "give less work and put up more swings."
Three things every student at Davidson should do before graduating are "go to Lake Campus, order food from Bonsai, and attend Thursday night worship."

Duke University

Address: Duke, 2138 Campus Drive, Box 90586, Durham, NC 27708-0586
Phone: 919-684-3214
E-mail Address: NA
Web site URL:
www.admissions.duke.edu
Year Founded: 1924
Private or Public: private
Religious affiliation:
Methodist
Location: small city
Regular Application
Deadline: 2-Jan
Number of Applicants:
19,386
Percent Accepted: 21%
Percent Accepted who
enroll: 41%
Number Entering: 1,687
Number of Transfers
Accepted each Year: 15–50
Mean SAT: NA
Mean ACT: NA

Middle 50% SAT range:
2,060–2,340
Middle 50% ACT range:
29–34
Early admission program
(EA/ ED/ NA): ED
ED or EA Acceptance Rate:
30%
Full time Undergraduate
enrollment: 6,197
Total enrollment: 12,824
Percent Male: 52%
Percent Female: 48%
Total Percent Minority:
42%
Percent African-American:
9.4%
Percent Asian/Pacific
Islander: 25.4%
Percent Hispanic: 6.9%
Percent Native-American:
0.3%
Percent Other: 0%
Percent in-state / out of
state: 14%/86%

Percent from Public HS:
67.7%
Retention Rate: 96%
Graduation Rate: 94%
Percent in On-campus
housing: 85%
Percent affiliated with
Greek system: 35%
Percent Varsity or Club
Athletes: NA
Number of official
organized extracurricular
organizations: 350
3 Most popular majors:
Biology, Economics, Psychology
Student/Faculty ratio:
11:01
Tuition and Fees:
$34,202.00
Cost for Room and Board:
$9,340.00
Percent receiving Financial
aid, first-year: 45%

Though snow might cause school to be cancelled, little else will get in the way of school spirit at Duke University. Located in Durham, North Carolina, Duke enjoys milder weather than its northeastern counterparts, thus providing for some confusion when snow does appear. Beyond that, the enthusiastic atmosphere that is Duke remains undisturbed. With its striking mix of gothic and Georgian architecture, thriving athletic programs, and challenging academics, Duke is an incredible place. Most importantly, "you can hold a great conversation with people, and they're not snobs."

Learning the Southern Way

Duke has undergone some serious changes since its founding in 1924. The Arts and Sciences curriculum was revised in 2000, and then refined in 2004 due to difficulties and student complaints. The 2000 revision made the liberal arts education at Duke "more complete;" increasing both the number of requirements and the areas they cover. Students report that they "appreciate the wide exposure" that the new curriculum provides. The requirements involve taking courses in the five Areas of Knowledge (Arts, Literature, and Performance; Civilizations; Natural Sciences; Social Sciences; Quantitative Studies), as well as the Modes of Inquiry (Cross-Cultural Inquiry; Ethical Inquiry; Science, Technology and Society; Foreign Language; Research; Writing).

The overall credits needed to graduate from Duke are 34, thus students have to complete at least two terms of five classes, while during the rest of their time they only have to take four. Students report that classes themselves are almost always challenging and engaging—in a good way. Average class size is about 30 people, while more specific classes such as seminars are even smaller, with about 12 students. Duke is strict about controlling class size in order to help facilitate student interaction with professors, though in the larger lectures it is still "pretty easy to get lost in the crowd." It may be easy to go unnoticed in larger classes, but professors at Duke are said to be good at both contacting students and responding to their queries and requests.

The grading is as easily evaluated. Though grading difficulty at Duke varies by major, in sciences there is very little grade inflation, while inflation in history and education is described as "pretty insane." Economics courses supposedly have no grade inflation at all, making it clear that GPA varies from major to major. The popularity of a given major does not necessarily correspond with the rate of grade inflation, as the most popular majors are said to be Economics and Public Policy and the least favored are English and foreign languages—a testament to the intellectual dedication of Duke undergraduates. The science program is very strong, and according to one science major, "is particularly good about helping students into medical school." The rate of medical school acceptance is high, and the very capable career center and strong alumni involvement makes the post-college transition smooth.

Life with the Blue Devils

Duke students have no complaints about the campus. The Georgian style housing of the East Campus and the gothic style of the West Campus give personality and individuality to campus dorms. The East Campus is home to freshman housing, with all the rooms surrounding a central quad. Five freshman buildings, however, are not on the quad: Blackwell, Gilbert-Adams, Randolph, Southgate and the new Bell Tower. Though they sacrifice the community fostered by the quad arrangement, three of these dorms do have air conditioning, which as one student aptly stated "is clutch." Gilbert Addoms and Southgate also don't follow much of the same architectural Georgian style. The one drawback of the freshman East Campus is that it is dry; there is no drinking allowed in the freshman dorms or on the quad, and the University is quite strict about these policies.

Duke also cracks down on alcohol at frats, which has become a point of contention in recent years. The West Campus, where the rest of the student body lives and most students are over the age of 21, is much less strict about alcohol and is not officially dry. Housing gets better as students advance through the ranks, and by junior year they can live in apartments in-between the East and West campuses, called Central. However, it is not until senior year that students are allowed to move off-campus, which many complain about.

Freshmen are required to eat in the dining halls, where the food is said to be "pretty good." Freshmen may again feel limited by the rigidity of the freshmen dining plan, as the restaurant scene in Durham continues to expand its desirable offerings. The restaurants are described as "amazing," often tempting students away from the dining halls. Whatever the limitations of the actual dining hall may be, it is made up for by the system called Duke Points, where students can use points much like dollars and patronize a variety of stores and restaurants where Duke Points are accepted. One student raved about how Duke Points are accepted at the Washington Duke Hotel, a five-star hotel and restaurant nearby. It is therefore easy to put "wine, champagne, and prime rib on your Duke points, making it that much easier to go out and have a good time on Mom and Dad." There are also places on campus where you can buy beer with Duke Points, for those late night moments when you run out of cash.

Dancing with the Devil

The party scene at Duke is not all about drinking, though it isn't hurting for alcohol, especially when you can charge your parents for booze. The most happening social scenes both on-campus and off-campus are at the fraternity houses. Because Durham is less than safe at night, not much partying goes on at bars or clubs in the city. Duke students frequent 9th Street, where George's and Charlie's are among the favorite haunts. Relations between Duke students and residents of Durham and there is growing overlap between the two groups, but the social scene primarily revolves around athletics and Greek life.

> "Though described as a 'pretty preppy school,' the Duke students are considered 'well-rounded and down to earth.' "

The immense popularity of the teams means athletes are high profile on campus, and the Greek houses provide a network within the larger community that many students chose to join. Indeed, the social scene is said to "really pick up in second semester, when rush begins." The big party nights are Tuesday, Thursday, Friday, and Saturday, demonstrating that for Blue Devils there is "always a good time to party."

According to one student, the people are what really define the social scene at Duke. Though described as a "pretty preppy school," the Duke students are considered "well-rounded and down to earth." It's easy to meet people freshman year, as everyone is on the same campus. Otherwise, being on a team or in a fraternity/sorority is a popular choice, and makes getting to know different people that much easier.

That said, the athletic scene is enormous at Duke. Blue Devil pride is unparalleled, and every year they show their best to the University of North Carolina at Chapel Hill in their competition for the Carlyle Cup. The Carlyle Cup is a trophy awarded at the end of the year to the school who has won the most games in all sports, and Duke won it in 2001, 2003, and most recently, 2004. Basketball is by far the most popular sport on campus, and both the men's and women's teams stand out in ability. The following of the men's basketball team is described as "prac-tically a cult," demonstrated in the popularity of Coach Krzyzewski, fondly referred to as Coach K "maybe just because his name is impossible to pronounce." Indeed, he is a "celebrity on campus," and the leadership class he taught this past year was nearly impossible to get into.

The Southern Way

No matter whom you ask about Duke, they will comment on the school spirit of the talented students. The pride comes hand in hand with an intellectual curiosity which drives the University. The Carlyle Cup, part of the rivalry between Duke and UNC, incites immense school spirit, but the campus is described as having electricity unlike any other that reaches far beyond athletics. Indeed, there is a self-described "Blue Devil magic about the school," which stirs all current and graduated attendees to keep alive special memories of Blue Devil times.—*Annemarie von der Goltz*

FYI

If you come to Duke, you'd better bring "a tent or sleeping bag to camp out for basketball games."

What's the typical weekend schedule? "Study, study, study, and then go to the bars in Durham or Chapel Hill."

If I could change one thing about Duke, it would be "the requirement that juniors have to live on campus."

Three things every student at Duke should do before graduating are "attend a basketball game in Cameron, walk through the Duke gardens, and eat brunch at the Washington Duke."

Elon University

Address: Elon, 2700 Campus Box, Elon, NC 27244
Phone: 336-278-3566
E-mail Address: admissions@elon.edu
Web site URL: www.elon.edu
Year Founded: 1889
Private or Public: private
Religious affiliation: United Church of Christ
Location: small city
Regular Application Deadline: 10-Jan
Number of Applicants: 9,200
Percent Accepted: 42%
Percent Accepted who enroll: 33%
Number Entering: 1,379
Number of Transfers Accepted each Year: 186
Mean SAT: NA
Mean ACT: NA
Middle 50% SAT range: 1,140–1,300

Middle 50% ACT range: 23–28
Early admission program (EA/ ED/ NA): ED and EA
ED or EA Acceptance Rate: 65%/48%
Full time Undergraduate enrollment: 4,850
Total enrollment: 5,200
Percent Male: 40%
Percent Female: 60%
Total Percent Minority: 21%
Percent African-American: 7%
Percent Asian/Pacific Islander: 2%
Percent Hispanic: 1%
Percent Native-American: 1%
Percent Other: 10%
Percent in-state / out of state: 30%/70%
Percent from Public HS: NA

Retention Rate: 89%
Graduation Rate: 74%
Percent in On-campus housing: 60%
Percent affiliated with Greek system: 32%
Percent Varsity or Club Athletes: 10–12%
Number of official organized extracurricular organizations: 148
3 Most popular majors: Business, Communications, Education
Student/Faculty ratio: 15:01
Tuition and Fees: $ 20,441.00
Cost for Room and Board: $ 6,850.00
Percent receiving Financial aid, first-year: NA

Founded by the Christian Church now known as the United Church of Christ in 1889, and tucked away in Elon, North Carolina, in the Piedmont region of the state, Elon University's beautiful wooded campus has been recognized by the *Princeton Review* as one of the nation's finest. An hour's drive away from Raleigh, Durham, Winston-Salem, and Chapel Hill, the classic Southern brick buildings intermingled with oak trees make Elon a pleasant living and learning environment. Students point to their unique academic experience, their campus-wide traditions, and the vibrant student life as the selling points of this picturesque southern school.

The "Elon Experience"

Elon places extraordinary emphasis on learning outside of the walls of the classroom. In 2005, Elon was named "America's Hottest College for Student Engagement" by *Newsweek*, a recognition that students are extremely involved in their education beyond simply attending class. This involvement is facilitated by the "Elon Experiences" program, in which students receive a transcript that tracks their study abroad, internships, service participation, leadership roles, and experiences conducting research. Elon's admissions office proudly boasts that the university sends more students abroad than any other masters-level university in the country through the Isabella Cannon Center for Study Abroad. Students also participate in large numbers in internships and volunteer service throughout their university careers. The John R. Kernodle, Jr. Center for Service-Learning facilitates many of the programs that Elon students enroll in as part of a service-learning experience, offering courses and housing service groups. Courses are often tailored to current events or needs of the region or the country; for example, a group of Elon students recently performed service in areas affected by Hurricane Katrina. An added bonus of the experiential learning program are the great town-gown relations at Elon. Because people do a lot of work within the community as part of their experiential learning, there is a lot of interaction with the local community. One popular yearly event is the Festival of the Oak. Lots of kids from the community come to Elon's campus for a day of activities run by many Elon students.

There are approximately 4,850 undergrads

at Elon and while the majority of them hail from North Carolina, Elon continues to draw students from 46 states and 42 countries. Although these numbers mark Elon as a small university, the school thinks large in terms of academics and facilities. Elon has worked hard in recent years to integrate technology in all areas of campus life. For example, the McMichael Science Center provides valuable lab space, high tech instruments, and over 70 computers to aid science students. Similarly, the Belk Library has nearly 200 computers available for public use. As the admissions office notes, "Elon's state-of-the-art facilities offer something for everyone."

Despite the large-scale technological offerings, Elon's education remains personalized to student needs: the student-to-faculty ratio is 1 to 14, and students are given many opportunities to work one-on-one with professors. Elon's year follows a "4-1-4" calendar, with a four-month fall semester, a one-month winter term, and a four-month spring semester. Many students use the one-month winter term for travel and fulfillment of the study abroad aspect of the "Elon Experiences." As one Elon senior remarked, "My winter term trip was centered around World War II and we went to France, the Netherlands, the Czech Republic, Germany, and Poland. Besides just the cultural aspects of the countries, we focused on this particular history and it was a more fulfilling experience than just traveling on my own."

Elon provides undergraduate education in four schools: Elon College, the college of arts and science; the Love School of Business; the School of Communications; and the School of Education. In total, students can choose from among 48 major fields of study, earning Bachelors of Arts, Bachelors of Science, or Bachelors of Fine Arts degrees. The most popular majors are business, communications, education, psychology and biology. A unique program at Elon is the dual-degree engineering program run in conjunction with North Carolina State University, North Carolina A & T State University, Georgia Tech, Columbia University, Virginia Tech and Washington University in St. Louis, in which students will graduate with one degree from Elon and a second from one of these affiliates.

Traditions at Elon

One of Elon's most beloved traditions takes place at 9:45 in the morning. Each Tuesday morning, students, faculty and staff gather around Fonville Fountain for refreshments and fellowship during "College Coffee." This is a great time to grab a bite to eat with a professor in a more relaxed setting, catch up with friends, or take a break before heading to class. "A lot of people go to refuel between classes," one Elon sophomore explained. "This was a great opportunity for me to meet new people as an underclassman."

> "Guys come in ties, and girls in sundresses, to tailgate and enjoy the game."

Another tradition revolves around the oak tree, the symbol of Elon. The campus is still heavily populated by oaks and is located on what used to be an oak grove, and "Elon" means oak in Hebrew. Newly arrived freshmen are given an acorn in the fall, and there is a special ceremony for seniors at the time of graduation around an oak tree, symbolizing the intellectual growth of Elon students.

Sports are also a major part of creating traditions at Elon. The university boasts 16 intercollegiate varsity sports, playing in the NCAA Division I as part of the Southern Conference. You don't have to be Michael Jordan to get involved in sports, however—Elon also has 18 intramural and 20 club sports that many students take part in. "Everyone comes out for club sports or intramurals," one junior agreed. Like kids at many Southern schools, Elon students dress up for the Homecoming football game, the biggest sporting event of the year. "This was a bit of a shock for me, coming from Indiana," an Elon senior said. "Guys come in ties, and girls in sundresses, to tailgate and enjoy the game." Although the tailgates at Homecoming have an undeniable southern flavor, many students say that Elon's general atmosphere is not as Southern as other schools in North Carolina. As one senior explained, "Prevailingly, the people that go here are not from North Carolina, we have a lot of people from the Northeast, California, as far away as Maine and North Dakota. It's not like the UNC schools, which are dominated by Southern students." Another student concurred: "I feel like it's a different experience than being at UNC Greensboro or Chapel Hill."

A New Way to Look at Dining

Elon has recently introduced an innovative new meal plan system that is based on the feedback of students. All nine dining halls on campus are participating in the new plan. Students can buy 5, 9, 11, 14, 17, or 19 meals per week; unused meals carry over from week to week until the end of the semester. There are no restrictive dining times or dining zones—students can eat whenever their stomach says it's time. According to one Elon senior, the best place to grab a bite to eat on campus is Harden dining hall in the bottom floor of the Moffit dormitory, because it has the biggest variety of foods. Most students would seem to agree—it's the largest dining hall on campus.

Most students at Elon end up living off campus by the end of their college careers. Freshman and sophomores live on campus unless they gain special approval to move off. Some juniors live on campus, and seniors who are involved in residential life, such as RAs, or athletes who are paying for housing, stay in campus housing, but the majority live in apartments or townhouses with friends. One dorm causing an exception to this rule is the newly constructed Danieley Center, a cluster of buildings boasting spacious suites and apartment-style housing. Many upperclassmen choose to live in this area. The university also owns apartment buildings such as Haggard Square and Elon Place that are technically still considered on campus housing but are a few blocks from the campus itself. As far as the dorms themselves, the best are Virginia Hall, which are single-sex by floor, and Moffit Hall, with its proximity to the dining area. Loan dorm also comes highly recommended. The Jordan Center area is considered the least desirable dorm on campus, but it is in the process of being renovated in the style of Danieley Center.

Get in the Zone

Elon students love to enjoy themselves when they're not having Elon Experiences or in the classroom. The Greek scene provides a lot of the social life of the campus, although students generally agree it's not dominant. There are 22 nationally recognized fraternities and sororities at the school, and they host a lot of social events, particularly on the weekend, but less than 20 members of the organization, usually sophomores, actually live in each of the houses that make up Greek Court. As one sorority sister put it, "You're not just in your sorority with 120 girls and that's the majority of what you do with your time. I'm still involved in my sorority but I have a ton of friends who aren't even in Greek life."

The University is also conscious about promoting the arts. Every semester get a program with all of the cultural events planned for the semester, such as musicals, plays, and concerts. There is a large annual concert for Elon students, where a well-known musical group performs for the whole student body. Maroon 5 was last year's act. "Movie runs" are a popular weekend activity, particularly for those students who don't drink. The university provides discount tickets and transportation to local theaters to see the latest blockbuster hits. The Zone—a large open space in the student center—is also popular for hosting dances and big events.

Elon students generally seem to have a great time learning in a wide array of settings, enjoying Elon's gorgeous weather, and making great friends. There are so many unique factors that make Elon a school that attracts people from all over the country an world. If you're looking for a balanced education, a college steeped in tradition, and an overall ideal college experience, you shouldn't look further than Elon University.—*Elizabeth Jordan*

FYI

If you come to Elon, you'd better bring "sunglasses, because even in the winter it's still sunny."

What is the typical weekend schedule? "Wednesday and Thursday is the bar scene, Friday and Saturday party at the frats or off campus, Sunday is usually a 'party' in the library with everyone doing all their homework."

If I could change one thing about Elon, "it would be the boy girl ratio, it's pretty high in favor of the boys."

Three things every student at Elon should do before graduating are "study abroad, take advantage of the opportunities for hands-on learning, get a minor degree."

North Carolina School of the Arts

Address: North Carolina School of the Arts, 1533 South Main Street, Winston-Salem, NC 27127
Phone: 336-770-3290
E-mail Address: admissions@ncarts.edu
Web site URL: www.ncarts.edu
Year Founded: 1963
Private or Public: public
Religious affiliation: none
Location: urban
Regular Application Deadline: 2-Mar
Number of Applicants: NA
Percent Accepted: 46%
Percent Accepted who enroll: 59%
Number Entering: NA
Number of Transfers Accepted each Year: NA
Mean SAT: 1,155
Mean ACT: 23

Middle 50% SAT range: 1,040–1,260
Middle 50% ACT range: 20–25
Early admission program (EA/ ED/ NA): NA
ED or EA Acceptance Rate: NA
Full time Undergraduate enrollment: 721
Total enrollment: NA
Percent Male: 59%
Percent Female: 41%
Total Percent Minority: 16%
Percent African-American: 10%
Percent Asian/Pacific Islander: 3%
Percent Hispanic: 2%
Percent Native-American: 0%
Percent Other: NA
Percent in-state / out of state: 48%/52%
Percent from Public HS: NA

Retention Rate: 75%
Graduation Rate: 48%
Percent in On-campus housing: 60%
Percent affiliated with Greek system: NA
Percent Varsity or Club Athletes: NA
Number of official organized extracurricular organizations: 3
3 Most popular majors: Cinematography and Film/Video Production, Music Performance
Student/Faculty ratio: 8:01
Tuition and Fees: $12,795.00
In State Tuition and Fees (if different): $2,195.00
Cost for Room and Board: $5,115.00
Percent receiving Financial aid, first-year: 64%

W ith some of the most talented students around—actors, dancers, musicians, filmmakers, and production designers—uniting behind their beloved mascot the "fighting pickle," the North Carolina School of the Arts (NCSA) defies categorization. This small, competitive arts conservatory is neither an ordinary college nor an ordinary arts school: quirky, intimate, and friendly, NCSA attracts applicants from all over the world and commands a respect among professional artists that rivals its more well-known competitors. For students truly passionate about their arts, NCSA provides intensive training with top-notch faculty for a fraction of the price of private conservatories.

Let's Go, Pickles!

The "School of the Arts," as locals sometimes call NCSA, is comprised of five arts schools: Dance, including modern and ballet, Drama, Filmmaking, Music, and Design and Production, which trains students in set design, costuming, wigs and makeup, sound, and lighting and is referred to as "D&P." Each school has its own culture and its own stereotypes—"you can usually tell what school someone is from by the way they're dressed," said a fourth-year Drama major—but the schools are united in the large quantity of work they demand. Some students chafe at the intense classes and rehearsals, which can run from 8 a.m. to midnight at peak times of year, but "the heavy workload tends to weed out those who are not up to standards."

While students from different schools may not see each other in their arts classes, General Studies classes are a different story. As NCSA's academic component, General Studies offers classes in the liberal arts and sciences, specially geared to students who care more about perfecting their plié than learning about Copernicus. That's not to say the classes are dumbed down. Students describe their academic professors as "better than you would expect for an arts school," but say it's hard to find time to do General Studies work when the arts classes are so demanding. For the most part, the faculty understands that students "are artists and don't want to major in math."

A Chance to Show Your Stuff

For a school whose goal is to teach students to create art, students say NCSA "realizes that the reason we attend is to actually do the work we are majoring in, not just to learn," and performance opportunities abound. In addition to participating in major performances, students have the option to perform chamber music, do outreach in the community, and participate in the annual summer production of *The Lost Colony* on Roanoke Island, assuring that graduates of NCSA have had plenty of chances to practice their art in "exceptional" facilities.

Most students come to NCSA because of particular programs or faculty members. In general, students say the arts faculty at NCSA is "stellar" and the standards that they expect of their students are high. Each member of the faculty is an expert—ballet students are taught by former principal dancers of the New York City Ballet and music students learn from teachers that have played with the world's major orchestras. Despite their prestige in the art world, in general teachers "make themselves ridiculously accessible." In addition to the level of know-how on staff, well-known artists are often brought in for classes or concerts. But no matter how good the faculty is, "at NCSA, hands-on experience is usually considered the best teacher."

Within departments, competition can sometimes be fierce; students must be invited by the faculty to return the following year. In some departments, students speak of an unofficial cut system in which a few students are not invited back after sophomore year. This practice seems to have recently subsided—facing state budget cuts, the school "needs the money"—but some students still worry that their spot "may be in jeopardy." For the most part, though, students tend to think positively and most say that they get along very well. After all, "a little competition can be healthy."

You Want Grits with That?

Set in the laid-back, small Southern city of Winston-Salem (often known to locals as "Winston"), NCSA provides its students with a very different experience from other arts schools, which are typically located in major urban centers. While the city may not be exciting, as one student said "it has its own charm." Students say they rarely interact with the locals, but Winston-Salem residents often make up a large percentage of the audiences at student shows. The NCSA pro-

duction of *The Nutcracker* is a holiday favorite in the city, selling out over a week of performances before going on tour and being shown on public television.

What is there to do in Winston? Students in search of a drink often head to the Black Bear and other bars on Burke Street, while shoppers find that Hanes Mall is "good-sized but nothing special." People looking to strut their stuff on the dance floor might not be so lucky, though: "There are no real dance clubs in Winston; you have to go to Greensboro for that," and students stress that having a car is necessary. "A car is important if you want to do *anything* off campus . . . like go out to eat, buy groceries, or go to a bar. Nothing is within walking distance and there is no ubiquitous college town shopping-eating-walking main street area," said one student.

Campus, for the most part, is "fairly safe" despite its location near some "creepy" areas. Nevertheless, "nothing really bad ever seems to happen, no matter how much people like to talk," and students say the area is improving. Straddling two neighborhoods, the campus connects the "beautiful, historic Washington Park area" with "what used to be the projects. Though they are no longer there, that neighborhood is still kind of sketchy."

Dorms like Prison Cells

All freshmen and sophomores are required to live on campus, either in the residence halls, which go by the letters A through F, or in apartment-style buildings. The residence halls get uniformly negative reviews, despite fostering a "nice feeling of camaraderie." One senior who has been an RA called the A-F buildings "gross" and mentioned the traditional rumor that they were built following the plans of a women's prison. "Though not disgusting or dirty, the rooms and halls are less than aesthetically pleasing. The walls are cinderblock and the floors are linoleum. My suggestion: get your mom/girlfriend/sister to help you decorate." Students looking to escape to the newer apartment-style buildings have to pay a bit more, but most juniors and seniors decide to live off campus. Competition is fierce for nearby houses, but students say apartments around the city are generally easy to get.

While some students complain that the dining hall food is lackluster, it has been improving since the recent renovation of the Hanes Student Commons. "I personally have seen the food go from bland to exotic," one student said. "They have a huge selection and really good vegetarian dishes." When venturing off campus for a change of taste, most students cite the nearby Acadia Grill as a popular choice, along with inexpensive Mexican restaurants.

NCSA operates a high school program on the same campus as the college, which garners mixed reactions from college students. While there is generally "no reason to interact with the highschoolers," it can be weird seeing them in the cafeteria. It's "more amusing than annoying, although on-campus life would be cooler if they weren't around," said one student.

Practice Hard, Party Harder

With the hectic schedule of classes and rehearsals which frequently spill over into the weekend, it can be difficult to find a moment to unwind. When students do get a moment, going to friends' performances is a popular choice. Generally free, the performances are "a great opportunity to see the nation's best up-and-coming artists." The Filmmaking school offers free screenings on the weekends and many students use the "well-equipped gym" to work out or play impromptu games. As for parties, most of them are off campus and students say they can get pretty wild: "there's a lot of rehearsal—we try to balance it with a lot of letting loose." Alcohol and drugs are fairly common—"it's an arts school"—but NCSA recently went to a dry campus, even for students over 21, so on-campus libations have to be fairly discreet.

The school organizes a few social events during the year, like skiing and hiking trips and Fall Fest, but most students agree that a lot of the on-campus events are "a joke." The ever popular exception is the annual Beaux Arts costume ball. Turning one of the film soundstages into a dance floor—lighting and sound designed by D&P stu-

dents and generally top-notch—the costume ball is an excuse to wear something completely outlandish or close to nothing at all. An NCSA degree serves as a lifelong Beaux Arts invitation, so the party is often a meeting place for young alumni that still live in the area.

Students describe NCSA as very accepting: "most students are progressive, open-minded, and busy . . . all sorts of things that would be considered weird or even bizarre are accepted as normal." Despite a state quota requirement that about half the students must be from North Carolina, NCSA manages to attract a fairly diverse student body with students from almost every state and several foreign countries. LGBT students feel welcome as well, as the school is "sexually diverse, and prides itself on being an open-minded environment."

> **"An NCSA degree could get you the job. Along with your talent, of course."**

"If your goals for college are to let loose, have fun, casually meet hundreds of people, and be the stud of your favorite fraternity, you're shit out of luck," said one senior. "Though the social life is not what you'd find at a larger school, the friendships made here are formed by a love of art and are deep and real. There is a huge amount of respect among students for each other as artists . . . and a strong sense of community." With its intimate size and friendly, anything-goes culture, NCSA belies a performing arts powerhouse. With well-known alumni appearing on stages and movie screens around the world and the reputation of the school steadily growing, "an NCSA degree could get you the job. Along with your talent, of course."—*Charles Cardinaux*

FYI
If you come to NCSA, you'd better bring "something with caffeine."
What's the typical weekend schedule? "Sleep in if you can, rehearse all day, and check out the parties or a film screening at night."
If I could change one thing about NCSA, I'd "allow more unexcused absences in General Studies classes!"
Three things every student at NCSA should do before graduating are "see the work of all the various programs at least once, watch a sunrise from the library or Performance Place rooftops (officially illegal—use the trellis), and choose having fun over work from time to time."

North Carolina State University

Address: North Carolina State, Office of Undergraduate Admissions, Campus Box 7103, Raleigh, NC 27695
Phone: 919-515-2434
E-mail Address: undergrade-admissions@ncsu.edu
Web site URL: www.admissions.ncsu.edu
Year Founded: 1887
Private or Public: public
Religious affiliation: none
Location: urban
Regular Application Deadline: 1-Feb
Number of Applicants: 15,541
Percent Accepted: 61%
Percent Accepted who enroll: 49%
Number Entering: 5,735
Number of Transfers Accepted each Year: 1,492
Mean SAT: NA
Mean ACT: NA

Middle 50% SAT range: 1,100–1,300
Middle 50% ACT range: 24–28
Early admission program (EA/ ED/ NA): EA
ED or EA Acceptance Rate: 55%
Full time Undergraduate enrollment: 22,879
Total enrollment: 30,149
Percent Male: 56.8%
Percent Female: 43.2%
Total Percent Minority: 18%
Percent African-American: 9.7%
Percent Asian/Pacific Islander: 5.3%
Percent Hispanic: 2.3%
Percent Native-American: 0.7%
Percent Other: NA
Percent in-state / out of state: 86.8%/13.2%

Percent from Public HS: 89%
Retention Rate: ~89–90%
Graduation Rate: 70%
Percent in On-campus housing: 35%
Percent affiliated with Greek system: 7–8%
Percent Varsity or Club Athletes: 13.1%
Number of official organized extracurricular organizations: 400
3 Most popular majors: Business Management, Communications, Electrical Engineering
Student/Faculty ratio: 15:01
Tuition and Fees: $4,783.00
In State Tuition and Fees (if different): $16,982.00
Cost for Room and Board: $7,041.00
Percent receiving Financial aid, first-year: 39%

If you're looking for science and technology, serious parties, and die-hard school spirit, North Carolina State University might just be the place for you. With more than 30,000 students, NC State also offers tons of different people, perspectives and opportunities. The campus is located next to downtown Raleigh, the capital of North Carolina. Both in-state and out-of-state students consider NC State quite a deal: The University is the largest research institution in North Carolina and fourth in the nation in attracting corporate research. And students are eager to point out that, in spite of its size, the campus doesn't feel that big, and can be walked across in 15 minutes. Additionally, Raleigh offers an ample selection of museums and events, though most students stay close to campus to participate in the vibrant campus life.

'Not Just a Cow College'
Although originally an agricultural school, NC State students are quick to point out that their school is now best known as a technical school. The design, textiles and engineering programs are particularly popular. In the words of one student, "There's no

question that there are a lot of engineers." This reputation has reached the point where humanities students complain that their disciplines don't get as much funding—meaning that it can be harder to get into the popular non-science classes, which are "more fun." In general, registering for classes can be really frustrating because of the sheer number of students at NC State, but "it does all get worked out in the end."

Before freshman year, students apply to the individual college within the university that contains their prospective major. For students who don't yet have a clue about what they want to do, there's the First-Year College, which requires them to take specific classes and specialized tests designed to help them settle on the right major. Students suggest, though, that if you have any idea what you want to do, it's better to go ahead and try it out since each college has faculty advisors to help you plan your academic career.

Students generally don't talk about their grades, a fact that contributes to NC State's laid-back atmosphere. Some assignments are actually optional, which also helps perpetuate this attitude among students. Optional tests are to the advantage of self-motivated students, but help disguise how much work there can be.

Introductory classes are usually very large, but students find themselves in smaller classes, as well. Although the larger classes are taught by professors, many teaching assistants—some of whom don't speak English well—are also present. Not all professors are particularly personable, but students do have the opportunity to talk to them, especially if they're willing to put forth some effort. Many of the majors, particularly the sciences, are demanding and leave little room in a student's schedule for exploration, sometimes only allowing one free course per semester outside of that major. Freshmen in particular have trouble getting into "fun classes" like Physical Education or Mythology.

Cheers, Beers and Wolfpack Pride

School pride is without a doubt a fundamental part of the NC State experience. With a history of nationally successful varsity basketball and football teams, students flock to games. As expected, tailgates for home football games are a major event, with up to 55,000 fans barbecuing, drinking and hanging out. At the games, which are "the most fun in the entire world," fans are clad in red (the school color), and notably "obnoxious, loud, fun and hilarious," particularly at games against rival UNC-Chapel Hill. It isn't all about winning, though; win or lose in the regularly sold-out stadium, NC State fans go to celebrate and party.

There aren't many schoolwide, school-sponsored social events other than athletic exhibitions at NC State. As one student said, "The administration assumes we can find ways to entertain ourselves." NC State students seem more than up to the challenge, hosting their own cultural and social events "all the time." There is a movie theater on-campus, and students have the opportunity to go to a play or concert every other night if they'd like. The administration even provides free tickets to students in the Honors or Scholars program. While there is no drinking at school-sponsored events, students definitely party hard every weekend. People typically party off-campus in friends' apartments, and students report that practically everyone drinks underage. One girl commented, "I think there are people who don't drink, but I don't pay attention." NC State has its fair share of frats and sororities, but students don't feel pressured to be

involved in them. One girl in a sorority noted that Greek life "can still be interesting even if you don't drink."

(A Few) Girls Gone Wild

While NC State's guy to girl ratio has been dropping, you "can still definitely notice that there are more guys." Unfortunately for wannabe Don Juans, this gives girls the advantage. However, don't let this hinder plans for romance; tons of students are dating, and there is plenty of hooking up. There is a very active gay, lesbian, bisexual and allies association, probably because campus is not a particularly accepting place. "It would be a rough place to be gay," one student said. With almost 90 percent of students from in state, you might expect the student body to be homogenous, but there are also students from all 50 states and 100 countries. While NC State has the demographics of a culturally diverse environment, some students complain that their school isn't very socially integrated. At the same time, one out-of-state student said he had expected more racism, but has found it to be a non-issue. While most students are physically active, making good use of the gym, one girl admitted, "You might find some beer guts" due to the hard partying.

NC State has an enormous variety of extracurricular clubs for students, ranging from political groups to club sports to community service groups. For example, the school has an enormous Habitat for Humanity chapter that meets each weekend and builds its own house every year. Religion also tends to be a "big force" at NC State: Campus Crusade for Christ is one of the largest student organizations. "But it is OK not to be religious," one student is quick to mention. Club sports are really competitive, often with serious tryouts, and if you just want to enjoy a casual game, intramural athletics is the place for you. Ultimate Frisbee and touch football are two of the more popular intramural sports. NC State also has a really popular outdoor adventures program through which students can learn how to rock-climb, hike or backpack. Not everyone at NC State cares about extracurricular activities, but those who do tend to pick one or two and get involved pretty seriously.

Sick of Brick

Campus architecture is dominated by red brick; the buildings and walkways are all brick and there is even a large open area called "The Brick Yard." One student jokingly insisted that the university receives a donation of brick every year and is obligated to use it. Just because campus looks like a brick factory doesn't mean it is ugly. On nice days, people flock to the open areas to sunbathe and play Frisbee. On the flip side, students warn that the brick walkways flood and overflow when it rains, so invest in a good pair of galoshes. One unique building on campus is Harrellson Hall, a round concrete building. Students report having been surprised when they went to their first class because all the classrooms are shaped like pie slices, "mak[ing] the blackboards really weird."

Most freshmen live on-campus in a variety of dorms. Some dorms are freshman-only, others are single-sex; some have suites, and others halls. The administration does a pretty good job pairing up roommates, but for those who really don't get along, it's not that difficult to change housing.

One thing that students living in dorms praise is the chance to meet many new people and sleep more, because they're closer to class. The dorms are grouped into three campuses: East, West and Central. West Campus is the most popular, probably because it houses several special academic programs such as the University Scholars, and learning and living villages such as the Women in Science and Engeneering (WISE) and Students Advocating for Youth (SAY). The university also offers an Honors Program which has recently moved to a new location on East Campus. One dorm, Alexander, has a program called the Global Village where every American student is paired with an international roommate.

Most upperclassmen, however, live off-campus in apartment complexes and houses. The school provides transportation between apartments and school (known by many as "the drunk bus"). Lots of students have cars and consider them important for their social life, since public transportation in Raleigh is a "joke." Students living off campus don't usually buy meal plans but instead cook at home or eat at the many nearby restaurants and cafes. Hillsborough Street, which runs through campus, is a favorite strip of eating and watering holes.

> **"I feel like I'll have a really strong background to do whatever I want when I graduate."**

With one dining hall on each side of campus, students can get tired of eating the same food. An on-campus food court with fast-food chains like Chick-fil-A and Taco Bell helps to break the monotony. Dining halls are not very social, but more like places to take care of business; students say they "get by" on the food there. If you want to watch sports with your meal, the Wolves' Den is the place to go—a student center where one might also go for a club meeting. The pervading campus style is very casual, including classes, and many students seem to be comfortable showing up in sweatpants and old T-shirts.

Although it has strong roots in agriculture, NC State is not just a "cow college" anymore. Among the huge student population one can find every type of person imaginable. With a lively social scene and countless activities available, students don't have trouble keeping themselves busy. On top of that, one student reported, "I feel like I'll have a really strong background to do whatever I want when I graduate."—*Alistair Anagnostou*

FYI
If you come to NC State, you'd better bring "red clothes and a Frisbee."
What is the typical weekend schedule? "Take a nap and party with friends Friday night; go to a sports event Saturday; party again Saturday night; and then catch up on work Sunday after sleeping in or going to church."
If I could change one thing about NC State, I'd "add a lot more parking."
Three things every student at NC State should do before graduating are "attend every football tailgate in a season, work for Habitat for Humanity and drink a pint in Mitch's Tavern on Hillsborough Street."

University of North Carolina / Chapel Hill

Address: UNC Chapel Hill, CB #2200, Jackson Hall, Chapel Hill, NC 27599-2200
Phone: 919-966-3621
E-mail Address: uadm@email.unc.edu
Web site URL: www.unc.edu
Year Founded: 1789
Private or Public: public
Religious affiliation: none
Location: suburban
Regular Application Deadline: 16-Jan
Number of Applicants: 19,728
Percent Accepted: 34%
Percent Accepted who enroll: 57%
Number Entering: 3,807
Number of Transfers Accepted each Year: 1,244
Mean SAT: 1,281
Mean ACT: 27
Middle 50% SAT range: NA

Middle 50% ACT range: 25–30
Early admission program (EA/ ED/ NA): EA
ED or EA Acceptance Rate: NA
Full time Undergraduate enrollment: 17,100
Total enrollment: 20,900
Percent Male: 40%
Percent Female: 60%
Total Percent Minority: 25%
Percent African-American: 12%
Percent Asian/Pacific Islander: 7%
Percent Hispanic: 5%
Percent Native-American: 1%
Percent Other: 4%
Percent in-state / out of state: 85%/15%
Percent from Public HS: 84%

Retention Rate: NA
Graduation Rate: NA
Percent in On-campus housing: 44%
Percent affiliated with Greek system: 0%
Percent Varsity or Club Athletes: NA
Number of official organized extracurricular organizations: 540
Most popular majors: Communications, Psychology
Student/Faculty ratio: 14:01
Tuition and Fees: $18,103.00
In State Tuition and Fees (if different): $3,455.00
Cost for Room and Board: $6,846
Percent receiving Financial aid, first-year: NA

Probably the highest-profile asset of UNC-CH is its incredible men's basketball team, which unites the whole campus in a flurry of baby blue and white. But Carolina is more than just a high-powered sports school; it is home to one of the best journalism schools in the country, an impeccably beautiful Southern campus, and countless international opportunities. Add the fact that UNC is one of the top few public universities in the nation, and one can easily see how it becomes *the* choice for so many high-spirited Tar Heels.

Carolina Academia

When students enroll at UNC, they're signing up for a broad and enriching academic experience. During freshman and sophomore years, all Tar Heels must fulfill eight to 12 distribution requirements, which cover academic "perspectives" from foreign languages to the natural sciences. Some of these requirements can be satisfied by certain high-school scores, and others require appropriate placement through tests during CTOPS, the mandatory freshman orientation session at Carolina. Around this time, students can also apply for the Honors Program, which is quite competitive.

At the end of sophomore year, students must declare their majors. Some of UNC's most reputable schools include business and journalism, which have programs that are notoriously difficult to get into. Other popular majors include biochemistry, environmental studies and classics. Of course, there are also some majors which Tar Heels consider more "laughable," including economics and recreation.

As could be expected, most of the introductory classes at Carolina are fairly huge, with enrollments as high as 400. As students move into later years and their respective majors, however, class size decreases considerably to an average of 20. Additionally, opportunities for small class sizes exist during freshman year through the optional freshman seminars, each of which enroll about 12 students and examine such topics as "Slave Literature."

Whether their classes are large or small, most Tar Heels are quick to praise the excellence and helpfulness of their professors. One journalism major commented that "professors have been extremely accessible, even when there are 150 people in a class." This quality of interaction between the professors and students is certainly a determining factor for those deciding between a smaller college and this large university. With such low in-state tuition and the close instruction of notables like Greg Gangi, Conrad Neumann, and Chris Martens, UNC is an incredible deal. One junior who had faced the small liberal arts school vs. public university dilemma concluded that "the value and reputation of this school is a bargain you can't deny."

Sometimes, professors themselves lead the recitation sessions for large classes, but usually these sessions, which weekly divide large classes into smaller groups, are led by teaching assistants (TAs). Though TAs are not always the most inspiring bunch, many Tar Heels seem very satisfied with their level of instruction. One environmental studies major summed up her experience: "All the TAs have been extremely interested with the students and their doing well, and they've also been flexible with grading." This is a good thing, because A's don't come easy at UNC. Grade-inflation, an issue at many colleges, "seems non-existent" at Carolina. "If you get an A, people are like, 'Wow, good job!'"

UNC also works hard to provide its students with many opportunities for national and international research; as one junior said it, "they put a lot of importance on trying to get students to gain a broader perspective." A good number of students apply for the Burch Fellows Program, which is set up to fund selected student research proposals. In fact, one environmental studies major gushed about her opportunity to take scuba diving courses in preparation for her summer research project, for which she will "get paid and get credit for being on the beach and scuba diving!" An even larger percentage of students opt to study abroad, and UNC encourages this through its diverse array of programs and easy credit-transfers.

On Being a Southern Socialite

Of the more than 16,000 undergraduates at UNC, about 80 percent are residents of North Carolina, fulfilling the state's quota. This means that for out-of-staters, gaining acceptance to Carolina is extremely competitive. As one junior from Tennessee said, "at the beginning of the semester when you are introducing yourself to the class there are almost always gasps from people when they hear you are out-of-state.

This is quickly followed by, 'You must be smart.'"

As far as stereotypes go, UNC students agree that the preppy Tar Heel is "pretty prominent." In comparing UNC to some of its neighbors, one student commented, "Duke is brainy, NC State is more for hicks, and UNC is preppy." Although typical Tar Heels are decidedly "upper-middle-class, white, skinny blond girls and guys with polo shirts," one student also noted that "every other [kind of] person is represented. . . . Carolina is a huge melting pot." Additionally, Tar Heels are known to be very friendly, engaging, and bubbling over with that Southern charm. "Everybody is on the up-and-up and folks aren't too worried about over-working and not having a good time. . . . It's a mix of the well-balanced individual and well-rounded friend that really defines the student population."

> "Everybody is on the up-and-up and folks aren't too worried about over-working and not having a good time."

According to the common conception, the social life at UNC is best defined by its Greek scene. And indeed, while only 20 percent of the campus is officially involved in a sorority or fraternity, "the Greeks like to think they're very big." Carolina's Greek life is very vibrant, with four main party nights a week (Tuesday, Thursday, Friday and Saturday) and numerous on-campus hangouts. For many, the Greek system is a convenient and fun way to make this huge school more intimate. As one frat brother commented, "It has been a great way for me to scale down the size of the school. For me, UNC is a school of about 1,000 people."

While some say that going Greek is "the best decision I've made since coming to Carolina," others emphasize that they've "never felt pressured into anything to make friends." One student recalls freshman year, when she had "two suitemates who did the sorority thing and would come home at 3 a.m. drunk, while the rest of us were watching movies." For those who don't opt for the Greek life, friends made in freshman dorms are often pals that stick around for the next four years. While it is hard to meet and sustain relationships through classes, social events put on by dorms are often great meeting places, as are events initiated by various clubs and organizations. Students agree that there is a social group that caters to anyone's definition of "having fun."

All the same, fun at Carolina often includes drinking. Reportedly, the ALE (Alcohol Law Enforcement) only busts obvious acts of stupidity, and these often only during first weeks of each semester. The off-campus scene can be somewhat stricter on alcohol, but even then only moderately. Nearby spots such as Bob's, Treehouse, The Library, W.B. Yeats, "La Rez," "Top O" and Spanky's are popular choices for late nights, as is the non-alcoholic Carolina Coffee Shop.

Wide Open Spaces and Living Places

UNC's campus in Chapel Hill is breathtakingly beautiful, with lawns that seem to stretch forever and Georgian buildings reminiscent of the 'Gone with the Wind' days. Characterized by three main campuses, UNC makes plenty of room for dormitories and student life buildings without sacrificing a classic, centralized atmosphere.

While a large number of Tar Heels move off-campus after freshman year, over 40 percent of students choose to live on campus. South Campus is home to the majority of on-campus students, as it has four high-rise, suite-styled dorms and four newer buildings with hall layouts. The older dorms, whose suite configurations make for tight quarters but seem to be "more conducive to making friends," are Hinton James (aka "Australia," as it's the farthest away from central campus), Craig, "E-Haus" (housing mainly sophomores) and Morrison. The latter, while known as the "party dorm," is also known for its renovation schedule: by the end of 2006, Morrison should be converted into apartment-style housing.

As one student observed, "once you're on South Campus, it's a little bit hard to leave." Upon matriculating, students can indicate housing preferences, including whether they'd like to live on Central, North or South campus. Although 10 percent of each UNC dorm is reserved for freshmen, most first-years get sent down under. One year later, upon using the seniority-based online housing system, South Campus residents find it can be hard to move with buddies from the most populated campus to one with more restricted housing. Therefore, to stay near friends, many students choose to remain on South Campus.

Partially because of Carolina's ban on providing parking for freshmen, some freshmen choose to live off-campus from the beginning, usually selecting Granville Towers as their makeshift "dorm." This independent, student-only apartment complex has AC (an amenity lacking in un-renovated dorms) and provides a personal parking spot for each resident. Besides freshmen, many transfer students also call Granville their UNC home. Granville residents often use the Franklin Street off-campus meal plan, which all students who frequent the street's many restaurants can purchase independently.

While there are only two dining halls on campus, they both offer a plethora of dining options. At either location students can purchase block meals of all-you-can-eat cafeteria fare, or flex dollars to be used at the various fast food eateries nestled inside the buildings. Students are most compelled to purchase the all-you-can-eat plan because of the socialization, though it's been said that "the food's not bad."

Nearby the two dining halls is the central cluster of the University. The main convening area, known as "The Pit," is the gathering place for any and all activists, whether they are promoting their clubs or raising money for a worldwide charity. Right next door is the hub of student activity, The Union. With its student government offices, computer clusters, bowling alley, coffee bar, study rooms, and various organizational headquarters, The Union is the hot spot for all types of Tar Heels.

Basketball and Other Attractions

It seems redundant to say, but the UNC Tar Heels are "seriously proud." With outstanding men's basketball and women's soccer teams, varsity sports at Carolina are "really exciting and definitely a source of pride for the school. . . . They create a lot of unity, and are great conversation starters."

A common conversation begins with, "Have you got tickets?" Because of the outlandishly high demand, students must get tickets through a lottery system where they "camp out at the Dean Dome, get a wristband, stand in line, watch a magic number get pulled, then get up the next day at 6:30." While there is not quite the same demand for other varsity games, women's basketball games, soccer, football, fencing and crew all draw a lot of fans—especially for matches against archrivals Duke and NC State. Most recently, the Tar Heels celebrated a victory over Duke in the 2004–2005 Carlyle Cup.

Even if they're not playing a varsity sport, most students at UNC are decidedly athletic. The Student Recreation Center, which offers free classes in everything from yoga to kick-boxing, is "always packed with people." While many Tar Heels choose to keep up their fitness by themselves, the rest are actively involved in junior varsity, club or intramural sports, all of which are popular.

Tar Heels put just as much energy into their various extracurriculars as they do into their athletics. One look into "The Pit" will satiate any cravings for community service, and a stroll through The Union shows off the *Daily Tar Heel*, literary magazines, theater groups, and even the Pirate Club. As one student commented, if the club "is not there, it's easy to make it up."

UNC is filled with opportunity, tickled with activity, and heaped with tradition. A beautiful, inspiring campus and small bill are just the beginnings of Carolina's path to academic excellence, international experience and incredible cohesiveness. And, don't forget the basketball.—*Elizabeth Dohrmann*

FYI

If you come to UNC, you'd better bring "a Carolina-blue shirt."
What's the typical weekend schedule? "Study, eat ALL over, party with friends."
If I could change one thing about UNC, I'd "create more parking!"
Three things every student at UNC should do before graduating are "see Carolina win a championship, experience Franklin Street, and sit in the pit."

Wake Forest University

Address: Wake Forest, PO Box 7305, Winston-Salem, NC 27109
Phone: 336-758-5201
E-mail Address: admissions@wfu.edu
Web site URL: www.wfu.edu/admissions
Year Founded: 1834
Private or Public: private
Religious affiliation: none
Location: suburban
Regular Application Deadline: 15-Nov
Number of Applicants: 7,484
Percent Accepted: 38.5%
Percent Accepted who enroll: 38.8%
Number Entering: 1,171
Number of Transfers Accepted each Year: varies
Mean SAT: NA
Mean ACT: NA

Middle 50% SAT range: 1,260–1,410
Middle 50% ACT range: NA
Early admission program (EA/ ED/ NA): ED
ED or EA Acceptance Rate: 34%
Full time Undergraduate enrollment: 4,138
Total enrollment: 6,716
Percent Male: 49%
Percent Female: 51%
Total Percent Minority: 14.7%
Percent African-American: 7%
Percent Asian/Pacific Islander: 4%
Percent Hispanic: 2%
Percent Native-American: 0.4%
Percent Other: 0.6%
Percent in-state / out of state: 28%/72%

Percent from Public HS: 66%
Retention Rate: 94%
Graduation Rate: 88%
Percent in On-campus housing: 71%
Percent affiliated with Greek system: 43%
Percent Varsity or Club Athletes: 19%
Number of official organized extracurricular organizations: 160+
3 Most popular majors: Business, Political Science, Communication
Student/Faculty ratio: 10:01
Tuition and Fees: $32,140.00
Cost for Room and Board: $8,800.00
Percent receiving Financial aid, first-year: 75%

Nestled in Winston-Salem, N.C., is Wake Forest University, a small private university whose spirit and resources rival its larger neighbors UNC-Chapel Hill and Duke. Wake Forest's undergraduate population of about 4,000 students reaps the benefits of close contact with a celebrated roster of professors and the glory of their Division I basketball team, while enjoying a beautiful campus. Wake students, known for an abundance of school spirit, play a crucial role in maintaining Wake Forest's position as one of the top universities in the state.

"Work Forest"

Wake Forest provides its students the perks of a larger university, in a more intimate academic environment suitable for the small undergraduate body. Class size, once past introductory lectures, is typically around 20 students. This intimate class size allows Wake Forest professors to cultivate intimate relationships with students and provide more individual attention. And with professors as prestigious as Maya Angelou, who teaches a popular poetry class, who can blame students for wanting more one-on-one time?

While professors allot a great deal of attention to their students, they also have high expectations. Wake Forest isn't known as "Work Forest" without good reason. Attendance and participation are significant factors in one's grade, so students must make a valiant effort in all of their classes. Professors are known for expecting a high level of preparedness. According to one student, some professors even "require an above average amount of work just to basically pass the course." The intimate academic setting makes it difficult to just slip by without notice, but Wake students agree the rewards are well worth the extra work.

Keeping with the "no pain, no gain" work mentality, the Calloway School of Business and Accountancy boasts a strong reputation and makes business one of Wake's most popular majors. But, it is also named one of the toughest majors, along with any of the sciences. Following in popularity are political science and communications. Many Wake students enter the pre-med track, as well. For those students looking to avoid taking up residence in the library, communications, psychology and sociology may be the paths to take. And those looking to flee the country for a semester, year, or just the summer will be happy to hear that Wake's study abroad programs are hugely popular and are run in such locales as London, Beijing, Peru and Moscow. In fact, sometime within their four years, more than 50 percent of students take advantage of the study abroad program at the University.

Part of Wake's academic rigor stems from its extensive distribution requirements. Students are required to take three courses in each of four divisions: fine and performing arts; history, religion and philosophy; language and literature; and social and behavioral sciences. Freshmen are required to take a first-year seminar, and students must complete two courses in health and exercise science before graduation. While this system was implemented to ensure that students received a broad education in the liberal arts, many complain that fulfilling the requirements eats up a large portion of time and can have an impact on schedules even beyond sophomore year. Yet the general consensus is that "the requirements may be tough but they give you a good base." This sentiment reflects the overall Wake attitude toward academics—in the end, the effort students put in is well rewarded.

Kiss Me, I'm Greek!

When it's time to put aside the books, students turn to the Greek system, which dominates the social scene. One student explained that, "The Greek system IS life, and almost everyone at least tries to rush." An estimated 50 percent of the student population is involved in the Greek system, and up to 65 percent rush at some point in their four years. A major event each semester is pledge night. Freshmen rushing a sorority or fraternity are required to run around campus kissing as many people as possible, while keeping track of their make-out madness in a notebook. Although fraternities do not actually have houses, they have specific sections of dorms set aside for them and "lounges" in those areas are designated for parties open to the entire campus. Typical weekends revolve around frat parties, and students will party from one frat's lounge to the next. Wednesday, Friday and Saturday nights are the main nights for going out. During the fall, students tailgate with the intensity of a larger state school thanks largely to their Division I status.

> "The Greek system IS life, and almost everyone at least tries to rush."

Students find that drinking is inevitably tied up with pledging a fraternity or sorority and Greek life in general. According to one fraternity brother, "Drinking is the primary activity of Wake Forest social life." The administration has reacted to this and has begun to come down on fraternities in particular. Many of the frats found themselves on probation for one reason or another during the past two years, which lead some of the weekend partying to move to off-campus locations. Nevertheless, for now frats continue to occupy the dominant campus social scene. And although there are regulations for drinking on campus and in dorms, residential advisors generally leave students alone unless they are disturbing others.

The social scene can seem very exclusive to those not involved in Greek life, but the school's budget for extracurricular activities is large. There are numerous clubs and groups satisfying almost every interest. And if you happen to find yourself without an extracurricular outlet, procuring a charter and funding for a new group is not difficult. The administration has attempted to host some social events—a recent and popular addition to the scene is Shag on the Mag, a themed dance. Unfortunately, Winston-Salem does not offer much in the way of alternatives to an on-campus scene. There are some bars, but they don't garner much traffic on weekends from Wake students. However, the city does provide a variety of restaurants popular with the undergraduate community.

Amenities, Please

Most students find residential life at Wake Forest satisfying. Dorms are characterized as "kind of old" and "small" but also "a lot of fun." Freshmen and sophomores are required to live on campus. In addition to the generic dorm, Wake also provides theme housing that creates an environment for people sharing particular extracurricular interests. For example, the Environmental House emphasizes environmentally friendly living and learning. No theme that appeals to you? Applications can be made for new theme housing. A great deal of Greek brothers move into their fraternity's section on campus, and one brother commented that he "had a blast living there." By senior year, though, many students move off campus into the numerous and inexpensive apartment complexes available. Off-campus living is facilitated by the fact that students are allowed cars all four years—and it is well advised to take advantage of that policy. Very few off-campus venues are within walking distance and there is a lack of public transportation. While complaints about public transportation are common, students give compliments of the campus facilities, including the top of the line athletic buildings. Campus technology is cutting edge, too. According to the school's Web site, "Upon enrollment students receive a ThinkPad and HP color printer/scanner/copier; computers are upgraded after two years and become the student's property upon graduation." As for the food, students say it's "not bad." There are two cafeterias on campus—the main one recently renovated in the summer of 2005. For hungry boys and girls, buffet-style options are available in the dining plan.

"Rolling the quad"

While the student body is deemed "friendly" and "approachable," it is also somewhat homogeneous. Most people are described as "white and preppy" and generally economically well-off. Students complain that diversity is somewhat lacking on campus and there is not much intermixing among various groups. In fact, students have been characterized as what one junior referred to as "cliquey." Nonetheless, approximately 14 percent of the student body is composed of multicultural students. And on a positive note, one student noted that, "There are rarely any racial problems and people are pretty appreciative of other cultures."

One common thread running throughout all Wake Forest students is the enormous amount of school spirit that is arguably disproportionate to their school's size. This can be attributed in part to Wake's status as a Division I school. The field hockey team has won numerous national championships and the football team is always competitive and well followed, if not wildly successful. And the Demon Deacons always come out in full force for the celebrated basketball team. Wake Forest basketball is consistently ranked in the top 25 and has prominent alumni such as NBA stars Tim Duncan, Josh Howard and Chris Paul. Students make an effort to attend games, which are held just a few minutes from campus. After each major athletic team win, students come back to campus and "roll the quad." All the students grab rolls of toilet paper and throw it all over the trees and cover the entire campus in mounds of Charmin. The enthusiasm of Wake students for academics and extracurriculars plays a key role in keeping Wake Forest unique.—*Janet Yang*

FYI

If you come to Wake Forest, you'd better bring "enthusiasm—we love our school!"

The typical weekend schedule is "get out of class, meet up, and start boozing with buddies, go out, pass out, wake up and sober up a little, then start all over again. Leave all your work until Sunday morning . . . eh afternoon . . . eh probably night."

If I could change one thing about Wake Forest, I'd "make it less Greek and less preppy."

Three things every student should do before graduation are "find the underground tunnel system, participate in pledge night, go to as many basketball games as possible."

North Dakota

Nestled along the banks of the Red River and on the periphery of the growing city of Grand Forks lies the University of North Dakota (UND). Already acclaimed for its fantastic aeronautics and technology programs, the school is continually improving its respectable facilities and faculty, as well as expanding the opportunities it offers to its students, both in the classroom and out. The University of North Dakota recently completed the Ralph Engelstad Arena, which is known on campus as "one of the best places to watch and play hockey in the world." The school has also raised new buildings for a variety of academic departments. UND seems to be on the cusp of a dynamic and exciting future, one in which the school will continue to play an ever-larger role in its community and in the world.

Academics Take to New Heights

The University of North Dakota has 10 colleges and 193 programs of study. In the College of Arts and Sciences, which enrolls about a quarter of the University's undergraduates, students can major in a variety of liberal arts fields. Some of UND's most popular courses of study include communications, nursing, and the health sciences. However, what truly separates UND from the rest of the crowd is the John D. Odegard School of Aerospace Science, touted by many as "the most technologically advanced collegiate environment for aerospace in the world." Students can major in any number of unique fields, including commercial aviation, airport management, and air traffic control. Students first go to "ground school" where they take classes in the mechanics of flying, aerodynamics, and regulations before they are paired one-on-one with flight instructors. Afterwards, the students take to the sky from the Grand Forks Airport, learning maneuvers in the air and going through takeoff and landing procedures at practice fields nearby or satellite airports as far away as Minnesota. Regardless of which school students are enrolled in, they must take courses in four core groups: communications; social sciences; arts and humanities; and mathematics, science and technology, in addition to requirements for their individual majors.

Class size never gets out of hand. According to one student, "Sometimes, I won't get into a particular section for a class, but I'm never not allowed to take the class at all because of the number of people taking it." Indeed, introductory lecture courses in the sciences may be home to around 150 to 200 students each day, but some upper-level courses and discussion classes sometimes don't make it above 10 students. Indeed, one of the assets to UND's curriculum is its favorable environment for lots of student-teacher interaction. One student explained that this was also attributable to the fact that the professors don't usually assign lots of work, preferring that their students "learn directly through discussion and contemplation." TAs offer additional help when the professor is not available, leading lab recitations and review sessions for those still struggling with yesterday's lecture.

Students who want to challenge themselves more with advanced work can apply for acceptance into the UND's Honors Program. The Program offers small, interdisciplinary classes and close faculty advising. Outside of the academic realm, the Honors Program Student Organization (HPSO) arranges trips, service projects, and a special publication for participating students. Special Honors housing is also available in the wings of two residence halls.

Winter Wonderland

In the winter, the UND campus looks like the North Pole. With temperatures dipping some 20 or 30 below zero coupled with significant snowfall, it's no wonder that the weather is the one thing many UND students want to change about their campus. However student perceptions of the wintry weather differ: "For out-of-state students who are used to a warmer climate, the winter may be a shock, but for North Dakotans and Minnesotans, it is nothing new," explained one student. According to one sophomore, the school has few underground tunnels to

provide protection from the elements and only a number of "plug-ins" that students can use to prevent their cars from freezing in the parking lot. However, in the spring, the landscape of UND changes completely. After the snow has melted, the groundskeepers plant "huge amounts of flowers."

Something Old, Something New . . .

Spread out on a stretch of the flattest land imaginable, the campus of the University of North Dakota is relatively small for a state school, requiring about 15 to 20 minutes to walk from one end to the other. The older buildings (including Merrifield Hall) are in matching brick and cluster around the center of campus. Although some of the facilities are fairly old, they aren't antiquated. One junior explained "they're still very clean and comfortable, and the school has been upgrading classes with multimedia equipment." Juxtaposed with these buildings are the more modern, glass-laden Aerospace complex buildings.

Students generally agree that the school's library system gives an adequate collection of publications, including special collections with historical records of North Dakota. The school recently launched a new online library system, making its resources more accessible to the student body. Students often go to the library of their particular department for serious studying. The second floor of the recently renovated Memorial Union Student Center is another hotspot for brushing up on one's academic pursuits.

Options Galore

Freshmen are not required to live on campus, and a substantial number of undergraduates choose to live off campus. Many opt to live just west of the UND campus or in the reasonably-priced apartments that can be found downtown. Those who choose to remain in the dorms are usually given suites, with three or four people sharing one bathroom. Though only available to upperclassmen, students mention "Swanson is by far the most comfortable dorm." Swanson has a glass elevator, bathrooms in every room, and a system that allows resident students to buzz in their guests. Each dorm also houses RAs who are said to vary in terms of strictness to UND policy. Most students find them to be "welcoming and friendly," though some are inevitably "too strict."

UND has 15 residence halls, most of which are connected to one of three dining halls. The university is also opening a new apartment-style facility in the fall of 2007. Students agree that the attitude toward the school food is bipolar: either students love it or they hate it. Those opting to live in campus dorms must purchase a meal plan; for those living off campus who decide to go without one, the choices are several local coffee shops such as the Wings Airport Café, few convenience stores and the Memorial Union Student Center, which houses a food court, ping-pong and pool tables, an arcade, and a lounge area. One of the most attractive qualities about UND, according to the students, is the feeling of safety on campus. The school provides a police force, emergency phones, and an escort service for its students. The down-to-earth atmosphere of medium-size Grand Forks adds to a strong feeling of closeness and community between the students of UND and locals.

Hockey on Center Stage

UND's University Program Council works very hard to provide quality social activities to the students and sponsors performances at the Chester Fritz Auditorium by musicians such as Reba McEntire and Travis Tritt. They also sponsor what is known as the Spring Concert, which has hosted such bands as Blues Traveler and Incubus. Council members also sponsor movie nights and a coffee bar at the Memorial Student Center. In addition, there are many places for students to hang out and get a bite to eat in Grand Forks. The most popular by far is a small "hole-in-the-wall" restaurant called the Red Pepper. Serving tacos and grinders, the students rave about the quality of the food and also the college-student-friendly prices it offers. Another popular place for students to eat is the local Applebee's, which offers buy-one-get-one-free appetizers if the UND hockey team won their game that night.

Much of the social life at UND revolves around attending the school's sports games. With the completion of the Ralph Engelstad Arena, every hockey game is sold out with 11,500 screaming students, faculty, and locals. Hockey attracts the biggest crowds when facing UND's chief rival, the University of Minnesota at Minneapolis. Other successful teams include men's and women's swimming, basketball, women's hockey and football. A large portion of students also participate in intramural tennis, soccer, basketball, and volleyball.

Those seeking social activity outside of the athletic scene also have options; "one doesn't have to look too hard to find a party every weekend," said one student. Students above the drinking age usually go to Whitey's, Cuckoo's Nest, Sledster's, Bonzer's, or El Roco, for a pitcher of beer. While the University is officially a dry campus, frats that decide to hold parties with alcohol can do so if they hire security guards to prevent underage drinking. Each year UND students look forward to the Springfest celebration, a party of over 5,000 students ("many of whom have a beer in their hand, or hands") that is held in University Park at the end of Spring term.

> **"At a party, it isn't unusual for two people who barely know each other through class to hit it off and spend the rest of the night hanging out,"**

Students describe their peers as friendly and open. "At a party, it isn't unusual for two people who barely know each other through class to hit it off and spend the rest of the night hanging out," said one student. Though the University enrolls nearly 13,000 students, the affable student body helps create a distinct sense of community.

The Great Balancing Act

Outside of partying, UND offers more than 220 chartered organizations on campus. Particularly popular among students is the Wilderness Pilots Club and Sioux Crew, a group dedicated to supporting UND's athletic teams. Others write for the *Dakota Student*, a biweekly campus newspaper with a weekly A&E section. Students can also participate in student government or the University Program Council. Large numbers of students are also part of the school's many musical extracurriculars, including the Men and Women's Choirs, the Concert Choir, the UND Orchestra, the Drum Band, and many others. The highest student involvement reportedly occurs with clubs that are associated with particular majors, including the Engineer's Council and the Medical School Club. An annual program called the Big Event allows students to reach out to the community through a wide range of service projects.

UND places a large emphasis on the health of its students. As one student said, "Athletics is what it is all about up here." The Hyslop Sports Center attracts many students who want to unwind after a long day of classes or just keep fit. It includes an indoor track, an Olympic-sized swimming pool, dance and aerobic classes, and an extensive exercise room with modern equipment. In addition, the University is opening the doors to a 106,000-square-foot Welness Center. This new building is designed to provide active learning opportunities in "the multiple dimensions of wellness." Amenities include such things as a suspended running track, three wood-floor courts, a Pilates/yoga studio, a meditation lounge, a nutrition bar, a massage studio, and much more.

UND is a fast-growing university, a school with potential that more than compensates for the ice-cold temperatures that it endures in the winter months. UND students come out well-prepared and eager to face whatever storminess they may encounter in the outside world. They've taken on the elements already.—*Darrick Li*

FYI
If you come to UND, you'd better bring "a snowsuit and hockey equipment."
What is the typical weekend schedule? "Party, go to the hockey game, party, recover."
If I could change one thing about UND, I'd "try to build a more diverse student body, geographically and ethnically. Oh, and build more tunnels for us in the winter."
Three things that every student at UND should do before graduating are "go to a hockey game, go fishing in the Red River, and go to the Red Pepper."

Ohio

Antioch College

Address: Antioch, 795 Livermore Street, Yellow Springs, OH 45387
Phone: 937-769-1100
E-mail Address: admissions@antioch-college.edu
Web site URL: http://www.antioch-college.edu
Year Founded: 1852
Private or Public: private
Religious affiliation: none
Location: rural
Regular Application Deadline: Rolling
Number of Applicants: 368
Percent Accepted: 60%
Percent Accepted who enroll: 15%
Number Entering: 46
Number of Transfers Accepted each Year: 43
Mean SAT: NA
Mean ACT: NA

Middle 50% SAT range: 1,050–1,310 (writing was not included here)
Middle 50% ACT range: 22–27
Early admission program (EA/ ED/ NA): EA
ED or EA Acceptance Rate: NA
Full time Undergraduate enrollment: 558
Total enrollment: 591
Percent Male: 32%
Percent Female: 68%
Total Percent Minority: 46%
Percent African-American: 7%
Percent Asian/Pacific Islander: 4%
Percent Hispanic: NA
Percent Native-American: NA
Percent Other: 35%
Percent in-state / out of state: 33%/77%
Percent from Public HS: NA

Retention Rate: 60%
Graduation Rate: 64%
Percent in On-campus housing: 95%
Percent affiliated with Greek system: 0%
Percent Varsity or Club Athletes: NA
Number of official organized extracurricular organizations: 16
3 Most popular majors: Area and Ethnic Studies, Interdisciplinary Studies, Liberal Arts
Student/Faculty ratio: 8:01
Tuition and Fees: $27,212.00
Cost for Room and Board: $7,004.00
Percent receiving Financial aid, first-year: 93%

Antioch students are known for their love of a good argument. Their campus, located in Yellow Springs, Ohio, is always politically charged, and its students are always ready to push the envelope, whether they're exploring "radical research on gender" at an annual drag-themed dance party or protesting the new president's curriculum reform. But all Antioch students agree their school is all the richer for its quirks and its conflicts. One freshman summed up his school like this: "Antioch is a strange, strange place...but wonderful nonetheless."

Growing Pains

The college, which implemented a new academic system and saw the arrival of a new president in fall of 2005, is undergoing what one student referred to as "a major period of transition." New academic guidelines have shifted its focus slightly, with 122 credits needed to graduate and only three required terms in the co-op program. The new academic system consists of "learning communities," in which a chosen set of professors teach a set of classes focused on a certain subject or area. The idea is to unite professors in an interdisciplinary course of study and to promote a core of classes. Yet some students feel that not all professors have responded enthusiastically to the curriculum changes.

"Things are shifting," explained one senior. "A lot of professors aren't entirely pleased with the new academic system. Some of them aren't so keen on participating in it, and we're having a bit of an exodus of professors."

Despite this, many feel that Antioch's changing academic landscape renders it an even more exciting place to spend four years than it was prior to the revamping. "Antioch is changing right now, really quickly," said one senior. "The people who go to this school will have a chance to determine where it goes. If you want to be involved in the rebuilding of a school, the change of an entire academic structure where the community is strong, this is the place to go."

"Co-op"-erating

Antioch students agree that one of their school's most unique features is its cooperative education program, designed to give students an opportunity to travel and live independently while still in college. Experiences during co-op term have ranged from helping to run a San Francisco-based theater company to working as a case manager at a mental health residential treatment facility in Pittsburgh to teaching English as a second language at a high school in Chicago. The entire program focuses on the idea of going out into an environment that is utterly unfamiliar.

While the college maintains a list of jobs and opportunities, much of the responsibility for ensuring the program's success lies with the students themselves. The experience was described by one senior as "almost being thrown to the wolves to a certain extent. They don't really help you find housing or adjust to the area at all, although not all of the jobs require you to go out and find your own place." Part of the school's new program, however, has established "co-op communities" in Ohio, New Mexico and Washington, D.C. These areas enable students to take jobs near groups of other Antioch students and thus act as a sort of support system for each other as they settle in to their temporary homes and communities.

No grades? No problem!

Like everything else about Antioch, academics at the school are unique. In place of letter grades, students receive "narrative evaluations" in their courses. Professors are amenable to providing students with letter grades upon request, but most students say that their peers rarely use this option. This laid-back approach has its benefits and its drawbacks. Some students find that, at times, the pressure-free atmosphere goes hand in hand with a certain laziness for some of their classmates.

"The system really draws people who may not have necessarily done so well in high school, because they weren't moti-

vated by the way a traditional high school works. But they're very bright people, and Antioch is a place with a lot of bright, critical thinkers," said one senior. "Whether they choose to use that or not...that's another matter."

Another student singled out Antioch's size, and in particular the extremely intimate size of the average class, as one of the highlights of attending the school. "Most classes are very small," he said. "If any class is larger than 12 students, I feel like that's too large."

Aside from the environmental studies department and the women's studies department, both popular in a student body known for its liberal, socially and environmentally conscious students, majors in the excellent communications department are the most popular. Antiochians are fond of saying that one of their communications professors, Anne Bohlen, "taught Michael Moore how to use a camera."

Costume Parties: What a Drag

Perhaps because few students have cars and because the town of Yellow Springs offers few opportunities for party-seekers, most students said that the social scene on weekends consists entirely of parties on-campus. Antioch students are generally as laid-back about their partying as they are about grades.

Students frequent the costume parties held in the student union each weekend; themes have ranged from "Cowboys and Robots" to "Mystery Prom" to "Jet-Setting Socialites A-Go-Go" to "That's Amazing...and Disgusting," for which past revelers have come attired in cellophane or even chocolate pudding. Another perennial favorite is "Gender F**k," an exploration ("it's become more than just a drag ball") of the more radical ideas on gender that "encourages gender-bending to the extreme" and for many students embodies the open, accepting and ever-inquiring nature of Antioch students regarding their own sexuality. "I think every Antioch student spends some time questioning, 'What gender am I? Am I really male?'" said one student. "This is also a very open community when it comes to transgender students. It's not uncommon to come back to school and see that someone has gotten a sex change."

Aside from these costume parties, however, the social scene on-campus is relatively easy-going and for the most part consists of gathering in friends' rooms or on The Stoop, a popular gathering place near the student union, to drink or smoke. Students described the presence of alcohol and some drugs on-campus, either due to administration policy or due to the make-up of the student body, as a relatively strong force in everyday life. One senior claimed that it was hard to stay away from the drug scene when living on campus, and that at least one student he knew had moved off campus to avoid that aspect of the social scene.

> **"It's not uncommon to come back to school and see that someone has gotten a sex change."**

Another student, however, said that regardless of the school's lenient alcohol policy, no Antioch student had ever gone to the hospital in her time there and that drugs were easy to avoid. "I do drink, but I don't feel pressured in the slightest," said one freshman.

Passionate About Politics
In general, students feel that the stereotypical Antioch student is defined not by how they he or she to party on the weekends—and certainly not by his or her athletic prowess. One student cited school shirts emblazoned with the slogan, "Antioch College: no football since 1929" as an example of the way the school's lack of interest in athletics "is almost a source of pride" on-campus. Rather, Antioch students feel that they are defined by their passions—and usually, by their liberal politics.

One senior described the classic Antioch student as "either the idealistic hippie who spends all their time in the garden talking about auras or the black-clad, angry liberal," while another joked that "if you go to Antioch, you have a few piercings and tattoos and have probably either colored or entirely shaved off your hair at least once in the past year." But all agreed that Antioch students are "ultra, ultra, ultra liberal" and that they love to debate, complain and protest for the causes about which they feel strongly.

"Any conservative who comes onto campus is pretty quickly driven off," said one student. "People just get so emotional and energetic about their causes and issues, and that's great to see. But sometimes it can end up as these constant clashes be-

tween people and personalities, and it can get extremely uncomfortable." Despite students' concerns with political issues and social injustice, however, one senior girl described the student body as "pretty white."

Perhaps due to the nature of Antioch's community, where "you pretty much know everyone" and everyone's ready to speak their mind and get into a debate with anyone else who does so, few students choose to move off campus at any point in their four years.

From "The Caf" to a Castle
In addition to the school's academic infrastructure, the physical campus is currently undergoing a transformation as well, with only three housing buildings open during the 2006-07 school year. Freshmen and seniors speak of the campus's 140-year-old main building, Antioch Hall, with awe and affection. It was described by one student as "a red brick castle-like building with a copper roof" and praised for "the really amazing view" from its towers by another. The student union, affectionately known as "the Caf," received fewer rave reviews; while one girl maintained that "it's getting a lot better" and another freshman praised "the vegan brownies," students agree that the food (and the hours of operation) are less than ideal.

Aside from the cafeteria, however, the student union is spoken of as a fairly popular gathering place, with one senior singling out the graffiti space in the top floor smoking lounge—one senior estimated that 70% of the campus smokes—as a favorite hangout spot.

Despite the amenities on campus, however, one senior recommends bringing a car as a means of occasional escape. "People can go so insane being around the same people on campus all the time," he said. "Bring a car or find a friend who has one pretty soon, so you're not always there in the whirlwind of Antioch drama."

In the end, students concur that "Antioch drama" is part of what makes their school such an unusual and one-of-a-kind place to spend four years. "It can be hard sometimes because of the nomadic nature of Antioch's educational program, but I don't think I could have gone anywhere else," said one senior. And one senior pointed to a common practice among professors as revealing of Antioch's general

philosophy. "Professors are fine with you leaving to drive to Washington, D.C. for a protest," he said. "They honestly are more understanding about you going to a protest than about being sick. They want you to get out there and be political, because, after all...that's what Antioch's all about."
—*Angelica Baker*

FYI

If you come to Antioch, you'd better bring "cigarettes, a strong sense of self, and a backpack—I've basically lived out of a hiking backpack for the past two years.

What is the typical weekend schedule? "Pick up some beer from the local beer shop on Friday, go to the party later on, wake up and go to brunch on Saturday, watch a movie or go into town and thrift shop for your outfit for that night's party...then play pool until two or three in the morning and dance your butt off."

If I could change one thing about Antioch, I'd "give us an endowment so we could pay our professors well. So many things that are bad here, are bad because we're such a poor school."

Three things every Antioch student should do before graduating are "get really angry at a community meeting, go hardcore at Gender F**k, and drink the yellow spring water from the Glen."

Bowling Green State University

Address: Bowling Green, 110 McFall Center, Bowling Green, OH 43403
Phone: NA
E-mail Address: choosebgsu@bgnet .bgsu.edu
Web site URL: http://go2.bgsu.edu/choose/
Year Founded: 1910
Private or Public: public
Religious affiliation: none
Location: rural
Regular Application Deadline: 16-Jul
Number of Applicants: NA
Percent Accepted: 90%
Percent Accepted who enroll: 35%
Number Entering: NA
Number of Transfers Accepted each Year: NA
Mean SAT: NA

Mean ACT: 22
Middle 50% SAT range: 1,000–1,200
Middle 50% ACT range: 19–24
Early admission program (EA/ ED/ NA): EA
ED or EA Acceptance Rate: NA
Full time Undergraduate enrollment: 15,875
Total enrollment: 15,875
Percent Male: 45%
Percent Female: 55%
Total Percent Minority: 14%
Percent African-American: 9%
Percent Asian/Pacific Islander: 1%
Percent Hispanic: 3%
Percent Native-American: 1%
Percent Other: NA

Percent in-state / out of state: 91%/9%
Percent from Public HS: NA
Retention Rate: 76%
Graduation Rate: 34% in four, 60% in six
Percent in On-campus housing: 43%
Percent affiliated with Greek system: 19%
Percent Varsity or Club Athletes: NA
Number of official organized extracurricular organizations: 280
Most popular majors: Marketing, Psychology
Student/Faculty ratio: 19:01
Tuition and Fees: NA
Percent receiving Financial aid, first-year: 56%

Bowling Green is the internationally revered home of the World Tractor Pulling Championships. But, don't let that fool you into thinking that there are no intellectuals in the city. The town of Bowling Green provides the students of Bowling Green State University (BGSU) with an enriching location to pursue their liberal arts degree.

Practical Learning

Unlike many universities, Bowling Green started off as a teaching school for women, but has grown into eight colleges today, the largest still being the College of Education and Human Development. One student says that the most popular major is education because of the flexibility and breadth of the curriculum. But there are more than 200 majors and programs to choose from. Additionally, BGSU has a competitive honors program and corresponding honors housing, with opportunities for graduation or departmental honors through a senior project. Getting into classes is not typically regarded as a problem. One student noted that being shut out is particularly unlikely "if you get on waiting lists immediately and actually talk to people to get strings pulled."

BGSU takes a very global view. Each year about 275 students study abroad, with programs ranging from a full year to a few weeks. The school provides extensive support for studying abroad, with opportunities available at 30 sites in 30 countries; as part of the National Student Exchange Program with 173 other colleges, you can go almost anywhere your imagination takes you. To top it off, BGSU is a leading partner in the Washington Center internship program, which provides excellent chances for students to work or study around D.C.

Students are guaranteed at least one hands-on, practical experience related to their major, whether through a study abroad, internship, or research fellowship. One exciting addition is cooperative education, which students refer to as "earn-while-you-learn," allowing participants to earn an average of $11 per hour at over 900 companies, while working towards graduation.

Dance Marathon

There are more than 280 student organizations to get involved with at BGSU. And because all are student-run, if you don't find one that fits your niche, you can also start your own. For such ambitious types, the Undergraduate Student Government may be the perfect place to start. The student body elects the members of this student council, which voices student concerns to the University Board of Trustees and the Faculty Senate. The governor of Ohio also appoints one undergraduate to the University Board of Trustees each year.

Other activities include working for *BG News*, the campus daily published each week covering community and national developments. Students also help plan and carry out campus-wide events such as homecoming, family weekend, black history month, sibs—kids weekend, and the dance marathon. The 32-hour dance marathon fundraiser benefits Mercy Children's hospital, ultimately providing the funds for research, treatment, and equipment to kids all over Northwest Ohio who suffer from serious diseases. The completely student-run event can really show you the impact of community service while providing valuable professional experience.

Engineers, Photographers, and Hockey Players

More than 16,000 undergraduates attend BGSU, making it one of the larger public universities in the country. And like many public schools, only 13 percent are non-residents, with around 500 international students. And keep in mind that BGSU has a relatively homogenous student body, with about 14 percent minorities. When describing the student population, most regard their peers as laid-back and typically friendly. "There is a stereotype of the khaki-wearing prep here, but honestly, no one really cares," noted one undergraduate. Diversity is "present, but very minor," although multicultural organizations on campus thrive.

BGSU has 18 NCAA varsity sports, and is one of 13 schools in the country to compete in Division I-A football and Division I ice hockey and basketball. Club sports abound for the rest of the students, everything from rugby to water polo and synchronized skating. "There is a good amount of school spirit, and it's nice to see it," one undergraduate noted. "However, it's not overdone." Most students attend the annual football game against rival school University of Toledo, where one student insists, "You must get your picture taken with Freddy and Freida Falcon!"

Pretty but Pricey

Underclassmen must live on campus unless they commute from home. But residential life really is quite luxurious, albeit in a public school sense. Each dorm has a computer lab, with one computer available for every 23 students, and an Ethernet connection in each room. Interestingly, professors also teach classes and hold office in many dorms. There are seven residence halls, each with its own personality; for instance, Harshman Quadrangle is known for having lots of fire alarm pranks pulled. The only entirely freshman dorm is MacDonald, which one freshman says produces a lot of horror stories stemming from the less than luxurious living conditions. One student says the nicest dorms are Offenhauer and Founders, partly because they are the only ones with air conditioning.

The campus is located in the suburbs of Bowling Green, a quintessential small college town 20 miles south of Toledo, and within short distances to all major cities in Ohio. "BGSU has a nice, safe campus, and everything is within walking distance," says a freshman. Students tend to be pleased with the overall experience and appearance of campus. The trees and landscape are frequently praised, and while the weather is notorious for being bitter cold, students note the natural beauty of the area. An old cemetery marks the middle of campus, which most students find interesting and compelling. There is a myth regarding the ghost of a woman who haunts Hanna Hall, "Supposedly," one student reported, "the ghost must be invited to every theater production or something bad will happen during the play, so every year they personally invite her."

There's something to eat here for everyone. You can eat at one of the dining centers, countless restaurants, snack bars, or the student union. "The Union is the best choice, with Starbucks, Wendy's, and Steak Escape, what more could you want?" says a student. Several convenience stores like the GT Express and Chily's Express are great places to go for midnight snacks or food on the run. And if you get really hungry, head to Commons which has all-you-can-eat meals. But one student warns that the worst choice is MacDonald's dining center, which has the same food all the time.

Where Weekends are for More than Bowling

The fraternity and sorority scene at BGSU is quite big, with over 36 to choose from for the 19 percent of students that join. More than food, the student union is a place for political debates, business discussions, educational programs, chats over cappuccinos, and just your good old, dependable hangout. The arts also have a wide presence at the student union where you can go to laugh at comedians, listen to musical performances, and view the artwork of fellow students and faculty. The Lenhart Grand Ballroom is a great place for club ballroom dancing or campus-wide dance parties.

> "Our colors may be poop and orange, but we're really cool, I promise!"

While Bowling Green is a dry campus and the residential halls strictly enforce the rules, undergraduates observe that being underage isn't really a problem, with the help of a fake ID or an older friend. For BGSU students, weekends can mean almost anything: partying at a frat or private apartment or clubbing in either Bowling Green and nearby Toledo. Others looking for a relaxing night might try the 250-seat movie theater with a 20-foot screen and surround sound. And wrap up the night with a slice of pizza from the Zzas at The Falcon's Nest food court. Bowling Green is a high quality university with a great number of opportunities, be it academic, extracurricular, social, or just plain everyday living. "Our colors may be poop and orange," exclaimed one student, "but we're really cool, I promise!"—*Jerry Guo*

FYI

If you come to BGSU, you'd better bring "common sense."

What is the typical weekend schedule? "It starts on Thursday, and goes until early Monday morning. We have a lot of clubs and bars here, more than I can count. And you can *always* find a party within a few blocks from campus. We have a lot of student apartments around campus, so parties here are 24/7; you can find one anytime, day or night."

If I could change on thing about BGSU, I "wouldn't change anything, honestly, people have the freedom to do what they want and I like that freedom of choice."

Three things every student at BGSU should do before graduating are "join the Greek life because you will always having something to do on weekends, and get help with homework. Ride the elevators in University Hall and try to make it out alive. And get to know your professors. Most are very nice and want to get to know you."

Case Western Reserve University

Address: Case Western, 10900 Euclid Avenue, Cleveland, OH 44106
Phone: 216-368-2000
E-mail Address: admission@case.edu
Web site URL: www.case.edu
Year Founded: 1826
Private or Public: private
Religious affiliation: none
Location: urban
Regular Application Deadline: 16-Jan
Number of Applicants: NA
Percent Accepted: 67%
Percent Accepted who enroll: 20%
Number Entering: NA
Number of Transfers Accepted each Year: NA
Mean SAT: NA
Mean ACT: NA

Middle 50% SAT range: 1,230–1,430
Middle 50% ACT range: 26–31
Early admission program (EA/ ED/ NA): EA
ED or EA Acceptance Rate: NA
Full time Undergraduate enrollment: 3,998
Total enrollment: 3,998
Percent Male: 58%
Percent Female: 42%
Total Percent Minority: 24%
Percent African-American: 5%
Percent Asian/Pacific Islander: 17%
Percent Hispanic: 2%
Percent Native-American: 0%
Percent Other: NA
Percent in-state / out of state: 55%/45%

Percent from Public HS: NA
Retention Rate: 91%
Graduation Rate: 58% in four, 77% in six
Percent in On-campus housing: 79%
Percent affiliated with Greek system: 52%
Percent Varsity or Club Athletes: NA
Number of official organized extracurricular organizations: 120
Most popular majors: Biomedical Engineering, Business Administration
Student/Faculty ratio: 9:01
Tuition and Fees: $30,240.00
Percent receiving Financial aid, first-year: 62%

Case is a place that "makes you proud of being nerdy and allows you to explore interests you never knew you had." It is a small community of some of the most hardworking students in America, who play just as hard as they study. In many ways, Case Western is "your traditional geeky tech school." Yet, nestled near America's Rock and Roll Hall of Fame in Cleveland, Ohio, Case has a dynamic character that distinguishes it from its other "geeky tech" counterparts.

Sleep? What's That?

Prospective students, be warned: "This just isn't a place for people who are looking for a constant party." Forbes rated Case as having the second-hardest workload of any school, surpassed only by famously workaholic M.I.T., and this rating was validated by the students as "absolutely true." If you're interested in Case, be prepared for four rigorous years, filled with many late-night study sessions and serious cramming. One student claims that 3 a.m. is the earliest he ever goes to bed. This is most often true in the engineering and hard-science majors.

Engineers, pre-med students, and hard-science majors constitute a whopping 65-plus percent of the undergraduates at Case.

Nurses and small pockets of arts and humanities majors make up the rest of the 3,500-some undergraduates. Engineers are expected to fulfill many requirements, including as many as 10 specific classes, such as thermodynamics, which is "worthless, if you're a civil engineer." Some students feel that there are too many requirements for certain engineering majors. The arts and humanities departments are reportedly much more liberal in terms of requirements.

Although the students are of high caliber and very hardworking, they do not report feelings of competition among themselves. "Everyone's competing to do well, but you don't get the sense that people are out to do better than everyone else," one student said.

Students at Case are generally happy, but "it's also pretty common to hear people complaining," frequently about the workload. "This isn't a school where you'd be able to find a scene if you wanted to go out on a Tuesday night, not that most of our students want to, but not having the option to makes people a little cranky at times."

Case professors received mixed reviews from "great" and "accessible" to "never available" and "too into their research." One student claimed that he "never had a bad teacher," while another says that he has "had some good ones and some arrogant ones." One student said, "The freshmen teachers are phenomenal, very energetic and very accessible." No other teacher embodies this description more than the extraordinary Dr. Ignacio Ocasio, better known as Doc Oc, who teaches intro chemistry. He has the entire freshman class send in pictures of themselves upon acceptance to the school and puts them on his screen saver along with their names. "Before we even get to campus, regardless of whether or not you're in his class first semester, he knows your name." Besides trying to know each of his 350 students, he draws on technological resources to be accessible and helpful to all his students, like having his lectures videotaped and available on the Internet, along with snapshots of the chalkboard to capture class notes. Although Doc Oc is an extraordinary rarity, at Case approachability and helpfulness are traits particularly found among the first-year professors. However, one junior noted, "As you get into higher level courses, there seems to be a lack of personality." Still, "The teachers are very helpful, if you seek them out yourselves." At Case there does not seem to be any prevalence of foreign professors who do not speak English well, with the exception of some physics TAs.

Interested in the Greek Scene?

Beyond classes and long hours of grueling studying, a vibrant social scene which revolves largely around the fraternities and sororities lies within Case Western. Beware, however; if frat parties and Greek letters don't get you enthused, you might feel a bit left out. Although "Greeks" constitute only 30 percent of the student body, "Greek life severely dominates the social scene on-campus, even though the number [of participants] is relatively low." There is a Greek Life Office, which even has an extensive Web site accessible from the main Case Web site. One of the biggest events on campus is Greek Week, which is described as "an intra-brotherhood bonding experience, which promotes a competitive atmosphere between different Greek houses." The week-long event is filled with many lighthearted activities, such as a human pyramid, egg toss, can castle for charity, an obstacle course, a root beer chug, a variety show and the biggest event of all, the rope pull, which is played with trenches and a human weight limit of 1,700 lbs. There are many different fraterni-

ties, each with different personalities, and "people end up generally where they fit best." For instance, Phi Delta and Sigma Alpha Epsilon are known to have predominantly athletes, while Zeta Psi and Sigma Nu have more of the "involved and fun guys." Different sororities have their own stereotypes as well, but many find that "while the stereotypes exist for a reason, they aren't always true." The Greek parties, which dominate the social scene, seem to be a good time until they get busted. As one student said, "Most houses get in trouble for stupid things." Greek house parties are not permitted to have kegs or hard alcohol, but it is reportedly still relatively easy to find alcohol, especially if you know a fraternity brother.

With the exception of Homecoming games or any match against Carnegie Mellon, the Spartan teams generally do not draw a huge crowd. Some of the highly ranked women's teams like swimming and soccer seem a bit more popular, but typically the sports teams receive little attendance. On the other hand, intramural sports (particularly soccer, flag football, basketball and softball) are hugely popular, with 75 percent of undergraduates participating at one time or another.

> "[Case] makes you proud of being nerdy and allows you to explore interests you never knew you had."

For off-campus entertainment, Case is fortunately located on Cleveland's University Circle, a one-square-mile area that offers students a multitude of cultural opportunities at incredibly low prices (for example, tickets to professional plays are $10). Although Cleveland as a whole is not as exciting as one might expect, between downtown and University Circle Case enjoys a vibrant area that is very accessible and caters to students. During the whole first week of school, there is a big street carnival for the feast of the Assumption. In addition, one can visit the Cleveland Museum of Art, admire the city's botanical gardens, watch a performance in Cleveland's impressive theater district, go to the Natural History Museum, or listen to the famous Cleveland Orchestra in Severance Hall. Then one can head down to Little Italy for dinner and late-night doughnuts. Beyond the downtown area, however, is "fairly ghetto" and not particularly receptive towards students.

The Dating Scene: The Good, the Bad, and the Geeky

With the female-to-male ratio hovering at around 40:60, one would think that the Case women have somewhat of an advantage in the dating scene. However, considering that "a large portion of the guys are already in serious relationships with their video game consoles," the number of eligible men and women are much more even than expected, or perhaps disadvantaging to the females. "We lost tons of men to video and computer games," one female student said.

The dating scene at Case seems to favor more serious dating and long-term relationships rather than random hook-ups. "The 'hey, I met someone cute last night' scenario just doesn't come up very often," one junior said, with the exception of some freshmen girls being pursued by single upperclassmen. All in all, the dating pool is very limited. Case is a small enough community for students to become familiar with all the eligible men and women in very short time. Have no fear, though. The dating scene does serve its purpose. One upperclassman says that she knows of four girls already engaged, and over half of her friends are in serious relationships. "People usually complain about how awful the dating scene is, but when they finally land a relationship, they're the kind that last."

Living at Case

Students are required to live on campus for the first two years of school, unless they at home and commute. Recently, the University has been completely renovating and rebuilding all student dormitories, including the 1960s housing complex on North campus. The new North campus development will include apartment-style housing, a 1,200 car garage, and renovations to university-owned apartments. The completion of these North campus projects is expected to conclude in 2006.

Sophomores have the choice of moving into fraternity or sorority houses, or into suites on coed floors on the south side of campus with the rest of the non-Greek student body. In the spring of 2004 a $4 million renovation of the University East Building (which serves as both a residential and retail facility) was completed, which is the first stage of the University's plan to create a four-corner College Town District. Additional, in-progress University projects include the planning of a new campus center, an upgrade to the Emerson gym weight room, and planning for a media-vision laboratory and a new SAGES cyber café in Crawford Hall.

A huge plus about living at Case is that it caters to each student's personal needs. There are many living arrangements available including priority housing for gay students and married couples. As for dining at Case, it is "nothing to write home about, but enough variety to not make it mundane and horrible," serving your traditional non-spectacular, yet fulfilling college meals.

With top-notch academics, a thriving social scene and a plethora of extracurriculars to keep them busy, students agree there's never a dull moment at Case. If you're the "work hard, play hard, or even the party hard type," explained one student, "you can be sure you'll find your niche here."
—*Margaret Scotti*

FYI
If you come to Case, you'd better bring a "computer—it's required."
What is the typical weekend schedule? "Friday, get drunk and party; Saturday, sleep late, attend a study session, then party at night; Sunday, go to review sessions, study, and do homework."
If I could change one thing about Case, it would be "the five months of snow."
Three things every student at Case should do before graduating are "explore University Circle, participate in Greek Week, and attend the Brain Bowl, Case vs. Carnegie Mellon."

College of Wooster

Address: College of Wooster, 1189 Beall Ave., Wooster, OH 44691
Phone: 800-877-9905
E-mail Address: admissions@wooster.edu
Web site URL: www.wooster.edu
Year Founded: 1866
Private or Public: private
Religious affiliation: none
Location: suburban
Regular Application Deadline: 16-Feb
Number of Applicants: 2,504
Percent Accepted: 91%
Percent Accepted who enroll: 25%
Number Entering: 493
Number of Transfers Accepted each Year: 36
Mean SAT: 1,217
Mean ACT: 26

Middle 50% SAT range: 1,100–1,320
Middle 50% ACT range: 23–29
Early admission program (EA/ ED/ NA): ED
ED or EA Acceptance Rate: 91%
Full time Undergraduate enrollment: 1,792
Total enrollment: 1,819
Percent Male: 51%
Percent Female: 49%
Total Percent Minority: 12%
Percent African-American: 5%
Percent Asian/Pacific Islander: 3%
Percent Hispanic: 2%
Percent Native-American: 1%
Percent Other: 11%
Percent in-state / out of state: 40%/60%

Percent from Public HS: 73%
Retention Rate: 87%
Graduation Rate: 73%
Percent in On-campus housing: 98%
Percent affiliated with Greek system: 30%
Percent Varsity or Club Athletes: NA
Number of official organized extracurricular organizations: 100
3 Most popular majors: English, history, Psychology
Student/Faculty ratio: 01/01/04
Tuition and Fees: $30,060.00
Cost for Room and Board: $0.00
Percent receiving Financial aid, first-year: 82%

"T he best kept secret in America." That's how many College of Wooster students describe their school. A small liberal arts school of nearly 2,000 students founded in 1866, College of Wooster is nestled in a rural northern-Ohio town outside of Cleveland. It is proud of its academics, Scottish heritage, and "Pipe Band," though many students feel the college does not receive the attention and respect it deserves.

A+ Academics

The College of Wooster is extremely proud of its capstone program called independent study (IS). Each Wooster senior creates an original project—whether it be a research project, written work, exhibit, or performance—with the one-on-one support of a faculty member. As for majors, English, Music, Biology, and International relations all receive good reviews, while Theater, Philosophy, and Communications are viewed as some of the slacker majors. Requirements for majors fluctuate between seven to 13 credits. Some have a required study abroad component—a popular option among students—that is usually fulfilled through a larger American university.

In addition, Wooster requires its students to complete a set of core requirements that are rather lengthy, but for which "there is plenty of choice, and you can finish by the end of first semester sophomore year." First-year students complete small writing-intensive seminars (FYS), which are taught by the students' academic advisors for the year. One student felt that a writing seminar is "great because it teaches you to think and write at the college level."

The harshest academic criticism is heaped on the registration process. Students are randomly given a number (in a lottery-style process) and according to the number, allowed into the registration building. "At this point, we run around like crazy signing up for classes. If a class is full, it's full, and you can't take it. Political science and Religion classes are usually the first to go."

Once actually enrolled in classes, students cannot say enough about their professors and the academics. As one International Relations major put it, "The professors are what make this school." Another student described professors as "very approachable and extremely willing to help. Without grad students at the college, professors can focus 100 percent on undergraduate teaching in small class settings. It's wonderful." There are 133 full time faculty members and the ratio of students to faculty is 12 to 1. Seventy percent of the classes offered have less than

20 students, while "large" classes tend to have no more than 30 to 35 students. Some classes have TAs, but they are not a large part of the academic structure at the College of Wooster. Students certainly must work hard, but "the work load is adequate; nothing more than you can't handle."

> **"The professors are what make this school."**

Where's the Town? Let's Climb the Chapel and Take a Look

The campus is described as pretty and fairly large for the size of the student body. One student summed it up: "the administration seems to love fresh brick." Others like the green and the tree-lined paths "of a picturesque college." One student was quick to point out McGaw Chapel as one of Wooster's most interesting buildings. This completely white building, finished in 1971 and with a seating capacity of 1,600, was built partly underground and partly above ground; the construction was half-completed when bedrock was discovered, and construction could not be completed as planned. The "oddly shaped" building is loved by some and hated by others, but almost everyone admits that the views from its roof are worth a glimpse. It is the site of many college activities. Guest speakers who have talked there have included Senator Bill Bradley, political analyst George Will, author David Halberstam and filmmaker Michael Moore.

Dorms are considered "fairly nice" in general. Armington Hall and Douglass Hall are both all-freshmen dorms, but students warn that rooms in those buildings "are like closets." Many of the halls have recently been renovated. Freshmen also have the option of living in all but four of the other dorms on campus. Many of these other dorms are program dorms, with some harder to get into than others.

Examples of programs dorms include science and humanities, international, smoke-free, chemical-free, and quiet dorm. Bissman Hall houses many of the colleges Greek organizations. The picturesque Kenarden, which features beautiful interior and exterior architecture, and Luce Hall are favorites of many upperclassmen. Compton is the only all-female residence on campus. Besides having the option of entering the standard room draw or applying to one of the special program dorms, upperclassmen are able to apply to live in one of the small houses owned by the University. These "program houses" are available to groups of students who share a commitment to serving the community. Residents of each house work with a group such as Habitat for Humanity, Goodwill, Planned Parenthood, or Ohio Reads during the course of the year. In general, most students live in doubles, with a few getting singles and even fewer sharing triples.

When asked about food, one student enthusiastically revealed, "It is good, surprisingly." There are two main dining halls on campus. Kitteredge is considered the "No-Fry Zone," while Lowry Center has more of the traditional stations and staples, including pizza, burgers, and fries. The center has a snack bar and a cyber café among other things as well. Dining Halls are open from 7 a.m. to 7 p.m., though students would certainly welcome more options. To break the monotony, students often are forced to look elsewhere. Matsos, a Greek restaurant, is a favorite of students; it is recommended to save time for a talk with Spiro, the owner, because "he loves students." The Old Jaol and C.W. Burgerstein's are also popular spots.

Students, however, do feel the effects of Wooster's small-town character, and complain about the lack of off-campus eateries. As one student said, "Besides a couple of tattoo parlors downtown, the town is dead." Most everything also closes by 9 p.m., though one freshman said, "C.K. (Country Kitchen) is good for late-night snacks, though you have to watch out as to what you order sometimes."

Something for Everyone

What the rural town of Wooster lacks, students feel the campus makes up for socially. The Greek system exists, but many students feel that its influence represents only one segment of the school's population. Many of the most enjoyable parties are thrown in various rooms, houses, and dorms—being underage is not considered a major problem. One student, however, commented that "drinking is not as prevalent as I thought it would be. There are many non-drinkers, and there is no pressure at all." There are plenty of campus-wide activities ranging from parties such as the 70s/80s Dance, Spring Fest, and 20s Prohibition Party, and for those who wish to volunteer and contribute to the community, blood drives and campus clean-ups.

Many students are also frequent visitors to Cleveland. Though parking can be a problem, cars remain the easiest and most accessible form of transportation. "Almost everyone has at least one friend who has a car on campus, so it's not at all a problem," said one freshman.

There are many active organizations and groups on campus and virtually every student takes part in at least one extracurricular activity. Some of the campus's favorite groups include Amnesty International, Peace by Peace, College Republicans, The Volunteer Network, and the student newspaper, *The Voice.* Wooster's most famous and respected student group, however, remains "the Pipe Band." Representative of the school's proud Scottish tradition, the Pipe Band is a group of Bagpipe players who, clad in kilts and knee socks, can be seen playing at various functions and at random spots across campus. "They're very cool and so good. The campus can rally around them and is extremely proud," said one student. The band also plays during half-time at football games.

Wooster's 22 sports teams compete in Division III of the North Coast Athletic Conference. Athletics aren't a huge part of the Wooster experience, but football and baseball usually post winning records. The gym is well-frequented by students, and was recently renovated. Intramurals are also a big draw and favorite method of relaxation for many students.

"More Diversity, Please"

The biggest criticism of the College of Wooster is a lack of diversity in its student body. There are very few non-Caucasian students, and almost everyone hails from a similar background. As one student said candidly, "We have a whole lot of diversity among white people, but almost no diversity among ethnic or racial groups. This needs to change." While there are some international students, most students come from Ohio and the Northeast. Interestingly, however, in the midst of this lack of diversity, it is hard to describe a typical College of Wooster student. "Jocks, freaks and geeks, treehuggers and nerds, you'll find them all here, and all are comfortable here," one student reported.

The College of Wooster is nestled in small-town USA and boasts a hard-working student body and an excellent teaching faculty. For small classes and individual attention, the College of Wooster is certainly recognized, but students warn "you have to be prepared to get to know the cows well."—*Nirupam Sinha*

FYI

If you come to the College of Wooster, you'd better bring "air freshener for the carpets in the dorms."

What is the typical weekend schedule? "Go to Common Grounds on Friday to hear music and drink coffee, sleep in on Saturday, do a little homework, watch movies at night, or hang out with friends; Sunday sleep even later, procrastinate some more, finally do more homework and try not to get depressed about going back to class on Monday."

If I could change one thing about the College of Wooster, I'd "bring more diversity to campus."

Three things every student at the College of Wooster should do before graduating are "eat at Matsos, fill up Kauke Arch with snow, and look at the stars from the golf course."

Denison University

Address: Denison, 100 Chapel Dr., Granville, OH 43023
Phone: 740-587-6276
E-mail Address: admissions@denison.edu
Web site URL: www.denison.edu/admissions
Year Founded: 1831
Private or Public: private
Religious affiliation: none
Location: small city
Regular Application Deadline: 15-Jan
Number of Applicants: 5,122
Percent Accepted: 39%
Percent Accepted who enroll: 26%
Number Entering: 622
Number of Transfers Accepted each Year: 14
Mean SAT: NA
Mean ACT: NA
Middle 50% SAT range: 1,150–1,330

Middle 50% ACT range: 25–29
Early admission program (EA/ ED/ NA): ED
ED or EA Acceptance Rate: NA
Full time Undergraduate enrollment: 2,292
Total enrollment: 2,329
Percent Male: 44%
Percent Female: 56%
Total Percent Minority: 14%
Percent African-American: 6%
Percent Asian/Pacific Islander: 3%
Percent Hispanic: 3%
Percent Native-American: 1%
Percent Other: 1%
Percent in-state / out of state: 39%/61%
Percent from Public HS: 70%

Retention Rate: 90%
Graduation Rate: 74.1%
Percent in On-campus housing: 98.5%
Percent affiliated with Greek system: 38%
Percent Varsity or Club Athletes: 78.3%
Number of official organized extracurricular organizations: 138
3 Most popular majors: Communication, Economics, Psychology
Student/Faculty ratio: 11:01
Tuition and Fees: $29,860.00
In State Tuition and Fees (if different): $29,860.00
Cost for Room and Board: $8,560.00
Percent receiving Financial aid, first-year: 93%

Nestled in the grassy hills of Ohio, 30 miles east of Columbus, lies the small town of Granville. Drive past the trees and vegetation, past the small Mom and Pop shops, and up a quaint, brick driveway, and there it lies: a hulking concrete-and-brick sign proclaiming "Denison University." "You see that sign, so big and permanent and you know you're home," said one student. "You're separated from the rest of the world. You know you're part of something special."

An Academic Support System

Denison prides itself on providing students with a comprehensive liberal arts education. The General Education Program includes requirements that run the gamut from fine arts and sciences to humanities and social sciences. Students agree that the sciences are quite popular, despite being notoriously challenging in the higher levels. Regardless, Denison hosts a strong science program, with several buildings and even a Biology-Reserve all devoted to this field.

Communications is also a popular major, though "it can be hard to get classes if you don't major or minor in it." Perhaps the most noticeable feature of Denison academics is the number of helpful and caring professors that comprises its academic staff. In addition to leading lectures and seminars, students report that professors also frequently work overtime in order to help struggling students understand challenging concepts. "I really love the professors here," one student said. "At the end of the year, one of my professors invited my class to her house and offered to cook us dinner!"

Denison students also recognize the importance of academic honesty. In such a small school, rumors spread quickly and "professors will find out about cheating." But at a college like Denison, why would anyone cheat in the first place? Students note that all are driven to do well, but never feel as though the atmosphere is competitive or smothering. "The mainstream idea of success here is that you don't feel pressure from other students; you do it for yourself." This feeling of encouragement and of friendship makes its mark on the social scene as well.

Diverse, but Divided

Denisonians love the community that the college breeds. "People here just genuinely care about each other," one student insisted. In a small school, located in a small town, students are bound to build tight-knit bonds with one another. Strong and lasting friendships seem to be a trademark of the Denison experience. But with such a small community, students voice the concern that the university also runs the risk of creating a "high school-like" feel, with a speedy rumor mill and many couples "going steady." While underclassmen usually just hook up, upperclassmen often settle down their junior year and fall into long term relationships. But even more than relationships or rumors, Denison's high school image is also perpetuated by the presence of "cliques." The fact that a large part of the Denison community draws from private schools causes some students to feel exasperated about the homogeneous but exclusive cliques within the school. Students report the "stereotypical Denison student" as being a wealthy, white, east-coast private school kids who like to "look nice" and wear preppy, Abercrombie-like clothes. One student commented that "there are a lot of different people, but they don't really interact with each other." Yet another student confirmed this fact, clarifying that "diversity at Denison is present, but not prevalent." Indeed, while Denison boasts students of different races, ethnicities, and nationalities, most tend to stick with their own kind. Addressing this phenomenon, one student said, "I've never seen anything like it. You look in the cafeteria and members of each race just sit with each other. I mean, you might have acquaintances that are of a different race, but most of your friends will probably be of your own race—and romantic interracial relationships don't really happen here." Students report that interracial relationships are extremely rare, and homosexual relationships are equally invisible on-campus. "You won't see two gay guys holding hands on this campus," a student explained.

Greek Life

"Greek life is pretty big, but not consuming," says one sorority sister. Students note that Greek parties do add a lot to the social scene, and "bar parties" are extremely popular as well. Fraternities and sororities often rent out a bar for the night, usually advertising a themed party that week on-campus. Students congregate outside the athletic center and are bussed to the bars in nearby towns to take part in drinking, dancing, and a healthy dose of debauchery. For those not into the Greek scene, on-campus parties are popular as well, in satellite housing or suites. Stu-

dents don't like the idea of quiet hour, however, which starts at 1am. RAs at Denison are usually pretty lenient and are described as decent enough to warn students about noise levels or alcohol before writing them up for their mischief. For most students, the nights to go out and have a good time are Monday, Wednesday, Friday and the weekend. Since most Denisonians have later classes on Tuesday and Thursday, Wednesday reigns as the logical choice for a midweek party break.

Housing Options Age Like Wine

Campus housing conditions have received a major facelift recently, which bodes well for incoming freshman. "The freshman dorms just got renovated and they're a lot nicer than when I was a freshman," an upperclassman said. Campus living is divided into four quads: North, South, East, and West; each has a different population and character all their own. North Quad holds the quiet, substance free dorms; West Quad houses juniors and sophomores; South Quad hosts seniors; and East Quad has both freshman dorms. Everyone agrees that housing at Denison, like a fine wine, only gets better with age. Juniors can opt to live with friends in suites with common rooms and private bathrooms, and seniors have the first dibs on the coveted Sunset dorms, described as apartment-like living spaces with fully-equipped kitchens. The quality of housing is crucial at Denison, as students are required to live on-campus all four years. This wouldn't be so hard for some students, if the food wasn't notoriously bad. "Something they could do to improve the meal plan," a student said, "is to not make us eat it."

> "You're separated from the rest of the world. You know you're part of something special."

Alternatives to the dining hall food in Slayter Student Union include Taco Bell and Pizza Hut, as well as other restaurants in nearby towns. Even though most students don't like the dining hall food, their empty stomachs and wallets force them to realize that constantly living off of these alternatives is really not an option.

Smallville, USA

Granville is an extremely small town, and that's just the way the locals like it. Denison students describe it as "quaint, with pretty much only one street," lined with charming Mom-and-Pop stores that close early and offer rustic attraction. But there just isn't much to do in this little Midwest town. To get around the area, "a car is essential." Cars allow students to go to bars, shop for necessities, or visit larger cities like Columbus. Easton, a nearby town is described as a "massive development" with a sprawling outdoor shopping complex, movie theaters, and other forms of entertainment. But while Granville's size doesn't offer much excitement, students appreciate its safety and quiet charm. "You can't imagine anything bad happening in Granville, of all places," a student said. A female student chimes in, "I've never felt unsafe in this town."

Beyond the Books

For those looking for something to do outside of class, Denison has plenty to offer. The musically inclined can audition for the male a cappella group (the Hilltoppers) or the female a cappella group (Ladies' Night Out). Those with a knack for writing should check out *The Denisonian*, the college's oldest and weekly newspaper, or *The Bullsheet*, a witty publication that pokes fun at Denison on an intermittent basis. Fraternities and sororities are also popular organizations within the student body. Each fraternity and sorority also sponsors a charity in order to emphasize the idea of giving back to the commu-

nity. Students report that hazing, a major fear on many college campuses, is "virtually nonexistent" at Denison. Because Denison is a Division III school, sports are a fun, but not all-consuming way to spend free time. The lacrosse, swimming, baseball, and softball teams are the most successful on-campus. Lacrosse reigns as the most popular spectator sport and the stands are always filled when the team is playing longtime rival Ohio Wesleyan.

The Denison Experience

Students at Denison are allowed to develop in many ways. While enjoying challenging academics, they are also building lifelong friendships, all in a beautiful setting. Life after Denison can prove to be exciting as well; Disney president Michael Eisner and *Alias* star Jennifer Garner both attended Denison. Yet the essence of this school that breeds both corporate visionaries and Hollywood stars can only be summed up by a current Denison student: "There's not many times in your life where you can be separate from the rest of the world, where you can see people every single day and be with your friends. You get a sense of belonging and community here at Denison. There are not a lot of times in your life that you can learn, have a good time, and be in a beautiful environment where people genuinely care about you. You get that here at Denison."—*Andrew Law*

FYI
If you come to Denison you'd better bring "your J.Crew gear."
What's the typical weekend schedule? "Students like to hang out with their friends drinking or just watching movies. Greek parties are big here on the weekends, too. But we all know that we can't put off our homework and just play on the weekends. There's way too much work here for that."
If I could change one thing about Denison I would change "the food."
Three things every student should do before graduating are "go to a bar party, skip school to go shopping at Easton (a city with a huge outdoor mall), and go to a lacrosse game against Ohio Wesleyan."

Kent State University

Address: Kent State, P.O. Box 5190, Kent, OH 44242-0001
Phone: 800-988-KENT
E-mail Address: admissions@kent.edu
Web site URL: www.kent.edu
Year Founded: 1910
Private or Public: public
Religious affiliation: none
Location: suburban
Regular Application Deadline: 1-Aug
Number of Applicants: NA
Percent Accepted: 84%
Percent Accepted who enroll: 38%
Number Entering: NA
Number of Transfers Accepted each Year: NA
Mean SAT: 1,040
Mean ACT: 22

Middle 50% SAT range: 460–580V, 460–590M
Middle 50% ACT range: 18–24
Early admission program (EA/ ED/ NA): NA
ED or EA Acceptance Rate: NA
Full time Undergraduate enrollment: 17,793
Total enrollment: NA
Percent Male: 41%
Percent Female: 59%
Total Percent Minority: 10%
Percent African-American: 8%
Percent Asian/Pacific Islander: 1%
Percent Hispanic: 1%
Percent Native-American: 0%
Percent Other: 6%
Percent in-state / out of state: 90%/10%

Percent from Public HS: NA
Retention Rate: 71%
Graduation Rate: 17%
Percent in On-campus housing: 35%
Percent affiliated with Greek system: 2%
Percent Varsity or Club Athletes: NA
Number of official organized extracurricular organizations: 204
Most popular majors: Nursing, Psychology
Student/Faculty ratio: 18:01
Tuition and Fees: NA
In State Tuition and Fees (if different): NA
Cost for Room and Board: NA
Percent receiving Financial aid, first-year: 63%

K ent State University, despite its place in history as a hotbed of political progressivism, is a quiet, laid-back institution. Kent offers a wide variety of academic opportunities, with a friendly atmosphere for an institution of its size. With over 24,000 students, Kent State is the second-largest university in Ohio. Although the campus is not very diverse—most of its students are in-state, Caucasian and middle-class—it offers its students various opportunities academically and socially. Kent State University also has a network of regional campuses across Ohio, catering to commuter students.

Liberal Education at a Large University

Kent State University gives its students some freedom to choose their own schedules within the constraints of Liberal Education Requirements, or LER. Every undergraduate student must attain credit in Composition, Mathematics, Logic and Foreign Language, Humanities and Fine Arts, Social Sciences, Basic Sciences, and Diversity. Most students seem to think that the LER is worthwhile, forcing them to explore classes they otherwise would not take.

"Human Sexuality" is a popular course, which one girl described as "one of the most fun classes I've taken in my life." Another popular class, a science class designed for non-science students, is called "Seven Ideas that Struck the Universe." Although most students seem to enjoy their classes, other students complain that the set of classes that complete the LER is too restricting.

Most introductory classes have 100 to 175 students, but the size can vary. Language classes and labs generally have less than 20 students, and class size drops once you start taking classes in the major. Professors teach all of the classes except labs, which are run by teaching assistants under the direction of a professor. Although there are no discussion sections to supplement lectures, professors have office hours set aside for helping students. The professors are for the most part approachable and helpful. Some professors even set time aside to help students on an Internet chat. These chats, as well as syllabi and class notes, are part of the Kent Web server.

The most popular majors at Kent are fashion, architecture, communications and business. The fashion program is outstanding and is ranked as one of the top fashion programs in the nation. Some of the less popular majors are still high quality and offer excellent experiences. Many majors offer study abroad programs: The fashion and architecture programs offer studies in Venice, the journalism program in London and Paris, and the conservation program in Australia and Mexico.

Suitcasers and Party Animals

The weekend social life at Kent State is, for most of the campus, admittedly lacking. Many students describe Kent State as a "suitcase campus," where half the on-campus students go home for the weekends. The students left on campus are left with a variety of things to do, though one must take the initiative to take advantage of the options.

> Many students describe Kent State as a "suitcase campus," where half the on-campus students go home for the weekends.

Partying is a big deal for those left on campus for the weekends. Because drinking is strictly prohibited in most of the dorms, most of the partying occurs off campus at the fraternity houses. The Greek scene is influential on campus, because the frats host most of the parties. Some of the more elite national fraternities are on Frat Row, but those are mostly dry. The party fraternities are located off of East Main Street, a main strip that is a center of off-campus life. There are a lot of fast food joints on East Main, where students can often be seen "getting their 3 a.m. Taco Bell."

For students who do not like the fraternity scene, there are a lot of other options. Upperclassmen usually hang out at their off-campus apartments. Wednesday is notorious for karaoke. On the weekends, those who are old enough go to the bars and clubs of downtown Kent. Many students spend their weekends participating in one of the multitude of extracurricular organizations. There are over 150 different organizations on campus, some of the more popular being community service organizations, the College Democrats, the Dive (a Christian youth group started only a few years ago), and Project Sound (a group that brings local bands to campus). Other students play sports, and for those who do not go home for the weekend, joining a traveling sports team is a great alternative.

Sports are a big deal on campus. Basketball is especially popular, since the men's team enjoyed recent success in the NCAA tournament, reaching the Elite Eight. The football team is not as good, but still enjoys the prevalent Kent State pride. Intramural sports are also very competitive; one intramural softball team was even sponsored by a local business. The recent rage has been club dodge ball, which is played in one of the indoor facilities. A new recreation center sports two pools, indoor basketball, volleyball and track, a spa area, and an indoor soccer arena.

On-Campus Housing: The "Freshman Experience" and More

Housing on campus is described as scarce. Not too long ago, a fire in one of the dorms caused students to be temporarily removed for cleanup, and the University had trouble finding space for the displaced students. Although there are some space issues, most students seemed satisfied with their experience in the dorms.

Freshmen have the option either to live in normal on-campus housing or to live in the special Freshman (or First Year) Experience dorms. Although the rooms in the Freshman Experience dorms are smaller, there are some benefits to staying in them. For one, only freshmen live in the dorms, so it makes it easy for new students to meet each other. Furthermore, they are smaller than normal dorms—at about 100 students, rather than about 750 students—which leads to a more intimate atmosphere.

Most students move off campus their junior years to apartments in the Kent area. The university requires that non-commuting students live on campus their first two years. The upperclassmen who choose to stay on campus have a pretty good choice of dorms. The standard room is a double, but some students pay more for a single, or buy out a quad with a friend for extra space. The housing has been going under renovation, and some "very elaborate" dorms were recently finished, which a senior called "an apartment on campus you don't have to clean." For this reason, there was an increase in upperclassmen living on campus a couple of years ago.

The security inside the dorms is fairly strict. One particularly annoyed student described the security guards as "pompous" and "self-righteous," but there is a general consensus that the policies are invasive. When an offense is committed, such as being caught drinking or partying, a strike is marked against a student. When a student accumulates enough strikes, they go to administrative courts. Although the police are not contacted, the process is still described as "irritating." Though alcohol is strictly prohibited in most dorms, there is "more [oncampus drinking] going on than people realize."

The food at Kent State gets mixed reviews from the students. One girl stated that the food is "OK, not as healthy as it could be," while another claims that "we have a very good variety." Students have a meal plan, which is based on credit that can be spent at a dining hall or at the food court. "The Hub" at the student center offers some fast food, including Quizno's, Einstein's Bagels, A&W, and Ambrosia. There is even a restaurant, which offers full-service meals—a popular place to take someone out for a date. A lot of students carry a Flash Cash card, which works with the meal plan and is also accepted at most local businesses.

May 4, 1970, and Kent State Today

The incident on May 4, 1970, when four student protesters were shot and killed at Kent State, is a stunning reminder of the tension between students and the government. Today, there is a memorial to the event, and every year the campus throws a big party on the anniversary. In recent years, the partying has been curbed because of problems in the past with rowdy crowds.

The campus today is surprisingly apolitical. There is still some bad blood between the city of Kent and Kent State University, but political protests are not very common on campus. Political activism is kept at a minimum because of a "general apathy" around campus. One junior girl stated that "everyone has their own opinions, but nobody makes the effort to do anything with it." There was some activity during the general election of 2004, but it is difficult to get the students interested in school politics. A "big protest" recently drew only 300 students.

Kent State University has a "pretty spreadout campus," with lots of open fields and sidewalks. There is a pretty forested area with a natural creek near the biology building. The architecture of the buildings varies. One can easily tell where they are by looking at the nearby buildings, as each area has a unique architecture. The art center in the center of campus is pretty and decorated with installation projects made by the students. Although a lot of students own cars, because of a parking problem most students walk around campus. The bus system has recently been revamped, and buses stop every seven minutes. Otherwise, it could take 30 minutes to walk across campus. During the "real bad-ass winter," the bus system becomes a serious boon to students, especially since the sidewalks do not always get plowed.

The campus is well-lit at night, and the students feel very safe, even when walking alone. Crime is a rare occurrence. There is an escort service available for those students who feel they need it. Overall, the campus receives high marks for atmosphere. The students are very comfortable, and all have loved their experiences there. One journalism major had misgivings when she came, but she soon changed her mind. She said, "Kent State grabbed me, pulled me in, and I never wanted to leave."—*Ryan Galisewski*

FYI

If you come to Kent State University, you'd better bring: "lots of extension cords, an umbrella, and a car."

What's the typical weekend schedule? "Thursday—dance club or frat party, Friday—going to class hung-over and chilling with friends at night, Saturday—homework during the day and clubbing in Kent at night, Sunday—recovering and doing homework."

If I could change one thing about Kent State University, I'd "change the way the security is handled on on-campus living."

Three things every student at Kent State University should do before graduating are "check out the May 4 memorial and get a good understanding of what happened, experience the nightlife downtown, and ride down a snowy hill on a cafeteria tray."

Kenyon College

Address: Kenyon, Ransom Hall, Kenyon College, Gambier, OH 43022
Phone: 740-427-5776
E-mail Address: admissions@kenyon.edu
Web site URL: www.kenyon.edu
Year Founded: 1824
Private or Public: Private
Religious affiliation: Episcopical nondenominonetiononel
Location: Rural
Regular Application Deadline: 16-Jan
Number of Applicants: 4,368
Percent Accepted: 148.8%
Percent Accepted who enroll: 32%
Number Entering: 458
Number of Transfers Accepted each Year: 10
Mean SAT: V–695, M–670
Mean ACT: 30.2

Middle 50% SAT range: V 640–750, M 630–710
Middle 50% ACT range: 28–32
Early admission program (EA/ ED/ NA): ED
ED or EA Acceptance Rate: 60%
Full time Undergraduate enrollment: 1,631
Total enrollment: 1,648
Percent Male: 48%
Percent Female: 52%
Total Percent Minority: 10.90%
Percent African-American: 3.30%
Percent Asian/Pacific Islander: 4.40%
Percent Hispanic: 2.70%
Percent Native-American: 0.50%
Percent Other: 0%
Percent in-state / out of state: 21%/79%

Percent from Public HS: 53%
Retention Rate: 92%
Graduation Rate: 84%
Percent in On-campus housing: 97%
Percent affiliated with Greek system: Frat 27%, Sor 9%
Percent Varsity or Club Athletes: 24%
Number of official organized extracurricular organizations: 103
3 Most popular majors: English, Political Science, Psychology
Student/Faculty ratio: 10:01
Tuition and Fees: $36,050
In State Tuition and Fees (if different): N/A
Cost for Room and Board: $5,900
Percent receiving Financial aid, first-year: 47%

A midst the valleys and rolling hills of Gambier, Ohio, lies the rural liberal arts paradise that is Kenyon College. With only 1,550 students, Kenyon has managed to carve out a reputation for itself as an academically challenging, artistically stimulating, and fun-loving place to spend those four formative years. And you can do it all surrounded by the pristine beauty of Kenyon's own nature preserve.

Comps but no Core

The small, intimate nature of the Kenyon community is definitely intensified when it comes to the academic community. Since the average class size is 14, students report that they definitely get a lot of one-on-one attention from their professors (and it's just professors—no TAs at Kenyon!). This can range from office hours to home visits, but professor accessibility is one of the highlights of academic life at Kenyon. In fact, one student said that, "There used to be a rule that all professors had to live on campus . . . It's not true anymore, but they're all still very close."

Rather than a standard set of core requirements, Kenyon students complete nine "units," or two semesters, of courses outside their own majors, whose requirements are of-ten rigorous enough without the added stress. And, instead of a thesis, Kenyon seniors prepare senior "exercises," more popularly known as "comps," in which they execute some kind of culminating project that encapsulates their studies during the last four years. The comps allow for a whole range of creative freedom, but can be stressful. One senior double-major in English and Dance and Drama said that she's excited about the original play she is writing, but admitted that she "pretty much lives in the library these days."

Yet, all of these requirements do not deter determined Kenyon students from double majoring or from enjoying their classes in popular majors like English, psychology, and political science. And there are popular courses that draw in students from all sorts of specialty areas, including an anthropology seminar on drinking culture and an English course entitled, "Strange Fish and Bearded Women." Overall, while students agree that academics are "challenging, they are also definitely what you make of it—you get out what you put back in."

Frats and "Phling"

Outside of the classroom, Kenyon students are sociable and easy to get along with. As one student asserted, "Compared to other places I've been, this place is incredibly friendly." The small community makes it easy to make friends. "If you sit on the bench on Middle Path, you can see everyone at Kenyon pass by. It's impossible to walk somewhere and not see everyone you know." Yet, there is definitely a downside, as one senior admitted. "Everyone definitely knows everyone else's business here . . . we call it the fishbowl," he laughed. While the Kenyon community is made up of people from all different states and countries, the majority of the students at Kenyon are admittedly white and upper-middle-class. Yet, students are quick to say that Kenyon is an accepting and welcoming place, regardless of background.

> **"It's impossible to walk somewhere and not see everyone you know."**

While Kenyon is a beautiful and safe campus ("we don't even lock our doors here," one student said), it can also get to be "pretty isolated." Luckily, nearby Ohio towns and cities provide a whole host of entertainment options, including movie theaters in Columbus and bands at schools like Ohio State. Students report that while a car is helpful, it is not necessary, since there are shuttles that can take undergrads to nearby towns, and the campus itself is navigable on foot. Of course, for those who choose to stay on campus during the weekends, there is an incredible amount of things to do, from shows and concerts, to film series and frat parties. And students report that while, "you can always go to a frat party," Greek life definitely does not dominate the Kenyon social scene.

Kenyon is not a dry campus and one student claimed that, "most of the campus does drink." However, other students contended that, "you definitely don't have to drink here to have a good time." For those who prefer their weekends dry, the Kenyon After-Dark Society sponsors a whole host of activities, including first-run movie premieres and an Iron Chef Dessert contest, for people to enjoy (soberly or not). In fact, campus-wide parties and activities are an especially prominent part of Kenyon social life. One of the most popular is "Philander's Phebruary Phling," an event that takes place the first weekend in February. With a different theme every year, students get together to dance, drink, and stay warm during the onset of winter.

Life in the "Fishbowl"

All students at Kenyon must live on campus, which helps to make the housing process easier to settle than at other schools. Housing is determined by lottery, which can often be a hit-or-miss process, yet students report that they usually manage to live with friends and form even tighter bonds with roommates by the time they graduate. While one student said that, "The best way to describe our living conditions is Spartan," others insisted that the school's neo-Gothic architecture is "simple, but pretty." The different dorms at Kenyon do have their own distinct characters and features; Old Kenyon, the oldest building on campus, is supposedly haunted, while Cables is the tallest building in Knox County. There are Community Advisers (CAs) who live on both freshman and upperclassman halls, but students say that they aren't too strict.

When it comes to food, students report that the college has made a conscious effort to improve its culinary standing in the last few years. One senior stated that, "The food started out awful, but it's gotten a lot better over the last few years—there's a sushi place at the gym, and there's a lot more of a focus on vegan and vegetarian options." There's not actually a meal plan at Kenyon— students just get all-you-can-eat meals at Pierce, the school's one dining hall that's currently undergoing extensive renovations. For those hoping to find food elsewhere, students say that the Gambier Grille offers yummy and affordable American fare, while the Kenyon Inn is nice but a bit more expensive. And, if you're willing to drive, the Chinese and Mexican restaurants at Mt. Vernon are usually worth the trip.

Students at Kenyon can choose from a plethora of extracurricular activities to occupy their time. There are a capella and theater groups galore—in fact, many shows traditionally leave a seat open during their performances for Paul Newman, one of the school's most famous alumnae, just in case he happens to turn up. Community service is another outlet—students say that Habitat for Humanity is growing into an increasingly popular way to spend a Saturday morning. From hosting a show on Kenyon's radio station to joining the Mock Trial team, there is no shortage of opportunity to stay busy.

For the more athletically inclined, one of

Kenyon's most famous Division III sports teams is the men's diving and swimming team, which has won 25 championships since 1980. The basketball and lacrosse teams are also growing in popularity, as is IM Ultimate Frisbee. In fact, the Kenyon College Ultimate Frisbee Team (KCUF) holds an event called the "Skivies Snow Bowl," in which players strip down to their underwear to play. One student admits that, "Student support for the sports teams tends to be a little lacking—we aren't a place with killer school spirit." Yet, the school's upcoming renovation of the gym and revamping of the intramural sports system leaves students optimistic about the future of Kenyon athletics.

Tradition!

Kenyon lore is rife with unique stories and enduring traditions. On the final night of freshman orientation, all freshmen stand on the steps of the theater building and sing Kenyon's four college songs as upperclassmen stand and jeer. Four years later, after their baccalaureate service, the seniors do it again, clothed in caps and gowns. It is this sense of community and continuity that binds Kenyon students together during their time together and makes the supportive and intimate atmosphere such a fun place to be, as one senior explained, "I love it here. I can safely say without feeling trite that this is truly a special place."—*Alexandra Bicks*

FYI

If you come to Kenyon, you'd better bring "a pair of boots—no one told me how cold Ohio would be and how much it would rain and snow!"

What's a typical weekend schedule? "Friday afternoon, finish up class, de-stress, dinner; Friday night, an a capella concert or a play, then a few different apt. parties (maybe the one bar on campus); Saturday, sleep in, work; Saturday night about the same (although maybe go out to eat one of those nights); Sunday, everyone does homework."

If I could change one thing about Kenyon, I'd "want there to be more diversity."

Three things everyone should do before graduating from Kenyon are: "Eat pie from Peggy Sue's (about 20 minutes away), go on Kim Shutt's ghost tour, go swimming in the nearby river down the hill."

Miami University

Address: Miami University, Ohio, 301 S Campus Ave, Oxford, OH 45056
Phone: 513-529-2531
E-mail Address: NA
Web site URL: www.muohio.edu
Year Founded: 1809
Private or Public: public
Religious affiliation: none
Location: rural
Regular Application Deadline: 2-Feb
Number of Applicants: 15,602
Percent Accepted: 78%
Percent Accepted who enroll: 30%
Number Entering: 3,166
Number of Transfers Accepted each Year: 239
Mean SAT: NA
Mean ACT: 26

Middle 50% SAT range: NA
Middle 50% ACT range: NA
Early admission program (EA/ ED/ NA): ED
ED or EA Acceptance Rate: NA
Full time Undergraduate enrollment: 14,471
Total enrollment: 16,700
Percent Male: 45%
Percent Female: 54%
Total Percent Minority: 14%
Percent African-American: 3%
Percent Asian/Pacific Islander: 3%
Percent Hispanic: 2%
Percent Native-American: 1%
Percent Other: NA
Percent in-state / out of state: 71%/29%
Percent from Public HS: NA

Retention Rate: 90%
Graduation Rate: 81%
Percent in On-campus housing: 48%
Percent affiliated with Greek system: 21%/20%
Percent Varsity or Club Athletes: NA
Number of official organized extracurricular organizations: 350
3 Most popular majors: Finance, Marketing, Zoology/Animal Biology
Student/Faculty ratio: 16:01
Tuition and Fees: $21, 011
In State Tuition and Fees (if different): $8,496.00
Cost for Room and Board: $7,810.00
Percent receiving Financial aid, first-year: NA

As one college sophomore at Miami University reflected on her college applications, "When I imagined college in high school, Miami is what I thought it'd be like. It's a traditional college town." Located in Oxford, Ohio, with picturesque red brick campus buildings surrounded by the countryside, Miami University is the ideal college for people who take pride in academics, still want to savor the college life of a thriving Greek system and experience a well rounded liberal education in a safe, yet daring atmosphere.

Academics

This "Public Ivy" takes education seriously. Every student at Miami University must complete the Miami Plan for Liberal Education which consists of foundation courses in the humanities, social sciences, fine arts, and formal reasoning, in addition to a thematic sequence of courses which provides an in-depth look into a subject other than your major. Culminating a student's program of study is the Senior Capstone Experience—a workshop, seminar, creative work, or project that is designed to meld a broad, liberal education with the specialized knowledge of a major. Miami boasts of nationally recognized programs in engineering, business and accounting. Students say that pre-med and business are the harder majors and that slackers tend to lean towards the education major. Architecture majors also handle a tough course load and actually bring "refrigerators, cots, and sleeping bags into the studio because they practically live there when projects are due."

The difficulty of classes depends on how hard one wants to make his or her schedule. One student explained that "only crazy people take 18 credit hours." Students appreciate the small class sizes (other than the large introductory classes) that Miami offers with a student faculty ratio at 17 to 1; however, students complain about the difficulty of getting into classes. It's a "huge problem" one student stated. Another student explained that "your scheduling priority for classes is by credit hours, so it only gets easier to get into classes." In-season athletes, graduate students and honor students have first choice for classes, followed by seniors, then juniors and so on. The best way to get into a class, one student explained, is "to stay for a week. A number of students will be discouraged that there is no room and someone will drop the class, leaving a spot open to you." Students do receive close attention from their professors, with only a limited number of TAs around the school. Miami also ranks among the top 10 schools in the country for the number of students who study abroad. The school has a European Center for students to attend in Luxembourg, but will accept nearly any other study abroad program from other colleges, as well.

Miami offers a number of honors and scholars programs for those seeking even more in-depth study. The Oxford Scholars Program automatically admits students who score a 29 or higher on the ACT and graduate in the top 10 percent of their class. Students live in the Honors and Scholars Hall, and benefit from close interaction with faculty, special courses, and guest lecturers. The University also offers a number of opportunities for undergraduate research.

Living Large (and Clean)

An adjective that students consistently use to describe their school is "clean." As one student commented, "The dorms reflect the campus. The cleaning system is amazing. Everything is clean." The self-contained college campus consists of colonial red brick buildings making up south, east, north, west, and central quads. "It's pretty," said a junior of the campus. "If you closed your eyes and thought 'college,' you would picture Miami." Dorms vary across the board from "big, but pretty dismal" to the all-girls' dorms which are like "posh hotels." Some dorms have air-conditioning, but for the most part dorms are typical, but clean college rooms. After sophomore year, most students choose to move off campus. As one sophomore said, "It's definitely rare for a senior to be in dorm."

Approximately half of the student body lives on campus in dorms and Greek houses. The Greek system dominates student activities on campus with a third of the school involved in a sorority or fraternity. "Everyone goes through rush," one student stated. While the Greek chapters "do party and have a good time," they each have their own philanthropy which supports "a higher cause." The Greek system also supports popular theme parties and the only semiformal and formal events on campus. One student said her Greek life is "enriching my experience. I don't think I would have met so many people had I not joined. The different sororities all live together and interact with one another." If not part of a Greek chapter, students may tend to feel left out. "If you're not in a Greek chapter and you're a business major, you don't have any friends," said one student. Western campus offers an alternative for the "hippie, artsy and eclectic people." Western Campus is a place to live and learn, separated from the main campus stereotype, said one architecture student.

Dining received rave reviews by students and is rated one of the best systems in the country. Students reported the dining halls were "immaculate" and easy to use. "The meal plan works perfectly," said a sophomore, "we can get snacks and eat whenever we want." While dining halls tend to close around seven, a convenience store located in the student center and numerous a la carte locations cater to a late-night attack of the munchies. Students say that bars and restaurants uptown, including Kona, Mary Jo's Cuisine, The Alexander House, and the classic Bagel and Deli, offer good dining alternatives.

Social Life Seekers

One has to actively search and carve a social life out of Miami's surroundings. Drinking is prevalent on campus. "We live in the middle of a corn field—what else is there to do but get hammered and pass out every weekend? Not much," said one student. Another student agreed with that sentiment, "It kind of sucks for non-drinkers. If you don't have a party to go to, you feel like a big loser." Students speak of freely flowing alcohol. For those who do not drink, Miami does offer an After Dark, a program that "gives kids something to do every Friday night from 10 p.m. to 2 a.m.," said a junior. The college also sponsors concerts and movies for the non-drinkers on campus. Students also make the occasional drive to Cincinnati or Dayton to encounter a larger social life. Dating is relatively non-existent at Miami due to the fact that there's nowhere to go, but students did attest to the frequency of random hook-ups.

Sports play a varied role on campus. Intramurals are a big draw, especially broomball, a game that Miami students invented, played on ice without skates. The only team most Miami students turn out in droves to

support is the hockey team. "Usually the games are standing room only," said one student.

The Skinny on Miami

The typical Miami student stereotype has been described as "the beautiful blonde, anorexic, wealthy, conservative, who wears Abercrombie, drives a black SUV, went to a Catholic high school, and got good grades in AP classes." Known to some as the "J. Crew University," most Miami students tend to dress with class for class. One student commented that "college students are supposed to come to class in pajamas. Well, not at Miami." Most students at the college come from white, upper-middle class, conservative backgrounds. Diversity on campus is definitely lacking, students report, even though the administration has tried to diversify the student body. Students also comment on the "health-craze" nature of the population. One student stated that "there are very few obese students. You will stick out if you do not at least appear athletic, in shape, or thin." Another student said that there are actually "lines in the recreation center to get onto exercise machines." Many students commented on the prevalence of eating disorders in the community.

> **"It's just the ideal environment to spend four years screwing up, having successes, and complaining about authority."**

Most students said that they would attend Miami again if given the chance due to its good reputation, its price, and the college-town feel of the campus. As one student said, "Most people think Miami, a midsize public university, is actually private and that can go a long way when you're out in the world. It's the ideal environment to spend four years screwing up, having successes, and complaining about authority."—*Lisa Siciliano*

FYI

If you come to Miami of Ohio, you'd better bring "khakis and sandals, for winter, summer, spring, and fall."

What is the typical weekend schedule? "Start getting drunk on Thursday and don't let up 'til Sunday when studying and laundry take over."

If I could change one thing about Miami, I'd "change the homogenous nature of everyone."

Three things every student at Miami of Ohio should do before graduating are "explore Uptown at night, play broomball, and walk through the hub in the fall when the leaves are changing."

Oberlin College

Address: Oberlin, 101 N. Professor St., Oberlin, OH 44074
Phone: 440-775-8411
E-mail Address: college.admission@oberlin.edu
Web site URL: www.oberlin.edu
Year Founded: 1833
Private or Public: private
Religious affiliation: none
Location: rural
Regular Application Deadline: 16-Jan
Number of Applicants: 4,000
Percent Accepted: 34%
Percent Accepted who enroll: 32%
Number Entering: 819
Number of Transfers Accepted each Year: 60
Mean SAT: 1,361
Mean ACT: 30

Middle 50% SAT range: 1,270–1,460
Middle 50% ACT range: 27–31
Early admission program (EA/ ED/ NA): ED
ED or EA Acceptance Rate: 60%
Full time Undergraduate enrollment: 2,829
Total enrollment: 2,841
Percent Male: 45%
Percent Female: 55%
Total Percent Minority: 19%
Percent African-American: 5%
Percent Asian/Pacific Islander: 8%
Percent Hispanic: 5%
Percent Native-American: 1%
Percent Other: NA
Percent in-state / out of state: 10%/90%

Percent from Public HS: NA
Retention Rate: 92%
Graduation Rate: 85%
Percent in On-campus housing: 86%
Percent affiliated with Greek system: NA
Percent Varsity or Club Athletes: NA
Number of official organized extracurricular organizations: 250
3 Most popular majors: Biology, English Language and Literature, History
Student/Faculty ratio: 10:01
Tuition and Fees: $34,216.00
Cost for Room and Board: $8,720.00
Percent receiving Financial aid, first-year: 53%

Oberlin's historical legacy as the first college to implement a number of revolutionary policies attracts an independent and diverse group of students to campus each year. The first college in the nation to admit students of color and the first to grant women a degree, Oberlin continues today to provide a freethinking atmosphere for its undergraduates.

Progressive Thinkers

Since its founding in 1833, Oberlin has always fostered liberal thinking. Just over 2,500 students attend Oberlin, with the majority enrolled in the College of Arts and Sciences and the remainder (about 500) enrolled in the highly regarded Conservatory of Music. "Obies" are required to fulfill basic distributional requirements in order to ensure a well-rounded liberal arts education. Students must take nine credit hours in each of three divisions (social science, humanities, and natural science), in addition to satisfying nine hours of cultural diversity classes (i.e. foreign language classes). Demonstrated proficiency in writing and quantitative reasoning are also musts, but these skills can be proven through a wide range of classes.

Oberlin prides itself on small class sizes averaging 18 students and an easily accessible faculty. History, biology, and English are reported to be the most popular majors. For a liberal arts college of its size, Oberlin also boasts strong science programs. While students report few problems fulfilling distributions, some complained that getting into popular classes "can be really hard, especially for first years." On the whole however, students are pleased with the quality of Oberlin's academics.

A number of alternative options for gaining credit are also available, and these unique opportunities are among most students' favorites. Winter Term, which takes place during the month of January, grants students an entire month to complete an independent or small group effort in one of three categories: academic study, personal growth, or field experience. A great deal of latitude is granted to students in designing projects, and the final results range from historical research presentations to a newfound love of skiing. Another of Oberlin's distinct offerings is ExCo, or Experimental College, which multiple students described as "a must-do" at Oberlin. ExCo is a completely student run department within the college that offers student taught classes in a wide variety of fields. ExCo subjects range from fishing to literature, and can be taught or taken for up to five hours of credit.

Horsecow Heaven

Oberlin is just about the furthest thing from a sports school. However, the Ultimate Frisbee team is nationally recognized and plays under quite a unique name: the Flying Horsecows. While the athletic scene may not be all that intense, music and the arts thrive at Oberlin. At the beginning of each semester, students are allowed to lease pieces of artwork by acclaimed artists such as Renoir and Warhol for a mere five dollars. As one student put it, "where else can students go to sleep with a Picasso above their heads?" Oberlin's reputation attracts a number of high quality music acts each semester, and it is possible to see a performance every night of the week.

> "A great deal of latitude is granted to students in designing projects, and the final results range from historical research presentations to a newfound love of skiing."

Oberlin, Ohio (pop. 8,600) provides only a few alternatives to the on-campus social scene, and most students spend their weekends at parties in the dorms or in off-campus housing. The campus dance club, The 'Sco, is another popular hangout, as well as a major part of the music scene. Almost the entire campus can be found at the Drag Ball and Safer Sex Night, annual parties that Obies go all out for. Older students often travel the 35 miles into Cleveland to seek an alternative to the campus social scene, but most weekends there is something to be found on campus.

Hippie Haven

All kinds flock to Oberlin, but the school is well known for its "hippie environment." Shirts and shoes are seen as optional on campus, although the dining halls require both. The student body at Oberlin is truly diverse, in all senses of the term. The campus was ranked as the 11th most politically active in the nation in 2005, and the student body is well informed and extremely socially active.

Freshmen live on campus, generally in two person dorm rooms. The living environment is relaxed, and advisors give their charges a great deal of leniency. In addition to college-owned housing, a relatively large group of students go independent, often living in co-ops or large off-campus houses. Additionally, there are a number of cultural houses for those who are interested in a foreign language. The dining system isn't ideal, but the food is reported to be "pretty good, surprisingly" although some students wish that there were more options. Overall, Oberlin's students are a relatively easy-going bunch who are happy with their college and chose it for its laid back attitude.—*Bob Casey*

FYI
If you come to Oberlin, you better bring "yourself. You as you truly are. You'll finally be in a place where you can be accepted. Not by everybody, of course, but by most of us."
What's the typical weekend schedule? "Stay up till the wee hours with friends, sleep in till the late morning/early afternoon, hip-hop dance practice Saturday evening, tumbling Sunday evening (immediately followed by fourth meal), and probably some other meetings and events in there, too. The time between all of that is full of work."
If I could change one thing about Oberlin, I'd . . . "make it easier to get into the classes you want."
Three things every student at Oberlin should do before graduating are "Take full advantage of the ExCo classes, meet lots of different people—it's an extremely diverse group with a great deal to share, and use Winter Terms to the fullest possible extent—they're a chance to learn about the things you want. It's a sweet opportunity."

Ohio State University

Address: Ohio State, 190 N. Oval Mall, Columbus, OH 43210

Phone: 614-292-3980

E-mail Address: askabuckeye@osu.edu

Web site URL: www.osu.edu

Year Founded: 1870

Private or Public: public

Religious affiliation: none

Location: urban

Regular Application Deadline: 2-Feb

Number of Applicants: NA

Percent Accepted: 68%

Percent Accepted who enroll: 51%

Number Entering: 6,280

Number of Transfers Accepted each Year: 3,133

Mean SAT: 1,194

Mean ACT: 26

Middle 50% SAT range: 1,090–1,310

Middle 50% ACT range: 24–29

Early admission program (EA/ ED/ NA): NA

ED or EA Acceptance Rate: NA

Full time Undergraduate enrollment: 37,239

Total enrollment: 47,312

Percent Male: 53%

Percent Female: 47%

Total Percent Minority: 20%

Percent African-American: 7%

Percent Asian/Pacific Islander: 5%

Percent Hispanic: 8%

Percent Native-American: less than 1%

Percent Other: NA

Percent in-state / out of state: 86%/14%

Percent from Public HS: NA

Retention Rate: 92%

Graduation Rate: 71%

Percent in On-campus housing: 24%

Percent affiliated with Greek system: 12%

Percent Varsity or Club Athletes: NA

Number of official organized extracurricular organizations: 800

3 Most popular majors: Political Science and Government, Psychology

Student/Faculty ratio: 13:01

Tuition and Fees: $20,193.00

In State Tuition and Fees (if different): $8,298.00

Cost for Room and Board: $6,720.00

Percent receiving Financial aid, first-year: 55%

O hio State has its own airport. Not every university can boast that, but then and again, not every university can say that it is the largest university in the United States. Ohio State stands as the flagship establishment of the state's public system of superior education, and is widely regarded as the best public university in Ohio. In this Big Ten School, everything is supersized—from the student body to the academic choices, the football games to the extracurricular activities. As one current sophomore said, "You cannot describe Ohio State without using a superlative."

Size Does Matter!

"When I tell people I meet that I go to OSU, the first thing they say is how big it is," said one undergraduate. Located in Columbus, Ohio State University is surrounded by over a million and a half people. Ohio's government, various professional sports teams, and various unique venues all surround the school and provide tons of possibilities for students to explore their environment and act as contributing citizens.

When the school was established in 1870, the founders intended to prepare students for a career in fields related to mechanics and agriculture. School administrators have extended this traditional curriculum to include both liberal arts and technical studies. Inside the walls of the school, almost 40,000 students intermingle, intellectualize, and enjoy the giant campus. With over 170 different majors and 23 different schools and colleges, students are hardly limited when it comes to class choice and student interest.

"We are literally surrounded by opportunities," one junior said. "If you want to do it, it's there." Another student agreed: "OSU's big size is what makes OSU such a great school."

For such a large university, classes tend to be relatively small. Only 7 percent of classes are over 100 students, and 43 percent of classes are capped at 20 students. Undergrads say that regardless of class size, "professors are accessible and are willing to meet. Many are especially good at responding to e-mails when students have questions regarding the class material."

Living in the Buckeye State

Freshmen are required to live on campus unless they are commuting. Students reside in what OSU refers to as "towers" and "houses." The difference between the two is that towers tend to be high-rise buildings of over 20 stories, whereas houses tend to stand only three floors high. There are 31 different residence halls on campus, and many are devoted to themed housing such as the First Year Collegian Learning Community, which offers math and science tutoring in the dorms, and the Spanish Language and Culture Halls, which feature conversation tables and a close relationship with the Ohio State Department of Spanish. Most students recommend the South Campus dorms for their location and atmosphere. One student said that "the three residential areas attract very different crowds, and all three have different vibes. South Campus definitely attracts the livelier crowd."

Ohio State offers four different dining plans, ranging from the Deluxe Plan (250 "swipes" or meals per quarter) to Commuter Plus (40 swipes per quarter). As for eating locations, students may choose from places such as all-you-can-eat North Commons and Merrill Commons, the take-out fast-food restaurant Buckeye Express, or even Viewpoint Bistro, which will cost two to three swipes in exchange for waiter service. Ohio State students also relish in the opportunity to enjoy the abundance of restaurants on High Street. As one former student said, "You can find anything your mouth desires on High Street. There are four-star restaurants and many small cafes. Food there, overall, is edible."

Greek Life and the Social Scene

Consistently ranked among the top party schools in the nation, Greek life plays a large part of the social scene at Ohio State. The biggest campus parties and events are sponsored and held by fraternities and sororities. The best place to find a good party on campus is on Indianola Street, where many of the Greek organizations are. Students tend to party-hop all night long, but the fun doesn't stop when the sun rises. During OSU football games, the streets are filled with people tailgating. Despite their killer keggers, most students agree that Greeks' contributions to the OSU community extend beyond their conspicuous penchant for partying—most notably, their involvement with community service.

> **"You cannot describe Ohio State without using a superlative."**

If the Greek scene doesn't sound appealing, there is no cause for worry. Ohio State offers more than 500 registered student organizations and the vast array of cultures, ethnicities, and religious groups make exploring new experiences at OSU an endless adventure. It's impossible to pass the Oval, which one student describes as "our huge kinda Central Park–ish thing," without seeing one student group or another promoting a cause. Ohio State students can always be seen playing football, debating, tanning, and maybe even attending an Earth Sciences class or a Tai Chi lesson smack in the middle of the Oval.

O-HI-OOOO!

"Football at OSU is almost a religion," said one junior. "Even if you don't like it coming in, you'll love it coming out." Another student said, "No one cares about hating [Michigan] the state, but definitely the school." Together, these two students are describing "The Game"—the annual Ohio State versus Michigan football game. The bitter rivalry is lived out through an intense week aptly titled "Beat Michigan Week," which is dense with partying and proud displays of the student body's hard-core school spirit, such as jumping into Mirror Lake with fellow Buckeyes while singing and chanting.

While the attachment that Ohio State students hold for their football team may be overwhelming for some, in the end, "what it comes down to is a deep love for our college and everything that endear us to it." —*Daniel Friedman and Christine Grace Lin*

FYI

If you come to OSU you better bring "a wardrobe that includes a lot of red and buckeye pride!"

What's the typical weekend schedule? "Kegs and eggs for breakfast, and football. Attend a game or watch it on TV. Either way, no exceptions."

If I could change one thing about OSU, I'd "change the police and parking rules . . . the police seem to pull people over a lot because they're bored. And parking is horrible!"

Three things every OSU student should do before graduating are: "attend an OSU football game with 100,000 ebullient people in scarlet attire, sit by Mirror Lake at night, and run across the oval naked at night."

Ohio University

Address: Ohio University, 120 Chub Hall, Athens, OH 45701-2979
Phone: 740-593-4100
E-mail Address: admissions@ohio.edu
Web site URL: www.applyweb.com/aw?ohio
Year Founded: 1804
Private or Public: public
Religious affiliation: none
Location: rural
Regular Application Deadline: 1-Feb
Number of Applicants: 12,417
Percent Accepted: 86%
Percent Accepted who enroll: 35%
Number Entering: 4,259
Number of Transfers Accepted each Year: 788
Mean SAT: NA
Mean ACT: NA
Middle 50% SAT range: 990–1,190

Middle 50% ACT range: 21–26
Early admission program (EA/ ED/ NA): NA
ED or EA Acceptance Rate: NA
Full time Undergraduate enrollment: 16,950
Total enrollment: 29,143
Percent Male: 47%
Percent Female: 53%
Total Percent Minority: 6%
Percent African-American: 3%
Percent Asian/Pacific Islander: 1%
Percent Hispanic: 2%
Percent Native-American: 0%
Percent Other: 0%
Percent in-state / out of state: 92%/8%
Percent from Public HS: 86%
Retention Rate: 80%
Graduation Rate: 71%

Percent in On-campus housing: 43%
Percent affiliated with Greek system: 12% M, 13% F
Percent Varsity or Club Athletes: 3%
Number of official organized extracurricular organizations: 360
3 Most popular majors: Recreation, Journalism, Biological Sciences
Student/Faculty ratio: 19:01
Tuition and Fees: $8,727.00
In State Tuition and Fees (if different): $17,691.00
Cost for Room and Board: $7,839.00
Percent receiving Financial aid, first-year: 29%

According to legend, Athens, Ohio, is one of the most haunted cities in the United States. Superstition holds that Athens, home to the Ohio University Bobcats, lies at the center of a pentangle formed by five cities where witches were hung in the 1700s. This geographic peculiarity supposedly causes the campus to be inhabited by a variety of spooks and spirits, in addition to its 17,000 students. Some Bobcats report that, while lying in bed while no one else is in the room, they have heard phantom typing on their computer keyboards. Others note that on the fourth floor of one Wilson dorm, the grains of wood on one door form a demon's face—this room has had so many reports of haunting that the University no longer assigns students to live there. Ghoulish stories, however, have certainly not scared students away from this school. Combining a well-deserved party school reputation with solid academic programs and a picturesque campus, it's no wonder that neither the ghosts nor the students want to leave OU.

Bobcats Hit the Books

OU, as one sophomore observed, is "more than just a party school; the academics are really good, too." Regardless of major, all OU students have to complete a series of requirements known as "tiers." Tier I consists of freshman English and math. Tier II involves 30 credit hours of classes in a cross-section of academic subjects. Tier III requires a junior-level English composition course. Students have mixed opinions about the tier system, some saying that they appreciate the opportunity to take classes outside of their major, while others complaining that "the extra classes are a waste of tuition money."

Luckily for those who don't enjoy completing their tiers, students only have to put up with each class for two and a half months. OU operates on the quarter system, so students enroll in three ten-week terms per academic year instead of two longer semesters like at most universities. As a result, school starts in late September, finishes in June, and provides a six-week break between the fall and winter terms that lasts from Thanksgiving until after New Years. Because of the short terms, classes meet either every day or in two-hour, twice-a-week sessions. One junior commented that a perk of the quarter system is that "we're on campus for the really nice weather in spring," while a sophomore said she liked the schedule because "if you've had a bad term, you get a fresh start in just a few weeks."

With 10 different colleges and an assortment of well-respected programs, there's something at OU to satisfy any academic interest. Boasting such standout graduates as *The Today Show*'s Matt Lauer, journalism is unanimously cited as OU's best program, and one of the most selective. Other strong majors include business, engineering, and pre-med, while majors in retail merchandising and in sports administration are considered somewhat less challenging. In order to begin taking upper-level classes, students must apply to the college in which they want to major. Most upper-level classes have about 20 or 30 students whereas intro classes can enroll up to 300 students. One sophomore cited this as a problem for freshmen undecided about their major, since the application process only takes place in the fall and "it can be hard to fit all your classes in four years, and lots of students end up staying for extra terms."

While students looking for an easy term can take guts like Health 101, Engineering Technology 280, art, or a "University College" class that teaches study skills and research techniques, science classes are said to be more challenging. Chemistry 151 is known to be the hardest class at OU, and rumor has it that nearly a third of students fail the first time they take it. Despite a few particularly hard classes, OU academics are generally found to be manageable. One junior described his course load as "moderate; it's not really easy but I can get my work done." Though some grumble about TAs who speak poor English, or annoying system backups during the online course-registration procedure, on the whole students are more than pleased with the quality of academics.

Good Dorms, Bad Eats

Despite occasional reports of poltergeists, most OU students are satisfied with their living arrangements. Students are required to live in the dorms for both freshman and sophomore years, in their choice of either single-sex or coed buildings. Most of the dorms have air-conditioning, and most rooms are doubles with common bathrooms on each hall. One of the major perks about living on campus is that each dorm room comes furnished with a computer with high-speed Internet access, so students don't necessarily have to purchase a computer of their own. Although dorms on the West Green quad are generally considered nicer than those on the New South quad, most students like living on campus in general because "it gives you the chance to meet people you'd never think to talk to otherwise," according to one sophomore. Most students move into off-campus housing for junior and senior years. These houses are in "student ghettos" where college students rent most of the houses, and none are more than a 10-minute walk from campus. "I love living off campus; it's cheaper and more relaxed," chimed in one student.

The rooms may be popular, but the dining halls are not. The major complaint about living on campus is the dining hall food. "It's horrible," said one sophomore, "I think they put laxatives in it because it just runs right through you." A senior commented that dining hall food is "really redundant, and you can't really eat healthily at all." Others complain about the dining halls' limited hours of operation. On-campus dining does have a few perks though. The super-20 meal plan option allows students to get cash for the meals they don't use, and the Grab-n-Go café lets students use their meal plan to purchase packaged food to take back to their rooms.

Life of the Party

The best aspect of OU, according to one student, is that "everyone goes out, and every night there's something to do." While the social scene caters to partygoers, there are enough options to ensure that every Bobcat has a great time. About a third of students join a fraternity or sorority at OU, making the Greek scene a powerful social force on campus. In addition to Friday—and Saturday-night frat house parties that draw large crowds, Greeks sponsor some popular annual parties. One such party is Derby Days, a party held in a cornfield one Saturday during spring term where bands play and kegs flow from morning until night. With the exception of a few invite-only parties, most Greek events are open to the general student body, although one sophomore noted that "girls are pretty much always welcome at frat parties, but sometimes they're stricter about non-Greek guys." Students agree that there's no pressure to rush. One male junior observed that "it's not like you're considered un-cool if you're not in a frat," and a female student agreed that "you don't feel obligated to be in a sorority." There's no real social division between

Greeks and non-Greeks, since "you have to live in the dorms for two years regardless, so you make a lot of friends both in and out of the Greek system."

OU has an equally vibrant non-Greek party scene. Upperclassmen enjoy hanging out at Athens bars, of which there are more than 20, especially during the Court Street Shuffle, when on the Saturday night of Mom's Weekend, students go from bar to bar with their mothers and have a drink at each one. House parties are frequent and open to everyone. According to one sophomore, "you can basically walk into any party even if you don't know anyone and have a great time; everyone's so cool and friendly." Every year, streets populated by student houses throw huge parties like Palmer Fest, Oak Fest, and High Fest, where the streets are closed off and filled with students while each house hosts a party.

> "The Halloween Party is insane; it's like nothing I ever expected!"

Given the supernatural legends surrounding OU, it is appropriate that the biggest of these block parties is the annual Halloween festivities. Court Street, the main street in Athens, shuts down completely as more than 30,000 students descend on OU from universities all over Ohio. "Everyone dresses up and gets trashed. It's a mile-worth of kids standing shoulder to shoulder," explained one sophomore. Another student raved, "the Halloween Street Party is insane; it's like nothing I ever expected!" Clearly, drinking is an important part of the OU social life. Despite recent administrative attempts to crack down on campus drinking, including increases in the police force patrolling the streets on weekend nights, alcohol is readily accessible to those who want it. Nondrinkers need not feel excluded from OU social life however. As one sophomore said, "I didn't drink much at all my freshman year and I still went to all the parties and had a great time."

Another remarkable feature of the social scene at OU is the friendliness of the student body. "Everyone is pretty close knit here," commented one junior. A senior described the average student as "preppy, but not stuck up, really down-to-earth, friendly, good people." About 90 percent of the student body hails from Ohio, which does lead a lot of students to hang out with high school friends at first, but most upperclassmen agree that by the end of freshman year they've met most of their friends through classes or the dorms. The University is also predominantly white—the third-whitest Ohio public university. One sophomore summed up the student body best: "students here are really chill; they're serious about school during the week so they can go out and party with their friends on the weekends."

A Red-Brick Beauty

Located in the wooded hills of Ohio, Athens was originally a manufacturing town that produced a large proportion of the country's bricks. Though most industry has since left the area, the legacy of the town's past is clearly visible on OU's campus, which many students name as their favorite feature of the school. One sophomore described the campus as "something you'd see in a movie," with large, tree-lined quads surrounded by beautiful, red-brick, colonial architecture. Students take advantage of their surroundings during the warmer fall and spring quarters by studying under a tree, sunbathing, "folfing" (Frisbee golfing), or just hanging out in the courtyards outside the dorms. Although the architecture remains old-fashioned, recent additions and renovations to science and political science buildings keep the campus updated. The Hocking River runs through the center of the hilly grounds, and the brick streets and sidewalks visually tie the campus and the city together.

The city is a "good mix between urbanism and trees," commented one junior, who added that one of the things he liked best about the small-town environment "is that Athens is basically a walking town—you can get anywhere in 15 minutes without a car." Though some students lament that Athens' small size makes them feel like they live in "the middle of nowhere," most are enthusiastic about the options available downtown. Since Athens is primarily a university town, many of the restaurants and bars cater to college students. In addition to the multitude of bars and clubs, popular late-night destinations include restaurants like the Pita Pit, Goodfellow's Pizza, Burrito Buggy, and a calzone restaurant called D.P. Dough, all of which are open until the wee hours of the morning so that students can grab a late-night meal. Policemen on horseback ensure the safety of the campus, and the mass of student housing surrounding the downtown area makes students feel at home off campus as well as on.

Athletics and Extracurriculars

After dividing their time between academics and partying, many students say they don't have much energy to devote to dozens of extracurricular interests. For those students who do wish to get involved in extracurriculars, OU offers a variety of opportunities. Many organizations relate directly to students' majors, like the business fraternity, the newspaper run by journalism students, or the radio station run by telecommunications majors. Other popular organizations include the Ski Club, which takes an annual trip to Colorado during winter break and a whitewater rafting trip in West Virginia during spring break, and the student government groups in every dorm. Many students opt to work, often in on-campus jobs in the library or dining halls. "The jobs start at minimum wage," said one sophomore dining hall employee, "but you get raises quickly and a discount on your meal plan." Intramural sports, or "IMs," are one of the most popular extracurricular options. With IM leagues in everything from flag football to Ultimate Frisbee to table tennis, students sign up in teams with friends, dorm mates, or members of their fraternity or sorority to engage in friendly competition once or twice a week.

In addition to participation in IM sports, athletically-inclined OU students have the opportunity to make use of one of the finest student gyms in the country. The Ping Recreation Center, over 168,000 square feet, houses everything you could possibly want, from weights to tennis courts to a swimming pool to aerobics classes. Although the Ping Center is one of the most popular and heavily used resources on campus, attendance at varsity sporting events is much sparser. As one junior observed, "the football team sucks, so no one goes to the games." Though the basketball, baseball, and club hockey teams are somewhat more popular, on the whole "there's not much school spirit in terms of athletics."

In spite of the lack of sports fans, OU students love their school and hardly mind the shoddy performance of the Bobcat athletic teams. One junior said that students enjoy being on campus so much that "no one wants to go home when classes are over in the spring!" From its wild parties to its beautiful campus, from the friendly students inhabiting it to the ghostly legends surrounding it, OU is a unique institution that inspires enthusiasm in its students. One sophomore said, "I feel at home here. It's a great atmosphere to learn in, and everyone makes you feel so comfortable. I wouldn't want to go anywhere else."—*Katherine Kirby Smith*

FYI

If you come to OU, you'd better bring "a beer bong, a fake ID, an iron stomach to handle the dining hall food, and a warm coat for the frigid winter quarter."

What is the typical weekend schedule? "Friday: pre-game in the dorms, go out to a house party or frat party, hit up the bars, get some pizza at Goodfellow's, go home and sleep until mid-afternoon. Saturday: do it all again. Sunday: sleep all day, try to do some work."

If I could change one thing about OU, I'd change the "strictness of the campus police."

Three things every student at OU should do before graduating are "party at Halloween, go to Derby Days, and do the Court Street Shuffle on Moms' Weekend."

Ohio Wesleyan University

Address: 61 S. Sandusky St.,
Delaware, OH 43015
Phone: 740-368-3020
E-mail Address:
owuadmit@owu.edu
Web site URL:
http://web.owu.edu
Year Founded: 1842
Private or Public: private
Religious affiliation:
Methodist
Location: suburban
**Regular Application
Deadline:** 2-May
Number of Applicants: NA
Percent Accepted: 63%
**Percent Accepted who
enroll:** NA
Number Entering: 565
**Number of Transfers
Accepted Each Year:** 48
Mean SAT: NA
Mean ACT: 27
Middle 50% SAT range:
1080–1320

Middle 50% ACT range:
24–28
**Early admission program
(EA/ED/NA):** ED and EA
ED or EA Acceptance Rate:
ED: 58%; EA: 89%
**Full time Undergraduate
enrollment:** 1,923
Total enrollment: 1,923
Percent Male: 48%
Percent Female: 52%
Total Percent Minority:
8%
Percent African-American:
5%
**Percent Asian/Pacific
Islander:** 2%
Percent Hispanic: 1%
Percent Native-American:
<1%
Percent Other: NA
**Percent in-state / out of
state:** 54%/46%
Percent from Public HS:
NA

Retention Rate: 79%
Graduation rate: 64%
**Percent in On-campus
housing:** 84%
**Percent affiliated with
Greek system:** 60%
**Percent Varsity or Club
Athletes:** NA
**Number of official
organized extracurricular
organizations:** 86
Most popular majors:
Business/Managerial
Economics, Psychology
Student/Faculty ratio:
13:01
Tuition and Fees:
$29,870.00
**In State Tuition and Fees
(if different):** NA
Cost for Room and Board:
$7,790.00
**Percent receiving Financial
aid, first-year:** 56%

While it's a little bit too cold for some, students at Ohio Wesleyan University always have good things to say about their school. Located in the small town of Delaware, Ohio, OWU offers a challenging academic program with the counterbalance of a vibrant Greek life.

The Right Stuff

Students praise the small classes and caring environment that OWU offers and OWU students are very quick to note the dedication of their professors who seem to be there for them whenever students need help. Don't get the wrong idea, though. OWU is not an easy school. One student commented, "OWU is a lot of work. It's easy to get in, but it's very hard to stay in."

OWU has some core requirements for graduation. While some students are not ecstatic about the guidelines, many think that the requirements are a helpful tool to direct their education. One student described the academics as "challenging, but not too much that you can't handle it. The distribution requirements make you experience things you wouldn't normally learn, and it makes for a well-rounded education." OWU

requires a freshman English class, two semesters of a foreign language, and classes in non-European culture, fine arts, social sciences, and natural sciences. The school also requires students to take 15 courses numbering 250 or above.

There are an incredible number of academic resources at OWU to help students through their difficult classes. One of the most popular is the Writing Resources Center. Open every weekday, students come with the sole purpose of becoming "more confident, effective writers." The WRC is only one of many different resources that are designed specifically to help students excel. The Ohiolink and CONSORT database systems in the library are also excellent academic tools for students.

While there are some school-wide resources outside of the classroom built for students' needs, students rank their classes and professors very highly. One student noted, "All intro science classes are capped at 50, and almost every class only has 20, 12, or as few as four students in them." Compared to many schools where huge, introductory classes are prevalent, these numbers are certainly boast-worthy. Students couldn't be happier with their dedicated professors. The personalized attention they give helps to make every class worthwhile. Students find that all of these things help contribute to their good experiences with the graduation requirements. There are enough courses offered that every student can find something that is both interesting and that fulfills a requirement although some students report missing some of the more diverse opportunities available at larger research institutions.

Behind the Scenes

Although students are kept busy by their classes, most note having plenty of time to kick back and get to know their peers. Most students point first to the fact that they have too much work to go out during the week, although on some days students will socialize a little bit with their friends, watch movies in their rooms, and generally hang out. Real partying is more or less entirely restricted to the weekends.

Many students point to the Greek life at Ohio Wesleyan as one of the key elements of their social life. A little less than half of the men, and slightly fewer women, associate themselves with the fraternities or sororities. Since girls don't live in the sorority houses, the pressure for them to join is not quite as strong as it is for guys. Many students find themselves walking up the hill on Friday and Saturday nights to the frats and sororities that are almost always throwing parties. One girl commented, "glittery, tight tops that show cleavage and tight jeans are a must." While each of the parties takes on a slightly different personality, everybody can find a good night on the hill. Additionally, in the small town of Delaware, Ohio, there are a couple of student-frequented bars that offer an alternative to students who are of age.

> "There just aren't many places to hang out in Delaware, Ohio."

Some students find Delaware life a little dull. As one student says, "There just aren't many places to hang out in Delaware, Ohio." There are a few shops and a movie theater in the town, but in order to really go out and find something interesting, students often say that they like to drive to larger towns nearby. Another student notes that Delaware is only 30 miles from Columbus and—as it is in the midst of a fast-growing residential area—Delaware is "almost becoming a suburb." During the few days a year when it is warm, many students enjoy hanging out on the green lawns of campus and playing Frisbee.

One complaint from many students is the lack of diversity at OWU. When asked what they might want to change about their school, answers ranged from the high cost of the school to the apathy of the student body. One student simply said, "They need to increase the number of non-white students."

The energy of OWU students seems to be dampened by the cold weather during the Ohio winters. Many end up inside, watching movies and studying instead of being as active as they might like in more community-oriented activities. One student expressed her frustration with the inactivity of students and professors alike, and the carelessness that can come with it: "Too many people, students and faculty both, couldn't care less about the appearance of our school. There is trash everywhere. Once, an entire pot of spaghetti was overturned on a sidewalk outside the campus center—it stayed there for four days before someone cleaned it up."

While some OWU students seem too involved in their work to care much about what's going on around them, others describe themselves as very involved in extracurricular activities. OWU certainly has opportunities for every interest. Additionally, the administration does a stellar job of planning open events for all students to attend. OWU students often comment on the incredible number of events, from parties to lectures that are held on a regular basis. Students recognize the Campus Programming Board as lying at the core of student life, planning and hosting "too many events to list." Sports, too, are for everybody at OWU. The University organizes intramural sports for people with little experience, and at the varsity level OWU has had recent success with several of its Division III sports. While OWU is not entirely focused on its sports program, many students mention that watching games is a lot of fun. As of 2007, the university is partaking in a fundraising campaign to improve the athletic facilities, including a gateway center to connect all of the athletic facilities.

While students seem to be pretty active outside of the classroom, many agree that little exists during the week except for their work. OWU students point to the Mean Bean Coffee House as a cool place to have some coffee (as well as the only coffee shop in Delaware) and get some work done. Students also like the Delaware Public Library as well as the on-campus libraries for quiet places to settle down to read.

Living and Eating

OWU offers a wide selection of dorms to choose from. There is an all-female dorm, an honors dorm, and four other co-ed dorms. Students seem to be happiest in Smith, a coed dorm that is the only air-conditioned dorm on campus. RAs are present on each floor of the dorms, and their attitude seems to vary significantly. While one RA claims that she is "as strict as can be," other students say that RAs are generally "pretty laid back, not very strict" and "for the most part, invisible." There are study rooms on each floor where students sometimes convene to hang out. Generally, parties appear to be fairly restricted to "The Hill," where all of the frats are located.

While students seem generally happy with their living conditions, the University's food doesn't garner such good marks. One student even says, "The dining hall food is horrible; I often get food poisoning from it." Although feelings are clearly quite strong regarding some of the dining halls, there do seem to be some good eating havens on campus. Smith dining hall is centrally located and all-you-can-eat, and the Bishop Café in the Hamilton-Williams Campus Center is widely recognized as having the best food on campus. Off-campus, Buns—which recently re-opened after it was destroyed in a fire—and Vaquero's—are popular spots to grab a bite.

Is OWU for You?

OWU students are hard working and dedicated to their studies. They put up with the freezing temperatures of Delaware, Ohio, to take advantage of small classes and caring professors. But, it's not all work. When they need some time off, they enjoy watching movies or going out to experience the standard, drunken Greek party life up on "The Hill." If you're not afraid of the cold, love to work, and enjoy the odd party, OWU is the place for you.—*Zane Selkirk*

FYI

If you come to OWU, you better bring a "Frisbee," a "big coat," and a "cookbook so you can make your own food."

What is the typical weekend schedule? "Driving in to Columbus, hanging out with friends, and sleeping."

If I could change one thing about OWU, I would "move the school to a bigger city."

Three things that every student at OWU should do before graduating are "slide down The Hill on a mattress, work hard, and go to at least one soccer game."

University of Cincinnati

Address: University of Cincinnati, PO Box 210091, Cincinnati, OH 45221-0091
Phone: 513-556-1100
E-mail Address: admissions@uc.edu
Web site URL: http://www.uc.edu
Year Founded: 1819
Private or Public: public
Religious affiliation: none
Location: urban
Regular Application Deadline: 2-Aug
Number of Applicants: 11,813
Percent Accepted: 76%
Percent Accepted who enroll: 39%
Number Entering: 3,914
Number of Transfers Accepted each Year: 1,580
Mean SAT: 1,118
Mean ACT: 24

Middle 50% SAT range: 1,000–1,230
Middle 50% ACT range: 21–27
Early admission program (EA/ ED/ NA): NA
ED or EA Acceptance Rate: NA
Full time Undergraduate enrollment: 19,977
Total enrollment: 27,342
Percent Male: 51%
Percent Female: 49%
Total Percent Minority: 23%
Percent African-American: 12%
Percent Asian/Pacific Islander: 3%
Percent Hispanic: 2%
Percent Native-American: <1%
Percent Other: 5%
Percent in-state / out of state: 91%/9%
Percent from Public HS: NA

Retention Rate: 80%
Graduation Rate: 52%
Percent in On-campus housing: 18%
Percent affiliated with Greek system: NA
Percent Varsity or Club Athletes: 5%
Number of official organized extracurricular organizations: 250
3 Most popular majors: Communications, Marketing, Psychology
Student/Faculty ratio: 14:01
Tuition and Fees: $23,904.00
In State Tuition and Fees (if different): $9,381.00
Cost for Room and Board: $8,286.00
Percent receiving Financial aid, first-year: 62%

L ooking for "hands-on-based knowledge" that gives you that extra edge with job placement? Look no further than Cincinnati. This "not-that-spread-out" campus located in scenic downtown Cincinnati, Ohio, has everything a student could want . . . at least, it will after the construction is finished.

More Songs About Buildings

Trying to overcome its reputation as a commuter school, UC is a campus marked by rapid change and construction intended to promote campus unity and spirit. Said one engineering student "UC stands for 'Under Construction' forever." She further explained that although the head of the University has attested that there are no plans for future projects, it was apparent that the campus would be under construction for some time to come. However, the construction is not all bad. Another student remarked "they are really trying to improve and create a nicer atmosphere for the students." To create a more central gathering place for students, a new recreational center is being built, as well as some more on-

campus dorms and buildings on Main Street. Currently, though, the best housing on campus are Turner, Jefferson and Schneider halls, which are only a couple years old. These dorms have suite-style rooms, with bedrooms adjoining a shared common space connecting them all. However, most students still live off-campus in the Clifton area of Cincinnati, across the street from campus. These apartment-style accommodations are also being revamped under the name of Stratford Heights. The end of 2005 saw the completion of the Van Wormer Library renovation project, complete with a new glass dome for the oldest building on campus. The University's renovation plans are detailed and extensive and cover virtually every aspect of campus life. Additionally, the surrounding neighborhoods joined together to restructure the urbanscape during 2006, aiming to produce a university area with renewed vitality and resources.

How 'bout Dem Bearcats?

What is a Bearcat? Well, it's one hell of a basketball player. Sporting events, as any good Ohioan could tell you, are enough to bring the community together and instill a sense of belonging and school pride. While football is the main sport at other schools in Ohio, the Bearcats actually have a strong tradition of basketball, fielding a nationally ranked team with a tradition of good play.. One might wonder if it is difficult to get tickets to the games. Absolutely. One student reported camping out overnight to buy tickets to a game that was three weeks away, understanding full well that student tickets to the game would be sold out in a matter of hours. So be sure to get a spot in line early if you want to root for the rowdy Bearcats.

Day by Day

How's the weather? "Schizophrenic," one student explained. According to another student, Cincinnati "doesn't like to make up its mind what season it's supposed to be." One day in winter it may be raining, and the next there might be a wind chill of minus 15 degrees Fahrenheit. "Be prepared for anything" is one motto of the Bearcats.

While the food is reputedly "decent for dorm food," there are plenty of different stations with different types of food in the dining halls. Meals are conveniently located within the dorm buildings so hungry students don't have to brave the unpredictable weather. And if you crave something more ethnic (or just better) and don't mind heading off-campus, you're in luck. Dining options are plentiful and good in Cincinnati. Indian, Chinese, Japanese and Italian restaurants are just a hop, skip and jump away. Make sure you have a car, though, because you will need it if you want to do anything off-campus.

"Diverse people like to do diverse things, and the people at UC are diverse," noted one student. Though perhaps not as much as some schools, UC does boast some diversity. This makes for an entertaining and full social scene. There is a strong Greek presence at the school, but there is also a large contingent of GDIs (God-Damned Independents). And actually, the two groups are fairly fluid, so students don't feel too pressured to join in the frat scene if it's not for them. House parties are generally held in the nearby Clifton area.

There are also plenty of bars and clubs in downtown Cincinnati that students frequent. Aside from partying, according to one student, "there are so many clubs and activities

that it's impossible not to do something." Students are very active around campus, doing everything from club sports to community service, although the former is a bit more popular than the latter. Also, there are on-campus alternatives to parties, such as "Friday Night Live," at which several comics from the show "Whose Line Is It Anyway?" have been known to perform.

> "While other schools may have one thing, there are three huge things that our campus has that others don't."

If you're wondering where you can take a date, the answer's actually Kentucky. Just across the Ohio-Kentucky line is an area called Newport on the Levee. This area has a lot of non-franchise, family-owned restaurants that lend themselves to the romantic atmosphere of a date. Another popular Kentucky destination is the Cold Stone Creamery in that same area.

On campus, be sure to check out McMicken Hall's stone lions that supposedly growl when virgins walk through them, the "haunted" Cincinnati Observatory Center, and the Crosley Tower, which was reportedly created from one continuous pour of concrete.

Class? Oh, Yeah! Class!

UC students have classes too, and depending on the program they are in, most get their money's worth on their education. "While other schools may have one thing, there are three huge things that our campus has that others don't," one student said. "CCM, DAAP and the Engineering School are all awesome programs." The first two stand for the College Conservatory of Music and Design, Architecture, Art and Planning. These three programs are the most competitive at UC, while the Business Program (CBA) and the Nursing Program, one student reported, are accorded less prestige among the students. The most interesting aspect of the academic program at UC, however, are the innovative co-op programs. Co-op is designed to give students real world experience in their program of study, reinforcing what they have learned in class. This experience renders students better equipped to handle their future jobs as well as gets their foot in the door with respect to potential employers. It "really helps with job placement" after school, one student said.

Fortune Telling

The University of Cincinnati does not have the school spirit of some of its other Ohio university brethren, but may get there soon.

The University of Cincinnati is doing a lot to improve itself, and is on the move to provide a well-rounded college experience—while it finishes construction.—*Ashley Elsner*

FYI

If you come to the University of Cincinnati, you'd better bring a "campus map. It's confusing with all the construction going on."

What is the typical weekend schedule? "Thursday through Saturday evenings are spent out and about, and the rest of the weekend is spent putting off work to Sunday."

If I could change one thing about the University of Cincinnati I'd "have better parking and make it less expensive. Even if you have a pass, that doesn't guarantee you'll get a spot in your assigned lot."

Three things every student at the University of Cincinnati should do before graduating are "go to Skyline on Ludlow for chili, talk to people and get involved."

Wittenberg University

Address: Wittenberg, PO Box 720, Springfield, OH 45501
Phone: 937-327-6314
E-mail Address: admission@wittenberg.edu
Web site URL: www.wittenberg.edu
Year Founded: 1842
Private or Public: private
Religious affiliation: Lutheran
Location: suburban
Regular Application Deadline: NA
Number of Applicants: 2,479
Percent Accepted: 82%
Percent Accepted who enroll: 29%
Number Entering: 590
Number of Transfers Accepted each Year: 60
Mean SAT: 1,166
Mean ACT: 24
Middle 50% SAT range: 1,050–1,290

Middle 50% ACT range: 22–24
Early admission program (EA/ ED/ NA): ED/EA
ED or EA Acceptance Rate: NA
Full time Undergraduate enrollment: 1,873
Total enrollment: NA
Percent Male: 45%
Percent Female: 55%
Total Percent Minority: 17%
Percent African-American: 6%
Percent Asian/Pacific Islander: 1%
Percent Hispanic: 1%
Percent Native-American: 0%
Percent Other: NA
Percent in-state / out of state: 75%/25%
Percent from Public HS: 78%
Retention Rate: 82%

Graduation Rate: 65%
Percent in On-campus housing: 85%
Percent affiliated with Greek system: 26%
Percent Varsity or Club Athletes: NA
Number of official organized extracurricular organizations: 130
3 Most popular majors: Biological and Physical Sciences, Business, General Teacher Education
Student/Faculty ratio: 12:01
Tuition and Fees: $29,280.00
Cost for Room and Board: $7,498.00
Percent receiving Financial aid, first-year: 71%

Wittenberg is a breath of fresh air for those tired of visiting colleges where the campus is packed with hordes of students grubbed out in last night's pajamas and sweats heading in every direction. If you want to attend a school where the students are dressed, always remember to accessorize with gleaming smiles, and where everybody knows your name, well then, Wittenberg is definitely the school for you.

We're talking Quality, not Quantity

When asked about why they chose Wittenberg, most students commented on the small class sizes and the atmosphere. One girl stated that, "From my visit and onward, everyone has been very friendly. Having small class sizes has been beneficial as well, because the professors are much more available when you may need one." As far as class sizes go, don't expect to be a nameless face in an auditorium lecture course. "Class sizes are wonderful! I've never been in a class with more than 30!" a student exclaimed. Class sizes generally range from 12 to 35 students, with basic introductory classes having 35. Higher-level courses are "generally in the teens, but sometimes even less."

The small size of Wittenberg presents

students with a lot of personal attention. One junior stated that, "Since I have been here, I have had countless meetings with faculty discussing future career plans and paths to take. Because the school is small, focus is more on the individual."

> **"Because the school is small, focus is more on the individual."**

Grading at Wittenberg is done on a 10-point scale. Classes are challenging, but students love to work together, and the faculty loves to help. "The students are intelligent, the professors are incredible," a campus newspaper boasted in an article, adding that, "We have more Professors of the Year than any other school in Ohio. We have 24 Fulbright Scholars. Our faculty is incredible." Since Wittenberg professors will know students on a first-name basis, it is hard not to work hard. "There is a lot more expected out of the students . . . students definitely strive to get good grades. The library is always packed and groups of students working on projects can be found all over campus."

As far as requirements go, there are prerequisites in each of the following seven areas: Integrated Learning; Natural World; Social Institutions; Fine, Performing, and Literary Arts; Religious and Philosophical Inquiry; Western Historical Perspectives; Non-Western Cultures. Further requirements dictate that you must cover areas of writing, research, foreign language, computing, speaking, and mathematics. There is also a physical activity requirement, which can be fulfilled by participation in intercollegiate athletics, or by taking various health and fitness courses. Community service is also mandatory. Sophomores must complete 30 hours of community service over the course of one term.

The most popular majors at Witt are Management and Education, but students also rave about Witt's English program. One senior pre-law English Literature major commented that, "the English department here is amazing. I get to work closely with professors; the entire English department knows me well, and is always willing to help." Be on the lookout for East Asian Studies, too, which was named as an increasingly popular major. For those students who aren't too eager to comply with a pre-arranged curriculum, there is also the option of designing your own major. Students can pick classes from a variety of disciplines to cater to their own interests and needs. Communications and Management are generally considered "the easy way out," while the sciences are considered to be toughest courses at the university. One student commented that, "Biology is a pretty difficult major, just because so many classes are required, but it's still totally worth it." And despite not being "remotely near any large body of water," one sophomore said that, "we actually have an excellent Marine Biology program."

While students love the small school, they are also encouraged to study abroad. "The program is excellent!" exclaimed one student. Offering more than 40 options in countries all over the world—from Buddhist temples to safaris in Kenya—the school is very supportive of students going abroad for a semester, or an entire year.

Dodgeball anyone?

Despite Wittenberg's small size, there is a huge selection of clubs and organizations to join. A female student explained that, "Most everyone is involved in at least one thing. It's just so easy because Witt offers something for everyone. We have everything from Student Senate to an improv comedy group called Pocket Lint. If you're interested in something, chances are we have something for it. And if not, it's so easy to create one." Don't believe her? Wittenberg's array sports include archery, cricket, and even dodgeball!

Despite the University's efforts to branch by implementing regional recruitment on the East Coast and in the Mid-West, "Wittenberg probably isn't as diverse as it would like to be," although students all agree that the school is actively working on rectifying the problem. Currently, the minority population is lower than most other schools, but there are still many campus groups promoting diversity, including the Concerned Black Students, Jewish Culture Club, Hispanic Culture Club, and Gay/Straight Alliance. The Polis House, a dorm dedicated to international awareness, promotes cultural awareness by hosting celebrations of holidays for different cultures.

The other six dorms on campus are Tower, Firesetine, Ferncliff, Meyers, New Residence, and Woodlawn. Dorms are assigned to freshmen based on when their applications and tuition fees are submitted. Post-freshman year, there are housing lotteries that students must attend in order to be placed in a dorm. After acquiring over 60 hours of credit, off-campus housing options are made available, though this is also done via a lottery process. Students have mixed feelings regarding whether on—or off-campus housing is better. One upperclassman stated that, "Most everyone lives on-campus, and it's so much more fun that way. People that live off-campus don't make as many friends as fast as those who live in the dorms. There are a few kids from the Springfield area who only live a few minutes away, but still choose to live on-campus anyway." (Wittenberg is located in the middle of Springfield, Ohio, which is described as being "pretty crappy on the south side, but really nice on the north side.") Most students agree that dorms are the easiest place to meet people. But while one student commented that the close proximity promoted by dorm life makes it "hard to not wanna get to know them," another student added that, "you might not always get along."

Greek-ing and Streaking

About one-third of students who live off campus at Wittenberg are in a Greek House. The six sororities and six fraternities on campus are responsible for most of the school's partying. Alcohol is allowed in dorms, but only as long as you are 21. (South Hall is the only substance-free residence hall). The school's enforcement of drugs and alcohol policies are "about middle of the road. Don't be stupid, and you won't get caught." Do not expect to see any frat boys doing keg stands here though—the school has banned beer kegs from all Wittenberg-owned housing, so fraternities do not generally provide alcohol, and parties are mostly BYOB. Despite the keg-ban, fraternities do throw parties "all the time," and "pretty good parties, actually . . . ." Aside from fraternity parties, students also enjoy hangouts such as the school's Student Union, which has yummy late-night food and a bar. The Ringside Café is also a student favorite; kids go throughout the week to unwind with a few drinks.

A description of Wittenberg is incomplete without mention of the Hollow, a grassy valley that is perfect for sunbathing and playing Frisbee on sunny days, sledding on snowy winter days, and streaking at night, regardless of the weather. The Hollow hosts Wittfest, the annual spring music festival sponsored by Union Board. Past Wittfest performers have included the Nappy Roots, American Hi-Fi, Hootie and the Blowfish, and 10,000 Maniacs. Springfield residents also attend the music festival, and there are carnival activities, such as inflatable obstacle courses, to provide amusement while the bands play.

Ultimately, students describe life at Wittenberg as "the perfect fit." The small-town feel of the school and the surrounding city draws people in. "The only bad thing about it being so small is that everyone knows everyone else's business. We tend to call it Wittenberg High School sometimes," explains one student. Wittenberg is a school where everybody knows your name—and then some.
—*Christine Grace Lin*

FYI
If you come to Wittenberg, you'd better bring "your own case of beer or a flask."
If I could change one thing about Wittenberg, I'd "make is just a little bit bigger. An extra 500 students would spice up campus life."
What's the typical weekend schedule? "Go to the football game if it's a home game, hang out at The Hollow if it's nice out, catch up on work, and hit a few frat parties."
The three things every student should do before graduating are "study abroad, study abroad, study abroad!"

Oklahoma

Oklahoma State University

Address: Oklahoma State, 101 Whitehurst Hall, Stillwater, OK 74078
Phone: 405-744-6858
E-mail Address: admit@okstate.edu
Web site URL: www.okstate.edu
Year Founded: 1,890
Private or Public: public
Religious affiliation: none
Location: urban
Regular Application Deadline: rolling
Number of Applicants: NA
Percent Accepted: 87%
Percent Accepted who enroll: 55%
Number Entering: NA
Number of Transfers Accepted each Year: 2,248
Mean SAT: NA
Mean ACT: 25
Middle 50% SAT range: 1,000–1,250

Middle 50% ACT range: 22–27
Early admission program (EA/ ED/ NA): NA
ED or EA Acceptance Rate: NA
Full time Undergraduate enrollment: 18,600
Total enrollment: 22,862
Percent Male: 51%
Percent Female: 49%
Total Percent Minority: 17%
Percent African-American: 4%
Percent Asian/Pacific Islander: 2%
Percent Hispanic: 2%
Percent Native-American: 9%
Percent Other: NA
Percent in-state / out of state: 78%/22%
Percent from Public HS: NA
Retention Rate: 79%

Graduation Rate: 60%
Percent in On-campus housing: 38%
Percent affiliated with Greek system: 30%
Percent Varsity or Club Athletes: NA
Number of official organized extracurricular organizations: 404
3 Most popular majors: Journalism, Management Science, Marketing
Student/Faculty ratio: 19:01
Tuition and Fees: $11,835.00
In State Tuition and Fees (if different): $3,263.00
Cost for Room and Board: $6,015.00
Percent receiving Financial aid, first-year: 44%

W hen you think of Oklahoma State University, what's the first thing that comes to mind? Cowboys? Well, contrary to the commonly-held perception, students at OSU come from diverse backgrounds, and the land and agriculture are perhaps the last things uniting the student body. Ranked as one of the top accounting schools in the nation, OSU has shed its agricultural image and offers its students a wide selection of academic, extracurricular, and social activities. The school's small-town atmosphere attracts many students, and its proximity to Oklahoma City and Tulsa provides additional venues for recreation and cultural activities.

Academics

Students are generally pleased with their academic experience at Oklahoma State University. Like many other colleges, OSU has academic requirements students must fulfill in order to graduate. The requirements vary within each major; however, every student must take courses in political science, English, American history, and American government. Hard majors include "anything that requires chemistry or physics," such as engineering and pre-med. Marketing and education are considered to be easy majors at OSU. Depending on the level of the course, the class size can vary. Most general education classes range from 20 to 75 students, but some science classes can have up to 250 students. In addition to classroom learning, students at OSU frequently have the opportunity to participate in projects and research conducted by professors and other staff members. "Freshman year I was involved in a research scholars program where I actually got to be in a lab with a professor after having little to no training. I got to do a lot of hands-on stuff that I would not have otherwise been able to do," recalled one student.

From time to time, OSU invites celebrities, politicians and other renowned figures to speak on-campus. Recent speakers include Phylicia Rashad, Suzanne Somers, and Magic Johnson. Students praise the faculty for their availability outside of class and are mostly satisfied with the quality of education at OSU. "I am most thrilled about the information I am learning in my classes, and my only grievance is that there is not enough time to do everything I need to be doing," said one student.

The Campus Experience

So what kind of student attends OSU? "The stereotype is that we are all hicks from small towns, but that is not the case at all!" said one student. In fact, the student body at OSU is fairly diverse. Students from both large cities and small towns attend OSU. The majority of the student body is Caucasian, with a moderate mix of minorities and international students. However, students agree that the student body is accepting of diversity and respects each other's beliefs. OSU is also home to many valedictorians, as well as multiple Rhodes, Truman, Marshall, and Udall scholars. It claims to be one of the best institutions of higher education in the western United States.

The Greek system is of great significance at OSU—15% of the student body belongs to a fraternity or sorority. There are currently 15 sororities and 20 fraternities at OSU. "Most of the time when you go somewhere, one of the first questions people ask you is, 'Are you in a house?'" said one student. Often, the best parties on campus are organized by fraternities, but in order to attend these events, you must either be a member of a sorority or fraternity, or be invited by a member. The Frontier, Destination, and Plantation Balls are a few of the parties hosted by fraternities.

For students who are not members of a Greek house, there is still a wide range of weekend and social activities to select from. "Though Stillwater is a small town, it is college-oriented, so there is always something going on and if not, there is always the option of going out to eat in the city or Tulsa," said one student. For the most part, freshmen and upperclassmen do the same things on the weekends. Some people drink and party; some people hang out with friends; and for those who live nearby, there is always the option of going home. The drinking scene is fairly big at OSU. However, students are not pressured to drink, and non-drinkers can fit in at any social event. OSU has many student organizations that are respected by both students and faculty. From intramurals to student government to community service projects, students can find just about any activity to suit their interests and passion. Many students agree that involvement in extracurriculars is a great way to make friends and to contribute to the school.

The Student Union Activities Board is considered one of the premier leadership organizations on-campus. The Board has sponsored visits from various prominent figures, such as former first lady Barbara Bush and sex therapist Dr. Ruth Westheimer. Many students are involved in committees for Homecoming festivities, which are said to be the third largest in the nation. Two campus-wide community service projects are held every year, one in the fall and one in spring. Called "Into the Streets" and "The Big Event," respectively, these projects require students to give up one day each semester to provide community service to those in need throughout Stillwater. Every year before the first home football game, students put on a big show called Orange Peel. Celebrities such as Bill Cosby, Faith Hill, and Sinbad have taken part in this event in the previous years. Depending on the organization and the student's interests, time commitment to extracurriculars can range from as few as five hours to as many as 30 hours a month.

The sports scene has a significant presence on OSU's campus. Basketball and football are perhaps the school's most popular sports, but the school is also known for its wrestling team, which won the national wrestling championship from 2003 to 2006. Referring to OSU's athletes, one student said, "Our guys are unbeatable." For those who are not on sports teams, intramurals and recreational activities in the fitness center are also popular. The Wellness Center and the Colvin Center are two athletic facilities open to students.

Grubbin' and Cribbin' Options

OSU students unanimously describe the campus as beautiful. "All of the architecture is modified Georgian architecture, so all the buildings look the same," said one student. Another student commented, "Our school is so pretty, I feel like I can be comfortable anywhere on-campus." The student union building is the largest in the nation, and many of the campus's facilities are under renovation. Five—and ten-year plans for $825 million of spending for academic, research, student life, and athletic facilities were recently approved. The master plan calls for the construction of new academic and student life buildings, revamping of all athletic facilities and the development of an athletic village, a campus irrigation system, four addition parking facilities, the reopening of the Hall of Fame Avenue, and construction of the west end zone of Boone Pickens Stadium.

There are plenty of restaurants and dance clubs (such as Tumbleweed and The Ozone) and a movie theater in the campus's vicinity. Students also have the option of traveling to Tulsa or Oklahoma City, which are each an hour away from OSU. The majority of the students have cars, but not having one should not preclude students from taking full advantage of all that the campus and its vicinities have to offer.

Students are required to live on-campus or in a Greek house their freshman year, unless their parents live in Stillwater and they want to live at home. Most freshmen live in standard dorms, which, according to many students, are "fairly nice." Freshman student housing continually evolves as dorms are replaced with apartment-type housing. The new system should be completed within the next few years. Most dormitories are air-conditioned and have a lot of storage space, leaving enough room to be comfortable. These new apartments and suites are embodied in Patchin-Jones Hall. The diversity of living styles among OSU students is mirrored by the diversity in living arrangements provided by the administration: besides apartment-style housing, there are also traditional high rises and Greek houses. Campus housing is available to all students, but most students choose to move to an apartment or a Greek house after freshman year. Marriage housing and honors dorms are a few of the other special housing options offered by OSU. "We also have a Spanish floor at one of our dorms, where student can only speak Spanish. I think it's a great idea!" said one student. RAs are present on every floor but are reportedly lenient and easy-going, for the most part.

Students at OSU are satisfied with the various dining options OU offers. "The cafeterias and places to use your meal plan are excellent. I never had a problem with not liking the food," said one student. Although students can choose from 10 different campus cafés, most eat at the non-cafeteria concessions on campus, which offer pizza, sandwiches, hamburgers, and "anything and everything you could possibly want." There are also a lot of restaurants in Stillwater. The most famous is Eskimo Joe's, which used to be a bar and is now a restaurant by day, bar by night. Thursday nights are big for Joe's—the place is almost always packed after 11 p.m. The Hideaway offers great pizza, Joseppi's offers Italian food; in addition, you have the typical Red Lobster, Chili's, Applebee's, and other small restaurants.

"The people at OSU are very friendly and down to earth!"

When asked to choose one thing that differentiated OSU from other schools, students replied that the student body is worthy of distinction. "The people at OSU are very friendly and down to earth!" remarked one student. Many students said they would choose to attend OSU again in a heartbeat. "OSU has opened up so many opportunities for me to excel. The Greek systems offer long-lasting friendships, the campus activities provide leadership opportunities, and international study programs broaden our view of the world. I never expected to walk away from OSU having had so many great experiences and memories."—*Soo Kim*

FYI

If you come to Oklahoma State University, you'd better bring a "desire to meet new people. If you leave OSU without meeting the people, you've missed out on one of the campus' best assets."

What is the typical weekend schedule? "Parties usually start on Thursday night and occur on Friday and Saturday night too. On weekends in the fall when we have football games, students tailgate and celebrate before and after the game."

If I could change one thing about Oklahoma State University, I'd "change the University's policy on bad weather. OSU never closes or cancels class, regardless of the weather."

Three things every student at Oklahoma State University should do before graduating are "go to all the athletic events possible, get involved in one of the many student organizations on campus, and participate in Homecoming festivities."

Oral Roberts University

Address: Oral Roberts, 7777
S. Lewis Avenue, Tulsa, OK
74171
Phone: 800-678-8876
E-mail Address:
admissions@oru.edu
Web site URL: www.oru.edu
Year Founded: 1963
Private or Public: private
Religious affiliation: Christian
interdenominonetiononel
Location: urban
**Regular Application
Deadline:** rolling
Number of Applicants: NA
Percent Accepted: 67%
**Percent Accepted who
enroll:** 61%
Number Entering: NA
**Number of Transfers
Accepted each Year:** NA
Mean SAT: 1,061
Mean ACT: 23
Middle 50% SAT range:
955–1,200

Middle 50% ACT range:
20–27
**Early admission program
(EA/ ED/ NA):** NA
ED or EA Acceptance Rate:
NA
**Full time Undergraduate
enrollment:** 3,303
Total enrollment: NA
Percent Male: 42%
Percent Female: 58%
Total Percent Minority: 26%
Percent African-American:
16%
**Percent Asian/Pacific
Islander:** 2%
Percent Hispanic: 6%
Percent Native-American:
2%
Percent Other: NA
**Percent in-state / out of
state:** 29%/71%
Percent from Public HS: NA
Retention Rate: 82%
Graduation Rate: 54%

**Percent in On-campus
housing:** 47%
**Percent affiliated with
Greek system:** NA
**Percent Varsity or Club
Athletes:** NA
**Number of official
organized extracurricular
organizations:** NA
3 Most popular majors:
Marketing/Marketing
Management, Mass
Communications/Media
Studies, Theology/
Theological Studies
Student/Faculty ratio:
16:01
Tuition and Fees:
$16,170.00
Cost for Room and Board:
$7,060.00
**Percent receiving
Financial aid, first-year:**
70%

S ixty-foot, thirty-ton bronze Praying
Hands grace the main entrance to Oral
Roberts University, indicating to all
visitors that ORU not only offers its students
academic guidance from the Ivory Tower, it
also directs students to depend on a lifetime's teachings from God. Due to its religious founding, students at the University
are encouraged to continually grow academically, physically, *and* spiritually. They
are given the unique opportunity to combine a top-notch education with a passionate religious and cultural experience. These
aspects of the ORU experience require students to adhere to strict rules such as a
dress code and as well as to refrain from the
partying that is characteristic of your "typical" college experience. Students are also
required to participate in mandatory chapel
services twice a week so they can continually live out the school founder's vision.
Evangelist Oral Roberts claims that God in-
structed him to found a university based on
"God's commission and the holy spirit."
Roberts obeyed this mandate and in 1965
opened Oral Roberts University in Tulsa.
Few universities can claim that they were
built as a result of a message directly from

God but Oral Roberts University is one of
the few that can.

Academics

As a Christian school, Oral Roberts University emphasizes students' personal spiritual
growth alongside a challenging academic
education. Students at Oral Roberts say academics are noticeably "above average" and
"top-notch." Students have the option to enroll in one of five undergraduate schools: the
School of Arts & Sciences, the School of
Business, the School of Education, the
School of LifeLong Education, or the Anna
Vaughn School of Nursing.

The five schools vary in difficulty but all
are known to be academically rigorous. According to one student, "The School of Education is very tough. There is a lot required of
education majors, but it is a good thing. We
have an exceptional program here and it
makes the hard work worth it, because I
know I am getting the best, top-of-the-line
education." The School of LifeLong Education provides flexible, quality education programs to adult learners and non-traditional
students. The business school is considered
"exceptional" and also offers a 5-year MBA

program. The School of Nursing is also "well-known and hard." Not surprisingly, the theology department within the School of Arts and Sciences is "incredible."

Especially attractive is the Honors Program, which admits 16 to 18 top applicants every year as Fellows. These students enroll in one three-credit hour Fellows Seminar each semester, in addition to one or two other Honors credit courses. Other highly qualified applicants are designated as Honors Program Scholars. Honors students are even invited to live in special dormitory wings with respected quiet hours, and a "quality academic atmosphere."

Faculty and staff at ORU devote themselves to building a university for God by actively participate in the lives of their students. ORU students appreciate this devotion and recognize its contribution to the successful academic environment. According to one undergrauduate, "All faculty are extremely willing to go the extra mile for their students." Many students even describe faculty-student relationships as their favorite aspect of ORU academics, specifically noting the "personal help [the students] receive."

The religious atmosphere at Oral Roberts emphasizes a non-competitive academic environment where "everybody would rather help you than compete against you." According to one student, competition is found "only in intramurals," an important part of campus life at ORU.

In Pursuit of Principled Social Life

ORU has been described as a place where students "get their learning and keep their burning." So life at the University goes well beyond academics. One unique feature of the ORU is an honor code which is taken very seriously and forbids the use of alcohol, tobacco, and drugs, as well as lying, cheating, cursing and pre-marital sex. The honor code, which is submitted with the application to the University, also requires students to attend all classes and chapel services and to participate in a physical fitness program. Unlike most universities around the country, weekend activities are not centered on drinking. This may be a result of the honor code, or it may just be a result of students' adherence to Christian values. Although drinking is not very common, it does occur, but usually off campus. According to one student, "nobody really drinks in the dorms unless they keep it on the down low." Drugs are even less prevalent than alcohol.

Instead of drinking, students who stay on campus spend their free time playing intramurals and attending dorm and sporting events. Most students do not stay on campus during the weekend. Instead, they tend to visit coffee shops, restaurants, and clubs, as well as commuter students' homes away from campus. Students usually have cars so they can visit these off-campus sites, as "Tulsa does not have a good public transportation system." According to one student, "Tulsa is very boring without a car."

One student said that stereotypical ORU students may be described "as Bible beaters and Jesus-freaks but also as hard-working, honest, respected people." While the student population at ORU boasts geographic diversity, in that the school attracts students from all 50 states and 55 different countries, all students are connected by their faith. "For the most part everybody has a relationship with God, which makes the people pretty much all the same. But as far as culture goes, there is a good mix," said one student.

Living as "brothers" and "sisters"

Most students will live in dorms unless they are commuters, married, or over age 25. Students generally do not mind that they are required to live on campus, because it creates a sense of "community spirit." Dorms are divided into wings, and freshmen are randomly assigned to a wing in a single-sex dorm. Each male wing is paired with a specific female wing, and "brother wings" and "sister wings" allow freshmen to meet members of the opposite sex. Brother and sister wings "plan events together, sit together in Chapel, and also have designated seats" together in the cafeteria. Freshmen may request a particular dorm if they have had family in that dorm, or they may be recruited by a particular wing. The wings that "recruit, draft on, and initiate people" are similar to fraternities, except the students live in dormitory halls, instead of separate houses elsewhere on campus. One of the oldest and most respected wings on campus is known as YoungBlood. Dorms are also known for their particular personalities. According to one student, "Claudius is the freshman, fun, social dorm. EMR is the fun, manly man's dorm. Michael and Wesley are for more of the pretty boys. Gabby is for the rich girls."

Freshmen generally find it easy to make friends in their own wings, or in their respective brother or sister wing. Additionally, freshmen do not feel excluded from upperclassmen's activities since, "everybody is included in whatever is going on." But according to one senior, the upperclassmen have much less free time for socializing. Every floor has an RA and a chaplain. RAs enforce curfews, notify students of events, and maintain general order on the floor. Chaplains provide students with spiritual support.

One thing ORU students all agree on is the strangeness and originality of campus architecture. One student describes it as "space age" and another describes it as "like the Jetsons." Most find it ugly at first, but all agree that it grows on them. Currently, roofs of buildings are being improved and construction for a new student center is underway.

Students generally hang out in and around the cafeteria and at the restaurants on campus, such as the Eagle's Nest or the internet café. When the weather is nice, they spend time on the quad as well. Favorite places on campus include the Prayer Gardens, surrounding the base of the 200-foot tall Prayer Tower which serves as the visitor's center and the Kenneth H. Cooper Aerobics Center (AC), a two-story building housing athletic facilities and exercise equipment. Located in a very safe neighborhood, ORU offers an extremely safe campus environment. There are no problems between the students and the residents of the surrounding neighborhoods. As one student put it, "They love us."

There is only one cafeteria on campus, but according to a student, it has "good variety. They try hard. You have to be creative sometimes." Another student agrees it is "better than most cafeterias I have eaten in, but it still gets old and is avoided most of the time." Students are required to be on a 17, 14, or 10-meal per week meal plan and each comes with a certain number of Eagle Bucks that can be used at different restaurants, as well as the coffee shop or bookstore. Even when the students tire of cafeteria food, it is not a problem since Tulsa boasts, "a huge restaurant variety—anything and everything you can imagine."

Sports as a Requirement

Oral Roberts University aims to "educate the whole man: spirit, mind, and body. Staying in shape and treating our bodies well is just as important as our mental state." In addition to most students' abstention from alcohol, drugs, and tobacco, students are all required to participate in some sort of physical activity. One way to do this is to participate in a varsity sport. The Oral Roberts Golden Eagles compete in eight Division I sports for both men and women. Though the school is fairly young and school pride and traditions are still developing, sporting events are well-attended. Basketball is especially popular at the 10,000-seat Mabee Basketball Stadium. For students who do not want the time commitment of Division I athletics, intramurals are popular as well. Intramural sports such as basketball, soccer, volleyball, flag football, tennis, badminton, and ping pong are extremely competitive.

> **"Staying in shape and treating our bodies well is just as important as our mental state."**

Outside of academics and athletics, students have many job opportunities on and off campus. Students are very committed to their extracurricular activities as well. Some students take part in mission trips, others write for the school newspaper, *The Oracle*, and some are involved in community outreach or the Leadership Academy. A unique group, called the Student Association allows students to play an active role in the decision-making and programming of the university.

ORU instructs its young people in how to combine morality with worldly endeavors like business and medicine and other professional arenas featured in its academic programs. The University's facilities, high tech amenities, and space age architecture contrasts greatly with the university's embrace of an old school mentality concerning academica life. Students all agree that devotion to God comes first; they love being in a strict academic environment where they are given the opportunity to "grow as a Christian." In the words of University President Roberts (who is son of the university's founder) ORU is a "ministry with a University not a University with a Ministry." If you are seeking a spiritual, as well as an academic, collegiate experience, you may be one of the growing number of applicants considering Oral Roberts University.—*Jessica Rubin*

FYI

If you come to Oral Roberts, you'd better bring "flip-flops" and "your bible . . . I guess."

What's the typical weekend schedule? "Friday: Coffee Shops, local concerts at Cain's Ballroom, out to eat and a movie. Saturday: maybe a basketball game or a drive-in movie. Sunday: Church, lunch and a nap. Next, the campus worship service."

If I could change one thing about Oral Roberts, I'd "get rid of the curfew and allow co-ed dorms" and "get more people to come here!"

Three things every student at Oral Roberts should do before graduating are "swim in the fountains, run the Howard Run (streaking around Howard Auditorium), and love our President."

University of Oklahoma

Address: University of Oklahoma, 1000 Asp Avenue, Norman, OK 73019
Phone: 800-234-6868
E-mail Address: admrec@ou.edu
Web site URL: www.ou.edu
Year Founded: 1890
Private or Public: public
Religious affiliation: none
Location: small city
Regular Application Deadline: 2-Apr
Number of Applicants: 7,471
Percent Accepted: 91%
Percent Accepted who enroll: 48%
Number Entering: 3,342
Number of Transfers Accepted each Year: 2,537
Mean SAT: 1,175
Mean ACT: 25
Middle 50% SAT range: NA

Middle 50% ACT range: 23–28
Early admission program (EA/ ED/ NA): NA
ED or EA Acceptance Rate: NA
Full time Undergraduate enrollment: 19,600
Total enrollment: 27,275
Percent Male: 49%
Percent Female: 51%
Total Percent Minority: 22%
Percent African-American: 5%
Percent Asian/Pacific Islander: 6%
Percent Hispanic: 4%
Percent Native-American: 7%
Percent Other: 2%
Percent in-state / out of state: 76%/24%
Percent from Public HS: NA

Retention Rate: 85%
Graduation Rate: 59%
Percent in On-campus housing: 28%
Percent affiliated with Greek system: 49%
Percent Varsity or Club Athletes: NA
Number of official organized extracurricular organizations: 359
3 Most popular majors: Journalism, Nursing, Sociology
Student/Faculty ratio: 19:01
Tuition and Fees: $11,295.00
In State Tuition and Fees (if different): $3,006.00
Cost for Room and Board: $6,863.00

Nestled in America's heartland, in the small town of Norman (just south of Oklahoma City) lies the University of Oklahoma. But OU, as the university is commonly called, is much more than the visible cluster of red brick buildings and bustling students. It is truly its own world, filled with incredible school spirit and rich tradition. Just two minutes at an OU football game (especially the "Red River Shootout," the face-off between OU and its arch-rival, the University of Texas) will lead any observer to realize that OU is no typical school. The "Boomer, Sooner" chant that fills the stadium will amaze visitors and excite students, alumni, and fans.

Who are the Boomers and Sooners, you ask? Well, the Boomers were pioneers who helped bring about Oklahoma's opening to settlers in the 1880s. The Sooners, on the other hand, were those unruly settlers who slipped in before President Harrison officially opened the territory. Today, the Sooners are the 21,000 plus students that make up the University of Oklahoma.

Party Like A Greek

In terms of extracurricular activities, Greek life and athletics rule the roost at OU. 50 percent of Sooners belong to a fraternity or sorority (it's no wonder, since there are 39 of them on campus!). For Greek women, the school year starts a week early with rush in August. To accommodate this, on-campus housing permits freshman girls to move in before rush begins, so they are comfortably settled for the hectic week. And no one need worry about being left out—in recent years,

President Boren reorganized the rush system to ensure that everyone who rushes all week will receive a bid to at least one sorority. Said one member, "Rush is a crazy process, but it's worth it in the end."

One aspect of Greek life that almost every participant appreciates is the exciting party scene. Theme parties, fraternity/sorority mixers, and date parties are just a few of the social events in the Greek world, and "rarely does a weekend go by without some kind of sorority/fraternity event." The Greek system is a major part of OU's social life, but it isn't the only part. "Obviously, there is a large fraternity and sorority life but not so big that it's hard to make friends without being in one," explained one freshman. Many students find friends in other extracurricular activities—sports, theatre, political or community service organizations—and others meet people just by "going to dinner, studying, and hanging out in the dorms." For those who are part of a fraternity or sorority, parties often take place in fraternity houses, but plenty of parties are held in non-Greek houses or apartments also.

The weekend usually starts on Thursday at OU, and Sooners know how to finish off each school week in style. Thursdays are often packed with fraternity parties and house parties. Fridays can be party nights too, but as one student explains, "Fridays are usually a little more low-key." Many students choose to just "hang out and rest up" for Saturday—and if it's a football weekend, that rest is much needed. "Everyone goes to the game at least four hours early to tailgate." School spirit abounds, with face paint, OU T-shirts, and flags everywhere. "There are a lot of die-hard Sooners out there—people who literally bleed crimson." Many alumni also attend each game. "Once a Sooner, always a Sooner" seems to be a motto most OU fans live by.

However, extreme school spirit has its downsides. If the Sooners lose, prepare to mourn. One freshman described the first OU loss she witnessed: "No one talked for about three days." Some students got angry, turning over trash cans and loudly lamenting the loss, but most just "walked around like zombies." But after a win, Norman rejoices. No one throws a better victory party than a Sooner, and campus is certainly alive on these Saturday nights (and, well, most Saturday nights). Although OU has recently cracked down on underage drinking, implementing an intimidating-but-rarely-enforced Three Strike System, students don't have to look very far to find alcohol. As one student puts it, "OU is a dry campus, but I haven't seen much dryness."

Still, while football and partying are like oxygen to many Sooners, there are many other weekend activities to appeal to every interest. Many students spend their weekends seeing productions at the OU School of Drama, watching movies, visiting Oklahoma City, or simply relaxing. And there is certainly no lack of clubs and activities at OU. "There are millions of organizations," commented one student. "Some students seem to do everything, and others do absolutely nothing." Whether you prefer to spend your free time saving the environment, playing Guitar Hero, or partying, you can do it at OU.

A More Academic Image

OU may have a student body of over 21,000, but that doesn't mean hundreds of students are packed into every class. "I had one class of about 100 kids," states one student, "but most of my classes have about 35 students." All classes are taught by professors, and most students claim that professors are remarkably accessible, considering the number of students they teach. "You can email professors anytime, even in a class of 200. They're really good about helping students out." However, getting into first-choice classes can be challenging. "I got into most of the classes I wanted," says one freshman, "but it's hard because freshmen register last."

> **"OU may have a student body of over 21,000, but that doesn't mean hundreds of students are packed into every class."**

The work at OU can be challenging, but "once you learn how to handle it, it's definitely manageable." In recent years, the university seems to be shooting for a more "academic image." Among the current Sooner student body are 700 National Merit Scholars; in fact, OU has the most National Merit Scholars enrolled per capita. The university is also among the top five in Rhodes Scholar graduates.

OU makes sure its top scholars are rewarded. Students in the Honors College (who must qualify with higher test scores and high school GPA) benefit from an early registration process, which allows them to enroll in "practically any class they want." Honors College students are the only ones who can graduate with honors, and they can enroll in small sections of about 20 students.

House Rules

On-campus housing is mandatory for all freshman students under age 20 (although there seem to be some exceptions to this rule), but many students choose to remain on campus all four years. OU's dorms are in the middle of a renovation project. Of the dorms, Couch and Walker are the most popular. "Couch is nice because it's been renovated, and all the furniture can be moved around." Couch also has the added bonus of the Couch Express, a small store and grill. Walker has a small convenience store named Etcetera, but it hasn't been renovated yet. Adams, another freshman dorm, is "not quite as nice." It has a Burger King on the ground floor, but "none of the towers connect, and the floor plan is really confusing." Freshman dorms are coed by floor, and upperclass dorms are coed by suite. RAs live on the floors with freshmen, and are "pretty helpful," although they do have to enforce the visitor rules, which state that coed visitors must leave freshman rooms by 12 a.m. on weeknights and 2 a.m. on weekends.

OU's on-campus dining facilities get mixed reviews, but most students agree that there is certainly plenty of variety available. Students can use meal points at the cafeteria, any on-campus convenience stores, and at the food court in the Student Union, which is a popular hangout. Many students move off campus after their freshman year, but plenty of students remain. "Some people think it's weird to live on campus after freshman year," explained one student, "but it's so much more convenient."

For students who live off-campus, finding parking on campus can a real pain. "You have to get to campus pretty early just to find a parking spot." Although there is public transit around campus and Norman, most students have cars. "I don't know what I'd do without my car," one student said. "If you want to go anywhere off campus, you pretty much need to drive."

And where do students go in their cars? One favorite in Norman is the Classic 50s Drive-In, which caters to Sooners with tasty hamburgers, shakes, and other staples. There are several other popular restaurants in Norman, as well as some "cute little shops" and a mall. "Biggest surprise about OU: I looooove Norman!" exclaimed one student. "To me, it is the perfect college town." One thing that is unique about Norman is that it is "all OU, all the time." And, if the small-town scene gets too repetitive, Oklahoma City is just 15 miles down the highway.

Southern Style

At first glance, OU's student body seems pretty homogeneous. "Most of the students are white, but there are a lot of African-American and Hispanic students also." Sooners have a reputation for being an unusually attractive bunch, but they don't necessarily flaunt it. "Most people are pretty casual—you know, T-shirts, jeans, flip-flops." In other words, no one is ostracized for wearing sweats to class. Still, in true Southern fashion, most OU students try to look good and keep fit, often using the university's gym facilities or intramural sports teams to help them along the way. One stereotype most Sooners would like to banish, however, is that "we are *not* rednecks." The majority of students come from Oklahoma, the Midwest, and Texas, but students come to OU from all over the country and even outside the country. And, because of OU's theatre and arts departments and on-campus museums, Sooners have plenty of cultural outlets. "There are lots of neat, cultured people here."

But, cultured or uncultured, majority or minority, Greek or non-Greek, all OU students have one thing in common: Sooner pride. Many students make up the fourth or fifth generation in their family to attend OU. And when they make the annual 187 mile trek from Norman down to Dallas for the OU/UT game, it doesn't matter where they're from or what they look like—all that matters is the color of their T-shirt and the cheer on their lips: "Boomer Sooner!"—*Elizabeth Bewley*

FYI

If you come to The University of Oklahoma, you'd better bring "your adventurous side, your pride, and sometimes a winter jacket."

What is the typical weekend schedule? "head to a frat party on Friday night (assuming you can get in), go to a football game Saturday morning after the tailgate, and sleep in Sunday."

If I could change one thing about The University of Oklahoma, I'd "change its proximity to outside life."

Three things every University of Oklahoma student should do before graduating are: "go to the UT/Oklahoma football game, take advantage of agriculture in the area, and join a fraternity."

The University of Tulsa

Address: University of Tulsa, Office of Admission, 600 S. College, Tulsa, OK 74104
Phone: 800-331-3050
E-mail Address: admission@utulsa.edu
Web site URL: www.utulsa.edu
Year Founded: 1894
Private or Public: private
Religious affiliation: Presbyterian
Location: urban
Regular Application Deadline: 15-Feb
Number of Applicants: 2,720
Percent Accepted: 75%
Percent Accepted who enroll: 32%
Number Entering: 825
Number of Transfers Accepted each Year: 314
Mean SAT: NA
Mean ACT: NA
Middle 50% SAT range: 1,070–1,380

Middle 50% ACT range: 23–30
Early admission program (EA/ ED/ NA): NA
ED or EA Acceptance Rate: NA
Full time Undergraduate enrollment: 2,712
Total enrollment: 4,125
Percent Male: 50%
Percent Female: 50%
Total Percent Minority: 19%
Percent African-American: 7%
Percent Asian/Pacific Islander: 3%
Percent Hispanic: 4%
Percent Native-American: 5%
Percent Other: 0%
Percent in-state / out of state: 54%/46%
Percent from Public HS: 78%

Retention Rate: 82%
Graduation Rate: 61%
Percent in On-campus housing: 60%
Percent affiliated with Greek system: 22%
Percent Varsity or Club Athletes: 30%
Number of official organized extracurricular organizations: 245
3 Most popular majors: Management, Marketing, Mechanical Engineering
Student/Faculty ratio: 11:01
Tuition and Fees: $20,738.00
Cost for Room and Board: $7,052.00
Percent receiving Financial aid, first-year: 52%

In the alphabet of life, the letter 'T' stands for many things: tortoise, telepathy, toiletries, tots. But when 't' stands for tenacity, talent, tradition, and togetherness, all in one setting, why that is when it also stands for TU, also known as the University of Tulsa. Now, you may be saying to yourself, TU? Did you say TU? Because then should it not be Tulsa University rather than the University of Tulsa? Perhaps yes. Perhaps no. And perhaps this grammatical flip-flop, though perplexing, perfectly demonstrates the small-size/big-time duality which TU actualizes.

Hackedemics

Across the board, TU is habitually known for its challenging academics (especially in the field of engineering.) And this can be attractive to strong-minded and/or intelligent young adults (indeed one of every ten students in the TU 2004 class are National Merit Scholars.) But we all know the most attractive attribute about a college to any young adult person is how that education will help him to land an eight-figure salary, become an icon, and/or hack into neighboring governments' intelligence computers. Yet, TU already knows all of that.

The University of Tulsa is "one of six pioneer institutions selected by the National Science Foundation to participate in the Federal Cyber Service Initiative (a.k.a. Cyber Corps) to train students for federal careers as computer security experts." This basically translates to "TU receiving $2.7 million to create a band of information security specialists who know how to defend the free-world and defend the internet from hackers." These students come out of the program not only with a degree in computer science and a couple years of their tuition paid for, but also "multiple federal-level computer security certificates as endorsed by the CNSS." They also get a new pick-up line: "excuse me, I seemed to have dropped my multiple federal-level computer security certificates around here . . ."

However, if computers are not your "bag," TU also receives funding for the "Tulsa Undergraduate Research Challenge, which lets students get involved in advanced research with faculty members as early as their freshman year." It is no wonder that in 2004, four students received Goldwater scholarships (the maximum awarded annually) and that in the past year, "nine University of Tulsa students won nationally competitive scholarships." But the "level of academic strain or prowess is totally dependent on what you want and your major—communication majors have it relatively easy, whereas students with majors like nursing and engineering can easily take up residency in the library."

Classes for Claustrophobics

Come to the University of Tulsa and never feel the restless constriction of cramming into a 500-seat auditorium with a bunch of pungent, pajama-wearing cohorts for the introductory lecture of Rocks for Jocks 101. Why? Because at TU, the average class-size is 20 students, 62 percent of classes are under 20 students, and only 1 percent of classes holds 50 or more students. This allows for one-on-one instruction in an environment that "feels like home," an environment where "the teachers become easy friends and mentors, who are so approachable, accommodating, and helpful." Sounds like a little slice of heaven, eh? Except in heaven you do not have to factor in that "attendance policies that can lower your grade making it so you can't skip class." In a class of 100, it is possible, but in a class of 12, hiding an absence can prove fruitless. Nonetheless, young adults (local, national, or international) continue to flock to TU in droves, thanks to the attentive faculty, the 11:1 student/teacher ratio, and the fact that "the school is small enough to not feel invisible, but also big enough where you are always meeting new people."

You and Me and Greek Makes Three

This constant confluence of new friendships may be in a large part related to how actively involved the students are within campus organizations. Ninety percent of students participate in some sort of club or organization—the "big ones" being: Young Democrats, FCA, Intramurals, or SA. SA is the Student Association which organizes most of the "big events" on campus, including Homecoming and Springfest—"a week of activities, free stuff, and concerts (Ben Folds, Hanson, 50 Cent, Vertical Horizon, etc.), with amazing tailgating on the 'U' before the football game."

Many of the other annual events are held by Greek frats or sororities, most have "philanthropy weeks that are way fun—usually games, competitions, and then parties on the weekends—all to raise money for their chosen organization." A favorite is the Lambda Chi's LUAU which is a "sand volleyball tourney where they cover a parking lot with sand

and anyone can play, it's kinda a big deal." At TU, only about a fifth of the students pledge a fraternity of sorority, making Greek life "an option but not a must." If a frat holds a party or philanthropic event, anyone can attend, "so people do not feel like they have to go Greek in order to have a social life."

> **"The school is small enough to not feel invisible, but also big enough where you are always meeting new people."**

In fact, if you want an ample social network, Intramurals might be a better bet. Eighty percent of the students partake of the intramural program, and "it is a common dream to win an intramural championship of some sort." The program is run through Collins Fitness Center, a brand-new fitness haven that came about during recent renovations (along with "amazing dorms—LaFortune is the best, the Twin dorms are the worst.") Most students describe the new fitness center as "unreal" though a few add "it is something that some huge rapper would own complete with plasma screens everywhere and every kind of workout machine you can imagine."

Running-Backs, Recorders, and Robots

We know TU students love to win academic awards and that they love to play intramurals, but what happens when you combine the two? You get student-athletes who love to win and student-athletic-supporters who love to watch them win! TU basketball games have "long been known as a Tulsa tradition" and "for once, the football team is doing well!" In fact, the Golden Hurricane (or so they are known because of a. their tendency to "roar through opponents" and b. Georgia Tech was already known as the tornado) has had recent success not only in football bowl games, but also in soccer. But in the words of an insightful fan, "winning is not the best part; the best part is that the school is small enough that you know most or a lot of the athletes and this personal connection makes cheering at sporting events or watching them on TV a lot more fun because you are watching your friends."

As touching as that is, what if you do not like watching sports? Not a problem! TU has a large visual and performing arts contingency, and with the city of Tulsa boasting a professional opera company, a national ballet company, and a symphony, the two share an intimate interaction. Often "kids have gotten to fill-in with the symphony" and recently the Tulsa Ballet adopted a 330-pound "fighting robot" built by TU students for a Battle Bots competition. Fortunately, "the bot had been stripped of its steel spikes and bullet-proof panels, allowing it to give a delicate ride to a full-length mirror and interact with the dancers."

Love and Leisure T-Town Style

If you are a TU student your hang-out is either the library or the "Ack-Ack." Funnily enough, at TU "the library is almost a social scene; it's fun," and ACAC is similar to a student union and the only place where you can use meal points outside of the cafeteria. Off campus, many students enjoy spending time at Utica Square, a trendy yet quaint outdoor shopping/eating/walking Mecca that is home to Santa's cottage during the winter months and Queenside's bakery year-round ("it has egg-salad to die for."). They also enjoy a trip to Phil brook Museum or the Tulsa Rose Garden, "where you can have a picnic at Woodward Park and watch a movie on your laptop."

But what if you are, perhaps, more nocturnal? Where do the creatures of the night hang out? Well, a typical TU Friday night could consist of "going to a bar then ending back up at a small apartment/house party." Apparently, there used to be more house parties, but because of recent University mandates, "the parties are now being regulated and have significantly decreased in size and quantity, as a result people frequent the bar scene more." The main watering-holes are Rehab, Hardwood's, or The Buccaneer (a dive-bar affectionately called The Buc). All are located across the street from campus, and "are always offering some kind of beer special or TU student discount."

Then there are other, more upscale restaurant/bar districts like Brookside, Cherry Street, or the Riverwalk (also a divine location to go for a jog). If you are not invited to a private apartment party, there are normally language house/frat parties, though those are known to "get kind of old after sophomore or junior year." Dorms also sometimes sponsor functions, and then "there are always City of Tulsa sponsored events like Mayfest or Oktoberfest (One fest has a lot of watercolors and live music and the other fest has a lot of potato pancakes, polka, and beer.)" If those combined with Springfest are not enough fests for you, there is even a Harley Motorcycle Festival "where they close down Brookside every year and have a huge party."

But what is a party if one is alone? The dating scene at the University of Tulsa is like a good male/female relationship—discordant. Boys will tell you "it is good, there is a range of different people around and you can find your athletic or partier or smart person and dates can be as simple as going to a party together." Girls will tell you "it's not bad, there are dating prospects although not too many of quality." But one thing is sure, "it is a small school so there is a clear understanding of who is dating who."

Max Forman once said: "Education seems to be in America the only commodity of which the customer tries to get as little he can for his money." Apparently, Max Forman has never seen the University of Tulsa, especially during its current booms of a growing international student population, continuing nationally recognized academic award winners, and improving athletic victors. But the special charm of the University of Tulsa is that "as cliché as this sounds, the school feels like one big family" no matter how it orders its name.—*Jocelyn Ranne*

FYI

If you come to TU you'd better bring "a variety of clothing (for all seasons) because it could be 70 degrees one day and snowing the next, and some cash. Things are expensive on campus, and campus police only know how to do one thing—and that's give out tickets."

What's the typical weekend schedule? "Friday night can start with dinner on Brookside, then parties start around 11 p.m. (most people check out frat row). Saturday you wake up (late) do some homework, check out a sporting event, and then repeat. You do work when you can, but it is mainly partying and catching up on sleep!"

If I could change one thing about TU, "I would get more quick and good food options on campus."

Three things that every TU student should do before graduating are "campout on the "U" (the big U-shaped grassy area in between the dorms, library, and classroom buildings), join an organization, and climb up on the roof of the library to go star-gazing."

Oregon

Lewis and Clark College

Address: Lewis and Clark, 0615 SW Palatine Hill Road, Portland, OR 97219-7899
Phone: 800-444-4111
E-mail Address: admissions@lclark.edu
Web site URL: www.lclark.edu
Year Founded: 1867
Private or Public: private
Religious affiliation: none
Location: urban
Regular Application Deadline: 1-Feb
Number of Applicants: 4,698
Percent Accepted: 58%
Percent Accepted who enroll: 19%
Number Entering: 571
Number of Transfers Accepted each Year: 142
Mean SAT: NA
Mean ACT: NA
Middle 50% SAT range: 1,840–2,030 (1,230–1,360)

Middle 50% ACT range: 26–30
Early admission program (EA/ ED/ NA): EA
ED or EA Acceptance Rate: NA
Full time Undergraduate enrollment: 1,940
Total enrollment: 3,433
Percent Male: 39%
Percent Female: 61%
Total Percent Minority: 15%
Percent African-American: 1%
Percent Asian/Pacific Islander: 6%
Percent Hispanic: 4%
Percent Native-American: 1%
Percent Other: 3%
Percent in-state / out of state: 21%/79%
Percent from Public HS: 74%

Retention Rate: 86%
Graduation Rate: 69%
Percent in On-campus housing: 66%
Percent affiliated with Greek system: 0%
Percent Varsity or Club Athletes: 27%
Number of official organized extracurricular organizations: 75
3 Most popular majors: Psychology, International Affairs, Biological Sciences, Sociology/Anthropology
Student/Faculty ratio: 12.5:1
Tuition and Fees: $29,556.00
Cost for Room and Board: $7,776.00
Percent receiving Financial aid, first-year: 74%

L ewis and Clark students love Portland. The passionate and worldly minds that attend the small classes of Lewis and Clark are also frequent visitors to downtown coffee shops and the famous Powell's bookstore. But it's not all about the city. Lewis and Clark's international focus, commitment to small classes and dedicated professors also draw students to this spectacular wooded estate.

Small Classes, Devoted Professors

Small classes and attentive professors are trademarks of Lewis and Clark's strong academic life. The average class size is 20 students, yet the biggest science class can hold around 70 students. While it varies among majors, most students agree that this small class size fosters discussion and "encourages students to think." Professors are "super passionate" and "want to be there and

connect with students." Because of this familiar interaction, and the fact that there are no TAs, students often develop close personal relationships with their professors.

Moreover, students explain that the closely knit nature of the academic community encourages them to be committed to their schoolwork, which they describe as "challenging." Nonetheless, while students generally "do well in school," grades are not widely discussed on campus. The sole academic complain seems to be that, being a smaller school, Lewis and Clark simply does not offer enough majors or courses from which to choose.

Perhaps to offset this disadvantage, Lewis and Clark students are encouraged to go abroad, and over half of the student take advantage of the school's programs in other countries. Students can choose locations all around the world, including England, Germany, France, India and Argentina. For the good or the bad, this ebb and flow of upper-classmen, as some leave to study and others return, creates what one student called a "transient school." Yet, students appreciate the experience of going abroad and the global perspective their comrades bring to discussions. Because of the interest in global affairs, popular majors include International Affairs and Languages.

> "This ebb and flow of upperclassmen as some leave to study and others return from studying abroad creates a 'transient school.'"

In terms of requirements, most students said they were "pretty standard" and not overly burdensome. All freshmen are required to take "Exploration and Discovery," a year long course meant as an overview of the most important works and topics of the diverse field of liberal arts. Students are split into small seminars, but each one regardless of professor is meant to cover the same material.. Professors of every discipline teach the course, so students' experiences in the course vary depending on their professor. When Lewis and Clark students need to hit the books, they use the "totally awesome" Watzek Library. There are study rooms for group study, long tables, and private carrels with computer hookups that allow students to check their email from a laptop.

Hippies and Hipsters

Students at Lewis and Clark form a homogeneously progressive and liberal community. Although there is an "overwhelming number of international students," people drawn to Lewis and Clark are generally interested in a lot of the same issues. Most are liberal and interested in change, taking on issues which range from sustainability to involvement in the community. Students express a tension between a desire for a more diverse campus and the appeal of their "Lewis and Clark bubble." Indeed, in some class discussions there is "little debate," and rarely a conservative or deeply religious belief voiced. Additionally, some pessimistically feel that students may superficially judge their peers "if you don't buy organic food you're not making the world a better place."

The social scene at Lewis and Clark is "intensely laid back." The Greek system was abolished in the 1970s with a donor's amendment, but students don't seem to miss it. Apparently the donor would not give the school her fortune unless the school promised to prohibit Greek houses, install an all-women's dorm, and serve ice cream at every meal.

Since freshmen and sophomores are required to live on campus, many of the underclassmen social events take place on campus. As a technically dry campus, students have to find ways around the prohibition on alcohol on campus to avoid write ups by the campus police. While Lewis and Clark is not your typical "party school," students do certainly have a good time. Underclassmen manage to drink in small groups in the dorms, and bigger parties are held off campus. Binge drinking, though, is not common. Some students smoke pot, but, much like drinking, drug use is a "private hang-out thing."

Finally, Portland is a big part of the social scene at Lewis and Clark. The campus is a 10-minute drive from the city or 30 minutes on the school—run shuttle. Students often make use of the shuttle that goes into downtown and surrounding areas every hour until 2 a.m. Once in Portland, the city has one of the most accessible public transport systems including a "great bus system." One of the major draws for many students is being able to explore the different areas of the city. Whether walking along Hawthorne Blvd. to find some new music, going to a film festival or attending "First Thursday," a program where all of the art galleries in Portland have new shows, Lewis and Clark students are drawn to the Portland scene. Coffee shops are a common place to do work or just hang out, and Powell's, the largest independent bookstore in America, is another big attraction.

"Summer Camp at a Park"

Lewis and Clark's campus is a lush, green area that used to be a rich donor's estate. As one would expect from a former estate, the buildings do not resemble typical college administrative buildings, but remind one of "snow white cottages." On the "fairly small" campus there is a looking pool, a rose garden, "lots of trees, and grassy space for people to lay out on sunny days." Unfortunately, those sunny days are few and far between. The charm of a lush campus with "spectacular" views of Mt. Hood make up for the wet and misty atmosphere.

LC students live in "typical college dorms" their first two years when they are required to live on campus. Many consider this a burden and would like to have the cheaper option of living off campus. There are, however, some perks to dorm living. As a way to meet people, some of the housing facilities have themed floors, such as an "environmental activism floor" and an "international floor." Room size varies from dorm to dorm, but almost all are coed by floor.

Upperclassmen commonly move off campus either into a house with friends or an apartment. Because the area surrounding Lewis and Clark is suburban and fairly isolated, many live in Portland proper. This move off campus can create a schism between the upper and underclassmen. Once students move off campus they "don't really see the people on campus" and sometimes become less involved in campus activities because "it's hard to get back to campus for a 7:00 meeting. You are probably only going to go if it's something really important to you." Some upperclassmen do not feel as connected to the college, but still prefer living off campus to the isolation they sometimes feel in the dorms.

The one dining hall on campus serves "reasonably good" food. Affectionately called "The Bon" after the college's catering company, Bon Appetite, it provides plenty of vegan and vegetarian options. Bon Appetite is considered one of the best food catering services in the Northwest and offers many types of food at different "stations." The meal plan is fairly flexible; students can choose the number of meals they want per week and also buy "flex points" that they can use as dollars at various a la carte places around campus.

Enjoying the Outdoors

With students living on such a verdant campus, it is no surprise that many of them enjoy outdoor activities. The "College of the Outdoors" is a college funded program that offers trips for everything from skiing, to backpacking, canoing and rock climbing. With the Oregon coast two hours away and Columbia River Gorge just an hour, there are plenty of spectacular sites to visit. Almost all students take advantage of these trips that can last a weekend or a day. Transportation is provided, and students can rent any gear that they may need.

Varsity and club sports are "not big" on campus, although the ultimate Frisbee and basketball teams do have a significant following. There are "quite a few athletes" on campus and those who do not play varsity sports can compete in intramural sports. These are fairly popular activities on campus, especially volleyball, skiing, and soccer.

Beyond athletics, students can also join a variety of clubs on campus or work in the student run co-op that serves as a popular social hang-out. The co-op is a place for students to sell their art, play music or just relax and have a cup of coffee. Social justice and activist clubs are big on campus, and other popular organizations include the women's center and the black student union.

Although students rarely display school spirit, their mascot, a Pioneer, is still a fitting symbol for Lewis and Clark students. Their attitude is reflected in one of the school's mottos, "Do not follow where the path may lead, go instead where there is no path and blaze a trail." Students enjoy the companionship of fellow well-traveled and independent students. Those committed to change and the generating new ideas thrive at Lewis and Clark—they can get a strong liberal arts education in a small school setting.—*Rachel Jeffers*

FYI

If you come to Lewis and Clark, you'd better bring "a raincoat, tofu and a pair of Chaco sandals."

The typical weekend schedule? "Brunch in your pajamas, work in a coffee shop downtown, and go to a movie or concert."

If I could change one thing about Lewis and Clark, I'd "diversify the student body in terms of background and ideology."

Three things every student at Lewis and Clark should do before graduating are "spend all day in Powell's, go to dinner with your professor, and go camping on the coast."

Oregon State University

Address: Oregon State, 104
Kerr Administration Building,
Corvallis, OR 97331
Phone: 541-737-4411
E-mail Address:
osuadmit@oregonstate.edu
Web site URL:
http://oregonstate.edu
Year Founded: 1858
Private or Public: public
Religious affiliation: none
Location: suburban
**Regular Application
Deadline:** 2-Sep
Number of Applicants: NA
Percent Accepted: 90%
**Percent Accepted who
enroll:** 35%
Number Entering: NA
**Number of Transfers
Accepted each Year:** NA
Mean SAT: NA
Mean ACT: 23
Middle 50% SAT range:
940–1,250

Middle 50% ACT range:
20–26
**Early admission program
(EA/ ED/ NA):** NA
ED or EA Acceptance Rate:
NA
**Full time Undergraduate
enrollment:** 15,196
Total enrollment: NA
Percent Male: 53%
Percent Female: 47%
Total Percent Minority: 14%
Percent African-American:
1%
**Percent Asian/Pacific
Islander:** 8%
Percent Hispanic: 4%
Percent Native-American: 1%
Percent Other: NA
**Percent in-state / out of
state:** 90%/10%
Percent from Public HS: NA
Retention Rate: 80%
Graduation Rate: 60%

**Percent in On-campus
housing:** 22%
**Percent affiliated with
Greek system:** 18%
**Percent Varsity or Club
Athletes:** NA
**Number of official
organized extracurricular
organizations:** 350
3 Most popular majors:
Business Administration/
Management, Health and
Physical Education, Natural
Sciences
Student/Faculty ratio:
19:01
Tuition and Fees:
$17,559.00
**In State Tuition and Fees
(if different):** $5,643.00
Cost for Room and Board:
$7,494.00
**Percent receiving Financial
aid, first-year:** 48%

Oregon State University is like your perfect date: it has beauty, intelligence, with a laid-back, fun-loving attitude. Nestled in quiet Corvallis, OSU offers its nearly 19,000 students solid academic programs complimented by a lively social life and picturesque surroundings.

A Natural High

OSU is situated in the middle of the stunningly beautiful Willamette Valley of Oregon Trail fame. For the outdoor enthusiast, a plethora of exciting activities abound: hiking and camping in the nearby woods, "little running trails" which wind through campus and cross "rarely used back roads," fly fishing and water sports on the many Oregon rivers, even snowboarding and skiing in the Cascade Mountains. If this is not enough, Corvallis is a mere 45-minute drive from the majestic Oregon coast. The Willamette Valley gives campus its "always green and beautiful" appearance, framed by mountains and trees. Students rave about the "gorgeous red brick" architecture and spacious, grassy quads. Students praise Corvallis, a subdued town of just 53,000 permanent residents, for being "super safe." Students comprise over 25 percent of the total population in this university town, and campus buildings occupy much of the city.

Because the University attracts a large international population, the city is remarkably diverse despite its relatively small size. What Corvallis lacks in big-city hustle and bustle it delivers in peaceful charm; there are "tons of flowers in planters" and students say the recently redone waterfront is "absolutely stunning." Town-gown relations range from "decent to good." There are occasional bouts of friction, but differences are forgotten when it comes time to cheer for Beaver sports teams.

Making a Beaver Outta You

School spirit runs deep, "especially during football season." The rivalry between the OSU Beavers and their archrival, the Ducks of the University of Oregon, is so intense that their annual football match up has been nicknamed the "Civil War." In addition to the numerous pep rallies in the week leading up to the War, one dining hall serves duck for dinner every night so that students can eat their rival's mascot as they prepare to devour them on the field. "Everyone's favorite" colors during Civil War week are orange and black—the school colors—as students go public with their Beaver pride; one recent graduate even remarked that she intends to use orange and black as her wedding colors. But you don't have to be a huge football fan to fit in at OSU. Even though it seems intense, "in practice, school spirit is fairly muted," a sophomore explained, except during the Civil War. Students continue to name Civil War week as a highlight of each year and OSU has won or tied versus the University of Oregon in three of the past five games between the teams.

Academic Buffet

When they're not cheering on their football team, Beavers are "very satisfied" with the academic offerings at their school. Boasting a staggering array of more than 200 academic programs and classes in everything from "crop and soil science" to "Japanese language" to "apparel, interiors, housing and merchandising," OSU has something for both the serious studier and the student looking for an easy A. The engineering and pre-pharmacy programs are widely considered OSU's best and most challenging. Communications, 20th-century studies, and sociology are great majors for the "very lazy," and one engineering student joked that the business department is the "shameful destination of most failed engineers."

All students have to fulfill a set of academic distributional requirements called the Baccalaureate Curriculum, more commonly known as "Bacc Core." One sophomore said he was frustrated that he had to take so many "easy and stupid" Bacc Core classes. Other students said they appreciated the educational diversity required by Bacc Core, and could "understand the thinking" behind receiving a "well-rounded education." A junior praised the unusual classes available in Bacc Core, and strongly recommended a "very interesting" class that focused on food in non-Western cultures.

Impersonal, gargantuan intro classes are a common cause of complaint for freshmen. Though recognized as somewhat "unavoidable" due to the university's size, these classes were assailed for lacking class participation and for having professors "who are more interested in their own research than in teaching a class." Fortunately, students report, by the beginning of sophomore year, students have a better grasp of their interests, and as they take more advanced classes, "class head counts thin considerably."

For students looking for challenges beyond the standard undergraduate curriculum, the University Honors College (UHC) was founded in 1995. With about 500 students, the comparatively small UHC has a unique identity, with access to all the benefits of a large university. Many students working toward their Honors Baccalaureate Degree live together in the McNary—or "McNerdy," as it is sometimes referred to—Complex and have to complete an additional thesis project. The "very intelligent" members of the UHC are highly respected by their peers, even though some are perceived to be "a little snooty."

Day In, Day Out

When not in their dorms, apartments, or classes, Beavers spend a significant amount of time in the "awesome" Dixon Recreation Center. This recently renovated rec center is equipped with a full gym, exercise rooms, and courts for games of basketball, volleyball, and racquetball. For slightly less athletic endeavors, the basement of the beloved MU building houses a popular bowling alley and game rooms. A senior recommended that students enroll in some of the "really fun" classes offered at the rec center, like "step aerobics, Pilates, bowling, fly fishing and country-and-western dancing."

Though many universities require freshmen to live in on-campus housing, OSU has no such rule. Even so, most freshmen opt to spend their first year living in traditional dorm-style housing, complete with "cramped" quarters and long hallways of identical double rooms. Upperclassmen who choose to live on campus find "stellar options" available, including well-lit spacious suites with several single rooms attached to common kitchen and living areas. Still, by sophomore year most Beavers elect to move out of the "expensive, mostly crappy" dorms into off-campus housing, which is readily available though, according to one junior, "still not exactly the lap of luxury." One freshman found the dining hall food "surprisingly" edible, but most students agree that cereal becomes a diet staple once the novelty of buffet-style meals wanes. Fast-food chains in the Memorial Union student center building accept meal plan points and offer a popular alternative to the dining hall. Otherwise, a grocery store and an array of coffee shops close to campus provide students with the sustenance to fuel their busy lives.

Animal House, Beaver Style

Many OSU students choose to live in one of fraternity or sorority houses on Greek Row, and Greek life is an important part of the campus social scene. The college boasts a whopping 42 fraternities and sororities. The "always packed" frat parties are a "great way to meet people" according to one social student. OSU frats are famous (or infamous, depending on your perspective) for their "Thirsty Thursday" parties, the weekly blow-outs that end each academic week. Some students head to these parties as early as 3:00 on a Thursday afternoon, and don't stumble home until the wee hours of the morning. Each Greek house has such a distinct personality that one student joked that it is easy "to judge a Greek by their letters." He said that each house has so "carefully purified its strain over the years" that it is like "some sort of convergent Darwinism run amok." A junior agreed that there is a Greek organization for nearly every type of person at OSU; "we've even got a 'hick' frat!" she exclaimed. Those who decide to go Greek are very attached to their houses. One sophomore described his fraternity as "a brotherhood based on friendship and acceptance." Non-Greeks have a less rosy view of the system. One particularly vehement junior described the overwhelming majority as either "inconsiderate Neanderthal frat rats or stereotypically dumb sorostitutes." Other students simply ignore Greek row; "it's just not my style," said one freshman girl, who didn't feel at all pressured to join a sorority.

> ## "We've even got a 'hick' frat!"

Everyone has an opinion about the Greek system at OSU, and its merits and demerits come under heated debate in the pages of student newspapers like the *Barometer*. OSU has a long-standing reputation as a party school, and merry-making is an activity both Greek and non-Greek students have in common. Beyond frat parties, every weekend features dozens of house and apartment parties for students looking to have a good time. For the over-21 crowd, a lively bar scene close to campus includes lots of student favorites like The Peacock and Platinum. Escape, an alcohol-free on-campus nightclub, opened in 2002. It emerged from an administrative effort to curb underage and binge drinking but was quickly deemed a "dismal failure" by much of the student body. Many students agree that "with the lack of ready-made things to do" in Corvallis, thought and creativity are often needed to find enjoyable alternatives to partying. Those students with a car find access to the many things to do in the nearby metropolis of Portland. Popular school traditions like Mom's Weekend and Dad's Weekend also help to break the study-party-sleep routine.

Just Chillin': A Lesson for Life

At OSU, where dressed up means "something other than jeans and a school sweatshirt" and professors "allow or even prefer students to address them by first name," the campus attitude can best be described as "laid-back." "People here are friendly," observed one senior; it's "a very cheerful place." Disputes over politics and school policy create "remarkably little tension" and generally remain confined to the "entertaining and enlightening arguments" in campus publications. Despite a "very diverse campus . . . ethnically, nationally, and linguistically," political beliefs which encompass "every point on the spectrum," and "clothing and hair that run the full gamut of possibilities," everyone here "just gets along," said a junior. OSU manages to maintain unity while promoting understanding, and many feel that is the hallmark of its education.—*Claire Gagne*

FYI

If you come to OSU, you'd better bring "an industrial strength umbrella and an orange Beavers sweatshirt."

What is the typical weekend schedule? "Drink, sleep late, study. In that order."

If I could change one thing about OSU, I'd "make the break between classes longer. Ten minutes isn't enough with a campus this large!"

Three things every student at OSU should do before graduating are "go to Thirsty Thursday, cheer for the Beavers at a Civil War game, and spend lots of time at MU."

Reed College

Address: Reed, 3203 SE Woodstock Blvd, Portland, OR 97202
Phone: 800-547-4750
E-mail Address: admission@reed.edu
Web site URL: web.reed.edu
Year Founded: 1911
Private or Public: private
Religious affiliation: none
Location: urban
Regular Application Deadline: 15-Jan
Number of Applicants: 3,054
Percent Accepted: 40%
Percent Accepted who enroll: 31%
Number Entering: 423
Number of Transfers Accepted each Year: 46
Mean SAT: NA
Mean ACT: NA

Middle 50% SAT range: 1,280–1,460
Middle 50% ACT range: 28–32
Early admission program (EA/ ED/ NA): ED
ED or EA Acceptance Rate: 69%
Full time Undergraduate enrollment: 1,365
Total enrollment: 1,436
Percent Male: 45%
Percent Female: 55%
Total Percent Minority: 22%
Percent African-American: 3%
Percent Asian/Pacific Islander: 9%
Percent Hispanic: 6%
Percent Native-American: 2%
Percent Other: 2%

Percent in-state / out of state: 13%/87%
Percent from Public HS: 60%
Retention Rate: 85%
Graduation Rate: 75%
Percent in On-campus housing: 65%
Percent affiliated with Greek system: 0%
Percent Varsity or Club Athletes: 10–12%
Number of official organized extracurricular organizations: 40+
3 Most popular majors: English, Biology, Psychology
Student/Faculty ratio: 10:01
Tuition and Fees: $34,530.00
Cost for Room and Board: $9,000.00

I f you dream of being either a frat brother or the girl who dates a frat brother, don't expect Reed College to be the place for you. Reed is a small school in Portland, Oregon, with a quirky student body, small class sizes, intense academic programs, and a beautiful campus. If you're an open-minded intellectual who doesn't like the prep or jock factor of many other prestigious, academically challenging schools, you will feel at home at Reed.

Academic Masochism

Reedies are quick to admit that the workload at their school is a serious challenge. One student explained that it's not uncommon to routinely spend seven hours straight working in the library. "I know that when I graduate, I'm going to have to learn how to function in the real world again, because I've been so immersed in academia," said one Reedie. However, students' academic loads are made bearable by their brilliant but approachable professors. There are no TAs at Reed since all classes are taught by professors. It's easy to get on a first name basis with them because classes are usually no bigger than 30 students. "It's great to be at a table with a few other students, sitting across from a professor who

wrote the book for the course," said one student.

Students say all majors and classes are difficult, and "there isn't anything you can slack off in." Popular majors include English, classics, and religion. Psychology is considered the major for the Reedie looking for a less arduous program, but students warn that this fact means it's overwhelming instead of incredibly overwhelming. Though Reed is thought of as more of a humanities-based school, science majors are becoming increasingly popular. "The sciences are strong at Reed as well" said one student, "we even have a nuclear reactor on campus now."

Two of the school's toughest courses, a writing-intensive freshman humanities course and the senior thesis, are required, but students have few complaints about them. The mandatory freshman course is "a common experience that unifies the student body and it's a great foundation for the rest of the Reed education," said one student.

Though free-spirited, Reedies are all focused and genuinely devoted to the pursuit of intellectual growth. "You go to Reed because you want to go to grad school," one student said simply. Whether they're designing their own physics experiments or writing their senior thesis on Shakespeare,

Reedies are always passionate about what they do. "It's cool to be in an environment where everyone's interesting it what they're studying," said one student. The students get to show off their laid-back side and introduce fellow students to their interests during Paideia, an event that takes place the week after winter break. During Paideia, everyone in the Reed community has the opportunity to teach a class except for professors. Reedies have taught everything from bike repair to politics during this week.

Study Hard, Party Hard

"The typical Reed student basically wouldn't fit in anywhere else. They're bookish, liberal hipsters, and also friendly and fun-loving" said one Reedie. Students explain that there is no social hierarchy at their school and everyone is accepting of each other. There are no cliques of popular jocks, since Reed doesn't participate in intercollegiate sports. Reedies instead use their competitive spirit in intracollege Ultimate Frisbee and rugby games.

Students only complaint about their fellow Reedies is the fact that there isn't enough racial diversity. "Reed is basically white and rich," one sophomore said. Despite the racial homogeneity of the current student population, students report that Reed is working to recruit a more multicultural student body. Others compliment Reed for its financial aid efforts that attract students from a variety of socioeconomic backgrounds.

Most Reed students are heavily involved in extracurricular activities and unique student organizations. Popular groups include the Bike Co-Op and the Reed Kommunal Shit Kollektiv, which organizes parties and gives out free goodies to students in the spirit of communism. When Reedies aren't studying or involved in student organizations, they are doing their other favorite activity: partying. "I put up with five days of shit for two nights of awesome," said one student. Most Reedies love a good party as much as they love a good lecture. "There's always something going on: parties, dances, or great concerts," said one enthusiastic student. The biggest party of the year is Ren Fayre, a three day party unanimously praised by Reed students that starts after the seniors turn in their theses. Alcohol and drugs are widespread at this and many other events, so much so that the other nickname for Reed students is Weedies. "There's really good pot in Oregon," explained one student.

Many students said that a great deal of the smoking of this really good pot takes place at the student union. "Though there is a fair amount of alcohol and drug use, people are responsible and there's no pressure to take part if you don't want to," said one freshman.

For those who don't want to socialize under the influence, there is a substance-free dorm and many substance-free activities sponsored on campus. Many students said that because of Reed's pot-smoking image, the administration is now trying to keep substance use in check. However, students assure that there will continue to be many good times to be had at Reed. Because of the schools liberal Honor Principle, students can't get busted for alcohol or drug use unless they harm or embarrass another student. "The focus of the Honor Principle is student responsibility instead of keeping us from having fun," said one student.

> At Reed we say that you can have only three of the following five: good academic performance, a relationship, a good group of friends, extracurricular activities, or sleep.

With their heavy workloads, many student organizations, and plentiful parties, most Reedies say that it is difficult to date seriously. "After you've been doing work all day, all you want to do is sleep. The last thing you want is to have to take someone out to dinner," explained one Reedie. Though some report having long-term relationships, most say that there are a lot random hookups. "At Reed we say that you can have only three of the following five: good academic performance, a relationship, a good group of friends, extracurricular activities, or sleep," concluded one student.

Eating in the Reed Bubble

Most Reedies report that there is so much to do on campus, they don't often venture into Portland. "Sometimes it feels like we're in a Reed bubble and not really in Portland," one student said. There is a good selection of restaurants to visit when students do take the short bike ride to the city, but students don't seem to suffer from a lack of good food on campus either. A private food contractor, otherwise known as a catering company, provides Reedies with their meals. The food is said to be "pretty damn good" with a plethora of vegetarian and vegan options.

The only complaint Reed students do have with their dining services is the way their meal plans are set up. Each student starts off the semester with a certain amount of points, known as Commons Cash. Each food item costs a certain amount of Commons Cash, meaning students must budget the amount of money they spend at each meal. Many students find themselves very close to the end of their Commons Cash before the end of the semester is in sight. This reality forces some to leave the Reed bubble and find their nourishment in Portland.

Pretty Sweet Campus
Reedies have praise for their college's campus. "It's really beautiful. There are tons of trees and the buildings are all brick and pretty. Some of the dorms are sort of strange looking, but they're all fine," said one student. Even if a few of the dorms look weird,

no one has any complaints about how they're set up inside. All dorms are coed and not segregated by grade. There are about 20 students per floor and one RA whose job is to offer advice and study breaks, not supervision. "Most rooms are divided doubles, which works well because everyone gets their own space," said one Reedie. Students report that the administration does a great job choosing roommates for freshmen. Old Dorm Block, which is prettier than it sounds, is one of the most popular residences. Students say that though Reed's dorms are popular, many upperclassmen live off campus. Suitable housing abounds, with plenty of apartments right across the street from campus.

Though they say that prospective students should definitely visit Reed before they make a decision, Reedies couldn't be happier with their college. As one freshman concluded, "If you're intelligent, ready to debate about anything, willing to be crazy, and not afraid of weird shit, Reed is the place for you.—*Keneisha Sinclair*

FYI

If you come to Reed, you'd better bring "the mental capacity for all the work and costumes for the theme parties."

They typical weekend schedule is "work all Friday afternoon and then party, work all Saturday morning then go to a concert or play and then party, and work like crazy all Sunday."

If I could change one thing about Reed, "I'd make it more diverse."

Three things every student at Reed should do before graduating are "go to the Rhody Gardens at night, chase the Doyle Owl, and write a great thesis."

University of Oregon

Address: University of Oregon, 1217 University of Oregon, Eugene, OR 97403
Phone: 800-232-3825
E-mail Address: uoadmit@uoregon.edu
Web site URL: www.uoregon.edu
Year Founded: 1876
Private or Public: public
Religious affiliation: none
Location: urban
Regular Application Deadline: 16-Jan
Number of Applicants: 10,012
Percent Accepted: 88%
Percent Accepted who enroll: 35%
Number Entering: 3,207
Number of Transfers Accepted each Year: 2,086
Mean SAT: 1,117
Mean ACT: NA

Middle 50% SAT range: NA
Middle 50% ACT range: NA
Early admission program (EA/ ED/ NA): EA
ED or EA Acceptance Rate: NA
Full time Undergraduate enrollment: 16,473
Total enrollment: 20,394
Percent Male: 53%
Percent Female: 47%
Total Percent Minority: 14%
Percent African-American: 2%
Percent Asian/Pacific Islander: 6%
Percent Hispanic: 4%
Percent Native-American: 1%
Percent Other: 1%
Percent in-state / out of state: 68%/32%
Percent from Public HS: NA

Retention Rate: 84%
Graduation Rate: 65%
Percent in On-campus housing: 22%
Percent affiliated with Greek system: 15%
Percent Varsity or Club Athletes: NA
Number of official organized extracurricular organizations: 250
3 Most popular majors: Business Administration/ Management, Journalism, Psychology
Student/Faculty ratio: 18:01
Tuition and Fees: $16,755.00
In State Tuition and Fees (if different): $4,341.00
Cost for Room and Board: $7,827.00

The University of Oregon is well-regarded for its academics, its athletics and the involvement of its students. Professors engage in thrilling research while constantly cultivating young minds, which go eagerly into the world and "move mountains," as the school's slogan says. With vast resources that include a museum of natural history, a marine biology station on the coast and a sports marketing center, the University also manages to give students personal attention. Located in the town of Eugene, UO has the benefit of a being in a dazzling city with small-town charm, set against the backdrop of Oregon's greenery.

Podcasts and Info Hell

The University of Oregon is comprised of seven different schools, although the Schools of Journalism and Architecture, as well as the Charles H. Lundquist College of Business, are considered particularly notable. Most freshmen begin their studies within the School of Arts and Sciences, and some choose to enter another school shortly thereafter. Those interested in a pre-professional major, such as journalism or business, must first complete the necessary prerequisites in order to be considered for acceptance into a specific school. The architecture major, a five-year program, is well-known for its difficulty and prominence, but prospective majors said they are generally excited about "the opportunities that open up after graduation."

Overall, the difficulty of classes depends on the student. Some find their classes sufficiently challenging, while others commented that "it's not a big change from high school." However, the general education requirements are diverse enough to ensure that each student is pushed out of his comfort zone at one point or another. To fulfill their requirements, students must complete 15 credits in three main categories: arts and letters, social sciences and natural sciences.

Survey class sizes are generally large, but with some effort, students say it's "easy to get a hold of" professors. To accommodate students' schedules, most hold office hours at various times during the week. And as an incentive to encourage these student-faculty relationships, if a student asks a professor to meet up in a University dining hall, the latter's meal is free. "This is a great opportunity to talk to your professors, and it's highly underused," one student reports.

For first-year students, journalism classes are very popular, particularly former broadcaster Al Stavitsky's course, "Mass Media and Society." Stavitsky creates podcasts, online audio files, that include information that bridges the assigned readings and his in-class lectures. Other professors across various departments have also expressed an interest in his method, including the implementation of podcasts. On the other hand, another journalism course, the so-called "Info Hell,' is notoriously intimidating and requires a 100-page research paper.

Students looking for a challenging academic opportunity might choose to apply to the Robert D. Clark Honors College, a selective program that provides its participants with an "intense" liberal arts education. It is the oldest four-year honors college in the nation, consisting of nearly 600 undergraduates. Classes are taught by some of the University's most prized professors and are capped at 25 students, allowing for plenty of personal attention. A senior thesis is required and the workload "never ever seems to end," but Honors College students agree that when all is said and done, "it's totally worth it."

Students with very specific academic interests in mind have the opportunity to choose from enrolling in over 50 Freshmen Interest Groups (FIGs). The groups vary in topic from "Introduction to Monkeys and Apes" to "Early Judaism to Mind and Society." Students say that participation in an FIG, which usually consists of about 25 students who take two core classes together in the fall term, is a great way to make friends right off the bat. Several of the FIGs even live together on campus.

Eating and Sleeping

Other than the specific building they will reside in, students living on and off campus have plenty of housing options to choose from. On-campus single and double rooms are both available, some with additional features such as a sink, a private bathroom or extra floor space. A single isn't guaranteed, but students who submit their housing forms earlier are more likely to get one. Special Interest halls attract those who wish to surround themselves with other honor students, musicians, athletes or international students, to name a few. Those interested in

joining a sorority or fraternity and moving into the chapter house soon into their freshman year may also sign up for a temporary housing option, to avoid breaking a residential hall contract.

Many UO dorms have their own unique characteristics. While Bean, for example, only houses freshmen, it's known for throwing the "craziest parties." However, the architect who created the dorm also designed prisons—a fact that does not seem to go unnoticed by students, one of whom referenced Bean's "small windows and poor lighting." The rooms in Carson all have sinks, and Barnhart houses a lot of athletes. Riley is the international dorm, with more than half of its students coming from overseas.

Students tend to move into cheaper apartments nearby after their first or second year, although on-campus housing is provided to all who request it. The Living-Learning Center, a large new housing complex that opened in 2006, includes classrooms in the basement and a central plaza serving as a café with outdoor seating and a setting for informal performances. The dorm rooms, primarily for first-year students, are reputed to be 50 percent larger than the current average rooms. University officials hope that the LLC will blur the distinction between residential and academic life.

Students who live on campus are required to purchase one of the University's three different meal plans. The dining program works on a weekly point system, and unused points may be rolled over. Carson and Barnhart offer all-you-can-eat buffets, while plenty of other venues around campus feature individual food items. "The food's not gourmet, but it could definitely be worse," one student said. The general consensus is that there are so many different kinds of food to choose from, it's easy enough to find something that suits the palate.

What to Do, What to Do

Greek life is relatively popular, as UO has 8 sororities, 14 full-fledged fraternities and 2 budding colonies—organizations that are similar to fraternities but that do not have chapter houses. While sororities have a more formal and structured recruitment process that takes place in the fall, fraternities recruit year-round. Students say that initiations are "enjoyable experiences," and no complaints have been lodged in recent years. All the chapter houses are dry, as is the rest of the campus. And while many students drink, there are plenty of other activities happening around campus to keep non-drinking or non-partying students busy at any given time. Drugs aren't extremely visible, but "if you look hard enough, you can find whatever you want."

Although the school sponsors dances, students note that attendance is poor: "I went to one during freshman year, and it was just a few people standing around," one complained. Since the no-alcohol policy is strictly enforced on campus, more parties take place in the surrounding area apartments.

Downtown Eugene is a popular and inspiring location, filled with working artists, writers and musicians. While students take advantage of amenities such as a nearby theater that offers admission for only $1.50, they also warn that "everything closes after dinner." UO's rival, Oregon State University, is only half an hour away and is often a common party locale. Outdoors activities are popular with many as well, as opportunities for some great skiing or sailing are just a couple hours away by car. Many students, especially those from in state, bring vehicles to campus. Although an overnight parking permit is "a hassle to obtain," enough students have cars on campus that "it's easy to find a ride."

UO students say they are extremely happy with the security measures provided by the University. The streets are well-lit, and blue phones are liberally distributed around campus. There are several safe transportation systems, such as the Assault Prevention Shuttle (APS) and the Drunk Driving Shuttle, which provide night-time and off-campus transport.

Go Ducks!

The majority of campus activities stem from the Erb Memorial Union (EMU), which headquarters all aspects of extracurricular organizations. While its claim to help students "discover new interests and tap hidden talents" may seem cheesy, students verify its importance on campus. Through EMU, one student discovered the Outdoor Program; another became a member of Alpha Phi Omega, the largest college service-based organization in the world; and yet another made plans to join the Peace Corps after graduation.

Opportunities to join organizations are plentiful at UO. The student newspaper, the *Oregon Daily Emerald*, has a huge staff of writers. A large intramural sports league, which is grouped into three skill levels, is fairly popular as well. Joining a team for a

season is highly recommended, and one student asserted that IMs are "the most fun" he's ever had. UO Debate is considered one of the best teams out of all the public universities, with two students recently placing among the top eight teams at the renowned World Universities Debating Championships. The University also hosts a plethora of music events, such as the Oregon Jazz Festival and the Oregon Bach Festival.

The Ducks sports teams inspire deep loyalty among students, which is eagerly expressed at every home game. The recently renovated Autzen Stadium is almost always packed with football fans who wait in line for hours to obtain tickets. Fans are born every day, as demonstrated by a student who commented, "I brought my roommate along once and she comes to all the games now!" Along the basketball court, thousands of students who call themselves the Pit Crew line up in bright yellow t-shirts to cheer on their favorite players. They are definitely the most visible and loudest supporters, and call themselves "the greatest student basketball fan organization in the nation."

Atmosphere

As a university renowned for its politically liberal student body, it is not unusual to see large groups of students dressed in hippie garb. "If you're not used to them, it's weird at first. But eventually, you realize that the hippies are an integral part of the campus image." Although UO has made a big push to promote diversity awareness on campus—it hosts at least one diversity-building event per week—students say that it has a long way to go. One student said she wished others were "more culturally aware," recalling an incident where another student transferred because the surrounding community was considered "too white." However, students also acknowledged that most people are generally open and accepting of others' beliefs and opinions.

> "It's easy to see why students of all backgrounds can sincerely call this campus 'home.'"

With such a broad spectrum of majors, political views and extracurricular options at students' fingertips, UO is a wonderful place to spend four years. Looking around, explained one student, "it's easy to see why students of all backgrounds can sincerely call this campus 'home.'"—*Catherine Jan*

FYI

If you're coming to University of Oregon, you'd better bring "an umbrella!"

What's the typical weekend schedule? "Wake up around noon, pregame, attend a sporting event, party hop at night, sleep, work, and work out."

If I could change one thing about the University of Oregon, I'd change "[the fact that] the roads have too many potholes."

Three things that every student should do before graduating are "paint your face for a football game, attend a charity event sponsored by a sorority or fraternity, and join a club about something that you've never heard about."

Willamette University

Address: Willamette, 900 State Street, Salem, OR 97301

Phone: 877-LIBARTS

E-mail Address: libarts@willamette.edu

Web site URL: www.willamette.edu

Year Founded: 1842

Private or Public: private

Religious affiliation: none

Location: small city

Regular Application Deadline: 1-Feb

Number of Applicants: 2,967

Percent Accepted: 75%

Percent Accepted who enroll: 22%

Number Entering: 541

Number of Transfers Accepted each Year: ~100

Mean SAT: NA

Mean ACT: NA

Middle 50% SAT range: 1,170–1,340

Middle 50% ACT range: 24–30

Early admission program (EA/ ED/ NA): EA

ED or EA Acceptance Rate: 32%

Full time Undergraduate enrollment: 1,823

Total enrollment: 2,642

Percent Male: 45%

Percent Female: 55%

Total Percent Minority: 20%

Percent African-American: 2%

Percent Asian/Pacific Islander: 7%

Percent Hispanic: 5%

Percent Native-American: 1%

Percent Other: 5%

Percent in-state / out of state: NA

Percent from Public HS: NA

Retention Rate: 88%

Graduation Rate: 74%

Percent in On-campus housing: 76%

Percent affiliated with Greek system: 27%

Percent Varsity or Club Athletes: 33%

Number of official organized extracurricular organizations: 94

4 Most popular majors: Politics, Biology, Economics, Spanish

Student/Faculty ratio: 11:01

Tuition and Fees: $30,018.00

Cost for Room and Board: $7,250.00

Percent receiving Financial aid, first-year: 77%

Located in the heart of Oregon, Willamette University, the oldest college in the West, is known not only for its strong academic reputation, but also for its student body, which challenges stereotypes on a daily basis. The school's gorgeous campus with historic red-brick buildings surrounded by a bustling city is just one manifestation of the diversity of interests and opportunities found at Willamette.

Where Professors Know Your Name

As one freshman girl commented, "So far, academics at Willamette have been one pleasant surprise after another." Willamette thrives not only on its reputation for a strong academic program, but also on the emphasis it places on fostering professor-student interaction. Class sizes are generally small (the same freshman commented that her largest class contains 17 students), and this allows professors and students to get to know each other, which students cite as an important aspect of academic life at Willamette. The student-to-professor ratio is 11:1, which allows for significant, meaningful relationships to form between teachers and students. One student remarked, "I have yet to have a professor that is not demanding yet reasonable, creative yet structured, and informative yet personal. The professors make themselves easily accessible to students and genuinely do care about us." The small class size also enables increased student participation and the occasional field trip for hands-on experience.

In addition to guidance provided by professors, Willamette itself provides a structure for students' course of study, as students are required to take courses in each of the following fields, or "modes of inquiry": qualitative thinking, quantitative thinking, analyzing arguments, creating in the arts, interpreting texts, thinking historically, understanding the natural world, and understanding society. In addition, Willamette students must take four courses designated as "writing centered." This set of requirements, though extensive, ensures that students leave Willamette with an education that is broad as well as focused in a particular major or area. Popular majors include economics, psychology, and the domains of science and music, which are also extremely popular but challenging due to the rigors of the requirements and the quality of those departments at Willamette. Though classes are challenging, the accessibility of the faculty members makes students feel at home and comfortable enough to speak freely, both in class and out. One senior commented, "I have never been taught by a faculty member whom I did not feel as though I could approach about absolutely anything."

Seeing Through Stereotypes

As Willamette is located deep in the Northwest and many students come from surrounding areas, they could all be extremely similar; however, students overwhelmingly maintain that this is not the case. Though the majority of the student body does come from similar backgrounds, which are mostly conservative, white, and middle-class, one freshman commented, "One cool thing about Willamette students is that we break a lot of stereotypes. What I mean by that is there could be a frat boy who is also a vegetarian, doesn't drink, and a Christian." Willamette students pride themselves on doing their own thing; this often doesn't fit into the stereotypical college mold, and that's OK by them.

> "I have never been taught by a faculty member whom I did not feel as though I could approach about absolutely anything."

The diversity of the student body's interests translates into a vast variety of opportunities offered at Willamette. There is a large array of organizations in which students can be involved, ranging from political groups, religious organizations, community service in Salem, and athletics. According to one female student, "The thing about this school is that there is diversity, so you are bound to find your niche." The Bearcats, a Division III team, compete in 12 different varsity sports, and a large percentage, in fact almost all, of the student body at Willamette participate in athletics in some capacity.

So Many Options, So Little Time

Like the student body, social life at Willamette is also extremely diverse—you can find entertainment at a frat party, bar, room party, or just by hanging out with friends or around campus. Though Willamette students do like to party, students are quick to reassure that Willamette is "not a party school." In terms of the Greek scene, there are eight Greek organizations on campus, five of which are fraternities. The frats have parties which are open to everyone, though two of the five are dry. Though they sometimes host events such as toga or blacklight parties, Greek life in general does not dominate the social scene at Willamette. Students, especially upperclassmen, often visit the surrounding bars in Salem, though the city itself is not known to have a particularly vibrant nightlife, and for this reason many students travel to nearby Portland for a fun night or weekend off-campus.

Dorm and room parties are also popular weekend attractions, and some dorms, such as Doney, Terra, Lausanne, and Matthews, are known to be the louder, more social than others. For quiet study, dorms such as Belknap, York, Lee, Wish, and Shepard are preferable. Off-campus "keggers" are also common weekend activities, whose popularity is due in large part to the ease with which alcohol can be served. At these events students do not have to worry about campus regulations, which are strict when it comes to drinking and drug use.

However, despite these parties, tamer on-campus socializing is preferred by many students, in part because "the campus is safe at night, although Salem is not." Though the campus is well-patrolled and protected by Willamette security forces, Salem itself is not known to be a safe place to walk around at night, and students, for this reason, often prefer to stay on campus, where they know they can get home safely and securely. However, students often take trips off campus for another reason: to get back to nature. The close proximity of natural beauty to the campus, such as the nearby mountains and west coast beach, allow students who want to get off campus for a day trip or a weekend the opportunity to get back to nature and enjoy the beauty of Oregon while at the same time getting a break from the city life of Salem.

Home Away from Home

Overall, Willamette, with its setup as a small community within the larger city of Salem, has all of the characteristics necessary to provide students with a home away from home. Freshmen and sophomores are required to live on-campus, which encourages them not only to form bonds when they first arrive, but to look upon Willamette as a comfortable, familiar place to come home to at the end of the day. In fall 2006, the new residential building Kaneko Commons opened for students, and promises to encourage more students to live on campus.

The small size of Willamette's classes and the student body itself allows students to feel a sense of community and connection that can be much harder to achieve on larger campuses. This sense of community, highlighted by the close relationships formed and emphasized between teachers and students, is commonly agreed to be what distinguishes Willamette from the many other universities all across the nation.

It is rare to find the kind of diversity Willamette presents at such a small university; however, Willamette provides the best of both worlds. It attracts students who break every type of mold, while at the same time fostering a sense of community and common bonds between students that are vital to a fulfilling, enjoyable college experience.—*Michelle Katz*

FYI
If you come to Willamette, you'd better bring "an open mind."
What is the typical weekend schedule? "A typical weekend at Willamette is perfect for going to the mountains or the beach."
If I could change one thing about Willamette, I'd "change the hypocritical administration."
The three things that every student at Willamette should do before graduating are "get in a food fight at Goudy during 'midnight breakfast', get thrown in Mill Stream on your birthday, and start the wave at a women's volleyball game."

Pennsylvania

Allegheny College

Address: Allegheny, Office of Admissions, Allegheny College, Box 520 North Main Street, Meadville, PA 16335
Phone: 814-332-4351
E-mail Address: admissions@allegheny.edu
Web site URL: www.allegheny.edu/admissions/apply
Year Founded: 1815
Private or Public: private
Religious affiliation: United Methodist
Location: small city
Regular Application Deadline: 15-Feb
Number of Applicants: 3,668
Percent Accepted: 63%
Percent Accepted who enroll: 25%
Number Entering: 599
Number of Transfers Accepted each Year: 48
Mean SAT: NA

Mean ACT: NA
Middle 50% SAT range: 1,130–1,300
Middle 50% ACT range: 23–28
Early admission program (EA/ ED/ NA): ED
ED EA Acceptance Rate: 80%
Full time Undergraduate enrollment: 2,048
Total enrollment: 2,095
Percent Male: 46%
Percent Female: 54%
Total Percent Minority: 7%
Percent African-American: 2%
Percent Asian/Pacific Islander: 3%
Percent Hispanic: 1%
Percent Native-American: 0%
Percent Other: 0%
Percent in-state / out of state: 64%/36%

Percent from Public HS: 84%
Retention Rate: 88%
Graduation Rate: 77%
Percent in On-campus housing: 78%
Percent affiliated with Greek system: 25%
Percent Varsity or Club Athletes: 44%
Number of official organized extracurricular organizations: 83
3 Most popular majors: Psychology, English, Biology
Student/Faculty ratio: 14:01
Tuition and Fees: $28,300.00
Cost for Room and Board: $7,000.00
Percent receiving Financial aid, first-year: 86%

Founded in 1815, Allegheny is one of the oldest colleges in the United States. With a history longer than that of some of the finest and most reputed universities in the country, Allegheny College features a beautiful, pastoral campus with great learning opportunities, for which it earned a place among the top 40 schools in *Colleges that Change Lives*. If you are looking for an excellent liberal arts education and do not mind living in a quiet, small town located hours away from any major cities, consider Allegheny as a potential college choice.

Meadville? Where is That?

Meadville is a small, "post-industrial" town in western Pennsylvania. It is home to a population of only 14,000 people. The closest metropolitan area is Pittsburg, PA, which is about 90 minutes away. Cleveland, the next nearest city, requires two hours of driving. As a result, although the school offers a quiet learning environment, it certainly has "neither the number nor the quality of activities that can be found in large metropolitan areas." While the Gator Activities Programming invites entertainers to perform on campus, it is obvious that "if you've always wanted to be in a city and have flashing lights and tons of things to do on the weekends, don't bother." Nevertheless, most students agree that "Allegheny has a beautiful campus." The college covers nearly 550 acres, including a natural reserve of 283 acres, as well as 203 acres dedicated to recreation. The campus offers great facilities such as an observatory, an art gallery, and a TV station, all for a small enrollment of about 2,000 students. With the nearby lakes and state parks, Allegheny is a great place for the enjoyment of nature and tranquility. As one student explained, "If you are looking for a small college in a rural and laid back community, Allegheny is the place for you."

The college's relationship with Meadville, however, remains rather detached. "There tends to be clash between 'townies' and us Alleghenians," said a student. "But we are truthfully working on the relationship." While most students in the college come from middle-class families, the formerly industrial Meadville has been facing economic difficulties since the 1980s. As a result, Allegheny students are sometimes just seen as "a bunch of rich kids." At the same time, one student remarked, "The campus is rather closed off to the town of Meadville, although there are some students that go to bars and go shopping." There are about 30 restaurants in the area and several small stores. Nevertheless, with the nearest mall about 30 minutes away, "the town doesn't really have anything interesting for us to go there," one senior said.

Despite being in an isolated location, however, the students are very content with the safety of both Allegheny College and Meadville. Few dangerous incidents ever occur in the area, and the students agree that Allegheny is "a peaceful residential campus."

Majorly into Minors

A top-100 liberal arts college according to *US News & World Report*, Allegheny provides its students with a well-rounded academic program. It is a relatively selective school, with average SAT scores between 1150 and 1300, and more than 70 percent of its students are in the top 20 percent of their high schools. The acceptance rate is generally around 60 percent, giving Allegheny a body of capable students. "Academics are the reason that everyone comes here," said a student.

Allegheny is well known for its science departments. "We have one of the best placements into med school in the nation," one Alleghenian said. "Our science departments are very hard. We don't curve grades like other colleges." Despite the belief that humanities and social science classes are less interesting and less difficult than science classes, most students agree that Allegheny "boasts excellent faculty in all fields." The construction of a $23 million state-of-the-art communications and theater center is in the works, and will help improve the school's reputation in humanities and arts.

The classes are based on hour credits. Most classes are four credits, and the students need 131 credit hours to graduate. People generally take four to five classes per semester. One of the distinctive elements of Allegheny is its requirement of both a major and a minor, which helps people to "achieve a more rounded education." The minor cannot be in the same academic division (humanities, natural sciences, and social sciences) as the major, meaning that the students have to take classes in very different fields, thus achieving the goal of a liberal arts education.

The school also has a vigorous set of requirements for its students. In addition to the mandatory classes in humanities, sciences, and social sciences, everyone is required to take three courses on academic planning, starting from second semester of freshman year to the end of sophomore year, to help prepare for the design of their programs of study and their activities. They also need to take three FS seminars during their freshman and sophomore years. These classes focus mostly on improving the students' ability to research and communicate ideas. There are more than 80 different seminars available to the students.

By the end of their sophomore year, students choose their majors among the 30 offered by Allegheny. The major requires anywhere from 32 to 48 hour credits and the completion of a junior seminar and a senior project. Students can also make their own major if they can justify the point of having their own course of study. The minor requires 12 credits.

> "I've babysat kids for professors before. We are all equals here and students help professors and professors help students.'"

The course load is often agreed to be challenging among Alleghenians. According to one student, "Allegheny College has one of the largest work loads for any class whether it be sciences, social sciences, or humanities. All areas are challenging—and encouraging—which Allegheny College facilitates its students to experience."

2,000 Students, One Tight-Knit Experience

Students at Allegheny maintain close ties with their professors. "Students and professors are all very close," said an Alleghenian. "Professors often invite students to their house for a meal." Indeed, the small classes give plenty of opportunities for the students to interact with the faculty. When asked about the relationship between the students and the faculty, one interviewee said, "I've babysat kids for professors before. We are all equals here and students help professors and professors help students."

The dorms are similar to most colleges. About 75 percent of the students live on campus. According to an Alleghenian, a typical room would be "double 17 by 15, no AC." "Only the more expensive, new dorms have AC," added another student who also pointed out that, "Bathroom and shower space is not an issue. There are plenty of those."

Greek life is an important part of Allegheny. Being part of a fraternity or sorority gives sisters and brothers access to a series of activities. Nevertheless, there are plenty of other activities on campus so that the students do not feel left out if they opt out of Greek life. Alcohol is an important part of parties, and it generally can be found by anyone.

Allegheny is trying hard to improve its diversity. Currently, less than 10 percent of Alleghenians are ethnic minorities. The administration is making it a priority to recruit more minority applicants.—*Xiaohang Liu*

FYI

If you come to Allegheny, you'd better bring "a Nalgene. We are big on those."
If I could change one thing about Allegheny, I'd "lower the cost of tuition."
Three things every student at Allegheny should do before graduating are: "Go to Eddie's Footlong for hotdogs, play pool in the Game Room, and take yoga classes."

Bryn Mawr College

Address: Bryn Mawr, 101 N. Merion Avenue, Bryn Mawr, PA 19010
Phone: 610-526-5152
E-mail Address: admissions@brynmawr.edu
Web site URL: www.brynmawr.edu
Year Founded: 1885
Private or Public: private
Religious affiliation: none
Location: suburban
Regular Application Deadline: 16-Jan
Number of Applicants: NA
Percent Accepted: 44%
Percent Accepted who enroll: 38%
Number Entering: NA
Number of Transfers Accepted each Year: NA
Mean SAT: 1,301
Mean ACT: 28

Middle 50% SAT range: 1,200–1,420
Middle 50% ACT range: 27–31
Early admission program (EA/ ED/ NA): ED
ED or EA Acceptance Rate: NA
Full time Undergraduate enrollment: 1,362
Total enrollment: 1,362
Percent Male: 3%
Percent Female: 97%
Total Percent Minority: 21%
Percent African-American: 6%
Percent Asian/Pacific Islander: 12%
Percent Hispanic: 3%
Percent Native-American: 0%
Percent Other: NA
Percent in-state / out of state: NA

Percent from Public HS: 64%
Retention Rate: 96%
Graduation Rate: 74% in four, 78% in six
Percent in On-campus housing: 95%
Percent affiliated with Greek system: 0%
Percent Varsity or Club Athletes: NA
Number of official organized extracurricular organizations: 100
3 Most popular majors: English, Math, Political Science
Student/Faculty ratio: 8:01
Tuition and Fees: $32,230.00
Percent receiving Financial aid, first-year: 56%

With an ideal location, beautiful campus, and hundreds of smart, motivated women, Bryn Mawr College may be home to one of the most satisfied student populations in the country. Located on the chic Main Line, just west of Philadelphia, Bryn Mawr has a lively party scene that incorporates nearby Haverford College. Students form close relationships with their professors, and they eagerly rise to the challenge of intellectually stimulating classes.

Ready, Set, Study

Don't come to Bryn Mawr if you're not ready to work. The students all say their workload is heavy, but they qualify it by gushing about how great their professors are and how interesting the material is for every class. What's more, academic competitiveness is almost entirely nonexistent. The honor code at Bryn Mawr is a strictly enforced set of rules that forbid the discussion of grades between students. This includes class rank as well, so no one knows how everyone else is doing until they graduate. The students describe themselves as "inwardly competitive," working to out-do themselves on each subsequent exam, not trying to beat their classmates.

As if the "amazing" classes at Bryn Mawr aren't enough, students also have the option to take courses at nearby Haverford, Swarthmore or UPenn. The hardest classes include some of the sciences (organic chemistry—no surprise), but also many art history courses, such as "Self and Other in the Arts of France." One of the best classes is said to be "Identification in Cinema," a film minor/art history major course taught by Homay King. Bryn Mawr students are required to take a Freshman Liberal Studies Seminar, as well as a set of core requirements that foster a broad, liberal arts education. The requirements include two labs, two natural sciences, two humanities and two social sciences. The Freshman Seminar focuses on writing skills, and prepares students for the popular English major. One unique major at Bryn Mawr is the Growth and Structure of Cities, which many students say has great course offerings. The most popular professors include Mary Louise Cookson—"even if you hate and suck at math you'll have a ton of fun in her calculus classes!"—Homay King, a film studies professor, and Gary McDonogh, the director of the Growth and Structure of Cities program.

Classes at Bryn Mawr are small and intimate. One sophomore has never had a class with more than 30 people, and classes are frequently found with fewer than 10. This atmosphere fosters the close student-to-professor bonds that students rave about. "You can send 10 e-mails a day to professors and they get back to you immediately," said one student. E-mailing is just the beginning—students not only meet with professors during office hours, but many baby-sit for their professors, walk their dogs or go to their homes for dinner on a regular basis. These relationships are more than just a nice bonus—they're vital. "It's impossible to do well if you don't meet with your professors. You won't get back a paper that doesn't have at least a page of comments on it; you can't get a good grade unless you have an intimate relationship with your professors." While specific office hours are the traditional time to talk with your professors, most profs at Bryn Mawr are available around the clock, inviting students to drop by any time. "Some teachers take the door off the hinges, literally."

Campus, City and Friends

When asked what she loved most about Bryn Mawr, one student replied sarcastically, "All the men!" But don't be fooled—despite the limitations of an all-female college, there is no shortage of men. Events and mingling at neighboring colleges like Haverford and Swarthmore make for lively social scenes and plenty of guy-girl interaction. The on-campus social scene is hugely varied; there's something for everyone. Political groups are extremely active, and there are tons of dance groups (everything from Asian fusion to classical ballet) and a cappella. Haverford tends to have the keg parties and dances, and the regular shuttle between the schools makes for easy access to parties.

> "Some teachers take the door off the hinges, literally."

The drinking policy at Bryn Mawr follows Pennsylvania state law, so the drinking age is 21. Nevertheless, the party scene incorporates underage drinkers without incident. One student sums it up: "No one gets in trouble for drinking because the campus is really responsible on its own. Public safety isn't an issue . . . no one is taken to the hospital, and it's really rare to see anyone throwing up." Thursdays and Saturdays are the big party nights on campus, while Fridays are more toned down since all the athletes have Saturday morning practice. "Thursday people party hard, and grin and bear it through their Friday classes," one student explained.

Beyond the party scene, students hang out in local coffee shops like Cosí or Starbucks, or go to hear live bands at The Point, a café just down the street. Nearby Philadelphia is extremely accessible by the local commuter rail system, which provides access to the Philadelphia Art Museum, clubs, and restaurants. Just 10 minutes away one can shop at King of Prussia Mall, which is one of the largest malls in the country. On campus most students hang out in their halls with friends, or in Carpenter Library, which is "open, well-lit, and has sofas everywhere." There's a café inside, and since students tend to be work-oriented this is a great way to do work and socialize at the same time.

Diversity on-campus is one of the greatest parts of Bryn Mawr. Students come from all around the country and the world. Campus is described as being virtually "clique-free," and students say that there is no segregation whatsoever. "It's very, very diverse economically, socially, politically and religiously. I'm the token white girl," one student said.

Housing and Food

Freshman housing doesn't get much better than what you will find at Bryn Mawr. First off, there are no "freshman dorms." Every dorm has women from all four years, and there is almost no difference in quality of rooms from freshman to senior year. Many rooms have bay windows, wood paneling, and fireplaces; some even have walk in closets. "Freshmen are taken care of really well."

Campus architecture is "gorgeous" classic Gothic, with beautiful stained-glass windows all over. There's a touch of modern style thanks to a new dorm, Erdman, designed by Louis Kahn as a modern Scottish castle. Students love the dorms and campus in general, and 98 percent of the women live on-campus. Safety isn't a concern for Bryn Mawr students, who feel totally safe, even at night. "You could walk around naked" and still be safe, jokes one sophomore. Many students don't lock their doors or their bikes, and lost wallets have been known to come back to their owners before they were noticed to be missing. This is just another way the students benefit from being in the suburbs.

Food on campus is "very good, and amazing in comparison to my friends' schools." There are tons of options for vegetarians and vegans, and while there are plenty of excellent restaurants in the area (and in Philadelphia), most students prefer to stick to the dining halls. Students who work as part of a financial aid arrangement are required to work in the dining halls, which are completely student-staffed.

Like the classes, dining halls are open to Haverford students as well, but since breakfast ends up being almost only Bryn Mawr women, you get lots of people in pajamas. In many cases, that's how they stay throughout the day. Designer brands can be spotted on campus, but for the most part, dress is casual throughout the week. On the weekends students get dressed up and made up, and head out for fun. Though there may not be guys enrolled at Bryn Mawr, there are generally quite a few on campus. The women decide as a floor at the beginning of the year whether their bathroom will be coed, and visiting guys are just expected to follow the Honor Code and be responsible.

Athletes We Are Not . . .

Sports at Bryn Mawr are "big but bad. We're incredibly passionate about how much we suck." School spirit is definitely not lacking in the least here, but unfortunately that doesn't carry over to achieving many victories. Nevertheless, students go out to support their teams (and Haverford's) even at away games. For the non-varsity athletic types, there are good gym facilities, a pool and plenty of safe places to run around campus. For almost every varsity sport there is a corresponding club team, so anyone can participate.

Student government is one of the largest organizations on campus, along with the *Bi-College News*, the Haverford-Bryn Mawr newspaper. There is also an active political community, with groups from every place on the political spectrum. An active Rainbow Alliance helps to promote an open, accepting atmosphere for LGBTQ students and their allies.

One of the things that make Bryn Mawr unique is the presence of the Traditions (with a capital "T"). These are four events held throughout the year, aimed at welcoming the underclassmen into the community. The first Tradition is Parade Night, which welcomes the freshmen to campus with the singing of the school song. Lantern Night follows, each class holding up a lantern of a different color to identify themselves. Third is Hell Week, during which the sophomores get freshmen to do all sorts of crazy things, which the upperclassmen help them evade. Finally, in May the college president rides a horse into campus to begin the May Day celebrations, which focus on the senior class.

Unspoken traditions can also be seen all over campus. "The party every weekend follows a scene," said one student, who explains that the second weekend of first semester is always a toga party, a Thursday in October is always a hurricane party, etc. One of the most clever party themes is the Traffic Light Party—you wear red if you're taken, yellow if you're casually seeing someone ("kind of taken"), and green if you're single and looking. Like alumna Katharine

Hepburn, Bryn Mawr women skinny-dip in the Cloisters as another unspoken tradition.

All in All

Bryn Mawr women love their school, and it's not hard to see why. Easy access to professors, small classes, a great location and a beautiful campus all make for a nearly ideal college experience. When asked if she'd choose to come to Bryn Mawr if she could go back to her senior year of high school, one student expressed an almost unanimous feeling: "I'd come here again in a heartbeat."—*Emily Cleveland*

FYI

If you come to Bryn Mawr, you'd better bring "a fierce work ethic."

What's the typical weekend schedule? "Friday: veg out with friends; Saturday: (as an athlete) get up early, get surprised by how many women are awake at 9 a.m. on a Saturday, party on your hall/in the dorms/at Haverford; Sunday: Sleep late, bemoan the fact that you haven't done enough work, sit in the library all day."

If I could change one thing about Bryn Mawr, "I'd make women leave their rooms more often."

Three things that every student at Bryn Mawr should do before graduating are "skinny dip in the Cloisters, go streaking in front of the president's house, and ring the Taylor bell."

Bucknell University

Address: Bucknell, Freas Hall, Bucknell University, Lewisburg, PA 17837
Phone: 570-577-1101
E-mail Address: admissions@bucknell.edu
Web site URL: www.bucknell.edu
Year Founded: 1846
Private or Public: private
Religious affiliation: none
Location: rural
Regular Application Deadline: 1-Jan
Number of Applicants: 9,021
Percent Accepted: 33%
Percent Accepted who enroll: 31%
Number Entering: 924
Number of Transfers Accepted each Year: 25–35
Mean SAT: NA
Mean ACT: NA

Middle 50% SAT range: v: 600–680, M: 630–710
Middle 50% ACT range: 27–30
Early admission program (EA/ ED/ NA): ED
ED or EA Acceptance Rate: 42%
Full time Undergraduate enrollment: 3,469
Total enrollment: 3,648
Percent Male: 48%
Percent Female: 52%
Total Percent Minority: 15.3%
Percent African-American: 3%
Percent Asian/Pacific Islander: 7%
Percent Hispanic: 2%
Percent Native-American: 0.3%
Percent Other: 3%
Percent in-state / out of state: 29%/71%

Percent from Public HS: 70%
Retention Rate: 95%
Graduation Rate: 90%
Percent in On-campus housing: 89%
Percent affiliated with Greek system: 37%
Percent Varsity or Club Athletes: 19%
Number of official organized extracurricular organizations: 135
3 Most popular majors: Management, Economics, Psychology
Student/Faculty ratio: 11:01
Tuition and Fees: $36,002.00
Cost for Room and Board: $7,366.00
Percent receiving Financial aid, first-year: 77%

Bucknell, a small liberal arts school situated in rural central Pennsylvania, offers the quintessential small campus feel. Small class sizes, close relationships between teachers and students, flexible and accommodating faculty, and beautiful new facilities are all qualities that create the charming and personable feel of this small community.

Accessible Academic Area

Like many small schools, Bucknell can boast an excellent 11 to 1 student teacher ratio that results in personal relationships between students and faculty. Students claim professors are flexible and almost always available, "You can just walk right into their office at almost any time and sit down and talk" says one student. Students' descriptions of professors have really revealed the faculty's involvement and investment in their students, "I really feel like the teachers are there to teach us, not just instruct us. It is a subtle but important difference." Only professors teach courses and teaching assistants, sometimes considered a nuisance when left in charge, are employed as a helpful supplement to lecture courses.

Perhaps one of the most impressive features of the academic curricula is the consistently small class sizes. The "large" intro level courses are sparse and usually have about 100 people. For the most part you will find yourself in more personal class settings of 20 to 30 people. As you move into the upper level courses classes are even more intimate, ranging from 13 to 20 people. Some classes are competitive to get into, especially those at the upper levels, but like one student said, "most of the time I haven't had a problem with getting into a class, the biggest problem I have had is fitting a class into my schedule when there are a lot of cool classes I want to take. The one time I had had a problem, I just spoke with the teacher and he let me in."

> **"I really feel like the teachers are there to teach us, not just instruct us. It is a subtle but important difference."**

The workload, like at any college "is what you make it. You can get by taking easy courses or you can challenge yourself. But to get an A you really have to work at it." The prestigious management and engineering schools draw in a lot of majors; however, economics, biology, English and psychology are common majors as well. Though Bucknell can boast a strong science and quantitative course program, its smaller majors like International Relations and Animal Behavior have strong reputations as well. Bucknell operates on a semester system and like any good liberal arts college, is invested in a well rounded education for its students based in a core curriculum. Core requirements for freshman year are one English, one math, and one "foundational skills" class, which is designed to develop persuasive writing skills. By the end of sophomore year two lab sciences must be taken, and by graduation students must have taken four humanities, two social sciences and three writing courses. However, there is no language requirement!

Out Late Livin' the Life

With the majority of the students living on-campus and being fairly isolated, the party scene is the center of campus social life and is hard to miss every Wednesday, Friday, and Saturday. Greek life at Bucknell is big; in fact 50% of sophomores, juniors, and seniors are in a frat or sorority. But students are not allowed to rush until their sophomore year, so a lot of underclassman partying occurs on campus in the dorms. Though membership in a sorority or fraternity will definitely improve your party options, if that is not your thing you can still make it onto the Register list (which is the list of invites for the select campus wide frat parties) if you have any friends in the house. Often in frats, specific sports teams will dominate the house. Perhaps this innate segregation within the student body leads to exclusive, tight-knit groups, but as one non-frat student said "the people are cliquey, but it is a big party scene and once you are out it is easy to meet people."

A good chunk of upperclassmen living is in off-campus housing; called "downtown houses," which gives students the freedom to host their own parties on their own property. But not all this wild partying goes unchecked. It has been the students's observations that police enforcement has been increasing in the last year or so, even in the downtown housing area. One needs to be aware that the school has in place a policy that discourages underage and out of hand drinking. It is a point system where, for example, 1 point may be received if an underage student is caught with an open drink, and where 10 points earn a suspension.

The school sponsors interesting non-alcohol related evening activities such as concerts and guest speakers, "just the other day Bill Nye the Science Guy came and the auditorium was completely full, which doesn't happen that often," said one student. However, concerts and speakers are much more of a rarity than parties and are not always students' number one choice.

There isn't much of a dating scene at Bucknell. Most students would generally agree that random hook-ups are much more common and dating is not the norm. As one freshman said, "Oh yeah, hook-ups are definitely popular. I've hooked up with six people already and it's only been a month and a half!" What a statement, but overzealous freshman status is not something that should be overlooked in this case!

Wait, Who Are You?

When asked to describe the student body with a stereotype, one student said "preppy white people. You look around and all the guys are wearing red shorts, or yellow shorts, or khaki shorts with a polo and popped collar." This view that there is a homogenous student population both racially, socio-economically, and even ideologically is consistent with student perceptions and diversity statistics. As one west-coaster put it, "there is a feeling of east coast pretension; the people are a little more self-centered than I am used to on the west coast." Though there is a fairly balanced pool of political views, that is obviously not enough to be considered truly diverse, and the school administration seems to be aware of this and has invested in long term plans to improve the diversity of the student population.

The Bucknell Bubble
The campus is an idyllic rural setting with beautiful, almost brand new, modern architecture. In fact, a new engineering building was added to the campus and is shared by undergrads and the small graduate population as well. Everything is easy to get to making "it the epitome of a walking campus." For the most part all the dorms are nice places to live, maybe with the exception of some freshman housing. The freshman housing is fairly spread out, but the central freshmen hall, as one can imagine, is the less desirable of the living spaces and is assigned to you ahead of arrival. Starting sophomore year students enter the room lottery. Bucknell has a unique system called "blockbooking rooms" which guarantees that you can live next to your friends no matter if you are in different rooms with different lottery numbers or not. It's also easy to do. Though not all dorms are a microcosm of the student body, there are two that have become the designated athlete dorms, one that is reserved for sorority living because there are no sorority houses, two dorms and one spe-cial interest house that are substance free, and one dorm that is more or less the quiet dorm, or "geeky dorm."

The meal plans and dinning halls are flexible and tasty. There is an assortment of meal plans to choose from catering to different eating habits that range from the unlimited plan to the declining balance where items are charged to your account individually. There are four main dinning halls each with a different taste and style and most of which are open from 7 a.m. to midnight (though not always serving hot food) which is a great convenience to late night studiers. Most students are satisfied with their on-campus cuisine and don't go out to the "downtown" area (which is misleading because it is really just a main drag) to eat out at the restaurants or bars.

Free Time . . . What?
Students have endless opportunities to get involved in clubs, volunteering, organizations, and sports. There are over 150 clubs and organizations operating through the school and twenty-seven men's and women's varsity athletic teams. Students seem to feel that the sports teams have a large presence on campus. To facilitate such interests, the school has built impressive athletic centers including a new field house, a new basketball arena for games and there are complete weight and exercise facilities for athletes and non-athletes alike. The student body has quite a bit of team spirit and pride for their school sports, with men's basketball definitely taking the cake. Almost every game is sold out. When asked what made Bucknell unique to him, one varsity athlete answered "the mix of a Division 1 athletic program and a small school environment."—*Shaughnessy Costigan*

FYI
If you come to Bucknell you had better bring a "good self esteem; every student on this campus is amazingly talented, and I still hold that Bucknell chooses students at least 50% based on looks."
A typical weekend at Bucknell consists of "procrastination, and a lot of it . . . even if you think there's nothing to do one weekend, by some miraculous turn of events, you find yourself socially booked until at least midnight on Saturday."
If you could change one thing about Bucknell, I'd "have there be a smaller Greek life."
Three things every student at Bucknell should do before graduation are "go to the Freeze and the Campus Theatre, walk around downtown Lewisburg, and go wild at least once!"

Carnegie Mellon University

Address: Carnegie Mellon,
500 Forbes Avenue,
Pittsburgh, PA 15213-3890
Phone: NA
E-mail Address:
undergraduate-
admissions@andrew.
cmu.edu
Web site URL: NA
Year Founded: 1900
Private or Public: private
Religious affiliation: none
Location: urban
**Regular Application
Deadline:** 2-Jan
Number of Applicants:
18,684
Percent Accepted: 34%
**Percent Accepted who
enroll:** 22%
Number Entering: 1,428
**Number of Transfers
Accepted each Year:** NA
Mean SAT: 1,380
Mean ACT: 30

Middle 50% SAT range:
1,300–1,500
Middle 50% ACT range:
28–32
**Early admission program
(EA/ ED/ NA):** ED
ED or EA Acceptance Rate:
NA
**Full time Undergraduate
enrollment:** 5,580
Total enrollment: 5,580
Percent Male: 61%
Percent Female: 39%
Total Percent Minority: 35%
Percent African-American:
5%
**Percent Asian/Pacific
Islander:** 24%
Percent Hispanic: 5%
Percent Native-American:
1%
Percent Other: NA
**Percent in-state / out of
state:** NA
Percent from Public HS: NA

Retention Rate: 94%
Graduation Rate: 69 in
four 86 in six
**Percent in On-campus
housing:** 66%
**Percent affiliated with
Greek system:** 17%
**Percent Varsity or Club
Athletes:** NA
**Number of official
organized
extracurricular
organizations:** 225
Most popular majors:
Computer Engineering,
Liberal Arts
Student/Faculty ratio:
10:01
Tuition and Fees:
$34,180.00
**Percent receiving
Financial aid, first-year:**
49%

It is midnight at Carnegie Mellon, and groups of students creep out of the libraries, computer clusters, and art studios. They are going to "paint the fence," a legendary activity in which students are allowed, between midnight and dawn, to paint the metal fence at the center of campus. The fence is used to advertise everything from frat parties, to memorials, to any of the range of activities hosted by the school's interesting mix of students, affectionately referred to as "the freaks and geeks."

Academics for Artists and for Techies

Carnegie Mellon is comprised of six undergraduate schools: the Mellon College of Science, the Carnegie Institute of Technology, the College of Fine Arts, the College of Humanities and Social Sciences, the Tepper School of Business, and the School of Computer Science. Each school and major has different requirements. "The requirements suck when you have to do them, but are great for applying to grad school," said a recent graduate. Students enjoy the wide range of courses offered. "It's hard to find such a

good business program, as well as computer science and theatre arts, all in one school," mused one senior. Said another student, "I have taken art and dance courses as well as engineering, computer science, and robotics courses." There is even a bagpipe major, which sets the school apart from others.

Undergraduates agree that the academics, though intense, are excellent preparation for further study. The most prestigious and the most difficult majors are generally in the arts, engineering, and computer schools. Classes are difficult and fast-paced, but the work often produces tangible results very quickly: "We learned how to build robots within the first three weeks of class, and then built a robot every week after that," said a student. On the other hand, some students refer to the School of Humanities and Social Sciences as "H & Less Stress." Students considered English, psychology, and modern languages to be the slacker majors. One student pointed to a divide in the quality of the teaching: "The caliber of the professors is nowhere near that of the other schools."

Class sizes range from below 20 for seminars and electives to about 100 people for introductory classes, although the size of some popular lecture classes can be in the 200s. A senior, having taken computer programming classes and humanities classes, identified the best part of CMU as having "such a diverse and good faculty."

Diversity in the Social Life

The diversity at CMU extends outside of the course catalogue. Freshmen find numerous ways to meet each other. A list of activities includes cruises, clubs, and "a crazy and silly night called Playfair where everyone runs around making fools of themselves in attempts to meet people." Freshman year is the best, according to a student, because "by sophomore year, a lot of people keep their doors shut." The social groups that form during freshman year often stay together over the four years. One junior said that Carnegie Mellon "is very cliquish—especially among the ethnic groups."

> "I have taken art and dance courses as well as engineering, computer science and robotics courses."

One way in which CMU lacks in diversity is gender. Almost two-thirds of the population is male. Although this might seem encouraging for females, students attest that "in terms of attractive people, the campus is limited," and they complain that a large percentage of the guys lack social skills. Nevertheless, those who want to randomly hook up have the opportunity to do so.

Frats and sororities are easy to rush and are an integral part of the social scene on campus, according to students. Parties are regularly held at the frats and sororities—especially Kappa Kappa Gamma, Phi Kappa Theta, and Theta Xi. Unfortunately, students claim that parties are often little more than crappy beer and bad music, except for the occasional beach party, jungle party, and foam party. "You can avoid Greek life if you just join other activities," said one student. However, according to some, freshmen usually only have the option of frat parties because they don't know enough people to go to other parties.

Underage drinking is officially not allowed on campus, and those caught doing it will be punished. However, "it's pretty easy to get alcohol if you want it," said one girl.

"As long as no one sees it and you're not being stupid, there haven't been many incidents involving underage drinking busts." Kegs are allowed on campus in the non-dry Greek houses, but no alcohol is allowed in student rooms.

Some students could ask for more from the social life. "Some weekends go by where there's not a lot to do," said a recent graduate. Outside the party scene, however, there are plenty of options. Movies play five nights a week in the University Center for $1. Over two hundred student clubs meet throughout the week. The drama school produces several plays that are given high ratings by students.

Suburbs of Pittsburgh

CMU is a small campus, with patches of grass and yellow brick buildings with copper roofs that have turned green over the years. "This is a beautiful and safe campus," said one pleased freshman. The art building is especially notable. One student commented, "every time I walk in the art building I see some new—usually odd, but amazing—work of art." "It's very pleasant here," said one student of the campus, but with a caveat: "unless it's a really nice day, you won't see anyone hanging out outside—we're notorious for hanging out in computer clusters."

CMU is located in the suburbs of Pittsburgh where it is considered safe, although "like any big city there are some shady areas." Students give Pittsburgh high ratings, and one student happily commented, "I love the fact that I am in a city but at the same time feel that I have an actual campus." Said another student, "there are many restaurants, bars, and museums within a mile of campus."

The food and the dining halls were given negative reviews in general. Upperclassmen warn future freshmen to get as small of a dining plan as possible. Those in the dining hall are either "cliques or loners," said one sophomore. People instead choose to eat off campus, at the Trucks, the Union Grill, or the numerous cheap restaurants near campus. For dates, students often leave campus and head over to Station Square, an area with nice restaurants.

Most students thought that their freshman housing was adequate. Students rated RAs in the dorms as considerate, helpful, and nice. Mudge, a converted mansion, is the students' favorite dorm, with suite-style, spacious rooms, and a gorgeous courtyard.

Donner, on the other hand, is "a dungeon, with small dingy rooms and shared bathrooms." Some dorms have air conditioning and CMU is always renovating to keep their dorms up-to-date. Despite the good reviews given to dorms, many students opt after the first year to live in the cheaper apartments off campus.

Computers Versus Athletics

Late night gaming sessions in the dorms are more popular than athletics at CMU, according to students. "People are too lazy.

Only about five people go to football games," said a freshman. Even at the Homecoming game, the stands don't fill up. Non-campus sports, such as the Super Bowl, also do not catch the attention of many CMU students. However, intramurals, where students compete in teams according to their school and major, are popular among the students.

If you prefer building robots to football, and if cutting-edge technology is as important to you as a great arts program, then CMU is the place to be.—*Andrew Hamilton*

FYI

If you come to Carnegie Mellon, you'd better bring "a warm coat and a computer."

What's the typical weekend schedule? "Friday night, party; Saturday, sleep until noon, do homework until dinner, party; Sunday, work."

If I could change one thing about Carnegie Mellon, "I would lessen the influence that Greek life has on campus."

Three things every student should do before graduating from Carnegie Mellon are "paint the fence, step away from a computer, and see a strange experimental play."

Dickinson College

Address: Dickinson, Waidner Admissions House, PO Box 1773, Carlisle, PA 17013
Phone: 800-644-1773
E-mail Address: admit@dickinson.edu
Web site URL: www.dickinson.edu
Year Founded: 1783
Private or Public: private
Religious affiliation: none
Location: suburban
Regular Application Deadline: 1-Feb
Number of Applicants: 5,298
Percent Accepted: 43%
Percent Accepted who enroll: 27%
Number Entering: 618
Number of Transfers Accepted each Year: varies
Mean SAT: NA
Mean ACT: NA
Middle 50% SAT range: 1,220–1,360

Middle 50% ACT range: 26–30
Early admission program (EA/ ED/ NA): ED and EA
ED or EA Acceptance Rate: 63%
Full time Undergraduate enrollment: 2,355
Total enrollment: 2,369
Percent Male: 44%
Percent Female: 56%
Total Percent Minority: 13%
Percent African-American: 5%
Percent Asian/Pacific Islander: 4%
Percent Hispanic: 4%
Percent Native-American: <1%
Percent Other: 1%
Percent in-state / out of state: 27%/73%
Percent from Public HS: 61%

Retention Rate: 91%
Graduation Rate: 82%
Percent in On-campus housing: 93%
Percent affiliated with Greek system: 21%
Percent Varsity or Club Athletes: 36%
Number of official organized extracurricular organizations: 140
3 Most popular majors: Political Science, Psychology, International Business and Management
Student/Faculty ratio: 12:01
Tuition and Fees: $33,470.00
Cost for Room and Board: $8,480.00
Percent receiving Financial aid, first-year: 96%

Located in the tiny town of Carlisle, Pa., Dickinson is a close-knit school with prestigious international business, foreign language, and political science programs. Dickinson is perfect for the student who dreams of traveling the globe, but wants to go to a college where everyone knows her name and Greek life abounds. It's also a great place for preps and those who love them.

Go to Class, Go Abroad

One of the first things that Dickinson students proudly mention about their school is its small class sizes. There are virtually no classes with more than 40 students, with many Dickinsonians happily saying that their classes have even less students. Students also praise their professors for being extremely approachable and helpful. "Our professors care a lot and are truly interested in what the students have to offer," said one freshman.

When your professors care and your classes are small, you better go to class. Dickinson assures that this happens with a strict attendance policy. Up to 20 percent of the grade for a course can be based on attendance, so those who care about their GPAs don't skip. Students say that it's relatively easy to get into classes that you want. Freshmen are encouraged to take 400-level courses with upperclassmen. Students said that you should expect to work at Dickinson, but that "it's the ideal workload. It's not too easy, but it's not too hard either."

Like most colleges, Dickinson has distribution requirements that students need to fulfill outside of their majors. The areas they must take courses in are philosophy, religion, environmental studies, social science, natural science, foreign language, comparative civilizations, physical education and literature. Dickinsonians say that the distribution requirements are easy to complete, and just like at the local Wal-Mart, you can often get a "two for the price of one" deal where one class fulfills two requirements. However, many students admit that people put off their distribution requirements and then have to cram them all into senior year. In addition to trying to knock out a few requirements, all freshmen take a Freshman Seminar. In these seminars, students build on the research and writing skills they honed before they got to Dickinson by studying topics that appeal to them.

Students are equally enthusiastic about Dickinson's study abroad program. Students can go abroad for a semester or a year to a variety of Dickinson-affiliated programs around the world. Students go to countries in Europe, Africa, Asia, and South and Central America simply to take classes in a setting more exciting than small-town Pennsylvania or to totally immerse themselves in a different culture. Most of the programs are not in big cities, but in small towns where students live with host families and can avoid annoying tourists. Dickinson's study abroad pro-

gram is so popular that one student said, "Every winter it's like a new class of people arrives because so many juniors are coming back from study abroad." International business, foreign language and East Asian studies classes are both extremely popular and renowned at Dickinson, further proving the international leanings of its students.

The Greekfest

Social life at Dickinson is dominated by Greek life. Fraternity parties are usually open to everyone and always very well attended. Students could not stress enough the importance of the frat scene. "Basically, if you're a guy, you have to join a frat or you'll be a social pariah," one student explained simply. There are four sororities on campus, including the infamous Kappas, who are known as "snobby and exclusive," but girls do not have to join them to be a part of the social life, since guys love girls to come to their frat parties.

> **"Basically, if you're a guy, you have to join a frat or you'll be a social pariah."**

Just like any other school with a huge Greek life, alcohol is abundant at Dickinson. In fact, Dickinson is sometimes called "Drinkinson." The administration is not at all happy with this nickname and is very tough on alcohol. They forbid kegs on campus and will take away the house of any fraternity that has a keg for fear that they promote binge drinking. The fraternities have found clever ways around the keg restriction by having cocktail parties. Students also say that the strict rules are often unsuccessfully enforced.

Dickinson is not all about drunken debauchery. Frequent dances and concerts are hosted at The Depot and The Quarry, two on campus hangouts. For such a small school, Dickinson attracts some big names to these events. "I was in the front row at the Death Cab for Cutie concert and there were like only 50 people there. It was amazing," said one satisfied student. A future concert will include Jay-Z. These kinds of events offer a fun occasional alternative to getting drunk at the frats.

Happy Little Preppy Family

Dickinsonians are pleased with the close-knit community that makes up their school. While one student complained that she feels like she "knows the entire student body," most students like the communal feel. Dickinson must do a great job of choosing roommates for freshmen, because the friends they make in their dorms their first year are the friends they have for the next three. "Most freshmen roommates stay together," one student explained.

The fact that it's a school where everyone knows your name really has an effect on the Dickinson dating scene. "By the time they're upperclassmen, most students are in relationships here, but many freshman are still in their high school relationships or having random hook ups," said one student. Some Dickinsonians utilize their study-abroad yearnings closer to home by hooking up in the East Asian studies room. Dickinson students are careful not to hook up too randomly, however, because the fear of running out of attractive partners in such a tiny school is real.

Dickinson students do more than party, hook up or make phone calls to their long-distance loves. They participate in varsity, club, or intramural sports with soccer, basketball and volleyball being the most popular. They are involved with student government, school publications, drama, comedy and foreign language clubs. Some students stressed that Dickinson needs to create community service organizations to add a giving-back element to student activities.

The typical Dickinsonian, students say, is a white, upper-middle class private school grad from the East Coast. "I really need to get a Polo shirt. I don't have one and everyone has them here," said one student when asked about Dickinson's prep factor. The administration strives for diversity, but like many things at Dickinson, it ends up having an international flavor. "Our diversity is from international students. Most of the black people you'll see on campus aren't from the United States but from Africa," one freshman explained.

Pretty Campus, Ugly City

Dickinsonians have little praise for the town of Carlisle. "It's a typical mid-Pennsylvanian town: boring, kind of trashy, and there's nothing to do," complained one student. Another summed up Carlisle by simply explaining that many residents have mullets. To escape the small town stuff, students can make the 20 minute trip to Harrisburg, Pennsylvania's capital.

Though they are displeased with the town, Dickinson students don't complain too much since their campus is beautiful. "It's just what a college should look like," said one student. Dickinsonians laud their campus's limestone buildings, wide open space and lush hills. The school is not only pleasing to the eye, but also pleasing to the stomach. Its meals are time and again rated among the best of college cafeteria food. Dickinsonians have slightly less praise for their dorms, at least the inside of them. Though most are renovated and some—like Goodyear, an upperclassman dorm—are legendary, some students complain about forced triples and huge differences in the amount of students housed in different dormitories. "My dorm has 40 people and the other freshmen one has 400. It's nice, because my dormmates are like my family, but sometimes I wish our dorm was bigger," explained one girl.

Dickinson seems to have it all. It offers its students the chance to be a part of a close-knit community but travel around the world, the chance to live in a small town but visit a big city, and the chance to party hard but challenge oneself academically. With all these options, Dickinsonians graduate feeling as if they made the right choice.
—*Keneisha Sinclair*

FYI

If you come to Dickinson, you'd better bring "a Polo or Lacoste shirt."
The typical weekend schedule is "Friday: watch a movie, then get dressed up and pregame before going to the frats; Saturday: sleep, do work, go out to dinner, then go to the frats; Sunday: sleep and do your work."
If I could change one thing about Dickinson, "I'd make it not so focused on Greek life."
Three things every student at Dickinson should do before graduating are "hook up in the East Asian Studies room, study abroad, and walk to the Wal-Mart."

Drexel University

Address: Drexel, Main Building, Room 212, 3141 Chestnut Street, Philadelphia, PA 19104
Phone: 800-2-DREXEL
E-mail Address: NA
Web site URL: www.drexel.edu/em/
Year Founded: 1891
Private or Public: private
Religious affiliation: none
Location: urban
Regular Application Deadline: 2-Mar
Number of Applicants: 12,093
Percent Accepted: 82%
Percent Accepted who enroll: 25%
Number Entering: 2,503
Number of Transfers Accepted each Year: 2,128
Mean SAT: 1,190

Mean ACT: NA
Middle 50% SAT range: 1,080–1,290
Middle 50% ACT range: NA
Early admission program (EA/ ED/ NA): NA
ED or EA Acceptance Rate: NA
Full time Undergraduate enrollment: 11,936
Total enrollment: 17,450
Percent Male: 61%
Percent Female: 39%
Total Percent Minority: 23%
Percent African-American: 5%
Percent Asian/Pacific Islander: 13%
Percent Hispanic: 4%
Percent Native-American: 1%
Percent Other: 7%
Percent in-state / out of state: 49%/51%

Percent from Public HS: 70%
Retention Rate: 80%
Graduation Rate: 60%
Percent in On-campus housing: 25%
Percent affiliated with Greek system: 10%
Percent Varsity or Club Athletes: NA
Number of official organized extracurricular organizations: 136
Most popular majors: Information Studies, Mechanical Engineering
Student/Faculty ratio: 10:01
Tuition and Fees: $25,450.00
Cost for Room and Board: $12,015.00
Percent receiving Financial aid, first-year: 74%

W ant a college experience where you can "go wireless" anywhere on campus, where you can enjoy the events, sights, and tastes of the City of Brotherly Love, and where the likelihood of having to stress about finding a job after you graduate is slim to none? Check out Philadelphia's Drexel University.

A "Real-World" College Experience

Drexel's co-operative education program was recently ranked in the nation's top 10 by *U.S. News & World Report.* The Drexel Plan, required by most majors, means each student will have completed three six-month stints of full-time employment (or "co-ops") before graduation. Students browse an online database of "many large, well-established companies," choosing from over 1,500 potential employers such as GlaxoSmithKline, Children's Hospital of Pennsylvania, Lockheed Martin, and Comcast Corporation. Although many co-ops are with Philadelphia-based companies, out-of-state and international opportunities with large companies make it so you can co-op "almost anywhere."

While some students are attracted to Drexel for its top-notch engineering pro-

grams, the fact that it offers a chance to "find out during college, rather than four years down the road, if what you're studying is what you want to do for the rest of your life" seems to truly be what sets Drexel apart from most other colleges. Almost all co-ops are salaried, and many students are offered employment upon graduation by former co-op employers.

Because most students follow the Drexel Plan, a five-year program is "pretty much standard." After attending class full-time for freshman year, these students will have a co-op each of their sophomore, pre-junior, and junior years. The regular classroom setting is standard, and most classes are structured with a lecture component and a smaller 15-20 student recitation section. One student said that while the University's engineering program (the nation's largest among private universities) is known to be tough, "most professors are well established in their fields and pride themselves" on demanding the most from their students. Although the college is known for its technology-based achievements (in addition to being a fully wireless campus since 2000, in 2002 Drexel was the first to launch a wireless Web portal service for students), the humanity department is also "pretty good, and provides a break from all of the engineering classes."

Drexel is divided into six colleges: the College of Arts and Sciences, the College of Business, the College of Media Arts and Design, the College of Engineering, the College of Information Science and Technology, and the College of Evening and Professional Studies. In addition, three schools offer undergraduate B.S. degrees: the School of Biomedical Engineering, Science, and Health Systems; the School of Education; and the School of Environmental Science, Engineering, and Policy.

Social Scene—On Campus and Around Philly

Drexel's location in the heart of Philadelphia, while limiting the "campus feel," does make for a variety of ways to spend the weekend. As with most college campuses, drinking is almost always involved in any social activity, and is sometimes enjoyed to excess. Drugs, while readily available in a city with a population of over 1.5 million, still play a comparatively limited role in campus life.

Freshmen are required to have full meal plans and to live on campus for their first three quarters of matriculation, unless a student is married or lives at home. Residence halls Calhoun, Myers, Kelly, Towers, and Van Resselaer are traditional freshman dorms, with East Hall designated as the all Honors freshman hall. Another unique housing feature Drexel offers are "learning communities," where students with similar academic interests can choose grouped together. Business, Engineering, Future Health Professionals, Information Science and Technology, and Media Arts and Design learning communities are offered.

Most upperclassmen are on limited meal plans, if any. All students seemed pleased with the options and set-up of the meal plan; Handschumacher Dining Center in the student center is the heart of the program, with a wide variety of food "stations" like the Mexican Bar and the Vegan and Vegetarian station. Other dining locations offer a la carte options and are spread throughout campus.

The majority of students opt to live off campus with a group of friends after freshman year, leading to plenty of time happily spent just hanging out, playing video games, or watching movies. Such a situation also leads to "lots of house parties, right in the city." "Even if you're under 21 you can find ways to party," remarked one minor, "whether it's at a house party or a frat party." And while the fraternity scene is present, it isn't as big as it once was. Campus events at Drexel are complemented by the proximity of St. Joe's, Temple, Villanova, and University of Pennsylvania. "Penn is a block from here, Temple's just a quick train ride away, and several others are also easily accessible by public transportation," noted one student. Given the school's male-heavy gender ratio, several students are grateful for the easy access to other schools.

For those of age, bars nearby like Cavanaugh's and Brownie's are popular college-student hangouts. Zocalo offers a tasty Tex-Mex dining option right near campus, and Bubble House serves up trendy, if overpriced, bubble tea and "funky" Thai fare. Overall, most students attest that there are "a lot of good little restaurants, especially ethnic places, all over the city." And of course, the corner in South Philly where Pat's and Geno's are located is "the place" to savor a bite of an "original" Philadelphia cheesesteak. Other not-to-miss activities include attending a concert by the Philadelphia Orchestra, visiting the famous Philadelphia Museum of Art, shopping on South Street, or watching an Eagles, Flyers, Sixers, or Phillies game. Finally, a local band scene thrives at restaurants and smaller venues, and bigger concert halls often host more mainstream attractions like OAR.

If you're worried your activities will be limited to watching, eating, and drinking, fear not. Leading a healthy lifestyle in the city once called the "No. 1 fattest city in America" by *Men's Health Magazine* has gotten a lot easier, thanks to recent improvements that made the city more bike-friendly. And "Boathouse Row is only a five-minute walk from campus and is a great place to run or bike along the Schuylkill River, and nearby Fairmount Park has plenty of trails as well."

Student Body

Diversity on campus is improving with Drexel's rising popularity among applicants, and many students note that there are many international students. However, both African-American and Latino populations are at or below 5 percent of the total student body, and several students observed that the campus still does seem to be "a lot of people from Pennsylvania, Delaware, or New Jersey."

Beyond the Classroom

Drexel's varsity teams play in a highly competitive league, and their traditionally strong basketball team provides the bulk of athletic-inspired school spirit for the Dragons. Many students lament the absence of a varsity football team, yet "intramural sports are popular, and people often sign up to play flag football, dodgeball, or basketball teams with their friends." Given its location in a city that offers opportunities to pursue a wide array of interests, Drexel's on-campus extracurriculars are low key, although it still has plenty of quirky clubs such as ASE, an architectural club whose mission is to design and race concrete canoes.

Students praised campus security, reporting that numerous alarm phones and campus and city security forces made for a safe feeling near Drexel, although because of its urban location most students agreed that being aware of one's surroundings was also key.

> "The co-op program works to the advantage of the college student. You realize it's much easier to learn through experience, from working with so many different people."

The range of experience offered by Drexel and its surrounding city is truly dazzling. "The co-op program works to the advantage of the college student. You realize it's much easier to learn through experience, from working with so many different people. And that's what employers are looking for after you graduate."—*Katie Matlack*

FYI

If you come to Drexel, you'd better bring "a beer funnel, an appetite for cheesesteak, and an appetite for learning."

What's the typical weekend schedule? "Going out on campus Thursday nights to various Thirsty Thursday events, going into the city Friday and Saturday nights, especially to Old City, and waking up late Sunday morning to do laundry and homework."

If I could change one thing about Drexel, "there would be more girls."

Three things every student at Drexel should do before graduating are: "Go to a giant house party and a giant frat party, run up the Art Museum steps Rocky-style, and visit Boathouse Row."

Franklin and Marshall College

Address: Franklin and Marshall, 637 College Avenue, Lancaster, PA 17603

Phone: 717-291-3951

E-mail Address: admission@fandm.edu

Web site URL: www.fandm.edu

Year Founded: 1787

Private or Public: private

Religious affiliation: none

Location: small city

Regular Application Deadline: 2-Feb

Number of Applicants: NA

Percent Accepted: 46%

Percent Accepted who enroll: 28%

Number Entering: 524

Number of Transfers Accepted each Year: 33

Mean SAT: 1,271

Mean ACT: NA

Middle 50% SAT range: 580–670V, 600–690M, 630–710W

Middle 50% ACT range: NA

Early admission program (EA/ ED/ NA): ED

ED or EA Acceptance Rate: 65%

Full time Undergraduate enrollment: 1,990

Total enrollment: 2,028

Percent Male: 48%

Percent Female: 52%

Total Percent Minority: 25%

Percent African-American: 5%

Percent Asian/Pacific Islander: 5%

Percent Hispanic: 5%

Percent Native-American: 1%

Percent Other: 75%

Percent in-state / out of state: 29%/71%

Percent from Public HS: 53%

Retention Rate: 91%

Graduation Rate: 81%

Percent in On-campus housing: 61%

Percent affiliated with Greek system: 27%

Percent Varsity or Club Athletes: NA

Number of official organized extracurricular organizations: 90

3 Most popular majors: Social Sciences, Business/Marketing, Interdisciplinary Studies

Student/Faculty ratio: 10:01

Tuition and Fees: $32,450.00

Cost for Room and Board: $8,540.00

Percent receiving Financial aid, first-year: 69%

Though they call themselves Diplomats, not many Franklin & Marshall students will be heading to Washington to write legislation. Despite its liberal arts reputation and mascot, Franklin & Marshall is a school that caters to the sciences. Double majors and extracurricular leaders thrive in the close community at F&M, where high expectations are found inside and outside the classroom. Students at the college jump headlong into community service, pursue hands-on academics and research opportunities, and take advantage of unmatched faculty interactions. However, their drive doesn't force them underground—Diplomats know how to have fun like students at any other college.

Small Classes, Big Research Opportunities

Though F&M specializes on the sciences, students can experience a diverse set of classes and departments before choosing a major. "In general, it's a liberal arts curriculum," one student said. "They have a core curriculum but they really try to promote freedom in choice of study." Students must take at least classes from each of the three realms of study in the "Foundations" program: Mind, Self and Spirit; the Natural World; and Community, Culture and Society. This core provides the base on which upperclassmen build their majors.

Many students arrive in Lancaster expecting to major in F&M's impressive pre-med program. The pre-med track often proves more to be more difficult than prospective students had imagined, as one biochemistry major pointed out: "There's a huge population of pre-med students here and that population decreases each year, pretty much exponentially." The same student, expressing a sentiment common among F&M science majors, said the only easy majors were "anything not science." Among non-science majors, the most popular concentrations include government, psychology, and business. But one English and neuroscience double major noted that "it's not unusual to see students majoring in two very different areas of study."

In either the sciences or the liberal arts, students agree that faculty interaction sets F&M apart. With a student to faculty ratio of 10:1, non-introductory classes are typically small and professors accessible. Even larger lectures often come to less than 50 students. One student doing chemistry research alongside his professor said that research opportunities at this small college "are readily available to the extent that they would be at any research university." Many students stay over the summer in nearby apartments to get involved with F&M faculty. Research, both during the year and over the summer, gives underclassmen the chance to contribute to groundbreaking work. "It's not just those in the sciences who want kids in their majors to take part in their research," one student said. "And I'm always invited over to the professors' houses for dinner afterwards to meet their families."

Lancaster Living

As one of the oldest colleges in the country, F&M is full of open spaces. In the fall and spring, Hartman Green swells with students playing Frisbee, reading, and generally enjoying themselves. Freshmen and sophomores are required to live on campus, all within a block or two of the Green. Most agree that the accommodations are comfortable but not exceptional. Hallways include both first-year and second-year students, with the latter having the option of living in doubles or suites. After sophomore year, most students move into the abundant and affordable off-campus housing across the street.

Lancaster provides F&M students with more than they usually expect when arriving on campus. Although small and relatively rural, the downtown area is full of fresh farm markets, affordable restaurants, and several clubs for students on the weekends. The restaurants become a tantalizing diversion from the typical college grub, about which one student reasoned, "I don't think college food is ever as good as home, but it won't kill you." And if you just can't resist a real home-cooked meal, many students from the East Coast use cars to escape to Philadelphia and Baltimore, which are both two hours away. "The campus doesn't become a ghost town on the weekend, but it is definitely convenient," one Philadelphian said.

The Weekend Wrap-up

Whether it's the weekend or not, students say that the campus is known to be cliquey. Fraternities and sororities are not officially recognized by the University but do exist in noticeable numbers. Nevertheless, Greek life does not dominate the social scene. "Greek life is an accessory," one student said. "By no means do you have to be in it to meet friends." Among the student body there is a clear divide between those who drink and those who do not. Those who don't drink argue that alcohol is only a small part of life at F&M: "What people say who came here 20 years ago is you have a miserable time here if you don't associate with Greek life, but what I see tells me that isn't the case." In contrast, those who do drink claim they can't imagine the school without it. Recently the administration has been increasingly strict in enforcing alcohol policies, including the prohibition of alcohol in dormitories of students under 21. In addition, local police have increased their watch over college night life—to the extent of breaking up parties and using undercover agents. Some say the police have taken it too far. "They're cracking down on us this year," said one frustrated student.

Much like frats, athletics play an accessory role on campus. Sports teams are a popular yet limited outlet for school pride. While the Division III squash, basketball and football programs are perennially solid, few students go crazy for them. Instead, Diplomats find other ways to show their school pride. "A lot of people walk around in F&M clothing," one student said.

The Typical Diplomat

Students insist diversity improves each year, but few have any difficulty in describing the average F&M student. Almost all are academically driven. Almost all are interested in getting involved in activities outside the classroom. And almost all are upper-middle class, white Northeasterners. "There's a distinct lack of diversity," one sophomore sighed. "The first thing you notice is it's a pretty homogeneous student body. You'll probably see rich and white, for one thing." In addition to a lack of racial and socioeco-

nomic diversity, several students added that religious and sexual diversity is relatively rare. But religious and social minorities that do exist emerge as a vocal faction of the student body. Hillel, the center for Jewish life, hosts events geared at all students regardless of faith, in part because F&M is "still predominantly WASP." The small gay population is visibly noticeable, but not very important in the social lives of straight students.

> "The first thing you notice is it's a pretty homogeneous student body. You'll probably see rich and white, for one thing."

Politically, F&M is not particularly vocal despite a fairly diverse collection of political leanings. While one sophomore suggested that there was an even split between conservatives and liberals, she added that most campus conservatives were liberal on social issues. For this reason, most students can be found in greater Lancaster volunteering. Tutoring, mentoring and volunteering with the elderly are popular options.

For most Diplomats, academics still come first. Each student comes to F&M interested in learning for learning's sake, and the drive of the typical F&M student reflects this interest. "There are a lot of competitive people here," one student conceded. "But the people who are competitive are competitive with themselves. I'd say students are definitely in it for the long haul together."
—*Andrew Bartholomew*

FYI
If you come to Franklin & Marshall, you'd better bring "the drive to take advantage of all the academic opportunities."
What's the typical weekend schedule? "Thursdays and Fridays: Parties start around 11:00. Saturdays: Quiet during the day. Parties start earlier. Sunday: Homework day."
If I could change one thing about Franklin & Marshall, it'd be "the police cracking down on us."
Three things every student should do before graduating are: "Pee on the Ben Franklin statue while drunk," "go to the Farmers' Market downtown," and "eat dinner with your professor."

Gettysburg College

Address: Gettysburg, 300 N. Washington St., Gettysburg, PA 17325
Phone: 800-431-0803
E-mail Address: admiss@gettysburg.edu
Web site URL: www.gettysburg.edu
Year Founded: 1832
Private or Public: private
Religious affiliation: Lutheran
Location: rural
Regular Application Deadline: 15-Feb
Number of Applicants: 5,310
Percent Accepted: 41%
Percent Accepted who enroll: 33%
Number Entering: 730
Number of Transfers Accepted each Year: NA
Mean SAT: 1,290
Mean ACT: NA

Middle 50% SAT range: 1,220–1,360
Middle 50% ACT range: NA
Early admission program (EA/ ED/ NA): ED
ED or EA Acceptance Rate: NA
Full time Undergraduate enrollment: 2,454
Total enrollment: 2,463
Percent Male: 48%
Percent Female: 52%
Total Percent Minority: 11%
Percent African-American: 5%
Percent Asian/Pacific Islander: 1%
Percent Hispanic: 2%
Percent Native-American: 0%
Percent Other: 1%
Percent in-state / out of state: 28%/ 72%

Percent from Public HS: 70%
Retention Rate: 92%
Graduation Rate: 78%
Percent in On-campus housing: 94%
Percent affiliated with Greek system: 40%
Percent Varsity or Club Athletes: NA
Number of official organized extracurricular organizations: 120
3 Most popular majors: Management, Psychology, Political Science
Student/Faculty ratio: 11:01
Tuition and Fees: $34,050.00
Cost for Room and Board: $8,260.00
Percent receiving Financial aid, first-year: 55%

A mention of Gettysburg College most often brings to mind the picturesque fields that served as a major battlefield during the Civil War and the location of Abraham Lincoln's famous Gettysburg Address. Come to Gettysburg though, and you will find more than just a campus steeped in history. On this site of enormous historical importance, Gettysburg students live and learn in the most thoroughly modern facilities. At this small liberal arts college, students are accomplishing more than war re-enactments and historical tours. They thrive in both the intimate academic atmosphere and the extensive social scene.

Integrated Learning

Classes at Gettysburg tend to be very small and with a student to faculty ratio of 11:1, it's no wonder classes rarely reach twenty students. Professors teach all classes and students agree that the professors are very accessible. According to one senior, "The professors here teach what they are passionate about. They really respect us and are interested in our minds." This type of enthusiasm appears to be uniformly present through the student body. Students start out freshman year with a unique Gettysburg experience,

the First Year Seminars. Freshmen pick from a variety of unique courses ranging from "The Makings of the Great American Musical" to "Got Porn? A Critical Approach to Pornography" and the "Critical Debates that Divided the Women's Movement." The learning experience does not stop at the end of the sixteen-person seminar, however. Residential Hall assignments for freshmen are directly linked to their freshmen seminar and college writing courses; that way informal discussion is facilitated outside the classroom setting. Students come to Gettysburg fairly aware of the requirements of the college, from the freshmen seminar to the course requirements mandating that students take courses in fields outside their major. Gettysburg students seem to agree that the requirements provide a broad liberal arts base without restricting their ability to explore. The part that draws the most complaints is the natural science requirement. But, as one student pointed out, "The science departments seem to understand and creates a few courses designed for seniors to meet their graduation requirements as painlessly as possible." These include courses such as "The Chesapeake Bay" and "Natural Disasters," which fill up within minutes of the beginning of senior course registration.

Gettysburg students cite the most popular majors as political science, history, psychology, and management, which is also named one of the easiest majors. Aspiring Management majors should be aware though that there is talk of the major being discontinued and its nearest replacement is economics. The Sciences are generally regarded as the hardest majors. Some of the more popular classes include "Philosophy of Food," "The Bible and Modern Moral Issues," and "Economics of Sports." Students here fall within a range of attitudes toward academics, ranging from the super motivated to the not motivated. Most students though "take academics pretty seriously and take an active stance in their education." According to one student, "The perfect description of Gettysburg College is that you work for a B, but you work your butt off for an A." In the words of another senior, "Gettysburg provides a great library and an amazing faculty. Anyone who claims he isn't get anything out of his academic endeavors isn't trying hard enough."

Immaculate Grounds

Students universally agree that Gettysburg provides world-class facilities. Musselman Library remains open twenty four hours Sunday through Thursday and provides tables for group studying, as well as quiet zones with a variety of seating and lighting options and even private rooms for studying. One student professes his love for the library's availability and says, "I don't think anyone can every truly appreciate how valuable the library hours are until your computer breaks at 2 a.m. when you have a paper due or when your roommate throws a party the night before an exam." The Breidenbaugh, where most English classes are held, is cited as a particularly beautiful building on campus. There are currently two gyms: Bream, the main gym with an indoor track and weightlifting room, and Plank, the smaller gym with a cardio and aerobics focus. There are complaints that both gyms fill up quickly because of the popularity of working out among students. But, there is work being done to provide a new gym to address this issue. There are also swimming pools and numerous sports fields on campus.

The town of Gettysburg itself is somewhat sleepy and isolated and caters mostly to tourism. Students often get involved in the town via tutoring or other forms of volunteer work. Students also benefit from some of the bars and restaurants, the local movie theatre, the outlet mall nearby and the proximity to Baltimore and Washington, DC.

Trapped On-Campus

Students regard residential life as above average. According to one student, "After visiting other schools, it seems Gettysburg has some of the nicest dorms." Housing gets better as you rise through the ranks. Freshmen life in standard doubles off a hallway, but upperclassmen dorms can be described as downright luxurious. Dorms have common rooms, often with big screen TVs. Many options are apartment style with a full kitchen, living room, and private bathroom. Seniors generally get suite style housing with all singles in The Quarry Suites. There are also theme houses owned by the college that are often closer to campus than dorms are. Many male students opt to live in their fraternity houses. Juniors and seniors are allowed to live off campus, but over ninety percent of students choose to stay on campus. On campus housing provides many parking options and there are even opportunities for coed living. There are Residential Advisors, but most understand the realities of college life and enforce rules reasonably. No alcohol is allowed in freshmen dorms, though.

Gettysburg food is often ranked in the top twenty nationally. One student goes as far as to call it "incredibly good for a college dining hall." One dining option, Servo, boasts a sauté line, grill and sandwich area, eggs made to order, and a vegan corner. In the College Union Building is a coffee shop, bookstore, and The Bullet Hole, another dining option that serves quick meals. Ike's serves made to order subs, soup and wraps and is open later than any of the other options. As satisfied as students are though, it is not uncommon to head off campus to eat on weekends at places such as Pizza House or nearby chain restaurants.

Popped Collars and Pearls

The Vineyard Vines and Vera Bradley sold in the school bookstore sums up the stereotype of the average Gettysburg student. Drawing its student population mostly from the Tri-State area and New England, students seem to feel that one thing Gettysburg does lack is diversity on campus, both racially and economically. Many are white and preppy and come from a privileged, private school background that is reflected by the BMWs, Jaguars, and Range Rovers littering the student parking lots. While students laud the administration for working to increase diversity on campus, there is still little intermixing between various groups. On the upside, one student remarks, "That is not to say there is an 'I'm better than you' attitude on campus and most students, regardless of income level, would feel comfortable at this school." Students are also universally described as friendly and approachable. The small, tightly knit campus means that people are welcoming and willing to lend a hand.

Students are also involved in a variety of extracurricular activities that draw people together. Division III sports are popular, although by junior year, many non-starters tend to drop out. Football is the most vocal and visible team because of its size, but lacrosse has also been nationally ranked for the past four years. Men and Women's soccer also been nationally ranked in the past year and were in the playoffs. Games often attract sports fans cheering their Bullets on. Intramurals, service organizations and various clubs also draw a large crowd.

To Be Greek or Not to Be

Gentlemen, you better step foot on campus ready to make friends with some girls! Greek life is the single largest affiliation on campus and accounts for over fifty percent of the campus population. Frat parties tend to dominate weekend activities, especially for underclassmen, and it is always advisable for guys to show up with a few extra girls in tow to ensure admittance. According to one student, "It's a safe bet that if you're not out at a frat sometime between Wednesday and Saturday, then you're probably not doing anything entertaining." On weekends, students frat hop with ease between houses located within feet of each other. Some popular fraternities include Phi Delt, Phi Sig, and FIJI. Sororities are also popular, but because they are not allowed to live in sorority houses together, they do not play the same role that fraternities do. Gettysburg students seem to agree that many groups of friends who may have split somewhat because of their choices to go Greek or not, often reunite as upperclassmen when both Greek and independents tend to seek out non-Greek activities.

> **"It's a safe bet that if you're not out at a frat sometime between Wednesday and Saturday, then you're probably not doing anything entertaining."**

Sports teams also play a prominent role on campus. Many students enter their freshmen year affiliated with one of Gettysburg's Division III teams and that is often reflected in the social scenes. Tuesdays are a popular night to attend "Pitchers", the weekly event at a local bar involving two-dollar pitchers of beer. Some of the other social options include campus wide activities and trips put on by the Campus Activities Board. Spring Fest is a yearly event that kicks off with a spring concert drawing students, alumni and faculty. Crab Fest is another popular event where the dining hall sets out a picnic of fresh crabs and beer set to music. Thanksgiving Dinner is eagerly anticipated during the fall semester because the dining hall organizes a family style Thanksgiving dinner for the entire student body. Snow Ball is the annual winter dance that provides free food and drink, as well as an opportunity to dress up.

Gettysburg College is a campus rich with historical buildings, significant Civil War sites and even rumors of hauntings. These traditions provide a background for the talented students who are drawn to both Gettysburg's history and its state of the art facilities and inspiring faculty. This beautiful school full of beautiful people boasts an intimate learning environment and social scene with something for everyone.—*Janet Yang*

FYI
If you come to Gettysburg you better bring "a bike in order to enjoy all the battlefields."
What's the typical weekend schedule? "Go to an outlet mall, go out for a nice meal with your friends off campus, drink at a frat party or somewhere else, and maybe watch a movie with friends."
If I could change one thing about Gettysburg, I'd "make it more diverse."
Three things every student at Gettysburg should do before graduating are "go on a GRAB (Gettysburg Recreational Activities Board) trip, swim in the fountain in the center of campus, and walk through the battlefields."

Haverford College

Address: Haverford, 370 Lancaster Avenue, Haverford, PA 19041
Phone: 610-896-1350
E-mail Address: admission@haverford.edu
Web site URL: www.haverford.edu
Year Founded: 1833
Private or Public: private
Religious affiliation: Quaker
Location: suburban
Regular Application Deadline: 15-Jan
Number of Applicants: 3,351
Percent Accepted: 19.4%
Percent Accepted who enroll: 36.1%
Number Entering: 314
Number of Transfers Accepted each Year: 3
Mean SAT: 1,400
Mean ACT: 32

Middle 50% SAT range: math: 650–740; verbal: 640–750; combined: 1,290–1,490
Middle 50% ACT range: 29–34
Early admission program (EA/ ED/ NA): ED
ED or EA Acceptance Rate: 40%
Full time Undergraduate enrollment: 1,168
Total enrollment: 1,168
Percent Male: 46.7%
Percent Female: 53.3%
Total Percent Minority: 28.7%
Percent African-American: 6.5%
Percent Asian/Pacific Islander: 12.7%
Percent Hispanic: 7.5%
Percent Native-American: 1%
Percent Other: 1%

Percent in-state / out of state: 15%/85%
Percent from Public HS: 58%
Retention Rate: 97%
Graduation Rate: 90%
Percent in On-campus housing: 98%
Percent affiliated with Greek system: 0%
Percent Varsity or Club Athletes: 40%
Number of official organized extracurricular organizations: 130
3 Most popular majors: Biology, Economics, Political Science
Student/Faculty ratio: 8:01
Tuition and Fees: $33,710.00
Cost for Room and Board: $10,390.00
Percent receiving Financial aid, first-year: 54%

Founded in 1833 by members of the Religious Society of Friends, this small liberal arts college—with a student body of only 1100—has never lost sight of its Quaker roots. A deep concern for social justice and a unique emphasis on an honor code that students say "fosters an environment of tolerance and acceptance" combine with rigorous academics, unusual traditions and a tight-knit community to give the quirky, driven students at Haverford College a truly one-of-a-kind educational experience.

On My Honor

Probably the most important single factor that shapes the Haverford experience, and one repeatedly cited by students as "what differentiates Haverford from other schools," is the Honor Code, a philosophy of integrity that is affirmed by the student body each year. The Honor Code governs all aspects of students' conduct, from academics to residential life, and all those interviewed stressed its important role in making the school "a very warm and welcoming place with an undeniable sense of community." Because it is maintained and enforced by the students (four members of each class are elected every year to serve on the Honor Council), Haverfordians have "tremendous self-governance" over the conduct of the student body: "We all have a common understanding of how we all want to be treated, and for the most part, we follow through with it." The power of the Honor Code at Haverford may seem unusual to an outsider, but students say over and over how the Honor Code affects every facet of their lives: "The Honor Code is a huge part of the school. Sure, it may create the HaverBubble, but most of the time when it comes down to it, trust, concern, and respect really flourish here."

Tough Love (It's Academic)

Most students say they came to Haverford primarily for the rigorous academics, and it certainly lives up to its reputation; descriptions of schoolwork range from "demanding" to "very challenging" to "incredibly heavy." As one student puts it, "The workload is such that it isn't too hard to just get by, but if you want to do really well it takes a lot of hard work, much more than what you expect from a college workload." Another notes that "around midterm time, a lot of people don't sleep."

But students agree that Haverford provides an excellent academic support system; its small size and accessible faculty enable students to receive much more personal attention and guidance than they would in a large research university. Furthermore, Haverford academics are unusual in that there is almost no feeling of competition between students, resulting from a tacit don't-ask-don't-tell policy regarding grades. Said one student, "Here at Haverford we have a sort-of rule where you don't talk about grades with people, because what we really want to avoid is one of these hyper-competitive academic scenarios."

> "The Honor Code is a huge part of the school. Sure, it may create the HaverBubble, but most of the time when it comes down to it, trust, concern, and respect really flourish here."

Like many aspects of college life, Haverford's academic requirements hearken back to its Quaker heritage. In addition to a standard set of distributional requirements—three courses each in the humanities, natural sciences and social sciences, a year of a foreign language, a freshman writing seminar and a physical education requirement—all students are also required to take a course in social justice, which "ties into our Quaker roots and an awareness of community issues." Students can satisfy these requirements with a wide range of courses; though Haverford can't in itself offer the broad course possibilities of a research university, it compensates by participating in a tricollege consortium with nearby Swarthmore and Bryn Mawr colleges, enabling Haverfordians to take courses at the other two institutions and receive credit through their own. Haverford's size also means that classes are much smaller and intimate: only 2% of classes have more than 50 students, and the average class size is 16. One senior reports that "even as a frosh, I was taking classes with 12 students in them. Now, as a senior, I regularly have 4–10 person classes."

Haverford professors garner high praise from students, both for their general knowledge and for their friendliness and accessibility to students. All classes are taught by full professors, and small class sizes enable professors to pay a great deal of individual attention to each person, both in class and out of it. According to one student, "Most of my friends have babysat, house-sat, or pet-sat for a prof at some point, and it's not unusual to see professors playing with their kids or dogs around the duck pond. Because profs live on campus, they're just as much a part of the community as we are . . . They really consider us their academic colleagues, and some of my favorite friends are professors." Some particularly outstanding professors cited by students include Ashok Gangadean in the philosophy department, Bill Hohenstein, who teaches sociology, and Bruce Partridge, the head of the astronomy department.

Overall, Haverford's small size proves to be a great advantage in providing students with an exceptional undergraduate education. Students consistently praise the small class sizes and emphasis on individual student-teacher relations, which provides a support system that helps students bear the workload with aplomb. Says a student, "Haverford is a highly rigorous but incredibly nurturing academic environment. It's impossible to get lost in the shuffle here, even if you try. If you come to Haverford, you will succeed."

A Sense of Community

In a school of Haverford's size and location—a well-to-do, wooded suburban area in the "middle of nowhere" half an hour outside Philadelphia—it is no surprise that the vast majority of students (estimated at between 95 and 99 percent) live on campus for all four years, either in a residence hall or in college-owned apartments. Housing is assigned through a lottery system with preference given by seniority, but students say that "freshman dorms are often nicer than upperclassman dorms; they're more centrally-located and are very cohesive." Some upperclassman residences have themes or personalities; the major themed dorm, dubbed "Drinker House" and home to a large number of athletes, lives up to its name by throwing regular parties.

And speaking of parties, Haverford does in fact throw them—though a student adds that "95 percent of the partying is done by 40 percent of the campus." Haverford's alcohol policy is fairly relaxed, and students say the college doesn't really stop people from partying in their rooms if they so desire. With no fraternities or sororities, Haverford's parties mostly go on in dorms or apartments, especially the so-called "party houses" like Drinker; if partying is your thing, it's only a matter of knowing where to look. One student calls Haverford the "kind of place where you can either do nothing or be doing everything depending on how much effort you put into your social life. . . . There's always something going on, but the onus is on you to figure out what's happening." Thus, students say that some people end up spending four years holed up in their rooms, while others throw themselves into extracurricular activities or parties. Socialization at Haverford, like many things in the college, is purely a matter of effort.

If you're more inclined to head off campus looking for fun, there are plenty of options in that realm as well. The local area features restaurants like Fellini's, Bertucci's and Kahurajo as well as a bar called Roaches, and though there is none of the bustling city life and the opportunities that are available at urban schools, Haverford does enjoy the advantage of being completely safe by day and night. Students also like to visit nearby colleges like Bryn Mawr—incidentally, dining at Bryn Mawr is an option for students on the Haverford meal plan—head into Philly for a night on the town, or shop at the King of Prussia Mall.

In terms of diversity, ethnic and otherwise, Haverford is rather limited by its size: "It is getting much more diverse ethnically in recent years. But it is still perceived to be a school dominated by rich white kids . . . but this perception is slowly changing." Socially speaking, Bryn Mawr students are fond of saying that the stereotypical Haverfordian is "short, hairy, Jewish, and named Dan," and while that characterization is far from universally true, 'Fordians do cheerfully acknowledge that "the typical Haverford student is nerdier than average [and] fairly awkward." Nevertheless, Haverfordians also tend to be friendly, tolerant and accepting, "pretty humble and down to earth. Students are chill and take life as it comes." And most agree that "making friends at Haverford is VERY easy," in large part because of the community spirit and cameraderie the small-college atmosphere fosters. "Once you meet people you know you're going to see them again at some point . . . you never go from one place to another without seeing someone you know."

School Spirit?
Perhaps not surprisingly, "rah-rah" school spirit and athletic pride aren't really Haverford's cup of tea. While around 40 percent of the student body plays varsity sports, with standouts being cross-country and track, students admit that athletics "aren't terribly large here in terms of school pride" and that "most people don't know when a game's going on." For those who are interested in sports, however, Haverford boasts a newly opened gym facility with state-of-the-art equipment.

Haverford also provides plenty of opportunities for extracurriculars, though on a rather small scale. While there are a number of organizations on campus—service groups and projects are particularly popular—they tend to attract a relatively small number of people, and students often pursue extracurricular involvement on an independent, individual basis. As with partying, students report, Haverford extracurriculars are what you make of them; some people focus exclusively on academics, while some throw themselves into outside activities. The campus also provides plenty of job opportunities for interested students, with a minimum wage of $8.50 for most positions.

On the whole, the main point students stress about life at Haverford is the unique freedom and the opportunities that they enjoy. Education, socializing and—thanks to the Honor Code—even policy enforcement are in the hands of the students, creating a sense of autonomy and responsibility unmatched at most other colleges. And nerdiness aside, Haverfordians really do know how to have fun. As one student admitted, "The only thing that surprised me about Haverford was how much fun everyone was. I expected there to be a lot of nerdy kids, and there are, but they know how to have a good conversation and a great time. I love meeting new people, and the quality and enthusiasm of those people makes the school feel much bigger than it might otherwise."—*Amy Koenig*

FYI
If you come to Haverford, you'd better bring "a dorky sense of humor, a North Face or EMS fleece, and lots of DVDs."
What is the typical weekend schedule? "Friday: have pastabilities in the DC, go to an a cappella or improv show, and make the rounds of the parties. Wake up late Saturday, hang out on campus or at King of Prussia Mall, have dinner out, and go to some parties. Sunday? Brunch at the DC, and then study all day!"
If I could change one thing about Haverford, I'd "have students relax a little more."
Three things every student at Haverford should do before graduating are "swim in the duck pond, go tunneling and sleepover in Magill (library)."

Lafayette College

Address: Lafayette, 118
Markle Hall, Easton, PA
18042
Phone: 610-330-5100
E-mail Address:
admissions@lafayette.edu
Web site URL:
www.lafayette.edu/
admissions
Year Founded: 1826
Private or Public: private
Religious affiliation:
Presbyterian
Location: urban
**Regular Application
Deadline:** 1-Jan
Number of Applicants: NA
Percent Accepted: 37%
**Percent Accepted who
enroll:** 28%
Number Entering: NA
**Number of Transfers
Accepted each Year:** NA

Mean SAT: 1,285
Mean ACT: 28
Middle 50% SAT range:
580–670v, 600–700M
Middle 50% ACT range:
25–30
**Early admission program
(EA/ ED/ NA):** ED
ED or EA Acceptance Rate:
NA
**Full time Undergraduate
enrollment:** 2,310
Total enrollment: NA
Percent Male: 52%
Percent Female: 48%
Total Percent Minority: 11%
Percent African-American:
5%
**Percent Asian/Pacific
Islander:** 2%
Percent Hispanic: 4%
Percent Native-American: 0%
Percent Other: 6%

**Percent in-state / out of
state:** 30%/70%
Percent from Public HS: 68%
Retention Rate: 93%
Graduation Rate: 87
**Percent in On-campus
housing:** 96%
**Percent affiliated with
Greek system:** 71%
**Percent Varsity or Club
Athletes:** NA
**Number of official
organized extracurricular
organizations:** 250
3 Most popular majors: NA
Student/Faculty ratio:
11:01
Tuition and Fees:
$31,501.00
Cost for Room and Board:
$9,864.00
**Percent receiving Financial
aid, first-year:** 37%

S ummer vacation draws near, and final
exams are within days, what do you
do? Go to All College Day! All College
Day is one of the biggest events held at
Lafayette College every spring on the weekend before exams start. With the quad and
tailgating areas packed with students, everyone joins in the festive atmosphere. All the
fraternities hold parties, while there are
bands and obstacle courses set up along the
quad, lending to a carnival-like scene. As
the school year ends, students go all out on
this last weekend before getting back to the
grind and preparing for exams. Strong
school pride and a liberal arts mindset define Lafayette, a small university tucked away
in scenic Easton, Pennsylvania. As students
become highly involved in campus activities, they generate a fervor that resonates
throughout campus.

Academic Exposure

Lafayette is a liberal arts school with a
strict core curriculum. From the start,
Lafayette immerses its students in rigorous
courses. As freshmen, students are required
to take a First-Year Seminar, a writing-intensive course that can cover a wide variety of subjects such as "Election Rhetoric"
and "The Human Animal." Continuing the

emphasis on writing, Lafayette asks for
completion of the College Writing course
that can be taken as a freshman or sophomore. In addition, the college offers Values
and Science/Technology seminars. These
seminars focus on writing and research
about issues in science. Besides these required courses, students also have to fulfill
a 32-credit requirement for graduation. The
core curriculum distributes these credits
among the humanities/social sciences, natural sciences, mathematics, and a writing
requirement that can be satisfied by the
First-Year Seminar, College Writing course,
and Values and Science/Technology seminar. One student maintained that the core
"is great because no matter what you study,
you get exposed to a little bit of everything."

While many of the freshman introductory
courses have about 100 students, all other
classes are capped at 35, and the seminars
are capped at 15. Students talk about
how there is competition to get into the
higher-level courses as a freshman or sophomore. For those who are strictly humanities
or science majors, there are courses that
will fulfill distributional requirements for areas outside one's major. For example, "A
Chemical Perspective" or "Baby Chem" is

made strictly for non-science majors looking to fulfill their natural science requisite. Of the workload, one student stated, "your professors will work you to the bone during the week, usually with small assignments, but for the most part, weekends are free with little to no work." With a strong balance between the sciences and humanities, Lafayette offers a limited range of majors that can be further expanded by tracks within each major. For example, a government and law major may direct his study along a political theory track. Engineering, government and law, and economics rank among the more popular majors, while art and physics are some of the unpopular ones. Mathematics and engineering are considered the more difficult majors.

The teacher-student relationship is an intimate one. Lafayette focuses on developing a close setting between faculty and students. At the end of each term, students fill out evaluations that the administration pays close attention to. In the small classes, students are able to interact with professors on a more personal level, and professors often run into their students on Lafayette's small campus. A student noted that "the teachers are always willing to sit down with you and will help you even if it isn't office hours." Despite the friendly atmosphere in the classroom, students find that it can be hard to get A's. Another complaint is that some classes only meet at 8 in the morning with no other possible times.

Bringing Students Back to Campus

Before freshman year, incoming students receive rooming cards that list out the different dormitories and allow them to pick out where they want to live. Lafayette then assigns students their list of preferred housing depending on when the cards are sent in and their tuition deposit made. Freshmen are divided among all the dormitories. The freshman rooms tend to be of good size, with South College having the nicest rooms. Most of dorms have been recently renovated while four new ones have just been built.

Sophomores, juniors and seniors are entered into a housing lottery in which seniors get first pick, and girls choose before guys do. Because of this system, sophomores get the short end of the deal as they are the last to pick and thus get the worst rooms as certain rooms are reserved solely for freshmen. In picking rooms, students can form a living group composed of people with the same interests. These living groups then live on the same floor of a building. These include cultural floors such as the French Floor and El Mundo, and there are also floors for special interests groups like the Volunteer Floor for those with strong interests in community service. Most of these groups are found in Keefe Hall, while Farber Hall and Ramer Hall also carry some. There is also the McKelvy House, a 19th-century stone mansion that holds 20 students of high academic distinction called McKelvy Scholars and residence is invitation-only. A common complaint regards the strictness of the RAs in the dorms. One student said, "Some have power trips," while another stated that dorm life becomes constricting because "you always have an RA breathing down your neck."

The choice location of living for upperclassmen is in off-campus apartments and houses or frat houses. However, Lafayette is changing its policy regarding off-campus housing in order to bring more students back to campus. Whereas juniors and seniors would be able to live wherever they wanted, the administration has now stated that students will no longer live in privately owned housing and will have to live in college-owned off-campus housing. These residences are reserved for juniors and seniors, and upperclassmen must first go through an application process and if they are accepted, they are put into a lottery for housing.

Lafayette features a relatively safe campus. The campus police patrol the grounds at night. However, the surrounding College Hill community can be dangerous at night, so caution is necessary. According to students, there is some tension between the community and college students as parties are generally held off campus, often leading to noise complaints.

There are two all-you-can-eat dining facilities and one a la carte food court with different restaurants. Farinon Student Restaurant features entrees ranging from Mediterranean cuisine to Tex-Mexican food, while Marquis Student Restaurant has a wood-burning pizza oven and cook-your-own stations. The late night café, Gilbert's, offers Seattle's Best coffee and grilled foods for students from early morning to wee hours of night. Students say that the food is very satisfactory, and the food court is preferred over others. Freshmen are required to have the full 20-meal-per-week plan, which also comes with 100 Flex dollars that can be used at local restaurants.

Afterwards, students can get different meal plans and Flex dollar plans.

Party Busters

If you had come to Lafayette during the 1970s, you'd have seen a campus rife with Greek life. Nowadays, there are only six frats and six sororities. The University has slowly been banning frats from campus. However, Greek life still holds some sway on the social scene. Starting freshman year, students are allowed to rush frats and are allowed to join them only after the beginning of sophomore year. The frats often hold parties for students throughout the weekend.

The administration focuses on public safety on campus. A series of probations are handed out to those caught with drugs and drug paraphernalia, and in some cases, students may be referred to the police. With a strict alcohol and drug policies, RAs are constantly on the lookout for underage drinking, and violations can result in probation and fines. Campus police, some of whom were former police officers, enforce the school's policies, while the liquor patrol searches for and looks to break up raucous parties. In response to the strict rules, one student stated, "In my opinion the school needs to lighten up a little bit. After all, most Lafayette students are hard workers and should be rewarded with the right to party just as hard as they work."

> "In my opinion the school needs to lighten up a little bit. After all, most Lafayette students are hard workers and should be rewarded with the right to party just as hard as they work."

Despite the policing of alcohol, students still have fun on the weekends. Starting on Wednesday, students head out to frats and parties held off campus and party on through Saturday. While underclassmen will head to off-campus parties, upperclassmen prefer to head to bars, which feature big college nights on Thursday. Sports teams often have their own parties as well as male athletes are not allowed to pledge frats, while females can join sororities. One student said about the social scene, "Everyone seems to be on the same cycle sometimes. On a good weekend it can seem like everyone is out, and the parties are amazing. Then everyone will be sick or doing work at the same time." Beginning the 2006–2007 year, students are unsure of how the partying scene will be. Most expect a sharp drop in partying at first as off-campus housing becomes limited because of new rules, but say it should come back to a normal level after adjusting to it.

For those not interested in the frat parties and off-campus parties, there are many fine Italian restaurants and stores within walking distance. Campus Pizza turns into a nightclub on the weekends, while another popular hang-out is a bar called Milo's Place.

Athletic, Not Athletic, Other?

Even though Lafayette is a small school, it is also a Division I sports school, meaning that of its small population, a large percentage are athletes. As a result, a common perception of the college is that it is very jock-oriented. While football and basketball play their games on campus, other sports have to travel off-campus in order to reach their sports facilities. As a result, the only games that most students attend are the football and basketball games. The biggest game of the year is the Lafayette-Lehigh football game; it is one of oldest college football rivalries with over 140 years of history.

While the athletes have their own gym, the new $35 million Allan P. Kirby Sports Center is available for non-athletes to use. The center features pools, an indoor track, billiards tables, ping pong and racquetball, just to name a few. In addition, intramural sports are huge at Lafayette. There is a competitive and a non-competitive league. Many students become highly committed to intramurals and play sports ranging from flag football to kickball to squash. Club sports also play a role in the active Lafayette student's life, with Frisbee, ice hockey and crew teams being especially popular.

For those whose palates are not satisfied by athletic activities, there are many other interesting clubs to participate in. The Lafayette investment club and academic clubs are among the most prominent. Many other groups are involved with community service. Students are very involved in their extracurricular activities and usually find one that they dedicate the bulk of their time to. For the working student, popular jobs include working at the library, fitness center or career services, or being a referee for the intramural leagues.

Getting Comfy With Each Other

Most people would typify Lafayette students as preppy, rich white kids. While there are not many minorities, Lafayette is making a significant effort to recruit people of other ethnicities. Despite the small percentage of minorities, many cultural groups are present such as the Association of Black Collegians and International Students Association. However, the lack of diversity is still very obvious. One student noted, "The international students only hang out with international students. . . . There's social segregation, but not on purpose."

Because of Lafayette's small size, students have no difficulty meeting new people and making close friends. Either through joining Greek life, hanging with the party crowd, or spending time with people in class, every student meets familiar faces each day on campus, and "you get close to people and hang out with them non-stop." The intimacy of Lafayette reveals no distinctions between upperclassmen and underclassmen, as everyone collectively forms a vibrant and energetic atmosphere. For many, there are no regrets about choosing a small school over a large state school, and students say that seeing the same people every day brings everyone together to form a secure network of friends that a larger school could not offer.—*Thomas Hsieh*

FYI

If you come to Lafayette, you'd better bring "a lot of backup food. You'll get sick of the food fast."

What's the typical weekend schedule? "Wake up on Saturday around noon, have lunch, do work if needed/relax and hang out, dinner, most partying generally starts at 10 or 11. Bars close at 2. Late night parties might open up then. Sunday—wake up, brunch at Farinon Dining Hall, again work if needed until it's done, or watch TV."

If I could change one thing about Lafayette, I'd "have public safety release their hold on the Greek system social scene."

Three things every student at Lafayette should do before graduating are "go to Porter's and get your own personal mug, eat the chili at Milo's Place, and buy a T-shirt that would be offensive to any student at Lehigh."

Lehigh University

Address: Lehigh, 27 Memorial Drive West, Bethlehem PA 18015
Phone: 610-758-3100
E-mail Address: inado@lehigh.edu
Web site URL: www.lehigh.edu
Year Founded: 1865
Private or Public: private
Religious affiliation: none
Location: small city
Regular Application Deadline: 1-Jan
Number of Applicants: 10,685
Percent Accepted: 60.8%
Percent Accepted who enroll: 29%
Number Entering: 1,215
Number of Transfers Accepted each Year: 300
Mean SAT: NA
Mean ACT: NA
Middle 50% SAT range: 1,290–1,410

Middle 50% ACT range: 28–31
Early admission program (EA/ ED/ NA): ED
ED or EA Acceptance Rate: NA
Full time Undergraduate enrollment: 4,679
Total enrollment: 6,500
Percent Male: 58%
Percent Female: 42%
Total Percent Minority: 21.2%
Percent African-American: 4%
Percent Asian/Pacific Islander: 7%
Percent Hispanic: 6.8%
Percent Native-American: <1%
Percent Other: 3.4%
Percent in-state / out of state: 78%/22%
Percent from Public HS: 65%

Retention Rate: 95%
Graduation Rate: 83%
Percent in On-campus housing: 80%
Percent affiliated with Greek system: 39%
Percent Varsity or Club Athletes: 15%
Number of official organized extracurricular organizations: 140
3 Most popular majors: Psychology, Marketing, Mechanical Engineering
Student/Faculty ratio: 9.5:1
Tuition and Fees: $33,470.00
Cost for Room and Board: $8,920.00
Percent receiving Financial aid, first-year: 50%

In the little town of Bethlehem, Pennsylvania, a bright and shining star lights the way for students as they climb the central campus hillside in search of a place where they can stop to rest for the evening. The star is a large statue built on the peak of this "Christmas city," and the site of repose is a collection of Greek houses at the top of the hill. Known for its unique balance between a challenging academic curriculum and a hardcore party scene, Lehigh University offers what one student called "a dynamic learning environment customized to individual interest" and a close-knit community where students are determined to learn as much as they can while still finding plenty of time to kick back and enjoy themselves.

What Kind of Engineer Are You?

The University is composed of four different colleges: the College of Arts and Sciences, the College of Business and Economics, the College of Engineering and Applied Science, and the College of Education (which is more focused on graduate work). While Lehigh is home to students with a wide variety of academic interests, the school is particularly renowned for its engineering and its business programs. About 35 percent of the student body majors in one of the 15 types of engineering, while another 30 percent chooses to study finance, accounting, or other aspects of economics. According to one student, "When people ask you what your major is, they generally just skip right to, 'What kind of engineer are you?'" It is common for students to take on a second major or a minor, and several people commented on the interesting propensity of engineers to minor in music. One psychology major confirmed the high majority of business and engineering students, but was also quick to point out that the College of Arts and Sciences actually has the highest enrollment. Almost half the student body is in arts and sciences, but because a good portion of those are only pursuing a minor in the arts, only about 20 percent have a true liberal arts major. Said another student, "They're trying to tweak admissions to get more academic diversity, but right now it's heavily geared toward business and hard sciences." The newly introduced Global Citizenship program lets students give their majors an international perspective.

Most students say that they have never had trouble registering for or getting into a course, except for some of the base classes, the extremely popular classes, and the easy classes (there aren't many of them), such as Intro Psych or Religion 101. Lehigh prides itself on its small class sizes; apart from a few large freshman lectures, most classes have between 15 and 20 students, with language classes being even smaller. Although the University is known for its academic rigor, most students say that competition among classmates is an extremely uncommon occurrence. "People are friendly here," said one sophomore. "Classes are small enough that you can really get to know people. We study in groups a lot, especially for projects in the business school that require us to work in teams." Said another student, "You really have to be able to work as a team and help each other out." In addition to great interaction between the students, everyone also has the opportunity to take advantage of an extremely dedicated, knowledgeable faculty. "We have great student-professor relations," comment one freshman. "No matter what time I walk into a professor's office, they've never not had time to talk to me." Added another student, "I like the professor enthusiasm. You can really tell that they love what they're doing, which makes something dull more bearable. I love that they're crazy about what they're teaching."

Students call the workload "decent, as long as you go to class and keep up with the work—otherwise you have to learn everything on your own!" Grading is strict and curving is rare, so "it's very difficult to get an A." Professors do expect a lot, but students are willing to work hard in order to learn the material and get the grade.

Bottoms-Up!

The competition at Lehigh, according to one student, seems to have more to do with the social scene than it does with the classroom. "It's a competition to see who can do the best while also drinking the most," she declared. Social life is dominated by the fraternities and sororities, with about 40 percent of the student body deciding to pledge at one of the 32 Greek houses. "If you're not in a fraternity or a sorority, you're usually on an athletic team," said one varsity runner. "Or you're just weird." Another student, when asked about Greek life, laughed and said, "It's a big part of Lehigh! It's a big deal and if that's your scene, then definitely take advantage of it; but if you don't join, you can easily find your own friends, your own group, and plenty of things to do on campus." Most parties take place

Thursday through Saturday on top of the hill where all the houses are, although there are a few special occasions during the year when students party all week (usually for the annual Lehigh-Lafayette football game in the fall and Greek Week in the spring). Seniors often go with friends to bars in the surrounding area.

Drinking policies are not strongly enforced. According to one student, "The administration doesn't do much because they know we balance partying with academics. As long as we care about school as well, they're willing to let some things slide." Another noted, "The people who are most highly respected are those who are at the top of their classes but who also drink; students take pride in being able to keep studies up but also party all the time." Lehigh was recently ranked the number three party school in the nation, and according to one upperclassman, "A lot of people feel the need to maintain that reputation."

> "You could hit copy and paste and 4,500 kids later you'd have Lehigh!"

Although parties are definitely enjoyable, they are not usually the best places to meet people. Most students say that they met their friends through classes or clubs, or because they lived near each other. "Classes are small and people are friendly, so it's easy to make friends," said one freshman. One major complaint about the Lehigh population is that it lacks ethnic and cultural diversity; even geographic diversity is low—even though there are a fair number of international students— since most students hail from the East Coast. "We're a pretty homogeneous place," said one student. "You could hit copy and paste and 4,500 kids later you'd have Lehigh!" Several students described themselves and their classmates as "preppy," with many in the upper-middle class and several with "Ugg boots, messy ponytails, and popped collars." Still, even though the minority population is small, everyone is inclusive and "people mix well together."

Life on the Hill

Freshmen and sophomores are required to live in dormitories on campus, while most upperclassmen move to Greek, athletic, or other residential houses in the surrounding area. Freshman dorms are randomly assigned, and several of the nicer ones are described as "palaces." There is no real separation between the campus and the town, so many "off-campus" houses are actually closer to university buildings than the dormitories are. Although underclassmen dorms are randomly assigned, they still have slight personality distinctions; usually, the quieter dorms are at the bottom of the hill and the rowdier dorms are at the top. In general, students enjoy living on campus in the "big, beautiful buildings," and many stay on campus as upperclassmen even though doing so is not a requirement. "I like the fact that campus is a small community where you see a lot of same people every day," said one freshman. Several people described campus architecture as "gothic, ivy-covered, with that classic college look." Another student added, "It IS built on a hill, though—that's the one drawback!" An additional disadvantage, according to some, is the drabness of the surrounding town. "I won't call it a dump," said one student, "but it isn't great." The huge difference between the economic status of the campus and the town does lead to a "bad relationship" between the students and the surrounding community, which is unfortunate but hopefully improvable through outreach programs and extracurricular community service.

When it comes to extracurricular activities, most students participate in community service programs through their Greek house or athletic team. Almost all student organizations, such as the newspaper or drama productions, are completely student-run. There are several musical organizations on campus, including the Philharmonic Orchestra, the marching band, the jazz band, and a variety of smaller ensembles. Varsity sports enjoy a popular following on campus, especially the football and basketball teams. According to one student, "Football games are the place to be on the weekends and people also go crazy at basketball games, but wrestling is the most revered sport on campus. Some of the wrestlers have gone to the Olympics!" Intramurals also constitute a big part of the sporting scene on campus. "Soccer and rugby especially are pretty big and pretty competitive, but everyone can play and lots of people really get into it," said one student.

When asked what differentiates their school from others, students again remarked on the apparently equal value conferred upon both drinking and academics. "It's a little unique in its magnitude," noted one student. "People go nuts for both! You study like a maniac, and then you drink like a maniac." Most people agree that the beautiful campus, the stimulating classes, and the friendly community all make them glad they chose Lehigh. Said one sophomore, "Fresh-man year is definitely an adjustment, as it would be anywhere. Definitely as you move up, you find more and more things you enjoy. It's a great place to spend four years!"—*Lindsay Starck*

FYI

If you come to Lehigh, you'd better bring "hiking boots, because you have to climb up that huge hill every day!"

What's the typical weekend schedule? "Thursday, drink; Friday, drink; Saturday, drink; Sunday, study."

If I could change one thing about Lehigh, I'd "do something about the homogenous student population."

Three things every student at Lehigh should do before graduating are: "Watch a football game on the grassy knoll, hike up to see the Bethlehem star, eat at Johnny's Bagels."

Muhlenberg College

Address: Muhlenberg, 2400 Chew Street, Allentown, PA 18104-5586

Phone: 484-664-3200

E-mail Address: admission@muhlenberg.edu

Web site URL: www.muhlenberg.edu/admissions/

Year Founded: 1848

Private or Public: private

Religious affiliation: Lutheran

Location: suburban

Regular Application Deadline: 16-Feb

Number of Applicants: 4,040

Percent Accepted: 44%

Percent Accepted who enroll: 32%

Number Entering: 559

Number of Transfers Accepted each Year: NA

Mean SAT: 1,220

Mean ACT: NA

Middle 50% SAT range: 1,120–1,320

Middle 50% ACT range: 26–29

Early admission program (EA/ ED/ NA): ED

ED or EA Acceptance Rate: NA

Full time Undergraduate enrollment: 2,443

Total enrollment: 2,443

Percent Male: 40%

Percent Female: 60%

Total Percent Minority: 10%

Percent African-American: 2%

Percent Asian/Pacific Islander: 4%

Percent Hispanic: 2%

Percent Native-American: 0%

Percent Other: NA

Percent in-state / out of state: 24%/76%

Percent from Public HS: 73%

Retention Rate: 93%

Graduation Rate: 86%

Percent in On-campus housing: 91%

Percent affiliated with Greek system: 13%/18%

Percent Varsity or Club Athletes: NA

Number of official organized extracurricular organizations: 1

3 Most popular majors: Business administration/ Management, Drama and Theatre arts, Psychology

Student/Faculty ratio: 12:01

Tuition and Fees: $30,490

Cost for Room and Board: $225.00

Percent receiving Financial aid, first-year: 45%

In the glow of unique candlelight ceremonies, students at Muhlenberg College celebrate both their entrance to and their exit from this close-knit college in Allentown, Pa. The college career that passes between these two ceremonies is no less unique, and students attest that the education and attention they receive during their years at Muhlenberg are second to none. Such an atmosphere is conducive to incredible growth and opportunity, and led one senior to say, "I can't imagine myself anywhere else."

A Supportive Academic Infrastructure

As one business and economics double major stated, "Muhlenberg's a strong academic school overall." With a variety of popular and well-respected programs, Muhlenberg's academics are solid across the board. According to one junior, "I have yet to encounter a department which I would consider sub-par, although there are some which could do with expansion."

Some of the strongest and most difficult programs of study at Muhlenberg include the pre-med track (which is "very highly regarded" and "more rigorous and time-consuming than anything else on campus") and the theater program, which "is growing in popularity with many critics." In addition to these disciplines, psychology, business and biology are also popular majors. Although some fields, like communications, are considered easier than others, students agree that the professor dictates each class's level of difficulty, and "some teachers are just easier than others."

If Muhlenberg students don't find the particular course they're seeking, they have easy access to courses at other Lehigh Valley Schools. This option is both helpful and convenient for students, especially since one can "shoot down I-22 to Lehigh in 20 minutes." Overall, however, students can find exactly what they want at Muhlenberg; some of the more unusual offerings in the past have included "Religions of Star Trek," a theater/English class on "Buffy the Vampire Slayer," and "that weird improv dancing class where the students are wrapped up in sheets and they dance all around the room."

The class sizes at Muhlenberg are quite small, with average enrollments between 12 and 24 (although entry-level science lectures can enroll around 100 students, which helps to weed out the uncommitted). Although most students seem to get into the classes they want, the registration process—which is alphabetically and seniority-based—can be frustrating for underclassmen. In the end, however, the benefits of having intimate class sizes outweigh any complaints about the process, as "there's a lot of one on one."

Muhlenberg students need 34 credits to graduate, and core requirements dictate that 12 of these credits signify completion of: a freshman seminar, two sciences, Literature, Religion, Philosophy, two semesters of a language, Reasoning, History, Culture and a behavioral science. One senior commented, "Overall, I am grateful for the . . . diverse group of general requirements." Another student mentioned that the requirements are manageable, "as long as you buckle down by the beginning of sophomore year." A junior, however, noted that she "could go without a few core requirements, like Philosophy."

What Muhlenberg students never have to go without is personalized attention from professors. Indeed, students recognize the incredible "teacher accessibility and credibility" as a treasured aspect of Muhlenberg's academic life. As one student said,

"The professors are our mentors, our challengers; our friends, they truly are a significant part of our community." From walking their dogs around campus to eating in the dining halls, Muhlenberg professors stay in close touch with their students. Within each department, students form close working relationships with their professors, who "provide a great amount of structure." One student remarked on the incredible brilliance of his economics and political science professors, recalling that "my teachers [went] to Princeton, MIT, and Wharton." Another student praised the personalized learning environment and its extensions into daily life, saying, "I even house-sit for my major advisor."

The Muhlenberg faculty further extends its influence in promoting study abroad, an opportunity that many students take advantage of in their junior year. In general, students at Muhlenberg are encouraged to expand their horizons, both academically and personally. As one senior commented, "I have had many experiences in courses that involved and encouraged learning outside of the classroom through service learning activities in the community, to hands-on experience in the field to attending theatrical performances."

On Being A Mule

At Muhlenberg, according to one student, "everybody has their own social scene." At the same time, students cite a few main groups that define the social life: the Greeks, the a cappella/theater/dance people, and the jocks. Frat life at Muhlenberg "used to be huge" before the school kicked two houses off campus in 2004–2005, but it still is pretty big. Now, with four recognized fraternities and the same number of sororities, some say the social life still "revolves around the Greeks." This seems especially true for underclassmen, who are not allowed cars on campus and find the many house parties convenient. As one freshman said of the social scene, "it's kind of hard as a freshman if you don't know upperclassmen."

While underage drinking is technically not allowed in the dorms, it is reportedly easy to get served, and the college administration's policies focus "more on safety and awareness/education than harsh punishment." Students are quick to say, however, that "there are still a good deal of non-drinking students at Muhlenberg who have no trouble mingling with drinking friends at any event." Hard drugs do not seem rampant at Muhlenberg, although one junior noted that there is "quite a lot of marijuana use and more coke going around than I would have expected."

Allentown, on whose hill Muhlenberg is located, is a small town with a bowling alley, movie theater and malls frequented by students. The "19th street experience," a street with privately owned shops and restaurants, is one of the nicer drags in town. Town-gown relations do not seem ideal, however; as one senior commented, "Allentown's got a very rough area downtown," and townies sometimes comment on the disparity between their town and "the rich kids on the hill."

Students nevertheless have some favorite haunts near campus, including the restaurants WaWa and Wegman's, Parma Pizza, Pistachio, and many popular chains. On the bar front, students frequent The Muhlenberg Cavern (affectionately known as "Woody's"); Stooges, which features Wing Night every Wednesday and has "great waitresses"; and Lupo's, which is the most lenient on underclassmen, but is also a little further away from campus. On average, students say they don't get into Allentown that much, "unless there are sponsored events," such as Senior Pub Nights, where Muhlenberg provides buses for senior bar-hopping. With their cars, however, upperclassmen can easily leave Allentown for Philly or NYC, both of which are just an hour and a half away.

> "Some would say that Muhlenberg students are sheltered and affluent, very Abercrombie or J.Crew-esque."

But most students stick around, especially during special events on campus. Annual Muhlenberg celebrations include Homecoming and "Midnight Breakfast," where members of the faculty, administration and staff serve a free breakfast to students on the midnight before spring finals. The Greeks also host annual galas, including the Gods & Goddesses Toga Party, Pole Dancing and Jello Wrestling. In addition, the campus hosts several bands each year, with such recent guests as 311, O.A.R. and Gavin De Graw.

As far as student stereotypes go, Muhlenberg seems to have several. One junior commented, "Some would say that Muhlenberg students are sheltered and affluent, very Abercrombie or J.Crew-esque." Most stu-

dents do come from upper middle-class and white backgrounds in the Northeast, with a large percentage hailing from private high schools in New Jersey, Pennsylvania and New York. One freshman noted, "I've never seen so many Uggs in my life." However, another student pointed out other types of diversity that exist at Muhlenberg when she said, "I feel as if diversity may be found in religious and political affiliations." With a large Jewish population, as well as Catholics and Protestants, this Lutheran-founded college is home to students of many faiths, as well as many political leanings, including an "outspoken conservative population."

Above all other descriptions, however, students describe each other as "very friendly and well-spoken . . . no one will ever turn their back on you." As one minority student said, "I think people at Muhlenberg tend to be independent free-thinkers, friendly, motivated and caring individuals."

Living on the Hill

Muhlenberg's campus is described as "very green and well-groomed," and is "really beautiful . . . everything is really close together." Noting the "warm, small-town feel," one student mentioned that the "buildings all have red doors to embody the Lutheran tradition of 'Welcome' which truly translates to the feel of the campus." Nowhere is this better felt than on Academic Row, the main stretch of buildings that includes the Haas bell tower, the modern Moyer building and the Student Union, which, along with the neighboring science building, has recently been renovated. The sprawling lawn in front of the Student Union is a favorite spot when the weather is nice, when students can be seen "enjoying lunch together under the sun."

Freshmen have five single-sex on-campus housing options: three for women and two for men. Both Walz and Prosser halls are coed, although Walz is smaller, air-conditioned and houses all early decision freshmen. The "social dorm" Prosser, with its three floors and four annexes, is next to the "quiet dorm" Brown, which is all-female and houses women of all years. Close by are the six upperclassmen dorms, the newest of which are South and Robertson.

In addition to these nine dorms, students can opt to live in nearby MILES (Muhlenberg Independent Living Experience) houses, which are owned by the college and have various community service and special interest themes. Not many students live off campus, as it is difficult to receive approval—but those who do rent houses or apartments within walking distance of the campus.

When it comes to dining, there are two main options at Muhlenberg, and both are housed in the Student Union building. General's Quarters (known as "GQ") is good for an a la carte meal, while The Garden Room is cafeteria sit-down style. The food is cited by most students as being "really repetitive" but "good." "Dining dollars" from meal plans can also be used at the coffee stand in the Student Union ("Java Joe's") or the small café in the newly renovated Life Sports Center ("The Powerhouse Café"), providing students with a little more variety.

"Go, Mules!"

While there is incredible variety in the extracurricular activities that Muhlenberg students pursue, athletics are certainly a staple. Especially evident from the new gym, which is "full of everything anyone could need," it is clear that "the school really places a great emphasis on athletics." As members of the Centennial Conference—which includes such rivals as Gettysburg, Dickinson, Haverford and Bryn Mawr—students have some exciting games to watch, and show a lot of school spirit. Popular spectator sports include women's basketball, men's soccer, track and field, football and women's rugby.

In addition to varsity and intramural athletics, students at Muhlenberg show a great interest in dance teams, a cappella (of which there are six groups) and theater production. There are also plenty of opportunities for work-study, and many students take advantage of positions in the Student Union, Library or theater box office. *The Weekly*, Muhlenberg's newspaper, and WMUH radio also pull lots of participants, as does the MAC (Muhlenberg Activity Council). While most everyone is committed to at least one or two organizations, one freshman noticed that "people usually manage their time well—I've never seen anyone stressed out."

With a lively and free-minded student population and an incredibly dedicated faculty, Muhlenberg College offers its students a beautiful haven to thrive during the four years between ceremonial candlelight. With such emphases on the undergraduate experience, it is no surprise that an enthusiastic senior raved, "Muhlenberg is an exceptional place where red doors never fade, bells always ring, and a friendly smile is never hard to find!"—*Elizabeth Dohrmann*

FYI
If you come to Muhlenberg, you'd better bring "a pair of Uggs."
What's the typical weekend schedule? "If you're a senior, go to Wing Night at Stooges on Wednesday; house parties Thursday night, followed by Lupo's; lay low on Friday night; go out Saturday."
If I could change one thing about Muhlenberg, I'd "take it out of Allentown and move it to a city."
Three things every student must do before graduating from Muhlenberg are, "study abroad, get wings at Stooges, and have dinner in the bell tower."

Penn State University

Address: Penn State, 201 Shields Building, Box 3000, University Park, PA 16804-300

Phone: 814-865-5471

E-mail Address: admissions@psu.edu

Web site URL: www.psu.edu/dept/admissions/

Year Founded: 1855

Private or Public: public

Religious affiliation: none

Location: urban

Regular Application Deadline: rolling

Number of Applicants: NA

Percent Accepted: 58%

Percent Accepted who enroll: NA

Number Entering: NA

Number of Transfers Accepted each Year: 667

Mean SAT: NA

Mean ACT: NA

Middle 50% SAT range: 1,080–1,280

Middle 50% ACT range: NA

Early admission program (EA/ ED/ NA): NA

ED or EA Acceptance Rate: NA

Full time Undergraduate enrollment: 36,613

Total enrollment: 42,793

Percent Male: 55%

Percent Female: 45%

Total Percent Minority: 13%

Percent African-American: 4%

Percent Asian/Pacific Islander: 6%

Percent Hispanic: 3%

Percent Native-American: less than 1%

Percent Other: NA

Percent in-state / out of state: 72%/28%

Percent from Public HS: NA

Retention Rate: 93%

Graduation Rate: NA

Percent in On-campus housing: 38%

Percent affiliated with Greek system: 23%

Percent Varsity or Club Athletes: NA

Number of official organized extracurricular organizations: 600

3 Most popular majors: NA

Student/Faculty ratio: 17:01

Tuition and Fees: $22,194.00

In State Tuition and Fees (if different): $11,646.00

Cost for Room and Board: $6,850.00

Percent receiving Financial aid, first-year: 49%

Even though students tend to refer to Penn State as one entity, it is actually a composite of 24 campuses that are scattered all over Pennsylvania. Nevertheless, the term "Penn State" has now come to be synonymous with the University Park campus, a vibrant academic, cultural and social center for students from all over Pennsylvania and the rest of the United States.

Options, Options, Options

Penn State was founded in 1855 when the state of Pennsylvania, responding to a request by the Pennsylvania State Agricultural Society, chartered a school that focused on farming and technology—a far cry from the Greek and Latin-based curriculum that was emphasized in most other colleges at the time. Throughout Penn State's long history, it has consistently been at the forefront of most higher education trends, such as the focus on engineering, research and even the Internet.

Penn State has general education requirements in social science and quantitative studies, and such requirements generally make up a third of a student's course load. While that may seem like a lot, one junior noted that, "Most students don't mind the bulk of them, and generally they are not that hard." "My experience was that I filled most of them up without even realizing it," another student added, perhaps thanks to Penn State's incredibly varied and diverse course catalog. One international politics major enthused, "The physical fitness requirement can be fulfilled with skiing, hip-hop dance, etc. There's even a major called Professional Golf Management." Nevertheless, she did bemoan the lab component of the required science sequence.

Penn State students agree that academics are "as difficult as you make them out to be." Even so, many recommend that prospective Penn State students should not be afraid to take more demanding classes, since those usually end up being the courses that have the most impact. For the academically ambitious, there is the Schreyer's Honors College, in which students complete a senior-year thesis. Individual departments may also have honors programs. A student enrolled in the Honors Program in economics said he took "one class dedicated to writing your senior thesis, and one honors seminar in which you get to read all these things that you would never read in any other class. If I didn't do this, I'd probably be pulling my hair out in

April." Said one student about the Honors Programs, "Personally, I was too lazy to apply, but through the years I have found that taking honors courses when able truly helps to avoid the B.S. work that normal classes might have. Plus you learn a lot more."

When it comes to freshman year classes, prospective students should expect to see lecture halls of 300 to 400 students and a wide range of quality. One student highly recommended the Psychology 100 course for its professor's nutty antics. Other students stress the importance of choosing classes based on the professor, not on the course itself, since one professor rarely teaches the same introductory course in consecutive years.

Priority for course registration goes to Honors students and student athletes, and then to the students with the most credits. Nevertheless, there are freshman-only sections and seminars, which one junior called "hit-or-miss." "For me, it was the hardest class of my freshman year," she explained. "For my roommate, she learned how to use the library card catalogue and that was about it."

When students come out of introductory classes, enrollment shrinks dramatically from 300 to about 25 or 30 students. Current Penn State students say that the grading might be a little bit skewed in the first year due to the different TAs, but it all evens out at the end. "Overall, grading is fair—not too harsh or lenient."

What's a Nittany, Anyways?

"When they founded Penn State, they decided to put it in the geographic center of Pennsylvania," one student said. "That means that everybody in Pennsylvania has equal access to Penn State . . . unfortunately, it also means that some would consider us in the middle of nowhere."

Despite Penn State's location, students do not lack for things to do. "Weekends are what you make of them here at PSU. You can stay in and do homework, see a movie, go out to eat, catch a concert, play pool on or off campus, or go to the bars or a friend's party. Anyone who claims that there is not enough to do in state college is, in my opinion, a toe-sucking liar."

Football is *huge* at Penn State. At this Big Ten School, the entire student population routinely turns out to support their beloved Nittany Lions. One junior echoed her classmates' sentiments when she said: "If you're on campus during game time on Saturdays, you're most likely the only person there. Not being a huge football fan myself, I was worried about this crazed reputation when I went in, but I found a lot of people use it as a chance to take a break from studying and socialize, making it more of a party than a football game."

As for weekend nights, a good majority of the student population parties—and parties hard. "After all, aren't we like, the number two party school in America?" one student mused. Students usually begin their weekends on Thursday and finish on Saturday. Frat parties are popular with freshmen, but upperclassmen gravitate towards the active bar scene downtown or house and apartment parties. Freshmen should be warned, however, that dorm parties rarely occur and are frequently shut down by the residential advisors. "With so much to do, it's really stupid to throw a dorm party. It's ridiculously easy to get caught," said one junior.

There are plenty of students who do not drink, and they say that they do not feel particularly ostracized for it. The HUB offers Late Night Penn State from every Thursday to Saturday, and people can catch comedians, musical performers, movies, arts and crafts, game shows, and so forth. However, that does not mean that the average Penn State student can avoid the presence of alcohol for all four years of college. "If you want a social life, you either have to drink or be around people who are drinking," said one non-drinker. "But the thing is, you'll never be pressured into doing it."

Besides football and parties, there is a notable Penn State event called THON. This is a student-run 48-hour dance-a-thon, and the proceeds go to benefit pediatric cancer. "It is the largest student-run philanthropy in the nation, and last year raised $4.21 million for the kids." It is an experience that you cannot miss. Students promise that feelings of community, camaraderie, and love are never stronger than during the 48 hours of THON every February.

State College and University Park

On the topic of on-campus living, opinions vary. On one hand, students agree that their mandatory first-year of on-campus living provided them with a lot of friends and companionship. However, the common problems with living on campus, such as dirty bathrooms, mismatched roommates and loud neighbors, still apply. "Though there is a lot of camaraderie between dorm-dwellers, the experience was often times discouraging and disgusting," one student said.

The result is that many students who remain on campus after freshman year prefer to move to the suite-style dormitory. East-view, South Halls, and West Halls tend to be the most desired dorms. Most freshmen (with the exception of Schreyer's Honors students, who live in South) are placed in the East Halls. One economics major said, "My second and third years were better than my first because I lived in a suite. In fact, that's probably why I stayed in the dorm. Suites are like apartments . . . it's not like sharing a room with somebody that you don't like all that much and then having to also share a bathroom."

> **"Well, I hate to resort to clichés, but Penn State is everything and more."**

Off campus, apartments and houses are pretty easy to find, especially if distance and convenience is not the most important factor. One graduate student said, "The buses that go off campus are pretty fast and reliable, and there are two enormous 24-hours grocery stores and a Wal-Mart that are easily accessible by these buses."

Penn State is racially representative of the state of Pennsylvania, but less diverse than it's peer universities. Students attest to the fact that because there are such large numbers of undergraduates on campus, "the numbers of minorities *look* big, but the percentage is actually pretty pitiful." There have been some racial incidents on campus the last few years, and students agree that what Penn State needs is more minority students.

Penn State's relationship with the town of State College can best be described as symbiotic—almost everyone who works in the town has some affiliation to Penn State. "If you go to an off-campus party and someone's from the town but not working for PSU, you look at him really strangely," one student said. There is almost no distinction between the town and campus: "If you live in South Halls, you just cross the street and you are 'downtown.' State College the town is filled with cheap restaurants and small shops, and you can get everything you need without ever setting foot inside a car or a bus."

That being said, the people of the town usually go out of their way to accommodate the needs of Penn State. When asked to describe town-gown relations, one student said, "Well, the first thing I noticed about State College is that for the kids, Halloween doesn't occur on October 31st! They go trick-or-treating two days before the actual date of Halloween. The reason for this is because the students tend to go a little crazy on Halloween, so it's not exactly safe for the kids to go door-to-door."—*Janet Xu*

FYI

If you come to Penn State, you'd better bring "a good winter jacket—waterproof, windproof, and breathable!"

What is the typical weekend schedule? "The weekend starts with Thirsty Thursday. Most seniors don't have classes on Friday, but most of the underclassmen do. Friday night everybody goes out, then Saturday is just complete oblivion. Sunday is . . . 'Oh crap, I actually have to get work done.' "

If I could change one thing about Penn State, I'd "get rid of all the red tape about taking classes— I think it's ridiculous that I can only take one finance class if I wanted, and that would be ntroduction to Finance."

Three things every student should do before graduating from Penn State are "Go to a football game; eat at the Creamery, because it's the best ice cream you will ever find; and go to Canyon Pizza at 2 a.m. at least one Friday or Saturday night to enjoy the enormously long line of drunk people waiting for their dollar slice."

Susquehanna University

Address: Susquehanna, 514 University Ave., Selinsgrove, PA 17870
Phone: 800-326-9672
E-mail Address: suadmiss@susqu.edu
Web site URL: www.susqu.edu/admissions/
Year Founded: 1858
Private or Public: private
Religious affiliation: Lutheran
Location: suburban
Regular Application Deadline: rolling
Number of Applicants: NA
Percent Accepted: 79%
Percent Accepted who enroll: 30%
Number Entering: NA
Number of Transfers Accepted each Year: NA
Mean SAT: NA
Mean ACT: NA
Middle 50% SAT range: V:530–610, M:520–620

Middle 50% ACT range: NA
Early admission program (EA/ ED/ NA): ED
ED or EA Acceptance Rate: NA
Full time Undergraduate enrollment: NA
Total enrollment: 1,928
Percent Male: 46%
Percent Female: 54%
Total Percent Minority: NA
Percent African-American: 3%
Percent Asian/Pacific Islander: 2%
Percent Hispanic: 2%
Percent Native-American: 0%
Percent Other: NA
Percent in-state / out of state: 59%/41%
Percent from Public HS: 85%
Retention Rate: 86%
Graduation Rate: 83%

Percent in On-campus housing: 78%
Percent affiliated with Greek system: 33%
Percent Varsity or Club Athletes: NA
Number of official organized extracurricular organizations: 121
3 Most popular majors: Business Administration/ Management, Communications Studies/Speech Communication and Rhetoric
Student/Faculty ratio: 14:01
Tuition and Fees: $27,620.00
Cost for Room and Board: $7,600.00
Percent receiving Financial aid, first-year: 66%

Georgian buildings and hundreds of trees create an ostensibly quiet and arcane setting for Susquehanna University in rural Pennsylvania. However, the 220-acre campus is anything but dormant. Students buzz with enthusiasm for Susquehanna's commitment to its close-knit community in which students partake of extensive academic and extracurricular opportunities.

Learning, Life Sciences, and Latkes

Academics at Susquehanna are all about options. Students can opt for one of six pre-professional programs or even design their own major with the help of a faculty member. Students attend one of three schools on-campus, the School of Arts, Humanities and Communications; the School of Natural and Social Sciences; and the Sigmund Weis School of Business. Students enjoy the fact that the exclusively undergraduate population can enroll in classes within any of the schools. One art history major gushed that "History and Culture of Jewish Cuisine" was her favorite class, while both

an early education major and a biology major chose to enroll in an honors philosophy course called "Thought and Civilization." Despite such tantalizing course options, Susquehanna does have a core of interdisciplinary requirements. Students say these core curriculum requirements are "easy to fulfill" and "comprehensive," but non-science majors dislike the requirement of one science class and one math or logic course.

Pass the Class (and the Gravy)

The core comprises approximately one-third of a student's courses and includes one class each in literature, fine arts, history, science or technology, writing, the social sciences, mathematics or logic, and philosophy or religion. Despite being mandatory, students report that all these classes fully engage students. With an average class size of approximately 18 and a student-faculty ratio of 14 to 1, Susquehanna cultivates the close relationships between professors and students for which small liberal arts schools are known. Many students call their professors by their first names and are even regularly invited to dinner at their professors' homes. At the Thanksgiving dinner offered in the dining hall, faculty members become waiters and serve turkey and stuffing to students, who typically rate the meal as their favorite campus event of the year.

Northeastern Exposure

The SU student body hails mostly from the Northeast, notably from Pennsylvania, New Jersey, and New York. Attempts to increase diversity have been only somewhat successful—only 8 percent of students are international or minority—but the University strongly encourages applicants of all economic, religious, and ethnic backgrounds. Indeed, Susquehanna offers need-based aid to over half of its students, has organizations affiliated with different races and religions, and boasts merit-based scholarships and an honors program to attract particularly talented applicants. A task force created by the Diversity Studies program is focusing on increasing diversity both in the curriculum and in the student body, in part through the creation of a Diversity Studies minor approved several years ago. Nonetheless, one African-American junior stated that he wishes "there were more diversity on-campus."

> "There's something for everyone, and if there isn't something for you, you can always start your own club or ask a professor for advice."

Despite the relatively homogenous population, Susquehanna students have interests ranging across the board. With over 100 organizations and activities and numerous opportunities for internships and jobs in the surrounding Susquehanna Valley, it would seem that students might find so many options daunting. In fact, the opposite is true. As one sophomore explained, "There's something for everyone, and if there isn't something for you, you can always start your own club or ask a professor for advice." Over half of students participate in some form of community service, including the Habitat for Humanity program, the University's Study Buddy program in which students tutor kids at local schools, and the Ronald McDonald House for hospitalized children.

Dining at "Deg"

Students often hang out at the Degenstein Campus Center that they dub "Deg," which includes the campus bookstore, the Evert Dining Room, the Encore Café, Charlie's Coffee House, a 450-seat auditorium, and the headquarters for both the student newspaper and radio station. Although students call Evert "crowded" with "numerous options that are nevertheless usually the same day-to-day," they also say that they "run into friends all the time" there and elsewhere on-campus. As on other college campuses, chicken wings, pizza, and a salad bar are staples in the dining experience.

The close-knit community can be attributed to the fact that 80 percent of students live on campus. It pays to be a veteran at SU when it comes to housing. Freshmen often find themselves in small triples, but upperclassmen have the coveted option of living in suites and townhouses in the Sassafras Complex, created in 1995 and substantially renovated in 2001, or in Hassinger Hall, an air-conditioned dormitory that some students refer to as "Hotel Hassinger." Upperclassmen may also apply to live together in one of the volunteer project houses where students volunteering for the same cause reside. Students conducting independent research can opt to live in the Scholars' House, which includes study areas, a seminar room, a resident assistant's quarters, and a visitor's apartment that allows students to informally interact with special university guests. A few students live in the sorority or fraternity houses near campus.

Where's the Party At?

A fifth of students are involved in Greek life, an aspect of SU that "divides the partiers and everyone else on the weekends," said a self-proclaimed "theater guy." The two biggest party events of the year are Greek Week, which consists of mostly fraternity— and sorority-sponsored events, and Spring Weekend, a four-day outdoor festival that is run by SAC (Student Activities Committee) and features music, games, and "general craziness." Students report that although mostly Greeks attend Greek Week, the majority of the campus turns out for Spring Weekend fun. Each year, SAC also sponsors one big annual concert; in recent years the campus has welcomed musical groups The Roots and Collective Soul.

One activity that virtually all SU students participate in is athletics. Home to 23 Varsity Division III sports teams and 14 intramural sports, "it seems like everyone does one sport or another," said a sophomore intramural volleyball player. The athletic student body can now enjoy two new sports facilities, the James W. Garrett Sports Complex and Lopardo Stadium, completed in 2001 and 2000, respectively. Garrett includes an impressive field house with an indoor track and courts for basketball, volleyball, and tennis, as well as a fitness center, a swimming pool, racquetball courts, and a student lounge and café.

Into the Future

The forward-looking administration at Susquehanna prides itself on offering its students resources usually found at schools twice its size. Its efforts have paid off in recent years, with the school extensively renovating its facilities and creating ambitious new academic programs like the Writers Institute, the Diversity Studies program, and the Arlin M. Adams Center for Law and Soci-

ety. Founded in 2001, the Law and Society Center holds an annual lecture series that sponsors renowned visitors, such as Nadine Strossen, the president of the American Civil Liberties Union, and Anthony Lewis, former *New York Times* columnist and two-time Pulitzer-Prize—winning author. The Center for Career Services provides another resource on campus that proves helpful to current and past students alike. A mandatory career planning course prepares second-year students for life after college, and the results so far have been impressive. The program is quite successful, as 96 percent of graduates enter a job or continue their education within six months of graduation.

With the administration's commitment to providing the benefits of a large university to its students, Susquehanna is a perfect environment for college applicants who also want the comfort of a small community. Recent improvements in facilities and programs and attempts to improve diversity make Susquehanna a school to keep an eye on. —*Abigail Reider*

FYI
If you come to Susquehanna, you'd better bring "lots of sweaters."
What's the typical weekend schedule? "Sleeping, eating, going to parties, and studying on Sunday."
If I could change one thing about Susquehanna, it would be "the cold or the lack of diversity."
Three things that every student should do before graduating are "take a trip to the Poconos to go skiing, attend a fireside chat with someone famous, and get a professor you don't like to wait on you during Thanksgiving dinner."

S w a r t h m o r e   C o l l e g e

Address: Swarthmore, 500 College Avenue, Swarthmore, PA 19081
Phone: 610-328-8300
E-mail Address: admissions@swarthmore.edu
Web site URL: www.swarthmore.edu/admissions
Year Founded: 1864
Private or Public: private
Religious affiliation: none
Location: suburban
Regular Application Deadline: 3-Jan
Number of Applicants: 4,852
Percent Accepted: 19%
Percent Accepted who enroll: 40%
Number Entering: 370
Number of Transfers Accepted each Year: 30
Mean SAT: 1,400

Mean ACT: 30.6
Middle 50% SAT range: V:660–770, M:660–760
Middle 50% ACT range: 28–34
Early admission program (EA/ ED/ NA): ED
ED or EA Acceptance Rate: 37%
Full time Undergraduate enrollment: 1,477
Total enrollment: 1,484
Percent Male: 48%
Percent Female: 52%
Total Percent Minority: 49%
Percent African-American: 8.7%
Percent Asian/Pacific Islander: 15.8%
Percent Hispanic: 10.4%
Percent Native-American: 0.8%
Percent Other: 13.6%

Percent in-state / out of state: 17%/83%
Percent from Public HS: 66%
Retention Rate: 96%
Graduation Rate: 92%
Percent in On-campus housing: 95%
Percent affiliated with Greek system: 70%
Percent Varsity or Club Athletes: NA
Number of official organized extracurricular organizations: 110
3 Most popular majors: Economics, Political Science, Government
Student/Faculty ratio: 8:01
Tuition and Fees: $33,232.00
Cost for Room and Board: $10,300.00
Percent receiving Financial aid, first-year: NA

Hundreds of acres of rolling lawns, hiking trails, and of course, a vibrant student body, make up Swarthmore's intimate college campus. Founded by the Quakers in 1864, Swarthmore is an "intellectual's haven," where grades are not dwelled upon and diversity is the norm. This liberal arts college, which is now non-sectarian and has always been coeducational, has a student body of just over 1500. The Swarthmore experience is centered on close friendships and a commitment to learning.

A senior said, "There's a wonderful, supportive community among students here." Swatties have a wide range of backgrounds and beliefs and come from all over the world. One student noted that her peers are praised for individuality, that it is cool to be different. Despite its small size, Swat "celebrates the life of the mind," with a strong global outlook and an education that prepares students to become "leaders for the common good."

Straight As Don't Mean Diddly

The intimate classroom environment at Swarthmore draws many students to the school. The eight-to-one student-faculty ratio allows professors to become more personally invested in their students' work. Many Swatties refer to their professors on a first-name basis, and one freshman said, "Professors have students over for meals in their homes and are incredibly interested to see students succeed." There are no teaching assistants at Swarthmore, meaning that professors—98% of whom have PhDs or other terminal degrees—or guest lecturers lead every class and discussion. Seminars are capped at twelve students in order to facilitate participation and dialogue between students and faculty members.

Swarthmore has majors and programs one would not expect of a liberal arts college, like an engineering program and programs in Peace and Conflict Studies, Film and Media Studies, Interpretation Theory, Cognitive Science, and Francophone Studies. About one-third of student majors fall within the social sciences, while majors in the physical sciences are the least popular. There are internship and research opportunities in a wide variety of fields, and student-faculty collaboration is common. If a student is having trouble finding a major that perfectly suits his or her interests, then designing a major is a great option that the faculty can help make possible.

A tutoring program and a writing center serve as helpful resources for students seeking extra help in academics. Additional student services include the Health and Counseling Services, Career Services Office, Intercultural Center, Black Cultural Center, and an on-campus bookstore. A state-of-the-art science center, solar energy laboratory, observatory, and a performing arts center are further examples of Swarthmore's facilities, which rival those of much larger universities.

The college has many connections overseas and the faculty encourages students to study abroad at some point during their Swarthmore experience. Swatties have completed over 100 different programs in countries around the world. The school also has a unique honors program modeled after the tutorial system at Oxford. This intensive program, centered on very small classes and dialogue, concludes with an examination conducted by outside scholars after two years of study.

> "Because everyone is smart, people can't just be intelligent—what counts here is being passionate about something."

For Swatties, learning does not end when class is dismissed. One student said, "Students carry their enthusiasm outside of class with them. Because everyone is smart, people can't just be intelligent—what counts here is being passionate about something." A senior added that a classroom conversation tends to spill over into lunchtime and sometimes keeps people talking until four o'clock in the morning.

While the students are academically driven, competition is not a factor. "No one knows anyone else's grades, or cares, even though everyone cares about doing well themselves," said one student. A freshman added, "This is the first time I've been around people smarter than me . . . and no way have I felt intimidated by people."

The mandatory pass/fail system in the fall semester of freshman year is a "life saver" that makes the transition from high school to college life easier on young Swatties. This program allows students to get involved in campus life without worrying too much about grades, since a student only

needs to get a passing grade. An academic advising program serves as an additional resource to students, although one senior warned, "The academic advising program is hit-or-miss for freshmen and sophomores . . . be pro-active about changing professors if you want to."

Both students and faculty at Swat take academics very seriously and the workload is intense. A freshman explained, "Some people complain about the fact that we don't have the same name recognition as some of the Ivies but we still have to do a ton of work."

Most Swatties have to come to terms with a GPA below 4.0. One senior explained, "No one does as well here as they did in high school—but it becomes very liberating once you realize you're learning more than you ever have before." Students spend much of their time doing school work, and students can be found studying all over the campus. Popular study spots for long hours of reading and writing papers of course include: Parrish Beach, an outdoor area with one-hundred year old oak trees; various coffee bars; the McCabe or Cornell libraries; or of course, dorm rooms.

Drunken Nights in an Arboretum

So what do Swatties do when an intense week of school work finally wraps up? One student described the weekend party scene as Pub Nites with all-you-can-drink beer every Thursday, and "sketchy, alcohol-soaked dance parties on Friday and Saturday nights." Students complain that the party scene gets monotonous and that costumes and fun themes are rare. Often, students have to find their own fun.

Alcohol is easy to come by, and underage drinking policies are rarely enforced. A Swarthmore senior claimed that the general rule of thumb is "Act like an adult and no one will bother you." A resident assistant at Swarthmore insisted that she and the other RAs are not meant to act as the "alcohol police," as long as students don't put themselves in danger.

Two fraternities form Swarthmore's Greek life, with only six percent of male students involved. A senior noted, "They're there for people who are interested, but social life certainly doesn't revolve around them." For those who prefer not to partake in the fraternity scene, there are plenty of party options.

Campus-wide social events are a fun option. There is the Pterodactyl Hunt, which a sophomore described as, "a campus-wide role playing game . . . a bunch of Swatties running around in a field dressed in capes and garbage bags and hitting each other with foam swords." One sophomore called the Sager Symposium the "wildest party of the year." It involves "a week of queer-themed speakers, workshops, and performances, culminating in the Sager Party (guys wear a dress, girls wear less)."

Some Swatties find that the campus starts to feel too isolated. One student explained, "It's a bubble . . . I think that's one of the biggest downsides of this school." But for a change of scenery, Swatties can easily hop on a train and end up in Philadelphia fifteen minutes later. A sophomore noted, "Most people like to get away at least once a

month, but hardly anyone orients their life around it."

Lifestyles of the Smart & Hippy
So where do Swatties fuel up for their long days of studying, arts, and activism? The main dining hall is Sharples, which one student called "edible, but barely. People go there for the atmosphere." Other dining options include Essie Mae's (an on-campus grill), or a handful of coffee bars and sandwich shops.

Swarthmore attracts individuals seeking an intimate, rustic campus community and a rigorous academic program. This undergraduate experience educates and prepares students for leadership and for life.—*Catherine Cheney*

FYI
If you come to Swarthmore, you better bring "dirty hippy clothes you never had the nerve to wear, comfy shoes so you can walk in the woods, and Tupperware to sneak food back from the dining halls since they close so early."
What's the typical weekend schedule? "Swatties party Thursday, Friday, and Saturday, but on Sunday you don't see anyone—they're back to the books."
If I could change one think about Swarthmore, I'd "want there to be more shops in the 'Ville', and I'd want them to be open later."
Three things every student at Swarthmore should do before graduating are, "Skinny dip in the creek, experience the Sager party, and date a fellow Swattie."

Temple University

Address: Temple, 1801 North Broad, Philadelphia, PA 19122-6096, NA
Phone: 215-204-7200
E-mail Address: tuadm@temple.edu
Web site URL: www.temple.edu
Year Founded: 1888
Private or Public: public
Religious affiliation: none
Location: urban
Regular Application Deadline: 39,173
Number of Applicants: NA
Percent Accepted: 60%
Percent Accepted who enroll: 35%
Number Entering: NA
Number of Transfers Accepted each Year: NA
Mean SAT: 1,053
Mean ACT: 22

Middle 50% SAT range: V:490–590, M:500–600
Middle 50% ACT range: 20–25
Early admission program (EA/ ED/ NA): NA
ED or EA Acceptance Rate: NA
Full time Undergraduate enrollment: NA
Total enrollment: 24,070
Percent Male: 45%
Percent Female: 55%
Total Percent Minority: 0%
Percent African-American: 18%
Percent Asian/Pacific Islander: 9%
Percent Hispanic: 3%
Percent Native-American: 0%
Percent Other: NA
Graduation Rate: 58

Percent in-state / out of state: 78%/22%
Percent from Public HS: NA
Retention Rate: 87%
Percent in On-campus housing: 20%
Percent affiliated with Greek system: 2%
Percent Varsity or Club Athletes: NA
Number of official organized extracurricular organizations: 182
Most popular majors: Elementary Education and Teaching, Psychology
Student/Faculty ratio: 17:01
Tuition and Fees: $17,724
In State Tuition and Fees (if different): $9,680

With a diverse student body, a dynamic city, and a multitude of liberal arts and pre-professional programs, Temple University in Philadelphia offers its undergraduates an incredible four-year experience. In fact, Temple Owls report that "an education from Temple is far more than class time and books—it's about culture . . . independence, and growth."

Build Your Core

Temple's required "Core Program," which is meant to help students acquire skills in areas ranging from math and science to arts and culture, demands a lot of class time. One frazzled freshman became overwhelmed as he listed some requirements, "an individual and society course, a race course, a science, a math, language requirements, international studies, etc." But students for the most part appreciate the rigorous liberal arts workout of the Core. As one student said, "It's good to have to take a class outside your major. I learned things I never would have otherwise." Besides, none of the core requirements are anywhere near as difficult as Temple's upper-level science courses. "We are infamous for our difficult science classes," one science major lamented. "It's a hard life. Being a bio major, it becomes your life if you even want to stand a chance." But Owls love a challenge because bio is one of the most popular majors, along with psychology, public health, education, and business. Music, tourism, and hospitality are not quite as popular. After the demands of the "Core Program," Owls can choose from over 120 undergraduate majors. Average class size is 26 and students reported that, "most professors are easily accessible." In terms of grading, one student said that, "some professors are more liked than others," but that "the grading is usually fair." Students can also study abroad at Temple's international campuses, which include Tokyo, Rome, and London, or partake in an honors program that offers smaller classes to its students and is taught by the most prestigious professors. Overall, students agreed that, "No one's going to hold your hand here, but the professors are accessible and the facilities are everything you could ask for."

Living on the Edge

Housing options at Temple include coed dorms, special housing for disabled students, and Living/Learning Centers Apartments for single students. "We are only provided housing the first two years, unless you are an athlete or an RA," one student explained. The luck of the draw is the only thing that separates the "nice, new suite dorms that have air conditioning, kitchenettes," and "the older community living dorms that are tiny." Owls don't complain though. One even swore by the tiny dorms, saying that "they are so much fun. They offer more of the dorm experience than the newer ones." RAs are usually cool, but students admit that some can be "pretty strict."

> "No one's going to hold your hand here, but the professors are accessible and the facilities are everything you could ask for."

Despite the dorm fun, most students live in apartments next to campus. When asked about quality of life in the apartments, one student said that, "They are nice, but also offer that college experience because you are surrounded by Temple students." Some popular apartment complexes include University Village, the Edge and YONO apartments.

As Scene on Campus

While there "are a good amount of commuters," students at Temple say that most undergrads don't own cars. "We are right smack in the middle of Philadelphia, there isn't much room for parking and public transportation, and shuttles are easily accessible." Together, Temple and Philadelphia offer a virtual playground of activity. On campus, there are tons of sports facilities, including the IBC, or the Independence Blue Cross Student Recreation Center, which is a 59,000 square feet building full of fitness equipment frequently populated by athletes. Other popular hangouts include the campus bell tower and The Wall, which is, "a collection of small food areas." Regarding the city, one female student put it, "Philadelphia offers fabulous history, art, dining and shopping, what's not to love?" Owls are happy with their campus design, as one student explained, "The SAC (Student Activities Center) is beautiful and new, as well as many of our older buildings like Mitten Hall and Conwell which maintain the classic beauty."

The University's jewel is definitely the new Teaching, Education, Collaboration, and Help Center, referred to as the "TECH

Center." Offering over 600 computer workstations, 80 loaner laptops, and wireless throughout the 75,000-square-foot structure, it's no wonder students "spend all Sunday at the Tech center doing work." Of course the 24-hour Starbucks, lounge furniture and cable channels only add to the atmosphere.

All that studying requires brain food, and Owls have their pick from the SAC, the dining halls in Johnson and Hedwick, and various other restaurants and fast food places on campus. A typical student food plan combines meal dollars for dining halls and "diamond dollars" for restaurants. One dining hall is buffet style and the other is restaurant/deli style and students generally reported that, "both are good." One expert eater added, "The food trucks rock, and be careful of the beef from the Taco Bell in SAC."

Greek Life

Even though only 1 percent of the male and female populations are Greek, sororities and fraternities rule Temple's nightlife. One student said that, "Greek life is huge, especially minority Greeks such as the African America and Latina fraternities and sororities." The university offers 24 recognized Greek organizations, but students wouldn't mind some more. As one student explained, "it's annoying 'cause there's always a line to get into the frat parties." If the frats are too crowded, Owls hit up the city scene with its laundry list of bars, such as "the Draught Horse, Maxi's, Pyramids, and *of course* Old City Clubs and Lounges." Although Temple University recently prohibited alcohol on campus, students aren't worried. "That only applies to the dorms on campus now...there are so many students in apartments and their parties aren't technically on campus." Alcohol is a mainstay of the party scene, but generally, "people don't call others losers if they don't drink, and drugs have never been an issue."

"Diversity University"

Temple University Owls are definitely a diverse and active group. Indeed, the Princeton Review ranked Temple University as the nation's second most diverse campus. One student explained, "I'm learning languages because it seems like I'm the only one speaking English!" Owls describe their campus as a friendly melting pot. "People are very nice, it's easy to meet people anywhere and everywhere. We are a big campus and there are crowds of people everywhere you look during the semester."

Temple University offers an incredible amount of extracurricular activities. One student bemoaned that, "The list is never ending! We have so many student organizations and clubs!" Sports are big on campus and Owls are dedicated fans. "Even though our football team has had a losing streak, their fans are so loyal." Basketball, soccer, fencing, and softball also draw crowds. For those who like to be in on the action, intramurals are "competitive and popular."

Temple is known for its vibrant student body, thriving city backdrop, and state of the art academic facilities. Most importantly, its students are happy where they are. As one asserted, "I have learned so much here, most importantly, to keep an open mind and to work to make the most of opportunities."
—*Eliza Crawford*

FYI
If you come to Temple, you'd better bring "an open mind and a smile on your face or you'd miss out on the amazing experience Temple offers!"
What's a typical weekend schedule? "Party, Party, Party, and then recover by spending your Sunday at the TECH center doing work."
If I could change one thing about Temple, I'd "offer students more individual attention, the university can be very unorganized sometimes."
Three things everyone should do before graduating Temple are: "Check out the free galleries offered the first Friday of every month, go to a concert at the Liacouras Center, and take a million and one pictures because you never want to forget your years here!

University of Pennsylvania

Address: U Penn, 1 College Hall, Philadelphia, PA 19104-6376

Phone: 215-898-7507

E-mail Address: info@admissions.ugao.upenn.edu

Web site URL: www.admissionsug.upenn.edu/

Year Founded: 1740

Private or Public: private

Religious affiliation: none

Location: urban

Regular Application Deadline: 2-Jan

Number of Applicants: 20,483

Percent Accepted: 18%

Percent Accepted who enroll: 66%

Number Entering: 2,373

Number of Transfers Accepted each Year: 231

Mean SAT: 1,413

Mean ACT: 32

Middle 50% SAT range: 1,330–1,510

Middle 50% ACT range: 29–33

Early admission program (EA/ ED/ NA): EA

ED or EA Acceptance Rate: 33%

Full time Undergraduate enrollment: 9,739

Total enrollment: 16,442

Percent Male: 50%

Percent Female: 50%

Total Percent Minority: 30%

Percent African-American: 7%

Percent Asian/Pacific Islander: 17%

Percent Hispanic: 6%

Percent Native-American: 0%

Percent Other: NA

Percent in-state / out of state: 19%/81%

Percent from Public HS: 52%

Retention Rate: 98%

Graduation Rate: 94%

Percent in On-campus housing: 64%

Percent affiliated with Greek system: 56%

Percent Varsity or Club Athletes: NA

Number of official organized extracurricular organizations: 365

Most popular majors: Finance, Nursing— Registered Nurse Training

Student/Faculty ratio: NA

Tuition and Fees: $34,156.00

Cost for Room and Board: $9,804.00

Percent receiving Financial aid, first-year: 44%

Founded in 1740 by Benjamin Franklin, the University of Pennsylvania has a long tradition of excellence. Although the workload is intense, academics are only one part of the Penn experience. As one student said, "This is the party Ivy; it's no lie!" Add to the mix a tremendous array of extracurriculars where you can do "anything you can think of", sports teams that routinely contend for Ivy League championships, and the vibrant city of Philadelphia, and it becomes easy to understand why Newsweek magazine has in the past rated Penn's students as the "happiest-to-be-there" in the entire country.

Pre-professionals Unite!

Applicants to Penn apply to one of four undergraduate schools: The College of Arts and Sciences, the world-renowned Wharton School, the School of Nursing, or the School of Engineering and Applied Sciences. The presence of the three professional schools sets Penn apart from most of the other Ivies (Wharton, for example, is the only undergraduate business school in the Ivy League), and the schools seem to contribute to a pre-professional attitude on campus. One senior noted: "Obviously, Wharton, engineering and nursing are all straight-up pre-professional, and even within the College students oftentimes have professions on their mind. But at the same time, in the College there's an opportunity for liberal arts."

Most prospective students apply to the College of Arts and Sciences. In addition to the 12 to 14 classes that fulfill their major, students in the College also take 20 elective courses, some of which must fulfill a set of distributional requirements. An entirely new set of distributional requirements took effect in the fall of 2006. To give students more freedom and flexibility in planning a course of study, the number of required distributional classes has been reduced from 10 to 7. Students take one course each in seven groups, including Society, History and Tradition, Arts and Letters, Living World, Physical World, Humanities and Social Science, and Natural Science and Math. There are also skill-oriented requirements, such as writing, foreign language and quantitative reasoning. Students should have no trouble at all with the new requirements. As one student notes, the requirements "are enough to give you a taste of a lot of different things, but at the same time, they let you do what you want to do." In terms of actually getting into the classes they want to take, students at Penn have mixed results. Class pre-registration occurs before the semester begins, but nonetheless many students use the course add/drop period at the beginning of a semester as a "shopping period" to tinker with their schedules. Students seem to get into their chosen classes if they sign up early, but "if you wait until shopping period to sign up for a class, it might be harder to get in." However, most students note that even when a class is listed as full, usually, if you express a genuine interest, the professor will grant you permission to take the class. In fact, students seem to indicate that professors are on the whole "extremely accessible" and really want to interact with students. Although talking to a professor can be "pretty difficult in a large class," all professors have designated office hours, and many professors, even in large lectures, "wish that more students would come to office hours."

In addition to the College of Arts and Sciences, Penn offers undergraduate degrees from the Wharton School, the School of Nursing, and the School of Engineering and Applied Sciences. The Wharton School is arguably the most prestigious graduate business school in the country, and it is almost certainly the most prestigious business school offering degrees to undergraduates. Thirty-seven courses are required for a Wharton degree, two of which must be taken outside of Wharton. All undergrads take classes such as Management 100, Law and Legal Processes, Accounting, Finance, and Human Resources Management. Wharton students pursue a Bachelor's of Science in Economics degree, but students can pursue many concentrations ranging from accounting to statistics. However, one Whartonite notes, "It's almost a joke here. They want kids to diversify, but almost everyone does finance." In the School of Nursing, students also pursue a more specialized course of study. In addition to several courses in the College of Arts and Sciences, candidates for the Bachelor's of Science in nursing degree pursue 28 classes in medicine. Finally, in the School of Engineering and Applied Sciences, also known as SEAS, undergraduates pursue a course of study similar to that of most engineering students nationwide. The curriculum is highly structured, and even from the begin-

ning students take mostly math, science and engineering courses.

Across the board, students note that undergrads at Penn work hard, with pre-med, engineering and business tracks being particularly intense. Although one student notes that "it's pretty evident when you walk past the library on a Friday that there are a lot of people who just work all the time here," this is not the norm. Students agree that "in order to survive, you do have to put in work and you do have to put in effort, but you don't have to work 24/7." However, if you want a 4.0, you had better be in the library on Fridays, because most classes in science, math, engineering and business are graded on a curve. One student said: "The curves encourage competition because your grade depends on how high everyone else does. I don't think people are vicious about it, but they're definitely aware of the fact that it's on a curve. If they want to get that A, they've got to study very, very hard."

> "The school really does try to look up to the ideals of Benjamin Franklin. They're really into this ideal of the cosmopolitan person who is educated in all sectors, and part of that is being able to go abroad."

Many students note that Penn offers many opportunities for interdisciplinary study that cannot be found at other universities. For example, two popular College majors are PPE, which stands for Philosophy, Politics and Economics, and also BBB, or Biological Bases of Behavior, a major that deals with the neuroscience of animal and human behavior. Students applying to Penn can also apply to special programs involving interdisciplinary study in two different schools, such as the Huntsman Program in International Studies and Business. This includes study in both the College and Wharton, and Management and Technology, which includes both Wharton and engineering. In addition, students agree that study abroad is "huge." According to one student, "The school really does try to look up to the ideals of Benjamin Franklin. They're really into this ideal of the cosmopolitan person who is educated in all sectors, and part of that is being able to go abroad." Study abroad is even encouraged in the professional schools and in the interschool programs (it is, in fact, required as a part of the Huntsman Program), and special study abroad programs designed for career-oriented majors are available. One can study finance in Madrid, or nursing in Bangkok.

The "Drinking" Ivy

Penn students might study hard, but they also like to have a good time. According to most undergrads, fraternities and sororities make up a major part of the on-campus social scene. Why the frats and sororities? As one senior said, "there's definitely a large part of campus that likes to have a good time at the end of the week," and most of the time that means going to parties where there is alcohol. As one student states, "This is a big drinking school. A party's not a party till you're drinking." Although officially Penn has a detailed alcohol policy that requires registration of parties over a certain size and forbids hard liquor and kegs in frat houses, students report that enforcement of the policy is very lax. Drinking is reportedly monitored more closely in underclassman dorms. While the freshman social scene revolves around the frat parties, upperclassmen indicate that "the older you get, the more you realize that frats aren't the only option." Many upperclassmen live off campus and host their own parties, and going to bars and clubbing are also popular. There may be parties every weekend, but students agree that the biggest event of the year is Spring Fling, a carnival with food, music, and games held every spring. Says one student, "Everyone is wasted; there's music, it's loud, and everyone goes."

If you aren't into the party scene, don't fret; you will still have a vibrant social life at Penn. The school newspaper, The Daily Pennsylvanian, publishes a list of weekend activities specifically geared toward nondrinkers every Thursday, and students report that there are always tons of shows, concerts and dances on the weekends. Going into downtown Philadelphia is also popular. According to one undergrad, "Philly is right here, and you'd have to be out of your mind to ignore it!" Students mostly go into Philly to go shopping, to go to restaurants, and to go out to bars and clubs. In addition, many people mentioned that Restaurant Week, a week in the fall when Philly's top restaurants drop their prices and offer bar-gain set menus, is very popular among students. One girl even reported that "because Philly has such an amazing restaurant scene, there might be a little more dating here than you would normally expect." As far as the dating scene in general, students note that random hook-ups and noncommittal relationships are prevalent at Penn. Of course, one student noted that this is not very different than at many other colleges, saying, "We're kind of the hook-up generation." However, students agree that there are "definitely a lot more people in relationships as years pass."

Varsity Blues (and Reds)

Besides partying, Penn students don their red and blue to support their varsity sports teams, the Quakers. The most popular sport on campus is men's basketball, and football is also well attended. Penn and Princeton are heated rivals, and thousands of screaming fans attend the Penn/Princeton games. Students report that the Penn-Harvard football rivalry also has become intense, since these two teams have repeatedly battled for the Ivy League title in recent years. As with everything at Penn, basketball and football have even developed their own traditions. Every year, students camp out overnight in the Palestra, Penn's revered hoops arena, to buy season tickets. However, the real excitement of "the line," as it is known, is that nobody knows when tickets are going to go on sale until about an hour beforehand, and so campus goes crazy as students rush to secure places.

In the third quarter of every football game, students sing a song called "Drink a Highball" and throw toast—yes, toast—onto the field. The song contains the line "Here's a toast to dear old Penn," and when the drinking age was 18, students would all take a drink at that line. When the drinking age was raised, students began to throw toast onto the field instead. As one student reports, students even hurl "muffins and pretty much any baked product, and they try and hit the cheerleaders." So much toast is thrown that a few years ago, an engineering student devised a "toast zamboni" to clean it all up.

In addition to varsity sports, the university also hosts the Penn Relays, a major track event that is a showcase for future Olympians. A "decent" percentage of the student body is involved in club and intramural sports, but students report that "everyone and their mothers" go to the gym, which is open from 6 a.m. to 1 a.m. Monday through Thursday, with slightly more normal hours on the weekends.

What Do *You* Do on Campus?

Besides cheering on their sports teams, Penn students express their spirit by getting involved in the Penn community. When asked if extracurriculars were a big deal on campus, one senior replied, "Yes, they're a big deal, period." Students agree that there are so many different clubs and organizations that "everyone finds their niche." Popular groups on campus include a cappella singing groups, Undergraduate Assembly (the student government), debate and Model UN, and The Daily Pennsylvanian (the student newspaper). Comedy is also big at Penn, and students applaud the all-male group Mask and Wig, which has been performing musical comedy since 1889. Penn students also get involved in the local community through community service, and everyone agrees that "there are a lot of opportunities for service in West Philly," where Penn is located.

The "Penn Bubble"

In addition to volunteering in the community, many Penn students live there. In fact, only about 60 percent of all students live on campus. Many upperclassmen live off campus because it is often cheaper than on-campus housing and also because they feel that it gives them more independence. Interestingly enough, though many Penn students do community service and live off campus, students agree that on the whole "students are hesitant to walk into the immediate community." The large socioeconomic disparity between Penn and the surrounding area seems to produce an isolating effect known as the "Penn Bubble." Some students are concerned for their safety in the local community, but most people agree that safety in the area has "really improved recently." One student said: "It's just like any city. You don't want to be walking around by yourself late at night." The university has large police and security forces and also offers shuttle and escort services to ensure student safety.

For the majority of students who reside on campus, Penn offers a variety of housing options. Most freshmen live in dorms around the Quad, which is meant to resemble the Oxford-Cambridge system of living. Each dorm contains about 400 people and has a dining hall close by. Other options include three high-rise dormitories, which offer apartment-style living with in-suite bathrooms and kitchenettes, and theme houses, in which students live with others who share similar academic or cultural interests. Residential advisers (RAs), who are usually juniors or seniors, live in underclassman dorms, along with Graduate Associates (GAs), who are grad students. RAs and GAs usually "lean toward the relaxed end, but there are definite exceptions to the rule." As for eating on campus, three main dining halls and a kosher kitchen offer a variety of "very flexible" meal plans, and there is also an a la carte food court. Most students agree that the food is "decent," but as one undergrad notes, "there are always healthy options, and the dining people here are very receptive to student input."

One thing that sets Penn apart from other schools is the Button. Right in the middle of Penn's campus is a giant sculpture of a button that is broken in two. As the story goes, Ben Franklin once ate such a huge meal that his pants button popped off and broke into two pieces; supposedly the Button has lain there ever since. Legend has it that many students hope to have sex under the Button before they graduate. While details are hazy, every student seems to know someone who has done "the Button tradition." The Button is just one way that Penn stands out from other schools.

Academically, Penn's excellence sets it apart from most schools, but what really distinguishes Penn is its unique blend of career-oriented education coupled with a broader liberal arts education. Students agree that few top schools share Penn's "work hard, play hard" attitude or the Quaker passion for extracurricular activities. Finally, there are the traditions. Penn is the only college where you can throw toast, party at Spring Fling and scream "Beat Princeton!" all while following in the legacy of Benjamin Franklin. Given all this, it's no wonder that "95 percent of students love being at Penn." If you seek an academic challenge coupled with a vibrant, tradition-filled on-campus community and the exciting city of Philadelphia, then Penn may be the place for you.—*Daniel Fromson*

FYI

If you come to Penn, you'd better bring "a copy of Ben Franklin's autobiography, because everyone here is obsessed with him."

What is the typical weekend schedule? "Thursday, go out to the frats; Friday, no class if you can help it, work, then go hang out with friends or go into Philly; Saturday, go to football, get some work done, go out and party; Sunday, scramble to finish work."

If I could change one thing about Penn, I'd "change the name. Everyone gets it confused with Penn State. People say it should be called Ben Franklin University."

Three things every student should do before graduating from Penn are "go to the Penn-Princeton basketball game, go into Philly, and take a class at Wharton so you can see what all the hype's about."

University of Pittsburgh

Address: U Pitt, Alumni Hall, 4227 Fifth Ave, Pittsburgh, PA 15260

Phone: 412-624-7488

E-mail Address: NA

Web site URL: www.pitt.edu/admissions.html

Year Founded: 1787

Private or Public: public

Religious affiliation: none

Location: urban

Regular Application Deadline: rolling

Number of Applicants: NA

Percent Accepted: 56%

Percent Accepted who enroll: 34%

Number Entering: 2,991

Number of Transfers Accepted each Year: NA

Mean SAT: 1,234

Mean ACT: 26

Middle 50% SAT range: 1,130–1,330

Middle 50% ACT range: 24–29

Early admission program (EA/ ED/ NA): NA

ED or EA Acceptance Rate: NA

Full time Undergraduate enrollment: 15,080

Total enrollment: 16,796

Percent Male: 47%

Percent Female: 52%

Total Percent Minority: 19%

Percent African-American: 9%

Percent Asian/Pacific Islander: 4%

Percent Hispanic: 1%

Percent Native-American: 0%

Percent Other: NA

Percent in-state / out of state: 85%/15%

Percent from Public HS: NA

Retention Rate: 89%

Graduation Rate: 73%

Percent in On-campus housing: 44%

Percent affiliated with Greek system: 9%/9%

Percent Varsity or Club Athletes: NA

Number of official organized extracurricular organizations: 450

3 Most popular majors: Marketing/Marketing Management, Psychology, Speech and Rhetorical Studies

Student/Faculty ratio: 16:01

Tuition and Fees: $20,686

In State Tuition and Fees (if different): $11,368.00

Cost for Room and Board: $7,800.00

Percent receiving Financial aid, first-year: 52%

In the early 1780s, Hugh Henry Brackenridge, newly elected to the Pennsylvania state assembly, sought funds from the state to build a new academy at the edge of the western frontier. In 1787, the Pittsburgh Academy was founded in a little log cabin. Today, University of Pittsburgh stands now as one of the oldest, most prestigious public universities in America. Located in the Oakland suburb of Pittsburgh, just a street away from the picturesque Schenley Park, the affectionately named "Pitt" has grown into a 132-acre mammoth of a university, boasting over 22,000 full-time undergraduates.

ABC, Pitt and Me

A little over half of undergraduates at Pitt enroll in the School of Arts & Sciences, and the rest are dispersed through the colleges of Engineering, Nursing, Business Administration, Health & Rehabilitation Services, Information Services, Social Work, Education and General Studies. In order to graduate from the School of Arts & Sciences, students must fulfill requirements in their major, general education and skills. Skills requirements were created to ensure that all Pitt graduates have competency in writing, algebra, quantitative and formal reasoning. Students are placed into or exempt from skills classes based on exams taken during high school or upon arrival at Pitt. The other, specialized colleges require that students fulfill a certain number of credits within the college and the rest through the School of Arts & Sciences.

Students at Pitt agree that their classes are generally pretty large—lectures often contain a couple hundred students, especially during the freshmen and sophomore years. However, these larger classes often have recitation once a week so that students can receive the individual attention that can be lost in a large university. Sometimes, though, all it takes is a little initiative. "I find that the professors are really accessible," says one engineering student. "They usually all have office hours, where you can just walk in and talk to them. Sometimes students get intimidated by them, but most of the professors honestly really enjoy being there and getting to know you better."

Pitt's size alone can make anybody—especially a freshman—a little overwhelmed academically, but students say the pressure dies down after a while. The trick lies in Pitt's many different schools and majors, which help break up a large student body into smaller academic environments. "Sooner or later, you start to connect with your department, and then it's like you're going to a small school," one recent graduate asserts. Indeed, there are over ninety registered academic-related organizations on campus, furthering the connections made in the departments.

Panther Central

Of course, Pitt wouldn't be Pitt without athletics. Football is arguably the biggest sport on campus. In its history, the Panthers have won nine NCAA national championships in football. Football games are often heralded by huge tailgates, pep rallies, and victory celebrations. In 2004, the University hired Dave Wannstedt, former NFL head coach and Pitt alumnus, as the new Panthers coach, hoping to bring back the football heydays of the 1970s and 1980s.

In the past few years, basketball has also grown into a major sport at Pitt. The men's basketball team won the Big East tournament in 2003, and has perennially been one of the most successful basketball teams on the East Coast. In fact, basketball tickets have become so coveted that they are now "impossible to get." To foster fledgling sports, Pitt has recently instituted a program of ticket distribution. Attendance at some of the lesser-known sport games,

such as certain women's sports, generates a certain number of points. Those points can then be used towards applying for tickets for a men's basketball game. The higher the number of points, the higher the priority. "That policy really helps ensure a rowdy ground at every home game, no matter what sport. Our student stands are never empty, and that really helps generate some serious school spirit," says one student.

It is no doubt that Pitt students also take the athletics of their new home city very seriously. "After the Steelers won the Superbowl, there were riots right on campus!" The successful athletics teams also contribute to a huge sense of school pride. Every time the football team wins a victory, the lights on top of the Cathedral of Learning shine blue and gold, an apt symbol of the close relationship of athletics and academics in this university.

All Night Long

Pitt students have their own underground, student-run Web site which functions as a giant Internet announcement board for campus parties. To date, over 8,000 users have registered, and a quick glance around the website turns up ads for frat parties, house parties, and even party reviews. This is hardly unusual for a college where the majority of students head out three nights a week, and some party it up every single day.

"House parties are by far the most popular, probably because it's really hard to get into bars underage," one student says. Another attests, "I went to this one party where they were playing beer pong on the front lawn. The cops were driving by and didn't even care!" Inside Pitt buildings, however, alcohol policy is much more stringent. One Pitt graduate explained, "Since we live in an urban environment, we do have a security guard who checks your Panther card before you go into your dorm, so if they can smell the alcohol on your breath or see you falling over, they *will* report you."

Even though Pitt is a relatively large state school, the Greek life is pretty subdued. The percentage of male students in fraternities hovers around 8 percent, and only 7 percent of girls are in sororities. Most students' social lives do not revolve around Greek letters. "Most sororities and fraternities have on-campus houses . . . Their parties are geared towards underclassmen and the people that live there or are part of the group," says one student.

> **"The great thing about Pitt is that one minute you can be on campus, in the hustle and bustle of Pittsburgh, and then you walk over a bridge, and all of the sudden you almost forget that you're in a city."**

Students at Pitt take full advantage of the fact that they are living in a vibrant city teeming with culture. "There are always concerts and other musical events going on, and there are a ton of bars in Oakland," says one undergrad. "And plus, CMU [Carnegie Mellon University] is almost right across the street, so a lot of CMU students come down to our frat parties and sometimes we go up to CMU. You really never get bored of the scene."

Besides weekly house parties and bar-hopping, Pitt also sponsors many big events. Not surprisingly, Homecoming Weekend is *"huge."* The Bigelow Bash is also spectacular. One weekend in late March or early April, Pitt closes down Bigelow Boulevard for a day of live music, games, and perhaps even some exotic animals and sumo wrestling.

Living at Pitt

Even though full-time undergraduate students are not required to live on campus, they are guaranteed on-campus housing for the first three years. Pitt owns many residential halls and apartment buildings on campus, and is currently in the midst of building more. The largest housing complex, Litchfield Towers, was finished in 1966 and encompasses three towers, each 22 stories high. The Towers are coed and house about 1800 students, many of them freshmen. Each residential hall room is equipped with furniture, telephone, cable TV, and online network service. Resident directors and assistants live in these halls to address any questions or concerns that may arise. The majority of Pitt's eateries are located in the lower level of the Towers, given its convenient and accessible location on campus. "Every student has to live in the Towers at some point," one student asserts. "You meet absolutely everyone there."

Besides the Towers, there are all-female dorms, Holland and Amos, with Amos hosting nine sororities. Sutherland Hall consists

of primarily athletes because of its close proximity to the Petersen Events Center and the major athletic facilities. Pitt also has Special Living Communities that cater to students who share a common academic or social interest. Some examples include Alcohol Free, Engineering Living-Learning Community, and the International Living Community.

Upperclassmen have the choice of apartment-style housing, which offers more self-reliability and independence than the traditional residential halls. They often include kitchens complete with stoves, refrigerators, garbage disposal, and dishwashers. Despite this, however, many juniors tend to move off-campus because of high housing costs. Dorms at Pitt usually run around $2,200 a semester, plus a required meal plan. Moving off-campus for students usually means cheaper rents, more freedom, and more control over food.

The Pitt meal plans work a little differently than those of most colleges, striking a very good balance between the two traditional types of meal plans. With every meal plan purchased, a student gets a certain amount of Meal Blocks and Dining Dollars. Meal Blocks can be best used in the Marketplace or for buying entrees. They are worth $5.40 per block. Dining Dollars can be swiped anywhere, for the exact amount of the purchase, and they are often used for smaller purchases. The Marketplace is located in the lower level of the Litchfield Towers, and it is an all-you-can-eat dining hall serving all three meals. Schenley Café, in the William Pitt Union, includes Pizza Hut Express, Freshens Smoothie Company, and Sub Connection. There are also a host of coffee carts and snack shops for those on the go. All in all, students don't complain much. "The food on campus is good—very good. It does get a little monotonous at times, but I think that's the same everywhere you go."

Log Cabins, Operas and Observatories

Perhaps the best-known piece of architecture at Pitt is the Cathedral of Learning. Soaring over 42 stories and 535 feet tall, the Cathedral is the second-tallest education-oriented building in the world. Its construction halted in the middle of the Great Depression, and the lore goes that it was only finished with the help of over 97,000 area school children who all chipped in a dime to buy a brick. The Cathedral of Learning is also famous for its two floors of

Nationality Rooms. The project started when John Gabbert Bowman, the tenth chancellor of Pitt, invited different national groups in Allegheny County to decorate a classroom in the Cathedral to reflect their own heritage. Today, the 26 Nationality Rooms boast palatial furniture from China, sixth-century mosaics from Israel, and an iroko wood entry door that portrays nine ancient and medieval African kings, among many others. "If you come to Pitt, even for a visit," says one student, "you have to see Cathedral Lawn and the Nationality Rooms."

The general feeling of the Pitt campus is urban. "No matter what time of the day it is, there's always going to be people walking around, doing things," one student proclaims. "We do live in Pittsburgh, after all." But those fond of the country do not need to worry. Just a bridge west of campus lays Schenley Park, the third-largest public park on the East Coast. This 400-acre park featuring hills, woods, walking trails, a botanical conservatory, swimming pool, tennis courts, golf course, nature center, and an ice skating rink, all within walking distance of Pitt.

The city of Pittsburgh also cannot be forgotten. In recent years, Pitt's administration has taken great efforts towards opening up the ample opportunities of Pittsburgh to the undergraduates of the University. Called Pitt-Arts, the program gives away thousands of free tickets to operas, ballets, theaters, films, and museums a year. Pitt students automatically receive free admission at the Andy Warhol Museum, the Phipps Conservatory and Botanical Gardens at Schenley Park, the Carnegie Museum of Art and Natural History, and the Mattress Factory museum. While it was only established ten years ago, PittArts now gives more than 30,000 students a year a chance to experience the vibrant city that they live in. Jokes one student, "See? We can be alcoholics *and* cultured!"

The original log cabin where Hugh Henry Brackenridge first built his Academy still stands today, wedged between the Cathedral of Learning and the Heinz Chapel. "It is the perfect spot," one student admits. "You can hardly believe you are still in a city." Perhaps that is the perfect portrait of the University of Pittsburgh—the crossroads of innovation and history, athletics and globalization, culture and education.—*Janet Xu*

FYI

If you come to Pitt, you'd better bring "Umbrella and waterproof shoes (it rains a lot and it will be muddy 50 percent of the time.)"

What's the typical weekend schedule? "Frat parties and house parties starting Thursday night, and maybe some bars if you're over 21, and maybe go into Pittsburgh on Saturday to catch a play."

If I could change one thing about Pitt, I'd change "the advising system for freshmen. They just don't give us enough info!"

Three things every student at Pitt should do before graduating are "look at the Nationality Rooms and then go to the top of the Cathedral, go to all the museums around campus that we get into for free, and go to a Panthers football game."

Villanova University

Address: Villanova, Austin Hall, 1st Floor, Villanova. PA 19085-1603

Phone: 610-519-4000

E-mail Address: gotovu@villanova.edu

Web site URL: www.villanova.edu/enroll/admission/

Year Founded: 1842

Private or Public: private

Religious affiliation: Roman Catholic

Location: suburban

Regular Application Deadline: 8-Jan

Number of Applicants: 12,913

Percent Accepted: 43%

Percent Accepted who enroll: 30%

Number Entering: 1,638

Number of Transfers Accepted each Year: 212

Mean SAT: 1,270

Mean ACT: 28

Middle 50% SAT range: 1,180–1,370

Middle 50% ACT range: 27–30

Early admission program (EA/ ED/ NA): EA

ED or EA Acceptance Rate: 44%

Full time Undergraduate enrollment: 6,877

Total enrollment: 9,726

Percent Male: 49%

Percent Female: 51%

Total Percent Minority: 17%

Percent African-American: 4%

Percent Asian/Pacific Islander: 7%

Percent Hispanic: 6%

Percent Native-American: 0%

Percent Other: NA

Percent in-state / out of state: 33%/67%

Percent from Public HS: 55%

Retention Rate: 95%

Graduation Rate: 87%

Percent in On-campus housing: 74%

Percent affiliated with Greek system: 21%

Percent Varsity or Club Athletes: NA

Number of official organized extracurricular organizations: 300

3 Most popular majors: Biological and Physical Sciences; Finance, General; Nursing—Registered Nurse Training (RN, ASN, BSN, MSN)

Student/Faculty ratio: 12:01

Tuition and Fees: $33,000

Cost for Room and Board: $9,480

Percent receiving Financial aid, first-year: 49%

A t Villanova, students take full advantage of everything their school has to offer. Students immerse themselves in their studies, a vast array of community service, all that the school's suburban Philadelphia location has to offer and of course, the school's wildly successful basketball team. While football's not much of a big deal, Villanova students "go crazy over basketball." "Hoops Mania" isn't just the season opener where the basketball team is introduced—it's a Villanova fever that has been contagious since the school was founded. Villanova's basketball team made it to the Elite 8 last year, and students say, "they're really good—that's why we are basketball crazy." In fact, during halftime at one of the games, it is possible to win a cruise or a brand new Mustang just for shooting a couple hoops.

Players, Greeks, and Saints

Basketball is just one of Villanova's many traditions. A Catholic university located only about 15 minutes away from Philadelphia, it is nestled right in the center of the Main Line—a well-known upscale area of suburban Philadelphia. While Villanova's campus is gorgeous, the University also boasts an exciting night life and a Greek system devoted to perpetual partying. However, whether or not you choose to go Greek, an active social life is a must. One student confessed, "As important as our grades are to us, [partying] is a really important aspect of our school." That said, forty percent of the student body belongs to one of 16 fraternities or sororities. They make their presence known during "Greek Week" when Greeks wear their letters and have contests and games around campus. Greek life is prevalent on campus, but since fraternities and sororities do not have houses, they do not consume the social life on campus and students say that anyone can survive without belonging to a fraternity or a sorority. But fraternities and sororities are not all about drinking and dancing the night away; they also avidly promote philanthropy. Each fraternity and sorority is affiliated with a different community service organization and organizes two events per year to raise money for their chosen charities. The service-based Greek life yields events like the Special Olympics on Villanova's campus, as well as a number of projects in Philadelphia city schools, shelters, and soup kitchens. "Habitat for Humanity is huge on our campus," one senior said, recommending that everyone go on mission trips during fall or spring break to build houses. "I know for some of my friends who go to big universities, it's not the cool thing to get involved in community service," she explained. "But here, it's the cool thing to do."

The Holy Grounds

For entertainment on college grounds, students go to Connelly Center, where free movies are shown on weekends. The school also hosts "Late Night Villanova" where students stay up all night doing various activities and all proceeds go to charity. Many also venture into Philadelphia. Railways line either side of campus and make it possible for freshmen and sophomores, who are not allowed to have cars, to explore the city. Weekend shuttles also run into the heart of Philadelphia and to the nearest mall. On the first Friday of every month and every Sunday, art galleries and museums are free for the public, and students often take advantage of this and swarm into the city. One sophomore recommended the popular South Street: "Shopping is fun because there are lots of random boutiques, but it's even fun just to sit and watch the people go by and see the random happenings." Another student agreed: "The people there are very different from what you see on campus; it's a breath of fresh air." South Philly, as it's known by locals, is "the place" to get an authentic Philly cheesesteak, the corner where Pat's and Geno's are located. Downtown Philadelphia also boasts several clubs, including "Shampoo" and "Envy" which host college nights for students and a bar called Brownie's. "When you turn 21," one senior said, "it's the rite of passage—you go to Brownie's."

> As important as our grades are to us, partying is a really important aspect of our school.

Villanova hosts a handful of annual campus-wide events. The St. Thomas of Villanova Day parade is held in the fall when students return from summer vacation. St. Thomas Villanova Day includes a feast and some speeches to recognize the founder of the University, St. Thomas of Villanova. A sim-

ilar carnival, NovaFest, is hosted at the end of the year. "NovaFest is a huge weekend party that we look forward to all year. We never really get good bands, but it's crazy and everyone drinks all weekend long." However, do not expect to obtain easy access to alcohol at these parties or at any other social gatherings; Villanova has a strict alcohol policy that is enforced by Resident Advisors. No alcohol is allowed for students under age, and students over 21 are only allowed to keep a certain amount of alcohol in their dorm room. Students say the RAs are "pretty strict on it. They make themselves very friendly, and very approachable, but we know that they're the arm of the law." However, students contend that while the university is strict on alcohol possession, "there are many ways to get around it." As for food and sustenance, Villanova offers a number of dining options in addition to regular dining hall meal plans. Meal plan points pay for items at the convenience store, the Italian kitchen, and the grill. Coffee shops like "The Holy Grounds" can be found all over campus, in libraries and in classroom buildings. The Bartley Exchange "has great sandwiches and meals which everyone agrees is the best place to eat on campus." There's also a traveling coffee cart that tries to capture customers from the nearby Starbucks.

Holy Wisdom

Applicants apply to one of Villanova's four colleges: Arts and Sciences, Commerce and Finance, Engineering, or Nursing. Students have the option of changing their college program once they are enrolled and are not required to declare a major until the end of sophomore year. Students in the college of Arts and Sciences must fulfill a number of distributional requirements. "They try to make you as well-rounded as possible," one senior said, listing the requirements in science, math, theology, history, foreign language, English, and ethics. "Our school is very much broken up by the college you're in," one senior said. "Academic-wise, you're very segregated." The freshman core, however—a survey of Western Literature and history from the ancient medieval period through the Renaissance and the Enlightenment to the present—is required of all freshmen and is "a big mixing pot." These core Humanities classes also have a very religious base. As an Augustinian university, "we read the bible as one of our books in them and also Augustine's 'Confessions.'"

Goin' to the Chapel

One amorously-minded sophomore noted the beauty of Villanova's on-campus church. "It's the most gorgeous chapel," she said, noting that couples are married there every weekend. The wait list to get married there is "so long there are at least two marriages a day on the weekends. Freshman year you're supposed to put your name on the list." While no one actually signs up to be married that far in advance, you might be able to arrange a marriage in a different way: couples who kiss under the arch in Coor Hall as freshmen are said to be destined for wedding bells in the chapel.

When it comes to other chapel-going, students say the Catholic tradition of the school is more like background noise than an omnipresent affiliation. "I was expecting it to be a whole bunch of Catholics," one freshman said, "But only some go to Mass." He soon discovered that Villanova was "more religiously diverse" than he had expected. The majority of students on campus are in fact Catholic, but as one sophomore noted, "they are not necessarily stringent Catholics; it is present, but I wouldn't say it pervades social life." The 8 p.m. and 10 p.m. masses are very popular times for students. Feel free to walk into Coor Hall or the chapel as you please, but watch your step at St. Mary's on West Campus. Not only do students tell great ghost stories about this and other buildings, they also warn that if you step on the seal in the floor there, you won't graduate in four years.

Posterchild for Preppy

"Basically everybody at this campus is out of an Abercrombie & Fitch catalog," one sophomore confessed. "But there are still some people who throw everybody on campus for a loop." Students describe the typical Villanova student as "upper-middle-class white—just your basic kid who grew up in the suburbs and whose parents are together . . . and they have brothers or sisters who go here or who've graduated from here; there's a lot of legacy at Villanova." While one sophomore concedes that many students come from a privileged background and "drive BMWs," "there are a lot of people who don't go with that crowd and who don't really care about that stuff." The homogeneity of the student population is a widespread complaint, although one sophomore optimistically reported, "The incoming class was far more diverse than ours," and "a lot more cultural clubs have popped up on campus recently."

Overall, students say the size and atmosphere of Villanova help make everyone feel at home. One sophomore remarked, "Villanova's big on community, and I think that's one of the things that really attracted me: leaving home I'd kind of have a new family as soon as I got here." Another student appreciated that Villanova is "not so big that you get lost in the masses, but not so small that everybody knows everything about everyone else; it makes for a comfortable feel." Remember, though, whether headed towards class, the chapel, or Philadelphia—watch out for those seals.—*Laura Sullivan*

FYI

If you come to Villanova, you'd better bring "readiness to work hard and party hard, a Louis Vuitton bag, and a fake ID."

What is the typical weekend schedule? "Friday nights party, Saturday sleep in, do some work during the day or watch football, Saturday night more parties, Sunday go to meetings and study with everyone in the Bartley Exchange."

If I could change one thing about Villanova, "I'd make the student body more diverse."

Three things every student at Villanova should do before graduating are "go to the basketball games, watch the chariot races, and go on a community service trip."

Rhode Island

Students considering Brown should not let its centuries-old Ivy League traditions fool them; Brown's history of progressive teachings has been a hallmark of its undergraduate experience since the school's founding in 1764. Today, you'll find that Brown has carried this tradition of intellectual and extracurricular curiosity into the 21st century, cementing its place as a true haven for fine academics and passionate interests in an environment that celebrates free thought.

So Chill and Satisfied

The absence of any general requirements at Brown is part of its overall atmosphere of freedom and experimentation. The "New Curriculum" allows Brown students to shape their own programs of study, which they said offers a number of advantages. One senior explained that "when you don't have requirements, it works for both people who don't know what they want to do and people who know exactly what they want to do; it helps

you structure your education for whatever fits you best." He added that, "you get a school full of people doing what they love." Brown also offers its famous Satisfactory/No Credit option, where students can opt to take as many classes as they like on a pass/fail evaluation basis instead of for a letter grade. While most students only choose to do this a few times a year, it lets them experiment in a subject outside their normal area of interest without having to worry about their numerical performance. One student said that it "goes in line with Brown's whole philosophy of giving you freedom to explore new fields without feeling that it all has to be related to your future success and your résumé."

Although many students choose to major in International Relations or Biology, they can specialize in more unusual majors or "concentrations," as well. Brown reportedly has the only Egyptology concentration in the Western Hemisphere, and the Neuroscience department is well-known for its professors and cutting-edge research. Professor Barrett Hazeltine's popular business management classes attract many students, and Biology professor Ken Miller was recently a leading witness in the Supreme Court case debating the teaching of evolution in schools. Adventurous students interested in the arts may cross-register at the nearby—and equally famed—Rhode Island School of Design.

Students agreed that while introductory courses can have up to a few hundred people in them, upper-level classes shrink in size considerably. Freshmen also have the option to sign up for First Year Seminars capped at 20 students, which offer an opportunity for first-years to get to know each other and a professor in a lively, intimate discussion setting. Professors are described as being very accessible if students need them to be. In addition to being required to host weekly office hours, many Brown professors get to know their students' names, even in large lecture courses. As one student put it, "If you're willing to take a little initiative, you can build really strong relationships."

The pervasive laidback attitude regarding academics is another strong characteristic of Brown. One senior confided that, "while it's really competitive to get into Brown, it's really not competitive when you get here." Although "the vast majority of people here are still working really hard," students say that it is rare for people to lose their cool about GPAs or class curves—in public, at least. This relaxed philosophy allows people to collaborate on work and generally to "stay away from bragging about how hardworking or stressed you are." Another senior explained that "it's hard to compete because everyone's passionate about their own interests and has their own achievements along different dimensions."

Conservative Commentators Need Not Apply

Every year at Brown, the Queer Alliance hosts Sex Power God, a wild party at which students are encouraged to wear as little clothing as possible. In 2005, SPG got some surprise attention when it was featured on the TV show "The O'Reilly Factor" as an example of Ivy League-sanctioned debauchery. Although Bill O'Reilly may not approve, students said that one of their favorite aspects of Brown is its liberalism and free-spirited atmosphere. Although they caution against giving in entirely to the conception of Brown students as "pot-smoking, flannel-wearing hippies," in general, students con-

curred that there's some truth to the image. The campus is "overwhelmingly liberal," although conservatives do have a voice, and students said that "everyone here is interested in making the world a better place."

In terms of encouraging diversity, students said that the admissions office is doing a good job geographically, but social divisions based on income and ethnicity are sometimes apparent. Students agreed that the mostly generous financial aid policy has improved in the past few years and has made attending an elite private school a reality for many low-income students.

Although the actual number of students in fraternities and sororities at Brown may be relatively small, their weekend parties are still very popular, especially among underclassmen. Everyone also finds themselves at parties in the dorms, usually earlier in the night, before they head out to some of the local bars and clubs in the downtown area or on nearby Thayer Street. The club Fish Co. is reportedly the place to be on Wednesday nights. Upperclassmen often attend parties at off-campus houses. Brown's policies on alcohol and drug use are described as "extremely loose," and campus police and Residential Counselors in the dorms "are really there just to make sure that you're being safe and not causing trouble." One girl said that she would often come back to her dorm hall at night and smell pot, but she said that "it's not at all something that people will pressure you to do, although it's definitely there if you want it."

Brown students find it easy to take the bus or train to Boston or New York on the weekends, but many find that just staying on College Hill in Providence is satisfactory. Brown's NCAA Division I teams usually have games, although few students reportedly attend them, even though the Bears' football team won the Ivy League in 2005.

Life on College Hill

Upon setting foot on campus, visitors to Brown immediately notice the striking colonial-style brick buildings and the wide, inviting Main Green. The campus is described as "very New England," complete with ivy and impeccable grounds. However, today's Brown students have adapted their school's austere backdrop to the 21st century. On sunny days, students crowd the lawns with lemonade stands, soccer games, back massage stations, and the occasional hookah.

Most freshmen live in Keeney Quadrangle, which houses about 600 students and is known as the "freshman zoo." The rest live in dorms that range from a few blocks to a ten-minute walk away. While Keeney is agreed to be the most social dorm, people said that the other dorms foster long-term relationships, as well. Everyone is assigned a roommate in a double, and the traditional long hallways are co-ed. The bathrooms are supposed to be single-sex, but some students reported having members of the opposite sex invade when their lines were too long. Freshmen are organized into units of 40 to 60 and are assigned undergraduate RCs. Students said they made the majority of their friends in their first-year units, since "it's a large enough group of people that you get a good variety of interests and personalities." After freshman year, students enter the Housing Lottery to draw for several different arrangements, ranging from triples to suites.

The two main all-you-can-eat dining halls, the "V-Dub" and the "Ratty," got mixed reviews, with most students agreeing that the fare quickly grows monotonous, even though the "V-dub" does have a vegetarian line. The meal plan was recently expanded to allow diners more freedom to use their plans at after-hours eateries on-campus, including the Ivy Room and Joe's. Nearby Thayer Street is an ever-popular option for a wide variety of food, from the famous falafels at East Side Pocket to Antonio's Pizza. If you want to venture off the Hill into the downtown area, the Dominican food gets good reviews for its affordability and exotic allure, while Café Paragon is "a good place to go for a good meal with your parents."

While one junior said she did not know why Brown students would need to leave College Hill to entertain themselves, the recently-renovated and revitalized downtown Providence is an enticing reason. The city has spruced itself up in the past several years, and its museums, events on the river, and "humongous" mall are attractive study breaks for students.

Campaigns and Cracked Pots

At Brown, students know how to balance ambitious activities with downtime. A sophomore said he thought that, "everyone here is involved in at least two or three extracurricular activities, usually very different from each other, and in a very driven way." Politics are a common interest, with the Brown College Democrats widely cited as the most popular organization. One sophomore even said that "a popular joke is that the Brown Green Party is bigger than the campus Republicans." No matter which party you pick, students say that the small size of Rhode Island is conducive in allowing them to get involved in local and statewide politics. "I have a lot of friends who feel like they're making changes in social policy and education reform—they really have an impact on who gets elected." The Queer Alliance draws many members, as do cultural heritage groups and a number of social activism organizations like the Brown Darfur Action Network and Amnesty International. A capella and dance groups also have a strong presence.

Recent years have seen an increase in the involvement of students in community service organizations in downtown Providence, challenging the belief that all Brown students avoid leaving College Hill. Some students also have jobs down the hill, although "Brown provides a lot of opportunities for employment, especially through Dining Services."

Brown students revel in a number of zany traditions that pervade the college's freeform atmosphere. Every finals period, a group of students organizes in secret and shows up on campus at a random time to run through the buildings, from the libraries to the dorms, in what is termed the "Naked Donut Run." "It's very Brown to think 'I'm free and naked and helping people by giving them donuts,' " one student remarked. A legend surrounding a mysterious figure from Brown's past has also become tradition. On Friday the 13th, students pay homage to the mythical professor Josiah Carberry, who supposedly studied "psychoceramics," or cracked pots.

> "It's very Brown to think 'I'm free and naked and helping people by giving them donuts.' "

"I don't think we conform to nonconformity but people are not afraid to express themselves," one student said. Indeed, Brown does leave its undergraduates many opportunities for freedom of expression, whether it is by letting students choose their own classes, run a medley of organizations, or spearhead campaigns. While it may be famous for its unstructured atmosphere, Brown students find that their self-motivation and passionate interests help them to shape unique college experiences.
—*Kimberly Chow*

FYI

If you come to Brown, you'd better bring: "liberal political beliefs and a scarf."

What's the typical weekend schedule? "Friday night go to a room party; Saturday sleep in then do community service in Providence; Saturday night go to a frat or a party thrown by an organization, then do work all Sunday.

If I could change one thing about Brown, "I would want people to venture off College Hill into downtown Providence more."

Three things that every student at Brown should do before graduating: "March against the University, like to protest the bookstore going corporate, take a completely ridiculous class that has nothing to do with your major, and try to get to the tops of as many buildings as you can."

Rhode Island School of Design

Address: University of Rhode Island, Two College Street, Providence, RI 02903

Phone: 800-364-RISD

E-mail Address: admissions@risd.edu

Web site URL: www.risd.edu/apply.cfm

Year Founded: 1877

Private or Public: private

Religious affiliation: NA

Location: urban

Regular Application Deadline: 15-Feb

Number of Applicants: 2,511

Percent Accepted: NA

Percent Accepted who enroll: NA

Number Entering: 398

Number of Transfers Accepted each Year: NA

Mean SAT: NA

Mean ACT: NA

Middle 50% SAT range: 1,080–1,330

Middle 50% ACT range: NA

Early admission program (EA/ ED/ NA): EA

ED or EA Acceptance Rate: 49%

Full time Undergraduate enrollment: 1,882

Total enrollment: 2,258

Percent Male: 35%

Percent Female: 65%

Total Percent Minority: 23%

Percent African-American: NA

Percent Asian/Pacific Islander: NA

Percent Hispanic: NA

Percent Native-American: NA

Percent in-state / out of state: NA

Percent in On-campus housing: 42%

Percent in Fraternities: NA

Percent in Sororities: NA

Retention Rate: NA

Graduation Rate: NA

Percent Varsity or Club Athletes: NA

3 Most popular majors: Fine and Studio Art, Commercial and Advertising Art, Industrial Design

Financial Information: NA

Tuition and Fees: $31,415

In State Tuition and Fees (if different): NA

Cost for Room and Board: $8,355

Percent Receiving Financial aid, first year: NA

P eople live, breathe, and dream art at the Rhode Island School of Design, affectionately called "Rizdee." Its students purportedly have the greatest workload in the country, surpassing even MIT. If you can make it through the 'grueling' freshman year, the rest of your time will be spent working creatively with renowned professors, many of whom are accomplished artists, and you will graduate with a diploma from one of the top art schools in the country. But it's not all work: from dressing up for the Artist's Ball, to cheering "Go Nads!" life is a little crazy and always unusual at RISD.

Art Is Life

RISD offers every imaginable artistic discipline, from illustration, architecture, and graphic design, the most popular majors, to the more unconventional glassblowing courses. Freshmen must take two courses in English, two in art history, and three studio courses both semesters, choosing from history, philosophy, and science classes second semester. Students also need studio credits to graduate, which consist of the creative core classes that "everyone spends hours and hours working on." The liberal arts courses are "informative and pretty good," and supplements (groups of 15 to 20 students from lecture courses) are "great because you can speak, have discussions about what you're learning in class, and can voice your questions." One girl complained, however, that the lectures were too large and disjointed, and that the schedule was too limited. But those who come to RISD are not looking for the typical liberal arts curriculum.

The workload at RISD is heavy, with students spending seven hours a day in the studio; says one student, "my roommate pulls all-nighters at least one night a week, every week." The first year is "one of the hardest workload-wise because you are fulfilling assignments, whereas later you are doing your own work and it is more specific for major requirements." In the imaginative environment of RISD, students say "it's easier to do the work because you are surrounded by other people doing it too, your peers motivate you."

Architecture majors are the hardest-worked of all; "you don't see them the first year," and many even sleep in the studio, emerging after 24-hour work sessions. The illustration major, on the other hand, "is very broad—you can do a lot of media, and people want to try their hand at a lot of different things." Those interested in double-majoring in some fields like printmaking and textile design will find that they are required to stay five years, yet the quality of the professors make it worthwhile for some.

RISD professors are not the usual bunch of tweed-jacketed scholars with thick-rimmed glasses sitting behind desks; many of them have made their names on the New York art scene, and eccentricity seems to be a requirement. One student divulged the story of a certain heartbroken professor who broke into the Providence sewer system, where he put all of his belongings, cast an exact replica of himself, left it there with everything he owned, and moved on. "It was a huge art piece, but there was no publicity, only people who had heard about it from others went to see it. He really made it for himself, it was a cathartic experience." Tom Mills is a professor famous for his exceptional drawing foundation class, and, like many professors at RISD, has studios in New York City. He also gives "mini art history lectures to supplement work in class to help his students."

Because of its focus on the arts, RISD does not have any major science facilities. Science classes can be taken in the Nature Lab, although some students take advantage of RISD's cross-registration program to take classes at Brown. The science requirement is very basic and no math is required, and one student confided that the Nature Lab was probably used more frequently for artistic purposes, as "the stuffed animals kept there make better models than live ones—they hold still."

The art facilities are stellar, as is to be expected from a school of RISD's prestige. Not surprisingly, "there are studios for anything you want to do, open 24 hours a day." Art supplies are conveniently located in the RISD store on-campus.

Party, Anyone?
There are plenty of options to choose from when deciding how to spend your meager free time at RISD. Thayer Street, only two blocks from the quad, is the local hangout for many students and has a wide variety of restaurants and bars to choose from. Whether you crave Italian food, Thai food, or cheesecake, it can be found on or near Thayer, home to Pizzeria Uno, O-Cha (meaning 'delicious' in Thai), The Cheesecake Factory, Paragon, the Andrea's, and a crepe place. Thayer is the place to see and be seen for freshmen and upperclassmen alike.

There is also the mall, an enormous complex with a cinema within walking distance of campus. Many students go to private parties at RISD and Brown, and though RISD has no Greek system, students can still enjoy Brown's frat parties, which host the wildest nights around. For those looking to dance, there are clubs, Viva being the most popular, and other venues that have themed events such as goth night, fetish night, and '80s night, by far the most popular: "'80s is a really big deal here."

For those without real over-21 IDs, there is still plenty to do—there are always concerts, dances, Broadway shows such as *Hairspray*, and art openings, as well as visiting speakers like Martha Stewart and the fashion designer Todd Oldham, among others. The highlights of the year are the three formal events thrown by the school. The Artist's Ball in first semester is "really, really crazy, everyone goes all-out on costumes, some people end up naked, and one girl, dressed as Sailor Moon from 'Anime' won a national contest for best costume and a trip to Cancún for two." Electroflow has a more "rave-like" atmosphere, and is held in a parking garage with DJs on each level, and Beaux Arts is held in the springtime down by the river. New York City and Boston are just a train ride away, and some professors organize trips for the class to look at shows in the cities. Ski trips are another option.

The school's alcohol policy is "supposedly strict, but most can get away with drinking. There are Public Safety people on patrol living in dorms who will look through your stuff if they suspect drinking and confiscate any substances, but it doesn't occur that often." Non-drinkers are equally comfortable, as there is no pressure at all to drink.

At RISD it is incredibly easy to meet people, and "everybody is pretty nuts; there are different personalities, and everyone is talented." The male to female ratio is "very weird," said one girl, "that's why we go up to Brown." Students report that many of the guys at RISD are gay, and that combined with the enormous workload makes having a love life difficult.

The Look and the Life

Students love the old New-England-style buildings and the nice, cozy little town just across the river from Providence. The campus is situated on top of College Hill, which can be "kind of treacherous in winter," so bring your snow boots! All freshmen live in dorms around Lower and Upper Quad, which are conveniently linked so "you can walk around the whole thing to visit friends (or go to the cafeteria) without venturing out into the cold." Each floor has a common room where people can hang out, as well as a work room where "you can paint big paintings, draw, or do big sculptures." Freshman year guarantees decent housing, usually singles or doubles. Due to the lack of housing, half the student body moves off-campus after their first year to live with friends, though there is a new dorm with a 500-person capacity. In addition, projects for a new student center, museum, and library are well underway to house the school's growing collections.

The main places to eat are the Met, which has a vegan bar, salad and sandwich bar, and the popular panini maker, as well as Carr Haus, which is "like a coffee shop with couches," and the Pit, a grill serving hamburgers and veggie burgers. The food at RISD is good, and the veggie options are particularly popular as they cater to the school's large vegetarian population.

Go Nads!

Sports are not taken too seriously at RISD, and this is reflected in the choice of team names: the hockey-playing Nads draw the biggest crowd, and one girl described the game as "hilarious—a lot of drunken people yelling and a large penis (the team mascot) skating around." The basketball team is the Balls, the swimming team the Strokes, and the school cheerleaders are known as the Jockstraps. To keep students fit, RISD has a gym and a small fitness center offering classes ranging from modern dance to yoga and the Brazilian dance capoeira, and students can always use the Brown facilities, which boast an Olympic pool, a huge gym, and a skating rink.

> **"It would be weird if you were normal."**

The emphasis at RISD is more on school spirit than sports prowess, and "people here are nuts, basically. We are all in our own little art bubble, we work a lot and don't mind the work, and we know that we can't party 24/7." One student raves, "you feel a part of everything, everybody is really different but nobody judges you for it. Everyone has their own style and personality . . . it would be weird if you were normal."—*Serena Hines*

FYI

If you come to RISD, you'd better bring "an incredibly open mind."

What is the typical weekend schedule? "Friday, you are usually tired from the week's work so you go out for a drink or to the movies; Saturday and Sunday, sleep in, spend the rest of the day in the studio, and later go down to Thayer Street, walk around, go to a party."

If I could change one thing about RISD, I'd "remove the hills."

Three things every student at RISD should do before graduating are "go to a Nads hockey game, go to the Artists' Ball, and try being a poor artist for a little bit."

Salve Regina University

Address: Salve Regina, 100 Ochre Point Avenue, Newport, RI 02840-4192
Phone: 401-341-2908
E-mail Address: sruadmis@salve.edu
Web site URL: www.salve.edu
Year Founded: 1947
Private or Public: private
Religious affiliation: Roman Catholic
Location: suburban
Regular Application Deadline: Rolling
Number of Applicants: 5,329
Percent Accepted: 56%
Percent Accepted who enroll: 19%
Number Entering: 567
Number of Transfers Accepted each Year: 118
Mean SAT: 1,098
Mean ACT: 23

Middle 50% SAT range: M:510–580,V:500–590
Middle 50% ACT range: 21–25
Early admission program (EA/ ED/ NA): EA
ED or EA Acceptance Rate: 61.7%
Full time Undergraduate enrollment: 2,079
Total enrollment: 2,589
Percent Male: 29%
Percent Female: 71%
Total Percent Minority: 18%
Percent African-American: 1%
Percent Asian/Pacific Islander: 1%
Percent Hispanic: 2%
Percent Native-American: 0%
Percent Other: 14%
Percent in-state / out of state: 16%/84%
Percent from Public HS: 65%

Retention Rate: 80%
Graduation Rate: 59%
Percent in On-campus housing: 58%
Percent affiliated with Greek system: 0%
Percent Varsity or Club Athletes: NA
Number of official organized extracurricular organizations: 42
3 Most popular majors: Business Administration/ Management, Criminal Justice, Elementary Education/Teaching
Student/Faculty ratio: 13:01
Tuition and Fees: $25,175.00
Cost for Room and Board: $9,800.00
Percent receiving Financial aid, first-year: 84.44%

S alve Regine College was founded under the tutelage of the Sisters of Mercy, and was originally intended to be a liberal arts college in the Catholic tradition. It changed its name to Salve Regina University in 1991, but it still remains a serious liberal arts college with a considerable Catholic bent. It started originally as a nursing program, and to this day it still boasts a popular and competitive nursing program. There are plenty of other majors to choose from, and all students receive a well-rounded liberal arts education, centered on an intensive core.

Liberal Arts with a Side of Catholicism

Salve Regina's most striking academic program is the Core Curriculum, which every student must complete in order to graduate. The core is extremely intensive, covering a wide range of subjects and disciplines. The Core Curriculum consists of the Common Core, five courses which every single student takes; and the Core Complement, for which there is a choice of which classes to take to meet the requirements. The Common Core includes Philosophy and Religious Studies courses, which are aimed at helping students understand the widespread influence of Judeo-Christian thought in the world, with a focus on Catholicism. One student described the curriculum as "definitely liberal arts by nature but with a very religious overtone." Some students do not take kindly to having religion "stuffed down their throats," but others accept it as part of the school's mission. There is also an introductory course taken freshmen year entitled "Portal: Seeking Wisdom," which serves to introduce students to the liberal arts. The core received mixed reactions from the students. One claimed that it was too restricting and the long list of requirements prevented her from going abroad for a semester. Another found the experience enlightening and instructive, albeit overwhelming at times. Although many of the core classes deal with very similar subjects, each new subject is somehow refreshing, as one will "get something different out of it looking it at a different angle from before."

Without a doubt, Salve's greatest academic strength is its commitment to student-to-professor interaction. One student earnestly said, "I absolutely adore my professors at Salve." When class sizes are so small and such a focus is placed on discussion and student participation, its no surprise that students and instructors share a strong bond. Most classes have fewer than 20 students, and only the most popular introductory classes have classes larger than 30 students. Such great emphasis on exploration leads to some very lively discussions; students are "always engaged in class." Even in the larger classes, "there's really good discussions that come up" and the professors are still accessible.

Salve students have many choices for their majors. Most liberal arts disciplines are covered, but the most popular majors are reportedly Nursing and Administration of Justice. The nursing program is one of the most difficult tracks at Salve. It has strict requirements; getting a C—in any nursing course is considered "failing" and results in expulsion from the major. The popularity of the nursing program may explain one of Salve's most interesting facets. The nursing department has "very few male students" and, seeing as it's one of the largest majors, the university as a whole has a high female-to-male ratio.

Salve Girls and Some Salve Guys

One student noted that, "Walking around it's pretty obvious that you run into more girls than guys," but she didn't feel that it was "very noticeable." Unlike many student bodies, Salve's seems very comfortable with itself. The school is markedly homogeneous. Naturally, the majority of students are affiliated with the Catholic Church in some way. Although there may be plenty of Catholics, one student warned that "the chapel is small and only a small percentage of students attends mass on Sundays." Furthermore, many of the students are described as white, preppy, and wealthy. One girl noted that, "Many people dress up for classes and carry around their Louis Vuitton and Coach bags." Only one student expressed an odious dislike of the stereotypical Salve kid, bemoaning their New England preppiness, although still admiring the school's quality of teaching. A word for the wise: although it may be difficult to fit into such a crowd, the students are for the most part pretty amiable and social. The typical student also "parties a lot and is very concerned with working out at the gym."

Salve students like to party. The campus is strictly dry, so most students have to go off campus, to the apartments of upper-classmen, in order to drink on the weekends. Even for being a dry campus, there are reportedly a lot of alcohol and drugs, and there is a prevalence along the more well-to-do of some "rich man's drugs." It remains difficult and somewhat a hassle for students to party, especially for those that are underage. Many students go to nearby Newport on the weekends to go clubbing and to escape the strict town of Newport. For those that do not want to stray far from campus or drink, the university hosts many dry events for the student body. Every spring the campus holds a concert, Brand New. On top of that, a comedian performs every week, and every once in a while bands or singers come to the weekly performance.

Newport: Bars, Beaches, and Villas

Salve Regina has "a beautiful campus." Located in the historic city of Newport, Rhode Island, the campus is well-known for the mansions it has acquired for university use—the school was originally founded when the gorgeous Ochre Court was donated to the Sisters of Mercy. Ochre Court is a Newport mansion, built to be the luxurious residence of a wealthy banker in the Gilded Age of the late nineteenth century. It is the heart of the campus, just as it has always been. When Salve was just a nursing school, it housed the faculty, the students, and the classrooms. Now, it is the location of the admissions office and a small chapel. Today, much of the campus shares the same historic grandeur of the Gilded Age. Classes are held in mansions; some of the main academic buildings, Wakehurst and McCauley, were also donated to the school by wealthy Newport families. The campus lies over the water and is described as "amazingly beautiful" by the students.

> **"Our classes are held in mansions . . . can you say that about another school?"**

Downtown Newport is rather touristy, there are a lot of places to shop and eat. Some favorite student eateries include the Brick Alley Pub, Sardella's, Puerini and the Red Parrot. Newport has a lot of unique stores and bars which are popular among Salve students on the weekends. The most popular beach for students is First Beach, which can be reached from campus on the Cliff Walk. The Cliff Walk stretches over three miles, and goes alongside a precipice overlooking the Atlantic Ocean. It is yet another one of the interesting vistas to be found at this uniquely Catholic liberal arts university founded in the historic city of Newport.—*Ryan Galisewski*

FYI

If you come to Salve Regina, you'd better bring "common sense, money (it would be a shame to put all those awesome stores downtown to waste), and a diverse sense of style."

What is the typical weekend schedule? "Go clubbing in Providence Friday night. Work during the day on Saturday and then go to a friend's party in Newport. Sunday either go to mass or sleep in, and then do work the rest of the day."

If I could change one thing about Salve Regina University, I would "make it a little bit more diverse. It gets boring having to see people who look exactly the same walking around campus."

Three things every Salve Regina University student should do before graduating are: "go for a drink at all of the bars on Thames Street and/or Broadway, visit the Breaker's Mansion before Christmas, and go for a drive on Ocean Drive—it's the most beautiful road in the world!"

University of Rhode Island

Address: University of Rhode Island, Newman Hall, 14 Upper College Road, Kingston, RI 02881	**Middle 50% SAT range:** NA	**Retention Rate:** 81%
	Middle 50% ACT range: NA	**Graduation Rate:** 56%
	Early admission program (EA/ ED/ NA): EA	**Percent in On-campus housing:** 40%
Phone: 401-874-7000	**ED or EA Acceptance Rate:** NA	**Percent affiliated with Greek system:** 18%
E-mail Address: uriadmit@uri.edu	**Full time Undergraduate enrollment:** 11,875	**Percent Varsity or Club Athletes:** NA
Web site URL: www.uri.edu	**Total enrollment:** 14,871	**Number of official organized extracurricular organizations:** 100
Year Founded: 1892	**Percent Male:** 44%	
Private or Public: public	**Percent Female:** 56%	
Religious affiliation: none	**Total Percent Minority:** 15%	**3 Most popular majors:** Communications Studies, Nursing, Psychology
Location: suburban	**Percent African-American:** 5%	
Regular Application Deadline: 2-Feb	**Percent Asian/Pacific Islander:** 2%	**Student/Faculty ratio:** 19:01
Number of Applicants: 13,497	**Percent Hispanic:** 5%	**Tuition and Fees:** $19,356.00
Percent Accepted: 74%	**Percent Native-American:** 0%	**In State Tuition and Fees (if different):** $5,656.00
Percent Accepted who enroll: 29%	**Percent Other:** 3%	**Cost for Room and Board:** $8,466.00
Number Entering: 2,780	**Percent in-state / out of state:** 53%/47%	
Number of Transfers Accepted each Year: 862	**Percent from Public HS:** NA	
Mean SAT: NA		
Mean ACT: 23		

While the URI administration tries hard to shed the school's "Animal House" reputation of old, collegiates at this public university still enjoy a fun-filled four years. Students are drawn to URI's strong academic departments, such as business and management, and to its low in-state tuition. Of course, its reputation as a party school "doesn't hurt, either."

The "School" Part of a Party School

While URI students certainly have their fun, academic requirements are a central part of each student's life. The University of Rhode Island requires students to complete a number of courses in order to graduate, including classes in the natural sciences, fine arts, mathematics, languages, and social sciences. While this subject load may seem daunting, current URIers say that prospective students have nothing to fear. "Really, as long as you go to class, you'll be fine," said one male junior. "Teachers here tend to understand that this is college . . . they let some stuff slide."

It's also pretty easy to skip class and get notes from a friend—especially since introductory classes here can be so large that a professor would never notice your absence. Some courses at URI enroll as many as 500 students. This can be a good thing—you can get into any class "as long as you have taken the prerequisites." Plus, according to students, the average class only has 40 to 50 students. Certain majors are also required to take specific classes. Students rave about the chemical engineering, German, and business departments, and URI has long been known for its marine biology programs. The most popular major seems to be communications, which is also ranked by students as one of the school's easiest. The human development/family studies major is also considered to be among the less demanding, while engineering is considered particularly difficult. The pharmacy major is also considered one of the hardest, as students must maintain a certain GPA to be allowed to continue in the program. Classes can be "as competitive as you want." It may be true that many students "don't care," but there is definitely some competition among those who are "top in their programs".

URI faces a common problem of many large universities—TAs teach more classes than students had hoped for. Despite this, students say that professors are "approachable, if you make the effort." Grading tends to be "pretty reasonable," although grade inflation and scaling of grades varies by course and department. According to several undergraduates, the same course taught in sections by different professors will have "totally different material, grading, and workload."

For the more academically inclined graduate of the Rhode Island public school system, the University offers an impressive and prestigious honors program. The class sizes are generally smaller and the courses more rigorous. Students can apply directly after high school or after their freshman or sophomore years. Like most other universities, URI extends to its students the possibility of study abroad, which, for some Rhode Island weary scholars, is a great chance to "escape and have a blast." URI also offers a "Centennial Scholarship" for motivated and qualified students, which provides the lucky chosen few with a full ride.

In terms of upgrades, the University of Rhode Island is in the process of building a new $9 million environmental studies center on the Kingston Campus. A new business building has also popped up recently, and new dorms and dining halls are in the works.

Home Sweet Home

URI's campus is a random smattering of gothic, colonial and modern architecture. The Quad, at the center of campus, is picturesque and a great place to "hang out or do work." While the Quad is home to a large number of academic buildings, the Greek houses are further away on the outskirts of the sprawling campus. Campus dorms, the student center, and the library are all nearby.

The dorms at Rhode Island get mixed reviews. While the dorms tend not to have specific identities—there is really no particular "party dorm" or "frat dorm" (though there is a discrepancy between more social and less social ones)—they vary greatly by condition and age. "Some dorms are really beautiful," said a senior, "but I was very disappointed freshman year to learn that mine was not one of them." All dorms, except one, are coed by floor. There is an all-female dorm, as well as a substance-free dorm, although the alcohol policy is "strictly enforced" in all on-campus housing. The policy states that students under 21 may not have any alcohol in their rooms, while those of legal drinking age may possess "only a small amount, like a six-pack." According to students, the RAs "vary, but are basically there to make sure things don't get out of control," although one student was convinced his RA was put in place "to ruin my life." Penalties are high for breaking the alcohol policy, helping to explain why most students not only prefer to party off campus, but also often opt for off-campus housing after freshman or sophomore year. Sorority and fraternity houses, as well as apartments and private houses near campus, are popular with upperclassmen. Since on-campus housing is not guaranteed after sophomore year, and students complain that, "there is a serious housing shortage at URI," off-campus living is a popular option. Of course, that also means that many students have cars to get around. Fortunately, the relationship with locals is described as "very good," and students generally feel very safe around campus and beyond it.

URI students can chow down at one of the school's three main dining rooms or the oft-praised "Ram's Den." Several meal plans are available to URI students, who praised the flexibility, if not the fare. "The dining hall food is okay," said one sophomore, "it just takes some getting used to." At the Ram's Den students use food points purchased at the beginning of the semester to buy the delectable goodies offered at "the best place on campus." The other dining halls vary, with some serving fast food while others offer more complete entrees. Several students complained about the selection of local restaurants, noting that "Kingston is not the place for five-star dining."

Kingston is a rather uneventful place, leading most students to feel that "drinking and partying is really the only thing to do here." While one student pointed out that "of course nothing important ever happens at URI—this is Rhode Island!" the administration tries to keep things lively with academic lectures and on-campus social events. When students need a night of hard drinking and wild fun, they turn to the Greek scene and to the bars and clubs of Providence to let off some steam.

Getting Soaked on a Dry Campus

After URI was named "America's Top Party School," the administration made the alcohol policy much tougher and started to be stricter with fraternity parties. Despite this, most students claim URI campus is "officially dry, but really, very wet." As with most large state universities, Greek life is the dominant form of social activity on campus, despite the fact that only about 10 percent of students are involved in the 20 fraternities and sororities. This is the case because parties, which must be registered with the university police, are generally open to the URI public. Despite the tendency of Greek life to dominate, students reported relatively little tension between Greeks and non-Greeks. While most students agreed that, "almost everyone here drinks," they also concurred that "not drinking doesn't necessarily mean you have no social life." Overall, students agreed that "everyone at URI is very friendly, and it's easy to meet people no matter what you're into."

Extracurricular activities are a major part of students' lives at URI, although the student body generally laments the lack of school spirit. Basketball and football games are popular draws, especially when URI heads out against rival Providence College.

Other notable sports teams are volleyball, baseball, soccer and sailing. Club sports are very popular, although for some, "it can be hard getting people to show up."

The student senate and the student-run newspaper, *The Good 5 Cent Cigar*, are also big campus extracurriculars. The Student Entertainment Committee is responsible for making sure that URI undergrads have plenty of fun, social options. A variety of other activities, including the Experimental Art Society and the Surf Club keep students' minds busy and their bodies outdoors. Yes, that's right, the Surf Club—the beach right near URI is "definitely one of the best parts of going to school here."

In addition to clubs and sports, a great number of students have part-time jobs. "It's pretty easy to get a work-study job at the event center, academic halls, or dining halls," remarked one senior.

Diversity is celebrated on the URI campus, with recent efforts by student groups, as well as the administration, to ensure that students of all backgrounds are tolerant of one another. As one student explained, "It would be hard to define a certain, stereotypical URI student. Basically everyone here has their own style." Students also spoke of the surprising geographic diversity, despite the fact that URI is a state school.

> **"It's much more fun than I ever imagined Rhode Island could be."**

Overall, URI collegiates seem content. While some undergrads wished there was slightly more emphasis on academics than on partying, most agreed that motivated students can combine a good learning experience with a lot of fun. Many echoed one senior's statement that, "I wouldn't change my decision to come here for anything in the world." In the words of one sophomore: "It's much more fun than I ever imagined Rhode Island could be."—*Erica Ross*

FYI
If you come to URI, you'd better bring "your smile, because everyone else here will have theirs."
What is the typical weekend schedule? "Start drinking on Wednesday. Continue through Monday morning."
If I could change one thing about URI "I'd build a parking garage."
Three things every student should do before graduating from URI are "swim at Narragansett beach, learn to surf, and spend an afternoon on the Quad with friends."

South Carolina

Clemson University

Address: Clemson, 105 Sikes Hall, Box 345124, Clemson, SC 29634
Phone: 864-656-3311
E-mail Address: cuadmissions@clemson.edu
Web site URL: www.clemson.edu/admission/
Year Founded: 1889
Private or Public: public
Religious affiliation: none
Location: rural
Regular Application Deadline: 2-May
Number of Applicants: 12,463
Percent Accepted: 55%
Percent Accepted who enroll: 40%
Number Entering: 2,903
Number of Transfers Accepted each Year: 1,105
Mean SAT: 1,217
Mean ACT: 27

Middle 50% SAT range: 1,130–1,320
Middle 50% ACT range: 25–29
Early admission program (EA/ ED/ NA): NA
ED or EA Acceptance Rate: NA
Full time Undergraduate enrollment: 13,959
Total enrollment: 13,959
Percent Male: 54%
Percent Female: 46%
Total Percent Minority: 18%
Percent African-American: 7%
Percent Asian/Pacific Islander: 2%
Percent Hispanic: 1%
Percent Native-American: 0%
Percent Other: 8%
Percent in-state / out of state: 68%/32%
Percent from Public HS: 89%

Retention Rate: 87%
Graduation Rate: NA
Percent in On-campus housing: 44%
Percent affiliated with Greek system: 25%
Percent Varsity or Club Athletes: NA
Number of official organized extracurricular organizations: 275
3 Most popular majors: Business, Engineering, Education
Student/Faculty ratio: 15:01
Tuition and Fees: $19,824.00
In State Tuition and Fees (if different): $9,400.00
Cost for Room and Board: $5,874.00
Percent receiving Financial aid, first-year: 64%

Six out of seven days of the week, Clemson, S.C., is the typical Southern town. With a population of 12,000, which is significantly lower than the number of students at Clemson University, the town's small, quaint, charming, and filled with "white upper-class Republicans." But on Saturdays, you're transported to a whole new color palette, as "the whole town just turns orange." At Clemson, football games are the main events, and students very rarely miss a home game. "Everyone falls in love with football, tailgating is a way of life, and you are late if you're not partying by noon for an 8 p.m. game." Fans, visitors, and alumni travel miles to see the orange and purple Tigers play in a gigantic stadium capable of seating 81,473 roaring fans.

A Smorgasbord of Majors

Students at Clemson report that there seems to be a major for everyone, even those individuals whose "major" interests do not include academics. " 'Party Right Through May'—that's what all the slackers and athletes major in," one student said. "I'm not really sure what they do." Believe it or not, "Party Right Through May" does have an official title, and those fun-loving students holding "Parks, Recreation, and Tourism Management" degrees are especially attractive to the U.S. Army recruiters seeking trip schedulers for soldiers.

At the opposite end of the spectrum, many students are drawn to Clemson for its excellent engineering program. Current undergraduates eagerly await the completion of an automotive engineering graduate center paid for by a $10 million endowment by BMW for automotive research and development. An excited freshman said: "BMW only has one American plant and it's here and that's sweet. Clemson is going to be one of the best places to study automotive engineering." However, prospective engineering students and car enthusiasts should be warned that the program is not easy. Students report that engineering's high number of requirements significantly cut down course options for underclassmen.

Clemson students apply to one of five different colleges: Agriculture, Forestry, and Life Sciences; Architecture, Arts, and Humanities; Business and Behavioral Science; Engineering and Science; or Health, Education, and Human Development. Each semester, students must take 12 to 17 hours worth of classes a week. However, not all classes last the full duration of the semester. The ever-popular "Camping and Backpacking" course in the leisure skills department, for example, consists of two 75-minute classes for five weeks.

Clemson is a big public school, but students consider the class sizes to be about average. While some courses, such as the general chemistry lecture, can number to up 150 students, the average class size is 29. In terms of grading policies, grade inflation won't be found at Clemson, and, as one student simply put, "There is no rounding up here." The University recently completed a controversial two-year trial period of a plus/minus grading system in 2004 and is currently considering whether or not to implement such a system.

Sweet Home South Carolina?

Not quite. According to its students, Clemson apparently isn't so Southern in its hospitality. The rooms and the food earn sub-par ratings, and, while there are new dorms, students complain that most on-campus facilities are "pretty run down and old." For this reason, it is not mandatory for freshmen to live on campus, but surprisingly "the 'horseshoe' is the place to be freshman year—on warm days the grassy area behind the highrises, 'Lever Beach,' is covered with bikini-clad girls tanning, and guys tossing the football around; at night there's tons of people hanging around outside—normally waiting for shuttles to the big frat parties going on that night." Those who do choose to stay and live in freshman dorms, including one not-so-affectionately called Shoeboxes, give the experience high acclaim. As one student put it, "You might rag on the rooms while you live there, but the social scene and good times make it a place you never stop missing and reminiscing about long after you have to move out."

Looking to foster intellectual and social relationships, Clemson tends to group students in dorms based on interests. Marveled one student: "My entire hall is engineering students. It makes it easier in terms of studying." Another emphasized, "It's better to be closer to the people in your field because you can get input and feedback from them more easily and vice versa." A few particularly sought out housing options are the Stadium Suites and the Lightsey Apartments, but such options are also significantly more expensive. Stadium Suites is a four-story building right by the stadium, making it an ideal location for football fans, though one student lamented, "there's one tree in the way that prevents you from seeing the game from your suite."

The food options at Clemson are far from gourmet. They consist mostly of retail food courts, and there are two dining halls—one for east campus and one for west campus. While some students say the food quality has improved in recent years, other complain that "the food gets old. They're the same thing everyday." A new student center called the Hendrix Center was recently erected in the year 2000. Along with other standard food court items, at Hendrix, students can purchase Clemson ice cream and Clemson's other, slightly more eclectic, specialty: blue cheese. Such delicacies are due in large part to Clemson's Department of Food Science and Human Nutrition, and students appreciate its contributions in the new center. "The Hendrix Center is the central spot. [Clemson] kind of centralized everything that was once a bit scattered. You used to have to walk really far to get good food."

Zoom Zoom

While the BMW engineering awaits completion, most students (freshmen included) satisfy their thirst for automotives by keeping their cars on campus. One student warned, "You absolutely need a car." Many students find Clemson isolated and a bit too "in the middle of nowhere." Anderson is the closest "decent-sized" town and Greenville is in the vicinity as well, but both are beyond walking distance. Other students defended the campus and one insisted that "it's beautiful. A lot of the colleges are in the city, but here, you have a real campus feel because you know everyone on campus is pretty much a student." Many bored students go off campus and into the town on weekends to party and go to bars. Since most of the Clemson population is from South Carolina, many also visit home on weekends but only if there's an away game. Stated one student, "If there's not a football game, it's pretty dead. . . . We become a suitcase college. Everyone packs up and goes."

"If there's not a football game, it's pretty dead. . . . We become a suitcase college. Everyone packs up and goes."

Where Is My Car?

So what's the catch to Clemson's being named the No. 2 party school in the nation in 2003? According to students, the boast-worthy reputation only holds for the 40 percent of guys and 70 percent of gals in fraternities and sororities. One dejected student lamented, "I don't know how welcome I'd be. They're not too inviting." Another said, "If you're not with a friend, for the most part, you can't get in [to the fraternities and sororities]." With only four bars and one on-campus pub around, one frat brother said, "I'm glad I pledged." So what's a fun-seeking non-Greek Clemson student to do? Turn to the strong athletic community, of course. Students note that some of the "big sports teams" step up and are known to throw their own parties and dances.

Alcohol is prevalent on campus, but if anyone gets caught, the university cracks down seriously for a period of time. "They know you're going to drink, but they want you to keep it inside. You can definitely get away with drinking." The university apparently prefers to being kept in the dark about its students' drinking habits. According to one student, "Signs around campus say 60 percent of students have 0–4 drinks a week, but I seriously don't believe that."

Southern Belles and Gentlemen

While the alcohol may flow freely, students report no need for beer goggles at Clemson. One male student raved that "the girls are hot. There are slightly more guys than girls, but there are a lot of good-looking girls. It's not like Georgia Tech." Are such claims too good to be true, or at least too good to last? Some Clemson students are upset at the university's recent attempts to make the admission process more difficult. One upset individual complained that "They're making entrances too hard. They're trying to get into the top 20 list because they're 27 right now on some list . . . so they're making everything ridiculous and we're just getting more and more engineering dorks."

Dorks included, the Clemson student body as a whole can be characterized as typically Southern and some say even a bit closed-minded. Students report very little diversity in terms of color and perspective. One student expressed that "the only black people here are pretty much athletes. Honestly, if I were black, I wouldn't want to go here." A minority student confirmed his sentiments: "The education is everything I expected. Clemson doesn't have the total package of college I was expecting, but I got the main thing I came here to get. I'd do the college thing over if I could." Yet another student stated that, in the dining halls, "It's a little bit self-segregated. Nothing new from high school." Students went as far to say that one campus building, the Strom Thurman Institute, proves disconcerting to the numerous students who pass it on their way to classes everyday and one student wondered, "I'm wondering what sort of message that sends to students."

While students report that Clemson may not provide the varying and stimulating perspectives a more diverse college might provide, they also stress its strengths and high quality of its education. "It would be almost impossible for someone to find a school with more pride than Clemson." Named the No. 1 public school in Time magazine in 2001, and praised by automobile and Tiger fans alike, Clemson is definitely the place to be.—*Robert James*

FYI

If you come to Clemson, you'd better bring "orange."

What's the typical weekend schedule? "Party or stay in with movies or go out to eat Thurs and Fri. "On football weekends, Saturday is entirely football—tailgates before and after the game, and usually a party afterwards, whether we win or lose. Sunday is the recovery and study day."

If I could change one thing about Clemson, I'd "make it snow in the wintertime, because it only gets cold enough to snow every so often."

Three things every student at Clemson should do before leaving are "go swimming off of the dam, play our Frisbee golf course and get involved with one of our student organizations."

Furman University

Address: Furman, 3300 Poinsett Hwy., Greenville, SC 29613
Phone: 864-294-2034
E-mail Address: admissions@furman.edu
Web site URL: www.engagefurman.com
Year Founded: 1826
Private or Public: private
Religious affiliation: none
Location: urban
Regular Application Deadline: 16-Jan
Number of Applicants: NA
Percent Accepted: 56%
Percent Accepted who enroll: 32%
Number Entering: 251
Number of Transfers Accepted each Year: 51
Mean SAT: NA
Mean ACT: NA

Middle 50% SAT range: V:590–690, M:590–690
Middle 50% ACT range: 25–31
Early admission program (EA/ ED/ NA): ED
ED or EA Acceptance Rate: 58%
Full time Undergraduate enrollment: 2,739
Total enrollment: 2,759
Percent Male: 41%
Percent Female: 59%
Total Percent Minority: 10%
Percent African-American: 7%
Percent Asian/Pacific Islander: 2%
Percent Hispanic: 1%
Percent Native-American: 0%
Percent Other: 90%
Percent in-state / out of state: 28%/72%

Percent from Public HS: 63%
Retention Rate: 94%
Graduation Rate: 86%
Percent in On-campus housing: 90%
Percent affiliated with Greek system: 75%
Percent Varsity or Club Athletes: NA
Number of official organized extracurricular organizations: 152
3 Most popular majors: Social Sciences, Business/Marketing, History
Student/Faculty ratio: 11:01
Tuition and Fees: $28,840.00
Cost for Room and Board: $7,552.00
Percent receiving Financial aid, first-year: 72%

Furman University's "gorgeous" campus and "stellar" academics make this small school in Greenville, South Carolina, a wise choice for students who are looking for a liberal-arts college, and one with a strongly Southern, traditional background. As one pleased sophomore business major put it, "Anyone who wants a great education, holds traditional moral views, and is accustomed to the South would love Furman."

Bread-and-Butter Courses

Academics at Furman are challenging and rewarding, students say, and the small size has its benefits: "Furman only focuses on undergrads so they definitely consume all of the attention." A psychology major commented, "Furman allows students to be active participants in class, and is the perfect size for individual attention and instruction."

Undergraduates here receive one-on-one attention from professors in classes of 20 or smaller, and encounter no teaching assistants except in administrative positions or as lab assistants.

For a school this small, academics provide a great deal of variety, but the bread-and-butter courses tend to be most in demand. The sciences, especially psychology, chemistry, and biology, are particularly strong and

perennially popular. Languages such as French and Spanish and education are also common majors. Although the most popular majors are fairly typical, there are some unique courses: one sociology class, Social Problems, studies local problems of food growth, racism and urban planning, and ventures on field trips to collect research data.

But intelligence is not enough to succeed without hard work, said one sophomore: "To get an A, you have to be willing to log some serious hours at the library." A communications and sociology double major added, "Furman's academics are very challenging. In order for me to make an A, I must spend about two to three hours studying a day per class."

Pearls and Heels

What sets Furman apart from its small liberal-arts cousins up North is the strongly Southern traditional culture, fed by a largely wealthy, well-bred majority. This conservatism extends to the sometimes "narrow-minded" conservative politics of its student body. The unofficial Furman tagline is "the country club of the South," and the unofficial dress code is pearls and stiletto heels. "When I went to class in my sweatpants one day," one girl said, "a classmate asked me if I was sick."

However, many students appreciate what they see as Southern politeness and gentility. One recently arrived freshman commented, "The people here are some of the nicest I have ever come across." Another student added that although Furman students are indeed wealthy, "Furman has a stereotype of being stuck up, but it isn't that true, and actually provides a lot of laughs."

> "When I went to class in my sweatpants one day, a classmate asked me if I was sick."

There are a variety of fun traditions at this Southern school that make up for its conservatism. During orientation week, boys find dates for an annual freshman picnic at the president's house by picking the girls' shoes out of boxes. Following the picnic, freshmen go "fountain hopping," attend the "my tie" dance, and finally the freshmen guys serenade the girls at midnight. Legend also says that if a couple kisses under the campus bell tower, they will marry.

Other aspects of Southern culture take getting used to for some students. The majority of the student body is white and Christian, and the Bible is listed as the most popular "favorite book" choice on Furman students' Facebook profiles. So many students go to brunch still dressed in church clothes after Sunday services that others will also dress up just to fit in.

Furman students generally enjoy a high quality of life. All undergraduates are required to live on campus for four years. Freshman and sophomore dorm complexes are "nothing to brag about," but the North Village apartments for juniors and seniors are enviable. Unfortunately, among Furman's downsides is the mediocrity of its food. According to one girl, "Southern cuisine in general is fattening, and the dining hall staff adds tons of butter and oil to make things better. So, right now, those wanting to avoid the freshman 15 have to make a conscious effort to eat healthy."

ROTC and Purple Body Paint

Outside academics, Furman students keep themselves busy with extracurriculars and social lives. There aren't many options for socializing on campus, however. "Outside the academic world, there are two types of people: those who go to frat parties and drink, and those who go out to dinner and then come back to watch a movie," said one sophomore. "There isn't much in between." Drinking is outlawed on campus, but off-campus fraternity houses and bars ensure that undergraduates do drink in great numbers. Drugs, however, are unpopular. In general, Furman students seem either to be in serious relationships or single.

The city of Greenville is nothing to scoff at; although it is one of the largest cities in northern South Carolina, it has a distinctly "college-town" feel. Greenville welcomes Furman students "with open arms" to its sizeable downtown, with a variety of restaurants set against the Reedy River. "The best ice cream I have ever had," one student added, "is located in a local hangout called Spill the Beans—on any given night the place is packed with students and members of the community alike."

Fraternities and sororities are popular for non-varsity athletes, as are Christian organizations. Intramural sports are also relatively well attended, although not everyone plays with the same level of seriousness. Sororities make a strong intramural presence; girls who don't belong to sororities can often be out of luck in trying to put a team together.

There are several more extracurricular options besides fraternities and intramurals, including plays and musicals and a large Army ROTC program. A fair number of students also have on-campus jobs in the library or the gym.

Varsity athletic teams are often successful, with a high-caliber football team, despite a lackluster show of school spirit. Students are making new efforts with organizations such as SWAC, "students who actually cheer" (and get decked out in purple body paint), but for the most part, "students are much more concerned with the pre-game tailgates" than attending the games themselves, said one student. Many would-be fans are so busy with schoolwork during the week that even the fan base for the popular football and basketball teams is quite small.

Southern Comfort

Despite the drawbacks of Furman's conservative, homogeneous student body, the tight-knit population and gorgeous campus grow on many students. But what some see as elite conservatism, others see as a legacy of moral values and Old South traditions. In the end, the excellent classes and the intimacy of the academic life here make all the difference and turn Furman into a valuable experience for many.—*Yotam Barkai*

FYI

If you come to Furman, you'd better bring "your pearls and heels if you're a girl and your bowtie if you're a boy."

What's the typical weekend schedule? "Friday: finish class, relax, and start partying; Saturday: wake up early to get dressed in your best for tailgating and a football game, Sunday: church followed by lunch and lots of studying."

If I could change one thing about Furman, "I'd change it to a slightly bigger size so it wouldn't have that high school feel."

Three things that every student should do before graduating are "steal a campus golf cart, run through the fountains, and go to the TKE Rockstar party in the fall."

South Carolina University

Address: University of South Carolina, 902 Sumter St. Access, Columbia, SC 29208
Phone: 800-868-5872
E-mail Address: admissions-ugrad@sc.edu
Web site URL: www.sc.edu
Year Founded: 1805
Private or Public: public
Religious affiliation: none
Location: urban
Regular Application Deadline: 2-Dec
Number of Applicants: 13,946
Percent Accepted: 63%
Percent Accepted who enroll: 42%
Number Entering: 3,697
Number of Transfers Accepted each Year: 2,058
Mean SAT: 1,172
Mean ACT: 25

Middle 50% SAT range: NA
Middle 50% ACT range: 23–28
Early admission program (EA/ ED/ NA): NA
ED or EA Acceptance Rate: NA
Full time Undergraduate enrollment: 18,648
Total enrollment: 25,950
Percent Male: 45%
Percent Female: 55%
Total Percent Minority: 19%
Percent African-American: 13%
Percent Asian/Pacific Islander: 3%
Percent Hispanic: 2%
Percent Native-American: 0%
Percent Other: 1%
Percent in-state / out of state: 83%/17%
Percent from Public HS: NA

Retention Rate: 86%
Graduation Rate: 62%
Percent in On-campus housing: 40%
Percent affiliated with Greek system: 29%
Percent Varsity or Club Athletes: NA
Number of official organized extracurricular organizations: 300
3 Most popular majors: Experimental Psychology, Public Relations/Image Management
Student/Faculty ratio: 17:01
Tuition and Fees: $19,836.00
In State Tuition and Fees (if different): $7,408.00
Cost for Room and Board: $6,520.00

I n spite of initial reservations "within a week I was obsessed," one senior summarized of her initial experience at South Carolina University. This passion seems to extend to most of USC students, who without hesitation, will sing their school's praises and show their collegiate pride at the drop of a hat or the blow of a whistle. Displays of devotion are especially evident at the ever-so-popular, and often over-the-top football games. But South Carolina University offers so much more than just grand sporting events. The academic programs, extensive extracurricular choices, and an exhausting party scene, all contribute to forming a memorable experience that most students, when given the choice, would wish to live all over again.

University 101

Despite South Carolina's large student body of 27,000, there are few complaints about becoming just a number. The class sizes at the University vary widely from 20 to 300, with intro classes generally on the high end of the spectrum. However, large lectures come equipped with smaller discussion sections to ensure that each student gets personal attention. "I have never taken a class that had more than 50 students," one Honors College student assured. Other students praised the numerous options for more intimate academic settings, often citing the professor for "making" the class. One senior raved that "[the professors] have been nothing but awesome," and students have generally described the professorship staff as being friendly, easily accessible and known to make great efforts to learn the names of all of their students. Among the faculty sit several famous names such as Don Fowler, the former chairman of the Democratic National Committee.

With 14 schools to choose from within the University, there is something for everyone. The major unanimously proclaimed as the most popular and also the most difficult is the number one nationally ranked International Business program. The major accepts only 50 people each year and attracts students from all over the country, and many from overseas as well. South Carolina also offers unique majors such as Sports and Entertainment Management or Hotel and Restaurant Tourism Management. And for the top qualified students of each year, there are programs such as the Honors Program and Capstone Scholars. For freshmen, an atypical class that is offered and sometimes required is University 101, a class that focuses solely on helping students adjust and make the best of university life. Aside from the required English, social science, and history courses (all of which students can place out of), there is a unique assortment of ways students can expand their knowledge, whether learning how to shag (the dance that is,) taking a wine tasting class or studying Super Bowl commercials (it's actually a class!) to vary their schedules. Overall the workload itself is generally deemed manageable. Some students complain about the large amounts of reading they receive, but as one sophomore explained, "People are not missing out on social life."

Where the Beer Is Green and the Beach Is Near

South Carolina offers many great ways to have a good time. Although many students contend that no particular social scene dominates, the Greek parties are the most common ones listed. For the 21+ crowd (or those with really good IDs) there are the Five Points downtown bars. People usually start going out on Thursday night, especially with Thursday being "college night" in the downtown area.

Even though only about 17 percent of students belong to a sorority or a fraternity, students generally agree that Greek life is "really noticeable." During the first week of school, one of the most prominent things on campus is the excess of flyers inviting people to rush.

And students estimate that a majority of the population does rush, especially girls. "During my freshman year half the kids on my floor rushed," one senior remembered. The Greeks, in addition to hosting regular weekend parties, also organize many exclusive theme parties and are the driving force behind Homecoming week festivities.

Nevertheless, as a senior pointed out, "you can have fun even if you're not Greek." Big annual celebrations include St. Patrick's Day at Five Points, when everything is blocked off from the city and the beer is green, and of course, Halloween weekend is "always fun." Many alternative entertainment options are provided by the student-run Carolina Productions. The group organizes main events on campus such as concerts, the Wacky Wednesday Booth that plans something new and fun for each Wednesday at the Student Center, and has even been responsible for bringing Bob Saget to campus. For a more low-key night, there are the dorm parties, which are especially popular for underclassmen. But be forewarned. Despite the abundance of partying on campus, the drinking rules are strict—SLED or undercover officers patrol the area and are quick to enforce the rules. All freshman dorms are labeled dry and all rooms in the upperclassmen dorms in which persons under 21 reside are dry, as well. However, as one freshman observed, "You can drink in the dorm—if you can get away with it." The ability to "get away with it" mainly depends on your RA and on how belligerent you become. One junior pointed out that although "we are not a dry campus," people are understanding of those who do not drink. As an alternative to partying, many students travel to Charleston on weekends where the beaches are plentiful.

Our Stereotypes Are Diverse

Many come to South Carolina with the expectation of a crowd of typical southern girls and frat guy types. But more often than not, students are pleasantly surprised by the diversity on campus. Although one junior described the day-to-day look as having "a beachy atmosphere—there are shorts and sandals everywhere," there is a greater stylistic range. But it doesn't mean there aren't stereotypes. As one sophomore put it, "You can definitely pick out the Greeks by their clothes, and you can definitely pick out 'emos' by their clothes." Nevertheless, there is a fair amount of geographic and ethnic diversity. Students hail from all 50 states and there is a well-represented international community at South Carolina. Some students acknowledge, however, that the campus often has segregation lines among groups—whites and blacks have their own separate frats and parties. "Walking around campus you [would] think it is segregated," said one student. Students, however, assure that there is no tension on campus, and that the relations among races are by no means "uncivil." Students are making strides to creating a more unified collegiate atmosphere, which even in its current state, is still generally described as very friendly.

Horseshoes and Pizza Huts

Due to numerous dorm renovation projects, one senior explained that, "housing right now is in limbo." Still, all freshmen are required to live on campus, spread out between the freshman-only dorms, many of which are single sex with strict visitation rules for members of the opposite sex. All freshman dorms feature suite-style rooms (two double bedrooms, a common room, and a bathroom). Due to dorm renovations, the upperclassmen are not guaranteed housing, however, this is not a problem as many, if not most, upperclassmen prefer off-campus housing—especially at the nearby university-exclusive apartment complexes. For those who choose to stay on campus, there are several coed options, including Roost, which mainly houses athletes and The Green Dorm, a completely environmentally friendly habitat, in addition to several themed communities such as the French community, the Spanish community (in each of which only that language is spoken), the International community, and the Music community. Currently, the University is also building a multi-million dollar Research community. The Greeks, especially in their sophomore year, often opt to reside in the multi-million dollar houses that populate the Greek village. All students are able to bring cars, and it seems like all do. Parking, or lack thereof, is the most common complaint heard from the students. "To get to class on time, you have to get there thirty minutes before to find a spot to park," one student warned.

South Carolina University students vote the campus food as "Most likely to make you gain the freshman 15." There are five dining halls, including the Russell House, which serves both as the student union and the grand marketplace, i.e. the main dining hall. Dining options include everything from a salad bar to an overabundance of fast food chains like Burger King, Chic-Fil-A, Taco Bell, and Pizza Hut where students can use their meal plans. Luckily, the city houses many privately owned restaurants that, all in all, "gives the city more character."

The campus itself is generally described as pretty with a smattering of modern industrial buildings, many newly renovated buildings, and of course, the horseshoe with "an old, traditional, southern feel to it." The horseshoe—you guessed it—is shaped like a horseshoe and it serves as the main, grassy hangout area for students looking to picnic or play Frisbee. Most importantly the campus is regarded as safe. "Considering the size of this university, they have done a good job of protected us," one student praised. Call boxes which are located throughout campus (you supposedly cannot turn around without seeing at least one), serve as emergency call services. A shuttle service also operates on campus.

The Loyal Gamecocks

Many students at South Carolina "rely on organizations to find [their] niche" a senior observed. Some of the more prominent groups include Student Government, the Triple A's (Association of African Americans), and of course Carolina Productions. For the politically aspiring there are the College Republicans and Young Dems; for the journalistically aspiring there is the *Daily Gamecock*, and for the socially aspiring, there are 14 sororities and 19 frats from which to choose.

> "Everyone here is obsessed with football, even those who are not athletic."

If all else fails, the uniting theme of the University seems to be sports. Club and intramural sports serve as competitive but very fun alternatives to varsity. But perhaps the most popular ways for being involved in the athletic life is actually just attending the varsity games. South Carolina's talented teams are fun to watch and support. The baseball and basketball games are both very well attended, but the king of all remains football and people fight for tickets, which sell out almost immediately. "Everyone here is obsessed with football, even those who are not athletic," one sophomore declared. The annual game against the archrival Clemson is among the most exciting and is preceded with a Tiger Burn—a pep rally and ceremonial burning of a paper-mâché Clemson's Tiger mascot. The proud Gamecocks attend the games always dressed in their best—pearls, cocktail dresses, blazers, and bow. The tailgates begin at noon and last for about five or more hours until the game begins. The Gamecocks are known for their loyalty; they cheer loudly until the last minute, win or loose.

It is easy to get swept up in the enthusiasm of the football crowd of the always-filled-to-the-brim William-Brice stadium. Such an exhilarating feeling is a good reflection of the mentality of South Carolina University's students. Any initial reservations incoming students might have are quickly replaced by feelings of school pride and affection. Because whether it be the campus, vast array of extracurriculars, or the friendly people, it is good to be a Gamecock.—*Dorota Poplawska*

FYI

If you come to South Carolina, you'd better bring "Rainbows (sandals that everyone wears) and dressy clothes for those football games."

What is the typical weekend schedule? "Thursday attend college night at Five Points and party on Friday. Saturdays are dominated by tailgates and football games that take up all day. Catch up on work Sunday after sleeping in or going to church."

If I could change one thing about South Carolina, I'd "change the efficiency of parking."

Three things every student at South Carolina should do before graduating are "Go to Five Points, stay till the end of a football game, and get to know a professor on a more personal basis."

Wofford College

Address: Wofford, 429 North Church St., Spartanburg, SC 29303
Phone: 864-597-4182
E-mail Address: boggsdw@wofford.edu
Web site URL: www.wofford.edu
Year Founded: 1854
Private or Public: private
Religious affiliation: United Methodist
Location: small city
Regular Application Deadline: 1-Feb
Number of Applicants: 2,089
Percent Accepted: 57%
Percent Accepted who enroll: 31%
Number Entering: 378
Number of Transfers Accepted each Year: 19
Mean SAT: 1,247
Mean ACT: 25

Middle 50% SAT range: 1,170–1,330
Middle 50% ACT range: 22–27
Early admission program (EA/ ED/ NA): ED
ED or EA Acceptance Rate: 60%
Full time Undergraduate enrollment: 1,228
Total enrollment: 1,240
Percent Male: 52%
Percent Female: 48%
Total Percent Minority: 10.5%
Percent African-American: 6%
Percent Asian/Pacific Islander: 2%
Percent Hispanic: 1%
Percent Native-American: <1%
Percent Other: 1%
Percent in-state / out of state: 37%/63%

Percent from Public HS: 70%
Retention Rate: 90%
Graduation Rate: 78.5%
Percent in On-campus housing: 91%
Percent affiliated with Greek system: 55%
Percent Varsity or Club Athletes: 23%
Number of official organized extracurricular organizations: 91
3 Most popular majors: Biology, Business Economics, English
Student/Faculty ratio: 11:01
Tuition and Fees: $26,110.00
Cost for Room and Board: $7,260.00
Percent receiving Financial aid, first-year: 53%

Wofford College offers a tight-knit community and strong teacher-student relationships for a student body that is smaller than the size of most high schools. With approximately 1,240 students, Wofford reserves a solid liberal arts education for a select group. Wofford's location in the traditional South impacts student culture and it's a known fact that "many of the ladies went to debutante balls." But Wofford especially stands out for its Division 1 Athletics. With such a small student body, "one in six guys plays football." Pearls, sports, and prep don't diminish the fact that Wofford is widely respected for a much raved about pre-medicine program and "many students go into politics" after graduation. There's no doubt that Wofford grads impact the lives of South Carolinians since "three of the South Carolina State Supreme Court justices graduated from Wofford."

Is There a Doctor in the Classroom?

Opened in 1854 and still affiliated with the Methodist Church, Wofford has remained small by choice. The administration reportedly has no plans to expand enrollment but instead plans to concentrate on providing a select group of students with a strong education in the humanities, arts, and sciences. Students say that "the small class sizes are really nice." One student warns, however, that due to Wofford's size, "there is not a wide variety of classes." Professors are especially accessible and maintain an "open door policy," according to students. "I didn't expect the professors to be so understanding, but they are like high school teachers in that sense. They want to help you out." Undergraduates are required to take courses in the humanities, English, fine arts, foreign language, science, history, philosophy, math, physical education and religion. These general education requirements are meant to ensure that by the end of their first two years, students have taken classes they normally would not have considered. Students are also required to complete four interim projects. The month of January is designated as Interim, a time between the two regular semesters when students can research, travel, take an internship, or work on an independent project. Interim projects on campus can include courses such as 'The Passion of the Christ' as Film, Sacred Art, Theology, and Cultural Maelstrom" or "Web Design For People Who Do Other Things For A Living." Off-campus travel programs in January 2006 included "A Cultural Tour of Ireland: From the Celtic Twilight to the Celtic Tiger" and "Scuba diving adventure on the Dutch Island of Bonaire, the fish capital of the Caribbean." Internship projects and service learning can even take you to Capitol Hill for a month. The Interim permits and encourages teachers and students to explore the new and untried, and most interim projects are graded Pass/Fail.

Among the most popular majors at Wofford are biology, business economics, political science, history, and English. "Business Economics is seen as a fairly easy program," one student said, and "sociology is picked on for having the easiest major." But "in general everyone respects each other because every major requires a lot of time and effort." The science department is reported to be particularly strong. One student said that as a physics major, "people tend to hold me in somewhat (unwarranted) high regard because there are so few of us. I have a class this semester where I am the only student in the class." But there is no doubt that the sciences and particularly the biology major are "top-notch" at Wofford and many students go on to medical school.

Tech Savvy

Wofford's efforts to provide cutting-edge technical services to its students are highlighted in a January 2006 article on "Coolest Campus Tech" on Forbes magazine's Web site (www.forbes.com). The article focuses on the Wofford program called FYI (First Year Interface), which allows freshmen to meet and greet via a MySpace-style Web site. After sharing profiles, photos, bedtimes and partying habits on the site, Wofford lets students who hit it off become roommates. They also may contact members of the Student Life staff with questions about what to expect when preparing to come to Wofford. The student profiles are searchable for similar interests, geographic areas and other information. Wofford also has begun posting podcasts to its Web site (www.wofford.edu) for listening and downloading audio recordings of campus programs and events. Wofford not only uses technology to help its students acclimate to campus. In 2002, Wofford began The Novel Experience—a program that asks incoming students to read an assigned novel over the summer and to write essays prior to arrival in Spartanburg. In early September, a town-gown exercise takes place when student groups and professors are assigned to eat at local restaurants through a lottery, discussing the novel over dinner. About a week later, the author comes to campus for a special address. "Talking with the author and the professors was definitely a highlight," one student said. "Because it happens in the first week of school, you go with your humanities class and you get to know them really well. It helped to make it more comfortable." Rising freshmen also have the option to attend a program called The Summit. This program takes place before the start of school, and new students spend a few days at a nice summer camp and go whitewater rafting. "It's where you first meet most of the people you come to hang out with."

Dorm Life: A Necessary Experience

An online lottery system sorts all dorm assignments and seniority is prioritized. Halls are coed in four of the dorms; two other dorms have two all-girl halls and all-guy halls per floor. The two freshman dorms accommodate men and women separately. Marsh Hall—the freshman dorm for men—is known as "particularly miserable, crazy and disgusting all at the same time. But all in all, a necessary experience." Greene Hall is the freshmen girls' dorm and "where freshman guys spend most of their time." All students living in dorms have the convenient advantage of a five or ten minute walk to classroom buildings. "If I wake up late at 9:20 I can still get to a 9:30 class." On the way, students enjoy the shade of many oak trees or stop to lounge on the benches near the central campus field. There are plans in the works to provide a type of campus "village" to students, comprised of apartment-like facilities in renovated houses Wofford purchased recently. Campus is "much safer" than the surrounding areas in Spartanburg. According to students, "it's kind of a rough town in places" and "people tend to stay within the 'Wofford bubble'."

Frat Row, Football, and More

"Greek life at Wofford is huge" and more than 50 percent of the student body is Greek. The Fraternity row (location on campus for fraternity houses and called "the row" by students) is the dominant social scene on campus. It's a popular site for a shaving cream fight and "you can't miss out on slip and slide at the row." "The frat row is a typical site of first-time meetings between folks." One of the most talked about days of the year is fraternity Bid Day when freshmen boys find out which fraternity they're pledging. A popular celebration follows. Spring Weekend has many activities and is a time when "you should party extremely hard." In addition to the popular varsity athletic teams, like men's and women's basketball, "we have an ultimate Frisbee team and a fly fishing organization—which is funded by the school for their equipment and trips." One student called it "a sweet gig."

Wofford and Spartanburg are not inter-changeable. With the exception of a few bars and the "gracious discounts" many local businesses offer to students, there is not much interaction. "I don't think that the two are intertwined unless there is an athletic event" one student said. Another student points out that "the town's heyday was gone years ago because it was once a big textile city." Wofford is located in "an underprivileged area so we interact with the community in a variety of ways through service learning and volunteer work," a student said. Wofford reportedly hosts two events during the school year for children in the area to attend. One student feels that "Wofford does a great job interacting with the surrounding community." Student groups on campus include Campus Ambassadors—students who volunteer their time to give tours to prospective students. The Fellowship of Christian Athletes (FCA) involves many students and "is held in high regard." The Outdoors Club is another option for bikers, hikers and climbers. "Most students are passionate about the clubs they are involved in" and "each group has their fanatic."

Southern Ladies and Gents

There's no getting around it. Most students say that "Wofford is typically viewed as a white conservative school." Students who attend Wofford are "particularly preppy and from 'old money' families or parents with white-collar careers." One student put it, "It seems like everyone's dad is either a doctor or an attorney." While some students admitted there is geographic diversity and students definitely come to Wofford from a variety of states in the Southeast—"there seems like there are as many out-of-state students as there are in-state"—ethnic diversity is not strong. "It's not diverse. Only about 10 percent of the school is made up of minority students." The "frat look" is very popular with "Sperry's, khakis and sunglasses with croakies making a dominant appearance all over campus" and "pastel colors are popularly worn by both guys and girls." According to another student, "the attitude is a positive and confident one. Students are proud to be at Wofford." While the Wofford student is stereotypically characterized as rich and preppy, "there are many people who do not fit this stereotype at all. In general, everyone here is friendly and you can always expect a hello when walking down the sidewalks on campus." The same mentality translates to the classroom where "there's always a comfortable setting. You just raise your hand if you have a question and the teacher will answer you."

"Students are proud to be at Wofford."

Any school that takes pride in its history as Wofford does is bound to have unique traditions. Old Main is the first building at the school's founding and the plaque is en-graved with the misspelling of the word "benificent" rather than "beneficent." For Wofford students, rubbing the mislaid "i" on a plaque at Old Main brings them luck on exams. If you're a student who desires personal attention at a small liberal arts college and who hopes for the benefits of an incredible network of alumni—"who are always there to offer jobs to the next graduates"—Wofford's luck is just waiting to rub off on you.—*Bess Hinson*

FYI

If you come to Wofford, you'd better bring "sunglasses with croakies, polo shirts, pearls and a flask."

What's the typical weekend schedule? "A sports game or workout during the day. Next, dinner or a movie with friends and then to fraternity row all night."

If you could change one thing about Wofford, it'd be "more diversity—a larger variety of students who are also more open-minded."

Three things every student at Wofford should do before graduating are "swim in the fountain after jumping in the mud on Guys' Bid Day, ring the bell in the Old Main building, date someone."

South Dakota

University of South Dakota

Address: University of South Dakota, 414 E. Clark, Vermillion, SD 57069

Phone: 877-269-6837

E-mail Address: admissions@usd.edu

Web site URL: www.usd.edu

Year Founded: 1862

Private or Public: public

Religious affiliation: none

Location: suburban

Regular Application Deadline: rolling

Number of Applicants: 3,044

Percent Accepted: 86%

Percent Accepted who enroll: 39%

Number Entering: 1,128

Number of Transfers Accepted each Year: 1,099

Mean SAT: NA

Mean ACT: 23

Middle 50% SAT range: NA

Middle 50% ACT range: 20–25

Early admission program (EA/ ED/ NA): NA

ED or EA Acceptance Rate: NA

Full time Undergraduate enrollment: 6,468

Total enrollment: 8,241

Percent Male: 38%

Percent Female: 62%

Total Percent Minority: 5%

Percent African-American: 1%

Percent Asian/Pacific Islander: 1%

Percent Hispanic: 1%

Percent Native-American: 2%

Percent Other: 0%

Percent in-state / out of state: 70%/30%

Percent from Public HS: NA

Retention Rate: 71%

Graduation Rate: 48%

Percent in On-campus housing: 31%

Percent affiliated with Greek system: 24%

Percent Varsity or Club Athletes: NA

Number of official organized extracurricular organizations: 130

3 Most popular majors: Business Administration/ Management, Psychology

Student/Faculty ratio: 15:01

Tuition and Fees: $7,569.00

In State Tuition and Fees (if different): $2,690.00

Cost for Room and Board: $4,964.00

The University of South Dakota simply refuses to allow its students to have the normal college experience. Residential assistants routinely inspect dorms for alcohol and fine guilty students $100 in addition to enforcing probation. Vermillion, the town in which USD is located, lacks the clubs and pubs college students live for in other states. And football games, held outdoors at most colleges nationwide, are held indoors in the Dakota Dome, where students report it generally "gets kind of warm." It may all sound a tad bit stifling, but a closer look at USD shows that in fact quite the opposite is true.

Live, Local, and Late-Breaking Majors . . .

USD is comprised of four different colleges: the College of Arts and Sciences, the School of Business, the School of Education, and the College of Fine Arts. The conveniently located School of Law and the School of Medicine also provide guidance and resources for students interested on a pre-law or pre-med track. Most USD students enter the College of Arts and Sciences and focus on a variety of majors within the wide-reaching and traditionally defined liberal arts realm. While there are many interesting majors to choose from, some concentrations, such as communications and business, rise to the top and attract the most students. And with distinguished alumni in media such as Tom Brokaw and Pat O'Brien, is it any wonder that most USD students flock to the strong mass communications department? While such large majors at USD dominate the spotlight, prospective students should also be aware of the comparatively smaller yet well-received concentrations that USD has to offer. Students sing the praises of the criminal justice department and describe the classes as "particularly interesting." Although USD is a state school, students are quick to point out that it's not overwhelming. With a student to faculty ratio of 14:1, USD rivals many state schools unable to boast such close interaction between students and staff.

USD students are generally described as "laidback" and "not stressed," which may be attributed to the lack of pluses and minuses in the grading system as well as the open opportunity to take classes satisfactory/unsatisfactory (known in other college systems as "pass/fail"). One student even suggested that on a given weekday, most students, depending on major, are "all out getting drunk." However, another student disagreed with this assessment, stating that classes can be "pretty tough" and that studying is "what a lot of people do during the week, mainly." Regardless of whether USD students are holding a pen or a bottle on most weekday nights, students warn about exercising caution in choosing classes, as confused students might find that advising at USD unable to meet their needs. As one student noted, "Even if you go down to talk to the advisors, they don't really help you all that much. You've got to do your own work and talk to older students."

More Tests?

Requirements at USD are atypical of the larger state university. Students are required to take a standardized test, the Collegiate Assessment of Academic Proficiency, before graduating, in addition to fulfilling a certain number of credit hours. These requirements, depending on college, focus on the study of mathematics, natural sciences, social sciences, and humanities and fine arts. Students are also required to take Introduction to Computers but can test out of it by taking an Information Technology Literacy Exam. All students are also required to take a test in Information Literacy. Non-compliance with taking these standardized tests, or failing them, results in an inability to graduate. With all these tests, you'd expect USD students to be nervous wrecks, constantly walking around with their noses in books or perhaps lined up at the nearest coffee shop. Quite the opposite is true, in fact, students report that few of their peers are even aware of them. "I'm not aware of any such tests," said one student. And anyway, USD students are in good company, as there are also exam requirements for students at the five other state schools in South Dakota.

The Return of the Native . . . or Not

Since USD offers so many areas of studies, students find that they have the opportunity to meet a lot of different types of people. According to one student, "The personality of the student body is split because of all the different colleges. There's a really good mix." However, another student noted, "In a state with so much Native American history and culture, you'd expect to see more Native Americans on campus, but there aren't. There are a lot in the state and the area, but not here." The mostly white student body tends to dress "preppy in winter coats." It is, after all, South Dakota, where parkas are hot and the weather is not. Students report that while "the beginning of the school year and a bit of the end of year has nice weather," the rest of the year can be quite rough. However, most students at USD are native to South Dakota and have already acclimated themselves to cold climates. With the non-South Dakotans on campus hailing from Minnesota, Nebraska, and Iowa, one can't expect too much complaining. The homogenous student body doesn't seem to bother many on campus. Overall, students state that USD is "big enough so that you get to know people and you can run into some people and have classes with them, but still get to meet new people."

And the Crowd Goes Wild

The Coyotes sure do know how to howl. Or maybe it's just the way the acoustics work inside the Dakota Dome. USD football players feel the love because in the Dome, "It gets loud really fast and that makes us more excited to play," said one football player. The dome is just a short walk for students on campus. Other sports, including softball, track and field, swimming, volleyball, and basketball, also hold events inside the Dome. For the winter basketball season, the basketball court is placed in the middle of the Dome, bleachers placed all around it, and the result is the largest basketball arena in NCAA Division II. While this might sound appealing, one student actually said, "It kind of sucks for basketball though, because you never get enough people in the big Dome for it to get pretty loud." But while the acoustics of the large space might sometimes hamper the cheers, overall, school spirit on campus is widespread. One student noted that "You always see people wearing red stuff and stuff always supporting USD."

> **"[The Dome] gets loud really fast, and that makes us more excited to play."**

During homecoming week, the school sponsors a week-long festival officially called Dakota Days but fondly dubbed D-Days by the students. Involving the whole college, D-Days is "pretty crazy and the weekend is even crazier." On the weekdays, there are concerts by various artists and events such as Jell-o wrestling and mechanical bull riding. On the Saturday, there is a parade and plenty of tailgating sponsored by booster clubs and local city businesses.

Runaway Students

After freshman and sophomore year, most students move off campus or into their fraternities or sororities. Why? Although residential assistants inform students about forthcoming alcohol searches and though "[residential assistants] don't want to get you in trouble," many students seek the freedom acquired from living off campus in houses. Students call their off-campus housing "a place of their own," and report that such residences are generally "fairly new, pretty big, and shared between six and eight people." These houses are also the epicenter of college life, with most non-fraternity and sorority parties taking place at them. Only some of the dorms are renovated, with Olson, Mickelson, and Beede Halls currently under construction. Most rooms are doubles in a hallway where 40–60 people share five or six showers. The dorms, according to one gloomy student, "are the smallest in the state." Thus, fraternities and sororities prove a promising solution to many unhappy, cramped dorm-dwellers and also provide social opportunities.

Dancing Greeks, Halloween Treats

Students see fraternities and sororities as places there "to make finding friends a lot easier" and even "get into parties that only girls are usually let into." Students at USD keep busy. Many students are active in the Greek scene, which is active with the local community. During "Strollers," the Greek groups get together for "not quite a dance-off, but you stay up for 24 hours straight and you try to raise money and see who can dance the longest." During Halloween, students are requested to stay in their dorms for a period of time so little kids from around town can trick or treat.

Speaking of frat parties, USD policy is stringent on drinking—on-campus drinking that is. One student said, "There are campus police walking around and if you get caught on college campus, the penalty's usually pretty stiff, so not that many people drink on campus." Elaborated another: "The cops are not nice. They're out to get us. They should let us have fun. They'll stop us if we're even wearing backpacks to a party." Yet another student explained that generally "People go out in the field, build a fire. Drink." Other students stressed that alternatives to the drinking/fire-building/mad cop scene include going "to parties, concerts, and shows. We're not too far from Sioux Falls." Many students who live close to home also go home for the weekends, which is not surprising given that most USD students voice the opinion that "Vermillion is boring."

A Bit of the Old and a Bit of the New

USD is a campus in transition, and with many building projects and renovations in the works, its face is constantly changing. Lazy students will be happy to note that academic buildings at USD are within close proximity of each other and the building facilities are "all pretty nice." With the exception of a few dorms, the campus buildings are relatively recent, and the fine arts building is "almost brand new." The medical school is currently under renovation, and a new Coyote Student Center is expected to open in 2007. Students report that campus overall is "pretty safe" and the "biggest crime is probably having parties and getting busted for underage drinking." Dining halls are also conveniently located around campus and even were reported to be "better than expected" by one student. Students have the option of eating at Lakota Marketplace in the student center, Commons Dining Hall, and Charlie's Grille. Most students avoid Commons and eat at Lakota or Charlie's where selection is said to be much better.

University of South Dakota is different from any other college. At USD, it is necessary to learn to balance an on-campus life of academics and community involvement with your off-campus life of cultural events and socializing in order to experience all that USD has to offer. Despite the apprehensions voiced about the size and isolation of Vermillion, strict RAs, and tests, students report that USD is still "better than expected."— *Anna Yu*

FYI
If you come to USD, you'd better bring "a ridiculously insulated winter coat."
What's the typical weekend schedule? "Study, sleep, and party."
If I could change one thing about USD I would have "nicer cops and more parking."
Three things that every student at USD should do before graduating are "attend Dakota Days, visit a frat, and visit upperclassmen houses."

Tennessee

Address: Rhodes, 2000 N. Parkway, Memphis, TN 38112
Phone: 901-843-3700
E-mail Address: adminfo@rhodes.edu
Web site URL: www.rhodes.edu/admissions
Year Founded: 1848
Private or Public: private
Religious affiliation: Presbyterian
Location: Suburban
Regular Application Deadline: 16-Jan
Number of Applicants: 3,844
Percent Accepted: 49%
Percent Accepted who enroll: 24%
Number Entering: 452
Number of Transfers Accepted each Year: 37
Mean SAT: 1,257
Mean ACT: 27

Middle 50% SAT range: M:590–680, V:590–690
Middle 50% ACT range: 26–30
Early admission program (EA/ ED/ NA): ED
ED or EA Acceptance Rate: 53%
Full time Undergraduate enrollment: 1,672
Total enrollment: 1,696
Percent Male: 41%
Percent Female: 59%
Total Percent Minority: 16%
Percent African-American: 6%
Percent Asian/Pacific Islander: 4%
Percent Hispanic: 2%
Percent Native-American: 0%
Percent Other: 4%
Percent in-state / out of state: 27%/73%

Percent from Public HS: 50%
Retention Rate: 86%
Graduation Rate: 78%
Percent in On-campus housing: 74%
Percent affiliated with Greek system: 48%/52%
Percent Varsity or Club Athletes: 25% varsity
Number of official organized extracurricular organizations: 90
3 Most popular majors: Business Administration/ Management, English Language and Literature
Student/Faculty ratio: 11:01
Tuition and Fees: $29,112.00
Cost for Room and Board: $7,180.00
Percent receiving Financial aid, first-year: 68%

In the midst of the bustle of Memphis, Tennessee lies the small liberal arts paradise of Rhodes College. Students from across the country flock to Rhodes to learn from talented professors, live in Gothic-style dorms, and play Frisbee on a tree-lined campus. The small, close-knit community provides a place where "Rhodents," as students are affectionately known, can thrive and grow for the four years they are there.

Not Just a Number

Academics at Rhodes are definitely challenging, yet students agree that the course load is manageable thanks in part to the small class size and individual attention each student receives. In order to graduate, Rhodents must fulfill requirements in seven different areas, ranging from English and social sciences to fine arts and physical education. Popular majors include biology, psychology, and business administration, which one student said, "has the beginner level courses with some of the largest number of students of any class, around 30."

No matter what you major in, you'll be working pretty hard. "I undoubtedly do more homework here than I did in high school," one student admitted. "Most classes are reading-intensive, and professors demand that students come to class prepared." Many professors even have strict attendance policies, which students cite as a downside to the smallness of most classes. Yet, overall, students say that the class size is a perk rather than a pitfall, since "small classes allow for complete engagement and a better relationship with the professor." Indeed, Rhodes professors are incredibly accessible. "All of my professors know me by name. I'm not a number." One senior even said that, "It is not unusual to go to dinner at a professor's home or enjoy coffee at our

Starbucks on campus. I love the student-teacher ratio here."

The "Rhodes Bubble"

When not hitting the books, Rhodes students are incredibly sociable and friendly. "Everyone I've met at Rhodes has been so nice," one first-semester freshman enthused. "I know so many people already!" The small number of students coupled with an intimate learning atmosphere makes for a tight-knit community in which people make fast friends. Historically, that community has always been a bit homogeneous. Students of color make up only 15 percent of the current freshman class. Yet students maintain that Rhodents are "all really open and interested in meeting new people" and support the college's commitment to building up the diversity of its population.

Regardless of background, sports and extracurriculars provide a plethora of opportunities for Rhodents to get to know one another. Although Rhodes has a whole host of Division III varsity sports teams, they don't often get enough student support. "If you want a school with killer school spirit, don't come to Rhodes," one student warned. "I don't think I even made it to our homecoming football game." Nevertheless, students insist that the school is making a concerted effort to boost attendance and school spirit, and many say that intramural and club teams are becoming more popular, especially football and basketball. Anyone just looking for a workout can take advantage of the newly renovated Mallory-Hyde gym and its variety of facilities, or simply join the multitudes tossing Frisbees on Rhodes' manicured lawns.

> "If you want a school with killer school spirit, don't come to Rhodes. I don't think I even made it to our homecoming football game."

Off the field, community service seems to be a typical Rhodent's pastime of choice. Students say that one of the most popular ways to become involved in service is through the Kinney Volunteer Program, which organizes and arranges volunteer service activities on campus and throughout the city of Memphis. From volunteering at soup kitchens to working with children at Memphis' famed St. Jude Children's Research Hospital, Kinney provides Rhodes students with a way to truly engage with the Memphis community and break out of what one student called "the Rhodes bubble."

The Land of the Delta Blues

The social scene at Rhodes is dominated by the Greek system—over half of the student body is involved in fraternities and sororities. But students are quick to stress that the Greek parties are open to the entire student body, and that, as one senior explained, "you do not have to go Greek to have a social life." One freshman female admitted though, that, "Joining a sorority has really helped me to meet people on campus . . . but of course, there are other ways." Despite the fact that Rhodes "is pretty strict about alcohol," drinking is prevalent on campus. "As long as you're careful about where you drink, you won't get in trouble," a junior said. Campus security is committed to protecting students. "Even if I walk across campus at late hours, I'm completely confident that I'll be safe." For those looking to party off campus and away from the frat houses, downtown Memphis has a whole host of bars and clubs, like the Flying Saucer and Silky's, that Rhodes students love to frequent. The school even provides buses that will take students downtown, to cut down on the risk of drunk driving on campus.

If you prefer your weekends dry, never fear—Rhodents maintain that "there is always an alternative to drinking." Memphis provides Rhodes students with many of these alternatives. One Memphis native enthused, "I was worried that [my experience] would be different than that of students from out of state . . . [but] Midtown and Downtown Memphis are full of exciting and new places and things that I'd never seen or experienced." Cars are a must for getting around the city, but, as one student explained, "A lot of people have cars, so someone can usually give you a ride . . . everyone I've met is really generous about giving rides." Music buffs can frequent the blues clubs on Beale Street, as well as the Rock and Soul Museum and, a bit further away, Graceland itself. Rhodes students often receive discount tickets to basketball games at the new FedEx Forum Stadium, and to local movie theaters, too. From eating soul food at Isaac Hayes' restaurant to seeing the pandas at the Memphis zoo, there is never a shortage of ways for Rhodes students to entertain themselves in the city around them.

Rat Snack Attack

Housing at Rhodes is, like many other aspects of campus life, intimate and community-based. Freshmen and sophomores are required to live on campus, but there is no difference in quality between any of the beautiful Gothic-style dorms. "When my friends [at other schools] saw my dorm, they got really jealous!" one freshman laughed. Juniors and seniors are able to live off campus, but many choose not to. In fact, three-fourths of Rhodes students choose to stay on campus with the community they have built. In terms of food, Rhodents all feast at one on-campus dining hall known as the "Rat." When describing the Rat, one student said that, "You can always get something you like, but sometimes you can get sick of the same stuff." The Lynx Lair provides a fast-food style alternative—some students say it's better than the Rat, which is mostly renowned for its omelets. For more tantalizing off-campus fare, the nearby Cooper-Young neighborhood boasts restaurants like the Young Avenue Deli and Café Ole that draw in students.

Whether playing Frisbee on the quad, studying in the newly renovated library, or wolfing down omelets at the Rat, Rhodes students are experts at carving out communities of their own and taking advantage of the resources around them. A nurturing liberal arts school in the middle of a big city, Rhodes offers its students the best of both worlds. "It's really nice to get off campus and leave the 'Rhodes bubble,' but it's also really nice to come back. It feels like home."—*Alexandra Bicks*

FYI

If you come to Rhodes, you'd better bring "A raincoat and umbrella, it rains a lot here!"

What's a typical weekend schedule? "When it's warm, people will be playing Frisbee on Friday afternoons. At night, there are some people downtown, some people hanging out in the dorms or fraternity houses, and some people off campus. Usually on Saturday or Sunday afternoons, people are relaxing or doing homework."

If I could change one thing about Rhodes, I'd "require students to live on campus all four years."

Three things everyone should do before graduating Rhodes are: "Ride the Lynx statue, enjoy Friday's Fried Chicken at the Rat, and attend at least one concert on campus."

University of Tennessee / Knoxville

Address: University of Tennessee, Knoxville, 320 Student Services Bldg., Knoxville, TN 37996

Phone: 865-974-2184

E-mail Address: admissions@utk.edu

Web site URL: www.utk.edu

Year Founded: 1794

Private or Public: public

Religious affiliation: none

Location: urban

Regular Application Deadline: 2-Feb

Number of Applicants: 12,372

Percent Accepted: 74

Percent Accepted who enroll: 46%

Number Entering: 4,244

Number of Transfers Accepted each Year: 1,766

Mean SAT: NA

Mean ACT: 25

Middle 50% SAT range: NA

Middle 50% ACT range: 23–28

Early admission program (EA/ ED/ NA): EA

ED or EA Acceptance Rate: NA

Full time Undergraduate enrollment: 20,619

Total enrollment: 26,641

Percent Male: 49%

Percent Female: 51%

Total Percent Minority: 15%

Percent African-American: 9%

Percent Asian/Pacific Islander: 3%

Percent Hispanic: 2%

Percent Native-American: 0%

Percent Other: 1%

Percent in-state / out of state: 87%/13%

Percent from Public HS: NA

Retention Rate: 82%

Graduation Rate: 60%

Percent in On-campus housing: 34%

Percent affiliated with Greek system: 32%

Percent Varsity or Club Athletes: NA

Number of official organized extracurricular organizations: 450

3 Most popular majors: English Language and Literature, Political Science and Government, Psychology

Student/Faculty ratio: 15:01

Tuition and Fees: $16,338.00

In State Tuition and Fees (if different): $5,072.00

Cost for Room and Board: $6,358.00

UT has it all—country, campus, and cityscape, with sky-high school spirit to match. Whether the Tennessee Volunteers are camping in the Rockies, singing about it in Neyland Stadium, or bar hopping in Knoxville, they know how to have a good time. They also know when to buckle down and study. Says one particularly dedicated junior, "My major concern with my classes is finishing on time with all A's by monitoring my work schedule with my study schedule."

Work Is What You Make It

Students at the University of Tennessee reiterate the fact that "it is the student that makes or breaks the academics." A given semester's load is "definitely manageable," and determined by the student's major, as well as his or her class attendance and effort. Some of the harder majors include nursing, engineering and architecture, while psychology and exercise science are less demanding. The General Education track demands 36 hours before graduation and basic core subjects like English, biology, and math—overall "a bit excessive," in the words of one sophomore.

The University requires a minimum GPA of 2.0. Failure to meet that minimum results in academic probation and eventually expulsion. One junior noted, however, that "the academic requirements at the University of Tennessee are very easy to abide by." Her classmate added that consistent class attendance yields a B average in most 100 and 200 level courses. (Many of the professors actually give five-point pop quizzes in lecture.) In higher-level courses, there is more work involved, and attendance itself is graded.

Big on School, Not on Student-Professor QT

According to students, one of the difficulties at a large university like UT, is that "getting into classes is difficult, and very frustrating" when you get shut out. A sophomore reported stories of students having difficulty with graduating on time because they could not get into the courses required to do so. However, her friend added that, "the system is improving." Lecture class size can be from 250 to 600 students, where discussions cap at 7 to 25. Though there are professor-student relationships in those smaller seminars, one sophomore finds them lacking in lecture. "I am having to get used to the fact that I am just a number in most of my classes," he said. To boot, many of the TAs employed to ease that feeling do not speak adequate English and make comprehension very difficult.

For its "mediocre" classification, the academic program at UT has many redeeming and unique qualities. For one, the University is making an effort to replace professors who can't manage the language barrier. Dr. Kris Koehne, who teaches human sexuality and child-family studies, is praised for teaching the "most interesting and hysterical class offered at the University of Tennessee." There are also some special programs for those with early ambitions. The Education program in particular is unique, as are the Volunteer Community and Design Community programs. Other students raved about outdoor projects in the nearby mountainside and one junior spoke of how much she valued an assignment in which she tried to prove the existence of God: "It was probably the hardest paper I have written in my entire life, but it taught me a lot about the human psyche and its perception of the outside world."

Living the Life

Social life at UT revolves around Greek system. Freshmen spend their weekend evenings at dorm, house, and frat parties where they are usually charged for a cup, but not for admission. Upperclassmen frequent "the Strip"—home of the Knoxville bar scene—but it is difficult to get in without being of age or having an expert fake ID. "UT is a 'dry' campus," explained one junior. "There is no alcohol allowed on campus, but there is always a lot available. The police department would say that there is a huge problem, but the students would say it's not." As a result, "cops are everywhere" and under-aged drinking has become an issue in the last few years, especially in light of recent citations and pedestrian accidents with drunk drivers. Drugs have a presence, too, but are generally kept "behind closed doors."

Outlets for non-drinkers include numerous organized activities throughout the week, including lectures, film screenings, and concerts. The *Ewing Gallery* and *McClung Museum* hold regular art exhibitions. Social and service-oriented organizations host formal events for their members throughout the year. For 10 years running the University has hosted a dance marathon to benefit the local children's hospital. The Student Center, which is home to the bookstore, computer store, three cafeterias, and a quick mart, is "one of the most popular places on campus during the day." Since the center also houses lecture halls and study areas, it is constantly in use.

Actual dating is rare at UT, but random hook-ups are commonplace. One student concluded that, "girls are better looking as a whole," while her classmate commented that, "it is an attractive campus simply because it is in the South, but it definitely could not compete with UNC, UGA, Ole Miss or SMU in the 'hot people' factor." According to one student who quoted the University Clinic, 80 percent of the school is sexually active and the STD rate is 50 percent (one out of two). One freshman noted that she has "yet to see a homosexual couple or interracial couple" on campus. A sophomore described the UT student population as middle-class "southern prep and granola hippie people." However, another student asserted that there are students from all walks of life, all income brackets, and many races and sexual orientations. Self-segregation is predominately in the form of ethnic fraternities.

As mentioned earlier, Greek life dominates most students' social debuts at UT. One frosh swore that she "cannot imagine going out not in a sorority. It has helped me meet so many new people and given me stuff to do such as pledge mixers and fraternity parties." The most popular sororities are AOPi, Tri-Delta, Chi Omega, Alpha Delta Pi, Kappa Kappa Gamma, Kappa Delta and Phi Mu. Getting into one of them is not easy: "Rush is very draining and exhausting, and sororities have grade cuts, so good grades are important," said one sorority-struck freshman. Fraternities like Pike, Sigma Chi and Kappa Sigma throw parties on the weekends and special events, like when Pike had Pat Green perform at their house. SAE has recently been kicked off-campus but still holds festivities and theme parties in line with its contemporaries. Some of the most highly anticipated parties include SAE's boxing tournament, Pike's Fall Fiesta, Volapalooza, Super Hero's Day Off, Peace Love Chi O, Casino Date party, Country clubbers mixers, Halloween parties and more themes than you can shake a stick at— "Wild Wild West," "Secs and Execs," Luau, "Lifestyles of the Rich and Famous," and— of course—'80s. Most of the cliques on campus are formed through the Greek system, though students also meet close friends through class and dorm assignments freshman year.

Ditch the Dorms

Freshman dorms are "small and old." They have air-conditioning, but students have no control over the temperature and "visiting hours" determines when friends can come over and only friends of the same sex are allowed to sleep over. All of the dorms have Residential Advisors, but they are only strict in the girls' dorms. "No limit" Clement, on the other hand, is known for its laid back RAs. South Carrick, Humes, North Carrick and Reese are the best freshman dorms because they surround a courtyard called the "Presidential" where the students can meet and socialize. Sophronia Strong, said to be the worst dorm, has small rooms and no air-conditioning. It's also rumored to be haunted. "Sophie" gets upset when she hears residents arguing on her birthday, one student explained. Hess, commonly known as "the zoo," is considered the craziest dorm on campus.

After freshman year, Greek and racial factors distribute students throughout the dorms. However, there are many off-campus options including sorority houses, apartments, and private houses that are within walking distance of campus. Rent is $350–450 a month on average and the most popular off-campus housing is in "The Fort," where there is usually a waiting list.

A Concrete Jungle

UT's campus is no architectural marvel, but it has the feel of a college atmosphere. One student maintained that "as long is there is a lot of school spirit, which Tennessee has, it really does not matter to me if it is not the prettiest campus." The campus also provides easy access to Knoxville, so students have the option of remaining in the campus bubble or venturing out into real life. In fact, as most have cars, University of Tennessee students frequently leave campus to rock climb, camp out, water ski or go rafting in nearby outdoor areas. Added one sophomore, "There are also lovely places like Gatlinburg and Dollywood just a few miles down I-40 which can be really fun if you are in the mood for a cheesy weekend!"

> "As long is there is a lot of school spirit, which Tennessee has, it really does not matter to me if it is not the prettiest campus."

Within the bubble, UT boasts great student facilities. "Exercising is very social and popular" and the gym, "T-Rec," features state of the art exercise and recreation equipment including "tons of machines, weights, weight equipment, an indoor track, four basketball courts, three racquetball courts, an outside intramural field [four actually] and an indoor and outdoor swimming pool." Not to mention the Smoothie King inside. Students rave about the library and surrounding movie theaters and parks available to them on the weekends. Neyland Stadium, of course, is the prize of UT. It seats over 100,000 football-lovers including just about every student on any giving Saturday. "The Hill" is the home of most science and math facilities and is currently under construction. One junior praised the work being done: "The University is finally making much needed changes to the physical structure of the buildings on campus."

All-Star Eats

Tennessee dining hall food is "great but fattening." All-Star plans are the best, as well as any plan (there are five) with "bonus bucks" that can be used outside of the dining halls. "The dining halls are very clean and the food is exquisite. Sometimes there are even theme parties! They cater to all appetites and are typically open at convenient hours but close around 8 p.m." Although UT dining has happy customers, the dining hall is not a social environment. When asked if she might go to the dining hall alone and find someone to sit with, one sophomore answered, "No way. Most people don't go to a dining hall without friends." And most people don't stay there longer than necessary. "There are lots of other places to go to hang out," or eat off campus. On a date you might go to the Tennessee Grill or the Riverside Tavern. "Sawyers and Vic and Bills Deli

are great little holes in the wall that you'll only know about or go to if you live around the area."

Venerable Volunteers

At a school as big as UT, "most everyone is in an organization of some sort; otherwise you would not meet very many people." Greek life and intramurals dominate student interest, but the Baptist Collegiate Ministries, Vol Nation (the pep club), and the Student Government Association are well-respected, too. One thing is for sure—community service has a high profile at UT. "We are the Volunteers for a reason," said an emphatic sophomore. For the more eccentric minds, there are also "funny organizations" like the fly fishing club which demand less time—two hours a week on average. Further, about half of the student body works a job on the side.

In accordance with their track records, football and women's basketball are most popular spectator sports on campus. "The football players are dumb and cocky but most everyone goes to the football games decked out in orange," said a student. Athletics are a source of pride at UT. Students participate in the Vol Walk, a procession before every game, sing "Rocky Top" at the top of their lungs during play, and tailgate religiously. There is even a large population of students who follow their football team as far as Florida for away games. Tennessee boasts celebrity status for a few coaches and former players. Peyton Manning, currently the quarterback for the Colts, retired his jersey on October 29, 2004 and Pat Summitt is the most winning coach in history. When it comes down to it, UT is defined by its "colors and school spirit."—*Lauren Ezell*

FYI
If you come to University of Tennessee, you better bring a "closet full of orange clothes."
What is a typical weekend schedule? "Sleep . . . drink . . . FOOTBALL . . . drink . . . sleep . . . drink . . . sleep . . . .study on Sunday night."
If I could change one thing about University of Tennessee, "I'd power-wash all the concrete buildings."
Three things every student at University of Tennessee should do before graduating are "paint the Rock, do a pub crawl, camp in the Smokies."

The University of the South (Sewanee)

Address: University of the South/Sewanee, 735 University Avenue, Sewanee, TN 37383
Phone: 800-522-2234
E-mail Address: admiss@sewanee.edu
Web site URL: www.sewanee.edu
Year Founded: 1857
Private or Public: private
Religious affiliation: Episcopal
Location: rural
Regular Application Deadline: 2-Feb
Number of Applicants: 1,932
Percent Accepted: 71%
Percent Accepted who enroll: 30%
Number Entering: 412
Number of Transfers Accepted each Year: 25

Mean SAT: NA
Mean ACT: NA
Middle 50% SAT range: NA
Middle 50% ACT range: 25–29
Early admission program (EA/ ED/ NA): ED
ED or EA Acceptance Rate: NA
Full time Undergraduate enrollment: 1,518
Total enrollment: 1,526
Percent Male: 48%
Percent Female: 52%
Total Percent Minority: 12%
Percent African-American: 4%
Percent Asian/Pacific Islander: 2%
Percent Hispanic: 3%
Percent Native-American: 1%
Percent Other: 2%

Percent in-state / out of state: 22%/78%
Percent from Public HS: 52%
Retention Rate: 92%
Graduation Rate: 77%
Percent in On-campus housing: 94%
Percent affiliated with Greek system: 69%
Percent Varsity or Club Athletes: NA
Number of official organized extracurricular organizations: 110
3 Most popular majors: NA
Student/Faculty ratio: 11:01
Tuition and Fees: $28,528.00
Cost for Room and Board: $8,160.00

In the midst of the beautiful rolling hills of East Tennessee lies the small liberal arts paradise of The University of the South at Sewanee. Sewanee, as it is more commonly known, offers a supportive learning environment coupled with a friendly and laid-back social scene. The small and intimate community allows Sewanee kids to spend four years learning from, and partying with, some of the most talented college students in the country.

Class Without TAs

One of Sewanee's biggest draws is its nurturing and accessible academic community. As one student describes, "Students are able to get valuable personal instruction from the professors in a very interactive environment where studies are based on discussion, not lecture." The school requires its students to fulfill a set of core requirements, including English, math, history and foreign languages. Some of the more popular majors include forestry and geology, even though they are "extremely challenging." English and history are also favorites, with physics and chemistry universally less popular.

Since Sewanee has no TAs, every single class is taught by professors, a move which elicits only praise from students despite the fact that "grading is fairly strict." Discussions are, as one student puts it, "fun and stimulating" due to the small class size, truly encouraging Sewanee kids to get the most out of their classroom experiences. Professors are described as "friendly and accessible" and "willing to meet with students at any time." One junior even goes so far as to say that, "Perhaps Sewanee's greatest academic strength is the relationship between students and professors . . . It is very difficult to find a bad teacher here."

Life in the "Bubble"

Outside of the classroom, Sewanee kids are incredibly sociable. As one junior said, "Sewanee people are some of the friendliest people on the planet . . . if there are any true stereotypes, it's that all Sewanee students are usually able to get along with everyone." One male student even asserts that "Some say we are all Southern hicks . . . but truth be told, I would rather be a Southern gentleman here [than anywhere else]." The stereotype that the population is made up of "privileged white students in a bubble" does admittedly "apply to many people," yet students are quick to defend their school's take on diversity. While the school may be "predominantly white," students insist that "we have a multicultural institute, and we try to promote racial awareness and cultural appreciation," recognizing the University's commitment to strengthening the diversity of the "close, but somewhat isolated community."

> **"Perhaps Sewanee's greatest academic strength is the relationship between students and professors."**

Regardless of background, sports and extracurricular activities provide a plethora of opportunities for people to get to know their peers. While Sewanee does have a large football team, one junior claims that "sports like basketball and football are not a huge draw for students," while soccer and especially rugby seem to be gaining popularity as they score more victories on the field. Intramural sports are also prominent at Sewanee, with women's field hockey and men's basketball described as the most "intense" in which students can participate. If you're just looking to stay in shape, the Fowler Center is a "fairly pleasant" gym with accessible facilities such as a pool, track and weight room. For non-athletes, Sewanee offers roughly 110 clubs, including community service organizations, publications and theater groups, giving students a variety of different social outlets.

The Sewanee residential community is made up of a variety of dorms and houses, each of which has its own unique character. Freshmen don't have separate housing, but are instead integrated into upperclassmen dorms from the very beginning, with the only difference being that singles are reserved for juniors and seniors. Most students live on campus, since Sewanee seniors are the only group permitted to apply for off-campus housing. Well-known dorms include Cannon Hall, the universally-recognized "party dorm," and Humphreys, which was finished in 2003 and "looks like a hotel, inside and out." There are also special language houses, in which students commit to only speaking the particular language of the house, as well as a few single-

sex dorms. Student proctors live in the dorms and fulfill the role of RAs, while Assistant Proctors (or APs) "work with freshmen to help them adjust to college life and enforce dorm rules."

Architecturally, students state that "most of the buildings at Sewanee are rather distinctive . . . think Oxford." The gorgeous All Saints' Cathedral, complete with stained glass windows, serves as a prominent campus landmark, while the towers of McClurg Dining Hall have earned it the nickname "Phallus Palace." Inside McClurg, Sewanee's only dining facility, students on a meal plan enjoy the "great number of choices" that the school has to offer. If the campus food starts to get old, Mi Casa Mexican restaurant and Shen Chinese buffet offer quick and easy alternatives.

It's All Greek To Me

The party scene at Sewanee is notorious for being one of the craziest in the country. One student admits, "Sewanee students work hard all week, and yes, we drink hard on the weekends . . . If you're against alcohol, you probably shouldn't go here." The prevalence of alcohol on campus is abetted by the Greek system, which essentially dominates the available social options. However, Sewanee kids are quick to assert that "the fraternity system promotes friendship in the community." The huge number of frats provides interested pledges with a variety of different alternatives, and they all have an open door policy, meaning that "anyone is allowed to party at any house on any given night."

However, some students warn that "lately the drinking policy has been getting stricter" and that officials have been cracking down on the amount of alcohol the fraternities and sororities are allowed to serve. To get around these regulations, people can also head off-campus for parties in senior residences, where the drinks continue to flow all night long. The University even has its own Tiger Bay Pub, a restaurant that serves beer until 10 pm and breakfast for the rest of the night, a sure sign of just how much alcohol serves as a hallmark of the school's social experience.

Despite Sewanee's self-proclaimed status as a wet campus, there are definitely weekend activities that don't necessarily involve alcohol. The Sewanee Union Theater offers sneak previews of upcoming films, while the nearby Lake Cheston club has occasional concerts and shows. Sewanee's proximity to the woods also allows students to enjoy outdoor activities like hiking and camping. The campus is incredibly safe, and town-gown relations are friendly, as many students comment that "[The town of Sewanee] generally tolerates the students, and the beer and liquor stores are especially appreciative of them." In terms of venturing off campus to explore the surrounding areas, Sewanee kids agree that "most people have cars." Indeed cars are necessary for everything from making Wal-Mart runs in nearby Cowen or Monteagle to making the treks to Nashville or Chattanooga. Popular off-campus clubs include Tubby's in Monteagle, while the coffee house Stirlings and Shenanigans bar and grill draw rave reviews from students. The Four Seasons even offers home cooking, but it is closed during the winter because it serves fresh food directly from nearby farms, a reminder of the advantages of Sewanee's rural location.

A Place Where Angels Dwell

Sewanee lore is rife with unique stories and enduring traditions. Students still "dress for class," meaning that they wear nicer clothes out of a sense of propriety and respect for the professors. Tour guides tell of nearby Civil War bombs and battles, while stories of ghosts and haunted buildings continue to circulate. Legend even has it that angels dwell at the gates of Sewanee, and many students admit to tapping the roof of their car when entering or exiting campus to "summon a 'Sewanee angel' " to protect them. Truly a charmed place, Sewanee offers prospective students a chance for a supportive and rewarding college experience, as one junior states, "Sewanee is just the greatest. Period."—*Alexandra Bicks*

FYI

If you come to Sewanee, you'd better bring "hiking boots, dress attire for class, a smile and sense of adventure."

What's a typical weekend schedule? "Friday night, party hard; Saturday morning, sleep; Saturday afternoon, go see some sports events; Saturday night, party hard; Sunday, go to church to make up for Friday and Saturday night, and then study!"

If I could change one thing about Sewanee, I'd "make it closer to a real city—it can get kind of isolated out here."

Three things everyone should do before graduating are "hike the perimeter trail, take interesting classes, and watch a sunset at Morgan's Steep."

Vanderbilt University

Address: Vanderbilt, 2305 West End Ave, Nashville, TN 37203
Phone: 615-322-2561
E-mail Address: admission@vanderbilt.edu
Web site URL: www.vanderbilt.edu
Year Founded: 1873
Private or Public: private
Religious affiliation: none
Location: urban
Regular Application Deadline: 4-Jan
Number of Applicants: 12,192
Percent Accepted: 34%
Percent Accepted who enroll: 39%
Number Entering: 1,590
Number of Transfers Accepted each Year: 162
Mean SAT: 1,370
Mean ACT: 30

Middle 50% SAT range: 1,280–1,460
Middle 50% ACT range: 30–32
Early admission program (EA/ ED/ NA): ED
ED or EA Acceptance Rate: NA
Full time Undergraduate enrollment: 6,378
Total enrollment: 11,607
Percent Male: 48%
Percent Female: 52%
Total Percent Minority: 19%
Percent African-American: 8%
Percent Asian/Pacific Islander: 6%
Percent Hispanic: 5%
Percent Native-American: 0%
Percent Other: NA
Percent in-state / out of state: 17%/83%

Percent from Public HS: 60%
Retention Rate: 96%
Graduation Rate: 89%
Percent in On-campus housing: 83%
Percent affiliated with Greek system: 42%
Percent Varsity or Club Athletes: NA
Number of official organized extracurricular organizations: 329
3 Most popular majors: Engineering Science; Psychology, General; Sociology
Student/Faculty ratio: 9:01
Tuition and Fees: $32,620
Cost for Room and Board: NA
Percent receiving Financial aid, first-year: 46%

Smack dab in the middle of Music City, USA, Vanderbilt University's idyllic brick buildings and grassy lawns are just blocks away from the good food and quirky culture of Nashville, Tennessee. Competitive both academically and socially, Vandy is a place for those who like to work hard, play hard, and eat great burgers.

Atypical "A's"

On Vanderbilt academics, one freshman concluded: "I am confident that the academics of Vanderbilt are perfectly balanced to allow its students to enjoy the college life, while still being rigorous enough to create respect in the job world and promote learning while on campus." But grade-grubbers be warned. Vanderbilt supports grade *defla*tion, an oft-forgotten phenomenon of a pre-SAT tutor America. As one junior elaborated, "B's are easy to get; A's are hard."

Students might have an easier time pushing 4.0's at the Peabody School of Education. The Human and Organizational Development major is one of the easiest on campus. Engineers, pre-med students, and economics majors have a tougher time. Some students argued, though that "each major is challenging . . . but not impossible. Accord-

ing to many students, "curriculum is an integral part of Vanderbilt."

Even in the more difficult majors, most Vanderbilt professors have an open-door policy and boast small class sizes. Upperclassmen say 30 students is the average campus wide, though large lectures border on 50. Freshmen seeking name-brand profs should enroll in Brian Griffith's Intro to Human Development, John Lachs' Intro to Philosophy, or Stephen Buckles' introductory economics courses.

Music City Madness

Vanderbilt has "top 20 academics according to *USNews* and a top 20 party scene according to *Playboy*." And Hugh Hefner certainly knows his parties—the entertainment options at Vanderbilt do not disappoint. Among fraternity parties, downtown Music City, movies on Peabody lawn, and on-campus concerts and lectures, Vandy students are never bored. "Being underage is only a problem if you want to go to bars downtown and you don't have a fake ID. Most take anything half-way legit," one junior said. Upperclassmen who are interested, however, can enjoy the Nashville nightlife courtesy of student-friendly cabs that frequent Vanderbilt's campus on the weekends. Underclassmen attend frat parties more often, and enjoy "cool live bands, literally every weekend."

> **"Vanderbilt has top 20 academics according to *USNews* and a top 20 party scene according to Playboy."**

There are many non-drinkers on campus, but they are well accepted and included in regular on-goings. As one freshman explained, "I know several of my closest friends and I don't drink, but we can still go to the frats and have fun." There is also a Christian fraternity that hosts dry parties. During the daytime, Vanderbilt has hosted many famous lecturers in years past including Maya Angelou and Tennessee native, Al Gore. Further, the "Chancellor's Lecture Series" is mandatory for freshman and open to the public, while the "Sarratt Student Center is a popular hang-out place." Students agreed that the highlight of Vanderbilt social life comes in April with the Rites of Spring. Just before finals, the school hires bands and performers for "a two-day orgy of music" on Alumni Lawn. Past performers include Ludakris, Maroon 5, and Robert Earl Keen.

On-campus dating is, for the most part, limited to formals, but there is a "small scene." It is mostly overwhelmed by "lots of random hook-ups." What does set Vanderbilt apart, according to one student, is that the "student body is unusually attractive," especially the women, he added.

The Vandy Vibe

The Vanderbilt stereotype is what you might expect at a southern school. One freshman listed the following perceived stereotypes: "Vanderbilt is an all wealthy white school. Girls are blonde, preppy, fake, and dependant. Guys are party animals and southern gentlemen. Everyone is from the South, and everyone dresses to impress." In reality, however, "there are more middle-class students than most people think. About half of the student body receives financial aid." Many students express satisfaction with the student body profile, but a considerable number wish there were more diversity.

Some of the homogeneity around Vandy campus is attributed to the "huge Greek system." One sophomore wrote that second semester rush is "stressful but fun!" Chi Omega, Delta Delta Delta, Kappa Alpha Theta, Kappa Kappa Gamma, and Kappa Delta are the cov-

eted sororities, while guys elbow to get into Sigma Chi, Sigma Alpha Epsilon, Kappa Alpha, and Pi Kappa Epsilon. The Greek system seems to be a significant forum for making friends at Vandy, and on the homogeneity that it creates, the same student argued that "smart and interesting people are definitely here . . . lots of students who actually care about political and social issues as well as what they look like!"

The Low-Down on Living

All Vanderbilt freshmen live on campus in one of three dorms. Kissam is the least well kept. Composed of single bedrooms, it is viewed as a "bookworm" area. Branscomb, neighbor to Greek row, boasts the best party scene. And Vandy-Barnard is the most popular dorm for freshmen. Most upperclassmen stay on campus, hopefully in Scales or Vaughn, the best upperclass dorms, while others live in fraternity or sorority houses or in other off-campus accommodations. There is an international house called McTyeire "where you have to speak a foreign language and eat dinner there four nights a week" and there is also a philosophy house.

On-campus dining plans are "decent . . . not great but not horrible." Rand, the main dining center, is a nice place to sit and chat with friends for hours on end. When students need a change of pace, however, they can use their meal points at surrounding restaurants: P.F. Chang's, Ken's Sushi, Pancake Pantry, and Bread & Company are all popular. Amerigo's is the hot spot for dates and Rotier's is home of the world's best cheeseburger. Vanderbilt also features a significant number of options for those with certain eating requirements, such as the Kosher and vegetarian establishments on campus.

Commodores in the Community

Vandy students are avid sports fans. Though basketball and baseball teams are the most successful, more students frequent weekly football games in the fall—often with a date and a dress. There is even a "Vanderbilt Fanatics" club that organizes the cheering effort. One nice tradition, according to students, "is for the students to stand and sing the alma mater after each game, win or lose".

For non-varsity athletes, there are a number of sporting options. One freshman said, "The club and intramural programs are popular and well run." Additionally, there are great facilities for recreational exercise such as swimming, weight lifting, tennis and basketball. On nice days, many students can be seen running "the loop," a three-mile course around campus.

In terms of non-athletic extracurriculars, Vanderbilt students are very community service oriented. Alternative Spring and Winter Break, which "take several hundred students to another state or country," and Habitat for Humanity are very well respected. Student who aren't involved in community service or the Commodore yearbook (another popular pastime), might take jobs on campus, although most students with jobs are part of the work-study program. Sororities and fraternities are the most time consuming extracurricular, but Vandy students insist that "academics come first."—*Lauren Ezell*

FYI

If you come to Vanderbilt you better bring "a sundress for football games."

What is a typical weekend schedule? "Study hard, play hard."

If I could change one thing about Vanderbilt, I'd "add more diversity to the student body."

Three things every student at Vanderbilt should do before graduating are: "Take a drunk picture with Chancellor Gee, take an ASB trip, and get painted up for a football game."

Texas

Imagine a day when classes are canceled for tug-of-war, stand-up comedians, free food, and . . . gospel choir? It's called Diadeloso, or "Day of the Bear," a yearly celebration that has been embraced by students at Baylor University for more than 70 years. Combined with strong academics and great school spirit, traditions like Diadeloso make attending the nation's largest Baptist university a unique experience.

Baylor Academics

Nestled in the suburban area outside Waco, Texas, Baylor provides undergraduates with a wide variety of educational opportunities. Upon admission, students may choose to pursue a bachelor's degree from the College of Arts and Sciences, the Hankamer School of Business, the School of Nursing, the School of Social Work, the Honors College, or the schools of Nursing, Education, Computer Science and Engineering, and Music. Baylor is known for its engineering program as well as its top-ranked entrepreneurship program. Pre-med and business are among the more popular courses of study.

The core curriculum is supplemented by two required chapel credits and two classes in religion, which most freshmen try to get out of the way during their first two semesters. One freshman said that she was surprised by the difficulty of some of her classes. However, the rigor of the academics varies from student to student, depending "on how much you want to challenge yourself." Many students agree that the teachers are very accessible and more than willing to help their pupils. Class sizes range from 20 students to over 100. Larger lectures are accompanied by separate discussion sections led by teaching assistants.

For those brave students seeking to challenge themselves, Baylor has an honors program that is open for admittance by special application. This four-year program involves conducting independent research and writing a senior thesis. One senior in the honors program said, "I had to work more, sleep less, take demanding courses on top of the required curriculum and write the longest paper I have ever composed." Despite the added work and stress, those who participate in the program still view it as a rewarding experience.

Religion, Regulations and Relaxation

When students at Baylor decide to take some time off from their studying, most look for entertainment off campus. The University has a strict policy on alcohol, so most of the partying takes place at fraternities and other venues away from the school grounds. While Greek life exists at Baylor, it does not dominate Baylor's social scene. As one undergrad commented, "You don't have to be in a fraternity to have a social life." In general, students say it is not too difficult to make friends, although "it helps if you know someone beforehand." One student remarked that "there's less drinking compared to other schools" and drug use is not prevalent. Popular hangout spots around the campus include Cricket's, a bar, and Common Grounds, a coffee shop.

Weekends at Baylor, however, involve more than just partying and catching up on sleep. Baylor is a Baptist University, and a large majority of students consider themselves Christian. One freshman mentioned that it's not rare to "go partying on Saturday night, then wake up on Sunday and go to church." The school emphasizes religion as part of the curriculum and part of Baylor's stated goal is to "reaffirm and deepen its distinctive Christian mission." And although some non-Christians go to Baylor, "most people believe in the same things." Students point to the school's spiritual roots as a key draw. As one undergrad said, "I love Baylor's Christian ideals. Where else can you listen to worship music in the dining halls?"

Life in Bear Country

Over 80 percent of students at Baylor hail from the Lone Star State. Diversity— whether geographic or racial—is not one of the University's strong points. One student said that the minority groups also tend to isolate themselves.

How do these Baylor students feel about living in Waco? Let's just say that most of them prefer to stay on or around campus rather than go into the city to spend their leisure time. In the words of one student, the area is "not exactly a rich community."

While one freshman noted that there is "not very much to do here," she also said that students may find entertainment in Austin and Dallas, which are both just an hour's drive from Baylor.

> **"I love Baylor's Christian ideals. Where else can you listen to worship music in the dining halls?"**

As for life on campus, students are generally satisfied with housing. One freshman was particularly happy with the situation, saying that "living in the dorms really makes you appreciate your space." All of the dorm buildings alternate between an all-girls floor and an all-guys floor. The rooms tend to be "pretty small, but in fairly good condition." Also living in the dorms are community leaders who are "mainly there to keep everything in order." CLs mostly keep an eye on drinking in the dorms and make sure there is no coed visiting after hours. Although dorm life can be a fun experience, almost all Baylor students choose to move to apartments after their freshman year. A brand-new complex called North Village is a popular place for upperclassmen to live.

Regardless of where they live, the students like to get involved in extracurricular activities, including intramural sports, volunteer work and any of the more than 300 student on-campus organizations. One popular event is "Steppin' Out," a day in which more than 3,000 students join together to do community service projects in Waco. The recently-built McLane Student Life Center, which hosts many of the intramural and club sports, has rock climbing walls, weight rooms, basketball and volleyball courts, and also pool tables and an indoor track.

Turning Out for the Home Team

School spirit is abundant at Baylor University, where many students turn out to support their Bears. At the football games the student section forms what is called the Baylor Line, where "all the freshmen sit in a certain section, wear these hideous bright yellow shirts, and cheer on the team." The strongest athletic programs at the school are baseball; men's tennis; and women's basketball, which won the national championship in 2005.

Undergrads also enjoy partaking in many

unique Baylor customs, including the Pigskin Revue, a song and dance festival that features the top acts from the student group All University Sing. At what is known as Christmas on 5th Street, students celebrate the holiday with "a full-on Christmas extravaganza with a real live manger scene and even camels." Baylor also proudly puts on the oldest and longest collegiate homecoming parade in the country.

Customs like these have built a strong sense of community at Baylor. Boasting a spirited student population and a beautiful campus, Baylor provides what one happy freshman called a "perfect college atmosphere."—*Henry Agnew*

FYI
If you come to Baylor University, you'd better bring "determination."
What is the typical weekend schedule? "Going out to dinner on Friday night, going to a football game and parties on Saturday, and church on Sunday morning."
If I could change one thing about Baylor, I'd "move it to a town other than Waco."
Three things every Baylor student should do before graduating are "see a play, run through the fountains at the science buildings, and take advantage of the gym."

Rice University

Address: Rice, Office of Admissions-MS 17, PO Box 1892, Houston, TX 77251	**Middle 50% SAT range:** 1350–1510	**Percent from Public HS:** NA
Phone: 800-527-6957	**Middle 50% ACT range:** 30–34	**Retention Rate:** 96%
E-mail Address: admi@rice.edu	**Early admission program (EA/ ED/ NA):** ED	**Graduation Rate:** 90%
Web site URL: www.futureowls.rice.edu/futureowls/Admission_Home1.asp	**ED or EA Acceptance Rate:** NA	**Percent in On-campus housing:** 71%
Year Founded: 1912	**Full time Undergraduate enrollment:** 2,964	**Percent affiliated with Greek system:** 0%
Private or Public: private	**Total enrollment:** 5,119	**Percent Varsity or Club Athletes:** NA
Religious affiliation: none	**Percent Male:** 51%	**Number of official organized extracurricular organizations:** 200+
Location: urban	**Percent Female:** 49%	
Regular Application Deadline: 10-Jan	**Total Percent Minority:** NA	**3 Most popular majors:** Bioscience, Economics, Psychology
Number of Applicants: 8,776	**Percent African-American:** 6%	
Percent Accepted: 24%	**Percent Asian/Pacific Islander:** 18%	**Student/Faculty ratio:** 5:01
Percent Accepted who enroll: 34%	**Percent Hispanic:** 12%	**Tuition and Fees:** $26,500.00
Number Entering: 715	**Percent Native-American:** 1%	**Cost for Room and Board:** $9,590.00
Number of Transfers Accepted each Year: 93	**Percent Other:** 6%	**Precent receiving Financial aid, first-year:** NA
Mean SAT: NA	**Percent in-state / out of state:** 51%/49%	
Mean ACT: NA		

W ith its cleanly manicured lawns, lush green vegetation and park-like atmosphere, one would hardly guess that Rice University is located just a few miles from downtown Houston, Texas. As one of the nation's top universities, it offers students an unmatched education in addition to a beautiful learning environment.

"We Study a Lot"
"We study a lot," was how one student described a typical Rice undergrad. "Some people study a lot all the time, even on weekends and nights, but if you want, you can be out Monday through Sunday having a good time." Even for those who choose the latter route, the University's academic requirements must first be met, which can vary in intensity depending on the major and the number of AP credits an individual has coming in. There are three areas of distributional requirements—humanities, social sciences and natural sciences. Students point out that the requirements have their "ups and downs," but one student said it is beneficial, since "taking classes outside of your major

really helps to open your mind." Many students take a lot of science courses anyway, and it seems like "half of the school is premed" to some students. In fact, it is common for students to continue their research at Rice over the summer. One of Rice's most well-known programs is the Rice-Baylor program, which means you have "guaranteed acceptance to Baylor College of Medicine." However, it only accepts approximately 10 undergrads into the program per year. Unfortunately, many premed students do not have the luxury of going abroad—a hefty sacrifice considering that about half the University's students do so for at least a semester.

> "Some people study a lot all the time, even on weekends and nights, but if you want, you can be out Monday through Sunday having a good time."

In terms of getting into classes, freshmen often have the most difficulty procuring a spot for the more coveted lectures. The upside for freshmen is that general education classes such as introductory humanities tend to be capped, so they range from 20 to 30 people. Other introductory courses, including biology, chemistry, physics and constitutionalism, are generally quite large, "which for Rice isn't that big—maybe 100 students." One Rice freshman bragged that "my smallest class is an amazing Introduction to Theater class, which only has about 10 students." Upper-level courses are extremely small at Rice, and they are typically less than 20 to 30 people. One upperclassman said, "I had four classes with fewer than 10 students last year."

While most Rice students "study a lot," most students would agree that mathematics, physics and computer science are the most challenging majors. However, "every discipline at Rice has very serious students, and those are the ones that study the most—it doesn't depend on the major."

The workload is more bearable when students have the opportunity to take classes from famous professors like Dennis Huston, a humanities teacher famous for lectures in which "he spits out obscenities left and right." People actually camp out in front of the registrar's office to ensure a spot in Huston's public speaking class. Bombs and Rockets, a class about the "Politics of American National Security," is another hot ticket.

Luckily, the class assignments are often as interesting as the lecturers. One premed student was assigned the task of creating artificial blood for one of his science courses.

Grade inflation doesn't seem to be a prominent concern at Rice, although some classes, such as chemistry, do have what are called "redemption points." In this system, if a student's score on a portion of the final exam is better than that of a test from the beginning of the year, the earlier test score replaces final questions pertaining to the earlier test, resulting in the higher grade. For more difficult classes, recitation sessions taught by the TAs are offered. Students seem to have mixed feelings about TAs, some complaining that they only muddle the information and that it can be "really hard to understand" those with foreign accents. However, one student praised the grad students at Rice: "This year I am taking a class taught by a TA and she's better than the professor." Whichever the case, "between the office hours of the TAs and professors, you can always get help if you need it."

Rice Lets Loose

Rice isn't all brains and no beer (despite its Greek-free status). Although most parties serve up alcohol, there are "always other things to do," one student emphatically pointed out, and "there's no real split socially between drinkers and non-drinkers." Plus, "you could always go to parties and just not drink." The residential colleges throw a lot of the parties. Well-known bashes include the Annual Night of Decadence, "which is basically a nude party," Disorientation (at the end of orientation week) and the Tower Party. Late-night games of powderpuff football and chilling "with the guys, playing some poker, and watching a movie" are options for those students who just want to veg out. The dating scene (or lack thereof) at Rice is often blamed on the common stereotype that "most of us guys tend to be shy," one male Rice student explained. And the males' shyness only works to their disadvantage, since "there's a good amount of cute girls on campus." The verdict is still out, however, because other Rice students feel that "you're either in a very serious relationship or you're not dating anyone at all."

Residential Colleges: Instant Family

The social life at Rice is greatly supplemented by the University's residential college system. About 400 people (100 from each grade) live in each of nine colleges, providing an instant family atmosphere ingrained in freshmen from the start of "a great orientation week." But not all students are as enthusiastic about what they call "O-Week." Freshmen from each college are divided into groups of eight to 10 students. "You're really tight with them from the start and you do all your activities with your group," a student explained. The colleges "make a very concerted effort to put people from very different backgrounds and with very different interests in each group," one student said. And yes, the residential colleges definitely do have different personalities, students said, which "are all brainwashed into us during our orientation week." But there are many positive things to be said for the residential college system, too. One student noted that "It's the best parts of a fraternity and a dorm all put together." And don't worry about meeting people outside of your residential college. Classes, parties or common friends are all ways to extend your circle of friends, although it does "take a little bit more effort."

Each college has its own master and staff of associates. The master is a tenured professor at the University and handles academic and personal matters, in addition to organizing social events. He or she lives and eats with the students in the residential college. The associates are faculty members, most of whom live outside of Rice, except for the two associates who reside in each college. They provide academic advice and help direct students' career choices.

Dorms vary from college to college, but most students would agree that none are shamefully terrible. They range from singles to quads, most of which are located on coed floors and share single-sex bathrooms. There are more singles in the newer colleges, but there's no reason to fear being lonely—usually four singles comprise a suite, with its own common room and bathroom. And don't worry about playing your music too loudly: the RA system is fairly lenient and the RAs "tend to be really cool here and enjoy hanging out with us."

Ode to Houston

What's green, flat, and pretty all around? Why, of course, the campus of Rice University. The campus has "lots of great facilities and big open quads" that students said "people are actually encouraged to walk on," al-though some prefer to utilize the plush grass for napping. The main local attraction is Rice Village, an outdoor mall with a mix of franchises and independent retailers that is "packed with restaurants." But who wants to walk when you can hitch a ride with any of the estimated 40 percent of Rice students who have cars on campus? Beyond campus, Houston has so much to offer, including the Theater District, Chinatown, and the Galleria—a "really famous really large mall." And if you get bored of the on-campus scene, venture to Houston for some "pretty good" clubbing or to catch a concert at The Engine Room. Favorite Rice bar hangouts include Bar Houston, Brian O'Neil's, Brock's Bar and Two Rows. Little Woodrow's is another popular bar in the Village (along with Brian O'Neil's). Luckily for students not blessed with the luxury of wheels, a rail system makes getting places a bit easier. Last year, Rice's President implemented "Passport to Houston," so now all undergraduates can ride the light rail for free, "which makes going to bars, baseball games and restaurants downtown, as well as the museum district and apartment complexes, very easy."

Get Your Grub On: More Than Just Rice

Each college has its own dining hall, and the quality varies slightly, although overall the food at Rice is "good by college standards." Even seniors opt to eat in the dining halls because "one of the great things about the college system is that students from all classes interact on a daily basis (primarily at lunch)." On Saturday nights, the serveries are closed for all students—a mixed blessing because "it forces one to go off campus." And there are more than enough places to choose from, with a great range in price and quality. When the clock strikes 2 a.m., Taco Cabana, "a better, cheaper version of Taco Bell," is the place to be for post-party munchies. House of Pies is another Rice novelty.

Salsa and The Thresher

"People game, take salsa lessons, play ultimate Frisbee" and do anything to "enrich themselves," one student said of the extracurricular scene at Rice. Although some organizations are more "official" than others, "as long as you have a group of people with a common shared idea, it can be made into an official club." The Cabinet, Parliament and Diet among others are the names of residential college student governments, and these are a popular activity, even more so than its counterpart, the University student government. Future journalists can take a stab at writing for Rice's widely read newspaper, The Thresher. High participation rates show more than just an interest to beef up the résumé. "Everybody does their own thing," one student explained.

Although Rice's athletics are not the pinnacle of the University, the school's baseball team won the College World Series in 2003, made the NCAA tournament last year and advanced to the NCAA Super Regionals. Rice students don't just cheer for the champs, though. A surprising number of people attend the football games "even though we're quite pathetic," one student said. College sports are another popular option—teams from various residential colleges compete against one another for the President's Cup. Although there are separate workout facilities for varsity athletes, the general public facility "pale in comparison to Duke's," as one student put it. "You're probably going to have to wait for cardio equipment anytime in the afternoon or evening, and most mornings as well. But the Board of Trustees has stated that a new Rec Center is a priority."—*Dana Schuster*

FYI

If you come to Rice you'd better bring a "sense of humor, good work ethic, lots of shorts, and an umbrella."

What is the typical weekend schedule? "Every weekend here is different than the next if you make it that way."

If I could change one thing about Rice, it would be "more on-campus housing."

Three things every student at Rice should do before graduating are "ride in Beer-Bike, sneak into Reckling Park or Rice Stadium after dark for an impromptu pick-up game or trot around the bases; and climb 180, 90, and 45 (giant stone statues in the engineering quad)."

Southern Methodist University

Address: Southern Methodist, P.O. Box 750181, Dallas, TX 75275
Phone: 800-323-0672
E-mail Address: ugadmission@smu.edu
Web site URL: www.smu.edu
Year Founded: 1911
Private or Public: private
Religious affiliation: Methodist
Location: urban
Regular Application Deadline: 15-Mar
Number of Applicants: NA
Percent Accepted: 54%
Percent Accepted who enroll: 33%
Number Entering: NA
Number of Transfers Accepted each Year: NA
Mean SAT: NA
Mean ACT: NA
Middle 50% SAT range: 1,760–2,010

Middle 50% ACT range: 24–29
Early admission program (EA/ ED/ NA): EA
ED or EA Acceptance Rate: NA
Full time Undergraduate enrollment: 6,296
Total enrollment: 10,941
Percent Male: 45%
Percent Female: 55%
Total Percent Minority: 21%
Percent African-American: 5%
Percent Asian/Pacific Islander: 6%
Percent Hispanic: 8%
Percent Native-American: 1%
Percent Other: NA
Percent in-state / out of state: 63.8%/36.2%
Percent from Public HS: 61%

Retention Rate: 88%
Graduation Rate: 74%
Percent in On-campus housing: 45%
Percent affiliated with Greek system: 32%
Percent Varsity or Club Athletes: NA
Number of official organized extracurricular organizations: 227
3 Most popular majors: Communications, Journalism, Social Sciences
Student/Faculty ratio: 12:01
Tuition and Fees: $26,880
Cost for Room and Board: $9,208
Percent receiving Financial aid, first-year: 78.8%

Many Southern Methodist University students are frustrated with the stereotypes associated with common perceptions of their beloved school, complaining that "everyone assumes because we go to SMU we must be rich and southern." But never fear. "SMU is really working to change its image from 'Southern Millionaires' University' to an academically charged, more demanding and well-respected and recognized university" asserted one proud Mustang. And while there are elements of that academic millionaire's club that still linger on campus (one sophomore insisted that every girl should know to bring "a Lily Pulitzer dress and pearls" to school), this is not by any means all that SMU has to offer. "SMU has top-notch academics, opportunities, professors, location and students," one senior explained.

Life on a Movie Set
SMU offers nationally recognized programs in fields ranging from business to dance. Although the offerings are rigorous, requirements are flexible enough to allow students to double major, to pick up minors, or to participate in one of the many study abroad programs that SMU offers. But between the wide variety of academic programs and extensive extracurricular involvements, students must quickly learn to balance their time. One Mustang observed, "There is always something to do but the library is also always packed!"

"First-years" (never call them "freshmen"!) are required to live on campus. There are a number of different housing options, including an Honors dorm. "I enjoy on-campus living because I don't have to drive much unless I'm going out to eat or shopping," a sophomore RA said. "It's nice being close to all of my classes." Another Mustang chimed in that he "loved living in the dorms! It can get a little loud in the freshman dorms at times, but it is essential to the freshman experience." After freshman year, the housing choices expand immensely. Sophomore males may decide to move into their fraternity houses (girls have to wait until their junior year to live in the sorority houses), but there are also on-campus, as well as off-campus apartments ("It's not cheap, but it's very doable"), and of course, various on-campus residence halls and houses.

The on-campus eating options, centered around the offerings of Umphrey Lee Center, are enough to keep most Mustangs happy. Its pasta bar has a loyal following amongst students, as do the omelets at Mac's Place. In general, on-campus dining offers enough variety that at least one item will please every student's palate. And, for at least one first-year, there's more than enough to keep her happy. "It's all pretty delicious," she said.

But even if the beauty of SMU is not in its dining halls, then the breathtaking campus landscape more than makes up for it. "The whole thing is amazing!" one senior raved. Another added, "It's like a movie campus!" Indeed, the school takes full advantage of the sunny Dallas weather. "The grounds keepers change all the flowers in the flower beds once a month so they're always in season and beautiful." All of this is encased in what one Mustang described as the "Highland Park Bubble." Highland Park, one of the wealthiest neighborhoods in Dallas, surrounds the campus. And while this may make things expensive for students, it also provides them with "small town shops and little diners." Furthermore, it provides an outstanding level of safety on campus. "I literally walked from one end of the campus to the other at midnight and felt extremely safe," one sophomore said. Indeed, thanks to the fact that the campus lies within the jurisdiction of four different police forces (Highland Park, neighboring University Park, SMU Campus Police, and the Dallas Police), students are well protected at all times.

TVs and Tailgating
On the surface, there is a large element of homogeneity within the student body. "SMU is really conservative. It's kind of like a scaled down version of UGA or Old Miss," one sophomore noted. However, there is a subtle streak of diversity that quickly becomes apparent upon closer investigation. For example, the campus boasts far more religious diversity than a school with the word "Methodist" in its name would be expected to have, with 31 religious groups, including the Hillel, Hindu Club, and the Baha'i Club, operating under the office of campus chaplain, including the Muslim Student Association. As one junior explained, "I would say the majority of campus often feels predominantly Christian. However, when you really start to meet people and talking to them, you will find out just how diverse we all really are."

There are a number of ways to get involved in athletics on campus, from intramural sports to the varsity level. And although the school is successful in a number of different sports, football is an undeniable favorite at

SMU. Some students complained that this favoritism can be to the detriment of other sports. "Our men's soccer team is ranked number one in our conference and many people do not have any interest."

> **"It's 'SMU tailgating.' People have big screen TVs, satellite dishes, leather couches, and other ridiculous tailgating items."**

Still, there's something to be said for the enthusiasm amongst students when it comes to supporting their football team. Aside from the requisite body-painting and jersey-wearing, Mustangs list tailgating amongst their favorite SMU traditions. Sure, this may sound like a relatively common pastime for a college campus, but don't be fooled. As one freshman explained, "It's 'SMU tailgating.' People have big screen TVs, satellite dishes, leather couches, and other ridiculous tailgating items." Indeed, tailgating draws crowds of Mustangs, alumni, and other fans to the 'Boulevard,' the road which runs north to south through the center of campus. Groups such as fraternities, sororities, and even different colleges rent out the red and blue tents that line the Boulevard to wait for the game to begin, aided by the large, digital countdown clocks that are scattered throughout the crowd. "Seeing friends, the free food, and the whole aspect of body-painting with fraternity brothers right before the game makes the whole experience a great one."

Going Greek

Despite the fact that only about one third of Mustangs are members of a fraternity or sorority, it is also true that Greek life has a disproportionately strong presence on campus. "At SMU Greek life is huge," one sorority sister asserted. "The school, particularly the admissions office, tries to play it down. But in reality, as proven by statistics, it is the students that are in sororities and fraternities that have the highest average GPA and are the most involved in other programs on campus".

But the Greek system's visibility does not end there. The rush process virtually takes over the entire campus during the week be-fore the start of spring semester in January. Rushees return early to SMU in order to participate in a full week of rush activities, described across the board as "intense." Sorority rushees, for example, have to dress for a different theme each day, whether it be business casual or formal. At the end of the rush process, all accepted sorority rushees participate in a "Pig Run," which entails the girls, dressed identically in white tops and jeans, to run from the center of campus to Sorority Row, all the while cheered on by the new fraternity pledges. And the enthusiasm extends well past rush. "In the spring everything kind of revolves around Greek life because everyone is so excited about it," a sophomore said.

The process is taken extremely seriously, to the point that potential pledges are not even allowed to interact with Greek members in the fall semester, for fear that groups will attempt to unfairly lure hapless first years into their sororities or fraternities. A small percentage of students, however, may take the process a little too seriously. "There's people who talk about girls transferring because they didn't get the house they wanted," one Mustang remarked, but later admitted to not knowing "how true that is."

The prominence of fraternities and sororities on campus often calls into question the issue of drinking on campus. In fact, aside from tailgates (at which those 21 and older wear bands indicating that they can drink), SMU is a dry campus. Campus police are strict in enforcing the rules. However, students do have the option of going to both fraternity parties and to the bars surrounding campus. And many actively take advantage of these opportunities. But at the same time, there are more than enough opportunities for those who choose to stay on campus and not to drink. "SMU does a great job of providing many things to do, such as sneak peek previews for upcoming movies." At times, Southern Methodist University may live up to its reputation "where rich white kids go to become Greek, party, and find their spouses." But that is far from all the school has to offer. From academics to tradition, SMU provides its students with the opportunity to have a world-class education within the "movie campus" that SMU calls home.—*Stephanie Brockman*

FYI

If you come to SMU, you'd better bring: a sundress for tailgating if you're a girl and a polo shirt if you're a boy.

What is the typical weekend schedule? Sleep almost all day on Saturday, wake up in time to tailgate, go pre-game and then tailgate, and then go to sleep. Sundays sleep in, shop, and do some studying.

If I could change one thing about SMU, I'd . . . "Dispel the negative stereotypes and rumors about SMU. I think many strong and focused students buy into the rumors and therefore believe SMU would not be a good fit for them."

Three things every student at SMU should do before graduating are . . . Go to Plucker's (a local restaurant with GREAT wings) late night, take Crime and Delinquency with Richard Hawkins, and explore, and probably get lost in, downtown Dallas

Texas A&M University

Address: Texas A&M, NA, College Station, TX 77843-1265

Phone: 979-845-3741

E-mail Address: admissions@tamu.edu

Web site URL: www.tamu.edu

Year Founded: 1876

Private or Public: public

Religious affiliation: none

Location: small city

Regular Application Deadline: 39,114

Number of Applicants: NA

Percent Accepted: 77%

Percent Accepted who enroll: 56%

Number Entering: NA

Number of Transfers Accepted each Year: NA

Mean SAT: 1,187

Mean ACT: 26

Middle 50% SAT range: V:520–630, M:560–660

Middle 50% ACT range: 23–28

Early admission program (EA/ ED/ NA): NA

ED or EA Acceptance Rate: NA

Full time Undergraduate enrollment: NA

Total enrollment: 36,473

Percent Male: 52%

Percent Female: 48%

Total Percent Minority: 0%

Percent African-American: 3%

Percent Asian/Pacific Islander: 4%

Percent Hispanic: 12%

Percent Native-American: 1%

Percent Other: NA

Percent in-state / out of state: 97%/3%

Percent from Public HS: NA

Retention Rate: 92%

Graduation Rate: 77%

Percent in On-campus housing: 25%

Percent affiliated with Greek system: 18%

Percent Varsity or Club Athletes: NA

Number of official organized extracurricular organizations: 727

3 Most popular majors: Biological and Physical Sciences, Multi/Interdisciplinary Studies

Student/Faculty ratio: 20:01

Tuition and Fees: $15,216

In State Tuition and Fees (if different): $6,966

Cost for Room and Board: $7,660

Percent receiving Financial aid, first-year: 38%

To call Texas A&M traditional would be a gross understatement. Located in College Station, Texas, this large state university is filled with traditional, conservative, proud Aggies. Although the undergraduate population is over 30,000, the school feels "homey" and the professors are "outgoing." Texas A&M is a school for those who are serious about football, those who want top-notch academics and those who want both.

Not as Large as it Seems

Although Texas A&M consists of 10 different colleges, Texas is a small school that "deceitfully comes off as a huge school." Most students agree that it is easy to find their niche. Like any school, intro classes can be large: some have up to 500 students. Texas A&M provides many smaller classes and special programs, however, to give students seeking a more intimate environment some outlet. Students enrolled in the honors program are enrolled in smaller classes from the beginning, and during the junior and senior years classes are frequently as small as 25 students. One sophomore described faculty members as "extremely approachable," also commenting, "Texas attracts proactive students. If you want attention you have to get it, but in return professors are excited to help." Still, other students note that it is easy to get lost in the crowd for those looking for that.

Students said one thing to note about Texas A&M was that academic experience can vary a lot by major. The bioscience departments as well as the business school have reputations for being somewhat rigid, while students agreed that most liberal arts faculty are more personable. Despite these variations, students said that advising is uniformly excellent, especially for those willing to look for it: "You just have to try out a few advisers."

Students from all of the colleges mix together. One senior commented, "The breadth of the university is one of the best things about it. I have lived with business majors, engineering majors, and English majors." Moreover, although Texas A&M students are serious academically, the environment is far from cutthroat.

Active, Friendly and Greek

Most students choose to live on or near campus, which furthers the sense of community. Freshmen generally live on campus, while sophomores, juniors and seniors often choose to live off-campus in sorority or fraternity houses or nearby apartment complexes described as "oversized dorm complexes." Campus is divided into the Northside and the Southside. Northside stereotypically houses "non-conformist" students, and Southside attracts Greek students and students involved in campus organizations. All on-campus housing is mixed and provides an opportunity for underclassmen to mix with upperclassmen.

While there is a Greek presence, students say Greek life does not dominate the social scene or student life. One senior in a sorority said: "The lack of focus on the Greek scene attracted me to the school. I love being part of a sorority, but it by no means dictates my life." She also noted Greek students' high level of involvement. "Those involved in fraternities or sororities do so much that it is another thing to add to the list."

Socially, students say there is a group for everyone. Fraternities and sororities are options, but by no means the only social outlet. "There is so much going on around the campus that it is hard not to find a group to identify with," said one senior. One student added, "Students are generally behaved and respectful." For the most part, students say the student body is conservative. Most students are "clean cut and have a good sense of morals," remarked one senior.

Another popular campus activity is the Corps, which draws many male students and is somewhat similar to a fraternity. The Corps is a "highly respected military organization that instills values in its members." Texas A&M was originally a military school, and in this sense, the Corps reflects Aggie roots and instills a high sense of tradition. Other clubs include student government associations (SGA) and freshman leadership organizations (FLO). With over 800 student organizations, it is obvious that Aggies do much more than just go to class. "The involvement of the students is astronomical. It's what makes Aggies Aggies," added one sophomore.

"Once an Aggie, Always an Aggie"

A sense of tradition is significant part of campus life, during college and after one graduates. One of the more prominent traditions is "class wildcats," which are distinct noises made by each class at football games. Another tradition is Muster, a ceremony that draws thousands to honor fallen Aggies. Dunking one's Aggie ring at the Dixie Chicken is also quite popular. The tradition entails dunking the ring in a pint of beer, chugging the beer, and catching the ring in one's teeth. Overall, tradition infiltrates many aspects of Aggie life; the most important one by far is football. A Texas A&M game is not your ordinary college football game. The entire town shuts down, thousands of fans travel in for the game, and the entire day is devoted to Aggie pride. The night before is the Midnight Yell, which is a pep rally run by "Yell Leaders." During the game, everyone is expected to stand and cheer for the team. As Aggies say it, "If Texas A&M loses, it is the crowd's fault for not cheering loudly enough."

All in all, the high sense of tradition, strong academic program, and enthusiastic student body make Texas A&M a unique college experience that turns students proud Aggies for life.—*Hilary Cohen*

FYI

If you come to Texas A&M you'd better bring "a cowboy hat and a willingness to embrace Texas culture."

What is the typical weekend schedule? "Thursday is club night, Friday is date night, and Saturday is bar night. Saturday afternoons are spent at the football games. On Sunday mornings, students go to church. Sunday afternoon is spent doing work."

If I could change one thing about Texas A&M, I'd "change the stereotype of an overly conservative student body. We are conservative, but by no means extreme."

Three things every student should do before graduating are "go pond hoping around campus, dunk your Aggie ring, and go to a Midnight Yell."

Texas Christian University

Address: Texas Christian, 2800 S. University Drive, Sadler Hall, Room 112, TCU Box 297013, Fort Worth, TX 76129
Phone: 800-828-3764
E-mail Address: frogmail@tcu.edu
Web site URL: www.admissions.tcu.edu
Year Founded: 1873
Private or Public: private
Religious affiliation: Disciples of Christ
Location: urban
Regular Application Deadline: 15-Feb
Number of Applicants: 8,667
Percent Accepted: 62%
Percent Accepted who enroll: 30%
Number Entering: 2,041
Number of Transfers Accepted each Year: 855

Mean SAT: NA
Mean ACT: NA
Middle 50% SAT range: 1,570–1,870
Middle 50% ACT range: 23–28
Early admission program (EA/ ED/ NA): EA
ED or EA Acceptance Rate: 60%
Full time Undergraduate enrollment: 7,269
Total enrollment: 8,865
Percent Male: 40%
Percent Female: 60%
Total Percent Minority: 23.7%
Percent African-American: 5.2%
Percent Asian/Pacific Islander: 2.3%
Percent Hispanic: 6.6%
Percent Native-American: 0.6%
Percent Other: 9%
Percent in-state / out of state: 73%/27%

Percent from Public HS: 95%
Retention Rate: 84%
Graduation Rate: 69%
Percent in On-campus housing: 46%
Percent affiliated with Greek system: 35%
Percent Varsity or Club Athletes: NA
Number of official organized extracurricular organizations: 200+
3 Most popular majors: Business, Nursing, Biology
Student/Faculty ratio: 14:01
Tuition and Fees: $23,028.00
Cost for Room and Board: $7,120.00
Percent receiving Financial aid, first-year: 68%

Texas Christian University lies in the heart of Dallas/Fort Worth, and it embodies the heart of Texas. From the football stands to the classroom, TCU students carry a "go get 'em" attitude and a horned frog football cheer. As one sophomore so eloquently put it, "I will bleed purple until the day I die."

The Perfect Fit

Texas Christian University offers its students a well-rounded liberal arts education that "gives you a broad experience but [doesn't] force you to delve too deeply into subjects you're not interested in," according to one sophomore. His classmate elaborated: "I revel in the academic life here." That life requires an "essential" core curriculum which consists of credits in the humanities, social science, natural science, mathematics, writing and oral communication. There is also a Heritage, Mission, Vision and Values requirement with emphasis in religion, culture and history. In addition, students at TCU must complete their majors' requirements. One sophomore explained that, "people in 'technical' majors like nursing or engineering have it much tougher than the liberal arts majors." Accordingly, students name biology, physics, mathematics, chemistry, accounting/finance, engineering and nursing as the difficult majors, and advertising/public relations, communications, interior design and nutrition as the less demanding ones.

The Neeley School of Business houses the most competitive majors, while hardcore studiers are found racing along the pre-med track. TCU also offers a highly praised Honors Program, which awards early class registration to students invited to the program upon acceptance to TCU, as well as those who prove themselves capable by first semester grades. In order to stay in the Honors Program, students must fulfill additional class requirements. Many pursue the Chancellor's Leadership Program and specialized programs in the business school in place of the generalized honors curriculum. Texas Christian University strives to maintain small classes of 30 to 40 students. Therefore, class registration for popular majors like communications can be difficult when many students compete for the same courses. (Athletes and honors students have the privilege of registering early). According to TCU students, the process, though potentially frustrating, results in "perfect" class sizes and a manageable workload. One sophomore stated that, "I feel like academics at TCU are challenging but not burdensome for the most part; students are still able to have a social life and keep a good GPA."

Although lacking worldwide fame, the professors at Texas Christian University are praised by their students. One student caringly described his favorite teachers: "Dr. Patrick Nuss is an amazing teacher in the business school. I particularly enjoy Dr. Blake Hestir of the Philosophy Department (the existentialist, he has a delightfully sinister sense of humor) and Dr. Timothy Parrish of the English Department (the classic ponytail, glasses, preoccupied, brilliant, bad-at-spelling English professor)." Other students reiterated the fact that they cherish their close relationships with professors and cite rare, yet positive, experiences with teaching assistants. "The only grievance I have with classes," one sophomore said, "is that sometimes there are not enough of them." However, the same student went on to explain the University's extraordinary focus on accommodating student concerns. For example, the School of Journalism recently added several classes in response to student demand.

Living It Up

TCU party life is divided in two ways: underclassmen and upperclassmen, and Greeks and non-Greeks. Underclassmen go to frat parties, house parties, and mixers on the weekends while upperclassmen prefer bars. However, obtaining alcohol is not much of a problem for anyone at TCU, even for those underage.

Since the University is a Christian school, there are many non-drinkers and more alternative social venues for them to enjoy. A number of concert venues are near campus, and the TCU theater has scheduled performances on most weekends. Further, the Bass Performance Hall provides musical performances and the Programming Council, part of the student government, plans movies and concerts for the collegiates. There is a student center on campus fit with a ballroom.

Most campuswide events at TCU are hosted by independent or Greek organizations. Thirty-five percent of the student body is involved in a sorority or fraternity. To no surprise, the rush process dominates a large amount of student energy. Though fraternity rush is relatively laidback at TCU, sorority rush is incredibly stressful, noted one sophomore. However, another added that 'cool' frats and sororities just depend on your preference of people. "Everyone has different ideas about which ones are the best," so there is no real hierarchy in the Texas Christian Greek society. The parties are usually fun and girls are rarely charged for admission or drinks. Most often, it's the fraternity members who fund alcohol purchases and theme parties, the best of which come at Halloween, Christmas and the end of the year—barring any police presence: "Fort Worth has the largest police force in Texas." The TCU administration is also tough on drinking. Kegs are allowed on campus only for tailgates and Greek organizations are held liable for any out-of-control events. However, the University has recently installed a "medical amnesty" policy that protects students with alcohol-induced sickness from punishment in order to insure their safe treatment.

A Deficit in Dating and Diversity

The dating life at TCU is minimal. "A lot of people joke that at TCU, you either have a boyfriend or you hook up, but there is little 'dating,' " said one sophomore. This phenomenon may make sense considering that the college is smack in the middle of a state famous for its attractive populace. Who wants to settle down when there's so much to go around? One male student elaborated: "The girls are hot. The guys aren't too shabby from what I hear either. Overall the campus is generally pretty gorgeous. It's easy to forget that there are unattractive people in the world." Aside from all of the ogling on campus, sex keeps a pretty low profile at TCU. There have recently been articles in campus publications about the lurking threat of STDs, but none of the interviewed students cited a significant presence.

In particular, homosexual and interracial couples are few and far between. "There are very few gays," said one student. Further, the school has a very small minority population. And although most students seem pleased with the student population, they do wish it were more diverse. The overwhelming homogeneity has made minority students somewhat exclusive. "The African-American crowd typically associates solely with each other," said one senior. "Many students assume that if a TCU student is black, he or she is an athlete, which is certainly not the case." The TCU stereotype is "white, rich and Greek." One student passionately described the "typical student" as a "sorority girl wearing her silly big sunglasses and carrying her Prada bag while she talks on her cell phone. She's probably driving her Mercedes, too." Since TCU was rated one of the fittest campuses in the country by Men's Health Magazine, and the Rec Center is one of the hottest daytime spots on campus, chances are she's probably worked hard enough to deserve those designer jeans.

Living On, Eating Off
The average freshman dorm at TCU provides "the basic necessities and nothing more." Space is tight, and visiting, alcohol and drug restrictions are even tighter, but students still find the overall dorm experience to be "fine." All dorms come with air-conditioning, heat, and RAs. Most students agreed that the best dorms are Moncrief Hall and Foster Hall. Could this be because they're also coed? They're also brand new and reserved for honor students, athletes, and upperclassmen. The worst dorm is reportedly Milton Daniel. "It has broken water

fountains and smells like puke and carrots on a fairly regular basis." Interestingly, binge drinkers and wild parties are mysteriously attracted to Milton's conditions.

TCU has a separate endowment dedicated to landscaping, so you can be sure that the physical campus is beautiful—and safe. "I absolutely feel safe at TCU," affirmed one student. The police are easily accessible and TCU has an all-male organization called "Froggie-Five-O" that gives rides to girls when they have to walk at night. Despite the friendly security services, most upperclassmen move off campus to enjoy apartment or house set-ups and lower prices. Added one sophomore, "Underclassmen are allowed to live off-campus, but it is strongly discouraged."

> "The campus is generally pretty gorgeous. It's easy to forget that there are unattractive people in the world."

Most students, even residents, eat a fair number of meals off campus, because of the dining halls' expensive prices and inconvenient timing (although the University is planning to improve the cafeterias in the near future). "The only thing that stays open past 2:30 in the afternoon is the Main which is really fattening and heavy food. Edens, Deco Deli and Sub Connection are all better options if you don't mind eating really early." The Main's main draw is its social appeal. Most campus cliques (fraternities, athletes) are represented there during the day, so groups of friends might appear just to socialize.

As for off-campus eateries, "the most famous restaurant in Fort Worth is undoubtedly Joe T. Garcia's. It's been around forever!" Italian Inn is also a great, but undiscovered date restaurant where the waiters serve and entertain. And although there is a local Starbucks for the corporation-friendly, the Panther City Coffee Co. is heralded as the best spot for an espresso shot.

Texas Is for Football
Football is the most popular spectator sport at Texas Christian University. The Horned Frogs recently won the Houston Bowl and draw much school spirit from students and

alumni alike. In face, TCU's traditional spectator chant, "Riff Ram Bah Zoo," is one of the oldest cheers in college history.

Unique to TCU are the Purple Hearts, a student organization that helps lure high school football players to the University. "We recruit senior football players for the TCU team through visits to the stadium and the athletic complex at home games," a student explained. For more recreational athletes, IM sports are prevalent at TCU and the Rickel Recreation Complex offers state-of-the-art athlete equipment. "Every cardio machine has its own flat-screen TV, and there are really nice weights and stuff. There are also aerobic classes and yoga every day, an indoor and outdoor swimming pool, and indoor and outdoor track."

According to one sophomore, "TCU students are very involved, and spend quite a bit of their time on other activities." About half of the student body works a part-time job, and most are identified by their extracurricular activities. Social organizations, performance groups, intramurals, academic organizations and service organizations are the most popular. The most heralded organization is Frog Camp, an orientation trip for freshmen for which upperclassmen are leaders. Also highly touted are the Student Government Association, Order of Omega Greek honors society, sports appreciation organizations, and the "eleven40seven" journal of written and visual arts.

Texas Tradition

One thing is clear: TCU is a University bathed in tradition. Along with legendary cheers, students are indoctrinated by a wealth of myth when they accept admission to the school. One student cited the following examples: "When the purple light is on in Frog Fountain, the Chancellor is on campus. If you kiss the nose of the iron Horned Frog statue, you will have good luck. The bodies of Addison and Randolph Clark (TCU's founders) are actually cremated inside their bronze statues. It is tradition to raise your right hand and make the horned frog sign with your fingers when the chapel bell rings the alma mater." Another noted that President Lyndon B. Johnson himself broke the ground of the Sid Richardson science building when it was built in the seventies.

TCU is a place that people fall in love with, from its glorious oaks to its cheesy mascot: "People take a lot of pride from being Frogs—we're the only Horned Frogs in the nation!"—*Lauren Ezell*

FYI

If you come to TCU, you better bring "a lot of Polos."

What is a typical weekend schedule? "Study by day, party by night."

If I could change one thing about TCU, I'd "make it more diverse."

Three things every student at TCU should do before graduating are "Study abroad, jump in Frog Fountain, and go to Joe T's and Ol' South."

Texas Tech University

Address: Texas Tech, Box 45005, Lubbock, TX 79409
Phone: 806-742-1480
E-mail Address: admissions@ttu.edu
Web site URL: www.ttu.edu
Year Founded: 1923
Private or Public: public
Religious affiliation: none
Location: urban
Regular Application Deadline: 2-May
Number of Applicants: NA
Percent Accepted: 70%
Percent Accepted who enroll: 40%
Number Entering: NA
Number of Transfers Accepted each Year: NA
Mean SAT: 1,096
Mean ACT: 24
Middle 50% SAT range: V: 500–590, M:520–620

Middle 50% ACT range: NA
Early admission program (EA/ ED/ NA): NA
ED or EA Acceptance Rate: NA
Full time Undergraduate enrollment: NA
Total enrollment: 23,838
Percent Male: 55%
Percent Female: 45%
Total Percent Minority: 0%
Percent African-American: 3%
Percent Asian/Pacific Islander: 3%
Percent Hispanic: 12%
Percent Native-American: 1%
Percent Other: NA
Percent in-state / out of state: 96%/4%

Percent from Public HS: NA
Retention Rate: 83%
Graduation Rate: 56%
Percent in On-campus housing: 24%
Percent affiliated with Greek system: NA
Percent Varsity or Club Athletes: NA
Number of official organized extracurricular organizations: 411
3 Most popular majors: Health and Physical Education, Mechanical Engineering, Psychology
Student/Faculty ratio: 18:01
Tuition and Fees: NA
Percent receiving Financial aid, first-year: 37%

A t a school with over 20,000 undergraduates, it's hard to define the "typical student." But students at Texas Tech are united by their commitment to the university and to the community at large. "This is one of the most exciting times to be a part of Texas Tech," explained one student, who sees a renaissance beginning for the school. "We're an emerging research university now," he said, citing several recently-hired faculty members and the acquisition of a new Vice President of Research for the University. "We want to become a top one."

Such ambition is characteristic of Tech students and is exemplified by the school's Student Government Association. Officers spend up to 40 hours per week at the SGA office, working to promote student needs and to develop and execute initiatives of their own. The SGA created programs such as Take a Kid to the Game, which allows local underprivileged kids to watch the Red Raiders play football and spend the day with a Tech student. The SGA has also worked with the university's career center to attract the attention of prominent Texas-based companies. "We want to do a better job of getting Tech's image out there," said a member of the SGA.

Academics on the Upswing

Students say they are generally happy with the courses offered at Tech, but deciding which classes to take can be a bit of a headache. Students criticized the advising program, claiming that counselors "aren't always helpful." One student, who complicated her degree plan by changing her major, said "it's hard for students who don't know what they want to do right away." While one student remarked that his interactions with advisors "left something to be desired," others reported that advisors can actually be helpful.

Small classes tend to give students the most positive academic experiences at Texas Tech. Introductory classes, particularly in popular departments like business, biology, architecture, and English, may have 400 or more students. One student called his experiences in these classes "disappointing," pointing out that he never got to actually meet his professors. Upper-level classes, however, which contain between 30 and 70 students, are "more fulfilling."

Regardless of class size, professors are "very accessible," offering regular, frequent office hours. Students also praised Tech's academic atmosphere. "It doesn't seem like a high-stress, competitive setting," said one student. "The professors and students are really friendly and open."

> **"This is one of the most exciting times to be a part of Texas Tech"**

One student highlighted Tech's recent academic improvement and potential for future growth. He said that while he is "not happy with where we are right now," the school has made a lot of progress in the past five years, as a greater number of small classes are offered and the quality of professors improves.

At Large in Lubbock

Most students at Texas Tech, especially non-freshmen, live off campus. However, a new on-campus option of two to three-bedroom apartment-style housing is popular among upperclassmen, one student said. Students said high-quality off-campus housing is relatively easy to find. In addition to the three apartment complexes across the street from campus (one of which is newer and more expensive than the other two), students also live in a residential neighborhood south of campus known as "Tech Terrace." Other popular apartment complexes may be found farther away from campus, but transportation to and from these locations usually requires a bus trip.

The university requires that freshmen live on-campus, and most students claimed that the experience of living in a dorm was valuable. One student noted that even though she moved off-campus by sophomore year, she was "grateful" for her on-campus experience because it was "a great way to meet people." Students also have the option of living on specially-assigned Intensive Study or Substance-Free floors (although technically, alcohol and other drugs are prohibited in all dorms).

Student attitudes are generally positive, but not extremely enthusiastic, about the town of Lubbock. One student said that she wishes she were in a bigger city—"though I love Lubbock," she added. Students say that the town is safe, and there is a separate on-campus police force. One student explained, "You either love Lubbock or you hate it, because there's not a whole lot to do, except get involved with things on-campus and in the town."

Gregarious Greeks

Getting involved is what Tech students do best. Whether it's involvement in a community outreach program, writing for Tech's newspaper, *The Daily Toreador*, or membership in a service sorority or fraternity, there is no shortage of extracurricular pursuits at Texas Tech.

While Tech's 400 student organizations cater to a variety of interests, Greek organizations are especially popular. "Greek life is really big, whether you're in it or not," said one student. Fraternities and sororities throw most of the parties at Tech, although because so many students live off-campus, non-Greek house parties are common as well. Greek students pointed out that by joining a fraternity or sorority, you are not only part of the single organization, but also a member of the greater Greek community at Tech. "It's nice to know that you can go to any local bar on a Thursday night and see all your friends," said one sorority member. Students at Tech are also attracted to Greek life for its service component, and some choose to join service sororities, which place an even greater emphasis on philanthropy. A student who joined both a Greek sorority and a non-Greek service sorority pointed out that while she enjoys Greek life, she has made closer friends through the service sorority because of its smaller size and more personal atmosphere.

The Center for Campus Life, which is the central office for all registered organizations on campus, is located in the Student Union Building. Since its recent renovation, the Student Union, which houses a bookstore, meeting rooms, TVs and a computing assistance center, has been especially popular among students. Furthermore, students are enthusiastic about the Student Union's food court, which includes a Chick-fil-A and a Starbucks.

The Center for Campus Life also provides a host of entertainment programs and events that range from concerts, interactive games, and movies to more academic-oriented programs like workshops and lecturers. TAB, the Tech Activities Board, also organizes events such as open mike nights, bowling, and foreign film screenings for those looking for an alternative to the Greek Life. When football season is in play, countless students participate in RaiderGate, co-hosted by the student government. RaiderGate is Texas Tech's version of tailgating, complete with live music and barbeque.

A "Dry" Town

Though Lubbock is a "dry" town and liquor stores are prohibited, bars are exempted from this law. In fact, Lubbock has a colorful bar scene—Bleachers Café, The Library, Rocky's, and Timmy's are student favorites. In order to purchase alcohol, students drive to an area called the Strip (apparently modeled after Las Vegas) outside of town. "It would be easier to go down to the convenience store and pick something up," one student griped.

While one student said that "a lot of partying goes on" at Tech, another pointed out that there is a "growing minority" that doesn't drink. In any case, students agreed that non-drinkers do not feel uncomfortable at Tech.

Red Raiders in a Red State

Students agree that the political climate at Tech and in Lubbock is "very conservative." One student put it this way: "If you don't love George Bush, you're in the minority." However, an officer of the University Democrats pointed out that liberal students are more common than you might expect, adding that liberalism is "an underground thing."

The student body at Tech is not very diverse, although students claim that the school is taking steps to increase racial diversity. While there is a Gay Straight Alliance at Tech, students agree that the gay community is not very visible. Of the 37 religiously-affiliated student organizations at Tech, 30 are Christian groups. One student pointed out that Bible studies are common and well-attended at Tech. Another student agreed that Christian groups are plentiful on campus but added that non-Christians "don't feel out of place."

Tech Takes the Field

Texas Tech is known for its high-caliber sports teams and enthusiastic fans. Cheering on the Red Raiders at football and basketball games is a central part of the Tech experience. Coach Bobby Knight has helped vault the basketball team into the spotlight, and women's basketball is drawing higher attendance than it ever has— higher, sometimes, than the men's team. Football, though, is the main attraction, according to students. The pre-game festivities alone are impressive, with fraternities, sororities, alumni groups, and even local rodeos sponsoring tailgates. On the Thursday before a game day, students decorate a statue of Will Rogers and his horse, Soapsuds, with red crepe paper. Even without the streamers, this Tech landmark is full of Tech pride. The horse's behind points straight in the direction of Tech's biggest rival, Texas A&M.

Non-varsity athletes at Tech are not just devoted fans; they are devoted players. Tech students are passionate about intramural sports, and since the expansion of the Student Recreation Center, IMs are more popular than ever. Student organizations, Greek organizations, and dorms field IM teams, and, as one student explained, "everybody plays; everybody wants to be the best." The Rec Center offers classes, workshops, and even massage therapy.

In the classroom, on the football field, or in the community, Red Raiders are proud to be part of the growth and improvement that characterizes Texas Tech. With a wide array of academic offerings, facilities that are constantly improving, and a rich extracurricular scene, Texas Tech is gaining popularity with Texans and non-Texans alike.—*Kathleen Reeves*

FYI

If you come to Texas Tech, you better bring "a dayplanner, because so many activities are offered on campus, and rain boots, because of the ineffective drainage system."

What's the typical weekend schedule? "Wednesday: Hit up a bar called South Beach; Thursday: Go to the Depot District of town; Friday: Hear a country band play at Wild West; Saturday: Football game day! Afterwards, head to a house party or the bars. Sunday: Wake up, spend all day at the library."

If I could change one thing about Tech, I'd "change the restrictive parking system."

Three things every student at Tech should do before graduating are "attend a football game, get involved in an on-campus organization, and go to Carol of Lights, an annual, nationally-recognized holiday lighting ceremony."

Trinity University

Address: Trinity, One Trinity Place, San Antonio, TX 78212-7200
Phone: 800-TRINITY
E-mail Address: admissions@trinity.edu
Web site URL: www.trinity.com
Year Founded: 1869
Private or Public: private
Religious affiliation: Presbyterian
Location: urban
Regular Application Deadline: 1-Feb
Number of Applicants: NA
Percent Accepted: 61%
Percent Accepted who enroll: NA
Number Entering: NA
Number of Transfers Accepted each Year: NA

Mean SAT: NA
Mean ACT: NA
Middle 50% SAT range: NA
Middle 50% ACT range: NA
Early admission program (EA/ ED/ NA): NA
ED or EA Acceptance Rate: NA
Full time Undergraduate enrollment: 2,449
Total enrollment: 2,693
Percent Male: 46%
Percent Female: 54%
Total Percent Minority: 40%
Percent African-American: 3%
Percent Asian/Pacific Islander: 7%
Percent Hispanic: 10%
Percent Native-American: 1%

Percent Other: 20%
Percent in-state / out of state: 83%/17%
Percent from Public HS: NA
Retention Rate: NA
Graduation Rate: NA
Percent in On-campus housing: NA
Percent affiliated with Greek system: 53%
Percent Varsity or Club Athletes: NA
Number of official organized extracurricular organizations: 130
3 Most popular majors: Business Administration, Modern Languages, English
Student/Faculty ratio: 10:1
Tuition and Fees: $23,136

Trinity University sits on the top of a hill, overlooking the beautiful San Antonio skyline. The attractive campus is ideally situated in a private setting in the midst of a growing, modern Texas city just minutes from the popular downtown tourist area, as well as the San Antonio airport. Year-round mild Texas weather, coupled with an equally "warm" campus community, allows students to party hardily while still partaking in a comparatively rigorous liberal arts education. Although the University is historically Presbyterian-affiliated, the religious feel of the campus is not as strong as the "family feel" that makes Trinity so unique.

High Educational Standards

Trinity University gives its students a strong liberal arts and science education and prepares them for "a lifetime of success in any endeavor." The school claims that compared to other universities, Trinity students receive a truly practical education. The academic program contains three components. The first component is the Common Curriculum, which provides a foundation in the arts and sciences. The Common Curriculum consists of a First Year Seminar Program and a Writing Workshop; proficiency in foreign language, computer, and mathematics skills; fitness education; a senior experience; and a

core liberal arts foundation consisting of "Five Fundamental Understandings." The second component of academic requirements is the major, which allows students to study a specific field in depth. Trinity offers its students 37 majors and 12 interdisciplinary minors. Thirdly, students must take elective courses in order to round out their curriculum and explore new areas.

Students generally agree that the "academic requirements are fairly stringent," but they also vary by department. According to one student, "Everyone is held to a high standard and the requirements are set forth to push even the brightest of students." Workload and class size all vary by department as well. Some students spend as much as 40 hours a week doing work, while many can get away with doing much less. Normal classes range in size from 25 to 80, but upper level courses in some departments have fewer than 10 students. One student observes that "the majority of the departments are well known on Trinity's campus, especially since it is such a small school." Because Trinity is small, it also allows for low faculty-to-student ratios. "Every student has the opportunity to get to know their professors very well if they wish. Many people take advantage of this and have developed extremely close relations with certain [professors]."

One unique aspect of Trinity's academic environment is the newly established Academic Honor Code. Initiated by students in 2004, the Honor Code is signed by all freshmen at new student orientation and requires that students sign every assignment, assuring that they have been honest in their academic endeavors.

Students at Trinity do not find much competition among their peers academically. According to one student, "The students at Trinity put more stress on their own academics rather than competing with others. There are some who do put stress on competition, but they are in the minority." Another student notes, "Everyone does their own thing academically, but there is a sense of competition in sports." For students who wish to go beyond the typical academic rigor, there are many honors societies at Trinity. These include Alpha Lambda Delta (a first year academic distinction), Golden Key National Honor Society, Phi Beta Kappa (general distinction; liberal arts and sciences), Alpha Epsilon Delta (pre-med honors society), and an honors society for about just every academic department. Students will find that most of the academic departments are well-known because it is such a small school. According to one student, "Although Trinity is considered to be a liberal arts school, the science department is very strong and continues to grow. The humanities aspect of Trinity is also thriving and new interdisciplinary majors are being added every year."

Sports and Frats Rule

On the weekends most students generally find themselves splitting time between fraternity parties and sporting events, as these tend to be the most popular social scenes on campus. According to one freshman, "Frats usually control the party scene on weekends." But a senior argues, "There is a large percentage of the student body involved in Greek life, but it doesn't dominate." In fact, the Greek scene incorporates about 25 percent of the student body and consists of six sororities and nine fraternities. An interesting fact about the Greek life at Trinity is that all of the sororities and fraternities are local; they are not affiliated with any national Greek organizations and as a result students do not have to pay high dues like at most other universities. The school does not allow Greek on-campus houses, but there are some "informal" off-campus houses.

Trinity University has 18 varsity sports teams, and they are some of the most competitive sports teams in the NCAA Division III and the Southern Collegiate Athletic Conference. Trinity has won 10 of the past 11 SCAC President's Cup Trophies, awarded to the conference's best overall sports program. According to one student, "Sports rule Trinity!" Students can often be found attending as many sporting events as they can on the weekends before going to the frat parties or local bars.

> ## "Sports rule Trinity!"

Many students at Trinity have cars, and there is "a good deal of parking on campus." Even so, since students are required to live on campus for three years, most of the weekend activity remains on campus. Only seniors live off campus, so according to one student, "they *do* have a different social life since most of their friends also live off campus and parties are off campus." Other students can use their cars on the weekends by going to local bars, one of the most popular being Bombay's Bicycle Club. San Antonio also provides many other opportunities for evening activity; students often go to Cowboys Dance Hall to see concerts or to the popular commercial River Walk, along the banks of the San Antonio River.

Alcohol at Trinity is very common, but probably just as common as at most universities—in the words of one student, "No more, no less." Drug use seems to the students to be just as widespread as at other schools as well. Students are aware that "there is a very strict drug and alcohol policy on campus and campus security responds very quickly to complaints." Even students who are 21 or older are only allowed to have beer in their rooms—no hard liquor.

Typical Trinity students have been described by their peers as "preppy" and "rich", but surprisingly, there "are not very many snobs." There is not much diversity at Trinity, but the diversity that is present is "well-represented." The students at Trinity are all very friendly and freshmen find it easy to meet others like themselves. According to one student, "Many people freshman year leave their doors propped open and hanging out in other people's rooms is very common."

Community Living

Living on campus is "integral to the educational experience" at Trinity and for this reason Trinity has imposed a Three-Year Residency Requirement on its students. Students are also guaranteed housing on campus senior year if they want it. As a result, nearly 80 percent of the student body lives on campus. First year students all live together in one area of campus, in one of seven dorms. This creates a freshman community. All residence halls are set up as suites, so two rooms share a bathroom and there are two students in each room. On-campus housing is considered "pretty decent" and this is not surprising given that students are required to live there for three years. About every 18 freshmen are assigned an upper-class Resident Mentor who guides them through New Student Orientation and "keeps the peace mostly." Trinity also offers its freshmen First Year Special Interest Housing, including options for Quiet Living and Substance-Free Living. After freshman year, students can request where they would like to live and may also request a roommate. Dorm personalities "change a little each year depending on who lives there," but often the upperclassmen dorms Thomas and Lightner are said to be party dorms. The dorms maintain their own traditions such as the annual baby-powdered covered Calvert Halloween "ghosts."

There are two places to eat on campus: Mabee Dining Hall and The Commons, a food court. The food on campus is, according to one student, "better than I thought it would be." The Commons is open until midnight, so students can buy late-night, fast-food snacks. There are also many good restaurants in nearby downtown San Antonio, if students get tired of the on-campus offerings.

Outside of the Classroom: Sports and More

At Trinity, athletics are much more than just a weekend diversion. In addition to the 18 competitive varsity teams, 65 percent of students at Trinity participate in club or intramural sports. Student-run club sports are very diverse, and include sports such as men's and women's lacrosse, equestrian, water polo, and even trap and skeet. Intramural sports give all students an opportunity to join in the athletic competitions, as there are teams for "almost anything you could think of."

Students also participate in many other activities outside of the classroom. About half of the students at Trinity participate in community service through the Trinity University Voluntary Action Center. There are also many religious groups on campus, as well as political action groups, and student publications such as the daily newspaper *The Trinitonian*. Some students also work during the school year and there are plenty of job opportunities for those students. Some of the most popular part-time work includes positions at local high schools, at Trinity's admissions office or work as a lifeguard. Again, accessibility to downtown San Antonio and its famed Riverwalk bars and restaurants is another perk of living in the middle of this modern city and popular tourist destination.

The sense of community resulting from Trinity's secluded campus, where most students live on campus, makes Trinity University a welcoming place. If that weren't enough, rigorous academics and stellar sports and social opportunities will likely satisfy almost anyone. Warm Texas weather and the University's nice facilities and private but accessible location in a modern city with great restaurants, bars, and professional sports nearby contribute to a very satisfied student body.—*Jessica Rubin*

FYI
If you come to Trinity, you'd better bring "lots of flip-flops."
What's the typical weekend schedule? "It's all about sports at Trinity. . . . You'd better be at the football, soccer, basketball, volleyball, and baseball games!"
If I could change one thing about Trinity, I'd "change the temperature of the classrooms . . . they are so chilly."
Three things every student at Trinity should do before graduating are: "Go abroad if you can, take advantage of the variety of student organizations on campus, and get to know a professor."

University of Dallas

Address: University of Dallas, 1845 E. Northgate Dr, Irving, TX 75062
Phone: 972-721-5266
E-mail Address: ugadmis@udallas.edu
Web site URL: www.udallas.edu
Year Founded: 1956
Private or Public: private
Religious affiliation: Catholic
Location: urban
Regular Application Deadline: 2-Aug
Number of Applicants: 876
Percent Accepted: 85%
Percent Accepted who enroll: 42%
Number Entering: 315
Number of Transfers Accepted each Year: 80
Mean SAT: 1,199
Mean ACT: 26

Middle 50% SAT range: 1,100–1,340
Middle 50% ACT range: 24–29
Early admission program (EA/ ED/ NA): EA
ED or EA Acceptance Rate: 71.4%
Full time Undergraduate enrollment: 1,188
Total enrollment: 2,941
Percent Male: 44%
Percent Female: 56%
Total Percent Minority: 33%
Percent African-American: 1%
Percent Asian/Pacific Islander: 6%
Percent Hispanic: 17%
Percent Native-American: 0%
Percent Other: 9%
Percent in-state / out of state: 56%/44%

Percent from Public HS: 45%
Retention Rate: 85%
Graduation Rate: 66%
Percent in On-campus housing: 62%
Percent affiliated with Greek system: 0%
Percent Varsity or Club Athletes: NA
Number of official organized extracurricular organizations: 35
Most popular majors: Business Administration, English
Student/Faculty ratio: 11:01
Tuition and Fees: $23,219.00
Cost for Room and Board: $7,615.00
Percent receiving Financial aid, first-year: 62%

Amidst the wide variety of colleges and universities in the greater Dallas area, the University of Dallas stands out for its combination of academic rigor and traditional Catholic sensibilities. With a strong emphasis on the Western canon, a comprehensive core curriculum, and a wildly popular study abroad program in Rome, UD offers its students a structured, traditional education that will serve them well both in and out the classroom.

Nerdy to the Core

UD has a reputation for being, as one student puts it, a "nerdy" school because of its comprehensive set of requirements known as the core curriculum. The UD core is mostly made up of primary sources that allow students to engage directly with the texts that shaped the foundations of Western thought. Of the credits needed to graduate, 15 are the same for everyone, made up of classes in English, math, theology, philosophy, economics and politics. In addition, there are science lab and language requirements that complete the core. English is one of the most popular majors at UD, despite the large amounts of reading, writing and memorization it requires. Psychology is also a favorite, even though majors have to complete a the-

sis over 100 pages long to graduate. Language and math majors are universally less popular.

No matter what you're majoring in, classes at UD seem to be challenging all around. As one student explains, "UD is hard, a lot harder than the other schools my friends go to . . . you can't find an easy class to shrug off." Though the University is generous with academic and athletic scholarships, they are difficult to maintain: "the academic demands for retaining any scholarships . . . are rigorous, so many students aren't able to slack off even if they don't care." Adding to the academic intensity, there is a very strict attendance policy at UD—missing four classes automatically means that you are dropped from the course. Luckily, students have the support of the faculty to guide them through the rough waters of UD academics; most students are happy with their professors, saying that they are "very accessible—they *want* you to contact them when you need them." Some popular ones include English professor Father Robert Maguire and economics teacher William Doyle, who help UD kids achieve their "number one goal" of truly learning and internalizing the material that they grapple with.

TGIT: Thank God It's Thursday

Of course, there is much more to life at UD besides its standout academic program. While sports admittedly "aren't the focus of UD," students enjoy participating in and cheering on the teams that they have, including the men's rugby and basketball teams, whose games draw a huge following. Support for women's teams is a little "less vigorous," but both genders play baseball, soccer and lacrosse. In fact, the UD lacrosse team is currently the only collegiate varsity lacrosse team in Texas. The newly renovated athletic center also provides lots of resources for students to stay in shape, including trainers and state-of-the-art equipment. Overall, as one student puts it, sports are "compatible" with the typical UD student way of life, even if they don't dominate it.

While there are over 35 extracurricular activities and clubs in which UD kids can participate, the consensus is that "club life isn't too popular in general, [since] a lot of students are busy studying." However, the student government and activities committee is large and attracts more and more people to their ranks in hopes of increasing the popularity of their events. Since there are no sororities or fraternities, on-campus social life at UD seems to revolve around parties in upperclassmen apartments either on campus or across the street in a group known as "Old Mill." Though some students say that "Student Apartment kids tend to stick to themselves," the parties they throw attract partygoers from all over the UD community. As one girl explains, "Younger and older students intermingle, making it easy for there to always be a party to go to if you have the right connections."

UD is a wet school, meaning that drinking is tolerated and prevalent throughout campus. While the drinking scene "never really gets out of control," one student admits that "technically, drinking policy is according to the law of the state of Texas, and if you get caught underage, you do get in trouble." Drinkers "tend to stick together" and congregate either at various parties or at a campus bar and grill called the Rathskeller that is actually on the student meal plan. For those who prefer their weekends dry, the student government sponsors a weekly event known as TGIT ("Thank God It's Thursday"), during which students party and dance to live music without the addition of alcohol.

Living in "the Convent"

Socially, UD provides a safe, friendly environment in which students can get to know each other. Despite the small size of the school (only about 1,100 total), most students claim that its nurturing environment is a help rather than a hindrance. "It's super easy to meet people your first semester, mostly because the school is so small . . . you immediately find your group of friends and settle in for the haul," said one junior. Diversity is a bit lacking at UD, since "most kids are white, hail from a Catholic (or at least Christian) household, and hold the same basic beliefs in common." However, some students claim that "there is a fair amount of diversity in religions and races," emphasizing that the University recognizes the importance of diversifying the student body and is making a conscious effort to do so. Either way, there is no lack of community at UD. As one junior raves, "That's one thing I love about this school . . . absolutely one hundred percent of [students] are genuine. Students are true to what they believe, kind and caring, and the farthest from a fake crowd you will ever find."

> "Students are true to what they believe, kind and caring, and the farthest from a fake crowd you will ever find."

The Dallas residential community is made up of a variety of houses, each of which has its own unique character. Freshmen and sophomores must live on campus in specific dorms, only one of which is coed. The prevalence of same-sex living "though it may seem like a bother, is actually pretty fun . . . dorm spirit is [awesome]." Of the eight dorms, the all-male Gregory and all-girl Jerome are known as the "party dorms" and Catherine, by contrast, is sometimes called "the Convent." All of them, however, have at least two RAs who are "strict" and "are pretty serious about their roles." While some upperclassmen continue to live on campus after sophomore year, most move to the Old Mill apartments across the street or into the Student Apartment complex, which are "a lot nicer . . . there's usually a waitlist to get in." The architecture on campus is "not very pretty to look at, but it serves its purpose"— some of UD's architectural standouts include the Braniff Memorial Tower, which is a "landmark for the University" and the newer Art Village, in which a whole group of buildings is "put on stilts, so . . . they pretty much [look like] they're in the trees."

All UD students who live on campus must be on a meal plan, and freshmen are assigned a 19-meal-per-week plan. After freshman year, you can choose between a plan of 19, 13, or 10 meals, and the declining balance can be used at the Rathskeller, which is located below the campus' only dining hall in the Haggar University Center. Most upperclassmen tend to get either the lowest amount of meals or no plan at all, since food-wise, "some days are better than others." Others are less diplomatic, saying, "Let's just put it this way—one of the most popular groups on Facebook is 'I starve myself to go to UD.' No one goes here for the dining services." Despite the lack of gourmet options, the dining hall and student center remain one of the central hangout locations on campus.

Dallas to Rome
Since there's "not much to do on campus," many UD students spend their weekends enjoying the restaurants and club scenes in the surrounding Texas areas. The town of Irving itself is "a little scruffy" and not quite as nice as the school itself, yet town-gown relations are so calm as to be almost non-existent, as one student describes: "Some people that live 15 minutes from the University have never even heard of it." To really get a taste of college town life, students recommend heading into the bigger city of Dallas itself for the best bar, shopping and restaurant scenes. They agree, however, that "[since] most places are a few miles away . . . if you want to hang out outside of campus, you need a car." Whether you want to party in downtown clubs, shop in the popular West End or Las Colinas districts or just grab dinner and a movie with friends, Dallas offers a plethora of opportunities for fun and relaxation off campus.

Perhaps the most well-known component of life at UD and the one that draws in the most students is its Rome program. Most sophomores spend at least one semester studying at UD's campus at Due Santi, just 20 minutes away from Rome itself. For many UD students, Rome is the highlight of their college career, as they take classes in subjects like ancient architecture and travel throughout Italy and Greece on weekends to see the very monuments they study. The Rome program, with its synthesis of Western tradition and Catholic values, and its application of the concepts learned in the classroom into real life, is the epitome of what makes the University of Dallas "a real, true, Catholic, strenuous liberal arts education that will influence all aspects of students' lives."—*Alexandra Bicks*

FYI
If you come to Dallas, you'd better bring: "a formal gown, cowboy hat and boots."
What's a typical weekend schedule? "Sleep it off from the night before, go to an occasional extra credit lecture on campus, do homework for a couple hours, hit Old Mill or the Student Apartments to do it again."
If I could change one thing about Dallas, I'd: "Make it a little bigger, and pretty-up some of that architecture."
Three things everyone should do before graduating are: "[participate in] all the activities you can, go to Rome, and attend mass at the Cistercian Abbey of Our Lady of Dallas."

The University of Houston

Address: University of Houston, Room 122 E.Cullen Building, Houston, TX 77204-2023
Phone: 713-743-1010 opt. 2
E-mail Address: NA
Web site URL: www.uh.edu/enroll/admis/
Year Founded: 1927
Private or Public: public
Religious affiliation: none
Location: urban
Regular Application Deadline: 2-Apr
Number of Applicants: 9,935
Percent Accepted: 74.51%
Percent Accepted who enroll: 46.4%
Number Entering: 3,435
Number of Transfers Accepted each Year: 5,080
Mean SAT: 1,054
Mean ACT: 21
Middle 50% SAT range: 950–1,190

Middle 50% ACT range: 19–24
Early admission program (EA/ ED/ NA): NA
ED or EA Acceptance Rate: NA
Full time Undergraduate enrollment: 26,959
Total enrollment: 33,426
Percent Male: 48%
Percent Female: 52%
Total Percent Minority: 69%
Percent African-American: 19%
Percent Asian/Pacific Islander: 24%
Percent Hispanic: 22%
Percent Native-American: <1%
Percent Other: <1%
Percent in-state / out of state: 98%/ 2%
Percent from Public HS: NA
Retention Rate: 78%
Graduation Rate: 42%

Percent in On-campus housing: 7%
Percent affiliated with Greek system: 3.48%
Percent Varsity or Club Athletes: NA
Number of official organized extracurricular organizations: 300
3 Most popular majors: Business/Commerce, Engineering, Psychology
Student/Faculty ratio: 20:01
Tuition and Fees: $15,159.00
In State Tuition and Fees (if different): $6,909.00
Cost for Room and Board: $6,418.00
Percent receiving Financial aid, first-year: 82.77%

Students who choose the University of Houston prepare for the professional world in a number of unique academic colleges, while enjoying the opportunity of living at home yet remaining involved on campus through intramural sports and numerous clubs. UH remains nearly unmatched among state universities in diversity of student background. Students travel from afar seeking Houston's requirement of a broad field of study, either with a liberal arts education offered by the Honors College or pursuing a mandated minor or double-major.

Renowned Academic Colleges

Opportunity for specialization abounds in the University's 14 academic colleges. In addition to the College of Liberal Arts and Social Sciences, numerous specialized colleges receive wide acclaim. The Conrad N. Hilton College of Hotel and Restaurant Management is "intense like the rest of the school," demanding much of its students in courses that include tours of restaurant and hotel facilities, economic theory, language and etiquette development, and food and beverage courses. Practicum courses put students in real-life employment situations to learn career skills. The C. T. Bauer College of Busi-

ness, a home to "great minds," ranks third among public Texas universities. The Colleges of Optometry and Pharmacy garner respect across the state as well. The Gerald D. Hines College of Architecture boasts amazing professors who are also known to solicit their students' help on projects and assist their students in finding internships.

The most selective of the colleges is the Honors College, a highly-ranked liberal arts program that enrolls 300 students to study literature and philosophy in a discussion environment. These students take a heavier-than-average course load, possibly 15-16 credit hours instead of a typical student's 12-13 credit schedule. Each semester, the Honors student must enroll in at least one course specific to the Honors College. They also must complete a Senior Honors Thesis to finish the program. The Honors College is located "in one of the better parts of campus" with classes held in the University's newly-renovated main library. Additional perks include priority registration, a private lounge and study space, and more structured advising. Advising within the Honors College does not require that you "hunt down an advisor" as meetings are preplanned for all Honors students.

For students who desire a less-intense experience than the Honors College, the Scholars Community, a supplementary course for which all students can apply, caters to the part of the student body that wants to be considered "more academic." The Scholars' Community is reportedly "not as intense" as the Honors College, and these students also enjoy priority registration and may take advantage of free tutoring sessions and special advising.

The University of Houston requires that all students take a core curriculum of 42 credit hours. This core curriculum does not limit students' freedom to explore possible majors, as students can and do change their major any number of times before junior year, when they must decide. Another distinctive aspect of the UH curriculum is that students within the College of Liberal Arts and Social Sciences must complete a minor or second major in addition to their first. Such a requirement ensures that all students study a diversity of topics.

Remarkable Courses

UH Colleges feature talented professors. "I've never had a professor I didn't like," reports one student. Even in comparison to the Honors College, professors are "just as good," but classes are larger. For example, one introductory chemistry course taught by the enthralling professor Dr. Simon Bott is one of the most interesting but one of the largest courses with an enrollment of approximately 600 students. Another popular course entitled "Principles of Drug Action" attracts a large number of students who ultimately find a seat in the class before graduating: "It seems like 80 percent go through it." "Beverage Appreciation," offered by the School of Hotel and Restaurant Management, is a popular winetasting course for juniors and seniors over 21 aspiring to become hospitality professionals. "Human Situation," an element of the Honors College curriculum, stands out from other courses as a "totally different" approach to reading works of literature and philosophy.

Students notice a constant flow of professors in and out of the University, which can enhance variety and opportunity, but can also make building relationships difficult. "I am having trouble finding professors who are still around to write letters of recommendation," laments one graduate school applicant. Although professors are easily reachable during office hours and by e-mail, "you would really have to work at a relationship" to get to know a member of the faculty.

Uncommon Diversity

The University of Houston has also been identified to its students as "one of the most diverse campuses in the nation." Indeed, few public universities can claim such a high number of international students and such a heterogeneous racial breakdown as the University of Houston. International students commonly hail from countries in Africa and Asia among others. Students say the University's generous financial aid policies contribute to a diverse student body.

The Commuter Lifestyle

Many students cite a close proximity to home and feasibility of living at home as major reasons for coming to the University of Houston. Alternatively, students who choose to live on campus avoid the stress of a morning commute. "Having to drive is a disadvantage because of traffic." In the past, parking space has been limited, but is expected to improve with the completion of a new parking garage.

In general, students feel that the student body is distributed fairly evenly between commuting students and students who choose to live on campus. Commuting students do not feel separated from their on-campus peers: "I practically live there. I stay so late that some of my classmates don't even know that I commute."

Constant Campus Improvement

The UH campus is set three-quarters of a mile away from a major freeway: "It's a great location because the campus is not totally downtown, so there is less traffic." One disadvantage of an urban campus, however, is that the UH campus adjoins economically troubled areas: "The area around it is not one of the nicest." Although students generally avoid the immediate vicinity, downtown Houston is always accessible. Still, the campus itself is peaceful and refreshing, featuring fountains and architecturally impressive structures. Also, construction seems to be constantly underway. Recent completions include renovations to the main library and a new Science and Engineering Center.

Living Options for Non-Commuters

Dormitories are the most common choice for housing at UH. "The Quads," which include the preferable Honors dorms, are regarded as the nicest dorm rooms. The basement of one building has a game room and kitchen equipment. Some regard Moody Towers as less appealing than the Quads. One student compares the dorms by the music they play in the cafeterias: nice classical music is standard for the Quads, while a visitor may hear "ghetto hip-hop" in the Towers. Each dorm features a lounge, computer lab with internet access, small convenience stores, and cafeterias for student use. Apartment-style living is also available in either university-owned or third-party buildings.

Dining options at UH are varied and commended. "UC Satellite," a newer dining area located underground, is "the best secret on campus." In addition to a deli with great sandwiches and a popular sushi bar, it features more commercialized restaurants like Smoothie King, Starbucks, Pizza Hut, Taco Bell, and Kim Son, serving Asian food. In addition, the Hilton Hotel on campus contains an upscale restaurant and a student-run café that operates during the night. Two dorm cafeterias serve "typical dorm food."

The Attractive Force of Activities

Clubs give many students a reason to stay on campus after class. Students remark that "there is a club for everything." Phi Theta Kappa, an honors society, is active and popular for résumé-building. Student Governing Board plans parties and fundraisers. Model UN, although not affiliated with UH, operates on the UH campus. Religious organizations have high membership. For example, the large Lakewood Church holds Sunday service and bible studies in a part of the campus recently bought out by the church. Interest groups and political organizations represent all sides. A unique Student Alumni Organization plans dinners and events to network undergraduates with alums. Guest speakers can also be arranged by department.

Recreational sports connect the student body outside of class. The three-year-old Rec Center features rock climbing, a competition swimming pool, a hockey area, and racquetball courts, among other activities. Students often take recreational sports classes and play intramural sports which sometimes go on to compete regionally. Flag football is known as one of the largest intramural programs. Respected varsity sports include competitive cheerleading and diving, which has generated Olympians.

School Spirit Sometimes Lacking

Although the effervescent competitive cheerleading squad is highly-ranked, their spirit does not always pour out into the rest of the student body. "Most people didn't even know what was going on during Spirit Week." One reason could be that many students leave campus: "It's a commuter school, so many students don't participate." Some students report that there is "hardly any school pride," but pride seems to be more "a matter of who you hang out with." In response to these complaints, the Cougar Club and the Bleacher Creatures, two pep squads, set out during games to amplify audience enthusiasm.

> **"Most people didn't even know what was going on during Spirit Week."**

One popular social event on campus is the Frontier Fiesta that occurs around the time of Homecoming. It involves tailgating, games, fire shows, and food. Most of the social life on campus revolves around the fraternities and sororities near the apartment buildings, which can be expected to host parties most weekend nights.

Downtown Action

One benefit of the University's location is that it allows access to the downtown, Richmond, and trendy Montrose, all of which are popular destinations for students seeking diversion. A shopping center near Rice University attracts UH students after school. Amy's Ice Cream and the 59 Diner also deserve a visit from every student. A collection of small, family-collection museums and theaters of the Theater District in downtown Houston offer student discounts.

Need of a New Reputation

UH is sometimes overlooked by Houston residents who are "in a hurry to get away from their parents." Because the University of Houston is located near the homes of many prospective students, they misjudge its value: "It's underestimated because it's in town." And so UH surprises many prospective students. To obtain an accurate perception of the University of Houston, one must investigate its numerous strong academic colleges and diverse and involved student body.—*Eric Klein*

FYI

If you come to the University of Houston, you'd better bring "workout clothes for the Rec Center and Intramural Sports."

What's the typical weekend schedule? "Either go to a restaurant or club in downtown Houston, or get a home-cooked meal if you commute."

If I could change one thing about the University of Houston, I'd "increase the level of school spirit."

Three things every student at the University of Houston should do before graduating are "Go to the Frontier Fiesta, see a play in the theater district, and take 'Principles of Drug Action'."

University of Texas / Austin

Address: University of Texas, Austin, P.O. Box 8058, Austin, TX 78713-8058
Phone: 512-475-7399
E-mail Address: NA
Web site URL: www.utexas.edu/student/admissions
Year Founded: 1883
Private or Public: public
Religious affiliation: none
Location: urban
Regular Application Deadline: 2-Feb
Number of Applicants: 23,502
Percent Accepted: 57%
Percent Accepted who enroll: 55%
Number Entering: 7,417
Number of Transfers Accepted each Year: 2,788
Mean SAT: 1,230
Mean ACT: 26

Middle 50% SAT range: NA
Middle 50% ACT range: 23–29
Early admission program (EA/ ED/ NA): NA
ED or EA Acceptance Rate: NA
Full time Undergraduate enrollment: 37,037
Total enrollment: 48,138
Percent Male: 48%
Percent Female: 52%
Total Percent Minority: 42%
Percent African-American: 4%
Percent Asian/Pacific Islander: 17%
Percent Hispanic: 17%
Percent Native-American: 0%
Percent Other: 4%
Percent in-state / out of state: 96%/4%

Percent from Public HS: NA
Retention Rate: 93%
Graduation Rate: 77%
Percent in On-campus housing: 19%
Percent affiliated with Greek system: 22%
Percent Varsity or Club Athletes: NA
Number of official organized extracurricular organizations: NA
3 Most popular majors: Economics, Political Science and Government
Student/Faculty ratio: 18:01
Tuition and Fees: $20,364.00
In State Tuition and Fees (if different): $7,630.00
Cost for Room and Board: $8,176.00

L ife at the University of Texas has something for everyone. With more than 48,000 students, the largest single campus enrollment in the nation, this flagship state school is a world unto itself. Not only is there an enormous range of quality course offerings, but students can enjoy a vibrant social life as well. In addition to the wealth of resources offered by the University, students can take advantage of the exciting scene in surrounding Austin. And, of course, there's nothing like a football game to get the weekend going. Life at UT is full of possibilities—according to one student, "If you make an effort to talk to people at the gym, on campus, at gatherings, you could have 47,999 friends." This vast array of opportunities offers students a wide range of experiences and options that is harder to find at smaller universities.

Charging into Classes

UT's size affords a wide variety of course offerings. While many introductory classes have Teaching Assistants, upper-level courses can have as few as 15 students. If you're in a popular major, signing up for courses can be difficult. UT anticipates that this can be a challenge to incoming freshman, and provides an orientation program to ease the transition to life at UT and help students navigate the class registration process.

All students must fulfill certain graduation requirements, including a foreign language requirement, writing proficiency, and a course on Texas government, politics, or history. Like most universities, classes at UT can range from "awesome to absolutely awful." The education major is generally regarded as one of the easiest; students in math and science departments tend to have the most rigorous academic programs. Several students double major to take advantage of the breadth of course offerings found at UT. A small and select group of students enroll in the Plan II Honors Program: a multidisciplinary liberal arts major offering small classes taught by some of the University's best professors. Students applying for this competitive program must fill out a secondary application in addition to their general application to UT. Plan II students live in separate dorms in the Honors Quad for their four years as an undergraduate. As a result, students in Plan II tend not to meet as many students outside their small program.

Several undergrads agree that one class everyone should take before graduation is Interpersonal Communications taught by Dr. John Daly. "The class is a blast," explained one student.

Longhorn Life

Though many freshmen live on campus, UT's large size necessitates that some students move off campus. Many high school seniors send in a housing application and deposit even before they are accepted to the school. Indeed, housing is limited, and competition for on-campus housing can be fierce. Jester, the largest dormitory—and often cited as the "worst" dorm—is a high-rise building housing almost 3,000 students. Jester has parts, East and West, and even has its own zip code! All dorms, however big or small, have air-conditioning, and students can elect to live in co-ed or single-sex dorms.

Most upperclassmen live off campus and seem to enjoy the opportunity to get to know the city of Austin a bit better. Off-campus housing options range from reasonable to costly; those students living particularly far away make use of a UT-operated shuttle service.

Although most Longhorns live off campus, there are extensive dining hall and eating options on campus. On-campus students usually purchase meal plans, allowing them to eat at any on-campus dining hall. Students tire of the options as the "choices are the same throughout the year," and many complain about the quality of the food.

Awesome Austin

Nestled in the heart of Austin, UT thrives on its location in the midst of a vibrant and exciting city. While some students complain that the campus "feels scrunched" and "lacks the big quads you see at Northern universities," there are "tons of activities" happening off campus. Many Longhorns enjoy Sixth Street for its nightclubs, bars, and trendy restaurants. "A slice of pizza from one of the streetside places on Sixth Street will even cure a hangover," said one UT senior. Known as "The Live Music Capital of the World," Austin also affords endless opportunities for listening to music. With a range of high-tech firms in the city and the State Capital building a few blocks from campus, students are constantly in the midst of activity. "One thing that differentiates UT from other schools is Austin" said one student. Indeed, after graduation, many students elect to remain in Austin, claiming that "you won't find a more exciting city to go to school in on the face of the planet."

> "You won't find a more exciting city to go to school in."

For those Longhorns who crave outdoor activities, Austin's weather is nearly ideal. Many students enjoy going to lakes and swimming areas like Barton Springs, Lake Travis, Lake Austin and Canyon Lake. Though the summer begins to heat up towards the end of the school year, winter temperatures rarely drop below freezing, so students can take advantage of the outdoors for much of the school year. Students feel safe on campus and regularly venture off campus for "camping, running, fishing, hiking, and mountain biking."

Longhorn Pride

"Texas is football, no ifs, ands or buts." Athletics are huge at UT—and why not? The football team consistently ranks in the top 15 and the school invests heavily in its athletic facilities. "The gym is gorgeous, albeit busy," said one student. "There are more than enough machines and weights to keep you busy and sweating."

Athletics are not the only things that unite students. The large Greek system also provides ample opportunities for socializing. Though many students "go Greek," those who don't can still attend the parties. Frat parties occur frequently, however, and some students feel that too much of the campus social life centers on such Greek-hosted social events. The Greek community also has political sway on campus; however, UT also has several activist groups and a large number of students who are driven to start their own if they feel passionate about a certain cause.

Some students work paying jobs either on

or off campus, but many spend time in extracurricular activities. Students participate in service, volunteer and faith organizations of all sorts. And since Austin is the state capital, students interested in politics can easily seek internships in government offices.

Being a UT student means having a lot of energy and pride—UT students are nothing if not spirited. With so many different opportunities at their fingertips, students can have an educational experience characterized by both breadth and depth. While the school's size may seem overwhelming at first, students agree that freshmen should jump right in and get involved: "The community is a welcoming one." According to one student, "If I had to choose again, I'd definitely take UT over any other school."—*Lucinda Stamm*

FYI

If you come to UT Austin, you'd better bring "a cowboy hat."

What is the typical weekend schedule? "Thursday, Friday and Saturday nights students tend to go out. During football season, Saturday is 'game-day' and most students start the day drinking with the masses of people at the game. By Sunday students are back to work."

If I could change one thing about UT Austin, I'd "make the social life less dependent on the Greek system."

Three things every student at UT Austin should do before graduating are "swim in the campus fountains, take John Daly's Interpersonal Communications class and take advantage of the music scene in Austin—they don't call it the 'Live Music Capital of the World' for nothing."

Utah

Address: Brigham Young,
A-153 ASB, Provo,
UT 84602
Phone: 801-422-2507
E-mail Address:
admissions@byu.edu
Web site URL: www.byu.edu
Year Founded: 1875
Private or Public: private
Religious affiliation: Church
of Jesus Christ of Latter-Day
Saints
Location: urban
**Regular Application
Deadline:** 2-Feb
Number of Applicants: NA
Percent Accepted: 78%
**Percent Accepted who
enroll:** 79%
Number Entering: NA
**Number of Transfers
Accepted each Year:** NA
Mean SAT: 1,241
Mean ACT: 27

Middle 50% SAT range:
1,220–1,310
Middle 50% ACT range:
25–29
**Early admission program
(EA/ ED/ NA):** NA
ED or EA Acceptance Rate:
NA
**Full time Undergraduate
enrollment:** 30,798
Total enrollment: 30,798
Percent Male: 51%
Percent Female: 49%
Total Percent Minority: 7%
Percent African-American:
0%
**Percent Asian/Pacific
Islander:** 3%
Percent Hispanic: 3%
Percent Native-American:
1%
Percent Other: NA
**Percent in-state / out of
state:** NA

Percent from Public HS:
NA
Retention Rate: 95%
Graduation Rate: NA
**Percent in On-campus
housing:** 20%
**Percent affiliated with
Greek system:** NA
**Percent Varsity or Club
Athletes:** NA
**Number of official
organized extracurricular
organizations:** 390
3 Most popular majors:
English, Political Science,
Psychology
Student/Faculty ratio:
21:01
Tuition and Fees:
$3,620.00
**Percent receiving Financial
aid, first-year:** 36%

Located in the heart of Utah, Brigham Young University combines strong academics, religion, and an alcohol-free environment, resulting in a college experience that is vastly different from those at other schools throughout the nation. While this may not seem appealing at first, BYU students say they love being in a place where "people go out and do some crazy things and just have a good time, and it's nice that they always remember what they did the night before."

A Different Kind of Education

BYU, named for Brigham Young, one of the founders of the Church of Latter-Day Saints, has long been known for its strong academics. It is becoming increasingly difficult to get into BYU, as one student commented, "It seems like they think they're in the Ivy League or something." Students cited exercise science, anatomy, and biology as popular majors, and the consensus was that the most popular, and the most competitive, was business. The business school at BYU is particularly strong, which makes the undergrad

business track extremely difficult, as many students hope to continue education after they graduate. In addition, many students express a desire to become dentists, so there is also a significant amount of competition in that department.

In terms of requirements, one junior commented that "academics are strict. Prerequisites are often extensive and classes are difficult to get into, and flagged classes keep people who aren't serious about the class from taking it." In addition to classes required for each of the many offered majors, BYU's academic requirements are unique in that each student is required to take a total of 14 religion classes before he or she graduates. Two of these classes must be on the Book of Mormon and one must be "Doctrine and Covenants." The rest of the classes can be filled with any number of electives, including classes on bible study, the New Testament, prophecies, and the study of marriage and family life. Though this religion requirement is substantial and marks a significant difference between BYU and other universities, most students maintain that the requirement is interesting rather than annoying. One student commented, "The religion requirement is as much as you want to make it. Many of the teachers are members of the Mormon Church, but they don't force doctrine down your throat. The classes focus on reading and sharing your point of view, and the teacher is more of a mediator than a preacher."

These different points of view represented in classes are due in large part to the experiences many of the students have had during the past few years on missions. The vast majority of male students at BYU attend college for a year, then head off to a foreign, often developing, country to spend two years there on a religious mission. These experiences allow them to learn not only language but culture, and their experiences bring a great deal of variety and diversity to their classes, helping to make up for the lack of diversity among the BYU student body.

Sober Fun?

In addition to its stringent religion requirements, BYU stands out among its peer universities for its strict policies regarding drinking, premarital sex, and student body appearance. The school has an honor code that is run by a board, and violations of the code can result in harsh penalties, even going as far as suspension or expulsion. As a result, the students take the honor code very seriously. In addition to several academic rules, the honor code prohibits alcohol consumption and premarital sexual relations of any kind, and it also includes a dress code for students which, among other rules, requires men to be clean shaven at all times. Male students cite this stipulation as by far the most annoying part of the honor code.

According to many, this sober policy does not prohibit students from having a good time on the weekends. Though there are a few fraternities and sororities, they are "a joke," and parties for the most part are in off-campus apartments, as the vast majority of the student body lives off campus. According to one junior, "The parties are different. The honor code keeps them fun and clean." Students characterized the social life at BYU as focused mainly around "hanging out" with friends. In addition, the student government is extremely active in creating activities on campus for the student body, so there are frequently school-sponsored dances on the weekends for those who want to let loose in a fun, sober way.

Another addition to the social life at BYU is its close proximity to the nearby Wasatch Mountains, part of the Rocky Mountain range. Many people have cars, and they often

go into the mountains to hike, snowboard, or ski. There is a big "Y" at the top of one of the mountain ranges to represent Brigham Young, and students like to "hike the Y" on sunny days. In addition, students frequently travel to nearby Provo Canyon, where they often take projectors and watch movies in the spring and fall. Nearby Salt Lake is also a popular weekend destination.

Go to School, Get Married

A wide variety of extracurriculars, ranging from sports, performance arts, politics, religion, and other clubs is offered at BYU. As one student said, "There are tons of clubs for every interest. There are political, religious, and sports clubs, as well as one called "The Quill and the Sword" for students who want to practice medieval fighting techniques." In addition to these standard offerings, a major focus of college life in Provo is the dating scene. According to one college sophomore, who had recently married, "They encourage dating because they want you to get married. Lots of kids go to church together, and many girls get married in their freshman and sophomore years." This constitutes a significant difference from most other universities, where dating can be virtually nonexistent.

> "People bend over backwards to help you out, and they are very accepting. A lot of times when there isn't a lot of variation in point of views, people become very close-minded, but that isn't the case here."

Partially as a result of this desire to find a mate, the student body at BYU is described as "open-minded and very friendly." One student was pleasantly surprised to find out that "People bend over backwards to help you out, and they are very accepting. A lot of times when there isn't a lot of variation in point of views, people become very close-minded, but that isn't the case here." Though the student body is predominantly white and many are from Utah and the surrounding states, students still manage to maintain a friendly and accepting mindset. A significant percentage of the students are Mormon; however, you do not have to be Mormon to attend BYU, and many non-Mormon students report that being in the minority did not dampen their college experience.

Picturesque Provo

Another draw to BYU is its location in Provo, located 20 minutes from the mountains and a mere 45 minute drive from metropolitan Salt

Lake City, which boasts concerts and other attractions for students on weekends. The campus itself is beautiful and exhibits architecture dating back from the foundation of the University all the way up to the newest buildings, renovated within the last five years.

Provo itself is a college town, focused around the University. According to one student, "There's not a whole lot to do in Provo, and there is a small-town feel to it." However, another student added that there are "restaurants and a few other attractions typical of a town."

Because they live in such a quaint, picturesque area, the vast majority of students live off campus. They are not required to live on campus at all, and those who do decide to are generally freshman. There are two dorm complexes, Deseret Towers and Helaman Halls, where many of the freshmen live. The rest of the student body lives nearby, as there is an abundance of affordable and nice housing, especially apartments, within a 10 minute radius of campus.

BYU is definitely not what a typical university whose social life is ruled by drinking and whose academics can go in any number of directions. The rules and regulations at BYU are strict; however, many students feel that they are worth it, and the experience they have at BYU helps them not only prepare for their future, but also create a complete life for themselves that starts while they are still in college.—*Michelle Katz*

FYI

If you come to BYU, you'd better bring "your Book of Mormon, and a heater because it gets pretty cold!"

What's a typical weekend schedule? "Hang out on Friday night, sleep late on Saturday, and hang out with friends again Saturday night."

If I could change one thing about BYU, I'd "would change the curfew rule and the fact that I have to shave every day!"

Three things every student at BYU should do before they graduate are "hike the Y, get married, and learn how to ski or snowboard.

University of Utah

Address: University of Utah, 201 S. 1469 E. Room 2505, Salt Lake City, UT 84112
Phone: 801-581-7281
E-mail Address: admissions@sa.utah.edu
Web site URL: www.sa.utah.edu/admiss
Year Founded: 1850
Private or Public: public
Religious affiliation: none
Location: urban
Regular Application Deadline: 1-Apr
Number of Applicants: 6,801
Percent Accepted: 84%
Percent Accepted who enroll: 81%
Number Entering: 4,682
Number of Transfers Accepted each Year: NA
Mean SAT: 1,120
Mean ACT: 24
Middle 50% SAT range: NA

Middle 50% ACT range: NA
Early admission program (EA/ ED/ NA): NA
ED or EA Acceptance Rate: NA
Full time Undergraduate enrollment: 15,174
Total enrollment: 28,619
Percent Male: 55%
Percent Female: 45%
Total Percent Minority: 10.7%
Percent African-American: 1%
Percent Asian/Pacific Islander: 5%
Percent Hispanic: 4.7%
Percent Native-American: 1%
Percent Other: 0%
Percent in-state / out of state: 84%/16%
Percent from Public HS: 72%
Retention Rate: 83%

Graduation Rate: 55%
Percent in On-campus housing: 31.5%
Percent affiliated with Greek system: 1%
Percent Varsity or Club Athletes: NA
Number of official organized extracurricular organizations: NA
3 Most popular majors: Political Science, Economics, Finance
Student/Faculty ratio: 15:01
Tuition and Fees: $4,662.00
In State Tuition and Fees (if different): $14,592.00
Cost for Room and Board: $5,604.00
Percent receiving Financial aid, first-year: 53.8%

The University of Utah is a commuter-based school set in Salt Lake City at the base of the Wasatch Mountains. On weekdays, students participate in a wide array of classes and activities, whereas on weekends it is common for students to head to their Utah homes.

Quality Education

The University of Utah offers over 100 undergraduate majors, spread among various programs including Architecture and Planning, Engineering, Fine Arts, Science, and Humanities. Students were generally happy with the quality of education, praising the "wide range" and "good selection" of classes. Professors were described as "helpful" and "accessible," with a student noting that some professors go out of their way to provide students with connections to various internships and community-service positions. While one student cited that there are "easier" classes with "multiple-choice tests," most students agreed that the pace and level of difficulty of classes was substantial and adequate. The English department in particular was praised for its "good faculty." Some of the most common majors at the University of Utah include communications, finance, psychology, political science and economics.

Students at the University of Utah must fulfill a set of General Education Requirements, including coursework in American Institutions, Lower Division Writing, and Quantitative reasoning, as well as two "Intellectual Exploration", or I.E., courses in each of the four following areas: Fine Arts, Humanities, Physical, Life and Applied Sciences, and Social Sciences. For the Bachelor's Degree they must also take credits in Diversity and Upper Division Writing. Most students agree that these requirements are relatively easy to meet and don't interfere with their major studies.

The University also offers more specialized academic programs, including LEAP, which fosters a more close-knit, academically-focused community among a diverse set of freshmen. The program enrolls approximately a quarter of the incoming class, and includes a small, year-long freshman seminar. There is an Honors Program at the University, which features classes capped at 30 students, distinguished professors, and specialized seminars and workshops. Students can obtain a Honors Certificate designation on their diploma by completing a set of approved Honors courses.

Commuters and Community

Students generally go to class wearing jeans and T-shirts. While "there is the occasional girl in high-heels," most people dress in a "relaxed" fashion. The dating scene is not very active at the University of Utah. Students report that while people do go on dates, the social scene mostly consists of "different groups of people hanging out" and "not really dating." There are a number of married couples, and some of the on-campus housing is allocated to them. In general, however, students feel that the "number of attractive people" on campus was "pretty good," potentially a contributing factor to what one student observed as "a lot of random hook-ups going on."

While the Greek system is present at the University, most people found that there is "not much pressure" to be part of it, citing classes and dorms (for those who live on campus) as potential spots for meeting close friends. As the University of Utah is largely a commuter-based campus with a large number of students coming from in-state, it is common for students to head home on the weekends. One student complained that it is "hard" to form lasting friendships because most people commute, despite people's propensity to be "pretty friendly." "It would be good if people could spend more time on campus and get to know people of different backgrounds." Students also report that it is common for students to hang out mainly with a circle of close friends from high school. Although students describe the ethnic background as "homogeneous in that it is predominantly white," they also feel that the student body's diversity is increasing: "You get to see minority and international students around." In fact, the Utah Opportunity Scholars Program awards 20 four-year scholarships covering tuition, books and fees to underrepresented, first-generation college students entering the university from high schools in the greater Salt Lake area.

> "It would be good if people could spend more time on campus and get to know people of different backgrounds."

Those students who do not live at home and commute to school daily, get to enjoy "generous" and "nice" on-campus housing conditions, which are generally spacious and "very comfortable." However, students were not as thrilled about on-campus dining, which they deemed as "overpriced" and "repetitive." One student added that, "If you're vegetarian, the options are severely limited." French fries, pizzas and grilled cheese sandwiches were mentioned as foods that students "had to live on." One student disparagingly remarked, "It's pretty impossible to mess up grilled-cheese sandwiches, but somehow they did." Students also noted that it is common to see people eating by themselves in the dining halls, since "people aren't too good about sitting with people that they don't know."

The options for off-campus dining are great, with "many fantastic restaurants" just a few minutes away from campus. Students can get downtown easily via the bus and train system, and enjoy substantial discounts at restaurants simply by presenting their student IDs.

The Grounds

Students described the campus as "fairly nice," with "grassy areas" and buildings of varied architectural styles. In particular the President's Circle was mentioned as an aesthetically pleasing spot, while the Union Building was praised as "a great place to hang out on a lazy Sunday afternoon."

In general, most students agreed that if they could choose all over again, they would still choose the University of Utah because of its range of classes, its proximity to home, and the number of cultural opportunities in Salt Lake City. While some students remarked that ethnic and religious diversity could use some improvement, most considered the University of Utah a "great and enjoyable place to be."
—*Wenshan Yeo*

FYI
If you come to the University of Utah, you'd better bring "a readiness to work hard."
What is the typical weekend schedule? "Clubbing, drinking and partying—period."
If I could change one thing about the University of Utah, I'd "have people spend more time on campus."
Three things every student at the University of Utah should do before graduating are "get to know the professors better, do some internships, try some of the great restaurants off campus."

Vermont

Bennington College

Address: Bennington, One College Drive, Bennington, Vermont 05201
Phone: 800-833-6845
E-mail Address: admissions@bennington.edu
Web site URL: www.bennington.edu
Year Founded: 1932
Private or Public: private
Religious affiliation: none
Location: rural
Regular Application Deadline: 4-Jan
Number of Applicants: 798
Percent Accepted: 66%
Percent Accepted who enroll: 24%
Number Entering: 127
Number of Transfers Accepted each Year: 36
Mean SAT: 1,193
Mean ACT: 26

Middle 50% SAT range: 1,670–2,000
Middle 50% ACT range: 23–28
Early admission program (EA/ ED/ NA): ED
ED or EA Acceptance Rate: 34%
Full time Undergraduate enrollment: 523
Total enrollment: 657
Percent Male: 31%
Percent Female: 69%
Total Percent Minority: 9%
Percent African-American: 2%
Percent Asian/Pacific Islander: 2%
Percent Hispanic: 2%
Percent Native-American: NA
Percent Other: 3%
Percent in-state / out of state: 3%/97%

Percent from Public HS: NA
Retention Rate: 85%
Graduation Rate: 59%
Percent in On-campus housing: 98%
Percent affiliated with Greek system: 0%
Percent Varsity or Club Athletes: NA
Number of official organized extracurricular organizations: 25
3 Most popular majors: Visual and Performing Arts, English, Foreign Languages and Literature
Student/Faculty ratio: 7:01
Tuition and Fees: $35,250.00
Cost for Room and Board: $8,730.00
Percent receiving Financial aid, first-year: 77%

Located in the Green Mountains of Southwestern Vermont, Bennington College boasts 300 wooded acres, five acres of tilled farmland, 15 acres of wetland, 80 species of trees and 121 species of birds. How's that for diversity?

Small and remote, Bennington attracts an equally intellectually diverse range of students, who come for the individualized academics and the intimate campus—not to mention the theme parties.

Flex Your Academic Muscle

Bennington's academic system is unique. There are no majors at Bennington; instead, students develop a "focus" or a "concentration" themselves with large input from a faculty adviser. Focuses can range from the more traditional, such as mathematics, to the absolutely untraditional, such as storytelling. With the help of a faculty adviser, students plan their course load to best suit their focus.

Some students relish this academic freedom, saying that it forces you to really "think about your education" and engage in your academic career. For example, one student, who is focusing on "painting and education," said he planned his course load to involve a lot of sciences so he could learn things like the chemistry used to make paint pigment. A junior with a focus in literature said, "The best students are the ones who do take advantage of the flexibility." Indeed, students agreed that the best academic careers are the ones that are cross-disciplinary, to use all of Bennington's resources.

But while many students laud this different take on academics, others say it encourages floundering, and in fact sometimes attracts "terrifically unmotivated" students. "No one is forced to get specific, so everyone is doing everything," one junior said. "Freedom is good for some people, but for most it is just too much." Along with no majors, grades are also optional at Bennington, with narrative evaluations available as an alternative option. Those with grad school plans typically opt for grades, but many other students opt out, helping to contribute to the somewhat misguided perception of Bennington as a "slacker school."

The most popular concentrations at Bennington are the visual arts, dance, writing and language programs. In fact, much of modern dance was developed at Bennington, whose program was founded by pioneer Martha Graham. The current faculty boasts many literature standouts, and a recent project brought a group of South African leaders to campus to lead classes in the social sciences.

Because of the "planning" system's built-in one-on-one time with faculty members, and because of the small size of the school, students are very close to professors. "I call most professors by their first name," said the student concentrating in painting and education. Other students say they frequently have lunch with their professors, and know their families. But again, this closeness seems to be a double-edged sword; some students complained that professors are almost "too nice," and as a result there is a kind of pressure to befriend all your professors to get ahead. "Something that goes hand in hand with extremely personal relationships is that there is favoritism."

One of the biggest draws to Bennington is the Field Work Term (FWT), a seven-week winter term during which students take internships at various institutions across the country and the world. An annual requirement for graduation, the FWT provides the opportunity to work at places such as the San Francisco Museum of Modern Art, the Pittsburgh Zoo and Houghton Mifflin Publishing Company. Many students enjoy the FWT as an opportunity not only to apply what they've learned to the real world, but also to take a break from life at Bennington's small and remote campus.

Do-It-Yourself Extracurriculars

Although it is a small campus, Bennington offers any extracurricular group you might want—if you're willing to create it. Because it is such a small school, most clubs come and go, with students forming new ones every year. Long-term groups include the school newspaper, the literary magazine SILO, the campus radio station WHIP, and the perennially popular Outing Club, which sponsors skiing, horseback riding, rock climbing and hiking trips in the neighboring

Green Mountains. There are also community service groups, including the Student Action Network (SAN) and the Community Outreach Leadership Team (COLT). One current club, sure to be a keeper, is Sugar Bush, in which students make maple syrup from nearby trees.

If you're looking for sports at Bennington, though, you're out of luck. As one junior bluntly puts it, "Why would anyone interested in sports come to Bennington?" There are no varsity sports team, and the only club team is coed soccer, which has been known to play nearby high schools. And forget about intramurals. Instead, Bennington students focus their energy on the great outdoors, the free fitness classes and the "great" rec center—complete with climbing wall and sauna.

The Birthplace of the Theme Party

What Bennington may lack in athletics it surely makes up for in theme parties. "Bennington is pretty much the birthplace of the theme party," one arts concentrator said. Another seconded, "You'll pretty much never go to a party at Bennington that isn't a theme party." Popular parties in the past include pirates versus ninjas, Pigstock (a pig roast with live music), the "office party," and the huge roller-disco party Rollerama. Every year, the college puts on SunFest, a music festival on the central lawn featuring 10 to 15 bands during the day. The recent addition of MoonFest the night before is also popular.

Although theme parties are truly the dominant social scene, there are a few other outlets for those not wanting to get dressed up. The campus brings in two to three live bands each week, most of which are small, indie-rock groups, most famously the White Stripes. There is also the occasional unthemed house party, though those are few and far between.

Drinking and drugs are both prevalent at Bennington, though not out of control. "Drugs are in your face if you look for them, they are not in your face if you are not," one male junior said. "They don't dominate the social scene. Parties are still fun if you aren't into that stuff—no one is going to force them on you, or think you're not cool if you're not into them."

From Colonial to Co-op

Bennington's version of student housing is similarly unique to its take on academics. Bennington offers five types of housing: a drug-free house on campus, an organic co-op off campus, colonial houses, 1970s modern houses and 2001 contemporary houses. Each house accommodates 25 to 30 students and is managed by two students selected by their peers. These students run Sunday evening "coffee houses" to discuss community issues or just to chat. Students across the board describe Bennington housing as "amazing." Not only are the houses beautiful, but the system guarantees that you'll end up living with your friends—and guarantees a single for junior and senior years.

Students are less unequivocally enthusiastic about the meal plan. Though the food is good by college standards, with plenty of vegetarian and meat options, all students must be on the same three-meal-a-day meal plan for all four years. So even though most houses come equipped with a kitchen, students rarely eat anywhere but the dining hall.

In fact, for the most part, students rarely venture far off the Bennington campus. Many students have cars, and thanks to a "ride board" cars are easy to find, but most choose to stay on what they consider a "really self-sufficient campus." That campus, while intellectually and increasingly socioeconomically diverse, is noticeably lacking in ethnic or cultural diversity. "It is sad," one student said. "This is one thing Bennington is—and needs to be—working on." The campus also has an overwhelming majority of women, running to around 70 percent of the undergraduate population. Female students say that this ratio is not as much of a problem as you might think, however, especially since they can meet people much more easily during the Field Work Term. "Ultimately people still have boyfriends, people still meet people."

If students are really itching to meet more people, they can go to nearby Hampshire or Williams Colleges. Most, however, stay in the area of North Bennington—the "ridiculously New England" town where Bennington College is actually located—or Bennington, a larger city. One especially nice aspect of such a remote lifestyle is that students never have to worry about their safety: "Vermont feels like the safest place in the world. I never worry."

> **"I feel like the main thing you learn at Bennington is how to educate yourself."**

Overall, a Bennington education is what you choose to make of it. It is unique, to be sure, but it is that unusual character that allows many students to flourish. For those expecting an easy ride, however, Bennington is not the place, nor is it the place for those who need much hand-holding: "I feel like the main thing you learn at Bennington is how to educate yourself."

And how to throw a damn good theme party.—*Claire Stanford*

FYI

If you come to Bennington, you'd better bring "roller skates, costumes and false eyelashes."

What's the typical weekend schedule? "Some sort of 'thirsty Thursday' celebration, class Friday, Friday night find out who is having a party in their room. Galavant around after, maybe see what band is playing. Saturday night, dress up in whatever you can find that remotely fits the theme of whatever party is going on and get drunk. Sunday, recover."

If you could change one thing about Bennington I'd "only admit students who would be terribly excited."

Three things every student should do before graduating are "go in the catacombs, take a private tutorial, and run naked across the Commons lawn."

Marlboro College

Address: Marlboro, NA,
Marlboro, VT 05344
Phone: 800-343-0049
E-mail Address:
admissions@marlboro.edu
Web site URL: www.marlboro
.edu/admissions/
Year Founded: 1946
Private or Public: private
Religious affiliation: none
Location: rural
**Regular Application
Deadline:** 15-Feb
Number of Applicants: 500
Percent Accepted: 75%
**Percent Accepted who
enroll:** 39%
Number Entering: 120
**Number of Transfers
Accepted each Year:** 30
Mean SAT: NA
Mean ACT: NA
Middle 50% SAT range:
1,720–2,040

Middle 50% ACT range:
24–30
**Early admission program
(EA/ ED/ NA):** EA&ED
ED or EA Acceptance Rate:
NA
**Full time Undergraduate
enrollment:** 330
Total enrollment: 370
Percent Male: 45%
Percent Female: 55%
Total Percent Minority: 8%
Percent African-American:
1%
**Percent Asian/Pacific
Islander:** 3%
Percent Hispanic: 4%
Percent Native-American:
0%
Percent Other: NA
**Percent in-state / out of
state:** 10%/90%
Percent from Public HS:
80%

Retention Rate: 73%
Graduation Rate: 50%
**Percent in On-campus
housing:** 88.0%
**Percent affiliated with
Greek system:** 0%
**Percent Varsity or Club
Athletes:** 10%
**Number of official
organized extracurricular
organizations:** 18
3 Most popular majors:
Social Sciences, Visual and
Performing Arts, Literature
and Writing
Student/Faculty ratio: 8:01
Tuition and Fees:
$29,240.00
Cost for Room and Board:
$8,600.00
**Percent receiving
Financial aid, first-year:**
86%

Located in rustic Vermont, a 20-minute drive from the nearest town, Marlboro College offers its students an academic sanctuary in the midst of the New England mountains and greenery. With a small student body and a focus on the outdoors and schoolwork, Marlboro provides an intimate environment perfect for those looking for a unique and self-driven collegiate experience.

An Intense Learning Environment

Marlboro, with its lack of athletics and scarcity of extracurricular activities, is primarily a learning-driven college. Students unanimously concur that most non-class time is spent on schoolwork. "It's a really rigorous setting," one junior said, "People just do work all the time. It really affects the social scene." Another junior agreed, "Work *is* our extracurricular activity."

The academic program is lauded as extremely strong all-around. Classes are small, with most classes consisting of about 10 students. "Eighteen students in a class is huge." If students are interested in a topic not offered, one-on-one tutorials can be arranged

with professors in fields such as Arabic or fiction writing. There are no required classes except for a writing seminar which must be completed during freshman year.

Because of the small classes and intellectual environment, it is easy for students to form strong bonds with the faculty members leading their classes. "It's up to the students to enhance the faculty-student bond," one junior explained. Another student said professors often eat in the dining hall and are for the most part extremely "affable and approachable." But another student pointed out the one downfall of small classes: students who don't do the reading generally stand out. "You can't hide," said one senior. "Professors will call you if you don't show up for class."

Classes are divided into five basic categories: humanities, social sciences, natural sciences, world studies and arts. In general, the humanities and literature departments are seen as the strongest, though there is also a notable "film culture," and political science is a very popular concentration. The math and science departments are "growing," though most students concede that those programs are slightly weaker. Recent additions to campus include the Serkin Arts Center and a new World Studies building.

"Work *is* our extracurricular activity."

Students choose a self-designed Plan of Concentration (known as the "Plan") to complete their studies at Marlboro. The plan can take many different forms: anything from a 120-page paper to an architectural model to writing a musical. Junior year is spent designing the plan and the project is executed during senior year. "Everything culminates in the Plan," one junior said.

Though most find the academic experience "intense" and "wonderful," for others it can be a little overbearing. "It can definitely be too much for some people," a junior said. In general, though, students say they appreciate the unique structure because it creates a non-competitive atmosphere, with the focus more on the "academic process." Some people transfer out, one sophomore said, because of the heavy workload, as they look for a college experience where the learning is "less individually driven."

An Intimate Community
The extremely small student body—there are only 330 students enrolled—makes for a unique collegiate social life. There are rarely huge on-campus parties and there are no frats or sororities to host gatherings. "Most of our parties are pretty mellow," one junior said. "People will dance; there will be a band playing; people will drink and smoke."

For some students though, living in such isolation can be restricting. "It kind of feels like we're living in a bubble," a senior said. Brattleboro, the nearest town, does offer "cool coffee houses and a co-op, which everyone loves because we're all hippies." Students also get off campus to participate in numerous outdoor activities in the surrounding Vermont mountains and lakes.

Despite the lack of prominent social activities, one junior said it was easy to find ways to have fun. "You just have to make things happen," she said. "There's not the consistent night life that you might find at a large university, but there's usually a few big parties every year and things to do."

Students at Marlboro tend to be of a certain mold. Most students hail from the mid-Atlantic and New England. A senior summed up the typical Marlboro student: "we tend to be white, of a similar socioeconomic category and—in general—people who didn't fit in during high school." The small community also means that everyone knows everyone's business. "You can't really avoid the gossip," one freshman said.

Dorms, "Cottages," and a Barn-turned-Building
The dorms that house Marlboro students reflect the intimate feel of the campus. The dorms are "really small," one senior said—each of the nine on-campus residence halls houses roughly 12 to 30 students with roughly 85 percent of students living on campus. In general, the rooms are large, though some of the rooms are arranged in an unusual fashion—some freshmen complained about having to live in triples.

While housing is guaranteed for freshmen, it is not guaranteed for the next three years. Typically, 50 or so students (usually sophomores) are forced to live off campus each year. The off-campus dormitories—only a quarter-mile away from central campus—offer an appealing option due to their intimate feel (students described them as "little cottages"). Other students choose to live in Brattleboro in an apartment. One senior who lives in Brattleboro said she enjoys the change of pace after living on the close-knit Marlboro campus for three years. "There's a huge art and music scene."

There is a residential adviser in every dorm, though they do not often take the disciplinarian role. "No one is policing you," a sophomore said. Instead, RAs serve as resources for students and are able to offer advice and answers.

In general, the campus itself is "pretty rustic." A junior said, "The landscape is definitely really nice with all the white buildings, though the architecture could use some work." The on-campus dorms—each built in a slightly different era—are marked by a variety of architecture styles. The main classroom building is a converted barn, and the campus center—marked by its huge wooden rafters—was designed by a student for his "Plan."

Food Complaints, Pride, and Broomball
One thing that all Marlboro students seem to agree on is the unappealing food on campus. There is one dining hall on campus and one basic meal plan for all students. A "big issue on campus" according to one junior, the food

is a constant source of consternation for students. "There is just no selection whatsoever," one junior said. Though some students said the food was passable and not as bad as it was made out to be, many students have taken to creating their own food options. Many students said the lack of vegetarian and vegan options forced even the most devout vegetarians to start eating meat again; vegetarians currently have the option of filling out forms to request chicken or fish.

In general, as one junior put it, "extracurriculars don't really exist" at Marlboro. Unlike other schools, where there are certain clubs that exist from year to year, students at Marlboro start up new clubs each year based on interests, which may fizzle and change at any given point in the year. "You can make happen pretty much whatever you want here," one senior said.

"Pride"—the campus shorthand for the Gay-Straight Alliance—is considered the most prominent on-campus organization. Music ensembles tend to attract a fair number of students as well. Many students also join committees to help plan events and deal with other Marlboro-related issues.

While there are no official sports teams, the club soccer team is a source of school pride, as the student body often comes out to support the soccer squad. Frisbee and fencing are other popular sports. The Outdoor Program also plans many trips and excursions every year. Every winter, the whole school participates in a "broomball" tournament—a kind of makeshift hockey game—on the frozen pond on campus, at which school spirit and enthusiasm is often at its highest.

Marlboro College certainly stands out from the endless list of colleges because of its small size and intense academic atmosphere. Though some students said it becomes suffocating and small at times, most students appreciate the closeness of the campus and the bonds they are able to form with faculty. As one student put it, "A typical Marlboro student is one who is interested in his or her education and wants to play a role in it."—*Josh Duboff*

FYI
If you come to Marlboro, you'd better bring "a winter coat, motivation, and a stick of deodorant."
What is the typical weekend schedule? "Eat brunch, read a few books, go to the pond/sledding, eat dinner, read more, party, dance, listen to music, have some good conversations, go to bed."
If I could change one thing about Marlboro, I'd "give the school a lot more money."
The three things every student should do before graduating from Marlboro: "play broomball, skinny-dip in South Pond, get to know each other well."

Middlebury College

Address: Middlebury, The Emma Willard House, Middlebury, VT 05753-6002	**Middle 50% SAT range:** 1,220–1,510	**Percent from Public HS:** 52%
Phone: 802-443-3000	**Middle 50% ACT range:** 29–32	**Retention Rate:** 96%
E-mail Address: admissions@middlebury.edu	**Early admission program (EA/ ED/ NA):** ED	**Graduation Rate:** 92%
Web site URL: www.middlebury.edu	**ED or EA Acceptance Rate:** NA	**Percent in On-campus housing:** 97%
Year Founded: 1800	**Full time Undergraduate enrollment:** 2,376	**Percent affiliated with Greek system:** NA
Private or Public: private	**Total enrollment:** 2,376	**Percent Varsity or Club Athletes:** NA
Religious affiliation: none	**Percent Male:** 48%	**Number of official organized extracurricular organizations:** 100
Location: rural	**Percent Female:** 52%	
Regular Application Deadline: 2-Jan	**Total Percent Minority:** 35%	**3 Most popular majors:** Economics, Psychology, English
Number of Applicants: 5,254	**Percent African-American:** 3%	
Percent Accepted: 42%	**Percent Asian/Pacific Islander:** 9%	**Student/Faculty ratio:** 9:01
Percent Accepted who enroll: 22%	**Percent Hispanic:** 6%	**Tuition and Fees:** $44,330.00
Number Entering: NA	**Percent Native-American:** 1%	**Cost for Room and Board:** NA
Number of Transfers Accepted each Year: NA	**Percent Other:** NA	**Percent receiving Financial aid, first-year:** 45%
Mean SAT: NA	**Percent in-state / out of state:** 7%/93%	
Mean ACT: NA		

Often described as the "picture-perfect New England campus," Middlebury College is truly the ideal environment for students who are active and outdoorsy, who appreciate a rigorous academic curriculum, and who want to enjoy delicious dining hall meals. Nestled within the famous green mountains in the cold, snowy, beautiful state of Vermont, Middlebury offers students a cozy environment where they can keep busy indoors with solid course schedules and a wide array of extracurricular activities, as well as amusing themselves outdoors in the natural beauty of their surroundings by skiing, hiking, or merely sitting back and enjoying the view of a sunrise over the mountains.

Parlez-vous Français?

Middlebury requires that all students fulfill 7 out of 8 distribution groups, which cover literature, language, deductive reasoning, math, science, art, history and philosophy/religion. In addition, everyone must fulfill four cultural distributions: Asian/Latin American, North American, European, and a comparative course, as well as taking two college writing classes and one freshman seminar. The majority of students say that the requirements are easy to fulfill; according to one junior, "I finished all mine freshman year." The top three majors are economics, English, and biology ("it's pretty nice to do pre-med here"), though other popular and interesting majors include environmental studies and international politics. "We have a lot of people who double-major," said one sophomore. "Basically, we all try to do as much as we can." Middlebury is world-renowned for its language program, and a large number of students study abroad for a semester or a summer program. The summer language program on campus is so intensive that it is possible to receive an M.A. in a language over the summer. The school year is actually split into three parts, with a fall semester, a spring semester, and a one-month interim period known as "J-term" where students take only one class (either getting an intensive course like organic chemistry out of the way as quickly as possible, or taking it easy with a light and fun class). As far as specific classes go, language classes are always highly recommended and organic chemistry is usually abhorred, but there are many unique courses such as an anatomy class that is also a dance class and an English/environmental studies class where students read Thoreau and

Emerson and travel to a farm where they learn to birth sheep.

Class size depends on subject; the largest introductory science classes have 75–85 people, but most classes have 20–25. Said one student, "I've had classes as small as 4 people!" All classes are taught by professors who "are always willing to sit down and talk to you about anything." Said one student, "I feel like our professors are teachers first and foremost—we are their priority, and it shows." Although registering for classes can be a frustrating process, students who don't get into the classes they want are often able to go talk to the professors, who are nearly always willing to make room for them. "Basically, if a student shows any interest whatsoever, a professor will bend over backwards trying to help them get into a course or better understand the material." The workload—though manageable—can be daunting, and sometimes students say that they feel overwhelmed. "Still," said one senior, "we work hard, we play hard. You learn a lot if you keep up, but if you fall behind you may never catch up again."

One particularly unique aspect of Middlebury is that in addition to the regular matriculating class in September, there is another group of about 100 students—"the Febs"—who start in February. They also graduate a semester later, and are therefore able to ski down one of the hills for their graduation tradition.

Something in Common[s]

Residential life at Middlebury is broken into five "commons," a system somewhat like the four houses in the Harry Potter books. Freshmen are assigned to a commons based on their choice of freshman seminars and the professor of the seminar becomes their advisor. Each commons has a certain number of residential buildings on campus, a dining hall, a game collection, different events and various speakers. Changing commons is simple to do and often just means a change in housing; the main benefit to staying in a commons are the housing points students receive when deciding where to live in an upcoming semester. Inter-commons rivalries are common, especially in intramural sports. These smaller communities within the larger community of Middlebury are designed to make life easier for incoming freshmen and foster a greater sense of belonging; while some students see this as an admirable objective, others complain about the housing discrepancy between commons

(although the college is currently undergoing major renovations in order to create a more balanced living situation) and the fact that they feel "punished" by the points system if they choose to live with friends instead of staying in their original commons.

Dorm quality increases with seniority, from basic singles and suites freshman year to apartment-style rooms senior year with a common room, kitchenette, and in-suite bathroom. The majority of students live on campus all four years—"We have great rooms, they get cleaned for us, and the dining hall food is amazing. Why would we want to leave?" Said one junior, "Sometimes we call this Club Midd, because we're really spoiled here. We're not ready for the real world." Dining hall food is, indeed, very delicious. Much of the food offered is locally produced, and the basic meal plan allows for unlimited trips to the dining hall and unlimited food while you're there. "The people who work there are really nice, too," said one sophomore. "When one girl said that she missed the salmon from her area of Alaska, they flew it in." The staff takes students' suggestions seriously (you can always fill out dining hall cards); many students have even given their own family recipes to the cooks, who have then proceeded to make that dish. Said one freshman, "We often end up at dinner for over an hour, and we keep getting snacks over the course of the evening. Plus, we always have Ben & Jerry's Ice Cream!"

When it comes to eating off-campus, students say that the greater Vermont area also "takes food very seriously, and it shows." One person cited a restaurant called Flatbread as having amazing pizzas, though the downside of living in rural Vermont is that there are no places that deliver pizza or Chinese late at night (and also no Starbucks!). Said one sophomore, "Food here is less expensive than in a big city and we go out occasionally, but when my parents come they always want to eat in the dining hall because it's so delicious!"

Work Hard, Play Hard

Students say that after a long week of studying, they are more than ready to party when the weekend rolls around. Drinking is prevalent on campus; "You always see everyone out at the same parties . . . dancing, drinking, and merrymaking." Instead of frats, Middlebury has social houses, co-ed groups of students (often affiliated with a commons) who throw parties. There are three bars that upperclassmen often frequent on Wednesday or Thursday nights, and since Middlebury is a small town, they will most likely run into other students at the same places. On campus, people socialize with friends in dorms or attend one of the many themed dance parties thrown by teams or clubs, such as eighties dances, contra dances, and the popular neon dance party thrown by the ski team. Non-alcoholic social activities include concerts by student bands, free movies on Friday nights, late-night snacks at the Grille (the union) and events organized by the Middlebury Campus Activity Board. Said one student, "On weekends people go out and party like crazy, then get up the next morning at 7 or 8 a.m. to go running!" Said another, "It's a varied but close-knit social scene. I've never been to a party where I didn't know someone." Annual parties include the Winter Carnival, when students go to cheer on the ski teams at home during the day and then dress up for a formal ball at night, and two other formals in fall and spring. Students also spend much of their free time at varsity hockey games, which draw fans from all over campus as well as the surrounding community.

> "Once we even ran into a professor's pond! It's dark, you're naked, it's fun!"

Middlebury boasts a wide variety of extracurricular groups, with everything from literary and art magazines to political organizations to Lovers of the Garden State ("I don't know what they do, but apparently they really like New Jersey"). There is a bird-watching club, a sign language club, religious and cultural groups, community service organizations, theatre, "too many a cappella groups for our size, in my opinion," dance groups, band and orchestra, the Middlebury Outdoors Club, and Sunday Night Group—a group that started out as an environmental activism group directed at climate change, but which has now "turned into a social justice group for anyone who wants to change the world." The list could go on and on. Particularly adventurous students enjoy the Polar Bear Club, where they drive to nearby lakes at night and run naked into the freezing water. According to one member, "Once we even ran into a professor's pond! It's dark, you're naked, it's fun!" Intramural sports, especially broomball, are also popular. "We were in the Wall Street Journal for

our Quidditch team," said one student. "The players wear capes and run around with brooms between their legs." This comment prompted another student to remark, "Everyone here is kind of quirky. Not weird or anything, just very social, very interesting, very open."

"Midd Kids" are definitely lauded as being friendly, outgoing, and outdoorsy individuals. "I met most of my friends in the dorm freshman year," said one senior. "But you can really sit down with anyone at mealtimes and you'll be welcomed." When asked to describe the typical student, people listed adjectives such as "athletic, health conscious, well-rounded, upper-middleclass, white, sometimes preppy, and good at something—whether it be playing an instrument or being a star athlete." Said one junior, "My little brother would tell you that I've turned into such a hippie since being here; I get food from an organic garden, talk about climate change all the time, and am always outside." The student body is extremely international, with students from all over the world, even "exciting places such as Burma, Kazakhstan, and Bhutan!" One senior commented, "The diversity in some areas is certainly lacking . . . and granted, it's hard to bring inner-city kids here, because who would want to come to Vermont?"

A Close-Knit Community

Although most students stay mainly on campus, people say it is good to know someone with a car because it is necessary to use one for skiing or grocery shopping. Everyone agrees that the campus is extremely safe at night. Said one student, "I mean, who could possibly attack you? . . . Cows, maybe?" Said another, "I never lock my door, and people always leave their stuff in the library unattended." Middlebury prides itself on its Honor Code, which is manifested in ways such as self-scheduled exams and the fact that the professor is never in the room when students take an exam. "There is a sense of community that everyone respects," said one senior. "You would never talk or cheat because it would be a violation of your respect for your professor and your peers. It's taken really seriously here."

The sense of community at Middlebury is indeed, for many students, one of the most distinctive aspects of the college. For others, the best part of the college is "the people—everyone is so passionate about what they do and about what everyone else is doing. You go to your friends' events, they come to

yours, you sit down and have crazy conversations all the time . . . there's just a lot of passion here!" Another student cautioned, "Sometimes Middlebury can turn into kind of a bubble that distances you from the outside world. As you long as you make an effort to stay in tune, you'll be okay." And as one junior summed up, "We all got into Middlebury because we were stellar in our high schools. Then you get to Midd where everyone is like that, you can face rejection for the first time, get grades you've never seen before, and it can be frustrating . . . but also invigorating, because you're surrounded by all these people who are going to change the world."
—*Lindsay Starck*

FYI

If you come to Middlebury, you'd better bring "a warm jacket."

What's the typical weekend schedule? "Sleep, brunch (order omelettes!), do work, sleep again, eat dinner, pre-game, go out."

If I could change one thing about Middlebury, I'd "make it less of a bubble from the outside world."

Three things every student at Middlebury should do before graduating are "streak the campus, study a language, watch a sunrise while sitting on a roof."

University of Vermont

Address: University of Vermont, Admissions Office, 194 So. Prospect Street, Burlington, VT 05401

Phone: 802-656-3370

E-mail Address: admissions@uvm.edu

Web site URL: www.uvm.edu/admissions

Year Founded: 1791

Private or Public: public

Religious affiliation: none

Location: small city

Regular Application Deadline: 15-Jan

Number of Applicants: 17,731

Percent Accepted: 65%

Percent Accepted who enroll: 19%

Number Entering: 2,551

Number of Transfers Accepted each Year: 948

Mean SAT: NA

Mean ACT: NA

Middle 50% SAT range: 1,080–1,250

Middle 50% ACT range: 22–27

Early admission program (EA/ ED/ NA): EA

ED or EA Acceptance Rate: 37%

Full time Undergraduate enrollment: 8,908

Total enrollment: 11,870

Percent Male: 44.6%

Percent Female: 55.4%

Total Percent Minority: 6.8%

Percent African-American: 1%

Percent Asian/Pacific Islander: 2.5%

Percent Hispanic: 1.5%

Percent Native-American: <1%

Percent Other: 1.5%

Percent in-state / out of state: 36%/64%

Percent from Public HS: NA

Retention Rate: 84.2%

Graduation Rate: 66.8%

Percent in On-campus housing: 52%

Percent affiliated with Greek system: 6%

Percent Varsity or Club Athletes: 20%

Number of official organized extracurricular organizations: 110

3 Most popular majors: Business Administration, Political Science, English

Student/Faculty ratio: 15:01

Tuition and Fees: $11,324.00

In State Tuition and Fees (if different): $26,308.00

Cost for Room and Board: $7,642.00

Percent receiving Financial aid, first-year: 67%

Why is University of Vermont abbreviated UVM? It actually comes from its Latin name *Universitas Viridis Montis*, which means "University of the Green Mountains." Founded in 1791, the same year Vermont became a state, the University of Vermont lives up to its Latin name, boasting both natural beauty and an environmental focus. With construction of modern suite-based resident halls, a new honors college, and the recent switch to dry dorms, UVM is shedding some of its party image in hopes of emphasizing its appealing academics and location.

ABCs the UVM Way

Undergraduate academics at UVM are broken down into seven different colleges. The most popular majors at UVM are environmental science, business administration, and psychology. While each major belongs to a specific college, every student is required to fulfill a six-credit Race and Culture requirement, as well as complete various education requirements in the other colleges, including two semesters of physical education. Luckily breaking a sweat isn't hard to do in Vermont. UVM owns a few natural areas like Mount Mansfield, which it uses for teaching, recreation and physical education classes.

Because of its close proximity to Canada (a one-hour drive to the border), UVM offers a Canadian Studies major. From classes in anthropology, to art history, English to business administration, UVM gives students a unique opportunity to learn about the USA's neighbor to the North. It even offers the class Due North that culminates in a week-long field trip to Canada to watch a hockey game and visit the parliament.

UVM offers an array of unique classes like the History of Rock and Roll, The Role of Drugs in Society, Films and Novels of Stephen King, Tolkien's Hobbits, and Pirates, Tacks and Seadogs. The two classes known for being easy are Introduction to English and Personal Health. But be forewarned. With all the varying courses UVM offers, most students wake up at 6 a.m. on registration day to get into the section they want. However, if students really want to get into a particular class or section, they can petition the professor for an override. Following the prevalent Vermont attitude, professors are required to let in students if the class is required for their major, but they almost let in all students who petition regardless of reason.

Classes tend to be on the rather large size in the beginning of freshman year and get smaller as students progress through their undergraduate careers. Introduction to Psychology has about 200 students, while most introductory classes range from 60 to 100. Upperclassman classes hover around 40 to 60 students, although most seniors will take two or three seminars, which are capped at 20. The main exception is with languages. All foreign language classes are kept small, at around 20 people. All classes are taught by professors, though sections and labs are taught by TAs. "I have had great experiences with TAs," one student said. "I have never had trouble communicating or finding times to meet outside of class with mine." Some professors, like Brookes Cowan who teaches Introduction to Sociology, are known for being laidback.

Professor Cowan lives in the student off-campus area and interacts very comfortably with her students. "Teachers are very professional, but they're not stuffy, they're very down to earth and very understanding. They understand if something is late due to a family function."

For those seeking an academically rigorous course load, the new Honors Program offers about 400 students such an opportunity. Honors Program students still belong to one of the seven academic colleges, but one class every semester is an honors program seminar of no more than 20 people. All freshmen in the program must take the Making Ethical Choices, Personal, Public and Professional seminar, but after their first year, they are allowed to choose their seminars. Along with the cohesion of living together in a Residency under a Dean in the new University Heights Complex, the Honors Program offers students special co-curricular and extracurricular opportunities, like field trips to Boston and Montreal, as well as small perks like early registration, extended library borrowing privileges and discounted tickets to performing arts events.

New Campus Living

UVM just recently finished building new residential halls on Athletic Campus. These residential halls are all LEED certified, which is the highest environmentally-sustainable construction certification a building can receive. All freshmen and sophomores are required to live on campus, and then are free to move off as juniors and seniors. Even so, housing is now guaranteed for all four years.

Campus dorms cluster in three places—North Campus, Athletic Campus and Redstone Campus—although there are a few dorms buildings on Central Campus, as well. North Campus is where most of the "shoebox" dorms are. Redstone campus is the southeast campus, named after the Redstone Residential buildings. Athletic Campus, the east campus, is noted for its close proximity to the Patrick Gymnasium and is home to the recently constructed new University Heights residential halls and the Living and Learning Buildings. Living and Learning (L&L) are theme dorms, either by suite or by floor. Some examples of themes range from the outdoor floor to the live music floor to the community service floor.

Although UVM is trying to make its dorms a new home away from home for students, most students view it as "a place where you live, not your home." Still, most students agree that they have made some of the most lasting friendships through the dorms.

Meal plans at UVM come in many variations with different amounts of points and blocks. Points are essentially dollars that you can use at à la carte cafés on campus, while blocks are swipes you use at one of the two all-you-can-eat dining halls that serve standard fare. While the points cafés are really well liked, points can also be used to order pizza from Dominoes and Pizza Hut any time of the day and late night, though most off campus places take Cat Scratch, the UVM student debit account instead. If students get tired of eating on campus, popular restaurants and cafés in Burlington include Three Tomatoes, Mountaintop Brew, American Flatbread and Red Onion Sandwich. Fitting in with the hippy image of UVM, most eateries are organic with many vegetarian options, but "are absolutely delicious and cheap!"

Residential Advisors (RAs) may be as young as sophomores and as old as graduate students and how strict your RA may be depends on who your RA is. However, one student reported that, "All RAs still adequately enforce the rules." UVM is not exactly a dry campus (the soon to be finished Davis Student Center will have a pub), but all residence halls are alcohol-free. "With respect to that rule, RAs make almost no exception." Response to the dry dorm rule has been mixed, because most students drink off campus at house parties and bars. However, "strict enforcement of rules by the administration and the police has diminished our reputation as a party school," one student said. There has been some counter effect where students have been turning to drugs in dorms as opposed to alcohol. While the person who phones in a drunken friend receives amnesty, anyone found drunk and underage will receive medical attention but will also have to attend counseling, perform community service and pay a fine after recovery.

Skis, Views and Booze

Burlington is a small, quaint city that feels like a town. With a population of about 40,000, and home to four colleges, Burlington is a true college town. "Almost all stores are mom and pop stores, and with UVM on the hill, and Burlington downtown by the shore of Lake Champlain, it's the most beautiful place to live." The center of downtown Burlington is Church Street, a cobblestone

paved, pedestrian-only eight square blocks, at the end of which sits a majestic old church.

Off-campus living and junior/senior years "is sort of an informal agreement ... it is ten times cheaper and a different scene." While there are a few frats and sororities at UVM, even some community service-based, different social groups tend to mingle and mix off campus at house parties or at bars. The five to six blocks between campus and downtown are where almost all upperclassmen live, and with all of it leading downhill to downtown and Lake Champlain, there is no bad view. Looking across Lake Champlain, students can see the Adirondack Mountains in New York State. Popular sports bars and pubs are RJ's, What Ale's You and Nectar's. Auggies on Tuesday nights serve Hurricanes for four dollars, massive alcohol drinks that make Auggies the most popular place for college students to beat the midweek blues. The main dance club is Rasputins, but newly opened club Plan B is gaining popularity, though mainly for an older crowd. Burlington's live music scene is always an option, as well as its many performing arts events for those seeking a different night out.

> "We all consciously choose this school. We didn't come here because we thought it was the best thing to do, it was what we were supposed to do next, or because we couldn't go somewhere else."

Of course, if arts are not your definition of a night out, UVM is part of the Division I athletics and "everyone attends the [men's] hockey games," one student said. All sporting event tickets are free to students, but since there are no season tickets available, students must wait in line for tickets to each game. Also highly attended are men's and women's basketball. UVM has not had a football team since 1974, "presumably to fund our other sports instead." Rather, rugby football remains a popular club sport. But for less competitive players, the big intramural sport is broomball. Over 100 teams sign up for broomball every year and students rave that "it's so much fun!"

Other popular extracurricular include Outdoor Club, Skiing and Snowboarding Club, and Volunteers in Action, the umbrella organization for most community service and social justice organizations, which sponsors the Alternative Spring Break Trip every year, where groups of ten students go on ten different trips, nine domestic and one abroad, to do community service. The Outdoor Club sponsors really cheap weekend trips every year that are publicized to all students via e-mails. And thanks to the proximity of the many great skiing locations and the discount provided by the club, the Skiing and Snowboarding club is always a popular activity to join.

A Different Diversity

"What we lack in racial and ethnic diversity, we make up for in a different type of diversity," a senior said. Vermont is the second whitest state, so the racial diversity at UVM is not surprisingly lacking. However students come from all different sorts of socioeconomic classes. Even though the University of Vermont is a public university, the majority of its students—64 percent, as a matter of fact—come from out of state. This is in part due to Vermont's small population, but it is also due to UVM's initial status as a private university, which was only changed in 1865. The result is that both UVM's in-state and out-of-state tuitions fall somewhere between private and public universities.

UVM students still have a liberal and environmental bent, living up to some degree to its "treehugger" stereotype. "Everyone buys local dairy and veggies," one student explained, while another student added that "there are recycling bins everywhere, and if you don't recycle, anyone on the street would stop to correct you." That's just the Vermont attitude toward life and nature. "That's what makes UVM special," one student said. "We all consciously choose this school. We didn't come here because we thought it was the best thing to do, it was what we were supposed to do next, or because we couldn't go somewhere else. It was because this was the University of Vermont."—*Jesse Dong*

FYI

If you come to UVM, you'd better bring environmental conscience."

What is the typical weekend schedule? "Attend a hockey game Friday night, go hiking or skiing Saturday afternoon, party with friends off campus Saturday night, and spend all of Sunday doing homework."

If I could change one thing about UVM, I'd "make the residences more of a home."

Three things ever student should do before graduating from UVM are: "go to the top of Mt. Mansfield, take part of the naked bike ride, and participate in the polar bear jump."

Virginia

College of William and Mary

Address: William and Mary, PO Box 8795, Williamsburg, VA 23187-8795
Phone: 757-221-4223
E-mail Address: admiss@wm.edu
Web site URL: www.wm.edu/admission
Year Founded: 1693
Private or Public: public
Religious affiliation: none
Location: small city
Regular Application Deadline: 1-Jan
Number of Applicants: 10,500–11,600
Percent Accepted: ~30%
Percent Accepted who enroll: ~40%
Number Entering: ~1,550
Number of Transfers Accepted each Year: ~300
Mean SAT: NA
Mean ACT: NA

Middle 50% SAT range: 1,280–1,430
Middle 50% ACT range: 28–32
Early admission program (EA/ ED/ NA): ED
ED or EA Acceptance Rate: 40%
Full time Undergraduate enrollment: 5,600
Total enrollment: 7,600
Percent Male: 45%
Percent Female: 55%
Total Percent Minority: 23.7%
Percent African-American: 7.8%
Percent Asian/Pacific Islander: 8%
Percent Hispanic: 6.8%
Percent Native-American: 1.1%
Percent Other: 11.2%
Percent in-state / out of state: 65%/35%

Percent from Public HS: NA
Retention Rate: 95%
Graduation Rate: 90%
Percent in On-campus housing: 76%
Percent affiliated with Greek system: 33%
Percent Varsity or Club Athletes: 85%
Number of official organized extracurricular organizations: 300+
3 Most popular majors: Business Administration, Psychology, Government
Student/Faculty ratio: 11:01
Tuition and Fees: $8,490.00
In State Tuition and Fees (if different): $25,048.00
Cost for Room and Board: $6,932.00
Percent receiving Financial aid, first-year: NA

The College of William and Mary, founded in 1693, is the second oldest university in the United States. As its tour guides are quick to tell you, it was the college that Thomas Jefferson attended, the college where George Washington was chancellor, and the college that gave birth to the Phi Beta Kappa society in 1776. Yet William and Mary isn't all about tri-corner hats and resting on past laurels, despite what its location in the touristy Colonial Williamsburg might make you think. What distinguishes William and Mary nowadays, aside from having Sandra Day O'Connor as chancellor, is its reputation for academic excellence. U.S. News & World Report ranked it first among public universities in terms of undergraduate teaching. Results like that have many students here proudly embracing their label of being a "public Ivy." But William and Mary isn't all about staying locked in the library. The school has a beautiful campus, a successful football team and serious cash flow from recent donations, which is funding a number of renovations and new buildings all around campus.

A Public Ivy

Most students here will freely admit that William and Mary is more focused on academics than anything else. As one senior put it, "even the most party-crazed people are capable of spending days locked in their room studying." To graduate, a student needs 120 credits, and the average course counts for three or four credits. In addition to this total, each undergraduate must satisfy the GERs, or General Education Requirements. These requirements include one course in mathematics and quantitative reasoning; two courses in natural sciences; two courses in social sciences; three courses in world cultures and history; one course in literature or art history; two credits in creative or performing arts; and one course in philosophical, religious, or social thought. Most courses at W&M fit into one of three categories in terms of size. There are the large introductory lectures with 100 to 250 people, average classes with 25 to 35 people, and seminars capped at 15. All freshmen are required to take a freshman seminar, and these are generally praised as being good courses. Registration for classes is relatively painless. The students who have more credits get to register first, and since AP credits count toward this total, the freshmen with the most APs have an advantage over their classmates.

William and Mary also rewards its freshman overachievers (generally the top 5 to 7 percent of each class) with its James Monroe Scholar Program. In addition to having one of the best dorms on campus (Monroe Hall) reserved exclusively for them freshman year, Monroe Scholars get first pick in freshman seminars, have a chance to apply for a $1,000 grant for the summer after freshman year, and are guaranteed $3,000 for an independent project the summer after their sophomore or junior years. It's a good deal for the Monroes, but it does have its tradeoffs. In an already intense academic environment, the Monroes feel the pressure even more than most.

> **"We really are the public Ivy, and not just because we're full of ourselves."**

Among the 35 concentrations offered at William and Mary, there is the usual mix of easy and hard majors. Some of the usual suspects like geology, psychology and anthropology are popular with the less academically motivated crowd, while biology, chemistry, physics and computer science are some of the hardest, best-taught of the majors. For those interested in economics, W&M offers a business major linked to their business school. One student in particular seemed almost indignant when asked whether or not W&M's academics lived up to their hype in U.S. News & World Report, saying "I think they're underrated. I don't think people are quite aware of how good they are. We really are the public Ivy, and not just because we're full of ourselves." Perhaps part of what makes the academics so good here is

that for the most part, classes are taught by full professors. In four years, one senior could recall having been taught by a TA only once. Students also seem quite enthusiastic about their professors, whom they call approachable, interested and even "brilliant."

Partying at a Deli?

So what do William and Mary students do when they're not in the library (which is, by the way, newly renovated and "really really nice")? There are a lot of options. Student organizations are popular, and most people belong to at least one or two clubs. There are numerous performing arts and a cappella groups; several publications like The DoG Street Journal (referencing Duke of Gloucester Street, the main drag known as DoG Street to students and locals) or *The Flat Hat*, W&M's weekly student newspaper; a number of Christian groups; and a whole host of others from Chess Club to Russian Club. Many students' social lives revolve around their organizations, as many clubs sponsor a number of parties and formals. Athletics, of course, play a big part in school life, especially a few years ago, when the Tribe football team made it all the way to the NCAA I-AA semifinals. Stands were more crowded than they had been in years, and Tribe Pride promises to stay inflated for years to come.

Greek organizations play a large role in the campus social scene as well. According to the W&M administration, 25 percent of undergrads are involved in Greek life, but according to one frat brother, the majority of those students belong to exclusive social service frats. The percentage of people who live in traditional party-oriented frat houses is much smaller, and continues to shrink as frats lose their charters or housing by infringing on alcohol and other policies. The frat parties still on-campus must be dry, and RAs reportedly get people in trouble for drinking. This is not to say that W&M is a dry campus by any means. Determined freshmen still drink on the weekends, but since they can't drink at the frats, they pre-game in their rooms first.

For upperclassmen, frats have largely lost their appeal, so many move to off-campus parties, which are often held by clubs or sports teams. Because of regulations, there are no bars near W&M, but three so-called "delis" in the area reportedly serve the same purpose. In recent years, the delis have started to card more strictly, but for the persistent, alcohol is still available. The best of these delis is the Green Leafe, which has Mug Night every Sunday, when you can bring in a mug and they'll fill it with beer for a small price. Aside from the delis, however, students report that there really isn't much off-campus nightlife, though there's always plenty to do on campus. In addition to the party scene, more toned-down events include forums with a host of visiting speakers: "In my years at the College I've seen Ralph Nader and Jon Stewart (he's an alum of ours) and even Kofi Annan and Supreme Court Justice Antonin Scalia."

Multinational Neighbors

In terms of housing, many students stay on campus all four years; as one student said, "I think people stay living on campus because it's very convenient and we have a really tight community." The dorms, which with a few exceptions are all coed either by room or by floor are generally pretty nice. Yates, Monroe and Barret may be a little better than average, and Dillard (now defunct, replaced by Jamestown North and Jamestown South) may be so far away that people dreaded getting placed there, but halls are actually in decent shape. The housing system revolves around a lottery that most agree "ends up being pretty fair." Freshman housing is generally pretty good, and friends made in freshman halls often end up being friends for all four years. For those into foreign languages, W&M offers the opportunity to live in houses geared toward a specific language, whether it be Russian, Spanish or French. Each house has a tutor from one of the countries where the language is spoken and hosts various cultural events. The language houses provide a warm, tight-knit community.

Dining Services at William and Mary reputedly used to be a lot better before a budget crisis a few years back led to cutbacks in quality. The university is, however, trying to remedy this: the main dining hall, "the Caf," recently received a facelift, with improvements including "amazing" food and an Internet café. Students can still find other good-quality offerings around, such as the daily-made sushi, which one student describes as "not sketchy. It's really good."

When the options feel limited, though, students can take a walk around town and find plenty of ways to spice up their dining.

Local restaurants like The Fat Canary, Aromas, Trellis and the Cheese Shop receive good ratings, though the ones in the tourist part of colonial Williamsburg are pretty pricey. There are also two convenience stores open 24-7 in Williamsburg, including the store WaWa, without which "students would go crazy."

What really sets William and Mary apart from most colleges, in the opinion of several students, is the sheer beauty of its campus. When these students talk about how spectacular their campus looks, they don't just mean the sites that every William and Mary tour guide points out: the colonial architecture of Old Campus, the famous Sunken Gardens, or even the Crim Dell pond with its storied bridge. (Supposedly, any couple who kisses on the bridge has to get married unless one of them throws the other one off.) These students mean places that are far less touristy, like the amphitheater at Lake Matoaka, which a couple of students said was honestly the most beautiful place they had ever been in their lives.

All students at William and Mary are fully aware of all the history and traditions they are privy to. As one student said, "We all know facts like the fact that the Wren Building is the oldest academic building in the country still in use. . . . Almost all of us can recite the great history of our college; almost all of us know the chorus to the alma mater. Our big tradition events such as the Yule Log and Convocation Ceremonies are incredibly crowded and bring us together."

So in the end, what does William and Mary have to offer? It has a beautiful campus, and thanks to a number of donations, William and Mary is also poised to complete a number of major renovations to the campus. People here are generally pretty studious folks, with a grasp on tradition. If you're looking for a gorgeous place to live and an Ivy League-level education for a public school price, the College of William and Mary is the place for you.—*Dan Hammond*

FYI

If you come to William and Mary, you'd better bring "your own entertainment."

The typical weekend schedule at William and Mary is "Friday night, frat or deli; Saturday, football game followed by studying followed by club party; Sunday, chill in your room."

If I could change one thing about William and Mary, "I'd bring back the old alcohol policies."

Three things every student at William and Mary should do before graduating are "ring the bell in Wren Hall, rock out at Blow Out and camp out a spring night in the Matoaka amphitheater."

George Mason University

Address: George Mason, 4400 University Drive, MSN 3A4, Fairfax, Virginia 22030
Phone: 703-993-2400
E-mail Address: admissions@gmu.edu
Web site URL: http://admissions.gmu.edu
Year Founded: 1957
Private or Public: public
Religious affiliation: none
Location: suburban
Regular Application Deadline: 16-Jan
Number of Applicants: NA
Percent Accepted: 61%
Percent Accepted who enroll: 36%
Number Entering: 2,458
Number of Transfers Accepted each Year: 3,460
Mean SAT: NA
Mean ACT: NA

Middle 50% SAT range: V:500–600, M:510–610, W:490–590
Middle 50% ACT range: 20–25%
Early admission program (EA/ ED/ NA): EA
ED or EA Acceptance Rate: NA
Full time Undergraduate enrollment: 17,812
Total enrollment: 18,221
Percent Male: 45%
Percent Female: 55%
Total Percent Minority: 31%
Percent African-American: 6%
Percent Asian/Pacific Islander: 18%
Percent Hispanic: 6%
Percent Native-American: 1%
Percent Other: 69%
Percent in-state / out of state: 80%/20%

Percent from Public HS: NA
Retention Rate: 86%
Graduation Rate: 55%
Percent in On-campus housing: 23%
Percent affiliated with Greek system: 10%
Percent Varsity or Club Athletes: NA
Number of official organized extracurricular organizations: 150
3 Most popular majors: Business/Marketing, Social Sciences, Engineering
Student/Faculty ratio: 15:01
Tuition and Fees: $18,552.00
In State Tuition and Fees (if different): $6,408.00
Cost for Room and Board: $6,750.00
Percent receiving Financial aid, first-year: 56%

Founded as an independent university in 1972 after originating as a branch of the University of Virginia, George Mason University is a rising star among American colleges. Its location less than an hour from the nation's capital affords students ample opportunities for work and play, and its three main campuses offer a wide array of curricular and extracurricular options. With a student body recently termed the most diverse in the nation by the Princeton Review and a faculty that brings practical experience as well as academic prestige to the table, GMU is perfectly suited to almost any type of student—and despite its relative youth, it's by no means short on college spirit.

Beyond the Books

George Mason students average around 15 credit hours, or about five courses, per semester, a workload that students find rigorous but manageable. Academic requirements vary depending on area of study, but every student must complete a set of general course requirements. Students add, however, that "it doesn't take as long to complete the general education requirements as it sounds like it does."

Of GMU's 100+ degree programs, those that are most popular with students include several offered by the School of Management, as well as history, economics, government and international politics, and the nursing program. Besides the main Fairfax campus, George Mason also offers classes and facilities in Arlington County, Prince William County (where the Freedom Aquatic and Fitness Center, "the largest fitness and aquatic center on the East Coast," is located) and Loudoun County, a location that just opened in 2005. The number and variety of programs available mean that GMU students have a plethora of options. Students do warn, however, that "GMU doesn't really allow students to double-major," though it is easy for those with diverse interests to pursue one or more minors. The university also caters to students transferring in from another institution; a significant percentage of incoming students hold associate's degrees from the neighboring Northern Virginia Community College.

GMU's faculty includes top names in their fields, such as Economics professors and Nobel laureates Vernon Smith and James Buchanan. Professors at Mason are generally deemed "very approachable," and students praise the fact that "many of the professors have real-world experience that they are able to bring in to their lectures, which is very helpful." Class sizes average around 30–40, and larger lecture courses are broken up into discussion sections taught by graduate teaching assistants. Many professors also communicate with their students using WebCT, an online program that allows students to upload assignments, check grades and discuss material on a class Web page. Students can also use the Internet to track their degree requirements using the PatriotWeb database, a convenience that means they "don't have to see an advisor constantly if they have questions."

A Capital Place to Be

The university's location close to Washington, D.C. and the large number of commuter students make George Mason's social scene truly unique. Proximity to the nation's capital gives Mason students a wide variety of options for term-time work and weekend fun, and students tend to be very involved outside campus. According to one junior, "Many students intern with political campaigns or work for government agencies or large corporations." Most GMU students either live in the surrounding area and commute to classes (many take advantage of the local Cue Bus system, which is free for students, and the Washington Metro subway system), or "live on campus during the week, but leave and stay with family or friends off campus for the weekend." Of 29,728 students enrolled in the fall of 2005, only 4,000 students lived on campus. As a result, students say that "most people socialize off campus" by taking advantage of the various opportunities for entertainment afforded by the university's surroundings, including local bars or clubs.

This doesn't mean, however, that the campus itself lacks a thriving social scene. GMU has 13 fraternities and 11 sororities, which are "either adored by their members or scorned and scoffed at by non-members" and often host parties open to all students, though the frats do not have separate housing on campus. The University also sponsors "Every Freakin' Friday," an event hosted, as per the name, every Friday that features "movies, food, comedians, live entertainment and much more" (including, recently, Adam Pas-

cal of RENT fame). A campus film committee also sponsors movies on weekend nights, "anything from United 93 to Thank You For Smoking to the Devil Wears Prada!" Partying in dorms and nearby student apartments is also popular, which sometimes leads to trouble with the administration. Despite enforcement policies that have recently become increasingly strict, students report that drinking is prevalent on campus. Overall, most students are happy with the social aspect of the university. Said one sophomore, "It is very easy to make friends at GMU."

Mason Madness

Because of the high percentage of commuters, students often meet most of their friends in classes and clubs, and student organizations function both as a way to get involved on campus and as a means of finding friends with similar interests in a large and extremely diverse student body. George Mason has a wide variety of "exceptionally organized and dedicated" extracurricular organizations, ranging from community service organizations and cultural interest clubs to art, theater and dance groups. GMU's weekly newspaper, *The Broadside*, is one of the top student publications in the nation and has a strong following on campus. The university also boasts a "very popular" radio station and literary magazine. On the whole, students are very committed to their extracurriculars: "People are always going to meetings, starting up organizations or planning activities."

Mason athletics, both varsity and intramural, also have a strong presence on campus. The campus offers a wide array of new and newly renovated athletics facilities, including the Aquatic and Fitness Center, where renovations are scheduled to end in 2007. Much of the university's athletic pride is centered around the basketball team, whose recent Final Four performance in the NCAA has brought it, and George Mason with it, into prominence. Said one student, "The nation fell in love with us and we were the Cinderella story of the year." Rather than having its homecoming in football season as is standard practice for many colleges, GMU's is centered around basketball and occurs in the spring semester along with the annual celebration of Mason Day. "Mason Madness" (formerly "Midnight Madness"), which kicks off the basketball season as students gather to watch the team's first practice of the season, is a well-attended event. Still, students tend to assert that "sports aren't that huge on campus," and that there is "more pride in the school itself, the reputation of the school," than in athletics themselves.

Living It Up, Off Campus or On

Because George Mason is a relatively "young" university, most of its buildings are either new or newly renovated, and it boasts a picturesque variety of modern architecture. A man-made lake near central campus provides a pleasant setting for students to walk and chat; the nearby, "beautifully sculpted" Center for the Arts and Patriot Center host a variety of events on behalf of both the university and outside organizations. Students also frequent the George W. Johnson Center (or JC), dubbed the "hangout for everyone," which houses the university bookstore, a food court, a movie theater, dance studios, study areas and "overflow from our already massive library."

Those who do live on campus reside in one of GMU's dorm complexes, though most students consider on-campus housing a "rip-off" and choose instead to commute from home or to rent apartments nearby. Freshmen live in President's Park, which has a very strict no-alcohol policy. The best rooms ("very nice, write-home-about quality") are in Potomac Heights, available only to upperclassmen. George Mason also has a number of dining options, with several dining halls, on-campus restaurants (including the JC's food court) and a cornucopia of local restaurants in the surrounding Old Town Fairfax.

> **"I'd say that students are focused academically and are very career-oriented, without being cutthroat or being overly uptight."**

More than any physical feature or facility, the characteristic that most sets George Mason apart in the eyes of its students is its diversity—one student termed the university "insanely diverse." Over 130 nationalities are represented on campus, and student interests run the gamut from politics to physics to dance. Mason students do have something in common, however: "I'd say that typical GMU students are focused academically and are very career-oriented, without being cutthroat or being overly uptight. The casual, friendly attitude is a constant." With dynamic professors, state-of-the-art facilities and convenient location, George Mason University is the perfect place for those who want to change the world and enjoy themselves while they're at it.—*Amy Koenig*

FYI

If you come to George Mason, you'd better bring "a Metro card. You'll probably need to use it more than once, especially if you work."

What's the typical weekend schedule? "Friday night: bar hopping in D.C. or Old Town Fairfax. Saturday: study. Sunday: parties in D.C. or at fraternities."

If I could change one thing about GMU, I'd change "the Orientation Program. Over the summer, they ran three large orientations during finals week. The orientation itself isn't a problem, but they should schedule more effectively."

Three things every Mason student should do before graduating are "go to Mason Day, take advantage of your resources, and go to the "The Price Is Right" taping in LA wearing your school colors."

Hampden-Sydney College

Address: Hampden-Sydney, P. O. Box 667, Hampden-Sydney, VA 23943
Phone: 434-223-6120
E-mail Address: admissions@hsc.edu
Web site URL: www.hsc.edu
Year Founded: 1775
Private or Public: private
Religious affiliation: Presbyterian
Location: rural
Regular Application Deadline: 1-Mar
Number of Applicants: 1,509
Percent Accepted: 430.7%
Percent Accepted who enroll: 33%
Number Entering: 346
Number of Transfers Accepted each Year: varies
Mean SAT: 1,122
Mean ACT: 22

Middle 50% SAT range: 1,040–1,210
Middle 50% ACT range: 20–25
Early admission program (EA/ ED/ NA): EA&ED
ED or EA Acceptance Rate: 69%
Full time Undergraduate enrollment: 1,100
Total enrollment: 1,100
Percent Male: 100%
Percent Female: 0%
Total Percent Minority: 8%
Percent African-American: 4%
Percent Asian/Pacific Islander: 1%
Percent Hispanic: 1%
Percent Native-American: 1%
Percent Other: 1%
Percent in-state / out of state: 66%/34%

Percent from Public HS: 58%
Retention Rate: 64%
Graduation Rate: 59%
Percent in On-campus housing: 95%
Percent affiliated with Greek system: 30%
Percent Varsity or Club Athletes: 90%
Number of official organized extracurricular organizations: 34
3 Most popular majors: Economics, History, Biology
Student/Faculty ratio: 13:01
Tuition and Fees: $26,344.00
Cost for Room and Board: $8,258.00
Percent receiving Financial aid, first-year: 85%

Since its 1775 founding, the creed of Hampden-Sydney College (HSC) has been forming "good men and good citizens in an atmosphere of sound learning." This small all-boys school maintains its tradition of excellence by holding students to the highest standards of character, curriculum, and climate. Tucked away in a small Virginian pocket of tranquility, HSC exudes a picturesque, old-school charm. Its effective and extensive honor system creates both a sense of citizenship and brotherhood.

The Core Curriculum, Liberal Arts at Its Finest

Hampden-Sydney has a broad core curriculum that ensures that each student has taken "at least two courses in every discipline" before graduation. Because these requirements are so extensive, it is common to find seniors still trying to fulfill the curriculum. For this same reason, many people double major. The curriculum within the majors is very broad, and each student must have a complete understanding of a subject. Popular majors include economics, political science, and history, although in the past few years, religion has become increasingly popular. While science may not be quite as popular, students rave about the "must-take class" of "Caveman Chemistry," a hands-on lab class in which students start off by making fire as the cavemen did, working their way though human history, and making plastic as their final project.

But when it comes to academics, Hampden-Sydney College is not all fun and games. Students must complete the Rhetoric Program, which consists of enrolling in challenging English classes, writing ten papers every semester, testing grammar proficiency, and taking an overall final exam. The Rhetoric Program is tough in the sense that "if you don't pass it, you don't graduate," but as a result, "everyone who graduates here can be proficient in writing, and write something that is worth reading." Furthermore, teachers are personally attentive and usually generous with extensions, "It's almost impossible to graduate with a 4.0 here because being perfect in your class is viewed as unattainable," one senior said. There is reportedly no grade inflation, and a C is often considered average.

We Eat Here, We Sleep Here, We . . . Fish Here?

A 1,100-member all-boys college, Hampden-Sydney allows for "an atmosphere where you leave your door open and get to know all of the guys in the hall." Before they arrive, freshmen can chose to live in one of three dorms. Most choose Cushing because of its large rooms and the sense of community fostered by its 16-person corridors. Sophomores and juniors have more options, and can even apply to live in college-owned off-campus housing. About 35 students per year do so, "but it's more convenient to live on-campus." Because the nearest town, Farmville, is a 10-mile drive away, hardly anyone chooses to live in apartments not affiliated with the college. The housing draws are done first by seniority and then by GPA.

The architecture is "old Georgian; red brick with white trim." And behind the commons area, at the foot of a hill, is a pond where students like to fish. Concerts, cookouts, pig roasts, and barbeque buffets are also hosted in that area. As far as the dining hall is concerned, food is said to be good, especially in comparison to other colleges. However, many students complain about "getting sick of the same good food by the end of the semester."

Intramural Life

The dominant extracurricular is most definitely intramural sports, with an 80 to 90 percent participation rate. Intramurals run all year round and essentials such as soccer, softball, flag football, and basketball are all offered.

With about 10 to 15 percent of the school participating, varsity athletics also receive much support, particularly the football team, whose homecoming game kicks off a week of partying with students from the competing school. The football team is also the only sports team large enough to be "a group unto themselves."

In light of the fact that forming clubs at Hampden-Sydney involves little more than "filling out a form," the football players have even formed the Tiger Athletic Club, an organization bearing likeness to its own frat, "especially due to the fact that they own a house." Other popular activities involve the Outsiders Club (which sponsors outdoor trips such as whitewater rafting), student government, the Young Republicans, and the debate society.

In Style and at Leisure

Although Hampden-Sydney is changing rapidly, it is still typecast as attracting "upper-middle-class white guys who drive SUV's." If dress is any indicator of anything, HSC boys are "not afraid to wear pink or rainbow sandals, year-round." Popped collars, khakis, and shaggy hair are also common sights. Students report that if you wear plaid, people will compliment your "cool pants." Dressing up during the day may not be the norm, but it definitely doesn't stand out.

As far as nightlife is concerned, an attendance policy prevents most students who have Friday classes from going out on Thursday nights. However, on Friday and Saturday nights, students will congregate in the off-campus apartments, or throw room parties. The alcohol policy is fairly lax. RAs do not go out to search and storm rooms, and most students feel comfortable with the degree of independence accorded them. Over 20 percent of students are members of frats. Fraternity Circle, the location of the frat houses, is the dominant (if not the only) social scene. But fraternity parties are not exclusive to the point where they throw parties only for themselves; they often host parties specifically for the entire student body. During Greek Week, fraternities open their houses to all students and host popular bands, including past acts such as Vanilla Ice and Galactic.

Contrary to popular belief, meeting girls is really not an issue at Hampden-Sydney College. Girls from other colleges, including the neighboring all-girls college Hollins, visit for the weekend just as boys from HSC visit the girls' schools. Also, the fraternities have frequent mixers with sororities from the University of Richmond and Virginia. The College Activities Committee also hosts mixers, and effort to increase the female presence at social events is definitely noticeable. When asked about girls, one student replied, "It enhances our situation being that we are all male. We certainly do form friendships with girls, but during the week when you have work to do, it's nice to hang out with the guys."

> **"The honor system sets us apart. It is really strong and plays a large role on campus."**

Southern Culture of Honor

Although some may be turned off by the "rolling hills and grazing cattle" that surround the school, others like the security of being able to leave their car doors unlocked and not having to swipe to access buildings. For the men of Hampden-Sydney, this sense of trust is a foundation for brotherhood. One student noted, "The honor system sets us apart. It is really strong and plays a large role on campus." Often, professors give tests and leave the room or give take home tests with the instructions not to use books and to return in two hours. This honor code is strictly enforced: the minimum punishment for lying, cheating, stealing (or tolerating those that do) ranges anywhere from one semester suspension to expulsion. An honor court maintains the code and is responsible for assigning any student accused of an infraction to an undergraduate lawyer while also determining the punishment. Albeit strict, "[The honor code's] effects benefit the entire community." According to one senior, the sense of trust and brotherhood "is really strong and plays a huge role on campus. On the whole, you can do what you want, but you have to grow up quick if you want to make it."—*Christine Kim*

FYI

If you come to Hampden-Sydney, you'd better bring "Seersuckers and loafers."

What's the typical weekend schedule? "Get out of classes, drink with the guys, and wait for the ladies to arrive from SBC, Hollins, and other schools. Go to the frats, dance and get obliterated. Wake up Saturday,(during football season, throw on the coat, go to the Founders lot and get completely drunk for free) wear off the hangover, start drinking again. Sunday: wake up, say goodbye to the weekend catch, watch football, do homework."

If I could change one thing about Hampden-Sydney, "We'd have girls. Just kidding. It would be slightly smaller. We're on the verge of becoming too big to be doing what we've been doing since we were founded, such as upholding our honor code."

Three things every student at Hampden-Sydney should do before graduating are "a bell run, a Hollins girl, and play rugby."

Hollins University

Address: Hollins, PO Box 9688, Roanoke, VA 24020
Phone: 800-456-9595
E-mail Address: huadm@hollins.edu
Web site URL: www.hollins.edu/admissions
Year Founded: 1842
Private or Public: private
Religious affiliation: none
Location: suburban
Regular Application Deadline: rolling
Number of Applicants: 686
Percent Accepted: 86%
Percent Accepted who enroll: 31%
Number Entering: NA
Number of Transfers Accepted each Year: NA
Mean SAT: 1,124
Mean ACT: 25

Middle 50% SAT range: V:530–640, M:490–590
Middle 50% ACT range: 22–27
Early admission program (EA/ ED/ NA): ED
ED or EA Acceptance Rate: 9700%
Full time Undergraduate enrollment: 818
Total enrollment: NA
Percent Male: 0%
Percent Female: 100%
Total Percent Minority: 12%
Percent African-American: 8%
Percent Asian/Pacific Islander: 1%
Percent Hispanic: 2%
Percent Native-American: 1%
Percent Other: 2%
Percent in-state / out of state: 52%/48%

Percent from Public HS: 77%
Retention Rate: 73%
Graduation Rate: 65%
Percent in On-campus housing: 80%
Percent affiliated with Greek system: 0%
Percent Varsity or Club Athletes: NA
Number of official organized extracurricular organizations: 46
3 Most popular majors: Communications, English, Psychology
Student/Faculty ratio: 10:01
Tuition and Fees: $23,800.00
Cost for Room and Board: $8,650.00
Percent receiving Financial aid, first-year: 71%

Respect for tradition and a love for tight-knit community are just some of the values held close to the hearts of students at Hollins University. Academics being no exception, the talented women at Hollins effectively utilize the honored ways of the past to explore and live bright futures as graduates of this distinguished institution.

Scales and Perspectives

A four-year women's university, Hollins divides coursework into four different categories including humanities, social sciences, fine arts and natural sciences. Rather than taking particular required courses, students must take eight credits from each of these divisions. Though some popular majors at Hollins include economics, history and psychology, English is by far the largest major. In fact, many students were drawn to Hollins by the reputation of their well-rated, well-funded creative writing program. A unique major is the interdisciplinary major, a program in which students work with two faculty members to compile a major from two or more disciplines suited to students' interests. Challenging classes at Hollins include upper-level political science classes, but all senior seminar 400-level classes, according to one senior, "have as much work as should be expected." While most students are humanities majors, the natural science facilities are still fairly up-to-date and a new visual arts center sparkles on campus. Hollins also offers a dance program that is always popular with students who must complete two zero-credit physical education courses before graduation. Second-semester freshmen also apply to enroll in the three-year Batten Leadership Institute, a non-curricular program designed for students to "go above and beyond" to focus on their leadership skills.

Germany in January?

Hollins divides its year into three parts—two semesters plus a four-week January short term. During short term, the university offers intense seminars, internships for upperclassmen, and study abroad opportunities in Greece, Spain, and Germany. Competition at Hollins is not cutthroat, but many students report a sporting competitiveness in classes. Students at Hollins feel this sense of competition enhances the spirit of sisterhood at the college. As one student noted, "You want to strive to be the best in your class or a particular class, but it's a natural, healthy competitiveness." The "Hollins family" also extends to the faculty. Many professors live on nearby "faculty row" and it is not uncommon that classes are moved there, sometimes just in time for dinner. It's no wonder that, with a low student-faculty ratio of ten to one and with 79 percent of classes under 20 students, by their fourth year, many students come to appreciate the special relationships forged with their faculty.

Good Living, Bad Food

Freshman dorms are unusually nice and new, often making the transition from home go much more smoothly. Each single or double is air-conditioned and each hallway of 15 girls shares a bathroom, kitchen, social room and study room. Upperclassmen reside in apartments and themed houses such as the Spanish house, French house or the fine arts house. Although these residences lack air-conditioning, most rooms are spacious singles, and one senior living in the Spanish house even boasted of her two closets and hardwood floor.

> "We have all kinds of girls here, from extreme liberal girls to true Southern belles who wear pearls, khakis and Oxfords."

The food situation at Hollins, however, does not receive such positive reviews. The dining hall has dinner hours (4:30–6:30 p.m.) that most find unusually early, and does not provide as much variation as many would hope for. However, Hollins is very sensitive to the needs voiced by various committees on religious and vegetarian sensitivity, and strives to ensure that an array of specific diets are accommodated. For those who need a quick fix (and we're talking of the fried variety), students can also eat at The Rat, a student center specializing in fast foods.

One to Two Beer Kind of School

Many freshmen spend Friday to Sunday at nearby Virginia schools to visit friends and boyfriends. And although Hollins is "a little bit on the outskirts of Roanoke," groups of girls sometimes frequent downtown clubs and bars. Students maintain that they "have all kinds of girls here, from extreme liberal girls to true Southern belles who wear pearls, khakis and Oxfords." Students note that Hollins is too small to be cliquish, and as students grow older, greater numbers of on-campus parties occur that are hosted in upperclassman apartments. Hollins girls have been known to occasionally get the party started on Thursday, but Friday and Saturday nights usually prove to be the most exciting. Some find it problematic that Hollins "shares its brother school," Hampden-Sydney College, with the four other women's colleges in the area. All boys aside, Hollins' own student body contains a good mix of partiers and "staunch sober girls" who choose not to drink. However, in general, Hollins students "play by the rules" and don't consider their campus to be a wild party school where students are "allowed to have open glasses anywhere, walking down the hallways . . . drinking themselves silly every weekend." As one student summed it up, "It's a one- to two-beer kind of school."

Let's Get Physical

Hollins' activity board is particularly strong, and "from concerts, to cultural events, to poker nights, there is always something to do no matter what your interests are." Many women are active in student government and community service. HOP, Hollins Outdoor Program, offers mountain climbing, whitewater rafting, and other outdoor excursions. As a Division III school, the sports teams at Hollins are not big enough to be too exclusive, socially or athletically. While no club sports are offered, Hollins gives interested students a chance to walk onto teams otherwise populated by mostly recruited athletes. For those disinterested in organized sports, Hollins has a gym equipped with a rock-climbing wall—donated by a Hollins alum, the first woman to climb mount Everest—a sauna, a pool, and a fencing studio that is also used for aerobics.

Sisterhood

Although sororities are prohibited by Hollins, the sense of sisterhood is campuswide, and many campus activities still revolve around tradition. On Tinker Day, the day of the first autumn frost, students wake up to the sound of seniors banging on pots and pans as they run down underclassman hallways. Students head to breakfast in the dining halls "in the craziest outfits imaginable," and afterward ditch classes for the day to trek up nearby Tinker Mountain for a picnic buffet at the summit, where the day is spent performing songs and skits. Another popular tradition is Ring Night, when juniors are officially inducted as seniors. This three-day celebration culminates with juniors receiving gift baskets full of senior "necessities" such as pots and pans (for Tinker Day) and four bottles of champagne from their secret senior sisters. Why four bottles of champagne at this "one- to two-beer school?" Another tradition, of course. One of the champagne bottles is used for the women's first-step tradition. Only seniors are allowed to walk on the front quad grass, and, on first-step day, seniors take their first steps on the beautiful front quad while popping the cork of their first bottle of champagne.

With so many fun yet meaningful traditions and a strong sense of community and support, it is no wonder that students grow to love Hollins for both its strengths and its weaknesses. As one student noted, "This school wasn't necessarily my top choice, but looking back on it, Hollins really was my perfect school."—*Christine J. Kim*

FYI

If you come to Hollins, you'd better bring "something unusual to wear for Tinker Day."

What's the typical weekend schedule? "Most classes will end around noon on Fridays. About a third of the students will jump in their cars and head for JMU, VMI or Virginia Tech. However, there's usually a party going on somewhere either Friday or Saturday, and these tend to follow all-day events like Arts Fest and the Hollins Theater shows. Sundays tend to be laid back and quiet with limited hours in the dining hall."

If I could change one thing about Hollins, "I'd alter the policies of the career development center to be more conducive to finding jobs rather than identifying possible career choices."

Three things every student at Hollins should do before leaving are "climb Tinker Mountain, see a Hollins dance performance, and participate in Ring Night."

James Madison University

Address: James Madison, MSC 0101, Harrisonburg, VA 22807
Phone: 540-568-5681
E-mail Address: admissions@jmu.edu
Web site URL: www.jmu.edu/admissions
Year Founded: 1908
Private or Public: public
Religious affiliation: none
Location: rural
Regular Application Deadline: 15-Jan
Number of Applicants: NA
Percent Accepted: 63%
Percent Accepted who enroll: 34%
Number Entering: NA
Number of Transfers Accepted each Year: NA
Mean SAT: NA
Mean ACT: NA

Middle 50% SAT range: V:520–610, M:530–620
Middle 50% ACT range: 21–26
Early admission program (EA/ ED/ NA): EA
ED or EA Acceptance Rate: NA
Full time Undergraduate enrollment: 15,653
Total enrollment: NA
Percent Male: 39%
Percent Female: 61%
Total Percent Minority: 11%
Percent African-American: 4%
Percent Asian/Pacific Islander: 5%
Percent Hispanic: 2%
Percent Native-American: 0%
Percent Other: 6%
Percent in-state / out of state: 70%/30%

Percent from Public HS: NA
Retention Rate: 92%
Graduation Rate: 63%
Percent in On-campus housing: 37%
Percent affiliated with Greek system: 18%
Percent Varsity or Club Athletes: NA
Number of official organized extracurricular organizations: 308
Most popular majors: Marketing, Psychology
Student/Faculty ratio: 16:01
Tuition and Fees: NA
In State Tuition and Fees (if different): NA
Cost for Room and Board: NA
Percent receiving Financial aid, first-year: 31%

In the midst of the stunning Shenandoah Valley lies a purple and gold gem, uncovered and raised from its modest beginnings as a Virginia teachers' school to become one of the leading schools in America. From the moment freshmen step onto James Madison University's campus, they are swept into the friendly bustle that defines the student body.

Academia Is Nuts (In the Good Way)

James Madison University offers a wide range of course offerings and lauded academic programs. Majors span from popular categories such as business and political science to the less popular (but nonetheless adored) social services program. Freshmen tend to attend larger lecture classes, while upperclassmen enjoy about a seventeen to one student-professor ratio. Almost all classes, large or small, are taught by full professors who hold consistent office hours and make themselves extremely accessible. In fact, there are "a ton of professors whom you can run into out on the town in bars and restaurants and they're almost always happy to chat."

Although some students complain about the general education requirements, there is no shortage of enthusiasm about particular departments. A senior describes the College of Integrated Science and Technology as "groundbreaking," a division with an entire portion of campus dedicated to it and a curriculum that incorporates biology, chemistry, physics, computer science, and technology. Students also love the School of Media Arts and Design (SMAD); one student remarked that "everyone should take at least one class in SMAD with Rusty Greene." JMU features a fantastic education program, in which education majors can earn their masters in JMU's five year program. Some Dukes will admit that "people have a lot of trouble with Elementary Statistics," Macroeconomics, and College of Business 300 (COB 300, which includes four separate classes taken at once), but add that even these are recommendable and very worthwhile. Almost all Dukes agree that, no matter what you take, there is still plenty of time to immerse yourself in extracurriculars.

Outside the Classroom

As one student aptly stated, "You'd be hard-pressed to find someone here who's not involved in some sort of student activity." The student body offers over 300 active student-run groups. Not necessarily the most popular but one of the most famed among these is IN8, JMU's secret society. Every year, it gives out eight letters to students and faculty who have significantly impacted their society to let them know that their work does not go unnoticed. In addition, in 2003, they donated a human sundial, a spot in the middle of campus where a person stands on a particular month's mark and casts a shadow on plaques six or seven feet away that designate the time.

When it comes to nightlife, fraternities and sororities provide a nice opportunity to make friends and get involved in the "party scene." Greek life only involves about 12 percent of students, but the ones who go Greek love it. Men rush only one fraternity, while women rush all eight sororities and slowly narrow down their options. Other people get involved with groups such as religious organizations, student government, the yearbook committee, activist groups, a cappella groups, or the sailing club, to name a few.

All sports at JMU are NCAA Division I, and, as demonstrated by the 2004 NCAA champion women's lacrosse team, some of JMU's athletic programs are particularly outstanding. Football, which hopes to be Division IA in the near future, and basketball provide nearly the strongest crowd draws, second only to the nationally acclaimed marching band. Although most Dukes do not attend all the games, everyone attends homecoming. The school annually provides a famous speaker to address a student body decked out in JMU's purple and gold, which proceeds to "tailgate all day and party all night." In general, students become involved in several activities over their four years and often still find time to work in local restaurants or as tutors, dining hall attendants, or teaching and information assistants. A stimulating environment succeeds in keeping Dukes, as one phrased it, "active and productive, and excited about what they're doing."

> "[Dukes are] active and productive, and excited about what they're doing."

Relaxing Down Under
JMU is incredibly friendly; its social graces tend to alleviate what might otherwise be a stressful academic lifestyle. Additionally, the campus accommodates students' busy schedules exceedingly well. JMU provides plenty of student facilities, including one of the most popular lounges on-campus, Taylor Down Under. Students can go to places like this and find access to computers, internet, billiards, board games, study areas, and comfortable futons ("Great for napping!"). The university also sends a constant flow of music over Taylor Down Under's PA system, interrupted only for common evening events such as "open mic nights," poetry readings, bands, comedy acts, and other entertainment. Other popularly frequented hangouts include the quad in the spring, where someone is always lying out doing homework or playing frisbee, or even the on-campus dining halls, some of which stay open until 10 p.m. on weeknights.

Well-Catered
Students who linger in the dining halls find everything from all-you-can-eat buffet style meals, to food courts, and more specialized sandwich bars and salad bars. The school "keeps experimenting with the menu" and actively responding to student complaints to keep its students satisfied. Recently the dining halls relieved the threat of student uproar by removing a certain beloved chicken wrap. For a different taste, Chick-fil-A and an Einstein Bros. Bagels are located on-campus, where students can use "dining dollars" that come with the standard 12-meal weekly plan. Of course, typical chain restaurants are scattered around Harrisonburg, especially after the recent addition of a new shopping center. Local favorites, however, include Mr. J's Bagels, known for its "AMAZING bagel sandwiches," El Charro, a Mexican restaurant, and Luigi's, an Italian pizzeria. When they leave the table, students will be happy to find that no eatery is too far from home.

In the Hall of the Mountain King: The Suite Life
All freshmen and many sophomores live on-campus in centrally located buildings, making "rolling out of bed three minutes before class starts incredibly possible (and done frequently)," according to one upperclassman veteran. In general, these residential halls vary from hall to suite style, and offer warm, beautiful, and historical dorms. Many Dukes claim that "Old Campus," a group of dorms constructed between 1908 and 1948 with blue stone, stands out as the nicest housing in the area, especially since all of its buildings have been renovated during the past decade. For those not lucky enough (or not inclined) to live there, the "Village" is available, offering advantages of its own. Its nine residential halls are standard cinderblock structures, including both standard freshman housing and

interest-related accommodations. Students can live in leadership communities, biology-themed communities, substance-free communities, international halls (where international students are paired with American roommates), and more. All dorms have remained co-ed since the last all-girls dorm opened its doors to men. The system seems to produce fast friends: one senior praised, "I still live with five girls from my freshman hall, and I've had the same (randomly assigned) roommate since freshman year."

On-campus housing is also available for upperclassmen, but most elect to enter the myriad of apartment and town-house complexes that have sprouted around the school in response to the quickly growing student population. This growth has created what one apartment dweller termed a "mini satellite campus off campus," consisting of various buildings. The student body has approximately doubled to 15,000 in the past 20 years, necessitating extra housing. Although parking spaces are generally scarce and the commute to class from the apartments is slightly longer than from on-campus housing, residents love where they live. Each of these complexes "has its own reputation and theme," providing off-campus essentials for their inhabitants.

Bust out the Party Hat

"Everyone from freshmen to super-seniors (5th years) show up at the apartment parties for mingling, dancing, flip cup, beer pong, and just some basic chatting over beer" when the weekend rolls around. Some Dukes start their nightlife on Wednesday or Thursday night, either in local bars or apartments. Mainstreet Bar and Grille, in particular, keeps some people dancing until 2 a.m. on Wednesday nights. Since no alcohol (JMU makes this very clear) is allowed in freshman dorms and no one underage can drink on campus, most partiers migrate to the apartments by Friday. Not everyone drinks, but those who do usually have the option to party hard: "At some universities, a cover is required by the owners of the house to pay for the alcohol, but at JMU, it's pretty much open and free to all, which is so nice to know that you're welcome everywhere." JMU students seem responsible about their habits, a trait best shown by the student-run "Safe Rides" program that offers free taxi service to those who have been drinking.

Moreover, the school's "three strikes" program forces them to proceed with relative caution, especially with respect to local police or higher-up administrators. Residential assistants purportedly "are always there for you, and do what they need to do to keep us all safe but let us enjoy ourselves, too." Some of the less strict ones "have even been known to play beer pong with us," says a freshman, though this occasion is rare. Dukes who would rather not party or drink can hit the student lounges, which stay open late, or go to a movie at the campus movie theater for only $2.50. Wherever students are, campus police, vigilant "campus cadets," and a "blue light system" (a series of blue lights all over campus, each within view of the next, that can be used to summon help or safety escorts) keep them safe all night.

The Bottom Line

As a recent student body president remarked in an interview, "I've never met a single person who left because they didn't like it here. The only ones who leave are the ones who think that maybe they wanted something different academically." As the school develops, however, this latter concern is becoming less and less prevalent. JMU provides a terrific liberal arts education and continues its history of producing successful alumni today, while fostering an inclusive and high-spirited atmosphere that complements its beautiful area. Most Dukes echo the testimony of one upperclassman: "If I had to choose all over again, I'd stick with JMU. Wouldn't change anything."—*Hugh Sullivan*

FYI
If you come to JMU, you'd better bring "a friendly attitude."
What's the typical weekend schedule? "Go to bars on Wednesday and Thursdays, apartment parties on Friday. Saturday, work out during the day; go to a frat party at night. Sunday, sleep in and study!"
If I could change one thing about JMU, I would "move it closer to a major city. JMU does a good job of bringing stuff down, and Charlottesville isn't too far away, but I would prefer to have the D.C. nightlife available."
Three things that every student at JMU should do before graduating are "swim in Newman Lake (not as pleasant as it may sound), ring the bells in the bell tower, and find the hidden underground tunnels that were originally built so that women could avoid the cold weather between classes but have since been shut down. (The bell tower is rumored to be haunted on foggy nights by the ghost of the girl whose death in the tunnels caused the tunnels' closing.)"

Randolph College

Address: Randolph-Macon, 2500 Rivermont Avenue, Lynchburg, VA 24503
Phone: 434-947-8100
E-mail Address: admissions@rmwc.edu
Web site URL: www.rmwc.edu
Year Founded: 1891
Private or Public: private
Religious affiliation: United Methodist
Location: small city
Regular Application Deadline: 1-Mar
Number of Applicants: NA
Percent Accepted: 89%
Percent Accepted who enroll: NA
Number Entering: 187
Number of Transfers Accepted each Year: NA
Mean SAT: 1,155
Mean ACT: 26
Middle 50% SAT range: M:490–630, V:520–630

Middle 50% ACT range: 23–27
Early admission program (EA/ ED/ NA): ED
ED or EA Acceptance Rate: 67%
Full time Undergraduate enrollment: 668
Total enrollment: 715
Percent Male: 0%
Percent Female: 100%
Total Percent Minority: 33%
Percent African-American: 9%
Percent Asian/Pacific Islander: 3%
Percent Hispanic: 5%
Percent Native-American: 1%
Percent Other: 15%
Percent in-state / out of state: 32%/68%
Percent from Public HS: 78%

Retention Rate: 78%
Graduation Rate: 65%
Percent in On-campus housing: 88%
Percent affiliated with Greek system: NA
Percent Varsity or Club Athletes: NA
Number of official organized extracurricular organizations: 40
3 Most popular majors: Social Sciences, Biology, Psychology
Student/Faculty ratio: 9:01
Tuition and Fees: $23,900.00
Cost for Room and Board: $8,800.00
Percent receiving Financial aid, first-year: 32%

Randolph College, formerly Randolph-Macon Women's College, is beginning a new chapter of its 115-year history. In fall of 2007, this small liberal arts college will admit its first coeducational class. The school also plans to release a new, enhanced curriculum starting in 2007. Yet with all these dramatic changes, the school insists that "the essential elements of the Randolph-Macon experience will remain constant."

A Close-Knit Community

Randolph College is described as a "gorgeous" college, set against the backdrop of the Virginia hills and distinctive for its classic redbrick buildings and a matching redbrick wall that surrounds the entire campus. The student body is made up of only about 1,150 students, and all of them are required to live on campus for their full four years. "I like that everyone lives here," said one student. "We have such a wonderful sense of community, and it only takes five minutes to get from one part of campus to another." Most people have "no real complaints" about the living situation, as the rooms are larger than those at many other colleges and each of the dorm buildings has a unique attribute such as air conditioning, elevators, larger rooms, a better location, or extended quiet hours. Freshmen dorms are assigned based on student preference forms, and upperclassmen draw for rooms in spring. Most of the dormitories are divided proportionally among the classes (except for the senior dorm and the mostly-freshmen dorm) in order to facilitate and encourage interaction among upperclassmen and underclassmen. One senior commented, "My first year, I had so many upperclassmen coming into my room, welcoming me, letting me borrow books, telling me about professors, giving me tips, asking me about my clubs . . . . people just take you under their wing!"

Another student commented, "It's really easy to meet people here because it's such a small school. There is only one dining hall and everyone has the same set meal plan, so "sometimes people will stay at dinner for hours, just talking. Of course there are a couple of cliques, but there will be groups in any community and no one is exclusive."

Students say they met their friends through athletics, clubs, classes, or freshman orientation groups. "There are a ton of mixers," said one student. "You'd have to live in a hole not to have any friends at Macon. And that's not possible to do here, either!" The college is very geographically diverse and boasts a large international student population, but ethnic diversity could use some improvement. "We could use more diversity, but I'm glad that we're at least as diverse as we are now," said one student. "It brings a lot to the classroom to have so many different vantage points."

From Homework to Happy Hour

The academics at Randolph are rigorous, to say the least. Students have a variety of requirements to fulfill, spanning such subjects as religion, philosophy, English, physical education, and a lab science. "Because of the liberal arts requirements, I get exposed to a lot of classes that may not be my strengths," commented one student. "But if you come in with an open mind and you push yourself to do well, they're really great." The most popular majors are psychology and biology, and if a student can't find a major that suits her among the list of more than 25 possibilities, she always has the opportunity to design her own major. Most students agree, "All the majors are difficult—[Randolph] definitely doesn't give anything out for free." Registration is based on seniority and usually people are satisfied with the system, but the popularity of certain majors (particularly biology), the limited selection of classes, and the small class size can sometimes make it difficult to get into certain courses. Class size varies from four or five students to thirty, although the average is nine. Workload, too, varies and depends on the class, the professor, and the preparation of the students. While some describe it as "pretty heavy compared to other colleges," another observed, "It's not too different from high school AP classes. It can be overwhelming at first, but it's definitely manageable." Said one student, "Standards are fairly high, but there's no animosity within the classroom. People just want to do their own personal best."

According to many students, grading can be stringent. "We have a saying here: 'Anywhere else it would have been an A,'" said one. "I don't know if that's true, or if that's just us complaining about it." Still, student-faculty relations are "amazing. There's a lot

of interaction with professors, especially on independent research projects." Another said, "A lot of professors have students babysitting, house-sitting, pet-sitting, whatever!" Most professors have an open-door policy, where students can come by and talk or ask questions even if it's not during office hours. "Professors want students to do well," noted one junior. The faculty is also highly involved in student extracurricular life, participating in award shows or other activities and often attending a Macon Community Happy Hour. Overall, students appreciate their professors and their academic opportunities, believing that the rigor of the curriculum is "worth it, because we're working hard for our education and becoming stronger women in the process."

We Like to Party?

The extracurricular activity at Randolph is centered around a wide variety of student clubs and organizations. "We're very involved in our clubs," said one student. "We're always out to save the world in one form or another." Several of the larger groups include the Global Aids Campaign, the Environmental Club, the Black Women's Alliance, various religious organizations, language clubs, and the Macon Activities Council, which brings in speakers and musicians and organizes events such as horseback riding or whitewater rafting. There are also multiple drama productions, musical ensembles, and a whole host of other clubs. "For our plays and shows, we don't play the male roles; we bring in men from the community," one student mentioned. "They always say they have a great time!" Said another, "We have upwards of 100 clubs for a student body of only 1,150 people, if that gives you any idea of how important clubs are to us."

> "You'd have to live in a hole not to have any friends at Macon. And that's not possible to do here, either!"

Varsity athletics, however, has a much smaller following. "The people involved are really dedicated and the faculty is supportive, but I don't know how much attention the student body pays to the WildCats," said one student athlete. Intramural sports are not big, either; most students get their exercise by working out on their own, lifting weights or going running. A large majority of students have jobs on campus, especially since many of them participate in the work-study program.

As far as the weekend social scene is concerned, Randolph is not a party school. "We go off-campus to party," said one student. "I'd say that on the weekends, almost half the campus goes home or goes to another college to party, while the other half stays behind to do work or club stuff." Another student said that weekend socializing can consist of a variety of activities such as drinking in people's rooms, going to a movie or out to dinner, going to see guest speakers or musicians, or going out to a club. "One club across the street has Wednesday college night, but generally, there's not a whole lot to do in Lynchburg," commented one sophomore. "Occasionally an organization on campus will host a bigger party, but for the most part people stick to smaller groups in rooms." One famous annual celebration is the "Never-Ending Weekend," with Friday night being the Tacky Party (the name is self-explanatory) and Saturday night being Fall Formal. Weekend activities in the surrounding town are limited, since Lynchburg "is not really a college town so you have to drive to get to a movie theatre and most good restaurants." When asked to comment on the town's relationship with the college, one student responded, "We're definitely a separate community, but the town respects Randolph students and they have no real reason to complain about us because we're not a party school."

Daisy Chains and Pumpkin Parades

One particularly distinctive tradition at Randolph is the inter-class rivalry. Students identify themselves as "evens" or "odds," depending on the year of their graduation, and they enthusiastically participate in a vast collection of activities—such as water balloon fights and painting each other's banners—associated with the even-odd rivalry. "Sister classes" (freshmen/juniors and sophomores/seniors) have a strong connection and they show their support for one another during Ring Week, when freshmen give small gifts to the juniors and create a scavenger hunt for them to find their class rings, and the Pumpkin Parade, where each senior receives a pumpkin carved by a sophomore. Right before graduation, sophomores make a huge daisy chain and pass it to the seniors. The class rivalry is even physically built into the school: a special staircase in the main lobby has one side for evens and one side for odds, and if a student goes up or down the wrong side, rumor has it that she won't graduate on time.

Randolph is certainly not for everyone. But for those who are willing to brave the tough academics and enjoy a somewhat quieter social scene, the college offers a vibrant community of dedicated, intelligent women who are working to better themselves and their society. One senior's final comment was, "It's a wonderful place. I've been exceedingly happy with what I've experienced there in the past four years."—*Lindsay Starck*

FYI

If you come to RC, you'd better bring "a whole lot of class spirit for the even-odd rivalry!"

What's the typical weekend schedule? "Relax, maybe party a bit or take a trip off-campus, then hit the books on Sunday."

If I could change one thing about RC, I'd "have more faculty available so that it's easier to get into popular or required classes."

Three things every student at RC should do before graduation are "join a club or several of them, ring the bell in May Hall, and participate in the traditional Dell Run (running naked across the Greek-style ampitheatre)."

Sweet Briar College

Address: Sweet Briar, PO Box B, Sweet Briar, VA 24595
Phone: 800.381.6142
E-mail Address: admissions@sbc.edu
Web site URL: www.sbc.edu
Year Founded: 1901
Private or Public: private
Religious affiliation: none
Location: rural
Regular Application Deadline: 1-Feb
Number of Applicants: 625
Percent Accepted: 79%
Percent Accepted who enroll: 40%
Number Entering: 200
Number of Transfers Accepted each Year: 30
Mean SAT: 1,130
Mean ACT: 25
Middle 50% SAT range: 1,030–1,250

Middle 50% ACT range: 24–26
Early admission program (EA/ ED/ NA): ED
ED or EA Acceptance Rate: NA
Full time Undergraduate enrollment: 739
Total enrollment: 751
Percent Male: 0%
Percent Female: 100%
Total Percent Minority: 12.5%
Percent African-American: NA
Percent Asian/Pacific Islander: NA
Percent Hispanic: NA
Percent Native-American: NA
Percent Other: NA
Percent in-state / out of state: 42%/58%

Percent from Public HS: 70%
Retention Rate: 79.6%
Graduation Rate: 69.8%
Percent in On-campus housing: 95%
Percent affiliated with Greek system: NA
Percent Varsity or Club Athletes: 22%
Number of official organized extracurricular organizations: 50+
3 Most popular majors: Business/Economics, Biology, Government
Student/Faculty ratio: 8:01
Tuition and Fees: $25,015.00
Cost for Room and Board: $10,040.00
Percent receiving Financial aid, first-year: 91%

Though small and rural, Sweet Briar College's quaint, historical college seems to house the best of everything—except for men, of course. According to a locally printed bumper sticker, at Sweet Briar College, "women are leaders and men are . . . *guests.*" That's an overstatement considering the male visitation privileges and security clearance they have to gain just to get on campus. They don't call Sweet Briar the "pink bubble" for nothing!

Workin' It

Don't think that all that pink means these girls aren't working hard. Academics are taken very seriously at Sweet Briar College. Writes one junior, "There is a lot of reading and paper writing, etc . . . and it can be really hard but we're all at Sweet Briar to gain an education and so we do what it takes." The girls are required to meet general education requirement including fulfilling certain "knowledge areas" and "skill areas," but course options allow for students do to so according to their own interests. For example, one junior took a course on the "History of Crime and Punishment in the West" to fulfill the "quantitative reasoning" requirement. Sweet Briar girls agree that there are no

"hard" or "easy" majors offered there. "Sweet Briar academics aren't for the faint of heart, no matter which major or minor you choose. We are a very small school . . . but it does ensure that none of our 40-something programs are weak." That may mean no coasting, but it also means that Sweet Briar students have full reign of their course options. Honors classes are available to all who are interested, and Sweet Briar offers certificate programs in Arts Management, Equine Studies and Leadership. Further, the average class size is 12 students! That kills all hopes of unnoticed absences on especially early—or late—mornings, but girls have no trouble working their way into capped courses. All they have to do is ask nicely.

The workload can be heavy at Sweet Briar but "girls learn to balance things quickly. Study parties are . . . a popular and fun way to get work done, but have a little fun at the same time." Professors are also very accessible for outside help and no classes are taught by TAs so girls enjoy lots of one-on-one time with their instructors. Further, they are able to complete special projects researching the local history in nearby Amherst and Lynchburg. Twenty-one of

Sweet Briar's thirty campus buildings are part of the "Sweet Briar College National Historic District" on the National Register of Historic Places.

Out on the Town

Social life at Sweet Briar is different than at other schools because girls have to go off campus to party. "The campus is pretty evenly split between the girls who like to go to other area school and girls who like to stay around SBC on the weekends." Shopping, dining out, and movie-going are popular. Though drinking is not unheard of, the Sweet Briar honor code disallows underage drinking, ensuring that non-drinkers are satisfied by a myriad of alternatives. The Campus Events Organization plans concerts and events on the weekends including two annual formal events, the "Fall Formal" and the "Junior Banquet." The CEO also organizes lectures, and exhibitions on a weekly basis. Recent guests include Salmon Rushdie, DanceBrazil, and the Roanoke Opera. Not bad for a small college town.

There's no Greek system at Sweet Briar College, but, as one T-shirt reads, "SBD: We're one big sorority." Tap Clubs are similar institutions, all but one of which are exclusive. Bum Chums and Ants N Asses are the most popular and many sponsor boathouse parties. However, on-campus cliques "change and morph frequently" so meeting new people is not a problem. In fact, most faces are familiar anyway on such a small campus.

According to a traditional jingle, "Diamonds are pretty and so are pearls, but nothing compares to Sweet Briar girls." It's not surprising then that boys come from nearby Hampden-Sydney to take Sweet Briar girls on dinner and movie dates in Lynchburg. Only about half of the student body is sexually active, however, so the jury's out on after-dinner activities. Says one junior, "a large percentage of the school is sexually active, but as educated women, I'm sure many, if not all of them make sure to use protection so STDs are not a perceived problem".

The Sweet Briar student body is "diverse in terms of personality types and backgrounds" but not much else. One girl writes that "Sweet Briar students are stereotyped as preppy girls who wear pearls, pink and green, and Vera Bradley bags." Most girls dress more casually than expected, however, and would prefer that the campus as a whole were more diverse.

Dorms and Dining

Unless they're married or over 25, Sweet Briar students are required to live on campus or at home. Freshmen are divided into floors and halls based on their chosen "male visitation option," but upperclasswomen are automatically allowed visitors at all hours. Meta Glass and Grammer Halls are for first-year students and are monitored by upperclasswomen called FYAs or First-Year Assistants and even the upperclass dorms have Community Assistants (CAs). Dew is the worst dorm and Manson has the best kitchen, but according to one student, "All of the dorms on campus are pretty nice . . . they all have nice big rooms and are really good compared to other college dorms I have seen." They better be if there's no way out of them.

Along with a four-year residential plan comes a 21 meal fixed dining plan. Sweet Briar girls can eat in the dining hall, or have wraps made at a station on the way to class. They can also purchase food from the "Bistro" or the "Café" at their expense . . . but the dining hall overlooks the mountain, so it's not to be avoided. "One could easily spend hours sitting in our dining hall and chatting, and I have on several occasions," says one student. Many student groups also hold meetings in the dining area. Girls who need a change of pace dine out at "The Briar Patch" in Amherst, or grab coffee at "The Drowsy Poet."

Loving the Locals

Sweet Briar students can't say enough about their campus—almost as beautiful as the girls. Writes one student, "[Sweet Briar] is the one college that I visited where I felt the pictures in the brochures didn't do it justice." The original campus buildings were built by Ralph Adams Cram and the recent ones emulate his style so that the architecture blends with the natural surroundings. "The campus feels very peaceful and is just a really pleasant place to be." At least there's something for these ladies to feast their eyes on.

The "Dell" is the grassy courtyard in the center of campus—a popular perch for students in search of a little sun. Other students, assured by the vigilance of the Campus Police, like to take walks around the "Dairy Loop." Those who want a break from nature can explore the shopping districts in Amherst and Lynchburg, both of which have healthy relationships with the College. Local elementary school students enjoy campus and gallery tours, science and art days given by Sweet Briar students. The girls also host a school supply drive and teach dance classes in town.

Down Time . . . Or Not

Sweet Briar girls don't take academics lightly, and the same goes for extracurriculars. One junior writes that "Sweet Briar student in general are extremely active in extracurricular activities, almost to the point of insanity." So when they're not in class, girls engage with respected groups like the student government, student newspaper, and intramurals. Tap Clubs are also popular but more fun that structured. Girls who need a good football fix have to travel to nearby Hampden-Sydney or VMI to catch a boy in uniform. The Sweet Briar Equestrian Team, however, is well-supported and fitted with a recruiting office. Less competitive souls get their workouts in the recreational gym, swimming pool or at the tennis court.

> **"It's like a four year slumber party with great classes interspersed!"**

When they're not excelling in the classroom or on the IM fields, the Sweet Briar Vixens are participating in one of the college's many traditions—or hiding from them. Daisy, the daughter of the College's founder is rumored to haunt the place. More wholesome rituals include "The Ring Game" which roots out those lucky girls who are engaged—yes, to be married—and the "Big/Little Sister" program which partners Juniors and Freshmen, not to mention Scream Night, Lantern Bearing, Step Singing, and Founder's Day. Wherever they choose to devote their energies, the girls of Sweet Briar College are wed to their alma mater. Quirky traditions and an idyllic campus are their favorite parts. One student comments, "It's like a four year slumber party with great classes interspersed!" Pillow fights anyone?—*Lauren Ezell*

FYI
If you come to Sweet Briar, you better bring "a car."
What is a typical weekend schedule? "Whatever you want!"
If I could change one thing about Sweet Briar, I'd "make the student body more diverse."
Three things every student at Sweet Briar should do before graduating are "go sledding on a dining hall tray, walk the dairy loop, and admire just how beautiful the campus is."

University of Richmond

Address: University of Richmond, 28 West Hamptom Way, Richmond, VA 23173
Phone: 804-289-8640
E-mail Address: admissions@richmond.edu
Web site URL: www.richmond.edu
Year Founded: 1830
Private or Public: private
Religious affiliation: none
Location: suburban
Regular Application Deadline: 16-Jan
Number of Applicants: 5,408%
Percent Accepted: 44%
Percent Accepted who enroll: 33.7%
Number Entering: 812
Number of Transfers Accepted each Year: 20–40
Mean SAT: 1,270

Mean ACT: 28
Middle 50% SAT range: 1,240–1,350
Middle 50% ACT range: 26–30
Early admission program (EA/ ED/ NA): ED
ED or EA Acceptance Rate: 20–25%
Full time Undergraduate enrollment: 2,920
Total enrollment: 3,685
Percent Male: 49%
Percent Female: 51%
Total Percent Minority: 10%
Percent African-American: 4%
Percent Asian/Pacific Islander: 3%
Percent Hispanic: 2%
Percent Native-American: less than 1%
Percent Other: NA
Percent in-state / out of state: 15%/85%

Percent from Public HS: 60%
Retention Rate: 92.5%
Graduation Rate: 84%
Percent in On-campus housing: 92%
Percent affiliated with Greek system: 45%
Percent Varsity or Club Athletes: NA
Number of official organized extracurricular organizations: 220
3 Most popular majors: Business Administration, English, Political Science
Student/Faculty ratio: 9:01
Tuition and Fees: $34,040
Cost for Room and Board: $6,060
Percent receiving Financial aid, first-year: 35%

When you head off to the University of Richmond, you'd better be prepared for a four-year marathon. The serene campus is bustling with activity, ambitious students and unique educational opportunities. Students throw themselves into every aspect of the Richmond experience and reap the benefits. A recently revamped library, gym and dining hall are just a few of the new perks at the already impressive school. Students come ready to work hard, play hard, and make the most of all that Richmond offers.

The Richmond Difference

The Robins School of Business at Richmond was recently ranked in number three by BusinessWeek. Most students agree that business is one of the most popular majors for students to pursue at UR. The Jepson School of Leadership Studies is one of a kind. If they don't choose business, students often select this interdisciplinary major in leadership studies that is unique to UR. "Anything in the science field is known to be killer," said one junior, "most people on campus are political science, business, or leadership majors." There is also praise for international business, which easily complements a language major. Students at Richmond must fulfill General Education requirements, the "gen-ed's," that range from science and math to literature and history. CORE, a combination of philosophy and literature that "not many people love" is one of the most notoriously hard requirements that everyone must suffer through explained one student. Students also take Wellness classes throughout the semester on various health and lifestyle issues.

Richmond students agree that the workload is challenging. "You'd be hard pressed to find an easy class at Richmond," said one junior. Students spend significant time in the library, which has almost become another location to socialize. "People are always in the library, you can find everyone there," one student described. Recent renovations to the main library make it an even more attractive destination. Richmond has a student-faculty ratio of 10:1 and most find it very easy to seek out help from professors. Small class size also aids in roundtable discussions and the free exchange of ideas in an intimate environment.

Students find it very easy to become involved on campus from Greek life to student government and an array of clubs and organizations. Richmond students approach their extracurriculars with the same intensity as their classes and often find it easy to become overcommitted. "I was surprised by how easy it is to become involved here," said a junior. Involvement, however, creates a close-knit community to which everyone can contribute.

From the Lodges, to Dhall

To balance out all that work, Richmond students never find their weekends dull. "Greek life pretty much rules here," said one junior girl. The lodges, where the fraternities are located, are known for their great throw-downs on Saturdays. Friday nights usually consist of going to the senior apartments and partying there. Drinking is prevalent but most agree that everyone is able to find his or her own comfortable social scenes.

In between parties, friends cherish their moments in the dining hall, affectionately known as "dhall," to debrief the past nights' events. All students living on campus must have a meal plan and the food is generally satisfactory. Some complain of a lack of variety or healthy options while others rave about new additions of brick oven pizza and a Mongolian grill. For those seeking more diverse options, venturing into the city of Richmond offers many local restaurants and two nearby shopping malls. Some students keep cars on campus, which is vital for escaping the "Richmond Bubble". One student complained of the contained campus, citing that "most students are too timid to get off campus and do their own thing".

If you're looking for a sports-oriented college, Richmond is not the place. "Nobody really cares about sports here" one sophomore declared. Basketball is perhaps the most popular team to follow, but attendance at most sporting events is low. Football also tends to bring students out, but only for the tailgates. Tailgating is a social event in itself. "Everyone gets dressed up as preppy as possible and drinks in the parking lot at the stadium," a senior described. After mingling in a mixture of pearls and popped collars, students head back to the dorms without making it to the game.

The Richmond Bubble

It may be a very contained world, but Richmond students are happy and quite comfortable in their bubble. "It's definitely sheltered away from the 'real world' " a student explained, "but it's a safe, friendly, and caring environment with every opportunity you would ask for." Students praise the beautiful campus and enjoy warm afternoons swimming or laying out by the James River. The Richmond community is friendly and fluid, making it easy to constantly meet new people. The student body lacks some diversity and despite university efforts to attract a more international crowd, everyone agrees that the majority of students appear to be preppy, middle-class northerners.

> "It's definitely sheltered away from the 'real world' but it's a safe, friendly, and caring environment with every opportunity you would ask for."

There is a prevalent sense of integrity within the student body due to a strong honor code that everyone signs freshman year. Freshman boys and girls take part in respective honor code signing ceremonies—Investiture for boys, and Proclamation for girls. The girls wear white dresses and the boys dress up as well, making each event a formal and special occasion. Crime is low and while most people agree you should not leave your laptop lying around, they feel very safe. For girls worried about walking home late at night or just looking to escape the cold, there is a campus shuttle service, but sorry boys, this one is strictly for the ladies so you'll be traveling on foot after your nights out.

The View Across the Lake

Students must live on campus until they are seniors when they have the option of moving to an apartment. Over 90% of students choose to remain on campus for all four years. "Nobody likes moving off campus because it's hard to stay in the social scene," said one junior. Housing is decent but some lament having to live in doubles until you are junior, as well as the single-sex dorms. Richmond was historically divided by the lake in the middle of campus into two separate colleges, Richmond College for boys and Westhampton College for the girls. Rumor has it that whomever you kiss on the gazebo in the middle of the lake will be the person you marry. Nowadays each sex lives on both sides of the lake but dorms remain single-sex. All of the freshman girls live in Laura Robbins and freshman boys are assigned to Grey Court. Solidarity easily forms within your class but the separation of sexes is said to have some negative effects. "Intermixing seems more forced and based around sexual attraction," one student complained, "if you see a guy in Laura Robbins you know he is there to see a girl."

The students relish several Richmond traditions that date back many years. Breaking out the traditional white dress again, the junior girls take part in "Ring Dance." This black tie event takes place at the old Richmond Hotel with each girl accompanied by her father and a date. A much less formal but equally important event is the Pig Roast, a campus-wide outdoor event. Pig roast takes place every March and is the "best day of the year" according to several students. The day commences early with a slew of students decked out in sundresses and ties, drinking mimosas. The party moves to the apartments and then continues at the lodges for this all day affair.

Overall, students are thrilled with their choice to attend Richmond, which is evident in the high level of enthusiasm and involvement in the school community. People are happy to take advantage of every aspect of their four years. One sophomore raved, "The people here are genuinely nice and excited about life! We really do all work hard and play hard." If you're ready to take it all in, be prepared to hit the ground running. —*Jennifer Hansen*

FYI

If you come to Richmond you'd better bring . . . "a polo shirt in every color, collar popped."

What is the typical weekend schedule? "Either apartment parties, or even better, fraternity lodge parties! Go shopping in Carytown, and every Saturday and Sunday afternoon, everyone piles into D-hall for brunch."

If I could change one thing about Richmond I'd . . . "make more apartment style or coed housing. Living in a dorm till you're a junior just sucks!"

Three things every Richmond student should do before graduating are "go all out at the pig roast, spend a few lazy afternoons by the James River, either attend Ring Dance (if you're a junior girl), or go with a junior girl to Ring Dance."

University of Virginia

Address: University of VA, PO Box 400160, Charlottesville, VA 22904

Phone: 434-982-3200

E-mail Address: undergradadmission @virginia.edu

Web site URL: www.virginia.edu

Year Founded: 1819

Private or Public: public

Religious affiliation: none

Location: small city

Regular Application Deadline: 2-Jan

Number of Applicants: 16,300

Percent Accepted: 38%

Percent Accepted who enroll: 50%

Number Entering: 3,100

Number of Transfers Accepted each Year: 789

Mean SAT: NA

Mean ACT: NA

Middle 50% SAT range: 1,220–1,420

Middle 50% ACT range: 28–32

Early admission program (EA/ ED/ NA): ED

ED or EA Acceptance Rate: 30%

Full time Undergraduate enrollment: 13,400

Total enrollment: 20,000

Percent Male: 46%

Percent Female: 54%

Total Percent Minority: 29%

Percent African-American: 9%

Percent Asian/Pacific Islander: 14%

Percent Hispanic: 5%

Percent Native-American: 1%

Percent Other: 0%

Percent in-state / out of state: 66%/34%

Percent from Public HS: 75%

Retention Rate: 97%

Graduation Rate: 92%

Percent in On-campus housing: 48%

Percent affiliated with Greek system: 30%

Percent Varsity or Club Athletes: 75%

Number of official organized extracurricular organizations: 500

3 Most popular majors: Economics, Government, Business

Student/Faculty ratio: 15:01

Tuition and Fees: $8,000.00

In State Tuition and Fees (if different): $26,000.00

Cost for Room and Board: $6,350.00

Percent receiving Financial aid, first-year: 25%

Nestled between the cosmopolitan, mid-sized city of Charlottesville, and the scenic beauty of the Blue Ridge, The University of Virginia (UVa) offers a combination of tradition and pride. UVa was founded by Thomas Jefferson, and both Edgar Allan Poe and Woodrow Wilson attended the University. Further tradition dictates in the fact that UVa has no "freshmen" and "sophomores;" instead, there are first-year and second-years and so on. This convention started because Thomas Jefferson, the school's founder, believed learning is continuous, and therefore a "freshman" is simply in their first year of a life-long education. Other idiosyncrasies include the "Wahoos'" reference to their campus as "Grounds" or simply calling UVa "the University." Learning the lingo as a first-year at the University is key to fitting in on Grounds.

A Lifelong Education and Free Lunches

The University breaks down undergraduates into six schools: the Architecture School, the Engineering School, the McIntire School of Commerce, the Nursing School, the Curry School of Education, and the College of Arts and Sciences. Each school has its own academic requirements determined by major. The academic requirements in the College are "basic:" 12 credits of math and science, six of humanities, three of history, six of social science, and three in non-Western perspectives. There are also additional foreign language and writing proficiency requirements. The Jeffersonian vision of academia is the cornerstone of the University, and requires students to "follow truth wherever it may lead," and it always leads to multiple disciplines.

Most students do not find the requirements burdensome "since they are really flexible, and you can space out anything that you detest so that you aren't stuck with a ton of courses that you hate in any given semester." Class sizes vary greatly "depending on which classes you take." The University offers a range of classes, from large lectures of 500 students down to a two-student seminar. Some classes are difficult to get into, such as Media Studies and Public Speaking, and during the beginning of class sign-ups "it is frustrating because it seems like everything is full and nobody can get the classes they want, but by the end of the drop period a lot of slots open up, so students just have to be patient and vigilant." UVa has "gut" classes like any other school, and Physics 105 (How Things Work), Mental Health, lower-level astronomy classes and physical education classes are considered to be a few examples.

Once students get into their courses, they say, professors "are very accessible." Most students are very happy with their professors; a UVa third year pointed out that "the professors here want you to learn, so they try and be available as much as possible." Students say "grading is usually tough but fair;" however, the Jeffersonian ideal definitely resonates with students. As one third year summed up, "I love it here. . . . [It is] challenging, but you always learn something."

In keeping with the University's tradition and history, Professors are either addressed as "Mr." or "Mrs." or "Professor," but never "Dr." because "Mr. Jefferson did not want that sort of division between students and faculty." Instead, as one student said, "Mr. Jefferson wanted students and professors to interact regularly and freely because that was how education was truly found." In response to this tenet, the College of Arts and Science Council has a "take your professor to lunch" program, in which the council will pay for your lunch with your professor as a way to increase interactions between students and the faculty outside of the classroom. One student even said, "I have been on a rowing machine at the Aquatic Fitness Center rowing next to my Organic Chemistry professor."

> "Mr. Jefferson wanted students and professors to interact regularly and freely because that was how education was truly found."

Students say the coursework at UVa is intense yet manageable. "There is still time for play, but the work comes first and during the week it takes a decent part of my schedule." While "tradition" and "history" resonate deeply with the Wahoos, the word "honor" has even more significance on Grounds. The Honor System attempts to provide students with substantial benefits dependent on self-governance, such as unproctored exams in their rooms or in a pavilion garden. Self-governance is a huge tradition at UVa; "not only do we have a completely student-run Honor System and University Judiciary Committeee, but the Student Council has a great deal of influence, distributing over $300,000 annually to student groups." However, the Honor System has become a "contentious issue here at UVa, especially the single sanction, which means automatic expulsion for anyone convicted by the Committee." Moreover, "a lot of professors give proctored exams and don't allow the freedom and trust promised in the prospectus. The University has done a good job of perpetuating the myths and there are examples of the benefits of the honor code, but they are the exception rather than the rule."

Life as a Wahoo

UVa students are known as "Wahoos" (or "Cavaliers") and Charlottesville is nicknamed "Hooville," an epithet said to originate from the legend of the wahoo fish, which can drink its weight in water. UVa students live up to these nicknames because "alcohol is everywhere on campus." However, "a student can go out and have a good time with or without alcohol." Between hanging out in the vibrant town of Charlottesville, going to a cappella concerts, intramurals, rock concerts and smaller parties, students boast that "there is something for everyone here." One first-year said, "I think that UVa is diverse when it comes to social scenes."

The University's policies on alcohol tend to be pretty strict, but "as long as you don't do anything stupid, you're fine." Students mostly go out on the weekends, "restricted to Thursday [through] Saturday or Sunday nights, but there are definitely places to go every night of the week." The fraternities lined up on Rugby Road tend to run the social scene "until students are of age to go to bars and purchase alcohol." Being underage is a problem at bars, but not at fraternities. Bid Night, Halloween and Springfest are reportedly the biggest parties on campus. Third- and fourth-year students frequent house and apartment parties, bars and other colleges, and often travel into Washington, D.C.

Dating among Wahoos is said to be "very common," and students agree "there are enough attractive people." Attractive or not, students love to dress up, and there are many occasions on Grounds. Besides the formal events for fraternities and sororities, another tradition at UVa is to get dressed up for football games. There has recently been a split among the student body with regards to wearing formal clothing to football games. Many students "now opt for donning orange-dominated school colors in an effort to create what's known as the 'Sea of Orange.'" Dress as you please, because UVa offers tons of other activities on the weekends besides football games.

There are always "local bands playing all over the place." The UVa movie theater showcases $3 movies every weekend: one old movie and one new movie. Big Hollywood names, including Anthony Hopkins and Sigourney Weaver, come to the annual Virginia Film Festival in Charlottesville. The Dalai Lama and Ralph Nader were among high-profile campus speakers in the last few years. Campuswide organized activities provide "good movies and amazing lectures."

Polos and Popped Collars?

While opinions on the student body differ from "very diverse" to "too homogeneous (predominantly white)," the stereotypical UVa student is: "white, preppy and well-groomed; wears khakis and polo shirts, or skirts with nice tank tops; probably upper-middle class." An aspect that most students agree on is that "there is a lot of self-segregation," which is "a big issue here." One student said: "There's definitely a lot of tension over the issue. I do think there has been minor progress over the years, however." Race relations aside, the University has the highest minority graduation rate, approximately 90 percent, of any public university in America.

One Wahoo said, "There is a reputation of pretentiousness and preppiness that seems to follow UVa everywhere, but I think that the school is very diverse and accepting; I know people who wear polo shirts each day, and I know people that wear T-shirts and jeans."

The Grounds

First-years live on campus and are divided between the New Dorms and the Old Dorms. Although rooms in the Old Dorms tend to be "small," they are also "more social." First-years in the New Dorms "get really big rooms with a suite area for every five rooms, and some rooms have air-conditioning." There is an RA for every 20 first-years, and each varies in strictness. Some are strict, some couldn't care less. "Most are strict when they need to be," one student said.

Lots of students move off Grounds after their first year and either relocate to fraternity and sorority houses or the two residential colleges on Grounds. The residential colleges, Brown and Hereford, "have personality, but other than that, the housing areas are pretty standard." There are also houses for students with common interests, including French, Spanish and Russian Houses. Living off-grounds is "very popular;" however, rents and proximity to the grounds can vary greatly. Students warn that off-grounds housing "is a ridiculous problem here in Charlottesville" because "most first-years are forced into signing a lease in October or early November with roommates they barely know yet."

While the dining halls tend to be "fairly clean," some students complain about dinner's ending too early. The dining hall food reportedly is "not terrible, but not good either, and the wait is often bad." The University just built a new "Observatory Hill Dining Hall," which serves mostly first-years, "and it sounds like the food will be better there as well." Students have "plus dollars" that come with their meal plans, and this allows students to eat at different stores, bakeries, or the Pav, Crossroads, and the Castle, which are food courts that house chain restaurants like Pizza Hut and Chick-Fil-A. There is a large food selection for vegetarians, and "the restaurants in Charlottesville are great, basically one from each cost category that are about five minutes away."

The Good Ole Song

People at UVa are "very devoted" to their extracurricular activities, and although "almost everyone belongs to some society or another, many belong to more than one." Some of the most well-respected organizations include the Madison House (community service), the Jefferson Society (debate), The Cavalier Daily and the University Guides. The Madison House "is the epicenter of volunteerism at the University." They run programs in tutoring, medical aid, pet care, elderly companionship and more. Some students also hold real jobs on the side, and the University also offers a lot of jobs for work-study students.

True to tradition and history, secret societies are "a large part of students' life here." These philanthropic societies are "very secretive about their workings in the community." While the IMP's are secret in their actions, everyone knows who they are. The Z's are secret until graduation, and the 7's are unknown until they die. "When individuals in the 7 Society pass, the chapel bell rings seven times at 7:07 p.m. then plays an eerie song on the seventh chord."

Although football is the most popular sport at UVa by far, soccer and basketball are also big. "There is so much school pride—especially with football." Both students and alumni go to football games, and "if you walk around campus on game-days, all you see is beer everywhere and everyone is dressed up," one student said. In sticking with tradition, Wahoos can be seen putting "their arms around each other and sway[ing] while singing 'The Good Ol' Song' after the team scores." Another tradition is the "fourth-year fifth," which is "a challenge of fourth-year students drinking a fifth of bourbon at the last football game of the season." Although the administration is working to curtail this last tradition, the Cavalier fans possess and express a great amount of team spirit. Students boast that their Aquatic and Fitness Center has great facilities for swimming, weight-lifting and the like. "The Aquatic Fitness Center is a top-of-the-line student and faculty resource." The University is due to complete the John Paul Jones Arena in May 2006. This $130 million arena will host to all basketball games as well as community events, such as major concerts and even circuses, in the hopes of continuing to draw members of the Charlottesville community into the life of the University. Aside from varsity sports, many students play intramurals, and there are always pick-up games around the grounds.

History and Beauty Unite

The grounds are "beautiful . . . hilly, open, historical architecture yet with a modern vibe." "Classic buildings" and "lots of trees and grassy area" contribute to the attractiveness of the campus. The University is centered around the Lawn, which neighbors the Rotunda, and hosts a statue of Homer and Frisbee games on sunny afternoons, and serves as a popular hangout on Sundays. "I love the Lawn. There are trees on the sides where you can sit and read or study," said one student. If you prefer studying indoors, UVa's main library, Alderman Library, is the backup to the Library of Congress. "Our libraries are pretty amazing."

UVa is a "really friendly place" where people are "generally enthusiastic and happy, and they don't stress out like at other schools." The "great thing about UVa is for a public university, you get an Ivy League education for about half price and the campus is great. . . . Plus, it's also a huge party school if you dig that sort of thing. There is something for everyone."—*Terren O'Reilly*

FYI

If you come to UVa, you'd better bring "a tie and polo shirts for guys and a sundress for girls."

What's the typical weekend schedule? "Everyone goes out Thursday through Saturday, and goes to fraternity parties or bars, depending on the weekend. Everyone tailgates all day on Saturday during football season."

If I could change one thing about UVa, it would be "the disproportion of in-state students (about 70 percent) to out-of-state students (30 percent)."

Three things every student at UVa student should do before graduating are "streak the lawn, learn the 'Good Ol' Song' and sing it at a football game, and enjoy the beauty of the lawn, gardens and architecture because you will not find them at other schools."

Virginia Polytechnic Institute and State University

Address: Virginia Polytech, 201 Burruss Hall, Blacksburg, VA 24061
Phone: 540-231-6267
E-mail Address: vtadmiss@vt.edu
Web site URL: www.vt.edu
Year Founded: 1892
Private or Public: public
Religious affiliation: none
Location: suburban
Regular Application Deadline: 15-Jan
Number of Applicants: 19,046
Percent Accepted: 66.3%
Percent Accepted who enroll: 41.1%
Number Entering: 5,176
Number of Transfers Accepted each Year: 800
Mean SAT: 1,231
Mean ACT: NA
Middle 50% SAT range: 1,130–1,330

Middle 50% ACT range: NA
Early admission program (EA/ ED/ NA): ED
ED or EA Acceptance Rate: 23%
Full time Undergraduate enrollment: 21,458
Total enrollment: 28,458
Percent Male: 57.7%
Percent Female: 42.3%
Total Percent Minority: 13.5%
Percent African-American: 4.7%
Percent Asian/Pacific Islander: 6.3%
Percent Hispanic: 2.2%
Percent Native-American: 30%
Percent Other: 10%
Percent in-state / out of state: 69%/31%
Percent from Public HS: NA
Retention Rate: 88%

Graduation Rate: 4 year 50%, 5 year 76%
Percent in On-campus housing: 41%
Percent affiliated with Greek system: NA
Percent Varsity or Club Athletes: NA
Number of official organized extracurricular organizations: 600
3 Most popular majors: Engineering, Business, Biological Sciences
Student/Faculty ratio: 16:01
Tuition and Fees: $19,049
In State Tuition and Fees (if different): $6,973.00
Cost for Room and Board: $4,700.00
Percent receiving Financial aid, first-year: NA

It is one fine winter day, and the snow is fresh. All of a sudden, the fire alarm goes off in Pritchard Hall and masses of students pour out of the dorm. The cadets and the members of the all-male dorm head off to the Drill Field and begin to engage in snow warfare. Other students begin to gather around the field to watch the groups duke it out. On one side, the disorderly males of Pritchard defend their territory, while on the other, the cadets gather in military formations and use their learned military tactics to attack the enemy. This epic snowball fight occurs every winter, only at Virginia Polytechnic Institute.

Virginia Tech, better known as "VT," is known mostly for its technical background, but it also provides for humanities as well. With its mascot, the HokieBird or Hokie (a large purple turkey) the University sets itself apart in the little town of Blacksburg, Va.

School Is for the Hokies

Freshmen who are sure of what they want to major in can enroll in one of Virginia Polytechnic's seven undergraduate colleges: Agriculture and Life Sciences; Architecture and Urban Studies; Pamplin College of Business; Engineering; Liberal Arts and Human Sciences; Natural Resources; and Science. Students who are undecided are placed in the University Studies program and have until the end of sophomore year to apply for a college. Students find it rather easy to switch from college to college, with only a few day's wait for the paperwork to be processed. However, with rigorous academic requirements, students are given very little time to explore other fields outside their major. Virginia Tech requires students to fulfill 36 to 44 semester hours distributed among the seven core areas: Writing and Discourse; Ideas, Cultural Traditions, and Values; Society and Human Behavior; Scientific Reasoning and Discovery; Quantitative and Symbolic Reasoning; Creativity and Aesthetic Reasoning; and Critical Issues in a Global Context. Of all the majors, engineering and architecture are the hardest with the most work and competition. One mechanical engineering major said that "the professors load you with work, while other majors don't." Communications, engineering, business and biology are the most popular majors, while some of the more unusual majors include wood science and forestry, as well as horticulture.

Virginia Tech also has a University Honors Program, which is made up of the top academic students. Incoming freshmen with excellent high school GPAs and high SAT scores are allowed to apply for the program. Current students can apply to the Honors program as long as they have a 3.5 GPA. Honors students have better access to faculty, intensive academic advising, priority in class registration, and honors-only courses. In addition, students in the program are given more opportunities for independent study and research. Upon acceptance, the program requires students to maintain a 3.5 GPA in order to keep their standing.

Introductory classes tend to have 200 to 300 people in each class, while the major-specific classes are much smaller with around 30 people. Because of the large classes and number of students, some students feel that the student-teacher relationship is not a good one. This tends to be especially true for the engineering and chemistry departments. One student said that "many professors just teach, and if you don't get it, they send you to a graduate student or teaching assistant." In addition, because there are so many students within these majors, many of the labs and sections are led by graduate students who often do not have a strong grasp of the subject and have poor English. However, many non-engineering majors feel the opposite way about their professors. An environment science major said: "You get to know all your professors really well. I had really good professors in geography and almost got into that because of them."

Keeping House

Students are required to live on campus for at least one year. The majority of on-campus students are freshmen, while some sophomores stay on campus. Most of the residences are coed with a few single-sex dorms. Pritchard, an all-male dorm, is the largest male dorm on the East Coast. Students say that female dorms are typically a lot better than the male dorms. One male student said, "Guy dorms are dirtier, and you have to deal with fire alarms every night. Plus, the bathrooms are gross." In addition, there are some complaints about RAs who can be really strict and dampen dorm life. Virginia Tech prohibits alcohol in the dorms and has visitation restrictions. Despite the downsides of dorm life, students enjoyed the ability to walk to wherever they want to go and the close proximity of the dining halls and gym. People enjoy hanging out on the quad outside of Pritchard when the weather is nice, and students can play a game of volleyball. Some of the dorms are GPA-oriented, while others are not. The athletes' dorm is near the gym and connected to the dining center, West End Market. The oldest dorms are for the ROTC cadets and are separated from the rest of campus.

After the first year, most students move off campus to townhouses and apartments in search of more private and cheaper living conditions. While many students bring their own cars, Virginia Tech provides a bus line that transports off-campus students to and from campus. Students note that while safety on campus is not an issue, the off-campus community can get a little more out of control. Often after big sporting events, crowds can get rowdy. The administration provides a Safe Ride program that will pick up students if they prefer not to walk somewhere, and emergency phone stations are available throughout the area.

The dining hall food receives great reviews from the students. The most preferred one is West End Market, where students can get fresh Maine lobster and London broil. The many other dining centers have all-you-care-to-eat buffets such as D2 and Shultz Dining Center. Virginia Tech also offers many food courts with restaurants such as Sbarro, Au Bon Pain and Chick-fil-A. In addition, there is an on-campus store for groceries. Students can select among many different meal plan options involving Flex dollars, which can be used to purchase food and for doing laundry. Even with the various dining plans, students have to watch how much they spend as they can easily run out of Flex dollars before semester's end and warn that "you have to read the fine print." Besides eating on campus, there are many bars and restaurant in nearby Christiansburg, where the mall and other retail stores are located, and the University provides transportation to and from the town.

Where's the Party at?

While not in the classroom, students are busy partying it up. Around 30 percent of the students at Virginia Tech are involved in Greek life. Many of the frats hold open parties and tend to dominate the social scene. The students who join frats find it to be a memorable experience and form a close network of friends that can aid in securing jobs and recommendations. Even though the frats are fun, students have to be able to balance the time commitments to the fraternity and to academics, and many drop out of the pledging process because of this.

Virginia Tech has a zero-tolerance policy for drugs and is also strict regarding alcohol. Alcohol is not allowed in the dorms and students are given judicial restrictions (JR) if they are caught with it. Three JRs result in suspension for one semester. While campus police do look out for violations of the alcohol policy, one student noted that "as long as you don't act stupid, you'll be OK."

> **"As long as you don't act stupid, you'll be OK."**

The parties tend to be held off campus, where all the frats and apartments are. Students head out starting Thursday and party until Saturday. Generally, underclassmen have no difficulty finding things to do and can usually be found at the different parties held at the apartment complexes. While underclassmen spend their time at off-campus parties, upperclassmen tend to enjoy their time downtown where the bars and clubs are. For those not interested in spending their weekends inebriated, students head off into the nearby Appalachian mountains where they go hiking and camping, and enjoy the beautiful scenery.

Passing the Time Away in Blacksburg

In Blacksburg, Va., people's minds are on one thing only during the fall: college football. With a perennially top-ranked team, a large amount of school pride is invested in Virginia Tech athletics. A student remarked, "Everyone, on their AIM profiles, has stuff from football and fight songs, too." Football is the most notable team on campus with players who are frequently in the media and have hopes of following in the paths of all-star alumni such as Michael Vick of the Atlanta Falcons. Many games are broadcast nationally and are always packed, giving Virginia Tech a reputation for being one of the toughest places to play. Fans congregate around campus and all that can be seen around Blacksburg is Virginia Tech paraphernalia. Tailgating is big, and all the alumni come down to party and barbecue.

The varsity athletes live in separate dorms and have their own gym. However, students say that the athletes "basically have their own fraternities and get in a lot of fights." For those not involved in intercollegiate athletics, there are also other venues to get out the competitive urges. The club lacrosse team is highly competitive because there is no varsity team. In addition, intramural sports are very competitive, and the frats and sororities get involved. There are different sports to participate in such as flag football, basketball, dodgeball and innertube water polo. There are also many student gyms. Some are located in the dorms such as Pritchard. The main gyms for students feature basketball courts, lifting machines and swimming pools.

While athletics can take up a significant amount of time, other clubs are also prominent on campus. The business clubs are very popular, and the Student-managed Endowment for Educational Development (SEED) group is notoriously difficult to get into. SEED manages over a million dollars from a portion of the Virginia Tech Foundation's endowment and uses it to invest in stocks, and usually, the group is able to turn a profit. Around 40 to 100 students apply for membership, but only 10 to 20 are accepted after an application and interview process. There are also many societies for each major that provide forums for the students of that major to meet their classmates and get to know each other better. Because the students in each major have similar interests, the societies help to form close friendships. In addition, social events are planned to help take students' minds off of academics. Plus, advisers help them with getting job offers, and events are planned to help students get to know the major better. One engineering major said, "I got to know many of my friends through engineering classes." A large percentage of the students are also involved with ROTC and Virginia Tech's Corps of Cadets program, which offers a structured military lifestyle for those looking for leadership development.

Red-blooded Hokies?

The students at Virginia Tech are typified as "hard-core football fans and very conservative." While the majority of students are from Virginia, there is a good blend of students from North and South. One student said of Virginia Tech's diversity: "It's mostly white, but there are many people from different countries and backgrounds. I see a lot of different people every day." Students find it easy to relate with their easygoing classmates and are able to meet new people often. Forums such as frats, societies and clubs help to further cement the friendships between all sorts of people. Because Virginia Tech draws its students mostly from neighboring states, some students know each other from home and therefore are able to network through friends' friends. Though the campus is big, the students all share the same interests and draw from each other's energy to create a friendly and home-like atmosphere for each other.—*Thomas Hsieh*

FYI

If you come to VT, you'd better bring "a map, because it is very big and you can easily get lost, and also to explore the beautiful mountains around the city."

What is the typical weekend schedule? "Typically stay out late Friday; sleep in Saturday, do some fun stuff during the afternoon, party at night; sleep in Sunday and do homework the rest of the day."

If I could change one thing about VT, I'd "change the dorm situation because Pritchard is an all-male dorm and is pretty bad."

Three things every student at VT should do before graduating are "go to a football game, go hiking and fishing in the Appalachian Mountains, and travel around Virginia because there are a lot of different schools nearby."

Washington and Lee University

Address: Washington and Lee, 204 West Washington St, Lexington, VA 24450-2116
Phone: 540-458-8710
E-mail Address: admissions@wlu.edu
Web site URL: www.wlu.edu
Year Founded: 1749
Private or Public: public
Religious affiliation: none
Location: rural
Regular Application Deadline: 16-Jan
Number of Applicants: 3,649
Percent Accepted: 27%
Percent Accepted who enroll: 39%
Number Entering: 460
Number of Transfers Accepted each Year: 13
Mean SAT: 1,385
Mean ACT: 20
Middle 50% SAT range: 1,310–1,460

Middle 50% ACT range: 28–31
Early admission program (EA/ ED/ NA): ED
ED or EA Acceptance Rate: 38.11%
Full time Undergraduate enrollment: 1,747
Total enrollment: 2,161
Percent Male: 51%
Percent Female: 49%
Total Percent Minority: 8%
Percent African-American: 4%
Percent Asian/Pacific Islander: 3%
Percent Hispanic: 1%
Percent Native-American: 0%
Percent Other: NA
Percent in-state / out of state: 15%/85%
Percent from Public HS: NA
Retention Rate: 94%

Graduation Rate: 86%
Percent in On-campus housing: 61%
Percent affiliated with Greek system: 79%
Percent Varsity or Club Athletes: NA
Number of official organized extracurricular organizations: 90
3 Most popular majors: Business Administration/ Management; Economics, General; History, General
Student/Faculty ratio: 10:01
Tuition and Fees: $27,960
Cost for Room and Board: $7,225
Percent receiving Financial aid, first-year: 36%

Just by knowing the name of Washington and Lee University, located in Lexington, Virginia, you already know a great deal about the school. Named for the two famous American generals, Washington and Lee boasts a rich historical tradition, an emphasis on honor and traditional American values, and a predominantly southern outlook. At Washington and Lee, you will find an extremely happy, though not particularly diverse, group of southern ladies and gentlemen.

A Liberal Arts Education That Covers All Bases

At Washington and Lee, a strong academic background is a main focus, and there is a large set of General Education Requirements to ensure that students receive the full benefits of attending a liberal arts institution. In addition to required classes in areas as widely varied as mathematics, social sciences, and foreign language, Washington and Lee students must fulfill a Physical Education requirement, though students praise the "really interesting" classes that fulfill this requirement. One student commented, "I took figure skating, skiing, and fitness—which pretty much just got me credit for going to the gym! They also have bowling, horseback riding, basketball, and many others." In general, the requirements are extensive, though the do have the benefit of allowing students to sample classes in several different fields as opposed to staying within their majors.

Popular majors at Washington and Lee include Politics, Business Administration, and Economics. English, Biology, and Neuroscience are generally considered to be harder majors, though all of the departments are considered comparable in terms of quality. Washington and Lee also houses the Williams School (also known as C-School), one of the few fully accredited undergraduate business schools in the nation.

Washington and Lee is a relatively small school, and as a result classes are usually not very big, thus fostering much closer professor-student relations. According to one male sophomore, "The student-faculty relations are generally very good. We have a speaking tradition that helps foster this. You can walk into a professor's office at any time for help or just to talk." Another student described the benefits of the small class size, saying, "The student faculty ratio is very low due to the extremely small size of the school. Also, the small classes mean that the professors really know who you are, and they take

attendance in almost every class. Lexington is a very small town and most of the professors live here. I had two that hosted cocktail parties for their classes at their homes." Despite the accessibility of the professors, grading is generally considered difficult, though fair. According to one student, "the work load is always doable." However, another comments that "Grading is hard. It is a very competitive school and they let you know first trimester freshman year that your GPA will go down."

In terms of schedule, Washington and Lee is divided into a trimester system, with a third "spring term" that lasts six weeks and during which students are only required to take two classes. Students enjoy this last term; one girl commented, "Although you finish later in the year, during the last trimester you only take two classes, so it's kind of a nice break from the rigorous five you take at most schools."

On My Honor

Another unique characteristic of Washington and Lee is its honor code, described by one male student as a "student governed, zero tolerance system." The honor code is an extremely strict code that prohibits students from only three actions: lying, cheating, and stealing. The code is taken extremely seriously, and a code violation can result in expulsion from the university.

> "Because of how seriously students take the honor code, professors are never present for tests and exams."

Many students appreciate the increased level of trust they receive from professors as a result of the code; one student described the test-taking situation at Washington and Lee, saying, "Because of how seriously students take the honor code, professors are never present for tests and exams. Many tests are self-administered anywhere (library, dorms, outside) and professors trust that the students will bring the exams back at the proper time. During exam weeks students may choose when and where to take their finals. Professors only write one copy of the exam, as they know students will not discuss the test." Another student described the seriousness of the honor code: "Every time you take a test or hand in a paper you have to sign it with the honor code. If you get caught cheating or plagiarizing, you're kicked out of the university, no questions asked." However, for most students, the benefits outweigh the risks, as the honor code allows them a far greater degree of freedom than most of their contemporaries at other universities.

An American Tradition of Beauty

The option of taking tests anywhere on campus is especially nice because Washington and Lee is widely known for its beautiful grounds. According to one current student, "the architecture of the campus is beautiful. The Colonnade is a national historic landmark." Washington and Lee's website confirms this statement: "Constructed between 1820 and 1842, Washington and Lee's Colonnade is a National Historic Landmark district and has been described by the National Park Service as forming 'one of the most dignified college campuses in the nation.' It is not only the heart of campus but also a symbol of Washington and Lee."

The school's historical traditions are described as "too many to name," though one sophomore explained, "Many buildings are thought to be haunted due to the age of the school."

Due to the beauty of the campus, freshmen enjoy their required first year on campus. Many older students elect to move off campus, as the surrounding areas are just as beautiful as the campus itself. One student commented, "Most juniors and seniors live off campus in apartments in town or houses out in the beautiful countryside." The town, Lexington, is "so small that on and off-campus living are not that different."

This beautiful campus is rich in history, and prides itself on reflecting the American tradition of higher learning. However, one potential disadvantage to the campus environment, students claim, is the student body's lack of diversity. One sophomore described the student body as relatively homogeneous, saying that "it would be characterized as conservative and upper middle class. Most students come from the south." However, another student went further into the problems of diversity, describing her freshman year experience. "[There is] almost none. Confederate flags are printed on some of the school shirts at the bookstore and students hang the flags in their dorm rooms. It is very hard for some people to understand and accept diversity. My freshman suitemate was from Africa, and her direct roommate was from Virginia and had a hard time adjusting to sharing a room with someone of a different race."

Go Greek or Bust

At Washington and Lee, the social life is almost exclusively focused on fraternities and sororities; one student conjectured that "almost 80% of kids are involved in Greek life." Greek life is the focus of most students to the exclusion of most else, as athletics are not all that popular, though lacrosse and soccer garner the most attention. Greek life starts from the moment students set foot on campus, which fosters not only an almost immediate sense of community, but also an opportunity to become friends with upperclassmen, which is unique to Washington and Lee. One student said, "Since freshmen are rushed the moment they step on campus, upperclassmen and underclassmen are mixed very well. Age and year doesn't really play a role in who your friends are." An upperclassman echoes this sentiment: "You will pretty much have the same social life from freshman to senior year because you will be in the same sorority or fraternity."

Social life is Greek or very little else; one student explained that "I never go to a bar. I always go to a fraternity house or an off-campus frat house." However, just because the social life is Greek-dominated doesn't mean there isn't always something to do. According to one proud student, "Washington and Lee is the second biggest party school in the country. There is somewhere to go almost every night." A sophomore comments, "The big nights are Wednesday, Friday and Saturday." Students generally attend either fraternity parties, which often feature bands, or house parties located out in the countryside. Drugs and alcohol are often a fixture of these parties; students describe drug and alcohol use as relatively common, though there is little use within the dorms themselves. More special parties include cocktail parties, semi-formals, and "fancy dress balls, due to the Greek social scene and southern values of the school."

Washington and Lee is the perfect place for future sorority girls and fraternity boys who want to immerse themselves in an environment rich in history and tradition, while at the same time enjoying the benefits of a school that offers an extensive education while housing seven-day-a-week parties. One student summed it up perfectly: "I expected a southern and conservative school and that's what I got. If I had to choose again, I would absolutely pick Washington and Lee over anywhere else!"
—*Michelle Katz*

FYI

If you come to Washington and Lee, you'd better bring "a collared shirt."

What is the typical weekend schedule? "Get out of class and start hanging out and go out to the country that night. Sleep in Saturday and watch college football and go out again Saturday night. Most students start their work Sunday evening."

If I could change one thing about Washington and Lee, I'd "make the administration realize that diversity isn't necessarily based on color."

Three things every student at Washington and Lee should do before graduating are "go tubing in the river, go for a drive out to Goshen, and sneak around the school's underground tunnels without getting caught!"

Washington

The Evergreen State College

Address: Evergreen State, 2700 Evergreen Parkway NW, Olympia, WA 98505
Phone: 360-867-6170
E-mail Address: admissions@evergreen.edu
Web site URL: www.evergreen.edu
Year Founded: 1967
Private or Public: public
Religious affiliation: none
Location: small city
Regular Application Deadline: 1-Mar
Number of Applicants: 1,534
Percent Accepted: 40%
Percent Accepted who enroll: 31%
Number Entering: 4,138
Number of Transfers Accepted each Year: 1,238
Mean SAT: 1,130
Mean ACT: 23
Middle 50% SAT range: 1,550–1,650

Middle 50% ACT range: NA
Early admission program (EA/ ED/ NA): NA
ED or EA Acceptance Rate: NA
Full time Undergraduate enrollment: 3,593
Total enrollment: 4,410
Percent Male: 46%
Percent Female: 54%
Total Percent Minority: 19%
Percent African-American: 5%
Percent Asian/Pacific Islander: 4%
Percent Hispanic: 5%
Percent Native-American: 5%
Percent Other: 0%
Percent in-state / out of state: 78.6%/21.4%
Percent from Public HS: NA
Retention Rate: 71%
Graduation Rate: 53%

Percent in On-campus housing: 25%
Percent affiliated with Greek system: 0%
Percent Varsity or Club Athletes: NA
Number of official organized extracurricular organizations: 50+
3 Most popular majors: Environmental Studies, Media Arts, Psychology/Pre-Med
Student/Faculty ratio: 21:01
Tuition and Fees: $4,128.00
In State Tuition and Fees (if different): $14,538.00
Cost for Room and Board: $6,924.00
Percent receiving Financial aid, first-year: 58%

A state school with a lush, thousand-acre campus just outside Olympia, Washington, Evergreen was founded in the 1970s and has been popularly known ever since as "that hippie school up north." As one student put it, "the stereotype is built up that there are a lot of hippies and we all eat granola and live in the woods." However, students insist that this is nothing more than a myth and that Greeners, as they are called, are much more than granola-eaters. One junior said, "[The stereotype is] that people here just smoke pot and talk about Buddhism, but I'm pretty positive I haven't had one conversation about Buddhism." While there is indeed a "liberal undertone" at the school, students emphasize that one can still find a rich diversity of ideas in the classroom. As one sophomore recounted, "In my seminar, I'm reading President Bush's favorite book (next to the Bible), and half of the class agrees with it and half of the class disagrees. You don't just have a bunch of liberal kids patting each other on the back." One senior added, "One thing we do have in common is that we're all pretty open-minded on campus. A lot of people recycle and you could say, 'Oh, you're a hippie,' but we're just normal people."

Although students maintain that Evergreen's population is as diverse as any other school, the Evergreen State College has not completely abandoned the liberal ideas (or types of people) from the era in which it was founded. In fact, one could say that Evergreen State continues to thrive on vestiges of the 1970s, giving it a unique educational style that grants students a sense of independence and interdisciplinary integration rarely found in the modern college.

Academic Liberation

Students at the Evergreen State College eagerly talk about the remarkable degree of freedom that their school allows them in their academic pursuits. "[The freedom] can be a beautiful thing for certain people," praised one student. "For students who have a drive to learn, and who don't need someone to be constantly on their back [about] turning something in, I really think Evergreen is a great place."

> **"[The stereotype is] that people here just smoke pot and talk about Buddhism, but I'm pretty positive I haven't had one conversation about Buddhism."**

Evergreen State's academic repertoire encourages students to be masters of their own scholastic destiny through four special features: academic programs, independent study contracts, internships, and study abroad. The bulk of Evergreen State's curriculum is in the form of academic programs, in which students register for a coordinated three-quarter set of classes centered on a unifying theme rather than signing up for several classes individually that, in all likelihood, would not be as integrated. One student focusing (Evergreen has no majors—only focuses) on environmental studies noted that the program Ocean Life and Environmental Policy, which he pursued in his first year at Evergreen State, has been his main academic inspiration. "That class was basically an introduction to marine biology and ecology, but we also did environmental policy and linked it to ocean life." In order to accommodate such cross-disciplinary studies as well as to satisfy the 25:1 student-faculty ratio that every class must uphold, programs are taught by more than one professor, with each professor specialized in the respective academic areas covered by the course.

This connection across the disciplines—such as biology, ecology and politics—is the distinguishing feature of Evergreen State's academic programs. Such integration allows the Evergreen State College to be lax when it comes to formal distribution requirements, without sacrificing an emphasis on basic skills. One student commented, "Whenever you put together a program at Evergreen, you're going to get the writing skills, the math skills, and you would have to search really hard not to get those things." Evergreen State students also can choose contracts, in which select students can set up independent study programs in coopera-

tion with a faculty member. "You specify the books you're going to read, where you're going to be, and how often you're going to contact your faculty member," one student said. "You could say, 'Hey, I want to do a contract about rainforest ecology.' " Students maintain that contracts are not an opportunity to avoid class, but instead, as the name suggests, they require a substantial amount of commitment of which not all students are deemed capable. "To get a contract they choose you. [Faculty] will talk to your old professors and ask, 'How good would they be?' "

Similarly, select students are allowed to take leave from Evergreen and study abroad or do internships for credit. "You'll say what you're going to do and what you're going to be learning, and the faculty will make sure that you're doing work and not just sweeping floors," one senior said. Such internships can lead to even bigger opportunities. "My friend worked on the movie S.W.A.T. and was offered a job," the senior said.

"No Grading," Not "No Work"

Perhaps the most striking feature of the Evergreen State education is the lack of numerical grading. Instead, at the end of each quarter professors write what is known as a narrative evaluation, which is essentially like the recommendation letters given to students at other colleges, but with painstaking detail to a student's improvement over the course of a quarter. Students value the flexibility that the narrative evaluation system offers as opposed to numerical grading. "Everything that you do extra in class reflects [in your evaluations] because your teacher can write about it, so you're not limited to an A." Another student praised the amount of detail that can go into an evaluation; he said that with Evergreen State evaluations, employers were probably more likely to get a "better impression of me and my work ethic and to judge me as a student better as opposed to with an A, B, or a C."

Yet with such a novel approach to academics, one might wonder whether there's the temptation just to slack off at Evergreen, or a necessity to be self-motivated and driven to take charge of their own work. Evergreen students insist that the case is mostly the latter. "I would say that people are very hardworking and [Evergreen's academic programs] force you to be very self-motivated," said one sophomore. Another student added, "There are not many students who just go to school. There's not really anyone who doesn't go to class. Everyone who is here wants to be here, and everyone who is here wants to learn. And if they don't, they leave."

In fact, one senior noted that Evergreen State is far from a slacker's dream. "I spent 40 to 50 hours a week doing homework my first year. It's pretty common, and my friends don't look at me funny when I say, 'I have to go do work now,' because they have to, too. I wouldn't say there's too much work, but there is a lot of work." Another student added: "School is hard here! But it's the attitudes of the people around you that help you relax and not feel overwhelmed." Students concurred that the work is manageable, especially because the academic program system allows professors to "coordinate so that they can assign a steady amount of homework." A senior noted that at one point during a program, "[Everyone] handed in their homework late, and the professors apologized and said that they had assigned too much work." The student concluded that this cooperation between the students and professors does help. "You can really get in the groove of a schedule that works for you," he said.

The Green and the Concrete

Evergreen State has a wide selection of rooming options. One student cited two examples, "They've got apartment-style living with four to six bedrooms with a furnished living area; they also have modular housing which is further down with their own parking lots. It's more secluded." Evergreen State offers several specialized dorms, such as "A Dorm," a freshmen-only building, and according to one sophomore, a sustainable living housing option is in the works, in which environment-conscious students can live according to the "concept of living without depleting your resources." Added another student, "Sustainable living rocks!"

Yet perhaps an inevitable consequence of having so many different housing options is variation in housing quality. While one student said, "The dorms are so much bigger than anyone else's dorms I've ever seen," another said, "I lived in housing my first year and I hated it. It's cramped and pretty rowdy."

Moreover, despite the multiplicity of housing options, students living on campus are in the minority. "I wish that there were more students living on campus," complained one sophomore. "There's 4,300 students, and only 1,000 kids live on-campus.

Some of them commute from their hometowns [in Washington]. A lot of people live in houses or apartments off-campus." She conceded, however, "It doesn't affect student life that much, but in terms of walking over to your friends' dorms to say hi, you can't really do that." In spite of this difficulty, however, the majority of the party scene takes place in the dorms. According to one freshman, "Awesome dorm parties are easy to have. You can register your parties and the cops won't come and bust it, unless it's really late and really loud."

Students generally agree that the dining hall food has improved leaps and bounds. Once catered by the Marriott hotel chain, Evergreen State now offers a dining option prepared by a business called Aramark. "They make crepes right in front of you," one senior raved. Evergreen State also prides itself on its organic farm, much of whose produce goes to the dining halls. "Seventy percent of the food is organic, and they're working their way up to making it 100 percent," one sophomore said. Evergreen State also offers a convenience store called The Corner, which is conveniently located near the dorms of Lower Campus and offers "fruits and breads, vegetables, juice, and the basic necessities—chips and candy."

Evergreen State also offers a good range of extracurriculars, including five intercollegiate sports and many clubs. Students explained that there are "lots and lots of student clubs, so many that you don't have time for them all!" One senior spoke of his involvement with the Student CD Project, which puts out a yearly collection of songs from Evergreen student bands. Students also have good things to say about Olympia and its vibrant nightlife and rich music scene, concentrated along streets such as the famous 4th Avenue Strip. Many people enjoy a one-day festival known as Super Saturday as well as events such as a Punk Rock Prom, sponsored by an animal-rights organization.

Greeners do admit that Evergreen State does not fit the mold of other colleges, yet they insist that that isn't a bad thing. As one senior said, "It's a shame that some students may be scared off by the hippie stereotypes that abound about Evergreen State." He concluded, "I really feel sorry for people who don't know how great Evergreen State is and who would do really well here."
—*Christopher Lapinig*

FYI

If you come to The Evergreen State College, you'd better bring "an umbrella. It's basically temperate rainforest, and it rains half of the year."

What is the typical weekend schedule? "Do work, go to the gym with my friends, go to basketball or soccer or volleyball games depending on what season it is, go up to Seattle or Olympia for concerts, eat out a lot, and do homework, of course."

If I could change one thing about The Evergreen State College, I'd "ask for more jobs off campus. It's really hard to find a job in Olympia, and I think most people at Evergreen work, but it's much easier to work off campus."

Three things that every student at The Evergreen State College should do before graduating are "go to the organic farm, rappel from the Clocktower, and go for a swim in the Sound on campus."

University of Puget Sound

Address: University of Puget Sound, 1500 North Warner Street, Tacoma, WA 98416-1062

Phone: 253-879-3211

E-mail Address: admission@ups.edu

Web site URL: www.ups.edu

Year Founded: 1888

Private or Public: private

Religious affiliation: none

Location: suburban

Regular Application Deadline: 1-Feb

Number of Applicants: 5,233

Percent Accepted: 64.7%

Percent Accepted who enroll: 20%

Number Entering: 749

Number of Transfers Accepted each Year: 195

Mean SAT: NA

Mean ACT: NA

Middle 50% SAT range: 1,165–1,340

Middle 50% ACT range: 25–29

Early admission program (EA/ ED/ NA): ED

ED or EA Acceptance Rate: 4.2%

Full time Undergraduate enrollment: 2,501

Total enrollment: 2,819

Percent Male: 42%

Percent Female: 58%

Total Percent Minority: 17%

Percent African-American: 3%

Percent Asian/Pacific Islander: 9%

Percent Hispanic: 3%

Percent Native-American: 2%

Percent Other: NA

Percent in-state / out of state: 30%/70%

Percent from Public HS: 76%

Retention Rate: 83%

Graduation Rate: 68%

Percent in On-campus housing: 62%

Percent affiliated with Greek system: 19%

Percent Varsity or Club Athletes: 18%

Number of official organized extracurricular organizations: 120

3 Most popular majors: Business, English, Psychology

Student/Faculty ratio: 11:01

Tuition and Fees: $30,060.00

Cost for Room and Board: $7,670.00

Percent receiving Financial aid, first-year: 88%

A re you interested in a liberal arts college that offers a rigorous curriculum, small classes and thoughtful professors? If so, the University of Puget Sound might be for you. Boasting 60 academic programs and more than 1,200 courses, UPS (as students call Puget Sound) is a mid-sized college that prides itself on its strong liberal arts foundation. It is situated on a lush green campus in the heart of the Pacific Northwest and is within driving distance of Seattle, Portland, Vancouver and Mt. Rainier.

Work Hard . . .

Every student at UPS will attest to the fact that "the workload is hard" and that "teachers expect a lot from [students]." However, most feel that the academic challenges they encounter at UPS are worthwhile and prepare them well for the real world.

Every matriculating student at UPS must complete a core curriculum and satisfy a foreign language requirement before graduation. The core curriculum consists of eight courses divided into three main subjects: argument and inquiry, five approaches to knowing, and interdisciplinary experience. Within each theme, students can choose from a wide variety of courses, which makes satisfying core requirements a relatively painless, and often enjoyable, experience.

Certain majors at UPS tend to be more popular than others; among these are psychology, English and business. In addition, a few new programs are rapidly growing in popularity, such as international political economy and theater. As if the tough workload at UPS was not enough, a few majors have earned the reputation of being especially difficult, such as politics and government, history, and biology. (Although in the case of biology, the main complaint was waking up in time for organic chemistry at 8 a.m.) For particularly strong students, UPS offers two special programs that accepted students can apply for. One is the Honors Program, which offers students a more in-depth liberal arts curriculum. The second is the Business Leadership Program, which emphasizes problem-solving techniques and provides students with unique internship opportunities.

With an average class size of 19, UPS offers an intimate learning environment for students. Nearly every class at UPS is seminar size, allowing students to have more discussions and participation opportunities than other universities' large class sizes allow. One disadvantage stemming from small class sizes is that students do not always get into the classes of their choice. However, if students are persistent and not overly rigid about their schedule, they are almost always able to take all the courses they wish to by the time they graduate.

Professors at UPS receive high praise. The consensus is that the professors are extremely approachable and interact frequently with students, both as mentors and as friends. As one senior said, "My favorite thing about UPS is probably the professors. These people truly cared about what I did, and they cared if I did well." It seems that the only negative thing students had to say about their professors was that they tended to "conspire" when setting test and due dates, which all inevitably occur at the same times. Finally, it should be noted that UPS has a "No-TA policy," meaning TAs are not allowed to teach or to grade major assignments.

Play Hard . . .

UPS students work hard when they have to, but they also know how to have fun. Although UPS is a "wet" campus in terms of allowing alcohol in students' rooms (as long as they're of age), the administration generally restricts any sort of drinking in a group setting on campus. As a result, most partying has been pushed off campus and into upperclassman houses and fraternity houses. One junior said: "These parties usually consist of dancing and casual drinking. There is a definite presence of alcohol, but I wouldn't characterize it as a problem. Most people know not to get out of control." According to another student, "There is a lot of drinking, but if you don't want to take part, you can always find something else to do." Several people cited poker games as being the activity of choice when everyone gets bored.

The Greek life at UPS is not as strong as at other schools and has had "declining interest over the last decade" or so. However, there are still four fraternities and five sororities on campus that all play an active role in the campus social life by hosting many parties throughout the year. Rushing at UPS is delayed until second semester of freshman year, which may account for the lower interest in Greek life. However, students recommend that everyone participate in the rush process to meet new people even if they do not plan to join a frat or a sorority. Two of the fraternities, Sigma Chi and Beta Theta Pi, regularly host parties. One of the most popular parties each year is "The Beach," at which the Sigma Chi house is filled with sand and the staircases are "turned into waterfalls." As you can imagine, cleanup for this fiesta is a colossal process, but "well worth it."

Apart from parties, UPS also sponsors many alcohol-free events. These include concerts, lectures, and karaoke or movie nights. The School of Music hosts their own concerts and attracts musicians from around the world. Several endowed lecture series exist on campus, with some recent speakers including New York Times columnist Thomas Friedman and Nobel Peace Laureate Oscar Sanchez. There is also the "Last Lecture" series, in which UPS professors speak as if they were giving their last lectures.

UPS students are very involved in extracurricular activities. There is "Hui-o-Hawaii," which hosts the largest luau in the Northwest. There is "Praxis Imago," which is a student-run film group that puts on a student film festival, "Foolish Pleasures," each year. Singing groups are also popular with notable ones being "Underground A Cappella," "Underground Rhythm," and "Underground Jazz." Several groups perform community service around campus, including "Kids Can Do" and "Circle K." In general, every student is involved with some sort of extracurricular activity, and most are involved in several. The student government at UPS is generous with funding and is usually willing to assist students with starting new clubs.

In athletics, UPS is a Division III school that does not offer athletic scholarships.

Although most students agree that athletics is not a major focus for UPS, support for sports teams is still strong. The top three varsity teams at UPS are crew, soccer, and swimming, all of which have been ranked near the top of their divisions in recent years. For students not on a sports team, intramurals are quite popular. In addition, the student fitness center is a top-notch facility with a rock-climbing wall, indoor tennis courts, basketball courts and a 25-meter pool.

Life on Campus

Most students at UPS live in doubles during their freshman year, although some are housed in triples or quads. Freshman rooms are located in two main residence halls, Todd/Phibbs and Anderson/Langdon, which have in them special themed floors such as the humanities floor, the substance-free floor, and the social justice floor. Some floors are co-ed while others are single-sex; all-girls residence halls are also available. In upperclass years, suites of six with common kitchenettes and bathrooms are available. In addition, UPS also owns approximately 60 houses on the outskirts of campus where students can live. UPS does have an RA system, but according to students, the RAs are generally not that strict. The easiest way for sophomores to get on-campus houses outside of the dorms is to apply for a theme house, which is a "good opportunity for people with the same interests to live together, similar to the theme floors in the dorms."

The UPS meal plan operates on a points system in which students pay for what they eat, rather than by number of meals. Dining is centralized in the Wheelock Student Center within which there are three places to eat: a main cafeteria, a café and a "pizza cellar." Students often praise the long operating hours of the dining service—the main cafeteria is open throughout the day until 10 p.m. Moreover, the pizza cellar, which also serves as a convenience store, is open into the wee hours of the morning. Finally, food quality was given a thumbs-up by all of the students interviewed with one student calling it "the best among colleges big and small."

When students tire of the on-campus dining options, they often walk a few blocks to the Proctor District where several shops and restaurants can be found. Some local favorites include the Metropolitan Market (gourmet grocery store) and Pomodoro's (Italian restaurant). For students with access to cars, The Waterfront is also an option.

When asked what UPS student stereotypes are, students inevitably mention Nalgenes and hiking gear. People often dress in "earthy" or "hippie" styles with fleeces and rain jackets quite popular (and appropriate to the climate). The student body at UPS is composed largely of middle-class Caucasian and Asian students, but the administration has made attempts in recent years to increase diversity on campus. The dating scene is relatively active, and students report that random hook-ups are quite prevalent, especially among freshmen and sophomores. Both homosexuality and interracial dating are present and accepted on campus.

Campus and Surroundings

The buildings at UPS have earned it the nickname of "Harvard of the West," thanks to their red-brick buildings with ivy running up the walls. There are grass and trees everywhere, although the ground can get quite soggy during the winter months. As one student said, "We have a bad rep for our weather, but it's really not that bad, even though it gets gray in November and stays gray until April."

> "We have a bad rep for our weather but it's really not that bad, even though it gets gray in November and stays gray until April."

The campus itself is situated in a residential neighborhood and is considered very safe. Indeed, many students at UPS refer to the "bubble" that encapsulates them and separates them from the rest of Tacoma and the outside world. "Life at UPS can be a retreat from the rest of the world or a conduit through which you connect to it," one student said. "In other words, it is secluded enough but not cut off from the real world." When the need for "big-city life" arises, most students head to downtown Tacoma, which has an assortment of theaters, museums, malls and restaurants, or to the bustle of Seattle. Occasionally, students also take advantage of Tacoma's proximity to Portland and Vancouver and drive to these cities for the weekend.

UPS is a challenging school that offers its students a strong liberal arts education. The University helps students realize their full potential, and in the process gain a solid foundation for life after college.
—*Anthony Xu*

FYI

If you come to UPS, you'd better bring "a rain jacket."

What is the typical weekend schedule? "Hang out or party on Friday night; sleep in on Saturday and lounge around or go shopping; sleep in on Sunday and do homework."

If I could change one thing about UPS, I'd "increase the diversity on campus."

Three things every student at UPS should do before graduating are "join a musical group, climb the big tree and go to a fireside dinner put on by the president."

University of Washington

Address: University of Washington, 1410 NE Campus Parkway, Box 355852, Seattle WA 98195-5852

Phone: 206-543-9686

E-mail Address: NA

Web site URL: http://admit.washington.edu/

Year Founded: 1861

Private or Public: public

Religious affiliation: none

Location: urban

Regular Application Deadline: 16-Nov

Number of Applicants: 11,339

Percent Accepted: 68%

Percent Accepted who enroll: 48%

Number Entering: 5,475

Number of Transfers Accepted each Year: 1,958

Mean SAT: NA

Mean ACT: 25

Middle 50% SAT range: NA

Middle 50% ACT range: 23–28

Early admission program (EA/ ED/ NA): NA

ED or EA Acceptance Rate: NA

Full time Undergraduate enrollment: 27,836

Total enrollment: 37,722

Percent Male: 48%

Percent Female: 52%

Total Percent Minority: 41%

Percent African-American: 3%

Percent Asian/Pacific Islander: 28

Percent Hispanic: 5%

Percent Native-American: 1%

Percent Other: 4%

Percent in-state / out of state: 82%/18%

Percent from Public HS: NA

Retention Rate: 93%

Graduation Rate: 75%

Percent in On-campus housing: 23%

Percent affiliated with Greek system: 0%

Percent Varsity or Club Athletes: NA

Number of official organized extracurricular organizations: 550

3 Most popular majors: Economics, Political Science and Government, Psychology

Student/Faculty ratio: 11:01

Tuition and Fees: $21,286.00

In State Tuition and Fees (if different): $5,988.00

Cost for Room and Board: $6,561.00

Nestled in the shadows of the Cascade and Olympic Mountain Ranges, the University of Washington embraces its Seattle location by combining the distinction of a prominent research institution with a "relaxed, west-coast atmosphere."

Living in Husky Territory

Despite the rumors, Seattle is far from being the rain capital of the nation. In fact, Seattle's annual precipitation is actually less than Miami, Boston, New York, Philadelphia, and Washington D.C! That being said, the city's rainy reputation stems from the dreary winter months, when for several weeks the region is enveloped in cloudy skies and light drizzle.

UW is a large university, enrolling more than 40,000 students on three campuses. The main location is in Seattle, Washington, with smaller campuses in Bothell and Tacoma. All three facilities serve an incredibly diverse student body, offering combinations of day and evening classes for either full-time or part-time students. Raved one junior, "The [Seattle] campus is absolutely gorgeous. We have over 700 acres of trees, grass, and amazing Gothic architecture. The people are amazing and it honestly doesn't rain that much!"

"UW is a very self-directed university," noted another student. "You need to know what you want in order to get it. Because it's so big, no one does it for you." With over 25,000 undergraduates on the Seattle campus alone, many incoming freshmen worry that they will become a nameless face in the crowd. However, current students repeatedly declared that friends are easy to find, and with "over 500 student groups, there's always something going on!"

Most students begin to associate with a

certain social circle early in their college experience. Social life at the UW, despite its diversity, was described as fairly segregated between the Greeks, the dorm kids, and the commuters. While the Greeks are sometimes described as "the rich white kids who wear Uggs and North Face jackets," the dominant campus fashion is decidedly practical: "fleeces, jeans, comfy stuff to stay dry and warm." One student cited the social groups as the main difference between underclassmen and upperclassmen; the older students tend to already have their social circles established, while the incoming freshman are much more open to hanging out with whomever.

Dorm Life and Coffee Breaks

Most UW students live on campus for their freshman year. The Hansee (all singles) and McCarty dorms are the two most popular. There are also theme dorms based on a student's interests, each occupying one or two floors inside the larger buildings. "I lived in the Honors House for two years, which was all the honors students. There's also a substance-free dorm, and an outdoor focus dorm," said one student. Even though the dorms are always full, UW is also "a huge commuter school."

"The campus is absolutely gorgeous, the people are amazing, and it honestly doesn't rain that much!

When it comes to dining, Huskies claim that "we have the best campus food service in the country!" The meal plan is fairly simple, as students place a certain amount of money in their dining accounts to spend like cash. Even though there are dining halls all over campus, Huskies may also choose to take advantage of the "cheap, amazing ethnic food places" in the U-District. As is to be expected in the birthplace of Starbucks, "The coffee shops are good, and there are tons of cute little secret ones all over, so go search for them!"

Upperclassmen often move off-campus into the surrounding neighborhoods. The Greek system occupies the north neighborhood, with 27 frats and 16 sororities owning off-campus houses. The area ten or so blocks north, Ravenna, is "nice, a little quieter." Despite the slightly higher rent, the U-District is a vibrant, diverse neighborhood, filled with cheap eateries, popular hangouts, and cool stores.

With eighty percent of the student body hailing from Washington State, the campus can often feel empty on Saturdays when students go home for the weekends. Most do not have cars, as parking is expensive and the bus system is easy, efficient, and free for students because part of their tuition goes toward a bus pass that allows for free rides on all Seattle public transportation. With the Sea-Tac airport, the ferry docks, and the Amtrak train station only a bus ride away, most UW students find they can travel fairly conveniently.

Sleepless in Seattle

In keeping with the diverse student body, there are many options for nighttime activities, though students listed a few particularly notable events. The residence halls throw a weeklong extravaganza called "Winterfest," complete with casino nights, dances, and bonfires. The annual "Pow Wow" and "Spring Cruise," in addition to the Greeks' annual Homecoming and "Anchor Splash" parties, also received high praise. On normal weekends, upperclassmen party more at bars or houses, while freshmen tend to flock to the larger frat parties.

UW's student body incorporates the complete spectrum of attitudes toward student drinking: some students go out every night of the week, while other students never touch alcohol. Students claim that, depending on one's social circle, there is not a lot of pressure to drink. Because the residence halls actually have a pretty strict alcohol and drug policy—including probation and mandatory alcohol counseling following certain offenses—most of the drinking takes place off-campus. These regulations, however, met with mixed reviews. According to one student, "if you get caught smoking pot by the campus police, you get in less trouble than you do for jaywalking."

Husky Fitness and Pride

Since Seattle has been named "the fittest city in the U.S" (according to rankings released by *Men's Fitness* in 2005), it comes as no surprise that the University of Washington is also recognized as one of the top athletic programs in the country. It is not unusual for the 11 men's and 12 women's varsity teams to earn national honors. If you are more inclined to cheer from the stands, Huskies hold the gold standard for the student cheering sections: "There is a lot of pride invested in being a Husky!" exclaimed a junior. All sports, except basketball and football, are free for students. During the fall, volleyball and football dominate the scene, as the "campus literally shuts down on football Saturday." During the annual Apple Cup, thousands of UW Huskies flock to the football stadium to cheer their school to victory over arch-rival, Washington State. During the winter, die-hard basketball fans camp outside the gym for days before games even if they already have tickets—just to show their support! This student section is one of the best in the country; affectionately called the "Dawg Pack", they even have their own locker in the men's locker room.

For the non-varsity athletes, there is a state-of-the-art gym called the "IMA". It has an elevated running track, a 5000 square foot weight room, over 300 machines, 4 basketball courts, racquetball, squash and tennis courts, a pool, saunas, and an indoor climbing wall. Free for all students, the gym also offers a diverse array of fitness classes, over twenty-five club sports, and the Dawg Bites Sports Café. Intramural sports are also a popular activity, ranging from very competitive to purely recreational: examples include inner-tube basketball, ultimate frisbee, rowing, and bowling.

There are over 550 student clubs on campus, ranging from living groups to multicultural societies to political associations to "just plain weird" groups. Students listed a medley of different organizations, including the Filipino American Students Association, the Amateur Porn Club, the Peanut Butter and Jelly Club, and Habitat for Humanity. A sophomore claims that the "funniest group" is an organization of extreme liberals called the LaRouches, who aggressively hand out pamphlets as students walk to class. "Do not take this group seriously," the sophomore laughs. "Many people joke about them." Extremist or not, students dedicate a lot of time to their organizations, and social groups are often defined by extracurricular activities.

Many students also manage to balance their studies and a job—either on campus as RAs or tutors, or in the local "U-District" neighborhood as waiters or store clerks. Since Huskies love their coffee, twenty-two espresso stands on campus supply students with part-time jobs, hang-out places, and delicious cheap coffee.

In the Classroom

With over 1,800 undergraduate courses offered every quarter, incoming freshmen might feel slightly overwhelmed. Freshmen may choose to join the FIG (Freshman Interest Group) program, where small groups of freshmen with similar academic interests share the same courses during their first quarter. The Honors Program is highly regarded, though a junior stressed that the program's diverse and interesting classes can be hard to get into.

Don't be surprised if many classes your freshman year are on the higher end of the student-to-faculty ratio. Said one sophomore, "My first quarter, all my classes had over 700 people in them, which was really daunting." Although the workload of a specific course almost directly corresponds the difficulty of a class, a sophomore noted an important exception in the introductory classes. "The introductory grading can be very hard," she noted, "as the main purpose of many of the intro classes is to 'weed out' those students who cannot handle the workload." However, once a student becomes more involved in a department, the focus is more on the material and the learning process. Said one student, "I didn't expect the professors to be as open to students as they were. They really made an effort to get to know us, so it wasn't at all impersonal."

The academics at the UW are extremely varied, as the requirements for graduation differ from college to college. The most competitive programs include the business school, the architecture school, and the college of engineering. The science majors were also widely cited as being difficult, due to the UW's top-tier medical school and the large number of students who enroll for UW's stellar scientific research facilities. Many other majors do not have any prerequisites for admission or a competitive admissions process. Several students testified to the discrepancy between the science and the humanities programs: "I have friends who take communications and history classes and they can easily get 3.6's or 3.7," said a sophomore, "while science majors often have GPAs an entire point lower." Students recommended Comparative History of Ideas, International Studies, and Near Eastern Languages and Cultures as being unique and intriguing majors.

Among UW's 3,500-plus faculty are seven Nobel Laureates, a National Book Award Winner, and 43 members in the National Academy of Sciences, not to mention many other widely-renowned scholars and scientists. Freshman seminars offer incoming students the opportunity to establish a relationship with these faculty members while exploring their field of study. But don't get too excited, a sophomore warns, as "in all honesty, the school is so big it is really hard to identify famous professors. There are celebrity profs, you just have to be part of the department to realize it." The competition for popular classes varies depending on the department, but as one student noted, "if you're a good enough student and stubborn enough, you can get into anything."

Even given the rare circumstance that a student does not find a niche on campus, Seattle and the surrounding area provide countless opportunities for adventure and entertainment. The school's proximity to both the Cascade Mountains and the Puget Sound leads to many diverting weekend trips. Seattle itself is a fascinating city, home to Starbucks, Microsoft, Amazon.com, REI, and Nintendo. Clearly, the University of Washington and the surrounding area can cater to the interests of all 40,000 students, whether athletes, baristas, scholars, or ski bums. One student's comment in particular emphasized the enthusiasm characteristic of all Huskies: "I love the UW. It's a fantastic education, I get exposed to a huge amount of cutting edge research, and there are so many opportunities I don't know where to start!"

FYI

If you come to UW, you'd better bring "a raincoat."

What's the typical weekend schedule? "Friday: hit up a party or lay low with friends; Saturday: shop, cheer on the Huskies at the football game, go out; Sunday: sleep till noon, get up and study, study, study!"

If I could change one thing about UW, I'd "make the registration process during freshman and sophomore year easier to get the classes you need."

Three things every student at UW should do before graduating are "jump off the bridge that goes to nowhere, eat at Burger Hut at 2:00 am, and take the bus to class even though it's only a 10 minute walk."

Washington State University

Address: Washington State, Undergraduate Admissions, Lighty 370, Pullman, WA 99164-1067	**Middle 50% SAT range:** V:480–590; M: 500–610	**Graduation Rate:** 34% (4 years)
Phone: 888-GO-TO-WSU (888-468-6978)	**Middle 50% ACT range:** NA	**Percent in On-campus housing:** 33%
	Early admission program (EA/ ED/ NA): NA	**Percent affiliated with Greek system:** M:15%; F:18%
E-mail Address: admiss2@wsu.edu	**ED or EA Acceptance Rate:** NA	**Percent Varsity or Club Athletes:** NA
Web site URL: www.wsu.edu	**Full time Undergraduate enrollment:** 19,554	
Year Founded: 1890	**Total enrollment:** NA	**Number of official organized extracurricular organizations:** 200+
Private or Public: Public	**Percent Male:** 48%	
Religious affiliation: none	**Percent Female:** 52%	
Location: rural	**Total Percent Minority:** 14.20%	**3 Most popular majors:** Mass Communications/ Media Studies; Education; Engineering
Regular Application Deadline: Rolling	**Percent African-American:** 3%	
Number of Applicants: 9,314	**Percent Asian/Pacific Islander:** 6%	**Student/Faculty ratio:** 15:01
Percent Accepted: 77%	**Percent Hispanic:** 4%	**Tuition and Fees:** $16,087
Percent Accepted who enroll: 40%	**Percent Native-American:** 1%	**In State Tuition and Fees (if different):** $6,447
Number Entering: 2,699	**Percent Other:** NA	**Cost for Room and Board:** $7,326
Number of Transfers Accepted each Year: 4,039	**Percent in-state / out of state:** 89%/11%	**Percent receiving Financial aid, first-year:** NA
Mean SAT: NA	**Percent from Public HS:** NA	
Mean ACT: NA	**Retention Rate:** 82%	

Pullman is a small and sleepy town, unless you happen to arrive when the WSU Cougars play the UW Huskies in the Apple Cup. Students suddenly stream out into the streets, and Pullman overflows with red, white, and cougar. Washington State University has always had a reputation for being the largest party school in the state. However, despite an ever-present party scene, WSU has also amped up its science programs to provide quality academics. Some claim that these changes are helping WSU shed its reputation and that the school is now becoming a well-respected university with numerous resources and the latest research facilities. But how much have they really changed?

Do you Wazzu?

The new president of the school restricted the printing of the slang term for the university, "Wazzu," on all endorsed clothing to discourage the reputation of being a party school. While it seems few would argue that this move changed the school's atmosphere, all agreed that the school's academics certainly weren't as easy as their party-hard reputation in the state made them seem. The school has a top-notch veterinarian program, and students agree that the most popular majors, in communications, business, and science, all have high-quality classes.

Remarked one student, "My overall experience with classes has proven that WSU has a rigorous academic structure. If you are thinking of becoming a veterinarian or working in agriculture, WSU is a definite prospect." Others argued that, while there were some hard classes, students who knew which courses to take could find a lighter workload. Although, if you are willing to work, some of the best and most challenging classes are in the science department. Most consider WSU a science school, and one junior said that he had yet to take a humanities class. However, there are a few required classes, such as a world histories course, a course in English composition, and some required math and science courses. Like most of the other classes geared towards freshman, the lectures are usually larger in number, with the average size of a general education class at 81 students. According to one student, some of the more popular classes can have a few hundred students, although English classes are generally capped at 30. There are teaching assistants to help out, though, and students said they were usually helpful.

If students need extra help, there are certainly ample resources. The professors have available office hours, and the college has a students' center on campus known as the "Q," where TAs wait inside to help you with any paper or problem set you're having trouble with. For many science and math lectures, there are also tutorial "classes," which aren't mandatory but are helpful to attend. In these classes, a teaching assistant will help further explain concepts and review material. Said one student "After freshman year, you kind of get it. They're there to help you, and it helps a lot to go."

Students say that you can generally get into the classes you want to, although it is sometimes hard as a freshman, because preference is given to upperclassmen. If a student makes it past the large introductory classes, they can generally get into whatever upper-level class they want, and those classes are usually much smaller. Students don't have to take required classes after freshman year besides those in their major, and they are more free to take classes they want to take. They can choose from a wide variety of classes not often offered at smaller colleges, or any college at all, such as billiards, scuba diving, hiphop, and for any would-be gymnasts, beginning tumbling. One student remarked "I love the broad class base." For students looking for vigorous academics, WSU also has much more intense courses. Freshmen can take a particularly unusual honors program; they live in an "Honors Dorm" and begin a thesis freshman year.

> "WSU's motto is 'World class, face to face.' So far the statement has proven to be accurate."

Majors are often career-based, and most students choose their classes and direction with careers in mind. The concepts of liberal arts and traditional education are much less popular than classes dealing with hard facts or specific skills. When asked about which was the worst major at WSU, a sophomore responded, "Philosophy is the worst. It might be taught well, but who have you heard of making millions with this kind of degree?" Overall, students are impressed by the quality of academics. One student said "WSU's motto is 'World class, face to face.' So far the statement has proven to be accurate."

Palouse-a-Palooza

Said one student: "You can't go home every weekend, and you're definitely more on your own because Pullman is so isolated." However, while the ten-county area known as the "Palouse," generally offers little but farmland, students certainly find enough to do in the small town of Pullman. While upperclassmen frequent bars such as Valhalla, the Coug, and Mike's, underclassmen are more likely to be found at popular coffee shops such as the Daily Grind and the Bookie. Many students are likely to hang out at the Rec, a giant gymnasium where students can play baskeball, lift weights, or head to the Jacuzzi. Although students used to hang out quite a bit at the Compton Union Building (the CUB), a student center with a bowling alley, movie theaters, and a cafés, the building is currently under renovation, and is scheduled to reopen in the fall of 2008. Most likely a migration back to the CUB will occur when it reopens.

Partying in the Palouse

Fraternities certainly throw a lot of the parties on campus, although students have mixed feelings about the entities themselves. One student claimed that Greek life was not a big deal, while another said that "[frats are] very important. There are a lot of negative stereotypes about fraternity men and sorority girls. Although there are some people who fit the criteria, the majority of those living on Greek Row are smart, goal-oriented individuals."

Most students don't feel at all pressured to drink. Those that want to will certainly have to go off campus. WSU has a strict alcohol policy on campus, and rooms are monitered by RA's who patrol the dorms at nine and midnight on weekdays, and additionally at three at night on weekends. Drugs are less prevalent, and one student remarked that some students do harder drugs, but that they formed a small minority.

The first time a student is caught with alcohol, there is a 50 dollar fine and a mandatory alcohol awareness class. The second time students are caught, the fine is larger, the student's parents are notified, and they have to meet one-on-one with a counselor to determine if they have a problem. After the third strike, a student is technically supposed to be sent home, but one sophomore claimed to know people on their fifth and sixth strikes. The same student said that the policy is "mostly to scare freshman," and that students didn't have to worry about the policy off campus.

All freshman are required to live on campus their first year, although they are also allowed to choose to live at a fraternity their second semester. About half of students decide to live on campus after freshman year. The ones that move off campus either get apartments with their friends or move into a fraternity or sorority. Most students didn't really like the freshman dorms, although they did say there was fun to be had there. Stevenson was usually the party dorm (party being a loose word as the dorms are dry), while Scott Cullman is more quiet. All of the buildings on campus are red brick buildings, which most students found very pretty. The campus is currently growing with renovations and new buildings. A new science building is in the works, and a Pacific 10 golf course will be finished in two years.

Cougar Pride

School spirit is rampant at WSU, and everyone is a die-hard Cougar fan. According to one student, Pullman and the campus are literally transformed on game day, with many more people out than are normally in town. The most exciting game of the year is the Apple Cup, in which the Cougars face off against their rivals, the University of Washington Huskies. Said one student "A football weekend is unlike any other. It's ridiculous with UW." Everyone sports Cougar t-shirts and sweathshirts, and Cougar license plates are also very popular.

However, for those students who aren't quite up to varsity level, Washington State still has a lot to offer. Intramural sports are the most popular extracurricular, and almost every sport is offered. One student said that people are "very passionate" about intramurals. The Outdoor Rec Center also has quite a bit to offer in the way of outdoor activities, and students can take river-rafting trips, go rock climbing, or even take one of the outdoor trips to Alaska. Pullman students are generally active, as a lot of the preferred activity involves the outdoors or hanging out at one of the recreation centers; at least, until it starts to snow.

Pullman prides itself in its friendly environment, and people are generally treated very well. Said one student "It's a pretty welcoming student body. If you randomly said hello to 20 people, you would easily get 18 hellos back."—*Molly Shepherd-Oppenheim*

FYI

If you come to WSU, you'd better bring, "Cougar gear, cougar gear, cougar gear."

What's the typical weekend schedule? "Friday: go to classes, work out, go to a party. Saturday: go to a football game, go to another party. Sunday: try to catch up on homework."

If I could change one thing about WSU, I'd "place it in a more vibrant location."

Three things every student at WSU should do before graduating are, "Go see the grizzly bears, go on one of the outdoor rec trips, and go to the Haunted Palouse, a Halloween haunted house and corn maze."

Whitman College

Address: Whitman College, 345 Boyer Avenue, Walla Walla WA 99362

Phone: 509-527-5176

E-mail Address: admission@whitman.edu

Web site URL: www.whitman.edu

Year Founded: 1883

Private or Public: private

Religious affiliation: none

Location: small city

Regular Application Deadline: 16-Jan

Number of Applicants: 3,000

Percent Accepted: ~45%

Percent Accepted who enroll: ~30%

Number Entering: ~400

Number of Transfers Accepted each Year: ~50

Mean SAT: NA

Mean ACT: NA

Middle 50% SAT range: V:620–730, M:610–700

Middle 50% ACT range: 28–32

Early admission program (EA/ ED/ NA): ED, 1 & 2

ED or EA Acceptance Rate: 65%

Full time Undergraduate enrollment: 1,455

Total enrollment: 1,455

Percent Male: 44%

Percent Female: 56%

Total Percent Minority: 21%

Percent African-American: 2.2%

Percent Asian/Pacific Islander: 9.80%

Percent Hispanic: 5%

Percent Native-American: 1%

Percent Other: 14.6%

Percent in-state / out of state: 41%/59%

Percent from Public HS: 76%

Retention Rate: 94.5%

Graduation Rate: 85%

Percent in On-campus housing: 70%

Percent affiliated with Greek system: 35%

Percent Varsity or Club Athletes: 25%

Number of official organized extracurricular organizations: 100+

3 Most popular majors: Psychology, Politics, English

Student/Faculty ratio: 10:01

Tuition and Fees: $42,690

Cost for Room and Board: $8,310

Percent receiving Financial aid, first-year: 81%

I f you love nature, the outdoors, and learning, then Whitman College in Walla Walla, Washington is the place for you. With a generally laid-back attitude and overall liberal mindset, Whitman students can take advantage of the abundance of activities offered on campus, as well as enjoy the outdoors in the beautiful Pacific Northwest.

Welcoming "Whitties"

Students say that one of the greatest perks of a Whitman experience is going to school in Walla Walla. Whitman students (called "Whitties") say that Walla Walla is the perfect college town—small and friendly with lots to do. One student remarked, "The campus and surrounding areas are so safe . . . I can leave my purse and belongings in a public place and know that when I return they'll be sitting right where I left them." Another described the campus and Walla Walla as,

"incredibly safe. You wouldn't believe it. I can trust anyone on this campus."

At Whitman, it's not uncommon to say hi or strike up a conversation with a stranger on the street. Freshmen at Whitman even said that the welcome they received on their first day at college was almost overwhelming. "Since it is a school of maybe 1,400 students, you end up meeting a lot of people pretty easily," one junior explained. "As far as friendliness goes, Whitman students are some of the friendliest people I have ever met." But the student population of Whitman is "not diverse." "There is not much diversity," and Whitties are "mostly white," with a very "small population of international students," one Whittie noted. Despite the lack of diversity, Whitties maintain that they are extremely accepting of any student. One Whittie summed up the student body by saying, "I was surprised by the kindness and acceptance I found here that I have never found anywhere else."

Love the Core

Many undergrads agree that one of the most important qualities of Whitman student is a "genuine interest in learning." Academics have always been central to life at Whitman, and many students say that the only thing Whitties love as much as the outdoors is learning.

> **"I can leave my purse and belongings in a public place and know that when I return they'll be sitting right where I left them."**

At the center of a Whitman education is the core curriculum. Students describe the Core program as one to "ensure some kind of exposure to all areas of the liberal arts." In addition to taking two semesters of Core classes ("Antiquity" and "Modernity") freshman year, Whitties are also required to fulfill a plethora of distributional requirements, including two social science classes, two humanities, two fine arts, two sciences, and a quantitative analysis course before graduating.

While the premed and science are popular majors, they are also known to be the most difficult. Of course, it is possible to be "challenged by any program you pursue," although reportedly there is a fair amount of grade inflation. And students maintain that it is hard to do poorly at Whitman because so many academic resources are available outside of class.

Whitties rave about their professors, describing them as "highly-regarded" and "very accessible." "I love the profs here . . . they are highly accessible people, and very friendly and helpful," one junior said.

What About the Weekends?

Whitties report a great social scene on campus. Students say that either unofficial on-campus parties, fraternity and sorority parties, or dances and events hosted by official Whitman clubs are the dominant activities for Friday and Saturday nights. One third of the student population is involved in Greek life. Sorority members live in the all-female Prentiss Hall. Frat parties are popular social events, but students report that they are "exclusive" or hard to get into.

Students say that, "like any other college," alcohol is very present on campus. The school's alcohol policy "is very laid back." Most students drink "in a private space that is somewhat contained (ie. in one's room with the door closed). If an RA catches you drinking in public, they pour out your drink, and that is all," one Whittie warned. However, many students stress that there are, "plenty of activities on campus if you don't drink." And students seem to agree that there are almost no drugs present on campus.

Whittie Winners

Whitties describe their campus as "beautiful." The campus is centered around Ankeny Field, which is pretty much "your typical college quad." Freshmen and sophomores live on campus and are required to have an on-campus meal plan. The biggest dorms on campus are Lyman and Jewitt Hall. There are also several smaller residence halls for juniors and seniors. In addition to the traditional dorm housing, Whitman also has many different theme houses, ranging from a volunteer house to a writing house, which, as one student described, "allow upperclassmen to live within a community of people with similar interests."

The meal plan at Whitman allows students to eat at two dining halls and the student center, Reid Campus Center. Students assert that Reid Center has better food than the halls, but the halls have "exceptional salad bars."

In terms of sports, jocks should take heart—Whitman has no football team or cheerleaders. However, students are quick to say that, "tennis, cross country, and skiing are very popular." There is also a biking team that is growing in popularity as well. Whitman's new tennis facility and indoor pool are proclaimed by most to be "high quality."

Because of the lack of varsity sports, Whitman students take intramural sports very seriously. Some of the most popular are bowling, flag football, ultimate Frisbee, basketball, and soccer. And despite a high level of competition, Whitties say that IMs are "fun!"

Whitman draws much of its appeal from its beautiful Pacific Northwest surroundings. While Whitties hold a great appreciation for nature, they are quick to refute common stereotypes that Whitman students care more about their hiking boots than their grades or extracurriculars. In truth, while the typical Whitman student is outdoorsy and free-spirited, he or she is also friendly, accepting, hard-working, and high-achieving. One student summed up his experience at Whitman by saying, "Being a 'Whittie' is an amazing experience, and if this school is the right place for you as a person, it's the best place in the world."—*Becky Bicks*

FYI

If you come to Whitman, you'd better bring: "Hiking boots, a Frisbee, a spirit of adventure and an open mind."

If I could change anything at Whitman, I'd "push the food service provider (Bon Apetit) to improve overall quality."

What's a typical weekend schedule? "Party on campus Saturday and sleep in and study on Sunday, or go on a camping trip Friday night and come back Sunday."

Three things everyone should do before graduating from Whitman are: "Run the Beer Mile, complete the Frisbee golf course, go on as many camping trips as possible."

West Virginia

Marshall University

Address: Marshall, Old Main 125, One John Marshall Drive, Huntington, WV 25755
Phone: 800-642-3499
E-mail Address: admissions@marshall.edu
Web site URL: www.marshall.edu/admissions/
Year Founded: 1837
Private or Public: public
Religious affiliation: none
Location: suburban
Regular Application Deadline: rolling
Number of Applicants: 2,577
Percent Accepted: 84%
Percent Accepted who enroll: 83%
Number Entering: 1,803
Number of Transfers Accepted each Year: NA
Mean SAT: NA
Mean ACT: 22
Middle 50% SAT range: NA

Middle 50% ACT range: 20–24
Early admission program (EA/ ED/ NA): NA
ED or EA Acceptance Rate: NA
Full time Undergraduate enrollment: 8,931
Total enrollment: 8,275
Percent Male: 44%
Percent Female: 56%
Total Percent Minority: 11%
Percent African-American: 5%
Percent Asian/Pacific Islander: 1%
Percent Hispanic: 1%
Percent Native-American: 0%
Percent Other: NA
Percent in-state / out of state: 83%/17%
Percent from Public HS: NA
Retention Rate: 73%
Graduation Rate: 37%

Percent in On-campus housing: NA
Percent affiliated with Greek system: NA
Percent Varsity or Club Athletes: NA
Number of official organized extracurricular organizations: NA
3 Most popular majors: Business Administration/Management, Elementary Education/Teaching, Psychology
Student/Faculty ratio: NA
Financial Information: NA
Tuition and Fees: $10,634
In State Tuition and Fees (if different): $3,932.00
Cost for Room and Board: $5,932.00
Percent receiving Financial aid, first-year: 45%

While Marshall University may seem like a bit of an extension of high school for some West Virginia residents, the University stands on its own, offering small classes, impressive scholarships, school spirit for the Thundering Herd, and a bustling social life.

Making the Grade

As a state school, Marshall is full of surprises. Many students say that the academic aspect of the University has exceeded their expectations. Students praise the array of interesting and challenging courses but warn that popular classes tend to be in the natural sciences or management departments, with a relatively low percentage of students majoring in humanities and foreign languages. Marshall also boasts several highly renowned graduate schools, including the school of journalism and the medical school, to which many students hope to apply after graduation.

The University is also liked for its small classes and approachable professors. A junior who transferred from Cincinnati State to Marshall after his freshman year is glad that the small size of the school "encourages student-teacher interaction." Another student added that "professors quickly get to know you by name . . . I've never been in a class larger than 100 people."

All students must complete distribution requirements known as the Marshall Plan, which stipulates that students fulfill a set number of classes per department—math, humanities, foreign language, and others. While the Marshall Plan is not considered overly burdensome, most students recommend starting it early, as it takes an average of three semesters to complete. Students are guided by assigned advisors, but usually a favorite professor becomes the main advisor.

Recently, the state of West Virginia put some cold, hard, cash down for a series of scholarships based on ACT scores and cumulative GPA, which provide in-state students partial or full tuition coverage. The University also runs the prestigious Yaeger Scholarship that provides tuition, room and board coverage, as well as extra perks, like early registration, to its recipients.

In 'n Out

Because of the scholarship deal set up by the state of West Virginia, Marshall attracts a lot of in-state students, a trait which affects student life on the weekends. "We're a suitcase campus," admits one student. By Friday night, people living nearby go home for the weekend, leaving a noticeable void on campus. However, more students stay on campus second semester, as the cold winter weather keeps people at school.

Although students are required to live on campus in their first two years, Marshall regulations allow students who live less than 50 miles away to live at home. This increases the commuter feel of the campus. The administration is trying to remedy the situation by upgrading the dorms and making Marshall a great place to live full time.

In the recent past, four modern dorms were built to address student complaints about old rooms. The Towers, as they are called, are a compound of two coed and two single-sex buildings. Their living spaces are designed as four or eight person suites, with air conditioning and a cafeteria (with "really, good food") connecting the two towers. However, one freshman warns, "these [Tower] dorms are largely assigned to athletes; you have to know someone in the administration to secure housing there." As a result, Marshall is also using its funding to renovate and build apartment buildings in the center of Huntington, which is getting a positive response from students.

All visitors must sign in and leave by curfew on weekdays, a rule that is widely disliked by students. Moreover, parties are not allowed in the dorms. RAs patrol the halls, upholding the dry campus rule, but the dorms are home to pajama parties and under-the-radar drinking nonetheless. In general, students find the RAs to be strict but understanding.

Get Your Herd On

When football season rolls around, the whole Marshall campus buzzes with excitement. Marshall students love their football team, the "Thundering Herd." To prepare for the games, fans "get their herd on," by putting on any piece of clothing with the school insignia on it and come out in full force to tailgate. One student recalls waking up at 4 a.m. in order to start the tailgate before the big 10 a.m. game got going.

In the past several years, however, the football team has lost its best players to the NFL, and is not as good as it used to be. Rugby, lacrosse, and basketball, on the other hand, still remain popular club sports. One junior exclaimed, "You have to go see the Marshall-WVU basketball game at Charleston!" The student body also keeps active with intramurals, but these do not have a dominating presence on campus.

And while athletics does seem to be a popular extracurricular, it is certainly not the only way to enjoy oneself at Marshall. The school sponsors many different clubs, like the skiing club (with the slopes only a couple of hours away), and white water rafting club (with the river also close by), as well as activities for the more sedate and spiritual, such as the Christian Crusaders, and Evangelical and Baptist groups, which enjoy a strong following on campus. The University also pulls in big comic talent in its annual Artist Series—even Whoopi Goldberg made an appearance.

When the Lights Go Out

In the off season, the social scene is dominated by the fraternities and the bars in Huntington. The Greek system is prominent on campus, with several fraternities and sororities. These houses host parties and weekly "gifs," or fraternity and sorority mixers, which are popular with the students. "There is always a frat party going on," one freshman said.

> "You tend to feel like you're in the 13th grade."

Students also head down to the town center, which "is very easily accessible" at one block from the campus and very welcoming of the student population who patronize a number of bars located on the main street. Popular choices range from The Union, which is strict on IDs and hosts a mainly upperclassman crowd, to 18+ bars such as Stumblers. Each bar has a unique atmosphere, and students can move from one with a dance floor to one with a pub decor. Each bar lures students with excellent drink specials, like a $5 all-you-can-drink deal.

In Need of Variety

But while the extracurricular scene is diverse, the student population is not. The percentage of white, in-state students is overwhelming, making for "a very homogeneous population." Students sometimes complain that it is hard to meet someone new, as "you spend time with people you went to high school with," and there are not that many large, open parties to mingle with new students.

One freshman noted that it is important to make new friends early on, because sometimes you "tend to feel like you're in 13th grade," since the population of students coming from nearby is so great. However, if a student takes the initiative to socialize with new people, the school provides great opportunities for exciting extracurricular activities. You just have to find your niche.
—*Agata Kostecka*

FYI
If you come to Marshall, you'd better bring "an appreciation of sports—we watch a lot of games."
What's the typical weekend schedule? "Party with friends on Thursday, hit the bars Friday, recover and relax Saturday, and catch up on homework on Sunday."
If I could change one thing about Marshall, I'd "reduce the number of people who commute."
Three things every student at Marshall should do before graduating are "tailgate at a football game, go to The Union when he/she turns 21, and go to the Marshall-WVU basketball game in Charleston."

West Virginia University

Address: West Virginia University, PO Box 6009, Morgantown, WV 26506
Phone: 800-344-WVU1
E-mail Address: go2wvu@mail.wvu.edu
Web site URL: http://admissions.wvu.edu/
Year Founded: 1867
Private or Public: public
Religious affiliation: none
Location: suburban
Regular Application Deadline: 2-Aug
Number of Applicants: NA
Percent Accepted: 92%
Percent Accepted who enroll: NA
Number Entering: NA
Number of Transfers Accepted each Year: NA
Mean SAT: NA
Mean ACT: NA

Middle 50% SAT range: NA
Middle 50% ACT range: NA
Early admission program (EA/ ED/ NA): NA
ED or EA Acceptance Rate: NA
Full time Undergraduate enrollment: NA
Total enrollment: 28,000
Percent Male: 45%
Percent Female: 55%
Total Percent Minority: NA
Percent African-American: NA
Percent Asian/Pacific Islander: NA
Percent Hispanic: NA
Percent Native-American: NA
Percent Other: NA
Percent in-state / out of state: 50% out
Percent from Public HS: NA
Retention Rate: 81%

Graduation Rate: NA
Percent in On-campus housing: 26%
Percent affiliated with Greek system: 25%
Percent Varsity or Club Athletes: NA
Number of official organized extracurricular organizations: NA
3 Most popular majors: Business, Communications, Engineering
Student/Faculty ratio: NA
Tuition and Fees: $9,106.00
In State Tuition and Fees (if different): $3,242.00
Cost for Room and Board: $6,630.00
Percent receiving Financial aid, first-year: 80%

I t is a fall Saturday morning, and everyone at West Virginia University is waking up early. The fun begins around 8, as students, donning yellow and blue shirts, make their way to the Pit to tailgate. Their final destination is Milan Puskar Stadium, where they will cheer the Mountaineers to victory. Whether or not the football team prevails, the students are always championship fans.

Any student will tell you football games are at the foundation of the WVU experience. The Pit, outside the stadium, is the gathering place for students before the game, where there are up to 50 kegs at once. WVU's football team consistently ranks among the top 25 teams in the country, and on game days, Morgantown temporarily becomes the most populated city in the state. Mongahela County has even been known to close its schools on the days of night games. Said one student, "I feel like the state of West Virginia is known for coal . . . and the Mountaineers." At WVU, school spirit isn't just limited to the stadium—students take pride in their academics as well.

Caring Professors

West Virginia University is known for its solid academic offerings and devoted professors. Beginning their junior year, students apply to a specific college, such as the College of Business and Economics or the School of Journalism, depending on their major. Students agree that professors are very clear about what they want and consistently accessible. One student raved about the "extremely good experiences" he has had with professors. He pointed out that professors at West Virginia "have seen everything" and are sympathetic and understanding. "They know how to handle every situation," he assured.. Teaching assistants are less reliable, though, and students have mixed feelings about the faculty adviser program. One student complained that his academic adviser was "clueless" and made no effort to meet with him. Other students praise the program, claiming that "your academic advisor is someone you can always go to, who is always available to meet with you."

> "I feel like the state of West Virginia is known for coal . . . and the Mountaineers."

While introductory classes contain up to several hundred students, with notes posted online, students do not feel invisible. The enthusiasm and involvement of professors ensures a personal academic experience for all.

Keeping Students Happy

While some of the classroom buildings in the historic downtown campus date back to the 19th century, the building that functions as the heart of WVU is strikingly modern. The Mountainlair, renovated in 1990, houses Student Administration, the food court, and "ballrooms" where concerts and lectures take place. It's also the site of WVUp All Night, the popular, weekly event that provides both entertainment and free food.. On Thursday, Friday, and Saturday nights from 7:00 p.m. to 2:00 a.m., students

stop by to enjoy snacks, movies, live music, video games, pool, and even bowling (there's an alley in the Mountainlair). Up All Night has been recognized as one of the best alcohol-free entertainment alternatives in the country, appealing to virtually all Mountaineers.

Another popular, school-sponsored entertainment event is FallFest. At the beginning of the fall semester, WVU welcomes its students back to school with an outdoor concert, often featuring a big-name act. Students are impressed with the effort and money the school expends on the event.

Goings On, On-Campus and Off

Drinking is still alive and well at WVU even with the non-alcoholic alternatives. Between the cornucopia of bars in Morgantown and the tradition of rowdy off-campus parties, drinking remains a popular pastime at the school. However, students point out there is no pressure to drink and some students choose to abstain.

Because drinking is strictly forbidden in the dorms, even for students over 21, parties happen off campus. Students say the school's policy on alcohol is very clear: If you are caught drinking in the dorms (by an RA, for example), you will get written up and fined. On the other hand, the school will not break up off-campus parties. This policy is one reason why the vast majority of students live off campus. "There are too many rules associated with the dorms—it can be restrictive to live there," one student said. Students also cited privacy and extra space as benefits of living off campus. All agree that off-campus housing is very easy to find, although the houses located downtown are taken quickly. Because West Virginia's campus is sprawling, this may mean a student ends up living a ways from classroom buildings. In fact, one student claimed, getting to the center of campus from most off-campus housing requires a 15- to 20-minute hike (literally—the hills at WVU are fierce). Furthermore, students warn that the off-campus houses are, in general, in worse condition than the dorms.

While students have mixed opinions about the food at West Virginia, they share an appreciation for the flexibility of WVU's meal plans. For students who live on-campus, there are five different meal plans to choose from and various large and small cafeterias, food courts, and cafés around campus. The many students who live off-campus can purchase the off-campus meal plan, which allows them to choose between several restaurants and fast-food places in Morgantown.

The frat scene is not very big at WVU, and parties tend to happen, instead, at students' off-campus houses. One street, Grant Avenue, located by the downtown campus, is famous for its parties (and occasional riots). Morgantown boasts a vibrant bar and club scene and is lax about carding, so the bars are a popular weekend (and weeknight) destination. Shooter's is described as the "freshman bar," while other popular places are Bent Willey's and Fin's. One student points out that, in general, bars are most popular with freshmen because by sophomore or junior year, students realize going to bars is an expensive habit.

Students enjoy more refined diversions, as well. The University Arts Series brings professional, touring musicals, concerts, and ballets to the school, while the Comedy Caravan presents nationally acclaimed comedians free of charge. The College of Creative Arts, one of WVU's undergraduate colleges, is always presenting art exhibits, concerts and plays.

The football team is not the only team attracting attention at WVU. Recently, the basketball team gained national prominence, rocketing into the Elite Eight in the NCAA playoffs in 2005. Attending basketball games has become the new obsession at West Virginia. In years past fans followed their favorite player, Kevin Pittsnogle. (Pittsnogle's allure was so strong that his fans invented a verb, "to pittsnogle." When a rival player or team is shown up, embarrassed, or just generally outdone, Mountaineers shout, "You've been pittsnogled!") The basketball team plays at the Coliseum, the site of concerts, facilities for other indoor sports, and even a few classrooms.

For non-varsity athletes, the Student Rec Center is a mecca, with free weights, aerobic machines; an elevated track; basketball, volleyball and badminton courts; and a 50-foot climbing wall. Students are enthusiastic about WVU's thriving intramural sports, which are based at the Rec Center. "It's nice that we have our own facilities," says one devotee of IMs and member of the team The North Spruce Street Bad Boys. "We have one of the best student rec centers in the country."

So . . . How 'Bout That Monorail?

West Virginia has two campuses, the Downtown campus and the Evansdale campus. The university built a monorail, called the PRT (Personal Rapid Transit), in 1972. The PRT runs until 10:15 p.m. during the week and 5:00 p.m. on Saturdays, and it is closed on Sundays. Students have mixed feelings about the PRT (some say it needs fixing up), but claim it is "necessary because it connects the two campuses." Still, getting around campus is not always easy, and the majority of upperclassmen have cars at school. While students allow that "you can get by without a car if you live downtown," they say that it's very important to have a car if you live on the Evansdale campus or off-campus. Because so many students have cars, traffic can be heavy and parking is scarce. For this reason, some say it's hard to get around *with* a car, as well. Students who live off-campus park on the street, and it can be difficult to find a space. Despite these drawbacks, students wholeheartedly recommend bringing a car to WVU, especially since, as one student points out, "West Virginia University is built on a mountain." Indeed, WVU is famous for its hills, which one student cited as a deterrent to attending class. At the same time, more active students enjoy the natural landscape of the school on the trails by the Monongahela River, which are perfect for strolls or jogs.

Despite the hills, students love WVU and Morgantown. Between its diverse restaurants, lively bars, and frequent concerts and shows, Morgantown is "the perfect college town." Furthermore, students say that the school and town truly go hand-in-hand, and that town-gown relations are "really good." Many locals attend WVU, but it doesn't take long for non-native West Virginians to feel at home. When asked if they would choose WVU all over again, most students claimed that they "definitely would." Students are not lying when they sing along with West Virginia's favorite son, John Denver, "Country roads, take me home, to the place I belong."—*Kathleen Reeves*

FYI

If you come to West Virginia, you'd better bring "your party shoes, and expect things to go as slow as the South." "Also, bring coffee—there are virtually no coffee shops in town."

What's the typical weekend schedule? "Take it easy on Friday, get up early on Saturday to start tailgating, go to the football game and root for the Mountaineers, and sing 'Country Roads' by John Denver."

If I could change one thing about West Virginia, I'd "change the ridiculous on-campus alcohol policy, or at least fix up some of the off-campus houses."

Three things every student at WVU should do before graduating are "go to WVUp All Night, go to a football (or basketball) game, and go whitewater rafting."

Wisconsin

Beloit College

Address: Beloit, 700 College Street, Beloit, WI 53511
Phone: 800-9-BELOIT
E-mail Address: invent@beloit.edu
Web site URL: www.beloit.edu
Year Founded: 1846
Private or Public: private
Religious affiliation: none
Location: urban
Regular Application Deadline: 16-Jan
Number of Applicants: 2,048
Percent Accepted: 67%
Percent Accepted who enroll: 25%
Number Entering: 347
Number of Transfers Accepted each Year: 54
Mean SAT: NA
Mean ACT: 27
Middle 50% SAT range: 1,160–1,380 (writing not included)

Middle 50% ACT range: 25–29
Early admission program (EA/ ED/ NA): EA
ED or EA Acceptance Rate: NA
Full time Undergraduate enrollment: 1,407
Total enrollment: 1,407
Percent Male: 40%
Percent Female: 60%
Total Percent Minority: 17%
Percent African-American: 3%
Percent Asian/Pacific Islander: 2%
Percent Hispanic: 4%
Percent Native-American: <1%
Percent Other: 7%
Percent in-state / out of state: 20%/80%
Percent from Public HS: 78%
Retention Rate: 86%

Graduation Rate: 71%
Percent in On-campus housing: 87%
Percent affiliated with Greek system: 8%/6%
Percent Varsity or Club Athletes: NA
Number of official organized extracurricular organizations: 85
3 Most popular majors: Social Sciences, Visual and Performing Arts, English
Student/Faculty ratio: 12:01
Tuition and Fees: $28,350.00
Cost for Room and Board: $6,162.00
Percent receiving Financial aid, first-year: 100%

Founded in 1846 in territorial Wisconsin with just $7,000 and a desire to bring education to the Midwest, Beloit College has now become an internationally recognized college famed for its liberal arts education and its distinctive atmosphere. A few students may whine about the cold winters of Wisconsin, but the environment at Beloit College is very welcoming. Strong academics with a focus on global relations and a thriving social life complete the beauty of a hip and enthusiastic campus.

Interdisciplinary Innovation

Although some students called the workload "challenging," most agree that it is quite rewarding, thoughtful, and interdisciplinary. Beloiters also rave that their professors are accessible and helpful. One freshman said that her professor offered her class an opportunity to work and learn in Africa with the professor over the summer.

A First-Year Initiatives program brings together all Beloit's freshmen through interdisciplinary seminars and orientation programs. This is complemented by a Sophomore-Year Initiatives program that works with sophomores to overcome the dreaded "sophomore slump" and helps them to become more aware of their aims and goals in college. Beyond that, there are few academic requirements—two courses in natural sciences or math, two in social sciences, and two in humanities. Additionally, each student must complete three writing-focused classes, and one interdisciplinary class. These requirements can be fulfilled through a variety of unique classes; the course catalogue has such offerings as Hieroglyphics, History of Physics, Whiffs and Sniffs: the Nature and Influence of Smells, and even Film Music. "The requirements are good in that they offer structure, but they are quite flexible and can be tailored to your individual interests," one undergrad explained.

To help students through difficult classes, Beloit offers a number of resources. The Learning Support Services Center often tutors students either individually or in groups, and the Writing Center, where tutors "work with students on a collaborative basis" is open until 9 p.m. on school nights. Students agree that the workload is just as intense as that at any first-rate university, regardless of the department. Classics is said to be a somewhat easy major, but one junior pointed out that the sciences tend to be more challenging "because of time and difficulty. There is certainly less wiggle room in [science majors] to take classes you are interested in" outside the major. Beloit's specialties, international relations and anthropology, are fairly difficult, but are both popular and renowned majors. Anthropology, in particular, received rave reviews. One student gushed that, "Indiana Jones was based on one of our archeology graduates named Roy Chapman. He donated all his artifacts to the school upon his death!" Luckily, living professors tend to be just as amazing. The reigning celebrity is Tom McBride of the English department, who is the creator of the annual "mindset lists" and described as "very Texan" with a "loud teaching style." There is also an archaeology professor, Dan Shea, who "frequently takes students along on his digs in Chile" and Pablo Tarol, a specialist on development and Latin America, a favorite of students.

The atmosphere at Beloit is intimate, considering that the college only has 1,300 undergraduates. Classes are usually less than 20 students and always under 30. Even the introductory survey classes are personal, although one philosophy major whined that they were "lacking in depth . . . but also unavoidable." Assignments, reflecting the students, tend to go beyond the standard papers. One student recalled "performing the entire *Paradise Lost* in front of an audience for an English class" while another said that, "In my African studies class we had to do oral presentations because African culture is more oral than ours."

Frisbee and Freak-Dancing

Beyond homework and classes, Beloit students keep busy. For those not writing for the *Roundtable*, the school paper, school nights are devoted to homework and other extracurriculars. Sports are very low key. When asked, a student said, "Sports? We have sports? Oh yeah, intramurals. I've heard rumors of varsity sports but never witnessed them. Kind of like ghost stories." When it's warm enough, Frisbee is surprisingly common on the grounds. Extracurricular groups include Young Democrats, Young Republicans, the Gay Alliance, Black Students United, Voces Latinas, and even fencing.

Thursday through Saturday nights, "everyone parties together on campus, which is awesome and friendly, but can always be awkward the next morning, since you know everyone," one female undergrad said. Freshmen tend to mix and mingle at larger and more formal functions, while upperclassmen parties are usually more private, "but they are still very much out in public with the rest of us mortals." The Greek scene, with only 8 percent of men and 6 percent of women involved, is small but key to the party circuit. One fraternity member commented that, "Greek life affects the community, but does not run it like on other schools. That's why I joined." All the parties have different themes, from a "Talking Heads" party to the soccer team's seventies-style "Playaz Ball" party, but students uniformly have a good time together. Beloit also organizes a Folk and Blues weekend (which everybody calls "Fuck and Booze") every fall that brings a number of bands to campus for two nights.

As part of the hippie environment, people do respect what alcohol can do to the body. Most people who do drink end up at Aldrich residential hall. One girl there said that, "when I didn't drink, I didn't feel out of the loop, but sometimes I feel that drinkers can be really inconsiderate about others, especially when it's a Wednesday night." Students said that IDs are rarely checked, and private parties are very common and very open. There is a zero tolerance policy on drugs. However, since there are a large proportion of hippies on campus, "there is certainly a lot of pot here, but you have to look harder to find stronger drugs." Coed dorms make hooking up and sex fairly common. "Students at Beloit can't be described as polyamorous," said one student, "they are just plain amorous." Of course, "there are also a fair amount of committed couples of all preferences."

Wild, Wonderful Wisconsin

The campus is very idyllic, thanks to its scenic location in the woods of Wisconsin. Beloit's greatest claim to landscape fame is its Native American burial mounds, which no other college in the States has. One of the burial mounds is shaped like a turtle, from which was derived Beloit's unofficial turtle mascot. "We're freaking Beloit College," one student exclaimed. "Everything begins and ends here! We also have a rich history of hippiedom." The campus incorporates Georgian and colonial architecture, and the woods add natural beauty. The city of Beloit is fairly unexciting, but just seven dollars buys a bus ticket to Madison, which is 45 minutes away.

> "Everything begins and ends here! We also have a rich history of hippiedom."

The campus residences are extraordinarily varied. One college radio announcer gave a quick rundown of the major dorms: "Peet is the stoner dorm. Aldrich is where the drunks go. 810 is where soccer players usually live. Avoid the '64 halls—they were built to be riot proof and thus are ugly as sin. The worst dorm would be Emerson 609, a freshman dorm with cinder block walls and dingy lighting."

The students, however, make up for the buildings. Of course, the student body can still easily fall into stereotypes. "You know those white kids with dreadlocks who are actually from the 'burbs of Chicago? A lot of those go here. A fair amount of indie kids/art students. But all the rest are pretty normal." There is some self-segregation, but the large number of international students really balances out the student body. A student government leader said, "I feel comfortable sitting with anybody" in the cafeterias.

From the campus to the classes to the night scene, there is a focus more on connections and understanding than just textbook learning at Beloit. It is "his emphasis on experiential learning and international perspectives," one freshman explained, "that makes Beloit truly excellent." Oh yeah, and it's fun, too!—*Jeffrey Zuckerman*

FYI

If you come to Beloit, you better bring "lots of costumes because people here LOVE theme parties"

What's the typical weekend schedule? "Friday night: party. Saturday: Sleep it off, do a little bit of homework. Party at night. Sunday: Do a lot of homework."

If I could change one thing about Beloit, I'd "get more diversity. Tons more. As in people who are not white and from Chicago."

Three things every student at Beloit should do before graduating are "Study abroad, have tea at a professor's house, and dance their ass off at as many campus parties as possible."

Lawrence University

Address: Lawrence, PO Box 599, Appleton, WI 54912
Phone: 920-832-6500
E-mail Address: excel@lawrence.edu
Web site URL: www.lawrence.edu
Year Founded: 1847
Private or Public: private
Religious affiliation: none
Location: small city
Regular Application Deadline: 15-Jan
Number of Applicants: 2,315
Percent Accepted: 56%
Percent Accepted who enroll: 29%
Number Entering: 399
Number of Transfers Accepted each Year: 40–50
Mean SAT: NA
Mean ACT: NA
Middle 50% SAT range: 1,200–1,430 (not req)

Middle 50% ACT range: 26–31
Early admission program (EA/ ED/ NA): EA&ED
ED or EA Acceptance Rate: NA
Full time Undergraduate enrollment: 1,442
Total enrollment: 1,442
Percent Male: 45%
Percent Female: 55%
Total Percent Minority: 18%
Percent African-American: 2%
Percent Asian/Pacific Islander: 3%
Percent Hispanic: 2%
Percent Native-American: 1%
Percent Other: 10%
Percent in-state / out of state: 38%/62%
Percent from Public HS: 82%

Retention Rate: 90%
Graduation Rate: 78%
Percent in On-campus housing: 99%
Percent affiliated with Greek system: 23% male, 10% female
Percent Varsity or Club Athletes: 75%
Number of official organized extracurricular organizations: 117
3 Most popular majors: Music Performance, Biology, Government
Student/Faculty ratio: 9:01
Tuition and Fees: $29,598.00
Cost for Room and Board: $6,382.00
Percent receiving Financial aid, first-year: 86%

I f you're looking for a traditional, private coed university in the Midwest, Lawrence University is just about the archetype. Founded in 1847, Lawrence University is situated along the Fox River in the middle of the small, but growing, metropolitan city of Appleton, Wisconsin. Students at Lawrence benefit from a rigorous academic environment and enjoy a thriving social community that makes good use of a nationally renowned conservatory of music.

Small Classes, Lots of Love

When talking about their university, students always rave about their animated professors and the comfortable class size that comes with a small liberal arts college. The class sizes include "one-on-one independent study, small group tutorials, and 'normal classes,'" which still stay under 40 students. As one student remarked: "I think my biggest class so far has been about 30, and I've had some as small as 11. Some of the higher-level classes and tutorials can be as small as four or five students." The small numbers mean that professors can really focus on individual students, a connection that most students value. One freshman

said, "The best part about Lawrence academics is that the faculty is not only extremely accessible but also enthusiastic to spend one-on-one time with students and form close personal relationships with them." TAs won't be found even in larger classes, and even freshmen can benefit from courses taught by some of the most distinguished Lawrence professors.

However, don't expect the dedicated faculty at Lawrence to ease up on the workload. Students often find themselves with stacks of books to read and pages of papers to write. Many find that there aren't too many "gut" classes, and that "even the dumb classes are still fairly intensive." So those looking for all party and no study get weeded out at Lawrence, because "the bar is set too high for slackers."

The liberal arts education that Lawrence offers pleases most students, especially students who have no preformed ideas of what their courses of study will be. Lawrence's unique curriculum requires freshman to take two terms of Freshmen Studies, one critical-thinking class and one "great books" course. This not only provides a good introduction to a liberal arts education, but also creates a core curriculum in which students of all disciplines can meet and converse.

It is important to note that Lawrence University operates on a trimester system, a schedule that pleases some but not others. The first trimester begins later in September and ends in beginning of December, while the second two trimesters extend from January through June. During each term the students usually take three courses. The later starting and ending dates can be considered inconveniences for students whose friends at other schools have different schedules. In general, students also find that their courses can become very intensive, since they are fit into the short 10-week terms.

All undergrads are required to live on campus, which contributes to the tight-knit community feel of the campus. Dormitories include buildings such as Ormsby Hall, with hardwood floors and a central location, and the substance-free Kohler Hall. Colman Hall offers a popular alternative to the campus's main dining hall. For upperclassmen, a brand-new hall with "enormous suites and in-suite bathrooms," along with comfortable singles, is the current favorite. In addition to the dorms, upperclassmen can choose to live in small residences owned by the University, which can house from eight to 27 people. Lawrence has three different types of houses in which students can elect to live. If a group of students is part of an established student organization and its members wish to live together (such as in the case of Greek organizations), they can apply for a Formal Group House, which is granted for three years (and can be renewed). Newer or unofficial student groups on campus can petition the student government for a Theme House, which lasts for one year. Finally, some small houses are set aside for general housing, so students can elect to live in them instead of the dorms after their freshman year. Approximately 15 percent of the campus lives in these small houses at any one time.

Where's Your Thermal Underwear?

Located in Appleton, in northeastern Wisconsin, Lawrence University sits atop a bluff overlooking the Fox River. Appleton and the surrounding cities comprise the Fox Cities, reportedly one of the fastest growing areas in Wisconsin, and "one of the best medium-sized metropolitan areas in the nation." According to one student, "Appleton is no great metropolis, but it's safe and, in its own way, quite charming. And there are some great restaurants within five minutes of campus." The areas around campus are mostly residential and middle- to upper-class. Students feel secure walking around campus, which is "not dangerous at all." Even students without cars can enjoy the restaurants and shopping places around Appleton. Breaking out of the academic bubble seems fairly easy, for "everything that you really need is within walking distance from campus, in either direction."

The climate in Wisconsin calls for puffy down jackets and thermal underwear, if you don't want to freeze on the way to class. In the winter, students can take advantage of Appleton's park system and sled or ice skate in the parks. In addition to the multitude of bars and shops downtown, Appleton has a downtown entertainment district that has made a sparkling new addition of a $5 million mega-screen theater.

The Sound of Music

Lawrence University's Conservatory of Music remains one of the leading music studies programs in the nation. The Conservatory consists of over 350 music majors and a dedicated faculty that gives individual attention to each composer, performer and scholar. Students in the conservatory combine the Conservatory curriculum with a liberal arts education, as at least one-third of the courses must be taken outside of the Conservatory. Students are also given the option to pursue both a Bachelor of Arts degree and Bachelor of Music degree in a special five-year program.

Students outside of the Conservatory can also take advantage of the multitude of music courses that it has to offer. Students feel that the Conservatory students, otherwise known as "Connies," are not completely separated from the rest of the University. While some feel that there are too many "Connies," students pursuing all studies are generally included in the community feel of Lawrence.

Because of the Conservatory, there are always performances, recitals and concerts around campus. Quite frequently, internationally renowned classical and jazz artists perform at the school. In Appleton, the recently built $45 million Fox Cities Performing Arts Center hosts many shows and concerts, from musical performances to Broadway plays. Students find that the new center "is excellent both aesthetically and acoustically. It's wonderful from both the performing and listening perspectives."

When the Weekend Rolls Around . . .

The Greek system at Lawrence is small, with only five fraternities and three sororities. As one student commented, freshmen "are more likely to be enchanted with the novelty of a frat party." But when annual bashes such as the "Foam Party," Beach Bash," or "Pimps and Hoes" roll around, upperclassmen flock to join in the fun. Underclassmen party in the dorms on campus, while the over-21 crowd has more options. One senior claimed, "Appleton's downtown boasts more bars than many cities twice its size." Around two dozen bars and clubs line College Avenue, a mere 10 minutes' walking distance and an even quicker ride by car. If you're feeling lazy, the "Viking Room," a campus bar, is also a popular choice. Students at Lawrence find that underage drinking is not a big issue. While Lawrence legally enforces "no underage drinking," students reported that the school tolerates drinking "as long as it is under control."

> **"The social life is perfect—something's always happening, but it's never overwhelming."**

At Lawrence, you don't need to drink and party to have fun on the weekends. According to one freshman, "the social life is perfect—something's always happening, but it's never overwhelming." Many students take advantage of the fantastic music programs and attend concerts and other theatrical shows. A trip to the enormous Fox Valley Mall nearby or restaurants, like the student favorite, Taste of Thai, in downtown Appleton add variety to a weekend. The trendy new late-night coffeehouse, Copper Rock, is a good place to cozy up with a date.

Positive Change and Improvement

For a small private university in central Wisconsin, Lawrence has a surprising amount of diversity, which stems primarily from its large international population. While nearly half of the students are from Wisconsin, the rest of the student population hails from almost every state. The school continues to recruit many international students as part of its initiative to bring a multicultural appeal to Lawrence. Lawrence International, the international students' organization, sponsors many activities, as does the Outdoor Recreation Club. Publications on campus include the weekly *Lawrentian* and the liberal publication *One Minute Left*, as well as *Tropos*, a yearly art and literary magazine. The openly LGBT population seems to be growing more and more comfortable on campus. From the Bonsai Club to the Students of Objectivism, students find that "there are always new clubs being formed and a good amount of action within student government."

The Division III athletics at Lawrence factor into the lives of students, but sports definitely don't dominate the typical student's schedule. Lawrence has strong men's and women's swim teams, and its volleyball and hockey teams also stand out. The fitness facilities are strategically located at the heart of campus, convenient for "ordinary students—not solely for athletes." Recently, an agreement with the local YMCA across the street from campus has allowed students access to these "top-notch" facilities as well. Students who like to jog or take scenic walks away from the studious environment of the campus can stroll on the many park paths and trails along nearby Fox River.

Lawrence has also renovated all of its science facilities, revealing newer buildings and classrooms. The University also plans to renovate its student union to create a place where students can relax and socialize. Currently, hungry students can visit the Grill, a greasy campus hangout open until 12 a.m. Lawrence students feel great pride for their school and generally reaffirm their decision to spend four years of their lives here. "It's hard to put down on paper. It just has a really nice feel to it," one senior said. At Lawrence, you can expect a small but friendly, supportive, musical and intellectually stimulating community.—*Karen Chen*

FYI

If you come to Lawrence, you'd better bring "a warm jacket. The wind can be especially biting."

What is the typical weekend schedule? "Party on Friday and Saturday, do homework on Sunday afternoon."

If I could change one thing about Lawrence, I'd "have the entire campus airlifted to a warmer climate with slightly better access to a big city."

Three things every student at Lawrence should do before graduating are "get to know several members of the faculty on a personal level, use a food tray from Downer as a sled, and attend a concert, orchestral or choral, in the Chapel."

Marquette University

Address: Marquette, PO Box 1881, Milwaukee, 53201-1881

Phone: 800-222-6544

E-mail Address: admissions@marquette.edu

Web site URL: www.marquette.edu/undergrad

Year Founded: 1881

Private or Public: private

Religious affiliation: Jesuit

Location: urban

Regular Application Deadline: 1-Dec

Number of Applicants: 14,000

Percent Accepted: 46.4%

Percent Accepted who enroll: 30%

Number Entering: 1,900

Number of Transfers Accepted each Year: 325

Mean SAT: 1,230

Mean ACT: 27

Middle 50% SAT range: 1,090–1,310

Middle 50% ACT range: 25–30

Early admission program (EA/ ED/ NA): NA

ED or EA Acceptance Rate: NA

Full time Undergraduate enrollment: 8,000

Total enrollment: 12,000

Percent Male: 49%

Percent Female: 51%

Total Percent Minority: 18%

Percent African-American: 5%

Percent Asian/Pacific Islander: 4.1%

Percent Hispanic: 4.3%

Percent Native-American: 0.5%

Percent Other: 4.1%

Percent in-state / out of state: 33% in / 67% out

Percent from Public HS: 65%

Retention Rate: 92%

Graduation Rate: 88%

Percent in On-campus housing: 95%

Percent affiliated with Greek system: 8%

Percent Varsity or Club Athletes: 8%

Number of official organized extracurricular organizations: 220

3 Most popular majors: Undecided, Engineering, Nursing

Student/Faculty ratio: 14:01

Tuition and Fees: $24,670.00

Cost for Room and Board: $8,120.00

Percent receiving Financial aid, first-year: 94%

Welcome to Milwaukee, the famous Brew City of Middle America. Cold weather, cold beer, and cheese are the staples of this lovely city, dotted with parks for hiking and picnicking, and situated on the edge of the sparkling Lake Michigan. Despite the icy weather and long winter, students of Marquette University are quite happy with their location and have plenty of school spirit to prove it. College unity transcends even the sports arena at this medium-sized urban university, as its Catholic affiliation pervades the student body, which takes pride in its religious traditions.

A Couple of Requirements

Marquette has much to offer in terms of academic variety across several schools, including colleges of Arts and Sciences, Com-

munication, Nursing, Business Administration, Engineering, Health Sciences, and Education. Students enjoy the many options and varied resources, but they sometimes feel overwhelmed with the amount of requirements: 36 credits in areas including Rhetoric, Literature, Math, Diverse Cultures, and Science. The university strives to maintain the Jesuit tradition of strong theological education, with six credit hours required in that field. One student lightheartedly commented, "I am not a huge fan of all theology, but, God dammit, we go to a Jesuit university," while another said it was hard to cram everything in her schedule in addition to her major requirements.

As for majors, the ones attracting most students are communication, business, and biomedical sciences (the latter being one of the hardest), along with journalism. Marquette has other strengths as well, such as its unique programs in dental hygiene, physical therapy, and its study abroad incentives. It is also associated with the Milwaukee Institute of Art and Design, a major perk for those into art.

Class size varies from major to major, but in general, courses range from large 200-person intro lectures to 12- to 30-student courses by junior and senior year as students further specialize. Even courses taken by first-year and second-year students are often small enough to foster a healthy, interactive relationship between the students and the professors. According to a current junior, "Every time I run into my old professors, even if I took their course my freshman year, they not only remember me but ask how I am doing. The professors are usually genuinely interested in your well-being as a student and a person."

There are virtually no complaints about the course load, as most students can afford to start partying on Thursday straight through Saturday, but spending up to 30 hours a week on school work is not uncommon at Marquette. In addition, it is very common for students to double-major. Many seem happy not only with the education they are receiving, but also with the personal growth afforded by close contact with professors and great study abroad opportunities. A junior political science and criminology major raved about her favorite professor: "She was very informal and had her office hours outside. She would always offer to go to the bars and things like that with us. She was great!" A couple classes that were praised were Dynamic Media and Politics and Juvenile Delinquency, which took students to juvenile court for a field trip.

Getting Better at Diversity

Besides doing schoolwork, Marquette students fill their time up with a diverse array of extracurricular activities. There are many clubs on campus that reflect a variety of interest groups, from the medieval reenactment club to community service groups. According to one student, service is "huge" at Marquette, and a large number of the student body comes out for Hunger Clean-Up, a day of cleaning up around Milwaukee. Basketball is definitely the biggest sport on campus and people holding tickets are referred to as "fanatics" for their enthusiastic school spirit. Games were described as "energetic, loud, lots of singing, lots of pride!

Just plain fun!" by one student, who also mentioned that Notre Dame and Madison were big rival teams.

> **"Most students are Christian so they share some sort of unity in that."**

Although the extracurriculars on campus may be diverse, the student body is slightly less so. Many students are from the Wisconsin and Illinois area, especially from Chicago, and are Caucasian and conservative. One student summed it up as "no diversity at all." But another said that the school isn't just a sea of "homogenous Midwestern white Republican Christians—some of the students are, but plenty aren't." The Marquette administration is striving to diversify their homogenous population while still maintaining the school's Jesuit traditions. Many students enjoy the comfort of a uniform student body and some frequently attend very traditional events like the Mass of the Holy Spirit at the Joan of Arc Chapel, located at the center of campus. Students take pride in this beautiful service and enjoy the Catholic affiliation of their school. Says one, "Most students are Christian so they share some sort of unity in that." Still, another pointed out that "Marquette isn't such a tight community because all the people are the same, but rather because they are committed to similar ideals and goals."

The Scoop on Brew City Living

Party all the way, dude. Yes, as you would expect at this Catholic school, the weekend starts on Thursday and no one follows the "strict" alcohol policy. In the Brew City, bars and clubs are never lacking, although a timeless favorite among the student body is Haggarty's Bar. Chilling with friends on campus often involves drinking, where keggers are common and often revolve around the hype of the basketball games. There is also a moderately-sized Greek system on campus that provides social outlets through a variety of theme parties. A notable annual party is the ABC: "anything but clothing." Such partying often leads to random hook-ups, but most agree that this is an underclassmen trend. There is more to the social life than drinking, however, since Milwaukee offers a wide variety of cultural events, concerts, art exhibits, and shows. Because many students are from the area and get internships in the area during the summer, local summer festivals provide great entertainment. They pervade the city, and Milwaukee residents make merry with music, parades, drinking on the streets, and dancing. Irish Fest week is always popular among college students.

No [Insert Opposite Sex Here] Allowed!

Although students reportedly do not abide by the no-alcohol rules, they do abide by the rules in the dorms. When living with RAs and priests, there is no escaping the patrols. Although several dorms on campus are co-ed, members of the opposite sex are not allowed to visit after 1 a.m. on weeknights or 2 a.m. on weekends.

Frosh dorms are small and cramped, and some students described them as "run-down" and "sorta ghetto," definitely "not the cleanest." But the architecture of the eight residence halls on campus, along with that of some other buildings, is quite remarkable. It has a modern touch that has received mixed reviews. McCormick, which maintains a reputation for crazy revelry at all times, is a round building with pie-slice shaped rooms. Tower and East are quieter and have typically-shaped, larger rooms.

The upperclassmen dorms get better, although a large number of students move off campus to nearby university-owned apartments after the first two years. Part of the draw of these more spacious quarters is the lack of living restrictions and RAs, not to mention the convenient nearby coffee-shops and laundromats.

Although many Marquette students move off the main campus, no one feels isolated. Everything on campus and in the vicinity is "clumped together." This is convenient because all the main classroom buildings, the library, the St. Joan of Arc Chapel, and even the main dorms are easily accessible—no trudging long distances in the icy weather! Marquette also receives much praise from its student body for its fantastic gym and athletic facilities.

Although the gym and the library got rave reviews, the food provided by the dining halls did not: "Perhaps the worst part of the university," as one student referred to it. Not only is the food not tasty, but it's also unhealthy, which means students often subsist on pizza, chicken nuggets, and burgers. However, if you're into Papa John's Pizza or Jimmy John's sandwiches, this could be the place for you. A car on campus is useful for grocery shopping if you decline to be on the meal plan, and it can also be convenient for shopping, road trips to Chicago (only an hour and a half away), or simply exploring Milwaukee. Marquette is the sort of school that does not become a ghost town on weekends. It's fun and alive and has a lot of pride, school spirit, and a strong alumni connection. Satisfied with the education and college experience they receive, most say they would do it all over again if they could.—*Carolina Galvao*

FYI

If you come to Marquette, you'd better bring "a good fake ID."

What is the typical weekend schedule? "Basketball games, bars, beer, enjoying the city of Milwaukee, and sleep."

If I could change one thing about Marquette, I would change "the food."

Three things every student at Marquette should do before graduating are "attend a game, attend at least one mass of the Holy Spirit, and study abroad."

University of Wisconsin/Madison

Address: University of Wisconsin, Madison, Armory & Gymnasium, 716 Langdon Street, Madison, WI 53706-1481
Phone: 608-262-3961
E-mail Address: onwisconsin@admissions.wisc.edu
Web site URL: www.admissions.wisc.edu
Year Founded: 1848
Private or Public: public
Religious affiliation: none
Location: small city
Regular Application Deadline: 1-Feb
Number of Applicants: 22,570
Percent Accepted: 58.5%
Percent Accepted who enroll: 42%
Number Entering: 6,800
Number of Transfers Accepted each Year: 1,200
Mean SAT: NA

Mean ACT: NA
Middle 50% SAT range: 1,770–2,010
Middle 50% ACT range: 26–30
Early admission program (EA/ ED/ NA): NA
ED or EA Acceptance Rate: NA
Full time Undergraduate enrollment: 28,458
Total enrollment: 41,480
Percent Male: 44%
Percent Female: 56%
Total Percent Minority: 14.5%
Percent African-American: 2.5%
Percent Asian/Pacific Islander: 5.4%
Percent Hispanic: 2.8%
Percent Native-American: 0.6%
Percent Other: 3.2%
Percent in-state / out of state: 78.4%/21.6%

Percent from Public HS: NA
Retention Rate: 94%
Graduation Rate: 78.1%
Percent in On-campus housing: 90%
Percent affiliated with Greek system: 10%
Percent Varsity or Club Athletes: NA
Number of official organized extracurricular organizations: 750
3 Most popular majors: Political Science, Psychology, English
Student/Faculty ratio: 13:01
Tuition and Fees: $6,730.00
In State Tuition and Fees (if different): $20,730.00
Cost for Room and Board: $6,920.00
Percent receiving Financial aid, first-year: 55%

Consistently rated among the top 10 public universities in the nation, the University of Wisconsin/Madison is a thriving, bustling campus happily situated between two beautiful lakeshores in the heart of the city. The University is well-known and widely respected for its challenging academics, its strong athletic teams, its ground-breaking research in a variety of fields, and—most importantly—its large and terrifically vibrant study body.

Work Hard . . .

Because Madison is such a large university, it has the resources and the faculty available to offer its students more than 4,000 courses in over 150 majors. Students can choose a major in any of the nine undergraduate colleges, which include the College of Agricultural and Life Sciences, the School of Business, the School of Education, the School of Engineering, the School of Human Ecology, the College of Letters and Science, the Medical School, the Nursing School, and the School of Pharmacy. Popular majors are psychology and economics (Madison has one of the best undergraduate business schools in the nation), while the majors of-fered in engineering are ruefully described as "ridiculous" in terms of their level of difficulty. Certain majors are sometimes referred to as "underwater basket-weaving majors" in reference to their being undemanding and not particularly useful, although most students generally do respect courses of study different from their own. As for unusual majors, the University boasts an amazing African language department with an extremely popular class on the African storyteller. The course is taught by Harold Scheub, one of the world's foremost experts in the field. Generally speaking, the variety of departments and majors available for study is so remarkable that one recent graduate commented, "Even during my senior year, I kept meeting people whose majors I had never heard of!"

Class sizes vary from large introductory lectures to smaller classes as students become more specialized in their studies. Large classes almost always meet in smaller discussion groups, and most students say that even in a big lecture they feel encouraged to ask questions without worrying about a professor being "insulted by the interruption." In addition, professors are available to talk to anyone who makes an effort to get to know them during office hours or through e-mail. Registration for classes can be frustrating; the system is based on seniority by number of credits, so it is often difficult for underclassmen to get into the classes they want. The workload is "manageable if you have a good work ethic," with "plenty of opportunities to excel," including the Honors Program, the Medical Scholars Program, study abroad, research, or any number of double majors, minors, and certificates. The motto at Madison has long been "Work hard, play hard," and most students can attest to the fact that "work hard" is no joke. As one junior noted, "People can overlook academics when they look at the school because they see us on TV during a badger game when we're all pepped up and when we're not representing the academic rigor that goes on here." In truth, however, classes can be very challenging, which means that when the weekend rolls around, students are always ready to close their books and focus instead on maintaining their reputation as one of the top party schools in the nation.

. . . Party Hard . . .
A typical Madison weekend runs from Thursday to Saturday and includes everything from frat parties and room parties during the evenings to barbecues and tailgating on a game day. Of course, as at any school, the amount of partying that goes on really varies from person to person. Drinking is definitely a big part of the social scene—especially at the very popular parties along Frat Row—though there are always other social activities for those who would rather stay sober. Memorial Union, a popular student hangout located on the edge of Lake Mendota, has recently initiated "Fashionably Late," a series of gaming nights, movies, concerts, and shows, "which are definitely an option if you don't feel like drinking." When asked if drinking was considered a problem on campus, most students felt that things usually settled down after freshman year when people began to solidify their groups of friends and stopped feeling like they had to go out every single weekend. Perhaps the craziest party night of the year is Halloween, when "out-of-towners flood into the city" and a crowd of 40,000 people celebrates all along State Street. Another famous Madison party is the Mifflin Street Block Party, a huge outdoor gathering right before the end of spring semester that boasts live bands and great barbecues.

A vast majority of students say they met their friends not at parties, but in class or through social organizations. Madison has hundreds of clubs and associations, including two great a cappella groups, a wide variety of intramural sports (including favorites such as badminton, dodgeball, and flag football in addition to the more commonly popular sports like Frisbee), and "clubs for everything." One well-known group is the Hoofers club, which offers a wide array of outdoor activities such as mountaineering, "outing" (hiking), riding, ski and snowboarding, SCUBA, and sailing. There are also a lot of political action groups and religious groups. Joining a club is a great idea, students say, because "once you find your place on campus, it stops feeling so big."

> **"The amount of school spirit at this university is incredible."**

The student body, however, is not quite as diverse as the extracurriculars. While the school does attract a large group of international students, the majority of students hail from Wisconsin or the surrounding area. As one student put it, "We're just a nice bunch of Midwestern kids." The University is currently working on Campaign 2008, a program geared toward attracting more minority students and therefore improving cultural and racial diversity. Diversity does exist in terms of interests and backgrounds, said one student, because "there are just so many people who all come here with different beliefs and different life experiences."

. . . Play Hard
According to one student, "Madison is truly a college sports town." The campus "goes nuts" over football, hockey, basketball, and volleyball, depending on the season. "The amount of school spirit at this university is incredible," one person said. According to one student fan, "We have the most formidable student section in the country, and we've definitely turned the tide in a lot of close games." A member of the old-school style marching band explained that game day rehearsals start at 7:00 a.m. and end at 9:00 a.m., at which point the band members often run to the dorms and loudly play school songs outside students' windows. "Usually it's pretty hard to sleep in on game day, no matter where you are," he said. Dur-

ing the week, Madison students display their school spirit by wearing school sweatshirts, hats, T-shirts, and anything else Badger-related. Even apart from the sports teams, students here have a lot of pride in their school and are always more than willing to show it off.

Life on the Lakes

The campus is situated on an isthmus between Lake Mendota and Lake Menona, a unique location that provides beautiful scenery as well as the resources for sailing, fishing, rowing, and a number of other outdoor activities. The University is also connected to the Capitol via State Street, which runs from the Capitol on one end to the library mall on the campus side, and offers visitors and students a wide variety of shops, restaurants, and theatres. State Street has everything from fine Italian restaurants such as Tutto Pasta to the quicker and more economical Noodles Inc., a multitude of other vegetarian and ethnic restaurants, a great cookies store, an impressive array of bars, vintage and off-beat clothing stores, and more commonly recognized stores like the Gap and Urban Outfitters. A walk through some of the shops on State Street can often be reminiscent of the University's "hippie days" of the '70s, when Madison was a hotspot for war protestors. Today the University retains its reputation as the stomping grounds for many liberal groups, and students say that there is always "some kind of protest happening on any given day on State Street." One student explained that a unique aspect of Madison is the variety of different environments in a small area. "You can walk through the whole campus in about 15 minutes, but within those 15 minutes you will cover everything from State Street and the downtown area, to the Capitol to the lakeshore where you'll feel like you're in the North Woods, to the agriculture part of campus that looks like typical dairy-farm Wisconsin, and then back to the middle of campus and the academic world."

Dorm living is divided into three basic areas: the South East dorms, known as the party area; the Lakeshore dorms, a quieter, calmer area right on Lake Mendota; and the private dorms, which are "slightly more expensive but have a lower people-per-bathroom ratio." Students are assigned to dorms based on a "preference system" where they rate their housing choices. Each dorm area "has its own little community" with eating places, workout centers, and a particular atmosphere. A lot of students move into nearby apartments or Greek houses after a year or two in the dorms. The area around campus is relatively safe, and while students point out that you need to be as careful at night as you should be anywhere, many feel perfectly comfortable walking to or from parties either alone or in a group.

Dining hall food is said to be "adequate" and "always hot and ready." One student observed, "The food is good for the first couple of weeks, then they start serving the same stuff over and over again!" The meal plan works through a prepaid card, which students can use to buy convenience-store style grocery items as well as to swipe in a standard cafeteria setting. The University is famous for its "wonderful" Babcock ice cream, made fresh right on campus in conjunction with the Food Science major in the College of Agricultural and Life Sciences. According to one student, "You can even visit the cows that they're milking!" Architecture on campus is described as a "random mix" of old and modern, and the University is currently undergoing several renovation projects.

On Wisconsin!

All things considered, most students at the University of Wisconsin-Madison are satisfied with their college choice. Its huge size provides students with a wealth of opportunities both inside the classroom and out, but everyone is still able to find his or her own smaller community of classmates and friends. One student commented, "At first I wasn't happy about going to a big state school because I thought I'd just be a number. But if you approach it as a challenge and as a place where there are opportunities for development and ways to distinguish yourself, the possibilities are limitless." And in a perfect example of the famous school spirit, when asked if she would choose Madison if she could do everything over again, one recent graduate replied, "Absolutely! Go Badgers!"—*Lindsay Starck*

FYI

If you come to the University of Wisconsin/Madison, you'd better bring "something red—school spirit here is huge."

What's the typical weekend schedule? "Friday night: party; Saturday: sleep in, then party, especially if there's a game; Sunday: study."

If I could change one thing about the University of Wisconsin/Madison, I'd "introduce a better bus system."

Three things every student at the University of Wisconsin/Madison should do before graduating are "go sledding down Bascom Hill, go to a Badger game and stay for the fifth quarter, and enjoy a cool evening at the Terrace on Lake Mendota—it's beautiful!"

Wyoming

I magine yourself amidst mountain ranges and grass plains. Look around and realize that you are engulfed in nature. Above you, nothing but sky; below you, nothing but solid earth. Then take several high-rise dorms, classroom buildings, and 10,000 students and plop them down in the middle of the wide-open prairie. What do you see now? The University of Wyoming in Laramie, Wyo.

Large Mountains, Large Classes
The class sizes at the University of Wyoming "really aren't bad, especially when your classes become more and more focused on your major," commented one senior. "I do have classes that go upward of about 200 students, but 90 to 95 percent of the classes have less than 50 kids in them." Don't let class sizes fool you, though; University of Wyoming has its share of caring and compassionate professors. "I have had so many professors that will really care about you as long as you show them you put in the time

and effort to show concern about their subject," one junior said. The TAs receive less-than-stellar marks and "have been known to blow off the students," according to one.

The students at the University of Wyoming take pride in their academic programs. Boasting fantastic engineering and research science departments, the U of Wyoming proves that it "can roll with the big kids." Wyoming's honors program is another strong point. High school students with at least a 3.8 GPA and a 1240 SAT score are selected to participate in the program and take five required classes, two in their freshman year and one each following year. One honors student commented on how diverse and interesting the class topics were: "The program offers several courses from chaos theory to English lit to AIDS/HIV awareness." Honors students are also given the option of living together in a special section of the dorms. The overall workload at the University of Wyoming varies. "The hardest majors by far are the engineering majors and classes in the honors program. Everything else is fairly manageable, but with frequent tests," commented one senior.

Renovated Dining Halls and "Mediocre Dorms"

Because the population of Laramie, Wyo., is so small, students often feel that it is hard to escape dorm life. Half of Laramie's 20,000 residents are Wyoming students, so when school gets out for summer break, the town "looks like an empty parking lot." Many students choose to live off campus, though the on-campus facilities are described as "very adequate." Wyoming's six dorm buildings are all located in the center of campus on a grassy field known as "Prexie's Pasture." Though each building has the same design and setup, some dorms are known by those who live in them. "The only bad thing about one of the dorms is that all the football and basketball players live there—it really begins to smell after a while," one freshman said. Though Prexie's Pasture itself is pretty, it is surrounded by "lots of cement buildings and sidewalks," one senior noted. "I sure wish the school would get rid of some of the cement and replace it with grass and trees."

Dining at the University of Wyoming is a college student's dream. The dining hall stays open all day until 11:30 p.m., and students can come and go as they please. The dining hall recently underwent renovations, and students are extremely happy about the variety of foods now available. "The renovations removed the 'one-size-fits-all' idea and made it more like a food court in a mall where you can walk up to the Mongolian grill or pasta bar and get whatever you want," boasted one senior. There are plenty of vegetarian options, and workers are extremely friendly. Off campus, students can charge food and coffee at participating restaurants to their Campus Expre$$ ID card. "The Expre$$ ID card allows us to grab a cup of coffee or late-night snack without having cash on hand," one sophomore said. "It really gives us an excuse to get out of the dining halls sometimes."

Saddle Up, UW!

The town of Laramie doesn't have much to offer students in the way of entertainment, though there are a few bars which upperclassmen frequent. Lovejoy's and Altitudes are two local favorites. A popular hot spot for freshmen and sophomores is Cowboy, a famous nightclub that hosts 18-and-older nights. However, the town and school are extremely strict about alcohol consumption. "Alcohol is very accessible but the administration and town do everything they can to stop [underage drinking]," commented one freshman. Wyoming offers plenty of non-alcoholic alternatives for students who opt not to drink. An organization called Friday Night Fever organizes movie nights, casino nights, and comedy nights where students can "have a really fun time without paying anything." For students who would rather hit the bottle on Fridays and Saturdays, on-campus parties are often hosted by one of the University's fraternities.

> "Our wildlife and nature are really a main focus at the University of Wyoming—not many college campuses can brag about their scenic locations."

However, the primary lure of Laramie isn't its cowboy-themed restaurants and on-campus parties. The scenic landscape is breathtaking, and the surrounding mountains inspire many students to seek out outdoor activities. Vedawoo (pronounced vee-da-voo) has the most popular rock climbing in the area, while Snowy Range and Happy Jack are known for their camping, hiking, and skiing. "[The mountains] require having a car to get to, but since most people here have cars on campus, it never seems to be a problem," said one senior. On weekends, many students take to the outdoors to appreciate the many gorgeous mountain views. "Our wildlife and nature are really a main focus at the University of Wyoming—not many college campuses can brag about their scenic locations," one freshman said.

The Student's Bodies

The students of the University of Wyoming take many things seriously: their sports teams, their school activities, and their fitness. One freshman said, "I was surprised to find so many people working out and participating in athletic activities." Several students noted that UW's Half-Acre Gym is a hot spot to hang out and one of the most noteworthy buildings on campus. "With so many athletes and nature-conscious people here, it's no wonder we have such a large population of fit people," said one sophomore. But students are definitely not image-conscious. When asked what the typical style of a UW student was, one junior responded, "A University of Wyoming sweatshirt and a pair of jeans," while another was quick to reply, "their pajamas." The relaxed atmosphere of the student body reflects their personalities. "I wouldn't want to be anywhere else—everything is just so easygoing here," one sophomore said.

Pride Runs Along the Plains of Laramie

At Wyoming, the professors care about the students, and the students care about the school. For many students, this sense of pride in their community is the best thing about UW. "First and foremost, I go to the University of Wyoming. I think that the fact that the entire state of Wyoming is behind it and all of its programs means a lot to the students here. Also, I think that the small community brings the students here closer together . . . and the people here are amazingly friendly," one freshman said. When asked if she would choose to attend the University of Wyoming again, she quickly responded, "Right now, I can't picture myself anywhere else. I love it here so much, it is like no place I have ever seen. I'm proud to tell my friends back home that I go to UW."—*Nate Puksta*

FYI

If you come to the University of Wyoming, you'd better bring a "warm coat and oxygen. At 7,500 feet above sea level, UW takes a toll on the lungs."

What is the typical weekend schedule? "Hiking, camping, climbing, studying, and drinking."

If I could change one thing at the University of Wyoming, "I'd make the shower heads higher in the bathrooms and lower the dorm-room temperature at least five degrees!"

Three things every student at the University of Wyoming should do before graduating are "enjoy the great area that surrounds Laramie (it is too unique and awesome to miss), go to a UW football game, and ski in the Snowy Mountain Range."

Canada

For the American student seeking the adventure of a foreign university but reluctant to travel halfway around the world, Canada may be the ideal location. A different culture, strong programs, and low tuition are just across the border. But there's more to Canada than mountain ranges, friendly people, and cold beer; before you pack your skis and buy a plane ticket, you should know what awaits you.

A Different Experience Across the Border

The greatest difference between Canadian and American universities is that in Canada there are no private colleges; all Canadian schools are government-funded. This has many implications, from overt funding problems to students' attitudes about the purpose of a university and a university education. As any administrator of a state school in the United States will tell you, legislators never seem to allocate as much funding as a school thinks it needs, and Canadian schools have suffered from budget cutbacks frequently just as American schools do. Many Canadian institutions have problems with their buildings and the quality of specialized equipment for science classes. Of course, this is not universally true, so it's important to find out which schools are strong in the subjects that interest you.

Although there are now more and more exceptions, Canadian universities often lack that elusive entity known as "school spirit" or "school unity." This can be explained in part by the size of most schools and the number of students who live at home or off campus. Unlike many Americans, most Canadians don't seem to be looking for the ideal "college experience." Instead, they are looking primarily for the right education for their future careers, and convenience is an important concern. By and large, Canadian students are unabashedly pre-professional. Students view a degree as a prerequisite for a job and attend university as a means to that end.

Admissions practices at Canadian schools also differ markedly from the American system. Acceptance is typically based more on students' cumulative high school grades than on other qualities, such as extracurricular activities and recommendations. However, standards still vary from school to school and from program to program.

To get a general overview of all Canadian colleges, it is helpful to know if the school is situated in a French-speaking province—it can make a big difference. Carleton University students benefit from having two provinces at their disposal—the bilingual Ontario and the primarily francophone Québec. With excellent academic programs in Journalism and Engineering as well as a prime location in the capital of Canada, the school abounds with opportunities for all types of students. Those seeking the bustle of city life may also want to check out McGill University, located in the cosmopolitan Montreal. In addition to offering an ideal urban location, the school boasts top-notch academics at an affordable tuition rate, even for foreigners. Canada's largest city is the playground for students at the reputable University of Toronto. The school relies on a residential college system to make the 40,000-plus student body a bit more manageable. Another school noted for its strong curriculum is Queen's University, located in the more rustic setting of Lake Ontario. As a smaller institution, Queen's provides a more tight-knit environment than many of its larger peer institutions. The University of British Columbia, which also offers an idyllic, outdoorsy campus, is known for its rigorous academics and diverse student body. For those seeking a less traditional academic program, the University of Waterloo offers a co-op system so students can pursue domestic or international internships. The picturesque McMaster University boasts innovative teaching, prestigious science departments, and a vibrant social life.

If you decide that a university in Canada is

right for you, there are certain procedures to follow and documents to obtain. Start early! Some schools may not be prepared to handle foreign students. For information, write or call the school and ask to be put in contact with their foreign students' office. Once accepted, you will need a visa and a student authorization. These must be obtained at a Canadian embassy or consulate in the United States, not in Canada. To get the documents, proof of U.S. citizenship is required (usually a passport or a birth certificate), a letter of acceptance to a Canadian institution, and proof of adequate funds to support yourself while in Canada. If you decide that it's for you, strap on a sense of adventure and get ready for a unique experience.— *Seung Lee and staff*

Carleton University

Address: Carleton, 315 Robertson Hall, 1125 Colonel By Drive, Ottawa, ON K1S 5B6 Canada
Phone: 613-520-3663
E-mail Address: NA
Web site URL: http://admissions.carleton.ca
Year Founded: 1942
Private or Public: public
Religious affiliation: NA
Location: urban
Regular Application Deadline: 10-Jan
Number of Applicants: NA
Percent Accepted: NA
Percent Accepted who enroll: NA
Number Entering: NA
Number of Transfers Accepted each Year: NA

Mean SAT: NA
Mean ACT: NA
Middle 50% SAT range: NA
Middle 50% ACT range: NA
Early admission program (EA/ ED/ NA): NA
ED or EA Acceptance Rate: NA
Full time Undergraduate enrollment: 16,740
Total enrollment: 23,839
Percent Male: 47%
Percent Female: 53%
Total Percent Minority: NA
Percent African-American: NA
Percent Asian/Pacific Islander: NA
Percent Hispanic: NA

Percent Native-American: NA
Percent in-state / out of state: NA
Percent in On-campus housing: NA
Percent in Fraternities: NA
Percent in Sororities: NA
Retention Rate: NA
Graduation Rate: NA
Percent Varsity or Club Athletes: NA
3 Most popular majors: NA
Financial Information: NA
Tuition and Fees: $6,167
In State Tuition and Fees (if different): $4,690
Cost for Room and Board: $7,091
Percent receiving Financial aid, first-year: NA

Located in southern Ottawa, Ontario, Carleton University combines the splendor of Canada's English-speaking capital city with the French-Canadian culture of nearby Québec. In addition to a treasure trove of national museums, government buildings, memorials, and celebrations of heritage, safe and scenic Ottawa offers trendy night spots, sidewalk cafés, hiking trails, the beautiful Rideau Canal that turns into the world's largest skating rink, and world-class research and development facilities in technology and medicine. Carleton students benefit from abundant opportunities for co-ops, internships, and real-world field experience as well as their school's challenging academic programs in a variety of areas.

Pre-Professionalism

Carleton is best known for its challenging professional programs in journalism, architecture, engineering, and public affairs. The school is one of only two universities in Canada to offer a degree in aerospace engineering, and the program has been growing quickly in recent years. Students within this major choose to focus on aerodynamics, propulsion, and vehicle performance; aerospace structures, systems, and vehicle design; or aerospace electronics and systems, and everyone must complete a final independent project before graduation. Many students take advantage of the option to take an aerospace engineering co-op internship instead of classes during their fourth year of enrollment, although this decision stretches the time required for graduation to five years. Carleton's program in criminology and criminal justice is also quite popular, and the proximity of the Parliamentary and other governmental buildings in Canada's capital city allows for a unique experience in field placement for internships. Criminology majors can choose to intern with attorneys, policy analysts, police, or victim counselors, to name a few of the options that present an exceptional opportunity to learn about the discipline from a front-line, hands-on perspective. The University's College of the Humanities offers a four-year, interdisciplinary Bachelor of Humanities degree focusing on the great Western canon. There students read a veritable "who's who" list of the most well-known historical works in Western civilization, including selections by Plato, Homer, Virgil, Shakespeare, Molière, and Kant. Although well-rounded, this major does not necessarily come with the best reputation, as one non-humanities student admitted to hearing that the program is "easy" and "basically for people who have less of a clue about what they want to do with themselves than people studying the arts." Carleton also boasts one of the "best journalism programs in Canada" that prepares students to become premiere journalists with an understanding of the responsibility of the press and that incorporates short apprenticeships as well as the possibility of specializing in the print or broadcasting media.

Carleton offers a program called ArtsOne for first-year students who have not yet chosen a major and who are undecided about which courses they should take when they arrive. This program offers several different sets, or "clusters," of four courses revolving around a particular theme contributes to the eventual awarding of a Bachelor of Arts degree. One hundred students enroll in each cluster and thus take all of the same classes, providing a smaller peer group within the larger university and a way to establish a home base of friends.

Professors at Carleton can be "eccentric," "enthusiastic," and "witty," and students generally find them to be easily accessible and very helpful. The most popular professors understandably tend to be the most dynamic and engaging: Professor Matthew Yeager of the Sociology and Anthropology Department, for example, asks his students to call him "Thunder" as a reflection of his unique, theatrical lecturing style (although as one student warned, "do not sit in the front rows, or even at the edge of any row, because he THUNDERS around the class!").

Students at Carleton are known for being welcoming and sociable, and according to one student, "it's easy to meet people because everyone at school is very friendly and willing to talk to people they don't know. Most people are in the same situation: they're in a new city where they don't know anyone and they are looking for friends to fill the loneliness of missing home." The school also prides itself on the carefully cultivated diversity within its student body and boasts a high rate of international enrollment with 147 different countries represented.

Tunnel Moles and Party Rats

Carleton offers underground, well-lit, heated tunnels that connect every building on campus and allow students to travel between their dorm rooms and classrooms in warmth and comfort as the outside temperatures drop to a January average of 13°F. The tunnels are appreciated by under- and upperclassmen alike, but as one student notes, this method of travel can become a way of life: "Some students living in the residence halls can go for months without actually seeing daylight! We call them tunnel-rats or tunnel-moles. But the tunnels do make going to school in one of the coldest cities (in this part of Canada) a lot easier." Luckily, the campus is fairly compact, and walking from one class to another takes only a few minutes.

"You don't mess with the R.A.s."

Housed in "institutional, modern, and artsy style buildings," undergraduates at Carleton can choose between two major options for dorm life: "Suite Style" residence halls such as Leeds and Prescott come equipped with various kitchen appliances in each room, while "Traditional Style" dorms do not permit in-room cooking and instead require students to buy a meal plan and eat in the Residence Dining Hall or in the variety of additional on-campus food outlets. The resident advisors in each dorm can be pretty strict about upholding the rules; as one of their undergraduate charges put it, "you don't mess with the R.A.s." Most students move out of the residence halls, or "res," after their first year and relocate to an apartment off campus. However, "there are a few lifers who love res too much to ever leave and go on to be Residence Advisors or just live in upper year residences for the duration of their schooling."

The drinking age in Ontario is 19, and students who have reached this birthday milestone are permitted to bring alcohol into their rooms within the residence halls but must refrain from carrying it outside or into shared dorm spaces such as stairways, lobbies, and elevators. Binge drinking exists as with any other college, but it is not especially prevalent; marijuana use, on the other hand, is "a big thing," and students "see people smoking weed pretty much every day."

The weeknight social scene revolves around Carleton's on-campus bar, Oliver's. Oliver's tends to be extremely popular on Tuesdays and particularly Thursdays, when "everyone from different social circles attends and intermingles" and provides an excellent opportunity for meeting new people. In contrast, weekends are "usually left for parties and other clubbing and bar experiences throughout the city." Because Carleton is located in the suburbs of Ottawa rather than in the middle of the city, "the social scene right around the school is a little lacking," but students can reach the downtown area very quickly thanks to the city's efficient transit system. Students also like to hang out in the food court in the University Centre, particularly in the student-run Rooster's Coffeehouse, which offers an assortment of coffees and teas as well as a seating area in front of a wide-screen TV. Underclassmen who have not yet reached Ontario's drinking age often journey into Hull Québec, about 15 to 20 minutes away by car, where the legal age of imbibing is only 18 and where "the bars are all skuzzy but promise a good time."

No Football? No Problem

Carleton does not have a varsity football team—it was disbanded in 1999—and instead, school pride rests with the successes of the "best men's basketball team in Canada," according to one enthusiastic student. Indeed, the Ravens seldom disappoint and have won many championships and titles, most recently the Canadian Interuniversity Sport (CIS) 2006 National Championship Tournament. The school's rivalry with the nearby University of Ottawa keeps the competition heated when the two basketball teams meet on the court. Carleton also hosts varsity fencing, golf, hockey, rugby, and water polo, among many other sports, as well as a variety of intramurals, including flag football for the pigskin enthusiasts who bemoan the loss of the varsity team. The Physical Recreation Centre, the largest facility of its kind in Canada, features two gymnasiums, a 50-meter indoor pool, a cardio center, a fitness testing lab, squash and tennis courts, a yoga room, and the brand-new Ice House (the skating and hockey rink), and serves the student body with training programs and services to accommodate everyone from professionals to beginner athletes.

As with many universities located in colder climates, the CU Ski and Snowboard Club is a popular organization on campus. Every fall, this organization generally sponsors a big hip hop show accompanied by ski and snowboard movie premieres that caters to "the hip hop community, the ski and snowboard community, and the drinking community (party people)." Carleton also offers over 150 student-run organizations, including the 60-year-old campus newspaper *The Charlatan*, the Sock 'n' Buskin Theatre Company, the community radio station CKCU-FM, and the Rideau River Residence Association (RRRA), which oversees students living on campus in the dorms. Generally, Carleton "frowns on frats and sororities," but they do exist off campus, and all Greek activities are carried out without University support.

Undergraduates at Carleton University generally exhibit enthusiasm and pride when discussing their alma mater and appreciate their school's efforts to keep them happy, from the underground tunnel system to the dedicated professors, from the friendly rivalry with the University of Ottawa to the co-op opportunities sponsored and arranged by the various academic departments. As one student summed up, "the atmosphere at Carleton is very positive. Everyone seems to really enjoy being at school and everyone is proud to be a student here."—*Kristin Knox*

FYI

If you come to Carleton, you'd better bring "a good supply of winter clothing."

What is the typical weekend schedule? "Attempt to do work on Saturday but instead choose to go to Ottawa and have fun. Then on Sunday, you really try to get work done."

If I could change one thing about Carleton, I'd "take away dry frosh week (no drinking events)."

Three things every student at Carleton should do before graduating are "climb all the stairs in Dunton Tower (if you don't, you're doomed to be jobless forever!), jump in the Alumni Park fountain during convocation, and hang out at Oliver's."

McGill University

Address: McGill, 845 Sherbrooke Street West, James Admin. Bldg, Room 205
Phone: 514-398-3910
E-mail Address: admissions@mcgill.ca
Web site URL: www.mmcgill.ca/applying
Year Founded: 1829
Private or Public: public
Religious affiliation: none
Location: urban
Regular Application Deadline: 15-Jan
Number of Applicants: 18,963
Percent Accepted: 54.6%
Percent Accepted who enroll: 45.2%
Number Entering: 5,362
Number of Transfers Accepted each Year: NA

Mean SAT: NA
Mean ACT: NA
Middle 50% SAT range: NA
Middle 50% ACT range: NA
Early admission program (EA/ ED/ NA): NA
ED or EA Acceptance Rate: NA
Full time Undergraduate enrollment: 17,972
Total enrollment: 30,333
Percent Male: 39.7%
Percent Female: 60.3%
Total Percent Minority: NA
Percent African-American: NA
Percent Asian/Pacific Islander: NA
Percent Hispanic: NA
Percent Native-American: NA
Percent Other: NA
Percent in-state / out of state: NA

Percent from Public HS: NA
Retention Rate: NA
Graduation Rate: NA
Percent in On-campus housing: 17%
Percent affiliated with Greek system: NA
Percent Varsity or Club Athletes: NA
Number of official organized extracurricular organizations: NA
3 Most popular majors: NA
Student/Faculty ratio: 16:01
Tuition and Fees: $13,088.00
In State Tuition and Fees (if different): $2,786.00
Cost for Room and Board: $7,694.00
Percent receiving Financial aid, first-year: NA

McGill University is "an old campus with new stuff being built and constant improvements being made, a beautiful campus in the middle of a downtown metropolis." Indeed, located in the heart of Montreal, McGill University is one of the most desirable university destinations for Americans as well as Canadians. It offers the best of both worlds: a safe college campus and a vibrant downtown just steps away. Students of McGill discover every corner of the city and make it their home, despite the constant academic demands and harsh winter weather. With a great combination of the collegiate and urban flavors, McGill has something to offer that few universities in Canada or the United States can match.

A Canadian Approach

Although McGill may not be as familiar to American students as Harvard or Yale, McGill is in fact one of the most elite universities in Canada. It attracts some of the best students from across Canada and beyond. McGill's academic structure is reminiscent of the programs of many graduate schools in the United States. When applying, students are required to choose an area of concentration and apply to the appropriate department, or "faculty." Each student needs 120 credits to graduate, but requirements vary within the departments. The first and second years consist mostly of core classes, which some students report are "pretty crappy to get through." The core classes are often bigger lectures, where getting to know the professor depends on the student's initiative. Once past the core requirements, however, students report that the courses are both entertaining and challenging. One student raved about his Human Anatomy class, where students perform hands-on study of cadavers: "We get to work with dead bodies, and no other university gets to do that!" Class size also tends to decrease, allowing for more contact with professors, although close contact with professors is generally "limited unless you want to hunt them down at office hours." Students are allowed to take some classes outside of their faculties, though this number is restricted.

Each faculty has its own personality. The Faculty of Arts was described by one student as "super easy," whereas the faculties of science, management, and law are considered the most challenging, both for the large number of work requirements and for the tough grading. One student commented that they felt particularly isolated in the Faculty of Management because of its location off the main campus. In general, the faculty system provides the opportunity for students to study their passions with greater specificity than is available in the American university system. The academic structure at McGill also minimizes the need to take subjects one does not enjoy. Indeed, for one literature major, "avoiding math has been a wonderful relief!"

Living in the City

McGill is a gem in the city, with green fields and trees a five-minute walk away from both St. Catharine and St. Laurent streets, right in the heart of Montreal's nightlife scene. These streets house an enormous array of nightclubs, bars, fantastic restaurants, and great shopping, making them the most popular destinations of the city. With such attractions so proximate, living on or near campus in first-year housing or in the housing offered to older students is an amazing opportunity. The campus grounds are considered very safe, and everything in Montreal is within walking distance and accessible through subway and bus.

On-campus housing is only guaranteed for first-year students at McGill. In the following years, most students live in off-campus housing or commute from home. The provided housing is located directly in the center of campus and each dorm is affectionately referred to as a "rez." Freshman year in the "rezes" is considered an amazing opportunity and an "awesome time." Each "rez" has a dorm head who lives in the building, and each floor has a floor fellow who is there more to be an aid to students than to get in their way. As far as parties and drinking on campus are concerned, the administration is described as pretty relaxed, and the floor fellows "pretty much leave you alone." This has much to do with the difference in legal drinking age, which is 18 in Québec. Non-smoking floors are available for those who have a preference, but smoking itself is not widespread and "quite avoidable."

The food at most dining halls is considered less than desirable. First years are expected to buy a "rez" food plan, which allows for three meals a day. Of all the residencies, the "new rez" just got outfitted with a new meal plan, rumored to now be the best on campus. However, once past the first year most students opt out of the meal plan, as one student observed that "it costs a lot for mediocre food, so my friends and I just buy our own groceries."

What to Do . . .

Beyond avoiding trouble with RAs, one of the greatest perks of McGill is the drinking age of 18. This allows a complete freedom when it comes to going out and partying, and it certainly makes drinking a big part of the social scene. Indeed, frats and sports teams, though they exist, find no prestige within the social scene. Hockey and football are the most popular sports, drawing the most attention and fan support from the student body. Despite this, there is an enormous range of activities, clubs, teams and organizations available to students. One inner-tube water polo player exclaims, "Even things you've never heard of you could probably do!" Despite the huge variety of extracurricular activities, however, they are not as popular among McGill students as at other schools. This is mostly because of the makeup of the student body, as more than 40 percent hails from greater Montreal and already enjoys a familiarity with the city and with some fellow students as well. As follows, the social scene is based on smaller groups of friends, acquired through the smaller communities of the faculties and "rezes," or the teams and organizations with which students actively choose to get involved. Though it is by no means difficult to meet people because of all the options available, it may be easy to become overwhelmed.

> "[Frosh week] is devoted to getting hammered and getting to know the school, but it's pretty much about getting hammered."

Annual events on campus are organized both within the faculties and as campus-wide functions, providing many chances to get to know people and have a good time. The faculties prove to be smaller communities and host annual events such as a carnival week in February, which offers "drinking games and organized events." The Open Air Pub is an event run by students and held in both September and April on a sectioned-off part of campus. Offering beer and games, it creates a great atmosphere to socialize and hang out. Last but not least, there is also the hugely popular "frosh week," the first week of freshman year, which is "devoted to getting hammered and getting to know the school, but it's pretty much about getting hammered." If you are looking for a social scene not confined to drinking, McGill certainly has plenty to offer. However, being directly in the city and having access to a great young nightlife, any incoming student should expect to be confronted with it.

The nightlife consists of parties on campus and going out in the city. Thursday nights are the big nights on campus, as few people have class on Friday. Friday and Saturday nights students go out more in the city, visiting bars and clubs with friends. The restaurants in Montreal are just as remarkable, running the gamut from high-end cuisine to quick joints open all night. One student raved about the Lebanese stands, which offer shish taouk, an after-hours favorite consisting of hummus, chicken and garlic sauce wrapped in a warm pita. Another dish worth sampling is poutine. Poutine is famous (and fattening) Québecois fare: French fries smothered with cheese curds and gravy. It may sound odd at first, but you can't experience Montreal without it!

With all of these amazing activities available, it seems difficult to think of anything that could hold students back . . . aside from the weather, that is. In Montreal, the winters get down to an average of 13 degrees Fahrenheit (or about minus-10 degrees Celsius), and the wind chill makes it feel even colder. Although prospective students should certainly be prepared for the cold, the academics and the bustling urban campus will keep most minds off of the weather year-round.—*Annemarie von der Goltz*

FYI

If you come to McGill, you'd better bring "a love of culture and city life."

What's the typical weekend schedule? "For some, it usually consists of getting some work done during the day, and chilling with some friends over good microbrewery beer (Unibroue, anyone?); for others, weekends are about partying it up."

If I could change one thing about McGill, "I'd get rid of the red-tape bureaucracy. But then again, I'm convinced that it's like that at any of the large, research-based institutions."

Three things every student should do before graduating are "watch the sunset from Mount Royal; check out Macdonald campus (it's beautiful—it houses our school of agriculture); and at least attempt to engage in a conversation en francais."

McMaster University

Address: McMaster, Gilmour Hall Room 108, 1280 Main St. W., Hamilton, Ontario L8S 4L8 Canada
Phone: 905-525-4600
E-mail Address: macadmit@mcmaster.ca
Web site URL: www.mcmaster.ca/
Year Founded: 1887
Private or Public: public
Religious affiliation: none
Location: suburban
Regular Application Deadline: 10-Feb
Number of Applicants: NA
Percent Accepted: NA
Percent Accepted who enroll: NA
Number Entering: NA
Number of Transfers Accepted each Year: NA

Mean SAT: NA
Mean ACT: NA
Middle 50% SAT range: NA
Middle 50% ACT range: NA
Early admission program (EA/ ED/ NA): NA
ED or EA Acceptance Rate: NA
Full time Undergraduate enrollment: NA
Total enrollment: NA
Percent Male: NA
Percent Female: NA
Total Percent Minority: NA
Percent African-American: NA
Percent Asian/Pacific Islander: NA
Percent Hispanic: NA
Percent Native-American: NA
Percent Other: NA

Percent in-state / out of state: NA
Percent from Public HS: NA
Retention Rate: NA
Graduation Rate: NA
Percent in On-campus housing: NA
Percent affiliated with Greek system: NA
Percent Varsity or Club Athletes: NA
Number of official organized extracurricular organizations: NA
3 Most popular majors: NA
Student/Faculty ratio: NA
Tuition and Fees: $15,156
Cost for Room and Board: $2,750.00
Percent receiving Financial aid, first-year: NA

Sprawling over three hundred green acres and studded with ivy-covered Gothic buildings, McMaster is regarded as one of the top universities in Canada. The University is named after Senator William McMaster, who, in 1887, bequeathed a large sum of money to found a "Christian school of learning." Today, the affectionately-named "Mac" is home to around 14,000 students, and stands as an undisputed center for ground-breaking research and innovation.

Bring on the Innovation!

If there is one thing that students agree on, it's the breathtaking variety of programs that McMaster offers, with majors ranging from anthropology and women's studies, to software engineering and Italian. Both basic three-year programs, as well as four-year "Honors Programs" are available. The Honors Programs usually require a higher GPA than their three-year counterparts, as well as an application.

McMaster is especially well-known for their health sciences, business, natural sciences and engineering departments. Not surprisingly, these are also some of the most difficult programs. "Math is ridiculously hard," said one fourth-year behavioral science major. "Sometimes the introductory classes become very difficult because they are designed to weed out students." But most science majors agree that it's worth it. Kinesiology, the study of human bodily movement, is especially acclaimed among undergrads.

Even if you're not into the hard-core sciences, McMaster still offers a great range of humanities courses. The limited-enrollment Art & Sciences program is touted by current students as a great way to get a broad-based, liberal arts education. "The Art & Sciences program offers a carefully constructed program drawing from both the sciences and humanities," explained one student. Approximately 60 students enroll in this program each year, and its small class sizes means that the students get plenty of attention from their professors.

Outside of the Art & Science program, McMaster's classes tend to be quite large, especially freshman year. "First year, three hundred in a lecture, easily," said one fourth-year. "But when you get into upper-level classes, they become more and more specialized. One of my current classes has 10 students." Another student agreed, advising newcomers not to be intimidated by larger lectures. "First year is full of lectures, but we have tutorials once a week with a TA. One of my favorite classes was Intro to Psych, which is a huge, impersonal class in most colleges. At Mac, we had the professor on video lecture, and when it's done, the TA's there to answer questions for us. It was really interactive and cool." Indeed, for a large research university, students agreed that professors and TAs were readily available and easy to approach, often giving McMaster the feeling of a small liberal arts college.

> "What defines McMaster really is the diversity of its students . . . [And we're] always on the cutting edge of teaching methods."

One of the more peculiar things about a McMaster education is its grading scale. Classes at McMaster grade on a 0-to-12 scale, 0 being fail, 1 being pass, and 12 being an "A+." Students are required to have an average of 7 (or a "B" in most colleges) in order to move up to the next level. In general, students seem to enjoy this method of grading, because it is more specific than simple letter grades. However, some lament that this results in a stricter curve, the disadvantages of which are especially felt within the science sectors.

McMaster is renowned, above all, for its innovative teaching. One of the most interesting facets is the "Inquiry" program, in which students can form an inquiry problem and explore their chosen problem with the help of an instructor, called a "facilitator." The "Inquiry" program has been expanded to most disciplines at McMaster. While inventive, there are downsides. One student complained that "Inquiry" projects are more like "giant independent study projects that most students put on the backburner until a few weeks before they're due." Others disagreed: "My two to three years of Inquiry have taught me an entirely different skill set compared to my traditional lecture based courses," said one third-year health student. "It really depends on what kind of facilitator you have," explained another.

Just Like John Belushi

The stress of a McMaster education shakes off pretty quickly during the weekends. After all, this is the school that graduated Ivan Reitman, one of the producers of *National Lampoon's Animal House*. In fact, a popular campus tale is that Reitman actually based some of the wild antics in the movie on actual events that occurred on the McMaster campus. Said one science student, "The Engs (engineers) work hard, but they party pretty hard too!" Indeed, that seems to be the social attitude of this friendly college.

The "weekend" starts on Thursday night, even though most students have class on Friday. A big component of the McMaster social life is the lack of Greek societies, which are prohibited under college rules. Thursday nights usually consist of clubbing or bar-hopping. Most students head over to either Quarters, a popular all-ages-allowed on-campus bar and club, or Hess Village in Hamilton, home to places like Elixir and Funky Munky. Those who are not yet 18 will frequent "keggers," even though kegs are technically not allowed in dormitories. Off-campus house parties are also popular. Friday is described by most students as "off day," but once Saturday rolls around, the McMaster students are back in true collegiate-partying form.

Since the legal drinking age is 19 in Ontario, drinking is a popular activity on campus. The students agree that the administration is very reasonable about the alcohol policy. Alcohol is allowed in dorm rooms, provided that the occupants are not under nineteen and the alcohol doesn't come in the form of glass bottles or kegs. At Quarters, the alcohol policy is said to be strictly enforced. Beyond alcohol, pot is the drug of choice for students, but very few actually partake in the so-called "heavier" drugs.

Not all of the partying needs to involve alcohol, though. The McMaster Student Union holds a Charity Ball every single year, which draws hundreds of students in formal attire. Nearby downtown Hamilton is also home to great live music venues, malls, and movie theaters. In addition to all of this, annual faculty formals, Homecoming, and Frost Week (the first week back after Winter Break) are yearly events conducive to an exciting campus life. Incoming freshmen can expect to get their first taste of the McMaster social scene at Welcome Week (also known as Frosh Week), which is, according to one student, "just really one whole month of partying. I don't think there was one night my entire freshman year in which I didn't have fun." One notable Frosh Week tradition is the "Pajama Parade." The new first-years don their best sleepwear and walk five or six blocks in broad daylight. Upperclassmen take their lawn chairs out and sit right at the street, greeting them and shaking their hands as they go past. Some upperclassmen get a little more affectionate, bestowing kisses on the new members of Mac.

Marauding Through Student Life

McMaster offers a host of extracurricular activities for its students. Recent success in sports has made athletic activities very popular at Mac. "The whole college comes out for the football games!" one student enthused. "It seems like *everybody* knows somebody on the team." Beyond football, basketball, volleyball, and men's rugby are all highly-regarded varsity teams. In addition to varsity, students can also participate in a range of intramural sports like water polo. "Ultimate Frisbee is *huge* here," a third-year political science major said. However, be prepared for a bit of dedication. "Athletics can be a little cultish at Mac," one student admitted. "Be aware that if you're going out on your own, and you run into your team, they might very well ostracize you."

If sports are not your thing, though, there are a host of other extracurricular activities in which to participate. A glance down the sprawling list of clubs yields the Chinese Commerce Association, the Jane Austen Society, the Trampoline and Power Tumbling Club, the Ismaili Student Association, and Students for Literacy. The major student-run organization is the McMaster Student Union (MSU), which does everything from running the design & copy center to publishing *The Silhouette*, McMaster's daily newspaper. However, the MSU's biggest job is to regulate all campus clubs. "The MSU is really meant to be the connection between the students and the McMaster administration," said one student. And to that extent, "They get the job done."

One of the most distinguishing features of McMaster is the diversity. "Mac is very culturally diverse," said one second-year. "It was a culture shock coming from a mostly white high school. Diversity is really promoted during Welcome Week in September. Mac does a good job of accepting everyone." Indeed, one of the biggest events on campus is Pangaea, a multicultural performance housed in a pavilion in which the campus groups get to showcase the food, beverage, history and traditions of their cultures.

Home, Home in Westdale

McMaster students who apply for residence choose from apartment-style or traditional-style dorms (in the latter, you can choose among a single, double, or triple). Mac has one female-only residence, and students can opt for substance-free floors or international-themed residences. Brandon Hall has a reputation for being the party dorm, but that is as far as the stereotypes go. "It really depends on who gets assigned to which dorm," one student explained.

About 3,000 undergraduate students live on campus every year, and 80 percent of dorm space is reserved for freshmen. Students often gush about their "residence." "It's a great experience. I lived on a French floor, and I met most of my friends through residence."

Freshman year, rooms are randomly assigned. McMaster's two apartment-style residences halls often go to the upperclassmen, international students, or students with medical issues. Priority for upperclassmen housing is given to those who make the Dean's Honor List (average of 9.5 or above) and students who show exemplary leadership in extracurricular activities. "However, even if you get DHL, you may not get your first pick of residence—for most, their first choice is Mary E. Keyes, the newest suite-style residence at McMaster."

At McMaster, Community Advisors (CAs) are assigned to each dorm. One of their biggest responsibilities is holding the "Connections" program, in which new students are able to air grievances, agree on overnight guest policies, and generally communicate with their roommates. How large a role a CA has on a first-year's life varies. "Are there residential advisors?" one student asked half-jokingly during his interview. "Probably. But if we did [have one], I didn't have much contact with her." A second-year commerce major, on the other hand, cited a "very good experiences with my CA. We are still friends and talk all the time."

Even though many students enjoy their time in residence, many others choose to live off-campus. Rents around campus are pretty inexpensive, and to some, it seems like a natural transition to share a house with several other classmates after their first year. All full-time students receive an eight-month bus pass free, which makes getting around a whole lot easier. A large number of students also commute from nearby Toronto and London.

But regardless of whether you live on campus or off, dining is an important aspect of campus life. McMaster offers five meals plans for students, and they operate on a debit-card (that is, à la carte) system. Students on a meal plan can use their plans in any of sixteen locations, including Commons Marketplace, which offers a host of healthy-food options, and the East Meets West Bistro in the Mary E. Keyes Residence. Few individuals, if any, complain about the quality of food at this university. McMaster features the only completely vegetarian college cafeteria in Canada, the Bridges Café. "Food at McMaster is perhaps one of the best among Canadian universities," boasted one student.

If there is one area to complain about, however, it is perhaps the price of food on campus. Students who live in campus dorms are required to subscribe to a minimum meal plan. Those who live off can choose from two meal plans. "Sometimes, however, it's just easier and cheaper to bring a sandwich from home," said a commuting student.

A Little Bit of Green

Despite the fact that McMaster is commonly listed as a part of Hamilton, Ontario, students are more likely to identify with upper-class Westdale, the village in which McMaster is located. "Nobody says it, but Westdale really is a university town," explained one McMaster student. "Hamilton? There are some people who have spent four years here but have never gone into downtown Hamilton." Other students agreed, one third-year stating that, "Hamilton's gotten a bad rap over the years, so I was actually a little bit apprehensive about coming to McMaster. But McMaster is pretty isolated—it's easy for it to become your entire life." Some argue that Hamilton has its charms, however. Surely it supplies McMaster with plenty of things to do in the form of bars, pubs, clubs and music venues. "Everybody should get out of Westdale at least once and hang out in downtown Hamilton. No, you will not get shot or robbed, and you'll find very interesting places to hang out or eat at," advised one student.

Of course, some will need that little bit of encouragement to leave campus. Current students rave about McMaster's grounds. "McMaster's campus is really beautiful, with lots of greenery and pathways, a rock garden, and picnic tables." It also doesn't hurt that it's surrounded by a conservation area known as Coote's Paradise. McMaster's pedestrian-friendly atmosphere extends even well into the night, since safety does not rate as a concern for students living on campus and in Westdale.

There is one complaint about McMaster's grounds, though. "Parking is a disaster!" exclaimed one commuter. Agreed another,

"My advice to first-years—definitely don't bring a car if you're living on campus."—*Janet Xu*

FYI

If you come to McMaster, you'd better bring "a healthy liver! You're going to be working it to death."

What's the typical weekend schedule? "Going to clubs or bars on Thursdays, just hanging out with friends on Fridays, then going out again Saturday night. On Sundays, you wake up, hit yourself on the head, and then go straight to work."

If I could change one thing about McMaster, I'd change "the corporate atmosphere. They're cutting back on the humanities programs because they don't make enough money, which I don't think is fair."

Three things every student at McMaster should do before graduating are "live in residence, go to Quarters, and get involved in a sport."

Queen's University

Address: Queen's University, 99 University Avenue, Kingston, Ontario K7L 3N6 Canada	**Mean ACT:** NA	**Percent from Public HS:** NA
	Middle 50% SAT range: NA	**Retention Rate:** NA
	Middle 50% ACT range: NA	**Graduation Rate:** NA
Phone: 613-533-2000	**Early admission program (EA/ ED/ NA):** NA	**Percent in On-campus housing:** NA
E-mail Address: NA	**ED or EA Acceptance Rate:** NA	**Percent affiliated with Greek system:** NA
Web site URL: www.queensu.ca	**Full time Undergraduate enrollment:** 14,130	**Percent Varsity or Club Athletes:** NA
Year Founded: 1841	**Total enrollment:** NA	
Private or Public: public	**Percent Male:** NA	**Number of official organized extracurricular organizations:** NA
Religious affiliation: none	**Percent Female:** NA	
Location: urban	**Total Percent Minority:** NA	
Regular Application Deadline: 16-Feb	**Percent African-American:** NA	**3 Most popular majors:** NA
Number of Applicants: NA		**Student/Faculty ratio:** NA
Percent Accepted: NA	**Percent Asian/Pacific Islander:** NA	**Tuition and Fees:** $3,551.00
Percent Accepted who enroll: NA	**Percent Hispanic:** NA	
Number Entering: NA	**Percent Native-American:** NA	**Cost for Room and Board:** $7,600.00
Number of Transfers Accepted each Year: NA	**Percent Other:** NA	
Mean SAT: NA	**Percent in-state / out of state:** NA	**Percent receiving Financial aid, first-year:** NA

Situated on the rustic northwestern shores of Lake Ontario, Queen's University is known for its beautiful location as well as its solid reputation for providing students with an unparalleled undergraduate experience. One of Canada's smaller institutions with approximately 14,000 undergrads, Queen's University has the atmosphere of an Ivy League institution without the Ivy League costs.

Slackers Need Not Apply

Academic requirements at Queen's are quite stringent. "Lazy students will not succeed academically at Queens," one undergraduate explained. The "Freshman 15" at Queens does not refer to weight gain, but to the expected grade deflation of 15 percent from one's high school GPA. However, students report that those who are not aiming for an honors B.S. degree tend to have an easier time with their workloads. Getting into desired classes is also generally not a problem, provided one registers early enough.

Queen's uses a grading system unlike the system in the United States. In most Canadian schools, including Queen's, 90 to 100 percent is an A+, 80 to 89 percent is an A, 65 to 79 percent is a B, 55 to 64 percent is a C, and, as a senior at Queen's reported, "if you get any grade below a 55 percent, you are pretty much boned."

With such distinguished graduates as John Roth, the current CEO of networking giant Nortel, the commerce, or business program at Queen's is considered one of the best in Canada. The program's rigorous entry requirements also mark it as one of the most competitive. Queen's also offers programs in nursing, engineering, and physical education.

Despite its relatively small overall student population, freshman classes tend to be quite large, often numbering in the hundreds. Students, however, report that the student-to-teacher ratio falls dramatically after the first year as students move beyond the necessary prerequisites. Upper-level courses and seminars tend to have no more than 20 to 30 students.

Students are generally happy with their professors, and some even go so far as to describe their professors as "cool." "My Classics 101 professor gave me a 10 percent bonus on a midterm because I could think up five references to Greek or Roman civilization from 'The Simpsons,' " one student said.

Queen's University offers a wide range of study-abroad opportunities. These programs are strongly encouraged, and most students participate in at least one of such programs in their four years at Queen's. Study abroad usually lasts a semester or a year. However, students also have the option of taking single classes for two to three weeks in different countries. The university even owns a castle in England, which students are encouraged to visit.

Drink to the Queen (or Don't)

Although Kingston, Ontario, is widely perceived as an affluent retirement community, there exists a vibrant social life both on and off campus. Alcohol is a big part of the social environment, but non-drinkers do not feel isolated. "There is always something to do for everyone," one student said. Even though the drinking age in Ontario is 19, freshmen typically take their parties off campus, as they are not permitted to bring beer bottles or kegs into the residences.

Queen's is proud of the fact that it does not have fraternities or sororities. Instead, most students enjoy bar hopping and clubbing on weekends at local hotspots including The Alehouse, Stages, and the campus bar, Queen's Pub. Smidgie's is the most popular bar for fourth-year students. Drug use among students is not conspicuous, nor is it seen by students as a major issue on campus.

However, the administration *is* strict in its alcohol policies. For example, it does not tolerate alcohol at university events unless it is in a licensed, fenced-off area. Furthermore, getting caught with a fake ID will get you banned from campus pubs for the rest of your academic career.

Besides the bars and clubs, campus events are generally well attended. Movie nights, concerts, dances, and boat cruises are some of the most popular events. The student center or the JDUC (John Deutche University Center) is well used by many different student organizations—including the central student governing council, the Alma Mater Society.

Beautiful People Abound

"There are many attractive guys and girls around," one undergraduate said. "There's always someone pleasant to adore." That said, some students complained that the student population is too homogeneous, with the majority of the student population hailing from white, upper-middle-class backgrounds. As one student explained, "We have a stereotype of the Gap-wearing, khaki-donning preppie school." Geographically, the majority of the students hail from various metropolitan areas of Ontario such as Toronto and Ottawa. Nevertheless, there is a sizeable international student population from countries such as Barbados, Jamaica, Trinidad, New Guinea, Saudi Arabia, China, and India. Meeting people at Queen's is not a concern. "It's really easy," one junior said. "People here are really friendly." However, that being said, another sophomore complained, "The school could use some more diversity."

Crammed Like Sardines in a Tin Can

Some students report being disappointed with the living arrangements. "I got an economy double that crammed two beds, two desks, and two metal hutches into a single-sized room my freshman year," one student lamented. "It was more than a little cramped." Despite the disappointing quality of the living arrangements, many students find that the residence system is amenable to a great social life. "I've met my closest friends through the residence system."

Each residence has "Floor Seniors" who are typically second-year students, as well as "Floor Dons," who are fourth-year students. The Floor Seniors tend to be strict, enforcing quiet hours during the weekdays, as well as guest and alcohol policies. "They just have bugs up their butts for the most part," one freshman complained.

Some of the dorms reportedly have different personalities. "For example, the McNeil girls are nuns, the Vic Hall kids party all the time, and the Leonard Hall boys are all rowdy and obnoxious," one undergraduate described. After first year, most students move out of the residence system into houses with four to six friends. There are many student houses in the area, as well as in an area affectionately known as the "Student Ghetto." Rent is reasonable, generally amounting to about $450 per month, and most student houses are within five minutes of campus.

The campus itself is fairly compact, only taking up three to four square blocks. The buildings tend to be a mix of modern and old, with the older buildings being based around designs from the University of Edinburgh. "The buildings are modern inside, yet historical on the outside—so it creates a nice contrast," one student said. The Queen's Learning Commons, which opened in 2005, unites the library with other student academic services such as the Writing Centre and ITS support.

> "If I could choose my university all over again, I would not even waste my time considering another institution— it would be Queen's all the way!"

As a result of being located in quiet Kingston, students reported feeling very safe at Queen's. Nevertheless, there exist various safety measures, such as the nighttime escort service, that bolster campus safety.

As for dining on campus, students considered the plan to be well-organized and flexible, though many complain that the offerings tend to be repetitive and bland. "The food is edible, but it's lower than prison quality," one hungry undergrad explained. There are vegetarian options available at all times, but it is "nothing spectacular." "I'm getting very sick of eating pasta all the time." Luckily, dinner times tend to be social hours, and students reported feeling very comfortable just sitting down with anyone and striking up a conversation. Of course, much finer dining options can be found off campus at one of Kingston's numerous upscale restaurants.

Tams and Gaels

Virtually all students tend to engage in a least one extracurricular activity during their academic career at Queen's. From debating to sports to writing for publications, Queen's has it all. "It depends on your personality," one undergraduate said. "If you like arguing, you hit the debate team. If you're athletic, you get in with the sports teams."

Tensions regarding sexuality and gender is not as big a problem at Queen's University as it is in other colleges. Queen's boasts a Queerientation Week, groups and publications for transgendered and gay students, women-friendly spaces, and a gender neutral bathroom that many students use.

The Golden Gaels, Queen's popular football team, draws in large student crowds to all their football games. "There is tons of school spirit with lots of traditions, including many songs and chants," one junior said. Homecoming is an especially festive occasion, as is the big annual game, which is usually against archrival McGill University. For those not skilled enough to hit the varsity ranks, there are numerous on-campus athletic facilities to satisfy students' desires to remain fit and active throughout college. Students can also join low-cost recreational clubs to learn a whole spectrum of sports, from break dancing to scuba diving. Scuba, in particular, benefits from Queen's proximity to the freshwaters of Lake Ontario.

Scottish traditions run deep at Queen's. All students are given Scottish berets called Tams and are taught how to sing the school song, the "Oil Thigh." Furthermore, Queen's is also known as the Canadian university with the best orientation week. "Other places have a paltry two or three days," an undergraduate explained. "We have a full week!"

All the different faculties also have their own traditions. The engineers, for example, are known to dye themselves purple and slam their leather jackets on the ground at certain times. Every year, the engineering freshmen have to climb a 24-foot-high greased pole and grab a hat off the top of it. "We have a lot of special and fun traditions around here," one student said. "It's what makes Queen's great!"

With its proud Scottish traditions, talented student body, and ideal location, it is no wonder that Queen's students are proud to announce, "I go to Queen's!"—*Christine Geiser*

FYI
If you come to Queen's University, you'd better bring "a lot of spirit and enthusiasm."
What is the typical weekend schedule? "Attending a Golden Gael's football game wearing your Queen's Coveralls and Tams, going to a post-game party at Stages or The Alehouse, going down to the lake and reading a book under a tree, and going out to dinner at a restaurant with friends."
If I could change one thing about Queen's I would "change the sport's team name—Golden Gael's just sounds sissy!"
Three things every student should do before graduating are "watch a homecoming football game, join the Queen's band, and jump into the lake wearing your Queen's coveralls."

University of British Columbia

Address: University of BC, 1200–1874 East Mall, Vancouver, BC V6T 1Z1 Canada
Phone: 604-822-9888
E-mail Address: international.reception@ubc.ca
Web site URL: www.welcome.ubc.ca
Year Founded: 1908
Private or Public: public
Religious affiliation: none
Location: urban
Regular Application Deadline: 1-Mar
Number of Applicants: 17,677
Percent Accepted: 58%
Percent Accepted who enroll: 48%
Number Entering: 4,937
Number of Transfers Accepted each Year: 889
Mean SAT: NA
Mean ACT: NA
Middle 50% SAT range: NA

Middle 50% ACT range: NA
Early admission program (EA/ ED/ NA): NA
ED or EA Acceptance Rate: NA
Full time Undergraduate enrollment: 19,934
Total enrollment: 43,301
Percent Male: 46%
Percent Female: 54%
Total Percent Minority: NA
Percent African-American: NA
Percent Asian/Pacific Islander: NA
Percent Hispanic: NA
Percent Native-American: NA
Percent Other: NA
Percent in-state / out of state: NA
Percent from Public HS: NA
Retention Rate: 92%
Graduation Rate: 78%
Percent in On-campus housing: 20%
Percent affiliated with Greek system: NA

Percent Varsity or Club Athletes: NA
Number of official organized extracurricular organizations: 250
3 Most popular majors: Psychology, Biology, Computer science
Student/Faculty ratio: 15:01
Tuition and Fees: CA$623.28 per credit (most programs) (1st year credit load: 30–35 credits) Fees CA$650–750 Books CA$1,200–1,400
In State Tuition and Fees (if different): Canadian citizens & permanent residents of Canada Tuition: CA$139.13 per credit (most programs) Fees CA$650–750 Books CA$1,200–1,400
Cost for Room and Board: CA$9,000

Students at the University of British Columbia will strongly urge you not to overlook the benefits of spending four years in a foreign country—even if it's only across the border in Canada. UBC's blend of stunning natural surroundings, thriving city life, and comprehensive academic offerings gives the Thunderbirds good reason to be proud of their global school.

Studying: Canadian Style

UBC is divided into several schools or faculties within which students may choose their majors. Some of the most popular are the Faculty of Arts, which encompasses much of the university's liberal arts programs, and the Faculty of Applied Sciences, which houses the Engineering departments and the School of Nursing. Other options include the Faculty of Forestry, the School of Human Kinetics, and the School of Journalism. "UBC really requires more of you than many other Canadian universities," one sophomore said. And although the general requirements are considered to be a nuisance, most students recognize the value of taking these core classes. In the Faculty of Arts, students must enroll in English, Literature, Science, and Language courses, although some of the requirements may be fulfilled by scores on standardized tests.

It may not be surprising that nearly all of the introductory-level courses at UBC consist of large lectures averaging 200 students a class, but students take comfort in the knowledge that these classes also feature small 15-person weekly discussion groups to go over the material. In addition, upper-level courses go down in size, and after one's first year, most students can find themselves in classes of 50 or fewer people. Although students lamented that, "it's easy with such big classes to get overlooked," professors generally make themselves very available through email and office hours. For freshmen looking for a gentler transition to the large university scene, UBC offers the Coordinated Arts Program, in which 100 first years have three of their five classes with the same group of people. Signing up for classes can pose a problem, particularly for first and second years, who get last pick, but one student reassuringly said that "if you really want to take a course, just go to the professor and they'll sign you up." For all years, the order of course signups is determined by grade point average.

The sciences, particularly engineering, are generally considered to be more difficult, and students described them as requiring more of a continuous workload than liberal arts courses. Within the arts departments, the International Relations major has a competitive application process. Highly-recommended courses include History 125, a comprehensive general history class starting in 1800, and Economics 101 and 102, taught by Robert Gateman, who writes his own textbook. Political Science professor Bruce Baum also gets high marks for "dressing up as Marx" during a lecture. Overall, UBC's position as a highly-regarded research community makes its students proud—one sophomore observed that the serious discoveries that her professors are making "really trickle down to the undergraduates they teach, and we benefit from their work."

No Need for a Fake ID
In this large of a university, which has an undergraduate population of 35,000, making friends as a first year might seem like an overwhelming task. However, students meet the majority of their friends in their residence halls through a variety of residence-sponsored activities and simple proximity to a large number of varied and interesting personalities hailing from all over the globe. Events hosted in the dorms include Totem Park's annual "Meat Market," where scantily-clad first years are the norm, and an assortment of theme parties like "Graffiti Night," which features a black light and the opportunity to use highlighters to create fluorescent works of arts on other students' shirts.

One of the advantages of going to school in Canada, as many students will inform you, is that the legal drinking age is only 19. This increased access to alcohol contributes to UBC's extensive bar and pub culture, a feature of the university's social life that is all the more exciting because of the city of Vancouver's renowned nightlife. However, undergraduates need not stray far to drink since the school itself has a number of drinking establishments on-campus. The most-frequented of these is the Pit Pub, which hosts "Pit Night" every Wednesday, an event that students describe as an opportunity to "get really drunk, fall over, and stumble home." A lot of drinking occurs in the residences, where the more-lenient RA's "don't crack down on underage drinking, but they can be hard on drugs," at least in the dorms. One girl claimed that "the best pot comes from British Columbia" and that this is reflected in the student body's affinities, but other students countered that "while [marijuana use] is a definite part of the UBC culture for many students, it's not over the top." The importance of having events and activities close to the dorms comes into play when it's raining, which "can get very dreary and usually lasts for several months at a time."

The social scene at UBC is characterized as being "generally very friendly," although students commented on certain cliques that form, particularly around ethnic groups and substance users. Not surprisingly, the campus is "extremely liberal" politically, although conservative students felt that the atmosphere was "not repressive." Even though it is a public school, many students are perceived to be upper-middle class and relatively affluent, which a girl speculated may stem from the fact that "tuition fees are higher for international students." More than 4,000 international students from 120 countries attend UBC, which creates a unique campus atmosphere. One sophomore even stated that she "can walk all the way across campus and not hear any English," an experience that she attributed to UBC's extensive international recruiting programs.

An International City

UBC is unique in that it does not require first years to live on-campus. Those freshmen who do choose to live in the residence complexes settle in either Totem Park or Place Vanier, living situations that are described as "incredibly convenient." Each dorm features an assortment of singles, doubles, triples, and quads, as well as a lounge, study area, small gym, cafeteria, and mini-mart. Totem has a reputation for being the party dorm, while Vanier is seen as "nicer and more sedate." There is a wider variety of residences available to upperclassmen including Walter Gage, featuring suites of six bedrooms and shared living space, and Fairview Crescent, which consists of townhouses. The distinct Ritsumeikan-UBC House, or "Rits," was built as a symbol of UBC's academic partnership with Ritsumekan University in Japan, and offers not only four-bedroom suites with shared kitchen and living room, but also a Japanese tatami room for "relaxing and meditation."

> "I can walk all the way across campus and not hear any English."

There is one RA on each floor in Totem and Vanier, each overseeing about 50 students. How strict they are depends on the person, but general consensus is that people get away with a lot in the dorms. Students say UBC does not make its substance policies clear, but the residences do have clear policies that forbid drinking in the hallway but allow it in the rooms. Drugs are not allowed in the dorms, although a single offense will not get you removed. When outside the residences, one junior girl claimed that "you can walk around campus with a joint and rarely get in trouble, and if you're drinking outside, campus security will just tell you to dump it out."

A large number of students choose to forgo UBC's provided housing, which only accommodates one-fifth of the undergraduate population, and instead look to off-campus options. Students who take this option claim that the advantages of these living situations, which vary in distance from campus and can be as far away as the other side of Vancouver, far outweigh the drawbacks, since the many attractions of the greater city are even more accessible, especially with the convenience of local public transportation. Students can purchase "U-passes" that give them unlimited access to the Vancouver bus system, which runs until four in the morning.

Thunderbirds find plenty to do on and around campus. The Student Union Building, also known as the SUB, houses a food court, the Pit, a number of small food vendors and restaurants, the Norm Theatre, and even clothing vendors on its multiple levels. The availability of these alternate eating opportunities can be a relief for students who find the cafeteria fare everything from "monotonous and unhealthy" to "disgusting." Meal plan money may be redeemed at other on-campus eateries besides those in Totem and Vanier, but many students choose to cook their own food.

While campus architecture is described as "incredibly eclectic but not very attractive at times," the scenic area surrounding UBC more than makes up for it. A junior gushed that "you're surrounded by forest, looking out on the water, with mountains on the other side—it's incredibly picturesque." Right next to campus, down a flight of stairs, is the famous Wreck Beach, where clothing is optional. Many students spend their wintry weekends at the famous Whistler resort to ski or snowboard. The city of Vancouver, however, is one of the main reasons students choose UBC. According to a senior: "You could manage by staying strictly on-campus all four years, but you'd be missing out on a whole world out there." From clubs and bars to pubs and restaurants, Vancouver seems to have everything in the way of culture and entertainment. Students' favorite joints to frequent include the Blarney Stone and the King's Head Pub for drinks, Numero Uno Pizza for cheap late-night slices, and the many ethnic cuisine restaurants, since "you name a country and you can probably find a restaurant that serves its food somewhere in Vancouver."

Thunderbirds Are Go!

UBC's varsity sports are apparently played down since, as a sophomore commented, "I'm not sure anyone attends many of the games at all." While they may not be following their fellow Thunderbirds closely, the rest of campus is reported to be pretty active, with students running outside whenever it isn't raining, or using the Birdcoop recreation center. Intramural sports are popular, as well. With over 275 student-run organizations, UBC students have plenty of choices. Many take advantage of nearby Whistler by joining the extremely popular "Ski and Board Club," which offers discount season passes to the slopes. Clubs centered around celebration of ethnic and cultural heritage are ubiquitous, due largely to the number of international students, as well as to the significant population of recent immigrants to Canada. These groups "put on a lot of events, like beer gardens and mixers."

A much-appreciated aspect of student life at UBC is the university's fun annual events. These include Day of the Longboat, when students gather in teams of ten to participate in a frantic canoe race, and Arts Country Fair, which is held on the last day of classes and offers a chance for students to unwind, listen to famous bands, and "basically start drinking around breakfast and keep it going all day." Daily surprises can include sightings of the many celebrities who film their projects in the Vancouver area, ranging from Jessica Alba to Al Pacino.

UBC offers its students the opportunity to live and study in a renowned research university setting bordered by a "wealth of natural beauty" and one of the most exciting cities on the West Coast, Vancouver. It may be large, but "everyone finds their place here in this laidback community," which is made even more attractive by its affordability. Students described UBC as a "completely comprehensive university," promising that "no matter what program you go into, you're going to get a great education out of it." Those looking for a truly international university in the top tier of Canadian education, might want to consider giving border-hopping a try.—*Kimberly Chow*

FYI

If you come to the University of British Columbia, you'd better bring: "a George Forman Grill for when you get tired of the cafeteria food, and rain boots."

What's the typical weekend schedule? "Friday night go to a residence party or a beer garden on-campus. Saturday play IM sports, go to Granville Island for its shopping market, at night go to downtown Vancouver for its pubs, bars, and clubs. Sunday play some sports and cram in the studying."

If I could change one thing about UBC, I'd "increase school spirit and promote clubs and organizations more."

Three things every student at UBC should do before graduating are: "Jump off the 10-meter high dive in your underwear or naked, gather your friends and race on Day of the Longboat, and go up the clock tower and appreciate the stunning view."

University of Toronto

Address: University of Toronto, 315 Bloor Street West, Toronto, Ontario MJS 1A3
Phone: 416-978-2190
E-mail Address: admissions.help@utoronto.ca
Web site URL: www.utoronto.ca
Year Founded: 1827
Private or Public: public
Religious affiliation: none
Location: urban
Application and Admissions Information: Depends on major
Regular Application Deadline: NA
Number of Applicants: 59,541
Percent Accepted: 65%
Percent Accepted who enroll: 32.9%
Number Entering: NA

Number of Transfers Accepted each Year: NA
Mean SAT: NA
Mean ACT: NA
Middle 50% SAT range: NA
Middle 50% ACT range: NA
Early admission program (EA/ ED/ NA): NA
ED or EA Acceptance Rate: NA
Full time Undergraduate enrollment: 44,349
Total enrollment: 69,711
Percent Male: 45%
Percent Female: 65%
Total Percent Minority: NA
Percent African-American: NA
Percent Asian/Pacific Islander: NA
Percent Hispanic: NA
Percent Native-American: NA
Percent Other: NA
Percent in-state / out of state: NA

Percent from Public HS: NA
Retention Rate: 95%
Graduation Rate: 76%
Percent in On-campus housing: 10%
Percent affiliated with Greek system: NA
Percent Varsity or Club Athletes: NA
Number of official organized extracurricular organizations: 200+
3 Most popular majors: Arts, Science, Engineering
Student/Faculty ratio: 20:01
Financial Information:, CAD, depends on program Tuition and Fees: NA
Percent receiving Financial aid, first-year: NA

A prestigious institution with three picturesque campuses spread around Canada's most vivacious and culturally diverse city, the University of Toronto has a wide selection of academic, athletic, and entertainment resources both on and off campus. The school is well known for its innovative research and academic prowess and has the best course selection in the nation. While most students are generally proud of the school and pleased with their choice, the intense workload and academic pressure can be overwhelming for many.

Competition in the Classroom
The professors at the University of Toronto are some of the most respected academics and experts in their respective fields. Faculty members have made major contributions to academia and research, including Sir Frederick Banting and J.J.R. Macleod, who won the Nobel Prize in 1923 for their discovery that insulin could control diabetes, as well as geneticist Tak Mak who was the first person to clone a T-cell gene.

A senior noted, however, that one of the drawbacks of having world-class professors is that the class sizes are usually extremely large with limited student-faculty interaction. With over 70,000 students, "it's hard to avoid feeling like a number," said a freshman. Courses at Toronto are extremely challenging, with professors who are noted to have higher standards than those at most other Canadian universities. Some students feel lost in the large classes and find the competitive nature among students and the overall academic intensity to be stifling.

One student expressed a desire to have professors "grade on academic achievement rather than academic achievement as compared to the rest of a class." But despite the high stress that comes with the academic prestige of the university, students don't regret the choice of attending; one student called his experience "an unparalleled educational opportunity," and said that the hard work is always worth it. Students are also encouraged to utilize on campus resources such as counseling, writing centers, and tutorials designed to help with rigorous course loads.

With the new waitlist feature that only allows students to sign up for a maximum of six courses, including waitlisted courses, U of T students are finding it more difficult to enroll in their classes of choice. But, prospects become brighter as students delve deeper into their majors. Class size reduces and student-faculty interaction increases with each year.

There are four main faculties at the U of T: engineering, music, arts and science, and physical education and health. Applicants to the university apply directly to the faculty of their choice. Co-op programs within faculties incorporate classroom teaching with real-world working experience, as students switch between university work and co-op jobs each semester. There are also specified tracks offered for students interested in science, as well as research opportunities that allow students to work side by side with their highly regarded professors.

The Toronto Triad

The University of Toronto is broken down into three campuses: the St. George Campus, the Mississauga Campus, and the Scarborough Campus. St. George Campus is the oldest of the three, established in 1827, and is nestled in a park-like setting in the downtown area. This, the primary campus, hosts over fifty thousand students. The nine thousand students at Mississauga are located west of downtown in a more modern environment, while the slightly larger student body of the Scarborough campus is part of a small, friendly academic community east of Toronto. Each regional section has its own student culture and campus pride, but a freshman expressed frustration with this division. "I'd have the three separate campuses together," she said. "There are rivalries between the campuses and I think U of T would be stronger as one."

Students explain that the buildings of all three campuses are aesthetically beautiful. One student said, "The buildings downtown are exquisite, old and new ones. The old ones are all so unique and detailed, and have such a history. The newer buildings also offer a modern type of uniqueness to the campus." The university has created a residential college system in order to create smaller communities within the overwhelmingly large student body. Seven of the nine colleges are located in the downtown campus, with the other residences are located within the two smaller campuses.

A senior explained that the dorm situation is largely traditional, with students housed in doubles their first year and singles in the following years; some students, however, live in suites or townhouses. One student explained that Toronto "does have a large commuter community, with many upper year students opting to live off-campus in houses or apartments in the downtown core." He added that some students live at home with their parents, which takes away from the student life aspect of the Toronto experience.

Opportunities for Involvement

The University of Toronto has over 175 officially recognized student clubs and opportunities for involvement are endless. Each of Toronto's three campuses has its own radio station, and there are over fifteen student newspapers as well as a number of artistic publications. Campus groups are an integral part of the student experience, from the Aeronautics team to Women in Life Learning. Hart House is a social, cultural, and recreational facility centered on cultural programming such as arts and music, and is a popular hangout for students.

First-rate athletic facilities include courts, pools, tracks, dance studios, beach volleyball courts, a sports medicine clinic, and facilities for weight training, aerobics and martial arts. There are free instructional classes each week as well as intramural sports leagues.

Students embrace the vast size of the campus and the opportunities available there, although it can be intimidating at first. "It is an urban metropolis that allows for anyone to explore culture, passions or interests," one senior said. "However, it can be alienating and overwhelming for newcomers." The cultural diversity and social acceptance at U of T is a perk for many. One student explained, "Social groups are really very non cliquey, with many students open to meeting friends that they normally would not have associated with in high school."

> **"It is an urban metropolis that allows for anyone to explore culture, passions or interests."**

The student body is diverse, with a multitude of international students and cultural events that expose students to different foods, traditions, and beliefs. One sophomore explained that he's met students from all over the map. "You really feel like you are part of the global village," he said.

In Search of a Social Scene

Students say that while there are a multitude of on-campus parties and events, the city is the best place for nightlife and weekend parties. "There's a lot to do in Toronto City," a student explained. "There are loads of activities going on all the time—parties, plays, shows, musicals, concerts..." Popular downtown clubs for the university crowd include Tonic and Joe, and the Duke of Gloucester on Yonge Street is often regarded as the best student hangout close to campus.

The drinking age in Canada is nineteen, a perk for students who can legally drink two years earlier than they would have been able to in the States. "Clubs and bars are spread out all over downtown Toronto," one student said. "That's what life is here!" One student said that "For a break from campus, U of T students generally go to one of the many nearby pubs to down a pint." Students explain that the general trend is pubs on Thursdays, clubs on Saturdays.

The Greek scene and sports scene are not key focuses at Toronto, falling far below the emphasis placed on academics. One student explained, "Toronto school spirit is generally lacking. Although students are proud of their academic and extracurricular life, generally that isn't parlayed into a strong school spirit." A senior said that many students at U of T spend much of their weekends studying, but there are opportunities for fun if schedules allow. Typical hangouts are Diablos at University College, the Understudy Café in the central campus area, and The Cat's Eye at Victoria College.

The City of Toronto is the largest in Canada and offers a plethora of resources for food, fun, and entertainment available to students at the university. Toronto has a wide variety of ballet, dance, opera, music, and theater companies. The world's first permanent IMAX movie theatre is in Toronto, as well as an open-air venue for music concerts, a popular pedestrian village, and a theater district. The yearly outdoor Shakespeare performances and international film festivals draw people from around the world, and sports fans will not be disappointed, as Toronto is the only Canadian city with teams in the NHL, NBA, and MLB.

The city is brimming with clubs, restaurants, sporting events, festivals, theater, and shops, and students don't run out of things to do in this multicultural and cosmopolitan city. Toronto's subway, bus, and streetcar systems are speedy and efficient, allowing students to get around town with general ease, and Toronto students have discounted rates to many events.

Despite student complaints about the "mountains of work," Toronto is said to hold the torch for education in Canada. With superior academics, distinguished professors, a wide range of on-campus organizations, and a city with endless opportunity for exploration and enjoyment, the Toronto experience is hard to compete with as long as you're willing to work.—*Catherine Cheney*

FYI

If you come to the University of Toronto, you better bring "Valium. Just kidding, but you need to be prepared not to let the competition get to you."

What is the typical weekend schedule? "It involves studying and essay writing. But when schedules are clear, pubs on Thursdays and clubs on Saturdays are popular social events, and allow for the much-needed blowing off of steam."

If I could change one thing about Toronto, I'd "combine the three campuses."

Three things every student at the University of Toronto should do before graduating are: "Attend a toga party at St. Michael's college, visit the U of T art gallery, and attend the special lectures offered, particularly those offered by visiting academics."

University of Waterloo

Address: University of Waterloo, 200 University Avenue West, Waterloo, Ontario, Canada N2L 3G1
Phone: 519-888-4567
E-mail Address: askus@uwaterloo.ca
Web site URL: www.findoutmore.uwaterloo.ca
Year Founded: 1959
Private or Public: public
Religious affiliation: none
Location: urban
Regular Application Deadline: 2-May
Number of Applicants: 31,741
Percent Accepted: 61%
Percent Accepted who enroll: 33%
Number Entering: 6,390
Number of Transfers Accepted each Year: NA

Mean SAT: NA
Mean ACT: NA
Middle 50% SAT range: NA
Middle 50% ACT range: NA
Early admission program (EA/ ED/ NA): NA
ED or EA Acceptance Rate: NA
Full time Undergraduate enrollment: NA
Total enrollment: NA
Percent Male: 49%
Percent Female: 51%
Total Percent Minority: NA
Percent African-American: NA
Percent Asian/Pacific Islander: NA
Percent Hispanic: NA
Percent Native-American: NA
Percent Other: NA
Percent in-state / out of state: 98%/2%
Percent from Public HS: NA

Retention Rate: 98%
Graduation Rate: NA
Percent in On-campus housing: NA
Percent affiliated with Greek system: 2%
Percent Varsity or Club Athletes: NA
Number of official organized extracurricular organizations: 80
3 Most popular majors: Computer Science, Kinesiology and Exercise Science, Mathematics, General
Student/Faculty ratio: 15:01
Tuition and Fees: $3,952
Cost for Room and Board: $5,950
Percent receiving Financial aid, first-year: NA

W here else can you get great academics, great work experience, and great bratwurst, all at Canadian prices? According to students at the University of Waterloo, all are within close reach.

A Taste of the Real World

The University of Waterloo is well known for its rigorous academic programs. Students keep busy fulfilling the 40 classes required for graduation (10 per year), while double majors are even more demanding. Academic programs are structured around Waterloo's six faculties: applied health sciences, arts, engineering, mathematics, environmental studies, and science; each has its own set of requirements and expectations. In addition, there is also an Independent Studies Program for those looking for something more specialized. While math and engineering have an especially strong reputation (Waterloo has more students enrolled in math than any other school in the world), the other departments are equally as demanding. There is little reported grade inflation, and professors are fairly accessible. One arts student, discussing the personal attention students receive, commented that he could not remember taking any English classes with more than 40 students per class, even freshman year.

One of Waterloo's biggest highlights is its well-developed, prestigious co-op program, where students divide the school year by alternating terms of school and employment. The co-op program is the largest of its kind in North America with over half of the student body participating. As a result, Waterloo operates on a trimester system, with classes in session all-year long to allow students in the co-op program to graduate within five years. Current undergrads highly recommend the program, saying, "not only can you get some much-needed cash, but you also get work experience, which is great for future employment." Being a part of the co-op system means having the opportunity to travel—not just to nearby Toronto, but to places outside of Canada as well. Students also report that coming back to school from the "real world" after working for a term provides a better perspective on classes and university life in general. One undergraduate said that, "sometimes it's nice just to get away for a change of scenery and to refocus my energies."

Building Friendships

Waterloo has no on-campus housing requirements, but almost all first-year students live in the dorms. Many second-years also try to stay on campus, but a recent housing shortage has made this difficult. The university's eight on-campus residences (primarily for first-year students) can be categorized into 2 main communities—the "UW residences" and the "University college residences." Each dorm has a resident advisor, nicknamed a "don," who is an upperclassman. The UW residences consist of Village 1, Mackenzie King Village, UW Place and Ron Eydt Village. University college residences include Conrad Grebel, Renison, St. Jerome's and Saint Paul's. They are small religiously-affiliated colleges with ties to the University. Many students are very enthusiastic about living within a residential college system. Offering both separate classes and housing spaces, the church colleges reportedly offer a "homier" atmosphere. Although each church college has a specific religious affiliation, students of any creed may apply for residence. Students say the church colleges have the most "spirit," and according to some, also have better food—try Conrad Grebel for Mennonite cooking. On the whole, dorm rooms are small and most students live in doubles, but are the place where "we start to build lasting friendships so it isn't so bad—in a sense, we are all in it together."

Upperclassmen tend to live off campus—there is plenty of available housing conveniently near the school, and the cost of living is more affordable. By living off campus, students are able to avoid the meal plan, which freshmen are quick to call "a total rip-off." Many find tasty food off campus at popular places like East Side Mario's, Subway, Campus Pizza, and University Plaza, which is open 24 hours a day.

Friendly, Outdoorsy Atmosphere

Students find the town of Waterloo, Ontario, a quiet kind of university town and are quick to differentiate it from nearby "gross, industrial, abandoned factory-like" Kitchener. For the outdoorsy types, the area around Laurel Creek provides the perfect opportunity to jog, swim, and bike. For those eager to explore the social scene, the Student Life Center organizes free movies and other recreational activities on campus and in the area. The area is also famous for its great Oktoberfest celebration every year: people come from all over to sample the bratwurst, take in the dancing, and absorb the unique atmosphere of the festival. Students enthusiastically recommend the event, even if it means just taking a tour of the local breweries.

As for the night life, students often head to Bombshelter. The student-run bar and club, also known as "Bomber," features popular Wednesday night parties, concerts, and infamous hot wings ("Our wings are so hot you need to sign a waiver!"). Other than that, there are the usual weekend parties with plenty of alcohol available. Waterloo may have the reputation for being a studious school, but as one student commented, "even the engineering students know how to relax once in awhile." Some students leave town on the weekends and head for Toronto, about an hour away, but most stay on campus, preferring to hang out with friends there.

Though not sanctioned by the University, fraternities and sororities do exist and are growing in size and number. Besides providing a social outlet, the groups organize a number of philanthropic events throughout the year. "Joining Kappa Kappa Gamma not only gave me the opportunity to do charity work, but it was also a great way to meet a fantastic group of smart, talented women," raved one fourth-year.

> **"We really know how to go after what we want."**

As a co-op school, the Waterloo campus is active year-round. Students on campus over the summer can attend the "huge" Canada Party held on the first of July at Columbia Lake. The event features concerts, carnival games, and fireworks, giving students a chance to enjoy the warm summer weather.

IMs and More

Due to the co-op system, many students do not have a lot of time to pursue other extracurricular activities. However, clubs and organizations number over 200, and include an active student government, the Federation of Orientation Committee (which runs frosh week), and *Imprint*, the main student newspaper. Intramurals are also strong with a number of fine facilities available. Any student with interest can play, and the lack of pressure on the field makes the experience enjoyable. By comparison, varsity sports are more on the periphery of students' interest. One senior had "never even thought about going to a sporting event!"

Quest for the Pink Tie
Waterloo, like all universities, has its own colorful traditions. Among them is the quest for the pink tie, which occurs during freshman week at the start of the school year. Math students, or "mathies" as they are called, enjoy the week-long activities and get the coveted pink tie. Later, a huge pink tie is hung over the side of the math building, and this often adds to the touch of rivalry between the math and engineering departments. During frosh week, engineering students try to steal the giant pink tie, while mathies try to sneak out the "tool," the engineering faculty's prized possession. As one student said, "we love to scheme and plot, but it is really just fun and games."

A Place to Grow
Waterloo students take their academic demands very seriously. "There are lots of smart people, especially in the sciences and engineering," says one undergrad. Students head to the Dana Porter Library to study, and computer clusters are readily available on campus. While the academic atmosphere may not be cutthroat, some complain that there are people who study compulsively. One student remarked that there exists a clear separation—"half the students study like crazy, and half have a life." Students at Waterloo can be cliquish, so school unity leaves room for improvement. However, the University of Waterloo still remains one of Canada's foremost educational institutions for the engineering, math, and the arts, and those who attend do take note of the formidable job placement rate after graduation. Above all, Waterloo students in general agree about the number of academic and social opportunities available. If there is one thing to remember about the people at Waterloo, it is that "we really know how to go after what we want." It is just that passion that keeps Waterloo growing and its students succeeding.—*Laura Sullivan*

FYI
If you're coming to Waterloo, you'd better bring "cleats and shin guards so you can play in the intramurals."
What is the typical weekend schedule? "Eat, play sports, party, STUDY."
If I could change one thing about Waterloo, I'd "improve the architecture."
Three things that every Waterloo student should do before graduating are "go tubing in Laurel Creek, go out for a team (competitive or intramurals), and check out Oktoberfest."

University of Western Ontario

Address: University of Western Ontario, Rm 165 Stesenson Lawson Bldg, London, Ontario N6A 5B8

Phone: 519-661-2100

E-mail Address: liaison@uwo.ca

Web site URL: welcome.uwo.ca

Year Founded: 1878

Private or Public: public

Religious affiliation: none

Location: urban

Regular Application Deadline: 2-Jun

Number of Applicants: 27,652

Percent Accepted: 59%

Percent Accepted who enroll: 25%

Number Entering: 5,871

Number of Transfers Accepted each Year: NA

Mean SAT: NA

Mean ACT: NA

Middle 50% SAT range: NA

Middle 50% ACT range: NA

Early admission program (EA/ ED/ NA): NA

ED or EA Acceptance Rate: NA

Full time Undergraduate enrollment: 28,513

Total enrollment: 30,000

Percent Male: 40%

Percent Female: 60%

Total Percent Minority: NA

Percent African-American: NA

Percent Asian/Pacific Islander: NA

Percent Hispanic: NA

Percent Native-American: NA

Percent Other: NA

Percent in-state / out of state: 96%/6%

Percent from Public HS: NA

Retention Rate: 95%

Graduation Rate: NA

Percent in On-campus housing: NA

Percent affiliated with Greek system: NA

Percent Varsity or Club Athletes: NA

Number of official organized extracurricular organizations: 171

3 Most popular majors: Digital Communications and Media/Multimedia, Medicine (MD)

Student/Faculty ratio: 12:01

Tuition and Fees: $3,920

Cost for Room and Board: $6,582

Percent receiving Financial aid, first-year: NA

Located just under two hours from Canada's largest city, which styles itself as "the center of the universe," the University of Western Ontario is one of the nation's most prestigious universities and a mecca in its own right. Outstanding professors, a beautiful campus, a world-renowned business school, and high-quality undergraduate programs draw many of Canada's top students to London, Ontario. The student who goes here will benefit from both a highly respected degree and from four years of "unparalleled fun."

Advancing Academics

The quality of the undergraduate academic experience at Western is, by most accounts, "steadily improving" as the administration tries to strengthen the school's academic credentials in order to attract top students. But though it is undeniably a "challenging" academic environment, for some students Western is "rightly known as a laid-back party school."

In general, classes are huge for most first-year students. Good professors are often found teaching underclassmen, but usually "there are about 500 of them [underclassmen] crammed into a room at one time." Upper-level classes, however, tend to be a lot smaller. Says one student: "Western is not exactly well-known for its graduate and doctorate programs, so you definitely get the sense in third- and fourth-year classes that the professors are trying to woo you over to their discipline to build up the school's postgraduate reputation."

Of course, a student's impression of Western's academic experience depends greatly on which program he or she pursues. Western offers a competitive BA/HBA program in conjunction with its Richard Ivey School of Business, an internationally ranked management school. One student in the joint degree program described it as "very elite and 10 times harder than the rest of Western's undergraduate program." The University also boasts smaller, affiliate colleges, such as Huron College, which set their own academic programs and offer smaller classes. Students in other majors report varying degrees of overall satisfaction. A social science major would give Western academic experience a "five or six on ten," saying that there are "only a handful of amazing profs," and that "it's hard to get individual attention." An actuarial science major, on the other hand, reported receiving a lot of academic guidance during her first year.

Other students complain about a lack of grade inflation in certain departments. Many frustrated students find themselves with 67–75 percent when they feel that their work deserves better. However, one proactive student noted that approaching the professor and complaining about the TA's ineptitude often can result in a higher grade. Like many other big schools, Western is "a heaven of finding loopholes."

A typical day at Western can stretch from early in the morning to late at night—one student reports having class from "9:00 a.m. to 10:00 p.m. with only a couple of hours of breaks in between." Engineering students sometimes have up to 35 hours of class a week. Ultimately, your schedule, your academic program, and your time at Western will be a product of your ability to make the most of what the enormous school offers.

A Good Deal—Unless You're Hungry

Despite its sprawling size, Western retains a "tight, close-knit feel, even though it's a huge school," perhaps because London is so "tiny" and "in the middle of nowhere." Many say that London is "beautiful and cheap to live in" although "like elsewhere in Canada, the weather is pretty shitty."

All first-year, full-time students are guaranteed housing. There are two main kinds of residences, "suite-style" and "traditional." The suites are generally quite spacious, often featuring two bedrooms, two bathrooms and a kitchen for four occupants. Rooms freshman year, says one student, are very clean. "We had cleaning service everyday and our own bathroom."

Residential life is extremely social. The largest dorm, Saugheen-Maitland Hall, nicknamed "The Zoo," made it onto David Letterman's top 10 list of best places to "get laid" in North America. Both guys and girls can be "pretty skanky," says one student. Though not everyone shares that sentiment, many find that the dorms are the center of the campus social scene.

Food on campus is purchased on a pay-per-item basis, and though it is "generally pretty healthy," it can also be prohibitively expensive. Students living in residences get a substantial discount on the dining hall food. The meal plan allows students to purchase a debit card for use anywhere on campus and even in some London restaurants. Students praise the variety of offerings, including sundae and salad bars and pizza in some dining halls, but complain about the cost. Students living off campus—including most upperclassmen—more often take advantage of London's numerous eateries. There are many sushi places, and Starbucks

shops abound. Says one student smugly, "the food around here is much better than at Queen's," Western's chief rival and sport nemesis.

Students mainly describe the overall financial burden of attending Western as "reasonable," although "this school will nail you on expensive books—but you don't have to actually buy them unless you're a science major!" When the vast majority of upperclassmen move off campus, there is a wide variety of high-quality, relatively low-cost housing. As one student said, "$500 a month can get you a pretty nice place." And despite the higher tuition charges for international students and the rising exchange rate, Western is still a bargain for Americans compared to U.S. schools of similar quality.

Primped and Primed

Students generally report that Western hosts a wide variety of people, and that every student can find their niche. Nevertheless, Western has a well-earned reputation as "Canada's private school" where many are the "children of wealthy families." There are "a lot of legacies," and "networking is really important here," says one student.

Another common observation about Western's student body is the GQ- and Vogue-worthy people who attend the University. There are some "very, very attractive women" who go here, and many students dress to impress. "I thought that everyone would go to class in their pajamas, but people really dress up here!" laments one student.

> "I thought that everyone would go to class in their pajamas, but people really dress up here!"

Like many other colleges, Western boasts an eccentric and resourceful group of engineering students. Recently a group of adept pranksters replicated a famous MIT stunt by dissembling a campus police car and reassembling it on the roof of a tall building. Each year several engineering students show their school colors by dying themselves purple for Homecoming Week. For one unfortunate student, however, the ink proved indelible for months. Students can join many extracurricular activities during their time away from class. Charity fashion shows are quite popular. One student says that her sorority was "a great way to meet people and become involved early on." Improv groups, student media organizations, and pre-professional clubs are also abundant on campus.

Nightlife at Western revolves mainly around campus bars and clubs. Though some city natives complain that all the bars "resemble Cheers'," most students report satisfaction with a bustling downtown scene. One bar even has a terrace which overlooks the library. Greek organizations can offer an important socializing venue for first-years, many of whom are underage and cannot drink in London unless they have a fake ID.

The Greek community, however, is not affiliated with the University, and some students lament the hostile attitude on the part of the administration towards fraternities and sororities, which has inhibited their presence on campus from becoming more widespread.

In general, a "very collegial atmosphere" prevails on campus. For the motivated students willing to seek them out, Western offers many wonderful academic and social possibilities that, for many, verify its reputation as one of Canada's top schools.—*Sara Schlemm*

FYI

If you come to Western, you'd better bring an "ironing board," "fancy clothes," and "independence."

What's the typical weekend schedule? "Go to bars on Richmond Street or frat parties. There may even be a toga party!"

If I could change one thing about Western I'd change "the expensive on-campus food."

Three things every Western student should do before graduating are "climb to the top of University College tower, follow the football team to Queen's, go to Jack's (the only on-campus bar where "everyone" goes)."

Index